To my wife Holly and my daughters Lizzie and Kat.
— R. A.

To my wife Lavinia, my son Daniel, my daughter
Carolyn, and Mom and Dad.
— L. K.

MASTERING MANAGEMENT SKILLS

SKILLS

A Manager's Toolkit

Ramon J. Aldag
University of Wisconsin–Madison

Loren W. Kuzuhara
University of Wisconsin–Madison

THOMSON
™
SOUTH-WESTERN

Australia · Canada · Mexico · Singapore · Spain · United Kingdom · United States

THOMSON

SOUTH-WESTERN

Mastering Management Skills: A Manager's Toolkit
Ramon J. Aldag, Loren W. Kuzuhara

VP/Editorial Director:
Jack W. Calhoun

VP/Editor-in-Chief:
Michael P. Roche

Senior Publisher:
Melissa Acuña

Executive Editor:
John Szilagyi

Developmental Editor:
Emma F. Guttler

Production Editor:
Tamborah E. Moore

Marketing Manager:
Jacquelyn Carrillo

Manager of Technology:
Vicky True

Technology Project Manager:
Kristen Meere

Media Editor:
Karen Schaffer

Manufacturing Coordinator:
Rhonda Utley

Printer:
Webcom Limited
Toronto, Ontario

Production House:
Trejo Production

Design Project Manager:
Anne Marie Rekow

Internal Designer:
Anne Marie Rekow

Cover Designer:
Anne Marie Rekow

Cover Illustrator:
Tivadar Bote

Brief Contents

TABLE OF CONTENTS

PART 2   INTERPERSONAL

Chapter 6
FOSTERING ETHICAL BEHAVIOR 249

Chapter 7
COMMUNICATING EFFECTIVELY 275

Chapter 8
LEADING EFFECTIVELY 323

Chapter 9
MANAGING POWER, SOCIAL INFLUENCE, AND POLITICS 363

PREFACE

The modern work environment—and life in general—demands a wide variety of behavioral skills: a skills portfolio. Traditional organizational behavior and management textbooks and courses in colleges and universities generally have continued to do a good job of surveying major concepts and theories and presenting examples of companies that apply them in some form. However, instructors, their students, and the employers who hire the students as they graduate from undergraduate and MBA programs increasingly want and need textbooks to do more. They call for books that emphasize "what to do to be an effective manager" and how to develop the right mix of skills needed to implement these behavioral strategies. In addition, students must learn how to apply these organizational behavior and management skills within complex, dynamic organizational and external environments while facing time, resource, political, and regulatory constraints. This vast array of challenges requires a new breed of textbook.

A BALANCE OF THEORY AND SKILLS APPLICATIONS

Mastering Management Skills: A Manager's Toolkit combines solid content with a rich integrated skills emphasis. It is appropriate for organizational behavior (OB) or management courses in which instructors prefer a very strong skills and real-world emphasis or for a management/OB skills course.

We believe the text offers a richer mix of skills and provides significantly more opportunities for skill development and mastery than current offerings, as well as greater use of Internet resources. The book has an open, clean, and integrated look and feel. Rather than provide a lengthy early discussion of theory in each chapter, we instead offer short presentations of theory as appropriate before introducing each skill-related exercise. We employ a broad variety of cases and examples, avoiding an overreliance on case studies in manufacturing settings. We strongly emphasize real-world examples and applications and use a wide variety of unique approaches to bring important theories and tools to life.

VISION OF THE TEXT

We designed *Mastering Management Skills: A Manager's Toolkit* to be unlike any other text on the market. It has the following distinctive personality:

> **Skills based.** Students appreciate, and increasingly expect, to learn concrete, practical, transferable skills. The text focuses primarily on skill development through skill assessment, awareness, attainment, and application.

> **Social learning perspective.** As we discuss in detail in Chapter 1, the text applies a social learning perspective. The generalized steps of the social learning perspective include preassessment, conceptual learning and modeling, conceptual and behavioral practice, and life application. Our terms for these, to emphasize the skills focus and offer an organizing framework (4 A's), are Skills **Assessment**, Skills **Awareness**, Skills **Attainment**, and Skills **Application**. All text features help students develop one or more of these steps.

> **Applications oriented.** The text has an applied focus. Descriptive and theoretical content are presented only as needed to provide the foundation or rationale for applied materials.

> **Complete.** The text provides a comprehensive set of tools and techniques needed for effective management in real-world situations.

> **Rich.** We try to avoid the flavor of a technical manual in which students are pushed mechanically through a series of steps. Instead, we provide a stimulating learning environment that truly interests students.

> **Engaging.** The text uses interesting examples, an open writing style, and humor where appropriate.

> **Real world.** We avoid widgets and hypothetical firms. We choose tools and techniques used in the real world. We regularly highlight the relevance of the text's content by explaining to students why it is important and how it is used in actual practice. We present interviews with practitioners in a variety of industries, organizations, and management levels to demonstrate the relevance of the content.

> **Current.** In today's environment, examples more than a few years old are stale, if not completely outdated and wrong. As such, our examples are as current as possible.

> **Accessible.** The text is friendly in tone, layout, and content.

TEXT PHILOSOPHY

Every textbook has an underlying philosophy that guides its content and presentation. Here are the key elements of our philosophy:

> Skills are the key to success in the modern environment. More sophisticated technology and more dynamic and complex markets require more sophisticated workers, which creates the need for a skills portfolio. In the modern workplace, it is skills, rather than firm-specific knowledge, that are most critical to career success.

> Skills do not flow directly from knowledge. The knowing–doing gap, discussed in Chapter 1, requires the actual application and practice of skills.

> The most valuable skills are broadly applicable, durable, and transferable. Students' career and personal growth will benefit from a portfolio filled with enduring and portable skills. Fortunately, unlike many technical skills, the

managerial skills we address will serve students well in many settings and over time.

> Critical management skills can be learned. Although some people may seem more gifted than others at skills such as communicating, leading, or dealing with conflict, these and other skills we address are primarily behavioral rather than trait based.

> Skill mastery requires a solid conceptual foundation. Skills can't be applied blindly. To be effective, students need to know *why* and *when* the skill is needed and *how* it should be used. Just as knowing without doing is futile, doing without knowing is potentially misguided and dangerous.

> Skills should be directed toward improving both personal and organizational outcomes. We view organizational behavior and management as having many goals. Although enhancing organizational performance and other outcomes of the firm are important goals, the lack of a clear, direct impact on organizational outcomes does not mean a skill is unimportant. Other goals, such as improving individual satisfaction and health or fostering positive workplace interactions, are significant in themselves. Further, we view personal and organizational outcomes as generally congruent or potentially congruent. That is, in some cases, personal and organizational outcomes move together. In other cases, companies can use reward systems and other policies and practices to help align personal and organizational consequences.

> Skill learning is a lifelong activity. Although many skills in students' portfolios will have enduring value, it will nevertheless be necessary to learn and apply new skills throughout one's career. Independent study, continuing education, on-the-job training, and professional associations may all help in this endeavor. This vital point is the primary theme of the final chapter of the text.

TEXT FEATURES

The text includes a variety of complementary features, consistent with our emphasis on skills assessment, skills awareness, skills attainment, and skills application.

> **Skills Objectives and Knowledge Objectives.** Each chapter begins with a set of specific skills (assessment, attainment, and application) objectives and related knowledge (that is, skills awareness) objectives.

> **Review of relevant content.** A solid overview of appropriate content is included in each chapter. Although this material reflects current theory, research, and writing, we emphasize research per se very little. In addition, our intent is not to catalog theories; we discuss specific theories only if they are major and have unique value. Multiple theories are presented only when they are complementary and/or cumulative. That is, we do not provide a series of critiques.

> **Pretest Skills Assessment.** This activity consists of brief scenarios based on actual dilemmas faced by real-world managers. They all focus on the bottom-

line concern of how to handle a management problem or situation. The exercises provide students with a baseline measure of how much they know about understanding and applying chapter concepts, and they also help students appreciate the difficulty of the particular challenge.

> **Self-Assessment materials.** Each chapter includes one or more self-assessments of communication styles, personality, leadership, conflict styles, stress levels, and so on. The text web site and instructor's resource manual contain additional information about scoring and interpreting these materials.

> **Skills Practice activities.** These activities—typically five to eight per chapter—provide intensive practice in applying the tools and techniques discussed, facilitating personal, interpersonal, and managerial skills development. Many of these exercises are meant to be applied in a team context or to offer that option. Two levels of difficulty are associated with these exercises—basic and challenging. The exercises will challenge students and prepare them for the work environment.

> **"Voice of Experience" practitioner interviews.** Interviews with a wide variety of managers, from recent graduates to seasoned professionals, capture the most difficult types of situations they have faced in the past, how they dealt with them, and what they learned from their experiences.

> **Focus on Management boxes.** These features provide discussions of company applications of chapter materials as well as related Web addresses.

> **Lighten Up features.** We use humor as appropriate. Lighten Up boxes at the ends of chapters focus on the lighter side of topics. Although humorous, each of these boxes reinforces key chapter content. More Lighten Up features are included in the textbook web site.

> **Bottom-Line features.** Students often ask about the bottom line associated with various concepts covered in organizational behavior and management classes; that is, "How do I apply this?" The Bottom-Line feature addresses this concern by translating discussions of key topics and skills into a set of steps for applying them effectively in an organizational context.

> **Real-world examples.** Drawn from a wide range of industries and situations, real-world examples are used extensively throughout the text.

> **Top Ten List: Key Points to Remember.** The Top Ten List, at the end of the body of the chapter, enumerates the key managerial guidelines. Students will not assimilate everything they learn from reading a textbook of course, but these lists reinforce important points that students should remember—and act on—in the future.

> **Questions for Review and Reflection.** Each chapter contains Review Questions that test knowledge of chapter content. In addition, thought-provoking Critical Thinking Questions require students to assess issues and controversies relating to chapter material. These questions often ask students to take and justify stands on chapter topics.

> **Chapter-end Web Exercises.** The two chapter-end Web-based exercises per chapter require students to access and use chapter-related Web material.

> **Chapter-end Cases.** We highlight recent events and challenges facing well-known companies and provide illustrations of chapter concepts in the chapter-end cases. Students develop critical thinking and analytical skills by thoroughly analyzing the situation and applying appropriate tools or techniques to address it.

> **Chapter-end Video Cases.** Each chapter includes a video case showing an actual organization dealing with management challenges. The video cases include introductory material and questions for discussion geared to chapter content.

TEXT ORGANIZATION

The text begins with a chapter emphasizing the importance of skills in the modern workplace and presenting the book's management skills framework. There are then 13 substantive chapters, a "looking ahead" chapter, and two appendixes. Each of the substantive chapters focuses on a particular skills cluster.

Chapter 2, "Understanding and Valuing Differences," stresses knowledge and skills required in increasingly diverse organizations, including personality, national culture, perceptions, and attitudes; together, these topics speak to the nature of diversity and the ways we may react to it.

In Chapter 3, "Solving Problems," we address skills needed for problem solving, creativity enhancement, and negotiating.

In Chapter 4, "Motivating Effectively," we focus on skills related to understanding employee needs, applying learning theories, setting effective goals, linking effort to outcomes, assuring fairness, and designing jobs to be intrinsically motivating.

Chapter 5, "Managing Stress," examines stress and burnout and offers personal and organizational guidelines for stress management.

In Chapter 6, "Fostering Ethical Behavior," we address ethics and business ethics, demonstrate the costs of ethical violations and the benefits of a strong culture of ethical behavior, and provide guidelines for enhancing our own ethical behavior and that of others.

Chapter 7, "Communicating Effectively," offers approaches to improving such critical skills as written communication, effective speaking, active listening, attending to nonverbal communications and informal communications, and use of electronic communication tools.

Chapter 8, "Leading Effectively," examines key leader skills and behaviors and provides guidelines and exercises to develop students' leadership knowledge and skills.

Chapter 9, "Managing Power, Social Influence, and Politics," addresses bases of interpersonal and subunit power and identifies specific social influence and political tactics.

In Chapter 10, "Managing Conflict," we examine causes, characteristics, and consequences of conflict and provide guidelines to resolve harmful conflict and to generate productive conflict.

Chapter 11, "Managing Teams," explores the management skills needed to create and lead teams effectively.

Chapter 12, "Building Human Assets," addresses key human resource skills associated with attracting, selecting, and developing employees, facilitating staffing and training and development, appraising employee performance, and compensating employees.

In Chapter 13, "Organizational Culture," we examine organizational culture, including its functions, elements, and impact on performance, and offer guidelines for assessing culture and managing cultural change.

Chapter 14, "Managing Change," addresses organizational change, presenting guidelines for fostering successful change and for developing change-oriented learning organizations.

Chapter 15 provides a summary of the skills addressed in the book and offers specific, detailed guidance for lifelong skills maintenance and learning.

Appendix A, "Strategic Management," focuses on a variety of skills needed to get the big picture of the firm and to ensure that strategies are consistent with overall organizational goals and environmental demands.

Finally, Appendix B, "Managing Careers," provides a variety of guidelines for the successful lifelong management of careers.

INSTRUCTOR RESOURCES

The following resources designed to aid instructors were developed entirely by the text authors.

Instructor's Resource Manual (ISBN: 0-324-29114-0). The Instructor's Resource Manual provides a high-quality and comprehensive instructional resource. It includes sample answers to Critical Thinking Questions, End-of-Chapter Cases, and Video Cases. It provides chapter outlines, sample course syllabi, and lesson plans for each chapter. In addition, it provides further information about text Self-Assessment exercises, including norm data developed specifically for the text to facilitate interpretation of student responses. It also offers additional exercises, cases, activities, and Web links to enrich students' learning experiences. The Instructor's Resource Manual gives instructors a confident grasp of all text material as well as providing extra information, tips, anecdotes, and examples to allow the instructor to demonstrate mastery of the material and to give "value added" to students beyond the text material.

Test Bank (ISBN: 0-324-29115-9). The Test Bank contains approximately 100 to 150 questions for each text chapter. These questions include all basic formats, including multiple choice, true and false, short answer, fill in the blank, and essay, as well as a significant number of scenario-type questions. The level of difficulty of each question is indicated next to the item. The Test Bank makes the design of a high–quality (relevant, challenging, and defensible) exam a simple and efficient process for instructors, and it also gives instructors leeway to tailor the exam to their preferred testing style.

Instructor's Resource CD-ROM (ISBN: 0-324-29118-3). Key instructor ancillaries (Instructor's Manual, Test Bank, ExamView, and PowerPoint slides) are provided on CD-ROM, giving instructors the ultimate tool for customizing lectures and presentations.

PowerPoint Slides. Approximately 40 PowerPoint slides are provided for each chapter, some drawn from text figures and others specifically designed for this resource. The PowerPoint slides include integrative figures, definitions of concepts, lists of important factors, practical implications, important conceptual frameworks, and other materials. Slides are attractively designed and fully animated to permit polished and professional presentations. Instructors may choose to use the presentations as provided or to add their own content and enrichment features. Available on the Instructor's Resource CD-ROM and the web site.

Videos (ISBN: 0324291191). Designed to enrich and support chapter concepts, each of the videos presents real business issues faced by a variety of service and manufacturing organizations. The video cases challenge students to study management and OB issues and develop solutions to business problems.

ExamView Testing Software. Instructors can create, deliver, and customize print and online tests in minutes with this easy-to-use testing and assessment system. ExamView offers both a Quick Test Wizard and an Online Test Wizard with a step-by-step guide through the process of creating tests; its unique WYSIWYG ("what you see is what you get") capability allows viewing the test on the screen exactly as it will print or display online. With ExamView's complete word processing capabilities, instructors can enter an unlimited number of new questions or edit existing questions. Available on the Instructor's Resource CD-ROM.

Text Web site at http://aldag.swlearning.com. The text Web site, developed and maintained by the authors, contains the following features:

> Downloadable PowerPoint slides and the Instructors' Resource Manual.

> Norm data for Self-Assessment exercises. As noted earlier, the norm data provided in the Instructor's Resource Manual will be regularly updated on the web site to provide a larger and more varied pool of comparison information.

> Devil's Advocate. This feature identifies and responds to some of the most common student concerns or questions about the content covered in the chapter. The Devil's Advocate feature addresses the issue of why chapter content is important.

> Web-Wise materials. Web-Wise boxes discuss resources and suggest associated Internet links students can explore.

> Additional Web links. Links to hundreds of problem-solving resources on the Web are provided and updated regularly.

> Talk to the Authors. This feature enables instructors to submit questions to the authors, request teaching tips regarding any aspect of the book, offer their own suggestions and examples, and so on. We will respond personally to e-mail queries.

> "Management Skills in the Movies." This unique feature offers a listing of movies (professional, training, and made in Hollywood) that illustrate skills discussed in the text. Many students enjoy watching videos that illustrate

course concepts. This web site feature provides a list of video clips that instructors have used effectively to illustrate important OB and management concepts and skills, as well as tips for their use.

> Regular updates. The Web site is actively maintained to provide new information concerning management tools, the real-world examples used in the text, new examples, and new exercises relating to the Web links. Again, the text, Instructors' Resource Manual, and web site each incorporates a variety of exercises relating to these links.

STUDENT RESOURCES

> **InfoTrac College Edition.** With InfoTrac College Edition, students get complete 24/7 access to full-text articles from hundreds of scholarly journals and popular periodicals such as *Newsweek, Time,* and *USA Today.* Thousands of full-length substantive articles spanning the past four years are updated daily, indexed, and linked. And because they're online, the articles are accessible from any computer with Internet access. InfoTrac College Edition is perfect for all students, from dorm dwellers to commuters and distance learners.

> **Interactive Study Center at http://aldag.swlearning.com.** The Student Web site, which we also develop and maintain, offers the following student resources:

- Interactive practice quizzes with feedback. The best way to prepare for exams is to get as much practice as possible answering questions that test mastery of each chapter's content. The Interactive Study Center includes multiple choice and true-false questions for each chapter.

- Challenging topics. This resource gives students easy-to-understand explanations of some of the most difficult concepts discussed in the book. Additional examples of each concept is provided with the explanations.

- Cyber review sessions. These offer concise overviews of the content covered in each chapter. Many students request review sessions from their instructors when it is exam time. This Web site feature provides students with a concise overview of the key topics covered in each chapter and helps students see how all of the topics fit together into a coherent whole. This is an extremely valuable resource for students when they are preparing for an upcoming exam.

AN INVITATION TO INSTRUCTORS

We have made every effort to offer in *Mastering Management Skills: A Manager's Toolkit* and its supplements a unique, comprehensive, accessible set of resources for instructors who hope to employ a strong skills emphasis in an organizational behavior or management course. Through the text's Web site, we hope to work with you as you use these materials, not only to provide information but also to learn your perspectives, insights, concerns, examples, and approaches. We invite you to take full advantage and contact us via e-mail, phone, or in any other way, and we look forward to interacting with you as you help prepare students for the Brave New World of organizational behavior and management.

ACKNOWLEDGMENTS

We'd like to extend our appreciation to those colleagues who contributed to *Mastering Management Skills: A Manager's Toolkit*. We have benefited from the detailed and constructive reviews provided by many people. In particular, we wish to thank the following educators who have served as reviewers: Susan Adams, Bentley College; Valerie Bacharach, Laurel Business Institute; David C. Baldridge, University of Connecticut; Brendan Bannister, Northeastern University; William Bommer, Georgia State University; Bill Brown, Montana State University; Jean Bush-Bacelis, Eastern Michigan University; Arch Darrow, Bowling Green State University; Roger Dean, Washington and Lee University; Robert Denhardt, Arizona State University; Peter Diplock, Clarkson University; William P. Ferris, Western New England College; Theodore Herbert, Rollins College; Jacqueline N. Hood, University of New Mexico; Fred Hughes, Faulkner University; James Jarrad, University of Dubuque; Michael Jolly, Idaho State University; David M. Leuser, Plymouth State College; Lynn Miller, LaSalle University; Ralph Mullin, Central Missouri State University; Marcella M. Norwood, University of Houston; Elizabeth C. Ravlin, University of South Carolina; Raymond T. Sparrowe, Cleveland State University; Robert Steel, University of Michigan-Dearborn; Gregory Stephens, Texas Christian University; John Wagner, Michigan State University; and Scott Williams, Wright State University.

ABOUT THE AUTHORS

RAMON (RAY) J. ALDAG

Ray Aldag holds the Glen A. Skillrud Family Chair in Business and is executive director of the Weinert Center for Entrepreneurship and past chair of the Department of Management and Human Resources at the University of Wisconsin–Madison. He received his BS in mechanical engineering, his MBA in production management, and his PhD in management from Michigan State University. Ray has worked as a thermal engineer on various *Apollo*, *Voyager*, and other aerospace projects at the Bendix Aerospace Division in Ann Arbor, Michigan. At Wisconsin, he has served as associate director of the Industrial Relations Research Institute and was the 1993 recipient of the Jerrod Distinguished Service Award. He is a member of honorary societies in business, engineering, and decision sciences, a fellow of the Academy of Management, and listed in *Who's Who in America*. He was the recipient of the 1995 Distinguished Service Award of the National Academy of Management.

Ray has 35 years of experience teaching management principles, organizational behavior, decision making, introduction to business, human resource management, business policy, and other courses. He has served on more than 60 PhD thesis committees.

An active researcher on such topics as leadership, culture, group decision processes, task design, and motivation, Ray has published more than 70 journal articles and book chapters in *Administrative Science Quarterly*, *Academy of Management Journal*, *Academy of Management Review*, *Decision Sciences*, *Journal of Applied Psychology*, *Journal of Management*, *Psychological Bulletin*, and elsewhere. He is coauthor of eight books, including *Business in a Changing World* (4th ed.), *Management* (2nd ed.), and *Leadership and Vision*. He is currently associate editor of *Decision Sciences* and has served as associate editor for organizational theory and behavior for the *Journal of Business Research*, as essays coeditor of the *Journal of Management Inquiry*, and as a consulting editor for the *Journal of Applied Psychology*. He currently serves on the editorial review boards of *Administrative Science Quarterly*, *Organization and Environment*, and the *Journal of Leadership and Organizational Studies*. He has served as a proposal reviewer for the Office of Personnel Management and the National Science Foundation and has received NSF funding for his research.

Ray served as the 1991–1992 president of the National Academy of Management, a professional organization with 10,000 members in more than 80 countries, and as the 1992–1993 president of the Foundation for Administrative Research. He has also served on the board of governors of the Academy of Management and in other Academy of Management positions in the Research Methods, Public Sector, Organizational Behavior, and Social Issues Divisions and in the Organizations and the Natural Environment Interest Group. He also has served as president of the Midwest Academy of Management and in various roles in the Decision Sciences Institute and the Industrial Relations Research Association.

Ray has consulting experience with a wide variety of public and private sector organizations in such industries as information processing, education, publishing, financial services, staffing, utilities, health care, heavy machinery, insurance, law enforcement, and pharmaceuticals.

LOREN W. KUZUHARA

Loren Kuzuhara is a teaching professor in the Department of Management and Human Resources at the University of Wisconsin–Madison School of Business. He teaches undergraduate courses in organizational behavior, management of teams, management consulting, and human resource management. In addition, Loren works individually with many students who are pursuing a variety of independent research projects focusing on management consulting and training and development.

Loren is the faculty adviser for the UW–Madison student chapters of the Society for Human Resource Management (SHRM) and Sigma Iota Epsilon (SIE). He also is the Sam Walton Fellow for the UW–Madison Students in Free Enterprise (SIFE) team and the coach for the student team that competes in the annual HR Games competition.

Loren earned his bachelor's degree in psychology from the University of Illinois at Urbana–Champaign and his MBA and PhD in management and human resources from the University of Wisconsin–Madison.

Loren has corporate experience working in the Strategic Research Department at American Family Insurance. He is an active management consultant as well.

Loren's research interests revolve around work motivation, leadership, team development, training and development, organizational effectiveness, and human resource management.

THE MANAGEMENT CHALLENGE:
CRITICAL SKILLS FOR THE NEW WORKPLACE

CHAPTER 1

Skills Objectives

> To analyze the key duties and responsibilities of a manager.

> To analyze the critical skills that distinguish between effective and ineffective managers.

> To develop basic action plans for addressing organizational problems and challenges.

> To develop a tree diagram to identify the goals, subgoals, and supporting tasks needed to implement action plans.

> To develop a personal learning plan for enhancing management skills.

KNOWLEDGE OBJECTIVES

> Identify characteristics of the modern workplace and the corresponding importance of management skills.

> Discuss reasons why you will need managerial skills during your career.

> Identify important differences between success in business and in school.

> Explain the knowing–doing gap.

> Discuss a management skills framework.

> Explain the stages of action planning and implementation.

The new world of work and organizations is complex, ambiguous, changing, diverse, and global. In today's organizations, hierarchies are flatter, deadlines are shorter, teams are pervasive, employees must manage themselves, and technology is transforming the nature, pace, and possibilities of work. The modern workplace demands speed, flexibility, creativity, cooperation, political savvy, proactivity, and attention to ethical behavior. It is a place where success requires the skills to react quickly and effectively at all times, often while working with others and with new technologies. These same skills also are increasingly needed for career and life success.

The job of a manager has become dramatically more complex over time. As such, we attempt in this text to do more than survey major concepts and theories. Rather, we emphasize what to do to be an effective manager and how to develop the right mix of skills to support the implementation of these behavioral strategies. We also provide tools to help you apply these management skills within complex, dynamic organizational and external environments while facing time, resource, political, and regulatory constraints.

This chapter lays the foundation for the text's skills focus. We begin by providing a brief overview of the nature of the modern workplace and the need for management skills in this new work environment. We then discuss ways that organizations are seeking to develop their employees' skills, and we argue that those skills are important for you in both work and life in general. Next, we note important differences between school and business and we address the "knowing–doing gap"— the inability to translate knowledge into appropriate action. Following this, we present the social learning perspective underlying the text as well as our managerial skills framework. Finally, we discuss action planning and implementation and provide a brief overview of the text's organization. Today's (and tomorrow's) work environment will require you to develop a skills portfolio—a set of valuable and transferable skills that you can carry from job to job and from company to company. This chapter shows how the text will help you build a solid foundation for your management skills portfolio.

Before reading on, complete the following Self-Assessment 1-1 to gain a greater understanding of your initial attitudes and beliefs about management. As you work through the various chapters of this book, some of your existing attitudes and beliefs about management may be reinforced. However, you likely will be surprised to learn about other management practices and principles and how they are implemented in real-world organizations. After you have completed the self-assessment, visit the text Web site to get feedback on your results.

SELF-ASSESSMENT 1-1

Attitudes Toward Management

Answer each of the following questions regarding your attitudes toward managing others in organizations. Answer each question as honestly as possible using the response scale provided.

1 Disagree strongly
2 Disagree somewhat
3 Neither agree nor disagree
4 Agree somewhat
5 Agree strongly

____ 1. I will only need management skills if I get a job as a manager or supervisor in an organization.

____ 2. Management skills will not be an important determinant of my long-term career success.

____ 3. Management skills are something that people either have or don't have—they cannot be learned.

____ 4. Once you become a manager, your job becomes easier because you are telling other people to do things rather than having to do them yourself.

____ 5. A person who demonstrates outstanding performance in an entry-level (nonmanagerial) job will almost always be an outstanding manager as well.

____ 6. Management is basically just a bunch of common sense ideas I already know anyway.

____ 7. Managers need to develop a big picture perspective of their work units and organizations in order to be effective.

____ 8. The study of management is really only relevant to business students who are majoring in management.

____ 9. Soft management skills, such as managing teams, communication skills, and leadership, are among the most important things needed for a person to be successful in real-world organizations.

____ 10. Poor management is responsible for a large percentage of company failures or bankruptcies.

Next, read the Pretest Skills Assessment and develop an "action plan"—that is, a set of things you would do—to address the key problems you see in the situation. After you are through, go to the text Web site to get feedback on your results.

PRETEST SKILLS ASSESSMENT

Using Management Skills to Address Organizational Problems

Note: This exercise is based on actual events encountered by managers in real-world organizations. Some information may have been modified in order to maintain the anonymity of the people and organization involved in the situation.

You just graduated from college in May and after taking a fabulous trip around Europe and Asia you are now ready to start your new job in the real world. You are excited about the prospects of being able to start doing more hands-on work in an actual organizational environment. Your new position is assistant store manager at a major department store located in Portland, Oregon. Your job is both to coordinate the activities of all the department supervisors and sales associates and to deal with customers. The pay and benefits you will be receiving are excellent, and you have been told that opportunities for advancement in the company are available if you do well.

A couple of weeks after starting the new job, your enthusiasm for the company is beginning to wear thin for a number of reasons:

> Many of the departmental supervisors and sales associates do not see you as having any credibility as a store manager because you just graduated from college, have no relevant work experience (other than a summer internship), and are significantly younger than most of the employees in the organization.

> Managers and sales associates in different departments are highly competitive with each other in terms of sales performance.

> The local economy is faring poorly, resulting in consumers having less money to spend on shopping.

> New competitors have been emerging on an ongoing basis. Consequently, the retail market is saturated with department stores.
> The department store recently laid off 20 percent of its departmental supervisors and sales associates because of declining sales and poor financial performance.
> Rumors are floating around that the department store may be acquired by a much larger department store based in San Diego.
> Employee satisfaction is at an all-time low (only 33 percent of the employees in the department store reported that they are satisfied with their current jobs), and the overall employee turnover rate has increased to 50 percent per year,

Develop an action plan for solving the problem in your work unit. Be sure your plan addresses both short-term and long-term issues. Be specific and be prepared to defend each element of the plan's feasibility and cost effectiveness.

MANAGEMENT SKILLS AND COMPANY SUCCESS

In an age of high technology and high finance, it is sometimes easy to forget the importance of management to company success. In fact, though, good management is critical to the prosperity, and even the survival, of firms. For example, one study of manufacturing firms over a five-year period considered a myriad of factors—such as firm size, market share, capital intensity, industry average return on sales, and the ability of managers to manage their people effectively—that might explain the firms' financial performance. The results were dramatic: Managers' ability was *three times* as powerful in explaining company profitability as all other factors combined.[1] Similarly, a study in the United Kingdom revealed management weaknesses to be the primary cause of most insolvencies, with poor management cited as at least a contributing factor in more than 80 percent of cases.[2] These and many other studies of large and small firms are consistent in pointing to management skills as critical to firm success.[3]

Recent examples of major companies facing difficulties because of poor management range from toy maker Mattel to underwear manufacturer Fruit of the Loom, from computer maker Gateway to the National Aeronautics and Space Administration (NASA), from computer software producer Baan to Chiquita Brands.[4] Similarly, the high mortality rate of dot-com firms is due in large part to management failures.[5]

Just as management has been implicated in company problems and failures, management success stories are abundant, cases in which management skills have created or transformed organizations in remarkable ways. Among the many we examine in future chapters, these cases include Herb Kelleher's development of a successful culture of fun at Southwest Airlines, Mary Kay Ash's inspirational leadership of Mary Kay Cosmetics, and Jack Welch's transformation of GE, all of which are widely known. Others are less visible but no less dramatic. We examine all of these stories and many more throughout this text.

Although successes and failures due to the quality of CEOs' management skills are often observed by outsiders, the same skills, such as the need to see the big picture, communicate effectively, interact well with others, and make good decisions, are becoming increasingly important at levels throughout the organization. The skills that help a CEO lead an organization can help a manager run a department or an employee deal with the demands of everyday work life.

The Voice of Experience feature presents an interview with Brad Pope and Jeff Millard, officers of the University of Wisconsin-Madison chapter of Sigma Iota Epsilon, the honorary and professional management fraternity. The interview explores how leaders of a student organization have learned valuable skills that help prepare them for the real world.

Now complete Skills Practice 1-1. This exercise requires you to draw from your own experience to identify your best and worst bosses, and to analyze why you feel this way about them. It will help you see the role of skills in determining a manager's effectiveness.

Before moving on, complete Skills Practice 1-2 by watching the movie *Office Space*. This is a comedy about corporate life that highlights some interesting and important management and organizational issues. Have fun with this one!

CRITICAL SKILLS ACROSS BUSINESS FUNCTIONS

Management skills are growing in importance for workers of all kinds. A study of financial staff identified as critical skills, in addition to financial leadership, these skills: strategic thinking, effective communication, and leadership.[6] Similarly, a survey of chief information officers found that more than three-fourths believe more widespread use of technology will require IT workers to communicate more effectively and articulately.[7] With more frequent information exchange, skills such as communication, diplomacy, and problem solving will grow in importance. As another example, a study of "Sales Management Competencies for the 21st Century" identified eight competencies consistently demonstrated by top-performing sales managers. Among those competencies are providing strategic vision, assembling teams of skilled employees, sharing information with employees, coaching, diagnosing performance, negotiating, and selecting high-potential employees.[8] Similarly, the American Institute of Certified Public Accountants (AICPA) Core Competency Framework identifies the skills and competencies accounting professionals need to be competitive now and in the years ahead.[9] Along with functional competencies, key competencies identified include such personal skills as communicating, handling personal relationships, and facilitating learning and personal improvement, as well as such broad business–perspective competencies as strategic thinking, critical thinking, and decision making.[10] In short, success in jobs of all kinds—finance, information technology, marketing, accounting, and others—now depends on the sorts of skills we address in this text.

SKILLS TRAINING IN ORGANIZATIONS

As evidence of the importance placed on skills in the modern workplace—and of the conviction that skills can be learned—American corporations spend more than $64 billion annually for the training of their work forces, about 85 percent of it in the area of management skills.[11] The world's best companies recognize the value of continuing skills training.[12] Dana Corp. requires all of its employees to complete 40 hours of education each year. The company spends about $32.5 million annually on employee training programs and has three Dana University schools. IBM invests 6

VOICE OF EXPERIENCE

THE VALUE OF MANAGEMENT SKILLS

Brad Pope and Jeff Millard, Past Presidents, Zeta Eta Chapter, University of Wisconsin–Madison, Sigma Iota Epsilon (SIE) Honorary and Professional Management Fraternity

1. Why are effective management and leadership important to the success of a student organization?

You have to remember that a student organization is a voluntary activity, so you need to work very hard to motivate members to join and get involved in the organization's activities. Leadership is needed to provide a clear sense of direction for the organization. Members will not remain involved if they fail to see the purpose and objectives of the organization. Finally, the leadership in a student organization must provide an effective structure that provides opportunities for other student members to assume responsibility for fund-raising, finance, membership development, and social activities.

2. What were some of the biggest management challenges you experienced in leading the SIE student organization?

The key challenges for our Sigma Iota Epsilon chapter were the management of organizational growth (i.e., a significant increase in membership), member turnover due to graduation, leadership succession, establishing an appropriate strategic focus for the organization, and defining appropriate roles for members who wanted to contribute to the organization.

3. How did you address these challenges?

One key change we have made in order to address the leadership succession issue was to create a vice president position in our executive team. The person who held this position served one semester as a vice president and then became the president the next semester. This provided the vice president with the time needed to learn the organization and to prepare for assuming the president's position. The issue of strategic focus was a major challenge for the organization given that management is such a broad field. After extensive discussion, we decided an appropriate focus for our chapter was leadership development. We selected this focus because it was a key management competency and we knew many employers look for leadership skills when they interview students for full-time positions after graduation.

4. What kinds of management skills did you develop through your leadership roles in SIE?

(Brad) One key skill I learned was how to delegate to others. At the beginning of the school year, I felt I had to do everything myself. It didn't take long for me to realize this was totally unrealistic so I had to delegate responsibility to others to handle certain issues and to trust them to get these things done. Fortunately, we had a *great* executive team that was very responsible and motivated.

(Jeff) Some of the skills I learned were problem solving, leadership, and teamwork. I was the head of the technology committee, responsible for creating a Web site for our chapter. In the beginning, my committee members and I had no idea what we needed to do to accomplish this task. However, we studied the problem and learned how to create Web pages by sitting around a computer together in the lab with a manual in front of us. Little by little, we saw the results of our efforts as the Web site began to take shape. It was a challenging, but rewarding, experience.

(Brad) One last thing I would add is that I learned the value of actively managing communication and following up with others so we are all on the same page. This takes a lot of time and effort, but it is absolutely critical to the success of any leader.

5. Did your management skills help you to be more competitive in terms of obtaining internships and looking for a job after graduation?

Definitely! Many employers use "behavioral interview" formats in which you must respond to questions by drawing from your personal experience. Our leadership experience with Sigma Iota Epsilon has greatly enhanced our ability to answer questions such as, "Tell me about a time when you added value to a team or organization." Based on our SIE experience, we can talk extensively about how we view our members as customers, try to understand what they want from their membership, and then look for ways to add value for them so their SIE experience contributes to their professional development.

http://sienational.colostate.edu/

percent of its profits on education. Merck & Co. spends 3.5 percent of its payroll, or about $100 million annually, on employee skills development programs. Abbott Laboratories offers one-week and three-week leadership development programs. Lucent Technologies is known for its dedication to learning. It knows that knowledge is all it has to sell, and it provides tuition reimbursement of up to $7,000 for undergraduate studies and $9,000 for graduate programs. Partly as a result, the company—with 120,000 employees—received 150,000 applications in a single year and has a voluntary turnover rate of just 1 percent.

Similarly, General Electric spends about $1 billion annually on education and training programs. GE executives and managers also volunteer time to talk with students at many grade levels, and they brainstorm with college faculty to identify which skills should be part of school curricula. GE's paid college internships are among its strongest programs.[13] The company seeks to help the students build technical and business skills in a hands-on setting; students do real work that is measurable and deliverable, are given performance reviews, and are assigned mentors. Read about skills training at AT&T Wireless Services in the Focus on Management feature.

A survey conducted by the Conference Board showed that a full 98 percent of respondents reported their skills training efforts reaped significant economic benefits for their firms.[14] Still, many companies are failing to develop key managerial skills.[15] For instance, in one study 72 percent of companies indicated their concern about being able to predict which skills will be missing from their organizations in a year, but just 21 percent of companies were able to identify where employees want to be in terms of skill development in a year.[16] Another study showed that 58 percent of managers had received no leadership training, 68 percent had not been trained in delegation, 72 percent had received no training in giving feedback on performance, and 87 percent had no training in stress management.[17] As such, you cannot assume every company will help you develop needed skills. Instead, you should seek out employers who are committed to helping you continuously develop

FOCUS ON MANAGEMENT

SKILLS TRAINING AT AT&T WIRELESS SERVICES[18]

AT&T Wireless Services, the nation's largest cellular service provider, is fighting to maintain its leadership in the face of intense competition and technological changes. The company is using a process called Managing Personal Growth (MPG) to help employees identify core competencies or critical skills, develop them with resources available through the company, and translate them into day-to-day decisions and actions that help the company meet its goals. Employees must take personal responsibility for developing those critical skills, not in company-mandated training sessions but on an ongoing basis. The MPG process forces employees to think about their personal values, what is important to them in life, what their current skills are, and what they hope to do in the future by acquiring new competencies. Employees then talk with their supervisors to develop an individual plan for their own development. A key function of the MPG process is to shift people to the idea of shared responsibility, making it clear they are responsible for their own careers. Their job security is grounded not in the company but in what they know and the value they can create around themselves.

http://www.attws.com/

VOICE OF EXPERIENCE

THE VALUE OF MANAGEMENT IN ACHIEVING ORGANIZATIONAL EFFECTIVENESS

Christopher (Kip) Frautschi, Director of Marketing, Webcrafters Corporation

1. Why is management important to the success of an organization?

The goal of an organization is to create the product or service successfully and do so while maintaining sufficient profitability to ensure a return of capital to investors, now and in the future. Most companies could, by firing all leaders and managers, improve their profit margin dramatically for about four months. Managers and leaders need to keep the firm focused on profitability and investment and ideas for the future. Also, competing demands for cash in different departments or areas need to be reconciled, along with what to invest in a product or service now, long before most nonmanagers see the need to change the operating and investing style and pri-orities of the present. Similarly, most firms could save money and increase their profitability by cutting out a direct sales force. But, of course, nobody would really take such a short-sighted action.

2. How would you respond to people who say the practice of management is nothing but common sense?

For the day-to-day operations of a company, perhaps it is only common sense; but that doesn't answer the question of why so few people have this common sense. To keep a team of people focused on the same goal at the same time seems easy when it is done well, but when it is, more commonly, done poorly, it is not difficult to observe the poor results and high costs that then occur.

3. What are the keys to being a good manager?

People are the key to any successful organization. Often, one finds two nearly identical companies, in the same industry, with similar market share, same founding year, all the top execu-tives in a given position went to school with their counterparts at the other company. But one firm is strongly profitable year in and year out, the other is barely profitable enough to stay in the business. Why? Because the strongly profitable firm has a successful culture—a can-do, on-time culture. Why? Because the managers have made the cumulative decisions that created over decades a better company. So successful management of people is the first point.

The second point blurs the line between manager and leader, but it is the willingness to lead. In the infantry the motto is "Follow Me!" The privates follow the second lieutenant up the hill into enemy fire because their second lieutenant is taking the risks too and leading and showing the way. Thus a good manager must see the ways things can be improved and lead his or her team into that vision so they all share that vision.

http://www.webcrafters-inc.com

and maintain those skills that will make you more valuable.[19] In addition, you must proactively identify and acquire key skills. A 2003 survey of training priorities conducted by *Training* magazine showed training for soft skills, including leadership, interpersonal skills, and teamwork, to top the list.[20] Kip Frautschi, an experienced marketing executive at the Webcrafters printing company, talks in the Voice of Experience feature about the importance of managerial skills in the business world.

Although most people are familiar with the term *management,* many do not really understand what managers do and the knowledge and skills they need to be effective. By completing Skills Practice 1-3, you will develop a much better idea of what a manager's job entails and why it is important to the success of an organization. As one indication of the importance companies are placing on identifying critical skills and hiring for them, read about IBM's "Manager Jam" in the Focus on Management feature.

FOCUS ON MANAGEMENT

IBM's Manager Jam[21]

With 319,000 employees across six continents, IBM is one of the world's largest businesses. For the company's 32,000 managers, it can also be a confusing place. With an increasingly mobile work force, many managers supervise employees they rarely see face to face. Some joke that IBM now stands for "I'm By Myself." As a result, Samuel Palmisano, IBM's new CEO, launched one of his first big initiatives: a two-year program exploring the role of the manager in the 21st century and needed management skills. The project's first event was "Manager Jam," a 48-hour real-time Web event in which managers from 50 different countries swapped ideas and strategies for dealing with problems shared by all of them, regardless of geography. An amazing 8,100 managers logged on to the company's intranet to participate in discussion forums.

DO *YOU* NEED MANAGEMENT SKILLS?

You may agree that firms need and want management skills in order to succeed, but may still question whether *you* personally need those skills. We believe there are at least three primary reasons why you will find management skills to be valuable: Companies want them, they are becoming more crucial in the changing business environment, and they will serve you well in life.

MANAGERIAL SKILLS AND HIRING

Quite simply, companies are hiring for skills, including managerial skills. A report released in 2000 by the U.S. General Accounting Office provided succinct advice for organizations: "Hire, develop, and retain employees according to competencies. Identify the competencies—knowledge, skills, abilities, and behaviors—needed to achieve high performance of mission and goals, and build and sustain the organization's talent pool through recruiting, hiring, development, and retention policies and practices targeted at building and sustaining those competencies."[22] Many companies go further, by tracking skills acquisition of their work force and tying pay to skills attained, even if they are not used.[23] This is a work force where competencies rule. It is absolutely critical that you learn what skills employers value and then work to develop them.

Students are sometimes surprised to learn of the criteria that firms and their interviewers use when screening job candidates. A study by the U.S. Department of Labor and the American Society of Training and Development of "Skills Employers Want" revealed 16 critical skills, as shown in Figure 1-1. We address directly almost all of these skills in subsequent chapters.

Similarly, a survey of human resource managers' perceptions of the importance of various skills, knowledge, and experience as employment criteria (with an evaluation of "1" meaning "Not a Factor" and "5" meaning "Extremely Important") yielded the results presented in Figure 1-2. Perhaps the most striking finding is that factors such as GPA, references, and college attended, although important, are rather far down the list. Skills in communication, problem solving, and human relations are all rated higher.

As another example, the National Association of Colleges and Employers reports that the top 10 qualities employers seek have little to do with technical skills.

FIGURE 1-1

The 16 Basic Skills Employees Need

Knowing How to Learn	Self-Confidence
Reading	Motivational Goal Setting
Writing	Personal and Career Development
Mathematics	Interpersonal Skills
Listening	Negotiation
Oral Communication	Teamwork
Problem Solving	Organizational Effectiveness
Creative Thinking	Leadership

Source: American Society for Training and Development and U.S. Department of Labor, Workplace Basics: Skills Employers Want, 1988.

Instead, employers want team players with strong verbal and written communication skills, honesty and integrity, interpersonal skills, motivation and initiative, a strong work ethic, and analytical skills.[24]

Now stop for a moment and consider this fact: The Bureau of Labor Statistics predicts the average 22-year-old college graduate in the year 2000 will have more than *eight* different employers before he or she reaches the age of 32; that's a change of employers every 15 months.[25] When you move to new employers, it will be your skills portfolio—not contacts in a past firm or firm-specific knowledge—that will be most important. As the information we've just presented indicates, soft skills, such as communicating, problem solving, motivating, leading, negotiating, and working with others, will make up a large and critical part of that skills portfolio. Read about how Merck and Company hires for competencies in the Focus on Management feature.

MANAGERIAL SKILLS IN THE NEW WORK ENVIRONMENT

Another reason to care about your managerial skills is that many developments in the new work environment are making such skills more important for career success.[26] Here is a sampling of those developments, each of which we explore in depth in future chapters:

FIGURE 1-2

Ranking of Human Resource Managers' Perceptions of Criteria for Evaluating Business Graduates

Criterion	Mean	Criterion	Mean
Oral communication skills	4.6	Nonverbal communication skills	3.7
Listening skills	4.5	Work experience	3.7
Résumé	4.4	Cover letter	3.6
Interpersonal communication skills	4.4	References (at interview stage)	3.4
Written communication skills	4.3	GPA, in major	3.4
Problem-solving skills	4.2	GPA, overall	3.3
Poise	4.2	Software application skills	3.2
Human relations skills	4.2	Office information systems knowledge	3.2
Job-related technical skills	4.2	College attended	3.1
Neat appearance	4.1	References (at initial screening)	2.7
Appropriate attire	3.8	Contacts within the organization	2.2

FOCUS ON MANAGEMENT

HIRING FOR COMPETENCIES AT MERCK[27]

When Merck and Company needed to fill a large number of field representative positions, it decided to focus specifically on competencies. Hiring managers were asked to identify the specific traits, skills, and behaviors most critical to job performance. A process was then developed to screen for those competencies at various steps of candidate assessment, including résumé screening, telephone evaluations, and the final interview. Each candidate then was scored on the criteria to give a rating of the candidate's potential. According to Merck chairman and CEO Raymond Gilmartin, the process was more efficient than previous approaches and yielded greater consistency across regions of the country. Gilmartin added, "There was another interesting effect: The people we hired were even more diverse than those we had hired as reps in the past. Diversity, in other words, was a welcome outcome of a process that was based entirely on business-directed criteria."

http://www.merck.com/

> **Entrepreneurship.** An increasing number of college graduates are becoming entrepreneurs, starting their own businesses.[28] A first-time entrepreneur faces many challenges, but perhaps the greatest is learning to become a boss. Recent evidence suggests that entrepreneurial success depends heavily on managerial skills, including social skills.[29] So, if you choose an entrepreneurial option, management skills are an absolute necessity.

> **Downsizing and delayering.** By one estimate, more than 43 million jobs have been lost in the United States since 1979 due to organizational downsizing—deliberate reductions of personnel.[30] This downsizing has served to make many organizations much leaner, often by eliminating many middle-level managers. One form of downsizing is delayering—the elimination of entire levels of the organizational hierarchy. For example, Champion International, a pulp and paper manufacturing firm, turned to delayering as part of its turnaround efforts, reducing management levels in its support functions from five to two.[31] Similarly, Dow Chemical embarked on a process of delayering in the mid-1990s that reduced its hierarchy from ten layers to six.[32] One important effect of such delayering is to push managerial responsibilities down to lower levels in the organization.

> **Job enrichment and empowerment.** As companies seek to make workplaces more satisfying and motivating, they are adopting a variety of approaches to giving workers more personal responsibility for their work. For instance, they are giving employees larger jobs, with more autonomy and greater opportunities to use valued skills. These job changes have many positive outcomes for employees and firms, but they also place additional demands on employees. In essence, these job changes "make every employee a manager," weaving the need for managerial skills into the fabric of jobs.[33]

> **Self-managed work teams.** Companies are making sharply increasing use of self-managed work teams.[34] These teams have responsibility not only for allocating tasks among members, deciding how to do their jobs, and carrying them out, but also in many cases for disciplining team members, evaluating members' performance, and even selecting and terminating members from the

team. As their name suggests, these teams have the responsibility and authority to manage themselves, and as such the teams' performance depends in large part on their members' managerial skills, including problem solving, persuasiveness, ethics, leadership, communication, motivation, and open-mindedness.[35]

> **Hiring for the second job.** Many firms are now taking a forward-looking approach to hiring. Rather than focusing just on the job candidates' ability to perform well in an entry-level job, they are considering whether candidates have the skills for subsequent, higher level positions. Thus, they are concerned relatively less with technical skills and more with the conceptual and interpersonal skills that will be needed in the future.

> **Growth in management positions.** Our earlier discussion of downsizing and delayering may give the impression that management ranks are shrinking. However, while specific firms have worked to trim their managerial numbers, economic growth and associated new firm formation have actually increased the overall number of managers in the United States. In fact, Bureau of Labor Statistics reports show that managers, administrators, and executives represent the *fastest growing* employment category.[36] In addition, an estimated 21 percent of top management and 24 percent of middle management positions across all functions, regions, and industries in the United States will become vacant in the next few years.[37] As such, whether you expect it now or not, there is a good chance you will end up in a management position.

Now complete Skills Practice 1-4 by watching the movie *Disclosure* starring Michael Douglas and Demi Moore. This is a corporate thriller about the drive for success, revenge, deception, and dirty politics. The film is intense, but it illustrates some important issues about key skills needed for success in real-world organizations.

MANAGERIAL SKILLS AND LIFE SUCCESS

Even a cursory look at the list of skills employers want and we address suggests a final reason to care about managerial skills: These are all skills that will serve you well in life in general. The abilities to communicate, to interact effectively with others, to negotiate, to solve problems, to lead, to think critically, to motivate others, to listen well, to deal with conflict, and to continue learning are valuable in social relationships, making daily transactions, and leading a fulfilling life.

Thus you will need an arsenal of managerial skills even before you formally enter a management position—or, indeed, even if you never enter one. As shown in Figure 1-3, those skills will remain important throughout your management career. In fact, the importance of conceptual skills increases at higher levels in the organization.

In the Voice of Experience feature, Troy Filipek, a recent college graduate now working as an actuary, talks about why he believes that management and organizational behavior (OB) are important for success in a real world organization.

SUCCESS IN SCHOOL AND BUSINESS

It is sometimes tempting—and perhaps comforting—to assume a successful college career will guarantee achievement in the business world. Although some of the same qualities, such as intelligence, conscientiousness, and drive, may be helpful in both settings, also be aware of many important differences between school and

FIGURE 1-3
Management Skills Needed for Success by Organizational Level

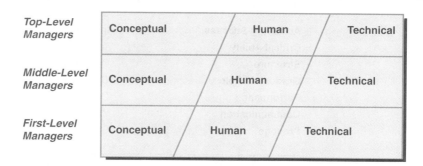

Top-Level Managers	Conceptual	Human	Technical
Middle-Level Managers	Conceptual	Human	Technical
First-Level Managers	Conceptual	Human	Technical

businesses. As shown in Figure 1-4, success in school is based largely on individual performance. Your communication to professors is primarily written, test taking is a critical ability, and performance criteria are generally well specified and relatively objective. Further, you are in two enviable positions: You are a customer whose satisfaction is important to your professors and school, and you are in a high-status position such as a senior or graduate student. As you enter business, you will see that success depends much more on teamwork. You will have to rely more on

VOICE OF EXPERIENCE

THE IMPORTANCE OF MANAGEMENT SKILLS IN THE REAL WORLD

Troy Filipek, Actuary and Recent Graduate

1. As a recent graduate, how have you applied OB/management principles in the real world?

At this point in my career, I have mainly applied teamwork principles in my day-to-day work. However, in the future, I will undoubtedly have to apply more managerial and leadership skills to be successful.

2. Why are OB/management skills important for people in a technical field?

Actuaries commonly are stereotyped as working in ivory towers, crunching numbers all day. But to be successful, we must be able to communicate highly technical concepts in a way that

new actuaries and nonactuaries understand. This requires the ability to work well with others, mentor recently hired employees, and get people to buy into what you are saying.

3. How would you respond to students who say a course in OB/management is of limited practical value?

Ultimately, to reach your full potential, you are going to need help along the way. To get this help, you must emphasize relationships, build social networks, and share your subsequent success with those who helped you attain it. All of these ideas stem from OB/management principles you learn in school.

4. What do you think are some key differences between success in school and success in the real world?

In the end, you'll be successful in both if you work hard and be responsible. However, in the real world, your success relies more on those around you than it does in school. Also, communication and leadership skills are far more prominent in the working world as a way to distinguish yourself.

5. What advice would you offer to students who are making this transition?

It is very easy to sit back and say OB/management is a lot of common sense, that everyone knows this stuff. But too often, these are the ideas most neglected in the workplace. Doing the little things like giving people a pat on the back, remembering their interests, and listening can go a long way in the long run.

FIGURE 1-4
Differences Between School and Business

	School	Business
Achieving Success	Individual	Teamwork
Critical Ability	Tests	Relationships
Structure	Quantified	Subjective
Graduate's Role	Customer	Employee
Performance	Objective	Judgments
Communication	Written	Verbal
Prestige	Senior	Trainee

Source: E. Taylor, *Graduates' Guide to Business Success: Solutions that Enable College Graduates to Excel in Business* (Hollywood, FL: Biography for Everyone, 1997), p. 13.

verbal communication, and handling relationships will emerge as a critical skill. Your job will be less structured, and your performance ratings will be more judgmental. Finally, you will often initially be in the low-prestige position of trainee, and you will be an employee rather than a customer.

In view of all these differences, you may not be surprised to learn that a wide range of studies show success in school does almost nothing to predict subsequent career success.[38] It is the growing evidence of this very weak link that has led many educators and managers to call for a greater emphasis on skills in the learning process. For example, the authors of a major study of management education sponsored by the American Assembly of Collegiate Schools of Business (AACSB) concluded, "The challenge of how to develop stronger people skills needs to be faced by both business schools in their education of their degree program students and by corporations and firms in their management development activities."[39]

THE KNOWING–DOING GAP
A common reaction of students studying management for the first time is that management is little more than common sense ideas and principles they already know. This sometimes leads to the perception of management in organizations as being easy or unimportant to the bottom line of an organization.

In reality, the study of management is deceptive in that much of it makes sense as you read it, but it becomes much more difficult once you try to apply these concepts and principles to actual case studies or work situations. This fundamental problem also occurs for many students when they take math classes. If they review for an exam by reading the textbook and their class notes, they can follow the logic of the sample problems that were solved. However, once they get into an exam and are required to solve an actual problem for themselves, they don't have a clue how to solve the problem.

The bottom line here is that simply *knowing*—recognizing or understanding what to do to manage an organization—is not enough to become a successful manager. Jeffrey Pfeffer and Robert Sutton from Stanford University became intrigued by the large number of managers and executives they worked with who knew what needed to be done to enhance the effectiveness of their organizations, but failed to implement it. Pfeffer and Sutton referred to this phenomenon as the "knowing–doing gap." For example, most managers agree it is important to reward employees for good performance and to link employee pay with job performance. However, in many organizations neither of these basic management principles is put into practice.

Many students wonder why the knowing–doing gap exists. Although there are many potential causes, Pfeffer and Sutton identified the following:[40]

> **Knowledge management efforts mostly emphasize technology and the transfer of codified information.** That is, the focus is on how to capture and distribute critical knowledge or information to management and employees. However, this does not address the issue of how the information can be used to make better decisions to enhance work-unit or organizational effectiveness.

> **Knowledge management tends to treat knowledge as a tangible thing, as a stock or a quantity, and therefore separates knowledge as a thing from the use of that thing.** The presumption is that simply possessing knowledge that can help make better decisions necessarily means the knowledge will be used. In many cases, this is not the case.

> **Formal systems can't easily store or transfer tacit knowledge.** Tacit knowledge refers to information important for doing something effectively that cannot be captured, measured, or codified by formal knowledge systems in organizations. Tacit knowledge tends to be acquired through specific experiences, observations of others, trial and error, and stories. Due to these characteristics of tacit knowledge, it becomes more difficult to transmit this knowledge to others in an organization and to get them to use it.

> **The people responsible for transferring and implementing knowledge management frequently do not understand the actual work being documented.** This is a common problem in that the designers of formal knowledge management systems do not comprehend the key underlying business processes, and therefore they may not have the capacity to design a system that facilitates the implementation of that knowledge by end users.

> **Knowledge management tends to focus on specific practices and ignore the importance of philosophy.** This refers to the tendency for people to want to know "what to do" to solve problems they face in their organizations. However, if the knowledge acquired by a manager or business professional is merely a collection of practices without a coherent, overarching philosophy, it becomes difficult to implement these practices. These individual practices may not be consistent with one another (that is, they do not make sense when implemented together). It is the philosophy that provides a framework for thinking about and implementing a set of strategies geared toward achieving specific business objectives.

Overcoming the knowing–doing gap represents one of the greatest challenges to managers in real-world organizations. Meetings, planning sessions, mission statements, and strategic plans with conceptual frameworks help develop the road map or blueprint for action in an organization, but the ultimate success of the firm is determined by its ability to implement or execute its plans in order to achieve organizational objectives and business results.

Pfeffer and Sutton offer the following recommendations for bridging the knowing–doing gap that exists in so many organizations:[41]

> **Why before how: Philosophy is important.** Make sure all members of an organization understand and are committed to a way of thinking about how to achieve given business objectives. This can be done through new employee orientations, formal training programs, and modifying the company's mission statement (formal statement of its purpose and values).

> **Knowing comes from doing and teaching others how.** Teaching through apprenticeships, coaching, and mentoring helps organizational members see how to "do the right things." From this emphasis on action comes a deeper understanding of what needs to be done and why (i.e., knowing).

> **Action comes before elegant plans and concepts.** Too many organizations have wasted far too much time attempting to develop elaborate conceptual frameworks and elegant strategic plans only to fail when it came to their implementation. The key is to focus on the bottom line of taking action and to ensure that talking about what to do is always coupled with specific actions.

> **There is no doing without mistakes.** What is the company's response? Every organization, no matter how successful, makes mistakes. The key is, does an organization possess a philosophy, approach, and culture that enables it to learn from its mistakes to reduce the likelihood of committing the same error in the future? Organizations that bridge the knowing–doing gap are able to learn and become smarter based on their successes and failures in the marketplace.

> **Fear fosters knowing–doing gaps.** So drive out fear. Fear often prevents people from doing what they know they should do in organizations. Management must create a value system, organizational culture, and policies and procedures that do not punish individuals for doing the right thing even if the results are less than optimal.

> **Beware of false analogies: Fight the competition, not each other.** Many organizations have created organizational cultures and systems that promote internal competition such as forced distribution performance appraisal systems and highly competitive reward and recognition systems. The presence of internal competition in an organization undermines cooperation and collaboration between individuals and work units. This results in a we versus they mentality in which important knowledge or information that one individual or work unit possesses may not be shared with others in the organization for the benefit of the overall firm. Clearly, management must promote a cooperative work environment where everyone is committed to working together in order to achieve the same business objectives.

> **Measure what matters and what can help turn knowledge into action.** The emphasis here is for management to identify a handful of critical measures of success for the organization and to track them on an ongoing basis. Focusing on these measures improves management's ability to identify and implement appropriate actions that will enhance the future performance of the company.

> **It matters what leaders do, how they spend their time, and how they allocate resources.** Ultimately, it is the responsibility of the leadership in organizations to create an organizational system and culture that value

creating, managing, and sharing knowledge as well as taking appropriate action to ensure effective implementation.

Now complete Skills Practice 1-5 to help you analyze why knowing–doing gaps may exist in a number of situations and then to develop specific strategies for eliminating these gaps. Remember, planning is important, but it is the implementation or execution of the plan that matters most in the end!

THE SOCIAL LEARNING PERSPECTIVE

To enhance your learning experience, we apply a social learning perspective in this text.[42] The generalized steps of the social learning perspective are presented in Figure 1-5.

We apply the social learning perspective through a "4 A's" organizing framework, as shown in Figure 1-6. Our steps, corresponding to the generalized steps of the social learning perspective, have the following content:

> **Skills assessment.** This first step in skill learning is to get baseline measures on important skills and to foster interest in those skills. We encourage this in each chapter through Pretest Skills Assessment exercises and a variety of other self-assessment scales. In addition, some Skills Practice exercises contain skills assessment elements.

> **Skills awareness.** This step includes discussion of important background material, such as why the topic is important, key approaches to mastering the skill, and other relevant information. This text employs a wide range of tools to facilitate this step. Along with thorough coverage of key concepts in the body of the chapters, several other features are incorporated. These include a Devil's Advocate feature to respond to commonly raised questions (available on the text Web site), Voice of Experience interviews with practitioners, Web-Wise features suggesting links to important Internet material (on the text Web site), Focus on Management segments illustrating current management applications of concepts, and Lighten Up boxes to showcase unique, creative, and sometimes humorous applications. In addition, Bottom Line figures provide visual summaries of important material, a Top Ten List summarizes some key lessons of the chapter, and chapter-end questions encourage review and critical thinking.

> **Skills attainment.** Here, through a variety of experiential methods, you develop the skill. Many of the text features facilitate skill attainment, but the several Skills Practice exercises in each chapter serve as the primary tools to help you in this critical step. You will see these take many forms, such as role playing, fieldwork exercises, development of action plans, and practice with specific techniques.

FIGURE 1-5
The Social Learning Perspective

FIGURE 1-6
The "4 A's" of Skill Learning

Skills Assessment → Skills Awareness → Skills Attainment → Skills Application

> **Skills application.** This final step involves life application. These include, for instance, using the skills in case analyses, life situations, field projects, and other applications. Text elements to support this step include many of the Skills Practice exercises and chapter-end material such as two Web exercises, two cases, and a video case.

The following Bottom Line lays out the basic step-by-step procedure that will help you master the key management skills needed for success in real-world organizations. You will see this process used throughout the book as the general framework for enhancing your skill development process. The Focus on Management feature discusses the importance of skills in the global labor market.

THE MANAGEMENT SKILLS FRAMEWORK

Many practitioners and scholars have attempted to list and classify key managerial skills.[43] The lists, generated from observing effective and ineffective managers, surveys

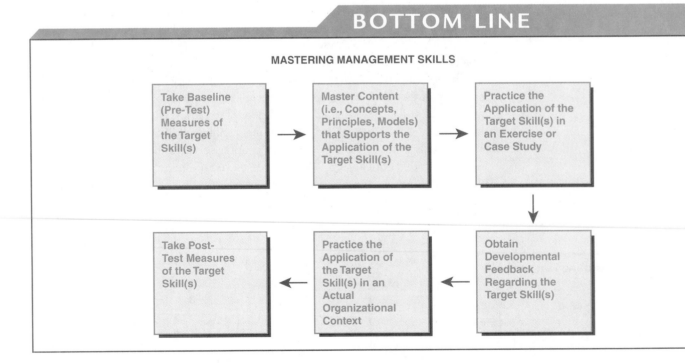

BOTTOM LINE

MASTERING MANAGEMENT SKILLS

Take Baseline (Pre-Test) Measures of the Target Skill(s) → Master Content (i.e., Concepts, Principles, Models) that Supports the Application of the Target Skill(s) → Practice the Application of the Target Skill(s) in an Exercise or Case Study → Obtain Developmental Feedback Regarding the Target Skill(s) → Practice the Application of the Target Skill(s) in an Actual Organizational Context → Take Post-Test Measures of the Target Skill(s)

FOCUS ON MANAGEMENT

SKILLS IN THE GLOBAL LABOR MARKET

With lowered trade barriers, the growth of electronic communications, and the search for new markets and labor forces, firms and their management are becoming increasingly global. As just one illustration of this, a record number of foreign CEOs are now running major companies in the United States.[44] Surveys show that the number of international assignments of employees is expected to accelerate in the next five years. However, many people fail in international assignments, and almost half say they would not work abroad again. Between 20 percent and 40 percent return to their home country early, and many quit their firms within a year of returning.[45] This all suggests that employees often lack the skills needed to succeed in international positions. For example, such assignments require employees to be especially attuned to cultural differences and to subtle nuances of nonverbal communication, to adapt to change, to work in diverse teams, to be sensitive to others' perceptions, and to tailor their leadership and motivational behaviors to fit national differences.

of CEOs, managers, and interviewers, and other methodologies, show rather remarkable similarities. For example, most lists contain the skills of communicating, interpersonal relations, planning and goal setting, problem solving, managing conflict, motivating others, managing change, and teamwork. Some lists contain additional skills such as stress management, time management, strategic planning, delegating, group problem solving, and building power and influence. We address each of these skills in this text.

Attempts to place managerial skills into categories generally yield three or four skills sets. For example, the skills may be classified as technical, interpersonal or human, and conceptual (as seen in Figure 1-3),[46] or as technical, human, political, and conceptual.[47] Technical skills include knowledge about methods, processes, and techniques designed to carry out some specialized activity as well as the ability to use tools and equipment related to the activity.[48] Interpersonal or human skills (sometimes split into human and political skills) deal with human behavior and interpersonal processes, communication, cooperation, and social sensitivity. Conceptual skills include analytical ability, creativity, efficiency in problem solving, and ability to recognize opportunities and potential problems. Thus the typology distinguishes among abilities to deal with things, people, and ideas and concepts.

Our management skills framework, presented in Figure 1-7, focuses on human and conceptual skills. We classify the skills as primarily personal (such as self-management and critical thinking); interpersonal (such as communicating and resolving conflict); and managerial (such as leading, motivating, managing teams, strategic planning, and creating a positive work culture). Thus, each of these sets contains some conceptual skills and some human skills. We view the three sets as at least partly sequential. For instance, the ability to think critically may facilitate valuing of differences or conflict resolution, and the ability to communicate effectively or to empower others may assist in leading, motivating, and managing teams. Be sure not to interpret the figure as suggesting the categories are completely distinct or that elements of one are not relevant to another. Instead, the intent is to provide a primary framework for classification of skills.

FIGURE 1-7

Management Skills Framework

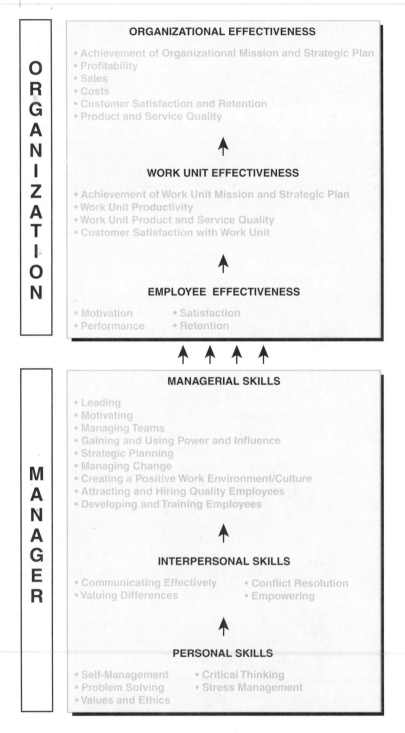

Further, our framework considers three levels of effectiveness—employee, work unit, and organizational. Employee effectiveness may be gauged by motivation, performance, participation behaviors (such as attendance and retention), and personal well-being and satisfaction. Work-unit effectiveness may relate to achieving the work unit's mission and strategic plan, productivity, quality, and customer satisfaction. Finally, organizational effectiveness may take such forms as achieving the organizational mission and strategic plan, profitability, customer satisfaction, and other criteria. We view organizational effectiveness broadly and do not consider it only in terms of profitability or shareholder returns. Again, we see these levels of effectiveness as sequential; employee effectiveness is an input to work-unit effectiveness that in turn fosters organizational effectiveness. We do not mean to imply these relationships are simple or automatic, or that, for example, an effective work unit cannot facilitate employee effectiveness.

ACTION PLANNING AND IMPLEMENTATION

Recall the action plan you developed in the Pretest Skills Assessment activity. You will be doing quite a bit of action plan development throughout this book as you work through the various exercises and learning activities in each chapter. Given this, let's talk a bit about what action planning is and what you need to do to apply it effectively.

Action planning is one of the most important activities you will engage in as a manager.[49] This refers to the process a manager uses to formulate the specific steps he or she takes when addressing business problems and challenges. In the real world, the issue of what needs to be done is always a bottom-line concern. The action plan becomes the blueprint or road map for actual implementation. We discuss action planning together with implementation, because they should be processes that are inextricably linked. Unfortunately, many organizations fail to recognize this important link.

Here are some basic guidelines for developing and implementing effective action plans. First, the process *must* be systematic and actively managed. A manager needs to start with a clear understanding of his or her objectives and how to achieve them through the implementation of specific action steps. In the real world, managers face complex and rapidly changing business environments, so a systematic process is needed. This is a challenge for many students who are more comfortable with an unstructured and spontaneous approach. Second, action planning requires a layering approach, in which action steps are translated into specific supporting actions in relation to each employee involved with implementation. The basic question here is, "Who will be responsible for doing what in the implementation process?" Finally, ongoing and systematic evaluation of your results after implementing the action plan is critical in order to maintain a focus on your bottom-line objectives as a manager. Again, this part of the process seems straightforward enough on the surface, but it requires ongoing effort on your part to evaluate the effectiveness of the action plan and to make appropriate modifications to ensure its long-term success.

A summary of the basic steps associated with developing and implementing an action plan is presented in the Bottom Line feature.

Now complete the action planning exercise in Skills Practice 1-6. This will give you an opportunity to apply the basic steps of the action planning process to a specific management situation.

BOTTOM LINE

ACTION PLANNING AND IMPLEMENTATION

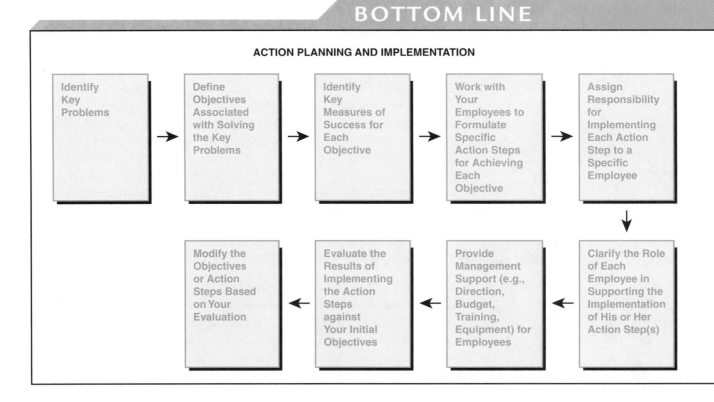

Next complete Skills Practice 1-7 by developing a tree diagram. This is a valuable tool that can help support the development of action plans. Finally, complete Skills Practice 1-8. It will help you evaluate your personal strengths and weaknesses and identify specific management knowledge and skill objectives you want to achieve after reading this text.

TOP TEN LIST: KEY POINTS TO REMEMBER

THE MANAGEMENT CHALLENGE: CRITICAL SKILLS FOR THE NEW WORKPLACE

10. Management effectiveness is a key determinant of organizational success or failure.

9. The skills needed for success in college and the skills needed for success in the business world are very different.

8. Managers must identify specific strategies for taking what they know about effective management and translating it into specific action.

7. The skills you learn from this book will be valuable to you even if you do not obtain a managerial or supervisory job immediately after graduating from college.

6. Action planning is a systematic process for identifying appropriate steps to take to address a given problem or challenge.

5. It is the implementation or execution of business plans that is key in determining the ultimate success of an organization.

4. Learning is a lifelong process.

3. Use your Management Skills Mastery Plan to keep yourself focused on achieving specific learning objectives by the time you complete this book.

2. Developing management skills will greatly enhance your preparation for the real world of business organizations.

1. Effective management in the real world involves much more than just common sense.

QUESTIONS FOR REVIEW AND REFLECTION

REVIEW QUESTIONS

1. How are management skills related to company success?

2. What is some evidence that companies are concerned about employees' managerial skills and believe those skills can be learned?

3. What are 16 critical "skills employers want"?

4. Identify seven primary differences between determinants of success in school and business.

5. What are six developments in the modern workplace that are making managerial skills more important?

6. What is the knowing–doing gap? How might it be overcome?

7. Describe the steps in the social learning perspective and indicate which text features address each step.

8. Discuss the management skills framework on which the text is based.

9. Identify the stages of action planning and implementation.

CRITICAL THINKING QUESTIONS

1. As noted in the chapter, the Bureau of Labor Statistics predicts the average 22-year-old college graduate in the year 2000 will have more than eight different employers before he or she reaches the age of 32. Consider the skills listed in Figure 1-1.
   a. Which of these skills might become more important because of frequent job changes?
   b. Which of these skills might be enhanced by frequent job changes?
   c. Which of these skills might be jeopardized by frequent job changes?
   For each answer, justify your choices.

2. The chapter discusses reasons for the knowing–doing gap. We indicated in our discussion of the text philosophy that you must have a solid understanding of concepts in order to apply skills properly. The lack of that understanding might constitute a doing–knowing gap. What characteristics of individuals and work environments might foster a doing–knowing gap?

3. Upon hearing that the Bureau of Labor Statistics projects young college graduates will stay with an employer an average of just 15 months, a CEO says, "We need to rethink the value of skills training. Why should we be spending money to train someone who

will probably only be here for a year or so?" How would you respond?

4. Consider the following characteristics of today's workplace: (a) globalization, (b) downsizing, (c) increasing diversity, and (d) increasing rates of change. For each of the trends, discuss how it might impact the importance of one of the skills listed in Figure 1-1.

5. When told a company has a policy of "hiring for the second job"—that is, of considering skill requirements not just of the entry-level job but also of higher-level jobs in making a selection decision—a job applicant says, "That's not fair. I'm applying for an entry-level job, and I have good qualifications for that job. I'm not applying to be a manager." Do you agree with the applicant's argument? Why or why not?

6. One philosophy of the text is that managerial skills should be directed toward enhancing both personal and organizational outcomes. Do you agree that managers should pay attention to factors that may have no direct impact on organizational outcomes? Why or why not?

EXPERIENTIAL EXERCISES

WEB EXERCISE 1-1: *FORTUNE* SKILLS ARTICLES

Go to the *Fortune* magazine Web site at **http://www.fortune.com/fortune**.

In the "Search Fortune" box, type "skills." You will be given a listing of more than 1,500 *Fortune* articles dealing with skills, with titles such as "Are You Smart Enough to Keep Your Job?," "What Team Leaders Need to Know," "How Safe Is Your Job?," "Really Important Things You Need to Know," and "You Are Absolutely, Positively on Your Own." Click on a title to access the full text of the article.

1. Select any two articles from the search.
2. Provide a one- to two-page summary of each article.
3. For each article, select one fact or idea you think is especially important for your future career. Discuss the fact or idea and indicate why you think it is important.

WEB EXERCISE 1-2: HUMAN PRINCIPLES FROM NINE PRIVATE-SECTOR ORGANIZATIONS

The U.S. General Accounting Office (GAO) is the investigative arm of Congress. GAO exists to support Congress in meeting its constitutional responsibilities and help improve the performance and accountability of the federal government for the American people. In January 2000, the GAO released the report "Human Capital: Key Principles from Nine Private Sector Organizations." It calls for federal managers to turn to the private sector to find examples they "may wish to consider as they steer their agencies toward higher performance." The report also discusses 10 "Principles of Human Capital" based on the experience of such private-sector firms as Federal Express Corp., Marriott International, Merck & Co., Motorola, and Southwest Airlines. Read the report at **http://frwebgate.access.gpo.gov/cgi-bin/useftp.cgi?IPaddress=162.140.64.21&filename=gg00028.txt&directory=/diskb/wais/data/gao**, and then respond to the following questions:

1. What are the 10 principles identified in the report?
2. Select and discuss any one of the principles, based on information presented in the report and your own knowledge concerning the principle.
3. Summarize one of the case illustrations related to the selected principle.
4. Do you think federal agencies would be able to implement the principle successfully? Why or why not?

CASE 1-1

BREAKTHROUGH: THE TRANSFORMATION OF CADILLAC

History of the Company
Cadillac, the luxury division of General Motors Corporation, the world's largest automaker, has been around for almost 100 years now. Most Americans considered it the "Standard of the World" during the 1950s and 1960s. In those days, owning a Cadillac, with its signature tail fins and

generous application of chrome, meant "you had made it." Cadillac was the choice of vehicle among celebrities such as Elvis Presley and Marilyn Monroe. At its peak in 1978, Cadillac sold 347,000 cars a year, making it the undisputed king of luxury cars in the United States.

The Decline of an American Icon (1970–2001)

However, in the late 1970s through the early 1990s, Cadillac began a gradual but dramatic slide in sales, profits, quality and prestige. The oil crisis in the 1970s motivated customers to seek more fuel-efficient vehicles. Foreign competition from Japanese automakers such as Toyota and Honda flooded the U.S. market with high-quality, reliable, and fuel-efficient vehicles. Later, Japanese automakers created luxury car lines, including Lexus, Infiniti, and Acura, that set new benchmarks for quality, performance, and luxury in the industry. Although European car makers (e.g., Mercedes-Benz, BMW, Audi, and Jaguar) experienced some setbacks from Japanese competition as well, large-scale transformations at these companies produced a wide range of new luxury "world-class vehicles." This has been especially true in recent years in the cases of Jaguar and Audi.

Meanwhile, Cadillac (and Lincoln, its domestic luxury car maker counterpart) clung to their traditional customer base by offering large, roomy sedans and coupes with powerful engines but "floaty" rides and sloppy handling that many drivers described as feeling like they were "sailing on a yacht." Increasingly the traditional vehicles that Cadillac offered such as the DeVille and Fleetwood became less and less appealing to younger and more sophisticated consumers.

Cadillac makers have often taken too many shortcuts in their product development. This has manifested itself in "badge engineering," in which they took a vehicle from another General Motors division such as Chevrolet or Oldsmobile, made some cosmetic changes to the vehicle (e.g., adding leather seats and a more powerful engine), and a Cadillac badge was attached to the vehicle. Savvy car drivers saw right through this strategy, though, and it further diluted and tarnished the Cadillac brand name. The most recent examples of this strategy included the Catera entry-level luxury sedan, based on an Opel (a GM subsidiary in Germany) platform, and the first-generation Escalade, a luxury sport-utility vehicle that was rushed to market in less than a year based on the Chevrolet/GMC Tahoe and Yukon.

Up until around 2002, when the name "Cadillac" was mentioned to consumers in their 20s and 30s, their common response was "these are cars for older people in their 60s" or a Cadillac is "their dad's car." Cadillac had lost its position as the top seller of luxury vehicles in the United States (BMW, Lexus, and Mercedes-Benz are ahead of Cadillac in sales volume) with sales stuck at around 180,000 vehicles per year.

In the area of quality and dependability, reviews from both auto analysts and closely watched annual surveys of consumers, such as JD Power and Associates and Consumer Reports, provided mixed results for the most part. For example, Cadillac rarely ranked among the top vehicles in JD Power and Associates initial quality surveys. None of its vehicles ranked among the top three in any category in the 2000 study. Although Cadillac has traditionally scored well in the JD Power Five-Year Vehicle Dependability Study, it fell to 11th place in the 2000 study from its more traditional ranking of 1st or 2nd (after Lexus).

The greatest threat for Cadillac was that many consumers didn't even consider it when they were in the market for a luxury vehicle. Moreover, the average age of a Cadillac customer was about 67 years. Cadillac's customer base was literally dying off.

The Revival of an American Icon (2001–present)

However, don't be so fast in counting out Cadillac in the global luxury vehicle race. Management at Cadillac has a plan that it hopes will revive Cadillac and once again make it the "Standard of the World." Although Cadillac has attempted to reinvent itself before, there is good reason to be cautiously optimistic this time. Michael O'Malley started the changes at the Cadillac division by freshening its corporate logo to give it a more contemporary look and creating new marketing concepts called "Art and Science" and the "Power of &." In 2001, Mark LaNeve took over as head of Cadillac. The new leadership and strategies have led to a radically different design philosophy, which has produced futuristic-looking vehicles with sharp edges and creases that resemble the stealth fighters used in the U.S. military. Some examples of vehicles designed with this new approach are the second-generation 2002 Cadillac Escalade and CTS sedan and the 2004 Cadillac Evoq roadster and SRX crossover vehicle. In 2005, a new STS (Sports Touring Sedan) to compete with the BMW 5-Series will hit the market. Cadillac also participated in the 24-hour LeMans race in 2000 for the first time since 1950. This was done to enhance the visibility of Cadillac as a global brand name and to associate the name more with high-performance racing. A high-performance version of the CTS called CTS-V will join the professional racing circuit in 2004 as well.

Cadillac's multi-faceted strategy for transforming itself is composed of the following elements:

Strengthening the Cadillac Image

Cadillac advertisements use rock music from Led Zeppelin, and Cadillac is displaying its cars at upscale events such as at the Oscars and at Times Square in New York and sponsoring high-visibility events such as National Football League games.

Improving Quality

Cadillac has shown significant improvement in a variety of quality rankings for automobiles in the last couple of years including JD Power and Associates. Its vehicles have also received favorable reviews from auto critics and magazines. Cadillac has a state-of-the-art production facility in Lansing, Michigan, that helps it increase productivity, reduce costs, and improve quality.

Enhancing the Performance Factor in its Vehicles

Cadillac will soon unveil new V Series vehicles that will emphasize performance. The first V Series vehicle will be a 2004 CTS-V. Other models such as the Escalade and SRX will also be available as V Series versions in the future.

Presentation

Cadillac dealers are being given incentives to upgrade the appearance of their showrooms to make them more luxurious.

Results

So far, Cadillac has achieved tremendous success in making Cadillac "cool again." Sales of its 2004 CTS and Escalade have both exceeded 35,000 each for the year 2003. Overall sales are expected to break the 200,000 unit mark in 2004.

The Escalade has become the vehicle of choice for many professional athletes and celebrities. The average age of a Cadillac customer has dropped into the mid 40s for the Escalade and the low 50s for the CTS. The residual value of Cadillacs has moved close to what a consumer would get for a BMW or Lexus. Quality scores are up for Cadillac vehicles. You may have even seen some Cadillac vehicles in chase scenes in some high visibility movies such as *Matrix Reloaded*, *Bad Boys II*, and *Italian Job*. The bottom line is that Cadillac management fully recognizes the stakes involved with their current turn-around strategy. In fact, some GM insiders have speculated that unless Cadillac can pull off its current turnaround, it could very well die. David Cole, the managing director of the University of Michigan's Office of Automotive Transportation, believes that Cadillac can come back, "if they execute well."

Discussion Questions

1. What kinds of management problems contributed to Cadillac's current situation?

2. What kinds of management skills will be needed at Cadillac in order to implement its turnaround strategy successfully?

3. Evaluate Cadillac's turnaround strategy. Do you think it will work? Why or why not?

4. What are the implications of this case for you as a future manager?

Source: D. Welch, "The Second Coming of Cadillac: Now Its Cars Are Cool. Will Bold Design and Lots of Horsepower Keep the Brand Rolling?" *Business Week*, November 24, 2003, pp. 79–80.

CASE 1-2

HOOTERS OF AMERICA, INC.—A BUSINESS SUCCESS STORY⁵⁰

Hooters of America, Inc. is an Atlanta-based operator and franchiser of 342 Hooters restaurant locations in 43 states, and 27 in other countries including Argentina, Austria, Brazil, Canada, England, Mexico, Puerto Rico, Singapore, Switzerland, and Taiwan. Its establishments are famous for their casual beach-themed dining environments filled with jukebox music from the 1950s and 1960s, sports programming shown on televisions, soups, sandwiches and buffalo wings, and the 15,000 Hooters Girls clad in T-shirts and orange shorts who serve the predominantly male customers. The Hooters concept can be summarized in its slogan: "Delightfully tacky, yet unrefined."

Hooters has two mission statements—one for its brand and one for its restaurants:⁵¹

This is the Hooters Brand Mission Statement:

To provide a family of hospitality services that achieves excellence and enhances lifestyles of all who come in contact with the Hooters brand.

The Hooters Restaurant Mission Statement is as follows:

We are committed to providing an environment of employee growth and development so that we can provide every guest a unique, entertaining dining experience in a fun and casual atmosphere delivered by attractive, vivacious Hooters Girls while making positive contributions to the communities in which we live.

Hooters: The Beginning

Hooters was started as a beach bar in Clearwater, Florida in October 1983 by a group of six friends originally from the

Midwest. They scraped together $140,000 to open the restaurant.

Finding the "Hooters Girl"

Ed Droste (one of the six founders) recruited the first Hooters girl in 1983. She matched his image of what the Hooters girl should be: bosomy but bubbly, knowledgeable about sports trivia, quick witted, an all-American girl, and interested in helping with charity fund-raising. One person described the Hooters girl as "naughty but not too naughty" or "PG-13."

Along Comes Hugh Connerty

Hugh Connerty was in Florida looking for locations for his steakhouse chain, but his plans quickly changed after one night at Hooters. Connerty offered to pay $50,000 to each of the six founders for the following deal. The original six could keep the Hooters trademark, earn three cents on each dollar his Hooters girls brought in and continue to expand throughout the six county Tampa Bay area, but Connerty could build anywhere else in the United States. In addition, the deal required him to remain faithful to every aspect of the original Hooters. The six founders accepted.

Introducing Bob Brooks . . .

Although Connerty had tremendous vision, what he lacked was the capital to back it up. So he approached Bob Brooks for loans. Not only was Brooks rich, but he also knew the restaurant industry quite well because several big-name restaurants bought from his food service company, Naturally Fresh. In 1988, Brooks called the notes (loans) and Connerty was not able to pay. So, Brooks took over Hooters development rights. Connerty got to keep two Hooters restaurants, one in Jacksonville and the other in Tallahassee.

Let the Feuding Begin!

Brooks had the capital to push Hooters into new territory, but what he lacked was the control to make decisions. The original six still had this power. This situation became problematic because Brooks did not like to be told what to do.

It started with Brooks pushing the restaurant to buy his Naturally Fresh products. For example, Brooks wanted Hooters to use his Naturally Fresh salad dressing. The originally six vetoed it, saying they preferred their original version.

The next big argument arose in the early 1990s, when the six founders wanted to abandon the midriff-baring shirts that the Hooters girls had always worn for a little less showy outfit: a tucked-in cotton tank top. Brooks felt the girls should wear Lycra. Again, the founders rejected this option, saying that Lycra was too tight and would taint their PG-13 image. They added that it would drive away their "family" crowd which contributed to about 30 percent of their total business.

These types of arguments continued throughout the decade.

The Hooters Girl Lawsuit

In 1995 the Equal Employment Opportunity Commission (EEOC) filed a lawsuit against Hooters, claiming that, employing only female servers, they were discriminating against men. Hooters counter-attacked by featuring an unshaven male restaurant manager, Vince, in a Hooters girl outfit and a blonde wig. This image replaced the previous one of the Hooters Girl in Hooters's billboard and ad campaigns. Underneath the picture read their anti-EEOC message: "Washington, Get a Grip!" Shortly after, the EEOC dropped the lawsuit, which created a brief truce between Brooks and the six founders, but not for long.

Going Too Far?

After the EEOC dropped the matter, Brooks launched a new campaign: a T-shirt proclaiming "She Survives!" The founders were furious, claiming Brooks had violated licensing agreements and sales needed to cease. This sparked one lawsuit after another between Brooks and the founders. The hostilities between the two camps were beginning to affect business.

A White Flag Is Finally Raised

The turn of the new century finally brought cooperation between the founders and Brooks. The founders reviewed some of Brooks's positive initiatives. In 1992, it was Brooks's idea to have Hooters sponsor Alan Kulwicki, who won the Winston Cup as NASCAR's top driver. In 1995, Brooks decided to drop NASCAR and start his own stock car racing series called Hooters Pro-Cup. He also started the Hooters minor golf league. In 2001, after much discussion, the founders decided to sell Brooks the Hooters trademark for $60 million. They retained the Tampa Bay, Chicago and Manhattan-area restaurants. They also held the rights to open a Hooters hotel and casino in Las Vegas and the rights if Hooters ever went to Hollywood (i.e., *Hooters: The Movie*). Brooks got everything else.

The Present and the Future

Hooters has sustained significant growth since its beginning in 1983. Its 2003 revenues are projected to be about $750 million. A major source of this revenue is the 30 million pounds of buffalo wings it sells each year. The company now has four lines of retail food, a golf tour, and two auto racing circuits. In addition, Hooters Air started in March 2003 with flights going from Newark, New Jersey, Baltimore, and Atlanta to Myrtle Beach, South Carolina. The plane sports the corporate colors of orange and white, with two Hooters girls on each flight reading sports trivia and giving away

Hooters merchandise. In the future, Bob Brooks, the CEO of Hooters of America, Inc., plans to expand to a thousand Hooters restaurant locations across the United States. When asked about the secret to Hooters success, Brooks's response is, "Good food, cold beer, and pretty girls never go out of style."

Discussion Questions

1. What types of management skills did the founders and subsequent leaders at Hooters need to establish the company and sustain its success?

2. What are the biggest opportunities for Hooters in the future? What actions should management take to address these opportunities?

3. What are the biggest challenges for Hooters in the future? What actions should management take to address these challenges?

4. What are the practical implications of this case for you as a future manager in a real-world organization?

VIDEO CASE: SUNSHINE CLEANING SYSTEMS, JIAN, AND ARCHWAY COOKIES

Running Time: 14:28

THE EVOLUTION OF MANAGEMENT

This video discusses three successful companies—SunShine Cleaning Systems, JIAN, and Archway Cookies—that face very different environments and have chosen to rely on distinct philosophies in managing organizational behavior.

The video shows executives and other employees from each of the companies as they discuss the ways their companies have met the challenges of their competitive environments. After viewing the video, answer the following questions:

1. In what ways, such as markets, technologies, available labor pool, and other dimensions, do the environments of SunShine, JIAN, and Archway differ?

2. According to the video, what are the respective philosophies adopted by SunShine, JIAN, and Archway? Describe each of these philosophies.

3. Why is a loyal and dedicated work force so important to SunShine? What steps has SunShine taken to earn employee loyalty and dedication?

4. How has the competitive environment faced by JIAN shaped its management approaches? What sort of employees does JIAN need? What has JIAN done to create an organization that takes advantage of its strengths?

5. What are some signs that Archway has been successful in developing a satisfied and effective work force?

6. What steps has Archway taken to ensure it produces and delivers quality cookies?

7. Could the approaches taken by SunShine, JIAN, and Archway be used together? Why or why not?

http://www.sunclean.com/outside_home.asp

http://www.jian.com/

http://www.archwaycookies.com/

LIGHTEN UP[52]

PERFORMANCE!

Companies are seeking creative ways to develop their employees' skills, and many are turning to literature, music, and the arts. When management consulting firm McKinsey & Company wanted to develop its employees' abilities to inspire, it hired outsiders to help the firm's consultants and partners write and stage an opera in three days. At Sears, Lockheed Martin, and Bristol Myers Squibb, a conductor and symphony orchestra rehearse Brahms to bring alive issues of leadership and teamwork for aspiring top managers. Kodak, Arthur Andersen, and Boeing have brought in poets to foster employees' creativity. Still other firms are using Shakespeare's *Henry V* as a case study on vision, strategy, and leadership skills, or are having employees act out playlets. Companies increasingly are coming to believe that, in an economy where firms such as Amazon.com have found ways to recombine resources to redefine whole industries, skills fostering vision, flair, and creativity are the new fuel. The arts are a natural reservoir for that fuel.

SKILLS PRACTICE

Best and Worst Managers

Skill Objective

To develop skill in evaluating how specific skills contribute to a manager's overall effectiveness.

Procedure

Note: Download the worksheet for this exercise from the text Web site. This will help guide you through the exercise.

1. This exercise can be completed individually or in groups of three to five students.
2. Think about the part-time jobs and internships you have held (or currently hold) and the bosses you have had for each of these jobs.
3. Now identify the boss who you feel is or was the *best* manager you have had as an employee.
4. Think about the specific things *(management practices)* your best boss did that made him or her so effective as a manager.
5. Given your answers in the previous step, identify the *skills* your best boss possessed in order to do the things that made him or her a highly effective manager. Be specific.
6. Now repeat steps 2 through 5 using the boss who you feel was the *worst* manager you have had. Use a separate piece of paper for recording your summary of this person.
7. Finally, place the summaries of your best and worst managers next to each other.
8. Answer the following questions.

Discussion Questions

1. How do your best and worst managers differ from one another in terms of the things they did (i.e., management practices)?
2. How do your best and worst managers differ from one another in terms of the management skills they possessed?

SKILLS PRACTICE

A Humorous Look at Corporate Life: **Office Space**

Skill Objective

To develop skill in identifying and analyzing a variety of management issues in an organizational setting.

Procedure

1. Obtain a copy of the movie *Office Space* starring Ron Livingston and Jennifer Anniston. It is available on VHS and DVD and can be rented or purchased from a local video store or retailer.
2. Watch the movie (in class or at home on your own). Note: Download the worksheet developed for this exercise from the Web site for this book. This will help you develop a list of scenes in the movie that are relevant for answering the discussion questions below.
3. Discuss the following questions as a class.

a. How would you describe Peter's (the main character's) job? Why does he dislike his job so much? Justify your answer using specific scenes and dialogue from the movie.
b. How would you describe Peter's boss (Bill Lumbergh)? To what degree is he an effective manager? Justify your answer using specific scenes and dialogue from the movie.
c. How would you describe the organization that Peter works for in terms of the work environment, his coworkers, the executives, and the company's policies and practices? Do these factors contribute to making the organization effective or dysfunctional? Justify your answer using specific scenes and dialogue from the movie.

SKILLS PRACTICE

Profiling the Job of a Real-World Manager (A Fieldwork Exercise)

Skill Objective

To develop skill in profiling the activities and skills associated with the job of a manager in an actual organizational setting.

Procedure

1. Identify a business professional you know who is currently in a managerial role in his or her organization and willing to be interviewed for this exercise.
2. Schedule a meeting of between 30 and 60 minutes with the manager.
3. In the interview, ask the manager the following questions:
   a. What is your position title?
   b. How long have you been in this position?
   c. What is the name of the work unit you manage?
   d. How many employees report to you?
   e. What are your primary duties and responsibilities in your position?
   f. What do you like most about being a manager?
   g. What do you like least about being a manager?
   h. What are the key areas of knowledge you need to be an effective manager?
   i. What are the critical skills you need to be an effective manager?
4. Summarize the results of your interview.
5. Answer the discussion questions below, based on the interview.
6. (Optional) Present a brief summary of your interview to your class and discuss what you learned from the exercise.

Discussion Questions

1. What did you learn about the job of a manager?
2. Which of the manager's responses, if any, surprised you? Why?
3. What do you see as being the most challenging aspects of being a manager?
4. What do you think you can do to develop the knowledge and skills needed to prepare yourself for a management position in the real world?

SKILLS PRACTICE

Dirty Politics in Action: **Disclosure**

Skill Objective

To develop skill in identifying and analyzing critical skills needed for success in a corporate environment.

Procedure

1. Obtain a copy of the movie *Disclosure* starring Michael Douglas and Demi Moore. It is available on VHS and DVD and can be rented or purchased from a local video store or retailer.
2. Watch the movie (in class or at home on your own).
   Note: Download the worksheet developed for this exercise from the Web site for this book. This will help you develop a list of scenes in the movie that are relevant for answering the discussion questions below.
3. Discuss the following questions as a class:
   a. What types of mistakes does Tom Sanders (Douglas) make throughout the film? What do these management mistakes cost him? Justify your answer using specific scenes and dialogue from the movie.
   b. What types of management and organizational skills does Tom Sanders need to use to survive in the movie? Justify your answer using specific scenes and dialogue from the movie.
   c. If you were Tom Sanders, what would you have done differently to handle the various challenges he encountered throughout the movie?
   d. What are the practical implications of this exercise for you as a future manager and leader in a real-world organization?

SKILLS PRACTICE

Bridging the Knowing–Doing Gap

Skill Objective

To identify sources of knowing–doing gaps and to develop strategies for eliminating them.

Procedure

Note: Download the worksheet for this exercise from the text Web site. This will help guide you through the exercise.

1. This activity may be done on an individual basis or in groups of three to five students.
2. Read the following list of common knowing–doing gaps that exist in many organizations in the real world:
   > (1) Managers who say they know employees should be rewarded for doing a good job, but fail to put this into practice with their employees.
   > (2) Managers who say they know they should solicit the input of their employees when making decisions that affect the entire work unit, but fail to put this into practice with their employees.
   > (3) Managers who say they know the use of teams can improve work-unit and organizational performance, but fail to put this into practice with their employees.
   > (4) Managers who say they know a well-trained and highly skilled work force is critical for the long-term competitiveness of a firm, but fail to put this into practice with their employees.
   > (5) Managers who say they know employee pay increases should be based on their job per-

formance, but fail to put this into practice with their employees.
   > (6) Managers who say they know a mission statement for an organization provides the overall direction and vision a company needs to be successful in the long term, but fail to put this into practice with their employees.
   > (7) Managers who say employees need to receive effective and thorough annual performance appraisals so they can develop professionally and improve their job performance, but fail to put this into practice with their employees.

3. For each knowing–doing gap, identify some reasons why this gap may exist. Record your answers on your piece of paper.
4. Now identify at least one action you could take to reduce or eliminate each knowing–doing gap listed. Record your recommendations on your worksheet.
5. Answer the discussion questions. (Optional) You can also present a summary of your results to the rest of your class.

Discussion Questions

1. Based on this exercise, why do you think knowing–doing gaps in management practices are so prevalent in organizations?
2. What kinds of things are most important in eliminating knowing–doing gaps in organizations?
3. Why isn't common sense enough for a person to be an effective manager in the real world?

SKILLS PRACTICE

Action Planning and Implementation

Skill Objective

To develop skill in creating action plans for addressing organizational problems and challenges.

Procedure

Note: Download the worksheet for this exercise from the text Web site. This will help guide you through the exercise.

1. This exercise can be completed on an individual basis or in groups of three to five students.

2. Select and read one of the management scenarios and develop an appropriate action plan using the action planning (Bottom Line) model described in the chapter. Record your plan on the worksheet.

Management Scenario 1

You are the manager of an upscale continental restaurant located in downtown Chicago. Although the restaurant has a good reputation in general, you have been experiencing a variety of operational problems. First, food quality has been declining. Part of the problem is that you have a new, less experienced head chef working in the kitchen. Second, you have been cutting some corners when ordering ingredients in order to reduce your costs. Third, customers have become increasingly frustrated with the 45- to 60-minute waits they have had to endure before being seated, even if they had reservations. The host who takes reservations has been overbooking reservations by 25 percent in order to ensure the dining room is full at all times and to account for no-shows. Fourth, you are concerned about the quality of service your servers are providing for guests. Some of them do not possess very customer service–oriented attitudes, which shows in their interactions with guests. The servers also have been experiencing a high level of job stress as the number of servers scheduled to work each shift has declined. Consequently, each server has to handle an average of 25 tables each night as opposed to the 15 tables considered standard in the past.

Based on this description, develop an action plan for addressing this situation and describe how you would manage the implementation process.

Management Scenario 2

You are the president of a business student organization suffering from a variety of problems. First, 20 students are considered members of the organization, but only about 4 (including yourself) are involved to a significant degree. Second, the organization really lacks a clear sense of what it is supposed to be (i.e., what are its objectives?). Although it is a professional business student organization, most of the organization's activities have involved socializing and going out to bars together. Third, the organization is virtually broke. The most recent bank statement you received showed an account balance of $10.

Develop an action plan for addressing this situation and describe how you would manage the implementation process.

3. (Optional) Present a summary of your action plan to the class and discuss it.

4. Answer the following discussion questions.

Discussion Questions

1. Evaluate the effectiveness of your action planning process. What were the most challenging aspects of the process? To what extent were you able to follow the steps in the action planning process model?

2. Identify and discuss the specific strengths and weaknesses of the action steps in your plan. Explain why you feel the issues you identified are strengths and weaknesses.

3. What are the practical implications of this exercise for you as a future manager in a real-world organization?

SKILLS PRACTICE

1-7   *Skill Level: CHALLENGING*

Developing and Using Tree Diagrams

Skill Objective

To develop skill in creating and using tree diagrams to support action planning.

Procedure

1. Download the worksheet developed for this exercise from the Web site for this textbook.

2. Form groups of five to seven people.

3. Develop a tree diagram by working through the following steps:

   a. **Step 1: Identify an overall goal for improving something of interest to the members of the group.** This could address issues such as how to improve a class, how to address an issue on campus (e.g., crime, employment), or how a business organization can enhance its performance (e.g., improving customer satisfaction, reducing costs, improving product or service quality). Write this goal in the appropriately labeled box in the worksheet for this exercise.

   b. **Step 2: Brainstorm as many supporting goals (subgoals) as possible that would support**

the achievement of the overall goal you iden-tified in step 1. For example, if the overall goal is to reduce costs, one example of a subgoal might be to "restrict business travel expenditures to essential business activities." The key is that each subgoal must support the overall goal. After the group has brainstormed as many potential sub-goals as possible, it should evaluate the pool of subgoals and try to identify the three to five the group feels are most important for supporting the achievement of the overall goal. Write the subgoals the group selects in the column of boxes to the right of the overall goal on the worksheet for this exercise.

c. **Step 3: Identify specific tasks that need to be completed in order to achieve each of the subgoals.** List these tasks in the order in which they need to be implemented. Fill in the tasks that support each subgoal in the column of boxes to the right of the subgoals.

d. **Step 4: Check the tasks and subgoals to make sure everyone feels they support the achievement of the overall goal.**

Discussion Questions

1. What is the value of tree diagrams? How can they be used to enhance managerial and organizational effectiveness?
2. What are the most important steps in designing an effective tree diagram? What are the barriers to this process, and how can you overcome them?
3. What are the most important steps in imple-menting a tree diagram? What are the barriers to this process, and how can you overcome them?
4. What are the practical implications of this exercise for you as a future manager and leader in a real-world organization?

SKILLS PRACTICE

1-8   *Skill Level:* CHALLENGING

Developing My Management Skills Mastery Plan

Skill Objective

To evaluate your personal strengths and weak-nesses and to identify specific management knowledge and skill objectives you want to achieve after reading this book.

Procedure

Note: Download the worksheet for this exercise from the text Web site. This will help guide you through the exercise.

1. Think about yourself in the context of how you have performed as a student and as an employee in your jobs. Try to identify your key personal strengths. For example, include the ability to get along with different types of people, teamwork skills, organizational skills, working well under pres-sure, analytical skills, and so on. Be as frank as pos-sible in making this self-evaluation. In addition, ask three to five people who know you well (such as friends, family members, coworkers, bosses, advi-sors, mentors, or professors) to give you some honest feedback about your personal strengths. Document these results on your worksheet.
2. Again, think about yourself in the context of how you have performed as a student and as an employee in your jobs. Try to identify your key per-sonal weaknesses. For example, include making deci-sions too quickly, not listening well to other people, failing to manage your time, not being open to dif-ferent viewpoints, and so on. Although it is more difficult to do when examining your personal weak-nesses (or "opportunities for improvement"), be as frank as possible in making this self-evaluation. In addition, ask three to five people who know you well (such as friends, family members, coworkers, bosses, advisors, mentors, or professors) to give you some honest feedback about your personal weaknesses. Document these results on your worksheet.
3. Now, looking at the personal strengths and weak-nesses you just identified, list three to seven key *knowledge objectives* (i.e., things you want to know or understand) you want to achieve by the time you have finished reading this book. These objectives should be things you feel will be important for you once you become a manager in an actual organiza-tion after graduation. Record these on your work-sheet.

4. Looking at the personal strengths and weaknesses you listed, identify three to seven key *skill objectives* (i.e., things you want to be able to do) you want to achieve by the time you have finished reading this book. These objectives should be things you feel will be important for you once you become a man-ager in an actual organization after graduation. Record these on your worksheet.

5. Keep this plan for future reference. You will use it as a basis for evaluating how much you have learned at the end of the book!

INDIVIDUAL

PART 1

UNDERSTANDING AND VALUING DIFFERENCES

CHAPTER 2

Skills Objectives

> To develop organizational plans for enhancing work force diversity.

> To assess individual differences in others and to develop strategies for dealing with those differences in a work group.

> To develop strategies for managing cross-cultural differences within a work group.

> To enhance perceptual accuracy in understanding situations and in making managerial decisions.

> To develop sensitivity to differences in others' perceptions of a situation.

> To assess employee job satisfaction and to identify strategies for enhancing it through managerial action and organizational policies and practices.

KNOWLEDGE OBJECTIVES

> Specify forms of diversity in organizations and why they are important.

> Describe approaches companies are taking to value and manage diversity.

> Identify and describe key personality dimensions on which employees may vary.

> Discuss why cross-cultural differences are relevant, and identify important dimensions on which cultures may vary.

> Understand the perceptual process and describe potential perceptual errors.

> Discuss the components of attitudes and indicate why attitudes are important.

The modern workplace is much more than a melting pot in which contents are transformed into a uniform mass. It is more like a rich stew, with ingredients varying in origin and properties, providing differing flavors, nuances, and textures, and retaining their character while contributing to the whole. We will see in this and subsequent chapters that many characteristics of these ingredients are important, including race and ethnic origin, gender, age, abilities, sexual orientation, personality, attitudes, and much more. As the ingredients become more varied, they offer the potential for an expanded, more exotic and exciting menu. Still, it is a challenge to blend the ingredients in ways that bring out their best qualities. And a stew that is a delight to one person may seem bland or bitter or simply unpalatable to another. In this chapter we explore the challenge of recognizing and capturing the best qualities of available ingredients—valuing diversity—while creating a successful stew—managing that diversity. We first explore company approaches to valuing and managing diversity, including efforts to bring more women and minorities successfully into the workplace. We then consider two further important elements of diversity—personality and national culture. Next we discuss perceptions and attitudes. We will see that perceptions as well as attitudes are important characteristics on which organization members may differ, and they are also key influences on reactions to diversity.

MANAGING DIVERSITY

The work force is becoming dramatically more diverse. Diversity refers to the membership mix in organizations in terms of gender, race, ethnic origin, and other characteristics. The Pillsbury Company defines *diversity* as "all the ways in which we differ."[1] Before reading on, complete Self-Assessment 2-1, "Attitudes Toward Diversity." After you have completed the exercise, go to the text Web site to get feedback on your results.

SELF-ASSESSMENT 2-1

Attitudes Toward Diversity

Answer each of the questions in this section using the following scale:

1 Disagree strongly
2 Disagree somewhat
3 Neither agree nor disagree
4 Agree somewhat
5 Agree strongly

____ 1. I enjoy working and interacting with people who have diverse racial/ethnic backgrounds.
____ 2. Older workers possess a lot of work and life experience that are of value to organizations.
____ 3. Men and women should receive the same treatment and opportunities in the workplace.
____ 4. A diverse work force can help an organization to be more innovative.
____ 5. Organizations have a moral responsibility to make their work forces more diverse.
____ 6. I am annoyed that organizations need to make so many changes in policies in order to accommodate employees with different religious affiliations.
____ 7. Different ideas or ways of thinking should also be considered a form of diversity.

     8. The emphasis that many organizations have been placing on helping employees better balance work and family life has gone too far.

     9. Gays and lesbians should have the right to work in an environment that is not hostile toward them.

     10. Diversity programs are often a form of "white male bashing" that results in reverse discrimination.

     11. In a hiring situation, the most qualified candidate should get the job even if it makes an organization less diverse in some way.

     12. Diversity in the workplace is just another management fad that will fade away in a couple of years.

     13. I understand the meaning of the term *work force diversity*.

     14. I understand how the effective management of work force diversity can help a firm enhance bottom-line results like profitability and customer satisfaction.

     15. Managers should emphasize what employees have in common rather than trying to accommodate so many differences between them.

Now, to get a basic idea of where you are starting in terms of some of the material covered in this chapter, try working through the following "Valuing Individual Differences" Pretest Skills Assessment. Don't worry if you don't know everything you'd like to know to complete the exercise; just do your best. Be as specific as possible in stating your recommendations. After you have completed the exercise, go to the text Web site to get feedback on your results.

PRETEST SKILLS ASSESSMENT

Valuing Individual Differences

Note: This exercise is based on actual events encountered by managers in real-world organizations. Some information may have been modified to maintain the anonymity of the people and organization involved in this situation.

You are the team leader for a business team charged with new product development for a company that designs and manufactures personal digital assistants (PDAs). These PDA devices have become extremely popular as a way to organize schedules, check and send e-mail, and surf the Web.

Your new team consists of people with very different backgrounds. Josh Kilzak, 23 years old, is a marketing specialist who will help your team figure out how to sell the new PDAs you design. He is very outgoing and creative and believes everything the team does must be based on what is best for the customer. Don Lee, 38 years old, is an electrical engineer at the company. His job is to provide technical expertise to the PDA development process. He is originally from Beijing, China. He is very bright but rather shy and quiet. He does not like confrontation or conflict with people. To Don, meeting the technical specifications of the product design is the most important issue, regardless of how long it takes or whether it will dissatisfy a customer. Kristin Pellegrin, 49 years old, is a financial analyst at the company. She is a hard-core numbers person who is most concerned with calculating and controlling costs. She views the success of the project solely in terms of financial measures of performance (e.g., development costs, return on investment, profitability). Her personality is very aggressive and can at times be abrasive.

The first meeting of the team was a disaster, because nobody could agree on what to do or how to do it. Each person had a different set of priorities and objectives. At one point, the meeting deteriorated into a shouting match between Josh and Kristin regarding the issue of meeting customer needs versus controlling product development costs. At the end of the meeting everyone left frustrated and pessimistic about the future chances of success for the team.

As the leader of this team, develop an action plan for handling this situation. Be specific, and focus on action. Be sure your plan addresses both short-term and long-term issues. Be very specific and be prepared to defend each element of your plan in terms of its feasibility and cost effectiveness.

Once you have completed your plan, go to the text Web site to find out how you did on this exercise.

Historically, many companies have focused on the potential problems created by a diverse work force. Managers believed there would be more misunderstandings and coordination problems as diversity increased. Further, very real prejudices against members of certain groups, such as blacks and women, could lead to conflict and mistrust.

Increasingly, though, organizations are learning to value diversity. Diversity can provide a powerful competitive advantage.[2] For one thing, a diverse work force brings more perspectives and a wider range of knowledge to bear on problems, increasing creativity and decision-making effectiveness. Diversity also helps a firm understand and meet the needs of diverse markets. As noted by former IBM CEO Lou Gerstner, "Our marketplace is made up of all races, religions, and sexual orientations, and therefore it is vital to our success that our workforce also be diverse."[3] Ted Childs, director of work force diversity at IBM, adds, "We think it is important for our customers to look inside and see people like them. If they can't, it seems to me that the prospect of them becoming and staying our customer declines."[4]

Kraft Foods spells out its commitment to diversity in metaphors:

A stellar meal requires contrasting and complementing textures and tastes. A winning sports team depends on the different talents of its members. A first-class orchestra needs many varied instruments. And a successful business team requires a variety of thought, energy and insight to attain and maintain a competitive edge. Kraft Foods is comprised of people from different backgrounds, different ethnicities, different work styles, different values and different ways of thinking. We invite these differences. We seek them /out. And we know that our business teams and the individuals thrive as a result.[5]

Companies successful at managing a diverse work force also find their recruiting prospects enhanced. As more females and minorities enter the work force, this advantage will become even more important. Figure 2-1 presents the top 10 firms in the 2003 *Fortune* ratings of the "50 Best Companies for Minorities."[6]

As described in the Focus on Management feature, Celanese and a handful of other firms—including Xerox, Avon, AT&T, Burger King, and Levi Strauss—have been at the vanguard of efforts to enhance work force diversity, even in the face of downsizing and severe competition. These firms have learned that, if their efforts to increase diversity—or to achieve any other human resource goal—are to be successful, they must be reflected in all facets of human resources management.

In the Voice of Experience feature, Karen O'Brien discusses her views on work force diversity and how those views drive her style for managing people at Bally's in Las Vegas.

FIGURE 2-1

The 10 Best Companies for Minorities

Company	No. of Minorities on Board	% Minority Officials & Managers	% Minority Employees	Comments
1. McDonald's	2 of 16	36%	52.6%	11 of 50 highest-paid employees are minorities. 35% of purchases are from minority-owned firms.
2. Fannie Mae	5 of 17	33%	44%	11 of 50 highest paid employees are minorities. Company offers diversity training to its partners, customers, and other businesses.
3. Denny's	3 of 9	29%	47%	46% of franchises are owned by minorities. Has the highest proportion of employees undergoing diversity training of all firms surveyed.
4. Union Bank of California	3 of 12	39%	55%	
5. Sempra Energy	4 of 14	29%	48%	
6. Southern California Edison	2 of 11	28.5%	44%	More than 20% of purchases are from minority-owned suppliers. Nine minorities are among 50 highest paid employees.
7. SBC Communications	3 of 21	—	38%	46% of new hires are minorities.
8. Freddie Mac	3 of 18	28%	32%	Eight minorities are among 50 highest paid employees.
9. PepsiCo	4 of 14	17%	27%	Eight minorities are among 50 highest paid employees.
10. PNM Resources	3 of 10	35%	48%	16 minorities are among 50 highest paid employees.

FOCUS ON MANAGEMENT

DIVERSITY AWARENESS AT CELANESE

Ernest H. Drew, the former CEO of Celanese (previously Hoechst Celanese), a large chemical company, became an advocate of a more diverse work force while attending a 1990 conference for Celanese's top 125 officers, mostly white men, who were joined by approximately 50 lower-level women and minorities.* The group split into problem-solving teams, some mixed by race and sex and others all white and male. The teams addressed the question of how the corporate culture affected the business and what changes might be made to improve results. When the teams presented their findings, one thing seemed clear to Drew. "It was so obvious that the diverse teams had the broader solutions," he says. "They had ideas I hadn't even thought of. For the first time, I realized that diversity is a strength as it relates to problem solving. Before, we just thought of diversity as the total number of minorities and women in the company, like affirmative action. Now we knew we needed diversity at every level of the company where decisions are made."† Drew also noticed that productivity was surging at the Celanese plants where the work force was becoming more diverse. As a result, Drew made Celanese a pioneer in attracting, retaining, and promoting women and minorities. It adopted a specific diversity target: at least 34 percent representation of females and minorities at all levels of the company by 2001, mirroring the company's prospective work force.

http://www.celanese.com/en/home.html

*This example is drawn from F. Rice, "How to Make Diversity Pay," *Fortune*, August 8, 1994, pp. 78–86.
†Rice, p. 79.

VOICE OF EXPERIENCE

VALUING DIFFERENCES

Karen O'Brien, Director of Player Development, Bally's Hotel Casino, Las Vegas

1. What kinds of work force diversity exist in your organization?

There is a lot of diversity in our employees. In terms of age, we hire a lot of younger and older workers for a variety of service and maintenance jobs. The younger and older workers tend to have different attitudes and personal values in many cases. In addition, our work force is very diverse in race, ethnicity, and nationality. We have employees who come to us from all over the United States as well as from European, Latin American, and Asian countries. From a guest's perspective, this gives our hotel and casino operations a very international feel.

2. What kinds of strategies do you use to handle work force diversity issues effectively?

I have a basic life philosophy that I try to put into practice. I believe it is critical to learn how to get along with people. This requires flexibility in your approach to handling work issues. People should be treated like people. That is, everyone should be given respect and treated fairly. I always try to do things to make people feel comfortable in their jobs and with their work environment in general. Managers really need to be very people oriented in order to be successful with all of this.

3. What advice would you give students in terms of how to manage work force diversity?

First, I think it is extremely important to "put yourself in another person's shoes." How would it feel if you were the one who was different in some way (e.g., being in a different country)? Wouldn't you feel out of place or maybe a bit awkward? It's really important to be sensitive to this issue. Try getting to know people before you make snap judgments about them based on stereotypes or a first impression. If you talk to them and get to know them, I'll bet you will see you have a lot more in common with them than you thought. Don't draw conclusions based on the fact that someone looks or talks differently than you do.

My managerial practice is to try and reach out to all employees by smiling, saying "hello," and offering assistance to them, if they need it. These practices have worked well for me over the course of my professional career.

http://www.ballys.com/

Companies must do more than accept and tolerate diversity; they must take active steps to foster diversity successfully in the workplace. Some of those steps might include training for tolerance, rewarding diversity efforts, changing employee attitudes toward diversity, and developing personnel policies that support diversity.

Now complete Skills Practice 2-1 by watching the movie *The Breakfast Club.* This film illustrates some interesting and important issues abut the meaning of diversity and learning how to value it. It will remind many of us of our high school days as well.

TRAINING FOR TOLERANCE

Firms are adopting many approaches to training for tolerance, sometimes with dramatic results. Nextel Communications conducted an ROI (return on investment) study of the diversity training program it offers to its 13,000 employees, coming up with an ROI of 163 percent.[7] As another example, at Celanese the top 26 officers are each required to join two organizations in which they are a minority. IBM's Systems Storage Division in San Jose, California (a city where 33 languages are spoken), launched an annual diversity day in 1993.[8] Employees dress in various ethnic costumes, perform traditional dances, and prepare authentic dishes for fellow workers. The festival has been so successful in defusing tensions, the plant's diversity council now prepares a monthly bulletin that lists diversity events in the city. The council will also produce a series of videos featuring a different culture monthly, to be played at gathering spots in the plant.

Firms are also providing training to integrate sexual orientation into ongoing diversity efforts. They explain that the reasons for valuing gay and lesbian employees are basically the same as for valuing women, religious minorities, and people of color: so all employees can contribute to their fullest potential, unhampered by prejudice, stereotypes, and discrimination.[9] In addition, many firms are "gender training" to promote tolerance between the sexes.[10] *Shades of Harassment,* a video and training program produced by Parallax Education with funding from Burger King Corp. and In-N-Out Burger, depicts a variety of scenes drawn from real-life examples of harassment or discrimination cases. The scenes include cases of racial, gender, age, disability and sexual orientation harassment or discrimination.[11]

REWARDING DIVERSITY EFFORTS

Some firms are tying performance appraisal to their efforts to increase diversity. At Celanese, the giant chemical firm cited earlier, four sets of outcomes are equally weighted in performance appraisals: attainment of work force diversity goals, financial success, customer satisfaction, and environmental and safety improvements.[12] As a result, managers at Celanese pay attention to diversity, knowing the success of their diversity efforts will be reflected in their salaries and bonuses.

As another example, Coca-Cola's chairman and CEO, Douglas Daft, announced in March 2000 he would tie his own compensation and that of others throughout the management ranks to diversity goals and would create an executive position for promoting minorities. Daft e-mailed employees worldwide, saying Coke would establish diversity goals and targets over the coming months and "everyone in the corporation, including the CEO, will be accountable for meeting them." He added that "success and compensation" will be tied to meeting diversity goals. The reforms followed recommendations by Coke's Diversity Advisory Council, created in 1999 after current and former Coke African American employees filed a lawsuit alleging discrimination in pay, promotions, and evaluations at Coke.[13]

CHANGING EMPLOYEE ATTITUDES TOWARD DIVERSITY

Companies are using a variety of innovative approaches to develop more positive employee diversity-related attitudes and skills.

As an example, US WEST Dex, a division of US WEST that produces white pages and yellow pages phone directories, trains its employees via a three-day diversity awareness workshop. Further, the majority of its managers have completed another diversity workshop, called "Managing Inclusion," which teaches them that praising, critiquing, and otherwise communicating with employees requires a variety of approaches, depending on the personality and background of each employee. Senior managers who have gone through training talk in the training sessions about how the training makes good bottom-line business sense, and how they learned ideas they can use on their jobs. US WEST Dex also uses "resource groups," volunteer-driven meetings that address the concerns of particular employees, such as women, blacks, Hispanics, gays, and lesbians.[14] Attendance is not limited to employees matching a particular profile. Instead, all employees are encouraged to attend, to better understand the feelings and viewpoints of coworkers regarding specific issues they are facing in the company and to offer suggestions. The company also does six-month follow-ups of programs, seeing if employees are applying their new skills to on-the-job situations. In addition, an annual companywide employee satisfaction survey incorporates questions on the state of diversity at US WEST Dex.

DEVELOPING PERSONNEL POLICIES THAT SUPPORT DIVERSITY[15]

One unfortunate consequence of the massive layoffs now taking place is setbacks in efforts to increase diversity in the work force. Many companies have found it difficult to achieve the dual goals of downsizing and diversity. One reason is that women and minorities hired to meet diversity goals often have little seniority, and thus they are among the first to be cut during downsizing. Another is that firms sometimes downsize by closing facilities in areas with large numbers of minority workers. As a result, the percentages of African Americans laid off in recent years at firms such as Dial Corp. and Pet Inc. have dramatically exceeded those for the overall work forces at those companies.[16] Some firms, such as AT&T, Xerox, and Burger King, have been successful in pursuing both diversity and downsizing. For example, AT&T, which has announced major job cuts every year since 1990, monitors work force reductions by department and finds creative ways to keep valued workers, regardless of their gender and color.[17] In some cases, large numbers of employees are retrained for work elsewhere in the company. Other workers are

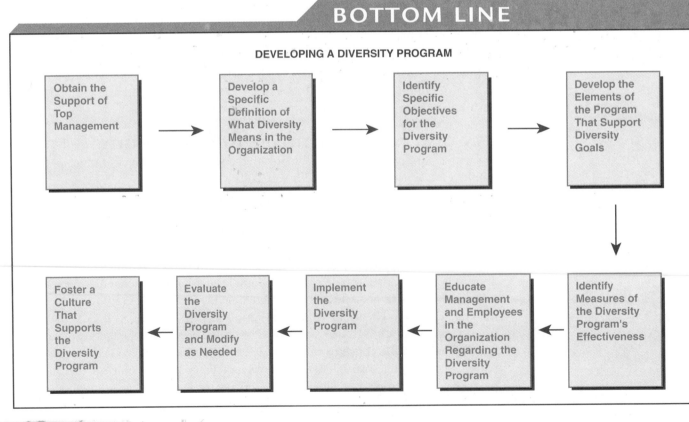

BOTTOM LINE

DEVELOPING A DIVERSITY PROGRAM

Obtain the Support of Top Management → Develop a Specific Definition of What Diversity Means in the Organization → Identify Specific Objectives for the Diversity Program → Develop the Elements of the Program That Support Diversity Goals

Foster a Culture That Supports the Diversity Program ← Evaluate the Diversity Program and Modify as Needed ← Implement the Diversity Program ← Educate Management and Employees in the Organization Regarding the Diversity Program ← Identify Measures of the Diversity Program's Effectiveness assigned to the in-house temporary agency and are loaned out to various departments until permanent jobs can be found for them. Further, AT&T offers valued laid-off employees an "enhanced leave of absence" in which the employee takes two years off to go to school or travel, with full benefits and assurance of reemployment at the same level and pay if a job in the company is available upon return.

To foster diversity in the workplace, managers need to design diversity programs that include training, reward programs, and policies that nurture diversity. Try designing a diversity program that includes these elements by completing Skills Practice 2-2. This is a very challenging activity, so don't be surprised if you struggle with it a bit. You are likely to be involved in the design and implementation of a diversity program once you get out into the real world, so this sort of practice—however difficult—is important.

The process model presented in the Bottom Line feature summarizes the basic steps associated with the development of a diversity program.

UNDERSTANDING PERSONALITY

Although we tend to think of diversity in terms of race, gender, and ethnic origin, the variety of personalities in the workplace is also critical. Personality determines how people respond to new situations, how they interact with others, whether they can work on their own, and much else. Personality also influences whether people behave ethically or unethically, are helpful or self-serving, are conscientious or try just to get by, feel in control of their situations or at the mercy of fate. For all of these reasons and many others, we must understand and be sensitive to personality differences in the workplace.

Personality is the organized and distinctive pattern of behavior that characterizes an individual's adaptation to a situation and endures over time.[18] The distinctive character of personality allows us to tell people apart—try to think of two people with identical personalities. The enduring character of personality permits us to recognize people and to anticipate their behaviors. Try to imagine a situation in which people had no enduring qualities. For instance, suppose your boss acted "like a different person" from day to day. This quirk could be interesting for a while, but it would soon lead to chaos.

In this section, we first consider emotional intelligence, a skill that includes the abilities to understand what motivates other people, how they work, and how to work cooperatively with them as well as to understand ourselves and to be able to use that understanding in our lives. We then address theories of personality as well as specific personality characteristics that are important in the workplace.

EMOTIONAL INTELLIGENCE

In *The Nicomachean Ethics,* Aristotle wrote, "Anyone can become angry—that is easy. But to be angry with the right person, to the right degree, at the right time, for the right purpose, and in the right way—this is not easy."[19] Aristotle called on us to manage our emotional lives with intelligence. Our passions, when properly managed, can help us act, prosper, and survive. Mismanaged, they can create havoc. The challenge, then, is to bring intelligence to our emotions.[20]

Most experts now agree that a relatively narrow range of linguistic and math skills heavily influence IQ scores. So IQ taps only a small part of the full human intellect. Further, the skills assessed by IQ tests may be relevant to classroom performance, but IQ scores do little to predict performance in the real world. This suggests the benefits of a broader view of intelligence. In one compelling demonstration of the need for this expanded view, children at age 4 were given an IQ test and the "Marshmallow Test." With the Marshmallow Test, the child is given a marshmallow and told that if he or she can put off eating it until later, he or she can have two. Twelve to 14 years later, this measure of ability to control impulse was twice as strong a predictor as IQ of how children did on the Scholastic Aptitude Test (SAT). It also predicted adjustment, popularity, confidence, and dependability.

When people—whether so-called experts or not—are asked to describe an intelligent person, they use phrases such as "solves problems well," "displays interest in the world at large," "accepts others for what they are," "admits mistakes," "is goal oriented," and "converses well." Such phrases suggest that people focus on the worldly side of intelligence, as opposed to just academic intelligence.

Howard Gardner, in *Frames of Mind,* discusses several forms of intelligence, including logical-mathematical, linguistic, bodily-kinesthetic, visual-spatial, musical, interpersonal, and intrapersonal.[21] Gardner argues that these intelligences are intrinsically equal in value and the degree to which people possess them helps explain how they learn and fare in the workplace. He further argues it is possible to hone these intelligences and that they wither with lack of use.

Only the first two of these intelligences fit into traditional conceptions of IQ. Gardner's "personal intelligences"—interpersonal and intrapersonal—are defined as follows:

> **Interpersonal intelligence** is the ability to understand other people: what motivates them, how they work, and how to work cooperatively with them.
> **Intrapersonal intelligence** is the capacity to form an accurate model of oneself and to be able to use that model to operate effectively in life.

Together, interpersonal intelligence and intrapersonal intelligence comprise emotional intelligence.

Daniel Goleman, author of *Emotional Intelligence* and *Working with Emotional Intelligence,* describes **emotional intelligence** as a different way of being smart. Emotional intelligence is not IQ; it's how we do in life, manage feelings, get along with others, and are empathetic and motivated.[22]

Whereas the sorts of intelligence gauged by IQ tests reside in the neocortex, or "rational" brain, EQ resides in the amygdala, in the deep recesses of the brain's limbic system. The amygdala's chemical surges produce everything from blind rage to fear to avoidance of pain to euphoria.

Emotional intelligence (EQ) is critical in answering questions such as these:

> Should you trust a coworker with a confidence?
> Is a friend on the verge of a nervous breakdown?
> How should you behave in an escalating argument?
> How should you respond to a racist joke?

EQ is important in organizations and in life in general for many reasons. For example,

> The emotional brain may highjack the rational brain. Fear, rage, and jealousy may prevent us from addressing problems rationally.
> EQ is especially important in higher-level jobs, including leadership roles. Technical skills may suffice in lower-level positions, but the ability to deal with others becomes key as we advance in the organization.
> EQ is critical for working in groups.
> EQ is needed to manage diversity effectively.
> EQ helps us adapt to new situations.

Emotional intelligence requires a rich set of abilities. These include self-awareness (recognizing an emotion as it engulfs us), emotion management (controlling reactions to emotion-laden events so our response fits the situation), self-motivation (directing emotions in the service of a desirable goal), empathy (recognizing emotions in others), and relationship management (managing the emotions in others).

EQ is critical in the real world. In business settings, EQ is related to leadership ability, group performance, individual performance, the quality of interpersonal exchange, change management skills, and the ability to conduct effective performance appraisals.[23] Throughout this book we address issues such as managing stress, self-motivation, coaching, and communicating to help you develop your emotional intelligence. Now assess your emotional intelligence along six dimensions by using the scale in Self-Assessment 2-2, "Emotional Intelligence." After you have completed the exercise, go to the text Web site to get feedback on your results.

SELF-ASSESSMENT 2-2

Emotional Intelligence

Answer each of the questions in this section using the following scale:

1 Disagree strongly
2 Disagree somewhat
3 Neither agree nor disagree
4 Agree somewhat
5 Agree strongly

____ 1. I try to manage my emotions and feelings in front of others.
____ 2. I am often able to resolve conflicts among others.
____ 3. My facial expression and conversational tone are important to me when I'm dealing with others.
____ 4. I have good people-handling skills.
____ 5. I am good at reading other people.
____ 6. I am sometimes paralyzed by my emotions; I get so angry or upset or depressed that I have trouble taking action.
____ 7. I think it's important to control my emotions.
____ 8. I wear my heart on my sleeve—I don't hide my emotions.
____ 9. I'm a good mediator in conflict situations.
____ 10. I sometimes don't realize how angry I am.
____ 11. When I get upset, I use the energy to help accomplish my goals.

_____ 12. I am good at recognizing other people's emotions.

_____ 13. I try to keep my emotions under control.

_____ 14. I am generally able to get others to calm down when they're upset.

_____ 15. I often don't recognize my emotions until someone else comments on them.

_____ 16. I am able to use my emotions to motivate myself.

_____ 17. I have a good poker face—people can't generally tell how I'm feeling.

_____ 18. In general, I'm not even conscious of my emotions.

_____ 19. I channel my emotions in productive ways.

_____ 20. In group settings I am often the person who helps everyone work together smoothly.

_____ 21. I can usually tell when people are trying to hide their true emotions.

_____ 22. I sometimes lose my temper.

PERSONALITY THEORIES

Many theories of personality have been proposed. Some early personality theories saw behavior as related to innate traits, such as independence, sociability, and humility. These traits were believed to be stable, enduring, and interrelated. The unique combination of these traits was seen as the clue to personality.

According to another early approach, Sigmund Freud's *psychoanalytic theory*, we are motivated by drives or instincts.[24] We may be unaware of these drives, and they are largely out of our control. In this theory, the unconscious mind plays an overwhelming role, sometimes revealed to us by "Freudian slips": inadvertent mistakes in speech or writing that suggest what is happening in a person's unconscious mind. The psychoanalytic model sees personality as a conflict between basic pleasure-seeking drives and a restrictive society. Unhappiness, neuroses, and psychoses are seen as the result of that conflict.

Humanistic-existential theories focus on the total personality of the individual instead of on the separate behaviors that make up the personality. They downplay the roles of the environment and biology and stress individual choice and personal responsibility. Instead of focusing on conflict, as in the Freudian model, they emphasize striving for awareness and fulfillment of the human potential. These strivings are seen as the basic force motivating human behavior. The work of Abraham Maslow, a key practitioner of this relatively optimistic approach, is discussed in Chapter 6.

Finally, *learning theories*—which we also discuss in Chapter 6—see personality as a set of patterns of learned behaviors. That is, personalities differ because people have different experiences in childhood and throughout life. According to this view, although personalities may be extremely complex, they are based on simple learning principles.

Each of these theories of personality makes different assumptions about things such as the role of the environment versus the role of biology, the degree to which people are active or passive, and motivating forces. Together, the approaches provide a variety of potentially useful perspectives for examining and predicting human behavior.

IMPORTANT PERSONALITY DIMENSIONS

It is especially important to understand how people with particular personalities may behave. In this section we review some personality characteristics related to behavior or performance. Before we consider these characteristics, complete Self-

Assessment 2-3, "Personality Dimensions." After you have completed the exercise, go to the text Web site to get feedback on your results.

SELF-ASSESSMENT 2-3

Personality Dimensions

Answer each of the questions in this section using the following scale:

1 Disagree strongly
2 Disagree somewhat
3 Neither agree nor disagree
4 Agree somewhat
5 Agree strongly

____ 1. I can often be persuaded to change my mind.
____ 2. In an ideal world, I'd know in advance the exact consequences of each of my actions.
____ 3. I tend to behave very differently depending on who I'm with.
____ 4. I look forward to changes.
____ 5. I'm a take-charge sort of person.
____ 6. I stick to my opinions pretty tenaciously.
____ 7. I generally like to play it safe.
____ 8. I believe authority relationships should be clearly defined.
____ 9. I often have trouble persevering.
____ 10. I generally find that what will be will be—my actions often make little difference.
____ 11. I like to know what the rules are, and then I try to follow them.
____ 12. Before I say something, I usually want to get a good idea of what my audience wants to hear.
____ 13. It's really important to look out for number one—if you're not careful, people will take advantage of you.
____ 14. I'm always trying to do several different things at the same time.
____ 15. I believe life is what you make of it—luck and fate are less important than how we behave.
____ 16. I often find myself getting angry when I'm tied up in traffic.
____ 17. I am pretty much of a risk taker.
____ 18. I think of myself as a go-getter.
____ 19. I generally show a lot of respect for people in positions of authority.
____ 20. If a goal is just and important, it may be okay to use some unsavory means to accomplish it.
____ 21. I generally see the bright side of the picture.
____ 22. I dislike ambiguous situations.
____ 23. I'm a pretty happy person.
____ 24. I generally say what I think, even in cases where the audience is likely to disagree.
____ 25. I take a lot of chances.
____ 26. I'm pretty laid back—I don't worry too much about time pressures.
____ 27. I believe hard work and skill are the keys to success.
____ 28. It is never acceptable to tell a white lie.
____ 29. I am generally satisfied with things.
____ 30. I am pretty stubborn at times.

RISK-TAKING PROPENSITY

People—even those in the same position in the same organization—differ markedly in their *risk-taking propensity*.[25] Some are risk averse. They like to play it safe, choosing alternatives that are likely to give a relatively low but certain return. Others—risk seekers—like to gamble. They prefer alternatives that may turn out very well or very poorly to those with little variance in outcomes. Risk takers tend to make fast decisions based on relatively little information. People with different levels of risk-taking propensity will make very different decisions in the same situation.[26]

PROACTIVE PERSONALITY

Proactivity is the extent to which people take actions to influence their environments. Proactive individuals look for opportunities, show initiative, take action, and persevere until they are able to bring about change. People with proactive personalities have been shown to engage in high levels of entrepreneurial activities and to have relatively high levels of job performance.[27] This is consistent with the idea that the modern workplace rewards take-charge, self-motivated individuals. As a result, proactive personality is a trait highly valued by employers.

AUTHORITARIANISM

Authoritarian individuals believe power and status should be clearly defined and there should be a hierarchy of authority.[28] They feel authority should be concentrated in the hands of a few leaders and this authority should be obeyed. So authoritarian leaders expect unquestioning obedience to their commands; authoritarian subordinates willingly give it. If a leader is authoritarian and his or her subordinate is not, frustration or conflict may result. Authoritarian individuals are likely to be most comfortable in organizations that emphasize rules and following the chain of command.

DOGMATISM

Dogmatic individuals are closed minded. They have rigid belief systems and doggedly stick to their opinions, refusing to revise them in the face of conflicting evidence. Dogmatic individuals make decisions quickly, based on relatively little information, and they are confident in those decisions. They like to follow the rules and are unlikely to consider novel alternatives. They may perform acceptably in well-defined, routine situations, especially if there are time constraints. In other cases, especially those demanding creativity, they do poorly.

LOCUS OF CONTROL

Locus of control refers to the degree to which individuals believe the things that happen to them are the result of their own actions. Those who believe such things are within their own control have an internal locus of control. Others have an external locus of control; they see their lives as being controlled by fate, circumstance, or chance. Externals are unlikely to believe they can do better if they try harder or the rewards and punishments they receive depend on how well they do. For each of these reasons, internals may be more highly motivated than externals. Internals have also been shown likely to respond in more positive ways to stress than externals, to behave in more ethical ways, to feel more empowered, and to be more entrepreneurial.[29]

TOLERANCE FOR AMBIGUITY

Individuals with high ***tolerance for ambiguity*** welcome uncertainty and change. Those with low tolerance for ambiguity see such situations as threatening and uncomfortable. Because managers are increasingly facing dynamic, unstructured situations, tolerance for ambiguity is clearly an important characteristic.

MACHIAVELLIANISM

Individuals with a ***Machiavellian*** personality think any behavior is acceptable if it achieves their goals. Machiavellians try to manipulate others. They are unemotional and detached. They "look out for number one" and aren't likely to be good team players. Not surprisingly, they also are relatively likely to be unethical.[30]

SELF-MONITORING

Self-monitoring is the extent to which people vary their behavior to match the situation and make the best possible impression on others.[31] High self-monitors pay close attention to their audience and tailor their behaviors accordingly. For instance, a high self-monitor may act humble and respectful when dealing with the boss but be boastful and ill mannered with subordinates. Similarly, a high self-monitor may present very different opinions to different audiences. Low self-monitors, in contrast, react to situations without looking to others for behavioral cues; they present the same face in different situations. High self-monitors are like chameleons, able to change their behaviors to fit the audience. Although this may seem devious, it could also be seen as sensitive to the demands of the situation. Evidence seems clear that high self-monitors tend to do better. For example, a study that tracked business graduates showed that high self-monitors got more promotions, either cross-company or within their original firm, than low self-monitors.[32] A recent review of research on self-monitoring concluded that high self-monitors receive better performance ratings and more promotions than low self-monitors and are more likely to emerge as leaders.[33]

TYPE A AND TYPE B

The ***Type A behavior pattern*** is characterized by feelings of great time pressure and impatience. Type A's work aggressively, speak explosively, and find themselves constantly struggling. The opposite pattern—relaxed, steady paced, and easygoing—is called the ***Type B behavior pattern***. Individuals with Type A behavior patterns are much more likely than others to experience high stress levels and to show a variety of symptoms of stress, including coronary heart disease. Type A's have trouble delegating responsibility to others, don't work well in groups, and are impatient with tasks requiring prolonged problem solving. Because of these limitations and the health risks of being a Type A, relatively few Type A's rise to high levels in organizations. We explore Type A behavior in more detail in our discussion of managing stress in Chapter 9.

THE BIG 5 PERSONALITY DIMENSIONS

Hundreds of personality characteristics have been identified, of which we have considered several of the most important. Evidence is accumulating that virtually all personality measures can be categorized into five consistent sets, now called the Big 5: extraversion, agreeableness, conscientiousness, emotional stability, and openness to experience. The Big 5 categories hold up remarkably well across national cultures and over time.[34]

> **Extraversion:** Extraverts tend to be outgoing and gregarious, dominant and ambitious, and adventuresome. They usually display positive emotions, have a large number of close friends, and take on leadership roles.

> **Agreeableness:** Agreeable persons are trusting, caring, good natured, cheerful, and gentle. Agreeableness is especially significant in careers where teamwork or customer service is important.

> **Conscientiousness:** Conscientious individuals are hardworking and persistent, responsible and careful, and well organized. Conscientiousness is related to success at work. Conscientious individuals have higher levels of job performance, engage in fewer counterproductive work behaviors, and they are more satisfied, absent less often, and less likely to leave the firm than those who are less conscientious.[35]

> **Emotional stability:** Emotional stability is best recognized by the absence of anxiety, hostility, depression, self-consciousness, vulnerability, and impulsiveness. Emotional stability is positively related to job performance.[36]

> **Openness to experience:** Individuals who are open to experience tend to be intelligent, imaginative, and unconventional. They do better than their opposites in learning new skills.

Take a few minutes now to rate yourself on these dimensions by completing Self-Assessment 2-4, "The Big 5 Personality Dimensions." After you have completed the exercise, go to the text Web site to get feedback on your results.

SELF-ASSESSMENT 2-4

The Big 5 Personality Dimensions

Answer each of the questions in this section using the following scale:

1 Disagree strongly
2 Disagree somewhat
3 Neither agree nor disagree
4 Agree somewhat
5 Agree strongly

____ 1. I am quite outgoing.
____ 2. I can get along with just about anyone.
____ 3. I think of myself as intellectual.
____ 4. I can sometimes be rude.
____ 5. I am a very warm person.
____ 6. I am shy.
____ 7. I am quite energetic.
____ 8. I would describe myself as temperamental.
____ 9. I am often envious.
____ 10. I am philosophical.
____ 11. I am generally quite relaxed.
____ 12. I am sometimes careless.
____ 13. I am unimaginative.
____ 14. I am often sloppy.
____ 15. I am sometimes withdrawn.

_____ 16. I would describe myself as creative.

_____ 17. I am quite practical.

_____ 18. I am a very kind person.

_____ 19. I am rarely jealous.

_____ 20. I am very organized.

Don't interpret our discussion of personality to suggest that people have no control over their actions. Instead, personality characteristics suggest tendencies to behave in certain ways. People's conscious decisions may help them overcome troublesome behavior patterns. For instance, employees may be able to take actions to alter Type A behavior patterns, to ensure they consider more information before making a decision, and to modify their risk preferences.

Still, throughout your career you will be working with people who react very differently from one another with respect to risk, uncertainty, new ideas, rules and regulations, and much else. Some of your colleagues are likely to be more manipulative, self-serving, and unethical than others. Some will be self-starters and some will need a push. Some will be driven and some will be laid back. These diverse personalities will provide opportunities and challenges as you build teams, try out new practices, and simply get through the workday. By recognizing this variety and its implications, you will have made a good start toward understanding, predicting, and influencing others successfully in the workplace.

Now complete Skills Practice 2-3. This exercise gives you the opportunity to administer some of the self-assessment measures of personality presented earlier in this chapter to a small sample of working individuals (managers or individual contributors), to develop a personality profile for each of these individuals, and to draw some conclusions about their work styles.

RECOGNIZING CROSS-CULTURAL DIFFERENCES

With *globalization*, the world's people are becoming more interconnected with respect to the cultural, political, technological, and environmental aspects of their lives. What does this mean for you?

> You are likely to spend at least part of your career in other countries—in fact, some companies now require international experience for their top managers.

> According to Andrew Grove, Chairman of Intel, with globalization "every employee will compete with every person in the world who is capable of doing the same job. There are a lot of them, and many of them are very hungry."[37]

> You may suddenly find yourself working for a foreign firm. About 25,000 international mergers and acquisitions took place in 2002, totaling $1.2 trillion.[38] Although U.S. companies have historically been the world's biggest buyers, United Kingdom firms have now taken over the lead. Increasingly, you may be working for a firm headquartered in Germany, Sweden, Japan, or almost anywhere else in the world.

> Your firm—and your job—will increasingly depend on international trade. Directly or indirectly, international trade now accounts for about 20 percent of all jobs in the United States.

> You will be managing a culturally diverse work force even if you never leave the United States. Consider the following: The Census Bureau estimates that by the year 2050, Asian Americans, Hispanics, African Americans, and other non-white groups will compose 47 percent of the U.S. population. The Hispanic population is projected to grow from 24 million (9 percent of the population) to 81 million (21 percent); Hispanics will account for 33 percent of the nation's population growth. In addition, the number of Asian Americans is projected to jump from 7 million to 35 million by 2040. The diversity provided by these groups is even greater than a listing of categories such as "Asian American" and "Hispanic" might suggest. For example, Hispanics represent many nationalities and ethnicities, including Mexicans, Cubans, Puerto Ricans, Spanish, Dominican Republicans, and people from 15 other Central and South American countries, all with different histories, labor force characteristics, and growth rates.

Organizations of all kinds must learn to manage cultural diversity effectively. Consider the New York Yankees. During the 1998 season Yankees pitching coach Mel Stottlemeyer did a masterful job of overseeing one of the most international pitching staffs in major league baseball. The staff—which included Graeme Lloyd from Australia, Orlando "El Duque" Hernandez from Cuba, Hideki Irabu from Japan, and Ramiro Mendoza and Mariano Rivera from Panama—led the Yankees to 114 wins, the most in American League history.[39]

So whether you are living in Lima, Ohio, or Lima, Peru, you will be managing a culturally diverse work force, dealing with global competitors, or even working for a foreign firm. What might we expect as we deal with people from other national cultures? Geert Hofstede, a Dutch researcher who worked as a psychologist for IBM, studied 116,000 people working in 64 countries and identified five important dimensions along which national cultures differ:[40]

> **Individualism versus collectivism.** In ***individualistic cultures***, such as the United States and Australia, the cultural belief is that the individual comes first—social frameworks are loosely knit and people are chiefly expected to look after their own interests and those of their immediate family. Individual achievement is emphasized. Society offers people a great amount of freedom, and they are used to making independent decisions and taking independent action. In ***collectivist cultures***, such as Colombia and Pakistan, there are tight social frameworks in which people expect their group members to look after them and protect them in times of trouble. In exchange for security, loyalty is expected. A saying that reflects the collectivist view is "The nail that sticks out will be pounded down."

> **Power distance** is the degree to which a society accepts the fact that power in institutions and organizations is distributed unequally. A high-power-distance society, such as the Philippines, Mexico, or India, accepts wide differences in power in organizations. Employees show great respect for authority, titles, status, and rank. Titles are important in bargaining. A low-power-distance society, such as Denmark, Israel, or Ireland, plays down inequalities as much as possible.

> **Uncertainty avoidance** refers to the way societies deal with risk and uncertainty. In low-uncertainty-avoidance countries, such as Switzerland and Denmark, people are relatively comfortable with risks and tolerate behaviors and opinions that differ from their own. In high-uncertainty-avoidance countries, such as Japan and Greece, there is a high level of anxiety among the people. Formal rules and

other mechanisms are used to provide security and reduce risk. Deviant ideas and behaviors are less tolerated, and people strive to believe in absolute truths.

> **Quality versus quantity of life.** Some cultures, such as Japan and Austria, emphasize the *quantity of life* and value assertiveness and the acquisition of money and material things. Other cultures, such as the Scandinavian countries, emphasize the *quality of life* and the importance of relationships, and they show sensitivity and concern for the welfare of others. In quality-of-life cultures, people stop to smell the roses. In quantity-of-life cultures, people try to get as many roses as possible.

> **Time orientation.** Citizens of some countries, such as Japan and Hong Kong, have a *long-term orientation*, derived from values that include thrift (saving) and persistence in achieving goals. Those from other countries, such as France and Indonesia, have a *short-term orientation*, derived from values that express a concern for maintaining personal stability or happiness and living for the present.

Another key factor is whether cultures are high or low context. In a *high-context culture*, such as most Asian, Hispanic, African, and Arab countries, the context in which a communication occurs is just as important as the words that are actually spoken, and cultural clues are important in understanding what is being communicated. The context includes the social setting, use of phrasing, gestures, and tone of voice, and the person's history and status. In a *low-context culture*, such as Germany or the United States, the words used by the speaker explicitly convey the speaker's message to the listener.

This suggests that nonverbal communications (see Chapter 5), although important in all settings, are especially critical in high-context cultures. Most immigrants to the United States are now coming from high-context cultures. Nonverbal communications have dramatically different meanings across cultures.[41] For instance, nodding your head means "Yes" in most countries but "No" in Bulgaria and Greece. The classic "OK" sign of thumb and forefinger forming a circle can imply "money" in Japan, means "worthless" in France, and is considered an obscene gesture in Brazil, Germany, and Russia. In Saudi Arabia, to cross your legs in such a way that you display the sole of your foot to your host is a grievous affront. North Americans often wave to signal "hello" or "good-bye," but this action signals "no!" in much of Europe.

There are also cultural differences in the meaning of eye contact. Whereas Americans generally expect eye contact in a conversation, many Asians and Hispanics consider eye contact, especially with a superior, to be utterly disrespectful. In countries such as Libya, looking a woman in the eye for more than a short time is considered a form of assault.

The Bottom Line feature presents a process model that summarizes the basic steps associated with managing cross-cultural differences.

MAINTAINING ACCURATE PERCEPTIONS

We all live in our own world. It is a world created by our attempts to sift through, to organize, and to interpret the tremendous number of things we see, hear, feel, and otherwise constantly sense. It is different from all other worlds—the unique product of a complex process.

Ms. Johnson, a fast-rising executive, exists in the world of one of her colleagues as hardworking and competent. In the world of another, she is driven and ruthless. The same job that in Sam's world is boring and routine exists in Carol's world as a source of challenge and opportunity. Mr. Bjornson's subtle messages to Mr. Peterson, carefully crafted and potentially powerful in Mr. Bjornson's world, are nowhere to be found in the world of Mr. Peterson.

The truth in our world depends on whether something is consistent with the rest of that world. Moreover, the nature of our unique world helps determine how we behave. How are these private worlds created? What makes each unique? How are we to deal with people living in other worlds?

In this section we consider the nature of the perceptual process, noting key influences at each step and associated problems. We then review the related process of causal attribution. Finally, we discuss ways to reduce perceptual errors.

THE PERCEPTUAL PROCESS

Knowledge of the world is sent to our brains through our sensory systems—seeing, hearing, tasting, touching, and smelling. *Perception* is the complex process by which we select, organize, and interpret sensory stimuli into a meaningful and coherent picture of the world.[42] As shown in Figure 2-2, perception involves several steps. In the first step, sensation, many stimuli impact on our sensory filters, but only some are sensed. Others are filtered out, perhaps because they are at very low levels or are not within a particular range. In subsequent steps, sensed stimuli are selected, organized, and translated. Let's consider what occurs at each of those steps.

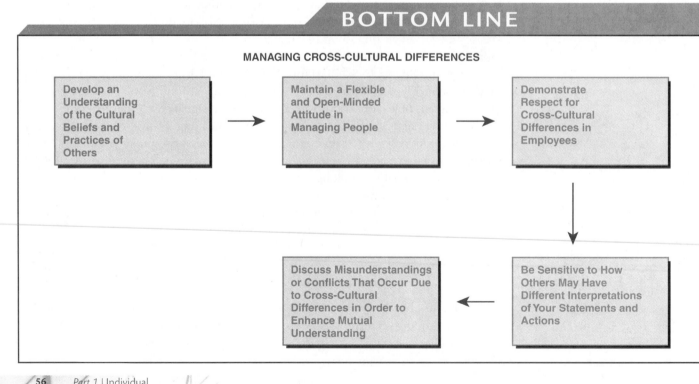

BOTTOM LINE

MANAGING CROSS-CULTURAL DIFFERENCES

Develop an Understanding of the Cultural Beliefs and Practices of Others → Maintain a Flexible and Open-Minded Attitude in Managing People → Demonstrate Respect for Cross-Cultural Differences in Employees → Be Sensitive to How Others May Have Different Interpretations of Your Statements and Actions → Discuss Misunderstandings or Conflicts That Occur Due to Cross-Cultural Differences in Order to Enhance Mutual Understanding

FIGURE 2-2
The Perceptual Process

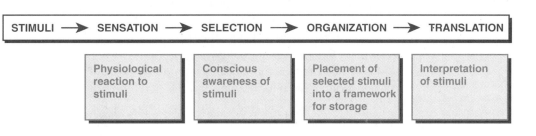

STIMULI → SENSATION → SELECTION → ORGANIZATION → TRANSLATION

| Physiological reaction to stimuli | Conscious awareness of stimuli | Placement of selected stimuli into a framework for storage | Interpretation of stimuli |

Selecting Stimuli. In this step, selection, some stimuli are selected for further processing. If our perceptions were not selective, we would be overwhelmed. For example, consider Figure 2-3. What do you see? An old man's face? A woman carrying a child? A woman's face? Another face? A gateway? A stooped old man? A hand? These and several other shapes can be found in the figure, but you would probably see only a few of them if you hadn't been prompted to search for more.

Ideally, we might select only the most important stimuli. However, many factors affect selection, some of which are potentially troublesome. For instance, we have all heard the saying "I'll believe it when I see it." The statement "I'll see it when I believe it" applies to perception. That is, we are more likely to see things we are expecting to see. This is called *perceptual readiness*. For example, executives in various

FIGURE 2-3
Nine Persons

Source: This is a black and white reprinting of a color painting by the Swiss artist Sandro Del Prete.

departments of a manufacturing firm read a detailed case study from a business policy course. Although they were told to analyze the case from a companywide perspective, they instead focused on their own areas—the areas where they were ready to see problems. Salespeople, for instance, saw marketing problems as needing attention, and production people identified organization and production problems as most pressing.[43] Thus perceptual readiness may cause us to fail to see the big picture.

Many other factors influence the stimuli we select. For example, different people will select different stimuli based on their needs and personalities. A hungry person is likely to focus on the food in an advertisement for china. Insecure people may focus on cues that imply threat. Also, stimuli that contrast with the surrounding environment are more likely than others to be selected. That contrast could be in color, size, flavor, or some other factor. The only person talking in a theater or the only blue shirt in a sea of Wisconsin red on a football weekend almost demands attention. In addition, repetition of a stimulus has an additive effect, making it more likely to attract attention. Advertisers, of course, make use of this fact, regularly repeating a message. And you have probably had an experience similar to the following: You say "hello" to a friend, Bob. Bob doesn't respond. You say "hello" again. Bob replies, "Oh, hi. Sorry, I didn't hear you the first time." In fact, of course, Bob *had* to hear you the first time to make that statement. Further, intense, changing, or novel stimuli are more likely to be selected.

Organizing Stimuli. Once stimuli have been selected, they must be organized in a useful framework. The way we organize stimuli is important. Things we group together tend to be recalled together, and their meanings tend to influence one another. In general, we are likely to group things that are somehow similar (for instance, in shape, size, or color) or that are close together in time or space (two accidents that occurred on the same day or two people seated together). Also, we tend to organize things so closure occurs. That is, we close up or fill in missing parts to create a meaningful whole.

Interpreting Stimuli. Finally, we interpret stimuli at the translation step in the perceptual process. The way we translate the stimuli we have selected and organized depends on the situation (for instance, whether it is friendly or hostile, relaxed or frantic), our characteristics, and characteristics of what we are perceiving. Many distortions of objective reality are possible at the translation stage. Some of these are simply due to quirks in the way our senses work. For instance, Figure 2-4 shows the "Hering Illusion," in which two parallel lines appear curved to us because of the nature of their background.

Other distortions are perhaps more subtle but certainly no less important. Some of the most important perceptual distortions are stereotyping, Pygmalion effect, halo effect, projection, primacy/recency effects, and perceptual defense.

> **Stereotyping**. Walter Lippmann coined the term ***stereotyping*** in 1922, describing stereotypes as "pictures in people's heads" that distorted their perceptions of others.[44] The term is now often used to mean the forming of an opinion of people based on group membership. Stereotyping, if accurate, may be useful, because it places information efficiently into categories. When we face new situations, stereotypes provide guidelines to help classify people. Unfortunately, stereotyping may lead to a distorted view of the situation if the

FIGURE 2-4
The Hering Illusion

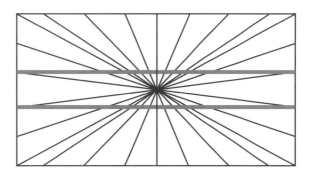

stereotyping is based on false premises. For instance, one study found that labeling a photograph as that of a management representative led to a different impression than when the same photograph was labeled as that of a union leader.[45] In another study, hiring decisions were made on the basis of matched pairs of dossiers.[46] The dossiers differed only in one way: One in each set had a male name and the other had a female name. The dossier with the male name was more likely to be hired. As another example, research shows that people have a variety of incorrect stereotypes about people with body piercing.[47] Research suggests that stereotyping in work organizations may be harmful to minority group members, older workers, and females.[48]

> **Pygmalion effect** We noted earlier that perceptual readiness influences the stimuli we select. It also influences how we interpret those stimuli. A prime example is the self-fulfilling prophecy, or ***Pygmalion effect***. The term comes from mythology. As told by Ovid, a sculptor named Pygmalion created a sculpture of a young woman so beautiful that he fell hopelessly in love with it. Venus, the goddess of love and beauty, was fascinated by this new kind of lover and brought the sculpture to life. Pygmalion named the maiden Galatea, and they had a son, Paphos. The Pygmalion effect, then, refers to creating something in the image we have of it. For better or worse, teachers, managers, and others often demonstrate this effect.[49] For example, teachers who were told certain students were especially intelligent (when, in fact, they were not) later perceived those students to show signs of greater intelligence and higher performance. As a result, they treated them differently. These "intelligent" students then showed gains in intellectual capacity while others did not. Similar findings have occurred when leaders were told (again, incorrectly) that certain of their subordinates were high performers. The leaders apparently saw "high-performing" subordinates differently and gave them considerable decision-making authority. They closely supervised "low performers." Thus perceptual readiness may cause us to color our perceptions based on our expectations.

> **Halo Effect**. ***Halo effect*** refers to a process in which a judge uses a general impression that is favorable or unfavorable (a "horns effect") to evaluate specific traits.[50] Because of this general halo, the judge doesn't evaluate each trait

independently. Sometimes one trait, such as a subordinate's honesty or enthusiasm, forms the halo. So if the boss feels the subordinate is honest, the subordinate may also be seen as loyal, efficient, and courteous, and so on.[51] That is, we have a tendency to perceive links between traits. If we make evaluations on the basis of a halo when the traits really aren't linked, halo error is the result. Of course, many traits are in fact related, so not all halo effect is really halo error.

> **Projection**. The term *projection* has taken on a variety of related meanings in which individuals project their own characteristics onto others. For example, people may relieve their own guilt by projecting blame on others. Fearful people tend to see others as fearful. People with certain undesirable personality characteristics, such as stinginess or obstinacy, tend to rate others as relatively high on those traits.[52]

> **Primacy/recency effects**. The time at which we receive a stimulus influences the weight we give it. Quite often, the first information we receive has a very great influence on our final impressions. This is called a *primacy effect*. It has important consequences when a sequence of alternatives is considered, such as in the case of job choice decisions or of job interviews. Sometimes, information we have received recently has a great influence—a *recency effect*. The bottom line for communication is that it's important to start strong and finish strong.

> **Perceptual defense**. When we face information we find to be threatening or unacceptable, our perceptions try to defend us. We may fail to perceive the troublesome stimuli, or we may distort our perceptions of the stimuli to make them less troublesome. Perceptual defense is especially evident when long-held beliefs or attitudes are challenged. To illustrate, in one study college students were given descriptions of factory workers.[53] These descriptions included the word *intelligent*. Because this description was contrary to the students' beliefs concerning factory workers, their perceptual defenses came to the rescue. Some students simply denied the workers were intelligent. Most frequently, they modified or distorted the description. Students, for instance, might accept the term *intelligent* but would couple it with another characteristic, such as lack of initiative, to maintain their overall perception of the workers. Clearly, perceptual defense can result in a very distorted and potentially biased view. For example, RJR Nabisco spent more than $300 million on a "smokeless" cigarette, Premier, before abandoning the project after eight years of research and testing. Researchers had simply continued to shrug off negative feedback, including the facts that the company didn't know how to make the product in a factory and the cigarette didn't taste right and caused a "hernia effect"—smokers had to inhale furiously to get much smoke. Rather than listen to the feedback, "Management would always say, 'We can fix this; we can fix that.'" A senior RJR executive said, "What happens is you get into a euphoria where you con yourself."[54]

Before moving on, complete Skills Practice 2-4, "Perceptual Accuracy: Do You Know Me?" This is a short but fun exercise that shows how we often possess at least some inaccurate impressions or perceptions of other people, especially those we don't know very well. Try it and you may surprise yourself with what you find out.

The process model shown in the Bottom Line feature summarizes the basic steps associated with increasing the accuracy of your perception of a situation.

IMPLICIT THEORIES

Implicit theories are theories in people's minds. For instance, we may believe jobs offering more challenge also provide more authority. Or we may believe leaders who let their subordinates participate in making decisions also care more about their subordinates. These implicit theories may be correct or incorrect. They may influence perceptions at the selection, organization, and translation stages. For instance, if we see evidence concerning one element of the theory, we will be likely to perceive other elements also. So if our boss lets us participate in decision making, we may also be more likely to see caring behaviors, to organize caring behaviors along with opportunities for participation, and to translate particular behaviors as more caring.[55]

Many working people—like many students—aren't big fans of formal academic theories they read about in textbooks. However, it is critical to recognize we all have our own personal, implicit theories that represent our beliefs about how things work. Complete Skills Practice 2-5 to get a better understanding of your implicit theories and how they influence your behavior.

BOTTOM LINE

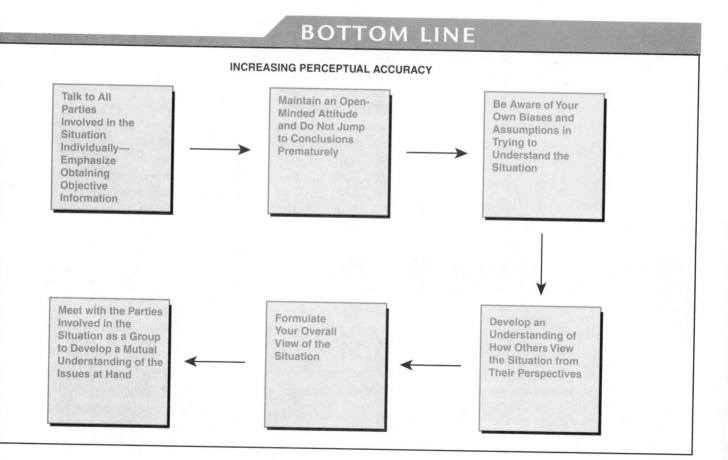

INCREASING PERCEPTUAL ACCURACY

Talk to All Parties Involved in the Situation Individually—Emphasize Obtaining Objective Information → Maintain an Open-Minded Attitude and Do Not Jump to Conclusions Prematurely → Be Aware of Your Own Biases and Assumptions in Trying to Understand the Situation ↓

Meet with the Parties Involved in the Situation as a Group to Develop a Mutual Understanding of the Issues at Hand ← Formulate Your Overall View of the Situation ← Develop an Understanding of How Others View the Situation from Their Perspectives

CAUSAL ATTRIBUTION

We must often form perceptions of the causes underlying others' behaviors. This process is called *causal attribution*. As an example, a district sales manager may want to determine what caused a salesperson's poor performance in the fall quarter. It may be especially important to determine whether the behavior was the result of internal factors, such as the person's motives or traits, or of external factors, such as luck or the situation. For example, if the sales manager feels her subordinate's poor performance is due to lack of effort (an internal factor), she may want to consider disciplinary actions. If she believes the poor performance is due to an economic downturn, such actions would seem unfair.

According to Harold Kelley's *attribution theory*, we try to sort out the causes of an individual's behavior by considering three factors.[56] For instance, in the case of our poor-performing salesperson, the boss might ask three questions. First, did others act the same way in this situation? That is, did others also have a poor period in the downturn? Second, does this salesperson always act this way in this situation? That is, does he always do poorly in economic downturns? Third, does this salesperson act differently in other situations? That is, does he do better in the absence of an economic downturn? If the boss answered yes to each of these questions, she would probably not blame her subordinate. If other people had done well in the downturn and this subordinate always does poorly, however, it would be hard to blame the situation. For an application of attribution theory, see the Focus on Management feature.

Unfortunately, causal attribution is a process prone to error. For instance, we tend to attribute the behavior of others to internal factors, even when this is not appropriate. That is, we often blame or commend people for things that are really outside their control. Also, the *self-serving bias*—the tendency to take credit for successes and deny personal responsibility for failures—is often seen.

REDUCING PERCEPTUAL ERRORS

Perception is so important and plays such a major role in determining our behavior that we must make every effort to do it right. For instance, people who are aware of their own characteristics make fewer errors in perceiving others and are less likely to see the world in black-and-white terms. Also, people who are able to accept themselves as they are can see a wider range of characteristics in others. They may also be less prone to projection. Further, simple knowledge of such tendencies as

FOCUS ON MANAGEMENT

ATTRIBUTION THEORY AT BOOTS THE CHEMIST

Boots the Chemist, a British pharmaceutical firm, wanted a test to select potential sales assistants. Dissatisfied with available tests, it developed a new questionnaire for its own use based on attribution theory (which, as noted in the text, looks at the ways in which people explain why events occurred). It was predicted—and shown in subsequent research—that the most successful sales performers and those rated most highly for their customer care would be more likely to attribute outcomes to internally controllable factors, such as their own effort or choice of sales strategy. The questionnaire is now used in the selection process for sales assistants and to help identify developmental needs.

http://www.the-times.co.
uk/news/pages/changing-
times.html?999

halo error, stereotyping, and self-serving bias may help avoid them. Finally, it is important to make a conscious effort to attend to relevant information and to test reality. Actively seek evidence of whether or not your perceptions are accurate. Compare your perceptions with those of others and try to account for any differences. Look for objective measures relating to the perceptions. If you think Mr. Tanaka is a poor performer, check his output levels.

You will encounter many real-world management situations in which the people involved have very different perceptions of an issue. Complete Skills Practice 2-6 to get some practice in dealing with such situations. Then complete Skills Practice 2-7, designed to help you develop a greater sensitivity toward others' perceptions of a situation or problem that may differ from your own.

ATTITUDES

Attitudes are the beliefs, feelings, and behavioral tendencies held by a person about an object, event, or person (called the *attitude object*). In this section we consider the nature of attitudes and look at some specific work attitudes. We also discuss how attitudes are formed and see how work attitudes are related to work behaviors.

THE COMPONENTS OF ATTITUDES

Our definition of *attitudes* indicates they have three components, as shown in Figure 2-5: cognitive, affective, and behavioral tendency.

> The **cognitive component** of attitudes is our cognitions, or beliefs about the facts pertaining to the attitude object. This is descriptive information rather

FIGURE 2-5
Components of Attitudes

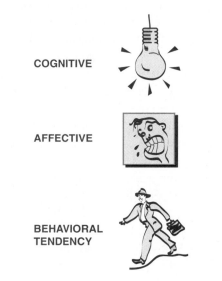

COGNITIVE

AFFECTIVE

BEHAVIORAL
TENDENCY

than liking or intentions. We may, for example, believe salespersons in our firm receive high pay or our firm is the oldest in the industry. These beliefs may, of course, be correct or incorrect.

> The second component of attitudes, the ***affective component***, is made up of our feelings toward the attitude object. The affective component (which shares the same root as *affection*) involves evaluation and emotion. For instance, we may think favorably or unfavorably about another employee or think a particular rule is good or bad.

> The third component, the ***behavioral tendency component***, is the way we intend to behave toward the attitude object. We may, for example, intend to tell off the boss or ask for a raise or outperform a coworker.

Sometimes, our cognitions may influence our feelings, which may, in turn, influence our behavioral tendencies. For example, our belief that pay is $7 an hour (cognitive component) may lead us to be dissatisfied with pay (affective component), which may lead us to decide to look for another job (behavioral tendency component). However, people with the same beliefs may develop different feelings (for example, some people may be satisfied with pay of $7 an hour), and different people with the same feelings may develop different behavioral intentions (some people, even though dissatisfied with pay, may never decide to seek work elsewhere). Also, there may even be cases in which our beliefs will be influenced by our feelings (as in the saying "Love is blind") or by our behavioral tendencies (as when, after learning we'll be required to move to another town, we begin to find things wrong with our current location). Further, as we discuss later, the components of our attitudes may even be influenced by our actual behaviors. The point, then, is that the various components of attitudes are rather intimately and intricately linked and may continually influence one another.

WHY CARE ABOUT ATTITUDES?

It might seem that managers should be concerned about employee behaviors, not their attitudes. After all, it's behavior, such as performance or absenteeism, that shows up on the bottom line. It could even be argued there is something sinister about trying to influence people's attitudes—what right do managers have to try to change (or even know) what people think?

In fact, though, managers should care about employee attitudes for several reasons. First, as we suggested earlier, attitudes may influence work behaviors. As shown in Figure 2-6, attitudes may influence such work outcomes as performance, turnover, and absenteeism (we'll see whether or not they actually do influence those behaviors later in the chapter). If so, managers may try to improve behaviors by bringing about changes in attitudes. Statements such as "A satisfied employee is a productive employee" show that many people do believe that attitudes (in this case, satisfaction) are related to work behaviors (here, productivity). So it is important to see what links, if any, really do exist between employee attitudes and their behaviors.

Second, work attitudes may influence things of direct concern to the employee, such as stress levels, ability to sleep, and attitudes toward other aspects of life. As we learn more about behavior in organizations, we realize no magic door separates work and nonwork life. Events at work have important consequences off the job and vice versa. As one example, research shows that fathers who have autonomy

FIGURE 2-6

Some Potential Relationships of Attitudes to Behaviors

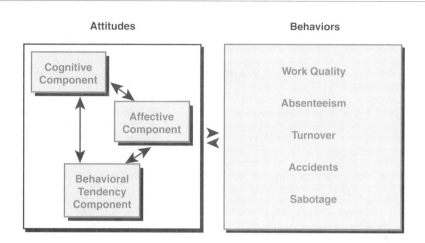

and supportive bosses at work tend to have higher self-esteem, to treat their children with greater acceptance and warmth, and to use less harsh discipline than do fathers with less autonomy and support at work.[57] When one father in the study, a trucker who had been working overtime, complained he hadn't seen his family for three days, his supervisor announced in front of 11 other drivers, "You can always get another family but you can't get another job like this one."[58]

Finally, attitudes are important for their own sake, independent of their consequences. Employees spend half their waking lives at work. Caring managers may want to learn how to make the working hours of employees more pleasant or how to make employees' jobs more involving. Further, managers may feel it is appropriate to reduce certain undesirable attitudes among their subordinates, such as prejudice.

JOB SATISFACTION

Job satisfaction is the best known and most commonly measured and studied work attitude. *Job satisfaction* is the affective component of work-related attitudes. Quite simply, it is how employees feel about their jobs.

Managers are often concerned about employees' satisfaction with specific facets of the job, as well as about overall job satisfaction. They may, for instance, want to know how employees feel about their pay and whether satisfaction with pay is higher in some departments than in others. Or they may simply ask, "Taking everything into consideration, how do our employees feel about their jobs?" Figure 2-7 shows the relationship of job facet satisfaction to overall job satisfaction.

MEASURING JOB SATISFACTION

Measuring levels of employee satisfaction is crucial. It provides important information concerning what is, and is not, being done correctly in the workplace. For example, if it is found that satisfaction with supervision is low, supervisory practices

FIGURE 2-7
Job Facet Satisfaction and Overall Satisfaction

might be carefully assessed. Similarly, if satisfaction is found to sharply increase or decrease in a department, the sources of that change should be explored. Further, of course, we would like satisfaction levels to be high in general. If they are not, some serious diagnosis is in order.[59]

The most popular approach to measuring satisfaction is to use standardized scales. These scales have generally been widely used and tested, so the user can be confident they provide accurate measures. In addition, norm data are often available for standardized scales. Norm data tell us how other people have scored on the scales. The data may, for instance, tell us the average score and distribution of scores of all past users of the scale, or they may provide such information for specific groups or industries. This provides useful comparative information.

The best known scale to assess facets of job satisfaction, the *Job Descriptive Index (JDI)*, measures satisfaction with the work itself, pay, coworkers, supervision, and promotions.[60] Figure 2-8 presents sample items from the supervision sub-scale of the JDI. By tapping satisfaction with particular job facets, a scale such as the JDI helps managers pinpoint sources of dissatisfaction and take appropriate actions. For example, if it is clear employees are satisfied with all aspects of their jobs except promotions, attention can be devoted to that area.

Overall job satisfaction, or general job satisfaction, is concerned with the overall feelings of an employee regarding the job. Examining facet satisfaction is very useful, but it may fail to see the forest for the trees. That is, measures of facet satisfaction can't give us the complete picture because employees may give differing weights to various job facets and may combine information about facets in different ways. For example, if an employee reports low satisfaction with promotional opportunities but doesn't really care about promotions, there will be little impact on overall job satisfaction. Also, there are probably many aspects of overall job satisfaction besides the specific facets measured in the JDI (suggested in Figure 2-7 by the fact that the satisfaction facets do not completely fill the job satisfaction circle).

FIGURE 2-8
Job Descriptive Index: Supervision Subscale Sample Items

The following adjectives and phrases describe five aspects of a job, the work itself, supervision, pay promotions, and coworkers. Carefully consider each adjective or phrase and indicate whether or not it is true of your job by circling:

> Y   for YES, this is true of my job.
>
> ?   for I cannot decide if this is true of my job.
>
> N   for NO, this is not true of my job.

The Supervision on My Job

		Y	?	N
>	Asks my advice	Y	?	N
>	Hard to please	Y	?	N
>	Impolite	Y	?	N
>	Influential	Y	?	N
>	Stubborn	Y	?	N
>	Knows job well	Y	?	N

Source: P. C. Smith, L. M. Kendall, and C. L. Hulin. *The Measurement of Satisfaction in Work and Retirement.* Chicago: Rand McNally, 1969.

Thus overall satisfaction measures provide useful additional information. In addition, it may be overall satisfaction with a job that most directly influences some behaviors, such as quitting. Many measures of overall job satisfaction are short and easy to use. One, the *Faces Scale*, asks employees to indicate how satisfied they are with their jobs by circling an appropriate face, ranging from one with a big smile to one with a big frown. Another, the Brayfield–Rothe scale, asks employees simply to indicate their degree of agreement with each of 18 statements about the job, such as "I find real enjoyment in my work" and "My job is like a hobby to me."[61]

In addition to paper-and-pencil tests, satisfaction may be assessed by use of the critical incidents method, interviews, or confrontation meetings. The *critical incidents method* as applied to the measurement of job satisfaction asks employees to recall incidents that were particularly satisfying or dissatisfying to them. Thus, rather than simply assessing levels of satisfaction, the specific determinants of satisfaction and dissatisfaction may be isolated. *Interviews* are useful because they allow in-depth questioning. That is, if signs are seen of satisfaction or of dissatisfaction, further probes can seek to better understand their nature and causes. Finally, *confrontation meetings* bring together groups of employees who are encouraged to express their feelings openly about their jobs. In such a group setting, employees may feel free to say things they might hold back if interviewed alone.

DETERMINANTS OF JOB SATISFACTION

There are two primary views concerning the determinants of job satisfaction—situational and dispositional. The *situational perspective* sees satisfaction as largely due to things in the environment of the employee, such as the nature of the job, reward system, and supervision. If this view is correct, it may be possible to influence satisfaction levels by changing such things. The ***dispositional perspective***, to the contrary, sees satisfaction as due to individual factors—some people are simply more satisfied in general than are others—and thus as relatively stable and more difficult to change. If this view is valid, varying the situation may have little impact on satisfaction.

Situational Determinants of Satisfaction. Many work-related factors influence job satisfaction. These are summarized in Figure 2-9. Among these, equitable rewards, work itself, and others in the organization (such as the supervisor) are often quite important. We examine the specific roles of many of these factors in detail in later chapters.

Dispositional Determinants of Satisfaction. As noted earlier, dispositional views see some people as generally satisfied and others as generally dissatisfied.[62] A direct approach to examining the dispositional perspective is simply to measure the degree to which people seem to be generally positive or negative in their outlooks; these are called ***positive affectivity*** and ***negative affectivity***.[63] Research consistently shows these measures to predict levels of job satisfaction.

The dispositional view is also supported by studies that follow people as they move across jobs through their lives. For example, one study tracked subjects from early adolescence to adulthood. It found that a measure of affective disposition—including items such as "cheerful," "warm," and "irritable (reversed)"—predicted overall attitudes from early adolescence through late adolescence and through two stages of adult life, a span of nearly 50 years.[64]

Another interesting approach to examining the dispositional view looks at identical twins who were reared apart. Such research—some of which considers more than 2,000 twins born in the state of Minnesota between 1936 and 1955—finds

FIGURE 2-9
Work-Related Influences on Satisfaction

Work Factors	Effects
❑ Work Itself	
> Challenge	Mentally challenging work that the individual can successfully accomplish is satisfying.
> Physical Demands	Tiring work is dissatisfying.
> Personal Interest	Personally interesting work is satisfying.
❑ Reward Structure	Rewards that are equitable and that provide accurate feedback on performance are satisfying.
❑ Working Conditions	
> Physical	Satisfaction depends on the match between working conditions and physical needs.
> Goal Attainment	Working conditions that promote goal attainment are satisfying.
❑ Others in the Organization	Individuals will be satisfied with supervisors, coworkers, or subordinates who help them attain rewards. Also, individuals will be more satisfied with colleagues who see things the same way they do.
❑ Organization and Management	Individuals will be satisfied with organizations that have policies and procedures designed to help them attain rewards. Individuals will be dissatisfied with conflicting roles and/or ambiguous roles imposed by the organization.
❑ Fringe Benefits	Fringe benefits do not have a strong influence on job satisfaction for most workers.

Source: Adapted from F. J. Landy, *Psychology at Work,* 4th Ed. Pacific Grove, CA: Brooks/Cole, 1989, p. 470.

considerable similarity in the satisfaction levels of the twins, despite different jobs.[65] The authors of a review of information on these twins concluded, "It may be that trying to be happy is as futile as trying to be taller, and therefore is counterproductive."[66] Such research, which suggests that people may have a satisfaction "set point" from which they may diverge but to which they quickly return, clearly supports a dispositional perspective.

Taken together, these research approaches provide some support for a dispositional view. So we must recognize that, even in an identical situation, people may have very different attitudes. The results certainly do not, though, argue that the situation is irrelevant. Instead, they suggest some people may have generally higher or lower levels of satisfaction than others. Situational factors are still very important.[67]

The Bottom Line feature presents a process model that summarizes the basic steps associated with enhancing employee job satisfaction.

Now complete Skills Practice 2-8, "Field Work: Analyzing Employee Job Satisfaction." The purpose of the activity is for you to get out into the field in order to assess the job satisfaction of an actual employee or manager and to propose specific actions that could be taken to enhance that person's job satisfaction.

BOTTOM LINE

ENHANCING EMPLOYEE JOB SATISFACTION

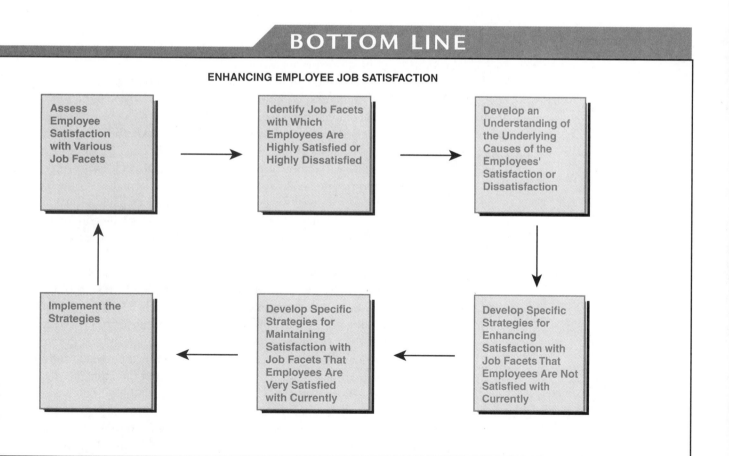

JOB INVOLVEMENT

Job involvement is the degree to which employees really are involved with—that is, get into—their jobs. Job involvement is high when the job is very important to the person's life or central to the person's self-concept. A person with a high degree of job involvement would agree with statements such as these:[68]

> The most important things that happen to me involve my job.
> The major satisfaction of my life comes from my job.
> I live, eat, and breathe my job.

Although companies want their workers to be involved in their jobs, overly high levels of job involvement may be undesirable. At the extreme, employees who are workaholics may neglect their families and outside activities and may even suffer health problems.[69]

A related attitude, *work involvement*, is the degree to which an employee is involved with work in general rather than with a specific job. There are some major differences in work involvement across cultures. For instance, Americans work longer hours and take less leisure time off than peoples of other advanced nations. The average hours worked per year during 2001 were 1,877 in the United States, 1,840 in Japan, 1,708 in Great Britain, 1,596 in France, and 1,480 in Germany.[70]

ORGANIZATIONAL COMMITMENT

Organizational commitment reflects the degree to which the employee shows (1) a strong desire to remain as a member of the organization; (2) a willingness to exert high levels of effort on behalf of the organization; and (3) a belief in, and acceptance of, the values and goals of the organization.[71]

Commitment can be classified in several ways. One important distinction is between affective commitment and continuance commitment.[72] *Affective commitment* is an emotional attachment characterized by strong affective ties to the organization and psychological identification with the organization. In other words, affective commitment flows from liking the organization, sharing its values, and caring about its fate. People with strong affective commitment *want* to stay with the firm. *Continuance commitment* results from considering the benefits of organizational membership and the perceived costs of leaving. It involves asking the questions "Can I afford to quit? What would I gain and lose?" As such, continuance commitment flows from the belief that one *needs* to stay with the firm because equal or better alternatives are not available elsewhere.

It might seem that a company would like to see very high levels of organizational commitment in its work force. For instance, as might be expected, employees with high levels of organizational commitment have low levels of turnover.[73] This relationship is strongest for younger employees, perhaps because they have less vested in the job than older employees do.[74] Evidence also suggests that commitment causes job satisfaction: Employees who are committed to their organizations apparently develop levels of satisfaction consistent with that commitment.[75]

Nevertheless, higher levels of commitment may not be desirable in some cases. For example, if low-performing employees are very committed to the organization, they may be reluctant to leave. If management is constrained from terminating low-performing employees, such commitment could be costly to the firm. Also, we have all heard of cases in which employees have been so committed to an organization or to a cause that they have been afraid to rock the boat or to criticize others in the firm. In extreme cases, commitment has led to the commission of illegal or unethical acts. As such, more commitment, like more of most things in life, is not necessarily better.

A subject of great current interest is how the massive downsizing of firms affects commitment. One stream of reasoning is that workers, recognizing that their firms treat them as expendable, will become disillusioned and stop caring about the organization, reducing commitment. Another is that in a climate of dramatic downsizing, workers will feel grateful for their jobs and cling to them fiercely. Perhaps it is the case that downsizing has counterbalancing effects, decreasing affective commitment but increasing continuance commitment.

REAL AND EXPRESSED ATTITUDES

We should pause here and make an important, if obvious, point: People's expressed attitudes may differ dramatically from their true attitudes. People may hide or falsely report their true attitudes because they feel the attitudes will be unpopular or somehow lead to retribution. Further, they may attempt to disguise their emotions because emotions reflect attitudes. In many cases, in fact, employees are required to express certain emotions as part of their work roles.[76] For example, employees at one chain of supermarkets are told to be friendly and courteous with customers and that "a friendly smile is a must." As such, these employees' smiles say nothing about their true feelings.[77]

FORMING ATTITUDES

We can form attitudes in a variety of ways—through direct personal experience, association, or social learning. Let's consider these in turn.

> **Direct experience.** For one, we may have direct personal experience with the attitude object. We may, for instance, have met a candidate for public office and liked what she had to say.
> **Association.** We may also form attitudes through association. That is, we may transfer an attitude about a particular attitude object to a new attitude object that is somehow similar. For example, if we like all of our current acquaintances who are runners, we may like a new acquaintance after learning she runs.
> **Social learning**. Finally, we may form attitudes indirectly through social learning. Here attitudes are influenced by information provided by others. We may read about the latest CD of the Indigo Girls, for instance, or may hear it discussed on MTV or listen to friends debating its merits.

Attitudes formed in any of these ways may be held intensely. However, those attitudes formed through direct personal experience are more clearly defined, held with greater certainty, more stable over time, and more resistant to counterinfluence than attitudes formed indirectly.

THE RELATIONSHIPS OF ATTITUDES TO BEHAVIORS

We said earlier that one reason managers may care about attitudes is that attitudes may be associated with important behaviors. If so, knowledge of the relationships of work attitudes to work behaviors could be valuable. Here we explore three possible ways they may be related: Attitudes may cause behaviors, behaviors may cause attitudes, or they may cause each other. Think carefully about the following issues—they are absolutely critical to understanding many issues in organizational life (and life in general).

Do Attitudes Cause Behaviors? Are you enjoying reading this chapter? Is there anything you'd rather be doing? If so, why don't you do it? Think about it for a minute and make a list of some of the reasons.

We said earlier that one reason why managers care about employee attitudes is that those attitudes may influence behaviors. This seems to make sense. If we have negative attitudes concerning the consumption of horsemeat, we might refuse to eat it. Similarly, if we don't like our jobs, it seems reasonable that we might not put our full effort into them. This general view, you'll recall, was suggested by Figure 2-6.

In fact, though, many researchers have found that the link between attitudes and behaviors is sometimes surprisingly weak. In the first major study of attitude–behavior relationships, R. T. LaPiere reported on his travels through the United States with a Chinese couple.[78] During those travels, the couple was almost always treated hospitably at hotels and restaurants. However, a survey of owners of the same establishments found their attitudes toward Asians to be very negative. In fact, 90 percent said that as a matter of policy Asians would not be served. Clearly, attitudes were not being translated into behaviors, at least in any simple and direct way.[79]

More recent attempts to sort out this puzzle have suggested reasons why the attitude–behavior linkage may be weak. For instance, even though people have certain attitudes, they may have no choice but to behave in certain ways. They may, for instance, have to keep a job they hate because no other job is available. We must recognize that a person's behavior is the result of many factors beyond attitude, including pressures exerted by others, the nature of the job market, and personality characteristics. For example, in the LaPiere research, the hotel and restaurant owners may simply have needed the money, they may have reported attitudes they didn't really hold, or they may have felt uncomfortable refusing service to actual people as opposed to hypothetical abstractions.

However, research may underestimate attitude–behavior relationships if, as we've suggested may sometimes be the case, reported attitudes or behaviors are false. For example, if employees falsely report how satisfied they are (perhaps from fear of retribution) or how they have behaved (perhaps because they were supposed to engage in the behavior but didn't), research on the link of satisfaction to that behavior will probably understate the strength of the relationship. Also, the strength of relationships will be understated if the instruments used to measure attitudes or behaviors lack validity or reliability.

In general, attitudes will probably best predict behavior when four conditions are present:[80]

> **The attitude is specific to the behavior.** An attitude such as intention to quit is probably a better predictor of turnover than a more general attitude, such as general job satisfaction.
> **The attitude is potent.** The stronger the attitude in our thinking, the more it will influence subsequent behavior. In general, attitudes from personal experience are more potent than attitudes based on secondhand information or less direct sources.

> **The attitude is salient.** Attitudes are more salient when they are more noticeable or prominent in our attention. Salient attitudes are more likely to be recalled and acted on. Attitudes may be made more salient by *priming,* using cues or reminders to bring them forward in our memory. For instance, a poster about workplace safety may prime or retrieve a worker's earlier opinions concerning safety. Once recalled, the attitudes are more likely to be acted on.

> **The behavior is not constrained or subject to other influences.** Attitudes will have little impact on behavior if the behavior cannot be varied or if many other things are affecting the behavior.

These factors suggest that attitudes will have the greatest impact on behavior if they are specific, formed through direct experience, made salient, and unconstrained. Clearly, these conditions don't always hold.

Now let's briefly consider evidence concerning the relationships between satisfaction and work behaviors. We focus here specifically on satisfaction, because it has certainly been the subject of more interest and research than other work-related attitudes. Before turning to research findings, let's consider Figure 2-10. According to that figure, continued dissatisfaction will lead to frustration. Because frustration is painful, we seek ways to reduce that pain. We can do this in a variety of ways:

> One way would be to *channel off the frustration.* For instance, after a bad day at work we might go home and yell at our children or spouse; this process of venting our frustration somewhere other than where it was caused is called ***displacement***.

> A second possibility is that we might *strike back at the source of frustration* by making accusations about people who are upsetting us, making negative statements about the company, joining informal groups that resist organizational

FIGURE 2-10
Some Potential Consequences of Dissatisfaction

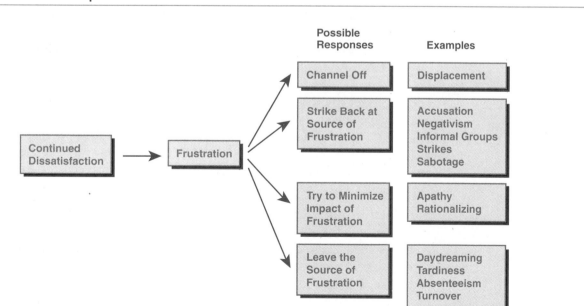

> rules and pressures, going out on strike, or even engaging in small acts of sabotage, such as intentionally denting a fender.

> Further, we might try to *minimize the psychological impact of the frustration* by becoming apathetic about the job—and thereby perhaps paying little attention to the quality of our work—or by convincing ourselves things aren't so bad.

> Finally, we might choose simply to *leave the source of frustration*. We can leave psychologically by daydreaming or physically through tardiness, absenteeism, or turnover.

Now let's look at some of these relationships in more detail. In particular, let's consider how satisfaction is related to turnover, absenteeism, performance, and work violence.

Satisfaction and Turnover. Retention simply means remaining with an organization. Its opposite—turnover—has many costs to firms, including disruption of the work process, the expenses of recruiting and training new employees, the loss of employees with valuable skills, knowledge, and experience, and low productivity of new employees during the training period. In some industries, turnover rates exceed 100 percent annually. Overall, voluntary turnover rates in the United States were 20.3 percent in 2002.[81]

Research clearly shows that more satisfied workers are less likely to leave the firm.[82] These studies find a little over 15 percent of the variance in turnover to be related to variance in satisfaction. Although that percentage may not seem like a lot, a decrease—or an increase—in turnover of even a few percentage points may determine the success, or even survival, of many firms.

Figure 2-11 presents a model of the relationship of satisfaction to turnover.[83] That model shows the link of satisfaction to turnover is indirect. That is, job satisfaction doesn't influence turnover directly. Instead, it influences things that may affect turnover, such as thoughts of quitting, intention to search for a new job, and intention to quit or stay.[84] In addition, the intention to quit or stay is also influenced by whether or not the employee thinks another acceptable job is available. Also, although not shown explicitly in the model, many sorts of pressures and factors, such as the wishes of one's family members and friends, feelings about the community, and aversion to change, may play roles.

In addition, economic conditions are important, because we're less likely to quit our jobs, even when we're unhappy with them, if times are hard and no other jobs are available. It is probably the case that satisfaction is a better predictor of turnover in good economic times than in bad.[85] In good times, a dissatisfied employee may feel confident other jobs will be available and therefore quit. In bad times, an employee may simply put up with dissatisfaction rather than take a chance on being out of work.

Satisfaction and Absenteeism. Attendance relates to whether an employee reports for work on a given day. Failure to attend—absenteeism—can be quite costly for companies. Typically, companies continue to pay absent employees. Further, absenteeism causes costly disruptions, such as the need to reschedule work and reassign employees. One estimate is that such disruptions cause productivity to drop by as much as 2.5 percent for every 1 percent increase in absenteeism.[86] Those

FIGURE 2-11

A Model of the Relationship of Satisfaction to Turnover

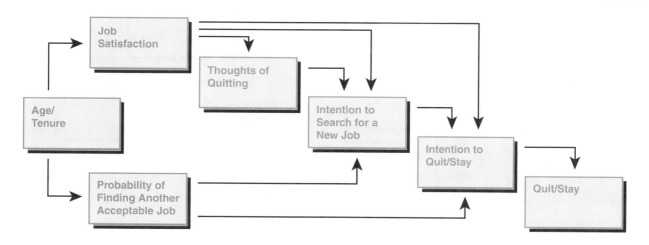

disruptions may also result in products of decreased quality, because regular employees are replaced by "swing" employees who move from one job to another. The defect-plagued "Monday car"—largely assembled by swing employees because of high absenteeism in auto assembly plants on Mondays—is an example.

An estimated 400 million person-days are lost annually through absenteeism—about four times the number lost in strikes. Total annual costs of absenteeism have been put in excess of $25 billion and are on the rise. In 2002, overall absence rates were 4.12 percent and absenteeism cost U.S. firms an average of $789 per employee, up from $593 in 1994.[87] Of course, it's hard to tell how much of this absenteeism is avoidable (that is, due simply to the employee's desire not to go to work that day) or unavoidable (due to factors such as illness or transportation problems). Because even if companies tried to keep track of such distinctions, there is one fairly safe bet in organizations: Nobody calls in bored. Instead, absent employees often invent more acceptable reasons for their failure to come to work. It is probably the case, though, that avoidable absenteeism makes up a large share of the total.

Research shows that satisfaction and absenteeism are negatively related, but the association is not as strong as we might expect. In fact, an analysis of many past studies that examined the relationship between job satisfaction and absenteeism found that little more than 2 percent of the variance in satisfaction is somehow associated with variance in absenteeism.[88]

However, satisfaction may play a larger role in determining absenteeism than such figures indicate. This is because, as we just indicated, much absenteeism is unavoidable because of illness and family emergencies. If the relationship of satisfaction to avoidable absenteeism could be assessed, it would probably be considerable. In addition, some facets of satisfaction may predict absenteeism better than others.

Figure 2-12 presents a model of the relationship of satisfaction to attendance. The model indicates that job satisfaction may influence motivation to attend, but motivation to attend also depends on other pressures to attend, such as a spouse or

FIGURE 2-12

A Model of the Relationship of Satisfaction to Attendance

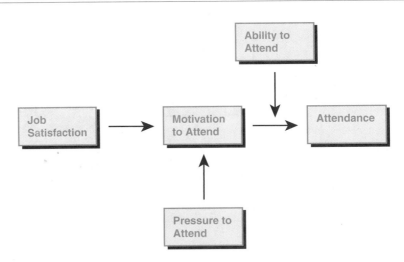

peer who tells us to get our lazy self to work. Further, whether or not motivation to attend results in attendance depends on the ability to attend. For example, we may want to go to work but be unable to do so because we are ill or our car breaks down. Perhaps the relatively low overall negative relationship between satisfaction and absenteeism is a reflection of the many pressures faced by employees and the many constraints on their behavior.

Satisfaction and Performance. A strong, and understandable, tendency is to assume satisfied employees will also be motivated and productive.[89] As we noted earlier in the chapter, this tendency is seen in statements such as "A satisfied worker is a productive worker." However, things are more complex than such statements would suggest.

Findings concerning the relationship of satisfaction to performance show us why research is often needed to augment common sense. It seems reasonable to expect that satisfied workers would be more productive, but many studies show this is really not the case, at least to any appreciable degree. Early reviews of the satisfaction–performance relationship concluded that the relationship of satisfaction to performance is so low as to be negligible, and satisfaction does not imply motivation for strong performance.[90] Further, a major statistical summary of previous research (including 74 studies with more than 12,000 subjects) revealed that only about 3 percent of variance in performance was associated with variance in satisfaction.[91]

To help make sense of these findings, consider Figures 2-13(a) and 2-13(b). Figure 2-13(a) presents the traditional view of the satisfaction–performance relationship: Satisfied employees exert more effort to perform and subsequently perform at higher levels. If this were an accurate picture of how satisfaction and performance are related, we would certainly expect to see a stronger relationship than is the case. Figure 2-13(b) suggests a different possibility: Performance may indirectly influence satisfaction. That is, performance levels affect the rewards employees receive. If employees feel their rewards are fair, they will be satisfied. If, however, they see the

FIGURE 2-13
Two Views of the Satisfaction–Performance Relationship

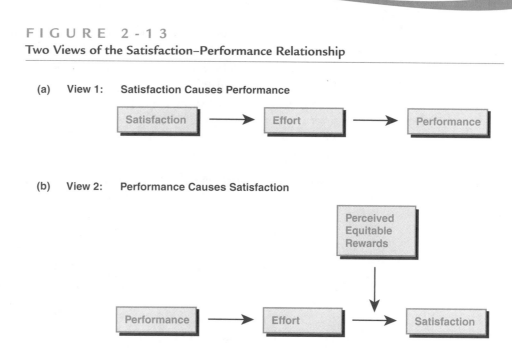

(a) View 1: **Satisfaction Causes Performance**

Satisfaction → Effort → Performance

(b) View 2: **Performance Causes Satisfaction**

Perceived Equitable Rewards

Performance → Effort → Satisfaction

rewards as unfair, they will be dissatisfied. This model, then, turns the traditional wisdom on its head, viewing satisfaction as a consequence of performance rather than a cause.

If this model is correct—and research suggests it is—why aren't satisfaction–performance relationships stronger? Quite simply, some companies don't reward their employees properly. For example, as we discuss in more detail in Chapter 6, if a company pays all of its employees the same amount, or if low performers get more than high performers, high performers will feel unfairly treated and low performers may be pleased. As such, high performers will be dissatisfied and low performers will be satisfied, resulting in a negative relationship between satisfaction and performance. Other companies may tie pay and other rewards directly to performance and may thus have very satisfied high performers, and vice versa, resulting in a positive satisfaction–performance relationship. This all says the relationship between satisfaction and performance among a firm's employees is important; if it is negative, the company should carefully examine whether it is rewarding employees properly. There is still another reason why firms would like the relationship of satisfaction to performance to be positive. Because absenteeism and turnover are negatively related to satisfaction, a positive relationship between satisfaction and performance helps ensure that a firm's high performers will continue to participate and absenteeism and turnover will be concentrated in low performers.

The question of the relationship of satisfaction to performance is still not settled. For instance, most studies of the satisfaction–performance relationship have used a narrow definition of performance, such as quantity of output or quality of craftsmanship. Broader performance behaviors—such as helping coworkers with a job-related problem, accepting orders without a fuss, making timely and constructive comments about the work unit or its head to outsiders, and protecting and conserving organizational resources—may in fact result from satisfaction.[92] Research shows that relationships between job satisfaction and these *organizational citizenship behaviors* (or *prosocial* behaviors) are much stronger than is typical of studies of the satisfaction–performance relationship where performance is narrowly defined.[93] The stronger relationships may be because citizenship behaviors generally represent actions more under the control of workers than conventional performance measures.[94] These citizenship behaviors have received little attention, but in many cases they may be just as important as narrower performance measures.

Satisfaction and Work Violence. Figure 2-10 suggested that dissatisfied employees may strike back at the source of their frustration. Unfortunately, we've seen what happens when this reaction to frustration becomes extreme.[95] Workplace violence, including homicides, is increasing. An estimated 1.7 million workers are injured in nonfatal workplace assaults annually and more than 1,000 are murdered, at an estimated total cost to companies of $35.4 billion.[96] Homicide is now the number-3 work-related cause of death, behind car crashes and other machinery accidents, and it is the *leading* cause of death for women in the workplace.

Certainly, not all of these murders are due to job dissatisfaction, but it appears that dissatisfaction does play a role. Violence is especially great in regimented settings, such as post offices, where employees feel they have no control over their work. In the face of dozens of killings in post offices, attention was focused on employees' jobs, described as treadmills of angry monotony, with labor–management hostility heightening tension.[97] The Centers for Disease Control and Prevention have formally declared workplace homicide an epidemic.

To deal with threats of violence, some firms are training managers to recognize aggressive behavior and effectively deal with it through communication and conflict management.[98] Some, such as IBM, have threat-assessment teams that meet to evaluate any threats that are made and to decide what action to take, including notification of law enforcement authorities. Firms must also recognize the danger of violence in the wake of downsizings and must be especially sensitive to the needs of those affected. Further, some organizations, such as the post office, now screen applicants in the hope of keeping out potentially aggressive individuals.[99]

Satisfaction and Nonwork Life. An intriguing, and important, question is how job satisfaction relates to satisfaction with nonwork life. For instance, perhaps job satisfaction somehow carries over to life satisfaction. Or perhaps employees who are satisfied at work devote so much time and energy to work, they ignore other aspects of their lives, resulting in low satisfaction with nonwork life. Still another possibility is that employees compensate for dissatisfaction at work by focusing more on home life and finding satisfaction there. If increasing employee job satisfaction were found to reduce nonwork satisfaction, such increases would be a mixed blessing. Happily, most research supports the spillover view: Satisfaction in one sphere of life, such as the job, seems to increase satisfaction in other spheres.

The Financial Impact of Attitudes. The failure to find that satisfaction causes better performance, at least in terms of traditional performance measures, does not mean attitudes don't influence financial performance. Instead, as we've tried to show, absenteeism, turnover, and many other employee behaviors also have substantial costs. The area of *behavioral accounting* is now trying to assess the financial impact of attitudes. It does this by examining the costs of such behaviors as turnover and absenteeism and the strength of their links to attitudes. Although this is still a relatively new field, and fraught with measurement problems, some of its conclusions are remarkable.

For instance, one study used behavioral accounting to estimate the costs of absenteeism, turnover, and balancing shortages of 160 bank tellers.[100] The study concluded that moderate improvements in attitudes averaging perhaps 0.7 on a seven-point scale would yield the bank total savings of $781,892, or $4,886.83 per employee. Another study has estimated that, on a national basis, a very modest improvement in employee attitudes of perhaps 0.15 on a seven-point scale would result in a total financial benefit of over $1 billion.[101]

THE ROLE OF MOOD

Our discussion to this point has focused on a number of work-related attitudes, such as satisfaction, organizational commitment, and job involvement, which we would expect to be rather heavily influenced by aspects of the job and to be at least somewhat enduring. However, some mental states are more ephemeral. *Mood* is a transient mental state or attitude, perhaps caused by something as fleeting as a sunny sky, convenient parking spot, pleasant odor, or good meal. Mood can affect job satisfaction as well as behaviors.[102] One of the most consistent findings in the literature of psychology is that happy people are helpful people. People who are in a good mood—whether because of finding change in a public phone coin slot, receiving a gift of free stationery, having access to sunshine, falling in love, or getting a cookie—do helpful things.[103] Interestingly, bad mood *also* often leads to helping behaviors. Helping others seems to be a way we can feel better about ourselves. Thus helping softens a bad mood and sustains a good mood.[104] As such, important work behaviors such as prosocial behaviors may be heavily influenced by mood.

DO BEHAVIORS CAUSE ATTITUDES?

The evidence we've reviewed shows that work attitudes often do influence work and nonwork behaviors, although sometimes in rather complex ways. Now we turn to the flip side of the question: Do behaviors cause attitudes? The answer is a clear "yes." Here we consider a few ways that behaviors may influence attitudes.

Dissonance Reduction. Leon Festinger proposed a theory of cognitive dissonance that suggests how behaviors may cause attitudes.[105] *Cognitions* are thoughts, and *dissonance* refers to lack of harmony. So *cognitive dissonance* is a situation in which we have conflicting thoughts. For example, if we don't like a coworker, Janet, but must treat her nicely because of job demands, we may experience such conflict.

As detailed by Festinger, cognitive dissonance is a tense, uncomfortable state.[106] People will do something to reduce that tension. One way to do so is to change one or both of the cognitions to make them consistent.

Furthermore, Festinger proposed, some cognitions are more resistant to change than others. For instance, cognitions based on physical reality, such as the fact that we just treated Janet nicely, are more resistant to change than are cognitions based on opinions and attitudes, such as our negative feelings toward Janet. The bottom line, then, is that we may change our attitudes to make them consistent with our behaviors. We may actually begin to like Janet.[107]

We said earlier that the high levels of reported job satisfaction may be artificially high. Dissonance theory suggests another reason why that may be the case. A set of thoughts such as "I continue to work on this job, yet it is dissatisfying" reflects dissonance. To reduce that dissonance, employees may convince themselves they are in fact satisfied with their jobs.

Consequences of Behavior. There are other important routes by which behaviors may influence attitudes. For one thing, as suggested by our discussion of the relationship of satisfaction to performance, behaviors may lead to consequences that affect attitudes. For instance, a high-performing employee may get a big raise, which may in turn increase satisfaction with pay. Or simply eating a food we've always shunned may lead us to like it.

Self-Attribution. Evidence indicates that behaving in a certain way can lead us to make corresponding attributions about ourselves. For example, smiling (for no good reason) can apparently induce a good mood and increase willingness to laugh at humorous material. Even though we are playing a role, we seem to internalize the attitudes and moods that maintain the role.[108]

Indoctrination. Brainwashing and cult recruitment are two forms of indoctrination that have proven to be effective. With brainwashing, torture or threat may be used to cause victims to yield to their oppressors' cause. Further, evidence suggests that brainwashing is most effective when pressures are withheld and the victim is induced, step by step, to behave more and more in agreement with the captors.[109] As the victim begins to engage in the behavior with pressure withheld, he or she comes to infer that the behavior was voluntary, and attitudes change accordingly.

Cults tend to bring about attitude change by isolating their members, shielding them from outside perspectives and influences and controlling their interpretations of events. Cults tend first to invite prospective members to inquiry meetings and then to ask them to make gradually stronger commitments by attending education sessions, doing favors for other members, or tithing larger amounts for cult support.[110] Over time, a momentum of compliance is established and the member's commitment to the cult grows.

Although indoctrination does not take these blatant forms in work organizations, these same actions may be seen there in weaker forms. Indoctrination tactics provide additional evidence that behaviors may cause attitudes.

TOP TEN LIST: KEY POINTS TO REMEMBER
UNDERSTANDING AND VALUING DIFFERENCES

10. Understand and adapt to personalities and working styles of others in your organization.

9. When making hiring decisions, assess the quality of fit or compatibility of an individual's personality with his or her job as well as with the culture of the work unit and the organization.

8. Remember that perception is the reality to which other people respond in organizations.

7. Perceptions of a given issue or situation can vary widely across people in an organization. Encourage others to share their perspectives with one another to develop a greater understanding of the issue and to move toward establishing a common ground.

6. Be aware of the biases you possess and the assumptions you make about others in your organization. Make a conscious effort to minimize the influence of these factors on how you perceive a situation or issue.

5. When dealing with perceptual differences between employees, be sure to get all sides of the story before making a decision.

4. When managing diversity, make sure you have a clear definition or vision of diversity for your organization that includes specific objectives and measures for assessing the effectiveness of your diversity program.

3. Take a systems view of organizations when implementing a diversity program. Implement diversity strategies that will enable your organization to attract, motivate, develop, and retain your target employees.

2. Maintain an open and flexible attitude in dealing with cross-cultural differences among your employees.

1. Assess employee job satisfaction on a regular basis, and develop specific strategies for either maintaining or improving job satisfaction through managerial and organizational policies and practices.

QUESTIONS FOR REVIEW AND REFLECTION
REVIEW QUESTIONS

1. What is diversity? What are specific steps (e.g., training, rewarding) that companies are taking to manage diversity successfully?

2. What is emotional intelligence? Why is it important in organizations?

3. Describe each of the following personality characteristics: risk-taking propensity, proactive personality, authoritarianism, dogmatism, locus of control, tolerance for ambiguity, Machiavellianism, self-monitoring, and Type A and Type B behavior patterns.

4. Discuss the Big 5 personality dimensions, including how they may be relevant at work.

5. Describe five ways that globalization is likely to affect you.

6. List six dimensions on which national cultures differ.

7. Describe the stages of the perceptual process.

8. Discuss each of the following perceptual distortions: stereotyping, Pygmalion effect, halo effect, projection, primacy/recency effects, and perceptual defense.

9. What is causal attribution? What are the three factors we consider when trying to sort out causes of an individual's behavior?

10. What are attitudes? What are the three components of attitudes? How are those components interrelated? Why are attitudes important?

11. What is job satisfaction? How is it measured? What are six work-related influences on satisfaction?

12. Define *job involvement* and *organizational commitment.* What is the difference between affective commitment and continuance commitment?

13. Discuss how job satisfaction levels are related to turnover, absenteeism, performance (including organizational citizenship behaviors), and work violence.

14. Identify four ways that behaviors may influence attitudes.

CRITICAL THINKING QUESTIONS

1. A colleague makes the following argument: "I can accept the fact I shouldn't discriminate against minorities. What I can't accept is that I have to change my attitudes toward minorities. The company can define unacceptable behavior at work, but it has no right telling me what to think." Take and defend a position for or against this argument.

2. Consider the dimensions on which national cultures differ (that is, individualism versus collectivism, power distance, uncertainty avoidance, and so on). Select one of those dimensions. Discuss consequences in the workplace if someone from another culture differing on the dimension from the United States were to take a job in a U.S. company. Then indicate what steps (policies, practices, training, etc.) you believe the U.S. company should take to help accommodate the differences.

3. Emotional intelligence is currently a very popular concept. However, as with many popular concepts, some people have dismissed it as a fad, seeing it as "just another call to get in touch with your feelings." Do you agree? Why or why not?

4. Take a position for or against the following statement: "Companies should have the right to refuse to hire people who have high levels of negative affectivity. Those people are going to be dissatisfied no matter what the company does, and they're likely to turn off customers and colleagues."

5. Consider the specific personality dimensions considered in this chapter (that is, risk-taking propensity, proactive personality, authoritarianism, etc.). Use those personality dimensions to describe each of the following: (1) a successful CEO of a large computer equipment retailer; (2) a successful entrepreneur; (3) someone you'd like for your boss; (4) someone you'd like for your subordinate. What are the reasons for any differences in the personality profiles across the four individuals?

6. After you tell a colleague about the Pygmalion effect, he replies, "It sounds to me like when we assign new subordinates to bosses, we should overstate their qualifications. That way, the bosses will treat them better, they'll perform better, and everyone will be happy." Do you agree? Why or why not?

7. One of your friends says, "I was torn about whether or not to quit my job here. Now that I've made the decision to quit, though, I've really started to see a lot of the problems here more clearly. This place really stinks." How might you want to counsel your friend about her changing perceptions of her current job?

8. The well-known saying "Nobody on her deathbed ever said, 'I should have spent more time at the office'" would seem to suggest people tend to be too involved in their work, at the expense of their personal lives. Do you agree? Why or why not?

9. A colleague says, "I guess I just don't get it with these organizational citizenship behaviors. As I understand it, they're behaviors that are good and useful but aren't included in the job description. I have two concerns. First, if they're really desirable, why aren't they in the job description? Second, should people be rewarded for engaging in organizational citizenship behaviors? On the one hand, they're doing something that helps the company, which is good. On the other hand, I've always believed people should be rewarded for doing their defined jobs as well as possible. Is it fair to reward people for things that are really outside the scope of their jobs? Won't that lead to favoritism?" How would you respond?

EXPERIENTIAL EXERCISES

WEB EXERCISE 2-1

Go to the following Web page, titled "Valuing Diversity: An Ongoing Commitment," which describes IBM's current diversity efforts:

http://www-3.ibm.com/employment/us/diverse/index.shtml

Write a three-page typewritten report on the material on this site. In your report, be sure to include a discussion of the following:

> Why IBM has an ongoing commitment to diversity
> IBM's policy on equal opportunity
> The ideals on which IBM's work force diversity "bridge" is built
> The challenges identified by IBM's Global Workforce Diversity Council

WEB EXERCISE 2-2

Using Google or some other search engine, do searches on one or more of the following topics: "diversity and training," "diversity and goals," "diversity and benefits," or "diversity and problems." In each case, you will get literally millions of hits. Select any *three* informative sites. Explore those sites and write a report discussing at least one interesting feature from each site.

CASE 2-1

EXCELLENCE THROUGH DIVERSITY: THE PFIZER APPROACH

The Case for Diversity

In today's competitive marketplace, more and more companies are realizing the link between organizational success and employee diversity. The desire for diversity goes beyond meeting the standards established by affirmative action. According to Business Week Online's article "Protecting Growth—the Business Case for Diversity Today,"[111] benchmarking has shown that "company diversity raises marketing opportunities, increases creativity and innovation, enhances recruitment and retention, boosts productivity, ups shareholder value, deepens customer loyalty, and increases employee commitment and morale."

Diversity reaps these benefits for a number of reasons. A more diverse organization can better relate to a large population base. Thus companies make fewer mistakes stemming from ignorance or misunderstandings about cultural differences. This creates better working relationships.

Moreover, if a workplace is diverse, it is more likely to attract broader talent. Because talent comes from a variety of sources, an organization that has broader talent may be able to make a better contribution to the industry.

The Company[112]

Pfizer is one of the world's largest health care companies, and it maintains a strong commitment to diversity. The company is based in New York. Pfizer discovers, develops, manufactures, and markets pharmaceuticals for humans and animals. It focuses primarily on three segments: health care, animal health, and consumer health care (e.g., Listerine mouthwash, Visine eyedrops). Its other (pharmaceutical drugs such as Lipitor for cholesterol reduction and Zoloft, an antidepressant) well-known products include Viagra and Zyrtec. Pfizer employs 120,000 people worldwide in more than 80 countries. Its products are available in over 150 countries. Its 2003 research and development budget was $7.1 billion. In 2002, it generated $32.4 billion in revenue.

The Mission of Pfizer is:
We will become the world's most valued company to patients, customers, colleagues, investors, business

partners, and the communities where we work and live.
The Purpose of Pfizer is:
We dedicate ourselves to humanity's quest for longer, healthier, happier lives through innovation in pharmaceutical, customer, and animals health products.
Pfizer's core values for supporting the achievement of its mission and purpose are:

- *Integrity—We demand of ourselves and others the highest ethical standards, and our products and processes will be of the highest quality.*
- *Innovation—This is the key to improving health and sustaining Pfizer's growth and profitability.*
- *Respect—We recognize that people are the cornerstone of Pfizer's success, we value diversity as a source of strength, and we are proud of Pfizer's history of treating people with respect and dignity.*
- *Customer Focus—We are deeply committed to meeting the needs of our customers, and we constantly focus on customer satisfaction.*
- *Teamwork—We know that to be a successful company we must work together, frequently transcending organizational and geographical boundaries to meet the changing needs of our customers.*
- *Leadership—We believe that leaders empower those around them by sharing knowledge and rewarding outstanding individual effort. Leaders are those who step forward to achieve difficult goals, envisioning what needs to happen and motivating others.*
- *Performance—We strive for continuous improvement in our performance, measuring results carefully, and ensuring that integrity and respect for people are never compromised.*
- *Community—We play an active role in making every country and community in which we operate a better place to live and work, knowing that the ongoing vitality of our host nations and local communities has a direct impact on the long-term health of our business.*

Pfizer's Approach to Diversity

Pfizer's formal statement on diversity is as follows:

Diversity of People, Diversity of Thought[113]

Pfizer is an equal opportunity employer, committed to the hiring, advancement, and fair treatment of individuals without regard to race, color, sex, sexual preference, age, national origin, ethnicity, disability, or veteran status, or any other protected status designated by federal, state, or local law.

Diversity of thought is critical to reaching the most innovative, customer-focused solutions to the many issues, problems, and challenges confronting our business. As such it is the responsibility of every manager to value and secure diversity of thought in his/her work unit by employing and developing the highest-caliber individuals differing from one another culturally, intellectually, and experientially, as well as by race, gender, and other factors.

Pfizer does not view diversity simply as the terms described in the Equal Employment Opportunity categories of race, gender and ethnicity, but diversity in its broadest sense: diversity of thought, of experience, and of background.

Pfizer's Diversity Initiatives

Pfizer has several initiatives in place to increase diversity within the organization.[114] These include providing support to school science programs, issuing scholarship and internship opportunities to college students, formal diversity training for employees, and a minority mentorship program.

Pfizer provides broad support for junior high education, primarily targeting females and minorities because they are typically underrepresented in the scientific community. The company offers training programs for science teachers, supplies for science laboratories, and hosts annual science fairs. The fairs are intended to expose students to the excitement of scientific research. A researcher from Pfizer's staff also demonstrates experiments like entertaining chemical reactions to pique student interest.

Another method that Pfizer uses to promote diversity is the Pfizer Cultural Diversity Scholarship Program. The program targets universities in each of its five geographic regions, donating four $2,000 scholarships at each school. The objective is to encourage students from diverse backgrounds to pursue a career with the company. Two scholarships are awarded to business students and two are given to biomedical science majors. Pfizer also provides internships for students prior to graduation and employment opportunities afterward.

One of Pfizer's objectives is achieving a global business perspective. Building diversity is one way to accomplish this. All employees at Pfizer must participate in a half-day training program, which works to increase employee awareness about the importance of diversity. The course, Creating a Culture of Inclusion, allows Pfizer to explain its diversity philosophy. Joe Bonito, vice president of Global Leadership, says the course will "explain how and why differences in employees are both respected and valued here. We compete in a marketplace that is diverse. Our customers are diverse and they are global. . . . The more we understand our customers, the more we will understand how to market to them. To do that, we need people who appreciate diversity and are diverse themselves."

Finally, Pfizer uses minority mentorship to ensure that new employees flourish in the company. Through this program, Pfizer hopes to break down the barriers that minority employees are likely to encounter. Mentors serve two primary roles: They assist minority employees in navigating the subtleties of corporate culture and help them develop the self-confidence they will need to succeed.

Discussion Questions

1. Why does Pfizer emphasize diversity so much? How does the company view the relationship between diversity and the long-term performance of the company?
2. To what extent do you feel that Pfizer's diversity initiatives are appropriate for demonstrating the company's commitment to diversity?
3. What recommendations would you give to Pfizer management in terms of addressing diversity issues effectively in the future?
4. What are the practical implications of this case for you as a future manager in a real-world organization?

CASE 2-2

OPRAH WINFREY'S MULTIFACETED PERSONALITY

Background[115]

Oprah Winfrey was born on January 29, 1954, in Kosciusko, Mississippi. She started her broadcasting career at the age of 17 when she was hired by a radio station in Nashville. Oprah attended Tennessee State University where she majored in speech communications and performing arts.

In January 1984, Oprah moved to Chicago where she helped turn around a struggling TV show called *AM Chicago*. This show was eventually expanded into a one-hour format and renamed *The Oprah Winfrey Show*.

The Oprah Winfrey Show went on to become the number-one nationally syndicated talk show in less than a year. The show has won many Daytime Emmy Awards including "Outstanding Host," "Outstanding Talk/Service Program," and "Outstanding Direction."

Oprah's love of acting and producing entertainment programs resulted in her creating her own production company called HARPO Entertainment Group that consists of Harpo Productions, Inc, HARPO Films, and HARPO Video, Inc.

Oprah has received many different awards, including being named one of the "100 Most Influential People of the 20th Century" by *Time* magazine. She was also listed as the first African American woman to become a billionaire in *Forbes* magazine.

Oprah's Personality[116, 117]

Oprah maintains an unconventional, but highly effective management style**.** The key dimensions of her personality and management style are discussed here.

Oprah the Perfectionist

Oprah has the reputation of being a perfectionist. When working on her magazine *O,* she examines every detail of the issue meticulously. If she finds a mistake, she feels frustrated with herself for not discovering it sooner. When reviewing previous issues, she is rarely satisfied with what she sees. She realizes she obsesses over her work.

Sometimes Oprah can be a difficult person to work with because of her overwhelming desire for perfection. For instance, in the launch of her magazine *O*, she insisted it reach all customers on the same day, in the same way her show reaches households every day at 4 P.M. When a distributor explained that magazines are still delivered by truck, she complained, saying magazine distribution needed to be updated.

Oprah the Inspiration

One way Oprah is able to inspire women is by being open about her own struggles and how she was able to overcome them. Whether discussing her humble beginnings, her childhood sexual abuse, or her struggle with her weight, Oprah makes people feel that, no matter what difficulties they are experiencing, they will be okay. She encourages people to find meaning in their lives and to seek out their purpose. Her empowering message is "You are responsible for your own life." Oprah encourages women to be true to their "authentic self" (a term coined by "life strategist" Dr. Phil). She emphasizes self-reliance. By sharing her personal struggles, she has won the trust of her audience.

Oprah has several forums in which she is able to deliver her inspirational message: her talk show, her magazine, and, most recently, her road show called "Living Your Best Life."

Oprah's show pushes viewers to work continually to better themselves. Oprah shares tidbits of inspiration through quotes, books, and her guests. One of her favorite quotes is by Ralph Waldo Emerson: "What lies behind us and what lies before us are tiny matters compared to what lies within us." She illustrates this through a segment entitled "Remembering Your Spirit." It features a brief story about a person who has undergone some type of crisis (e.g., death of a child, divorce) and how he or she discovered a truth about life as a result. It demonstrates how we can triumph over trials and become a better person because of them. The name was later changed to "Remembering Your Joy" after some viewers complained Oprah was trying to toy with their religious beliefs.

Her magazine, the anti-*Cosmopolitan,* encourages women to accept themselves as they are and to have the courage to take risks and realize the power that lies within them. Oprah is on the cover of each magazine, not a tall, beautiful model or a glamorous image of perfection that readers could never reach. Although readers accept they could not afford the designer gowns Oprah wears, they believe Oprah's goals and aspirations emulate their own. Her magazine is more than a magazine. Readers say it's a "personal growth manual." Oprah wants to provide women with the tools to find themselves.

Oprah's "Live Your Best Life" road show was another medium through which she declared her message of spiritual empowerment and inspiration. Even with ticket prices close to $185, she sold out every event.

Oprah the Humanitarian

Oprah gives millions each year to charity (at least 10 percent of her income). She is building a school to educate girls in South Africa. She would like to bring at least a dozen additional schools and perhaps medical clinics to the same area. Oprah's three main causes include women, children, and education. She says, "When you educate a woman you set her free."

Her philanthropy also extends to her talk show. Even though her ratings were lowest on her Book Club days, she continued this feature for several years because she felt it encouraged people to read.

Oprah the Shrewd Businesswoman

Oprah insists on having as much control as possible over the empire she has built. She signs all checks over $1,000 and examines smaller ones that others sign. She makes all employees sign a lifelong confidentiality agreement. When advisers wish to meet with her for fifteen minutes, she gives them five. When negotiating her magazine deal, she insisted she not only be involved, but also have the final say on every decision. Most magazines place nearly 22 pages of advertising between the cover and the table of contents, but Oprah refused to do so. In a meeting with advertising executives, Oprah announced the table of contents in *O* would be on page 2. The advertising firms protested, but Oprah would not budge.

Oprah the Down-to-Earth Businesswoman

Oprah makes decisions based on her gut. When deciding whether or not she would like to work with someone, the first question she asks is, "Can I trust you?" She describes her business decisions as "leaps of faith" and says her management style is "management by instinct" above anything else. She laughs at phrases like "strategic planning" or "multipurposing content." She is extremely selective about who she employs. Individuals who do make the cut receive excellent pay and benefits, including six weeks of vacation time their first year. After an interview with *Fortune* magazine she decided she will no longer be doing business interviews, claiming, "I'm uncomfortable talking about money and money issues."

Oprah the Success

Oprah has approximately 22 million viewers watching her show in the United States alone. Her show brings in over $300 million in revenue annually. Oprah was ranked as one of *Business Week*'s top 25 managers. For 16 consecutive years *The Oprah Show* has ranked number one among talk shows. *O* magazine pulled in over $140 million in revenue last year with 2 million copies sold. The first day the magazine was released, it sold 100,000 copies, which makes it the most successful magazine launch ever. (The *Sports Illustrated* swimsuit edition featuring Elle Macpherson on the cover was a distant second, selling 81,000 copies.) The "Live Your Best Life" road show raked in $1.6 million in ticket sales, with 8,500 women in combined attendance at the four events.

Discussion Questions

1. Assess Oprah Winfrey's personality in terms of the traits discussed in this chapter. Which personality traits are relevant for explaining Oprah's personality?

2. Evaluate the degree to which Oprah's personality is appropriate given the demands of her job. Support your answer using information from this case and material from this chapter. What are the strengths of her personality? Weaknesses?

3. What can you learn from Oprah's personality and management style that can help you become a more effective manager in a real-world organization in the future?

VIDEO CASE: HUDSON'S

DIVERSITY AND COMMUNICATION IN BUSINESS

Running Time: 12:00

Hudson's, with 22 stores, is part of Target Corporation. The fourth largest retailer in the United States, with more than 1,200 stores in 44 states, Target Corporation (formerly Dayton-Hudson Corporation) is a Minneapolis-based firm that also includes Dayton's, Target, Mervyn's, and Marshall Fields.

Founded in 1881, Hudson's has shown a strong commitment to the well-being of the communities where its stores are located. Today, Hudson's continues its tradition of more than half a century of contributing 5 percent of federally taxable income to support the communities in which it operates. Over the last 15 years, Hudson's has awarded over $20 million to nonprofit organizations for programs designed to enrich the quality of life.

The video shows President and CEO Dennis Toffolo and other Hudson's executives as they discuss diversity issues at Hudson's. After viewing the video, answer the following questions.

1. According to Dennis Toffolo and other Hudson's executives, why is Hudson's committed to diversity?

2. How does Northland store manager Larry Williams describe the meaning of diversity at Hudson's?

3. What is the role of each Hudson's store's Diversity Committee?

4. What are some specific ways Hudson's shows its commitment to diversity?

5. How has Hudson's modified its stores to facilitate diversity?

6. How does Hudson's address stereotyping in its diversity training?

http://www.hudsons.com/

LIGHTEN UP

JUST FOR FUN TESTS

You can find many personality and other tests on the Web. For a broad selection, go to:

http://www.queendom.com/test_frm.html

This site includes personality tests, general health and lifestyle assessment, career choice and preparation, mental and emotional health assessment, and other tests. Check out the "Just for Fun Tests" for "The Risk Test," "The Sense of Humor Test," "The Vanity Test," and 98 others.

SKILLS PRACTICE

2-1　　　　　　　　　　*Skill Level:* BASIC

Dealing with Diversity: **The Breakfast Club**

Skill Objective

To develop skill in analyzing perceptual and attitudinal processes as they relate to issues of diversity between members of a group.

Procedure

1. Obtain a copy of the movie *The Breakfast Club* starring Molly Ringwald and Emilio Estevez. It is available on VHS and DVD and can be rented or purchased from a local video store or retailer.

2. Watch the movie (in class or at home on your own). Note: Download the worksheet developed for this exercise from the text Web site. This will help you to develop a list of scenes in the movie that illustrate relevant diversity issues.

   As you watch the film, identify the different types of diversity issues that exist in terms of perceptual biases and attitudes demonstrated by the various characters. Document your notes from the film on your worksheet.

3. Discuss the following questions as a class.
   a. What types of diversity exist among the five main characters in the movie?
   b. How do the characters perceive one another early in the film? Were their perceptions of each other accurate or inaccurate? Why was this the case?
   c. How do the characters' perceptions of each other change over the course of the movie? Why does this occur?
   d. What is the key lesson that the group in the movie learns about diversity?
   e. How are the diversity issues illustrated in this movie also relevant to diversity issues in real-world business organizations?
   f. What are the practical implications of this exercise for you as a future manager and leader in a real-world organization?

SKILLS PRACTICE

2-2　　　　　　　　*Skill Level:* CHALLENGING

Developing an Effective Diversity Program

Skill Objective

To develop skill in designing and implementing an effective diversity program in an organization.

Procedure

Note: Download the worksheet developed for this exercise from the text Web site.

1. Form groups of five students each.
2. Using the characteristics of effective diversity programs listed below and material from the chapter, design a diversity program for an organization. It could be the college or university you attend, a student organization, or a real-world organization that you have worked in part time or on an internship. Be as specific as possible about which elements you would integrate into your program.

Characteristics of Effective Diversity Programs

   a. A clear definition of diversity as the organization sees it
   b. Integration of diversity into the organization's mission and strategic plan
   c. Support of top management
   d. Involvement of employees in the design of the program
   e. A long-term perspective
   f. Identification, tracking, and communication of critical measures of success for the program
   g. Diversity training
   h. A supportive organizational culture
   i. A systems perspective that aligns HR systems (recruiting, selection, training and development, performance appraisal, and compensation) with the goals of the diversity program (e.g., attraction, development, and retention of underrepresented groups)

3. Develop an action plan for implementing your diversity program effectively.
4. Answer the discussion questions.

Discussion Questions

1. What are the benefits of diversity programs in organizations? How can a concern for diversity help an organization be more successful in the long run?
2. Evaluate the diversity program you created for this exercise. What are its strengths? Its weaknesses?
3. What are the major barriers to the successful implementation of your diversity program? What actions could be taken to overcome these barriers?
4. What are the practical implications of this exercise for you as a future manager in a real-world organization?

SKILLS PRACTICE

2-3   *Skill Level: CHALLENGING*

Field Work: Assessing Personality Factors

Skill Objective

1. To develop skill in using self-assessment data to better understand personality factors and differences between individuals.

Procedure

Note: Download the worksheet developed for this exercise from the text Web site. This will facilitate your working through the steps below.

1. Make copies of Self-Assessments 2-2 (emotional intelligence), 2-3 (personality dimensions), and 2-4 (Big 5 personality dimensions) from this chapter or download them from the text Web site.
2. Administer these self-assessments to three to five working people, who can be managers or individual contributors in real-world organizations.
3. Score the results of the completed self-assessments using the scoring key (download it from the text Web site).
4. Download the worksheet developed for this exercise from the text Web site. This document will be used to summarize the results of the self-assessments.
5. Answer the discussion questions below.

Discussion Questions

1. Based on the results of the self-assessments, how would you describe the personality of each individual? What are the most important results?
2. In what ways might each individual's personality (based on question 1) influence his or her behavior in the workplace?
3. How could the three self-assessments utilized in this exercise be used in a real-world organization to enhance the effectiveness of individual contributors or managers?
4. What are the practical implications of this exercise for you as a future manager or leader of a real-world organization?

SKILLS PRACTICE

2-4

Skill Level: BASIC

Perceptual Accuracy: Do You Know Me?

Skill Objectives

1. To develop skill in understanding one's biases in perceiving people, issues, and so on.

2. To develop strategies for making perceptions more accurate.

Procedure

Note: Download the worksheet developed for this exercise from the text Web site.

1. Find a partner in your class who you do not know. Take two or three minutes to get acquainted with one another.

2. Using the nine-point scale provided on the worksheet, do the following:

   a. Respond to each of the five statements in Round 1 (see below) in terms of the extent to which *you* agree or disagree with it (there are no right or wrong answers here, so please be honest!). Record your responses on the worksheet.

   b. Respond to each statement in Round 1 in terms of how you think *your partner* answered it. Record your responses on the worksheet.

Round 1 Statements

   i. I like the TV show *Friends.*

   ii. I like drinking wine more than beer.

   iii. I enjoy reading books in my leisure time.

   iv. I would love to own a BMW automobile.

   v. I am an animal lover.

Round 2 Statements

   i. Money is the number-one motivator of people.

   ii. Downsizing and employee layoffs should be avoided at any cost.

   iii. I do not like working in teams.

   iv. The key to success in business is personal relationships.

   v. Managing people is just a matter of common sense.

3. Once you and your partner have completed your ratings, share your responses with each other. Using the scoring summary on the worksheet, determine the total difference score between your predicted ratings of your partner and your partner's actual responses. A lower score (approximately 0–10) means your predictions of your partner's responses to the statements was very accurate, whereas a higher score (approximately 20 or more) means your predictions were very inaccurate.

4. Now discuss with each other what information you used as a basis for making your predictions of your partner's ratings.

5. Repeat steps 2 through 4, but use the Round 2 questions this time.

6. Answer the discussion questions below.

Discussion Questions

1. What are your reactions to this exercise? Were you surprised by the results?

2. What information did you use as a basis for predicting your partner's responses to the statements? In retrospect, was it appropriate to use this information as a basis for predicting your partner's responses? Why or why not?

3. Did your perceptions of your partner become more accurate from Round 1 to Round 2? Why was this the case?

4. How could this type of exercise be used in a real-world organization to enhance the effectiveness of workers in dealing with individual differences?

5. What are the practical implications of this exercise for you as a future manager in a real-world organization?

SKILLS PRACTICE

Skill Level: CHALLENGING

Implicit Theories of Personality

Skill Objective

To develop skill in understanding how individual differences affect work behavior.

Procedure

Note: Download the worksheet developed for this exercise from the text Web site.

1. Brainstorm a list of the personality characteristics you feel are important at work.

   List all the characteristics you identified down the rows and across the columns of the table on your worksheet.

2. Discuss each personality trait you identified in terms of why you feel it is important.

3. Now think about how the various traits you identified are related to one another. Indicate the relationships between the various characteristics in your "implicit theory" by putting a "+" if you feel the trait in a given row has a positive effect on the trait in a given column. If you feel the trait in a row has a negative effect on the trait in a column, indicate this with a "−". Finally, if you feel there is no relationship between a trait in a given row and another trait in a column, indicate this with a "0."

4. In the last row of your table, write "job performance" in the lefthand column in that row, show with a "+", "0", or "−" whether you feel performance is positively related, unrelated, or negatively related to each corresponding trait.

5. Based on the implicit theory you have identified, discuss specific strategies employers could use to find and/or develop the kinds of individuals who are likely to be effective employees.

SKILLS PRACTICE

Skill Level: CHALLENGING

He Said, She Said

Skill Objective

To develop skill in managing different perceptions of a situation.

Procedure

Note: Download the worksheet developed for this exercise from the text Web site.

1. Read the following scenarios.

2. Using the general guidelines for reducing perceptual errors discussed in the chapter, identify specific strategies for managing the perceptual differences in each scenario.

Scenario 1: The Team Slacker

You are the manager of a team of sales associates at a large department store. One day, Lisa, one of your high-performing employees, comes to talk to you about a problem she is experiencing. She states that Phil, one of the other sales associates, is not being a team player. Specifically, he never does his fair share when it comes to performing the nonsales responsibilities and duties of his job (e.g., stocking the shelves with new products, doing inventory, putting tags on products). Lisa perceives this as grossly unfair because she feels it affects her ability to perform her job effectively. What would you do?

Scenario 2: The New Process

You are the manager of a team of production workers at a manufacturing facility. In order to enhance overall work unit efficiency and effectiveness, you have decided to adopt some new technology that will automate certain aspects of the production process. You believe this will enhance quality and productivity while reducing costs. However, at a recent departmental meeting, many of your employees expressed negative views of the new technology as a "management trick" to get them to worker harder for the same pay and then to eliminate their jobs altogether. What would you do?

Scenario 3: Obtaining the Commitment of a Senior Executive

You are the director of marketing at a medium-sized financial services firm. Six months ago, the vice president of your division requested that you conduct a study to identify strategies for enhancing customer retention. The results of your study have clearly revealed that your customers view the company as stale and outdated and the quality of customer service provided as low. Based on this, you need to recommend some fundamental changes in the firm's marketing strategy. The major barrier is that you must make a presentation of your findings and recommendations to your vice president at the next Marketing Division meeting. In particular, the vice president is a strong advocate of maintaining the status quo. She also does not like hearing bad news and has been known to "shoot the messenger" when bad news is presented to her. Given this, how should you approach the situation?

Scenario 4: Butting Heads on the Cross-Functional Team
You are the manager of a product development team at a computer corporation. The goal of the team is to develop highly innovative products that exceed consumer expectations in terms of cost, quality, and features. You are experiencing some serious clashes of personalities and perspectives on your team. Specifically, marketing and engineering team members have very different perceptions of what the team's goals should be and how it should work toward achieving its goals. Marketing team members place great emphasis on understanding the needs and wants of customers and capitalizing on market opportunities in an aggressive manner. Engineering team members are more concerned with technical issues of new products (e.g., making sure the design is right) and are not willing to compromise their technical standards in order to meet short-term customer needs. How would you handle this situation?

SKILLS PRACTICE

2-7
Skill Level: BASIC

Walking a Mile in the Shoes of Another
Skill Objective
To demonstrate the importance of testing your understanding of how others perceive a given situation.
Procedure
Note: Download the worksheet developed for this exercise from the text Web site.

1. Select an employed individual to follow ("shadow") for at least half a day. Ideally, this should be a person whose job you are only familiar with at a general level.
2. In a couple of paragraphs, write a description of what you think this person's job entails. Do this before you meet with the person. Be sure to address the following questions:

   a. What are the tasks and responsibilities associated with this job?
   b. Why is this job important to the organization?
   c. What kinds of knowledge and skills are important in order to be successful at this job?
   d. What are the most difficult aspects of this job?

3. Spend half a day observing the person you selected performing his or her job. Ask the person the questions you listed in item 2.
4. Compare the description of the job you wrote in item 2 (before observing the job) versus item 3 (what you actually learned about the job). How similar or different were they? What are the practical implications of this exercise for you as a future manager?

SKILLS PRACTICE

2-8
Skill Level: BASIC

Field Work: Analyzing Employee Job Satisfaction
Skill Objectives
1. To develop skill in analyzing employee job satisfaction data.

2. To develop skill in formulating action plans for enhancing job satisfaction.

Procedure

Note: Download the worksheet developed for this exercise from the text Web site.

1. Identify an employee or manager currently working in an organizational setting who is willing to be interviewed for this activity.

2. Ask the following questions in the interview.

   a. What is your job title? What are your primary tasks, duties, and responsibilities?

   b. How satisfied are you with the *work you perform* as part of your job? Why do you feel this way?

   c. How satisfied are you with the *supervision* you receive in your job? Why do you feel this way?

   d. How satisfied are you with your *coworkers* in your job? Why do you feel this way?

   e. How satisfied are you with the *compensation and benefits* you receive as part of your job? Why do you feel this way?

   f. How satisfied are you with the *opportunities for advancement* in your organization? Why do you feel this way?

   g. How satisfied are you with the *organization* you work for? Why do you feel this way?

   h. How satisfied are you with your *overall job*? Why do you feel this way?

3. Discuss the results of the job satisfaction assessment you just performed.

4. Develop an action plan to enhance the job satisfaction of the person you interviewed for this activity. Be specific.

5. Optional: Present a brief summary of your analysis and action plan to your class for discussion purposes.

PROBLEM SOLVING

Skills Objectives

> *To apply the general problem-solving process to analyze and resolve organizational challenges systematically.*

> *To use problem-solving tools to enhance the effectiveness of business decision making.*

> *To take appropriate actions to overcome common constraints on the problem-solving process.*

> *To use creativity-enhancement techniques to generate innovative ideas and solutions to business problems.*

> *To apply the basic principles of bargaining and negotiation in order to achieve desired agreements between two or more parties.*

KNOWLEDGE OBJECTIVES

> Understand why decision making is important in organizations.

> Discuss the five stages of the problem-solving process.

> Identify influences on problem solving and ways that people make decisions in the face of those influences.

> Discuss the many faces of intuition.

> Explain the stages of the creative process.

> Discuss techniques for enhancing creativity.

> Identify characteristics of creative organizations.

> Discuss five strategies for negotiating.

> Discuss guidelines for attaining win-win solutions.

Decisions are constantly being made at all levels of organizations. Corporate strategists plot mergers, devise financial and market gambits, and determine plant locations. Middle managers consider motivational tools, planning and control techniques, and ways to reduce subordinates' resistance to change. Lower-level employees decide whether to go to work, to produce at a certain level, to join informal groups, and to follow company procedures. Decisions are the fabric of organizations.

Can you think of some examples of companies where management is faced with tough decisions about how to solve organizational problems? Well, what if you were Edward Breen, the new CEO of Tyco International, a global firm with thousands of products relating to security, health, electronics, and communications and more than 250,000 employees worldwide? What decisions would you make to help the global firm regain the trust of employees, shareholders, and customers after it was run, according to prosecutors, as a "criminal enterprise"?[1] The former CEO and CFO were accused of looting the Bermuda-registered company of nearly $600 million. Tyco was also in the midst of a liquidity crisis, with big debt repayments due within months. What if you were John Eyler, CEO of Toys "R" Us, the toy retailer that has struggled and watched as Wal-Mart surpassed it as the number one toy retailer in the United States?[2] How would you get Toys "R" Us back on track? Or what if you were a top official of NASA, facing criticism that NASA's management problems led to the *Challenger* and *Columbia* disasters and are now seeking ways to prevent future fiascoes?[3]

There are many reasons why you should care about problem solving. For example,[4]

> Organizational members are increasingly being evaluated on their problem-solving ability. So decisions may affect your career, rewards, and satisfaction.
> The quality and acceptability of your decisions will affect how well you perform and the degree of your satisfaction with work.
> Solving problems takes considerable time and effort and is often uncomfortable. It makes sense to try to do well on something on which you will spend so much time and psychic energy.
> Activities in organizations are generally the results of decisions. By examining how decisions are made, you will better understand how organizations work.

In this chapter we examine the problem-solving process and offer guidelines for each step of the process. We then discuss the PDCA (plan, do, check, act) cycle. Next we consider a variety of factors that influence our problem solving and then consider how we solve problems in the face of those factors. We next study the nature of creativity and address techniques for enhancing creativity and for developing creative organizations. Finally, we discuss negotiating and bargaining, including strategies for negotiating and guidelines for attaining win-win solutions. Together, the chapter material offers a framework and tools for understanding and improving problem-solving skills.

Before reading further, complete Self-Assessment Exercise 3-1 regarding attitudes toward problem solving. This self-assessment will give you some insights into your attitudes and beliefs about problem solving in general as well as into your problem-solving style. Then, as a way to introduce the material in this chapter and for you to assess your general problem-solving skills, read the case in the Pretest Skills Assessment and develop a plan for how you would handle the situation. After you have completed these activities, visit the text Web site to learn more about your responses.

SELF-ASSESSMENT 3-1

Attitudes Toward Problem Solving

Answer the questions that follow about your attitudes toward solving problems in the business world. You will learn more from this chapter if you become more aware of your beliefs and feelings about problem solving. Answer each question as honestly as possible using the following response scale:

1 Disagree strongly
2 Disagree somewhat
3 Neither agree nor disagree
4 Agree somewhat
5 Agree strongly

____ 1. Solving business problems is mostly a matter of just using your common sense.
____ 2. Problem solving should involve the use of a systematic procedure.
____ 3. People spend too much time analyzing problems, which takes away from doing what is needed to solve them.
____ 4. Identifying problems in a given situation is usually the simplest part of the problem-solving process.
____ 5. Problem-solving tools should be used only when other methods for solving a problem have failed.
____ 6. The key measure of problem-solving effectiveness is efficiency in resolving the problem.
____ 7. An ideal or perfect solution to a problem can be implemented in most situations.
____ 8. In most cases, determining a solution to a problem is easier than implementing it.

PRETEST SKILLS ASSESSMENT

Solving Problems

Note: This exercise is based on actual events encountered by managers in real-world organizations. Some information may have been modified in order to maintain the anonymity of the people and organization involved in this situation.

You are the hotel manager of a 200-room luxury resort located in Chicago that is part of a global lodging corporation based in the United States. Your resort provides lodging for business travelers who desire luxurious but affordable accommodations. In the past, your resort has earned a favorable reputation from guests and your annual occupancy rate has been approximately 75 percent, which is considered good by general industry standards.

Recently, the corporate office has announced a new measurement system that will be used to assess the performance of various aspects of each hotel in the chain. The primary measure in the system is the Guest Satisfaction Index (GSI). This measure will be obtained by asking each customer to complete a survey at the time of checkout to assess his or her overall satisfaction with the hotel. Questions will also cover guest satisfaction with specific units including front desk, room service, housekeeping, bell services, restaurants, maintenance, and the concierge. A detailed summary of all scores will be sent to each hotel manager on a quarterly basis. Each hotel manager's job performance and annual merit pay increase will be based on the GSI scores obtained for his or her hotel.

You receive the first GSI score for your hotel, and it indicates that only 30 percent of customers in the past quarter stated they were satisfied or highly satisfied with their overall stay at your hotel. You are obviously alarmed about these disappointing results. What is the problem? How will you explain this to your boss? How will you fix the problem?

Develop an action plan for solving the problem at your hotel. Be sure your plan addresses both short-term and long-term issues. Be very specific and be prepared to defend each element of your plan in terms of its feasibility and cost effectiveness.

Now complete Skills Practice 3-1. This exercise will provide you with in-depth exposure to some real-world managers and how they solve challenging business problems.

THE PROBLEM-SOLVING PROCESS

Successful problem solvers recognize making a good decision is more than just choosing one option over another. Instead, they follow the five steps in the problem-solving process shown in Figure 3-1.

DEFINE THE PROBLEM

Careful problem definition is crucial. Unless proper time and care are taken at this stage, we may solve the wrong problem. A problem occurs when there is a gap between the desired and the actual situation. Declining profits, high scrap rates, or inability to increase market share are all possible problems. Too often the problem is defined in terms of symptoms. For instance, management may define the problem as employee apathy instead of seeing that apathy as a symptom of a deeper problem, such as an inadequate pay structure. Or the problem may be defined in terms of a preferred solution. A problem statement such as "Gloria is a poor manager" focuses on proposed solutions relating to Gloria rather than directly addressing the criterion of interest, such as declining performance in Gloria's department.[5] Here are some guidelines for writing a good problem statement:

FIGURE 3-1
The Problem-Solving Process

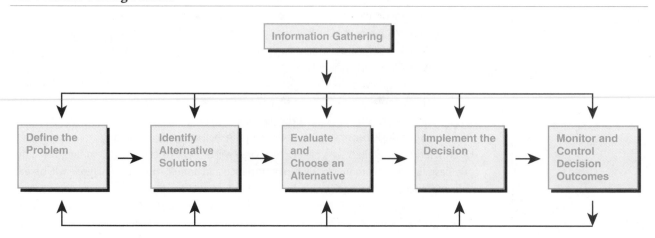

> **State the problem explicitly.** We have a tendency to assume the problem is too obvious to require an explicit statement. However, even so-called obvious problems are seen differently by different people or not seen at all.

> **Specify the standard(s) violated.** There are many different types of standards that may be violated. These could be personal (such as violation of privacy or trust), group (such as violation of equal treatment or lack of opportunity to participate), organizational (such as poor quality or high scrap rates), or even societal (such as socially irresponsible behavior).

> **State the problem in specific behavioral terms.** Don't use broad generalizations such as lack of communications, personality conflicts, or the like. What specific behavioral standards are being violated? What specific behavioral change is desired? What behavior would constitute a solution to the problem?

> **Specify whose problem it is.** This helps identify who must be involved in problem resolution. That is, who owns the problem? The problem statement should make clear the perspective being taken. For instance, is the problem statement from the perspective of a particular manager? Of a team?

> **Avoid stating the problem merely as an implied solution.** For instance, suppose productivity has declined. A problem statement such as "The plant manager must find ways to motivate employees to improve productivity" implies a solution—motivating employees. In fact, though, the problem may lie in equipment problems, management decisions, or much else. Prematurely focusing on employee motivation inappropriately narrows the scope of inquiry.

> **Avoid stating the problem as a dilemma.** People sometimes state a problem as an unsolvable predicament. They may say, "The problem is that we will lose no matter which action we take" or "We've been handed a hopeless situation." This may come from a desire for sympathy or attention or to gain vengeance or avoid effort, but it does nothing to solve the problem.

IDENTIFY ALTERNATIVE SOLUTIONS

Alternatives are the various approaches taken to solve the problem. Good solutions require good alternatives. Unfortunately, in their rush to judgment, problem solvers often slight the alternative-generation stage. At this stage *divergent thinking* is needed. That is, problem solvers must stretch their minds, seeking new possibilities. Creativity, which we discuss in detail later in the chapter, is especially important at the alternative-generation stage. In the business world, divergent thinking is sometimes referred to as "thinking outside the box," where the "box" is the conventional approach to thinking and acting.

EVALUATE AND CHOOSE AN ALTERNATIVE

Once alternatives are thoroughly generated, they can be evaluated and a choice can be made. This stage requires *convergent thinking*, a narrowing in on a solution. There are two general approaches to evaluation and choice. With *screening approaches*, each alternative is identified as satisfactory or unsatisfactory. Unsatisfactory alternatives are screened out, leaving only those that can clear all hurdles. *Scoring approaches* assign a total score to each alternative. Then the alternative with the best score can be chosen.

The screening table in Figure 3-2 is an example of a screening approach. Alternative solutions (in this case, digital cameras) are listed in the left-most column. Important attributes of the alternatives are listed along the top row, from most important to least important. Entries in the matrix are the scores of the alternatives on the attributes. Finally, constraints are presented for each attribute. These constraints represent the hurdles, or cutoff scores for acceptable levels, of each attribute. The nature of the constraints will depend on the attributes. For some attributes, such as price, lower levels are better, and the constraints specify maximum acceptable levels. For others, such as mega-pixels, included memory, and optical zoom, higher levels are better, so the constraints specify minimum levels. For some decisions it is even possible that constraints will specify acceptable ranges, such as a comfortable temperature range.

Once this table is developed, it can easily be used to make a choice. One approach (called *elimination by aspects*) would be first to screen out those alternatives not satisfying the constraint for the most important attribute, then to screen out those remaining that don't satisfy the constraint for the next most important attribute, and so on. We can continue this method until only one alternative remains or until no attributes remain. If more than one alternative remains after all constraints are considered, we could add further attributes and corresponding constraints, could make constraints more stringent and recheck, or could choose from among the acceptable alternatives on some other basis, such as looking at the degree to which each exceeds the constraints or even flipping a coin. In the example given in Figure 3-2, we would start with the most important attribute, mega-pixels, and screen out no alternatives, because all exceed the 2.0 mega-pixel minimum. We would then see whether the alternatives satisfy the second constraint, price, and so on. In this case, the Olympus camera fails the price constraint, so it is eliminated. This leaves the Fujifilm and HP cameras. These cameras satisfy both the included memory and optical zoom constraint, so either would be acceptable. In looking at attribute levels and the constraints, though, it is evident the HP is better than, or as good as, the Fujifilm camera for *every* attribute. It has lower scores on the attribute for which low levels are desirable (that with a "less than" constraint—price) and higher or equal scores on those for which high levels are desirable (those with "greater than" or "greater than or equal to" constraints—mega-pixels, included memory, and optical zoom). Because of this, the HP is said to *dominate* the Fujifilm for the attributes considered and should always be chosen.[6]

FIGURE 3-2
Screening Table

Alternatives	Attributes			
	Mega-Pixels	Price ($)	Included Memory	Optical Zoom
Olympus Camedia E-10	4.1	1100	32	4X
Fujifilm Fine Pix 601 Zoom	3.0	550	16	3X
HP Photosmart 850	4.0	500	16	8X
Constraints	> 2.0	< 800.00	> 8	≥ 3X

Another screening approach is to check the alternatives against the constraints, one alternative (rather than one attribute) at a time. That is, we would first check to see if the Olympus satisfies all the constraints. Because it doesn't (i.e., it costs too much), we would then see whether the Fujifilm satisfies all the constraints. It does, so we would choose it. This approach, which selects the first acceptable alternative, is called *satisficing*. Satisficing simplifies and speeds the decision process because we can collect information on alternatives one at a time; if we find an acceptable alternative, we don't have to gather information on others. Unfortunately, satisficing makes us slaves to the order in which alternatives are considered. In this case, we would choose the Fujifilm camera, although the HP camera (which we wouldn't consider if using satisficing) is better or as good for *every* attribute considered. Thus satisficing represents a common trade-off in decision making between ease of choice making and decision quality. Now complete Skills Practice 3-2 to help develop your skill in using a screening table to make choices.

Scoring approaches add levels of complexity to choice making. First, instead of assigning cutoff levels for each attribute, the attributes are given weights according to their relative importance. Second, the attribute levels are assigned utilities according to their relative levels of satisfactoriness. For example, the best level of an attribute could be assigned a utility of 100 and the worst attribute level a utility of 0. Other attribute levels are then assigned utilities corresponding to their respective satisfactoriness relative to the best level. Once these weights and utilities are assigned, the utility of each alternative can be determined by multiplying the alternative's utility for each attribute times the weight of that attribute and summing across all attributes. That is, the utility for alternative *i* is calculated across the *n* attributes as follows:

$$U_i = \sum_{j=1}^{n} (W_j \times U_{ij})$$

Where

U_i is the overall utility, or satisfactoriness, of alternative *i*
W_j is the relative weight given to attribute *j*
U_{ij} is the utility, or satisfactoriness, of alternative *i* on attribute *j*

Then the alternative with the highest overall utility (i.e., the highest level of satisfactoriness) can be chosen. As you can see, this is a more complex process than a screening approach. It does, though, give the opportunity of finding a "best" solution, as opposed to just a satisfactory one.

Some decision situations are even more complicated because they contain elements of risk, uncertainty, or conflict. With *decision making under risk*, the quality of outcomes associated with alternatives depends on which of multiple events (such as levels of rainfall, changes in the Dow Jones Industrials Average, or levels of student enrollments) occurs, *and* we are somehow able to attach probabilities to those events. In the case of *decision making under uncertainty*, the quality of outcomes associated with alternatives depends on which of multiple events occurs, but we are unable to attach probabilities to the events. In the case of *decision making under conflict*, the quality of outcomes of alternatives (sometimes called *strategies*) depends on the actions taken by a competitor. These situations require additional tools, such as decision trees, decision matrices, and game theory.[7]

IMPLEMENT THE DECISION

Together, the first three stages of the problem-solving process are called *decision making*. The problem-solving process isn't over once we complete these stages, however. Unfortunately, decisions do not implement themselves. Necessary resources must be available for implementation. Also, those who will be involved in implementation must fully understand and accept the solution. For that reason, implementers are often encouraged to participate in the earlier stages of the process.

A fundamental question at this stage is how long to persist in trying to implement the decision successfully. It is easy to err in either direction. The many difficulties that typically arise when trying to implement a major decision can lead to frustration, discontent, and the temptation to throw in the towel. As noted by Rosabeth Moss Kanter, "Everything looks like a failure in the middle."[8]

At the same time, decision makers are also prone to *escalation of commitment*. This is the tendency to "throw good money after bad," continuing to pour more time and resources into a failing project. Some powerful forces lead to escalation of commitment.[9] For instance, we find it hard to ignore "sunk costs," the resources that are already "down the drain." Also, as long as we are putting more resources into a project, we don't have to admit we've failed. Further, there are many social rewards for persistence; people tend to praise managers who "stick to their guns" in the face of opposition and bleak odds. For these and other reasons, escalation of commitment is a tempting, and dangerous, tendency. Decision makers in organizations, like other gamblers, have got to "know when to fold 'em." Here are some guidelines for minimizing the dangers of inappropriate escalation of commitment:[10]

> Create *stopping rules* prior to launching a project. These stopping rules specify the conditions under which the project should be abandoned.[11]
> Specify objective criteria for evaluating the status of a project.
> Actively gather information on project performance, and accept warning signals when they occur.
> Make it clear that "pulling the plug" is a viable option, and don't be afraid to follow through when needed.
> Be wary of penalizing managers if their projects fail. If managers feel their careers will be damaged by failure, they may escalate commitment rather than admit failure.
> Seek objective views on project status, such as from external auditors.

MONITOR AND CONTROL DECISION OUTCOMES

The final step in the problem-solving process is to monitor decision outcomes and take necessary corrective action. If decision control is to be effective, steps must be taken to ensure that necessary information is gathered. Contingency plans must be developed to permit changes if the decision does not turn out well. *Contingency planning* is the process of developing alternative courses of action that can be followed if a decision, perhaps because of unexpected events, does not work out as planned. Contingency plans ensure that backups are available, and they help remove the panic element in unforeseen situations. The book and movie *The Perfect Storm* describe a situation in which a series of freakish weather conditions came together in the worst possible way to create a horrendous storm. Contingency plans

FOCUS ON MANAGEMENT

ESCALATION OF COMMITMENT IN THE NATIONAL BASKETBALL ASSOCIATION

Examples of escalation of commitment can be found everywhere. In one interesting study, new players in the NBA were examined. The researchers found that players for whom the initial investment was greater, as measured by their higher draft position, had more playing

time and longer NBA careers, independent of their performance. The NBA draft is highly visible, and team managers may have expected criticism if they failed to field their expensive players. As such, they gave their higher draft choices more opportunities to play, even when their performance didn't justify it.*

*B. M. Staw and H. Hoang, "Sunk Costs in the NBA: Why Draft Order

Affects Playing Time and Survival in Professional Basketball," *Administrative Science Quarterly*, 1995, 40, pp. 474–494. See also C. F. Camerer and R. A. Weber, "The Econometrics and Behavioral Economics of Escalation of Commitment: A Re-Examination of Staw and Hoang's NBA Data," *Journal of Economic Behavior and Organization*, May 1999, pp. 59–82.

are sometimes developed to deal with a "worst-case" scenario, the situation in which events fall together in the worst possible way to create the organizational equivalent of the "perfect storm."

Thus contingency planning requires preparing for the worst even while hoping for the best. The need for contingency planning was seen in the September 11, 2001, attack on the World Trade Center. The law firm Sidley Austin Brown & Wood LLP was hit directly. The firm occupied floors 54 through 59 in the North Tower, the building hit first. Less than an hour after getting the news in the firm's main office in Chicago, the firm's disaster recovery plan was distributed to all key personnel. The disaster recovery plan began with employee contact and information lists, which Chicago employees used to call all New York employees to ensure they were accounted for. Emphasis in subsequent days and weeks focused on such issues as communication, computer system consolidation, procurement of new office space in New York, and providing Employee Assistance Plan (EAP) counselors. Because a contingency plan was in place, the firm was able to survive an unimaginable disaster, providing help to its employees while keeping its vital records intact.[12]

FOCUS ON MANAGEMENT

THE ROAR OF THE CROWD

Bill Walsh, formerly the offensive coordinator of the Cincinnati Bengals football team, recalls a close game where the Bengals trailed the Oakland Raiders 31–28 with three minutes left in a playoff game at Oakland. The Bengals had the ball, but the noise of the home crowd

was deafening. In addition, the phone system Walsh used to communicate with his spotter in the press box began to malfunction. Between the roar of the crowd, the mechanical difficulties, and the excitement of the players, coordination broke down and the Bengals lost. Walsh says this experience taught him the importance of con-

tingency planning. He wrote, "We lost the game, and I decided that I would never again be confronted by circumstances I hadn't prepared for, no matter how unlikely they might seem."*

*See B. Walsh, "When Things Go Bad," *Forbes*, March 29, 1993, pp. 13–14.

Now that we have examined each of the steps in the general problem-solving process, complete Skills Practice 3-3 to develop skill in applying the process to business problems.

THE PDCA CYCLE

Many teams involved in decisions relating to quality improvement or other issues involving large, complex processes have found it useful to apply the PDCA (plan, do, check, act) cycle, sometimes called the Deming cycle, shown in Figure 3-3.[13] The PDCA cycle can be applied to any recurring activity, such as annual planning processes or everyday work such as materials handling, billing, and order taking.

The PDCA cycle permits learning, thus helping make sense of problems that may at first seem overwhelming. As suggested by the name, there are four steps: a plan is developed (**p**lan); the plan is tested on a trial basis (**d**o); the effects of the plan are evaluated and monitored (**c**heck); and appropriate corrective actions are taken (**a**ct). In the Plan stage, the team's purpose and goals are identified, a theory is developed, measures of success are defined, and activities are planned. In the Do stage, the plan is executed by undertaking activities, introducing interventions, and applying the best knowledge to the pursuit of the desired purpose and goals. In the Check (or Study) stage, outcomes are monitored by testing the validity of the theory and plan. Results are studied for signs of progress or success or unexpected outcomes. The team searches for new lessons to learn and new problems to solve.

FIGURE 3-3
The PDCA Cycle

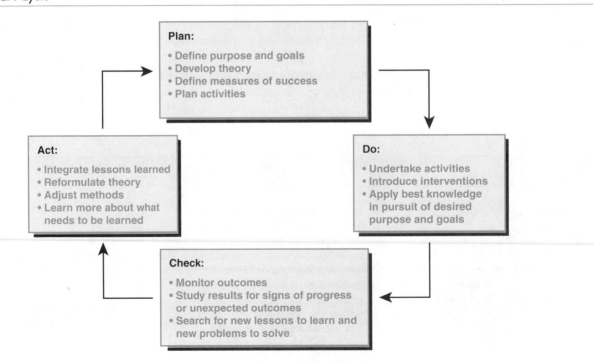

Finally, in the Act stage, the lessons learned are integrated, the theory reformulated, and methods adjusted. The team learns what more it needs to learn. And the cycle continues, providing a constant dialogue of theory and application.

Time to go to the movies! Complete Skills Practice 3-4 by watching *October Sky,* an inspiring and heartwarming film about a group of high school boys who set out to build a rocket that will actually fly. The movie, based on a true story, illustrates problem solving.

Now complete Skills Practice 3-5 to practice applying the PDCA cycle to a specific problem.

INFLUENCES ON PROBLEM SOLVING

Figure 3-4 provides a rough outline of the steps information goes through as it is used for problem solving. That is, the individual must perceive and process cognitively the available information. A decision is then made and implemented. Finally, the consequences of the decision are evaluated and stored for use in future problem solving.

Ideally, the decision maker would have all the information needed—and no more—when it was required and in the desired form. The perceptual processes would select and process the information in an unbiased way. The cognitive processes would quickly, accurately, and objectively evaluate the information and arrive at an optimal choice. Subsequent evaluation of consequences would be unbiased and storage would be efficient. The "real-world" situation is far from this idyllic scenario, however. Many factors may impede a successful decision-making process, as described in this section.

FIGURE 3-4
Factors Influencing Decision Making

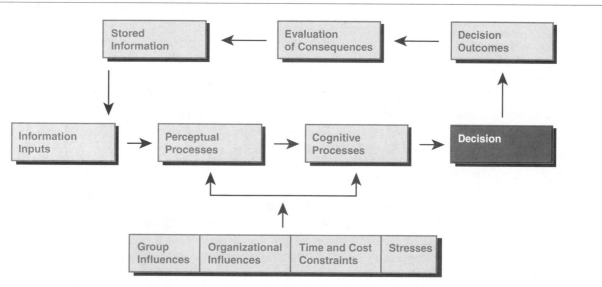

INFORMATION INPUTS

We must often act on the basis of less-than-perfect information. It may be incomplete, late, or in the wrong form. There may be too much of it, and it may simply be wrong.

Information may be imperfect for many reasons. For one, there simply may be too little time to carry out a full information search. And rapidly changing, complex situations make it especially difficult to get good information. Some types of problem solvers—including those who are young, risk takers, or dogmatic—act on the basis of relatively little information. Those with opposite characteristics feel especially uncomfortable when information is not abundant.

It is important to recognize that "perfect information" may simply not be attainable. In reality, information is often badly flawed, but decisions must still be made.

PERCEPTUAL PROCESSES

As we saw in Chapter 2, our perceptual processes can result in distortions. Recall, for instance, that we tend to perceive what we're expecting to perceive. Our perceptual selection is influenced by needs and personality characteristics and many factors other than the nature of the object being perceived. When we interpret information, we are subject to stereotyping, halo error, projection, perceptual defense, and a host of other troublesome influences.

COGNITIVE PROCESSES[14]

We as human problem solvers also face a variety of cognitive constraints. These include the following:

> We have very limited short-term memories, with a capacity for only a few pieces of information.

> We are basically serial-information processors, rather than parallel-information processors. That is, we find it difficult to deal with multiple problems simultaneously. As a result, we process information relatively slowly.

> We have limited computational ability. The sorts of calculations implied by theories of maximization, such as the rational economic man so popular in microeconomics, cannot be handled without assistance.

> Unlike a computer, we care about the outcomes of our decisions. This causes us to have doubts about whether our decision is correct.

> We evaluate information differently depending on how it is presented to us. Consider the following example to illustrate these **framing effects**. One group of people was asked the following question:

Imagine you have decided to see a play and paid the admission price of $10 per ticket. As you enter the theater, you discover you have lost the ticket. The seat was not marked and the ticket cannot be recovered. Would you pay $10 for another ticket?

Another group was asked this question:

Imagine you have decided to see a play where admission is $10 per ticket. As you enter the theater you discover you have lost a $10 bill. Would you still pay $10 for a ticket to see the play?

The outcomes for both situations are identical: a $10 cost with no ticket or a $20 cost with a ticket. But of those faced with the first question, most (54 percent) said they would not buy another ticket. Of those asked the second question, only 12 percent indicated they wouldn't buy the ticket.

To explain this apparent paradox, decision theorists Tversky and Kahneman proposed a psychological account in which people keep track of transactions. The loss registers in the "ticket account" in the first case but not in the second.[15]

GROUP INFLUENCES

Groups influence problem solvers in several ways. For one thing, they exert pressure for conformity to group norms. For another, they influence the individual's risk preferences, generally in the risky direction for most business-related decisions. We consider group influences in Chapter 11, "Managing Teams."

ORGANIZATIONAL INFLUENCES

Problem solvers act within the context of the organization and are continually influenced by it. For instance, the organizational reward system influences the way decisions are made. If it rewards cautious decisions, employees will learn to play it safe. If it rewards taking chances, employees will learn to take risks. Rewards for creativity will reinforce the making of creative decisions.

TIME AND COST CONSTRAINTS

Obviously, time and cost constraints restrict our ability to get good, thorough information. Less obviously, time constraints also may cause us to change the nature of our decision processes. When pressed to make a quick decision, for instance, we may seek negative information about alternatives to screen them out quickly instead of carefully balancing positive and negative aspects.[16] Many managers face strong pressure from their organization to "be decisive" and to take action as quickly as possible (to be "a doer") rather than to analyze an issue at length (to be "a thinker").

STRESS

Decision makers often act under great psychological stress. Especially when the stakes are high, we may find it difficult to react with cool rationality. For example, the events of 9/11 created a situation of enormous stress for many decision makers.

FOCUS ON MANAGEMENT

DEEP BLUE

There is ongoing debate and controversy over whether computers can "think" and whether computers can really outperform humans at challenging mental tasks. One battleground in the human–computer skirmishes is the chessboard. In 1997, a much-watched match between world chess champion Gary Kasparov and IBM's Deep Blue supercomputer ended with Kasparov's resignation in the sixth and final game and his losing the competition to Big Blue by a score of 3½ to 2½. This was the first time any chess champion had been beaten by a machine in a traditional match and the first time Kasparov had lost a multigame match against an individual opponent. A dispirited Kasparov said, "I'm a human being. When I see something that is beyond my understanding, I'm afraid."*

*For updates on this man-versus-machine saga, see G. Kasparov, "Man vs. Machine: Deep Junior Makes the Fight Worth It," *Wall Street Journal*, February 10, 2003, p. A14; and S. Levy, "Man vs. Machine: Checkmate," *Newsweek*, July 21, 2003, p. 51.

Chemical disasters, nuclear incidents, plane crashes, and product tamperings are other notable examples, but executives face less visible "hot decision" situations regularly. We will see that such situations may lead to inadequate decision making.[17]

PROBLEM SOLVING IN THE FACE OF CONSTRAINTS

The many barriers faced by decision makers have a variety of consequences, some obvious and others not. In view of all the difficulties people face in problem solving, we do remarkably well. For instance, studies show that humans do a very good job of making statistical inferences.[18] Further, we may do even better in the "real world" than lab experiments suggest.[19] Nevertheless, the various barriers we have discussed do hinder problem solving in some important ways. Figure 3-5 presents some of the consequences of decision barriers.

Before reading further, complete the problem-solving quiz in Self-Assessment Exercise 3-2. It illustrates several issues we consider in the following section.

SELF-ASSESSMENT 3-2

Problem-Solving Quiz

The following questions present a variety of types of problem-solving situations. Respond to each question.

1. Which of the following sequences of outcomes of 10 flips of a fair coin is more likely:
   SEQUENCE A: HHHHHHHHHH or
   SEQUENCE B: HTTHTHHTTT?
   ____ Sequence A is more likely.
   ____ Sequence B is more likely.
   ____ The two sequences are equally likely.

FIGURE 3-5
Consequences of Decision Barriers

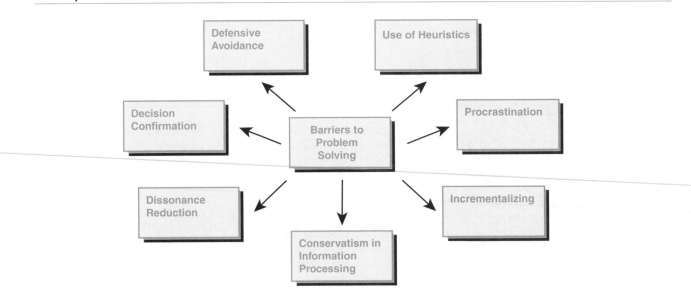

2. A number of pairs of causes of death in the United States are listed. For each pair, indicate which cause is responsible for more deaths annually in the United States.

   PAIR A: ____ Motor vehicle accidents

   ____ Lung cancer

   PAIR B: ____ Strokes

   ____ All accidents

   PAIR C: ____ Tuberculosis

   ____ Fire and flames

   PAIR D: ____ Emphysema

   ____ Homicide

3. Would days with over 60 percent male births be more common in a maternity ward with 15 births per day, or in a larger ward with 45 births per day, or about the same in the two wards?

   ____ More common in the smaller ward

   ____ More common in the larger ward

   ____ Equally likely in the two wards

4. A gas station charges $1.50 for a gallon of gas if the customer pays with a credit card, but gives a five cent discount for a cash payment (that is, the price is $1.45 a gallon if the customer pays cash). Do you think it is fair that the gas station has these different prices?

   ____ Yes, it is fair.

   ____ No, it isn't fair.

   Now suppose the gas station charges $1.45 for a gallon of gas if the customer pays with cash, but adds a five cent surcharge for a credit card payment (that is, the price is $1.50 a gallon if the customer pays with a credit card). Do you think it is fair that the gas station has these different prices?

   ____ Yes, it is fair.

   ____ No, it isn't fair.

5. Athletes who are at their peak are frequently shown on the cover of *Sports Illustrated* magazine. After appearing on the cover, they often do less well. This has been referred to as the "*Sports Illustrated* jinx." Assuming that athletes do in fact perform less well after appearing on the *SI* cover, do you think this is evidence of a jinx?

   ____ Yes

   ____ No

6. Linda is a bright 31-year-old woman who majored in philosophy in college, where she was actively involved in issues of social justice. Rank the following statements from most likely (1) to least likely (3).

   ____ Linda is a feminist

   ____ Linda is a bank teller

   ____ Linda is a feminist and a bank teller

USE OF HEURISTICS[20]

Heuristics (from the Greek word *heuriskein*, meaning "to find or discover") are devices we use—often without knowing it—to simplify decision making. They are simplifying rules of thumb. Although they typically do make things easier for the decision maker, they generally result in less than optimal solutions. Heuristics have proven to be so important in their impact on decision making that a pioneer in the field—Daniel Kahneman of Princeton University—was awarded the 2002 Nobel

Prize in Economics, making him the first psychologist to win economics' highest honor.[21] Here are some important heuristics:

> *Satisficing* (as noted earlier in the chapter) means choosing the first acceptable alternative rather than looking for the best. So instead of trying to find the sharpest needle in a haystack, we may stop searching once we have located the first needle.[22] Satisficing is certainly a time-saver, because we don't have to gather information about all alternatives, only those we consider before making a choice. A problem with satisficing, of course, is that a far better candidate may be one or two or three alternatives down the list. That alternative will never even be considered.

> Often when we face a great amount of information, such as the full résumés of many job candidates, we may simply ignore most of the information and focus on only one or two attributes, such as previous experience and physical appearance.

> *Representativeness* is the tendency to place something in a class if it seems representative of the class. So if someone looks like an astronaut to us, we might classify that person as an astronaut, although there are very few astronauts. Representativeness can have serious consequences because it is closely related to stereotyping. For instance, if we perceive that men "look like" executives and women "look like" administrative assistants, we may behave accordingly. This could result in hiring or promotion biases against women.

> *Availability* is the tendency to estimate a probability of an event on the basis of how easy it is to recall examples of the event. To illustrate: Is it more likely that a word in the English language starts with the letter *r* or that it has *r* as the third letter?[23] Most people incorrectly guess that *r* is more common as the first letter. The reason for this is that we store information by the first rather than the third letter (witness the phone directory) and can thus retrieve it more easily on that basis. As another example, because certain causes of death are more likely than others to receive publicity in the newspapers and elsewhere, they are more available in our memories than are others. As a result, we tend to overestimate their probabilities.[24]

> When we face a sequence of information, it is often difficult to combine it all properly to come up with a solution. For instance, in one study two groups of high school students had five seconds to estimate a numerical expression on the blackboard. One group was told to estimate the following product:

$$8 \times 7 \times 6 \times 5 \times 4 \times 3 \times 2 \times 1$$

The other group estimated the following product:

$$1 \times 2 \times 3 \times 4 \times 5 \times 6 \times 7 \times 8$$

The two products are of course identical, although computed in reverse order. However, the median estimate for the first group, with the descending sequence, was 2,250. For the second group, with the ascending sequence, it was 512. The correct answer is 40,320.[25] *Anchoring and adjustment* is the tendency to use an early bit of information as an anchor and then use new information to adjust that initial anchor. If we weighted all that new information properly, this would be fine. However, we tend to give too little weight to new information. So in the example, insufficient revision resulted in estimates being too low for both groups. The first group started with a higher initial anchor and thus came up with a higher, but still insufficient, estimate.

Heuristics, although potentially harmful, may not be all bad. For one thing, the problems that heuristics cause in laboratory experiments may be less severe in actual job settings. We often receive continuous feedback concerning our performance; for instance, as we trim a hedge, we can see what remains to be trimmed, whether we need to trim a section further, and so on. So if a heuristic "points us in the right direction," we can often then use feedback later to make adjustments. For this and other reasons, heuristics may actually be helpful in some cases. A weakness is that, even though we often use heuristics, we may not know it. For instance, one study found that job interviewers were unaware they used simplifying procedures in making their judgments.[26] Inadvertent use of heuristics, especially in onetime decision situations, may be dangerous.

PROCRASTINATION

Because we find decision making to be uncomfortable, we may put off making and announcing a decision as long as possible. This procrastination delays the time at which we commit ourselves to the decision and thus makes it more difficult for us to reverse that decision. We may justify our delay on the grounds that we are using the time to gather additional information. Secretly, we may be wishing the problem would simply go away. Procrastination can cost time, money, reputation, and opportunity. Procrastination can also lead to scrambling to meet deadlines and even to cheating or other unethical behaviors.[27]

Careers have been ruined and companies destroyed by chronic procrastination.[28] When Blimpie International submarine shops teetered on the brink of insolvency in 1988, founder Anthony Conza identified procrastination in decision making as a major cause. In response, he set specific goals for improvements and provided firm dates for task completion. Within five years, Blimpie's had rebounded; it more than tripled in size, to more than 700 restaurants, and its share price rose from $0.125 to $11.50.[29] Blimpie's now has more than 2,100 restaurants in 16 countries.

INCREMENTALIZING

Suppose you wanted to design a perfect mousetrap. How would you begin? Most people would think of the best currently available mousetrap and then begin to revise it bit by bit, adding a better spring or disposal mechanism. This procedure of changing one attribute a little and then another is called *incrementalizing*.[30] Incrementalizing may be appropriate if only a "somewhat better" product is needed, but it can seriously stifle truly creative alternatives. To learn more about creative mousetraps, see Web Exercise 3-2.

CONSERVATISM IN INFORMATION PROCESSING

We tend to show *conservatism in information processing*. This means that when we get new information, we don't revise our past estimates as much as we should. For instance, if we initially believe the probability of an event is 0.5 and are presented with new information that should increase the probability to 0.8, we are more likely to revise our estimate to only 0.6 or 0.7. Conservatism can have serious consequences for decision making because we don't fully respond to changing situations.[31]

DISSONANCE REDUCTION

Most decisions require us to make difficult choices. Although we make the choice that seems best overall, we may still like some things about the alternatives we reject and may not care for some things about the chosen alternative. This creates a condition of conflicting thoughts, called *cognitive dissonance* ("I've rejected something, yet it has some good characteristics; I've accepted something, yet it has some undesirable characteristics"). Cognitive dissonance is uncomfortable. We take a variety of actions, including a search for confirming information, a distortion of attitudes, and an avoidance of disconfirming information, to justify our decisions. As a result, we are likely to overestimate the quality of our past decisions; consequently, we underestimate the need to improve our decisions.

DECISION CONFIRMATION

Dissonance reduction that occurs before the announcement of a decision has been called *decision confirmation*. Peer Soelberg showed, for instance, that by studying students' decision processes, he could identify their job choices weeks before they announced them. According to Soelberg, the students actually made a decision fairly early in the process. The remainder of the process was spent building a case for the preferred alternative. Then when they finally announced a decision, they could present a strong argument in its favor.[32]

DEFENSIVE AVOIDANCE

Psychological stress in hot decision situations may result in errors in scanning of alternatives.[33] When a hot decision situation—such as a major decision, an impending attack, or major surgery—occurs and it looks like important goals cannot be met, stress increases. This stress is especially great if someone—such as a confirmed smoker hearing the Surgeon General's warnings—is committed to a course of action challenged by new information. As stress grows, there is a tendency to lose hope of finding a better solution to the decision conflict, and *defensive avoidance* occurs. This is a condition in which the individual avoids information about risks of the chosen alternative or opportunities associated with a rejected alternative.

A state of defensive avoidance is characterized by the following:

> Lack of vigilant search
> Distortion of the meanings of warning messages
> Selective inattention and forgetting
> Rationalizing

Because of defensive avoidance and other undesirable reactions to hot decision situations, many large industrial companies have formal crisis planning and management teams. These teams are trained to ask hard questions before situations occur. George Greer, former vice president and coordinator of the crisis management team at H. J. Heinz Co., stated, "We try to say, 'What would we do if the president of the company were kidnapped, if a plant burned down, if somebody allegedly tampered with a product?' "[34] The apparently chaotic response of Exxon to its huge Alaskan oil spill demonstrates the dangers of failure to consider such questions carefully.

THE MANY FACES OF INTUITION

We face so many difficulties when trying to make good decisions that we may ask, Why not just rely on intuition? After all, we don't want to make "sterile" decisions, based solely on numbers and formulas and computer programs. And we can all think of cases when a gut decision worked well. Unfortunately, the term *intuition* is used in so many ways, with so many different—and often opposing—implications and varying levels of empirical support, it has become almost meaningless. Nevertheless, you will repeatedly encounter calls to "use your intuition," so you need to think through this issue. Here are some ways intuition is used.[35]

> **Intuition as paranormal power or sixth sense.** People using intuition in this sense believe intuitive managers succeed because they use extrasensory powers that their nonintuitive counterparts lack or haven't fully developed.

> **Intuition as a personality trait.** Some people treat intuition as a personality characteristic that a person is born with or acquires in early childhood, which is then essentially fixed for life. This personality type is seen as preferring to rely on hunches, inspiration, and insight to solve problems.

> **Intuition as an unconscious process.** According to this view, intuition is a set of processes that occur at the unconscious level at the same time that analysis is proceeding at the conscious level. Those seeing intuition in this way generally believe we can learn to attend to our unconscious (i.e., to decide intuitively) and that this will lead to better decisions.

> **Intuition as a set of actions.** Sometimes intuition is seen as a set of observable methods or actions used by decision makers. These are evident in the ways decision makers gather, process, and use information. For instance, successful intuitive decision makers are said to often skip levels and seek information directly from key individuals, to meet face to face with those individuals, and to probe subtly for information in a way that is unlikely to trigger defensive reactions.[36]

> **Intuition as distilled experience.** Here intuition is seen as "analyses frozen into habit and into the capacity for rapid response through recognition."[37] That is, a manager who makes the same sorts of decisions many times over the years can identify an appropriate course of action without conscious information processing.

> **Intuition as a residual.** This perspective says essentially that any choice that isn't a product of systematic, conscious data gathering and analysis must be intuition.

It seems obvious that statements such as "Managers should rely on intuition" are meaningless unless we know how the term is being used. Here are some guidelines regarding the various uses of the term:

> If someone refers to *intuition*, be sure to ask what he or she means by the term.

> There is simply no support for the "intuition as paranormal power" perspective and no reason to believe such abilities could be developed if they did exist.

> There is no value in treating intuition as a residual category (that is, as anything that doesn't look like systematic problem solving). Such a perspective—telling us what intuition is not—gives absolutely no guidance on how better "intuitive" decisions could be made.

> If intuition is seen as a personality trait, it may be possible to select managers based on their intuitive ability, but training will have little impact. There is, though, relatively little evidence to suggest certain personality traits are associated with more *effective* "intuitive" decisions (although it is possible to identify people who prefer to make decisions in nonsystematic ways).

> If intuition is seen as distilled experience, it is learnable but not teachable; developing intuition will require years of practice. Evidence supports the contention that some decision makers (such as chess masters) are able over time to learn patterns and otherwise make what appear to be good "intuitive" decisions.

> If intuition is conceptualized as an unconscious process, it may not be possible to develop the unconscious, but it may be feasible to train decision makers to rely more on its "often-faint whisper."[38] Unfortunately, there is little solid guidance for how this might be done.

> If intuition is viewed as a set of actions taken by certain types of decision makers, it may be possible to study those decision makers and learn from them. To a great extent, this chapter deals with actions that successful decision makers take to get information, behave creatively, make good choices, properly implement decisions, and so on. Much of what some people call intuition is simply use of good, learnable decision techniques.

In general, though, it seems clear that intuition is a complicated—if not confusing—concept. Much more must be learned about the nature of intuition, its effects, and the ways it may be learned before it will be possible to make confident claims for its ability to improve decision making.

IMPROVING PROBLEM SOLVING

Despite the obstacles that managers face in solving problems, techniques—summarized in Figure 3-6—are available that can enhance the problem-solving process. We have already examined some of these techniques and address others in subsequent sections and chapters.

Skills Practice 3-6 gives you an opportunity to observe and analyze a problem-solving process that was implemented by a team of NASA engineers in the movie *Apollo 13*. In particular, focus on the conditions under which this problem-solving process was implemented. Enjoy!

The Voice of Experience feature presents an interview with Dale Gavney, a management consultant at the CUNA Mutual Group. It offers one practitioner's views on problems he has faced in a corporate environment and how he has learned to handle thesse problems over time.

FOSTERING CREATIVITY

Good problem solving occurs when managers have many viable, creative alternatives to consider. To inspire employees to approach problems creatively and to nurture a creative environment, organizations follow three general approaches. These include hiring creative individuals, applying specific creativity-enhancement techniques, and

FIGURE 3-6
Guidelines for Improving Problem Solving

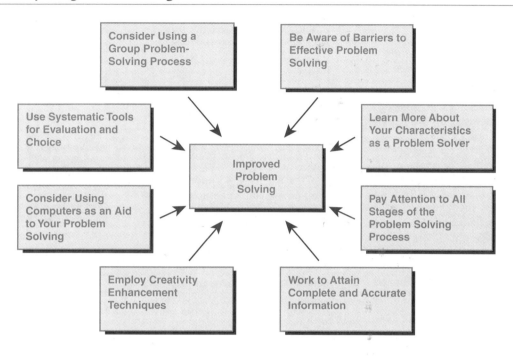

developing a creative organization. After discussions of the nature of creativity, the creative process, and views of creativity, we consider these approaches in turn.

THE NATURE OF CREATIVITY

Creative behavior is defined as production of ideas that are both new and useful. *Creative ability* is the ability to produce ideas that are both new and useful. These definitions may seem constraining because the usefulness of some truly creative alternatives might not be immediately evident. One scholar has addressed this dilemma by differentiating between originality and creativity. He wrote, "7,363,474 is quite an original answer to the problem 'How much is 12 + 12?' However, it is only when conditions are such that the answer is useful that we can also call it creative."[39] Thus the answer 7,363,474 is original but not creative. As we discuss in Chapter 4 and elsewhere, ability may not translate into behavior. Both motivation and a proper setting may be necessary if innate creative ability is to blossom into creative output.[40]

THE CREATIVE PROCESS

Creativity involves more than the sudden moment of inspiration in which a cartoon light bulb flashes in the brain. Instead, as shown in Figure 3-7, there are four stages to the creative process: preparation, incubation, insight, and verification.[41]

> *Preparation* involves gathering, sorting, and integrating information and other materials to provide a solid base for a later breakthrough. The discoveries of penicillin, the benzene ring, or gravity, although each involved a moment

VOICE OF EXPERIENCE

SOLVING PROBLEMS

Dale Gavney, Management Consultant—People and Change Management, CUNA Mutual Group

1. What are some of the most difficult problems you have experienced on your job?

There's no rocket science in this answer—I've found the most difficult problems are the complex problems. For example, managing a large project is like an ongoing exercise in problem-solving. I've found factors such as the number of people who care about the outcome (i.e., the stakeholders) and the number of functional areas involved in the project to be predictors of complexity and difficulty.

2. What specific actions have you taken to solve these problems?

I've developed and borrowed frameworks that help me assess ambiguous situations. For example, I've used project definition documents (see PMI, the Project Management Institute, for more information). These documents have given me a series of questions which have helped me define the problem, an important step in solving a problem. I've also borrowed from others who develop research in the social sciences. My favorite resource, since my work focuses on people at work, is the HPT (Human Performance Technology) framework from the International Society for Performance Improvement. This framework addresses the "problem" of how to improve human performance and competency. I've taken this framework and modified it to fit my own particular needs. Specifically, I have a number of key questions I'll typically ask clients at the beginning of a

project. I also have surveys that have been developed from this framework. One key in effective problem-solving is asking your customer the right question at the right time to get the information you need to solve the problem.

3. How important is creativity in problem solving?

Creativity is very important. Problem-solving and decision-making require people who can take a multitude of factors, consider which are most relevant, narrow the factors down, create options, and propose or take action. Your employer and customers will expect you to be able to arrive at conclusions that will benefit the business even when no clear alternative is present. This calls for creative problem-solving. The phrase "think outside the box" has become cliché because it has been used over and over in the work place. The fact that it has been used over and over shows that there is increasing pressure on business to develop innovative, customer-focussed products and services. In short, a rote, pre-determined problem-solving process will not always deliver the best solution.

4. How do you balance data and intuition in problem solving?

It depends on the problem. I feel that decision making without data is like gambling—or worse. There are two major challenges when using data. One is making sense of a large amount of data that may be available and culling the data down to a manageable number of discrete variables. The other is recognizing which data are actionable data—the most important type. That is, data that allow you to make informed decisions that lead to the desired

business results. I still occasionally refer to my old college statistics texts, mostly for refreshers on general descriptive statistics, correlation coefficients, and regression analysis.

If you want to effectively maximize your intuition, make sure you've properly defined the problem. Next, you need to have the ability and time to absorb many relevant facts related to the problem. Then, sleep on it, or just let some time pass, or meditate, etc. There needs to be some time for the facts "percolate" and mix with your experience, values and experience or wisdom. Bounce the problem off of trusted peers to gain different perspectives. At some point, your intuition will help you in arriving at a solution. I would stress that I've become better at listening to my intuition over time. Also, the more confident you are in your abilities the better your intuition will serve you. That is, a person easily swayed by others often doesn't listen to their intuition.

5. What advice would you give to students regarding how to analyze and solve business problems effectively in the real world?

- Develop a network of peers and mentors to help you with the most difficult decisions. When you have a particularly challenging problem, explain your situation to these individuals and ask for their perspective and help. When the opportunity arises, return the favor. Along the same lines, when wrestling with a decision, don't be too proud. I made the mistake in the early part of my career of asking too few

VOICE OF EXPERIENCE (continued)

questions. Ask for help often, especially with people with whom you enjoy a trusting relationship.

- Recognize when you're burned out or stuck. There's nothing like stepping away from a problem or sleeping on it to clarify your mind. Recognize this may happen over the course of your career, and develop some other approach to clear your

mind. I have friends who use meditation, exercise, or more spiritual outlets to achieve this effect.

- Finally, take a cue from your doctor, who looks at your body as a system. When you visit your doctor for an upset stomach, she will ask you a number of questions—"What have you eaten recently?", "Have you been hit in the abdomen recently?", "Has anything stressful happened to you

recently?" As shown by these questions, she is looking at multiple possible causes of the pain in your stomach. Depending upon the answers to your questions, she can narrow down all the possible reasons for your upset stomach, perhaps order certain tests, and then prescribe a solution that will make you feel better. So, take a systems approach to problem-solving for better results.

of insight, would have been impossible without a firm grasp of related information.

> During the *incubation* stage, the mind is not consciously focused on the problem. The individual may be relaxed, asleep, reflective, or otherwise involved. A. E. Housman wrote, "As I went along, thinking nothing in particular . . . there would flow into my mind, with sudden and unaccountable emotion, sometimes a line or two of verse, sometimes a whole stanza at once."[42]

> The *insight* ("Eureka!") stage is the familiar, sudden moment of inspiration. This is what we often think of as creativity, but it is only one step in the creative process.

> Finally, *verification* is necessary. Here the individual carries out the chores involved in carefully checking facts to support the insight, carrying out research to determine that the DNA molecule is in fact a double helix or that a meteorite did really create a dust cloud that led to the extinction of the dinosaurs. This process further supports the contention that creativity does not just happen. It is a thorough and often painstaking activity.

TECHNIQUES FOR ENHANCING CREATIVITY

A wide variety of popular techniques have been developed to enhance creativity, as described in this section. We address additional techniques in Chapter 11, "Managing Teams."

FIGURE 3-7
The Creative Process

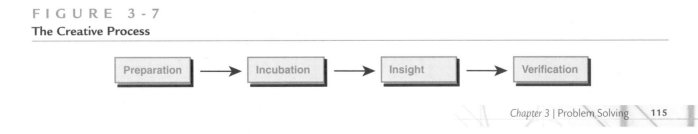

GORDON TECHNIQUE[43]

William J. J. Gordon worked with creative-thinking groups and had a creative variety of other pursuits, among them salvage diver, horse handler, ambulance driver, college lecturer, and pig breeder ("a lot of bone and not much bacon, but they were the fastest pigs in the East").[44] He was concerned that people, when asked to come up with a creative new idea, would instead incrementalize. That is, they would take an available alternative and improve it bit by bit. Although this might lead to marginally better alternatives, the alternatives probably would not be real breakthroughs.

Gordon decided that one way to avoid this problem would be simply not to tell people what they were inventing. Thus the *Gordon technique* uses an initial focus on function. Rather than being told to build a better mousetrap, the group might first be told the focus was capturing. Instead of the group being instructed to design an improved knife, the function could be given as severing.[45]

SYNECTICS

Gordon also developed a well-known technique called *synectics*, which means "the joining of apparently unrelated elements." It means this in two senses. First, very different sorts of people are put together in synectics groups in order to achieve a great diversity of perspectives. Second, synectics relies heavily on the use of analogies. Three synectics tools are direct analogy, personal analogy, and fantasy analogy.

> *Direct analogy.* This involves looking for parallel facts, knowledge, or technology in a different domain from the one being worked on. For instance, can we think of anything similar that occurs in nature? Alexander Graham Bell's words illustrate this approach:

> *It struck me that the bones of the human ear were very massive, indeed, as compared with the delicate thin membrane that operated them, and the thought occurred that if a membrane so delicate could move bones relatively so massive, why should not a thicker and stouter piece of membrane move my piece of steel? And the telephone was conceived.*[46]

> *Personal analogy.* With personal analogy, synectics group members try to identify psychologically with key parts of the problem. In one case, for example, the group was asked to design a mechanism that would run a shaft turning at 400 to 4,000 rpm so the power-takeoff end of the shaft would turn at a constant 400 rpm. To address this question, members of the group metaphorically entered the box and tried to use their bodies to attain the required speed without undue friction.

> *Fantasy analogy.* Sigmund Freud saw creativity as the fulfillment of a wish or fantasy. Fantasy analogy asks, "How in my wildest dreams can I make this happen?" Gordon gives the example of a synectics group with the task of inventing a vapor-proof closure for space suits. The solution was a spring mechanism based on the fantasy analogy of rows of trained insects clasping claws to hold shut the closure.

There is more to synectics than just the use of analogy. The technique follows a structured problem-solving sequence in which a client and other participants interact to develop a workable solution to the client's problem. For instance, after the problem has been introduced and discussed, there is a "springboards" stage in which the problem is opened up by asking the client to convert concerns, opinions, and desires into statements such as "I wish . . ." or "How to . . ." Later, after an initial idea has been developed and refined, an "itemized response" stage requires the client to think of three useful aspects or advantages of the idea and to generate key concerns. Still later, after the group works to modify the suggestion to overcome these concerns, the "possible solution" is checked for elements of newness and feasibility and whether there is sufficient commitment to the solution to take additional steps. Finally, the client lists actions to be taken to implement the solution, including timing and the personnel to be used.

Synectics techniques have been widely adopted by both businesses and educational institutions.[47] American Express, 3M, Audi, Citigroup, the Harvard Medical School, IBM, NATO, Nabisco, and Shell are among organizations applying synectics. Use of synectics is credited by Betty Means, Citibank's director of global marketing, with helping sign up more than 2 million new customers for Citibank's Visa and MasterCard.[48] Now complete Skills Practice 3-7 to develop your skill in using the synectics technique for generating creative solutions to problems.

IDEA CHECKLISTS

Several *idea checklists* have been developed to enhance creativity.[49] These involve asking a series of questions about how we might use something that we already have. For example, one checklist of idea-spurring questions is called SCAMPER (for Substitute? Combine? Adapt? Modify or magnify? Put to other uses? Eliminate or reduce? Reverse or rearrange?). Here's an example of adapting: Clarence Birdseye worked as a fur trader in Labrador before World War I. He noted that Inuit preserved fish by quick freezing and the fish, when thawed, were flaky and moist. Birdseye adapted this process to make quick-frozen food available to the general public. This replaced the old slow-freeze process that left food dry and tasteless. The huge success of quick-frozen food led to the creation of General Foods.

And here's an example of eliminating: Kiichiro Toyoda, the founder of Toyota, sought ways to eliminate large inventories and the need for warehouses. American supermarkets fascinated him, and he noted they require vast amounts of food that can't be stored on site because of spoilage and space considerations. When supplies run low, the staff contacts the appropriate supplier and items arrive "just in time." Toyota adopted this concept and streamlined its operation, eliminating waste and warehouses and reducing costs dramatically. Toyota's "just-in-time" approach gave it a huge competitive edge. Just-in-time is now being adopted worldwide.

George Washington Carver asked the question, "How can peanuts be put to other uses?" and came up with over 300 applications. Many creative ideas have resulted from asking how waste products could be put to other uses. Rubber bands are made from surgical tubing; garbage is compressed into construction blocks; petrochemical waste is sold as Silly Putty; the Goodyear Tire Company has a pollution-free heating plant in Michigan that uses discarded tires as its only fuel.

Perhaps the best known listing technique is the "73 idea-spurring questions" devised by Alex Osborne.[50] This checklist can be applied to any alternative. Here are some of the questions.

> Put to other uses? New ways to use as is? Other uses if modified?
> Adapt? What else is like it? What other ideas does this suggest? Does past offer parallel? What could I copy? Whom could I emulate?
> Minify? What to subtract? Smaller? Condensed? Miniature? Lower? Shorter? Lighter? Omit? Streamline? Split up? Understate?
> Substitute? Who else instead? What else instead? Other ingredient? Other material? Other process? Other power? Other place? Other approach? Other tone of voice?
> Rearrange? Interchange components? Other pattern? Other layout? Other sequence? Transpose cause and effect? Change pace? Change schedule?
> Combine? How about a blend, an alloy, an assortment, an ensemble? Combine units? Combine purposes? Combine appeals? Combine ideas?

ATTRIBUTE LISTING

According to the developer of *attribute listing*, Robert Crawford, "Each time we take a step we do it by changing an attribute or a quality of something, or else by applying that same quality or attribute to some other thing."[51] There are two forms of attribute listing: attribute modifying and attribute transferring.[52]

With attribute modifying, the main attributes of the problem object are listed. Then ways to improve each attribute are listed. For instance, the technique might be used to concentrate on ways to improve the running shoe attributes of weight, stability, cushioning, and durability. Attribute transferring is similar to direct analogy in synectics. Attributes from one thing are transferred to another.

CHECKERBOARD METHOD

The *checkerboard method*, also called *morphological analysis*, is an extension of attribute modifying. Specific ideas for one attribute or problem dimension are listed along one axis of a matrix. Ideas for a second attribute are listed along the other axis. If desired, a third axis (and attribute) can be added. The cells of the matrix then provide idea combinations. For instance, the axes for a vehicle might be *type of energy source* (e.g., steam, magnetic fields, compressed air, nuclear), *medium of travel* (e.g., rollers, air, water, rails), and *type of vehicle* (e.g., cart, chair, sling, bed).[53] Figure 3-8 shows a simple application of the checkerboard method to the design of paper clips.

The benefit of the checkerboard method is that it makes us aware of all possible combinations of the attributes. Many, of course, will prove to be of little value, but others may be worthwhile. Like other creativity-enhancement techniques, the checkerboard method makes us view the world from a different perspective. It is very useful for producing large numbers of new ideas.[54] Skills Practice 3-8 will help you develop skill in applying the checkerboard method to specific business scenarios.

RETRODUCTION

We are the slaves of our assumptions; they dictate the way we behave.[55] *Retroduction* involves changing an assumption. This may serve two purposes. First, our

FIGURE 3-8
The Checkerboard Method

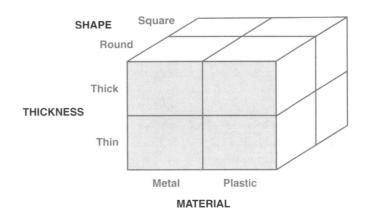

assumptions may be wrong. Second, even if our assumptions are correct, we may gain valuable new perspectives from looking at things from a different angle. Albert Einstein, for instance, revised Isaac Newton's assumption that space is flat to the assumption that space is curved and developed a new perspective on time and space.

As a simple example of the power of assumptions, consider paper clips, the subject of Figure 3-8. The standard Gem paper clip, invented in 1899, accounts for most of the 20 billion paper clips sold every year. More than 100 alternative designs have been patented, varying in size, material, and shape. "Ring" clips, "owl" clips, "arrowhead" clips, "butterfly" clips, and many others have been offered, and their inventors present compelling cases for their superiority. Nevertheless, they haven't made a noticeable dent in Gem's market superiority. Why? It would seem the inventors share a common—and incorrect—assumption: that paper clips are used to clip sheets of paper together. In fact, though, research shows that only 20 percent of paper clips are used to hold papers. The rest are twisted or broken by people during phone conversations, unwound to clean pipes, nails, or ears, used to reinforce eyeglasses, or put to other creative uses. The Gem, unlike its competitors, can easily be taken apart and reshaped.[56]

One retroduction technique says, "Suppose *X* were *Y*." For instance, "Suppose custodians were chief executives." Another technique pairs apparently distinct concepts, such as **power** and **satisfaction** or **perception** and **structure**, and sees what new alternatives might be suggested. Yet another asks "What if?" For example, what if employees could design their own jobs? What if we viewed customers as owners of the firm?[57] One individual who applied these retroduction techniques generated such questions as "What are the structural irregularities of semiconductors?" and "Can arteries have rashes?" Each of these questions is now the subject of study and debate, the first among physicists and the second among researchers on disease processes.[58] Henry Ford questioned the practice of moving workers to material, asking, "What if we moved the work to the people?" This questioning led to the birth of the assembly line. Retroduction offers new perspectives and helps free people from mental ruts.

Here's a final example: For years, bankers assumed that customers preferred human tellers. In the early 1980s, Citibank decided that installing automatic tellers would help it cut costs. However, because Citibank executives assumed people would prefer not to use machines, they reserved human tellers for people with large accounts and relegated smaller depositors to the machines. The machines proved unpopular and Citibank stopped using them, believing the failure was proof that its assumption was correct. Later, another banker challenged this assumption. He asked, in effect, "What if people really like to use automatic tellers? What if the Citibank customers who used the machines simply resented being treated as second-class citizens?" He brought back the automatic tellers with no "class distinctions," and they were an immediate success.[59] Skills Practice 3-9 is designed to develop your skill in applying the questioning of assumptions and what-if approaches to retroduction.

The accompanying Bottom Line feature shows the key steps of each of the creativity-enhancement techniques we have considered. It also shows how alternatives generated by the techniques can serve as inputs to later steps in the problem-solving process.

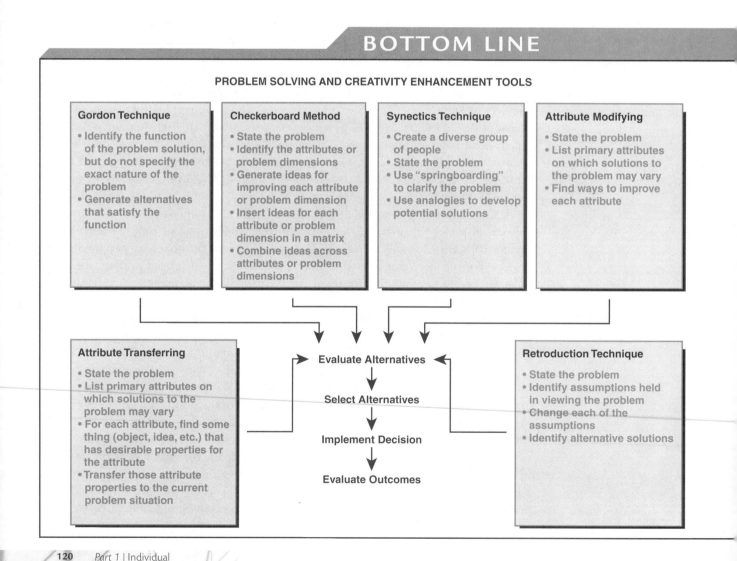

BOTTOM LINE

PROBLEM SOLVING AND CREATIVITY ENHANCEMENT TOOLS

Gordon Technique

- Identify the function of the problem solution, but do not specify the exact nature of the problem
- Generate alternatives that satisfy the function

Checkerboard Method

- State the problem
- Identify the attributes or problem dimensions
- Generate ideas for improving each attribute or problem dimension
- Insert ideas for each attribute or problem dimension in a matrix
- Combine ideas across attributes or problem dimensions

Synectics Technique

- Create a diverse group of people
- State the problem
- Use "springboarding" to clarify the problem
- Use analogies to develop potential solutions

Attribute Modifying

- State the problem
- List primary attributes on which solutions to the problem may vary
- Find ways to improve each attribute

Attribute Transferring

- State the problem
- List primary attributes on which solutions to the problem may vary
- For each attribute, find something (object, idea, etc.) that has desirable properties for the attribute
- Transfer those attribute properties to the current problem situation

Evaluate Alternatives

↓

Select Alternatives

↓

Implement Decision

↓

Evaluate Outcomes

Retroduction Technique

- State the problem
- Identify assumptions held in viewing the problem
- Change each of the assumptions
- Identify alternative solutions

THE CREATIVE ORGANIZATION

Along with use of specific creativity-enhancement techniques, an organization may try to choose appropriate structure and processes to foster creative behavior. Some writers have studied creative individuals and their desires and have drawn a picture of an organization that would seem to suit them best. One such picture is shown in Figure 3-9. The loose, free-flowing, adaptive nature of this organization is quite similar to the organic structure discussed in other chapters. Such a structure seems appropriate in dynamic, complex, uncertain situations—exactly those most requiring creativity. We'll see later in this section what companies are doing to create such structures. Creative organizations also provide rewards and support for creativity while encouraging employees to believe they are capable of generating creative ideas.[60]

The importance of these dimensions is perhaps best seen in their absence. For instance, Japan has in recent years been losing its best and brightest young pure scientists to the United States and other countries. The reason: the scientists are unwilling to accept a system that relies on bureaucratic constraints and seniority and stifles individualism, job mobility, and open debate. In the Japanese system, young scientists are expected to plug away patiently under the close supervision of older scientists. If they are unhappy, they can't easily move because the notion of lifelong employment is powerful in Japan and job hoppers are seen as pariahs. Open debate

FIGURE 3-9
Characteristics of a Creative Organization

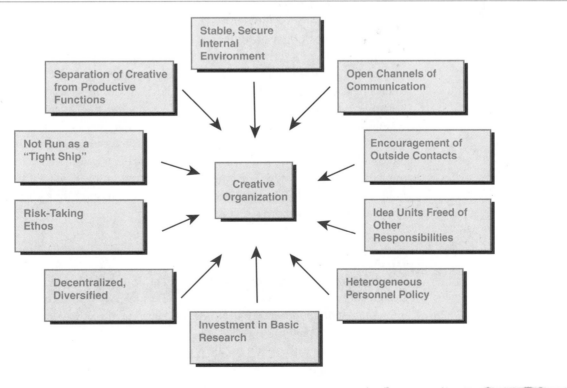

is so rare that when one speaker was challenged at a conference, he froze, unable to answer. In another case, a young scientist held back from questioning the data of an elderly, influential author because the elder "would have lost face and . . . I would have been indirectly punished some day when I filed an application" for a grant. Bureaucratic rules regularly crimp freedom; for instance, scientists must apply months ahead for government consent to leave the country. Rather than taking risks and exploring new areas, scholars search Western journals to find research topics. One consequence of this uncreative environment is that only a handful of Japanese scientists have ever won Nobel prizes, compared to more than a score of French scientists and about 150 Americans.[61]

If it is not possible to change the organization markedly to make it more conducive to creativity, another option is to free some units from bureaucratic entanglements by setting up relatively autonomous units. For instance, when General Motors launched its Saturn project, the first new nameplate in the GM line since 1918, it wanted a clean-slate approach without unnecessary ties to past ways of designing, engineering, manufacturing, or selling the product. As a result, it set up a new organization in order to free Saturn from the inefficiencies and overstaffing of the then-current GM bureaucracy.[62] Complete Skills Practice 3-10 to develop an action plan for promoting a creative organization.

VENTURE TEAMS

A *venture team* is a temporary grouping of organization members to generate new ideas.[63] So creative thinking is not stifled, team members are freed of the organization's bureaucracy and in many cases have a separate location and facilities known as *skunk works*.[64] Major corporations such as IBM, 3M, Dow Chemical, and Texas Instruments have used venture teams to solve technical problems and promote change. Ford Motor Company used skunk works to keep the new Mustang alive.[65] Faced with tight budgets, tough time constraints, and an uncertain vision of the new Mustang, Ford formed the 400-member "Team Mustang." Team members thought of themselves as independent stockholders of the "Mustang Car Co.," which happened to be financed by Ford. They set up Mustang Car Co. in a converted furniture warehouse, received approval to move Ford engineers from various locations to the warehouse, and grouped employees into "chunk teams," with responsibility for every "chunk" of the car. Mustang Car Co. did away with many elements of the traditional hierarchy and many restrictive rules and procedures. The result: the fundamentally redesigned new Mustang was completed in three years and for about $700 million—25 percent less time and 30 percent less money than for any comparable new car program in Ford's recent history.[66]

IDEA CHAMPIONS

An **idea champion** is a member of the organization assigned responsibility for the successful implementation of a change. The idea champion may be a senior manager or a staff member, such as the inventor of the idea that has prompted the change. An idea champion is devoted to the change and is willing to spend time and energy to see that the change takes place. Idea champions will fight resistance to

FOCUS ON MANAGEMENT

METROJET

Two dozen mechanics, flight attendants, dispatchers, and reservation agents of US Air, selected by senior managers and union leaders, were offered an unusual assignment: Help start a low-fare airline for US Air. US Air had decided it needed the low-fare airline to help counter the expansion of Southwest Airlines into the east, and it put the project into the hands of its front-line employees. In the unusual experiment in worker empowerment, the employees—each of whom knew his

or her job well, but none with experience starting a business, much less an airline—worked under the code name US2. They priced peanuts, conducted focus groups, and argued over everything from how fast to fly the planes to whether to keep pillows and blankets aboard. Taking just one day off (to watch the Super Bowl) the team completed its assignment in only four months. Named MetroJet, based on 4,200 entries in an employee contest, the airline achieved great initial success but was terminated as part of US Air's cost-cutting moves following the 9/11

tragedy and its devastating effects on the airline industry.*

*S. Carey, "US Air 'Peon' Team Pilots Start-Up of Low-Fare Airline," *Wall Street Journal,* pp. B1, B8. See also A. L. Velocci, Jr., "MetroJet's Expansion Tests Rivals' Mettle," *Aviation Week and Space Technology,* April 12, 1999, p. 57; and S. Carey, "US Air Sets Plans to Restore Profitability—Heavy Cost Cuts in Strategy Quickly Spur the Wrath of the Carrier's Unions," *Wall Street Journal,* August 16, 2001, p. A3.

change and will actively pursue resources necessary to carry out the change. Idea champions may be critical to the success or failure of change. For example, Texas Instruments reviewed 50 successful and 50 unsuccessful technical projects. One consistent finding was that every failure also lacked an idea champion. As a result, Texas Instruments set up as its number one criterion for project approval the presence of an idea champion.[67]

INTRAPRENEURSHIP

Many people have praised the flexibility, creativity, risk taking, and energy often associated with small firms and entrepreneurship and have asked how these elements might be instilled in larger organizations. *Intrapreneurship* is the name given to entrepreneurial activities within a larger organization, and *intrapreneurs* are essentially internal entrepreneurs.[68]

Intrapreneurs and entrepreneurs have much in common.[69] For instance, they value creativity and autonomy and have a strong desire to achieve. Because intrapreneurs work within a corporate system, however, they face the benefits and constraints of that system. Unlike entrepreneurs, intrapreneurs operate under a corporate accounting system and must report to hierarchical superiors. They do not personally face the financial risks that entrepreneurs do, nor do they enjoy the same rewards. They can draw on the rich financial resources of the corporation.

Intrapreneurs may need different competencies to succeed than do entrepreneurs. For instance, intrapreneurs must be somewhat skilled at organizational politics, which entrepreneurs may find reprehensible and that may, in fact, motivate them to work for themselves. Further, whereas entrepreneurs must provide their own goals and rewards, intrapreneurs are within the reward system of the formal organization.

Freedom factors serve as scissors to cut away excessive paperwork controls and to create a nurturing environment for intrapreneurship. Here are some "freedom factors":[70]

> **Self-selection.** Intrapreneurs appoint themselves to their role and receive the corporation's blessing for their self-appointed task. Management cannot appoint someone an intrapreneur, tell him or her to become passionately committed to an idea, and then expect success. The self-selection process often begins with bootlegging: The intrapreneur works nights or weekends or on time borrowed from approved projects to build the case for sanction of self-appointed tasks.

> **No handoffs.** Innovation is not a relay race in which an idea can be handed off from runner to runner. When a developing business or product is "handed off" from a committed intrapreneur to whoever is next in line, dedication to the project may suffer.

> **The doer decides.** The intrapreneur's job is to visualize a new business reality and then make it happen. The primary problem in big organizations is not blocking the vision, but blocking the action. The solution lies in letting the doer decide; the intrapreneur must be allowed to act.

> **Corporate slack.** When all corporate resources are committed to what is planned, nothing is left for trying the unplanned. Yet innovation is inherently unplanned. Intrapreneurs need discretionary resources to explore and develop new ideas. Employees should be given the freedom to use a percentage of their time on projects of their own choosing and to set aside funds to explore new ideas when they occur.

> **Ending the home-run philosophy.** Today's corporate culture favors a few well-studied, well-planned attempts to hit a home run. But nobody bats a thousand, and it is better to try more times with less careful and expensive preparation for each. Companies that demand projection of the huge payoff before entering a market rarely get in on the ground floor of new industries, and even if they do they rarely find the high-profit segments.

> **Tolerance of risk, failure, and mistakes.** Innovation cannot be achieved without risk and mistakes. Even successful innovation generally begins with blunders and false starts.

> **Patient money.** Innovation takes time, even decades, but the rhythm of corporations is annual planning. Sophisticated investors in innovation have the courage and patience to let their investments prove themselves or go bust.

> **Freedom from "turfiness."** Executives' emphasis on beating their peers in the race to the top leads to an obsession with turf. Because new ideas almost always cross the boundaries of existing patterns of organizations, a jealous tendency to turfiness blocks innovation. An effective organization must focus competition on performance and contribution, not politics.

> **Cross-functional teams.** Small teams with full responsibility for developing an intraprise solve many of the basic problems of bigness in innovation. Whenever a new idea begins, it encounters resistance from other functional areas, and each idea needs the support of all functions before it can be a success. But some companies resist the formation of cross-functional teams.

> **Multiple options.** Entrepreneurs live in a multioption universe. If one venture capitalist or supplier can't or won't meet their needs, there are many more to

choose from. Intrapreneurs, however, often face single-option situations that may be called *internal monopolies.* They must have their product made by a certain factory or sold by a certain sales force. Too often these groups lack motivation or are simply wrong for the job, and a good idea dies an unnecessary death. Intrapreneurs should have the freedom to select from all possible ways to get the job done—internal or external.

In addition to these "freedom factors," two other factors foster intrapreneurial success. First, sponsorship of intrapreneurs is important. Sponsors ensure that the "intraprise" receives the required resources and help temper the grievances of those who feel threatened by the innovation. Many intrapreneurs have several sponsors: lower-level sponsors to take care of day-to-day support needs and higher-level sponsors to fend off threatening strategic attacks. Second, there must be suitable rewards for intrapreneurship. Traditional rewards for success don't match the risks of innovating or intrapreneuring. Also, the basic reward in most companies is promotion, which doesn't work well for most intrapreneurs; they seek freedom to use their intuition, take risks, and invest the company's money in building new businesses and launching new products and services. For this reason, a key reward for intrapreneurs is *intracapital*, a discretionary budget earned by the intrapreneur and used to fund the creation of new intraprises and innovation for the corporation.

Hoping to grow and compete in a fast-paced market, Bell Atlantic turned to intrapreneurship with great success. Within a few years, more than 130 intrapreneurs had championed more than 100 projects, at least 15 products were on or near the market, and 15 patents had been awarded. Potential revenues estimated from the projects total a minimum of $100 million within five years.[71] Similarly, at Xerox, many creative ideas were lost before being turned into marketable products. As a result, Xerox recognized the need to nurture entrepreneurs within the corporation. The company formed Xerox Technology Ventures (XTV), a venture-capital group that allows Xerox to bring creative products to the market through intrapreneurship. XTV has become so successful that it is now a role model for other firms.[72]

CREATIVITY AND DIVERSITY

People differing in gender, age, race, disability status, and sexual orientation bring to organizations a variety of attitudes, values, and perspectives as well as a broad, rich base of experience to address a problem.[73] As a result, while the group becomes more diverse, the potential for creativity is enhanced. Innovative organizations have generally done a better job than others in eradicating racism and sexism, and they tend to employ more women and nonwhite men than do less innovative firms.[74] In addition, brainstorming groups consisting of diverse ethnic and racial groups produce higher-quality ideas than do homogeneous groups.[75] Further, the presence in groups of individuals holding minority views leads to critical analysis of decision issues and alternatives, resulting in consideration of a larger number of alternatives and a more thorough examination of underlying assumptions.[76] And because homogeneous groups tend to value conformity and agreement and are reluctant to rock the boat, such groups often discourage critical thinking. Because of this, diversity may foster more open, honest, and effective decision making.[77]

Taken together, this all suggests that diversity can yield many benefits for decision making and creativity. However, diversity may also increase the potential for misunderstandings and increase conflict and anxiety among members.[78] The challenge is to manage cultural diversity in such a way as to capture its benefits while minimizing potential problems.[79]

COMPANY PROGRAMS TO ENHANCE CREATIVITY

Firms are using special programs to foster their employees' creativity. Many send their employees on retreats and outings to jolt them out of routine ways of thinking.[80] Quaker Oats Co. executives go horseback riding when they need fresh approaches to budget and marketing problems. American Greeting Co.'s licensing unit, Those Characters from Cleveland, which created Strawberry Shortcake and the Care Bears, has a half-dozen weekend retreats in the woods each year, where its creative personnel brainstorm, play games, and sketch to be inspired with new ideas.

Mattel Inc., the world's largest toy manufacturer, uses its "Project Platypus" to invent original new toys. To stimulate new ways of thinking, the company brings together 15 or 20 employees from different disciplines such as engineering, design, marketing, and copywriting to participate in each session. To begin, participants "cleanse their palates," or leave the rigidity of the corporate world behind, by interacting with guests such as an improvisational artist, a Jungian psychoanalyst, and an expert on brainwave frequencies. Those guests may encourage the participants to devise a method to prevent an egg from breaking if dropped from 14 feet or to watch a Japanese tea ceremony. Platypus sessions take place at a large building separate from headquarters. There are no internal walls, desks are on wheels to encourage spontaneous collaboration, and a chalkboard wall invites team members to doodle or write sayings. Once a project is under way, team members post their sketched ideas on the walls. If a designer fastens an orange sticker to the drawing, it is an invitation to others to "make it juicy" and add suggestions to the idea. The sessions encourage creative thinking, cross-functional cooperation, and group bonding. The first session, which concluded at the end of 2001, produced Ello, a construction and activity toy for girls. Based on the Ello experience, Mattel plans to use Platypus to develop two or three new toy brand ideas each year.[81]

The growing emphasis on creativity is evident worldwide. For example, independent thinking and improvisation have historically been stifled in many Japanese firms. As a result, Japanese companies have excelled at improving on existing products but have rarely been pioneers. Now, though, competitive pressures and rapid change are demanding greater creativity to invent new products, markets, and businesses, and Japanese firms are trying to respond.[82] For instance, Shiseido, Japan's largest cosmetics maker, has implemented a series of four seminars to enhance the creativity of its managers. The four-day seminars, held at resorts on Mount Fuji, cover such topics as "Time and Space," "Expression and Language," "Beauty and Truth," and "Body and Soul." In one session, managers are told that the company needs to become a "living system" that adapts to its surroundings much as an organism does. Then they are asked to ponder a goldfish and a crab, answering a series of questions about each and deciding which of the animals' characteristics would be desirable for Shiseido. In another session, participants are told to change their mannerisms in order to act and speak like Americans; they walk around the room with exaggerated movements, talking loudly and flailing their arms. In yet another gathering, which focuses on the importance of equilibrium and patience, the managers watch the leader of a renowned dance troupe slowly contort his body.

At Omron Corp., a maker of electronic controls, midlevel employees attend a monthly *juku*, or cram school, where they think and plan as if they were 19th-century warlords, private detectives, or Formula One race car drivers. Fuji Film asks its senior managers to study topics such as the history of Venice and the sociology of apes. Although such exercises may sometimes appear bizarre or even humorous, they encourage the employees to break out of the corporate shell and think in different ways.

NEGOTIATING AND BARGAINING

Decision making is difficult enough when we must "simply" choose alternatives. When our decision making is in the face of another party who may have opposing interests, things become even more complicated.

STRATEGIES FOR NEGOTIATING

Parties to negotiation (or, in general, to a conflict situation) tend to adopt one of five negotiation strategies, each with its own objectives, behaviors, rationale, and probable outcomes. These strategies reflect differing levels of emphasis on assertiveness (attempting to satisfy one's own interests) and cooperativeness (attempting to satisfy the other party's concerns), as shown in Figure 3-10.

> **Forcing.** With forcing, the negotiator is assertive and uncooperative, attempting to satisfy his or her own needs at the expense of those of the other party. If the negotiator is successful, this results in a form of "win-lose" outcome, with a clear winner and loser.

FIGURE 3-10
Negotiating Styles

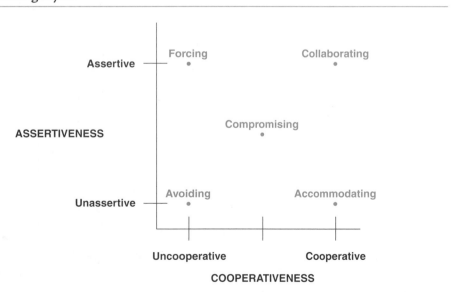

> **Avoiding.** A negotiator adopting an avoiding strategy is neither assertive nor cooperative, neglecting the interests of both parties by trying to sidestep the conflict or put off making a decision. Regular use of this strategy may lead to frustration, uncertainties, and stalemates, yielding a "lose-lose" outcome, with neither party's needs being satisfied.
> **Compromising.** A compromising negotiator shows moderate levels of both assertiveness and cooperation. The compromise doesn't fully satisfy the needs of either party, but the pain is shared.
> **Accommodating.** Some negotiators are cooperative without being assertive, thus satisfying the other party's needs while neglecting their own. The accommodating party may thus become a "sucker," being taken advantage of and losing stature and self-esteem. Thus this creates another "win-lose" situation, with the accommodating party being the loser.
> **Collaborating.** A negotiator adopting the collaborating style is both cooperative and assertive, focusing on satisfying the needs of both parties. This style—sometimes called a problem-solving style—has the potential for yielding "win-win" outcomes, satisfying the needs of both parties.

Another way to view these styles is in terms of their emphasis on distribution—dividing a fixed-size pie among the parties—or integration—with the parties finding ways to enlarge the pie. As shown in Figure 3-11, *distributive styles* are zero-sum, with any gain to one party coming at the expense of the other. Conversely, *integrative styles* are non-zero-sum, with the joint decisions of the parties dictating the ultimate size of the resources to be shared. Of the styles considered earlier, only

F I G U R E   3 - 1 1
Distributive and Integrative Approaches

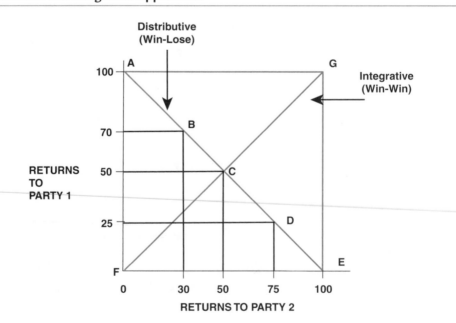

the collaborating style is integrative, or "win-win." All others involve suboptimal outcomes for one or both parties. It may not always be possible to find an integrative solution, but we won't find one if we don't try.

Note in Figure 3-11 that with a distributive approach the sum of the two parties' outcomes is 100. If Party 1 gets 70, Party 2 gets 30 (Point B); if Party 1 gets 50, Party 2 gets 50 (Point C); and so on. That is, any gain to one party is a corresponding loss to the other. With an integrative approach, in contrast, the sum of the two parties' outcomes depends on their mutual choices. At Point F, neither party gets anything; at Point C, each gets 50; at Point G, each gets 100.

GUIDELINES FOR ATTAINING WIN-WIN SOLUTIONS[83]

Here are some specific guidelines for reaching win-win, integrative agreements.

> **Think win-win.** In the heat and emotion of negotiations, it's often difficult to focus on mutual gain. Instead, we begin to think about outmaneuvering the other party, coming out ahead, or simply venting our feelings. As such, it is critical to keep focused on the goal of a mutually acceptable, integrative solution.

> **Plan for the negotiations.**[84] Invest the time to determine the who, what, when, and why of negotiations. That is, *who* will you be negotiating with, and what can you learn about them, their personalities, motivations, and interests? *What* is the subject matter of the negotiations, and what strengths and weaknesses do you and the other party bring to bear in addressing that subject matter? *When* must the negotiations commence and be completed? If the parties have different deadlines, the party with the longer deadline has an advantage. If there are no specific deadlines, it may be useful to develop a time line to keep negotiations on track. *Why* are we negotiating? What are the desired results? By focusing on these desired results, rational negotiations and integrative outcomes are more likely.

> **Know your BATNA.**[85] *BATNA* stands for "the **B**est **A**lternative **T**o a **N**egotiated **A**greement." This gives the minimum outcome we require of a negotiated settlement. Any negotiated alternative that gives us a better outcome than our BATNA is better than an impasse; any negotiated alternative that is less than the BATNA should be declined. Thus the BATNA determines our reservation point, the point at which we are indifferent between a negotiated agreement and an impasse. If you don't have a clear BATNA, work to develop one. If you don't have the ability to walk away from a deal, you'll have the least power and leverage in bargaining.

> **Work to understand the other party.** Although you hope to be objective in the negotiating process, you will be dealing with other humans, who bring their own emotions, values, motivations, beliefs, backgrounds, and perceptions. Win-win solutions demand a relationship of trust and respect. Such relationships are based on mutual understanding and sensitivity.

> **Focus on a common objective and depersonalize the problem.** Throughout the negotiations, remain focused on a central question: How can we mutually achieve our common objectives? The problem—not the other party—becomes the adversary. If negotiators act as adversaries in personal confrontation, it will be impossible to separate substantive issues from personal

relationships. Comments may be interpreted as personal attacks, and each side may become defensive and stubborn. Consider the following analogy.

Like two shipwrecked sailors in a lifeboat at sea quarreling over limited rations and supplies, negotiators may begin by viewing each other as adversaries. Each may view the other as a hindrance. To survive, however, those two sailors will want to disentangle the objective problems from the people. They will want to identify the needs of each, whether for shade, medicine, water, or food. They will want to go further and treat the meeting of those needs as a shared problem, along with other shared problems like keeping watch, catching rainwater, and getting the lifeboat to shore. Seeing themselves engaged in side-by-side efforts to solve a mutual problem, the sailors will become better able to reconcile their conflicting interests as well as to advance their shared interests.[86]

> **Negotiate from interests, not positions.** Negotiations may stall if each side pushes for its position and fights the other party's position. When negotiators bargain over positions, they tend to start with an extreme position, hold fiercely to it, hide true motivations, and yield ground only grudgingly. Try to focus instead on underlying interests. If positions are stated, what are the interests that explain the positions? Ask "why" questions, such as "Why do you need to have a one-year limit on the contract?" or "Why do you need the parts to meet that specific standard?" And ask, "Why not?" What stands in the way of the other party accepting what you're asking for?

> **Build on differences.** It might seem that negotiations would be easiest when all parties to the negotiations had common interests, perspectives, and so on. In fact, though, successful negotiations may flow from differences. For instance, if I need money now and you don't need it until later, we have the potential for a deal. If I think one of my ballplayers is past his prime and you think he has the potential for further years of productivity if he joins your team, we both have incentive to make a trade. If you think one of your investments is too risky to keep and I'm trying to build additional risk into my portfolio, we might both benefit if I were to acquire the investment. As such, differences in time preferences, estimates of the probabilities of future outcomes, and risk preferences may each provide the impetus for a successful transaction.

> **Work to control emotions.** As noted in our discussion of emotional intelligence, emotions may short-circuit rational thinking. Negotiations can be frustrating, and they may even invoke anger. Avoid the temptation to lash out. Try to understand your emotions and those of the other party, and treat them as legitimate. If your side feels anger about an issue or the negotiating process, let the other party know, and treat this as a topic for discussion. Similarly, give the other party the opportunity to identify and release feelings of frustration.

> **Use active listening.** Active listening gives you what the other person really wants and is willing to concede, and it ensures that you recognize the flow of the negotiations. Careful listening also conveys to the other party that you are serious about working together toward a solution. And sometimes a period of silence induces the other party to open up, giving away information to fill the void.

> **Be creative.** For instance, challenge your assumptions about available resources, the other party's motivation, and the scope of the bargaining. The

next section provides some specific guidelines for creatively achieving integrative, win-win agreements.

TECHNIQUES FOR REACHING INTEGRATIVE AGREEMENTS[87]

Here are five techniques to help reach an integrative agreement. Each somehow encourages us to think creatively about the negotiations process, by challenging our assumptions, broadening our perspectives, or encouraging the development of innovative new options.

> **Obtaining added resources.** Earlier in this chapter we said we are slaves to our assumptions. If we're faced with the challenge of negotiating for resources, such as personnel or funds, we may simply assume that additional resources aren't available. Because this assumption may not be true, we should ask whether additional resources might in fact be available. So if two departments are negotiating to get authorization to purchase a new computer system this year, and it appears that only one system will be authorized, they might first try to make the case that two systems should be approved. Although obtaining added resources may not always be feasible, we should at least consider the possibility.

> **Providing nonspecific compensation.** With *nonspecific compensation*, one party gets what it wants and the other is paid on some unrelated issue. For instance, if only one computer system is approved, the department that gets the system might agree to purchase a database needed by both departments.

> **Trading issues.** *Trading issues* means each party concedes on low-priority issues in exchange for concessions on higher priority issues. Thus each party gets the part of the agreement it considers most important. Perhaps Department A feels it is critical to have physical control of the computer system and Department B, although it would like to have physical control, is concerned primarily with having access to the system at certain peak times. The system could thus be located in Department A, but with guaranteed access for Department B as negotiated.

> **Cost cutting.** With *cost cutting*, one party gets what it wants and the other gets the costs associated with the concession reduced or eliminated. For instance, if one department gets a computer system, the department that doesn't get the system might nevertheless get restricted access to the system.

> **Bridging.** With *bridging*, neither party gets its initial demands, but a new option that satisfies the major interests of both parties is developed. This might involve, for instance, using the funds that would be applied to a single computer system to find two lower-cost systems or jointly controlling the system and agreeing on a time-sharing arrangement.

TACTICS TO ENCOURAGE SHARING OF INFORMATION[88]

Productive negotiation and problem solving require the sharing of information. However, people are often reluctant to provide information because they may fear it will be used against them or will put them at a competitive disadvantage. Here are some tactics to encourage sharing of information:

> **Decide on a distribution rule in advance.** Often, full and open sharing of information would help the parties to negotiation to find a good solution. However, each party may be afraid to share information because it might permit the other party somehow to "win" or to get more than a fair share. In such cases, it may be useful to agree on a distribution rule in advance. For instance, both sides might agree that if an agreement following information sharing results in some "surplus" over the best solution that could be found prior to sharing of information, each party will get half of the surplus. This clearly demonstrates the benefit of sharing while minimizing vulnerability.

> **Ask questions.** People often use negotiating situations primarily to try to influence others. As a result, they spend a lot of time talking and relatively little time asking questions and listening. Even when the other party is talking, we may be thinking about what we're going to say next rather than really trying to understand what is being said. In communication situations, we should consider what information we need from the other party and then ask the questions necessary to get that information. We may not get answers to all our questions, but we're more likely to get answers if we ask than if we don't.

> **Strategically disclose information.** To develop trust, it is often important to create a climate of openness. One way to do this is to provide some useful—but probably not critical—information to the other party. In communication, behaviors are often reciprocated. If we scream, others may scream; if we apologize, others may apologize. Similarly, if we give information, the other party is likely to share information in turn. Continued reciprocity can result in full sharing of important information.

> **Make multiple offers simultaneously.** When dealing with someone in a bargaining situation, we tend to make a single offer or proposition and then wait for a response. If the offer is rejected, we may "go back to the drawing board," fashion another, and hope for a better result. However, an option is to put together a set of offers. Ideally, the offers would be equally desirable to us but may differ in their attractiveness to the other party. This gives the appearance we are flexible, and it also lets us collect useful information. If one of the multiple offers is accepted, we have an agreement. If not, we can at least ask which of the offers was most desirable and use that information to craft further offers.

> **Search for postsettlement settlements.** People are often reluctant to "put all their cards on the table" until they have an agreement. Prior to that agreement, they may feel full disclosure could be harmful. A very useful approach is to search for *postsettlement settlements*. That is, once the parties have found a mutually acceptable agreement, they can employ a third party who is given full information and told to search for another agreement that is better for both parties. Either party to the initial agreement can veto any new such postsettlement settlement proposed by the third party. The initial settlement is essentially insurance in hand, and it leads to an increased willingness to seek a carefully crafted, preferable alternative.

Skills Practice 3-11 will help develop your skill in negotiating in a business context by applying negotiating techniques to one of two specific negotiating situations.

TOP TEN LIST: KEY POINTS TO REMEMBER

EFFECTIVE PROBLEM SOLVING

10. Be aware of the problem-solving process and take care to properly address each of its stages.

9. Use data to drive the problem-solving process.

8. Identify the root cause of a problem as a basis for developing appropriate solutions.

7. Use problem-solving tools to ensure that a systematic approach to problem solving is being used.

6. Follow up on decisions to evaluate outcomes and to take corrective action if needed.

5. Implement a Plan-Do-Check-Act approach to problem solving that incorporates an emphasis on the use of data, experimentation, evaluation, and modification.

4. Be aware of your use of inappropriate heuristics that may diminish the quality of your problem-solving process.

3. Foster a work environment and work culture that support creative thinking and exploration of ideas.

2. Create and leverage work force diversity as a means for promoting creativity and innovation.

1. Be aware of alternative negotiating styles and work to achieve integrative solutions.

QUESTIONS FOR REVIEW AND REFLECTION

REVIEW QUESTIONS

1. Discuss the five steps in the problem-solving process.
2. Identify six guidelines for problem definition.
3. Differentiate between screening approaches and scoring approaches.
4. Discuss the four steps in the PDCA cycle.
5. Identify seven influences on problem solving.
6. What are seven consequences of barriers to problem solving?

7. Identify eight guidelines for improving problem solving.
8. What are the four stages of the creative process?
9. Discuss six techniques for enhancing creativity.
10. Identify 10 characteristics of the creative organization.
11. Discuss venture teams, idea champions, and intrapreneurship.
12. Describe 5 strategies for negotiating and 10 guidelines for attaining win-win solutions.

CRITICAL THINKING QUESTIONS

1. In view of the various problems we, as humans, face in making decisions, some people have suggested we use computers to help us. For instance, the computer can calculate its choice of an optimal decision based on the best available data and specified criteria. We can then decide to use, somehow to revise, or to reject that decision. This use of computers as inputs to our decision making is called *clinical synthesis*. What do you see as potential benefits and difficulties associated with clinical synthesis?

2. You mention to your boss that you have learned what you think are very useful guidelines for defining a problem. She answers, "Defining a problem! I *know* what my problems are. I need solutions!" How would you defend the need for careful problem definition?

3. We have seen that creativity is especially important in situations that are complex and dynamic. Do you think it is worthwhile to devote resources to enhancing creativity in firms in more stable, traditional industries? Why or why not?

4. We have examined some characteristics of creative individuals. Suppose someone said to you, "We really need creativity in our company. Let's put together a checklist of characteristics of creative individuals and use that in our hiring." What do you see as some potential benefits and costs of a policy of hiring "creative types"?

5. One difficulty with introducing creativity-enhancement techniques is that some people just don't feel comfortable using them. The techniques seem "different," and most people haven't given much thought to increasing their creativity. Sometimes they are afraid that using the techniques will make them look

foolish. What are some things you might do to encourage your team members to try some of the creativity-enhancement techniques discussed in this chapter?

6. Told about the benefits of "win-win" solutions, your colleague says, "That's fine if the other guy is willing to go along. But if I'm trying for integrative solutions and he isn't, I'll get killed." How would you respond?

EXPERIENTIAL EXERCISES

WEB EXERCISE 3-1

Go to the Mind Tools home page at **http://www.mindtools.com/index.html**. Click on either "Creativity Tools" or "Techniques for Effective Decision Making" and select one tool from the corresponding page. Write a one-page executive summary describing the tool and indicating how it might be useful in a managerial career.

WEB EXERCISE 3-2

Feeling creative? Think you have a patentable idea? Go to the home page of the U.S. Patent and Trademark Office at **http://www.uspto.gov/**. Click on "Search Patents" and then click on "Quick Search" under "Issued Patents." This source permits you to search and view patent documents from the United States since 1790. Remember our discussions of paper clips? Type *paper clip* in the search engine and you'll find more than 790 patent documents relating to paper clips (some may be new kinds of paper clips and others may somehow involve paper clips). Or you could search for *toothpick* and find more than 1,000 patent documents, including patents for a "combination writing implement and toothpick dispenser," a "therapeutic toothpick for treating oral and systemic diseases," a "prismatic light transparent toothpick," a "tobacco-impregnated toothpick," and a "nicotine-containing toothpick." Have an idea for a better mousetrap? You'd better check out the mousetrap patents first—you'll find a "magnetic computer-ized mousetrap," a "low oxygen scented mouse trap," a "marbles counterweighted repeating mousetrap," and many more. Or check out the 22,000 robot-related patent documents or the 200 harmonica-related documents.

Do patent searches on topics that interest you. Look for patents that strike you as especially interesting.

1. Select three patents, describe them, and indicate why you chose them.
2. Which of the patents do you think is most creative? Why?
3. Try to identify a creativity-enhancement technique that may have inspired each of the patents. For instance, could the patent have been inspired by a form of analogy, by a listing technique, or by retroduction?
4. Select one of the patents and use a creativity-enhancement technique such as listing to revise the patented item in a creative way.

CASE 3-1

PROBLEM SOLVING AT MCDONALD'S: REBUILDING THE GOLDEN ARCHES[89]

The Company

McDonald's, the fast-food company, is truly an American icon. The company was founded by Ray A. Kroc in 1955 when he opened the very first McDonald's restaurant in Des Plaines, Illinois. Since then, McDonald's, with its core menu of Big Macs and fries, has grown to become the world's largest and best known food service retailer with more than 30,000 locations in 110 countries. Over 46 mil-lion customers are served in McDonald's restaurants around the globe each day.[90]

At the core of McDonald's business philosophy is its vision for corporate social responsibility. This includes the following areas:

- Community: This provides support for local schools, youth sports, and other community programs in times of need. This includes the Ronald McDonald Houses that provide housing for the families of children who are receiving treatment for serious illnesses at nearby hospitals or clinics.

- Environment: The company has a strong commitment to environmental protection. It has developed innovative programs for recycling, resource conservation, and waste reduction.
- Marketplace: The company works with experts to ensure the quality and safety of its products and restaurant environments, and the protection of workers' health, safety, and human rights. This also includes the improvement of animal handling practices and the preservation of life-saving antibiotics.
- People: The company seeks to be the best employer in each community in which it does business around the world. This includes a strong commitment to the principles of respect, recognition, openness, and employee development. Work force diversity is also highly valued in company operations around the world in terms of recruiting, hiring, and job promotion practices.
- Resources and recognition: The company seeks the advice of independent experts to ensure that its overall social responsibility efforts are appropriate and effective.

The CEO of McDonald's is Jim Cantalupo. He has been in this position since January 2003. Cantalupo has been with the company for 28 years and has served as chief executive officer of McDonald's International and, most recently, as president and vice chairman of McDonald's Corporation.

Problems at McDonald's

Despite the strength of McDonald's past performance, the company has encountered some serious problems that threaten to damage or destroy its reputation for value, cleanliness, quality, and service. For example, the company has experienced declining revenues and profits for six to seven successive quarters and it had to lower its earnings expectations for the year 2002.

Menu Innovations

A major concern for McDonald's is that it has failed to develop any successful new menu items since the creation of Chicken McNuggets back in 1983. Even the idea for Chicken McNuggets did not come from the corporate headquarters—but from a McDonald's franchisee. The company's experiments with dollar value menus and other special pricing schemes were also perceived by customers as being confusing and not a good value.

Store Design and Layout

McDonald's has always been known for the cleanliness of its restaurants. However, this is not the necessarily the case any longer. Many customers have complained that the McDonald's restaurants they go into look run down, dirty, and old. Moreover, the overall design of the restaurants (the interior and exterior) is seen as being rather dated. All of this has made them less appealing as a dining option for fast-food diners.

Food Quality

Studies of food quality at fast-food restaurants have consistently found that McDonald's ranks near the very bottom when compared to other fast-food establishments. In fact, a study by the research firm Sandelman & Associates in 2001 found that McDonald's ranked dead last for taste and quality of ingredients among 60 restaurant chains. These results were especially disappointing to company management, given that it had just implemented a new food preparation system to dramatically improve the efficiency of food preparation and the taste and freshness of the food. The reality of the new food preparation system was that it did not increase the freshness of cooked food and it actually was a less efficient method for making food than the old system it replaced. It was also very costly to franchisees who purchased the system. This strained relations between the company and many of its franchisees.

McDonald's menu has also been criticized for being too unhealthy. A number of lawsuits were filed against the company alleging that McDonald's food was unhealthy, addictive, and caused children to become morbidly obese.

Customer Service

McDonald's was once known for the consistently fast and friendly customer service provided by the workers in its restaurants. However, in recent years, the company's reputation for service has deteriorated badly as customer complaints about rude and inefficient service from McDonald's workers accumulated. For example, one consultant who works with McDonald's franchisees has documented over 300,000 customer complaints about quality of service received during visits to the company's restaurants.

Competition

A major factor that has driven many of McDonald's problems is competition. Some competitors such as Burger King and Wendy's have developed more innovative and tasty menus. These fast-food companies consistently earn high marks for food quality from customers. However, other types of restaurants have also emerged to challenge

McDonald's supremacy in fast-food. These include Subway and its submarine sandwiches and the Atlanta Bread Company. These restaurants have provided more upscale menus and dining environments that have made them very attractive alternatives to McDonald's more traditional burger and fries menu. In short, these new competitors have "raised the bar" for quality in the fast-food industry.

Customer Tastes

With obesity becoming a major problem in the United States and many customers becoming more concerned with healthy eating, many of the items on McDonald's menu are perceived as being too unhealthy. For the most part, McDonald's menu does not offer much in terms of healthy selections such as salads or sandwiches.

Customers today also want more variety in their menu options when they dine out even if it is for fast food. Despite this, McDonald's menu has maintained its focus on a traditional burger and fries menu.

Acquisitions of Other Restaurants

McDonald's has attempted to expand beyond its core focus on its McDonald's restaurants by acquiring a variety of restaurants including Donato's Pizzerias, Boston Market, and Chipotle Mexican Grill. So far, the company has seen little growth from these acquisitions and has failed to develop any significant synergies between these restaurants and the McDonald's restaurants.

Management's Response

Presently, McDonald's has implemented a wide range of initiatives in an attempt to solve its problems and to reinvent itself. The following list presents a summary of the actions that have been taken so far.

- Some franchisees have redecorated their restaurants to include marble bathrooms and Ralph Lauren wallpaper
- The company is experimenting with new restaurant formats (e.g., sit-down formats)
- New menu items such as premium salads and McGriddle breakfast sandwiches have been added.
- Dual drive-thru lanes at restaurants have been added.
- Mystery shoppers visit locations to evaluate customer service
- A 1-800 number has been set up to capture customer comments and complaints about food, service, etc.
- The company will work harder to improve or phase out weak franchise operators
- Smaller menus and bun burners will be implemented to reduce food preparation time by up to 30 seconds

- A new advertising campaign with the slogan, "I'm Lovin It" will be launched along with another Monopoly game promotion
- Happy Meals for children can now be ordered with a salad
- Some franchisees (e.g., New York, Texas) are offering Wi-Fi wireless access for customers to entice them to stay and spend more money on food
- Cantalupo has unveiled a new "McDonald's Plan to Win" that emphasizes people, products, place, price, and promotions
- E-Learning and hospitality workshops for employees are being implemented

The Future

Some of the recent results indicate that McDonald's turnaround strategies are having a positive impact on the company's performance. For example, In June 2003, sales at McDonald's U.S. stores rose 7 percent. However, Cantalupo admits this is just the beginning. What needs to be done to sustain the positive gains realized so far? Will McDonald's be able to find the right formula to revitalize its menu for the long term? How will the company "get back to the basics" (value, quality, service) that made it a world-class company? How will it respond to the onslaught on new competitors and the changing tastes of American consumers? How can McDonald's continue to export its business model to other parts of the world? The challenges for McDonald's are tremendous and the stakes have never been higher.

Discussion Questions

1. How did the problems at McDonald's occur in the first place? Could they have been prevented? If so, how?

2. What types of strategies has McDonald's implemented in an attempt to better understand and solve the problems facing the company? To what extent have they been effective? Why?

3. Based on this case, develop a set of recommendations for McDonald's management that specifies the actions they should take to support short-term improvements in McDonald's operations and financial performance. Make sure that each of your recommendations is specific and action oriented. Also, be sure to address what needs to be done to ensure the effective execution of your recommendations.

4. Based on this case, develop a set of recommendations for McDonald's management that specifies the actions

they should take to support *long-term* improvements in McDonald's operations and financial performance. Make sure that each of your recommendations is specific and action oriented. Also, be sure to address what

needs to be done to ensure the effective execution of your recommendations.

5. What are the practical implications of this case for you as a future manager?

CASE 3-2

CREATIVITY AT NOKIA[91]

The Company

Nokia Corporation is a world leader in the design, development, and manufacture of digital wireless phones. Its fundamental business objective is "to strengthen our position as a leading communication systems and products provider." Its strategic intent is "to create personalized communication technology that enables people to shape their own mobile world." Nokia's business strategy focuses on the following areas:

- Innovating technology to allow people to access Internet applications, devices, and services instantly
- Capitalizing on its leadership role by continuing to target and enter segments of the communications market that it believes will experience rapid growth
- Expanding in these segments during the initial stages of their development
- Leading the development and commercialization of the higher capacity networks and systems required to make wireless content more accessible and rewarding to the end user
- Contributing to the development of new technologies, products and systems for open communications
- Establishing alliances with other device providers in order to make mobile access to services easier to the end user[92]

The company is based in Espoo, Finland, and employs more than 56,000 people worldwide. Nokia is composed of two business groups: Nokia Mobile Phones and Nokia Networks. In addition, the company has separate divisions called the Nokia Ventures Organization and the Nokia Research Center. The company maintains research and development centers in 14 countries and manufacturing operations in 10 countries. Its mobile phones are sold in 130 countries.

In 1998, Nokia passed Motorola to become the world's number one maker of mobile phones. As of 2003, its global market share stood at approximately 39 percent; this is expected to grow in the future.[93] The company has experienced particularly strong growth in the U.S. market

and in the global CDMA (This stands for Code Division Multiple Access, and it is an emerging wireless phone technology that provides a superior call quality and reliability.) market due to the aggressive development of new models containing a rich array of multimedia features. In the near future, Nokia will even move into the arena of handheld gaming when it unveils the N-Gage, a gaming device with an integrated wireless phone.

The Nokia Approach

Given the tremendous success of the 135-year-old corporation, Nokia has been subjected to a great deal of scrutiny and analysis, with the focus being on trying to explain how Nokia has survived and prospered (that is, "its secret code").

A major element of Nokia's approach has been to cooperate with competitors by signing deals that would provide for the sharing of common technologies and standards used in mobile phones. Consequently, the strategic challenge for Nokia is to be more innovative than its competitors in terms of coming out with more stylish and technologically advanced mobile phones.

In the 1990s, Nokia was generally very successful in offering more innovative products than its competitors. Its phones had logical user interfaces and stylish designs with desirable features, and it was able to get the right products to market on time and in sufficient quantities.

Nokia CEO Jorma Ollila attributes a major part of the company's success to the way in which the organization creates a "meeting of the minds." Specifically, he tries to create an environment that rewards merit, is fun to work in, encourages unconventional thinking, and does not punish failure.

Moreover, just about every important project is assigned to a team. And Ollila and his senior management team do not play "political games" with each other.

Another key player in Nokia's success in the mobile phone business was a young marketing executive named Anssi Vanjoki. His major contribution was that he studied successful brands such as Nike and Phillip Morris and concluded that the critical factor in explaining the success of those brands was that they shared a "holistic approach," in that everything from design, production, distribution, and advertising needed to be driven by a deep understanding of the function and overall vision of the product. What made Vanjoki's insight especially important for Nokia was that he was the first to apply this holistic approach to mobile phones.

Pertti Korhonen, the vice president of R&D, was put in charge of the project to develop a digital phone for the three major standards around the world (GSM, TDMA, and PDS). He coordinated a global, cross-functional team composed of designers, marketers, manufacturing specialists, and suppliers in pursuing the team's objectives. One of the team's major breakthroughs resulted from its struggle to design a user interface for the Japanese market. Based on extensive brainstorming, this led to the development of a large screen with a text menu.

Other dominant characteristics of the work environment at Nokia are the degree to which people are given the freedom to make their own decisions about how to perform their jobs and the lack of formalized systems in the organization. Sometimes this approach makes it difficult to figure out who is in charge. To balance the lack of formal controls, there are certain individuals whose role is to impose some degree of structure in the company.

Nokia's 18,000 engineers, designers, and sociologists scattered around the world make up a federation that values rule breaking and risk taking. One research and development manager described the work environment as being like a "jazz band" that has a leader, but where each individual can improvise his or her contribution to the larger group.[94] Nokia's success in innovation is in large part due to its annual research and development budget of $3 billion and the fact that 40 percent of its employees are involved in activities related to this area.

In 2002, the Nokia Mobile Phones Unit divided itself into nine small, autonomous business units in order to reassign its people to new areas such as entertainment and imaging. Each of these units is a profit and loss center that has the autonomy to build its own business model, conduct its own research and marketing, and develop its own long-term plans for product development.[95]

The company's approach to innovation includes internal and external venturing activities in the form of initiatives such as its Mind and Foresight teams that identify new technologies, business models, and entrepreneurs from outside of Nokia's research and development function. Within Nokia, its New Growth Businesses unit serves as an incubator for new stand-alone businesses that are closely related to the company's core activities.

Finally, Nokia holds annual meetings called the "Nokia Way" that use global brainstorming sessions, involving all employees at all levels in the organization, about what Nokia's strategic priorities should be in the future. These meetings have produced strategic priority statements such as "Bring the Internet to everybody's pocket" that serve to inspire and focus the activities of Nokia workers around the world.

A Major Challenge

Despite its success, a major challenge that Nokia will need to respond to is that the company is becoming less "Finnish" because over 50 percent of its employees come from other countries. This could pose a threat to the unique "Nokia Way" that has helped the company prosper. How will Nokia be able to sustain its momentum in the mobile phone business given its innovation strategy? How will it stay ahead of old competitors like Motorola and new ones such as Samsung and Sony Ericsson?

Discussion Questions

1. What kinds of creativity tools does Nokia use to support its product innovation strategy?
2. Which characteristics of a creative organization are illustrated by Nokia? Which are not? Why?
3. Based on this case, develop a set of recommendations for Nokia management that specifies the actions they should take to sustain Nokia's *short-term* success. Make sure that each of your recommendations is specific and action oriented. Also, be sure to address what needs to be done to ensure the effective execution of your recommendations.
4. Based on this case, develop a set of recommendations for Nokia management that specifies the actions they should take to sustain Nokia's *long-term* success. Make sure that each of your recommendations is specific and action oriented. Also, be sure to address what needs to be done to ensure the effective execution of your recommendations.
5. What are the practical implications of this case for you as a future manager?

VIDEO CASE: NEXT DOOR FOOD STORE

A STUDY IN DECISION MAKING

Headquartered in Mount Pleasant, Michigan, Next Door Food Store is a family-run business with more than 30 outlets in Michigan and Indiana. The stores sell gasoline and a wide variety of grocery and general merchandise items. Along with many other challenges, Next Door must deal with a diverse customer base as well as the convenience store industry's remarkable 100 percent average annual turnover rate.

The video shows Next Door Food Store's president and CEO, Dave Johnson, other Next Door executives, and representatives of Next Door's channels of distribution as they discuss key decisions faced by the company. After viewing the video, answer the following questions.

1. What are the two fundamental decisions faced by the Next Door Food Store?
2. How does the nature of the convenience industry influence Next Door's goals and constraints? What has Next Door identified as its goals? As its constraints?
3. What were the alternatives considered by Next Door in regard to distribution channels? Which of those alternatives did Next Door choose? Why?
4. Do the decisions made by Next Door seem to be based more on use of screening approaches or more on scoring approaches? Why do you conclude that?
5. Why does Next Door consider the product mix to be risky? How does the Coca-Cola example illustrate that risk?
6. What were factors that led Next Door to decide to allocate cold vaults to such products as bottled waters, teas, and sports drinks?
7. How might you determine whether Next Door's problem solving has been effective?

http://www.nextdoor1.com/

LIGHTEN UP

THE WORLD'S EASIEST QUIZ

Was our discussion of difficulties in decision making getting discouraging? Take a few minutes to complete "The World's Easiest Quiz." The answers follow.

1. How long did the Hundred Years' War last?
2. Which country makes Panama hats?
3. From which animal do we get catgut?
4. In which month do Russians celebrate the October Revolution?
5. What is a camel's hairbrush made of?
6. The Canary Islands in the Pacific are named after what animal?
7. What was King George VI's first name?
8. What color is a purple finch?
9. Where are Chinese gooseberries from?
10. How long did the Thirty Years' War last?

Answers

1. 116 years, from 1337 to 1453.
2. Ecuador.
3. From sheep and horses.
4. November. The Russian calendar was 13 days behind ours.
5. Squirrel fur.
6. The Latin name was Insularia Canaria—Island of the Dogs.
7. Albert. When he came to the throne in 1936 he respected the wish of Queen Victoria that no future king should ever be called Albert.
8. Distinctively crimson.
9. New Zealand.
10. Thirty years, from 1618 to 1648, of course.

LIGHTEN UP

THE IG NOBEL PRIZE

Each year, 10 individuals whose achievements "cannot or should not be reproduced" are honored with Ig Nobel Prizes. At the ceremony (held in 2002 at Harvard University), more than 1,000 spectators watch the winners step forward to accept their prizes, handed out by bemused genuine Nobel laureates. Some recent winners:

Peace: Charl Fourie and Michelle Wong of Johannes-burg, South Africa, for inventing an automobile burglar alarm consisting of a detection circuit and a flamethrower.

Interdisciplinary research: Karl Kruszelnicki of the University of Sydney, for performing a comprehensive survey of human belly button lint—who gets it, when, what color, and how much.

Hygiene: Eduardo Segura, of Lavakan de Aste, in Tarragona, Spain, for inventing a washing machine for cats and dogs.

Economics: The executives, corporate directors, and auditors of Enron, Adelphia, Rite Aid, Tyco, Arthur Andersen, and selected other firms, for adapting the concept of imaginary numbers for use in the business world.

Managed health care: The late George and Charlotte Blonsky, for inventing a device (U.S. Patent 3,216,423) to aid women in giving birth—the woman is strapped onto a circular table, and the table is then rotated at high speed.

Chemistry: Takeshi Makino, president of the Safety Detective Agency in Osaka, Japan, for his involvement with S-Check, an infidelity detection spray that wives can apply to their husbands' underwear.

Environmental protection: Hyuk-ho Kwon of Kolon Company of Seoul, Korea, for inventing the self-perfuming business suit.

Medicine: To Patient Y and to his doctors, Caroline Mills, Meirion Llewelyn, David Kelly, and Peter Holt, of Royal Gwent Hospital, in Newport, Wales, for the cautionary medical report "A Man Who Pricked His Finger and Smelled Putrid for 5 Years" (*The Lancet,* November 9, 1996, p. 1282).

Nutrition: John Martinez of J. Martinez & Company, Atlanta, for Luak Coffee, the world's most expensive coffee, which is made from coffee beans ingested and excreted by the luak, a bobcat-like animal native to Indonesia.

http://www.improbable.com/ig/ig-top.html

Skills Practice

3-1   *Skill Level: BASIC*

Field Experience: Interviews with Real-World Problem Solvers

Skill Objectives

To develop a better understanding of how management practitioners actually solve challenging business problems.

Procedure

1. Identify three managers who work in different business organizations. Ask the managers if you can interview each of them for approximately 30 to 45 minutes.
2. When you meet with each manager, ask the following questions.
   a. How would you describe your problem solving style? Why do you feel this is an effective way to solve the problems you face as part of your job?
   b. Tell me about the greatest success you have achieved in your job in terms of solving a problem. Why was your handling of this problem such as success? How did you go about solving this problem? What was the outcome of the implementation of your solution?
   c. Tell me about the most difficult problem you had to deal with in your job. Why was this such a challenging problem, and how did you go about solving this problem? What was the outcome of the implementation of your solution?
   d. What kinds of strategies do you use to enhance your creativity in solving business problems?
   e. What advice would you give students regarding specific things that they can do to become better problem solvers in the real world?
3. Summarize the results of your interviews.

Discussion Questions

1. Based on the summary of your interviews, is it possible to identify one best approach to problem solving or does it depend on the situation? Why?
2. Based on the summary of your interviews, what do you feel are the most important things to remember about solving problems effectively in real-world business organizations?

SKILLS PRACTICE

Developing and Using a Screening Table

Skill Objective

To develop skill in applying a screening table to make choices.

Procedure

1. Select a choice-making exercise that is relevant to you. This could be, for instance, a job-choice decision, a choice among alternative products or services, a choice about daily activities, or so on. Specify the choice.

2. Identify alternatives. For instance, if you are considering alternative jobs, list those jobs. If you are thinking of purchasing a new bicycle, go to a source (such as *Consumer Reports*) that provides information on bicycles and identify four or five from among which you'd like to choose.

3. Identify at least four attributes of the alternatives (but as many attributes as you'd like). For example, for a job choice this could include starting salary, job type, location, benefits, or whatever attributes you think are most important.

4. Rank the attributes from most important to you to least important to you.

5. For each attribute, select a cutoff level. Recall that this is the level that must be satisfied if the alternative *is not to be rejected.* As such, this is more than just a "want" level; it is a level that, if not satisfied, would cause you to reject the alternative. Recall too that the nature of the cutoff will vary with the attribute. For instance, for price you would typically want a "less than" constraint, causing you to reject alternatives that have prices above the constraint. For quality or durability or warranty, you would typically want a "greater than" constraint. You may even have constraints saying that only certain ranges, or even only certain levels, are acceptable (for instance, you might say that location is acceptable only if the job is in the Southwest).

6. For each alternative, determine a score on each attribute. These may be hard data, such as prices, salt content, or calories, drawn from a source such as *Consumer Reports,* or your own subjective evalua-

tion (for instance, for appearance of a car you might use your own taste to classify the appearance as "very attractive," "somewhat attractive," "somewhat unattractive," or "very unattractive").

7. Use a screening table like the one shown in Figure 3-2. On the left-hand (vertical) axis, list the alternatives you are considering. Along the top (horizontal) axis, list the attributes you are considering, arraying them from most important to least important.

8. On the last row of the table, fill in the constraints you have specified for each attribute. Be sure to indicate the nature of the constraint (e.g., less than, less than or equal to, equal to, greater than or equal to, greater than).

9. Fill in the table using the scores you have developed for each alternative on each attribute.

Discussion Questions

1. How did you select the alternatives you considered?

2. How did you select and rank the attributes you considered?

3. How did you select the cutoff score for each attribute?

4. What choice would you make using the elimination-by-aspects screening approach (that is, eliminating on an attribute-by-attribute basis)?

5. What choice would you make using the satisficing screening approach (that is, considering one alternative at a time and selecting the first acceptable alternative)?

6. Are your choices the same using elimination by aspects and satisficing? Would your satisficing choice have been different if the alternatives had been ordered differently?

7. Are you comfortable with the choices you made using these methods? Why or why not? If not, what might you do to make yourself more comfortable with your choices?

8. What are three practical implications of these screening approaches for you as a future manager?

SKILLS PRACTICE

Applying the General Problem-Solving Process

Skill Objective

To develop skill in applying the general problem-solving process to business problems.

Directions

Note: Download the worksheet that was developed for this exercise from the Web site for this textbook. This will facilitate your working through this exercise.

Step 1: Identify a problem you are dealing with in your organization or school or something you have heard about in the news. Then write a one-paragraph statement of the problem you select. Some example problems follow.

   a. The Harley Davidson motorcycle manufacturer is experiencing challenges in making its motorbikes more appealing to younger consumers and consumers abroad.

   b. The U.S. Armed Forces cannot recruit enough new people to meet its demand for labor.

   c. Eastman Kodak, the film and digital camera manufacturer, is experiencing challenges from a shrinking market for traditional camera film and intensified competition from other digital camera manufacturers such as Sony and Canon.

   d. Motorola, the wireless phone manufacturer, has been slow to develop new phones that incorporate emerging technologies such as integrated digital cameras into their phones.

   e. Ford Motor Company's Mercury division is experiencing problems with its identity and market positioning as luxury brands come out with lower-priced vehicles and less expensive brands come out with more luxurious models. The effect of this is that Mercury, which is supposed to be positioned between the more basic brands and luxury brands, is getting squeezed on both ends.

   f. A student organization has a low level of member involvement in the organization's activities.

   g. A business school is struggling to identify what it needs to teach students in preparing them for the real world.

   h. Traditional retailers are losing market share to Internet-based retailers.

Step 2: Define the problem.

Guidelines (See this chapter for more information):

   a. State the problem explicitly.

   b Specify the standard(s) violated.

   c. Specify the problem in specific behavioral terms.

   d. Specify whose problem it is.

   e. Avoid stating the problem merely as an implied solution.

   f. Avoid stating the problem as a dilemma.

Step 3: Identify alternative solutions to the problem.

Step 4: Identify the criteria you will use to evaluate your alternative solutions and evaluate your alternative solutions on the basis of those criteria.

Step 5: Select the best alternative solution to your problem.

Step 6: Identify the action steps you would take to implement your decision and to monitor and control the outcomes associated with the decision.

Step 7: Evaluate your problem-solving process.

Discussion Questions

   1. What aspect(s) of the problem-solving process did you handle effectively in this exercise? Why?

   2. What aspect(s) of the problem-solving process did you not handle effectively in this exercise? Why?

   3. What are the barriers to the problem solving process that you encountered in this exercise? To what extent do these barriers also occur when solving problems in real-world business organizations?

   4. Why is the problem-solving process much more challenging to implement than it is to learn and understand in a textbook?

   5. What are the practical implications of this exercise for use as a future manager and leader in a real-world organization?

SKILLS PRACTICE

3-4

The Problem-Solving Process and the PDCA Cycle in Action: October Sky

Skill Objective

To develop skill in analyzing a complex problem and in evaluating a problem-solving process.

Procedure

1. Obtain a copy of the movie *October Sky.* It is available on VHS and DVD and can be rented or purchased from a local video store or retailer.

2. Watch the movie (in class or at home on your own). Note: Download the worksheet that was developed for this exercise from the Web site for this book. This will help you to develop a list of scenes in the movie that illustrate various problem-solving issues. As you watch the film, identify specific scenes in which the actions of the characters address various aspects of the problem solving process and/or the PDCA cycle. Document your notes about these scenes on your worksheet.

3. Discuss the following questions as a class.

   a. Based on the problem-solving process model discussed in this chapter, evaluate the problem-solving process used by the group of boys in the movie as they attempted to build a model rocket that would fly.

   b. Based on the discussion of the PDCA model in this chapter, evaluate the degree to which the group of boys in the movie implemented the PDCA model as they attempted to build a model rocket that would fly.

   c. What are the practical implications of this exercise for you as a future manager and leader in a real-world organization?

SKILLS PRACTICE

3-5

Applying the Plan-Do-Check-Act Model

Skill Objective

To develop skill in applying the PDCA model in order to solve problems.

Procedure

1. Form teams of three to five people each.

2. The teams are to develop a process that will enable them to build the tallest house of cards. Each team will need to demonstrate its process from start to finish at the end of the exercise as a basis for evaluating the team's process and for awarding the first-place prize (if one is to be awarded). You must apply the PDCA model to your developmental process. That is, think of a possible approach, try it, evaluate it, modify your approach, and then try that.

   Materials You Will Need to Provide:

   > One standard deck of cards for each team

   > A ruler

   > A reward for the winning team (optional)

3. Teams have about 20 minutes to work on their process.

4. At the end of the 20-minute trial period, each team should demonstrate its process for building a house of cards. The prize will be awarded to the team with the tallest house of cards.

Discussion Questions

1. How did your team apply the PDCA model to its process? To what extent was this model helpful in accomplishing your task?

2. What kinds of real-world tasks or processes could benefit from the application of the PDCA model?

3. What are the practical implications of the PDCA model for you as a future manager?

SKILLS PRACTICE

3-6   *Skill Level: CHALLENGING*

***Problem Solving Under Adverse Conditions:* Apollo 13**
Skill Objective
To develop skill in analyzing a complex problem and in evaluating a problem-solving process that was implemented under extremely adverse conditions.
Procedure
   1. Obtain a copy of the movie *Apollo 13*. It is available on VHS and DVD and can be rented or purchased from a local video store or retailer.
   2. Watch the movie (this can be done in class or at home on your own). Note: Download the worksheet that was developed for this exercise from the Web site for this book. This will help you to develop a list of scenes in the movie that illustrate various problem-solving issues. As you watch the film, take notes regarding the problem-solving strategies used by NASA engineers to develop and implement a solution to the problem facing the astronauts on *Apollo 13*. Be sure to document your notes about all relevant scenes on your worksheet.

3. Discuss the following questions as a class.
   a. Based on the problem-solving process model discussed in this chapter, evaluate the problem-solving process used by the NASA engineers in the movie as they attempted to build a device that would save the lives of the astronauts on *Apollo 13*. To what degree was this problem-solving process effective? Why?
   b. What were the constraints facing the NASA engineers that made it more challenging for them to solve the problem facing them? How did they overcome these constraints?
   c. In what ways is business problem solving similar to the conditions under which problem solving occurred in the *Apollo 13* movie?
   d. What are the practical implications of this exercise for you as a future manager and leader in a real-world organization?

SKILLS PRACTICE

3-7   *Skill Level: BASIC*

Applying Synectics Analogies
Skill Objective
To develop skill in using the synectics technique for generating creative solutions to business problems.
Directions
   1. Read the following scenario:
      The Case of the Christmas Crunch
      You are the product designer for a major toy manufacturer based in the United States. One of the keys to success in the toy business is the ability to design and develop innovative products that capture the interest and imagination of children. Your boss has given you the task of developing a big smash toy for the next holiday season. In the past, these kinds of big hit toys have included the Nintendo 64 video game system, Tickle Me Elmo, Furby, and Pokemon. (Note: If you prefer, you can use your own problem for completing this exercise.)

2. Apply the various synectics analogies to address the problem in this case. For example:
   a. Use direct analogies by completing the following sentence stem: The problem I am working on is like . . .
   b. Use personal analogies by completing the sentence following stem: One thing I can do to identify with this problem is . . .
   c. Use fantasy analogies by completing the following sentence stem: In my wildest dreams I could solve this problem by . . .

Discussion Questions
   1. To what extent do you think the synectics analogies were effective?
   2. Discuss some examples of real-world problems that could be solved through the use of synectics.
   3. What are the keys to the successful implementation of synectics in real-world organizations?

SKILLS PRACTICE

Skill Level: CHALLENGING

Applying the Checkerboard Technique
Skill Objective
To develop skill in applying the checkerboard technique for enhancing creativity.
Procedure

1. Select one of the following scenarios. Based on the scenario you select, identify two relevant product or service attributes and brainstorm levels/types for each attribute. (Note: Use more than two attributes if appropriate.)

   Problem Scenario 1

   The McDonald's Corporation has been faced with the challenge of expanding its traditional burger-and-fries menu in order to support the continued growth of the company. Use the checkerboard technique to address this issue.

   Problem Scenario 2

   General Motors Corporation has been trying to identify new types of cars and trucks that consumers will find appealing. It is critical for GM to do this in order to strengthen its market share in North America as well as in global markets. Use the checkerboard technique to address this issue.

   Problem Scenario 3

   Amazon.com is interested in identifying new opportunities for growth beyond its core Internet bookstore business. This is critical for Amazon.com, given growing competition in Internet-based bookstore retailers.

2. List your two attributes along with the list of attribute levels/types you brainstormed.

3. Develop a checkerboard matrix with levels/types for attribute 1 on the horizontal axis and levels/types for attribute 2 on the vertical axis.

4. Evaluate the various ideas identified by the checkerboard. Circle the ideas that appear to have merit.

Discussion Questions

1. How effective was the checkerboard as a tool for enhancing creativity?

2. If you were really using the checkerboard to address the issue you analyzed for this exercise, what would be the next step?

3. What would be the key strategies for using this technique effectively as a manager in a real-world situation?

SKILLS PRACTICE

Skill Level: CHALLENGING

Applying Retroduction Techniques
Skill Objective
To develop skill in using the questioning of assumptions and what-if approaches to retroduction in order to identify creative solutions to business problems.
Directions

1. Read the following scenario:

   The Relentless Pursuit of Academic Excellence

   Suppose the department chair of the field in which you are majoring at your college or university has asked you to help her to develop a list of creative ways to enhance the quality and effectiveness of the academic program in which you are enrolled. This is a critical strategic issue for the department chair because it has long-term implications for the future of your academic program. Use the retroduction techniques of challenging assumptions and asking "what if" to generate a list of ideas. Remember, the chair is counting on you to deliver, so don't disappoint her! (Note: You may also use your own problem for this exercise, if you wish.)

2. Carefully consider the scenario and identify at least four assumptions you would typically make when developing creative alternatives for your department chair. Now see what new alternatives you can generate if you change each of those assumptions.

3. In addition, try to generate alternative solutions to the problem by responding to each of the following what-if questions (or to any other what-if questions you can devise): What if unlimited funding were

available to enhance the program? What if you could use *any* resources you want—people, techniques, technologies, programs, or whatever—to develop an "ideal" program? What if students could design their own courses? What if it were no longer possible to use books, lectures, or classrooms?

Discussion Questions

1. To what degree were the retroduction techniques helpful in generating creative solutions to your problem? Why?
2. Discuss some specific ways in which retroduction techniques could be applied to real-world managerial problems.
3. What are the keys to the successful implementation of retroduction techniques?

SKILLS PRACTICE

3-10   *Skill Level:* BASIC

Developing Creative Organizations

Skill Objective

To develop skill in formulating an action plan for fostering a creative organization.

Directions

For each of the following characteristics of a creative organization, brainstorm a list of actions that could be taken by management to incorporate it into a firm.

Characteristics of Creative Organizations

> Open channels of communication
> Outside contacts
> Freeing idea units of other responsibilities
> Heterogeneous personnel policies
> Investment in basic research
> Decentralized and diversified organization

> Risk-taking ethos
> Not running the organization as a "tight ship"
> Separating the creative and productive functions
> Promoting a stable and secure internal environment

Discussion Questions

1. How would your proposed strategies help an organization to be more creative?
2. What kinds of challenges might you encounter in actually implementing the strategies you identified?
3. How does this exercise demonstrate the value of theoretical frameworks?
4. What are the practical implications of this exercise for you as a future manager?

SKILLS PRACTICE

3-11   *Skill Level:* CHALLENGING

Applying Negotiating Techniques

Skill Objective

To develop skill in negotiating in a business context.

Procedure

1. Work with one other student in this exercise.
2. Select one of the following negotiating scenarios. Apply the tactics for sharing of information and attaining a win-win solution discussed in the chapter.
3. Role-play the scenario, with the goal of negotiating an acceptable agreement.
4. Discuss the questions that follow the scenarios.

Scenario 1: Negotiating an Employment Contract

This scenario involves a negotiation process between a job candidate and an employer regarding the terms of a job offer for a management trainee position.

Role 1: The Job Candidate

Your goal is to maximize your salary and benefits (bonuses, flexible work schedules, stock options, a private office, holidays and days off, etc.). Overall, you feel an appropriate starting salary would be somewhere around $40,000 to $50,000. You are very interested in the job and you like the company. Although you have no prior work experience, you have graduated from a top-notch university where you did very well academically (GPA of 3.5/4.0). You know there is intense competition among employers for the best workers.

Role 2: The Employer

Your goal is to get the job candidate to accept the job offer while minimizing costs. You are very interested in this job candidate, and you are willing to add some reasonable perks in order to entice the job candidate to accept your offer. The salary range for the management trainee position is $30,000 to $45,000.

Given the job candidate's lack of work experience, you feel it is appropriate to provide a starting salary near the bottom of the salary range. This is consistent with your previous practice with new hires.

Scenario 2: Negotiating a Merger Deal

This scenario involves the heads of two companies who are attempting to merge their companies.

Role 1: CEO from Company 1

You are the CEO of a major auto company based in the United States. Your company designs and manufactures a full line of cars, trucks, minivans, and sport-utility vehicles. The corporate headquarters of your firm is in Detroit, Michigan, but you have international operations (research and development, assembly, dealerships) in Europe, Asia, and Latin America.

The company has a strong market position in the United States but is still trying to establish itself abroad. The company is currently implementing an aggressive plan to increase its presence in other countries around the world.

Because of weakness in global demand for autos and the tremendous long-term investments needed to design and manufacture vehicles, many firms in the industry are scrambling to develop strategic alliances, to merge, or to acquire other firms.

Due to a string of extremely profitable years, your firm has deep pockets and is anxious to acquire another firm. You will base the amount you are willing to spend on the prices of recent acquisitions in the industry (checking these prices should be part of your preparation).

Role 2: CEO from Company 2

You are the CEO of a major auto company based in Asia. You design and manufacture a full line of cars, trucks, minivans, and sport-utility vehicles. You have a reasonably strong position in international markets but have been losing ground to other competitors in your home markets.

You are interested in exploring a possible merger with another firm, but due to cultural differences and national pride you are hesitant. Ideally, you would like to form a strategic alliance with an appropriate firm that would enable you to reduce costs and to strengthen the market position of the company in international markets.

Discussion Questions

1. How would you describe the negotiating style you used in your negotiating scenario (that is, which tactics discussed in the chapter did you apply)? To what extent was your negotiating style effective? Why?

2. How would you describe the negotiating style of the other person in this scenario (that is, which tactics discussed in the chapter did that person apply)? To what extent was that person's negotiating style effective? Why?

3. In retrospect, what actions could each individual have taken to enhance the effectiveness of the negotiating process (for example, to come to a better agreement)?

4. What are the practical implications of this exercise for you as a future manager?

MOTIVATING EFFECTIVELY

CHAPTER 4

Skills Objectives

> To assess employee needs and develop strategies for increasing work motivation.

> To use operant learning techniques to facilitate the acquisition of desired employee behaviors.

> To use operant learning techniques to eliminate undesired employee behaviors.

> To set appropriate goals for employees that will increase work motivation.

> To develop skills in self-management.

> To use expectancy theory principles to increase work motivation, job performance, and job satisfaction.

> To use fairness theories to create a positive work environment and to increase work motivation.

> To design jobs that satisfy the active needs of employees and increase work motivation.

KNOWLEDGE OBJECTIVES

> Identify special challenges of motivating in the modern workplace.

> Understand the nature of motivation, including need theories and process theories of motivation.

> Be able to apply learning theory, including forms of learning, contingencies of reinforcement, and schedules of reinforcement.

> Understand key characteristics of effective goals.

> Understand how jobs can be designed to foster intrinsic motivation.

In Chapter 1 we described the modern workplace as complex, ambiguous, changing, diverse, and global. In this new world of work, hierarchies are flatter, deadlines are shorter, teams are pervasive, employees must manage themselves, and technology is transforming the nature, pace, and possibilities of work. The new world of work demands speed, flexibility, creativity, cooperation, self-management, and political savvy. Facilitating effective behaviors has probably never been more difficult, and never more important. In this chapter we cover a variety of topics and associated skills that can help you with these challenges. Specifically, we address issues relating to motivation, including understanding employee needs, applying learning theories, setting effective goals, applying self-management techniques, linking effort to outcomes, and ensuring fairness.

Before reading on, complete Self-Assessment 4-1. It gauges your attitudes toward a variety of motivation-related issues we address in this chapter. Then complete the Pretest Skills Assessment to get an indication of your initial level of skill in managing motivation. After you have completed these exercises, visit the text Web site to learn more about your responses.

SELF-ASSESSMENT 4-1

Attitudes Toward Motivation

Answer the questions that follow regarding your attitudes toward motivating others in organizations. You will learn more from this chapter if you develop a greater awareness of your beliefs and feelings about work motivation. Answer each question as honestly as possible using the following response scale:

1 Disagree strongly
2 Disagree somewhat
3 Neither agree nor disagree
4 Agree somewhat
5 Agree strongly

____ 1. For all practical purposes, managers cannot influence employee motivation.
____ 2. Employee motivation has surprisingly little impact on the company's bottom line.
____ 3. Money is the key motivator for the vast majority of workers.
____ 4. Most managers have a good understanding of what motivates their employees.
____ 5. Managers shouldn't have to worry about how to motivate their workers because workers should be motivated on their own.
____ 6. The most effective goal for employees is a "do your best" goal.
____ 7. Using rewards and incentives to motivate employees is morally wrong because it represents a form of bribery.
____ 8. Even highly motivated employees often aren't able to perform at a high level.
____ 9. Although employees may be upset if they feel they are getting less than they deserve, they will be happy if they think they are getting more than they deserve.
____ 10. The sole objective of job design is to maximize worker efficiency.
____ 11. Fairness in the treatment of employees has a significant impact on the level of worker motivation.
____ 12. Giving workers rewards and incentives for doing a good job is not generally feasible because it is too costly and time consuming to implement.

Motivation

Note: This exercise is based on actual events encountered by managers in real-world organizations. Some information may have been modified in order to maintain the anonymity of the people and organization involved in this situation.

You are the director of operations at a major amusement park located in Florida. You are experiencing some serious problems with the employees you hired for the busy summer season. These are college students looking for summer internship experience. The jobs these seasonal employees perform include working in concessions, park maintenance, and ride operations. The hourly wages offered for these jobs are below average compared to other seasonal jobs in the area, but raising employees' pay is not a feasible option at this time. Housing is provided for all of these workers for the summer.

Your experience with these seasonal employees has revealed that many of them have an "I don't care" attitude, they want to do as little work as possible, they routinely come to work late or not at all, and they even leave their work areas during their shifts if they think there is nothing to do. Many of them just want to party and they don't care much about the job itself. Clearly, all of this is incompatible with the park's goal to create a friendly, fun-filled experience for all of its customers.

Your task is to develop an action plan, including a set of motivational strategies you can use to address the problems that exist in the scenario just described. Be sure your plan addresses both short-term and long-term issues. Be very specific and be prepared to defend each element of your plan in terms of its feasibility and cost effectiveness. Remember that increasing worker pay is not an option, and more "parties" for workers would just make the problem worse in this case.

FUNDAMENTALS OF MOTIVATION

Motivation comes from the Latin *movere,* "to move." Motivation is about moving ourselves and others to some goal. Motivation requires arousal to initiate behavior toward a goal, direction to focus that behavior properly, and persistence to ultimately attain the goal. In the following sections we examine a variety of approaches to motivation. Think of these as a toolkit. Some of the approaches (called *content theories* or *need theories*) help us understand what people want. Others—called *process theories*—focus on the motivation process. The questions asked and the corresponding theories we address are these:

> How can valued outcomes be tied to behaviors in order to reinforce desired behaviors and eliminate undesired behaviors? This is the domain of *learning theory*.

> How can goals be set to motivate behavior properly? This is the question addressed by *goal-setting theory*.

> What elements must be present in a situation if a person is to be motivated? *Expectancy theory* addresses this issue.

> What causes a person to see a situation as fair or unfair and be motivated accordingly? *Equity theory* and related theories of fairness examine this question.

VOICE OF EXPERIENCE

MOTIVATING EFFECTIVELY

Lisa Stone, Head Coach, University of Wisconsin–Madison Women's Basketball Team

1. **What is your general philosophy regarding the best ways to motivate basketball players and people in general?**

   My philosophy is "Team Unity." "We are only as strong as our weakest link." The best way to motivate players is to first have them **BELIEVE** in themselves. Self confidence and inner strength are the beginnings of a strong team. Everyone then understands their role and competes to the best of their abilities. Communication, presentation and representation are also keys to strong teams. Unity does not happen without them. Team members must be able to communicate with each other, must represent themselves as a unit and must present themselves with class. Positive reinforcement and an enthusiastic approach help further motivation.

2. **What are the biggest challenges you face in motivating your players? What do you do to address these challenges?**

   Some players have difficulty because they do not believe in themselves. "Strengthen yourself so you are then able to share yourself with others." To address these challenges, an open-door policy must be there in order to communicate. As a coach, you must instill confidence in each student-athlete by demonstrating confidence in yourself!!!

3. **In what ways are the strategies that can be used to motivate basketball players effectively similar to the strategies that can be used to motivate workers in a business environment?**

   A team is a team! Whether it is a basketball team or a major corporation. We all are members of a team. For example, our family is a team. We all must work together to achieve our goals. We all must agree to disagree and still love one another. We must communicate. We must work through good and bad and maintain balance in our lives. "We are only as strong as our weakest link!" Help each other, share ideas and put the TEAM ahead of yourself.

4. **What advice would you give students regarding the things they will need to do to motivate people effectively once they get out into the real world?**

   Believe in yourself and what you have to offer. Keep learning and surround yourself with people who will help you succeed. Never stop learning and always COMMUNICATE!

> How can jobs be designed to make them intrinsically motivating? That is, how can the jobs themselves provide motivation without use of external rewards? *Job characteristics theory* provides one useful approach to the design of jobs that are motivating.

It is important to recognize that these are not really competing theories. Instead, they provide an arsenal of tools to address the many aspects of motivation.[1]

Before moving ahead, complete Skills Practice 4-1. This exercise will give you an opportunity to learn about the strategies that real-world managers use to motivate their workers and provide a solid foundation for the rest of the chapter.

UNDERSTANDING EMPLOYEE NEEDS

All people have needs. A *need* is something that people require. *Satisfaction* is the condition of need fulfillment, such as when a hungry person eats or when a person driven by the desire for success finally achieves that goal. Motivation is the attempt to satisfy a need. The need satisfaction process is shown in Figure 4-1. The practice

FIGURE 4-1
The Need Satisfaction Process

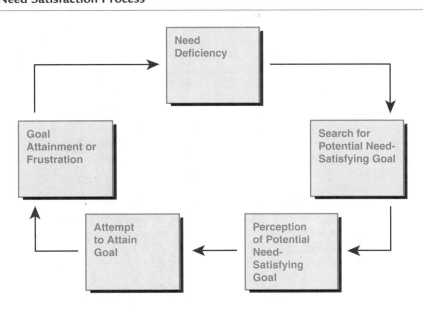

of management is largely concerned with motivating employees to work harder, more efficiently, and more intelligently. We look at five theories of motivation and at how each relates to motivating people in the workplace. We will see that these theories have some similar implications for rewarding employees.

MASLOW'S NEED HIERARCHY

Psychologist Abraham Maslow did much of the classic work on motivation theory. He believed the key to motivating people is understanding that they are motivated by needs, which are arranged in a hierarchy of importance. This hierarchy is known as *Maslow's need hierarchy* (see Figure 4-2).[2] Maslow theorized that people seek to satisfy needs at the lowest level of the hierarchy before trying to satisfy needs on the next-higher level. What needs motivate a person depends on where that person is on the hierarchy at that time. In particular, Maslow believed motivation should be examined in terms of five sets of needs:

1. **Physiological:** the need for food, sleep, water, air, and sex
2. **Security:** the need for safety, family stability, and economic security
3. **Social or affiliation:** the need to belong, to interact with others, to have friends, and to love and be loved
4. **Esteem:** the need for respect and recognition from others
5. **Self-actualization:** the need to realize one's potential, to grow, to be creative, and to accomplish

Maslow argued that as we satisfy any one of these five sets of needs, that set becomes less important to us and motivates us less. Eating, for example, satisfies the physiological need of hunger and leaves us less interested in food. In the same way, the need for affiliation and friendship is strongest for someone who feels excluded. Once this person makes friends, the need to belong becomes less important.

FIGURE 4-2
Maslow's Need Hierarchy

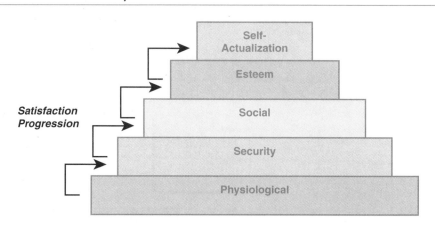

Climbing the Hierarchy. Maslow believed these needs were arranged in a hierarchy from "lowest" to "highest," as shown in Figure 4-2. He suggested we "climb" the hierarchy. That is, we first satisfy our basic physiological needs. Only when we have done so are we motivated by the needs at the next-higher level of the hierarchy: the needs for safety and security. When this group of needs is met, we move on to the next level, and so on. This move up the hierarchy as needs are satisfied is called *satisfaction progression*.

Lessons from Maslow's Hierarchy. Maslow's view of motivation shows that people have a variety of needs. People work for many reasons besides the paycheck that buys them food and shelter. We work so we can be with others, gain respect, and realize our potential. Management must consider these needs when it designs reward systems for employees. Also, Maslow's hierarchy emphasizes that people differ in the needs that are currently most important to them. For example, a worker faced with heavy mortgage payments may focus primarily on security needs. Another, with the mortgage paid off, may be more concerned about social needs. The former employee might be strongly motivated by money, whereas the latter may be more motivated by being included in a group. Finally, the hierarchy also makes it clear that need importance and need satisfaction are very different things—need importance (which drives motivation) often flows from dissatisfaction.

Maslow's need hierarchy provides useful perspectives for understanding motivation, and it has been widely accepted. However, more recent research suggests it is only partially correct. For instance, satisfying needs at the top of the hierarchy generally does not lead to a decrease in motivation. Instead, people who are able to self-actualize become *more* motivated to take on self-actualizing activities. Further, instead of five sets of needs, people's needs seem to cluster in just two or three sets, as discussed later. Also, the climb up the hierarchy is rather unpredictable; once we've satisfied needs at the lowest levels, needs at any of the other levels may become more important to us.

ALDERFER'S ERG THEORY

Maslow's need hierarchy provided an important starting point for an improved theory of human needs. Clayton Alderfer developed the ***existence-relatedness-growth (ERG) theory***, which revised Maslow's theory to make it consistent with research findings concerning human needs.

Let's examine the three key differences between Alderfer's ERG theory and Maslow's need hierarchy. First, because studies have shown that people have two or three sets of needs rather than the five Maslow hypothesized, Alderfer collapsed his needs into three sets:

> **Existence needs.** These include all forms of material and physical desires.
> **Relatedness needs.** These include all needs that involve relationships with others. Relatedness needs include anger and hostility as well as friendship. For instance, we may feel the need to yell at one person and befriend another. Isolation from others would cause deprivation of relatedness needs in either case.
> **Growth needs.** These include all needs involving creative efforts that people make toward themselves and their environment.

Alderfer revised Maslow's theory in other ways as well. First, he argued that the three need sets form a hierarchy only in the sense of increasing abstractness, or decreasing concreteness. As we move from existence to relatedness to growth needs, the ways to satisfy the needs become less and less concrete.

Second, Alderfer recognized that, although satisfying our existence and relatedness needs may make them less important to us, such is not the case for growth needs. Instead, our growth needs become increasingly important as we satisfy them. As we are able to be creative and productive, we raise our growth goals and are again dissatisfied until we satisfy these new goals. Recall that this is consistent with the evidence we reviewed concerning Maslow's need hierarchy.

Finally, Alderfer reasoned that we are likely to focus first on needs that can be satisfied in concrete ways. We then attend to those with more abstract means of satisfaction. This is similar to Maslow's idea of satisfaction progression. However, Alderfer added the idea of frustration regression. ***Frustration regression*** occurs when our inability to satisfy needs at a particular level in the hierarchy causes us to regress and focus on more concrete needs. If we are unable to satisfy our growth needs, we will drop back and focus on relatedness needs. If we are unable to satisfy our relatedness needs, we will focus on existence needs. Alderfer's needs, as well as satisfaction progression and frustration regression, are illustrated in Figure 4-3. The combination of satisfaction progression and frustration regression can result in cycling as we focus on one need, then another, then back again.

MCCLELLAND'S MANIFEST NEEDS

Management theorist David McClelland offered another way to look at motivation. Whereas Maslow argued that people were born with a particular set of needs, which become more or less important over time depending on their satisfaction, McClelland believed needs were acquired through the interaction of the individual with his or her environment.[3] Because these needs are not innate but rather become

FIGURE 4-3
Alderfer's ERG Theory

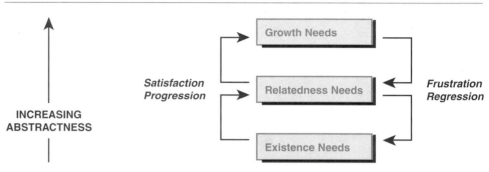

apparent (that is, manifest themselves) over time, they are called *manifest needs*. McClelland focused primarily on three manifest needs: the need for achievement, the need for affiliation, and the need for power over others.

> **Need for achievement.** People with a strong *need for achievement* want to do well no matter what goal they pursue. They also desire personal responsibility and want quick feedback about how well they have done at a given task. Some jobs, such as those in sales, are best for people with a strong need for achievement because of the responsibility and feedback they provide. Strong need for achievement, however, is not necessary in all work situations. For example, McClelland tested a large number of scientists, including several Nobel Prize winners, and found them to be only about average in need for achievement.[4] He reasoned that people with high need for achievement would not be drawn to such jobs, because research is conducted over many years and feedback may be very slow.

McClelland argued that the need for achievement can be developed in people by getting them to believe they can change and by helping them to set personal goals. This process also includes learning to "speak the language of achievement." By this we mean that people can be taught to think, talk, and act as if they were achievement-oriented.

In practice, McClelland was successful in developing the need for achievement. For example, after he conducted training sessions for 52 businesspeople in Kakinada, India, the achievement activity of the trainees nearly doubled, and that of people who couldn't participate in the programs because of space constraints remained about the same.[5] Achievement activity meant starting a new business or sharply increasing company profits. One trainee raised enough money to put up the tallest building in Bombay—the Everest Apartments.[6]

> **Need for affiliation.** The *need for affiliation* is the desire to establish and maintain friendly and warm relations with other people, much like Maslow's social need. People with a strong need for affiliation welcome tasks requiring interaction with others, whereas those having less of this need may prefer to work alone.

> **Need for power.** The *need for power* is the desire to control other people, to influence their behavior, and to be responsible for them.[7] McClelland saw the need for achievement as most important for entrepreneurs and the need for power as most important for managers of large organizations. Those who have a strong need for power can try to dominate others for the sake of dominating, deriving satisfaction from conquering others. Or they can satisfy their need for power through means that help the organization, such as leading a group to develop and achieve goals. McClelland felt that the need for power, when exhibited in ways that help the organization, was the most important factor in managerial success. People who have a strong need for achievement might be overly concerned with personal achievement, and those with a strong need for affiliation might not take necessary actions if they might offend the group.

Lessons from McClelland's Perspective. McClelland's work gives us an expanded view of workers' needs. It also suggests that appropriate training might actually develop employees' needs in ways that could benefit both their careers and the organization. Whereas Maslow essentially viewed needs as buckets to be filled, McClelland saw them as seeds to be grown. This is an important difference from Maslow's theory. Also, McClelland's perspective helps identify the characteristics of people who may be most suitable for particular kinds of jobs in organizations.

IMPLICATIONS OF NEED THEORIES

Taken together, the three need theories we have considered have a number of important implications for managing.

> **Different people have varying need structures as well as differing needs that may be salient at a given time.** Some people generally care more about a particular need or set of needs, such as relatedness needs, than others. In addition, people at a given point in time will vary in the level to which the needs they care about are satisfied.
> **Whereas satisfaction occurs when needs are met, motivation flows from lack of need satisfaction.** We must be careful not to fall in the trap of equating satisfaction with motivation. Some things that are very satisfying may be *demotivating*. For example, an employee whose pay is so high that she can afford anything she wants may not be motivated to gain an incentive for reaching a particular performance goal.
> **A reward may satisfy multiple needs.** It is sometimes tempting to assume that a particular reward, such as pay, will satisfy only certain needs, such as lower-order needs. However, such a viewpoint is simplistic. For example, employees may use money to buy food, pay the mortgage, go on a date, purchase a prestigious automobile, or finance a hobby or self-improvement class.
> **Needs appear to form two clusters (lower order and higher order) or three (existence, relatedness, and growth).** It is useful to understand how needs cluster in order to find ways to satisfy needs in a particular set. For example, recognizing that employees tend to have a cluster of needs called growth needs permits us to explore ways to satisfy that cluster. Conversely, if employees had a very large set of clusters of needs—say, 10 or 20—we would need to look more narrowly at ways to satisfy each salient need set.

> **Although most people focus first on existence needs when those needs are not satisfied, it is not possible to say which needs will next become most important.** Again, there is no lockstep climb up a fixed need hierarchy. We should not expect that we can easily predict which needs an employee will focus on next.

> **Both satisfaction progression and frustration regression are important.** Not only do employees move from a focus on one need to a focus on another, but they somehow move back again. This is a continuous, dynamic process in which multiple needs are likely to be somehow salient at the same point in time.

> **The "top" cluster of needs, sometimes called *growth needs,* behaves differently from others.** Although most needs become less motivating as they are satisfied, growth needs become more motivating. Thus, designing jobs or otherwise rewarding employees in ways that satisfy growth needs may cause people to place more emphasis on those needs rather than less. This is encouraging, because it suggests there is no "cap" on growth needs.

> **It may be possible to develop people's needs.** The structure of needs may not be fixed. For example, some employees who never placed much emphasis on growth needs may develop those needs when given the opportunity to satisfy them. Thus employees may grow into jobs offering challenge and responsibility, giving greater importance to growth needs in the face of enriched job demands.

The Bottom Line feature presents a process model showing how need theories can be applied to manage employee motivation.

Skills Practice 4-2 will help you develop skill in analyzing employee needs and use creative motivational strategies to satisfy those needs.

BOTTOM LINE

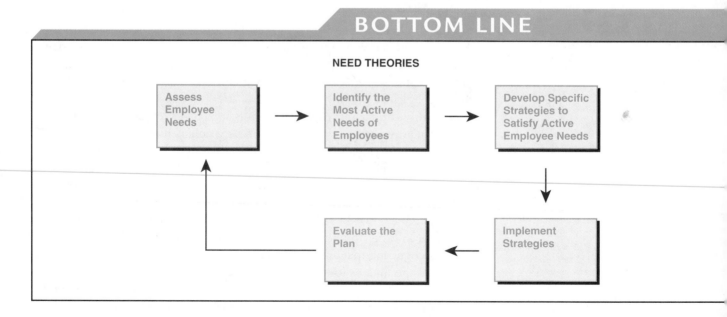

NEED THEORIES

Assess Employee Needs → Identify the Most Active Needs of Employees → Develop Specific Strategies to Satisfy Active Employee Needs → Implement Strategies → Evaluate the Plan → (back to Assess Employee Needs)

APPLYING LEARNING THEORIES

Learning is any relatively permanent change in behavior produced by experience. Changes in behavior due to physical variations, such as growth, deterioration, fatigue, and sleep, are not learning. Similarly, temporary changes are not true learning. Also, the changes may not be desirable; we have probably all learned some behaviors that have caused us to be less effective or less adaptive than before. Here, we briefly review three types of learning: classical conditioning, operant conditioning, and social learning. Together, these learning theories help explain how our behaviors are determined through our own experiences as well as the experiences of others.[8]

CLASSICAL CONDITIONING

To many people, mention of learning theory brings to mind thoughts of Pavlov's dog. In his experiments, Pavlov taught a dog to salivate in response to any of a variety of stimuli, such as a touch on the paw or the sound of a bell.[9] He did this by continually pairing the bell or other stimulus, which originally produced no increase in saliva, with food. Salivation was a normal physiological response to food in the mouth. The repeated pairing of the bell with the food caused the dog to salivate simply upon hearing the bell. Figure 4-4 shows this process.

The learning that took place in these experiments is called *classical* or *Pavlovian conditioning*. It occurs when, through pairing of stimuli, a new stimulus is responded to in the same way as the original stimulus. The thought of dangling rewards in front of salivating employees is a bit unseemly. Happily, this is **not** the sort of learning that is most relevant in organizational settings. There are at least three reasons for this:

> It is often difficult to use classical conditioning.

> There are ethical concerns about its use.

> It can't be used to teach a new behavior—it is useful only for transferring an existing behavior from one stimulus to another. Because the point of applying learning theory is often to teach and change the strength of current behaviors, other approaches are needed.

FIGURE 4-4
Classical Conditioning

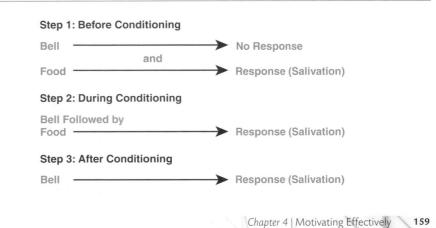

Step 1: Before Conditioning

Bell ⟶ No Response

and

Food ⟶ Response (Salivation)

Step 2: During Conditioning

Bell Followed by
Food ⟶ Response (Salivation)

Step 3: After Conditioning

Bell ⟶ Response (Salivation)

OPERANT CONDITIONING

Most learning in organizations relies on the law of effect. The *law of effect* states that rewarded behavior will tend to be repeated; unrewarded behavior will tend not to be repeated. So if we want someone to continue acting in a certain way, we should see they are somehow rewarded for acting in that way. If we want them to stop particular undesirable behaviors, we should make sure we are not rewarding them for those behaviors. The sort of conditioning that relies on the law of effect is called *operant conditioning* or, after its best known researcher and theorist, *Skinnerian conditioning*.[10] Figure 4-5 illustrates operant conditioning.

Individuals enter organizations, and particular situations within organizations, with very different histories of reinforcement. That is, they have learned different things. Some have learned that working hard is the way to get ahead. Others have learned to be stubborn in the face of challenge. Still others have learned to avoid troublesome situations. Thus many differences in behaviors among employees may be due to the different ways their behaviors have been rewarded or punished in the past.

SOCIAL LEARNING

Both classical conditioning and operant conditioning focus on learning as something that develops out of our own experiences. However, much of what we have learned comes from the experience of others. Because others have been burned by a hot stove or have failed in their attempts to start a new company or have found that certain leader behaviors are ineffective, we don't have to get burned ourselves to learn what they learned. Instead, we can benefit from social learning. *Social learning* is learning that occurs through any of a variety of social channels—newspapers, books, television, conversations with family members, friends, and coworkers, and so on. Social learning accounts for much of our knowledge. Coaching and mentoring are important organizational examples of social learning.

USING CONTINGENCIES OF REINFORCEMENT

We said earlier that operant conditioning uses rewards or unpleasant consequences to strengthen desired behaviors or to weaken undesired behaviors. The various ways we can tie consequences to behaviors are called *contingencies of reinforcement*. Figure 4-6 shows three contingencies of reinforcement—positive reinforcement, escape learning, and avoidance learning—used to strengthen desired behaviors.

Positive reinforcement involves giving a reward when desired behavior occurs, in order to increase the likelihood that the behavior will be repeated. A bonus for a job well done or a pat on the back for a good effort are examples. In many jobs, bonuses and other forms of merit-based compensation are very important, often exceeding base salaries.

FIGURE 4-5
Operant Conditioning

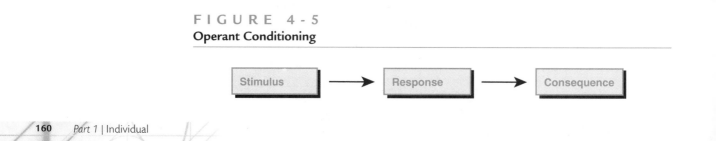

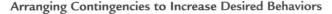

FIGURE 4-6
Arranging Contingencies to Increase Desired Behaviors

Positive Reinforcement

Escape Learning (Negative Reinforcement)

Avoidance Learning

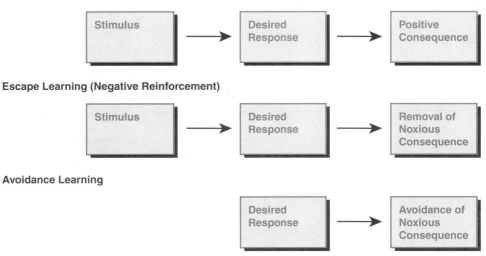

Another way to increase the likelihood of desired behavior is to remove some unpleasant consequence when that behavior occurs. For example, suppose a rat is subjected to a loud, irritating noise until it presses a lever. Once it presses the lever, the noise stops. The rat would soon learn to press the lever to escape the grating noise. This is called *escape conditioning*. If pressing the lever would actually prevent the onset of the noise, this would be called *avoidance conditioning*. In some companies, there are certain jobs that employees feel are very good, and others that are clearly "the pits." If employees believe they will be transferred from the bad jobs if they perform well, we have an example of escape conditioning. If employees in good jobs think they can avoid being transferred to bad jobs if they continue to perform well, we have an example of avoidance conditioning. Skills Practice 4-3 will give you the chance to develop skill in thinking strategically about identifying employee behaviors you want to promote in your work unit and in linking appropriate consequences to the behaviors so employees will continue to engage in them.

As seen in Figure 4-7, undesired behaviors may be reduced by nonreinforcement or by punishment. *Nonreinforcement* causes extinction of an undesired behavior by removing the reinforcing consequence that previously followed the behavior. Consider the case of Sam. We have (unintentionally) been teaching Sam to make unwarranted demands by regularly giving in to those demands. How can we get him to stop? One answer is simply to stop rewarding him for that undesired behavior. That is, don't give in to the demands. He will learn that unwarranted demands aren't rewarded, and he will eventually stop making them.

A second way to reduce undesired behavior, *punishment*, is defined as presenting an unpleasant consequence, or removing a desired consequence, whenever an undesired behavior occurs. So when Sam makes his demands, we could put a letter of reprimand in his file (an unpleasant consequence), or we could stop

FIGURE 4-7
Arranging Contingencies to Reduce Undesired Behaviors

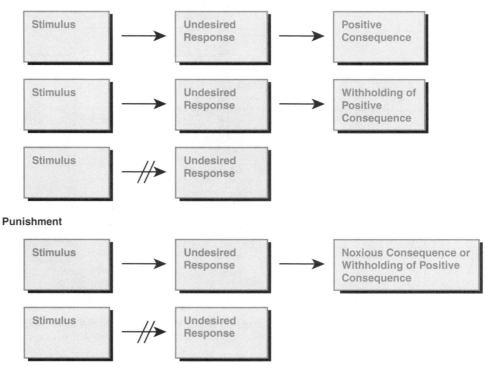

Nonreinforcement (Extinction)

Stimulus	→	Undesired Response	→	Positive Consequence
Stimulus	→	Undesired Response	→	Withholding of Positive Consequence
Stimulus	⫫	Undesired Response		

Punishment

| Stimulus | → | Undesired Response | → | Noxious Consequence or Withholding of Positive Consequence |
| Stimulus | ⫫ | Undesired Response | | |

interacting with him socially (removal of a desired consequence). Note that both nonreinforcement and punishment can involve removal of a desired consequence. With nonreinforcement, the reward we would withhold (agreeing to demands) was the one previously tied to the behavior. With punishment, the reward withheld (social interaction) was not previously a reinforcer of that behavior.

It is often tempting to apply punishment, and there are certainly situations in which punishment can't be avoided. However, punishment should be used only as a last resort. Problems with punishment include the following:

> Managers don't like to punish others.
> Managers may feel constrained from using punishment because of company policy or threat of reprisal.
> Punishment may engender resentment.
> Punishment may lead to revenge and retaliation.
> Punishment leads to adherence only when the person administering the punishment is present or monitoring.
> Others may misinterpret the reasons for punishment.
> Punishment may reduce an undesired behavior, but it doesn't directly teach a desired behavior.

As an example of the application of punishment, Russia punished several senior military commanders on September 7, 2002, for "gross negligence" that contributed to the crash of a military helicopter in Chechnya that killed 119 soldiers and civilians a little more than two weeks earlier.[11] The commanders were said to have defied orders and violated basic safety rules. Russian president Vladimir Putin, who was strongly criticized for his halting response to the sinking of the nuclear-powered submarine *Kurst* in August 2000, was sharply disparaging of the commanders after the crash. Putin apparently felt that rapid punishment was needed to clearly demonstrate that such behavior would not be tolerated. The Focus on Management feature discusses Goodyear's decision to stop labeling its 'worst' workers, a process it had used in order to weed out poor performers.

APPLYING REINFORCEMENT SCHEDULES

One learning theory issue, which we've just addressed, is *how* outcomes should be tied to behaviors to motivate desired behaviors and minimize undesired behaviors. However, suppose we decide we are going to use money to reward employees for high performance. How do we decide *when* we should give the money? Should we give it immediately after the desired behavior? After the desired behaviors have continued for a week? Every 10 times the desired behavior occurs? That is, what should be our *schedule of reinforcement*?

In choosing a schedule of reinforcement, we might seek several outcomes:

> **Rapid learning.** Ideally, we would use a schedule of reinforcement that very quickly teaches desired behaviors.

> **High response rate.** We would like a high "bang for the buck." That is, we would like to choose a schedule of reinforcement that yields high levels of motivation at relatively little cost.

> **High response stability.** We would like to encourage employees to engage in desired behaviors on a regular basis. We wouldn't, for instance, want an employee to work hard only the day before he or she will be paid or to take safety precautions only before a scheduled inspection.

> **Low extinction rate.** Once a desired behavior is learned, we would like it to be maintained even if we might have to stop rewarding for a while.

FOCUS ON MANAGEMENT

GOODYEAR TO STOP LABELING "WORST" WORKERS*

Goodyear announced in 2002 that it would stop asking managers to identify the 2,800 employees who make up the worst-performing 10 percent of the company's salaried work force. It had used the so-called ABC system—in which the top 10 percent of workers got A's, 80 percent got B's, and 10 percent got C's—to weed out underperforming workers. The move to eliminate the system came following an age discrimination lawsuit saying Goodyear was singling out too many older employees as bad workers. In doing so, Goodyear became the latest company to put the brakes on such systems, following others including Ford Motor Company; Ford quit handling out C's to its bottom 10 percent after paying $10.6 million to settle an age discrimination suit.

* D. Jones, "Goodyear to Stop Labeling 10% of Its Workers as Worst," *USA Today*, September 12, 2002, p. B1.

There are many ways to arrange schedules of reinforcement, and we will see they vary in terms of the degree to which they might satisfy the conditions we've just discussed. One basic distinction is whether or not behavior is reinforced every time it occurs (such as for every unit produced). ***Continuous reinforcement*** occurs if every behavior is reinforced. Continuous reinforcement leads to rapid learning. However, if for some reason it is necessary to stop reinforcing (for instance, if the supervisor must leave the room), rapid extinction occurs. Most of the time, it is simply impractical to reinforce on a continuous basis, so a partial-reinforcement schedule is used.

Partial-reinforcement schedules can be time based or behavior based. Also, they can be administered on a fixed, unchanging basis, or they can be varied around some mean. There are four basic partial-reinforcement schedules.

With a ***fixed-interval schedule***, a reinforcer is given at fixed time intervals, such as once a week. Weekly paychecks and monthly inspections are common examples. Fixed-interval schedules, although easy to use, result in slow learning and a moderately fast extinction rate. They also have a low response rate (that is, frequency of response per reinforcement) and very low response stability (people speed up just before the time of reinforcement and then slow down).

A ***variable-interval schedule*** is also time based. However, a reinforcer is administered randomly around some average interval. For instance, an instructor might announce there will be four pop quizzes during the semester, but will not say when they will occur. Learning rate, extinction rate, response rate, and response stability are all better for the variable-interval than for the fixed-interval schedule. However, they are generally not as good as for ratio-based schedules.

A ***fixed-ratio schedule*** provides a reinforcer after a given number of acceptable behaviors. Commissions given on the basis of sales levels (such as for every 10 sales) and bonuses given for every three meritorious behaviors are examples. Fixed-ratio schedules have very high response rates and response stability. They have high learning rates, but, unfortunately, rapid extinction rates as well. Fixed-ratio schedules can be stretched to foster learning and increase response rate. For instance, we might want to teach a new behavior by first reinforcing every instance of that behavior (that is, by using a continuous-reinforcement schedule), then stretch the schedule so a reward is given for only two instances of the behavior (called a 2:1 schedule), then for three instances (a 3:1 schedule), and so on. By stretching schedules in this way, Skinner trained pigeons to peck at rates faster than machine-gun fire.

Whereas a fixed-ratio schedule reinforces after every *n* responses, a ***variable-ratio schedule*** reinforces ***on average*** every *n* responses. For instance, a "one-armed bandit" might have a payoff an average of once in every 10 pulls of the handle. However, precisely when the payoff will occur is unknown. Response rates and response stability are similar to those for fixed-ratio schedules, but learning is slower. However, extinction is very slow. Companies have made some very creative attempts to use variable-ratio schedules. For instance, in one firm, names of employees who didn't use their sick leave were placed in a lottery for a large prize. Sick-leave costs fell by 62 percent.[12]

Figure 4-8 compares the various schedules of reinforcement. It is clear in looking at the figure that there are some trade-offs when using the various schedules of reinforcement. For example, a variable-ratio schedule is very powerful in most ways, but results in slow learning. So it may be desirable to combine schedules. For example, as noted earlier, a behavior might be taught by initially using

FIGURE 4-8
Comparing the Schedules of Reinforcement

	SCHEDULE OF REINFORCEMENT				
Measure	Continuous	Fixed Ratio	Variable Ratio	Fixed Interval	Variable Interval
Learning Rate	Very fast	Fast	Slow	Very Slow	Moderate
Response Rate	Very low	Very high	Very high	Low	Moderate
Response Stability	Very high	High	High	Very low	Low to moderate
Extinction Rate	Very fast	Fast	Very slow	Moderately fast	Slow

continuous reinforcement, followed by stretching of the schedule to yield a fixed-ratio schedule, and then adding a variable element.

Of course, there are other practical considerations in choosing schedules. The Focus on Management feature illustrates how schedules of reinforcement are used at Lincoln Electric. For instance, employees need to pay their bills regularly and may count on a weekly paycheck (a fixed-interval schedule). Also, it is easy to administer a fixed-interval schedule. Nevertheless, the relatively greater power of other schedules suggests we should seek creative ways to employ other schedules of reinforcement whenever possible.

ORGANIZATIONAL BEHAVIOR MODIFICATION

Organizational behavior modification (OBM) uses the principles of learning theory to manage behavior in organizations. Organizational behavior modification

FOCUS ON MANAGEMENT

INCENTIVES AT LINCOLN ELECTRIC

Founded in 1895, Lincoln Electric is the global leader in the arc welding industry, with operations, manufacturing alliances, and joint ventures in 18 countries and a worldwide network of distributors and sales offices covering more than 160 countries. Lincoln Electric attributes much of its success to its dedicated, highly talented work force. On its Web site, Lincoln notes that "people are Lincoln's fundamental advantage—the source of all our other strengths. Our people are highly trained and motivated. They are productive and team

oriented." To foster that motivation, Lincoln has developed a unique incentive performance system. In 1923, Lincoln Electric was among the first companies in the United States to offer workers paid vacations, and in 1925, it was one of the first to provide an employee stock ownership plan. Lincoln has one of the oldest "pay-for-performance" systems in the country. Lincoln provides piecework incentives for all production work—that is, pay is tied directly to output levels. In addition, Lincoln has an annual profit-sharing bonus plan and offers guaranteed employment after three years of service—it has not

laid off an employee in U.S. operations since 1948. Lincoln's Web site states, "Through this well-defined group of incentives, Lincoln encourages and compensates individual initiative and responsibility. Employees work together to reduce costs and improve quality. These individual and cooperative efforts create a more profitable company, the success of which each person shares according to his or her own contribution."

http://www.lincolnelectric.com /corporate/career/default.asp practitioners and theorists typically use some combination of operant conditioning techniques and social learning to achieve their goals.

Here are some guidelines for effectively using learning techniques in organizations:[13]

1. **Don't give the same reward to all.** Reward those who exhibit desired behaviors (such as high performance) more than those who don't.

2. **Recognize that failure to respond to behavior has reinforcing consequences.** Managers must remember that inaction, as well as action, has reinforcing consequences. They should ask, "What behavior will I reinforce if I do nothing?"

3. **Tell a person what behavior gets reinforced.** Make the contingencies of reinforcement clear to employees. Don't make them guess which behaviors will be rewarded or punished.

4. **Tell a person what he or she is doing wrong.** If the manager does not make clear to an employee why, for instance, a reward is being withheld, the employee may attribute the action to a past desired behavior rather than the behavior the manager wants to extinguish.

5. **Don't punish in front of others.** When employees are punished in front of others, they lose face and are doubly punished. This can cause resentment and a variety of problems.

6. **Make the consequences equal to the behavior.** Overrewarding desired behavior makes an employee feel guilty. Underrewarding desired behavior or overpunishing undesired behavior causes anger. Underpunishing undesired behavior seems like a slap on the wrist and may have little impact.

7. **Reinforce behaviors as soon as possible.** As suggested in the Focus on Management feature, immediate rewards can be very powerful.

Note that some of the rules we've listed rely heavily on cognitions. This recognizes that employees can learn through observation and advice as well as from their own experiences.

Organizational behavior modification often uses behavioral shaping. *Behavioral shaping* is the learning of a complex behavior through successive approximations of

FOCUS ON MANAGEMENT

HACIENDA BUCKS

Rewarding a person in June for a job well done in January does little to reinforce the behavior. Recognizing this, Hacienda Mexican Restaurants hires "mystery shoppers" to pose as customers and report back on employees who have gone out of their way to serve a customer or help one another. When either these "mystery shoppers" or supervisors in the firm see such behaviors, employees are immediately rewarded with "Hacienda Bucks" that can be redeemed for food or beverages in any of the restaurant's locations.* In general, the more immediately a reward is given, the more powerful is its motivating effect. For another example of the power of immediate rewards, see this chapter's Video Case, Motivating for Performance: A Study of Valassis Communications, Inc. *http://www.haciendafiesta.com/*

*S. Nelton, "Saying 'Gracias' on the Spot," *Nation's Business*, May 1993, p. 12. See also A. Perlik, "State Fare," *Restaurants and Institutions*, October 1, 2002, pp. 50–57.

the desired behavior. Initially, the employee gets a reward for any behavior that is in any way positively related to the desired behavior. Subsequently, responses are not reinforced unless they are more and more similar to the desired behavior. Responses are "shaped" until the desired complex behavior is achieved.

Properly applied, learning theory works very well. Many firms, including Emory Air Freight, General Electric, and Weyerhaeuser, have implemented very successful programs. In fact, some critics worry that learning theory works *too* well, possibly pushing the employee to exhaustion or to other undesirable outcomes. They see this as especially troublesome, because this behavior—particularly when noncognitive, operant conditioning is used—is to some extent outside the control of the employee, overriding free will. From this perspective, learning theory has Orwellian overtones.

When used with intelligence and caution, we believe learning theory can be extremely useful. After all, managers are reinforcing behavior all the time; the trick is to do it right. Cognitive approaches, in which employees know why they are being rewarded or punished and are aware of the contingencies of reinforcement, overcome some of the concerns that employees are being ruthlessly manipulated. In addition, proponents of learning theory are essentially unanimous in advocating positive reinforcement (the carrot) over punishment (the stick). As such, proper application of learning theory helps guarantee that employees get the rewards they want while fostering desired organizational outcomes. The Bottom Line feature shows how organizational behavior modification can be systematically implemented to encourage the learning of desired behaviors as well as the unlearning of undesired behaviors.

Skills Practice 4-4 gives you another opportunity to develop skill in applying learning theory principles. In this case, you are asked to apply the principles to reduce levels of undesired work behaviors.

BOTTOM LINE

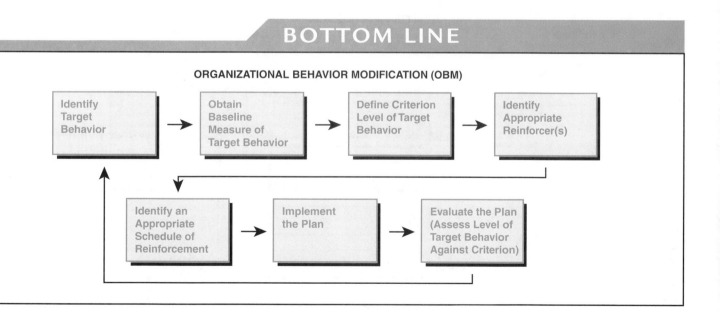

ORGANIZATIONAL BEHAVIOR MODIFICATION (OBM)

Identify Target Behavior → Obtain Baseline Measure of Target Behavior → Define Criterion Level of Target Behavior → Identify Appropriate Reinforcer(s)

Identify an Appropriate Schedule of Reinforcement → Implement the Plan → Evaluate the Plan (Assess Level of Target Behavior Against Criterion)

EFFECTIVE GOAL SETTING

A *goal* is simply a desired end state, that is, something we want. Certainly, employee behavior often seems to be goal directed. Employees may strive to reach quotas, to win contests, to make it through the workday, or to outperform their coworkers. Sometimes their goals are difficult, sometimes easy. Sometimes they are very specific and sometimes vague. As we will see, the nature of employee goals, and how they are set, can be very important. Goal setting is also simple and inexpensive.

FUNCTIONS OF GOALS

Goals serve a variety of important functions. For instance:[14]

> Goals let employees know what they are expected to do.
> Goals relieve boredom. Consider how boring most games would be if you didn't keep score and try to reach goals.
> Reaching goals and getting positive feedback leads to increased liking for the task and satisfaction with job performance.
> Attaining goals leads to recognition by peers, supervisors, and others.
> Attaining goals leads to feelings of increased self-confidence, pride in achievement, and willingness to accept future challenges.

EFFECTIVE GOAL SETTING

Research on goal setting has yielded some clear and useful findings. Here are some guidelines for effective goal setting (see Figure 4-9):

> **Set specific goals.** Quite simply, specific goals lead to higher performance than just "do your best" goals. In fact, do your best goals have about the same effect as no goal at all. Imagine a runner circling a track, shouting to her

FIGURE 4-9
Important Goal Characteristics

coach, "How much farther do I have to go?" A reply from the coach of "Just do your best" won't help much.[15] Specific goals are so powerful as to overwhelm other things. In one study, subjects were assigned to either a low-motivation or a high-motivation group based on performance, ability, and attitude ratings.[16] The low-motivation group received specific task goals, whereas the high-motivation group was told to "do your best." Performance of the low-motivation group quickly caught up to that of the high-motivation group. Of course, goals must be appropriate. If some goals are specific and others are not, the nonspecific goals will not receive much emphasis. Also, there is a danger that a manager may really care about X but, because Y is easier to quantify, will set goals for Y instead. The Focus on Management feature provides an example.

> **Set difficult goals.** There is a positive, linear relationship between goal difficulty and task performance. That is, the more difficult the goal, the better the task performance. This relationship holds for various kinds of tasks, time horizons, and ages of subjects. However, employees must believe the goal is attainable. If not, they will not accept it. Also, people pursue many goals at the same time. If they believe one is too difficult, they will focus on other, more attainable goals. Interestingly, when people face difficult goals, they engage in more problem analysis and creative behavior than when faced with simple goals. So they both work harder and work smarter.

> **Give feedback on goal progress.** Feedback keeps behavior on track. Feedback may also stimulate greater effort (we see later in this chapter that feedback from the job itself is a major determinant of the motivating potential of a job). A video game without a score would soon be abandoned. And when people get feedback concerning their performance, they tend to set personal improvement goals. The nature of the feedback makes a difference. As we discuss later in the chapter, feedback from the job itself is generally better than that provided by others. Finally, feedback is clearly more important for some

FOCUS ON MANAGEMENT

TO CUT FAILURE RATE, SCHOOLS SHED STUDENTS*

Schools should clearly be concerned with helping students learn and successfully complete their education. One easily quantifiable measure of student performance is the dropout rate. However, New York City's school system was sharply criticized in 2003 for trying to directly reduce dropout rates rather than dealing with the underlying causes for dropouts. Specifically, it was learned that schools were counseling, or even forcing, students to leave school early. These "pushouts" were then classified under bureaucratic categories that hid their failure to graduate. As a result, it was estimated that the city's dropout rate—given as about 20 percent—would be as high as 30 percent if these "pushouts" were included. Under the federal No Child Left Behind Act, schools with low graduation rates risk being deemed failing schools, and the temptation to push out students to manipulate graduation rates is increasing. Nevertheless, it seems clear that such actions are a way to distort levels of goal achievement rather than to improve students' educational experience.

* T. Lewin and J. Medina, "To Cut Failure Rate, Schools Shed Students," *New York Times*, July 31, 2003, p. A1.

people than for others. We've seen elsewhere, for instance, that people with a high need for achievement have especially strong desires for feedback.

> **Consider peer competition for goal attainment.** If employees are working toward individual goals, such as salespeople pursuing independent sales goals, competition for goal attainment may be useful. Its impact is especially great in zero-sum situations, that is, where there is a fixed pie to divide. However, competition can hurt if tasks are interdependent. In such a case, an employee's attempts to excel may harm the performance of another. Also, if competition focuses on the quantity of output, quality may suffer.

> **Use participation in goal setting.** Participation isn't a panacea. Some people simply don't like to participate, and in some situations (such as under severe time constraints) participation may be inappropriate. In general, though, participation increases understanding and acceptance of the goal. Participation often leads to setting of more difficult goals, which may in turn lead to higher performance.[17]

> **Encourage goal acceptance.** *Goal acceptance* is the degree to which individuals accept particular goals as their own. If a goal is not accepted, the other goal attributes don't matter. Goal acceptance is likely to be lacking if the individual sees goals as unreachable or sees no benefit from reaching the goal.

> **Encourage goal commitment.** *Goal commitment* is the degree to which individuals are dedicated to trying to reach the goals they have adopted. Like goal acceptance, it is a necessary condition for goal-directed effort. Goal commitment is affected by the same factors as goal acceptance. Those factors influence goal acceptance before the goal is set and goal commitment once the individual is pursuing the goal.

Of course, most goal setting involves changes in a number of goal attributes. As one example, consider a field experiment in the logging industry. Trucks carrying logs from the woods to the mill varied in the number of trees they hauled from one time to the next because the trees varied in size. As a result, considerable judgment entered into the decision of what was a full load. However, analyses showed that trucks were carrying an average of only about 60 percent of their legal net weight. Eventually the researchers, management, and the union decided that a goal of 94 percent of legal net weight was difficult but reachable. The drivers, who were responsible for loading the trucks, were assigned this 94 percent goal. After about a month, performance increased from the initial 60 percent to about 80 percent of capacity. It then dipped to 70 percent for another month before rising to 90 percent, where it remained for the next six months. Company accountants estimated the results translated into a savings to the company of a quarter of a million dollars' worth of new trucks alone. Several goal attributes had been changed—goals were difficult, were more specific than in the past, and had apparently been accepted.[18]

MANAGEMENT BY OBJECTIVES

Management by objectives (MBO) is a motivational technique in which the manager and employee work together to set employee goals. The employee's performance is later measured against these goals. Management by objectives combines many of the goal-setting principles we have just described. The MBO process begins by identifying general areas of responsibility important to the firm. Once this has been done, the employee and manager get together and agree on specific objectives that the employee will meet during some future period of time. For example, one key responsibility area in sales management might be sales volume, and the objective might be to increase sales by 35 percent over the next six months. Once the manager and the employee have agreed on specific objectives, they develop a strategy together for meeting these objectives. The manager and the employee then meet periodically to review how the employee has done relative to the agreed-upon objectives. If there is a problem, they discuss why objectives have not been met. The final step in the MBO process is either to set new goals for the next time period or to develop new strategies to meet the previously agreed-upon goals. The entire procedure then begins anew.

Management by objectives was one of the most popular motivational tools in the 1960s and 1970s, and it is still widely used in various forms. However, MBO is not perfect. For example, it may be difficult and time consuming to implement. Sometimes the agreed-upon goals are not specific enough, resulting in employee frustration. Also, MBO has been faulted for encouraging people to focus only on goals that can be easily expressed in numbers (such as the number of units produced in a week or the average number of sales calls made per day), ignoring goals that are hard to measure (such as quality of products or creativity).

MBO does encourage planning and goal setting, however, and it lets employees know how they are doing on the job. Also, it allows employees to participate in setting goals, which is good for morale and motivation. It helps spot deviations from performance goals before it is too late to do anything about them. Because MBO combines three elements that have been found to improve productivity—goal setting, feedback, and participation—it might be expected that MBO would also be successful. In fact, one review found that 68 of 70 major studies on the issue showed

BOTTOM LINE

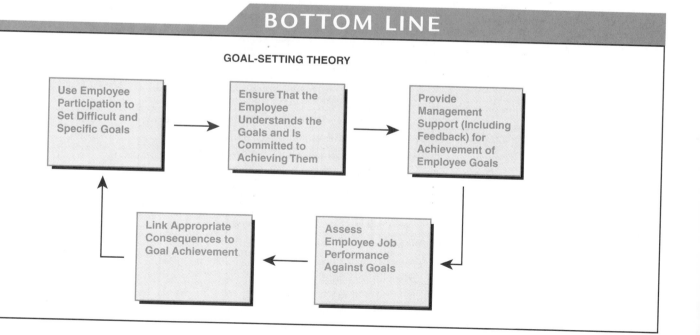

GOAL-SETTING THEORY

MBO to result in productivity gains.[19] These studies also demonstrate that top-management commitment to MBO is critical for success. When top-management commitment was high, MBO resulted in an average productivity gain of 56 percent. When top-management commitment was low, the average gain in productivity was only 6 percent. The process model presented in the Bottom Line feature on the previous page illustrates how goal-setting principles can be applied in order to enhance employees' motivation and job performance.

Skills Practice 4-5 will encourage you to think more systematically about the process of identifying specific goals you want to achieve and the processes needed to achieve them. Then complete Skills Practice 4-6 by watching the movie *Jerry Maguire* and analyzing Jerry's motivations throughout the film. Enjoy!

MASTERING SELF-MANAGEMENT

The 1st-century Roman philosopher, author, and statesman Lucius Annaeus Seneca wrote, "He is most powerful who has power over himself." As a manager and in other roles in organizations, you must be able to motivate yourself and to teach others this critical skill. Self-management is the process of managing oneself. Instead of relying on others to reward and punish, to direct, to set goals, and to provide feedback, we must learn to use these tools to manage our own behavior.

Self-Assessment 4-2 will give you some baseline information as a foundation for your later self-management goals. In the Voice of Experience feature on page 175, Ann and Jim Cue discuss the challenges and strategies related to self-management.

SELF-ASSESSMENT 4-2

Self-Management Attitudes and Practices

Answer each of the questions in this section using the following scale:
1 Disagree strongly
2 Disagree somewhat
3 Neither agree nor disagree
4 Agree somewhat
5 Agree strongly

____ 1. I regularly set goals for myself.
____ 2. I keep track of how well I've been doing.
____ 3. I generally keep the resolutions that I make.
____ 4. I often seek feedback about my performance.
____ 5. I am able to focus on positive aspects of my work.
____ 6. I'll sometimes deny myself something I want until I've met my goals.
____ 7. I use a to-do list to plan my activities.
____ 8. I have trouble working without supervision.
____ 9. When I set my mind on some goal, I persevere until it's accomplished.
____ 10. I'm a self-starter.
____ 11. I make lists of things I need to do.
____ 12. I'm good at time management.
____ 13. I'm usually confident that I can reach my goals.
____ 14. I am careful about how I manage my time.

____ 15. I always plan my day.

____ 16. I often find I spend my time on trivial things and put off doing what's really important.

____ 17. Unless someone pushes me a bit, I have trouble getting motivated.

____ 18. I reward myself when I meet my goals.

____ 19. I tend to dwell on unpleasant aspects of the things I need to do.

____ 20. I tend to deal with life as it comes rather than to try to plan things.

____ 21. I generally try to find a place to work where I'll be free from interruptions.

____ 22. I'm pretty disorganized.

____ 23. The goals I set are quite specific.

____ 24. Distractions often interfere with my performance.

____ 25. I sometimes give myself a treat if I've done something well.

____ 26. I am able to focus on positive aspects of my activities.

____ 27. I use notes or other prompts to remind myself of things I should be doing.

____ 28. I seem to waste a lot of time.

____ 29. I use a day planner or other aids to keep track of schedules and deadlines.

____ 30. I often think about how I can improve my performance.

____ 31. I tend to lose track of the goals I've set for myself.

____ 32. I tend to set difficult goals for myself.

____ 33. I plan things for weeks in advance.

____ 34. I try to make a visible commitment to my goals.

____ 35. I set aside blocks of time for important activities.

THE NEED FOR SELF-MANAGEMENT

Self-management is needed particularly when employees are relatively isolated, such as with telecommuting. It may also be useful when supervision is lacking or when employees must be self-directing, as with enriched jobs and self-managed work teams.[20] In such cases, self-management may serve as a potent "substitute for leadership."[21] The movement in organizations toward what some have called *self-organization*—freeing employees to figure out how to get the job done without central planning or control—assumes that employees will have the skills to proactively deal with workplace uncertainties and demands.[22] As we have discussed in other chapters, such companies as General Electric, Xerox, Hallmark, Ben & Jerry's, and Eastman Kodak are abandoning traditional top-down organization and moving toward self-organization.[23]

In addition, self-management may be less expensive than reliance on organizational reward-and-control systems and, once self-management skills have been learned, they are transferable across a vast array of tasks and settings. Finally, self-reinforced behavior is generally maintained more effectively than if it had been externally regulated.[24] In view of all these potential benefits, it isn't surprising that self-management is often presented as a distinguishing characteristic of "best" and "most admired" firms.[25] It's also no surprise that self-motivation is among the key characteristics sought by employers. Use of self-management at W. L. Gore and Associates is discussed in the Focus on Management feature on page 176.

CONSEQUENCES OF SELF-MANAGEMENT

Self-management works. Early evidence came from clinical settings, where self-management techniques have been very successful in programs dealing with weight loss, smoking cessation, and phobia reduction.[26] In academic settings, they have led to improved study habits and enhanced academic performance. In organizational settings, they have reduced absenteeism, increased satisfaction with work, enhanced commitment to the organization, and improved task performance.[27]

FORMS OF SELF-MANAGEMENT

There are two broad approaches to self-management. The first, termed *behavioral self-management*, is to learn to manage our own behaviors, deciding what we want to achieve and setting up appropriate systems of goals, rewards, and controls. The second, termed *cognitive self-management*, involves the development of effective thinking patterns. These approaches can best be used together to achieve effective and satisfying patterns of thought and behavior.

GUIDELINES FOR BEHAVIORAL SELF-MANAGEMENT

Here are concrete steps to take to change or maintain behaviors:

> **Pinpoint the specific behavior you want to change or maintain.** One way to do this is through self-observation. You may decide, for instance, that you are working on jobs you should delegate to others, you need to lose weight, or you spend too much time chatting with people who walk into your office.

> **Set specific goals for behavioral change.** As we discussed earlier in the chapter, effective goals should be specific, difficult, and measurable. Further, if the goals are to be effective, our acceptance of and commitment to them must be sincere. Some specific goals might include:
> - Exercise at least four days a week for at least 30 minutes per day.[28]
> - Spend at least two hours with my children every evening.
> - Quit smoking for three months.

> **Keep track of the frequency, duration, and any other dimensions of interest, such as the time and place at which the behavior occurs.** Use diaries, graphs, or timing devices as needed. Sometimes self-monitoring itself is sufficient to change the behavior. For instance, if you really identify how much time you spend watching television, you may simply watch less. Here are some examples of monitoring techniques:
> - Weigh in once a week at the gym.
> - Each time I eat fast food, write down what I ate and how much the meal cost me.
> - Write on my calendar what time I arrive at school each day.
> - Put project due dates on a calendar and track what has been done for projects each week leading up to the due date.

> **Modify cues.** Sometimes the behavior we want to change is preceded by other events that serve as cues or signals for the behavior. By altering or controlling the cues, you may be able to change the behavior. For example, you may find you can't get your work done because you're constantly answering the phone. A solution might be to activate your voice mail or have an assistant hold calls. Or you may increase desired behaviors by as simple a prompt as a to-do list. Some cue modifications might include:
> - Plan a menu for the week ahead.
> - Bring my work-out clothes to school so I can work out immediately after class.

VOICE OF EXPERIENCE

SELF-MANAGEMENT

Ann and Jim Cue, Multilevel Distributors, Sunrider International

1. **What are the most significant challenges you face in managing yourselves in running a Sunrider distributorship?**

We are a Multi-Level Distributor for Sunrider International, a major direct marketer of personal health care products. We have approximately 3,000 distributors that operate under our umbrella. In setting up our business operations over 10 years ago, we decided to locate our business office in one section of our home.

One of the biggest challenges we face regarding self-management is the issue of deciding how much time to give to our business. We are the owners of our distributorship so we really don't report to anyone in the Sunrider hierarchy. Given this, we have to decide for ourselves what our business hours will be and how we will operate. It can be really tough trying to figure out exactly where to "draw the line" between your personal and business lives.

A second big challenge we have encountered is deciding how to balance the need to have some structure and formalization in our system versus the need for flexibility. This is especially difficult since we need to set some guidelines for ourselves about procedures or policies for things like ordering products and documenting business transactions.

On the other hand, we need the flexibility to be able to handle a wide variety of issues that come up on a day-to-day basis as well as to help us strike some balance between work and family.

2. **What kinds of self-management strategies have been effective for you?**

Given that our business office is actually part of our home, space management is critical. We keep all our business and personal issues completely separate from each other. For example, we only do business with our distributors in the business area of our home. When the mail comes each day, we physically separate it into work vs. personal piles and put them in different parts of the house. We have two computers—one for all of our Sunrider business and the other for personal stuff.

We have learned that you must have some formal policies and procedures so that you ensure that key tasks get accomplished and you have time for your personal life. For example, we have created policies for ourselves that specify that we will not do business on Sundays and that the deadline for our distributors to place orders is 2 P.M. on the Thursday of each week

Ongoing planning meetings are absolutely critical for us to manage ourselves. Every Monday morning, we hold a planning session where we set goals for the week and a list of things to do. This is the basis for focusing our

time and effort throughout the week. Every three months or so, we hold a planning meeting that focuses more on the overall direction and long-term goals of our business.

We feel that a big part of self-management is rewarding yourself for your accomplishments. When we meet or exceed our sales goals for a given period of time, we make a point of doing something to reward ourselves (e.g., buying new software for our personal computer).

3. **What kinds of advice would you give students regarding the best ways to develop self-management skills?**

First of all, recognize that this is not common sense and it is not easy to do. You must become a master of the fundamental skills of goal setting, time management, and self-motivation. Take courses, read books, or go to seminars to learn these critical skills. It's not enough to just learn these skills, though. You must actually apply these principles and make them work in terms of your job. How can you do this? Write the key principles of success down on a piece of paper and post it in a place where you will see it every day. Think about how everything you do in your job can be related back to these principles. The bottom line here is to keep these principles visual and salient for yourself.

http://www.sunrider.com

FOCUS ON MANAGEMENT

SELF-MANAGEMENT AT W. L. GORE & ASSOCIATES

W. L. Gore & Associates is regularly named as one of the "100 Best Companies to Work For in America." Lauded for its innovative technologies and fluoropolymer expertise, the company is probably best known for its GORE-TEX fabrics. Gore has a unique culture that fosters self-management and worker empowerment. As noted on its Web site,

How we work sets us apart. We encourage hands-on innovation, involving those closest to a project in decision making. Teams organize around opportunities and leaders emerge. Our founder,

Bill Gore, created a flat lattice organization. There are no chains of command nor pre-determined channels of communication. Instead, we communicate directly with each other and are accountable to fellow members of our multi-disciplined teams.

How does all this happen? Associates (not employees) are hired for general work areas. With the guidance of their sponsors (not bosses) and a growing understanding of opportunities and team objectives, associates commit to projects that match their skills. Everyone can quickly earn the credibility to

define and drive projects. Sponsors help associates chart a course in the organization that will offer personal fulfillment while maximizing their contribution to the enterprise. Leaders may be appointed, but are defined by "followership." More often, leaders emerge naturally by demonstrating special knowledge, skill, or experience that advances a business objective.

This is a culture that rewards, fosters—and demands—self-management skills.

http://www.gore.com/corp/ about/culture.html

- Eat small meals throughout the day so I don't get very hungry and overindulge.
- Study on the second floor of the library so I don't see my friends who study on the first floor.
- Keep low-fat snacks in my office so I don't get snack food from the vending machine.

> **Modify consequences.** This can involve self-reward or self-punishment (or both). You might, for example, reward yourself for quitting smoking by spending the savings on purchases of musical CDs. Or you may decide that you'll skip a concert if you don't meet your goal. Here are some consequences that may serve as rewards or punishments:

- Each time I complete a project before it's due, I'll buy myself a new CD.
- If I get up on time, I can have my favorite breakfast (raspberry toaster strudel).
- I will award myself four hours of free time on Sunday night to spend having fun if I complete all my tasks.
- I will save the money I would have spent on cigarettes for six months and apply it to a trip to Negril, Jamaica.
- I will have pictures of me with a flabby belly if I don't keep up my exercise routine.

Some consequences, such as the CD purchase, are relatively immediate, whereas others, such as the trip to Jamaica, must wait until the behavior has been exhibited for a lengthy period of time. It is generally best to use a combination of such consequences, such as a reward for each week you don't smoke with a longer-term reward, such as the Jamaica trip.

> **Reorder behavior.** We often do relatively enjoyable tasks in order to put off others we don't care for. As a result, the things we put off may never get done or may get done poorly. To prevent this, make pleasant behaviors depend on completion of the noxious task. For instance, if you enjoy reading your mail but find writing reports to be unpleasant, put off reading the mail until you have finished the project reports. Here are further examples:
>   • Exercise before dinner rather than after.
>   • Make lunch the night before, rather than in the morning as I usually do, and read the paper in the morning, so I'll be sure to have lunch.
>   • Eat my vegetables before I eat the meat. This way, I should be more full before I eat the meat.

> **Write a contract with yourself** (see Skills Practice 4-7 for a sample contract). In the contract, specify the behavior you will change, the length of the contract, how you will monitor progress, the rewards or punishments you will use, and so on. Write the contract clearly and post it in a conspicuous spot. Have others witness the contract, sign it, and agree to help to monitor your behaviors.

> **Rehearse.** Physically or mentally practice activities before you actually perform them. Rehearsal may suggest you should rethink your goals.

> **Check your progress on a regular basis.** If you're not doing as well as you'd like, take corrective action, such as changing prompts or rewards or making sure you are rewarding yourself promptly.

> **Plan strategies to maintain a successful change.** If not, you may fall back into your old habits. But don't become wedded to the same system of rewards and punishments on which you relied to bring about the change. Consider something such as a maintenance diet, or give yourself a bit more slack regarding leisure activities.

Use Skills Practice 4-7 to apply self-management to your own behaviors. Try it first with a behavior that you can easily observe and in which you may quickly see results, such as an exercise schedule or a program to cut down on distractions at work. Then apply it to a longer-term goal, such as learning a new skill. Once you master these techniques, you can draw on them to help with almost any task. The Bottom Line feature presents a process model that summarizes the basic steps associated with implementation of the self-management process.

COGNITIVE-FOCUSED STRATEGIES FOR SELF-MANAGEMENT

Behavioral self-management works best when accompanied by effective thinking, as shown in Figure 4-10.[29] One step to effective thinking is to redesign tasks physically and mentally to make them more naturally rewarding. This involves creating ways to do tasks so the enjoyment of performing the task itself creates significant natural reward value. Natural rewards come from performing tasks in a way that allows us to experience a sense of competence, a sense of self-control, and a sense of purpose. In addition, effective thinking is fostered by establishment of constructive and effective habits of thinking, such as "opportunity thinking" as opposed to "obstacle thinking." By studying and managing our beliefs and assumptions, we can start to

BOTTOM LINE

THE SELF-MANAGEMENT PROCESS

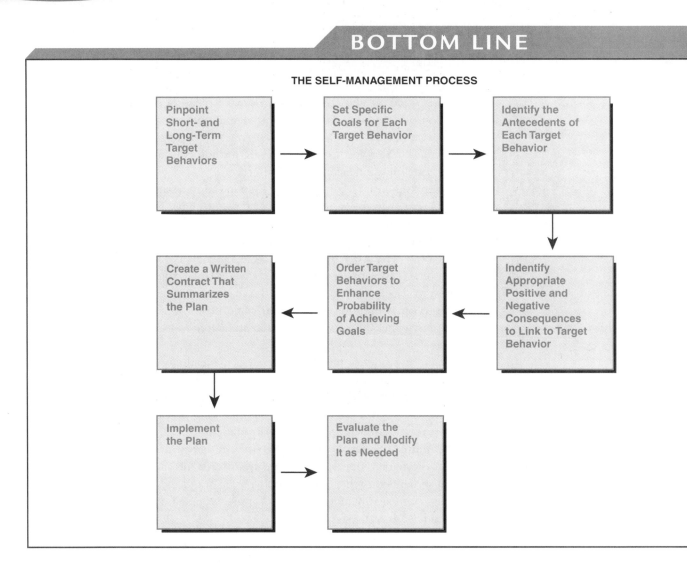

develop the ability to find opportunities in new work challenges. Use of mental imagery techniques and positive internal self-talk aids this process. Effective, positive thinking patterns are necessary for successful self-management and are also helpful for dealing effectively with stress, the topic to which we address in Chapter 5.[30]

LINKING EFFORT TO OUTCOMES: EXPECTANCY THEORY

If someone is going to try to engage in some behavior, three conditions have to be satisfied. First, the person must believe his or her efforts are somehow tied to the behavior. If not, why try? Second, the behavior must somehow be tied to outcomes. If not, why attempt the behavior? Third, those outcomes must be *valent* (that is, valued). If the outcomes aren't valued, why try to attain them? If any of these three conditions isn't satisfied, the individual has no reason to try. This simple idea is the essence of

FIGURE 4-10
Strategies that Promote Effective Thinking

FIGURE 4-10
Strategies that Promote Effective Thinking

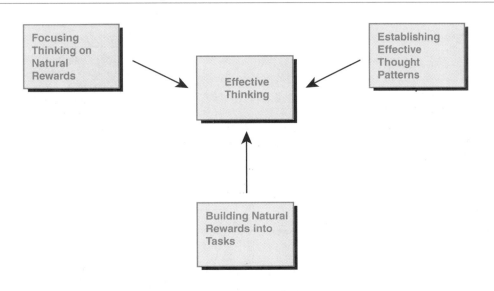

expectancy theory. *Expectancy theory* is an approach to the understanding of motivation that examines the links in the process from effort to ultimate rewards.[31]

EXPECTANCY THEORY CONCEPTS

The key elements of expectancy theory are as follows (see Figure 4-11).

> **First-order outcome.** A *first-order outcome* is the direct result of effort. The first-order outcome may be performance, creativity, low absenteeism, low turnover, or any other desired behavior. There may be more than one first-order outcome.

> **Second-order outcome.** A *second-order outcome* is anything, good or bad, that may result from attainment of the first-order outcome. Typically, there are many second-order outcomes, such as pay, esteem of coworkers, and approval of the supervisor.

> **Expectancy.** *Expectancy* is the perceived linkage between effort and the first-order outcome. There is an expectancy for each first-order outcome. If a worker feels that trying harder won't improve his or her performance, the expectancy of effort for the attainment of performance would be low. If a worker feels that more effort will translate directly into higher performance, expectancy would be high. Expectancies are often expressed as probabilities. Figure 4-12 shows some of the factors that may affect the actual linkage between effort and the first-order outcome of performance. One of these, of course, is ability. If ability is completely lacking, effort won't help much. Another is the situation. In some situations, such as the assembly line, the employee is constrained. Greater effort simply won't speed up the line. A final factor is role perceptions. If employees don't know what their roles are (that

FIGURE 4-11
The Components of Expectancy Theory

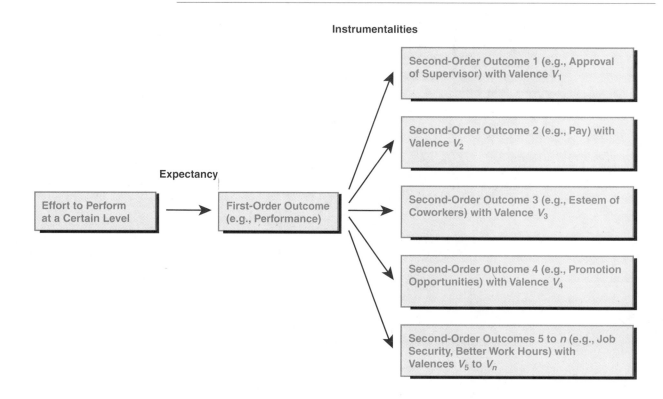

is, what management expects of them), they will probably misdirect their efforts. Each of these factors is likely to influence expectancies.

> **Instrumentality.** *Instrumentality* is the perceived linkage between a first-order outcome and a second-order outcome. There is an instrumentality for each combination of first- and second-order outcomes. Like expectancy, instrumentalities are often expressed as probabilities.[32] If an employee feels that

FIGURE 4-12
The Linkage of Effort to a First-Order Outcome

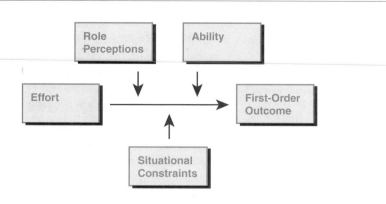

higher performance will lead to pay increases, the instrumentality of performance for the attainment of pay increases would be high. If an employee feels that performance and pay are unrelated, that instrumentality would be zero.

> **Valence.** *Valence* is simply the value an individual attaches to an outcome. The valences of second-order outcomes are the values of such variables as pay increases, supervisory approval, security, and esteem of coworkers. The valence of a first-order outcome, such as performance, depends on the valences of second-order outcomes and on the instrumentalities of the first-order outcome for the attainment of those second-order outcomes. In particular, it is the sum of the products of the valence of the first-order outcomes and the instrumentality of the first-order outcome for the attainment of the second-order outcomes. That is,

$$\begin{pmatrix} \text{Valence of} \\ \text{First-Order} \\ \text{Outcome} \end{pmatrix} = \sum_{i=1}^{n} \begin{pmatrix} \text{Valence of} \\ \text{Second-Order} \\ \text{Outcome } i \end{pmatrix} \times \begin{pmatrix} \text{Instrumentality of First-Order} \\ \text{Outcome for the Attainment of} \\ \text{Second-Order Outcome } i \end{pmatrix}$$

> **Force to perform, or effort.** As Figure 4-13 shows, the degree to which an employee exerts *force to perform, or effort,* to attain a first-order outcome depends on both the expectancy that effort will lead to an increase in that first-order outcome and the valence of the first-order outcome. For instance, expectancy theory would predict that an employee would exert no effort to perform at a higher level if he or she either saw no possibility that effort would lead to higher performance or did not value higher performance. Formally,

$$\begin{pmatrix} \text{Effort to Attain the} \\ \text{First-Order Outcome} \end{pmatrix} = \text{Expectancy} \times \begin{pmatrix} \text{Valence of the} \\ \text{First-Order Outcome} \end{pmatrix}$$

Expectancy theory is at base, then, a theory that focuses on values and perceived (sometimes called subjective) probabilities. People may place different values on outcomes, and they may have very different perceptions about probabilities. Expectancy theory suggests that managers should not assume they know what employees want or think. Instead, they should directly assess valences, expectancy perceptions, and instrumentality perceptions. Questionnaires can be used to make these assessments. In those questionnaires, valence is usually rated on a scale of −10 to +10. Expectan-

FIGURE 4-13
Determinants of Effort to Perform

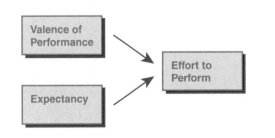

cies and instrumentalities are usually rated on scales of 0 (no chance the outcome will occur) to 1 (the outcome will definitely occur).

IMPLICATIONS OF EXPECTANCY THEORY

Expectancy theory provides a variety of important implications for managers. For example,

> **Recognize that three conditions are necessary for motivation to perform:** valued rewards, a perceived link of effort to performance (expectancy), and perceived links of performance to valent outcomes (instrumentalities). If *any* of those elements is missing, motivation will be low.

> **Assess perceptions of each of those conditions,** which can provide extremely useful information. For example, you may find that employees don't really value some of the rewards you have been using or they don't believe their efforts will translate into performance or their performance into rewards. Conversely, you may be surprised to find that employees place great value on rewards that could be easily and inexpensively provided or that employees have surprisingly strong expectancy or instrumentality perceptions.

> **Identify gaps between employee and management perceptions.** For example, a common response of management upon learning that employees don't believe their rewards are tied to their performance levels is "They're wrong! We tightly link pay and other rewards to performance." From an expectancy theory perspective, whether or not the employees' perceptions are wrong is irrelevant; perceptions drive behavior. If rewards actually are tied to behaviors in ways that employees don't recognize, management's job is to convince employees of that fact.

> **As suggested earlier, and consistent with our discussion of need theories, make sure you are giving employees rewards they value.** One option is to employ *cafeteria-style benefit plans*. In these plans, employees can choose from a range of alternative benefits. For instance, employees of differing ages or marital status may desire different benefits. One employee may choose all salary with no other benefits; another may choose the total allowance for pension and insurance contributions. As an example, Du Pont's U.S. employees can choose from a menu of medical, dental, and life insurance options as well as financial planning.[33]

> **Ask what factors may be weakening expectancy perceptions.** Do employees know what they are supposed to do? Have they been properly trained? Are there characteristics of the situation—resource constraints, poor tools, or whatever—that make it difficult for employees to perform well regardless of their efforts?

> **Ask what factors may be weakening instrumentality perceptions.** Is it true that rewards really aren't tied to performance? Is management simply not communicating well with employees about the nature of the reward system?

> **If employees appear to be poorly motivated, work backward.** Try to determine which of the expectancy theory conditions may be lacking.

Which of the expectancy theory components appears to be especially weak in the company depicted in the nearby Dilbert cartoon? The process diagram in the

BOTTOM LINE

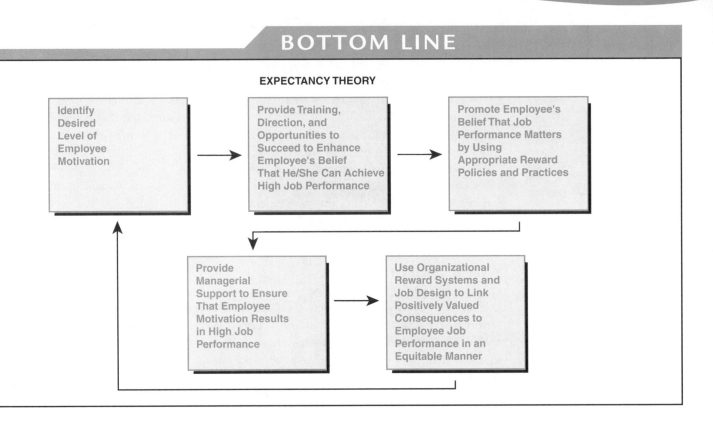

EXPECTANCY THEORY

Identify Desired Level of Employee Motivation → Provide Training, Direction, and Opportunities to Succeed to Enhance Employee's Belief That He/She Can Achieve High Job Performance → Promote Employee's Belief That Job Performance Matters by Using Appropriate Reward Policies and Practices → Provide Managerial Support to Ensure That Employee Motivation Results in High Job Performance → Use Organizational Reward Systems and Job Design to Link Positively Valued Consequences to Employee Job Performance in an Equitable Manner

Bottom Line feature shows how expectancy theory can be applied to manage employee motivation and performance effectively.

Skills Practice 4-8 will help you develop skill in conducting a comprehensive analysis of worker motivation and performance using expectancy theory. This exercise is a bit more work than some others, for you need to actually go into the field to interview a working person in order to conduct your analysis. The insights you will gain will justify the effort!

DILBERT reprinted by permission of United Feature Syndicate, Inc.

ASSURING FAIRNESS

It goes without saying that we should treat people fairly. What, though, do we mean by fair? Certainly, fairness has something to do with not cheating others or blatantly playing favorites. But fairness is more complex than that. There are at least two important types of fairness: distributive fairness and procedural fairness. These deal, in turn, with fairness in regard to the sorts of things we get and the processes used to allocate rewards.

Equity theory, which focuses on distributive fairness, is one of a family of theories based on the idea that people want to maintain balance. By focusing on the balance of the inputs, or contributions, people make to the outcomes they receive, equity theory helps us understand how employees determine whether they are being treated fairly.

WHY BE FAIR?

According to equity theorists, people want to maintain distributive fairness. *Distributive fairness* exists when someone thinks people are getting what they deserve—not less, certainly, but *not more either.* According to equity theory, people feel uncomfortable when they get less than they deserve (because they feel cheated) or more than they deserve (because they feel guilty). Research evidence supports this contention.[34] Some people—called *equity sensitives*—are especially focused on equity considerations.[35] People want distributive fairness for several reasons.[36] For instance,

> When people experience a situation they feel is not fair, they experience an unpleasant state of tension. Restoration of distributive fairness reduces that tension.
> Some people try to be fair because they think others will reward them for being fair.
> Behaving fairly may bolster a person's self-esteem.
> Most people find it comforting to believe life is fair. By giving others what we think they deserve, we strengthen that belief.

Employers may have other, more specific reasons for wanting to treat their employees fairly.[37] They may, for instance, want to do the following:

> **Conform to business norms.** For example, people in business generally agree that employees who do better work should get more rewards.
> **Attract superior workers to their company and weed out inferior workers.** If rewards are fairly tied to performance, a positive relationship between satisfaction and performance should result. Thus high performers should be satisfied and disposed to stay with the firm, and low performers should be dissatisfied and leave the firm.
> **Motivate employees to produce.** As expectancy theory indicates, tying rewards to performance should enhance instrumentality perceptions and thus increase motivation to perform well.
> **Develop trust.** A trusting environment is extremely important to workers, especially in turbulent job environments. Managers who don't treat their employees fairly will not be trusted.

As an example of the resentment engendered by inequity perceptions, IBM in the mid-1990s confronted the worst crisis in its history. In the previous eight years, it had cut more than 180,000 of its 405,000 jobs, and by the end of the year it would report an annual loss of more than $8 billion. In the face of these cutbacks and the threat of further belt tightening, employees were dismayed by the perks the company maintained for managers and top salespeople—country clubs with golf courses and skeet shooting; a large fleet of private jets; a Rose Bowl Parade float; and elaborate sales meetings featuring a five-act circus, Bob Newhart, Larry King, Liza Minelli, and others. Whatever the merits of such expenses, they created a sense of great inequity and led to many angry complaints.[38]

Similarly, there has been a global debate over CEO pay, with the levels of CEO compensation skyrocketing relative to that of the average hourly worker—today's average U.S. CEO makes more than 530 times the pay of the average hourly worker, compared to 85 times in 1990 and 42 times in 1980.[39] Further, 90 percent of stock-option plans for Standard & Poor's 500 companies don't attach performance conditions to option grants. The growing compensation gap has led to charges of greed and concerns about the impact of perceived inequities.[40] Further, U.S. employees aren't the only ones complaining about inequities—CEO compensation packages are beginning to rise worldwide as foreign executives are eyeing the staggering sums received by their U.S. counterparts.[41] The Focus on Management feature shows the dramatic consequences of perceived inequity at American Airlines.

FOCUS ON MANAGEMENT

INEQUITY AT AMERICAN AIRLINES*

On April 24, 2003, under fire for the lavish compensation packages received by executives in the face of huge losses by the airline, Donald McCarty resigned as CEO of AMR, the parent company of American Airlines. McCarty's career began to crumble on the night of April 15, when American made a filing with the Securities and Exchange Commission disclosing that the company had decided in March to give seven executives cash bonuses equal to up to twice their base salaries if they stayed until January 2005; McCarty's bonus would have been more than $1.6 million. The same filing showed that American had made a $41 million pretax payment to protect executives' bonuses if the

company went into bankruptcy. American's unionized workers, who had just finished voting to accept $1.62 billion in annual concessions, were outraged at the news in the filing. Not only did they see the executives' bonuses and perks as excessive, but it appeared to them that McCarty had delayed the securities filing by at least two weeks to hide information that might have jeopardized their votes for concessions. Following news of the filing, union members decided to vote again. Facing the new vote, and fearing the company would be forced into bankruptcy if the concessions were not approved, McCarty met for 12 hours with union leaders and four local congressmen in Dallas, near AMR's headquarters. The result was that McCarty resigned in return

for persuading the unions to accept the concessions. The new agreements would, among other changes, provide for contracts for five years, rather than six, and a new cash incentive plan. For McCarty, a 31-year veteran of the company, the costs of inequity were high.

* Based on S. McCartney and J. S. Lublin, "AMR Addresses CEO's Future—Anger Mounts over Failure to Disclose Pay Packages; $1.04 Billion Loss Is Posted," *Wall Street Journal*, April 24, 2003, p. A3; E. E. Schultz and T. Francis, "Executives Get Pension Security While Plans for Workers Falter," *Wall Street Journal*, April 24, 2003, p. A1; and E. Wong, "Under Fire for Perks, Chief Quits American Airlines," *New York Times*, April 25, 2003, p. C1.

DETERMINING EQUITY

How do people determine whether outcomes are equitable? J. Stacey Adams proposed the following equation for an equitable relationship.[42] It is based on the writings of Aristotle, an earlier student of behavior:[43]

$$\frac{O_p}{I_p} = \frac{O_o}{I_o}$$

Where:

O_p is the person's perception of the outcomes he or she is receiving.
I_p is the person's perception of his or her inputs.
O_o is the person's perception of the outcomes some comparison person
(called a *comparison other*) is receiving.
I_o is the person's perception of the inputs of the comparison other.

This equation says that equity exists when a person feels the ratio of his or her outcomes to his or her inputs is *equal to* that ratio for some comparison other. Neither is seen as getting less or more than his or her inputs justify. Note that *each* of the elements in the equation is a perception. Although actual conditions may (or may not) influence those perceptions, they do not directly enter the equity calculations.

The comparison other may be another individual (such as a coworker or friend), a group of other people (such as workers on another job), or some abstract combination of people. It may even be the perceiving person at an earlier point in time.

INPUTS AND OUTCOMES

At base, inputs are anything employees believe they are contributing to the job. Outcomes are anything they believe they are getting from the job. So inputs might include such things as seniority, time, performance, appearance, dedication to the organization, effort, intelligence, and provision of needed tools. Outcomes might include pay, promotional opportunities, job status, job interest, esteem of coworkers, monotony, praise, fatigue, and dangerous working conditions. Note that employees may view some outcomes of the job negatively, such as fatigue and dangerous working conditions. Obviously, different people care about different inputs and outcomes. An input for one person may even be an outcome for another. For instance, one worker may value increased responsibility, viewing it as an outcome. Another may see that same increased responsibility as a burdensome input. In the Dilbert cartoon, it is clear that Alice and her boss have very different perceptions about what factors should weigh into the equity equation.

RESTORING EQUITY

If an individual perceives a situation to be inequitable, there are many ways to restore equity. For instance, suppose that Frank feels underpaid relative to his coworker Karen. He could try to restore equity in each of the following ways:

> **He can raise his actual outcomes.** For instance, Frank might demand and get a raise.

DILBERT reprinted by permission of United Feature Syndicate, Inc.

> **He can lower his inputs.** Frank might slow down on the job, withhold important information, or stop doing unpaid overtime work.
> **He can perceptually distort his inputs and/or outcomes.** Frank could reason that he was actually getting things out of the job he hadn't been considering, or he could downgrade the values of his inputs.
> **He can perceptually distort Karen's inputs and/or outcomes.** Frank could devalue the nonpay outcomes Karen is receiving, or he could increase his estimates of Karen's inputs.
> **He can leave the situation.** With a big enough feeling of inequity, Frank might psychologically withdraw from the situation or might actually apply for a transfer or quit.
> **He can act to change Karen's inputs and/or outcomes.** Frank could try to convince Karen to raise her inputs, could talk to the boss about lowering Karen's pay, or could take steps to try to make Karen leave her job.
> **He can change his comparison other.** Frank could begin to compare his situation to that of Paul rather than to that of Karen.

People do use these mechanisms to restore equity. For instance, field studies and laboratory experiments have shown that individuals withdraw from tasks when they are inequitably treated—even, in some cases, when they are overpaid.[44] Considerable evidence also indicates that people change their perceptions to restore equity.[45] Underpaid workers often perceive they have made relatively low inputs and begin to see themselves as less qualified than others.[46] Some also exaggerate their outcomes, rating their jobs as far more interesting than others do.

As an example of the ways employees may take action to restore equity, consider the case of a manufacturing plant that made small mechanical parts for the aerospace and automotive industries. When important contracts were canceled, the company announced a 15 percent pay cut for all employees in the plant. Compared to employees in another plant, whose pay was not cut, the affected employees reacted by doubling their normal theft rate of tools and supplies from the company, and turnover jumped to 23 percent (compared to a normal 5 percent). When the pay cut ended after 10 weeks, theft returned to normal levels.[47] Apparently, employees in the plant experienced underpayment inequity, and some reacted by stealing. Others apparently decided simply to leave the inequitable situation.

Equity theory would permit any of a wide range of adjustments to restore equity, but it would be useful to know specifically which change is most likely to occur. Adams has provided the following set of propositions concerning how people choose from among the alternatives available to reduce inequity:[48]

> They will first try to maximize valued outcomes.
> They will be reluctant to increase inputs that are difficult or costly to change.
> They will resist actual or perceived changes in inputs or outcomes that are central to their self-concept and self-esteem.
> They will be more resistant to changing perceptions about their own inputs and outcomes than to changing perceptions about their comparison others' inputs and outcomes.
> They will leave the situation only when inequity is great and other means of reducing it are not available. Partial withdrawal, such as absenteeism, will occur more frequently and under lower conditions of inequity.
> They will be reluctant to change their comparison others.

The process model presented in the Bottom Line feature shows how equity theory can be systematically implemented to establish and maintain an employee's sense of perceived equity in his or her work situation.

OTHER RULES FOR DETERMINING DISTRIBUTIVE FAIRNESS

Equity theory is based on the contributions rule. The ***contributions rule*** says distributive fairness is determined by equating contributions (inputs) with outcomes.

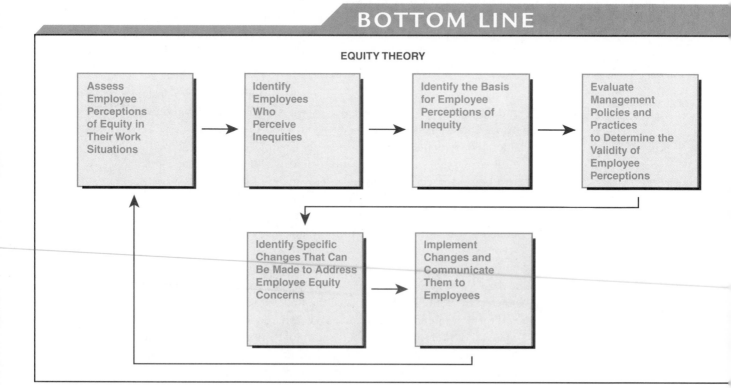

BOTTOM LINE

EQUITY THEORY

Assess Employee Perceptions of Equity in Their Work Situations → Identify Employees Who Perceive Inequities → Identify the Basis for Employee Perceptions of Inequity → Evaluate Management Policies and Practices to Determine the Validity of Employee Perceptions → Identify Specific Changes That Can Be Made to Address Employee Equity Concerns → Implement Changes and Communicate Them to Employees

However, people may use other rules when determining distributive fairness. They may, for example, employ the ***needs rule***, feeling it is fair to give people what they need rather than what they contribute. Or they may employ the ***equality rule***, arguing it is fair for everyone to get the same amount.

A variety of factors determine the weights we give to these various rules, including the following.

> **Self-interest.** People tend to assign higher weights to rules that favor them. A high performer will likely favor the contributions rule, whereas a needy person will favor the needs rule.
> **Conformity.** People tend to conform to the beliefs and behaviors of others with whom they regularly interact. So if all of a manager's coworkers favor the equality rule, the manager may also apply that rule.
> **Availability of relevant information.** People are reluctant to use a rule for which they don't have sufficient information. For instance, if a manager doesn't know what subordinates need, the needs rule probably won't be applied.

In addition, some things affect the weights given to specific rules. For instance, if it is important that high performers maintain their output levels, the contributions rule will be weighted heavily. When someone feels responsible for the receivers' welfare, the needs rule is likely to be applied. And the equality rule is easy to apply. People may also turn to the equality rule when needs and contributions are hard to assess.

PROCEDURAL FAIRNESS

Distributive fairness depends on whether receivers get what they deserve. People may also be concerned with procedural fairness. ***Procedural fairness*** is whether the process used to allocate outcomes is fair.[49] If procedures seem unfair, people may also question the distribution of rewards. But even if people don't get what they want, they may be satisfied as long as they believe the allocation process was fair. Procedural fairness seems to have important consequences. Research has shown, for instance, that survivors' reactions to a major reorganization depended on perceptions of procedural fairness, with procedural justice predicting organizational commitment, job satisfaction, intentions to stay with the firm, and trust in management.[50] Similarly, job satisfaction and organizational commitment of untenured management professors subsequent to their tenure and promotion processes were found to be related to perceptions of both distributive and procedural fairness.[51]

Not surprisingly, people tend to think procedures are fair when those procedures favor their interests. They also believe procedures to be fairer when they have some control over the allocation process. Further, they are likely to consider a procedure to be unfair when it uses questionable means to get information about the receivers' behavior (such as the use of hidden cameras) or if the evaluations of receivers seem to be based on unreliable or irrelevant information (such as faulty performance appraisals).[52]

IMPLICATIONS OF FAIRNESS THEORIES[53]

Equity theory and related theories of fairness have important implications for managing behavior in organizations, including the following:

> **Fairness is absolutely critical to employees.** Fairness influences both employee attitudes and their behaviors.

> **Perceptions play a central role in determinations of fairness.** Whether or not management thinks something is fair, employees will react negatively if they perceive it to be unfair.

> **Fairness involves a comparison process.** Employees don't decide whether something is fair by looking only at their own paychecks and other rewards. Instead, they compare their rewards and contributions to those of relevant others. As such, it is critical to make sure that rewards are equitably distributed across employees.

> **Both distributive fairness and procedural fairness are important.** Employees obviously care about whether they're getting what they think they deserve, but they also are very concerned about whether the process used to determine rewards was fair. Even if employees are pleased with what they received, they may have qualms if they think the allocation process was unfair. They may, for instance, feel guilt, or they may question whether the process will give them what they deserve next time. If employees get less than they feel they deserve, a clear explanation of exactly how rewards were determined may temper their reactions. This, of course, puts the onus appropriately on management to actually use a fair allocation process.

> **Both overreward and underreward may cause problems.** Whereas underreward may cause anger, overreward may cause guilt.

> **Employees may consider inputs and outcomes that are different from those we may expect.** Indeed, what some employees consider inputs, others may see as outcomes.

> **We need to find what people really value and what they think they are contributing.** We cannot assume people value what we expect them to value or that they see their contributions as we do. Perhaps the best way to find what people see as inputs and outcomes is to ask them.

> **Employees may find many ways to reduce perceived inequity.** In the case of underreward inequity, these might include producing less, producing lower-quality work, quitting, or even sabotage or theft.

> **Although the exact means employees will use to reduce inequity may be difficult to predict, almost all are harmful to organizations and perhaps to the individuals themselves.** Not only may inequity lead to bad outcomes for the organization, it may also generate stress in employees and perhaps even cause them to question their self-worth.

Skills Practice 4-9 will help you develop skill in translating the concept of equity into managerial practice through a systematic process of analysis, evaluation, and action planning.

DESIGNING MOTIVATING JOBS

Jobs are central to the lives of most people. They consume a large part of our days and often our nights. To a great extent, many of us rate our success in life on the basis of the status, pay, and other characteristics of our jobs. And others often size us up by our response to "Tell me, what do you do?" Indeed, it is hard to imagine not working. Albert Camus has written, "Without work, all life goes rotten. But when work is soulless, life stifles and dies." What is it about jobs that makes them important to people? What makes them exciting? Why are some soulless? What makes jobs "good" or "bad"? Does everyone want the same things from jobs? And what can management do to improve jobs and increase their motivating potential?

THE CASE FOR SPECIALIZATION

Frederick Taylor introduced scientific management in the early 1900s.[54] According to scientific management, the "one best way" to perform a job should be found. That "one best way" usually results in job simplification, with each worker performing the same few activities over and over. Advantages cited for specialization include the following:

> The worker should be better able to perform the task and should find it to be easier.
> Time is not lost moving from one piece of machinery to another.
> The use of specialized machinery is encouraged.
> Replacement of employees who are absent or who leave the organization is easier, because the job is simpler and easier to learn.
> Especially where assembly lines are used, the worker will adjust to the required pace and be drawn along by "traction."

Scientific management was credited with some notable successes. For instance, application of its principles in one case increased the number of bricks laid per worker-hour from 120 to 350. Further, scientific management permitted the worker to maximize performance by focusing on a narrow range of activities. If the worker was paid on a piece-rate basis, this would result in higher pay. As a result, scientific management was widely adopted in the United States and elsewhere.

However, Taylor is now often criticized for his emphasis on efficiency at the possible expense of employee satisfaction. He did consider the human element, but many of his views today seem inhumane. He wrote, for instance, that the kind of person who made a good pig-iron handler was "of the type of the ox." Whether or not criticisms of Taylor are correct, it does seem that the simplified, routine jobs he proposed may have some unforeseen results. For instance, they may lead to boredom, dissatisfaction, or other negative outcomes, as shown in Figure 4-14.

JOB SIZE

If we believe "small" jobs are demeaning and dissatisfying for workers, a logical question to ask is how we can make jobs larger. There are at least two major dimensions to job size. They are job depth and job scope, or range.

Job depth refers to the degree to which employees can influence their work environments and carry out planning and control functions. *Job scope* is the number of different activities the worker performs, regardless of their content. Increases in job depth are usually called *job enrichment*; increases in job scope are referred to as *job enlargement*. Most job changes are likely to influence both depth and scope, but these are separate dimensions and can be independently changed.

The following are among the suggested advantages of increases in scope:

> There should be less fatigue of particular muscles, because a greater variety of muscles may be used.

FIGURE 4-14

Potential Reactions to Specialized Jobs

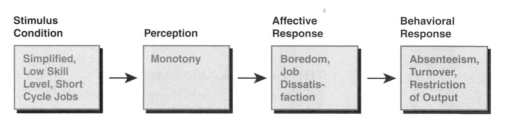

Stimulus Condition	Perception	Affective Response	Behavioral Response
Simplified, Low Skill Level, Short Cycle Jobs	Monotony	Boredom, Job Dissatisfaction	Absenteeism, Turnover, Restriction of Output

> Because the employee will complete a larger part of the task, there may be more of a feeling of accomplishment.

> The employee may exercise a greater variety of skills.

> Large increases in scope may enhance managerial flexibility. For instance, if a company uses assembly teams rather than assembly lines, it can shut down a small number of the benches used by assembly teams rather than the entire line.

The presumed benefits for increased depth are primarily psychological. For instance, Chris Argyris has suggested that because small routine jobs are frustrating to the drives of "mature" individuals, they may result in use of a variety of defense mechanisms.[55] Those *defense mechanisms* are ways in which the employee may try to reduce the tensions caused by frustration. They might involve physically leaving the source of frustration (such as through absenteeism or turnover), mentally leaving (through apathy or daydreaming), or striking back (perhaps by slowing down on the job or by making negative comments about the company). As shown in Figure 4-15, Argyris has argued that the typical firm's response to such defense mechanisms is to make jobs even more specialized, tighten up on rules, and emphasize authority relationships. These actions further frustrate maturity drives, and a self-reinforcing cycle occurs. Argyris reasons that to break out of that cycle, it is necessary to treat employees as mature individuals. Giving them more opportunity for planning and control is one step in that direction.

Others made similar arguments.[56] For instance, M. Scott Myers said the assumption underlying work simplification is that there are two groups of employees. One group, responsible and highly motivated, is known as *managers.* The other, irresponsible and in need of close supervision, is called *workers.* Because of those assumed differences, companies call on managers to plan, direct, and control. They expect workers simply to carry out orders. Myers argued that companies must break down this artificial dichotomy and "make every employee a manager." This would involve turning many planning and control functions over to workers. That is, it would require enriching their jobs. Such job enrichment would be expected to enhance *intrinsic motivation*. Unlike things such as pay, which are forms of *extrinsic motivation,* intrinsic motivation comes from the job itself—just doing the job is motivating, independent of other rewards.[57]

Companies in many industries are using job enrichment. In the hotel industry, for instance, front-desk clerks, housekeepers, bellhops, and other employees are being

FIGURE 4-15
The Argyris Maturity Drive Frustration Cycle

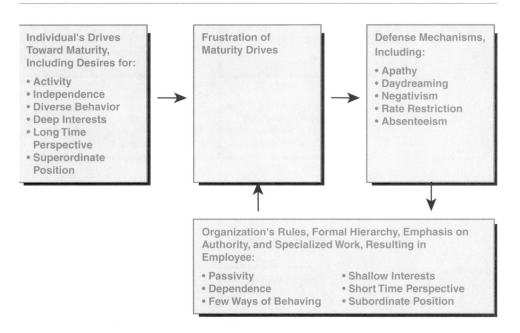

given more authority to make decisions on their own and to handle disputes with customers. At the Ritz-Carlton Hotel Company, for instance, front-desk clerks can now take off up to $2,000 from a guest's bill if the guest feels service was not up to par.[58] At John Deere & Co., workers who assembled parts for machines are now, after six months of training, traveling around the Midwest speaking to groups of farmers as part of the Deere marketing team. Other hourly workers routinely give advice on cost cutting and improving product quality. Job enrichment is part of Deere's plan to use its workers as a source of competitive advantage.[59] And truck drivers for Ryder System Inc., which has a contract with Xerox to deliver and install that firm's copying machines, now are fluent with computers and fax machines. Sporting the title of "service associates" and carrying business cards, they fax invoices, train office workers in how to use the latest office technology, and generally help customers solve problems.[60]

THE JOB CHARACTERISTICS MODEL

If we want to change jobs, we need to know which job dimensions are important to employees. In particular, before we can enrich jobs, we need to know what makes a job enriched. The examples we have just cited provide some clues. The jobs might, for instance, involve more responsibility, freedom, and challenge and a richer set of job duties. But are these necessary conditions for enrichment? Are there additional elements to enrichment? The *job characteristics model*, shown in Figure 4-16, describes jobs as having five core task dimensions and two interpersonal dimensions.[61]

CORE TASK DIMENSIONS

The *core task dimensions* are characteristics of the job itself believed to be key influences on employee motivation. They include the following:

FIGURE 4-16
The Job Characteristics Model

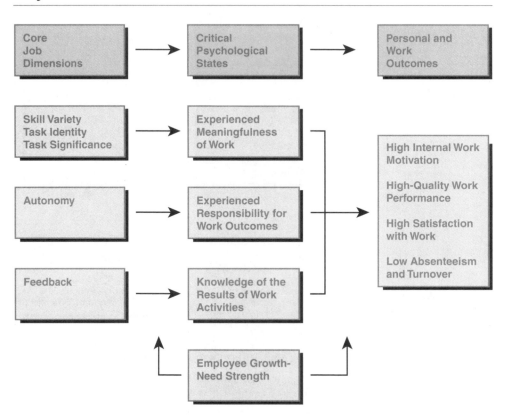

> **Skill variety.** The degree to which the job requires employees to perform a wide range of operations in their work and/or the degree to which employees must use a variety of equipment and procedures in their work.

> **Autonomy.** The extent to which employees have a major say in scheduling their work, selecting the equipment they will use, and deciding on procedures they will follow.[62]

> **Task identity.** The extent to which employees do an entire piece of work and can clearly identify the result of their efforts.

> **Task significance.** The extent to which the job has a strong impact on the lives and work of other people.

> **Feedback.** The degree to which employees receive information while they are working that reveals how well they are performing on the job.

INTERPERSONAL DIMENSIONS

The ***interpersonal dimensions*** (not shown in the figure) are job characteristics that influence the degree to which employees engage in relationships with others on the job. They are as follows:

> **Dealing with others:** the degree to which a job requires employees to deal with other people (inside or outside the firm) to complete their work

> **Friendship opportunities:** the degree to which a job allows employees to talk with one another on the job and to establish informal relationships with other employees at work

Sample items measuring each of the core task dimensions are shown in Figure 4-17. Can you match each item to the appropriate dimension?

According to the model, the core task dimensions have an impact on three *critical psychological states*: experienced meaningfulness of work, experienced responsibility for work outcomes, and knowledge of the actual results of work activities. Further, the model indicates that perceptions of the core task dimensions fit together to yield the *motivating potential score* of the job. This model implies that if any of the three components are very low, overall motivating potential of the task will be low. Further, as long as any of the three remain at very low levels, increases in the others will do little to improve overall motivating potential.

EVIDENCE REGARDING THE JOB CHARACTERISTICS MODEL

The job characteristics approach has dominated recent job design efforts. Questions have been raised concerning whether all employees actually view their jobs on these specific dimensions.[63] It does seem, though, that the dimensions may serve as useful guides for understanding reactions to jobs and for planning redesign strategies.

Studies show that perceptions of the core task dimensions are related to job satisfaction, job involvement, organizational commitment, and other favorable attitudes. However, those perceptions are usually not related in any consistent way to quantity of performance.[64] Employees on enriched jobs typically get the benefits of enrichment simply by carrying out the task, regardless of their performance levels. So we would expect the core task dimension perceptions to translate into increased performance only when persistence on the task is important.[65]

Research shows that the combinatory model proposed by the job characteristics model (in which a very low level on one dimension would neutralize the impact of

---

FIGURE 4-17
Measuring the Core Task Dimensions

Listed here are five statements that may (or may not) describe your job. You are to indicate the degree to which each statement is an accurate description of the job on which you work. Do this by writing the appropriate number in the left-hand margin, based on the following scale:

1	2	3	4	5	6	7
Very untrue of the job	Mostly untrue of the job	Slightly untrue of the job	Uncertain	Slightly true of the job	Moderately true of the job	Very true of the job

Please make your descriptions as objective and factually accurate as possible, without regard for whether you like or dislike your job.
1. The job requires me to use a variety of complex or high-level skills.
2. The job gives me considerable opportunity for independence and freedom in how I do the work.
3. The job provides me with the chance to finish completely the pieces of work I begin.
4. Just doing the work required by the job provides many chances for me to figure out how well I'm doing.
5. The job is one where a lot of other people can be affected by how well the work gets done.

Source: Adapted from J. R. Hackman and G. Oldham, *Work Redesign*. Reading, MA: Addison, Wesley, 1980, pp. 300–301.

changes in other dimensions) is probably not valid. That is, task dimension percep-tions somehow seem to "add up" to influence reactions rather than representing a series of hurdles.[66] This is a welcome finding because it suggests that improvements on any of the dimensions may help.[67]

THE FOCUS ON PERCEPTIONS

Remember that the job characteristics approach focuses on employee perceptions of task characteristics. This is appropriate because we act on the basis of our percep-tions. However, many things may affect perceptions. For instance, in one study stu-dents were asked to perform a simple assembly task.[68] The task was the same for all students, but the way they perceived the task depended on their ages and person-alities. As an example, older students felt the task offered more skill variety and feedback but less task identity than did younger students. In general, we might expect that an employee with considerable experience and training on a task would see it very differently than would a rookie.[69]

This makes the job of job design more difficult. It is not enough to make objec-tive changes in feedback, skill variety, or the other task dimensions. We must also discover how those objective changes translate into perceptions.

IMPLEMENTING JOB ENRICHMENT

Implementing principles for job redesign are job changes that might influence the core task dimensions.[70] Figure 4-18 presents those implementing principles. As our previous examples suggest, implementing principles include such actions as giving workers tasks to perform that require a larger variety of skills, letting workers do a larger part of the job in order to increase task identity and task significance, permit-ting employees to have increased contact with clients in order to increase skill variety, autonomy, and feedback, vertically loading the job (that is, giving more "management" responsibility) to enhance autonomy, and opening new feedback channels. Another, related, way to enhance the core task dimensions is through job rotation. With *job rotation*, employees systematically move from one job to another, getting a change of pace and duties, learning more about the company, and often developing a broad foundation for future advancement.[71]

These principles may be useful in providing suggestions for how companies can change jobs to increase levels of the core task dimensions. However, their use must take place as part of a systematic assessment of the particular situation. For instance, if job enrichment is to be successful, it must fit with the organization's employees, practices, structure, and technology.

THE CONDITIONS FOR SUCCESSFUL REDESIGN

A family of jobs should be considered for redesign in the following situations:[72]

> The employees perceive their jobs to be deficient in the core task dimensions. It is important to stress here that worker perceptions, not just the assumptions of management or consultants, are crucial.
> Employees are fairly well satisfied with pay, fringe benefits, and working con-ditions. If workers are unhappy with these factors, they are likely to resent and resist job redesign.

FIGURE 4-18
Implementing Principles for Job Redesign

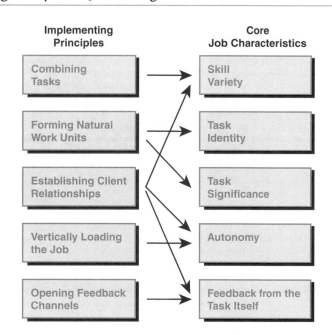

The current structure and technology of the unit where the jobs are housed are hospitable to enriched jobs. If the overall organization has a mechanistic structure or technology such as assembly lines, redesign attempts may be expensive and hard to implement. They are also likely ultimately to fail.

> Employees want the sorts of things—variety, autonomy, feedback, and so on—that enriched jobs provide.

These conditions suggest that job redesign should be undertaken carefully and selectively. It may be appropriate only in a limited set of situations and, as we discuss in the next section, it must be carefully and systematically implemented.

WHO WANTS JOB ENRICHMENT?

You probably know some people who would like more challenge, variety, and responsibility from their jobs and others who might be indifferent to them. Still others might say, "If you're going to give me all the decision-making responsibility of my boss, give me my boss's pay." The direct measure of the degree to which an employee wants an enriched job is called ***growth-need strength (GNS)***. This is basically the degree to which an individual wants such things as challenge and responsibility. Most employees respond positively to high levels of the core task dimensions, and those with strong GNS react most favorably. This suggests a simple and reasonable way to determine who wants job redesign: If we don't know whether employees are likely to react favorably to job enrichment, we can ask them. The process model presented in the Bottom Line feature illustrates how job characteristics theory can be applied in order to enhance employees' intrinsic motivation and yield desirable personal and organizational outcomes.

BOTTOM LINE

JOB CHARACTERISTICS THEORY

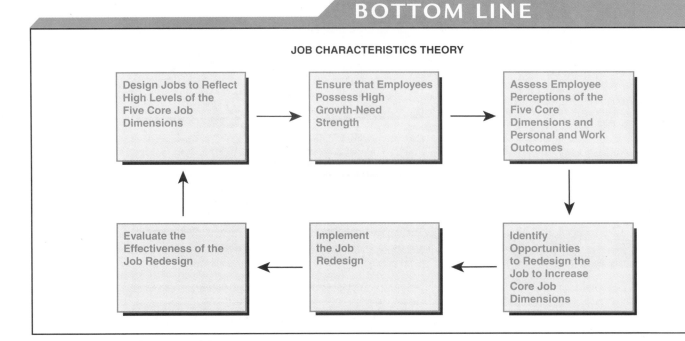

Skills Practice 4-10 will show you how to apply job characteristics theory in order to enrich a job and achieve higher levels of satisfaction, motivation, and performance from employees. Skills Practice 4-11 will give you an opportunity to apply a very popular motivational framework called FISH! to the issue of enhancing the quality of your worst job/work environment. See why there is so much buzz about this concept by completing this exercise!

We have presented several theories of motivation in this chapter. One of the most common questions we receive about this material is this: "How do we put all of these theories together in a way that we can apply them in the real world?" Skills Practice 4-12 asks you to think about how the various theories discussed in this chapter are similar and different from one another in order to identify the key things to remember about motivating workers based on all of the theories. This is a very challenging exercise, but highly beneficial. Go for it!

TOP TEN LIST: KEY POINTS TO REMEMBER

HOW TO MOTIVATE EFFECTIVELY

10. Assess employee needs and identify those that are most active (unsatisfied). Take specific actions to satisfy these needs through an employee's job and overall work experience in your organization.

9. Align the satisfaction of employee needs with the achievement of organizational goals through your managerial policies and practices.

8. Demonstrate to employees that good job performance makes a difference by linking positive outcomes or rewards to performance.

7. Demonstrate to employees that poor performance will not be tolerated by linking negative outcomes with poor performance or by eliminating positive outcomes that inadvertently led to the poor performance.

6. Develop and implement personal and job-related strategies for managing yourself more effectively

5. Set specific and challenging goals and objectives for your employees and ensure that they are aligned with the goals of the overall work unit. Monitor progress toward goal achievement and take appropriate corrective action as needed.

4. Develop and maintain employees' motivation by ensuring that they feel they have the ability to be successful on their job, that consequences are linked to performance, and that these consequences are appropriately valued by employees.

3. Provide managerial support for employee motivation so it results in high levels of job performance.

2. Monitor employee perceptions of their treatment by you and the organization. Take action to ensure that employees feel they are treated fairly.

1. Design jobs so the characteristics of the job provide a good fit with the knowledge, skills, abilities, goals, and values of each employee.

QUESTIONS FOR REVIEW AND REFLECTION

REVIEW QUESTIONS

1. Define *need, satisfaction,* and *motivation* and describe the need satisfaction process.

2. Identify the five needs in Maslow's need hierarchy, the three needs in Alderfer's ERG theory, and the three manifest needs considered by McClelland.

3. Discuss eight implications of need theories.

4. What is learning? Discuss classical conditioning, operant conditioning, and social learning.

5. Describe three contingencies of reinforcement to increase desired behaviors and two contingencies of reinforcement to reduce undesired behaviors.

6. Compare continuous reinforcement and four partial-reinforcement schedules in terms of learning rate, response rate, response stability, and extinction rate.

7. Provide seven guidelines for the effective use of organizational behavior modification.

8. Give five reasons why goals are important, and provide seven guidelines for effective goal setting.

9. What is behavioral self-management? Present ten guidelines for behavioral self-management.

10. What is cognitive self-management? Discuss three strategies to promote effective thinking.

11. Discuss the elements of expectancy theory as well as seven implications of the theory.

12. Discuss reasons why people seek fairness in general as well as why employers may want to treat their employees fairly.

13. According to equity theory, how do employees determine if they have been treated fairly? What are seven ways an employee may attempt to restore equity when underrewarded?

14. Present nine implications of fairness theories.

15. Discuss the job characteristics model, including the five core task dimensions and two interpersonal dimensions.

16. Identify approaches to implementing job enrichment and the conditions for successful job redesign.

CRITICAL THINKING QUESTIONS

1. A manager says, "We pay our employees to do their jobs, and we pay them well. That should be motivation enough." How would you respond?

2. When you say you have been reading about learning theory and are hoping to apply it in the workplace, a colleague expresses alarm. She says, "There's enough stress in this place without having people playing mind games to jack up performance." Do you agree with this position? Why or why not?

3. Larry Bird upon retiring as coach of the Indianapolis Pacers commented on the difficulty of motivating professional basketball players. A common reaction to his comments was this: "These players make tens of millions of dollars. How can they *not* be motivated?" Use the theories discussed in this chapter to give some reasons why it might be difficult to motivate such players.

4. For decades, many people have questioned attempts to use learning theory to motivate employees. Now some people are raising similar concerns about company efforts to teach employees behavioral self-management. They reason, "It's bad enough that we try to drive employees to work beyond their limits. Now we're teaching them to push *themselves*. Where will it all end?" Do you agree? Why or why not?

5. A production worker says, "They say they're going to enrich my job. From what I've heard, it looks to me like I'm being asked to learn more things and take more responsibility. If that's enrichment, I don't want it." Discuss this response in view of the theories presented in this chapter. Do you believe it is right to require employees to accept enriched jobs? Why or why not?

6. When you suggest using a lottery in your plant in order to reduce absenteeism, your boss replies, "No way. We're not going to have any gambling here while I'm in charge." How would you respond?

7. Describe a situation in which avoidance learning might be effectively and ethically used in an organizational setting.

8. Perceptions are central to expectancy theory, equity theory, and job characteristics theory. Do you think it is the responsibility of managers to try to influence employees' perceptions? Can you envision situations in which it would be inappropriate or unethical for them to attempt to alter employees' perceptions?

9. We discussed concerns about potential inequity raised by the extremely high ratio of U.S. CEOs' pay relative to that of blue-collar workers (and to that of most others in organizations). Ben & Jerry's was one company that tried to keep CEO pay quite low relative to that of operative-level employees (initially the ratio was capped at 5 to 1, then it was raised to 7 to 1). From the perspective of Ben & Jerry's, what might be some of the benefits and some of the problems associated with this low ratio?

EXPERIENTIAL EXERCISES

WEB EXERCISE 4-1

Go to the Funderstanding "About Learning" page at:

http://www.funderstanding.com/theories.cfm

This section of the Funderstanding site provides links to resources exploring how learning can be enhanced. Click on the "About Learning" link to access a dozen theories of how people learn. Select any four of the theories and provide a one-page summary of each.

WEB EXERCISE 4-2

Go to the Web site of the Psychology Centre of Athabasca University, "Canada's Open University," and access the page on "Demonstrations and Tutorials" at:

http://server.bmod.athabascau.ca/html/aupr/demos.shtml

You will find links to many resources at Athabasca University and elsewhere relating to learning theory and other topics in psychology, including many interactive demonstrations. Click on one of the following: "Classical Conditioning Demonstration," "Heuristics: Cognitive Rules of Thumb," "Learning by Observation," "Operant Conditioning," or "Pavlovian Conditioning" and investigate the associated materials. Write a one-page report on the principles demonstrated and what you learned from them that might be useful on the job.

CASE 4-1

MOTIVATIONAL PROGRAMS AT THE AGENCY FIELD OFFICE OF A MAJOR INSURANCE COMPANY[73]

Note: This case is based on an actual business unit in a real-world organization. Because of concerns regarding the potential sensitivity of issues presented in this case, some information has been modified to protect the anonymity of the company and the members of the teams.

The Agency Field Office

The Agency Field Office is part of the USA International Insurance Company (USAIC) based in Los Angeles, California. A major function of this office is to develop, implement, and evaluate a variety of motivational and reward programs for the company's 211 agents based in their territory in the northwest United States (Oregon, Washington State). USAIC's agents are independent contractors who run their own businesses. This results in some tension between the corporate offices and the agents because the agents are fiercely independent and resent being told what to do or how to do it. These agents have a contract to be the exclusive providers of USAIC products. The company cannot control the exact business practices of its agents, but it can influence them through the type of training provided.

Motivational Factors of USAIC Agents

The USAIC agents in the Northwest territory are older and very experienced for the most part. The average age of an agent is 50 years-old with 17 years of experience as an agent. There is a small contingent of young and inexperienced agents, but they make up only about 15 percent of the agent force in this territory.

One of the biggest challenges in motivating USAIC agents is that many of them already make very high salaries ($150,000 to $250,000 per year) by just maintaining their existing customer bases. Consequently, many agents were not motivated to change their business practices, sales tactics, or other behaviors when motivational programs have been implemented in the past. However, USAIC has expanded its product portfolio to include new financial products such as annuities and mutual funds. The company wants its agents to push the selling of these new products, but many agents have not been motivated to do so. Agents often want to focus on the products they are familiar with (e.g., home, auto, and life insurance products) and have a lot of experience selling rather than going through the tedious and time-consuming process of learning about and selling new products.

Methodology

Management consultants were hired by management at the Agency Field Office in USAIC's Northwest territory to evaluate the motivational programs (promotions) being implemented with the agents in the territory and to make recommendations for enhancing their effectiveness.

Consultants conducted a series of interviews and administered paper-and-pencil surveys with agency office management and field agents to obtain the data needed to support the objective of the project.

Results

The key results from the interviews and surveys are shown here. Note that the motivational programs (promotions) run by the Agency Field Office focused on providing incentives for agents to sell more of the new financial products such as mutual funds and annuities.

Key Results: Agent Awareness of Motivational Programs (Promotions)

Promotion Month	Percentage of Agents Who Were Aware of Promotions Being Run This Month
March 2004	31%
April 2004	28%
May 2004	32%
June 2004	30%
July 2004	27%
August 2004	30%

Key Results: Agent Understanding of Motivational Programs

Question	Strongly Disagree	Disagree	Agree	Strongly Agree
1. I am motivated by the current promotions being offered by USAIC.	11%	34%	35%	20%
2. I understand the qualifications for receiving rewards associated with current USAIC promotions.	23%	40%	30%	7%
3. The Agency Field Office is effective in informing me of promotions.	50%	25%	15%	10%
4. The Agency Field Office is effective in explaining promotions to me.	60%	20%	20%	0%
5. Current USAIC promotions motivate me to learn more about the new financial products being offered by the company.	5%	20%	42%	33%
6. I support USAIC's decision to start offering new financial products.	57%	20%	10%	13%
7. I am committed to selling USAIC's new financial products	45%	36%	11%	8%

Discussion Questions

1. Now it's your turn to be the consultant. Based on the information provided here, analyze the results of the various assessments of the agents' reactions to the promotions being offered by USAIC. Download the worksheet created for this exercise from the text Web site to help you structure your approach. Be sure to document your key findings on this worksheet.

2. Based on your key results, develop a set of *short-term recommendations* (actions that should be taken immediately or in the next few months) for the Agency Field Office team to help them to enhance the effectiveness of their motivational programs (promotions). Make sure each of your recommendations is specific and action oriented. Be prepared to justify each of your recommendations to management at the Agency Field Office in terms of merit, feasibility, and cost effectiveness. Also, make sure you address what management needs to do to ensure the effective execution of your recommendations.

3. Based on your key results, develop a set of *long-term recommendations* (actions that should be taken after the next three to five years) for the Agency Field Office team to help them enhance the effectiveness of their motivational programs (promotions). Make sure each of your recommendations is specific and action oriented. Be prepared to justify each of your recommendations to management at the Agency Field Office in terms of merit, feasibility, and cost effectiveness. Also, make sure you address what management needs to do in order to ensure the effective execution of your recommendations.

4. Make a five- to ten-minute presentation of your results and recommendations to the class.

5. What did you learn from this case study in terms of motivation issues in the real world and what must be done to enhance their effectiveness? Which concepts discussed in this chapter were helpful to you in conducting your analysis and in formulating your recommendations?

CASE 4-2

MOTIVATING THE "CELEBRATION OF CHILDHOOD" AT GYMBOREE CORPORATION

The Company

The Gymboree Corporation, started in 1976 by Joan Barnes, designs, contract manufactures, and retails a line of unique and high-quality apparel and accessories for children from birth to 8 years of age. The company operates over 570 retail stores in the United States and a number of other countries, including Canada, the United Kingdom, and Ireland.

In terms of recent financial performance, net sales from Gymboree's retail operations for the second fiscal quarter of 2003 were $110.4 million, an increase of 5 percent compared to net sales from the previous year. Comparable store sales for the second fiscal quarter increased 1 percent.. Total net sales, including sales from Gymboree Play & Music operations, were $113.1 million, an increase of 5 percent over last year.

The company's brands include the following:

- Gymboree Play and Music Programs: These include parent and child classes that support the development of children from newborn to 5 years of age.
- Gymboree Retail Stores: Offer upscale, stylish apparel for children ages newborn to 8 years of age. Gymboree's retail stores are known for being "child and parent friendly." Each store possesses features such as full-length mirrors, stroller-sized aisles, and various children's videos that make it easier for parents to shop.
- Janie and Jack Shops: Offer distinctive and stylish clothing, accessories, and gifts for babies sized preemie to 3T sold in a boutique setting with great attention to detail.

The Gymboree Vision Statement

The vision statement at Gymboree reads as follows:[74]

The Gymboree Corporation provides children, parents, and communities around the world with products and services that enrich, support, and celebrate childhood.

We succeed by knowing our customers and exceeding their expectations for quality and customer service. We grow by drawing on the strengths and abilities of every member of the Gymboree team. We build our brand through creativity and innovation in developing and delivering a unique array of products and services.

We at Gymboree are committed to stakeholder value. We are inspired by children and dedicated to growing the most respected children's company in the world.

Gymboree's Operating Values[75]

Gymboree's core values as a company include the following:

We are passionate about quality. Gymboree Corp. represents quality. We are obsessed with exceeding our customers' expectations in our products and services. We build and respect our brand by maintaining stringent stan-

dards. We require authenticity in what we do. We continuously improve ourselves and look for new businesses to enhance the lives of our customers.

We are connected. We are connected with our customers, employees, stores/shops, business partners and shareholders. We are unified to achieve common goals and are committed to maximizing our profitability. We grow our business by removing roadblocks and respecting each other while always remaining genuine to ourselves.

We are creative. We create something from nothing. We harness the imagination, talent and creative expression of our teams to bring the best products and experiences to our customers. We challenge our teams to search for unique solutions, we learn by doing, and we recognize success with creative rewards.

We are unique. The Gymboree Corporation is unique. Simply stated, our customers deserve for us to give them the best possible products and services. We do this by providing the best environment for our employees so they can deliver the most innovative products and best service to our customers. We contribute to our Company by freely expressing our opinions and trusting each other.

We are playful. We play with a purpose. As an organization, we are flexible and enjoy the challenge of change. We strive to enrich the lives of our customers and our employees by infusing the curiosity, laughter, and joy of being a child into all that we do.

Employee Benefits

Gymboree seeks to hire and develop a diverse work force. Employee benefits include the following:[76]

- Medical, dental, vision, life insurance and disability coverage
- Paid flex-time off, holidays and parental leave
- 401(k) savings plan
- Funding of approved educational courses
- Team Member Assistance Program
- Adoption assistance
- Pager program for expectant parents
- Stock purchase plan
- Bonus plan
- Direct payroll deposit
- Snack time
- Sabbatical program
- Team member discounts
- Flexible spending account

The Challenge

One of the corporate values that has been central to the "Gymboree Way" is the "celebration of childhood." Given that the company is in the business of creating innovative and high-quality children's apparel, this is quite appropriate. In a nutshell, Gymboree management wanted to create a work environment that supported "playfulness," "creativity," and "spontaneity." The challenge was how to do it. What kinds of specific company policies, practices, procedures, and so on, would motivate employees to fulfill Gymboree's vision?

Management Strategies to Motivate Gymboree Employees

Gymboree management implemented a wide range of innovative employee policies and practices to motivate employees to "celebrate childhood" each and every day of work. Every Thursday at 3 P.M., the company rings a bell over the intercom system indicating it is time for employee's to go to "recess." Recess?! During recess, employees play with rubber balls, skip rope, play hopscotch, and draw on the sidewalk with chalk. On Wednesday afternoons, employees take a "snack time" break by munching on root beer floats, chips and dips, and pretzels.

The company also implemented special benefits for employees who are pregnant or who have spouses that are expecting. The company has a "Pager Program" that provides all moms- or dads-to-be with pagers to maintain an emergency communications link with their spouses or doctors during the last three months of a pregnancy. Other benefits include on-site diaper-changing rooms and paternity or adoption leave for employees. Finally, the company created a "GymCares" program that links employee volunteers from Gymboree with specific community service opportunities involving children.

Discussion Questions

1. How does Gymboree Corporation use an understanding of need theories of motivation to effectively motivate its employees? To what extent do you feel these strategies are appropriate? Justify your response.

2. How does Gymboree Corporation use an understanding of process theories of motivation to motivate its employees effectively? To what extent do you think these strategies are appropriate? Justify your response.

3. To what extent do you believe the Gymboree Corporation would be a motivating place for you to work? Justify your response.

4. Develop an action plan for senior management at Gymboree that provides recommendations for sustaining and enhancing the effectiveness of the motivational strategies currently being implemented at the company, Make sure your recommendations are specific and action oriented. Be able to justify your recommendations in terms of their feasibility, effectiveness, and cost.

5. What are the practical implications of this case for you as a future manager?

Source: K. Hein, "Gymboree," *Incentive,* January 1999, pp. 42–44. For more on the philosophy and success of Gymboree, see C. Canabou, "Time for a Turnaround," *Fast Company*, January 2003, pp. 55+; and L. Lee, "Thinking Small at the Mall: To Keep Growing, Chains Have to Keep Chasing Niches," *Business Week*, May 26, 2003, p. 94.

VIDEO CASE: MOTIVATING FOR PERFORMANCE

A STUDY OF VALASSIS COMMUNICATIONS, INC.

Running Time: 13:17

Based in Livonia, Michigan, Valassis Communications, Inc. (VCI) is a leading publisher of freestanding, four-color coupon booklets distributed in Sunday newspapers. It also offers consumer samples bundled with newspapers, creates single-advertiser promotional materials, and puts clients' ads directly on the pages of newspapers. VCI is expanding onto the Internet through 50 percent–owned save.com to provide online coupons and a stake in Independent Delivery Services, which offers e-commerce software to grocery stores. In 2002, Valassis had 1,556 employees and a net income of $95.3 million on $853 million in sales.

Valassis Communications is rated by *Fortune* magazine as one of the 100 Best Companies to Work For in America. *Fortune* notes that "Celebrations are big at this newspaper-insert printer. When the stock hit a target price, employees partied at an airport hangar and were given flights on a vintage B-17 bomber. The company has an on-site hairstylist, manicurist, and doctor, and new parents are given an infant car seat."

The video shows chairman and CEO David Brandon and other Valassis officers as they discuss motivating strategies at Valassis and as they interact with employees. After viewing the video, answer the following questions:

1. Why is employee motivation important in the creation of a corporate culture where people are performing at a high level?

2. What sort of people does Valassis try to hire to achieve its goals?

3. To what does Valassis attribute its extremely low turnover?
4. What sorts of monetary rewards does Valassis use to motivate employees? To what does it tie those rewards?
5. What is Champion Pay? According to learning theory, what aspect of Champion Pay should make it a very powerful motivator?
6. Other than monetary rewards, what approaches does Valassis use to motivate its employees?

http://http://www.valassis.com/

LIGHTEN UP

SNIFFY, THE VIRTUAL RAT

Many experiments on conditioning use laboratory rats, often teaching them to navigate through mazes. Now you can use Sniffy the Virtual Rat to explore operant and classical conditioning by performing experiments that demonstrate most of the major conditioning phenomena discussed in textbooks on the psychology of learning. To use this very realistic simulation, go to

http://www.wadsworth.com/psychology_d/ special_features/ext/sniffy/about.htm

and click on "Download" at the bottom of the page. You'll be taken to a page where you can download a free trial version of the program.

SKILLS PRACTICE

4-1

Skill Level: BASIC

Field Experience: Interviews with Real-World Managers About Strategies for Motivating Workers

Skill Objective

To develop a better understanding of what management practitioners in the real world do to motivate their workers.

Procedure

1. Identify one or two managers who work in different business organizations. Ask the manager(s) if you can interview each of them for approximately 30 to 45 minutes.
2. When you meet with each manager, ask the following questions:
    a. Why should managers be concerned with managing the motivation of their workers? What is the cost of not addressing employee motivation issues?
    b. What are the most challenging employee motivation problems you have experienced in your career? How did you handle them?
    c. What types of strategies do you use to motivate your workers? What kinds of barriers exist to implementing these strategies? What do you do to overcome them?
    d. How difficult is it to link rewards to the level of employee job performance? Why is this the case?
    e. Which rewards do your employees value the most? Does everyone value the same rewards for the most part, or does it depend on the person?
    f. What advice would you give students regarding specific actions they can take to motivate workers effectively in the real world?
3. Summarize the results of your interviews.

Discussion Questions

1. Based on the summary of your interviews, what are your key findings about employee motivation? Why?
2. What are the practical implications of this exercise for you as a future manager and leader of a real-world organization?

SKILLS PRACTICE

Developing Motivational Strategies Using 1001 Ways to Reward Employees *and Content Theories*

Skill Objective

To develop skill in analyzing employee needs and linking them to appropriate motivational strategies from the best-selling book *1001 Ways to Reward Employees*.

Procedure

Note: Download the worksheet developed for this exercise from the Web site for this textbook.

1. Form groups of three to five students each.
2. Read the employee profiles that follow and identify what kinds of motivational strategies you might use to satisfy each employee's active needs, based on the sampling of innovative motivational strategies identified by *1001 Ways to Reward Employees* as well as on your understanding of the need or content theories of motivation. Develop your strategies into an action plan that specifies exactly what you believe should be done to motivate the employee effectively. Be prepared to defend each of your strategies in terms of its feasibility, effectiveness, and cost.
3. When your team is done, have one person from the team present to the class a summary of your motivational plan for each employee.
4. The class should then evaluate each team's motivational plan and offer suggestions for improving it.

Employee 1

Mike recently received his bachelor's degree in finance from the University of Michigan. He has accepted a position as a financial analyst at a major commercial bank in New York. Mike's starting salary is $35,000 per year.

Mike possesses a high need for achievement; he wants the opportunity to work on the high-impact projects at the firm. Mike excelled in his course work at Michigan, so he knows he is good. He will work hard for the company, but he expects to be rewarded handsomely for his work. On the negative side, Mike tends to be high on introversion and low on agreeableness.

What is your assessment of Mike's active needs? As a manager, what kinds of strategies would you use to satisfy those needs?

Employee 2

Susan is a single mother of two children. She has been employed as a financial analyst with the same bank as Mike

for 10 years. She possesses a bachelor's degree from the University of Wisconsin—Madison. Susan's work has always been very good. She is responsible, a good team player, and high on conscientiousness and extraversion. Given that Susan has two children, she is especially concerned about maintaining her employment with the company in order to meet her family's financial needs. In addition, Susan has been struggling to balance her work and family schedules (e.g., picking kids up from school, doctor's appointments). Susan's current salary is $47,000 per year.

What is your assessment of Susan's active needs? As a manager, what kinds of strategies would you use to satisfy those needs?

Examples of Motivational Strategies from 1001 Ways to Reward Employees

- Call an employee into your office to thank him/her
- Send an e-mail message to an employee expressing your appreciation of his/her efforts
- Assign an employee to an important company task force or committee
- Order a pizza for a communal lunch
- Put a thank you note on an employee's cubicle or office door
- Send an employee to a professional conference or training program of his/her choice
- Give an employee a round of golf
- Give an employee more autonomy
- Acknowledge individual achievements by using employee names when preparing status reports for top management
- Give an employee a weekend trip
- Grant an employee an extra day off
- Give an employee a special project to work on
- Create a Hall of Fame wall with photos of outstanding employees
- Arrange for an employee to have lunch with an executive
- Grant an employee an extra break or a two-hour lunch
- Make a donation to an employee's favorite charity
- Award dinners for two to employees when they do something special
- Give employees tickets to a sports or cultural event

- Give an employee a gift certificate for something that he/she likes
- Give an employee a computer/laptop to use at home
- Take an employee out to lunch
- Give an employee his/her choice of assignments or projects
- Give an employee $50 in cash with a thank you note
- Pay for an employee to get a free manicure or massage

- Buy an employee something to use in his/her hobby
- Give an employee responsibility for a key product
- Schedule a staff meeting off-site in a more relaxed atmosphere
- Feature an employee in a company publication

Source: B. Nelson, *1001 Ways to Reward Employees* (New York: Workman, 1994), pp. 4–75.

SKILLS PRACTICE

4-3   *Skill Level:* **CHALLENGING**

Reinforcing Desired Work Behaviors

Skill Objective

To develop skill in identifying target behaviors and linking appropriate consequences to them in order to reinforce appropriate work behavior.

Procedure

Note: Download the worksheet developed for this exercise from the Web site for this textbook.

1. Select one of the following work scenarios to use for this exercise. If you prefer to substitute a situation from your current or past work experience, that will be fine as well. You may work in groups of three to five individuals for this exercise if you wish.

Scenario 1: Rotten Airline Customer Service

Customers of a major airline are very dissatisfied with the quality of service they have been receiving from flight attendants. Specifically, they find many of the flight attendants rude, unresponsive, and uncaring. Using the procedure presented in the chapter, describe how you would handle this situation.

Scenario 2: Botched Orders at the Fast-Food Drive-Thru

The manager of a fast-food (burger and fries) restaurant is experiencing major problems, with the wrong orders being given to drive-thru customers. Customers have been absolutely furious when they discover after they have driven away that they received the wrong order. Using the process presented in the chapter, describe how you would handle this situation.

Scenario 3: Motivating Managers to Complete Their Employee Performance Appraisals

The director of human resources at a large manufacturing company is trying to develop some strategies to motivate the 30 production supervisors on the line to take the time to complete their annual performance appraisals of employees by each employee's anniversary date (when he or she started working for the company). Presently, only 50 percent of employee performance appraisals are completed at all each year, and only 20 percent of them are done on time. Using the procedure presented in the chapter, describe how you would handle this situation.

Scenario 4: Motivating Sales Representatives to Push Sales of a Specific Product

The district manager for a pharmaceutical company based on the East Coast has 25 sales representatives that work under her in a sales territory in Cleveland, Ohio. Her sales representatives are responsible for selling a variety of cholesterol- reducing and high blood pressure medications to doctors. The company has just come out with a new drug called Genecotrol that it wants the sales representatives to start focusing on in order to establish the drug in the market. Using the procedure presented in the chapter, describe how you would handle this situation.

2. Using the following steps, apply the basic process for reinforcing desired behaviors.

   a. Identify the target behavior. Be as specific as possible.

   Examples of general types of work behaviors:
   > Attendance
   > Quality of work
   > Safety practices
   > Thinking creatively ("out of the box")
   > Timeliness
   > Customer service
   > Sales calls
   > Attention to detail
   > Productivity
   > Teamwork
   > Risk-taking behavior

Examples of specific target behaviors:

> To achieve an attendance rate of 95 percent over the next three months

> To achieve a rate of timeliness (i.e., getting to work on time) of 100 percent over the next six months

> To achieve an average productivity rate of 50 units/hour over the next 12 months

> To achieve a defect rate of 1 percent over the next quarter

> To return all phone calls from customers within 24 hours

b. Identify appropriate consequences to link to the desired behavior.

> If you want to use *positive reinforcement,* then identify positively valued consequences that could be linked with engaging in the desired behavior.

> If you want to use *avoidance learning,* then identify specific negative consequences that would be avoided (not experienced) as a result of engaging in the desired behavior.

> If you want to use *escape learning,* then identify the specific negative stimulus that would be removed or eliminated as a result of engaging in the desired behavior.

c. State how you will link the consequences you identified to the target behavior.

3. Present your plan to the class. Be very specific in terms of the elements of your plan and be prepared to discuss why your plan will be feasible and effective.

SKILLS PRACTICE

4-4   *Skill Level: CHALLENGING*

Managing Undesired Employee Behaviors

Skill Objective

To develop skill in identifying undesired employee behaviors and linking appropriate consequences to them in order to eliminate inappropriate work behavior.

Procedure

Note: Download the worksheet created for this exercise from the Web site for this textbook.

1. Select one of the following work scenarios to use as a basis for applying the process.

Scenario 1: The Problem Team Member

You are the project leader of a product development team at a computer firm. The team itself is composed of 10 employees representing various functional areas in the firm, including marketing, engineering, finance, and human resources. The objective of the team is to develop new and innovative computer hardware in a cost-effective and efficient manner.

The team has been meeting on a weekly basis for a number of months. Although the overall product development process has been fairly smooth so far, you are experiencing a problem with one team member who consistently shows up for meetings 15 to 20 minutes late or fails to attend meetings at all. This employee's behavior is slowing the progress of the team because some key decisions have been delayed.

What would you do to handle this employee?

Scenario 2: The Rotten Customer Service Provider

You are the manager of a high-end restaurant located in a luxury hotel in Seattle. Although the restaurant has long held a reputation for its outstanding international cuisine, satisfaction with customer service has been declining.

Your wait staff is very professional and service oriented as a whole, but the tight labor market has made it increasingly difficult to find qualified employees. You have received a number of complaints from customers about one employee in particular. This employee has made a number of mistakes: serving the wrong orders, overcharging customers, and even making some rude comments to customers. You believe this employee has the potential to be a good server, but you need to address some of her behavioral issues immediately.

What would you do to handle this situation?

Scenario 3: The Hypercompetitive Sales Associates

You are the supervisor of the housewares department at a major department store in Atlanta. You manage a staff of 25 sales associates who work on a commission system based on sales volume. Your sales associates are given sales goals they are expected to meet each day they work. Employees who meet or exceed their sales targets receive a variety of rewards, including higher commissions, recognition, and a more attractive work schedule.

One problem that has emerged from the commission system used at your company is that sales associates are highly competitive with each other, sometimes even stealing sales from one another. Moreover, there is no cooperation or teamwork among the sales associates, because they feel the work environment is one of "survival of the fittest."

You are not happy with the work environment that has evolved in your department. You believe competition among sales associates will ultimately damage the quality of service they provide to customers.

What would you do to eliminate the competitive behavior in this situation?

2. Apply the following steps to develop a systematic plan for addressing the problem behavior in the scenario you have selected.

   a. Identify the undesired employee behavior (e.g., unsafe work practices, poor customer service). Be as specific as possible.

   b. Decide whether you want to use punishment or nonreinforcement to address the problem behavior.

      > *If you decide to use nonreinforcement,* identify the specific actions you would take to ensure that the employee's behavior is not reinforced in any way, Your action plan would stop here, and there is no need to go through the remaining steps.

      > *If you decide the use of punishment is appropriate,* identify negatively valued consequences (e.g., verbal reprimands, less desirable work assignments). Make sure these outcomes are negatively valued by the employee.

   c. Identify the schedule of reinforcement you think would be most appropriate for the situation.

   d. Link the negatively valued consequences to the target behavior.

   e. Identify the new (desired) employee behavior you want to replace the undesired behavior. Reinforce this behavior. Such reinforcement is important so employees understand what they should do instead of the undesired behavior.

3. Answer the following discussion questions as a class.

Discussion Questions

1. Describe your action plan for dealing with the problem employee behavior in the scenario you selected. Be prepared to defend your plan in terms of its feasibility, effectiveness, and cost.

2. What steps would you take if the plan you just described did not work?

3. What are the practical implications of this exercise for you as a future manager?

SKILLS PRACTICE

4-5   *Skill Level: BASIC*

Applying Goal-Setting Theory to Motivate Employees

Skill Objective

To develop skill in setting goals that provide appropriate direction and enhance goal-directed effort. Use goal-setting theory when identifying desired ends to be achieved at the organizational, work unit, team, and/or individual level.

Note: Download the worksheet developed for this exercise from the textbook Web site.

Steps in Using Goal-Setting Theory

1. Identify your ultimate goal in terms of the following:

   a. What you want to accomplish in specific, measurable terms

   b. When you want to accomplish it

      Make sure your goal is something you believe will be challenging but not impossible to accomplish (e.g., General Motors capturing 30 percent of the U.S. auto market in 2004). If you are setting work unit or organizational goals, involve relevant managers and employees in the process. Here are some examples:

      > To complete our group project assignment by the due date

      > To accomplish a 20 percent reduction in operating costs by the end of the 2004 fiscal year

> To increase worker productivity by 10 percent within the next quarter
> To increase customer retention by 30 percent within the next three years

2. Given your overall goal, identify what you will need to do to achieve it (e.g., subgoals). These subgoals deal with the process you will use to accomplish your goals. Here is an example:

Overall goal: To increase worker productivity 10 percent by December 31, 2004.

Subgoal	Completion Date
Analyze our current work process and develop a flowchart to describe it.	June 15, 2004
Develop a list of three to five key action steps for eliminating inefficiencies in the process.	July 1, 2004
Pilot-test action steps and perform evaluation in terms of impact on productivity.	August 15, 2004
Identify modifications to action steps or additional action steps that may support the overall goal.	September 15, 2004
Implement modified or new action steps.	October 1, 2004
Monitor results and evaluate in terms of impact on productivity trends for the year.	November 30, 2004
Conduct final evaluation of work process and communicate results to senior management.	December 31, 2004

Key Tips for Effective Goal Setting

1. Always keep the ultimate (long-term) goal in mind.
2. Keep your subgoals (process) in alignment with your ultimate goal.
3. Summarize your goals in a formal document. Make sure everyone involved in implementing the plan understands it and is committed to it.
4. Monitor your progress toward achieving your goals on a regular basis. Make adjustments to your goals as needed.

Now it's your turn. Using the principles of goal setting discussed in this exercise and in the chapter, do the following.

1. Identify a class project you are or will be working on this semester. This can be an individual or group project. An especially complex or challenging project would be ideal for this exercise. Alternatively, this could be any project you are working on for a student organization or part-time job/internship.
2. Develop an appropriate goal-setting plan for the project you identified in Step 1. Document your plan on a piece of paper. As shown in the earlier example, this plan should contain your overall goal, subgoals, and dates for completion.
3. Identify and discuss any barriers to the implementation of the plan and how you will address these issues. Optional: Present your plan to the class and have them critique it.

Discussion Questions

1. Why does goal setting work? Why is it beneficial to form a goal-setting plan?
2. Why is goal setting much more difficult to implement than many people think?
3. To what extent is effective goal setting a challenge or problem for real-world managers and employees? Why is this the case? What can be done about it?
4. What are the most important actions to take to ensure that a goal-setting plan will be successful?
5. What are the practical implications of this exercise for you as a future manager and leader of a real-world organization?

SKILLS PRACTICE

Motivational Analysis: **Jerry Maguire**

Skill Objective

To develop skill in analyzing the goals, needs, and motivations of an individual and how they can change over time as seen in the movie *Jerry Maguire.*

Procedure

1. Obtain a copy of the movie *Jerry Maguire.* It is available on VHS and DVD and can be rented or purchased from a local video store or retailer.

2. Watch the movie (in class or at home on your own). Note: Download the worksheet developed for this exercise from the text Web site for this book, which will help you to record your notes from various scenes in the movie. As you watch the film, take notes regarding the goals, active needs, and other motivations of Jerry Maguire throughout the movie. Be sure to document your notes about all relevant scenes on your worksheet.

3. Discuss the following questions as a class.

a. Based on the need theories of motivation, which need(s) were most active for Jerry Maguire early in the film? How did this influence his behavior? Which need(s) were most active for Jerry Maguire at the end of the film? How did this influence his behavior?

b. Based on goal theory, what were Jerry Maguire's goals early in the film in comparison with the end of the film? Why did his goals change?

c. Based on learning theory, which of Jerry's behaviors were reinforced or not reinforced throughout this movie? How did these reinforcements influence Jerry's behaviors?

d. What kinds of motivational issues shown in this movie are similar to the types of issues that many people face in real-world business organizations?

e. What are the practical implications of this exercise for you as a future manager and leader in a real-world organization?

SKILLS PRACTICE

Applying Self-Management

Skill Objective

To apply behavioral self-management techniques to two behaviors. Note: Download the worksheet developed for this exercise from the textbook Web site.

Procedure

Apply the self-management guidelines we have discussed to your own behaviors. Start by pinpointing two behaviors you would like to change. One of these should be short term, such as your physical exercise or eating habits or time spent on the telephone during the next week. The other should be for a longer period, such as the amount of work you will take home at night over the next six months. For each pinpointed behavior, go through the steps we have discussed. It may help to have friends or colleagues provide support with the self-management process. For example, they may sign your contract and check on a regular basis to see that you are maintaining the desired behaviors.

1. *Self-analysis*
   A. Pinpointing
      (i) What is a short-term behavior you would like to change?
      (ii) What is a longer-term behavior you would like to change?
   B. Self-set goals: For each of the selected behaviors, set a specific goal.
   C. Self-monitoring: How do you plan to monitor each of these behaviors?

2. *Modifying antecedents:* For each of the behaviors to be changed, identify events that precede and serve as cues or signals for the behavior and might be altered. For example, if leaving your door open leads to your spending excessive time talking with friends, you might keep your door closed. If you smoke when in certain settings, you might want to avoid those settings.

3. *Modifying consequences:* What rewards or punishments will you use to alter each of the behaviors identified?

4. *Reordering of behavior:* For each behavior, identify one or more ways that reordering of behaviors may help. For example, if you put off an unpleasant task until you have completed more pleasant tasks, can you change the order so the pleasant task becomes a reward for completion of the unpleasant task?

5. *Contracting:* For each of the behaviors you have selected, write a brief contract specifying the behavior to be changed, how you will monitor the behaviors, what rewards and punishments you will use to encourage desired behaviors, and so on. In addition, if feasible, identify an individual or individuals who might help to monitor the behaviors. A contract follows for your use with the short-term behavior you have chosen. Develop a similar contract for your selected long-term behavior.

6. *Evaluating program effectiveness*

7. *Maintaining the desired change:* How will you know whether your behavioral change program was effective? If your change attempts aren't initially successful, what steps will you take? Also, how do you plan to maintain the desired behaviors once they are attained?

SELF-MANAGEMENT CONTRACT

Short-Term Behavior

Effective dates: From _____ to _____ .

The following behavior will be monitored by: _____ .

Behavior: _____

Monitoring will occur: _____
(when or in what situations)

Whenever _____ *occurs at* _____ ,
(behavior)   (specified level)

_____ *will award* _____ _____ .
(self or other)   (consequence)

Whenever the behavior does not occur at the specified level, the following consequence will occur: _____

Contract may be revised on: _____
(date)

Signatures: _____

                   _____

                   _____

SKILLS PRACTICE

4-8   *Skill Level:* **CHALLENGING**

Applying Expectancy Theory

Skill Objective

To develop skill in applying expectancy theory to the effective management of employee motivation. Note: Download the worksheet developed for this exercise from the textbook Web site.

Procedure

1. Form groups of three to five students (optional).

2. Identify an individual who is currently employed full time. This person can be an employee or a manager and can work for any type of organization. Ask

if you can interview him or her for about 15 minutes.

3. Based on expectancy theory, ask the person you are interviewing the following questions.

Expectancy Theory Assessment Interview Questions

> What is your position title?
> What is the name of your company?
> What business(es) is your company involved in?
> What are the key tasks and responsibilities that your job entails?
> Overall, to what extent are you motivated to perform your job at a high level?
> To what extent do you believe you can perform your job at a high level, if you make an effort? Why is this the case? Be specific.
> To what extent do you think there are positive consequences (e.g., rewards) associated with performing your job at a high level? Why is this the case? Be specific.
> How do you feel about the consequences you believe are linked to performing your job at a high level? Do you like them, feel indifferent toward them, or dislike them? Why?
> To what extent do you think there are negative consequences (e.g., verbal or written reprimands) associated with performing your job at a low level? Why is this the case? Be specific.
> How do you feel about the consequences you believe are linked to performing your job at a low level? Are you indifferent toward them, or do you dislike them? Why?

4. Once you have completed the interview, assess the person's level of work motivation based on his or her expectancy, instrumentality, and valence perceptions.

5. Now develop an action plan consisting of a set of specific actions that could be taken to increase this person's motivation. Be sure to discuss how your recommendations address the various components of expectancy theory.

6. Present your assessment and action plan to the class. Be sure to present your recommendations in terms of specific actions you would take to enhance the motivation of the employee in the scenario.

SKILLS PRACTICE

4-9   *Skill Level: CHALLENGING*

Applying Equity Theory

Skill Objective

To develop skill in applying equity theory to real-world work situations. Note: Download the worksheet developed for this exercise from the textbook Web site.

Procedure

1. Select one of the following scenarios.

Scenario 1: The Unbalanced Workloads

You are the supervisor of the bill-processing department at a large utility company based in Boca Raton, Florida. You have 16 clerical workers who are responsible for processing the payment of incoming bills from the company's customers. Everyone in your work unit has a cubicle in an open work environment where employees can see each other easily. As the supervisor of the department, you have an office located adjacent to the area where your clerical employees perform their jobs.

All of the clerical workers in your department are relatively new, so their job tenure and compensation all fall within a narrow range. Merit pay increases are supposed to be given each year, but management has decided just to give everyone a standard 3 percent pay increase each year rather than differentiate pay increases based on performance.

A recent job satisfaction survey administered to your employees revealed that many of them perceive tremendous inequities in the amount of work they have to do relative to their coworkers in the department. On the survey, many employees commented that some employees always get a lot of work to do while others sit around having personal conversations on their phones, surfing the Internet, or playing electronic blackjack on their computers.

This situation has resulted in a high level of frustration for many of the clerical employees. Some employees have been talking about transferring to other departments or finding employment with another company altogether.

Based on equity theory, what would you do to handle this situation?

Scenario 2: The Compensation "Outlier"

You are the director of software applications at a medium-size business software firm based in California. You have a team of 10 software programmers who work to develop new software for the firm. Your current staff members have an average of seven years of programming experience and make an average of $50,000 per year.

Recently, the company has experienced a dramatic increase in the need for new, talented programmers for entry-level positions. Given a tremendous shortage of qualified computer programmers graduating from the top universities, the starting salaries for new, entry-level programmers has risen to $45,000 to $50,000 per year. Although this is generally accepted as the norm among employers hiring computer programmers in today's job market, it has created significant frustration and dissatisfaction among your existing staff. Specifically, your experienced staff does not feel it is fair for new programmers straight out of college to be making almost as much money (or in some cases the same amount) as they do. In addition, they know the new programmers are not capable of han-

dling the kinds of advanced projects they are working on at the present time.

Nobody has quit over this issue yet, but you are concerned about the adverse effect it has had on some current employees' morale and motivation. Using equity theory, how would you handle this situation?

2. Develop an action plan (i.e., a list of steps you would take) for establishing and maintaining payment equity in the scenario you selected.
3. Answer the following discussion questions as a class.

Discussion Questions

1. Why are perceptions important in equity theory? Why are perceptions important in the real world?
2. What was the problem in the scenario you selected? What were the relevant perceptions of the employees in your scenario?
3. What kinds of actions did you recommend in order to establish and maintain payment equity in your scenario?
4. What are the practical implications of this exercise for you as a future manager?

SKILLS PRACTICE

4-10   *Skill Level:* CHALLENGING

Applying Job Characteristics Theory to Increase Employee Motivation

Skill Objective

To develop skill in using job characteristics theory to enrich jobs and enhance employee motivation, performance, and satisfaction.

Procedure

1. Select one job you are familiar with. Ideally, this will be a current job or one you held in the past.
2. List the major tasks and responsibilities associated with the job you selected. This does not need to be exhaustive; just try to identify the most important aspects of the job.
3. Below your list of job tasks and responsibilities, rate the job in terms of the following:
   > Perceived levels of each of the five core job dimensions (i.e., low, moderate, or high)
   > Your satisfaction with the job
   > Your motivation to perform the job
   > Your actual performance on the job
4. Now take another piece of paper and write the

name of each core job dimension on it with some space underneath each one. Brainstorm a list of things (two or three strategies) that could be implemented in order to increase your perceived level of each core job dimension. Remember: you want to perceive that the job possesses a high level of all five of the core job dimensions. Be as specific and action oriented as possible.

5. Present to the class your job redesign plan from the preceding step. Explain why each of your strategies would help increase the perceived level of each core job dimension and the personal and work outcomes identified by the theory.
6. Answer the following discussion questions.

Discussion Questions

1. Why should a manager be concerned about job design?
2. How is job characteristics theory useful in designing good jobs?

3. What are the keys to the successful implementation of job design and job redesign in organizations? What are the major barriers to making job design work?

4. What are the practical implications of this exercise for you as a future manager?

SKILLS PRACTICE

Developing Motivational Strategies Using the FISH! Philosophy

Skill Objective

To develop skill in creating employee motivational programs based on Lundin, Christensen, and Paul's FISH! Philosophy.[77]

Overview

FISH!, developed by Lundin, Christensen, and Paul, is a motivational framework for energizing work environments in organizations. It is based on the researchers' observations of the spirit and enthusiasm of workers throwing fish around at Seattle's Pike's Place Fish Market. While standing in a drizzle and handling cold dead fish might seem like a nasty way to make a living, the fish mongers at Pike's Place decided they would enjoy their work. The focus of the FISH! philosophy is to identify the characteristics of the work environment at the fish market that make it so motivating and determine how to export them to the work environments in other organizations. This exercise will give you an opportunity to apply FISH! and to evaluate it as a motivational framework.

Procedure

Note: Download the worksheet developed for this exercise from the Web site for this textbook.

1. Read the following brief description of the four principles of the FISH! philosophy presented by Lundin, Christensen, and Paul in their best-selling books (S. C. Lundin, H. Paul, and J. Christensen, *FISH!* [New York: Hyperion Press, 2000]; and *FISH!Tales* [New York. Hyperion Press/ChartHouse International Learning, 2002]). To learn more about the FISH! philosophy, go to:

http://www.charthouse.com/product_film_fp.asp

The Fish! philosophy says a work environment that will energize and motivate workers possesses the following four characteristics:

- **Play.** Make the work environment fun and people will be energized and more creative in their work. Serious tasks can benefit from fun if they are performed in a spontaneous and light-hearted manner.

- **Make Their Day.** Special memories in a work environment can be created when people practice small acts of kindness or unforgettable engagements with their coworkers and customers.

- **Be There.** This refers to the concept of truly being present for one another in everyday encounters with coworkers and customers. This can help fight employee burnout because it does not result in the loss of energy associated with just "going through the motions" in performing one's job.

- **Choose Your Attitude.** When you look for the best in a situation and maintain a positive attitude, you give yourself the power to choose your response to that situation and to realize opportunities that may not have been present otherwise.

2. Describe the worst job you have ever had during your career in a few paragraphs. Be sure to explain why this job was so bad in as much detail as possible.

3. Based on step 2, brainstorm a list of actions (an action plan) that you could take to create a new work environment that possesses each of the four elements of the FISH! philosophy. Be specific and action oriented.

4. When you are finished, present your action plan to the class in a three- to five-minute presentation. Be sure to explain how you would ensure that your action plan gets implemented effectively. In addition, make sure you justify why your plan would work in terms of feasibility, effectiveness, and cost.

Discussion Questions

1. Evaluate the FISH! Philosophy. Do you believe it has merit? Why or why not?

2. How are the elements of the FISH! philosophy related to the various theories of motivation discussed in this chapter? How is the FISH! philosophy similar to other motivation theories? How is it different?

3. What kinds of strategies would need to be used to motivate managers and employees in a large

organization to embrace the elements of the FISH! philosophy and to put them into practice on a daily basis?

SKILLS PRACTICE

Making Sense of Motivation Theories

Skill Objective

To develop skill in integrating and synthesizing various theories of motivation into a coherent overall understanding of motivation that can ultimately facilitate the management of workers in a real world organization.

Procedure

Note: Download the worksheet developed for this exercise from the Web site for this textbook to facilitate your work.

1. Form groups of three or five individuals.
2. Briefly review this chapter in order to make a list of the following theories of motivation that were presented. This should include Alderfer's ERG theory, operant conditioning, goal setting, expectancy theory, equity theory, and job characteristics theory.
3. Try to think of these theories as the pieces of a puzzle. Your task is to try to fit them together in a way that makes sense to you. Draw a basic diagram of each model (or download the worksheets for this

4. What are the practical implications of this exercise for you as a future manager and leader of a real-world organization?

exercise from the Web site for this textbook) and place them side by side on the wall with some tape.
4. Brainstorm a list of the similarities and differences among the theories on your worksheet.
5. Now brainstorm a list of what you feel are the most useful elements of all of these theories on your worksheet. Draw a diagram that shows of these elements together in a visual format. This can just be a listing of each element with a box around it and having an arrow pointing toward another box called "motivation."

Discussion Questions

1. Present the results of your work based on completing this exercise. What were your most significant findings? Why?
2. Clearly, this was a *very* challenging exercise, but why it is important to do this kind of an activity, especially for the topic of motivation?
3. How can doing this exercise help you become a better motivator of workers in the future?

MANAGING STRESS

CHAPTER 5

Skills Objectives

> *To develop skill in assessing your personal and work stressors and how they are related to your stress reactions in various situations.*

> *To develop and implement strategies to enhance your ability to cope with stressful work situations.*

> *To develop skill in designing and implementing stress management programs for workers in real-world organizational settings.*

KNOWLEDGE OBJECTIVES

> Discuss the prevalence and nature of stress.

> Identify key stressors.

> Discuss personal characteristics that influence stress.

> Recognize signs of stress.

> Identify components and consequences of burnout.

> Understand personal approaches to managing stress.

> Understand organizational approaches to managing stress.

How important is stress? One indication is that a September 1, 2003, Google search yielded a remarkable 8,430,003 hits on stress. Why all this interest? Stress is a cause of psychological problems as well as physical reactions, such as high blood pressure, backaches, and heart disease; an estimated 75 to 90 percent of visits to doctors are somehow stress related.[1] Stress is associated with high levels of dissatisfaction, absenteeism, turnover, lost productivity, and lawsuits. It may also result in a climate that stifles creativity. It has been implicated in workplace violence and employee suicide.[2] Total stress-related costs to U.S. business are estimated at $200 to $300 billion annually.[3] An estimated 65 million Americans suffer symptoms of stress, spending more than $370 million a year on stress-busting fitness routines and stress-related pharmaceutical drugs and books.[4]

The Microsoft Lexicon is an online "compilation of slang peculiar to the Microsoft working environment." Here is the lexicon's definition of "Death March":

Death March: The long, lingering final countdown to a ship date, involving 16–25-hour days, catnaps on couches, and plenty of "flat food" (food, mostly from vending machines, that you can slip under people's doors so they can keep working).

Although the term **death march** is used in a tongue-in-cheek fashion at Microsoft to refer to the stress of meeting looming deadlines, stress is, in fact, a very real killer.[5] For instance, **karoshi**, three Japanese characters that literally mean "excessive," "labor," and "death," is a term used to describe sudden death from heart attack or stroke induced by job stress. Japanese work, on average, 225 hours, or almost six workweeks, more per year than their American counterparts. One in six male Japanese workers puts in more than 3,100 hours annually—or about 60 hours a week, 52 weeks a year. Their overwork is driven in part by employers' demands and expected loyalty to the company and by the weakness of Japan's labor unions and the country's strong work ethic. It appears that karoshi results primarily from feelings of depression and helplessness combined with overwork. Karoshi is now recognized by the Japanese government as a cause of death under the country's workers' compensation law. Dentsu, Japan's largest advertising agency, was ordered to pay the equivalent of $1.2 million to the family of Ichiro Oshima, an employee who killed himself after working exceptionally long hours. In the eight months before his death, Oshima, a radio-commercial planner, had worked from early in the morning until well past 2 A.M. for 105 days and beyond 4 A.M. for 49 days. Although only about 75 Japanese per year have been formally identified under the law as succumbing to karoshi, some estimates place karoshi deaths at 10,000 to 30,000 annually, with tens of thousands of others suffering serious physical and mental health consequences.[6] Recognizing the dangers of karoshi, the Japanese Labor Ministry has asked the Japan Federation of Employers' Associations, Nikkerien, to join in efforts to prevent stress-related deaths, in part through reduced overtime demands. In addition, Japan's prime minister has proposed legislation aimed at encouraging citizens to reduce their work hours and to take more holidays.[7]

This chapter examines stress and burnout, including the nature of stress, primary stressors, signs of stress, the characteristics of burnout, and personal and organizational approaches to stress management. As a way to assess your initial level of skill in managing issues related to stress in organizations, read the Pretest Skills Assessment and develop an action plan for handling this situation. Be as specific as possible in stating your recommendations. After you are through, visit the text Web site to get feedback on the exercise.

PRETEST SKILLS ASSESSMENT

Managing Stress

You are the head nurse supervisor for the evening shift in the emergency room at a large hospital located in Atlanta, Georgia. You oversee 15 nurses who work from 11 P.M. until 6 A.M. Because the hospital is located in a large city, a high volume of patients comes in for various reasons. The work environment is fast paced, and the workload is tremendous. In fact, some of your nurses have worked double shifts in order to help care for the flow of patients who come into the hospital.

In the last year, the morale of the nurses in the emergency room has plummeted. The absenteeism rate for the night shift has tripled because many nurses are calling in sick. Turnover has risen to 70 percent per year as well. Some nurses have left for other nursing jobs that provide better working hours, a more reasonable workload, and greater opportunities for personal and professional development. Other nurses have left to pursue careers in different fields. All this comes at a bad time because of the national shortage of nurses.

As the supervisor of this work unit, develop an action plan for handling this situation. Be specific and focus on action.

Now take a few minutes to complete Self-Assessment 5-1, "Tension and Anxiety." It will provide you with information about the degree to which you currently experience symptoms of stress. After you have completed the self-assessment, visit the text Web site to see how your results compare to those of other people.

SELF-ASSESSMENT 5-1

Tension and Anxiety

Answer each of the questions in this section using the following scale:

1 Disagree strongly
2 Disagree somewhat
3 Neither agree nor disagree
4 Agree somewhat
5 Agree strongly

____ 1. I have trouble relaxing at home.
____ 2. My workload is under control.
____ 3. I use alcohol or other drugs to help me relax.
____ 4. I have trouble sleeping.
____ 5. When I get up in the morning, I look forward to the day.
____ 6. I feel nervous under pressure.
____ 7. I have a constant fear of failure.
____ 8. I feel short-tempered and irritable.
____ 9. I find myself angry with people I care about.
____ 10. At the end of the day, I usually have a sense of accomplishment.
____ 11. I find fault with all sorts of things.
____ 12. I don't find much pleasure in life.
____ 13. I haven't been happy lately.

_____ 14. I'm not exercising as much as I used to.

_____ 15. I often feel extreme irritation over small things.

_____ 16. I look forward to meeting new people and doing new things.

_____ 17. I often feel hounded, cornered, or trapped.

_____ 18. I lack energy.

_____ 19. I often feel I just can't cope.

_____ 20. I sometimes have feelings of hopelessness.

_____ 21. I am unable to stop thinking about my problems.

_____ 22. I often feel preoccupied and indecisive.

_____ 23. My muscles often feel tense and achy.

_____ 24. I often feel I can't do anything right.

_____ 25. I engage in a variety of pleasant hobbies and other activities.

Next let's consider the nature of stress and methods to recognize and manage stress at both a personal and an organizational level.

THE NATURE OF STRESS

As shown in Figure 5-1, we must consider three concepts—stressors, stress, and stress reactions—when trying to deal effectively with stress.

Stressors are environmental factors (deadlines, noise, rules, demanding bosses, and the like) that raise stress levels. **Stress** is a physiological state resulting from stressors. As shown in Figure 5-2, when faced with stressors, our body undergoes a complex set of reactions aimed at preparing us to engage effectively in "fight or flight"—striking back at the stressor or escaping it. Finally, as we discuss shortly, **stress reactions** are mental and physical responses to stress.

The processes involved in stress may be effective in countering immediate threats, but they also burden the body's resources. Hans Selye has described a *general adaptation syndrome* of the body's responses to a stressor. As shown in Figure 5-3, the general adaptation syndrome has three stages. First, in the alarm stage, the body gears up for action. Then, in the resistance stage, the body tries to fight back at the stressor. Finally, in the exhaustion stage, the body's resources are drained, and resistance is no longer possible.

STRESS REACTIONS

As suggested by the general adaptation syndrome, not all stress is bad; stress may help us prepare for a challenge. However, prolonged exposure to stressors may be debilitating. As shown in Figure 5-4, at low levels stress is an activating force, called *eustress*

FIGURE 5-1
Concepts Involved in Stress Management

FIGURE 5-2
Physiological Reactions in Stress

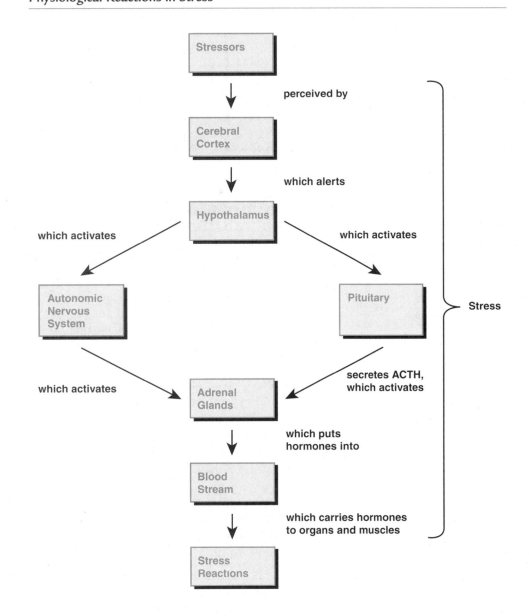

from the Greek "eu," meaning good. However, excessive levels of stress, called *distress*, have negative consequences. Most employees already face at least moderate levels of stress. American doctors write 25 million prescriptions a year for sedatives such as Valium.[8] So almost any increase in organizational stressors is likely to cause distress.

STRESSORS

Almost anything can be a stressor: job insecurity, poor working conditions, excessive responsibility, job loss, office politics, family concerns, and so on. In this section, we consider some primary stressors.

FIGURE 5-3
The General Adaptation Syndrome

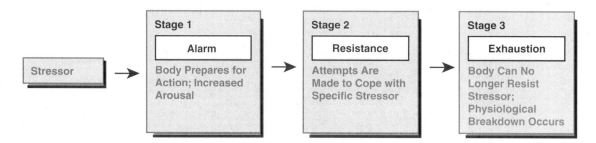

WORK ENVIRONMENT

The key stressors faced by our early ancestors came from the physical environment, such as hostile weather, threatening animals, and uncertain food supplies. Civilization has expanded the range of stressors, but the work environment continues to provide challenges. For instance, some jobs are by their nature risky. In the United States, commercial fishing is the most dangerous job, with Alaskan crab fishing topping the list; in recent years, it has had an average of one injury per employee per year (a figure rendered more remarkable by the fact that the crab-fishing season lasts only a few weeks), and the fatal accident rate is 100 times the national average.[9] Police work, fire fighting, and timber cutting are other highest risk jobs. The Focus on Management feature discusses the stress experienced by members of the New York City Fire Department following the awful events of September 11, 2001.

Many other jobs pose subtler dangers, such as prolonged noise, glaring or inadequate lighting, excessive temperature variations, poor air quality, or required repetitive motions. For instance, building-related illness and sick building syndrome[10] are now cited as major stressors. After the energy crisis of the 1970s, buildings were

FIGURE 5-4
Eustress and Distress

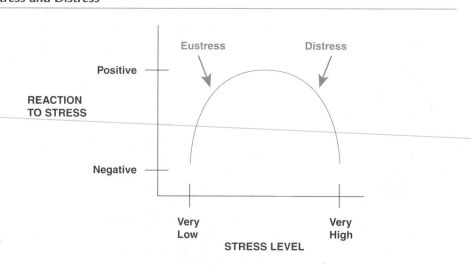

FOCUS ON MANAGEMENT

FDNY Tries to Rescue Its Own[11]

Members of the New York City Fire Department (FDNY) played heroic roles following the September 11, 2001, terrorist attacks on the World Trade Center. Now the FDNY is facing another rescue attempt, this time trying to find and treat emotionally troubled firefighters. In late 2002, full-page newspaper ads began appearing, bearing the simple plea, "SAVE THE FDNY." The ads, sponsored by the Uniformed Firefighters Association, brought attention to the fact that New York firefighters were retiring at twice the previous year's rate, with the force losing 40 of its

most experienced firefighters each week. In the wake of 9/11 the firefighters in the New York City Fire Department face incredible stress. Many firefighters had died during rescue efforts after the attacks. Many more suffered severe health problems, including a lung inflammation called allergic alveolitis, from breathing the dense plumes of dust and debris after the Twin Towers collapsed. The nightmarish events of the day haunt surviving FDNY members, causing more than 100 to take stress leaves and many more to seek psychological help at an FDNY counseling unit. The unit, with 22 clinicians and 33 counselors, is a six-day-a-week operation, and people

service the phones 7 days a week, 24 hours a day. Michael O'Keefe, a battalion chief who helps administer the unit, says, "In the days and weeks following [9/11] all we had were tasks. We worked 24 hours. Then we attended funerals—there were days of ten to twelve funerals. There is more time now," he says, to remember and think, which inevitably leads to even greater stress. There are simply not enough counselors. The head of the unit, Malachy Corrigan, says, "We are bursting—literally—in terms of space, and also bursting in terms of patient load. How many can you see in one day? Clients are telling us about body parts. It is very difficult work."

made tight. Windows were sealed in commercial buildings, and the buildings depended solely on mechanical ventilation to supply heating, cooling, and humidity. Now mildew, fungi, viruses, and bacteria abound, as do chemicals from carpet, paint, photocopier toner, radon and its decay products, and many other contaminants.[12] Indoor air is much more seriously polluted than outdoor air in even the largest and most industrialized cities.[13] Building-related illness and sick building syndrome have been implicated in respiratory/lung problems; asthma; stroke; eye, ear, nose, and throat irritation; headaches, dizziness, and fatigue; emphysema; heart disease; cancer; organ damage; and acute toxicity.[14]

INTERPERSONAL CONFLICT

We have all encountered people with whom we simply can't get along; we find them to be somehow offensive or irritating. Generally, we try to avoid such people. In the workplace, though, we may have coworkers, subordinates, or even superiors we can't stand and with whom we must deal on a daily basis—and may have to do so for years into the future. Worse, we may have to depend on such people for our jobs, salary increases, or promotions. It's not surprising that this can serve as a very debilitating stressor.[15]

SPECIFIC JOB DEMANDS

By their nature, managerial jobs and many other jobs in organizations require specific activities that may be stressors for many people. For instance, the manager's job is full of demands to communicate with individuals or groups. When people are asked to list their greatest fears, death usually shows up somewhere in the top five.[16] For many people, public speaking is at the top rung on the fear ladder. The thought of standing in front of others, possibly looking nervous, boring the audience, being laughed at, or saying something foolish paralyzes many people. Generally, audience members aren't aware of a speaker's stage fright, and nervousness may actually enhance the vitality and enthusiasm brought to the situation.[17] Nevertheless, the stress induced by the fear of speaking is very real.

EMOTIONAL LABOR

Imagine you are in a bad time in your life. Perhaps a loved one has died or your child has a chronic illness or you're concerned about the emotional health of a friend. Suppose, too, that you have to go to work every day during those hard times and your job requires you to be upbeat: you must smile at customers, greet them enthusiastically, interact with them warmly, and leave them with the admonition to "have a nice day." Such work demands *emotional labor*, the required public display of emotions that employees may not feel privately.[18] The consequences of this emotional labor include a deadened emotional state and burnout.[19]

LIFE EVENTS

Another stressor is life change (or even imagined change).[20] Our bodies see changes, whether good or bad, as stressors requiring some reaction. As shown in Figure 5-5, many common organizational actions—geographical reassignments, promotions, early retirements, reprimands, firings—can have tremendous cumulative life impacts. For instance, experts have identified two peaks in death rates for retired men: one at age 65 and one in the mid-80s. The first peak corresponds to the postretirement adjustment period.[21] Note that the stressors listed in Figure 5-5 aren't all bad. Even desirable changes, such as a promotion or vacation, are stress inducing. Research shows that people experiencing very high levels of life change as measured by this scale experienced much higher levels of stress and were more likely to have health problems than those with low levels of life change.[22]

FIGURE 5-5

Stressful Life Events

Event	Relative Stressfulness
Death of a spouse	100
Divorce	73
Marital separation	65
Jail term	63
Death of a close family member	63
Personal injury or illness	53
Marriage	50
Firing from a job	47
Retirement	45
Pregnancy	40
Death of a close friend	37
Son or daughter leaving home	29
Trouble with in-laws	28
Trouble with boss	23
Change in residence	20
Vacation	13
Christmas	12
Minor violations of the law	11

HASSLES

Big things, such as deaths and disasters, are clearly stress inducing, but so are daily hassles. A troublesome neighbor, home renovations, a long daily commute, financing children's education, and even dealing with a malfunctioning teller machine can all add to our stress levels.[23] What these situations lack in severity they make up in frequency.

ROLE STRESSORS

Jobs with conflicting expectations (called *role conflict*) or unclear expectations (called *role ambiguity*) about what an employee is supposed to do at work serve as major stressors. Role conflict and role ambiguity have been shown to lead to dissatisfaction, absenteeism, turnover, poor performance, and a host of other undesirable outcomes.

Role ambiguity occurs when people:

> lack clear information about what they are expected to accomplish;
> know what outcomes are expected but don't know how to achieve those outcomes; or
> don't know what personal costs or benefits are associated with meeting particular expectations.

Role conflict may take many forms:

> **Intersender role conflict** results from conflicting expectations of different role senders. For example, supervisors sometimes find that their subordinates expect them to identify with labor while their superiors expect them to see themselves as part of management.
> **Intrasender role conflict** occurs when a single role sender transmits incompatible expectations. This situation might occur, for instance, if a boss says to place more emphasis on quality while at the same time demanding greater quantity.
> **Inter-role conflict** comes about through incompatible demands of different roles. A person's role as operations manager of a company that needs wetlands to expand production capacity may conflict with her role as officer of a local conservation group.[24]
> **Person-role conflict** results from clashes between role demands and personal values and expectations. A police officer called on to evict an aging tenant or a manager who must fire loyal employees because of budget cuts may experience person-role conflict. Or consider shelter workers at the ASPCA. People are drawn to work at the shelters because they love animals, but they must often kill young, healthy animals. It's not surprising that shelter workers suffer a wide range of distressing reactions, including grief, anger, nightmares, and depression.[25]

In addition, when the level or nature of job demands is inconsistent with an employee's capabilities and interests, *role overload* or *role underload* may occur. As shown in Figure 5-6, either role overload or role underload may be quantitative or qualitative. We may be overwhelmed with too much to do (quantitative overload) or bored with too little to do (quantitative underload). Similarly, we may be frustrated

FIGURE 5-6
Role Overload and Underload

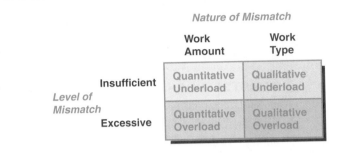

by being given types of tasks beyond our capabilities (qualitative overload) or by being faced with simple, tedious, perhaps demeaning work (qualitative underload).

RESPONSIBILITY FOR OTHERS

It is often stressful enough to have to take care of ourselves. When we must also accept responsibility for the welfare of others, the level of our stressors escalates. Managers may feel responsible for the welfare of their subordinates and mentors for the welfare of their protégés. Similarly, employees may have to care for children at home or for elderly relatives. The latter set of responsibilities—called *eldercare*— is a growing problem both for employees and employers. A study by the American Association of Retired Persons found that people with heavy eldercare responsibilities reported feelings of depression about six times the national average.[26] A growing number of baby boomers—members of the so-called *sandwich generation*—find themselves pressed on one side by child-care responsibilities and on the other by the need to care for elderly parents and relatives.[27] Companies lose an estimated $25 to $30 billion a year because of employees' caregiving responsibilities.[28]

DEALING WITH OTHERS' STRESS: THE TOXIC HANDLERS

In the Martin Scorsese movie *Bringing out the Dead*, Nicholas Cage plays a New York paramedic working the graveyard shift in Hell's Kitchen.[29] The nightly horrors of his job take an exhausting toll on his life; he cannot bring himself to eat, and his sleep is haunted by visions of a young woman who died as he tried to revive her. Cage's character is one form of *toxic handler*, someone who must deal regularly with the sorrows and ill fortune of others as part of the job. Many managers in organizations also are toxic handlers, voluntarily shouldering the sadness, frustration, bitterness, and anger of others to help the organization accomplish its goals.[30]

PERSONAL CHARACTERISTICS THAT INFLUENCE STRESS

Some people bounce back better in the face of stressors than others do. These resilient individuals tend to share some personality characteristics, including low levels of the type A behavior pattern, high levels of hardiness and optimism, and rapid tension discharge rate.

> **Type A behavior pattern.** As we discussed in Chapter 2, the *Type A behavior pattern* is characterized by feelings of great time pressure and impatience. Type A persons work aggressively, speak explosively, and find themselves constantly struggling. The opposite pattern—relaxed, steady paced, and easygoing—is called the *type B behavior pattern*. The type A is much more likely than the type B to experience high stress levels and to suffer negative stress reactions, including fatal heart attacks.[31] It appears that one dimension of type A behavior—hostility—is the key culprit in leading to negative stress reactions.

> **Hardiness.** Hardy individuals have high levels of commitment to their jobs, believe they can control their outcomes, and see stress as a challenge. These three components of commitment, control, and challenge combine to provide resistance to the adverse effects of stress.[32]

> **Tension discharge rate.** Suppose your boss has humiliated you in front of your coworkers, blaming you for the department's failure to meet a critical deadline. You feel the missed deadline is the boss's fault but know you can't strike back at him. Instead, you keep quiet, silently seething. What then? Would you continue to dwell on this injustice, replaying it in your mind and getting more and more angry, or would you be able to let it go? Those who can let it go—who have high *tension discharge rates*—deal better with stress.[33]

> **Optimism.** Someone has said, "Whether you believe you can succeed or that you can't, you're right." Life is often a self-fulfilling prophecy. People who believe events will turn out well are more self-confident, set higher personal goals, adopt problem-focused coping styles, persist in the face of difficulties, and generate enthusiasm in others. As a result, they do better than those who anticipate bad outcomes. Optimists assume their troubles are temporary ("I'm tired today") rather than permanent ("I'm washed up") and specific ("I have a bad habit") rather than universal ("I'm a bad person"). Also, they give themselves credit when things go right and often externalize their failures ("That was a tough audience" rather than "I gave a bad speech").[34]

Signs of Stress

The many signs of stress include the following:

> Trouble concentrating.
> Working excessively but not effectively.
> Feeling you've lost perspective on what's important in life.
> Angry outbursts.
> Changes in sleeping patterns.
> Loss of interest in social and recreational activities.
> Prolonged fatigue.
> Increases in smoking, drinking, and eating.
> A feeling you just can't face the day.

Burnout

The constellation of stress reactions is sometimes called *burnout*, a process of emotional exhaustion, depersonalization, and diminished accomplishment, with low job satisfaction and a reduced sense of competence.[35] As shown in Figure 5-7, the four major components to burnout are physical exhaustion, emotional exhaustion, attitudinal exhaustion, and feelings of low personal accomplishment. Of these, emotional exhaustion seems to have the strongest links to undesirable personal and organizational outcomes. For instance, emotional exhaustion is positively related to turnover intentions and negatively associated with commitment to the organization, job performance, and willingness to engage in so-called good citizenship behaviors.[36]

Burnout is a serious threat not just to performance but also to health and life. In the following section we turn to guidelines for managing stress and burnout.[37]

GUIDELINES FOR MANAGING PERSONAL STRESS

What can you do about stress?

> **Take it seriously.** Act as if stress is a matter of life and death—because it is.
> **Manage your time.** Here are some guidelines for time management:[38]
>   • **Conduct a time analysis.** Make a list of all the routine activities you perform and record the time you spend on each activity. After a month, add up the totals and see what things are making the greatest demands on your time. You'll probably find time-consuming activities that can be trimmed.[39]
>   • **Set priorities and plan a time budget.** Schedule activities, being sure to leave some slack time (perhaps 10 to 15 percent of your time) for unexpected emergencies and opportunities. Plan your work and work your plan.
>   • **Schedule leisure activities.** Build time into your schedule for relaxation and recuperation. If not, they'll be driven out by other things.
>   • **Ask which tasks can be curtailed.** Categorize tasks in terms of their urgency and importance. Sort mail and other tasks into A—urgent and

FIGURE 5-7
Major Components of Burnout

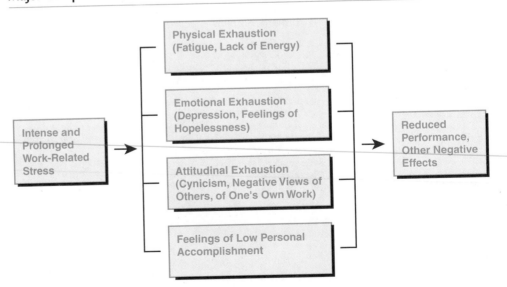

important; B—not urgent but important; C—urgent but not important; and D—neither urgent nor important. Focus on you're A's and B's.

- **Try to accumulate similar tasks and handle them together.** For instance, set aside one block of time to write letters, another to return phone calls, and so on.
- **Learn to say no.** Trying to do everything for everyone will hurt both you and others. Unless you learn to say no, you'll be overwhelmed, and the work you do will suffer.
- **Don't procrastinate.** Procrastination may be the single most common time management problem. Apply self-management tools to overcome tendencies to procrastinate.[40]
- **Learn to delegate.** Often we are overwhelmed because we are reluctant to pass on work to others. Delegating work is a key component of effective management. It permits you to help develop team members' skills while concentrating on matters of importance.[41]

> **Develop effective coping strategies.** People cope with stress in very different ways. Some run away from stressors, either physically or mentally. Some turn to colleagues or friends for help. Others roll up their sleeves and do their best to deal with the stressor. Still others rethink the stressors, finding ways to view them as opportunities. And some turn to alcohol or other drugs to ease the pain. In general, coping strategies that deal directly with the stressor work better than those that rely on avoidance or treatment of symptoms.[42] Now complete Self-Assessment 5-2, "Coping with Stress." It will help identify the ways you tend to deal with stressful situations. After you have completed the self-assessment, visit the text Web site to see how your results compare to those of other people.

SELF-ASSESSMENT 5-2

Coping with Stress

Answer each of the questions in this self-assessment using the following scale:

1 Disagree strongly
2 Disagree somewhat
3 Neither agree nor disagree
4 Agree somewhat
5 Agree strongly

When I am faced with a stressful situation, I:

____ 1. Do my best to get out of the situation gracefully.
____ 2. Try to address the situation directly and promptly.
____ 3. Try to get additional people involved in the situation.
____ 4. Tell myself that I can probably work things out to my advantage.
____ 5. Avoid being in this situation if I can.
____ 6. Try to see this situation as an opportunity to learn and develop new skills.
____ 7. Work on changing the things that caused this situation.
____ 8. Try to think of myself as a winner—as someone who always comes through.
____ 9. Try to be very organized so I can keep up on things.

____ 10. Turn to others for support.
____ 11. Tell myself that time takes care of situations like this.
____ 12. Ask others to help out.
____ 13. Separate myself as much as possible from the people who created this situation.
____ 14. Remind myself that other people have been in this situation and that I can probably do as well as they did.
____ 15. Seek help or advice from friends or colleagues.
____ 16. Think of ways to use this situation to show what I can do.
____ 17. Work hard to resolve it.
____ 18. Request help from other people who have the power to do something for me.
____ 19. Devote more time and energy to dealing with the situation.
____ 20. Accept the situation because there is nothing I can do to change it.

Next complete Skills Practice 5-1. This exercise will give you an opportunity to get out into the real world and interview some managers about how they handle their own stress and the stress of their employees.

> **Get fit and stay fit.** Physically fit individuals are better able to master stressful situations. Exercise reduces tension, strengthens the cardiovascular system, and sends feel-good drugs, including dopamine and beta-endorphin, to the brain. Also, do your best to get a good night's sleep. When we sleep well, we wake up feeling refreshed and alert and ready to face daily stressors. The National Science Foundation estimates the total annual cost of sleep deprivation and insomnia to U.S. businesses, including absenteeism, accidents, hospitalization, medical costs, and decreased productivity, is as much as $107 billion.[43] Although there are individual differences in how much sleep we need, research shows that people sleeping an average of eight hours a night live longer than those sleeping significantly more or less.[44] Recognizing the costs of employee fatigue, some companies are now permitting their employees to take short "power naps."[45]

> **Let it go.** As we said earlier, people who have high tension discharge rates (i.e., who can quickly let go of a stressful situation) suffer fewer negative stress reactions. Letting go of stress is often difficult. If someone has cut us off in traffic or yelled at us at work, we often continue to stew about it. The more we do this, though, the worse we feel and the greater the likely health consequences. Although it's hard to let it go, we can at least tell ourselves that the longer we dwell on the stressor, the more we let the person or thing bothering us win. Living well is the best revenge.

> **Get a little help from your friends.** People with the support of colleagues, friends, families, and loved ones experience far fewer symptoms of stress than do those without social support. *Social support* helps in at least three ways. First, it can directly reduce the impact of stress by fulfilling critical human needs, such as security and social contact, and by emphasizing positive life and work aspects, such as affiliation and approval. Social support may also buffer the impact of stressors because members of the social support network provide resources to help the individual cope with them.[46] Third, just knowing others are available to help us has positive effects. For example, research

shows that, after controlling for factors such as age and smoking, individuals who believe they have more social support have higher levels of natural killer (NK) cell levels, increasing immune function.[47] If you are lacking social support, seek it out. Work on friendships, keep family ties strong, and find a place to belong: Social groups, local support organizations, and churches, mosques, or synagogues are possibilities.

> **Think positively.** Don't dwell on the worst possible scenario. Treat a stressful situation as an opportunity to show your skills and abilities.

> **Learn to relax.** Use relaxation techniques including the following:

1. The ***Relaxation Response*** is an anti-stress response in which muscle tension, heart rate, and blood pressure decrease and breathing slows. Here are the steps of the Relaxation Response:[48]

   a. Sit quietly in a comfortable position.

   b. Close your eyes.

   c. Deeply relax all muscles, beginning at your feet and progressing up to your face. Keep all muscles relaxed.

   d. Breathe through your nose. Become aware of your breathing. As you breathe out, say the word "one" silently to yourself. For example, breathe in . . . out, "one," in . . . out, "one," and so on. Breathe easily and naturally. You might also say the words "calm" or "let go" as you exhale.

   e. Continue for 10 to 20 minutes. As you feel yourself relax, try to visualize your favorite place—a beach, lake, or a mountain stream. Try to picture it in detail and recall feelings of peace and contentment while being there. You may open your eyes to check the time, but do not use an alarm. When you finish, sit quietly for several minutes, at first with your eyes closed and later with your eyes open. Do not stand up for a few minutes.

   f. Don't worry about whether you are successful in achieving a deep level of relaxation. Maintain a passive attitude and permit relaxation to occur at its own pace. When distracting thoughts occur, try to ignore them by not dwelling on them and return to repeating "one." With practice, the response should come with little effort. Practice the technique once or twice daily, but not within two hours of any meal because the digestive process seems to interfere with the elicitation of the relaxation response.

2. ***Transcendental meditation,*** or ***TM***, is a popular form of meditation that involves sitting comfortably with eyes closed and engaging in the repetition of a special sound for 20 minutes twice a day. Studies show TM is related to reduced heart rate, lowered oxygen consumption, and decreased blood pressure.[49] Medical evidence indicates that practicing TM may help unclog arteries, especially in African Americans with high blood pressure.[50] Meditation has also been shown to alleviate lower back pain, headaches, and arthritis, decrease absenteeism, tardiness, and turnover, increase brain-wave activity, and improve concentration.[51]

3. ***Progressive muscular relaxation,*** or ***PMR***, is a systematic technique for achieving a deep state of relaxation. Developed more than 50 years

ago, PMR is based on the finding that we can relax a muscle by first tensing it for a few seconds and then releasing it. As such, PMR involves tensing and relaxing various muscle groups throughout the body to achieve a deep state of relaxation. PMR is especially helpful for people feeling uptight and experiencing tension headaches, tightness around the eyes, muscle spasms, high blood pressure, and insomnia.[52]

4. *Biofeedback* is a treatment technique in which people are trained to improve their health by using signals from their own bodies. A machine detects, amplifies, and displays small changes in a person's body and brain. For instance, heart rate, blood pressure, temperature, and brain-wave patterns might be displayed. Physical therapists use biofeedback to help stroke victims regain movement in paralyzed muscles. Psychologists help tense and anxious clients learn to relax and specialists in many different fields help patients cope with pain using biofeedback. In a sense, a biofeedback machine acts as a sixth sense that allows us to see or hear activity inside our bodies. One type of biofeedback machine picks up electrical signals in the muscles and translates them into a form that patients can detect. It may, for instance, trigger a flashing light bulb or activate a beeper every time muscles grow more tense. If patients want to relax tense muscles, they try to slow down the flashing or beeping.

> **Manage change.** Avoid unnecessary change and think through the cumulative impact of planned changes.

> **Avoid self-medication.** Those who deal with stress by treating its symptoms—especially by use of alcohol or other drugs—often find themselves in a downward spiral.[53]

> **Practice self-management.** The self-management techniques we discussed in Chapter 4 can be applied effectively to stress management. You could, for instance, use self-management to modify stressors, build social support networks, improve coping styles, or better deal with stress reactions.

> **Get professional help.** Especially if stress is severe, seek out professional guidance. Most campuses and many firms have people whose key role is to provide assistance in times of crisis. Take advantage of them.[54]

Now complete Skills Practice 5-2. This exercise will show you some basic techniques that can really enhance your ability to manage stress more effectively in the real world. Next complete Skills Practice 5-3 to develop a personal stress management program.

ORGANIZATIONAL POLICIES AND PRACTICES FOR MANAGING WORKPLACE STRESS

As a leader, you can do more than manage your own stress; you can help to develop a less stressful work environment. You can do this by clarifying expectations, providing needed coaching and social support, empowering, encouraging family-sensitive work practices (such as on-site child-care facilities and flextime), and teaching stress management skills. We address family-sensitive work practices elsewhere in the book. Let's now consider some other company policies and practices that help manage employees' stress.

STRESS MANAGEMENT PROGRAMS

Many companies now offer programs specifically directed toward stress management. For instance, when Chase Manhattan Corporation was anticipating a 12 percent work force reduction, it initiated a program of lunchtime support groups, led by professional therapists, for employees feeling stress. Ovation Marketing Inc. even provides an in-house professional masseuse to reduce employees' stress and increase their creativity. Ovation also offers a complete exercise room, a sauna, warm yellow lighting, and a large office filled with nothing but soft feather beds and huge down cushions. That area, called the *Pillow Room*, is used for collective brainstorming, solitary daydreaming, and afternoon napping.[55]

WELLNESS PROGRAMS

Today's health care costs are astounding. In the United States, they now total more than $1 trillion annually, or 14 percent of the gross national product. According to *Workforce* magazine, health care spending by employers worked out to $5,266 per employee in 2001.[56] An estimated 50 percent of corporate profits go to health care costs versus only 7 percent three decades ago.[57] For every 100 workers in the country, an average of 27 have cardiovascular disease, 24 have high blood pressure, 50 or more have high cholesterol, 26 are classified as obese, 26 smoke, 10 are heavy drinkers, 60 don't wear seat belts regularly, 50 don't get adequate exercise, and 44 suffer from excessive levels of stress.[58] A study at Steelcase Corporation determined that for every employee who had excessive alcohol consumption, the company paid $597 more per year in health care. The corresponding figures were $488 more for sedentary employees, $327 more for employees with hypertension, and $285 more for smokers.[59] Partly as a result of such figures, 91 percent of organizations now have some sort of health promotion program in place.[60]

FOCUS ON MANAGEMENT

SUCCESSFUL WELLNESS PROGRAMS*

Two notably successful wellness programs are offered by Sentara Healthcare and Chevron Corporation. Both programs were winners of the C. Everett Koop National Health Award. Chevron has an on-site fitness center, coaches who lead stretching exercises during breaks in the offices, and staff specialists who facilitate such "energizers" as stretches and laughter before meetings. Employees can also set "ergonomic breaks" every 15, 30, or 60 minutes on their computers to remind them to take a break and stretch. The company provides healthy choices for snacks and meals at all-day meetings. Sentara began its Healthy Edge program in 1995 for employees at its 60-plus hospitals, nursing homes, and pharmacies. The program incorporates awareness of health risks, handbooks about common disorders and how to treat them, and between 50 and 100 fitness programs on site each month, including aerobics and stretching. Sentara also encourages "power naps" during work hours.

http://www.sentara.com

http://www.chevron.com

*Information from W. Atkinson, "Employee Fatigue," *Management Review,* October 1999, pp. 56–60.

As suggested by the examples just cited, wellness programs take a variety of forms:[61]

> **Assessment activities.** Assessment activities help employees learn their fitness levels and health risks, often through a health screening when people have their height, weight, cholesterol, and blood pressure checked. Assessment may also include a computerized analysis, called a ***health risk appraisal***, which consists of a confidential questionnaire in which employees report their smoking and alcohol consumption levels, weight, age, family history of various illnesses, and so on. This is used to compute a "health age"—the actual age adjusted up or down by health risks and healthy lifestyle practices—as well as specific suggestions for change.

> **Communication materials.** These include such publications as newsletters, paycheck stuffers, posters, and other communications regarding wellness.

> **Self-help materials.** The advantage of self-help is that people can alter their behavior on their own time and in the privacy of their own homes. Some wellness vendors also provide toll-free counseling for employees trying to quit smoking, lose weight, or manage stress on their own. A study conducted for Ford Motor Company by the American Institute of Preventive Medicine showed a 45 percent quit rate for 622 employees who participated in a self-help smoking cessation program. All Ford employees were able to request a self-help kit and, in the materials, they were given a toll-free number they could call to speak at any time with a health educator regarding questions or problems with quitting.

> **Group programs.** Group programs are generally classes conducted by an instructor who comes on site to a union hall or the workplace. These programs permit interaction with a professional and other attendees. Unfortunately, participation rates tend to be low for such programs.

> **Medical self-care instruction.** An estimated 25 percent of the 735 million annual visits to physicians in the United States are unnecessary, as are more than half of the 90 million emergency room visits. As such, medical self-care—teaching employees to become wiser consumers of the health care system—is a promising way to reduce health care costs. Medical self-care programs often include a self-care guide, self-care workshops, a nurse advice line, and promotional materials to reinforce self-care recognition and behaviors.

Wellness programs often incorporate incentives for healthy behavior. These might take the form of charging less for health plan contributions, offering lower coverage charges, providing reimbursement for wellness programs, giving premium discounts to employees who engage in healthy lifestyles, and giving gifts such as T-shirts, water bottles, or golf equipment to participants in wellness programs.[62] At Pitney-Bowes, about 40 percent of employees earn credits each year by participating in wellness programs. These employees get a 5 percent reduction in their health insurance costs. The company estimates that each employee who participates in the program saves the company from $291 to $375 in annual health care costs versus a $40 annual cost to administer the program.[63] Other companies using incentives in their wellness programs include Honeywell, Hoffman-LaRoche, and Coors Brewing Company.[64]

FOCUS ON MANAGEMENT

HEALTH INCENTIVE PROGRAMS AT HOME DEPOT

Ruth Flott, an audit and controls specialist for the Atlanta-based Home Depot, used to feel stressed during much of her first seven years working for this hardware giant. According to a study by the New York Business Group on Health, each employee who, like Flott, suffers from stress, anxiety, or depression misses 16 days of work per year. Listening to Flott testify to the success of the company's health incentive programs is like listening to an evangelist preach at the pulpit. Thanks to the company's stress management, nutrition enhancement, and exercise programs, she is not only less stressed but has lost 62 pounds. "There is no excuse for anyone to be overweight or unhealthy at Home Depot," she says. Her productivity has also improved. "Now I have all this energy. I'm zipping around. I'm alert. I told my boss since I've been working out I'm getting double the work done so how about double the salary," she jokes.[65] Through the company's Better Health wellness program, employees can also get a variety of educational materials, access to local wellness representatives and dieticians, and screening for cholesterol levels.[66]

EMPLOYEE ASSISTANCE PROGRAMS

The line between wellness programs and employee assistance programs (EAPs) is now blurring. However, EAPs have historically been used to help employees with serious personal and organizational problems, often relating to alcoholism and substance abuse. The programs now touch on other serious stressors, including sexual harassment, financial planning, child care and eldercare, depression, and domestic violence.[67] Several organizations now educate their employees about

BOTTOM LINE

THE STRESS MANAGEMENT PROCESS

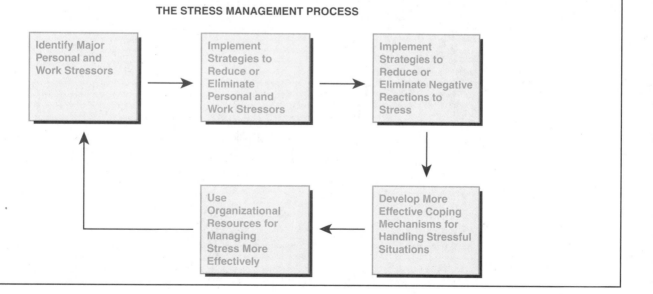

domestic violence and provide in-house assistance programs, including counseling and referrals to community domestic violence programs. Both Polaroid Corporation and Liz Claiborne, Inc., have EAPs that offer treatment and support to employees facing violence in their homes.[68]

It's movie time again. Stop and complete Skills Practice 5-4. The exercise involves watching the movie *Pushing Tin*, about air traffic controllers, and conducting a basic analysis of the film in terms of the job stressors and stress reactions you identify in its various scenes. Enjoy!

The process model in the Bottom Line feature summarizes the basic steps associated with implementation of the stress management process.

Now complete Skills Practice 5-5. This exercise will help you learn how to design and implement an organizational stress management program.

TOP TEN LIST: KEY POINTS TO REMEMBER

MANAGING STRESS

10. Develop and implement personal and job-related strategies for managing yourself more effectively.
9. Always seek to achieve some balance between work and leisure in your life.
8. Enhance your ability to cope with stress by eating right and exercising regularly.
7. Develop and maintain a personal and professional support network.
6. Conduct a formal assessment of the job and life stressors that your employees are experiencing and implement specific strategies to prevent or minimize high levels of employee stress.
5. Monitor yourself and your employees for symptoms of burnout and take corrective action immediately to address the problem.
4. Provide organizational support (e.g., access to employee assistance programs, support groups, fitness programs, stress management workshops) for employees who are experiencing high levels of stress.
3. Remember that very low and very high levels of stressors are both associated with high levels of employee stress.
2. Calculate and monitor the costs associated with employee stress and use this information to justify the development and implementation of a formal stress management program.
1. Remember there will always be some bad days, setbacks, and hassles associated with any job and organization. Recognizing this will help you let go of the negative experiences in a job and to move forward constructively and positively.

QUESTIONS FOR REVIEW AND REFLECTION

REVIEW QUESTIONS

1. Define stressors, stress, and stress reactions.
2. Discuss the set of reactions involved in the physiological state of stress.
3. Explain the three stages of the General Adaptation Syndrome.
4. What is the difference between eustress and distress?
5. Identify four costs of stress.
6. Identify nine primary stressors.
7. What are the three components of hardiness?
8. Identify four types of role conflict.
9. Discuss the various forms of role overload and role underload.
10. Discuss four personal influences on stress.
11. Identify nine signs of stress.
12. What are the major components of burnout?
13. Present 12 guidelines for managing personal stress.
14. List 8 guidelines for time management.
15. What are wellness programs? Describe forms of wellness programs.
16. What are employee assistance programs (EAPs)?

CRITICAL THINKING QUESTIONS

1. After listening to a presentation on company programs for managing stress, your boss says, "This really bothers me. Stress is a natural part of any job. When employees take a job as a telemarketer or customer service representative or manager or whatever, they know the job's demands are likely to be stressful. If people can't handle the stress, they should look for other jobs. The company shouldn't have to spend time and money to compensate for employees' weaknesses." Take and defend a position for or against your boss's arguments.
2. A colleague says, "I just can't accept the idea that desirable changes are stressful. They're exciting and stimulating, but I see that as something very different from stress." How would you respond?
3. Some companies are now giving incentives to employees who engage in healthy behaviors. Consider the

following argument: "What matters to employees and companies is the state of the employees' health, not just whether they're currently engaging in certain types of healthy behaviors. Companies should be rewarding employees for their health status, not their healthy behaviors." Present your views on this argument.

4. A friend says, "It's easy to say that optimistic people deal better with stress. But what if optimism isn't war- ranted? Am I supposed to try to kid myself? That seems dangerous. It seems better to me to be realistic than optimistic." Do you agree? How would you respond?

5. One response to complaints about high levels of job stress is to say, "Welcome to the 21st century. Stress isn't going away, and it will only get worse. Get over it." Do you agree stress is an inevitable consequence of the modern workplace? Why or why not?

EXPERIENTIAL EXERCISES

WEB EXERCISE 5-1

Stress Management and Emotional Wellness Links

The following Web site offers hundreds of links to stress management and emotional wellness resources, including cognitive approaches to stress management, humor and health, relaxation techniques, time management strategies, approaches to increasing social support networks, nutri- tional approaches to stress management, exercise and stress management, emotional self-help, and much more:

http://imt.net/~randolfi/StressLinks.html

Visit the site and then complete the following tasks:

1. Select three links from the site that seem potentially useful and/or interesting to you (for instance, Bio- feedback Webzine, Mantra Meditation, and Panic Coping Skills).
2. Visit those three sites and examine the resources, pro- viding a short (two-paragraph) discussion of each.
3. Provide your reactions to each of the sites. Were they interesting? Useful? Would you use them again? How might they help you as a manager?

WEB EXERCISE 5-2

Mind Tools

The MindTools Stress Management Techniques page pro- vides tools for dealing with stress. Go to the MindTools page at:

http://www.mindtools.com/smpage.html

On the page you will find recommendations and exer- cises relating to personal stress management, including Stress Diary, "Psyching Up," Anticipating Stress, Time Man- agement, Physical Relaxation Techniques, Health and Nutrition, and other stress management approaches.

1. Read the "Stress Diary" section and keep a stress diary for a week, following the guidelines provided.
2. Write a one-page summary of your analysis of the diary. What were the key things you learned in keeping the diary?
3. Choose two of the other approaches and discuss ways in which you could personally use each. Provide specifics about application to your personal life.

CASE 5-1

THE WORK/LIFE BALANCE PROGRAM AT DELOITTE & TOUCHE

The Organization

Deloitte & Touche is a leading professional services firm that offers assurance and advisory, tax, and management con- sulting services to clients. As of September 2003, the firm employed a professional staff of almost 23,000 people working at approximately 100 U.S. offices. The firm works with clients in a wide range of industries, including financial services, energy/utilities, technology, communications, man- ufacturing, and transportation. On a global scale, Deloitte & Touche is part of Deloitte Touche Tohmatsu, a professional services firm with more than 119,000 employees who work with clients in more than 140 countries. In 2002, the firm had revenue of over $12.5 billion.

The corporate mission of Deloitte & Touche is "To Help Our Clients and Our People Excel." The core values of the firm include the following: outstanding value to clients, commitment to each other, integrity, strength from cultural diversity, and recognition of the importance of people.

The Situation

In 1992, Deloitte & Touche identified two alarming realities with respect to its work force. First, the turnover rate for women at the firm was much higher than for men. Female employees perceived that the firm was male dominated and limited opportunities were available for advancement. Second, both men and women reported they were experiencing major challenges in balancing work with their personal commitments.[69]

The Work/Life Balance Program

One of the key human resource standards at the firm is "respecting the personal lives of our people and supporting them in balancing multiple commitments and interests." On the basis of this principle and the results of the 1992 surveys, Deloitte & Touche implemented a work/life balance program in 1993 to enable its employees to establish and maintain high-quality professional and personal lives. The rationale behind this was that employees who have more meaningful and satisfying personal lives would be more effective at work.

The major feature of the work/life balance program is flexibility. The firm offers flexible work schedules to employees so they have greater control over which days they work and how many hours they work on those days. Flextime provides workers with the option of starting their workday earlier and finishing earlier. This enables some employees to pick their children up after school or to have time to handle business during the day. The telecommuting component of the program makes it possible for employees to work at home and to have the flexibility to pursue other personal interests, such as writing a book, running for public office, or training to compete in a sporting event.

Another unique component of the program is called *LifeWorks*. This program is administered by Ceridian Perfor-

mance Partners. It provides resource and referral services that help employees with child care and eldercare, school selection, adoption assistance, and locating a variety of personal and convenience services.

Results

In 1997, at least 650 employees were using flexible work arrangements. Over 70 percent of the employees using these arrangements indicated they would have left the firm if these options were not available to them. Deloitte & Touche estimates the increased retention of administrative professionals due to the work/life balance program has saved it over $11 million. The program has also helped the firm hire high-quality professionals. Specifically, 76 percent of women and 60 percent of men said the work/life balance program strongly influenced their decision to accept a job offer with Deloitte & Touche.

The results of the 1999 Human Resource Standards Survey and Flexible Work Arrangements Survey indicated that the work/life balance program at Deloitte & Touche has been highly beneficial for its employees, its clients, and the firm as a whole. The 1999 results of these surveys showed that an all-time high of 83 percent of the firm's employees said they would recommend Deloitte & Touche to their friends as a place to work.

Finally, Deloitte & Touche was listed among *Fortune* magazine's 2003 ranking of the 100 Best Companies to Work For. This was the seventh consecutive year the firm received this recognition.

Discussion Questions

1. Why has the issue of work/life balance in organizations become so significant in the last decade?
2. From a business perspective, what case can be made in support of implementing work/life balance programs in organizations?
3. What are the strengths of the work/life program at Deloitte & Touche? What about weaknesses?
4. What are the short-term and long-term challenges associated with the success of the work/life program at Deloitte & Touche?
5. What are the practical implications of this case for you as a future manager?

Source: http://www.deloitte.com.

CASE 5-2

CONDUCTING A JOB STRESS ASSESSMENT AT A MAJOR NOT-FOR-PROFIT ORGANIZATION

Note: This case is based on actual events in a real-world organization. Because of concerns regarding the potential sensitivity of issues presented in this case, some information has been modified to protect the anonymity of the company and its employees.

The Company

The Omega Chapter of the Global Humanitarian Initiative (GHI) is based in New York City. Its primary mission is to provide food, shelter, and services to sustain quality of life for the poor and homeless. The fundamental operating values of the chapter include the following: compassion, respect, care, fairness, unity, and sincerity. This chapter was established in 1901, making it one of the oldest and largest chapters in the GHI organization.

The chapter consists of a team of 15 administrators, a staff of approximately 425 individuals, and a huge volunteer force of over 1,700 people. The staff is a mixture of professionals (e.g., information technology, accounting, training) and support staff (e.g., clerical, maintenance).

Methodology

A management consultant was hired by the senior administrative team to conduct a formal assessment of the job stressors that employees (nonvolunteers) experienced in relation to their jobs and to identify appropriate recommendations for reducing the level of the most significant stressors. This decision was driven by a concern that many employees were stressed out and increasingly unable to perform their jobs effectively.

The consultant, working with members of the administrative team and the director of Human Relations (HR) at the company, designed and administered a survey that asked staff employees (not volunteers) a variety of questions about job stressors they were experiencing. The survey was a paper-and-pencil assessment composed of 17 questions that used a combination of structured rating scales (e.g., strongly agree, strongly disagree) and open-ended questions. The consultant administered the survey through interdepartmental mail to 425 employees and asked them to return the surveys within one week. In the end, a total of 350 completed surveys were returned that resulted in a response rate of 77.8 percent.

Results

The consultant analyzed the survey responses from participants using basic statistical procedures. The results are shown in Table 1.

Discussion Questions

1. Now it's your turn to be the consultant. Based on the information provided in the table, analyze the results of the survey regarding job stress. Download the worksheet created for this exercise from the Web site for this textbook to help you structure your approach to this exercise. Be sure to document your key findings on this worksheet.

2. Based on your key results, develop a set of *short-term recommendations* (things that should be done immediately or in the next few months) to help the administrative team at the Omega chapter reduce employee job stress or enhance the ability of employees to cope with stress. Make sure each of your recommendations is specific and action oriented. Be prepared to justify each of your recommendations to the administrative team in terms of merit, feasibility, and cost effectiveness. Also, make sure you address what the administrative team needs to do to ensure the effective execution of your recommendations.

3. Based on your key results, develop a set of *long-term recommendations* (things that should be done in the next three to five years) to help the administrative team at the Omega chapter reduce employee job stress or enhance the ability of employees to cope with stress. Make sure each of your recommendations is specific and action oriented. Be prepared to justify each of your recommendations to the administrative team in terms of merit, feasibility, and cost effectiveness. Also, make sure you address what the administrative team needs to do to ensure the effective execution of your recommendations.

4. Make a five- to ten-minute presentation of your results and recommendations to the class.

5. What did you learn from this case study about stress management issues in real-world organizations?

Source: Based on a management consulting project completed by L. McVicker and C. Smith, May 2000.

Table 1. Summary of Key Results from the Survey of Job Stress

Question	Strongly Disagree	Disagree	Neutral	Agree	Strongly Agree
1. I use effective time management methods such as making to-do lists or prioritizing tasks.	3%	3%	10%	53%	31%
2. I maintain balance in my life by pursuing a variety of interests outside of work.	0%	11%	17%	47%	25%
3. I have a close relationship with someone who serves as my mentor or adviser.	19%	17%	23%	28%	13%
4. I have some time during each day when I can work uninterrupted.	23%	43%	21%	9%	4%
5. The work environment I am in is hectic, busy, and disorganized.	14%	10%	16%	43%	17%
6. I experience a lot of pressure to complete my work by a certain time.	6%	4%	13%	47%	30%
7. The physical work environment I am in is unpleasant.	51%	37%	5%	3%	4%
8. I feel prepared to handle changes in technology that occur in the company.	11%	8%	23%	37%	21%
9. I am experiencing changes in my personal life that affect my ability to perform my job.	4%	7%	15%	42%	31%
10. My boss maintains good communication with me regarding issues that affect me.	34%	28%	26%	8%	4%
11. My boss provides me with clear expectations of what I need to achieve to perform my job well.	28%	37%	10%	17%	8%
12. I receive appropriate direction from my boss regarding what I need to do to be successful in my job.	21%	30%	23%	16%	10%
13. The workload associated with my job is reasonable.	62%	30%	8%	0%	0%
14. The compensation and benefits I receive are fair considering what I contribute to the success of this organization.	31%	37%	20%	10%	2%
15. There is too much gossiping among employees in this organization.	27%	24%	25%	14%	10%
16. I have flexibility in terms of when I start and finish work each day.	51%	27%	12%	8%	2%
17. I have flexibility in terms of which days of the week I work.	57%	21%	10%	10%	2%

LIGHTEN UP

THE MICROSOFT LEXICON

We wrote earlier in the chapter about jargon at Microsoft. To learn more about the special language of Microsoft, access The Microsoft Lexicon:

http://www.members.tripod.com/jeeem/mslex. htm

There you'll find the definitions of buzzword bingo, dogfood, facemail, klugey, open the kimono, permatemp, self-toast, weasel user, and about 150 more Microsoft terms.

SKILLS PRACTICE

5-1   *Skill Level: BASIC*

Field Experience: Interviews with Real-World Managers About Stress Management Strategies

Skill Objective

To develop a better understanding of what management practitioners in the real world do to manage their stress and the stress of others in their organizations.

Procedure

1. Identify two managers who work in different business organizations. Ask the managers if you can interview each of them for approximately 30 to 45 minutes.

2. When you meet with each manager, ask the following questions:

   a. What sources of stress exist in your job?

   b. What types of strategies do you use to cope with the stress you experience in your job?

   c. Tell me about the most stressful job experience you have ever had. Why was this experience so stressful? How did you handle it?

   d. What are the most significant stressors that your employees (direct reports) are experiencing in their jobs? Why is this the case?

   e. What types of strategies do you use as a manager to help your employees cope better with job stress?

   f. What advice would you give students regarding specific actions they can take to manage their own stress effectively as well others' stress in the real world?

3. Summarize the results of your interviews.

Discussion Questions

1. Based on the summary of your interviews, what are your key findings about stress management? Why?

2. What are the practical implications of this exercise for you as a future manager and leader of a real-world organization?

SKILLS PRACTICE

5-2   *Skill Level: BASIC*

Tools for Effective Stress Management

Skill Objective

To learn how to apply basic tools to enhance your ability to manage stress.

Procedure

1. Read the description of each of the stress management tools here.

2. Work through the step-by-step instructions for using each of the tools.

3. Answer the discussion questions as a class.

Stress Management Tools

Note: Download the worksheet developed for this exercise from the Web site for this textbook.

1. The Job Analysis Technique

The job analysis technique lowers job stress by letting you know what you have to do to be successful on a job. That is, the technique reduces the stressor of role ambiguity.

a. *Select a job you have now.* This should be a job you have held long enough to answer the questions here.

b. Based on your understanding of this job, write a very basic job description that includes a list of the major duties and responsibilities of the job, and the knowledge, skills, and abilities needed by a person who is qualified for this job.

c. Review the job description and identify the key objectives and priorities for the job, the criteria used to evaluate job performance, incentives and rewards associated with the job, and any training the company provides for the job.

d. Examine the mission statement of the company in which this job exists and develop an understanding of how the job contributes to the achievement of the company's mission. Note: If you have a basic understanding of the company's mission, you can write a basic summary of it for this exercise. If you do not know what the mission of your company is, you will need to obtain this information outside of your class time.

e. Assess the culture of the organization associated with the job in terms of its values, norms, rituals, taboos, and so on. How does the job fit into this culture and support? Note: If you need more information to answer this question, talk to your boss or a coworker from your company outside of class time.

f. Identify the top performers in the job and find out why they are so successful in terms of specific knowledge, skills, and so on. Note: If you do not know who these individuals might be, ask your boss or a coworker from your company outside of class time for more information.

g. Assess the degree to which you have the support you need to be successful on the job (e.g., staff, budget, direction).

h. Confirm your understanding of the priorities of the job with those of your boss. Make sure they are consistent with each other. If not, discuss these issues with your boss.

i. Take action by performing the job and prioritizing the things you and your boss agree are critical to the success of the job.

2. Physical Relaxation Techniques

a. Deep Breathing

> Take 10 deep breaths and try to relax your body as much as possible after each breath.

b. Progressive Muscle Relaxation

> Start at the top of the list of target muscle groups below (right foot) and tighten that target muscle group as much as possible for a few seconds before releasing it. Now focus mentally on relaxing this muscle group even further.

> Go to the next target muscle group (right lower leg and foot) and repeat the procedure of tightening that muscle group and then releasing it.

> Repeat the tighten-and-relax procedure for the rest of the target muscle groups in order until you complete the last one (face). The recommended sequence for target muscle groups is as follows:

- Right foot
- Right lower leg and foot
- Entire right leg
- Left foot
- Left lower leg and foot
- Entire left leg
- Right hand
- Right forearm and hand
- Entire right arm
- Left hand
- Left forearm and hand
- Entire left arm
- Abdomen
- Chest
- Neck and shoulders
- Face

c. The Relaxation Response

> Sit in a chair in a quiet and comfortable environment.

> Close your eyes.

> Start by relaxing your feet and move up your body relaxing your muscles as you go.

> Pay attention to your breathing as you work through this process.

> Breathe in deeply and then let your breath out. Do this for ten or twenty minutes.

3. Performance Plan

> *Select a job you have now,* a job you have held long enough to answer the questions below.

> Make a list of everything that could go wrong and interfere with completing your job successfully.

> Estimate the likelihood of each of the things going wrong actually occurring. If the likelihood of something going wrong is very low, eliminate it from the list.

> For the remaining things that could go wrong, identify specific actions you could take to address them through appropriate preparation (e.g., better planning and goal setting), things you can avoid by not taking unnecessary risk (e.g., trying to do too much at once), and things you can eliminate through better time management, a stress management strategy, or some other general strategy.

> Document your plan and refer back to it during the performance of your job.

Discussion Questions

1. What is your reaction to the Job Analysis Technique for stress management? Was it effective? Why or why not? What are the keys to implementing this technique successfully with a job in a real-world organization?

2. What is your reaction to the Physical Relaxation Techniques for stress management? Were they effective? Why or why not? What are the keys to implementing these techniques successfully with a job in a real-world organization?

3. What is your reaction to the Performance Plan Technique for stress management? Was it effective? Why or why not? What are the keys to implementing this technique successfully with a job in a real-world organization?

4. What are the practical implications of this exercise for you as a future manager and leader in a real-world organization?

Source: http://www.mindtools.com

SKILLS PRACTICE

| 5-3 | Skill Level: BASIC |

Developing a Personal Stress Management Program

Skill Objective

To develop skill in designing and implementing a personal stress management program.

Procedure

1. Follow the steps given to identify the stressors in your current situation and to develop an action plan for reducing these stressors and managing them more effectively. Download the worksheet created for this exercise from the Web site for this textbook.

    Step 1: Using a simple 10 point scale with 1 = "no stress at all" to 10 = "extremely stressed out," rate your current situation in terms of the overall level of stress you are experiencing currently. Write down your overall rating.

    Step 2: List the major stressors you are experiencing in relation to your work.

    Step 3: List the major stressors you are experiencing in relation to your life in general.

    Step 4: How do you tend to respond to the stress you experience in your work and in your life in general? Note some of your most common physical and psychological reactions to the stressors you listed in steps 2 and 3.

    Step 5: Develop a list of actions you might take to reduce the level of life and work stressors you identified.

    Step 6: Identify a list of actions you might take to deal with or cope with stressful situations more effectively.

Discussion Questions

1. Evaluate your personal stress management plan. What are its strengths and weaknesses?

2. If you were to implement your personal stress management plan, what would you need to do to make it successful?

3. What factors would create barriers to the success of your personal stress management plan? What could you do, if anything, to overcome these barriers?

4. What are the implications of this exercise for you as a future manager or supervisor?

SKILLS PRACTICE

| 5-4 | Skill Level: BASIC |

Analyzing Job Stressors in the Movie Pushing Tin

Skill Objective

To develop skill in analyzing job stressors, stress, and stress reactions of workers in a particularly stressful job.

Procedure

1. Obtain a copy of the movie *Pushing Tin* starring John Cusack and Billy Bob Thornton. It is available on VHS and DVD and you can rent or purchase it from a local video store or retailer.

2. Watch the movie (in class or at home on your own).
     Note: Download the worksheet developed for this exercise from the Web site for this book. This will help you record your notes from various scenes in the movie.

   As you watch the film, take notes regarding the various types of stressors, stress levels, and stress reactions of the air traffic controllers. Be sure to document your notes about all relevant scenes on your worksheet.

3. Discuss the following questions as a class.
   a. What major job stressors did the main characters in the film experience?
   b. What types of stress reactions did the main characters exhibit throughout the film?
   c. What type of personality describes each of the main characters, and how did this personality influence the level of stress and type of stress reactions he experienced in the movie?
   d. If you were to develop a formal stress management program for these air traffic controllers, what would it include?
   e. What are the practical implications of this exercise for you as a future manager and leader in a real-world organization?

SKILLS PRACTICE

5-5   *Skill Level: CHALLENGING*

Designing and Implementing Organizational Stress Management Programs

Skill Objectives

1. To develop skill in designing organizational stress management programs.

2. To develop skill in implementing organizational stress management programs.

Procedure

Note: Download the worksheet developed for this exercise to facilitate working through the steps here.

1. Break up into teams of three to five students.
2. Read the description of the scenario provided.
   Note: This example is based on a real firm and actual events that took place at the firm.

   The partners at a medium-sized management consulting firm of 100 employees are concerned that many of their consultants are simply burning out on the job. A number of consultants have reported that everyone on the front lines is "overwhelmed" and "demoralized" from the workload and the pressure to achieve results. In addition, two senior consultants just resigned today, stating they needed more time for their personal lives and family.

   Consultants typically work 60 or more hours per week and travel about 50 to 70 percent of the time. Compensation for entry-level consultants is $60,000 to $75,000 with senior consultants easily earning more than $175,000 per year. Benefits include life insurance, basic health insurance, and a 401(k)

   retirement plan. The work performed by consultants provides tremendous variety and challenge. Many of the clients of the firm are Global 500 companies.

   The consulting business is very competitive so everyone in the firm is under tremendous pressure to look continually for new clients and other sources of revenue. Consultants often have only a few days to transition to a new project once they have completed an assignment. This is considered necessary given the need to be responsive to client needs.

   The consulting firm has been growing rapidly the last two years with the addition of several major clients. However, a serious concern is whether the firm will be able to handle the increased workload and sustain the quality service it has become known for in the industry.

3. Develop a formal stress management program that will be administered organizationwide to address the stress-related issues facing workers in the organization in the scenario. Use material from this chapter to help you design your program.
4. Develop an action plan for implementing your organizational stress management program. Be specific and action oriented. Also, be sure to do what you feel is needed to ensure the program actually gets implemented.
5. Optional: Prepare a five-minute presentation of

your organizational stress management program for your class.

Discussion Questions

1. What are the keys to the effective design of organizational stress management programs?

2. What are the keys to the effective implementation of organizational stress management programs?

3. How can the effectiveness of an organizational stress management program be evaluated? Why is this important to do?

4. What are the practical implications of this exercise for you as a future manager or leader of a real-world organization?

INTERPERSONAL

PART 2

FOSTERING ETHICAL BEHAVIOR

CHAPTER 6

Skills Objectives

> To develop skill in encouraging ethical employee behavior.

> To integrate ethical considerations effectively into the managerial decision-making process.

> To develop skill in resolving ethical dilemmas in the managerial decision-making process.

> To develop skill in creating programs for enhancing ethical behavior in an organization.

> To develop skill in creating a code of ethics.

> To develop skill in creating an ethics training program.

KNOWLEDGE OBJECTIVES

> Recognize forms of unethical behavior in organizations.

> Understand whistle-blowing.

> Be aware of forms of legal remedies for unethical behaviors.

> Discuss guidelines for ethical behavior.

> Identify ways to encourage ethical behavior in others.

Time magazine's "Persons of the Year" for 2002 were Sherron Watkins, Coleen Rowley, and Cynthia Cooper, three prominent "whistle-blowers."[1] Sherron Watkins is the Enron vice president who wrote a letter to chairman Kenneth Lay warning him that the company was using improper accounting procedures. When a congressional subcommittee investigating Enron's collapse released the letter, the Year of the Whistle-blower began. Coleen Rowley is an FBI staff attorney who caused a sensation with a memo to FBI director Robert Mueller about how the bureau ignored pleas from her field office to investigate Zacarias Moussaoui, now indicted as a September 11 co-conspirator. Cynthia Cooper disclosed to WorldCom's board of directors that the company had covered up $3.8 billion in losses through fraudulent bookkeeping.

Over the last few years, numerous major corporations, including Enron, Arthur Andersen, Tyco, and WorldCom, have been the subject of huge scandals, leading to disastrous results for the firms and their employees and shareholders, to jail sentences for some officers, and to a dramatic erosion of public trust in major corporations.[2] Even Martha Stewart and the venerable *New York Times* found themselves at the center of scandals.[3] A Doonesbury cartoon shows President Bush defending the business world against attacks in the press and Congress, saying "It's just unfair to the 30 percent of CEOs who are honest."[4] White-collar crime—and the harsh sentences to which it may now lead—has become so commonplace that a 2003 television comedy, *Arrested Development,* centers on the family of an executive who is imprisoned for crafty accounting.[5] Pictures of handcuffed executives being roughly treated like "common criminals" fill the news.[6]

In this chapter, we address ethics and business ethics. We see that ethical violations can be devastating for organizations, and strong cultures of ethical behavior can foster employee morale, reputation, and performance. We offer guidelines both for fostering our own ethical behavior and for encouraging ethical behavior in others.

In the Voice of Experience feature, Marsha McVicker discusses the importance of ethics in her company, Errand Solutions. As a way to introduce the material in this chapter and for you to assess your skill in handling situations involving ethical issues, develop a plan for how you would handle the scenario in the Pretest Skills Assessment. Then complete Self-Assessment 6-1 regarding your attitudes toward organizational ethics. After you are done, visit the text Web site to learn more about your responses.

PRETEST SKILLS ASSESSMENT

Managing Ethics

Note: This exercise is based on events encountered by managers in real-world organizations. Some information may have been modified in order to maintain the anonymity of the people and organizations involved in this situation.

You are the manager of a team of 15 sales representatives for a major copier and office equipment manufacturer. This is a highly competitive industry in which profit margins are razor thin. Consequently, operating costs must be carefully monitored. Your sales representatives travel around by car within a sales territory of about 100 square miles. Oftentimes, they meet with current or prospective clients for lunches or dinners to talk business and to negotiate deals. They also give clients a variety of promotional items such as mugs, mouse pads, and pens. You are concerned that these sales representatives appear to be abusing the reporting of their expenses each month by "expensing" (requesting a reimbursement from the company) personal (not for business purposes) expenses such as meals, gas used in their cars, and overnight stays at hotels. Although the company does possess some guidelines for what the sales representatives can and cannot report as reimbursable expenses, there are still a lot of items on monthly expense reports that appear to be suspect. You are extremely concerned that charging personal expenses to the company has become an accepted practice among the sales representatives because they have rationalized it in terms of "everyone does it."

Develop an action plan for addressing the ethical issues in this situation. Be sure your plan addresses both short-term and long-term issues. Be very specific and be prepared to defend each element of your plan in terms of its feasibility and cost effectiveness. Once you have completed your plan, go to the Web site for this textbook to find out how you did on this exercise.

SELF-ASSESSMENT 6-1

Attitudes Toward Organizational Ethics

Answer the following questions regarding your attitudes toward ethics. Try to respond to each question as honestly as possible using the following response scale:

1 Disagree strongly
2 Disagree somewhat
3 Neither agree nor disagree
4 Agree somewhat
5 Agree strongly

____ 1. The ethics of employees cannot be changed by managerial action or organizational policies and practices.

____ 2. Employees' cultural backgrounds may shape their views on whether a specific behavior is ethical.

____ 3. The degree to which employees behave in an ethical manner does not impact the organization's long-term financial performance.

____ 4. Dealing with business ethics effectively is a major concern to managers today.

____ 5. Business ethics are not important so long as an organization is achieving its bottom-line objectives.

____ 6. Many consumers admire and are more likely to purchase products and services from organizations that are ethical.

____ 7. Ethical standards vary so much across individuals, it is impossible for an organization to develop a set of ethical standards that apply to all of its members.

____ 8. The cultures of some organizations actually discourage their members (managers and employees) from behaving ethically.

____ 9. Top management must be a good role model for ethical behavior in order to support the creation of a more ethical organization.

____ 10. The reward systems in some organizations reinforce unethical behavior among their managers and employees.

VOICE OF EXPERIENCE

FOSTERING ETHICAL BEHAVIOR
Marsha McVicker, CEO, Errand Solutions

1. Are ethics a major consideration in your day-to-day decision making as the CEO of a major errand, convenience, and travel assistance service?

Ethical behavior is the cornerstone of the mission statement of Errand Solutions: "Our goal is to make friends and fans out of all we interact with by bringing energy, integrity and enthusiasm to all we do." It is also a critical component of our success, as evidenced by our growth in the hospitality industry. This steadfast adherence to consistent ethical conduct has certainly been tested on more than one occasion.

2. Can you give specific examples of situations where you faced challenges relating to ethics?

In September 2001, a large Chicago hotel dismissed its internal concierge staff and outsourced the operations of the department to Errand Solutions. This decision was driven by two major concerns.

1. Revenue made in the form of commissions was unreported to the management of the hotel. Concierges received kickbacks for referring guests to certain establishments and for recommending various service providers.

2. The level of customer service was poor. The hotel did not feel that it had any control over the desk activities.

Errand Solutions was hired to end the "under the desk" business and make the concierge service more efficient and customer service oriented. We immediately implemented several new processes and procedures to resolve the dilemma the hotel faced. Contracts with vendors were formalized, software was developed to monitor, capture, and assist with all activities, and a detailed training program was established that promoted team-based solutions, guest feedback, and unbiased referrals. Most importantly, the concierge hiring process was overhauled.

In order to be an employee of Errand Solutions, a prospect goes through a series of intensive interviews that include a "day on the job" and discussions with other employees. One of the key components on which we evaluate a potential employee is ethical conduct. Many of the questions test how an individual would respond if he or she was offered a free dinner or special access to parties.

At Errand Solutions we feel very strongly that in order to provide objective advice to guests at the hotel, the concierges must experience the city in the same manner a guest would, and that means they cannot tell local restaurants or entertainment venues who they are or what they do. Historically, restaurants and entertainment venues cater to concierges. They throw them elaborate parties under the guise of educating them about their establishment. In addition, the concierges get preferential treatment, free meals, gifts, and often cash rewards for sending guests to these establishments. The concierges are therefore encouraged to send guests to whatever establishment will result in the most personal profit. Although there are many ethical concierges in the hospitality business, the existing system did not encourage ethical behavior.

All Errand Solutions employees are required to sign a gifts and gratuities policy that reads as follows:

*As an Errand Solutions employee you are not allowed to accept "incentives" from vendors and/or potential vendors in exchange for referrals, implied or actual. This includes free meals and gift certificates. These "incentives" are inclusive of monetary, service, or product gifts. Any and all complimentary items offered to the concierge desk are to be immediately turned over to the Concierge Manager, who will return them **immediately** to the vendor. Additionally, no Errand Solutions employee shall attend any non-company-sponsored function that provides any free product or services. If there is ever any doubt, consult with the Concierge Manager.*

You are absolutely never to mark up a product or service unless you are instructed to do so by your supervisor. Additionally, all deposits for tours or events received at the concierge desk shall be entered as revenue. This applies to all venues whether they are a designated "vendor" or not.

*As a service provider, you **are** allowed to accept gratuities from guests. This income must be reported for tax purposes and should be noted on your weekly time sheet.*

Failure to adhere to any of the above policies is cause for immediate termination.

As a result of implementing these new processes and procedures, especially the Gifts and Gratuities Policy, Errand Solutions met resistance from many area restaurants and concierges at other hotels. Some concierges

VOICE OF EXPERIENCE (continued)

threatened to boycott doing business with any hospitality organization that did business with Errand Solutions. A small handful of restaurant owners and concierges who were very comfortable with the kickback system initiated a negative public relations campaign in the press based on fears and misinformation. One local restaurateur even went so far as to issue a death threat, claiming that if Errand Solutions continued to do business in the city of Chicago he would kill not

only the business, but those most closely associated with it.

In spite of the threats, Errand Solutions has never wavered from its principles. As a result, our clients have benefited from dramatically improved customer service, and we continue to grow based on our ethical, objective approach.

3. **Do you have ethics-related advice for students about to enter the workplace?**
   One of the best pieces of advice that the Errand Solutions

team ever received was that if you compromise your ethics, you compromise your credibility. Once your credibility is in question, so is the future of your endeavor. So hold on strong to what you believe to be right. Passion and perseverance will pull you through.

http://www.errandsolutions .com/

THE NEED FOR ETHICAL BEHAVIOR

Ethics are principles of morality or rules of conduct.[7] *Business ethics* are rules about how businesses and their employees ought to behave. Ethical behavior conforms to these rules; unethical behavior violates them. Business ethics help guide an organization's efforts and offer a foundation for its culture.

The need for ethical behavior in organizations has been dramatized by some very visible ethical violations, including use of kickbacks, bribes, and myriad other forms of corruption. Consider these facts:

> In one study, 65 percent of managers claimed to have personally seen or had direct evidence of fraud, waste, or mismanagement within their organizations. Of these people, however, only 50 percent reported what they had seen to appropriate authorities.[8]

> In a survey of more than 1,000 randomly selected adults, 24 percent reported they had been asked to do something at work that went against their ethical standards. Of those, 41 percent reported carrying out the order.[9]

> The U.S. Chamber of Commerce estimates that workplace theft costs U.S. businesses up to $40 billion each year and employees are thought to be responsible for much of the theft.[10]

> By one estimate, the yearly business costs of internal fraud in the United States are somewhere between the annual GDP of Bulgaria ($50 billion) and the GDP of Taiwan ($400 billion).[11]

> A study of restaurant workers found that 12 percent of those surveyed admitted to having intentionally contaminated food they prepared or served to a customer. Twenty-six percent admitted to touching a coworker in a sexually inappropriate way, and 24 percent took illegal drugs before coming to work.[12]

> *Bribes*—payments up front to influence a transaction—have reached such epidemic proportions that 34 industrial nations have forged a multinational

treaty to address them.[13] In some countries, gifts and gratuities are seen as an acceptable part of doing business—much as we give tips for good service—and aren't viewed as bribes. However, in other cases, ethical and legal violations are more clear cut. Bribery in overseas dealings has increased sharply in the last two decades. Bribes paid to acquire large contracts in developing countries are estimated now to exceed 15 percent of the contracts' value.[14] Outright bribes and payments for *quanxi,* or "connections," total $3 billion to $5 billion in China, costs largely borne by consumers.[15]

> *Kickbacks,* which occur when someone who has won a contract or made a sale through favorable treatment gives back part of the profits from the transaction to the party providing the favor, are proliferating.[16] For example, in the so-called IBM affair, the computer giant's arm in Argentina was charged with paying $37 million in kickbacks and bribes to land a $250 million contract with the state-run Banco de la Nación.[17]

> Many U.S. companies have been charged with running inhumane *sweatshops*, most of them in developing countries, with low wages, long hours, and unhealthy conditions and often employing children or forced labor. In late 1999, more than 50,000 protesters descended on the meetings of the World Trade Organization in Seattle to protest sweatshops (as well as such issues as human rights violations, environmental degradation, and genetically engineered food).[18] John Sweeney, president of the AFL-CIO, said that corporate interests are well looked after "while 250 million children around the world go to work, not school, and tens of thousands of workers are chained into forced labor and prison camps."[19] Activists charge that many of the products sold by the Gap and Nike, among others, are made in such Third World sweatshops.[20] The Fair Labor Organization is an anti-sweatshop group that counts 12 manufacturers (including several, such as Nike, Liz Claiborne, and Reebok that make apparel and footwear) and nearly 200 colleges among its members. Members agree to accept the group's code of conduct and to accept external monitoring of their compliance with the code. A 2003 report by the group cited violations of its code in countries such as Thailand, China, and Turkey by members including Reebok, Phillips-Van Heusen, and Nike.[21] In September 2003, Nike agreed to pay the Fair Labor Association $1.5 million in a settlement relating to working conditions in its foreign factories. The funds will be used by the group to improve the quality of independent monitoring in countries where apparel is made and to help workers in those countries improve their skills.[22]

Skills Practice 6-1 gives you a chance to gain firsthand experience with ethical issues. Complete the exercise by interviewing managers about their perspectives on ethical issues and suggestions for handling them more effectively.

Now complete Skills Practice 6-2 by watching *Wall Street,* the classic film about corporate greed. This is an excellent example of important ethical challenges that face many organizations today.

ETHICS AND FIRM PERFORMANCE

It is very difficult to document the relationship of ethical behavior to organizational performance. There are many reasons for this, including disagreements over what behavior is ethical. However, some attempts have been made to explore the relationship. For instance, one study found that companies that had an "ethical commitment"—as evidenced by the inclusion of ethics codes in the management reports within annual reports—had much higher levels of financial performance than did those without such codes in the reports. Also, those companies with an "ethical commitment" had higher scores on *Fortune* reputation ratings.[23] Further, the last decade has been a period of "ethical consumerism," with an increasing number of consumers making their purchase decisions on the basis of firms' ethical reputations; one study showed that in a recent one-year period, over half of consumers reported having purchased a product or recommended a company on the basis of its reputation.[24] As another example, evidence suggests that ethical values are related to characteristics of "excellent" companies.[25] In addition, as we discuss a bit later, committing specific unethical acts may have disastrous consequences for organizations and their officers.

THE WHISTLE-BLOWING RESPONSE TO UNETHICAL BEHAVIOR

An employee who learns his or her company engages in an illegal or unethical activity can keep quiet, report the incident to others in the firm, or go outside the firm with the information. By going outside the firm, the employee is said to be "blowing the whistle." **Whistle-blowers**, those individuals who report to the press, government, or other parties outside the firm illegal activity occurring in a firm, may find their jobs and careers threatened. About 35 states now have laws protecting whistle-blowers.[26] Note that the three women cited in the chapter's opening example are not truly whistle-blowers by this definition because they did not intentionally go outside the firm with their concerns.[27]

The federal False Claims Act allows whistle-blowers to sue government wrongdoers in the name of the United States. The False Claims Act was strengthened in 1986, bolstering whistle-blowers in three important ways. It gave them more power to initiate and prosecute claims, offered them up to 25 percent of any money recovered by the government, and provided protection against employer retaliation. Since enactment of the act, the number of whistle-blower complaints received by the Department of Justice has skyrocketed, and the government has recovered more than $1.8 billion in false claims cases.[28]

Advocates of whistle-blower protection note that without protection, those reporting wrongdoing may face (and have faced) harassment, demotion, firing, or other retribution (including death). Even under the current laws, half of whistle-blowers get fired, half of those fired lose their jobs, and most of them then lose their families.[29] Randy Robarge was a well-respected nuclear power supervisor chosen by his company, ConEd, to narrate the company's training video on safety, which is used throughout the industry. He lost his job after raising concerns about improper storage of radioactive material at ConEd's Zion power plant and has been unable to find new work in the subsequent six years. Robarge says, "This is my livelihood, what I love to do. But I'm off limits. No one wants to touch me. I was labeled as a whistle-blower."[30] Without protection, according to advocates of such protection, employees would never be willing to expose important wrongdoing.

Opponents of such protection argue that whistle-blowing causes employees to circumvent companies' internal mechanisms for ethical resolution, may encourage malcontents who will take every opportunity to complain, and may lead to abuse of the law. For instance, they argue, a marginal employee afraid of being dismissed because of poor performance may find gossip about someone in the firm (or make some up), report it outside the firm, and then evoke whistle-blower protection laws when the company threatens dismissal. Opponents of protection laws also argue that such laws may encourage "dialing-for-dollars" whistle-blowers who care more about personal gain than about justice. For instance, whistle-blowers have received awards of more than $30 million for reporting on illegal activities in their firms.[31]

Whatever the merits of whistle-blowing and of whistle-blowers' protection laws, whistle-blowing without a doubt can have devastating consequences for the targeted firms. Further, the need for whistle-blowing generally suggests both that unethical behaviors have reached unacceptable levels within the firm and that appropriate internal mechanisms to correct such behaviors are lacking.

LEGAL REMEDIES FOR UNETHICAL BEHAVIOR

For millennia, we have turned to legal codes for guidelines for dealing with unethical behavior. Of the several codes of law and conduct surviving from the ancient Middle East, the most famous after the Hebrew Torah is the Code of Hammurabi, sixth king of the Amorite Dynasty of Old Babylon from 1792 B.C. to 1750 B.C.[32] Hammurabi developed a code consisting of 282 rules outlining all aspects of public involvement and sorted into groups such as family, labor, personal property, real estate, trade, and business. This was the first time in history that laws had been categorized into various sections. Here is a sampling of the laws:

6. If any one steal the property of a temple or of the court, he shall be put to death, and also the one who receives the stolen thing from him shall be put to death.

55. If any one open his ditches to water his crop, but is careless, and the water flood the field of his neighbor, then he shall pay his neighbor corn for his loss.

102. If a merchant entrust money to an agent (broker) for some investment, and the broker suffer a loss in the place to which he goes, he shall make good the capital to the merchant.

106. If the agent accept money from the merchant, but have a quarrel with the merchant (denying the receipt), then shall the merchant swear before God and witnesses that he has given this money to the agent, and the agent shall pay him three times the sum.

115. If any one have a claim for corn or money upon another and imprison him; if the prisoner die in prison a natural death, the case shall go no further.

196. If a man put out the eye of another man, his eye shall be put out.[33]

In more recent years, this search for legal guidance has continued. A 19th-century English judge, Edward Baron Thurlow, lamented in a court decision: "Did you ever expect a corporation to have a conscience when it has no soul to be damned and no body to be kicked?" Then he whispered, "By God, it ought to have both."[34] Increasingly, governments are finding a "body to be kicked." They are applying criminal laws to companies and company executives. For example, the Foreign Corrupt Practices Act of 1977 was enacted in response to disclosures that American corporations were paying bribes to high governmental officials in foreign countries in an attempt to win contracts and sell products and services.[35]

Further, Congress created a U.S. Sentencing Commission to issue new guidelines for white-collar crime, such as bribery, fraud, and tax evasion. The commission's guidelines—the 1991 Sentencing Guidelines for Organizations—provide tougher sanctions, including jail sentences and fines in the millions of dollars, for those convicted of corporate lawbreaking. Many businesspeople who paid small fines, if anything, for wrongdoing are now serving mandatory prison terms.[36] Sentencing under the guidelines for an offense committed by an organization depends on the nature of the crime, the amount of loss suffered by victims of the crime, and the amount of planning evidenced by the offense. In addition, such factors as the organization's history of criminal activity and whether high-level organizational personnel were involved in or tolerated the activity are considered in determining a penalty. Depending on such considerations, a $25,000 bribe paid to a city official could result in fines ranging from $17,500 to $1.4 million.[37]

In response to the recent financial scandals, Congress passed the Sarbanes-Oxley Act of 2002, intended to increase the transparency, integrity, and accountability of public companies. This act created a new agency to police the accounting industry. It also requires that CEOs personally sign off on documents they put out, such as quarterly and annual reports. In addition, the act provides additional protections for employees of publicly traded companies who report violations of federal securities law, the rules of the Securities and Exchange Commission, or "any provision of Federal law relating to fraud against shareholders."[38] The act states that a protected employee may not be discharged, demoted, suspended, harassed, or discriminated against in any way because of a protected disclosure, and it specifies a variety of damages that may be awarded to the employee.

Companies must do more than rely on whistle-blowing and legal mechanisms to ensure ethical behavior (and having corporate sins publicized or corporate officers thrown in jail are rather drastic and painful approaches to ethical compliance). If they are really serious about encouraging ethical behaviors, managers and companies must take concrete actions, establishing and following guidelines for ethical behavior.

GUIDELINES FOR ETHICAL BEHAVIOR

Mark Twain advised, "Always do right. This will gratify some people, and astonish the rest." As a manager, it is absolutely critical that you behave ethically. One reason is obvious and overwhelming: It is the right thing to do. Another is perhaps less evident: If you do not, you will lose respect for yourself and from others as well as credibility and trust and, as you do, you will lose the power to lead. Research shows that trust in leadership is positively related to such important outcomes as job performance, altruism, conscientiousness, job satisfaction, and organizational commitment.[39] Here are some guidelines for ethical behavior:

> *Be honest*, direct, and open in your dealings with others. Jim Kouzes and Barry Posner, authors of *The Leadership Challenge,* surveyed more than 20,000 people on four continents to identify the characteristics they most look for and admire in a leader. Only four characteristics were identified by more than 50 percent: competent (63 percent), inspiring (68 percent), forward looking (75 percent), and honest (88 percent). Honesty's top rating suggests it is perhaps *the* essential ingredient of successful leadership.[40]

> *Take ethical stands* on difficult issues. Confucius said, "The superior man understands what is right; the inferior man understands what will sell." The willingness to stand up for your beliefs is one mark of a transformational leader.

> Ask whether your actions reflect the *rights of others*, including such rights as due process, free speech, and privacy.

> Ask whether your actions are *just*. An act is unjust if it involves unequal treatment of individuals or inconsistent administration of rules.

> Ask how you would feel if the act was done to you.

> Use your power in ethical ways. If you have power because you control rewards, deliver on your promises. If you have power because of your ability to administer punishments, fully inform people who work for you of the rules and penalties for violations, provide warning before punishing, and administer discipline consistently and promptly. If your power flows from expertise, do nothing to endanger those relying on the expertise. If your power results from others' respect and admiration, take actions to justify and maintain that power: Treat people fairly, be considerate of their needs and feelings, show your appreciation when they do things that please you, and defend their interests when acting as a group representative.

> Apply the *sunlight test*. How would you feel if your actions were brought to the light of day? Would you be proud to have your children read about them in the newspaper? Now complete Skills Practice 6-3. The exercise will help raise your awareness of ethical issues and how to deal with them more effectively in the future.

ENCOURAGING ETHICAL BEHAVIOR IN OTHERS

It is not enough that managers behave ethically; they must also encourage ethical behavior in others. To do this, you can:

> **Promote, communicate, and reward ethical behavior as a key value.** About half the respondents to a 2003 Business Ethics Survey conducted by the Society for Human Resource Management (SHRM) and the Ethics Resource Center said ethical conduct is not rewarded in business today.[41]

> **Model ethical behavior.** Both in public and private, act in ways you hope and expect others to act. If others see that you don't walk the talk, your speeches about ethics will be dismissed as hypocrisy.

> **Speak out against unethical behavior when you see it.** Don't wink at it or ignore it, and certainly don't reward it. Remember that if employees can get ahead by acting in unethical ways and nothing is done about it, that behavior is being rewarded and will probably be repeated.

> **Communicate expectations regarding ethical behavior.** For instance, make sure employees are aware of the organization's *code of ethics*.[42] The code of ethics should be a living document embodying principles that show up in performance appraisals and the reward system. A code of ethics is most meaningful when employees help draft and revise it. For instance, Herron Communications Corporation had the company lawyers draft a code of ethics to govern many facets of employee behavior. The employees' response to the many "thou shalt nots" was so negative, the code was never implemented. The company then got employees involved in developing a new code. It was worded in terms of acceptable behavior rather than forbidden actions, and response was much more favorable.[43] The Focus on Management feature discusses codes of ethics in the National Collegiate Athletic Association (NCAA).

Companies should do more than just remind employees of the code of ethics. Employees should regularly receive messages of various sorts concerning the importance of ethical behavior. The 2003 National Business Ethics Survey of 1,500 workers nationwide found that in firms where management talks about the importance of ethics, informs employees, keeps promises, and models ethical behavior, 15 percent of employees report having observed misconduct. When employees think management only talks about ethics or does nothing, 56 percent report observing misconduct.[44] Unfortunately, one study found that regardless of organizational rank, no more than one-third of employees of *Fortune* 1,000 firms received any sort of message regarding ethics, other than a reminder of the code, more than once a year.[45]

Now complete Skills Practice 6-4. This exercise will illustrate how to develop and implement an effective code of ethics for an actual organization.

> **Make sure goals don't push employees into unethical behavior.** Unreasonable goals are often the motivation for lying, cheating, and stealing. Twenty-four percent of respondents to the 2003 Business Ethics Survey reported they feel pressured to compromise ethical standards all the time,

FOCUS ON MANAGEMENT

ETHICS CODES IN THE NCAA

In October 2003, more than 300 of the 326 Division I major college head basketball coaches gathered to create a higher standard in their profession. In the wake of a series of severe scandals in the game, the National Association of Basketball Coaches (NABC) announced a plan to help create NCAA legislation to guide conduct of coaches. Each coach agreed to customize a code of ethics to his program and have it ready within three weeks. An ethics committee was charged with creating sanctions for coaches that could include suspensions or ineligibility for awards. Duke coach Mike Krzyzewski, president of the NABC Foundation, said, "For me, this is a historic day for the game of basketball. And there will be other historic days, hopefully, as a result of us being able to show we need teamwork to take care of the game."[46]

fairly often, or periodically—up from 13 percent in 1997. The five top causes for pressure to compromise ethical standards were following the boss's directives (49 percent), meeting overly aggressive objectives (48 percent), helping the organization survive (40 percent), meeting schedule pressures (35 percent), and wanting to be a team player (27 percent).[47] Research shows that employees facing pressure from their organizations to engage in unethical behavior are likely to experience internal conflicts, be less satisfied and committed to the company, and leave the firm.[48]

> **Encourage ethics training.** Tie ethics training to the legal, behavioral, and policy needs of organizations and their members.[49] Make sure employees know about laws, policies, and expectations regarding ethical behavior. Ethics training is most often used to address conflicts of interest, personal conduct, public conduct, use of official information, and responsibilities to those in authority.[50] It can also reinforce codes of ethics so employees can see how the generality of codes can be used in specific day-to-day situations.[51] Ethics training might include such things as video material, role playing, board games with ethical scenarios, conferences on ethical issues, and use of current newspaper reports of real-life occurrences relating to ethical issues.[52]

At GE, videos and seminars are used to encourage employees to report ethical violations. Employees are even subjected to pop quizzes in hallways with questions such as, "What are the three ways to report wrongdoing?" A correct answer wins a coffee mug.[53] The Focus on Management feature discusses training and other efforts at MCI to enhance ethical behavior.

Unfortunately, no more than one-fourth of all employees in *Fortune* 1,000 firms receive ethics training and education at least once a year. About the same number receive no ethics training or education of any sort.[54]

> **Give employees ways to voice their ethical questions and concerns.** Don't force employees to ignore unethical behavior, to accept it, or to jeopardize their careers by going outside the firm with their concerns (that is, by whistle-blowing).

For instance, IBM has had a "Speak Up!" program for more than 25 years. It allows an employee to appeal any supervisory action and get a mailed response without having his or her name communicated to the supervisor. A meeting between the employee and management is arranged if necessary.

FOCUS ON MANAGEMENT

ETHICS AWARENESS AT MCI

At MCI—the company formerly known as WorldCom that had admitted to the largest financial fraud in U.S. history and was forced into bankruptcy—ethics are an overwhelming concern of new CEO Michael Capellas. He peppers his speeches with references to one of the company's guiding principles: "Do the right thing because it's the right thing to do." All 55,000 MCI employees must complete an online ethics training course. More than 2,000 MCI managers and finance employees have gone through full-day ethics training seminars, considering ethical issues and addressing ethical dilemmas. Capellas also appointed a chief ethics officer who will report directly to him: Nancy Higgins, former ethics vice president at Lockheed-Martin.[55]

About one-half of the *Fortune 1,000* firms have adopted some kind of *ethics hotlines*—telephone-based systems employees can use (anonymously if they prefer) for ethics and compliance complaints and questions. For example, Sundstrand Corporation has an ethics hot line that receives an average of 1,500 calls per year.[56]

In addition, many firms, including Rockwell, Johnson & Johnson, Herman Miller, Inc., and Volvo, encourage workers to report ethical problems to ombudsmen's offices. The *ombudsman*—an old Norse term for "people's representative"—is a neutral third party designated by the firm to check out and help resolve employee complaints.[57] Ombudsmen are also helpful in preventing miscommunication and misunderstanding between management and employees.[58] Deborah Cardillo, corporate ombudsman since 1985 for Eastman Kodak, says employees often find themselves in a difficult situation they'd like to handle themselves but are stuck, not knowing how to proceed. The ombudsman's role, she says, is "to get someone unstuck."[59] Companies must make clear to employees which discussions can be treated as confidential and which cannot. For example, if an employee tells the ombudsman of a situation involving an "imminent threat of serious harm" or potentially illegal behavior, the information cannot be held confidential.[60]

> **Set up internal programs to resolve ethical conflicts.** Develop clear routines and procedures for dealing with any complaints or allegations brought against employees under the ethics policies of the firm.

> **Create a culture of ethics.** To foster ethical behavior, organizations must create ethical cultures, characterized by strong ethical values, with an emphasis on honesty and openness. Ginger Graham, group chairman in the office of the president at Guidant Corporation, a medical device manufacturer, argues that organizations must first understand why they deny problems and promote dishonesty. She suggests stressing honesty as a key value and using stories and rituals to celebrate honesty, showing how the organization openly faces difficult challenges. In addition, she says leaders must model honest behavior by following through on their promises, avoiding finger-pointing, and owning up to mistakes and weaknesses.[61]

The Bottom Line feature presents a process model summarizing the basic steps associated with encouraging ethical behavior in organizations. Now complete Skills Practice 6-5. This activity will help you develop skill in thinking about and dealing with difficult ethical dilemmas in various managerial situations. Finally, complete Skills Practice 6-6. This exercise provides you with an opportunity to develop an ethics program for an actual organization. After you finish, you can go to the Web site for this text and compare what you created with the actual program the company developed and implemented.

BOTTOM LINE

ENCOURAGING ETHICAL EMPLOYEE BEHAVIOR

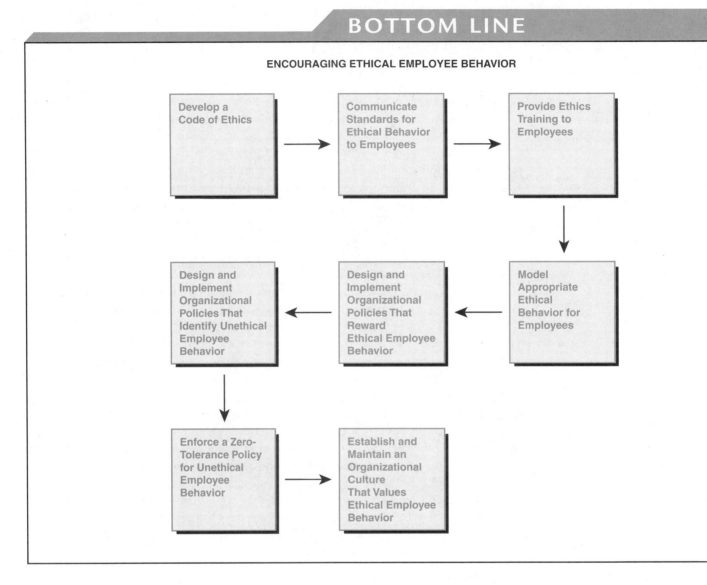

Top Ten List: Key Points to Remember

FOSTERING ETHICAL BEHAVIOR

10. Establish what "ethical behavior" means for your firm.
9. Translate your general standards for ethical behavior into specific actions that employees can take to be ethical in performing their jobs on a daily basis.
8. Create a formal code of ethics for your organization and integrate it into new employee orientation programs.
7. Provide formal ethics training for all managers and employees in your organization.
6. Ensure that the leadership of the organization models high standards for ethical behavior for other members of the organization.
5. Provide ongoing opportunities (e.g., meetings, conferences, town hall meetings) for employees to ask questions and to voice concerns about ethical issues.
4. Develop a clear sense of why being ethical matters to your organization in terms of its objectives or the means it is using to reach desired ends.
3. Use managerial and organizational policies and practices to reward ethical behavior and to punish unethical behavior.
2. Communicate the ethical standards of your organization to employees using a variety of mechanisms (e.g., employee handbooks, mission statements, annual reports, memos).
1. Develop a "system" and a culture that value the importance of ethical behavior in the workplace.

Questions for Review and Reflection

REVIEW QUESTIONS

1. Define business ethics.
2. Give examples of unethical or illegal behaviors in organizations and their costs and consequences.
3. What is the difference between bribes and kickbacks?
4. What are sweatshops? Why are they garnering so much attention?
5. How are ethical behaviors related to organizational performance?
6. What is whistle-blowing? What are arguments for and against whistle-blower protection?
7. What are some legal remedies for unethical behavior?
8. Identify seven guidelines for enhancing your own ethical behavior.
9. Discuss eight guidelines for encouraging ethical behavior in others.
10. What is an ombudsman? What is the purpose of ethics hotlines?

CRITICAL THINKING QUESTIONS

1. Consider the following argument: "We can't change people's ethical values; those are learned early in life. As a company, we should simply expect complete integrity from our employees and then punish unethical behavior promptly and appropriately." Do you agree? Why or why not?
2. One response to calls to stop using sweatshops in foreign countries is that the wages paid by the sweatshops are not low by the standards of the nations in which they are found, and shutting down the sweatshops would simply deprive needy workers of their incomes. Do you agree? Why or why not?
3. This chapter has presented positions for and against enhanced whistle-blower protection. Take and defend a position for or against such enhanced protection. In your defense of the position, be sure to address arguments made by those opposing your view.
4. A concern is sometimes raised that by focusing on issues such as ethics, companies may lose sight of "the bottom line." Based on the material presented in this chapter and your own experience and perspectives, discuss ways that *failure to pay attention* to ethics may harm a firm's financial performance.
5. In the wake of the recent plague of corporate scandals,

EXPERIENTIAL EXERCISES

WEB EXERCISE 6-1: OMBUDSMEN

Go to the Ombudsman resources on the University of Colorado Conflict Research Consortium Web site at:

http://crinfo.org/masterresults.cfm?pid=263

You will find Web resources such as "The Role of Ombudsmen in Dispute Resolution," "The Corporate Ombudsman: An Overview and Analysis," and "Neutrality in Listening." Select any three ombudsman Web resources that interest you. Write a two- to three-page report summarizing what you learned from the resources.

WEB EXERCISE 6-2: CODES OF ETHICS

EthicsWeb.ca offers a wide variety of ethics resources. Click on the following link to find codes of ethics of about 50 organizations (as well as guidelines for writing your own code of ethics):

http://www.ethicsweb.ca/resources
professional/codes-of-ethics.html

1. Select three company codes of ethics from the site (or from other Web sites you identify).
2. Identify one topic covered in each of the three codes of ethics (e.g., conflicts of interest, accepting gifts, or use of company facilities). Provide summaries of each of the relevant sections.
3. Compare and contrast the coverage of the topic across the three codes of ethics. What might account for similarities and differences? Do you think one of the codes would be more effective than the others? Why or why not?

CASE 6-1

DECLINE (AND COMEBACK?) AT LEVI STRAUSS & CO.

The Company[62]

Levi Strauss & Co. is a manufacturer and marketer of branded jeans and casual sportswear. Its brand names include Levi's, Dockers, and Levi Strauss Signature. The company was founded in 1853 by Levi Strauss, a Bavarian immigrant. It has about 1,500 employees who work at its corporate headquarters in San Francisco, California, with approximately 12,400 employees worldwide. It maintains 21 production facilities and 25 customer service centers around the world. Levi Strauss & Co.'s corporate structure is divided into three geographic divisions: Levi Strauss, the Americas, Levi Strauss, Europe, Middle East, and Africa; and Levi Strauss, Asia Pacific.

The vision of Levi Strauss & Co. is as follows:

"People love our clothes and trust our company. We will market the most appealing and widely worn casual clothing in the world. We will clothe the world."

The company's core values are empathy, originality, integrity, and courage. Specifically, the formal statement of these values is as follows:

Empathy—Walking in Other People's Shoes
Empathy begins with listening . . . paying close attention to the world around us . . . understanding, appreciating, and meeting the needs of those we serve, including consumers, retail customers, shareholders, and each other as employees.

Originality—Being Authentic and Innovative
Levis Strauss started it and forever earned a place in history. Today, the Levi's brand is an authentic American icon, known the world over. . . . Its jeans are young at heart, strong, adaptable, they have been worn by generations of individuals who have made them their own. They are symbolic of frontier

independence, democratic idealism, social change, and fun. Levi's jeans are both a work pant and a fashion statement. Collectively, these attributes and values make the Levi's brand unlike any other. . . . Now, more than ever, constant and meaningful innovation is critical to our commercial success. . . . As the "makers and keepers" of Levis Strauss' legacy, we must look at the world with fresh eyes and use the power of ideas to improve everything we do across all dimensions of our business.

Integrity—Doing the Right Thing

Ethical conduct and social responsibility characterize our way of doing business. We are honest and trustworthy. We do what we say we are going to do. Integrity includes a willingness to do the right thing for out employees, brands, the company, and society as a whole, even when personal, professional, and social risks or economic pressures confront us. This principle of responsible commercial success is embedded in the company's experience. It continues to anchor our beliefs and behaviors today, and it is one of the reasons that customers trust our brands. Our shareholders expect us to manage the company this way. It strengthens brand equity and drives sustained, profitable growth, and superior return on investment.

Courage—Standing Up for What We Believe

It takes courage to be great. Courage is the willingness to challenge hierarchy, accepted practices, and conventional wisdom. Courage includes truth telling and acting resolutely on our beliefs. It means standing by our convictions.

Socially Responsible Worldwide Sourcing[63]

Levis Strauss & Co. maintains global sourcing and operating guidelines as one reflection of its long history of commitment to ethics and social responsibility. Management uses country assessment guidelines as a basis for making business-related decisions within the company's framework for ethics and social responsibility. Specifically, all business opportunities (e.g., places where the company may do business or set up production facilities) are evaluated in terms of health and safety conditions provided for employees, the quality of the human rights environment, supportiveness of the legal system, and the overall political, economic, and social environment.

In evaluating potential business partners, Levi Strauss & Co. assesses the degree to which these parties demon-strate a commitment to high ethical standards, compliance with legal requirements, concern for the environment, and employment standards (e.g., avoiding the use of child labor and prison labor and concern for working hours, wages and benefits, and health and safety).

The company's commitment to ethics and social responsibility can be seen in the creation of committee involvement teams that encourage employees to be active participants in their local communities. In addition, the company and the Levi Strauss Foundation maintain a global giving program that makes contributions to community organizations in over 40 countries. These contributions are used to address problems related to AIDS and discrimination and racism. The company has also taken a strong stand on protecting worker rights by actively participating in the Fair Labor Association and the Ethical Trading Initiative.

The organizational culture that exists at Levi Strauss & Co. is very values driven. Some specific elements of the culture include a strong belief in ongoing employee rewards and recognition, flexible work arrangements (e.g., leave of absence programs, a business casual dress code), employee empowerment, and concern for ethics and social responsibility as a driver of behavior every day.

The Situation: Decline of the Levi's Brand Name[64]

The CEO of Levi Strauss & Co. was Robert Haas, a Harvard MBA whose previous experience involved working in the Peace Corps and for McKinsey, the management consulting firm. Haas's vision for Levi Strauss was to create a company driven by social values and concern for the communities in which the company did business. This led Haas to create a business process/re-engineering initiative that he thought would greatly enhance the responsiveness of the company to changing markets and customer preferences.

The beginning of the decline in the Levi's brand name began around 1990 as its market share among young male consumers dropped significantly. Other problems included poor in-store displays, missed deliveries to retailers (e.g., JCPenney), and high manufacturing costs. Between 1990 and 1998, the situation only got worse for the company. The company's market share of male consumers 16 years old and up went from more than 48 percent in 1990 to 25 percent in 1998. Suddenly, Levi's was no longer cool among the influential younger crowd.

The search for answers as to how the venerable Levi's name could have experienced such a dramatic slide pointed to a number of underlying causes. First, Robert Haas did not possess any relevant retailing experience, raising questions about how he could lead an apparel firm. Some employees noted that he demonstrated a concern for every employee's ideas and opinions to a fault. Although employee participation and involvement made sense in a wide range of situations, some employees felt this resulted in tremendous inefficiencies, long meetings, endless discussions, and an inability to eventually make a decision and move forward.

An overemphasis on addressing the issues of ethics and social responsibility may have also played a role in the company's problems because significant time and resources were spent integrating these issues into the "Levi Strauss Mission and Aspirations Statement." Also, the company's compensation system was redesigned so a third of executive bonuses were based on "managing aspirationally." Finally, considerable time was spent in task forces and committees that were formed to address issues related to work force diversity.

Other management problems not necessarily linked with the ethics and social responsibility issue also contributed to the company's problems. In short, the company refused to change its product line as customer preferences and markets changed despite data that retailers showed to Levi Strauss management demonstrating how customer buying patterns were shifting. In the end, Levi Strauss ended up attempting to sell the same basic 501 jeans to a market that had fragmented into multiple niches.

Management also did not do an effective job of managing change. For example, the implementation of its customer service supply chain program involved rewriting hundreds of job descriptions. Employees were asked to reapply for new jobs based on this system. In some cases, employees did not get the jobs for which they had applied, creating chaos. In addition, an employee attitude survey dealing with organizational change contained questions that many employees viewed as inappropriate or offensive. The company lost some of its best employees, who decided they had tolerated enough and quit their jobs.

Finally, there was the issue of lack of accountability. Now that Levi Strauss was privately owned, Haas didn't have to worry about responding to shareholder concerns.

Management's Actions

Levi Strauss management has taken a number of actions in an attempt to turn the company around. It created a new mission statement for itself: "To be the casual company authority." The company has created a new brand management structure and has increased external recruiting to bring new blood into the organization. It also brought out a new specialized brand called *Red Line* in an attempt to regain an image of being cool among young urban consumers.

In the fall of 1999, Philip Marineau became the new CEO at Levi Strauss, with Robert Haas moving to chairman. Marineau's job has been to develop and implement a three-year turnaround strategy for the company. He has focused on reducing the company's $3.6 billion debt and launching new lines of apparel, including Engineered Jeans, 569s, and Silver Tab Label for women.

So far, there is reason to be somewhat optimistic. Third-quarter sales for 2003 increased 6 percent to $1.1 billion from $1 billion for the same period in 2002. Gross profit was $404 million. Part of these results were due to a successful introduction of the Levi Strauss Signature line into 3,000 Wal-Mart stores and strength in its Asian business. This is part of Marineau's consumer segmentation strategy: marketing distinctive jeanswear products to a much broader range of consumers to drive sales growth for 2004. However, the future is far from certain for this 150-year-old company as the retail industry becomes more challenging owing to intense competition from such companies as Tommy Hilfiger, the Gap, Nautica, and Calvin Klein.

Discussion Questions

1. What are the most significant challenges facing Levi Strauss & Co.? Explain your reasoning.
2. What recommendations would you give to CEO Phil Marineau regarding the actions he must take to sustain the turnaround?
3. Evaluate Levi Strauss's emphasis on ethics and social responsibility in relation to its past and current performance. To what extent are the two related to each other? Justify your answer.
4. What are the practical implications of this case for you as a future supervisor or manager?

CASE 6-2

REBUILDING TRUST AND INTEGRITY AT TYCO INTERNATIONAL LTD.

The Company[65]

Tyco International Ltd. is a leading producer of products and services in a variety of businesses including electronics (e.g., passive electronic components, private radio systems); fire and security (e.g., anti-theft systems, video surveillance systems); health care (e.g., surgical, respiratory imaging, and pharmaceutical products); plastics and adhesives (e.g., polyethylene-based films, disposable dinnerware products); and engineer products and services (e.g., industrial valves, control products). The CEO of the company is Edward D. Breen. In 2002, Tyco employed 267,500 people in its various businesses. The company had sales of $36.8 billion and a net income of $979 million in 2003. Tyco is based in Portsmouth, New Hampshire.

> The mission of Tyco International Ltd. is as follows:
> *We will increase the value of our company and our global portfolio of diversified brands by exceeding customers' expectations and achieving market leadership and operating excellence in every segment of our company.*
>
> The company's key goals are as follows:

- Governance—Adhere to the highest standards of corporate governance by establishing processes and practices that promote and ensure integrity, compliance, and accountability.
- Customers—Fully understand and exceed our customers' needs, wants, and preferences and provide greater value to our customers than our competition.
- People—Attract and retain, at every level of the company, people who represent the highest standards of excellence and integrity.
- Operating Excellence—Implement initiatives across our business segments to achieve best-in-class operating practices and leverage company-wide opportunities, utilizing Six Sigma measurements.
- Financial Results/Liquidity—Consistently achieve outstanding performance in revenues, earnings, cash flow, and all other key financial metrics. Establish a capital structure that meets both long- and short-term needs. Tyco's people and values include the following:
- Integrity—We must demand of ourselves and each other the highest standards of individual and corporate integrity. We safeguard company assets. We comply with all company policies and laws.

- Excellence—We continually challenge each other to improve our products, our processes, and ourselves. We strive always to understand our customers' businesses and help them achieve their goals. We are dedicated to diversity, fair treatment, mutual respect, and trust.
- Teamwork—We foster an environment that encourages innovation, creativity, and results through teamwork. We practice leadership that teaches, inspires, and promotes full participation and career development. We encourage open and effective communication and interaction.
- Accountability—We honor commitments we make, and take personal responsibility for all actions and results. We create an operating discipline of continuous improvement that is an integral part of our culture.

Corporate Scandals

Dennis Koslowski, the former chairman and chief executive officer of Tyco International who resigned for what he cited as personal reasons, caused tremendous damage to the image, credibility, and trustworthiness of his company. He, along with Mark Swartz, the former chief financial officer at the company, are accused of looting $600 million in unauthorized compensation from the corporate treasury.[66] Prosecutors in Koslowski's larceny trial were also shown a 30-minute video of a lavish $2 million birthday party he threw for his wife on the island of Sardinia using $1 million of Tyco's funds. The video was used to show Koslowski was guilty of using Tyco's funds for his personal needs. If found guilty, Koslowski and Swartz could face up to 30 years in prison.

Rebuilding the Company: Enter Edward Breen[67]

On July 29, 2002, Edward D. Breen took over the helm of an embattled Tyco International that, according to prosecutors, was a "criminal enterprise." On his first day on the job, a group of investors showed up unexpectedly, demanding the entire Tyco board be replaced immediately. Then, on his one-year anniversary as CEO, the company disclosed it was restating its results back to 1998 when it had originally stated it would not be making any such restatements.

Breen's single biggest challenge has been to remove the ghost of Dennis Koslowski and to rebuild trust and credibility in Tyco International. Achieving this goal will not be easy because the company's accounting practices are being investigated in response to allegations that Tyco had been cooking its numbers under former CEO Koslowski. This has strained relations with the company's customers and investors. Moreover, the Securities and Exchange Commission (SEC) and the Internal Revenue Service (IRS) are also investigating Tyco's financial records regarding the way in which the company handled cancelled contracts in its security alarm business (ADT) and whether it was using its incorporation in Bermuda as a way to hide taxable income.

Many insiders and analysts believe Breen is the right person to get the job done. Specifically, Breen is seen as a down-to-earth team player, who does not believe in providing lavish benefits for himself such as the $6,000 shower curtains, $15,000 umbrella stands, and two personal gourmet chefs his predecessor valued so greatly. In addition, Breen is an optimist who projects a can-do attitude and confidence in the success of his turnaround plan. This has earned him the trust and respect of many members of the organization. Breen has taken the following actions to help steer Tyco in the right direction:

- Planned and implemented "centralized efficiency programs" (e.g., Six Sigma) to provide better monitoring and control functions over key business systems and processes (e.g., accounting, information).
- Set aggressive, but not impossible goals for Tyco in the next two years (10 to 12 percent earnings growth, 4 to 6 percent revenue growth).
- Terminated the entire board of directors and most of the members of the executive team.
- Hired a vice president of corporate governance who reports directly to the board.
- Created an ombudsmen office where employees can report concerns confidentially.

- Gave more authority to the lead director of the board of directors and prohibited all corporate loans to senior executives.
- Reduced executive compensation including his own (about $3 million in 2003).
- Plans to move Tyco's corporate headquarters out of its current extravagant location on 57th Street to a more modest location in Princeton, New Jersey.

The Future

Nobody knows for sure if Ed Breen will actually be successful in enabling Tyco to regain its former glory and stature as one of the most respected companies in the world. However, many feel that if anyone can pull off this turnaround, it is Ed Breen.

Discussion Questions

1. How are the scandals and investigations of Tyco International damaging its credibility and reputation in the eyes of its stakeholders (e.g., employees, investors)?
2. Evaluate Tyco's value statements that were presented in this case. To what extent will they actually help Tyco be a more ethical company?
3. Evaluate Breen's handling of the situation in trying to eliminate the perception of Tyco International as a "criminal enterprise." Be specific.
4. Based on the discussion of guidelines for encouraging ethical behavior discussed in the chapter, identify and describe some additional actions that Breen could take to encourage more ethical behavior at Tyco. Be specific.
5. What are the practical implications of this exercise for you as a future manager in the real world?

VIDEO CASE

WORKPLACE PRIVACY: STRONG TALK, STRONGER MEASURES

Running Time: 4:08

Ethical questions surrounding declining workplace privacy in the face of burgeoning computer surveillance are highlighted in this video, narrated by CNN correspondent Wolf Blitzer. Among those taking positions on the issue are Scott Liebowitz, president of That Fish Place/That Pet Place; Roy Young, vice president for sales and marketing of Adavi Inc., maker of Silent Watch surveillance software; and law professor Jeffrey Rosen, author of *The Unwanted Gaze: The Destruction of Privacy in America.*

As discussed in the video, an American Management Association survey showed that 54 percent of companies now monitor their employees' Internet use, and 38 percent review employees' e-mail. With programs such as Silent Watch, managers can monitor every keystroke made by employees, even those keystrokes subsequently deleted. Based on computer surveillance, companies such as Xerox and the New York Times have fired employees found to be using their computers for unauthorized reasons.

After viewing the video, answer the following questions:

1. What arguments do Scott Liebowitz and Roy Young present in favor of workplace surveillance? Do you agree with those their arguments? Why or why not?

2. What arguments does Jeffrey Rosen present in opposition to workplace surveillance? Do you agree with his arguments? Why or why not?

3. What rights appear to be in conflict in this case? What factors do you think should be considered in deciding which of those rights should prevail in a given situation?

4. What long-run consequences, positive and negative, do you think computer surveillance of employees will have on workplaces?

5. A survey found that 90 percent of the nation's workers admit to surfing recreational Web sites during office hours, and 84 percent say they send personal e-mails from work. How, if at all, does such widespread behavior affect the feasibility and desirability of disciplining workers for unauthorized computer use?

http://www.thatpetplace.com/

http://www.adavi.com/testimonials.cfm

SKILLS PRACTICE

6-1   *Skill Level: BASIC*

Field Experience: Interviews with Managers About Managing Ethics

Skill Objective

To develop a better understanding of what management practitioners in the real world do to manage ethics effectively.

Procedure

1. Identify three managers who work in different business organizations. Ask the manager(s) if you can interview each of them for approximately 30 minutes.

2. When you meet with each manager, ask the following questions.

   a. Why is being ethical important for a manager? For an organization?

   b. Can you give me some examples of the types of ethical issues you encounter in your job? What types of strategies do you use to handle these ethical issues?

   c. Which of the strategies you use to manage ethical issues tend to be the most effective? Why?

   d. What specific actions can a manager take to encourage his or her employees to behave more ethically?

   e. What advice would you give students regarding specific actions they can take to manage ethical issues effectively in the real world?

3. Summarize the results of your interviews.

Discussion Questions

1. Based on the summary of your interviews, what are your key findings about managing ethics? Why are these findings so significant?

2. What are the practical implications of this exercise for you as a future manager and leader of a real-world organization?

SKILLS PRACTICE

6-2   *Skill Level: CHALLENGING*

Ethics in the Business World: Wall Street

Skill Objective

To develop skill in analyzing how individual differences and business environments can influence ethical (or unethical) behavior.

Procedure

1. Obtain a copy of the movie *Wall Street* starring Michael Douglas and Charlie Sheen. It is available on VHS and DVD and can be rented or purchased from a local video store or retailer.

2. Watch the movie (in class or at home on your own). Be sure to note specific scenes and dialogue that illustrate issues of ethics and how various factors in the business environment portrayed in the film influence the ethical behavior of the main characters.

    Note: Download the worksheet developed for this exercise from the Web site for this book. This will help you document your notes regarding relevant scenes from the movie.

3. Discuss the following questions as a class.

    a. To what extent was the behavior of the two main characters, Bud Fox and Gordon Gekko, ethical or unethical? Support your answer using scenes and dialogue from the movie.

    b. What aspects of the corporation in the movie contributed to making the behavior of the Fox and Gekko more or less ethical? Support your answer using scenes and dialogue from the movie.

    c. If you were advising Bud Fox, what would you have recommended he do to handle the situation more effectively?

    d. How are the ethical issues in this movie similar to the issues that some real-world organizations have had to deal with today?

    e. What are the practical implications of this exercise for you in dealing with ethical issues in real-world organizations?

SKILLS PRACTICE

6-3   *Skill Level:* BASIC

Ethical Reflections

Consider each of the following questions and respond as honestly as possible. There are no right or wrong answers. Instead, these reflections are intended to encourage you to think about some important ethical issues facing people in businesses today. Download from the text Web site the worksheet developed for this exercise.

1. Think of a situation in which you had to make an important ethical choice (at school, at work, with friends, etc.). Describe the choice and identify why you made the choice you did.

2. Thinking back on your choice, are you now satisfied with it? Was there anything you wish you had done differently? Were there things that others could have done that would have helped you "do the right thing"?

3. What lessons do you draw from your answers to questions 1 and 2?

4. Identify a situation (preferably one in which you were personally involved) in which someone did something you felt was unethical. Describe the situation and indicate why you feel the behavior was unethical.

5. What do you think were some causes of the unethical behavior you just described? Try to think of as many feasible causes as you can. For instance, did the behavior reflect the values or personalities (or both) of the person or people involved? Demands of the situation? The sorts of things that were rewarded? A culture that encouraged the behavior? A lack of mechanisms to prevent the behavior? Other factors?

6. What happened to the person who engaged in the unethical behavior you have described? Did he or she gain or lose by engaging in the behavior? Should anyone have done anything differently to ensure the individual wouldn't profit from the behavior?

7. The following list contains a series of questions about ethical behavior. Answer each of these questions. Then meet with at least one other student in your class and compare your answers. Explore reasons why you may have had different answers. Use the following scale when responding:

1 Disagree strongly
2 Disagree somewhat
3 Neither agree nor disagree
4 Agree somewhat
5 Agree strongly

____ 1. In general, people who engage in unethical behavior get ahead in organizations.

____ 2. Most organizations encourage unethical behavior if it helps profits.

____ 3. Things considered to be unethical in one culture (e.g., bribery or child labor) may be considered ethical in another.

____ 4. Whether a behavior is ethical or unethical is in the eyes of the beholder.

____ 5. When dealing with people from other cultures, we shouldn't try to impose our ethical standards on them.

____ 6. Most people try to be ethical.

____ 7. In general, I believe worthwhile ends may justify some cutting of ethical corners.

____ 8. Ethical behavior pays off on the bottom line.

____ 9. If I see people engaging in unethical behavior, such as stealing office supplies or making inappropriate use of company resources, I am morally obligated to report it.

____ 10. Virtually everyone will do unethical things if the situation demands it.

____ 11. When people behave in unethical ways, it is more often because of the situations in which they find themselves rather than their values or personalities.

____ 12. The degree to which employees behave ethically should be part of formal performance reviews.

____ 13. Ethics isn't something that can be taught.

____ 14. I wouldn't work in a company if I thought it would require me to engage in unethical acts.

____ 15. Some people are inherently unethical.

____ 16. It's generally not possible to decide what is or isn't ethical.

____ 17. If I worked in a company at which I saw people breaking the law in ways that endangered public safety, I would report the wrongdoing to law enforcement officials or others outside the firm if necessary.

____ 18. It's not the company's responsibility to encourage ethical behavior; employees have the responsibility to be ethical.

____ 19. Companies should have a zero-tolerance policy for unethical behavior; any unethical behavior should be grounds for dismissal.

____ 20. Employees shouldn't be held responsible for unethical behaviors that aren't addressed explicitly in the company's code of ethics.

SKILLS PRACTICE

6-4

Skill Level: **CHALLENGING**

Developing a Code of Ethics

Skill Objective
To develop skill in creating an effective code of ethics that specifies the standards for ethical behavior in an organization.

Procedure

1. Form teams of approximately five people.

2. Download the worksheet developed for this exercise from the Web site for this textbook. This will provide a useful template for completing this exercise.

3. Review the general guidelines provided here regarding the development of a code of ethics. Note: It would be helpful to complete Web Exercise 6-2 before doing this exercise.

   a. Step 1: Make a list of the key values of the organization based on its mission, culture, and primary objectives.

   b. Step 2: Narrow it down to a short list of five to seven core values that represent the factors of the greatest importance to the organization.

   c. Step 3: Develop a set of specific behaviors that reflect each of the core values of the organization.

   d. Step 4: Create the code of ethics by listing the core values and the supporting behaviors in a single document.

   e. Step 5: Send the code of ethics to relevant stakeholders of the organization (e.g., management, employees, customers, board members, etc.) to ensure it is appropriate and clear.

   f. Step 6: Finalize the code of ethics and integrate it into the employee handbook, new employee orientation training programs, and so on.

4. Based on the general guidelines, draft a code of ethics for an organization with which the members of the group are familiar. This could be the college or university they attend, a student organization, or a company they know.

5. Develop a set of strategies for actually implementing the code of ethics in the organization used for this exercise.

6. Answer the discussion questions below as a class.

   a. Evaluate your code of ethics. Why do you feel it is appropriate? What difficulties might you en-counter in trying to actually implement it in the organization you used for this exercise? Why or why not?

   b. What other strategies does management need to implement with a code of ethics in order to increase the ethical behavior of employees in an organization?

   c. What are the key practical implications of this exercise for you as a future manager in a real-world organization?

SKILLS PRACTICE

6-5	Skill Level: BASIC

Handling Ethical Dilemmas

Skill Objective

To develop skill in evaluating managerial situations with ethical implications.

Procedure

Note: Download the worksheet developed for this exercise from the Web site for this textbook.

1. This exercise can be completed individually or in groups of three to five students.

2. Select one of the following scenarios and develop an action plan for dealing with it effectively as a manager.

3. Optional: Present your action plan to the class and defend it.

4. Discuss the questions that follow as a class.

Scenario 1: Jobs—to Export or Not to Export?

The Americana Corporation, a leading U.S. manufacturer of a variety of consumer electronics products such as personal digital assistants, digital phones, pagers, and digital cameras, has taken great pride in its tradition of being an "All-American" company committed to designing and manufacturing all its products in the United States. This strategic emphasis has been incorporated into the company's mission statement and its product advertising.

Recently, the company's financial performance has begun to decline, owing to intense foreign competition, value-oriented consumers, and severe upward pressure on costs. For the first time, you are contemplating the idea of moving some or all of your production overseas to a developing country with cheap labor. However, you don't know how such a move will be received by employees and customers, who may perceive this move as unethical or irresponsible given the company's All-American image. What would you do?

Scenario 2: Managing a Staff of Financial Advisors

Linda Jones is the manager of a group of financial advisors at a mutual fund company based in New York. Her staff does a lot of its work out in the field, meeting directly with customers to develop appropriate investment plans for achieving their financial goals. The relationship between the financial advisor and the client is critical for the long-term success and profitability of the firm. This relationship must be based on mutual trust and respect.

The financial advisors receive a base salary, but a major portion of their overall compensation comes from sales commissions. For her financial advisors, Linda sets specific sales targets they are expected to meet. Failure to do so consistently leads to disciplinary action or termination.

The environment at the firm clearly stresses the importance of prospecting customers and selling as a core activity. Recently, it has come to Linda's attention that some of her staff members have been using high-pressure sales tactics on elderly people and recent widows in order to get them to invest in high-risk mutual funds that generate large commissions for themselves. The problem here is that the very aggressive and volatile high-risk mutual funds are generally not a good investment option for elderly people and recent widows. Given this situation, what would you do?

Scenario 3: Does Integrity Matter?
Keisha Anderson, the CEO of Austin Corporation, needs to fill the position of vice president of marketing. The candidate he likes is Bill Scott, who has been with the firm for 15 years and is viewed as highly competent. He possesses excellent technical skills. Bill is very outgoing and personable. He has tremendous energy and charisma, and he would bring a lot of experience and expertise to the position.

But Keisha is concerned that although Bill is married with two children, he has developed a reputation in the company for being a "womanizer." In fact, rumors have been circulated about affairs he has had with female employees.

Given the family-oriented and very conservative culture that prevails in the firm, this issue could be problematic in terms of giving the job to Bill. What would you do?

Discussion Questions
1. Why is it important to consider the ethical implications of decisions that managers make?
2. To what extent should managers make tradeoffs between handling ethical issues appropriately and achieving bottom-line business objectives and results?
3. What are the practical implications of this exercise for you as future manager in a real-world organization?

SKILLS PRACTICE

6-6   *Skill Level:* **CHALLENGING**

Developing an Ethics Program

Skill Objective
To develop skill in designing an ethics program for an organization.

Procedure
1. Form teams of approximately five people.
2. Download the worksheet developed for this exercise from the Web site for this textbook. This will provide a useful template for working through this exercise.
3. Read the case study below and develop a formal ethics program to help this organization encourage the practice of "personal and business integrity" among all of its employees.
4. Develop a set of strategies for actually implementing the ethics program you developed earlier.
5. Answer the discussion questions at the end of this exercise.

Case Study: *Implementing an Employee Ethics Program at Quorum Health Group*

The Situation
Quorum Health Group, Inc. owns and operates 21 acute care hospitals and local/regional health care systems in nine states in the United States. Quorum employs a workforce of more than 20,000 employees. The basic mission of the company is as follows:

Quorum Health Group, Inc. owns and manages health care systems and is committed to meeting the needs of consumers and providers through innovative services that enhance the delivery of quality health-care.

One of the key values at Quorum is "personal and business integrity." This issue has become increasingly important to health care organizations as regulation of the overall industry intensifies and the business practices of health care providers are subjected to greater scrutiny by the federal government and payers of health care services.

Given the concern for compliance with complex regulation, Quorum identified the need to develop a comprehensive business ethics program for its management and employees.

The purpose of the program was to reinforce the values of the company and to ensure that employees possessed the knowledge and tools to make ethical decisions in performing their jobs on a day-to-day basis.

Discussion Questions
1. Suppose that you were put in charge of developing the business ethics program at Quorum. What would you do? Be as specific as possible in developing the various elements of your program.
2. What are the practical implications of this exercise

for you as a future manager or leader in a real-world
organization?

http://www.quorumhealth.com/

Source: C. F. Batts, "Making Ethics an Organization Priority," *The Healthcare Forum Journal*, January/February 1998, pp. 38–41.

COMMUNICATING EFFECTIVELY

CHAPTER 7

Skills Objectives

> *To enhance the accuracy of communications with others through the effective management of the basic communication process.*

> *To overcome barriers to effective communication.*

> *To enhance the effectiveness of speaking within a management context.*

> *To use active listening in order to enhance understanding of communication with others within organizations.*

> *To use nonverbal communications effectively to support and understand communications with others.*

> *To encourage and manage informal communication with others.*

> *To enhance communication with others in a cross-cultural context.*

KNOWLEDGE OBJECTIVES

> Identify the functions of communication.

> Explain the steps in the communication process.

> Discuss communication channels, including key channel dimensions.

> Identify communication networks differing in centralization and relative centrality and discuss the relative merits of each.

> Discuss principles of supportive communication.

> Explain guidelines for understanding and overcoming communication barriers.

> Present guidelines for effective speaking and active listening.

> Understand guidelines for effective use of e-mail.

> Identify approaches to e-commerce.

> Discuss ways to read and use nonverbal communication.

> Discuss the importance of informal communication, including the grapevine.

> Identify tips for effective cross-cultural communication.

Tom Peters and Robert Waterman sought in their book *In Search of Excellence: Lessons from America's Best-Run Companies* to discover the secrets of America's truly excellent companies.[1] Their findings led them to argue that the amount, nature, and uses of communication in the excellent companies were remarkably different from those of their nonexcellent peers. Peters and Waterman found that the excellent companies they examined use a variety of philosophies, practices, and structures to encourage communication. At IBM and Delta Airlines, open-door policies were pervasive. At Hewlett-Packard and United Airlines, versions of "management by wandering about" were practiced, in which managers were encouraged to get out of their offices and informally communicate. Corning Glass installed escalators rather than elevators in its new engineering building to increase the chance of face-to-face contact. At Citibank, the desks of operations officers and lending officers were moved to the same floor and intermingled to encourage communication. Intel's new buildings in Silicon Valley were designed to have an excess of small conference rooms, filled with blackboards to facilitate communication, where people can eat lunch or solve problems. What these examples have in common, according to Peters and Waterman, are "lots of communication" (p. 122).

This emphasis on communication is not surprising. Communication affects virtually every area of work. Communication with employees about plant closings, performance appraisals, organizational goals, probable salary increases and job changes, and even the date of the company picnic are essential to the proper functioning of the firm. If communication is inaccurate or inadequate, uncertainty, apprehension, errors, and dissatisfaction may ensue.

Organizations also must communicate effectively with parties outside their boundaries. And, as we discuss later in the chapter, companies regularly find themselves communicating with the public to quell rumors. Increasingly, they also must pay heed to their "word of mouse" reputations, responding to angry customers' critical postings on Internet forums.[2]

Further, much of a manager's time is spent communicating. In a classic study, Henry Mintzberg observed chief executive officers on a daily basis to see how they actually spent their time. He found CEOs to spend 78 percent of their time on communication-related activities involving direct contact with others, including scheduled and unscheduled meetings, telephone calls, and tours of facilities. Even the 22 percent of time spent on what was called "deskwork" included answering mail and was thus related to communication. Also, the CEOs said activities involving direct communication with others were more interesting and valuable than more routine activities. The chief executives regularly communicated with peers, clients, suppliers, associates, subordinates, members of the board of directors, and others. And face-to-face communication appears to demand large amounts of time at all managerial levels. Mintzberg estimated such communication to take 59 percent of the time of supervisors and 89 percent of the time of middle managers.[3]

In this chapter we examine a variety of important issues relating to communication. We first consider functions of communication and the nature of the communication process. We then address communication channels, including important dimensions on which channels may vary, followed by a review of communication network types. Next we examine communication barriers and ways they can be overcome. We then present guidelines for effective written communication, effective speaking, and mastering active listening. Following this, we address forms and functions of nonverbal communication. Next, we consider important issues in electronic communication, including e-mail, the Internet and the World Wide Web, teleconferencing and videoconferencing, and e-commerce. We close with discussions of informal communication, coaching and counseling, and cross-cultural communication.

Before continuing, complete Self-Assessment Exercise 7-1 to evaluate your personal communication style. Then complete the Pretest Skills Assessment. After you are through, you can learn more about your responses by visiting the text Web site.

SELF-ASSESSMENT 7-1

Your Personal Communication Style

Answer each of the following questions using the following scale:

1 Disagree strongly
2 Disagree somewhat
3 Neither agree nor disagree
4 Agree somewhat
5 Agree strongly

In discussions with others:

_____ 1. I tend to speak my mind in a direct and straightforward way.
_____ 2. I argue my points fully and thoroughly.
_____ 3. I would rather say nothing than hurt someone's feelings.
_____ 4. I believe in carefully discussing things before making decisions.
_____ 5. I quickly "cut to the bottom line" in getting my point across.
_____ 6. I really enjoy the process of conversing.
_____ 7. I am a good listener.
_____ 8. I am sometimes accused of being long-winded.
_____ 9. I am very concerned with others' feelings.
_____ 10. I rarely interrupt others.
_____ 11. I value brevity and frankness.
_____ 12. I hesitate to offer advice or criticism.
_____ 13. I expect others to appreciate my input and to deal with it in a constructive way.
_____ 14. I feel it is best to say what I think and to avoid emotion.
_____ 15. I offer a lot of detail in support of my position.
_____ 16. I am soft-spoken.
_____ 17. I enjoy debating others.
_____ 18. I think it is better to say what I really believe than to "pretty up" my views to try to make people feel comfortable.
_____ 19. I give very complete, precise directions to others.
_____ 20. I use as few words as possible.
_____ 21. I try to keep things warm and supportive.

Note: This exercise is based on actual events encountered by managers in real-world organizations. Some information may have been modified in order to maintain the anonymity of the people and organization involved in this situation.

You are the vice president of the Organizational Development Division at a major manufacturing firm. Your division is composed of two departments—total quality management and organizational research. Each department is headed by a manager. The function of the total quality management department is to work with management throughout the company to embrace total quality management principles and to implement them in their work units. A major objective of the department is to get managers to use data to drive their decision making regarding the operation of their work units.

The organizational research department has the goal of working with management to identify research projects that will enhance the long-term competitiveness of the firm. These projects cover issues ranging from strategic analysis to quality, human resources, marketing, and administration.

One of the most significant challenges facing your division is that there is no communication between the total quality and organizational research departments. Part of the problem is that your two departmental managers have very different styles and do not get along at all. Although the two departments are physically located next to each other, the staff from both units (10–15 employees in each department) are not communicating with each other about opportunities to collaborate on mutually beneficial projects. This problem has resulted in a significant reduction in the overall effectiveness of the division and increases costs associated with the need to hire external consultants and research firms to perform work that could be done internally by one of the departments.

Develop an action plan for solving the problem at your company. Be sure your plan addresses both short-terms and long-terms issues. Be very specific and be prepared to defend each element of your plan in terms of its feasibility and cost effectiveness.

Stop here and complete Skills Practice 7-1. This skills practice involves the analysis of communication issues among a group of individuals who end up in the same lifeboat after their ship is sunk. The classic Hitchcock film on which it is based offers valuable insights regarding communication.

FUNCTIONS OF COMMUNICATION AND THE COMMUNICATION PROCESS

Communication is the transfer of information from one person to another. It may serve several important functions.[4]

> **Information function.** Communication provides information to be used for decision making. Managers require information concerning alternatives, future events, and potential outcomes of their decisions to make reasoned choices. For example, when United Airlines entered bankruptcy in December 2002, CEO Glenn Tilton e-mailed its Mileage Plus members to assure them the firm had filed to reorganize under Chapter 11 "in order to make the fundamental

changes necessary to remain one of the world's premier airlines. While United undergoes reorganization, please know that our commitment to providing you with safe and reliable service remains unchanged." He then went on to assure that tickets would be honored, refund and exchange policies unchanged, and accumulated miles honored.[5]

> **Motivational function.** Communication encourages commitment to organizational objectives, thus enhancing motivation. For instance, former New York City mayor Rudolph Giuliani's calm, reassuring, and inspiring communications after the attacks of 9/11 were credited with motivating New Yorkers to pull together in the face of disaster.

> **Control function.** Communication clarifies duties, authority, and responsibilities, thereby permitting control. If there is ambiguity concerning such things, it is impossible to isolate sources of problems and to take corrective actions.

> **Emotive function.** Communication permits the expression of feelings and the satisfaction of social needs. It may also help vent frustrations. After the breakup of AT&T, there was a marked increase in the number of customers who yelled at operators, a convenient target for anger.

Communication is a process involving several steps, as shown in Figure 7-1.[6] The first step is the development of an idea that the sender wishes to transmit. Step 2 is to encode the idea into words, charts, or other symbols for transmission. Step 3 is to transmit the message by the method chosen, such as memo, phone call, e-mail, or personal visit. Step 4 is the receipt of the message by another person. The receiver of the message must play an active role at this stage. If the message is oral, the receiver must be a good listener. Step 5 is to decode the message so it can be understood. Such understanding occurs only in the mind of the receiver, and no guarantee exists that the message as intended by the sender will be the same as the message understood by the receiver. That is, the message must successfully cross the "bridge of meaning." Once receivers have obtained and decoded a message, they may accept or reject it, which is Step 6. Whether or not the message will be accepted depends on such factors as perceptions of the message's accuracy, the authority and perceived expertise of the sender, and the implications of the message for the receiver. Finally, in Step 7, the receiver uses the message. This may involve discarding it, storing it for future use, or taking action consistent with the message.

Although Figure 7-1 shows feedback, not all communication includes such feedback. As we discuss in the next section, communication may be one way or two way; there are relative benefits and costs to each, depending on the situation.

Skills Practice 7-2 provides an opportunity for you to develop skill in effectively implementing the various elements of the basic communication process in order to enhance the likelihood that others will properly receive your message.

As Self-Assessment 7-1 demonstrated, people tend to use different styles when communicating. For instance, some are careful to explain their views, and others are not. Some are more assertive than others. Some are very concerned about the other person's feelings; others say we should keep emotions out of our discussions. Some rely more on nonverbal communications than others, and so on. The Focus on Management feature on page 281 discusses the effective use of communications in a crisis situation.

FIGURE 7-1

The Communication Process

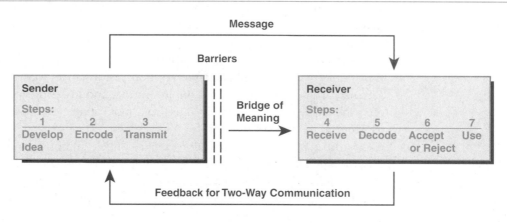

COMMUNICATION CHANNELS

As noted earlier, a communication channel is the medium through which a message is sent. This would include both human channels, such as speech and body movements, and mechanical channels, such as computer networks, the mail, and the telephone. In choosing appropriate channels, you may want to consider several channel dimensions.[7]

CHANNEL DIMENSIONS

Important dimensions on which channels may differ include capacity, modifiability, duplication, immediacy, one-way versus two-way flow, number of linkages, appropriateness, and richness.

> **Capacity.** Channel capacity is the amount of information that can be sent through a channel over a given period of time without significant distortion. A telephone, for instance, has greater capacity than a memo, since the memo is constrained by reading speed.

> **Modifiability.** Modifiability is the degree to which the rate of transmission can be varied. Modifiability of a memo or other written message is high; the recipient can read at a chosen speed and even set the memo aside for a while. A televised message is typically less modifiable (although VCRs are changing this).

> **Duplication.** It is sometimes useful to use subchannels to reiterate or elaborate on a message, especially when it is complex or novel. A television commercial, for instance, may use both visual and auditory subchannels to sell a product.

> **Immediacy.** Immediacy is the speed at which a message can be transmitted. E-mail now transmits reports and other information almost instantly. The U.S. Postal Service may take a few days, or more, to deliver the same message.

> **One-way versus two-way flow.** Some channels, such as a memo and a videotaped lecture, are essentially one-way. *One-way communication* gives a message without opportunity for immediate feedback, such as when a plant manager sends a memo to all employees in the plant. In contrast, *two-way*

FOCUS ON MANAGEMENT

COMMUNICATING AFTER THE OKLAHOMA CITY BOMBING*

Kerr-McGee Corp. is an Oklahoma City–based oil and gas exploration and production company with assets of approximately $7 billion. The Kerr-McGee Corp. building complex is located just two blocks from the site of the April 1995 bombing of the Murrah Federal Building in downtown Oklahoma City. Although Kerr-McGee has extensive crisis communication plans for all its facilities, nothing like the bombing had ever been anticipated. After the initial bomb, it was thought a second bomb was about to explode. The Kerr-McGee buildings were designated as part of the "crime scene," complete with yellow tape. That designation brought many questions from employees, such as these: Were any of our people hurt or killed? Can we help? When can we move our cars? When can we go back to work? How can we get our paychecks if we can't get back to work? With the buildings evacuated, how can we know what's going on? The problem Kerr-McGee faced was how to communicate with 900 scattered, confused, concerned employees in the face of chaos. Within minutes after the bombing, Kerr-McGee's executive management group was transformed into a corporate communications team. About a dozen top executives combined with three members of the corporate communications staff to develop and implement strategic plans to let employees know what was going on. Among the many steps taken were the following:

> One hour and 17 minutes after the bombing, a brief employee bulletin was sent by e-mail to all downtown employees. The e-mail said there had been some minor injuries in the McGee Tower as well as some office and window damage and a doctor was standing by.

> At about the same time, rumors of a second bomb caused evacuation within a two-block radius of the Murrah building, including the Kerr-McGee complex. A public address announcement asked employees to clear the building in an orderly manner and to gather at a nearby convention center. There they were told to return home to await further information.

> A "calling tree" was formed, whereby top executives would contact their direct reports, who would contact their direct reports, and so on, until all employees were contacted. The message said in effect, "We don't know when we can get back in the building, but we'll try to keep you posted."

> A "command center," complete with 15 phone lines, was set up in another Kerr-McGee facility in Oklahoma City. The executive/communications team staffed the phones round the clock for four days in order to respond to employees' questions.

> On the Monday employees returned to work, Kerr-McGee's top executives stationed themselves at all entrances to the building. They handed out "memorial ribbons" to returning employees and gave them each a hug.

> Kerr-McGee's management hired Crisis Management International (CMI), a firm composed of psychologists and psychiatrists who specialize in personal counseling following tragic events. Their first order of business was to have mass meetings with all employees. These were followed by "Let's talk about it" sessions with groups of 20 employees. Finally, the CMI people were made available to employees and their family members on a one-to-one basis for several weeks.

http://www.kerr-mcgee.com/

*D. Dozier, "Case Study: Employee Communications at Kerr-McGee in the Aftermath of the Oklahoma City Bombing," *Public Relations Quarterly*, Summer 1998, pp. 13–18.

---

communication, such as a telephone conversation or a face-to-face chat, allows the message recipient to ask questions and provide feedback. Research shows the following:[8]

- One-way communication is faster than two way.
- Two-way communication is more accurate than one way.
- Receivers are more sure of themselves and make more correct judgments of how right or wrong they are with two-way communication.
- The sender may feel less secure in two-way communication. The message recipients can point out errors, interrupt a stream of thought, disagree, or otherwise challenge the sender.

- Two-way communication is relatively noisy and disorderly. One-way communication appears neat and efficient to an outside observer, but the communication is often less accurate.

> **Number of linkages.** Some channels provide direct contact between a sender and the ultimate recipient; others involve intermediate linkages. Longer channels invite omission and distortion. Use as few linkages as possible.

> **Appropriateness.** Some channels are "made for" certain types of messages and may be completely inappropriate for others. A billboard may be fine for an advertising message, but it is probably not the place to reprimand an employee.

> **Richness.** Richness is the potential information-carrying capacity of data. If the communication of an item of data, such as a wink, conveys substantial new information, it is considered rich. If it provides little new understanding, it is low in richness. Face-to-face communication is the richest form of communication. It provides immediate feedback; with that feedback, understanding can be checked and interpretations corrected. Face-to-face communications also permit the observation of multiple cues, including body language, facial expression, and tone of voice, as we discuss later in the chapter. Face-to-face communications are followed, in declining order of information richness, by the telephone, written personal communications, written formal communications, and computer output.[9]

SELECTING CHANNELS

When sending messages, consider the characteristics we have just presented. How much information must be transmitted? How fast? Does the message require elaboration? Is speed of the essence? Is feedback necessary? Are certain channels unsuited to the nature of the message? You may decide after weighing these factors that available channels somehow must be modified or that multiple channels are needed. Whatever the result, the choice of channels should be carefully weighed.

COMMUNICATION NETWORKS

Communication channels may be linked in a variety of ways to form ***communication networks***.[10] These networks are used to structure the information flows among network members. Whether you realize it or not, you will be making decisions about communication networks on a regular basis. You will need to decide, for instance, who should be in the loop to receive certain types of messages and to whom they should be instructed to respond. In making such decisions, you will determine who has direct and speedy access to information, who is most central in communication networks, who will be able to get information only after others have received it, and so on. Communication networks influence decision quality, member satisfaction, message quality, and other variables. Figure 7-2 shows six common networks.

The chain network links members sequentially. The Y network modifies the chain to have one member communicating to three others. With the wheel network, all communication must flow through a central individual. The circle network permits each member to communicate with two others. With the star network, any member can communicate directly with any other. A variant of the star, called the com-con network, permits all members to communicate directly but also has a central member who is considered the leader.

FIGURE 7-2
Communication Networks

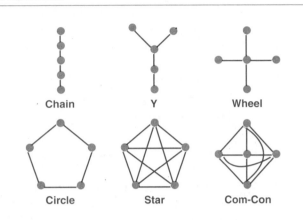

These networks clearly differ on a number of dimensions. For instance, with networks such as the chain and the circle, it may be necessary for a message to pass through multiple links to reach its destination. With the star and com-con networks, one link is sufficient. The networks also vary in degree of centralization. The circle and star networks are decentralized—everyone is as central as everyone else. The wheel and the com-con networks, in contrast, clearly have central members.

Relative centrality is the degree of to which an individual is central in a network. In the wheel network, there is clearly a central member. Because information more often flows through central members, they are likely to be perceived as leaders and to have high status. They are also likely to be more satisfied than their less central counterparts. Again, in the circle and star networks, all members are equally central.

Along with the degree of relative centrality of members within a network, the overall centralization of the network is also of interest. ***Centralization*** is a measure of the degree to which some members of the network are more central than others. So the wheel, with one relatively central member and all others much less central, is highly centralized. The star, with equal member relative centralities, is completely decentralized.

Centralized networks tend to permit rapid decision making, but average member satisfaction is low. Centralized networks may be efficient for simple problems. But as complexity increases, more decentralization (and thus more participation in decision making) is needed, so the wheel network might be appropriate for routine, well-structured tasks, especially if there are time constraints. However, a network such as the circle or star would probably be better for tasks requiring creativity and a wide range of member inputs.

UNDERSTANDING AND OVERCOMING COMMUNICATION BARRIERS

Unfortunately, many things can interfere with effective communication. Such breakdowns can have disastrous consequences. For example, communication failures at the *New York Times* were blamed for the failure of top editors to be aware of the fact that a staff reporter, Jayson Blair, had made errors or the equivalent of journalistic fraud in dozens of articles. The resulting furor led to two top editors' resignations and permanent scars of the paper's reputation.[11] Some of the more common barriers to effective communication include semantics, distraction, misrepresentation, information retention, and perceptual factors.

SEMANTICS

Semantics, or **code noise**, occurs when the meaning of a message to the sender differs from its meaning to the recipient. Too often, this may be the result of "jargon," involving pretentious terminology or language specific to a particular profession or group. Here's an example of pretentious terminology: The **Wall Street Journal** reported on a federal tax case in which a fire alarm was described as a "combustion enunciator," a door as a "removable partition," a manhole as "equipment access," and windows as "decorative fixtures."[12]

Here is a sampling of jargon relating to computers and the modern workplace:

> *Salmon day:* Fighting uphill; swimming against the current.
> *Blamestorming:* Discussing a project failure with coworkers.
> *PEBCAK:* "Problem exists between chair and keyboard." That is, an operator error.[13]
> *Easter eggs:* Undocumented bits of code hidden in computer applications and operating systems that, once accessed, provide a bit of information or entertainment, such as a game, a joke, or the names of people who developed the program.[14]
> *Sticky eyeballs:* People who spend a lot of time at a Web site.
> *Cube farm:* Rows of cubicles instead of private offices.
> *RTM:* Read the manual.

Deloitte Consulting, an arm of the accounting firm Deloitte Touche Tohmatsu, has developed a new software program, Bullfighter, that identifies jargon in documents. Its goal is to make it easier for investors to decipher what companies are trying to say. The program, available for free download at http://www.dc.com/insights/bullfighter/, can also be used by firms to help ensure that their messages are jargon free.[15]

DISTRACTION

Distraction, or **psychological noise**, occurs when a recipient does not understand the sender's message because he or she is simply thinking about something else. For instance, the recipient may be distracted by financial worries or upcoming deadlines. Often, of course, recipients don't understand senders' messages, because they are thinking about their own replies rather than concentrating on the message to which they are going to reply. Thus active listening is an important communication skill, as explained later in this chapter.

MISREPRESENTATION

Misrepresentation may also cause the failure of communication and may take various forms. Deliberate lies are an extreme example. People sometimes lie on their résumés (sometimes called *padding*), in their advertising messages (sometimes called *puffery*), and in their campaign promises (sometimes called *politics*). More often, information may be subtly distorted to the sender's benefit. A memo that focuses on sales increases but downplays drops in profit, an annual report that tries to hide changes in accounting format, and a brochure from a drug manufacturer that ignores hazardous side effects would be examples of this kind of misrepresentation.

Indeed, some forms of misrepresentation are so common that examples to the contrary are newsworthy. For instance, it is almost "common practice" for company annual reports to present the year's events in a favorable light. The "Dear Stockholder" letter in an annual report of poultry producer Holly Farms Corp. broke that mold. It began, "You already know the Bad News about our past fiscal year. We were wrong about chickens. The chicken market did not recover from salmonella publicity and we entered a sharp chicken depression. We lost money in chickens—our worst year in history. And the poor performance was mostly our fault."[16]

INFORMATION RETENTION

Information is a valuable resource. Those who control it are in positions of power. Some employees may retain specific sorts of information, such as a formula or a filing system, and thereby make themselves more necessary. Others are in positions that give them the ability to channel—or not to channel—information to various individuals inside and outside the organization. Still others are in positions in which they process information, sending only some of it along. Each of these sorts of individuals has the potential to create barriers to proper communication.

PERCEPTUAL FACTORS

Most perceptual errors are directly relevant to communication. Stereotyping, as discussed in Chapter 2, may cause us to ignore or distort the messages of people we have classified in certain ways. A manager may, for instance, feel that union representatives are not trustworthy. As a result, the manager may misinterpret conciliatory gestures from the union. Selective perception may cause us to ignore communication that conflicts with our beliefs and expectations. Halo error may lead us to bias our evaluation of a message because of some unrelated characteristic of the message sender, such as physical appearance. Projection may lead us to infer information in a message we receive based on our own feelings. If we are angry, for instance, we may see anger in the message. Primacy and recency effects may cause us to give differing weights to various communications, depending on when we receive them.

"The Voice of Experience feature is an interview with Sandra Bushue, Vice President of Business Development at Siemens. The interview provides valuable insights regarding communication problems in organizations and recommendations for becoming a more effective communicator."

OVERCOMING COMMUNICATION BARRIERS

There are many approaches to overcoming the causes of communication failures. For instance, feedback, repetitions of the messages, use of multiple channels, and simplified language may reduce problems due to semantics, selective perception, and distraction. Simplified language includes use of simple words and phrases, short and familiar words, personal pronouns (such as *you* and *them*), short sentences and paragraphs, active verbs, and illustrations, examples, and charts.

VOICE OF EXPERIENCE

COMMUNICATING EFFECTIVELY

Sandra K. Bushue, Vice President, Business Development, Siemens

1. What are the barriers to effective communication with the general public?

Since each of us is different, every person has his or her own barriers for communicating effectively. The biggest mistake that communicators usually make is not taking the time to understand their audience. In order to be an effective communicator, you must have some knowledge of the audience's interests, and you must understand your role as a facilitator to reach your goal or outcome. What is your role or what kind of goal or outcome are you looking to achieve? The outcome could be to inform, to persuade, or to sell. It is important to have a sense of what that is up front so you can communicate appropriately. Communicators must use their authentic voice. Oftentimes you hear a speaker presenting in a different tone that comes off sounding like a lecture or a sermon. Using your own voice and having self-confidence are always winning strategies.

Another important point is the ability to winnow your thoughts to the essentials. Communicators who go on and on without getting to the point are boring and ineffective. Develop your premise and use the prominent details that support it. Work to be informative, and remember that an audience always appreciates a dash of humor.

The inability to make eye contact is a barrier. A presenter needs to be able to connect with the audience through eye contact. A speaker must look at the audience and not through or around them. Making eye contact gives a speaker authority and lends the information credibility.

2. How do you handle communicating a message with which you may not entirely agree?

Personally, this is a difficult question. I am not effective if I do not agree with the message I am presenting. However, if you find yourself in this situation, the best advice is to remain factual and to the point. This is not a good time to give your opinion, for it may dilute or even contradict the message. Think professionally and be professional. However, if it is a topic that completely comprises your principles and core beliefs, ask to be removed from the assignment. You don't want to get into the situation where you are asked to defend or explain something if you believe you will not succeed.

3. How do you deliver a consistent message in the face of public scrutiny?

This is easy. Keep your message simple and ensure it supports your core beliefs. Your core principles will keep you grounded and preclude an inconsistent message. For some, the difficult task is developing core beliefs or principles. Developing these ideas is a process you begin early in life. It is not something you write down on a paper napkin as you are having drinks at the local bar. If you are a politician, you must search to develop what you believe in, and once you know, that becomes the foundation. All of your ideas and policies work around that center.

The same principle applies to business. In any given communications-related situation, once you've developed strong and reliable core message points, stick to those and find concrete examples to help these points stand up to scrutiny. Keep these points and examples in mind as you answer your critics, and stay the course in your message delivery.

4. What three core communication skills should students work to develop most?

The three core communication skills a student should work to develop are writing, writing, and writing. This skill cannot be stressed enough. You must be able to express yourself in writing, not only to become an effective speaker, but an effective leader as well. If you think of great orators, you will find they were good writers. Here are some examples: prime ministers Winston Churchill and Margaret Thatcher, and presidents Thomas Jefferson, Abraham Lincoln, and Ronald Reagan. Each of these leaders were good writers and good communicators.

The ability to write is the key to success in any profession. Writing has become more prominent in the age of the Internet and electronic communications. Because of the proliferation of easy communications mediums like e-mail, instant messaging, and SMS text messaging, people are writing more than ever. But at the same time, the craft itself seems to be suffering. It is a skill you must work to perfect in order to succeed. A few years ago, I had a young man who worked for me. His responsibilities included organizing trade shows and events for the company. Through reading his e-mails about the organization of these events, I noticed this employee was a very

VOICE OF EXPERIENCE (continued)

clear and concise writer. Eventually, I gave him the responsibility of writing letters to Congress and other public relations materials.

Today, at a young age, he is the manager of corporate communications for our company, writing press releases and letters for the

company's president. He has a very bright future. Writing is important for effective communication.

Communication overload may be reduced by careful review of the material needed by the recipient and by use of the exception principle. The ***exception principle*** states that only exceptions should be reported—there is no need for messages stating the production line didn't break down or that absenteeism or competitive conditions are unchanged. Short-circuiting may be reduced through careful consideration of who has a "need to know" the material. Electronic data-processing techniques that automatically route messages to certain people may also help.

Information retention and misrepresentation are more difficult problems and have led to some very different prescriptions. Some call for tightened formal controls and even organizational audit groups. An ***organizational audit group*** is designed to ferret out the points at which omissions or distortions are taking place. Others have argued just the opposite, saying that fewer formal controls and a more open, trusting organizational climate are needed.

These suggestions make it clear there is no free lunch when dealing with communication. Things that lessen one problem are likely to worsen another. For instance, feedback, redundancy, and multiple channels may make communication overload worse. The exception principle makes misrepresentation and information retention easier. This does not mean the situation is hopeless, only that we must pay serious attention to these problems and carefully weigh the resultant trade-offs.

In Korea and Japan, some companies are taking a novel approach to reducing communication overload. They specify one hour in the morning when no one— including the chief executive—is to be interrupted by phone calls, coworkers, or meetings. Some corporations, including Samsung and Hyundai, say the system has enhanced creativity and produced major administrative productivity gains.[17]

Now complete Skills Practice 7-3. This exercise requires you to get out into the real world to interview a manager about communication issues. It will give you additional foundation for the content of this chapter.

GUIDELINES FOR EFFECTIVE WRITTEN COMMUNICATION

Written communication is required when the action called for is complex and must be done in a precise way. Written communication also provides a permanent form of record keeping and can reach a large number of people easily. Here we briefly discuss six forms of written communication in organizations—three for communicating downward and three for communicating upward.

FORMS OF DOWNWARD COMMUNICATION

Downward communication involves messages from senders relatively high in the organizational structure to receivers in lower-level positions, such as from a supervisor to a subordinate. It is used for such purposes as giving instructions, providing information about policies and procedures, giving feedback about performance, and indoctrinating or motivating. In addition to letters and memos, three written forms of downward communications are manuals, handbooks, and newsletters.

A company manual is an integrated system of long-term instructions, brought together between covers, classified, coded, indexed, and otherwise prepared to maximize its reference value. Manuals have a high degree of authority. They deal primarily with policy, procedure, or organization. Because manuals are technical and complex, employees should be trained to use them.

Handbooks are usually less authoritative, formal, and lengthy than manuals and generally apply at lower organizational levels. The employee handbook, for example, outlines the duties and privileges of the individual worker. Handbooks generally have a low-key, friendly, personal approach.[18]

Company newsletters are usually issued biweekly or monthly. Informal in tone, they are used to disseminate information to many employees. Newsletters might announce company social functions, contain stories about employees cited for superior performance or attendance, or provide answers about employment issues. Unlike a manual, a newsletter has a mix of personal, social, and work-related information. Japanese firms sometimes send out newsletters in the form of comic books. Comic books, or *mangas,* are widely read in Japan, and dozens of Japanese companies now use this form to convey information to employees.[19]

Another interesting form of downward communication is the Weblog, or Blog for short. Some corporate executives now use Web pages to talk informally with employee, customers, and vendors. They see "blogging" as a way to provide a direct voice, sidestepping public relations firms and glossy brochures.[20] An innovative approach to downward management is discussed in the Focus on Management feature.

FORMS OF UPWARD COMMUNICATION

Upward communication involves communication from sources in lower-level positions to receivers in relatively higher positions. It is often used to give information on achievement or progress, to point out problems that are being encountered, to pass on ideas for improvement of activities, and to provide information about feelings on work and nonwork activities. Three techniques that are especially useful in upward communication are suggestion systems, grievances, and attitude surveys.

A *suggestion system* permits employees to submit ideas or suggestions for improving company effectiveness. The suggestions are then evaluated, generally by a panel of managers, and the valuable ones are acted on. The initiator of the idea may get a cash award, a letter of commendation, or an insignia. The idea behind a suggestion system is that employees are in the best position to contribute ideas to make their jobs more effective.[21]

Grievances are formal, written complaints submitted by employees regarding alleged unfair treatment on the job.[22] They may cover such topics as working conditions, promotions, pay, disciplinary action, supervision, and work assignments. Grievance procedures often involve several steps. In the first step, the employee's immediate supervisor reviews the grievance. Failure to resolve the grievance at that

FOCUS ON MANAGEMENT

PATHFINDERS AT LLOYDS TSB*

The merger of Lloyds and TSB created a single British bank with 77,000 members and 15 million customers. The newly consolidated bank won a Marketing Society Award for the care it took to launch and explain the merged organization to its employees. Lloyds TSB realized it needed to win the hearts and minds of its personnel if they were to be motivated to "deliver the brand" to customers. It ran a comprehensive and sustained internal program, highlighted by a live event called "Your Life. Your Bank." Staff nominated colleagues to act as brand ambassadors, called "pathfinders," whose role was to attend the event, absorb the key messages, and pass them on to 15 of their colleagues. A total of 5,000 staff acted as pathfinders. The event comprised a 28-stand exhibition, representing each of the bank's departments, with interactive elements to show how Lloyds TSB is aligning itself with the customer. A morning session explored how Lloyds and TSB are coming together; in the afternoon the focus was on brand understanding. Following the event, pathfinders passed on what they had learned to their colleagues in prearranged, structured cascade sessions. They were supplied with a pack containing bullet-point summaries, visual support on overhead transparencies, a computer disk, and a video summary. On customer launch day, the bank's chief executive addressed the staff live on business TV. All staff received a letter welcoming them to their new bank. Subsequent research revealed very positive employee responses to the process.

http://www.lloydstsb.co.uk/

*"Internal Communications," *Marketing,* June 6, 2000, p. 19.

step might lead to appeals at higher levels, perhaps including the company's industrial relations office or an outside mediator. Grievances allow employees to channel their frustrations and feelings of injustice in productive ways.

Attitude surveys are often conducted annually or biannually. The surveys provide information about employees' feelings and attitudes on many employment issues, such as satisfaction with pay and supervision. Responses are usually anonymous so employees can feel free to speak their minds. Results of the surveys are tabulated and a report is prepared. The company then acts on the information provided.[23] About half of large firms use surveys, often for a wide range of purposes. For instance, at Wells Fargo & Co. in San Francisco, employees have been asked about such things as the effectiveness of the bank's advertising, the quality and innovation of its products, and its responsibility to the community.

Skills Practice 7-4 gives you an opportunity to develop skill in designing and implementing employee attitude surveys in organizations. Be careful: Some students initially think this is an easy activity. In reality, this is a very complex and challenging process, if you want to do it right.

Whatever form written communications take, they must be easy to understand. Figure 7-3 presents some guides for readable writing.

GUIDELINES FOR EFFECTIVE SPEAKING

Effective speakers communicate logically, clearly, and confidently.[24] Effective speaking requires thorough preparation. Knowing your purpose and your audience are critical; 2,800 years ago Aristotle said that outstanding communicators must first understand their audiences and gear their language and persuasive appeals to them. Physical delivery, including presence, voice control, eye contact, and other nonverbal cues, discussed in the next section, may make the difference between success

FIGURE 7-3
Guides for Readable Writing

- Use simple words and phrases, such as *improve* instead of *ameliorate* and *like* instead of *in a manner similar to that of.*
- Use short and familiar words, such as *darken* instead of *obfuscate.*
- Use personal pronouns, such as *you* and *them,* if the style permits.
- Use illustrations, examples, and charts. These techniques are even better when they are tied to the reader's experiences.
- Use short sentences and paragraphs. Big words and thick reports may look impressive, but the communicator's job is to inform people, not impress them.
- Use active verb forms, such as "The manager said . . . ," rather than passive verb forms, such as "It was said by the manager that . . ."
- Don't use unnecessary words. For example, in the sentence "Bad weather conditions prevented my trip," the word *conditions* is unnecessary. Instead, write, "Bad weather prevented my trip."

Source: From *Human Behavior at Work: Organizational Behavior,* 7th ed., by K. Davis and J. W. Newstrom. Copyright 1985 by Mc-Graw Hill Book Company.

and failure. The way you speak reflects your intelligence, ability to think, and ability to organize. These abilities are highly valued in business and in society in general and can be crucial in social relationships and job opportunities.

What follows are guidelines for effective speaking. Because speaking involves both verbal and nonverbal aspects, some of these guidelines touch on issues we explore in more detail in the next section.

> **Determine the purpose of your communication.** Is it to explain ideas to others? To recognize outstanding efforts? To entertain? To induce an emotion? To instill a belief? Your speech should be tailored to facilitate the desired purpose of your communication.

> **Consider issues of time and space.** Determine the best time and location for delivering your message. Consider how much time you will have and how your message might relate to other messages delivered before and after it. Think about what recent events might be in the minds of your listeners and whether you should refer to those events.

> **Adapt to your listeners.** Consider the size of the audience as well as factors such as audience age, gender, interests, level of knowledge about the subject, and values. You'll need to prepare very differently for a one-to-one talk, a small-group presentation, and a lecture to a large audience. Also consider audience expectations. For example, is the audience expecting an entertaining after-dinner talk, a stirring inspirational message, or how-to tips? Consider as well if there may be hearing-impaired audience members or an international audience that cannot speak fluent English.

> **Use appropriate vocabulary.** Speak at the proper level for the particular audience. Seek clarity. Avoid use of words that may have different meanings to various members of the audience, and avoid unnecessary jargon.

> **Practice voice control.** Consider proper speech volume, pitch, and speaking rate. Avoid mumbling and awkward pauses. It is helpful to listen to yourself on an audiotape and to observe your mannerisms on videotape. Ask others to critique your presentations.

> **Use appropriate gestures.** Properly used, gestures can make a presentation more engaging, and they may help disguise anxiety. Avoid short, jerky move-

ments that may appear as nervousness, and use a variety of gestures so you don't seem to be in a rut. Use gestures to reinforce spoken points or even as substitutes.

> **Organize your presentation.** Any oral presentation can be divided into three parts: gaining attention, presenting the information, and closing effectively. The amount of time devoted to gaining attention will depend on the audience members' familiarity with, and interest in, the subject. A personal greeting, a stunning statement or opinion, a suspenseful question, or humor may help gain attention. To share information effectively, ask how you can give the subject high priority in the minds of listeners, how you can bring the subject more clearly into focus, and how you can develop it in a form that satisfies your listeners. Finally, an effective closing gives a sense of completion and reinforces key points.

The step-by-step process model shown in the Bottom Line feature identifies the basic actions that a manager would take in order to use speaking skills to make effective speeches or business presentations in an organizational setting.

Skills Practice 7-5 will increase your skill in tailoring your business presentations to characteristics of your audience. This is a critical skill that you will need to possess in the workplace.

BOTTOM LINE

DEVELOPING EFFECTIVE SPEAKING SKILLS

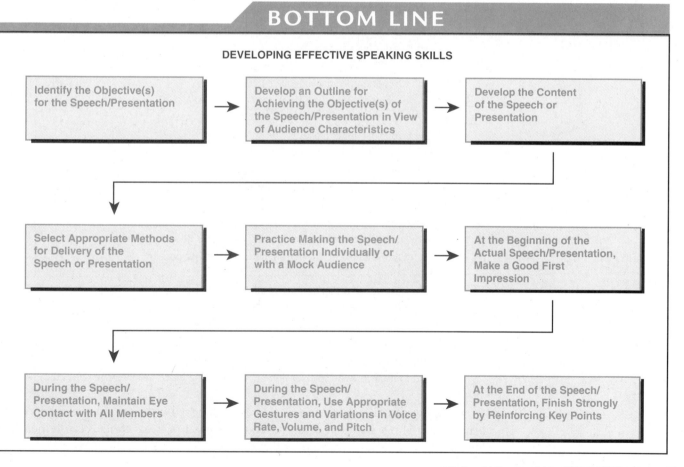

Identify the Objective(s) for the Speech/Presentation → Develop an Outline for Achieving the Objective(s) of the Speech/Presentation in View of Audience Characteristics → Develop the Content of the Speech or Presentation

Select Appropriate Methods for Delivery of the Speech or Presentation → Practice Making the Speech/Presentation Individually or with a Mock Audience → At the Beginning of the Actual Speech/Presentation, Make a Good First Impression

During the Speech/Presentation, Maintain Eye Contact with All Members → During the Speech/Presentation, Use Appropriate Gestures and Variations in Voice Rate, Volume, and Pitch → At the End of the Speech/Presentation, Finish Strongly by Reinforcing Key Points

MASTERING ACTIVE LISTENING

Obviously, face-to-face verbal communication involves speaking. More than that, though, it also requires listening.[25] Unfortunately, most people would rather talk than listen. According to one old joke, the opposite of talking isn't listening, it's waiting to talk.[26] Before reading on, complete Self-Assessment 7-2, "Active Listening." After you are done, visit the text Web site to learn more about your responses.

SELF-ASSESSMENT 7-2

Active Listening

Answer each of the questions in this section using the following scale:

1 Disagree strongly
2 Disagree somewhat
3 Neither agree nor disagree
4 Agree somewhat
5 Agree strongly

When listening to someone:

____ 1. I ask questions to be confident I understand.
____ 2. I am able to keep quiet.
____ 3. I pay attention to the other person's nonverbal cues.
____ 4. I often find my mind wandering.
____ 5. I often paraphrase what was said to make sure I've understood.
____ 6. I often find myself interrupting.
____ 7. I tend to think about what I'm going to say next.
____ 8. I tend to get emotionally involved.
____ 9. I generally try to make eye contact.
____ 10. I am often impatient.
____ 11. I tend to lean forward, toward the speaker.
____ 12. I often doodle, tap my pen, or shuffle papers.
____ 13. I am able to stay focused.
____ 14. I try to understand the speaker's feelings as well as the intellectual content.
____ 15. I often sit with my arms crossed.
____ 16. I often make comments to show I understand.
____ 17. I am generally looking for an opening to get the floor.
____ 18. I tend to evaluate and make judgments about the speaker.
____ 19. I sometimes look at my watch.
____ 20. I use gestures of understanding, such as nods of the head.
____ 21. I often succumb to distractions, such as ringing telephones or activity in the hallway.
____ 22. I sometimes express irritation at the speaker's speech patterns or hesitancy.
____ 23. I pay attention to signs of emotion in the speaker's voice.
____ 24. I maintain a relaxed posture.
____ 25. I periodically ask the speaker if I'm understanding his or her message correctly.

Listening can take many forms. Casual or marginal listening, such as when colleagues chat about sports over lunch, requires only a passive effort, because there is little pressure to learn or remember the message. With attentive listening, as when a manager is delivering a performance appraisal, the listener is motivated to hear, understand, and remember. With active listening, such as counseling situations and conflict interviews, it is important to listen to more than just the content of the message. Attention to nonverbal cues will also be important. Active listening requires that you convey to the speaker a sense of trust, identify with his or her feelings and thoughts, and encourage him or her to be as specific as possible about feelings and concerns.

Here are some guidelines for active listening.[27]

> **Control the physical environment.** Try to minimize noise and other distractions, such as an uncomfortable room temperature or improper lighting. Don't sit near doorways or under air-conditioning vents. If the location is noisy or uncomfortable, move to a quieter setting. Take steps to minimize unnecessary distractions.

> **Be alert.** Give your full attention, and allot the necessary time to listen.

> **Be mentally prepared.** Do your homework in advance of the conversation. Anticipate the encounter by learning new terminology and background information about the persons, organization, or issues.

> **Be emotionally prepared.** Keep an open mind about what is being said, even if it is unpleasant. Give the speaker the opportunity to complete his or her message before raising questions.

> **Be attentive.** Continually review the speaker's message, and tie the various ideas or segments of the message together. Think of each idea as a link in a chain. Take notes if necessary, but record only main points. Develop an effective system of note taking.

> **Read nonverbal cues.** Pay attention to the speaker's tone of voice, expressions, gestures, and other nonverbal cues. We discuss nonverbal cues in more detail in the next section.

> **Distinguish among facts, inferences, and value judgments.** Try to sort out whether what is being said is a fact that can be verified, an inference (that is, a conclusion reached after consideration of a set of facts), or a personal judgment based on the speaker's value system. These may all be important, but you should do your best to determine which is which.

> **Offer and solicit feedback.** The best form of feedback in a listening situation is to paraphrase the speaker's message. This allows the speaker to verify the

BOTTOM LINE

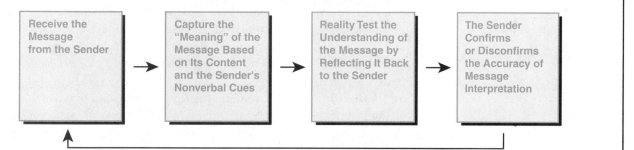

DEVELOPING ACTIVE LISTENING SKILLS

Receive the Message from the Sender → Capture the "Meaning" of the Message Based on Its Content and the Sender's Nonverbal Cues → Reality Test the Understanding of the Message by Reflecting It Back to the Sender → The Sender Confirms or Disconfirms the Accuracy of Message Interpretation accuracy and completeness of what was transmitted and to make necessary changes or additions.

The step-by-step process model shown in the Bottom Line feature identifies the basic actions that a manager would take in order to use active listening skills to enhance communication with others in an organizational setting.

Skills Practice 7-6 focuses on helping you to develop the ability to listen to others more effectively. This is a critical skill for managers, but is often not put into practice very well.

USING AND READING NONVERBAL COMMUNICATION

Nonverbal communication uses no words or uses words in a way that conveys meaning beyond their strict definition. It may take place through such channels as the body, the face, the tone of voice, and interpersonal distance. A wink, a touch, or a change of body position can all convey worlds of meaning. Further, that meaning may vary markedly depending on the situation, the gender of the parties, and the culture. Studies generally suggest that a substantial amount of information transmitted during a conversation—perhaps 80 or 90 percent—is nonverbal.[28] It was clear from our discussion of speaking and listening that it's impossible to talk about face-to-face verbal communication without also introducing issues of nonverbal communication.

FUNCTIONS OF NONVERBAL COMMUNICATION

Nonverbal communication provides five functions: accenting, contradicting, substituting, complementing, and regulating.[29]

> **Accenting** is adding emphasis to a verbal message. For instance, an angry boss who pounds on the desk and slams a door while reprimanding a subordinate is using nonverbal communication to reinforce the verbal scolding.

> **Contradicting** is signaling the opposite of the verbal message. Sometimes, an interviewee, salesperson, or boss will say one thing but, through eye movements, hand gestures, smiles, posture, or some other means of nonverbal communication, relay a very different message. For instance, a police chief noted, "Eyes move in patterns. They move differently when you're remembering and when you're creating. And if you're creating when you're talking to me about a crime, you're lying."[30] Nonverbal cues are typically more spontaneous and less consciously controlled than verbal cues, and they are viewed as more accurate. So when verbal and nonverbal communications are contradictory, the nonverbal communications tend to be given most weight.

> **Substituting** is replacing the verbal message with a nonverbal message. Some nonverbal cues have distinct and widely recognized meanings, so they may appropriately substitute for their verbal counterparts. For example, a nod may replace a spoken "yes."

> **Complementing** involves sending the same message nonverbally that is sent verbally. A hug accompanying a statement of "I love you," a pat on the back accompanying "Good job!" and a "high five" accompanying "Congratulations!" are all examples of complementing.

> **Regulating** is using nonverbal communication to control the flow of the verbal message. For instance, a boss who is becoming impatient with an overly long presentation by a subordinate and wants him to speed up may begin to conspicuously look at her watch or may start tapping a pencil on the desktop.

FORMS OF NONVERBAL COMMUNICATION

Nonverbal communication can take many forms, as shown in Figure 7-4, including paralanguage, hand movements, facial expressions, eye contact, posture, touch, dress, and proxemics.[31]

Paralanguage concerns how something is said rather than what is said. It includes all vocal aspects of speech other than words.[32] For example, voice qualities—such as pitch, rhythm, tempo, and volume—influence interpretation of a verbal message. A soft, low-pitched voice and a slow rate indicate liking, whereas a high-pitched voice indicates anger. Moderate rate, pitch, and volume indicate boredom.[33] Similarly, *vocal characterizers*, such as coughing, yawning, clearing the throat, and grunting, may be important. Although they can sometimes be used effectively, they generally are distracting and annoying, and they should be avoided. *Vocal qualifiers* are variations in tone or intensity of speech. For example, increases in rate or volume may indicate impatience or anger, respectively. The power of verbal qualifiers can be seen by repeating the sentence "I didn't say he stole your car" seven times, stressing a different word each time. Finally, vocal segregates are pauses between utterances and may include "ahs" and "ums." In situations such as interviews, prolonged pauses suggest a lack of confidence and organization.[34]

There are several types of hand movements. Some have a specific meaning that is understood in a particular culture or occupation, such as a thumbs-up gesture. Others, such as touching oneself or others, may be associated with anxiety, guilt, hostility, or suspicion. For example, interviewers are sometimes taught that a hand-to-face movement is a sign of deception.[35]

FIGURE 7-4
Forms of Nonverbal Communication

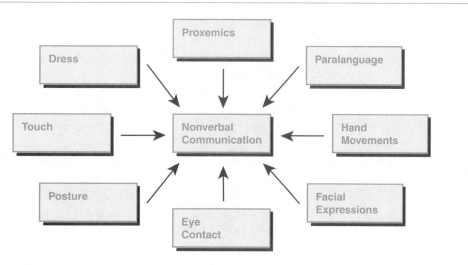

By one estimate, the human face can make 250,000 different expressions.[36] The Roman scholar Pliny the Elder wrote more than 2,000 years ago that "The face of man is the index to joy and mirth, to severity and sadness." Facial expressions are generally understood to have a particular meaning. For example, facial expressions communicating six emotions—happiness, sadness, anger, fear, surprise, and disgust—are recognized worldwide. Even when people try to suppress facial expressions, they may make very short expressions lasting a fraction of a second that will reveal true meaning.

Eye contact is a major regulator of conversation. Generally, eye contact suggests understanding and interest.[37] Seeking eye contact connotes the desire to open a conversation. Conversely, someone hoping to avoid communication—such as an unprepared student in class—will avoid eye contact. Also, some characteristic eye-contact patterns have specific meanings. For instance, the slow blink—a pattern in which an individual closes his or her eyes for two to four seconds and then slowly opens them—indicates doubt or suspicion. When combined with a condescending or impatient tone of voice, it communicates superiority or disinterest.

Posture is the way people position their bodies with respect to others. For example, if a customer's arms are relaxed and open and she leans forward as she talks to a salesperson, her posture reflects approval and acceptance of the salesperson's message. If she leans back with arms tightly crossed, her posture suggests rejection or disagreement.[38]

Touch can convey warmth, understanding, and intimacy. Touch may also enhance positive feelings about the touching person and the situation. For example, studies show that when a store assistant, server in a restaurant, or product demonstrator lightly touched a customer on the arm, the customer saw the touching person more positively, had a more positive attitude toward the situation, and was more likely to comply with the toucher's suggestions.[39] Note, though, that this research involved casual touching of the arm. To the contrary, many other forms of touching may be resented, and unwanted touching can be a form of sexual harassment.[40]

When we encounter others, one of the first things we notice is the way they are dressed. Dress can convey characteristics such as image, mood, identity, power, wealth, and authority.[41] People who are dressed formally are better able to command respect. For instance, research has shown that pedestrians are more likely to cross against traffic lights when led by a well-dressed person than when led by a poorly dressed individual.[42] People in positions of authority, such as doctors and police officers, often wear distinctive uniforms to reinforce their status.[43] In addition, we all wear our own uniforms, that is, the particular way we choose to dress to communicate something about ourselves to others. Because of the importance of dress, many companies have a dress code to ensure that appropriate signals are conveyed to customers and others, and violation of a dress code may even be a cause for dismissal.[44]

Increasingly, though, companies are relaxing dress codes in order to create a more relaxed and egalitarian climate. Others are instituting "dress-down days," often Fridays, when employees can wear more casual clothes.[45] These dress-down days are very stressful for many people. Deciding what to wear—once not a real option—has become complex, controversial, and perplexing. Many companies are, in fact, quite formal about what is considered to be acceptable casual dress. For example, Southland Corp. put on a "fashion show," with employees modeling what is—and isn't—acceptable to wear for casual day, compiled a two-inch-thick binder of catalog clippings, with sections marked "appropriate" and "inappropriate," and formed an eight-member "Employee Dress Code Committee" to resolve disputes over questionable dress.[46] Casual dress day at American General Corp. got the ax after employees arrived dressed as—among other things—Santa Claus, the Easter Bunny, and a duck.

Proxemics is the use of interpersonal space (that is, proximity) to convey status or degree of intimacy. Sitting at the head of a table conveys status, standing close to another conveys intimacy, and sitting behind a desk (as opposed to alongside it) indicates a superior–subordinate relationship. Two elements of proxemics—personal space and seating arrangements—are especially relevant in organizational settings.[47] We discuss proxemics in more detail in Chapter 11.

Skills Practice 7-7 is designed to help you see the role of nonverbal sources of information in the overall communication process. Remember, nonverbal communication can provide large amounts of information to the receiver, so it must be actively managed along with verbal forms of communication.

ELECTRONIC COMMUNICATION

Computers are transforming communication. In this section we consider e-mail, the Internet and the World Wide Web, teleconferencing and videoconferencing, and e-commerce.

E-MAIL

The exploding technology of **electronic mail**, or **e-mail**, the electronic transmission of written information, provides a very fast, inexpensive, and efficient means of communicating. Nestle SA, a Swiss-based multinational food corporation, installed an electronic mail system to connect its 60,000 employees in 80 countries. Nestle's European units can use the system to share information about production schedules and inventory levels in order to ship excess products from one country to another.[48] About 70 million employees in the United States now use e-mail, and they send billions of e-mails daily.[49] E-mail can help speed up communications, build and maintain business relationships, cut mailing costs, and create a sense of community.[50] Programs can now translate e-mail messages into a variety of languages, and wearable PCs let users read e-mail while on the move.[51] Soon, the vast majority of mobile phones will offer Internet access.[52] Here are some simple guidelines for using e-mail.

> **Be careful.** Both sending and receiving e-mail demand caution. Don't send sloppy or hastily reasoned messages simply because e-mail seems informal. Also, a simple "slip of the finger" can be devastating. For example, a corporate chief executive hit the wrong key while on a public e-mail network and misaddressed a note intended for the firm's head of product development. As a result, he sent a total stranger the company's product plans for the next year and a half.[53] As yet another reason for caution, opening e-mail attachments can introduce harmful viruses to a computer, sometimes causing irreparable damage.

> **Recognize privacy issues.** "Privacy in the digital age is dead."[54] People often treat e-mail as private and impermanent, but it actually may remain on servers for years, and it can later be made available for public inspection, criticism, or ridicule. Many companies routinely monitor employees' e-mail, and the e-mail administrator of most systems has the ability to read all e-mail messages.[55] In

fact, someone has called using e-mail the digital equivalent of shouting out the window. Scott McNealy, CEO of Sun Microsystems, when asked how transmissions could be made more secure said, "You have zero privacy anyway. Get over it."[56] As such, don't write anything in e-mail messages that you would not want to be widely read.[57] Further, theft of personal information can result in many problems, including identity theft. As such, you should consider privacy software and other tools to help guard your privacy.[58]

> **Keep messages clear, simple, and short.** Use a subject line that clearly conveys the content of the message. Be concise. Some experts suggest that e-mails should not exceed 25 lines. Avoid lengthy attachments; they may take many minutes to download, and some readers' computer systems can't handle attachments at all. Also, resist the temptation to use fancy formatting, such as multiple fonts and colors—messages that look beautiful on your computer screen may be a jumbled mess when received.

> **Reply only to appropriate persons.** Resist the temptation to "reply to all" or to copy your message to everyone you can think of. Ask yourself who really needs the message.

> **Personalize your e-mail as appropriate.** E-mail doesn't give the opportunity for personal social interaction, including nonverbal communication. To help compensate for this, people sometimes use forms of emotional punctuation, called smileys, to convey their feelings. Smileys can add a personal touch to e-mails. However, they shouldn't be overused, and they may be inappropriate in some formal e-mails.[59] See the chapter-end Light Up for more on Smileys.

> **Be considerate.** Avoid using e-mail to vent frustration and anger through hostile messages. This practice, known as *flaming*, can create a climate of distrust, fear, and anger.[60] Unfortunately, flaming is common, and e-mail is also sometimes used to harass others, including for sexual harassment and to make threats of violence or blackmail.[61] E-mail is more likely to be irresponsible and to contain profanity and negative sentiment than face-to-face communication. This is probably because e-mail is conveyed in the form of text by a person who is physically removed from the recipient and because e-mail messages are erroneously seen as fleeting in nature and thus as permitting greater freedom of expression and self-disclosure.[62] Because of these factors, "Netiquette" (that is, *Net etiquette*) is especially important. Netiquette is addressed in Web Exercise 7-2.[63]

> **Check e-mail at least once a day.** Respond as quickly as possible to messages. If your response will be delayed, let the sender know you have received the message and when you will respond.

> **Manage your e-mail with folders and filters.** E-mail can lead to the equivalent of electronic junk mail, with employees receiving dozens of unwanted messages—called spam—daily.[64] Also, e-mail users often join lists to share information with people with common interests, such as project management, labor law, or communications. Remarkably, surveys reveal that an average office worker gets 190 messages daily.[65] Set up folders to organize e-mails. Use filters to eliminate junk e-mail and to transfer low-priority messages to designated folders.[66]

THE INTERNET AND THE WORLD WIDE WEB

In an IBM ad, a group of nuns is walking through a Prague convent; subtitles tell us that they are discussing their computers' operating system. One nun's face lights up as she says, "I'm dying to surf the net."[67] The "Net" referred to by the nun is, of course, the *Internet*—a worldwide collection of computer networks permitting access to libraries, news sources, and groups with special interests. Dubbed the "Information Superhighway" by the popular press, the Internet was born in 1969 when the ARPANET (Advanced Research Projects Agency Network) was developed under contract with ARPA, the Advanced Research Projects Agency of the U.S. Department of Defense. The ARPANET was constructed so researchers could share information with university, military, and defense contractors and to study how communications could be maintained in the event of nuclear attack.[68] When, after a series of developments, the National Science Foundation took over management of the Internet in the mid-1980s and subsequently increased the capacity of its circuits, the number of users exploded. The Internet is growing faster than any other telecommunications system ever built, including the telephone network.[69]

Perhaps the most exciting part of the Internet is the World Wide Web. The *World Wide Web*, or Web as it is sometimes called, is a collection of standards used to access the information available on the Internet.[70] A key feature is that Web documents include links to other Web documents. With the Web, users can leap from one computer database to another at the click of a mouse, following ideas, color photographs, interactive diagrams, sound, and video clips, all linked by a technology known as *hypertext*.[71] The Web was conceived in 1989 at the European Laboratory for Particle Physics (known as CERN, from an earlier French name), in Geneva, Switzerland. The creators saw it as a way to distribute and evaluate document-based information among high-energy physicists around the world. Since the development a few years later of Mosaic, software to navigate the Internet using the Web's coding system, and then of Netscape and other browsers, growth of the Web has been dramatic.[72]

Companies are now taking advantage of the Web by developing *corporate portals*, which provide access to internal company information via a Web browser. They take one of two forms.[73] Most common is a workplace community portal. This displays many types of information that may be interesting or important to employees, such as notices of employee gatherings and information about job postings and benefits packages. The second form, taken by the new generation of portals, displays information from virtually all of the company's most important databases, including financials, sales and marketing, inventory, supply-and-demand tracking, human resources, procurement, and research and development. A Merrill Lynch report called portals "the Yahoo of company information." Data can easily be accessed, integrated, and entered into various applications. A wide range of companies, such as Staples, Inc., and General Electric Appliances, are installing portals to better access and manage information, cut costs, free up time for managers, and add to the bottom line. Du Pont estimates it will save up to $66 million from the first phase of its portal.

TELECONFERENCING AND VIDEOCONFERENCING

As another example of electronic communication, *teleconferencing* permits a group of people to confer simultaneously via telephone or electronic mail. Teleconferencing that also has the capability to let participants see each other over video screens is called *videoconferencing*. Such technologies offer businesses tremendous savings in time, energy, and money. Many firms conduct sales meetings, editorial conferences, and job interviews via teleconference.[74] In addition, these systems enable companies to form work teams able to overcome the barriers of time and space. For instance, following 9/11 and then the Severe Acute Respiratory Syndrome (SARS) outbreak, many firms increased their use of videoconferencing, as discussed in the nearby Focus on Management.[75] Dan Denardo, manager of global videoconferencing for Dow Chemical Company, says videoconferencing improves customer service, helps deliver products faster, and slashes travel costs. Denardo, who supervises more than 160 video cameras at Dow's headquarters, estimates the company saves more than $7 million annually on travel costs alone.[76] Further, videoconferencing permits meetings on the spur of the moment, and prices are plummeting.

According to AT&T Bell Laboratories president John Mayo, videoconferencing components based on light waves should start to augment slower electronic parts by early in this century. This will permit seamless networks of data, voice, and moving pictures. In AT&T's vision, videoconferencing with built-in language translation across national borders will be as common as today's word processing programs.[77]

E-COMMERCE

E-commerce is defined as "the sharing of business information, maintaining business relationships, and conducting business transactions by means of telecommunications networks."[78] As this definition suggests, e-commerce is more than buying and selling over the Web, although that aspect has certainly exploded in recent years. Instead, e-commerce involves using network communications technology to engage in a wide range of activities up and down the value-added chain, both within and outside the organization.[79] That is, it might include use of electronic communication technologies for purchasing of materials, hiring employees, collaborative planning and scheduling of production with suppliers and customers, and much more.

E-commerce can be initiated by business and aimed at business (business to business, or B2B), consumers (business to consumer, or B2C), or government (business to government, or B2G). It can be initiated by the consumer and aimed at business (consumer to business, or C2B), consumers (consumer to consumer, or C2C), or government (consumer to government, or C2G). It can be initiated by government

FOCUS ON MANAGEMENT

EXECUTIVES ON A LEASH*

At the height of the SARS outbreak, Bangkok-based executive-search firm The Wright Company faced a dilemma: For a typical search it might fly in as many as eight candidates to its regional offices for interviews. However, travel bans to parts of Asia were threatening its business; candidates were simply unwilling to fly in. In response, the company tripled its use of videoconferencing. With the subsequent ebbing of SARS, though, the company didn't go back to business as usual; it had saved so much time and money that it is replacing many of its preliminary face-to-face interviews with videoconferencing. It is also investing tens of thousands of dollars in a videoconferencing suite in its Bangkok office.

Heavy use of videoconferencing represents a substantial change even in the United States. It is remarkable in tradition-bound Asia, where face-to-face meetings have been seen as necessary to conduct business. However, when people realized face-to-face meetings weren't possible, they quickly adapted to the new reality and are now embracing videoconferencing.

*Based on S. Neuman, "Executives on a Leash," *Far Eastern Economic Review*, July 10, 2003, pp. 35–36.

and aimed at business (government to business, or G2B), consumers (government to consumers, or G2C), or government (government to government, or G2G). B2B transactions account for the majority of e-commerce sales volume.

Here are a few examples of the impact and promise of e-commerce:

> **Online retail sales.** Internet retailers (called ***e-tailers***) are among the more visible players in the Internet economy. The Web has revolutionized retailing in many ways, including by blurring the boundaries between types of companies. For instance, Amazon.com began as a bookseller and is now expanding far into other markets. Some e-tailers, such as Amazon.com, are Internet based (and known as ***dotcoms***). Others are traditional firms, such as Dell and Barnes & Noble, that have developed a Web presence (these firms are sometimes referred to as "click-and-mortar" retailers). In the latter case, an emerging question is how to coordinate the efforts of the Web business and of the traditional retail element (known as the ***legacy business***).[80] In addition, collections of retailers sometimes operate out of a common Web site in electronic malls, or "cybermalls."[81]

> **Online recruiting.** There are now dozens of major job sites on the Web.[82] A 30-day classified ad in a major newspaper costs an average of about 20 times that of a 30-day posting on a major job board. Further, businesses can place job ads on the Web and start receiving résumés within minutes. Those résumés can then be forwarded to managers, screened out, or otherwise processed. In addition, companies can use the Web to offer job prospects a wealth of information about the job and company culture.

> **Collaborative planning.** An ***extranet*** is a Web-based platform that controls the exchange of data with outside parties. Companies are using extranets to share internal company information with outside parties, such as a manufacturer with its suppliers, distributors, and other collaborators.[83] Extranets determine who has access to data and the nature of their access (for instance, whether they can edit data or only have viewing privileges). Heineken, with its headquarters in Europe, faced delays between order placement in the United States and delivery of 10 to 12 weeks.[84] To reduce that time, Heineken recently implemented an extranet to connect with its customers and suppliers. Called HOPS (Heineken Operational Planning System), the system allows for real-time forecasting and ordering interaction with distributors. Distributors log on to customized Web pages, enter identification and a password, and then can view sales forecasts and modify and submit orders by pressing a button. Order submissions are immediately available at the Heineken brewery in Europe, which can then adjust brewing and shipment schedules. HOPS has helped Heineken cut delivery times to distributors in half while reducing inventories and cutting costs. It also provides a calendar permitting Heineken to notify distributors of events and e-mail to broadcast new products, newsletters, or problems.

E-commerce in Japan is growing less rapidly than that in the United States and Europe, because many fewer people own computers. However, NTT DoCoMo may be Japan's last, best hope in the global Internet race. The company's name is based on the Japanese word for "anywhere." The firm's "I-mode" cell phones provide cheap and continuous wireless access to the Internet as well as voice-recognition technology. Users don't have to make new dial-up connections to get on the Internet; they are always connected as long as they have a signal and a charged battery. Subscribers can swap e-mail and pictures and access more than 4,000 specially formatted Web sites. It is said that there are three things a Japanese teenage girl won't leave home without: her six-inch platform shoes, touch-up toner for her hair color of the day, and her colorful I-mode phone (which is worn like jewelry). In part as a result, DoCoMo is now the world's most valuable cell phone company.[85]

INFORMAL COMMUNICATION

Although formal communication channels are important, much information flows in other, officially unrecognized ways. *Informal communication* is information shared without formally imposed obligations or restrictions.[86]

In organizational settings, information communicated informally among employees is referred to as the *grapevine*. Over three-fourths of the information sent over the grapevine is accurate. However, because even one error can change the whole meaning of a message, such a figure may be misleading. Further, grapevine information is often incomplete, giving a partial picture. As a result, many people view the grapevine negatively. Studies show that people see the grapevine as a primary source of information, but rank it very low as a preferred source.

Despite their problems, grapevines do fill needs. They often carry messages that formal systems do not. They are fast and flexible, and they provide messages that are understandable to employees. Further, the tendrils of the grapevine wind their way around often formidable barriers, seeking out information from people in the know. Whatever the accuracy of information carried over the grapevine, employees tend to view it as accurate. Because of this, grapevine information is often powerful.

The importance of the grapevine varies with national culture. For example, the grapevine and associated rumors are especially important in Mexico. In the office, the grapevine is often the most important source for employees to find out about new changes, especially those affecting personnel. There are probably several reasons for this. For one thing, rumors tend to be formed when uncertainty is high and formal channels of communication fail to provide good information; these conditions prevail in Mexico. In addition, Mexico has a strong oral tradition, and Mexicans have developed a suspicious attitude toward "official" information.[87]

Whatever managers think of the grapevine, they must accept the fact that it exists. Smart managers try to learn who is on the grapevine and how it works. They act to reduce misunderstandings and other negative effects of the grapevine. They may, for instance, provide accurate information to squelch unfounded rumors. They may also harvest the grapevine, using it to get feedback about employee attitudes and ideas. Managers may also use the grapevine as a message channel to carry information that is somehow inappropriate for formal channels.[88] Skills Practice 7-8 will help you to recognize the value of informal communication in organizations and to develop some strategies for managing it more effectively. The nearby Focus on Management demonstrates the power of rumors.

FOCUS ON MANAGEMENT

RUMORS OF SATANISM

Procter & Gamble Co. has struggled for decades to fight rumors that its moon-and-stars trademark is linked to Satanism. Lawsuits, changes in the P&G trademark, and responses to up to 200 concerned callers a day have not halted the persistent rumors.* Now P&G has gone to the Web to fight back. It has set up a Web site specifically to combat the rumors. The site contains a discussion of the history of the P&G moon-and-stars logo, claims that Amway distributors were spreading the rumors, and provides letters of support from the Billy Graham Evangelistic Association, Jerry Falwell, and the archbishop of Cincinnati (P&G's hometown) refuting the rumors.†

http://www.pg.com/about_pg /overview_facts/trademark _facts.jhtml

*Z. Schiller, "P&G Is Still Having a Devil of a Time," *Business Week*, September 11, 1995, p. 46.

†N. Kulish, "Still Bedeviled by Satan Rumors, P&G Battles Back on the Web," *Wall Street Journal*, September 21, 1999, p. B1.

COACHING AND COUNSELING

One key function of communication is that of coaching employees to improve their performance and career development. Here are some guidelines for effective coaching.[89]

> **Create a situation where you are prepared to coach and the employee is open to coaching.** Develop a climate of trust and mutual respect where employees feel open to share their views, needs, and concerns and to try new ideas.

> **Use reflective listening—focus both on words and their emotional content.** Facilitate self-discovery by letting employees think for themselves and present their opinions. Ask, "What do you think?"

> **Talk to your employees, not at them.** Avoid phrases like "You should . . ." and "I want . . ." and instead ask questions such as "What can we do about this?" and "How can we get this done?"

> **Value different perspectives.** Try to understand the differing motivations, work values, goals, and capabilities of individual employees. Learn what tasks interest them, what they find difficult, and to what they aspire.

> **Mutually identify goals.** Focus on behaviors rather than attitudes; behaviors can be changed, whereas attitudes tend to be inflexible. If you feel an employee has a "bad attitude," give feedback on behaviors that might be changed rather than criticizing the attitude.

> **Ask questions.** Use questions to open new possibilities, explore perceptions and assumptions, and provide new ways of examining the same information.

> **Give useful feedback.** Focus both on outcome feedback and on how behavior change can lead to improved outcomes. Ask the employee what he or she thinks should be worked on. Then suggest one of more of those areas on which the employee might concentrate.

> **Track, follow through on your promises, and reward improved behavior.** Recognize and reinforce changed behavior.

The step-by-step process model shown in the Bottom Line feature identifies the basic actions that a manager would take in order to use coaching skills to handle job performance issues in an organizational setting.

GUIDELINES FOR CROSS-CULTURAL COMMUNICATION

Interdisciplinary teams bring together individuals with different training, expectations, experience, and attitudes. These differences in background are one reason for communication problems in teams. But if teams made up of individuals from the same company (or at least the same country) have difficulty communicating, you can imagine how much greater the differences and problems that occur when representatives of different cultures must work together. Here are some guidelines for more effective cross-cultural communication.

> **Learn all you can about the other party's culture.** Sometimes a person thinks he or she is communicating well but is too ignorant of the message receiver's culture to know that he or she is not. For example, communications professors in the United States tend to emphasize the need for *writer-responsible* written work. This means the writer takes responsibility for making the message so simple and transparent that the receiver could not possibly read in anything other than the direct message. But in Chinese society,

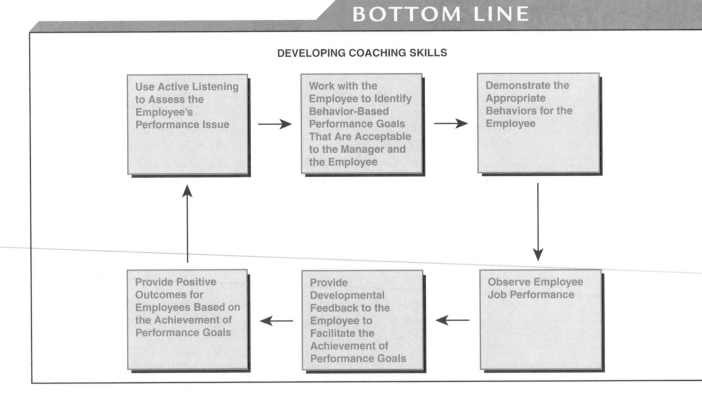

BOTTOM LINE

DEVELOPING COACHING SKILLS

Use Active Listening to Assess the Employee's Performance Issue → Work with the Employee to Identify Behavior-Based Performance Goals That Are Acceptable to the Manager and the Employee → Demonstrate the Appropriate Behaviors for the Employee

Provide Positive Outcomes for Employees Based on the Achievement of Performance Goals ← Provide Developmental Feedback to the Employee to Facilitate the Achievement of Performance Goals ← Observe Employee Job Performance communication, including business communication, is much more indirect.[90] Chinese communications are intended to have more than one level of meaning and interpretation. Unlike countries such as the United States and Canada, which are considered relatively low-context cultures, countries of the Pacific Rim are high-context cultures. In a ***high-context culture***, the real meaning of the message is immersed in the context of the communication.[91] In such a culture, the burden is placed on the receiver to uncover the full meaning of the message from the context in which it was sent; the sender provides pieces of a puzzle, and the receiver must provide the missing links. In a ***low-context culture***, the fundamental meaning of the message is in the explicit statement made. Therefore, translating from one language to another or writing a business letter in one culture versus the other involves much more than substituting Chinese for English words.

> **Try to speak the language.** We learn much about a culture, and certainly facilitate communication, by speaking its language. By speaking the language—even if haltingly—we are more likely to recognize subtle nuances of meaning, to avoid gaffes, and to show a sense of caring and commitment. Lack of adequate knowledge of another language can lead to many problems. Horror stories even of "simple" translation are common. Coca-Cola had to change the name of its soft drink in China after discovering that in Chinese the words mean "Bite the wax tadpole." The new name translates to "May the mouth rejoice." Microsoft Corp. had to issue apologies after it released a Spanish-language version of its Word 6.0 program. The thesaurus accompanying the program suggested that "vicious" and "perverse" could substitute for ***lesbian*** and that "bastard" is a synonym for ***people of mixed race***.[92]

Children in many European and Asian countries begin learning English in elementary school. In the last three decades more than 40 million Japanese have taken the Society for Testing English Proficiency (STEP) exam to demonstrate their competence in the English language. In addition, many thousands annually take proficiency exams in Korean, Indonesian, and—increasingly—Chinese.[93] American business students have only recently been realizing the benefits of learning a second, and perhaps a third, language. The more progressive colleges of business have developed language classes to meet the special needs of international commerce. For example, some students can now take a course called Italian for Business.[94] Instead of reading classics of Italian literature, they read Italian advertisements and learn in class how to open a bank account or apply for a credit card in Italy.

> **Challenge your stereotypes and assumptions.** Even when a person speaks the language, stereotypes and assumptions can get in the way of good communication. To avoid this, constantly challenge your own stereotypes about the culture when dealing with another society.[95] The goal is to replace your original assumptions and beliefs about the society in question (often acquired from watching movies or television) with information received from actual members of that society. If you do not challenge your stereotypes, you may find you have unknowingly offended an international business representative.

> **Withhold evaluation.** In your interactions with people of other cultures, try to gather facts while avoiding evaluation. Too often, we interpret words or

BOTTOM LINE

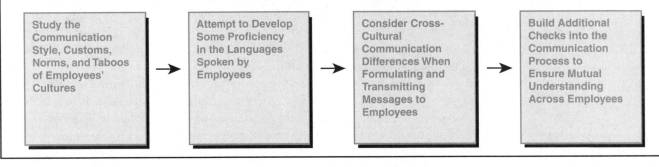

CROSS-CULTURAL COMMUNICATION SKILLS

| Study the Communication Style, Customs, Norms, and Taboos of Employees' Cultures | → | Attempt to Develop Some Proficiency in the Languages Spoken by Employees | → | Consider Cross-Cultural Communication Differences When Formulating and Transmitting Messages to Employees | → | Build Additional Checks into the Communication Process to Ensure Mutual Understanding Across Employees |

behaviors from the perspective of our own culture. Put on the other party's hat (or beret, fez, conch hat, bowler, sombrero, or whatever) and try to understand the situation from his or her position.

The step-by-step procedure presented in the Bottom Line feature shows the basic actions a manager should take to handle cross-cultural communication issues effectively when working with people from other cultures in multinational teams and/or organizations.

Skills Practice 7-9 will give you a number of opportunities to analyze cross-cultural differences in communication within a variety of business settings.

TOP TEN LIST: KEY POINTS TO REMEMBER
HOW TO COMMUNICATE EFFECTIVELY

10. Stay focused on communicating a very specific idea to your receiver(s).
9. Make sure your message captures the key meaning of your idea.
8. Consider the type of message and the communication style of your receiver(s) when sending your message.
7. Analyze verbal and nonverbal cues from the sender when receiving a message.
6. Establish and maintain communication networks to create formal communication linkages and to institutionalize key patterns of interaction.

5. When making presentations, be especially concerned with adapting your message to characteristics of your audience.
4. Use active listening to test your understanding of what others are communicating to you.
3. Take steps to encourage more informal interaction among your employees and between your work unit and other key players in your organization.
2. Be sensitive to differences in communication styles across cultures.
1. Actively manage communication with your employees to keep them up to date on issues that affect them.

QUESTIONS FOR REVIEW AND REFLECTION
REVIEW QUESTIONS

1. What are the four primary functions of communication?
2. Describe each of the steps in the communication process.
3. Describe eight key dimensions of communication channels.
4. Draw three communications networks (e.g., wheel, circle, star), and indicate how they are likely to differ in terms of the satisfaction of each of the members, the speed of decision making, and the ability to deal with complex tasks.
5. Identify and briefly discuss five major barriers to communication.

6. Identify three forms of upward communication in organizations and three forms of downward communication.
7. Provide seven guidelines for effective speaking.
8. Provide seven guidelines for active listening.
9. Give five functions of nonverbal communications and eight forms of nonverbal communication.
10. Discuss eight guidelines for effective use of e-mail.
11. Identify nine guidelines for coaching and counseling.
12. Discuss four steps to effective cross-cultural communication.

CRITICAL THINKING QUESTIONS

1. In anticipation of a pending merger between their firm and another, employees have been showing signs of growing stress and concern. Many are worried about whether they will lose their jobs, face cuts in pay and benefits, or otherwise be hurt by the merger. Management has communicated nothing to employees about likely consequences of the merger, saying, "We don't know everything ourselves yet about how things will play out." How might you advise management regarding its response?
2. A human resources manager refuses to use e-mail, saying it doesn't offer an opportunity for nonverbal communication. Take a position either in support of or in opposition to her view. In defending your position, be sure to

indicate arguments in support of the position and your anticipated reactions to criticisms of the position.
3. You are the founder of a small computer software company that derives most of its revenue from a video-editing program. The program has been commercially successful, but you have learned that a few users have experienced problems and have apparently suffered damage to many of their video files as a result. You are concerned that if you notify other adopters of the problems and provide either a "patch" to fix the bug or a replacement program, the publicity could cripple sales. How would you proceed? What might be some dangers associated with your proposed course of action?

4. Your company is concerned about anecdotal evidence that employees are abusing their Internet access, "surfing" the Web for sports and entertainment sites during work hours. A number of alternatives have been proposed, including:

   > Prohibit Internet access during work hours.
   > Monitor employees' Internet use with surveillance software.
   > Place "blocking" software on the company's computer network to severely restrict access to certain types of sites.
   > Develop a policy on appropriate Internet use, and put employees on an honor system to follow the policy.
   > Do nothing.

   Select one of these options—or develop an alternative of your own. Justify your choice, and indicate how you would notify employees of your selected option.

5. Management is aware that informal communication—the grapevine—is rampant in the organization. Rumors about pending events, leaks of management plans, gossip about office romances, and torrents of other information are swelling the grapevine and extending its tendrils. During a recent meeting of the top man-agement team, one manager recounted a story he had overheard two employees discussing. He expressed concern that the story, which contained sexual innuen-does, could be viewed as contributing to a hostile work environment and could potentially lead to charges of sexual harassment against the firm. "We need to stamp out these sorts of stories," he argued. Another manager responded with caution, saying there was no way to stop informal communications and any management action could lead to a backlash. Yet another said management should somehow "tap" the grapevine, asking a trusted employee to pass on to management any informal communications that might be viewed as inappropriate or harmful. What would be your inputs to this discussion?

6. As director of training you are committed to making employees aware of cross-cultural issues and have implemented related training and education pro-grams. However, several employees have vocally com-plained that this sort of "touchy-feely stuff" is a waste of time. "I'm planning to work right here in Dubuque for the rest of my career," one said. How might you respond to such concerns from employees who antic-ipate no international assignments?

EXPERIENTIAL EXERCISES

WEB EXERCISE 7-1

Go to the following site, titled "A Beginner's Guide to Japan":

*http://www.shinnova.com/part/99-japa/
abj17-e.htm*

   This site provides access to a wide variety of information about Japan and its language and culture and about traveling and doing business in Japan. This link takes you to the "Non-verbal Communication" material. Write a two-page memo to your boss, who will soon be traveling to Japan. In your memo, discuss the roles in Japan of silence and the meaning of specific facial expressions, touching, and gestures. Also, indicate how objects are shown respect in Japan.

WEB EXERCISE 7-2

Etiquette is important any time we communicate. As we have seen in this chapter, electronic mail offers wonderful opportunities for communication as well as unique chal-lenges. Etiquette—in this case, Net etiquette, or "Neti-quette"—is especially critical with e-mail. Conduct a Web search on "Netiquette," and prepare a one-page memo-randum giving 10 guidelines for Netiquette. One excellent Netiquette resource can be found at:

http://www.dtcc.edu/cs/rfc1855.html

CASE 7-1

SALES TEAM COMMUNICATION ISSUES AT A REGIONAL NEWSPAPER*

Note: This case is based on an actual team in a real-world organization. Due to concerns regarding the potential sensitivity of issues presented in this case, some information has been modified to protect the anonymity of the company and the members of the teams.

The Company

The *Sun Post* is a regional newspaper based in the southwestern United States. It was established in 1970 and has a circulation of over a million. The newspaper employs over 700 employees. The mission statement of the newspaper is as follows:

> *To be an indispensable print and Internet information provider in the Southwest. We will build our business through the highest quality journalism, advertising, customer service, and community involvement in order to support our objectives of long-term growth. Our success will ultimately be driven by our highly committed and well trained workforce.*

The *strategic objectives* of the *Sun Post* are as follows:

1. To maximize long-term profitability
2. To maximize long-term market share in terms of circulation volume, Internet usage, and advertising
3. To minimize long-term operational costs
4. To maximize process efficiency in terms of production and distribution

These are the *strategies* being employed to support the achievement of *Sun Post*'s strategic objectives:

1. To grow circulation through better products, promotions, and service
2. To grow advertising revenue
3. To grow Internet audience through enhanced production, promotion, and service
4. To enhance operational efficiency by introducing cost-effective, integrated technologies, accessing and improving work processes, and managing costs

The *Sun Post* has two types of customers: readers and advertisers. The demographic profile of a *Sun Post* reader is very diverse in terms of age, occupation, racial/ethnic background, and socioeconomic status.

Competitors of the *Sun Post* include three other regional newspapers, television stations, and Internet Web sites that provides regional and national news. Based on circulation figures, the *Sun Post* is number two relative to other regional newspaper competitors.

The Advertising Department Sales Team at the *Sun Post*

The *Sun Post* sales team consists of 15 members—12 regular team members (sales representatives, graphic designers) and 3 supervisors. The basic function of this team is to sell and design print advertisements to a wide range of customers.

The sales representatives and graphic designers on the team must coordinate their communications with each other in order for the team to be effective in selling and designing high-quality and profitable advertisements.

Sales representatives spend their time selling print ads to advertisers in their territory. The individuals who hold this position have a mean age of 27 years-old. They all possess a bachelor's degree in marketing or business administration, The mean job tenure of people in this position is 3.7 years. Sales representatives spend a significant amount of time on the road prospecting for new customers and meeting with existing customers to sell new advertisements.

Graphic designers take the advertisements that have been sold to customers and create the actual print advertisements that will meet the customer's specifications. These individuals have a mean age of 31 years-old and possess college degrees in graphic arts.

The sales supervisors work with the sales representatives to set and meet specific sales quotas for each quarter. They also provide training, coaching, and developmental feedback for sales representatives to enhance their job performance. The sales supervisors also work with the graphic designers to create attractive, imaginative, and cost-effective print ads for customers.

Compensation varies by the type of position on the team. Sales representatives earn a base salary of $30,000 plus commissions based on sales. Graphic designers are paid a base salary of $38,000 and are given a variety of incentives for reaching the team's monthly revenue goal, for working with sales representatives to support sales team growth targets, and achieving advertisement productivity targets.

Source: Based on a management consulting project completed by A. Almeida, S. Alper, K. Korevec, D. Schmitt, and E. Storck, May 2003.

The culture of the advertising department sales team is very informal and relaxed. Team members say they feel like part of a family. The team also holds social get-togethers on a regular basis.

Methodology

Consultants were hired by the managing editor of the *Sun Post* to evaluate the effectiveness of communications between members of the team and to make recommendations for enhancing its effectiveness. This action was motivated by the managing editor's concern that communication problems may be reducing the effectiveness of the sales team.

Consultants conducted a series of interviews with members of the management team and administered an in-depth battery of paper and pencil self-assessments to capture their perceptions of the team and its functioning. These questionnaires asked about each team member's perceptions of the team's management of conflict, meeting effectiveness, and overall team functioning (defining of roles and responsibilities, decision making, communicating, etc.) These data were supplemented with a series of ongoing observations of the management team during its meetings.

Results

The consultant's observations of the sales team revealed the following:

- The team has a supportive and informal work environment
- The team is very cohesive and it has a fun culture
- Each individual feels like a valued member of the team
- Sales representatives hand in advertisements at the last minute to the designers, which causes conflict and frustration on the team
- Sales representatives always try to maximize the number of ads sold, but this overwhelms the graphic designers who must create the ads
- Team members do not inform each other when they will be out of the office
- No formal system for tracking team member schedules exists
- The team does not hold regular team meetings due to tight schedules and deadlines of team members
- The team lacks formal processes to ensure that work gets done
- Graphic designers feel they are not being compensated fairly relative to the sales representatives
- Sales representatives feel they are under too much pressure to get into the field and to sell ads all the time

Overall results of the sales team's responses to the self-assessments revealed the following:

Team Meeting Effectiveness Results: Mean Scores

Note: The response scale ranged from 1 to 7 with higher scores reflecting greater degrees of team effectiveness.

Goal Clarity and Under-standing	Member Involvement in Team Discussions	Members Consulted When Making Decisions	Communica-tions Open and Honest with Good Listening	Can Team Members Be Candid with Each Other?	Group Decision Making	Commitment of Individuals to the Team	Do Team Members Help Each Other?
5.9	4.6	5.1	4.7	5.1	4.7	5.8	6.3

Conflict Management Effectiveness Results: Mean Scores

Note: The response scale ranged from 1 to 7 with higher scores reflecting greater degrees of conflict management effectiveness.

Listening	Acknowledging Other Views	Objectivity	Norms	Proper Approach to Conflict	Trust and Openness	Conflict Aftermath
4.1	4.5	5.3	4.3	4.1	4.8	4.7

Team Performance Assessment Results: Mean Scores

Note: The response scale ranged from 1 to 7 with higher scores reflecting greater degrees of team performance effectiveness.

Goals and Results	Communi- cation	Collaboration	Team Competencies	Emotional Climate	Leadership	Planning and Coordination
5.5	2.8	6.0	5.8	6.3	5.6	3.1

Discussion Questions

1. Now it's your turn to be the consultant. Based on the information just provided, analyze the results of the various assessments of the sales team's functioning focusing on communication issues. Download the worksheet that has been created for this exercise from the Web site for this textbook to help you to structure your approach to this exercise. Be sure to document your key findings on this worksheet.

2. Based on your key results, develop a set of *short-term recommendations* (things that should be done immediately or in the next few months) for the sales team to help them to enhance the effectiveness of their communications. Make sure that each of your recommen- dations is specific and action oriented. Be prepared to justify each of your recommendations to the managing editor in terms of merit, feasibility, and cost effectiveness. Also, make sure you address what the managing editor needs to do to ensure the effective execution of your recommendations.

3. Make a five- to ten-minute presentation of your results and recommendations to the class.

4. What did you learn from this case study in terms of communication issues in real-world teams and what must be done to enhance their effectiveness? Which concepts discussed in this chapter were helpful to you in conducting your analysis and in formulating your recommendations?

CASE 7-2

CRISIS MANAGEMENT COMMUNICATIONS AT THE COCA-COLA® COMPANY

Background

The Coca-Cola Company is the largest manufacturer, mar- keter, and distributor of nonalcoholic beverages in the world. It is considered the most recognized and most valuable global brand among consumers as well. Many of its numerous brand names (e.g., Coke, Diet Coke, Minute Maid Orange Juice, Dasani bottled water) are sold in nearly 200 countries around the world. Coke's corporate headquarters is in Atlanta, Georgia. The company employs over 31,000 employees.

The Coca-Cola Company's fundamental vision is as follows:

> *To bring refreshment, value, joy, and fun to all of our stakeholders. We successfully nurture our brands, especially Coca-Cola. This is key to our ultimate obli- gation to provide consistently attractive returns to the owners of our business.**

The company believes that nurturing relationships with all of its stakeholders is absolutely critical to its long- term success and survival. It seeks to accomplish this by being a "good corporate citizen." Specifically, Coca-Cola is committed to managing all of its businesses around the globe with a common value system and set of operating principles called "The Coca-Cola Promise." It emphasizes the highest standards of integrity and excellence. These values are put into practice in relation to the company's actions with its bottlers, the marketplace, the workplace, the environment, and the community.

The dimensions of Coca-Cola's corporate citizenship model include the following:†

The Marketplace
- Highest ethical standards
- Quality of products
- Integrity of brands
- Dedication of employees
- Innovation
- Superb customer service
- Respect for the unique customers and cultures in the communities where we do business

* **Source:** http://www.cocacola.com.
† **Source:** http://www.cocacola.com.

The Workplace

- Treat each employee with dignity, fairness, and respect
- Foster an inclusive environment that encourages all employees to develop and perform to their fullest
- Commitment to human rights

The Community

- Contribution of time, expertise, and resources to develop sustainable communities
- Improving the quality of life through local initiatives

The Coca-Cola company's CEO (during the incidents described in this case) was Douglas Ivester. He joined Coca-Cola in 1979 as assistant controller and director of corporate auditing, and then he went on to assume positions as vice president in 1981 and chief financial officer in 1985. Ivester was born in New Holland, Georgia, and graduated cum laude from the University of Georgia with a BBA.

The Situation

In June 1999, 120 people in Belgium became ill (e.g., vomiting, headaches) after drinking Coca-Cola. More than 50 of these people, many of them children, needed to be hospitalized.

The Belgian health ministry immediately launched an investigation of the incident and demanded that Coca-Cola remove all of its Coke-branded drinks as well as its other brands, such as Nestea and Minute Maid, from store shelves. The governments in France, Spain, and the Netherlands imposed bans on products produced by Coca-Cola in response to this crisis.

Coca-Cola Management's Handling of the Crisis

Two Days after the Crisis Began

Two days after the first reports that people were becoming ill from drinking Coke emerged, the company made the decision to withdraw 2.5 million bottles of Coca-Cola, Coca-Cola Light, Fanta, and Sprite from store shelves in European countries. This action was taken in an attempt to reassure the governments and customers that the problem was being handled by the company. However, the company did not provide any formal explanation to the general public as to why drinking Coke had made the individuals sick. There were no news conferences, press releases, or advertisements designed to set the record straight on what really happened with the tainted Coke, why it happened, and what the company was going to do to prevent the problem from recurring in the future. Coca-Cola also refused to establish and maintain an open dialogue with the Belgian Health Ministry immediately after the incident. Rather, it elected to launch its own independent, internal investigation of the issue.

One Week After the Crisis Began

About a week after the beginning of the crisis, Douglas Ivester issued a brief statement regarding the tainted Coke in Belgium and the people who had become ill after drinking it. Specifically, he stated, "I want to reassure our consumers, customers, and governments in Europe that the Coca-Cola company is taking all the necessary steps to handle this situation."

Coke published its formal apology in Belgian newspapers, set up a consumer hotline to answer questions from customers, and offered to pay all medical bills for the individuals made sick by drinking Coke.

The two explanations Coca-Cola offered for the crisis were that a small number of bottles from its Antwerp plant contained defective carbon dioxide and that some cans from its French factory had been contaminated by a fungicide. The company indicated that a small number of the contaminated cans might still be on sale at small independent retailers in the United Kingdom. Coca-Cola stated that it had no plans to inform the general public of this issue because it believed media coverage had already taken care of this.

The Aftermath of the Crisis

Coca-Cola management has received mixed reviews from analysts and customers in Europe for its handling of the Belgian crisis. Some analysts believe Coca-Cola has done irreparable damage to its brand image and has lost the confidence of customers, and they estimate the episode cost Coca-Cola more than $200 million in expenses and lost profits. The company's management, however, believes strongly that the company will rebound in Europe with no long-term negative impact on sales and profits resulting from the incident.

Discussion Questions

1. Evaluate Coca-Cola management's handling of the crisis in Belgium and other European countries. What did they do well? Where could they have improved?

2. To what degree, if any, do you feel this crisis damaged the image and sales of Coke products in Europe and other parts of the world? Why?

3. Which specific principles of effective communication discussed in the chapter were either implemented or not implemented?

4. Suppose you were Doug Ivester in this case. Write a formal apology to the public regarding what you feel would be an appropriate way to handle the issue of the tainted Coke. How would you deliver this message? Be specific.

5. If you were the CEO of the Coca-Cola Company at the time of this crisis, what would you have done to handle the crisis?

6. Suppose Coca-Cola experiences another incident of tainted Coke, but this time it is in China and thousands of people have fallen ill or even died after drinking Coke. The Chinese government is absolutely furious and demanding responsible action from your company. How would you respond? Develop an action plan for handling this situation. Be specific and action oriented and remember the importance of building

and maintaining trust in the Coca-Cola Promise.

7. What are the practical implications of this case for you as a future manager?

http://www.thecoca-colacompany.com/

Source: S. Bell, "Coke Pays the Price of a Mishandled Crisis," *Marketing,* June 24, 1999, p. 15; "Coke's Hard Lesson in Crisis Management," *Business Week,* July 5, 1999, p. 102; and V. Johnson and S. C. Pappas, "Crisis Management in Belgium: The Case of Coca-Cola," *Corporate Communications: An International Journal,* 2003, 8(1), pp. 18–22.

Video Case: Bank of Alma
A Study in Listening and Communicating

> Running Time: 10:02

The Bank of Alma is a small community bank emphasizing customer service and individual attention. The video presents John McCormack, the bank's president and CEO, and other officers as they describe the importance of listening and communicating at the Bank of Alma and as they interact with customers. After viewing the video, answer the following questions.

1. Why are communications so important at the Bank of Alma?

2. What communications techniques are used at the Bank of Alma to provide personalized customer service?

3. What are some specific obstacles to effective communication in a bank setting?

4. What are some guidelines for good listening as practiced at the Bank of Alma?

5. How are nonverbal communications important at the Bank of Alma? What nonverbal communications do bank employees use in their interactions with customers?

Lighten Up
Bad Mickey

A hipo, a Wallenda, and an imagineer order drinks at a bar. They do a little work—edit a violin, nonconcur with a wild duck, take care of some bad Mickey—and then ask for the bill. "This is on the mouse," says one of the three. Who picks up the tab?

It's not uncommon to hear chatter like this from the mouths of corporate employees. Sometimes translating it requires knowing the jargon, not of MBAs, industries, or regions, but of particular companies.

For instance, an employee at IBM who is fluent in IBM-speak knows that a "hipo" is an employee on the fast track to success—someone with "high potential." (According to one IBMer, an employee with low potential is known as an "alpo.") IBM speakers don't disagree with their bosses—they nonconcur. And anyone who nonconcurs often and abrasively, but constructively, is a "wild duck" in IBM-speak. Former chairman Thomas Watson, Jr., borrowed that tag from Kierkegaard.

Like other tribal entities, corporations develop their own dialects as a way of linking members of the tribe and delineating their ranks. "It has the double purpose of bonding the user to the group and separating the user from general society," says Robert Chapman, editor of the *New Dictionary of American Slang.* "It makes us feel warm and wanted. This works in any society—a company, a school, a family, a saloon."

Slang often occurs in offices where words are the company's business, such as newspapers and magazines. *Newsweek's* top editors are known as *Wallendas,* after the famous family of aerialists—a reference to the precarious nature of their jobs. *Newsweek* writers also call each week's top story the "violin." A spokesman says that's because the story is supposed to "reflect the tone" of the news.

Walt Disney Co., one of the world's shrewdest manufacturers of cultural imagery, is a rare example of a company that has consciously invented its own jargon. It calls the division that plans its theme parks "Walt Disney Imagineering." At orientation sessions (at Disney University), new theme park employees are carefully told to say they are "on stage" while at work and "backstage" while taking a break. They are also told to consider each other not as employees but as "cast members."

Jack Herrman, a former Disney World publicist, recalls that his colleagues would brand anything positive "good Mickey" and anything negative—like a cigarette butt on the sidewalk—"bad Mickey." He also remembers putting lunch on the Disney World expense account and calling it "on the mouse." "You're immersed in the jargon they impose upon you as a way of life," he says.[96]

LIGHTEN UP

THE SMILE TRAINERS

The Japanese are too serious, says Yoshiko Kadokawa, author of the book *Power of a Laughing Face* and president of the Smile Amenity Institute. At a seminar for managers, his students bite on a chopstick or pen. Kadokawa then instructs them to "lift the edge of your mouth higher than the edge of the chopstick. Hold your cheeks and count: *idi, ni, san.* This is how you form your mouth shape." Smile trainers in Japan use techniques such as "underwater training," in which students put their faces in water and then exhale when laughing. Some firms in Japan look for smiling faces in the hiring process. Yurchiro Koiso, dean of McDonald's Japanese training programs, explains that job applicants are asked to describe their most pleasant experience, and then managers evaluate whether their faces reflect the pleasure they are discussing. Applicants who don't have genuine smiles are banished to making burgers rather than greeting customers. "Service is smile and hustle," says Koiso.

LIGHTEN UP

SMILEYS

E-mail takes away much of the opportunity for nonverbal communication. You can't raise your voice, gesture, pound on the desk, or wink. You can, though, use *emoticons*—series of symbols that, when read sideways, resemble little faces and convey emotions. These emoticons are better known as *smileys*. There are thousands of smileys. Here is a sampling:

:-) I'm just kidding
:8) I'm a pig
:-(I'm sad
:-o I'm bored (yawn)

B-) I'm cool
:-* Kiss
:-# My lips are sealed
=8) I'm a baboon
:-& I'm tongue-tied
':-) I accidentally shaved off one eyebrow
;-) Wink
C=>:*')) I'm a drunk demonic chef with a cold and a double chin[97]

To check out hundreds of smileys, go to:

http://members.aol.com/bearpage/smileys.htm

LIGHTEN UP

HAVE YOU HEARD?

Have you heard:

> About the African consumers who were horrified by an American baby food company's packaging? When they saw a picture of a baby on the jar's label, they assumed the jar contained babies!

> About the customer who picked up some fried chicken from a fast-food outlet and discovered an unusual-tasting piece was actually a batter-fried rat? The victim sued the restaurant and won a six-figure award.

> That the Chevrolet Nova sold poorly in Spanish-speaking countries because its name translates as "doesn't go" in Spanish?

> That colleges and universities have regulations specifying that a student whose roommate commits suicide will automatically receive a 4.0 grade point average for the current school term? The institutions believe the stress caused by the suicide would make it impossible for the roommate to perform well in class, unfairly resulting in poor grades.

> About the schoolchildren who were given cartoon character tattoos laced with LSD?

> That an early experiment in subliminal advertising at a movie theater resulted in tremendously increased sales of popcorn and Coke?

> That Finland once banned Donald Duck because he wears no pants?

> About the thriving colony of large alligators that lives deep in the bowels of the New York City sewer system? Apparently, baby alligators brought back as pets from Florida by tourists were dumped into the sewers.

> That colleges and universities have regulations specifying how long students must wait in the classroom before leaving if the instructor fails to appear and that these wait times vary depending on the academic rank of the instructor?

> That designer Tommy Hilfiger shocked the world when he appeared on *Oprah* and said, "If I knew that Blacks and Asians were going to wear my clothes, I would have never designed them"?

> That rice thrown to wish newlywed couples well can kill birds? The rice expands explosively in the birds' stomachs.

If you've heard any of these things, you've heard an **urban legend**. Urban legends are compelling stories that appear mysteriously and spread spontaneously in varying forms. They often contain elements of humor or horror. And—like *all* of the preceding stories—they are often false (but persist nonetheless). To learn more about these urban legends and many others (and about some wild stories that actually *are* true), go to the Urban Legends Reference Pages at:

http://www.snopes2.com/

SKILLS PRACTICE

7-1   *Skill Level:* **CHALLENGING**

Analyzing Interpersonal Communication Dynamics: **Lifeboat**

Skill Objective

To develop skill in analyzing patterns of communication within a group context.

Procedure

1. Obtain a copy of the old classic Alfred Hitchcock movie *Lifeboat*. It is available on VHS and can be rented or purchased from a local video store or retailer.

2. Watch the movie (in class or at home on your own). (Note: Download the worksheet that was developed for this exercise from the Web site for this book. This will help you record your notes from various scenes in the movie.)

   As you watch the film, analyze the patterns of communication between the various members of the lifeboat. Document your notes about these scenes on your worksheet.

3. Discuss the following questions as a class.

   a. What are the communication styles of the various characters? To what extent are these styles compatible or incompatible with each other? Why?

   b. How would you describe the patterns of communication between the various characters in the movie? Why?

   c. Is the overall communication process between the characters in the film effective? Why or why not?

   d. In what ways are the communication issues in this film similar to those that you might encounter in a real-world business organization?

   e. What are the practical implications of this exercise for you as a future manager and leader in a real-world organization?

SKILLS PRACTICE

7-2   *Skill Level: BASIC*

Managing the Communication Process

Skill Objective

To develop skill in effectively applying and managing various aspects of the communication process.

Procedure

Note: Download the worksheet that has been developed for this exercise from the Web site for this textbook. This will help you to better structure your answers to each of the scenarios below.

Read each of the brief scenarios that follow and identify how you would address the communication issues in each by applying the steps in this communication process model:

1. What is your idea?
2. What is your message?
3. Which channel of communication will you use?
4. How will you ensure that the receiver gets the message and decodes it properly?

Scenario 1: Informing Employees of a Layoff

Your company has just announced a round of employee layoffs that will have a significant impact on your work unit. Specifically, your boss has told you that you need to reduce your staff by 50 percent. After a very difficult process, you have decided which employees will be laid off.

Using the communication process model, how would you communicate your decision to the employees who are going to be laid off?

Scenario 2: Explaining a New Policy or Procedure to Your Staff

Your company has just adopted a new performance appraisal system that requires employees to evaluate the performance of their bosses. You believe many of your employees will resist any required participation in this process because they are concerned about confidentiality and potential repercussions associated with any critical remarks they may make about you. You would like to obtain their commitment to this new performance appraisal system.

Using the communication process model, how would you deal with potential employee concerns about the new system?

Scenario 3: Making Recommendations to Senior Management

You are the director of marketing research at a large consumer products corporation based in New York City. Your job is to manage teams of researchers who work on identifying market opportunities for new or existing products and to assess customer satisfaction with your products. Recent research has indicated that the majority of customers are dissatisfied with your products and view them as being of low quality relative to comparable products from competing firms.

Senior management has asked you to present the findings of your department's research at the quarterly cabinet meeting. Your challenge is how to break the bad news to them given the tendency at your company for management to "shoot the messenger" when bad news is being delivered.

Using the communication process model, how would you communicate the news about customer dissatisfaction?

Scenario 4: Dealing with a Crisis

You are the director of public relations for a large dairy coop based in California. On Monday morning, you receive a phone call that three children and five elderly people died in Chicago after drinking the milk produced at one of your company's facilities. In addition, there are reports that hundreds of other people have become ill from drinking milk from the same facility. TV coverage and the national newspapers are providing full coverage of this breaking story. You do not have all of the information about the situation, but you know the company has launched an immediate investigation into the matter.

Using the communication process model, how and what would you communicate to the media, the general public, and your own employees?

Scenario 5: Dealing with an Ugly Lawsuit Against Your Company

You are the director of human resources at a highly successful department store based in San Antonio, Texas. You just learned that a female manager is filing a lawsuit against the company's charismatic CEO for sexual harassment. This employee is alleging that the CEO "came on to her" at a company social and told her she would lose her job if she did not sleep with him that night. You know this situation will be a disaster once the media, the public, and your employees hear about this.

Using the communication process model, how would you communicate the news about the lawsuit to everyone?

Discussion Questions

1. Evaluate your plan for dealing with each of the scenarios. Which aspects would be the most challenging to handle and why? Exactly how would you communicate your messages in the scenarios to the relevant players inside and outside the organization?

2. In the real world, these issues would most likely be far more complex to handle. Why?

3. What are the implications of this exercise for you as a future supervisor or manager in a real-world organization?

SKILLS PRACTICE

7-3   *Skill Level: CHALLENGING*

Field Experience: Analyzing Communication Issues in Real-World Organizations

Skills Objectives

1. To develop a better understanding of the type of communication issues that people in real-world organizations have to deal with.

2. To develop a better understanding of how managers handle communication issues in the real world.

Procedure

1. Identify two or three managers who work in a real-world business organization. Ask the managers if you can interview each of them for approximately 30 to 45 minutes.

2. When you meet with each manager, ask the following questions.

   a. How would you describe your communication style? Can you give me an example of a situation you were in that illustrates this communication style?

   b. What are the most difficult challenges you face in terms of communicating with various people you deal with in your organization? How do you handle them?

   c. Why is communicating effectively with people in organizations challenging? What is the cost of poor communication to the effectiveness of an organization?

   d. What do you think are the most important things for an individual to do to be an effective communicator in a real-world organization? Why?

3. Optional: Repeat questions 2a–d by interviewing one or two employees of the manager you interviewed earlier.

4. Summarize the results of your interviews.

Discussion Questions

1. What did your interview(s) illustrate about why communication can be such a difficult challenge for managers in real-world organizations?

2. Based on the summary of your interviews, what do you feel are the most important things to remember about communicating effectively in real-world business organizations?

SKILLS PRACTICE

7-4   *Skill Level: CHALLENGING*

Designing and Implementing Employee Attitude Surveys

Skills Objectives

1. To develop skill in designing an employee attitude survey.

2. To develop skill in administering an employee attitude survey.

Procedure

Note: Download the worksheet that has been developed for this exercise. This will facilitate your working through the steps below.

1. Break up into teams of three to five students.

2. Select an organization you are familiar with based on general knowledge or past or present work experience. If you can't think of a "real-world" organization to use, select a student organization that someone is involved with.

3. Suppose the president of the organization you selected has asked you to design and administer a survey to assess employees' perceptions and atti-

tudes toward their jobs and the general work environment. The purpose of the survey is to identify specific strategies for enhancing the quality of the work environment for employees.

4. As a team, design your survey by brainstorming a list of 10 to 20 appropriate questions. Try to include at least 10 structured questions and one or two open-ended questions as well.

Examples of Structured Questions

Question	Strongly Disagree	Disagree	Neutral	Agree	Strongly Agree
1. I am satisfied with the kind of work I do in performing my job.	1	2	3	4	5
2. My supervisor provides the direction I need to be successful in my job.	1	2	3	4	5
3. The environment in this organization motivates me to do my best work.	1	2	3	4	5

SKILLS PRACTICE

7-5   *Skill Level: BASIC*

Effective Speaking

Skill Objective

To develop skill in making effective presentations to different types of audiences.

Procedure

1. Select a topic (e.g., a theory or concept) to use as a basis for your speeches from any content area in this book.
2. Read the following case scenarios.
3. Select one scenario, and prepare a three- to five-minute speech to present to your class.
4. Present the speech, and obtain feedback from your classmates regarding the effectiveness of your speech.
5. Talk about the discussion questions that follow.

Skill Practice Scenarios

Case 1: Senior Executives

You have been asked to make a brief presentation of your topic to a group of senior executives at your company.

Your goal is to explain your topic to them in an appropriate manner and to convince them that your chosen topic is important to the success of the organization.

Case 2: Entry-Level Supervisors with Little Formal Education
You have been asked to make a brief presentation of your topic to a group of entry-level supervisors with little formal education. Your goal is to provide them with a clear understanding of the topic and to see why it is important to them in their jobs.

Discussion Questions

1. What kinds of adjustments did you make in order to take into consideration the characteristics of your audience?
2. What are the practical implications of this exercise for you as a future manager in a real-world organization?

SKILLS PRACTICE

Active Listening Skills

Skill Objective

To use active learning to develop skill in capturing the meaning of messages communicated by others in order to enhance one's understanding of a work situation or issue.

Procedure

1. Find a partner in your class. Try to work with someone you do not know, if possible.
2. Work through the following exercise.
3. Answer the discussion questions at the end of this exercise.

Active Listening Exercise

Step 1: One person should assume the role of the "speaker" (storyteller) and the other person should play the role of the "listener." After one round of the exercise is completed, the roles should be switched.

Step 2: (The Speaker) Think about the best (or worst) job you have ever held. Tell your partner why you liked (or disliked) this job so much (e.g., coworkers, type of work, pay). Try to provide as much detail as possible by using specific examples.

Step 3: (The Listener) Try to use active listening in listening to your partner's description of his/her favorite/worst job. You can do this by trying to capture the *meaning* of what your partner is saying rather than just the words spoken. This means you should consider nonverbal cues (e.g., facial expressions, posture) as well as the emotions you observe in the other person as he or she is speaking (e.g., enthusiasm, frustration). Occasionally, you should try to "reality test" your understanding of what the other person is saying by making a statement such as "So what I hear you saying is . . ." or "So what you mean is . . ." This is to ensure that your understanding of what the speaker is trying to communicate to you is accurate. Sometimes this is called "being on the same page." When the other person has completed his or her story, try to summarize, in your own words, the main ideas or points made. This is an excellent test of whether you actually understand the main ideas contained in the message.

Step 4: Switch roles and repeat Steps 1 and 2.

Discussion Questions

1. What is your reaction to this exercise in terms of trying to listen more actively? Why do you feel this way?
2. How can active listening skills help you to become a more effective manager in the real world? What are the problems associated with not using active listening when you communicate with other people?
3. What are the practical implications of this exercise for you as a future manager and leader in a real-world organization?

SKILLS PRACTICE

Understanding and Managing Nonverbal Communication

Skill Objective

To develop skill in managing nonverbal forms of communication.

Procedure

Note: Please download the worksheet that has been developed for this exercise and use it to record your observations of the other individuals who are participating in this exercise.

1. Form groups of five to seven people.
2. Write your first and last name on the name sticker provided and stick it on your shirt.
3. Now spend one minute engaging in small talk with each member of your group on a one-on-one basis. You can talk about anything you want to including movies, weekend plans, major, career objectives, your hometown, hobbies and interests, and so on. Relax and have fun with this! Be sure to pay attention to the nonverbal cues (see later) that you observe from each person you talk to during the exercise. Write down your observations on your worksheet. Be sure to continue rotating from

person to person until you have talked to everyone in your group. Here are some examples of nonverbal cues to observe:

> Dress
> Touch
> Posture
> Eye contact
> Facial expressions
> Hand movements
> Paralanguage
> Proxemics

4. Answer the discussion questions.

Discussion Questions

1. Share your observations of nonverbal behavior with the other members of your group. Be sure to talk about the specific nonverbals you observed and what you feel they communicated to you. Discuss whether your analysis of other people's nonverbal behavior was accurate.

2. What types of nonverbal behaviors did you find to be the most informative about the people you talked with during the exercise? Why?

3. What types of nonverbal behaviors should you be aware of when communicating with others in a real-world organization?

4. What would be some general guidelines for managing nonverbal communication when you deal with many different types of people, that is, different genders, races, ethnicities, or functional backgrounds (e.g., marketing, engineering)?

5. What are the practical implications of this exercise for you as a future manager or leader in a real-world organization?

SKILLS PRACTICE

7-8 | *Skill Level:* BASIC

Managing Informal Communication

Skill Objective

To develop skill in managing informal communication in organizations more effectively.

Procedure

Go through the following steps to develop some general strategies for managing informal communication:

1. Identify the work unit you will use as a focus for this exercise. This can be a work unit from a part-time or summer job you held or have now, a student organization you are a member of, or any other work unit with which you are familiar.

2. Brainstorm some specific strategies for enhancing informal communication with respect to the work units you just identified. Try to be as creative as possible!

3. Evaluate your ideas and decide on three to five specific strategies you would like to implement within your work unit.

4. Develop a list of the steps you would take to support the implementation of your strategies.

5. Finalize your plan into a concise summary of your strategies for enhancing informal communication.

Discussion Questions

1. In what ways can informal communication contribute to the success of a work unit beyond the use of formal methods of communication? That is, why should we care about managing informal communication?

2. What might be some barriers in a real-world organization to the successful implementation of the strategies you identified?

3. What are the managerial implications of this exercise for you as a future manager?

SKILLS PRACTICE

Skill Level: CHALLENGING

Managing Cross-Cultural Communication

Skill Objective

To develop skill in managing communication in a cross-cultural context.

Procedure

1. Form groups of three to five people.
2. Assign one scenario to each group.
3. The task of each group is to develop a set of steps it would take to handle the issue of cross-cultural communication in relation to its particular scenario. Be as specific as possible in developing your guidelines.
4. Make a brief three- to five-minute presentation of your plan to the class for discussion purposes.

Mini-Case 1: "Up a Creek Without a Paddle"

You are the marketing manager at a U.S. computer corporation that designs and manufactures personal computers, software applications, mainframe computers, and computer peripherals. You have been asked by your boss to pick up a group of five Chinese businessmen at the local airport. Your company is attempting to negotiate a deal with this Chinese company to become one of their major suppliers of computer peripherals (e.g., disk drives, modems). If the deal can be made, this would provide your firm with a tremendous opportunity for long-term growth.

The major obstacle you face is that although the Chinese businessmen you are meeting speak some English, they are not fluent in English. And you don't know a word of Chinese.

What would be your plan for overcoming the communication problems you are sure to encounter in this situation?

Mini-Case 2: "Leading a Global Team"

You are a manager of a U.S. multinational corporation based in Chicago. Your firm specializes in offering management consulting services (e.g., information technology solutions, change management, total quality) to clients all over the world.

You have just been assigned to lead a newly formed consulting team that will work with a client in France on managing a merger or acquisition. The composition of your team is multinational, consisting of consultants from France, India, Brazil, Japan, and the United States. Although everyone on the team is fluent in English, there are many "stylistic differences" in communication.

Although the multinational diversity on your team is a strength in many ways, you know you will need to work hard to maintain effective communication with the various team members.

What would be your plan for dealing with the communication issues in this situation?

Mini-Case 3: "The Yankee in Jakarta"

You are a U.S. expatriate from a consumer food and beverage company based in San Francisco. You have been assigned to assume the manager position at a new marketing office in Jakarta, Indonesia. The objective of this new office is to capitalize on the emerging food products market in Indonesia and Southeast Asia. There are 20 local Indonesians (mostly professionals with college degrees) who report to you.

Fortunately, you are semifluent in the Indonesian language. In addition, your staff understands a fair amount of English. The key challenge is that your communication style is very direct and explicit (characteristic of a low-context culture), whereas your staff's communication style is very indirect and implicit (characteristic of a high-context culture). You realize the differences in communication styles will create some significant challenges for you and your staff.

What would be your plan for dealing with the communication issues in this situation?

LEADING EFFECTIVELY

Skills Objectives

> To match appropriate leadership styles to the needs of the situation.

> To develop and implement leadership strategies that address substitutes and neutralizers of leadership in a given situation.

> To develop and implement leadership strategies that support the transformation of organizations.

> To evaluate the performance of a leader systematically and to develop recommendations to enhance a leader's effectiveness.

> To develop skill in thinking holistically about leadership theory and practice.

KNOWLEDGE OBJECTIVES

> Understand emerging perspectives on leadership.

> Discuss traits related to success as a leader.

> Explain key leader behaviors, including consideration and initiating structure.

> Understand the path–goal theory of leadership.

> Identify substitutes for, and neutralizers of, leadership.

> Discuss leader–member exchange theory.

> Understand transformational leadership, including specific transformational leader behaviors.

> Identify key elements of the language of leadership.

Steve Jobs has been called "a classic comeback kid" and "the Lazarus of the PC world."[1] With his friend Steve Wozniak, Jobs founded Apple Computer in his father's garage in the 1970s and gave birth to the microcomputer revolution. Jobs had a passionate vision that many described as a near religion, challenging engineers to build, not good, but "insanely great" products that would "make a dent in the universe." But Jobs had no management training and no business skills, and his style wasn't suited to building a stable corporation. He was ousted from Apple in 1985, his reputation apparently forever tarnished. Jobs resigned himself to smaller ponds, founding NeXT, which made an elegant black computer for the university market, and buying Pixar Animation Studios. Under his leadership, Pixar became a powerhouse, with blockbusters including *Toy Story, A Bug's Life,* and *Toy Story 2.* In 1995, just after *Toy Story*'s release, Jobs took Pixar public and became a billionaire.

Meanwhile, for a decade after Jobs' departure, Apple floundered, with its market share falling to single digits and its prospects dim. In 1997, Jobs was invited back to Apple as interim CEO. In the next two years, he helped restore Apple's pride, quadruple its market share, and bring it back to solid profitability. He has introduced new products such as the iMac, iBook, and G3 Cube, launched a "Think Different" ad campaign, signed a pact with Microsoft, unveiled an ambitious Internet strategy, and helped dispel feelings of anxiety and helplessness. Although he appears to have mellowed somewhat, Jobs is still described as temperamental, driven, dashing, charismatic, erratic, eccentric, brilliant, pompous, and given to wild bouts of infectious enthusiasm. With the "interim" now removed from his Apple title, he continues his quest, viewing both Apple and Pixar as embodying his vision of the computer as an empowering cultural force. Still, some wondered if the mercurial Jobs was what Apple needed now that it has emerged from the edge of crisis. To date, signs are positive: Pixar's profits are up sharply, Apple has introduced the iPod, the iTunes Music Store, and powerful new computers, and Jobs continues to reap praise.[2]

Men and women have sought since the beginning of recorded history to become leaders and to succeed in leadership roles. The fact that some leaders have been remarkably successful while others—although often intelligent, well meaning, and conscientious—have failed dismally suggests that becoming an effective leader may not be easy and the ways to do so are far from obvious. The realization that some leaders—like Steve Jobs—have bounced back and forth between success and failure makes the task seem even more daunting.

In this chapter we provide guidelines and exercises to develop your leadership knowledge and skills. We first define leadership and distinguish between *leading* and *managing.* We then examine emerging perspectives on leadership to see how views of leadership have evolved to meet the demands of the modern workplace. Next, we consider whether it is possible to identify traits of successful leaders—that is, whether there are "born leaders." Then we explore how leaders can develop power bases and employ social influence tactics. We then turn our attention to leader behaviors, including theories to help explain when those behaviors are needed. Following this, we examine transformational leadership, including both transformational leader behaviors and how leaders can employ the "language of leadership" to inspire followers. We conclude the chapter with some suggestions for choosing a leadership style.

Take a moment to complete Self-Assessment 8-1 then learn more about your responses by visiting the text Web site. You will learn more from this chapter if you start off with a greater awareness of your beliefs and feelings about leadership.

SELF-ASSESSMENT 8-1

Attitudes Toward Leadership

Answer the questions that follow regarding your attitudes toward leading others in organizations. Answer each question as honestly as possible using the following response scale:

1 Disagree strongly
2 Disagree somewhat
3 Neither agree nor disagree
4 Agree somewhat
5 Agree strongly

____ 1. A person needs to be feared by his or her employees in order to be an effective leader.
____ 2. There is one best way to lead people in organizations.
____ 3. A major part of leadership is providing direction for employees.
____ 4. A person needs to consider the characteristics of the situation in order to become an effective leader.
____ 5. Leaders should rely on the use of their formal authority or position in the organization as the best way to influence their employees.
____ 6. Leadership ability is something that cannot be developed, because you either have it at birth or you don't.
____ 7. Leadership effectiveness should be measured solely in terms of the financial performance of the organization.
____ 8. Effective leaders must be trusted and respected by their employees.
____ 9. Workers in today's modern business environment don't value or need leadership from management.
___ 10. The knowledge and skills needed to perform well in a nonmanagerial position are pretty much the same as those needed to be an effective leader in an organization.

As a way to assess your initial level of skill in leading others, read the scenario in the nearby Pretest Skills Assessment and develop an action plan for how you would handle this situation. Be as specific as possible in stating your recommendations. After you are through, learn more about your responses by checking the text Web site.

PRETEST SKILLS ASSESSMENT

Leading

Note: This exercise is based on actual events encountered by managers in real-world organizations. Some information may have been modified in order to maintain the anonymity of the people and organization involved in this situation.

You are the new production supervisor at a global computer corporation based in San Antonio, Texas. You have a team of 500 employees who assemble different models of laptop computers using a variety of components. The work requires a high level of worker knowledge and skill, for workers must custom-build these computers based on specifications from customers.

Your employees are a mix of young, inexperienced people who possess marginal work skills and limited formal education, part-time college students who want to get their feet wet and are anxious to move up in the organization and develop careers for themselves, and very experienced people who have worked on the company's assembly line for more than 20 years but are not comfortable with all the new technology they are required to learn for their jobs.

Your work unit has been experiencing problems with quality (i.e., high defects and customer return rates), high costs, and low productivity. In addition, the previous supervisor of this unit had to be terminated because his leadership style was so abrasive, many employees threatened to quit if the company did not get rid of him.

Develop an action plan for solving the problems in your work unit. Be sure your plan addresses both short-term and long-term issues. Be very specific, and be prepared to defend each element of your plan in terms of its feasibility and cost effectiveness.

WHAT IS LEADERSHIP?

We define *leadership* as the ability to influence others toward the achievement of goals. Leadership, then, relates to the ability to influence others. This suggests that leaders may not always be influencing but can do so when needed. It suggests, too, that leadership is about dealing with others and, as such, that a variety of interpersonal skills may be needed by effective leaders. Finally, leadership is related to goal achievement; the leader exerts influence not for its own sake but to yield desired outcomes.

Leadership may sound like another name for *management*, but the terms and related functions are generally viewed as distinct. Whereas management aims at providing consistency and order to organizations, leadership seeks to produce constructive and adaptive change. Management is focused on accomplishing activities and mastering routines; leadership involves influencing others and creating visions for change. Management is directed toward coordinating activities in order to get a job done, and leadership is concerned with the process of developing mutual purposes. Both management and leadership somehow involve influencing others toward goal attainment, but management relies more on a one-way authority relationship, whereas leadership relies more on a multidirectional influence relationship. In the words of leadership experts Warren Bennis and Burt Nanus, "Managers are people who do things right and leaders are people who do the right things."[3]

Now complete Skills Practice 8-1, "Fieldwork: Interview with a Leader." The purpose of the exercise is to give you the opportunity to get out into the real world and learn about leadership issues by interviewing an individual who is a leader in an organization. This exercise will literally bring to life many of the issues discussed in this chapter.

Next complete Skills Practice 8-2, "Profiling a Great Leader." The purpose of the activity is to get you to formalize what you already know and believe about what it takes to be a good leader. This will provide a nice foundation on which to build as we move through the chapter. The Focus on Management feature provides *Business Week*'s rankings of the best and worst managers of 2002.

EMERGING PERSPECTIVES ON LEADERSHIP

The field of leadership is dynamic. Recent decades have seen rather remarkable changes in how we think about leadership. Those changes reflect both continued

FOCUS ON MANAGEMENT

THE BEST (AND WORST) MANAGERS OF THE YEAR

Historically, *Business Week* has picked the "Top 25 Managers of the Year." For 2002, it felt compelled to rank both the best *and* the worst managers. According to *Business Week,* the "year 2002 will be remembered as the *annus horribilis* of business. It was a time of tumult and reassessment, high drama and low comedy. Corporate crime and greed were spectacularly exposed in companies that had once been praised, run by executives who had once been trusted. . . . Chief executives seemed startled by the ridicule, distrust, and outright contempt they faced. At the same time, they had to contend with an economy that edged ever-so-slowly toward a recovery but kept falling short. If ever there was a year to examine the ways in which managers succeed—and fail—this was it." Topping the list of the best managers were Susan Kropf and Andrea Jung of Avon Products, Michael O'Leary of Ryanair, Fujio Cho of Toyota, and Michael Dell of Dell Computer. Leading the list of worst managers were Sandy Weill of Citigroup, Dick Brown of Electronic Data Systems, Bill Harrison of J. P. Morgan Chase, and James and Charles Dolan of Cablevision. Read about the Best and Worst Managers of the Year and how they earned their rankings at:

http://www.businessweek.com /magazine/toc/03_02/B38150 302best.htm

development of leadership theory and practice and awareness of the need to adapt leadership to the demands of the modern workplace. Figure 8-1 presents some facets of the changing look of leadership.

Let's look at these in turn. First, whereas early leadership approaches emphasized the traits of successful leaders—who successful leaders *are*—newer approaches ask how successful leaders behave—what successful leaders *do.*

Second, early approaches to leadership tended to take a universalistic perspective, asking, "What works?" Newer approaches, recognizing that characteristics of the situation, such as followers' needs and skills, and various characteristics of the

FIGURE 8-1
The Changing Look of Leadership

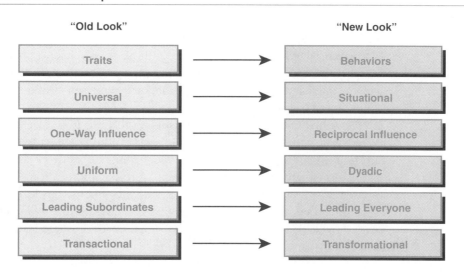

"Old Look"	"New Look"
Traits	Behaviors
Universal	Situational
One-Way Influence	Reciprocal Influence
Uniform	Dyadic
Leading Subordinates	Leading Everyone
Transactional	Transformational

task must be considered, ask instead, "What works when?" Considering the situation may complicate the leader's life, but it is a necessary complication for effectiveness.

Third, early leadership approaches considered primarily one-way influence. In particular, they asked how a leader influences followers. Newer perspectives recognize that the influence process is reciprocal—just as leaders are influencing followers, followers are also influencing leaders. Effective leadership resides in the complex interplay of these mutual patterns of influence.

Fourth, early leadership approaches tended to assume that leaders treat their various followers in similar ways—some leaders are nice, others "bossy," others strict, and so on—but more recent approaches recognize that leaders may—for good or bad reasons—treat different followers differently. They may be more considerate with some followers than with others, give some more direction than others, let some participate more in decision making, and so on.

Fifth, whereas leadership approaches initially focused on the relationship of leaders to their subordinates, modern views of leadership are more inclusive. They recognize that the "others" whom leaders influence may include not just subordinates but also many others, including team members and perhaps even hierarchical superiors. Leadership does not have to face downward.

Finally, most early approaches to leadership tended to consider how a leader might influence others in a series of transactions. That is, they viewed leaders and followers as engaging in exchanges in which the leader would offer certain things—rewards, support, protection, for example—in return for desired follower behaviors. Newer leadership approaches recognize that, although important, this transactional view is incomplete. Leaders must take actions to transform followers and organizations by communicating values, inspiring, intellectually stimulating, and showing confidence in the face of crisis. Such transformational leader behaviors may often be critical to the life of an organization.

LEADER TRAITS

The earliest approach to the study of leadership was to try to identify characteristics, or traits, of successful leaders. For instance, one early study found links between leadership success and intelligence, education, preferences for high levels of risk, desire for independence, and other variables.[4] Literally thousands of studies have now explored leadership traits. Some of those traits relate to physical factors, some to ability, many to personality, and still others to social characteristics. Of the traits, activity, intelligence, knowledge, dominance, and self-confidence are most often found linked to leader success.

Unfortunately, most reviews of studies relating to leadership traits have concluded that the trait approach has not been fruitful.[5] One early survey of this literature noted that of all traits that showed up in one study or another as related to leadership effectiveness, only 5 percent were common to four or more studies.[6] In another early study, some high school students emerged as leaders on one type of task and others emerged on other tasks.[7] These findings suggest that the traits needed by leaders may depend on the situation. To illustrate how traits of successful leaders may vary, consider the following leaders: Mohandas Gandhi, Mary Kay Ash, Kemal Ataturk, Herb Kelleher, Henry Cisneros, Thomas Jefferson, Ho Chi Minh, Bill

Gates, Margaret Thatcher, Cochise, Nelson Mandela, Lech Walesa, Winston Churchill. How are they similar? How do they differ?

Despite the generally unsuccessful search for leader traits, the hunt continues. Perhaps the most promising approach is to focus on the roles of the "Big 5" personality dimensions, discussed in Chapter 2. For example, one statistical review of past research examined relationships of the Big 5 dimensions to leader emergence and leader effectiveness.[8] That review concluded that extraversion, openness to experience, agreeableness, and conscientiousness were positively related to leadership, and neuroticism was negatively related. Extraversion had the most consistent links to leadership across study settings and leadership criteria.

A basic concern with the trait approach relates to the question of how the findings can be used. Because traits are relatively stable, it is unlikely that leaders can develop them through training. So although information concerning traits of successful leaders might be useful to select leaders and place them in suitable positions, it is otherwise of limited value. In part, this is because the trait approach considers only characteristics of the leader while ignoring the characteristics of followers and situations.

This doesn't mean we should abandon the trait approach. For instance, it may be useful to determine which traits are associated with success in particular situations. However, it is safe at this point to say that more is likely to be gained by looking directly at what successful leaders *do* than at what they *are*. Before moving on, complete Self-Assessment 8-2 to gain some insights into yourself as a leader. After you are done, visit the text Web site to learn more about your responses.

SELF-ASSESSMENT 8-2

Thinking About Yourself as a Leader

"He who knows others is wise; he who knows himself is enlightened." —Lao-tzu (c. 604–c. 531 B.C.)

"It is much more difficult to judge oneself than to judge others." —Antoine de Saint-Exupéry (1900–1944), The Little Prince (1943)

If we are to understand and perhaps alter our leader behaviors, it's important to give some serious thought to our past leadership accomplishments, current leader behaviors, and leadership goals. Often it is helpful to articulate our thoughts and feelings concerning these issues. With that in mind, respond to the following:

1. Describe some leadership role you now hold or have held (e.g., at work or in a social organization). How long have you been, or were you, in the position?
2. Describe some leadership situation for which you are especially proud of your performance. What about your leadership characteristics or behaviors do you think contributed to that accomplishment?
3. Describe some leadership quality you would like to have that you think you are now lacking.
4. Consider a leader who has influenced you or motivated you. Describe the techniques he or she used to engage you as a follower.
5. Think of a situation in which a leader disappointed you. What did he or she do, or not do, that was disappointing?
6. Suppose you were to retire from your firm tomorrow and one of your direct reports (or peers) was asked by your replacement to describe your leadership traits, behaviors, and/or effectiveness. What three or four words or phrases do you think he or she would be most likely to use?

KEY LEADER BEHAVIORS AND SKILLS

The legendary Green Bay Packers coach Vince Lombardi is credited with once having said that leaders aren't born, they are made, and they are made just like anything else: through hard work. In the Voice of Experience feature, Rich Frohmader, partner at Virchow, Krause & Co., LLP, an accounting and consulting firm, shares his insights and advice regarding effective leadership. He notes he is self-trained, with an evolving style. What behaviors are evident in his leadership style?

In the search for leader behaviors that make a difference, several kinds of behaviors have been examined. In this section, we first consider autocratic and democratic styles, reflecting the degree to which the leader lets followers participate in decision making. We then address the degree to which the leader exhibits behaviors that are relationship oriented and/or task oriented. Following a look at these sets of behaviors, we consider some characteristics of the situation that may help determine when those behaviors are needed.

AUTOCRATIC AND DEMOCRATIC STYLES

An early approach to the study of leadership considered the degree to which leaders are autocratic or democratic. *Autocratic leaders* make decisions themselves, without inputs from subordinates. *Democratic leaders* let subordinates participate in decision making. Thus, as shown in Figure 8-2, autocratic and democratic styles are at opposite ends of a single continuum, differing in degree of delegation of decision-making authority. They differ *only* on this dimension, not necessarily on other variables, such as sensitivity and caring. Although there may be a tendency to think of democratic leaders as more caring than autocratic leaders, there are "benevolent autocrats" who sincerely believe—correctly or not—that they are in the best position to make decisions that will benefit their subordinates and the organization. There are also uncaring democratic leaders who delegate responsibility in an attempt to avoid taking personal responsibility for decisions.

Democratic style is consistently linked to higher levels of subordinate satisfaction. However, the relationship of style to performance is more complex. Democratic style is usually positively, but weakly, related to productivity. Many factors determine whether a democratic style is appropriate, including the nature of the task and the personalities of subordinates. When tasks are simple and repetitive, participation has little effect, because "there is little to participate about."[9] When subordinates are intelligent and desire independence, participation is especially important.

Deciding on the appropriate level of participation is extremely important. Participation is empowering and satisfying, and it generates enthusiasm for the decisions reached. However, participation takes time away from other activities. Also, some people don't like to participate, and most people don't want to get involved

FIGURE 8-2
Autocratic and Democratic Styles

Lower	Degree of Participation	Higher
Autocratic		Democratic

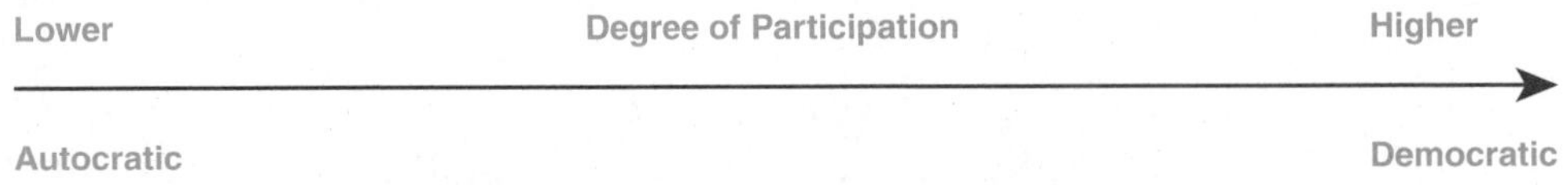

VOICE OF EXPERIENCE

LEADING EFFECTIVELY

Rich Frohmader, Partner, Virchow, Krause & Co. LLP

1. As a leader and manager in your organization, how is leadership different than management?

Well, as a partner in a CPA firm, management has to realize that we are in a people business. Our only real assets are our people. Yes, we spend a great deal of money on computers and software, but we are way ahead if we can hire good people. Therefore, managing and leading our people is key to our success. I don't think about leadership vs. management when I'm working with my staff and peers on a daily basis. However, there is a difference, although the terms have "overlap." I see leadership as a visionary and motivational role that usually involves change, whereas management tends to involve controlling or directing people. Leadership requires the foresight to see opportunities that will grow the practice or improve efficiencies and then leading the effort and motivating people to carry out the change. Identifying the need to hire tax specialists in the state and local tax area, or in the research and development tax credit area, devising a strategy to locate or train those specialists, and then leading the charge to help them market their services so they are successful is an example of how leadership can work. Managing people can be more methodical and administrative. For example, management might need to make sure employees are making their personal charge budgets each week, completing time reports on time and getting the training they need to be great assets to the organization and to our clients, as well as meeting professional licensing standards. Personally, I have more fun when I'm leading.

2. What type of leadership style do you most often use?

I chair the tax services committee, a group of six tax partners from various geographic regions within our firm. I lead by building consensus and getting all parties to buy in to a particular concept. The dictatorial style just would not work with this group of people. For example, last year I heard of an outsourcing opportunity that would help us flatten out our peak workload a bit. It amounted to a quality of life issue for our employees who work a lot of overtime during our busy season. Initially, the group did not appreciate the concept and summarily dismissed the idea. However, I saw the advantages and brought it back to the group and asked the vendor to come in and demo his product. The second time the group saw the advantages immediately and we are now ready to implement this concept. If I had forced the concept through a year ago, I would have experienced problems with them being committed to implementation and may not have even received the firm's executive committee approval. Professional talented people tend to have a mind of their own! They are great assets, but you have to lead them by building consensus.

3. What is the most challenging part of being a leader? How do you handle these challenges?

Most accountants find communications their biggest stumbling block. We are educated in the fine art of analyzing numbers and researching technical rules. Therefore we analyze and calculate, but we frequently fail to explain and communicate adequately. I need to consciously remember to communicate as often and as clearly as possible. Many organizations have the same problem. The leaders talk about a new initiative for days, but when it comes to driving it through their business, they don't understand why everyone's not on the same page. We need to communicate our messages several different ways and follow up.

For example, recently I purchased a license to access education courses over the Web. Our tax committee reviewed the courses, the cost, and decided on the number of users. We signed up the users on the product and notified them via e-mail. Three months later I asked a group of users how the product was working and I got blank stares (it's the same look I get when I talk to my teenage sons). Lesson learned—communicate often and follow up.

4. What advice would you give students about developing their leadership abilities?

Leadership probably is best developed outside of the classroom. Most school classes give you little opportunity to lead, although some group projects can provide leadership opportunities. Remember, not everyone is equipped to be a leader. Many people have personal characteristics that make them better followers. That's okay. If the world was filled with leaders, there would be no one to follow the leader. However, if you think you have leadership characteristics and you want to start refining them, look for opportunities to join a nonprofit board or school group. While a member, observe how others lead these groups, and then be bold enough to volunteer to be the president or vice president of the group, or

chair a subcommittee, when the time is right. Find something you're interested in so you stick with it. It could be your accounting association at school,

your church's youth group, or your local United Way organization. Good luck!

in decisions they care little about. In Chapter 11, "Managing Teams," we address more thoroughly the question of when participation is most useful.

Also, we noted in Chapter 2 that people vary their behaviors depending on their perceptions of others; recall that this is a cause of the Pygmalion effect. So we might expect managers who see their subordinates as high performers to treat them differently, giving them more responsibility. As a result, the relationship between democratic style and performance could be due to the impact of performance on style rather than vice versa. That is, leaders may be more willing to delegate to high-performing followers than to low performers.

CONSIDERATION AND INITIATING STRUCTURE

For about half a century, researchers have examined a wide variety of leader behaviors, and one conclusion is clear: Effective leaders show concern for *both* the task and the people they lead. Without concern for the task, the job won't get done. Without concern for people, satisfaction, motivation, and team spirit will plummet and performance will ultimately suffer.

Two sets of leader behaviors—consideration and initiating structure—address these concerns:

> **Consideration** is behavior that shows friendship, mutual trust, respect, and warmth. Considerate leaders are friendly and approachable, look out for the personal welfare of team members, back up the members in their actions, and find time to listen to them.

> **Initiating structure** is behavior that helps clarify the task and get the job done. Initiating leaders provide definite standards of performance, set goals, organize work, emphasize meeting deadlines, and coordinate the work of team members.

It is easy—and wrong—to assume these are somehow conflicting sets of behaviors. That is, it might seem that considerate leaders don't provide a lot of structure or that structuring leaders tend to be inconsiderate. In fact, there is no trade-off between consideration and initiating structure. As shown in Figure 8-3, skillful leaders can exhibit *both* sets of behaviors. *Should* you as a leader exhibit both? The answer is that you should exhibit them *as needed*. For example, if team members are highly motivated, know their jobs, and have worked well together in the past, initiating structure may not help much. It may, in fact, be resented. The key is that you must show *concern* for people and the task, assess the situation, and then draw on your arsenal of behaviors as needed.

FIGURE 8-3
Consideration and Initiating Structure

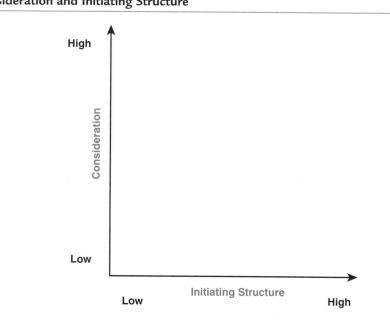

THE ROLE OF THE SITUATION

We have repeatedly said that leaders must fit their behaviors to the nature of the task, followers, and other characteristics of the situation. Many factors may influence the way leader behaviors affect subordinate responses, including the following:[10]

> **Pressure.** When the situation involves stress, time pressures, task demands, and physical danger, subordinates view leaders' initiating structure more favorably than in calm, secure situations. Historically, subordinates have accepted autocratic, structuring leaders in times of war or other national emergency.

> **Task-related satisfaction.** When jobs are not intrinsically satisfying, leader-initiating structure may increase performance, but it leads to resentment and dissatisfaction. If subordinates don't like the job, they see little to gain from being told how to do it. Also, when the task is not intrinsically satisfying (that is, satisfying in itself), leader consideration becomes more important. A friendly, supportive boss may not be very important if you really enjoy your work, but a bit of warmth and comforting helps ease the pain of an unsatisfying job.

> **Subordinate need for information.** When subordinates lack knowledge about the task, perhaps because they are new on the job or because the job is very ambiguous, they like initiating structure. Quite simply, they are glad to get advice and structure when they need it.

> **Subordinate expectations.** Subordinates react more positively to levels of consideration and initiating structure that they expect than to unexpected levels of those behaviors. For instance, subordinates may even initially react warily to high levels of consideration from a usually inconsiderate boss. Perhaps they are suspicious about this unexpected behavior. This certainly doesn't mean the boss shouldn't show consideration, just that there may be a "feeling out" period after the changed behavior.

FOCUS ON MANAGEMENT

RECYCLING PEOPLE AT OMNI COMPUTER PRODUCTS*

Gerald Chamales is founder, president, and CEO of fast-growing Omni Computer Products, a company that manufactures printer ribbons and recycles toner cartridges under the Rhinotek brand. Chamales provides an example of a leader who cares about his employees as well as profits. A college dropout and a recovering drug and alcohol abuser who spent six months in a psychiatric facility and bottomed out as a homeless youth on the streets of Venice, California, more than 25 years ago, Chamales now recycles both people and laser cartridges.

In 1979, Chamales decided to rebuild his life. He set up a card table, borrowed $1,300 on his credit card, and started selling computer products. Now Chamales is inspired to help people with similar rough backgrounds. A full third of his 250 employees, including managers, are drawn from the welfare rolls and

halfway houses of Los Angeles. Before Chamales will hire anyone with a troubled past, he demands 30 days of sobriety in a treatment program. After they join the payroll, Omni supports them with training programs, motivational seminars, and even short-term loans. A mentor is also assigned to each new employee—ex-addicts often need help with such basic etiquette as shaking hands and looking people in the eye.

This concern for people has been coupled with a strong focus on the bottom line. Chamales says, "When you get the right people, they give you 300 percent because they're so desperate to rebuild their lives. They're really hardworking people. They're street smart. If their energies are channeled properly, they can be some of the best employees." Turnover of recovering alcoholics and drug addicts in Omni's work force is significantly lower than that of other employees. Omni was named to *Industry Week*'s list of the

Growing Companies 25—America's Most Successful Small Manufacturers. Chamales was named Ernst & Young's Los Angeles Area Entrepreneur of the Year for 2001. 350 of the *Fortune* 500 companies currently purchase Rhinotek products.

http://rhinotek.com/index.html

*Based on E. Leibowitz, "Clean, Sober, and Good for Business," *Business Week,* March 1, 1999, p. ENT12; M. Marchetti, "Selling Saved Their Lives," *Sales and Marketing Management,* February 1999, pp. 36–42; J. Maybury, "The Homeless CEO," *Forbes,* June 1, 1998, p. 32; C. Hymowitz, "Bosses Need to Learn Whether They Inspire, or Just Drive, Staffers, *Wall Street Journal*, August 14, 2001, p. B1; and "High-Technology Giant Duels with Nimble Knock-Off Artists—for Hewlett-Packard, a Fight over Lowly Ink Cartridges Concerns Key Profit Source—Rhinotek's Bootleg Prototype," *Wall Street Journal*, September 25, 2002, p. A1.

Together, these findings suggest some straightforward and logical guidelines for leaders. If the situation calls for structure, provide it. If it doesn't, subordinates will see structuring behaviors as redundant and bothersome. If subordinates clearly could use some support, consideration would be especially helpful. If not, consideration may be less important (although it rarely hurts). And subordinates (and others) value some predictability in behavior. If leaders behave erratically, subordinates are likely to react with suspicion and caution.

This recognition of the importance of the situation is reflected in theories of leadership we examine in the following sections. Each of these theories somehow considers the fit between the leader and the situation, and each gives the leader ways to achieve effective fit.

PATH–GOAL THEORY OF LEADERSHIP

Because so many things can affect the effectiveness of leader behaviors, it would be helpful to have a systematic framework in which to consider them. Path–goal theory provides one such framework. Robert House developed the *path–goal theory of leader effectiveness*, an extension and revision of the work of Martin Evans.[11] House based this approach on expectancy theory (discussed in Chapter 6). The theory essentially says leaders are effective because of their impact on subordinates' motivation, ability to perform effectively, and satisfaction. The theory is called path–goal because it focuses on how the leader influences the subordinates' perceptions of their goals and paths to goal attainment. According to path–goal theory, a leader's behavior is motivating or satisfying to the degree that it increases subordinate goal attainment and clarifies the paths to these goals. To couch these statements more explicitly in expectancy theory terms, the path–goal theory sees the leader as having the following three motivational functions:

> The leader can increase valences associated with work-goal attainment.
> The leader can increase instrumentalities of work-goal attainment for the acquisition of personal outcomes.
> The leader can increase the expectancy that effort will result in work-goal attainment.

In short, path–goal theory says leader behaviors are unlikely to have a positive effect unless they somehow help the subordinate attain desired outcomes.

Path–goal theory examines how the effectiveness of each of four sets of leader behaviors is influenced by two sets of contingency factors.

PATH–GOAL LEADER BEHAVIORS

Path–goal theory considers the following four kinds of leader behaviors:

> **Directive leadership** is characterized by a leader who lets subordinates know what is expected of them and tells them how to do it. This is similar to initiating structure.
> **Supportive leadership** is characterized by a friendly and approachable leader who shows concern for the status, well-being, and needs of subordinates. This is much like consideration.
> **Participative leadership** is characterized by a leader who consults with subordinates and asks for their suggestions, which he or she seriously considers before making a decision.
> **Achievement-oriented leadership** is characterized by a leader who sets challenging goals, expects subordinates to perform at their highest level, and shows confidence that subordinates will meet such expectations.

Path–goal theory tries to explain how each of these types of leadership affects the following:

> The satisfaction of subordinates
> The subordinates' acceptance of the leader
> The degree to which subordinates feel their effort will result in performance (expectancy)
> And the degree to which subordinates feel their performance will result in rewards (instrumentalities)

Again, the theory essentially argues that subordinates will see each style of leadership as acceptable, satisfying, and motivating if they believe it either is an immediate source of desired outcomes or is useful in leading to such outcomes in the future.

CONTINGENCY FACTORS

The model considers two contingency factors—personal characteristics of the subordinates and the nature of the task to be performed. As an example, subordinates who don't feel they have the ability to master their tasks will probably react positively to directive leadership. And if the job is highly structured, subordinates will see directive leadership as unnecessary and will resent it. The elements of path–goal theory are shown in Figure 8-4.

Path–goal theory offers concrete guidelines concerning potentially important leader behaviors and situational variables and provides a logical framework to examine how they might interact to influence follower satisfaction and performance. Also, it emphasizes the need for leaders to be sensitive and flexible. That is, it encourages leaders to be sensitive to the characteristics of their subordinates and the task and to recognize they may need to tailor their behaviors accordingly. This is a point we will stress again—the effective leader asks not "What works?" but "What works when?" The ability to adapt leader behaviors to the demands of the task and subordinates is a critical skill.

Skills Practice 8-3 is a group activity that will help you see how path–goal theory works in action. After completing this exercise, you should have a much greater mastery of how to apply path–goal theory in an organizational context. The process model shown in the Bottom Line feature summarizes the basic steps associated with the application of the path–goal theory of leadership.

SUBSTITUTES FOR LEADERSHIP AND NEUTRALIZERS OF LEADERSHIP

We have said that particular leader behaviors are needed in particular situations. In other situations, those same behaviors may be useless or even harmful. This fact is the basis for the notions of **substitutes for leadership** and **neutralizers of leadership**. Figure 8-5 lists some of these substitutes and neutralizers. The figure indicates, for instance, that subordinates with high levels of ability or tasks that are well

FIGURE 8-4
Elements of Path–Goal Theory

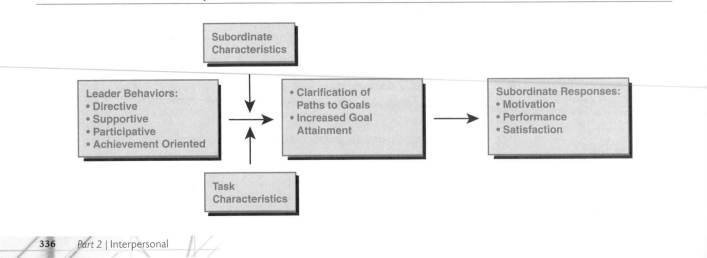

BOTTOM LINE

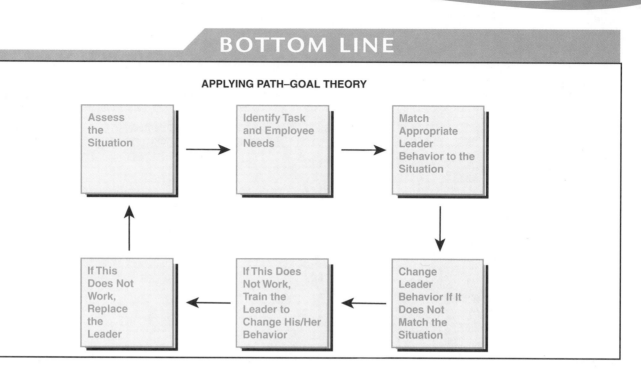

APPLYING PATH–GOAL THEORY

structured serve as substitutes for structuring leadership, and a considerable distance between the superior and subordinate neutralizes the effects of such leadership. Similarly, relationship-oriented, supportive, considerate leadership will be neutralized when subordinates have high needs for independence, and tasks that are intrinsically satisfying and cohesive work groups serve as substitutes for such leadership.[12]

The process model shown in the Bottom Line feature on page 339 summarizes the basic steps associated with the effective management of substitutes and neutralizers of leadership. Skills Practice 8-4 will give you an opportunity to identify substitutes for leadership and neutralizers of leadership and to develop appropriate strategies in a work situation.

LEADER–MEMBER EXCHANGE THEORY

We have already seen that leaders may appropriately behave differently in different situations. So asking whether a leader is autocratic or democratic, considerate or inconsiderate, is a bit simplistic. We have also seen that leaders may behave differently with some subordinates than with others. They may, for instance, let subordinates whom they feel are high performers have more say in decision making than others. A good deal of evidence indicates that leaders do treat various subordinates differently. There may be some good reasons for this. Some subordinates may, for instance, need more guidance or reassurance or supervision than others. The *leader–member exchange (LMX) theory of leadership* examines other factors that may cause leaders to treat some subordinates differently than others.[13]

According to leader–member exchange theory, leaders establish a one-on-one relationship with each follower. These relationships vary in terms of the quality of

FIGURE 8-5
Leadership Substitutes and Neutralizers

	SUBSTITUTE OR NEUTRALIZER ROLES	
	Relationship-Oriented Supportive, Considerate Leadership	Task-Oriented Directive, Structuring Leadership
Characteristic		
Of the Subordinate		
1. Ability, experience, training, knowledge		Substitute
2. Need for independence	Neutralizer	Neutralizer
3. "Professional" orientation	Substitute	Substitute
4. Indifference toward organizational rewards	Neutralizer	Neutralizer
Of the Task		
5. Unambiguous and routine		Substitute
6. Standardized methods		Substitute
7. Provides its own feedback concerning accomplishment		Substitute
8. Intrinsically satisfying	Substitute	
Of the Organization		
9. Formalization (explicit plans, goals, and areas of responsibility)		Substitute
10. Inflexibility (rigid, unbending rules and procedures)		Neutralizer
11. Closely knit, cohesive work groups	Substitute	Substitute
12. Highly specified and active advisory and staff functions		Substitute
13. Organizational rewards not within the leader's contract	Neutralizer	Neutralizer
14. Considerable distance between superior and subordinate	Neutralizer	Neutralizer

Source: S. Kerr and J. M. Jermier, "Substitutes for Leadership: Their Meaning and Measurement," *Organizational Behavior and Human Performance,* vol. 22, 1978, pp. 375–403.

the exchange. Some followers—members of the in-group—have a high-quality relationship with the leader, characterized by mutual trust, liking, and respect. These followers enjoy the confidence of their leader and are given interesting and challenging assignments. In exchange for the benefits of in-group status, these members have a role to carry out—to work hard, be loyal, and support the leader. Other followers—the out-group—have a lower quality relationship with the leader. The leader tends to see them as lacking motivation or competence or loyalty, interacts with them less, and offers them few chances to demonstrate their capabilities. These out-group members, in turn, may "live down" to the leader's expectations, carrying out the tasks defined in their formal job descriptions and facing no real expectations of loyalty, creativity, or high performance. Figure 8-6 shows how the leader may treat some followers as members of an in-group and others as out-group members.

Life is full of self-fulfilling prophecies, and the relationships described by the leader–member exchange model certainly are among them. Members of the in-group are given support and opportunities and viewed by the leader with a positive eye. Members of the out-group are—for whatever reason—placed in constraining boxes in which they have little chance or motivation to do well. Sadly, followers

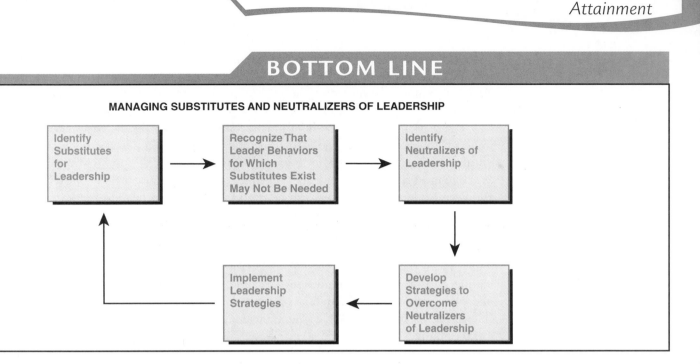

BOTTOM LINE

MANAGING SUBSTITUTES AND NEUTRALIZERS OF LEADERSHIP

may sometimes find themselves as members of in-groups or out-groups due less to their abilities and potential than to favoritism, stereotypes, or personal conflicts.

In an ideal world, there would be no in-groups or out-groups—all followers would enjoy the rich exchange relationships of in-group status. In the real world, in-groups and out-groups are common and perhaps cannot be avoided. Nevertheless,

FIGURE 8-6
Leader–Member Exchange Model

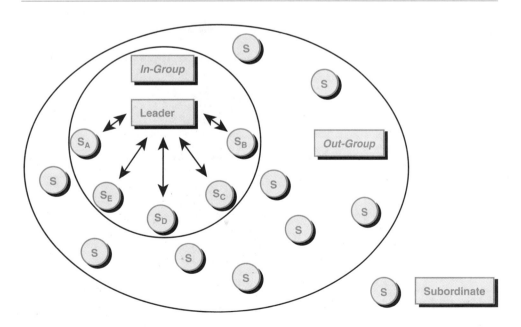

leaders must do all they can to ensure that in-group membership is based on ability and motivation rather than favoritism or prejudice. They must also ensure that followers can move between the groups, having access to in-group membership when it is earned and falling from such status when it is no longer justified.

The process model in the Bottom Line feature summarizes the basic steps associated with application of the leader–member exchange model. It emphasizes the ideal of moving all followers to in-group status.

The most recent focus of leader–member exchange theory is on how exchanges between leaders and followers can be used for "leadership making."[14] *Leadership making* is an approach to helping the leader develop high-quality exchanges with all of his or her followers rather than just a few. It tries to make all followers feel like part of the in-group and thus to avoid the inequities and negative implications of being in an out-group. Leadership making seeks to promote the development of partnerships in which the leader tries to build effective dyads with all employees in the work unit as well as networks of partnerships throughout the organization.

As shown in Figure 8-7, leadership making develops over time in three phases: (1) the stranger phase, (2) the acquaintance phase, and (3) the mature phase. In the *stranger phase*, exchanges between the leader and follower are low in quality, like those of out-group members. The follower complies with the formal leader, who enjoys hierarchical status, controls rewards, and is motivated primarily by self-interest rather than the good of the group. The *acquaintance phase* begins with an "offer" by the leader or follower for improved career-oriented social exchanges that involve sharing more resources and personal or work-related information. This phase is a testing-out period to see whether the follower is interested in taking on more roles and responsibilities and the leader is willing to offer new challenges. Quality of relations improves as leader–follower dyads develop trust and mutual

BOTTOM LINE

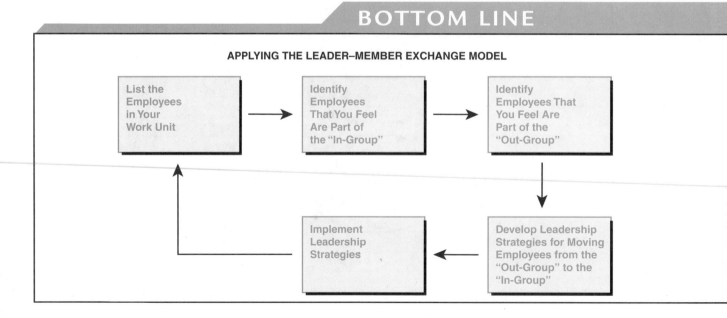

APPLYING THE LEADER–MEMBER EXCHANGE MODEL

List the Employees in Your Work Unit → Identify Employees That You Feel Are Part of the "In-Group" → Identify Employees That You Feel Are Part of the "Out-Group"

Implement Leadership Strategies ← Develop Leadership Strategies for Moving Employees from the "Out-Group" to the "In-Group"

FIGURE 8-7
Phases in Leadership Making

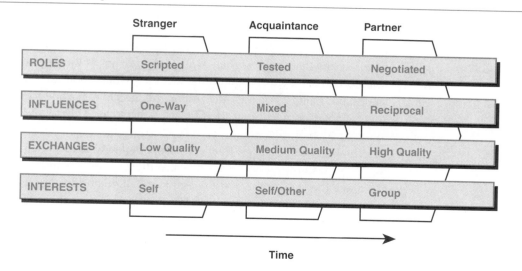

respect and begin to focus more on the purposes and goals of the group rather than self-interest. Finally, the *mature phase* is characterized by high-quality leader–member exchanges. Relationships that have progressed to this stage show high levels of trust, mutual respect, and mutual obligation. The leader and follower have tested the relationship and found they can rely on each other. Each member of the dyad influences the other, and each may ask the other for favors and special assistance. The leader and follower are tied together in productive ways, and they move beyond their own self-interest to focus on the greater good of the team and organization.

TRANSFORMATIONAL LEADERSHIP

The behaviors we have discussed to this point are critical to the effective functioning of teams and organizations. When we think about great leaders, though, we usually picture something more: We expect inspiration, conviction, and vision. These are the essence of *transformational leadership*, which is based in the personal values, beliefs, and qualities of the leader. Transformational leaders broaden and elevate the interests of their followers, generate awareness and acceptance of the purposes and mission of the group, and stir followers to look beyond their own interests to the interests of others. Transformational leaders display the following five sets of behaviors:

> **Attributed charisma.** *Charisma* is a Greek word meaning "divinely inspired gift." More than 60 years ago, Max Weber wrote that charismatic leaders reveal a transcendent mission or course of action that may be itself appealing to the potential followers but is acted on because the followers believe their leader is extraordinarily gifted. Mary Kay Ash of Mary Kay Cosmetics, Jack Welch of

General Electric, and Herb Kelleher at Southwest Airlines were known for their charisma. Leaders are seen as being charismatic when they display a sense of power and confidence, remain calm during crisis situations, and provide reassurance that obstacles can be overcome.

> **Idealized influence.** Walter Bagehot, a noted 19th-century economist and editor, wrote that strong beliefs win strong men, and then make them stronger. Leaders display idealized influence when they talk about their important values and beliefs; consider the moral and ethical consequences of their decisions; display conviction in their ideals, beliefs, and values; and model values in their actions.

> **Intellectual stimulation.** Intellectually stimulating leaders help followers recognize problems and find ways to solve them. They encourage followers to challenge the status quo. They champion change and foster creative deviance.

> **Inspirational leadership.** Napoleon Bonaparte is reputed to have said that a leader is a dealer in hope. Inspirational leaders give followers hope, energizing them to pursue a vision. They envision exciting new possibilities, talk optimistically about the future, express confidence that goals can be met, and articulate a compelling vision of the future.

> **Individualized consideration.** Transformational leaders do more than just "be nice." They show personal interest and concern in their *individual* followers, and they promote their followers' self-development. They coach their followers, serve as their mentors, and focus them on developing their strengths.

Transformational leadership will require new sets of skills, including the following:[15]

FOCUS ON MANAGEMENT

TRANSFORMATIONAL LEADERSHIP AT GENERAL ELECTRIC*

Jack Welch, former CEO of General Electric, is a notable transformational leader. "We have found what we believe to be the distilled essence of competitiveness. It is the reservoir of talent and creativity and energy that can be found in each of our people. That essence is liberated when we make people believe that what they think and do is important—and then get out of their way while they do it." Prior to stepping down as CEO, Welch described his successor: "I want somebody with incredible energy who can excite others, who can define their vision, who finds change fun and doesn't get paralyzed by it. I want somebody who feels comfortable in Delhi or Denver."

When Welch retired in 2001, Jeff Immelt, 47, won a tough succession battle to become the ninth CEO of the corporate giant. Immelt took over at a difficult time, with the U.S. economy moving into recession. Still, he has earned high marks from most observers, making structural changes at GE, eliminating GE businesses that didn't fit well with the company's core competencies, changing GE's governance policies, and asking hard questions about what GE should be selling. Like some other CEOs who recently succeeded visible leaders, though, Immelt has adopted a relatively low profile, rejecting celebrity status. Whether this style will provide the vision and presence GE needs in the future remains to be seen.

http://www.ge.com/index.htm

*See J. Schlosser, B. Cherry, and M. Tran, "Jeff Immelt," *Fortune*, August 11, 2003, p. 66; P. Sellers, "First-Class Reunion," *Fortune*, May 26, 2003, p. 56; and D. McGinn and K. Naughton, "The CEO's Challenge," *Newsweek*, April 28, 2003, pp. 50–54.

> **Anticipatory skills**—the ability to scan intuitively and systematically the changing environment
> **Visioning skills**—the process of persuasion and example by which an individual or leadership team induces a group to take action in accord with the leader's purposes or, most likely, the shared purposes of all
> **Value-congruence skills**—the ability to be in touch with employees' needs so they can engage employees on the basis of shared motives, values, and goals
> **Empowerment skills**—the ability to share power with employees effectively so they can share the satisfaction derived from accomplishment
> **Self-understanding skills**—introspective skills as well as frameworks with which leaders understand both themselves and their employees

These are precisely the sorts of skills we seek to develop and reinforce throughout this text.

We close this section with two important points. First, these ways of behaving have consistently been shown to influence team performance, the satisfaction and motivation of followers, and many other important outcomes.[16] Second, these are all behaviors you *can* change. You can, for example, choose to pay more attention to those who work for you, to set inspirational goals, to model the values you espouse, and to provide reassurance in the face of obstacles. The process model in the nearby Bottom Line summarizes the basic steps associated with the application of transformational leadership.

Now assess your own transformational leader behaviors by completing Self-Assessment 8-3. After you have answered the questions, go to the text Web site to learn more about your responses. Then complete Skills Practice 8-5 to develop skill in applying transformational leadership to a work situation.

BOTTOM LINE

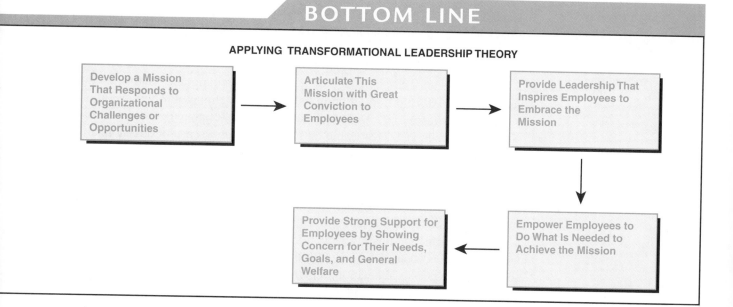

APPLYING TRANSFORMATIONAL LEADERSHIP THEORY

Develop a Mission That Responds to Organizational Challenges or Opportunities → Articulate This Mission with Great Conviction to Employees → Provide Leadership That Inspires Employees to Embrace the Mission → Empower Employees to Do What Is Needed to Achieve the Mission → Provide Strong Support for Employees by Showing Concern for Their Needs, Goals, and General Welfare

Your Transformational Leader Behaviors

Indicate your degree of agreement with each of the statements provided by using the following scale:

1 Disagree strongly
2 Disagree somewhat
3 Neither agree nor disagree
4 Agree somewhat
5 Agree strongly

____ 1. I take stands on difficult issues.
____ 2. I am able to remain calm in difficult times.
____ 3. I encourage others to challenge the status quo.
____ 4. I treat others as individuals.
____ 5. I talk optimistically about the future.
____ 6. I assure others that obstacles can be overcome.
____ 7. I stand up for my beliefs and values.
____ 8. I look for multiple perspectives when solving problems.
____ 9. I coach others to develop their individual strengths.
____ 10. I am able to display an aura of power and confidence.
____ 11. I think about the ethical and moral aspects of my decisions.
____ 12. I encourage others to question assumptions.
____ 13. I present clear and persuasive visions of the future.
____ 14. I tailor my advice to others' particular needs.
____ 15. I talk about exciting new beginnings.

THE LANGUAGE OF LEADERSHIP

Transformational leaders must be able to inspire; communicate their vision, ideals, and beliefs; provide compelling reassurance; and challenge followers to think in new ways. To do all this, they must be masters of communication: They must "speak the language of leadership."

Two aspects of the language of leadership—framing and rhetorical crafting—are crucial.[17] *Framing* is presenting the message, defining the purpose in a meaningful way. *Rhetorical crafting* is using symbolic language to give emotional power to the message. That is, the message provides a sense of direction, and rhetoric heightens its emotional appeal and makes it memorable.

Two key elements of framing are amplifying values and belief amplification. *Amplifying values* is the process of identifying and elevating certain values as basic to the overall mission. *Belief amplification* is the process of emphasizing factors that support or impede actions taken to achieve desired values.

Rhetorical techniques of inspirational leaders include using metaphors, analogies, and stories, gearing language to the particular audience, and employing such speech techniques as alliteration, repetition, and rhythm.

Martin Luther King, Jr., in his famous "I Have a Dream" speech, delivered on the steps of the Lincoln Memorial in 1963, sculpted a masterpiece of language in service

FOCUS ON MANAGEMENT

REBUILDING THE GARAGE AT HEWLETT-PACKARD*

Carleton (Carly) Fiorina majored in medieval history and philosophy at Stanford University and later dropped out of UCLA's law school after one semester. In 1999, she was named CEO of Hewlett-Packard, the first outsider selected for a top position at the company. HP, started in a garage in 1938 by Bill Hewlett and Dave Packard with $538 in working capital, rode a history of innovation to become a leading global provider of computing and imaging solutions and services, with 86,500 employees worldwide and $42.4 billion in 1999 revenues. Fiorina became the first female CEO of one of America's 20 largest corporations and was ranked by *Fortune* magazine as the most powerful woman in American business (beating out Oprah Winfrey).

As a Stanford undergraduate, Fiorina worked as an HP temporary shipping clerk. After graduation, she joined AT&T and rose through many positions ultimately to lead the spin-off of Lucent Technologies from AT&T. Her early success, high energy, fearless leadership, and a personal touch that inspires intense loyalty made Fiorina an American business legend.

When Fiorina took the reins, HP was awash in question marks, with lackluster financial performance and a dearth of recent innovative offerings. Fiorina saw the company as sick and endangered—slow, complacent, and risk averse. Seeking to reinvent HP, Fiorina evoked its original "garage" spirit and launched a $200 million brand and advertising campaign that included a new logo with the word "invent." Saying, "Preserve the best, reinvent the rest," Fiorina has pushed through more drastic changes in a short period of time than HP has ever seen before. She drew up a "rules of the garage," based on how the original HP operated. Among its mantras are "No politics, no bureaucracy" and "Radical ideas are not bad ideas." Along with many other changes, Fiorina has revamped salary structures to tie pay more closely to performance, reinforced key values, restructured the company to encourage independent product groups to work together, and realigned the upper ranks of the firm. She is seeking to make the company more agile, moving it to "Internet time."

In the first months of Fiorina's rein, HP showed strong revenue growth, sharply increased its presence in the heavy-duty computing market, and won the admiration of Wall Street analysts. Fiorina has grand visions for the computer industry, predicting that "computer-driven appliances and services will be as pervasive as oxygen, as reliable as the sun and moon, and as invisible as radio waves." In 2002, she succeeded through cool, persistent persuasion with her plan to "reinvent" HP by merging it with Compaq in the face of fierce opposition. Fiorina still has doubters; some view her as ruthless and question the long-run effectiveness of her past decisions. Still, Fiorina relishes the challenges she faces, and few doubt that she has the skills and determination to meet those tests head on.

http://www.hp.com/

*This discussion is based in part on "Business: Rebuilding the Garage," *The Economist,* July 15, 2000, pp. 59–50; "Wake-Up Call for HP," *Technology Review,* May/June 2000, pp. 94–100; N. Watson, "The Lists," *Fortune,* April 17, 2000, pp. 289–295; and Q. Hardy, "All Carly, All the Time," *Forbes,* December 13, 1999, pp. 138–144.

---

of transformational leadership. He spoke of values he held dear—"the inalienable rights of life, liberty, and the pursuit of happiness," "the riches of freedom and the security of justice," the need to "forever conduct our struggle on the high plane of dignity and discipline."

King envisioned exciting new possibilities, speaking with passion of the day when "on the red hills of Georgia the sons of former slaves and the sons of former slave owners will be able to sit down together at a table of brotherhood." He assured his listeners that "with this faith we will be able to hew out of the mountain of despair a stone of hope." He recognized the individual needs and perspectives of his audience members, speaking of the "marvelous new militancy that has engulfed the Negro community" but also of "our white brothers." "We cannot walk alone," he warned. He used words of inclusion, hope, and faith, ending with his vision of the day when "all of God's children . . . will be able to join hands and sing, in the words of the old Negro spiritual, 'Free at last! Free at last! Thank God Almighty, we are free at last!'" He repeated key phrases again and again, and his voice rose in volume and emotion as the speech progressed. Martin Luther King, Jr.'s famous speech can be found at many places on the Web, including: http://www.mecca.org/~crights/dream.htm.

REFLECTIONS ON LEADERSHIP

As a manager or team member, you will often find yourself in positions of leadership or of potential leadership. Your leadership role will sometimes be formally prescribed, and at other times may develop informally. In either case, your actions may affect the performance and satisfaction of your subordinates and others. Give your leadership behaviors the attention they deserve.

When selecting people for leadership positions or assigning them to leadership tasks, consider such traits as intelligence, self-confidence, decisiveness, and need for occupational achievement. However, be sure to ask whether the position really calls for such traits. It is illegal to use selection criteria unrelated to task performance.

Remember that a leader must show concern for both task accomplishment and fulfillment of subordinate needs. This does not mean that as a leader you will always need to emphasize each of these factors. Often the nature of tasks or of subordinates will take care of some concerns or make them less important. However, you must be ready to step in to see that these dual needs are somehow satisfied.

Remember too that the same style or behavior may not work in every situation. In deciding how to behave, consider the maturity and needs of your subordinates, the structure and other characteristics of the task, and the nature of the organization. The models discussed in this chapter should be useful in highlighting factors to keep in mind. Treat them as guides rather than as absolute rules. If you are using styles or behaviors that violate the suggestions of the models, ask yourself why. Do you disagree with the model? Is it ignoring variables you feel are important, or are you somehow failing to assess the situation properly?

In general, behaviors reflecting consideration on the part of the leader are satisfying to subordinates and don't harm productivity. Further, consideration makes initiating structure more palatable. So if the situation is one that calls for a leader to initiate structure, consideration will be important.

Leadership can be frustrating. Structured tasks, separation of superiors and subordinates, bureaucratic constraints, and other factors can sometimes handcuff the leader. Try to be aware of such substitutes and neutralizers for leadership. If they seem helpful to the satisfaction and performance of your subordinates, it may be best to accept them. If you feel they are constraining performance or satisfaction, you may want to try to circumvent them. For instance, if your subordinates are indifferent toward organizational rewards, you may try to determine which rewards are important to them. You may also need to rely on alternatives to constrained power bases.

Also, as a leader do not accept the situation as fixed. You may be able to change task structure, your power, relations with subordinates, and other dimensions. Before accepting the constraints, try to loosen them. Before fitting your behaviors to the situation, tailor the situation to your liking.

Perhaps more than anything else, the models reviewed in this chapter show that leader sensitivity, critical thinking, and flexibility are crucial. Leaders must be sensitive to the characteristics of tasks, workers, and other dimensions of the situation. They must choose suitable behaviors, avoiding those that are inappropriate or redundant. Finally, they must then have the flexibility to adopt those behaviors. These are difficult attributes to develop, but they will become increasingly important. You would be wise to try to cultivate them.

Finally, remember that vision and inspiration are important. Don't let a narrow focus on structuring of tasks and dealing with subordinates' needs on a day-to-day basis cause you to ignore broader, more transformational aspects of the leadership role.

Well, it's movie time again! Complete Skills Practice 8-6 by watching the movie *Gandhi* or *Mother Teresa*. These are classic films and do a nice job of illustrating why these two individuals were among the greatest leaders of all time. The ultimate question is this: "What can we learn about the leadership of organizations from these two extraordinary people?"

Skills Practice 8-7 gives you an opportunity to put the pieces of your leadership puzzle together and to think about leadership in an integrative manner based on the theories and concepts discussed in the chapter.

TOP TEN LIST: KEY POINTS TO REMEMBER

HOW TO LEAD EFFECTIVELY

10. Learn as much as you can about the work unit, organization, and industry associated with your leadership position.
9. Identify the needs of the leadership situation based on your goals and strategies, the motivation and skill of employees, and the complexity of the task.
8. Match the appropriate leadership style to the needs of the situation (that is, establish a leader–situation match).
7. Identify factors that can reduce the need for leadership (substitutes) and as well as factors that will make it more difficult to provide leadership (neutralizers) in a situation. Develop strategies to overcome neutralizers of leadership.
6. Develop leaders by identifying individuals with leadership potential and providing them with formal and informal work and networking opportunities to develop relevant knowledge and skills.
5. Educate and guide your followers so they understand their specific role in contributing to the success of the organization and are committed to it.
4. Establish and maintain good working relationships with your followers based on the principles of mutual trust and respect.
3. Measure the success of a leader in terms of employee outcomes such as motivation, satisfaction, and job performance as well as work unit or organizational outcomes.
2. Be aware that timing is critical and you will only have a certain "window of opportunity" to establish the credibility of your leadership within an organization.
1. Remember, no single leadership style is universally effective: Effective leadership depends on the situation.

QUESTIONS FOR REVIEW AND REFLECTION

REVIEW QUESTIONS

1. What are six differences between the "old look" and the "new look" of leadership?
2. Which traits have been most consistently linked with effective leadership?
3. Define *consideration* and *initiating structure.*
4. Identify four characteristics of the situation that influence the way leader behaviors affect follower responses.
5. Discuss the path–goal theory of leadership, including the leader behaviors, contingency factors, and outcomes it considers.
6. What are substitutes for leadership and neutralizers of leadership? Identify five substitutes or neutralizers, and indicate how each affects the role(s) of task-oriented and/or relationship-oriented leader behaviors.
7. Discuss leader–member exchange theory.
8. What is transformational leadership? Identify five transformational leader behaviors and five skills needed for transformational leadership.
9. What is meant by "the language of leadership"? What are four characteristics of the language of effective transformational leaders?
10. Give five guidelines for becoming a leader.

CRITICAL THINKING QUESTIONS

1. Take a position either for or against the following statement: "Different skills are needed to become a leader than to be successful once in a leadership role." Defend your position.
2. We said in this chapter that transformational leadership requires five sets of skills. Which of those skills do you think is most difficult to develop? Easiest? Why?
3. When told about path–goal theory, a manager says, "They've got it backward. The trick is to decide on what behavior I want to use and then to tailor the situation to fit those behaviors, not vice versa." What do you think of his argument?
4. When a supervisor is accused of treating some of her subordinates better than others, she says, "If some

employees are in the in-group, it's because they've earned a place in the in-group." How would you respond to her statement?

5. A colleague says, "I really don't agree with the idea of substitutes for leadership. It never hurts to provide a little more guidance or to show a little more caring." Do you agree? Why or why not?

6. In accepting the Democratic Party's nomination for president of the United States, Al Gore responded to criticisms that he lacked charisma, saying, "I know that sometimes people say I'm too serious, that I talk too much substance and policy. . . . But the presidency is more than a popularity contest. It's a day-to-day fight for people." Suppose you had been a political adviser to Gore and wanted to make him appear more charismatic. What advice might you have given him?

7. A manager says, "Don't give me this talk about the 'language of leadership.' That's putting style over substance. I want my employees to be swayed by the power of my arguments, not by speech tricks." How would you respond?

EXPERIENTIAL EXERCISES

WEB EXERCISE 8-1

TDIndustries, the premier construction and service company in the Southwest, is employee owned, debt free, and profitable. It was chosen national "Contractor of the Year" by Associated Builders and Contractors, a national construction association representing 18,000 firms across the United States. TDIndustries was ranked seventh in the year 2003 on *Fortune* magazine's "100 Best Companies to Work For in America." The company's CEO, Jack Lowe, Jr., attributes the company's success to a set of basic values that include concern for and belief in individual human beings and the valuing of individual differences, as well as to adherence to the philosophy of servant leadership. As described by Robert Greenleaf in *The Servant as Leader*,[18] the tenets of servant leadership include the views that leaders are people who have followers because they have earned recognition and respect, and leaders are first servants of those they lead. Servant leadership sees the leader as a teacher, a source of information and knowledge, and a standard setter, more than a giver of directions and a disciplinarian. Jack Lowe is a noted proponent of the philosophy of servant leadership. Read more about servant leadership on the TDIndustries Web site at

http://www.tdindustries.com/AboutUs/Culture.asp

Then go to the Web site of the Robert K. Greenleaf Center for Servant-Leadership at

http://greenleaf.org/index.html

Read the sections titled "About Us" and "What Is Servant-Leadership?" and sample readings from the "Read About Servant-Leadership" section. Then click on the picture of Robert Greenleaf to read material on "Who Was Robert K. Greenleaf?" Based on your reading on the two Web sites, answer the following questions:

1. Describe the servant leader in terms of the dimensions of consideration, initiating structure, and democratic versus autocratic style.

2. What power bases would the servant leader be likely to employ or avoid?

3. What might be primary social influence processes used by servant leaders?

4. Do you think the philosophy of servant leadership should be more widely adopted? Why or why not?

WEB EXERCISE 8-2

Go to the Web site of the Quotation Center at:

http://www.cyber-nation.com/victory/quotations/

At this site you will find links to thousands of quotations, searchable by subject, author, or keyword. Click on "View Quotes by Subject." You will see a listing of the letters of the alphabet. Click on "L" to get to a page showing subjects beginning with *L*. Then click on "Leaders and Leadership." You will be shown more than 80 related quotes. Read through the quotes. Select five or more of the quotes you think capture your views on leaders and leadership. Discuss those quotes and why you selected them.

CASE 8-1

EVALUATING A LEADERSHIP DEVELOPMENT PROGRAM AT OPTIMAX PUBLISHING[19]

Note: This case is based on an actual program in a real-world organization. Because of concerns regarding the potential sensitivity of issues presented in this case, some information has been modified to protect the anonymity of the company and the members of the teams.

The Company

Optimax Publishing is a mid-sized publisher of textbooks in a wide range of disciplines for the K–12 market. The company is based in Boston, Massachusetts, and has approximately 500 employees. The company was started in 1980 and has established itself as a top publisher of high-quality and innovative textbooks.

Optimax Publishing has grown significantly in the last few years based on its expanding portfolio of books and strong sales from abroad. This led Christine Potter, the president of the company, to become concerned with the issue of leadership development. Specifically, she was worried about how the company's short-term and long-term leadership needs will be satisfied. The company was growing so quickly, it simply did not have enough people with the right kinds of knowledge and skills to step up into leadership positions.

Potter decided to create a leadership development program to provide a process for grooming high-potential individuals for future leadership positions at Optimax. Participants in this leadership program met four times a year to eat dinner, to discuss company issues, and to listen to an outside speaker talk about some issue related to effective leadership (e.g., managing change, strategic planning). Participants were selected based on job performance and leadership potential. An attempt was made to include people from a cross-section of the organization. The president and other members of senior management also participated in this program as advisers, mentors, and speakers. A total of 64 individuals were selected to be participants in this program.

The formal objectives of the leadership development program were as follows:

- To recognize the important role that participants play in the company
- To give participants the opportunity to learn more about other departments in the company
- To give participants the opportunity to network and socialize with other leaders at the company
- To provide participants with senior management's vision and strategic plan for the company
- To offer the potential for additional financial rewards in the form of bonuses for participation in the program

Methodology

A management consultant was hired by senior management at Optimax to evaluate the effectiveness of the leadership development program and to make recommendations for enhancing its effectiveness.

The consultant, working with the director of HR at the company, designed and administered a survey of participants in the leadership development program. The survey was a paper-and-pencil assessment composed of 25 questions pertaining to participant attitudes toward various elements of the leadership development program at Optimax. Questions used a combination of structured rating scales (i.e., strongly agree, strongly disagree) and open-ended questions. The consultant administered the survey at the end of one of the leadership development program meetings, so she was able to achieve a 100 percent response rate.

Results

The consultant analyzed the survey responses from participants using basic statistical procedures. The results are shown in the table.

Discussion Questions

1. Now it's your turn to be the consultant. Based on the information provided in the table, analyze the results of the survey regarding the effectiveness of the leadership development program. Download the worksheet created for this exercise from the Web site for this textbook to help you structure your approach to this exercise. Be sure to document your key findings on this worksheet.

2. Based on your key results, develop a set of *short-term recommendations* (things that should be done immediately or in the next few months) to help senior management at Optimax enhance the effectiveness of the leadership development program. Make sure each of your recommendations is specific and action oriented. Be prepared to justify each of your recommendations to the senior management in terms of merit, feasibility, and cost effectiveness. Also, make sure you address what senior management needs to do to ensure the effective execution of your recommendations.

Summary of Key Results from Survey of Leadership Development Program (LDP) Participants

Question	Strongly Disagree	Disagree	Neutral	Agree	Strongly Agree
1. I am satisfied with the format used for the LDP at Optimax.	6%	13%	21%	48%	12%
2. The LDP at Optimax has provided me with new knowledge that has enhanced my leadership abilities.	12%	14%	32%	26%	16%
3. The LDP at Optimax has provided me with new skills that have enhanced my leadership abilities.	22%	27%	31%	15%	5%
4. The length of the LDP meetings is just about right.	0%	0%	8%	35%	57%
5. The location of the LDP meetings creates a positive environment for discussion and learning.	0%	0%	23%	45%	32%
6. I feel I have a better understanding of Optimax's vision and strategic plan as a result of the LDP.	17%	26%	31%	15%	11%
7. Members of senior management are supportive of the LDP at Optimax.	0%	12%	22%	38%	28%
8. I am more motivated to develop my leadership abilities as a result of participating in the LDP at Optimax.	8%	14%	36%	24%	18%
9. I am able to interact with and discuss issues with members of senior management at the LDP meetings.	3%	11%	41%	28%	17%
10. I am able to interact with and discuss issues with members of other Optimax departments at LDP meetings.	16%	15%	26%	28%	15%
11. I have a better understanding of my role at Optimax as a result of the LDP program.	12%	19%	37%	16%	16%
12. I am satisfied with the monetary bonus I receive based on my participation in the LDP at Optimax.	7%	10%	18%	38%	27%
13. I believe my chances of being promoted to a leadership position have increased based on my participation in the LDP at Optimax.	13%	24%	24%	27%	12%

3. Based on your key results, develop a set of *long-term recommendations* (things that should be done in the next three to five years) to help senior management at Optimax enhance the effectiveness of the leadership development program. Make sure each of your recommendations is specific and action oriented. Be prepared to justify each of your recommendations to the senior management in terms of merit, feasibility, and cost effectiveness. Also, make sure you address what senior management needs to do to ensure the effective execution of your recommendations.

4. Make a five to ten-minute presentation of your results and recommendations to the class.

5. What did you learn from this case study about leadership development issues in real-world organizations?

CASE 8-2

BILL FORD'S LEADERSHIP AND THE TURNAROUND AT FORD MOTOR COMPANY

Background

The Ford Motor Company, based in Dearborn, Michigan, is the world's second largest automaker. It designs, manufactures, and markets cars and trucks under the following brand names: Ford, Mercury, Lincoln, Volvo, Jaguar, Land Rover, and Aston Martin. The company also has a controlling ownership of Mazda. Ford has over 350,000 employees who work at its various offices and facilities on 6 continents and in over 250 global markets. In the second quarter of 2003, Ford Motor Company reported net income of $417 million, or 22 cents a share. The company had pretax profits of $718 million based on revenue of $40.7 billion.[20]

Ford Vision and Values[21]

The vision, mission, and values that define the Ford Motor Company are as follows:

Our Vision

To become the world's leading consumer company for automotive products and services.

Our Mission

We are a global family with a proud heritage passionately committed to providing mobility for people around the world. We anticipate consumer need and deliver outstanding products and services that improve people's lives.

Our Values

Our business is driven by our consumer focus, creativity, resourcefulness, and entrepreneurial spirit. We are an inspired, diverse team. We respect and value everyone's contribution. The health and safety of our people are paramount.

We are a leader in environmental responsibility. Our integrity is never compromised and we make a positive contribution to society.

We continually strive to improve everything that we do. Guided by these values, we provide superior returns to our shareholders.

Bill Ford[22]

Bill Ford is the CEO and chairman of the board at Ford Motor Company. His great-grandfather was Henry Ford, the founder of the company. He joined the company in 1979 as a product-planning analyst and went on to hold a variety of positions in manufacturing, sales, marketing, product development, and finance. In 1987, he was elected the chairman

and managing director of Ford Switzerland and then to the board of directors in 1988. Ford assumed the role as head of business strategy for the Ford Automotive Group in 1990 and then became general manager of the Climate Control Division in 1992. He became the vice president and head of Ford Motor's Commercial Truck Division Vehicle Center in 1994 in order to become the chairman of the board of directors' Finance Committee in 1995. He also served as the chairman of the board's Environmental and Public Policy Committee in 1997 and chairman of the Nominating and Governance Committee in 1999. He assumed his current position as CEO on October 30, 2001.

Bill Ford's personal vision for Ford Motor Company is to "build a stronger business, and make a better world" based on the company's tradition of improving people's lives.

Ford was born in Detroit on May 3, 1957. He has a bachelor of arts degree from Princeton University and a master of science degree in management from Massachusetts Institute of Technology (MIT).

The Situation at Ford[23]

Bill Ford's two-year tenure as CEO at Ford Motor has been challenging, to say the least. In fact, Ford readily admits he did not want to be CEO and was doing it out of a "sense of responsibility" to his family and the company. As a result, some have referred to Bill Ford as the "reluctant CEO."

When Bill Ford assumed leadership of Ford Motor Company in October 2001, the company was in the worst shape it had been in since the 1970s. Many of the problems were created by former CEO Jacques A. Nasser, who was fired for poor performance. The problems included the following:

- **Declining profits** (e.g., the company lost approximately $6.4 billion in 2001–2003). Ford has been losing money on each car or truck that is sells due to its bloated cost structure and poor production efficiency.
- **Other financial pressures.** The company will need $5 to $8 billion to meet its employee pension obligations over the next five years. In 2002, it needed $2.3 billion to cover employee health care benefits, a 21 percent increase over the previous year that is expected to continue increasing in the future.
- **Poor product quality**. *Consumer Reports* magazine rated Ford Motor dead last in quality and reliability among major automakers. Numerous recalls on popular vehicles

such as the Focus sedan, Escape sport-utility vehicle, and Explorer sport-utility vehicle damaged the company's reputation for quality. The Firestone tires recall in which Explorers with Firestone tires on them demonstrated a tendency to blow out and cause accidents and injuries cost the company $3.5 billion and further damaged consumer confidence in Ford Motor Company. Although the focus of this case was on the Firestone tires, some evidence suggested that a design flaw in the Explorer could have contributed to the problem as well.

A major cause of quality problems has been the use of dated factories that do not use flexible manufacturing processes. This has made it difficult for the company to be competitive with General Motors, not to mention its European and Japanese competitors.

- **Lack of new cars and trucks in the product development pipeline.** Financial constraints and a lack of focus on product development left little in the product development pipeline. Some of the vehicles in development may also be delayed. Meanwhile, other automakers such as Toyota, Honda, Nissan, and General Motors were spending billions of dollars developing new cars and trucks with fresh designs and cutting-edge technologies.

- **Lack of a clear road map to drive the turnaround.** Major challenges still exist in terms of what to do with Ford Motor Company's array of car and truck brands. For example, what should be done with the more upscale Mercury division that is positioned between the Ford and Lincoln brands? What should be done with the Lincoln luxury brand now that the company owns other luxury brands with more cachet such as Jaguar, Aston Martin, and Land Rover?

- **Global operations.** Ford's European operations have been struggling for a number of years now. Jaguar has been experiencing problems with quality and overextending itself with too many vehicles being targeted toward too many people. Jaguar's X-Type sedan, its most recent offering, has achieved very mixed results in terms of sales and customer reactions. Some analysts are concerned that Jaguar is tarnishing its exclusive image by growing its portfolio of vehicles in the lower price ranges of automobiles. In China, a market with huge long-term potential for growth, Ford Motor Company is far behind other automakers in terms of formulating a strategy, setting up joint ventures with local partners, and establishing itself in the market.

- **People problems.** Bill Ford's predecessor, Jacques Nasser, did a lot of damage to relations with dealers and to employee morale based on his leadership style. Bill Ford will have to work hard to rebuild goodwill with these stakeholders.

Ford has spent a lot of energy assembling a management team he thought would provide the needed mix of knowledge and experience to support the turnaround strategy. However, this team has experienced significant problems with political infighting and interpersonal conflict. In particular, David Thursfield, the person hired to be in charge of cost cutting, has had serious problems working with the rest of the management team, which has damaged its cohesiveness. Thursfield is very good at what he does, but his style in dealing with other members of the team has become problematic. In addition, the company desperately needs a "car guru" like Bob Lutz at General Motors to provide the leadership needed to support Ford Motor Company's product revival. Bill Ford intentionally maintains a "hands off" approach to managing the details of the product design process, so an executive car guru is critical to the company's success.

All of the problems just described have put Ford Motor Company into a position in which it must "fight for its life." Rumors have even circulated that the company may be forced to file for bankruptcy protection in the future.

The Turnaround Strategy[24]

Since taking over the helm at Ford Motor Company, Bill Ford has certainly not sat idle. He has held meeting after meeting with employees to convey a sense of urgency to the company's situation and to inspire them to work hard and give their best to return Ford Motor Company to its glory days. This has provided a "consistency of purpose" for the organization.

Ford does not care about hierarchy. He regularly meets with managers and employees at all levels in the organization to discuss issues. He also eats in the company cafeteria so he can "take the pulse" of the work force about their concerns and any ideas they have for improving operations.

Bill Ford tries not to force his opinions on his employees whenever possible. He has also been reluctant to terminate poor performing managers. This has generated some concern among insiders that he is not tough enough to make the decisions and the changes necessary to turn around the company.

Ford is an excellent communicator, who is seen by his followers as a "down to earth" kind of guy who is likable and trustworthy. However, sometimes he wishes he had someone to talk to about dilemmas he is facing or about where he should steer the company in the future.

The company has been moving forward with the development of some new products it hopes will revive its sales, increase market share, and improve its image in the marketplace. These new models include the GT40 sports car, the Ford Five Hundred sedan, and the Cross Trainer car/SUV hybrid. A major goal of these new vehicles is for each one to be targeted toward a specific set of customer needs and wants. In addition, Ford Motor has entered into a cooperative arrangement with General Motors to develop six-speed automatic transmissions that can be used in future vehicles.

Ford has set some aggressive goals to support the company's turnaround. These include reducing costs by $3.5 billion and closing up to six plants. So far, Bill Ford's plan has achieved a few encouraging results, such as a 10 percent reduction in warranty claims, better quality, and no major recalls associated with new product launches.

Bill Ford's greatest concern is that the company is simply not moving forward with its turnaround fast enough to keep up with changing customer tastes, technology, and other competitors in the auto industry.

Discussion Questions

1. Based on path–goal theory, evaluate the degree of leader behaviors exhibited by Bill Ford that are likely to fit the current situation of the Ford Motor Company. Do his behaviors seem appropriate? Why? What should be done to maintain or improve the match of Bill Ford's behaviors to the situation at Ford in the future?

2. Based on transformational leadership theory, assess the degree to which Bill Ford is a transformational leader. What recommendations would you give to Bill Ford to sustain or enhance his effectiveness as a transformational leader at the Ford Motor Company? Why?

3. What are the substitutes and/or neutralizers of leadership that exist in this case? What can Bill Ford do to eliminate or reduce the neutralizers of leadership?

4. Develop an overall action plan for Bill Ford that specifies the actions he needs to take in the short term (immediately or within the next few months) to support the turnaround at Ford Motor Company? Make sure each of your recommendations is specific and action oriented. Be prepared to justify each of your recommendations in terms of merit, feasibility, and cost effectiveness. Also, make sure you address what needs to be done to ensure the effective execution of your recommendations.

5. Develop an overall action plan for Bill Ford that specifies the actions he needs to take in the long term (within the next three to five years) to support the turnaround at Ford Motor Company. Make sure each of your recommendations is specific and action oriented. Be prepared to justify each of your recommendations in terms of merit, feasibility, and cost effectiveness. Also, make sure you address what needs to be done to ensure the effective execution of your recommendations.

6. Make a five- to ten-minute presentation of your results and recommendations to the class.

7. What did you learn from this case study in terms of leadership issues in real-world organizations and what must be done to enhance their effectiveness? Which concepts discussed in this chapter were helpful to you in conducting your analysis and in formulating your recommendations?

VIDEO CASE: SUNSHINE CLEANING SYSTEMS

LEADERSHIP IN AN ORGANIZATION

Running Time: 11:50

This video presents issues relating to leadership at SunShine Cleaning Systems, one of the largest contract cleaning companies in the state of Florida, with $10 million in annual sales and about 1,000 employees. SunShine's CEO, Larry Calufetti, and others discuss and demonstrate the nature and consequences of leadership at SunShine. SunShine has been financially successful and has maintained low turnover rates in an industry faced with unique challenges. After viewing the video, answer the following questions:

1. Based on information presented in the video and your own knowledge, what are likely to be some special difficulties associated with leadership in the cleaning industry?

2. CEO Larry Calufetti was formerly a catcher and a manager with the New York Mets baseball team. How has his baseball experience influenced his leadership philosophy?

3. What are eight characteristics of the "coaching leadership style" at SunShine?

4. What are some examples of reward power at SunShine?
5. What does Steve Ketchum mean when he says, "I can't see the fences anymore"? What does this anecdote say about Larry Calufetti's leadership style?
6. The video states that all managers at SunShine have adopted Larry Calufetti's leadership style. Based on information presented in this chapter, what might be some benefits of a uniformity of leadership styles across all managers? What might be some costs?
7. What is the purpose of "Larry's Dream Team"?

LIGHTEN UP

THE LINK TO LINKS

In the continuing quest to understand leadership, researchers have linked leaders' effectiveness to their performance on the golf links. A recent study of golfing and leader effectiveness conducted by the *New York Times* compared golf handicaps of corporate heads to their companies' stock market performance over three years. The pattern was clear and statistically significant: The lower (that is, the better) the leader's golf handicap, the better his or her company's performance. For instance, executives whose companies were in the top performance group had handicaps that were about five strokes better than did executives whose firms showed the poorest performance.

What could explain such findings? Perhaps natural leaders also tend to be natural athletes. Perhaps perseverance or high need for achievement pays off in both golf and business. Perhaps early life experiences—such as caddying for executives—built golf skills while it provided exposure to business banter. Whatever the explanation, the study provides one more excuse for taking the time to improve one's golf game.

LIGHTEN UP

BOSSES FROM HELL[25]

In his *Dilbert* cartoons, Scott Adams lambastes "pointy-headed" bosses who are amazingly insensitive, unqualified, vindictive, fail to deliver on promises, or are simply clueless. These bosses may seem too bad to be true, but Adams actually gets most of his ideas from the tens of thousands of messages he receives from readers of his strips. Annual "best boss/worst boss" contests also generate far more "worst boss" than "best boss" nominations.

Consider the following examples of actual bosses:

> An elderly engineer passed away at his desk at approximately 3 P.M. The boss told office workers not to call 911 until 5 P.M. because it would disrupt the routine and be nonproductive.

> A boss told a programmer, "Give me a list of the unknown bugs in this system."

> An employee's boss sent him a bouquet of balloons with words of praise on each one after closing a major account the company had romanced for months. But the message on the card said, "Good luck on your new job." When the employee, confused, asked, "What new job?" his boss replied, "The job you are looking for today. You're fired. I decided two months ago to cut overhead and let you go, but waited until our big account was secure."

> An employee's father was scheduled for hip surgery, which had already been delayed by pneumonia. The employee's boss insisted she call the surgeon and reschedule so she wouldn't miss work.

> A supervisor for a *Fortune* 500 chemical manufacturer would announce at 3 P.M. he was leaving early, say his good nights, and leave, only to sneak up the back stairway to hide in the supply closet with the lights off to spy on employees for two hours.

> A boss who was a control freak imposed two-minute limits on his subordinates' bathroom visits—and went in after them if they remained overtime.

SKILLS PRACTICE

8-1   *Skill Level: BASIC*

Fieldwork: Interview with a Leader

Skill Objective

To understand the types of challenges faced by leaders of organizations and the tactics they use to handle those issues effectively.
Note: Download the worksheet developed for this exercise from the Web site for this textbook.
Procedure

1. Identify someone who is in a leadership position in an organization and willing to be interviewed for this assignment. The organization may be of any type; the main issue here is to select a firm that interests you in some way.

2. In the interview with your leader, ask the following questions:
   > What is your position title? What are the primary tasks and responsibilities associated with your job?
   > Describe your organization in terms of its products and services, mission, structure, and any other characteristics you think are important.
   > How would you define *effective leadership* as it relates to your job?
   > What have been the most difficult leadership challenges you have experienced in your job? How did you handle them?
   > What kind of advice would you give students regarding the best ways to develop their own leadership skills for the future?

3. Summarize the results of your interview, and either make a brief presentation to your class or submit a brief written summary of your findings.

SKILLS PRACTICE

8-2   *Skill Level: BASIC*

Profiling a Great Leader

Skill Objective

To develop a profile of the traits an individual should possess and the behaviors he or she should exhibit in order to be a great leader.
Note: Download the worksheet developed for this exercise from the Web site for this textbook.
Procedure

1. Think of an individual you consider a truly great leader. This person may come from business, politics, religion, or any other field.

2. Record the following information on your worksheet:
   a. Leader's name and position
   b. Leader's greatest accomplishment(s)
   c. The traits or qualities this individual possessed that make him or her a great leader
   d. The behaviors or actions of this individual that make him or her a great leader

3. Answer the following discussion questions.

Discussion Questions

1. If you had to select one or two items from the leadership profile you just prepared that you think are the most critical to effective leadership, what would they be? Why?

2. Would the leadership profile be effective in all types of situations? Why or why not?

SKILLS PRACTICE

8-3   *Skill Level: CHALLENGING*

Role Immersion Exercise: Using Path–Goal Theory to Establish Leader–Situation Match

Skill Objective

To develop skill in applying path–goal theory to a work situation.

Procedure

1. Form groups of four to five students each.
2. Assign one student to each of the following roles:

a. Team leader

b. Employee 1

c. Employee 2

d. Employee 3

e. Observer

Note: If your group has only four members, you can eliminate the observer role.

3. Each student should read the following general scenario and their individual roles. Students should not read each other's role sheets.

a. The Setting

Williams & Associates is a leading advertising firm based in New York City. The firm specializes in the development of advertising campaigns for many *Fortune* 500 corporations. It employs approximately 75 advertising specialists and support staff at its main headquarters.

Williams & Associates faces fierce competition from other advertising firms from around the United States and the rest of the world. Speed and responsiveness to tough customer demands are critical for success in this industry. In the end, however, everything hinges on the effectiveness of advertising campaigns in generating business for their clients. This reality puts tremendous pressure on these firms to leverage every advantage they can find.

Recently, the firm has won a contract to develop an advertising campaign for Cobra Motor Corporation, a new luxury car manufacturer that aims to compete directly with world-class luxury car manufacturers such as Lexus, BMW, Mercedes, Audi, Jaguar, Cadillac, and Lincoln. Cobra is new to the luxury car market, so it needs to establish its name in the highly competitive U.S. market and enhance its name recognition. In the future, Cobra wants consumers to associate its name with the attributes of quality, exclusivity, elegance, performance, and sportiness.

The challenge for Williams & Associates is to create an advertising campaign that will make consumers remember the name of Cobra Motor Corporation.

b. Role 1: The Leader

You are the leader of the advertising development team in charge of the Cobra account. Your task is to effectively lead the various members of your team in completing the task of developing a high-quality advertising campaign for Cobra. Use path–goal theory as your primary guide in helping you lead your team through the process of developing the ad campaign.

Key Tips for Playing This Role

1. Remember, you want to develop an advertising campaign for Cobra that meets their requirements of establishing the name of the company and getting consumers to view it as a legitimate player in the luxury auto industry.

2. Apply the basic logic of path–goal theory in leading your team in this situation. That is, assess the needs of your employees and the nature of the task. Then match the appropriate leadership behavior (directive, supportive, achievement oriented, participative) to each employee.

3. Don't forget you only have 30 minutes to develop your advertising campaign.

c. Role 2: Employee 1

You are one of the advertising specialists on the team developing an advertising campaign for Cobra Motor. You are a recent graduate of Billingsworth College, where you majored in English. You were an excellent student in college, maintaining a 3.7/4.0 GPA. However, you have had only one introductory course in advertising, and you have no prior work experience in the business world.

Key Tips for Playing This Role

1. Repeatedly state that you just started and don't have a clue what's going on or what you are supposed to be doing.

2. Ask for a lot of clarification on issues the leader brings up, and act confused by the explanations. The bottom line is that you need structure and direction from the leader.

d. Role 3: Employee 2

You are one of the advertising specialists on the team developing an advertising campaign for Cobra Motor. You have over 15 years of experience on the job, so you are a seasoned veteran. You don't need direction from the leader, because you believe you already know how to perform your job. However, you have a strong need for recognition for your contributions to the project and to the firm in general.

Key Tips for Playing This Role

1. Emphasize repeatedly that you have bent over backward for the firm in the past, but the firm has never shown any appreciation for your contributions.

2. Also state that the management has not provided enough support for advertising development teams in the past and you believe management doesn't really care much about its employees.

e. Role 4: Employee 3

You are one of the advertising specialists on the team developing an advertising campaign for Cobra Motor. You have been with the firm for about three years now. You are highly committed to the success of the firm, and you want to excel at your job in order to have a chance of being promoted in the future.

Key Tips for Playing This Role

1. You want the leader to inspire you, to fire you up, and to lead the team to victory. The bottom line is that you demand strong leadership.

2. State that you expect the leader to communicate his or her vision or mission for the project to the team. Ask the leader why employees should give 150 percent of their effort to this project. You want your leader to be someone who has a clear sense of his or her goals and can get others to become committed to achieving those goals as well. Make "Why should we care?" or "Why is this important?" statements during the process.

f. Role 5: Process Observer

Your job is to observe the process and to document what the leader does to handle the situation and how employees react to the leader's behavior.

4. Each team will have 30 minutes to conduct the exercise.

5. When time has expired, each team should address the following discussion questions.

Discussion Questions

1. What were the characteristics of each of the employees and the task?

2. What types of behaviors was the leader using in dealing with each of the employees? Were they appropriate?

3. What suggestions would you make to the leader to enhance his or her effectiveness in this situation?

4. What are the practical implications of this simulation for you as future leaders in organizations?

5. Optional: The observer from each team can present a brief summary to the class of personal impressions of the process, what the leader did, and how employees reacted.

SKILLS PRACTICE

8-4   *Skill Level: BASIC*

Managing Substitutes for Leadership and Neutralizers of Leadership

Skill Objective

To develop skill in identifying substitutes for leadership and neutralizers of leadership and to match appropriate leadership behaviors to these situations.

Note: Download the worksheet developed for this exercise from the text Web site.

Procedure

1. Analyze the following information and identify the substitutes for leadership and the neutralizers of leadership for the employees in the scenario.

The Situation

You are the manager of a team of four video game devel-

opers for a major software company called X-GAMES based in California. Your team's task is to create highly innovative action and fighting games for the major video game systems in the industry. X-GAMES has a very informal and flexible operating structure designed to foster creativity in the organization. Information regarding your employees is summarized in the accompanying table.

2. Develop an action plan for managing the substitutes and neutralizers of leadership in this scenario. What type of leadership behavior, if any, is needed to lead each individual effectively?

Employee	Experience and Qualifications	Need for Independence	Professional Orientation	Attitudes Toward Organizational Rewards	Task Structure	Intrinsic Task Satisfaction
Josh Kanvik	High	Low	High	Positive	High	High
Blake Williams	Low	Low	Low	Positive	Low	Low
Kenisha Divine	High	High	High	Indifferent	High	High

SKILLS PRACTICE

Skill Level: CHALLENGING

Role Immersion Exercise: Using Transformational Leadership to Support Organizational Change

Skill Objective

To develop skill in applying transformational leadership to a work situation.

Note: Download the worksheet developed for this exercise from the Web site for this textbook.

Procedure

1. Form groups of four to five students each.
2. Assign one student to each of the following roles:
   a. CEO
   b. Vice president of marketing
   c. Vice president of manufacturing
   d. Vice president of finance
   e. Observer

   Note: If your group has only four members, eliminate the role of the observer.
3. Each student should read the following general scenario and his or her individual role. Students should not read each other's role sheets.

a. The Setting

GCX Computer Corporation is a manufacturer of mid-level to high-end desktop and laptop computers. The company established itself as a leader in the industry in the 1980s with its innovative product design, cutting-edge technology, value pricing, and outstanding technical support. The company is based in Denver, Colorado, where it employs 2,000 employees in administration, marketing, finance, and human resources. Manufacturing operations are located in Tuscaloosa, Alabama, where 1,000 production employees assemble its products on three separate shifts that run six days per week.

GCX sells its computer systems in more than 60 countries throughout the world. It is ranked fourth in the computer industry on the basis of market share.

In the past few years, GCX corporate performance has slipped significantly. Production costs have been increasing at 20 percent above the industry average, quality has declined dramatically, customer satisfaction has dropped 35 percent, and profitability has dropped by 70 percent. In addition, competition from other U.S. companies and foreign firms from Taiwan has intensified, and many customers have flocked to basic computer models that cost less than $1,000. In addition to these negative results, employee job satisfaction and retention throughout the company have decreased by 50 percent in just two years.

b. Role 1: The Chief Executive Officer

You are the CEO and the leader of the senior management team at GCX. Your general objective is to lead your team by taking appropriate action to effectively turn around the organization's performance. Your specific task is to develop a turnaround plan for GCX that specifies the company's future goals and strategies for achieving them.

You should take specific actions that reflect the following behavioral dimensions of transformational leadership theory:

> *Attributed charisma*—Try to inspire your team by showing great confidence that a turnaround at the company is possible and obstacles can be overcome.
> *Idealized influence*—Communicate your beliefs and values to the management team.
> *Intellectual stimulation*—Encourage team members to challenge the status quo and to support change.
> *Inspirational leadership*—Articulate a compelling vision of the future to your team.
> *Individualized consideration*—Show personal interest in and concern for each member of your team.

Don't forget that you only have 30 minutes to develop a turnaround plan for GCX Corporation.

c. Role 2: Vice President of Marketing

You are the vice president of marketing at GCX. You believe the company's recent poor performance is just a fluke and nothing is fundamentally wrong with the company. You should focus your attention on the customer satisfaction data and emphasize that the numbers will improve over time. Your initial position should be that you don't see any point in developing a turnaround plan because the company is not in a crisis at all. If you think the CEO does an effective job of convincing you otherwise, feel free to modify your position. However, do not change your position unless you believe there is a compelling reason to do so.

d. Role 3: Vice President of Manufacturing

You are the vice president of manufacturing at CGX. Your major concern is the product quality results, which have declined significantly. Your initial position should be that you agree with the CEO: A turnaround plan is needed for the company, but you are not sure what it should look like.

In short, you need direction and structure from the CEO regarding the specifics of the turnaround plan.

e. Role 4: Vice President of Finance

You are the vice president of finance at GCX Corporation. You are a fence sitter, in that you haven't decided whether a turnaround plan for GCX is a good idea or not, but you are willing to discuss it with the other members of the team. You believe the cause of the company's declining profitability is inefficiencies in the manufacturing plant.

f. Role 5: Process Observer

Your job is to observe the process and to document what the leader does to handle the situation and how employees react to the leader's behavior.

4. Each team will have 30 minutes to conduct the exercise.

5. When time has expired, each team should address the following discussion questions.

Discussion Questions

1. What types of behaviors was the leader using in dealing with each of the employees? Were they appropriate?
2. What suggestions would you make to the leader to enhance his or her effectiveness in this situation?
3. What are the practical implications of this simulation for you as future leaders in organizations?
4. *Optional:* The observer from each team can present a brief summary to the class of personal impressions of the process, what the leader did, and how employees reacted.

SKILLS PRACTICE

8-6 *Skill Level: CHALLENGING*

Great Leaders in Action: **Gandhi** *and* **Mother Teresa**

Skill Objective

To develop skill in creating and analyzing an in-depth profile of a great leader.

Procedure

1. Obtain a copy of the movie *Gandhi* or *Mother Teresa.* They are both available on VHS and DVD and can be rented or purchased from a local video store or retailer.
2. Watch the movie (in class or at home on your own). Note: Download the worksheet developed for this exercise from the text Web site. This will help you record your notes from various scenes in the movie.

   As you watch the film, develop a profile of the leader (Gandhi or Mother Teresa) in terms of leadership traits, leadership behaviors, and the specific situations in which the leader demonstrates why he

or she was such a great leader. Document your notes from the film on your worksheet.

3. Discuss the following questions as a class.
   a. Why was Gandhi or Mother Teresa such a great leader? Give examples of scenes from the movie you watched that support your reasons.
   b. Which leadership theory or theories discussed in this chapter explain why Gandhi or Mother Teresa was a great leader?
   c. What can leaders of business organizations learn from Gandhi or Mother Teresa about effective leadership? How can this be put into practice in a real-world organization?
   d. What are the practical implications of this exercise for you as a future manager and leader in a real-world organization?

SKILLS PRACTICE

8-7 *Skill Level: CHALLENGING*

Putting the Pieces Together: Developing an Integrative Approach to Leadership

Skill Objective

To develop an effective leadership style based on an integrative (trait, behavioral, and situational) approach to leadership theories.

Note: Download the worksheet developed for this exercise from the text Web site. This will help structure your approach to the exercise.

Procedure

1. Based on the leadership theories you read about in this chapter, identify the following on a separate piece of paper:
   a. The general traits or qualities you consider important for effective leadership.
   b. The general behaviors you believe an individual should exhibit in order to be an effective leader.
   c. Situational factors you think are important to consider for effective leadership.
   d. The general outcomes you see as measures of leadership effectiveness.
2. For each of the mini-cases that follow, discuss the type of leadership you believe would be needed to handle the situation effectively.

Integrative Leadership Case 1

You are the manager of a group of 20 recent college graduates who have been hired as sales representatives for your firm. Their job duties include selling computer networking software systems to corporate clients around the United States and the world. This job requires in-depth product knowledge and an understanding of customers' complex and constantly changing needs.

Your employees are bright, but they have little or no experience in sales. Each new hire is required to go through a six-week training program to learn the basics of sales techniques and gain product knowledge. However, many of them are still very intimidated by the thought of having to apply all of this knowledge in working with real clients.

How would you apply the leadership style you developed to the handling of this situation?

Integrative Leadership Case 2

You are the manager of a team of seven experienced food science researchers working for a consumer foods corporation. These scientists all have master's degrees or doctorates in their field. They possess an average of five years of work experience in the food industry, and they are highly competent at what they do.

The team works on a project basis in developing new products for the company. Members of the team have a strong need to run their own show with a minimal amount of guidance from management. Specifically, they maintain strong opinions about what should be done and how it should be done.

How would you apply the leadership style you developed to the handling of this situation?

Integrative Leadership Case 3

You are the manager of a team of 50 production workers at a consumer electronics company that manufactures TVs, boom boxes, and other stereo equipment. The team works together to assemble these products on a fairly traditional production line. The work is fairly routine, and your employees have enough experience to understand how to perform their jobs effectively. The challenge for you is that you were just promoted from production employee to manager. That is, until recently you were a coworker of the people you now must manage as their new boss. Some members of the team are happy for you and your promotion, but others resent that you were promoted over them and are now a part of management and not to be trusted.

How would you apply the leadership style you developed to the handling of this situation?

Integrative Leadership Case 4

You are the president of Premiere Hotels, a company that provides basic lodging and accommodations for business travelers at a reasonable price. Your company has over 500 locations throughout the United States and Canada. Although your company has done well financially in the past 20 years, the hotel industry has become extremely competitive. Customers are more demanding now, and they expect more services and better accommodations for a lower price. Competition is intensifying, and new, more upscale hotels have been created that cater to consumers in your traditional niche.

These environmental changes are starting to affect Premiere Hotels' bottom line. In addition, a recent study of customer satisfaction with various hotels placed Premiere well below the industry average. Rumors are starting to circulate among employees that the company will announce mass employee layoffs in the near future and possibly close some of its hotels. These concerns are having a devastating effect on employee morale and job satisfaction.

How would you apply the leadership style you developed to the handling of this situation?

3. Answer the following discussion questions.

Discussion Questions

1. What do the various leadership theories have in common with each other? How do they differ from one another?
2. Which leadership theory (or theories) was most valuable to you in developing your overall leadership style?
3. To what degree did you modify the overall leadership style you developed, based on the scenarios in this exercise?
4. What are the implications of this exercise for you as a future organizational leader?

MANAGING POWER, SOCIAL INFLUENCE, AND POLITICS

CHAPTER 9

Skills Objectives

> To develop and implement strategies for enhancing leader power and influence.

> To develop the tools and abilities to empower others effectively.

> To apply political strategies and tactics to manage work situations effectively.

> To develop skill in applying impression management strategies in different types of organizational situations.

> To apply strategies for reducing political activity in an organization.

KNOWLEDGE OBJECTIVES

> Identify bases of interpersonal power and subunit power.

> Discuss the stages of the empowerment process.

> Explain social influence tactics.

> Identify causes and consequences—including costs and benefits—of political behaviors.

> Recognize political strategies and tactics and learn guidelines for minimizing political activities.

When *Fortune* magazine in 2003 selected its "25 most powerful people in business," it used as its guiding definition the ability to influence others, whether in a company, an industry, or the world at large.[1] Topping its list were Berkshire Hathaway's Warren Buffett, Microsoft chairman and cofounder (and world's richest man) Bill Gates, Wal-Mart Stores CEO Lee Scott, Citigroup CEO Sandy Weill, and News Corporation CEO Rupert Murdoch.

Fortune noted that "power is in business's soul" and people acknowledge power's presence in ways they're not even aware of. For instance, when two people are put in a room together, the less powerful seeks more eye contact while listening and less eye contact when speaking. The more powerful smiles less, sits in weirder positions, and does more steepling of fingers (that is, touching them together in a raised position, à la Sherlock Holmes).

Fortune further noted some "immutable laws" of power, including the following:

> Power, like gravity, can't be observed directly. Only its effects can. Absolute power, although it may corrupt absolutely, doesn't exist in business. Instead, everyone exerts power over someone else.

> Power flows from a variety of sources. For example, *Fortune* noted that some people in business (which it termed "king-makers") gain power by making other people powerful, others ("disrupters") by developing a novel concept that shakes up an industry, and still others ("zeit-geisters") by influencing what others think.

> "Comparing Apples to Microsofts ain't easy. . . . Well, is the most powerful person (1) the megacompany CEO whom 100,000 employees salute as boss, (2) the bond trader who cuts the mega-company's value in half whenever he blows his nose, (3) the economist whose ideas subtly dictate the bond trader's moves, or (4) Lockheed Martin CEO Vance Coffman, who has enough air power to ionize all of the above? Rock, scissors, paper, Hellfire missile."[2]

This all suggests that power and related phenomena are complex, subtle, relative, and hard to assess. In this chapter we address the elusive—but immensely important—topics of power, social influence, and politics. We address bases of interpersonal and subunit power, discuss steps in the empowerment process, and identify specific social influence and political tactics.

Take a few minutes now and complete Self-Assessment 9-1. You will learn more from this chapter if you start off with a greater awareness of your beliefs and feelings about how to manage power and politics. After you have completed this exercise, visit the text Web site to learn more about your responses.

SELF-ASSESSMENT 9-1

Attitudes Toward Managing Power, Social Influence, and Politics

Answer the following questions regarding your attitudes toward managing politics in organizations. Answer each question as honestly as possible using the response scale that follows.

1 Disagree strongly
2 Disagree somewhat
3 Neither agree nor disagree
4 Agree somewhat
5 Agree strongly

____ 1. Effective managers do not use political tactics to get their jobs done in organizations.

____ 2. You don't really have power until you use it.

____ 3. People who have authority automatically possess power.

____ 4. The best strategy for responding to people who behave in a highly political manner is to ignore them.

____ 5. Political factors are not important to my personal success in an organization as long as I perform my job well and mind my own business.

____ 6. A person needs to be feared by his or her employees in order to be an effective leader.

____ 7. Leaders should rely on the use of their formal authority or position in the organization as the best way to influence their employees.

____ 8. If you give your subordinates more power, you are left with less.

____ 9. It is best to draw power from a variety of sources (such as rewards and expertise) rather than sticking to a single power base.

____ 10. Rather than rely on politics, it is better to use tools such as committees, outside experts, and objective decision criteria.

As a way to assess your initial level of skill in managing power, social influence, and politics, complete the Pretest Skills Assessment. Read the scenario and develop an action plan for how you would handle this situation. Be as specific as possible in stating your recommendations.

PRETEST SKILLS ASSESSMENT

This exercise is based on events encountered by managers in real-world organizations. Some information has been modified to maintain the anonymity of the people and organization involved in this situation.

Managing Power, Social Influence, and Politics

You are the director of marketing at XBKE, a company that designs and manufactures high-end racing bicycles. You lead a team of seven bright but relatively inexperienced marketing specialists responsible for building the sporty image of the brand through a variety of promotional campaigns. In the past, your team was fairly successful marketing the company's products when it only had three basic models. However, the company's explosive growth, changing customer preferences (desire for greater off-road capability and for a wider variety of styles and colors), and intense foreign competition have made your team's job infinitely more complex.

The company recently announced a new empowerment program in which employees are to be given greater freedom to work in teams to manage themselves. Your job as the leader is to serve more as a coach or resource person as opposed to serving as a manager providing specific direction to the team. When you announce this to your team, the reaction is very mixed. A few employees like the idea, but others are not comfortable with the lack of structure associated with the new program. A major concern of everyone is that they don't really understand what empowerment means or how they are supposed to behave under such a program. In addition, you are concerned that some of the personality differences among your employees will become problematic without a clear structure for the team. Specifically, some employees have been very competitive with each other so they may increase their chances for a promotion in the company.

Develop an action plan for addressing the issues in this situation. Be sure your plan addresses both short-term and long-term issues and is specific. Be prepared to defend the feasibility and cost effectiveness of each element of your plan. Once you have completed your plan, go to the text Web site to get feedback on the exercise.

DEVELOPING AND USING POWER BASES

In Chapter 8 we defined leadership as the ability to influence others toward the achievement of goals. But what exactly is influence? How does it relate to authority, power, and control? How does a leader gain the ability to influence? These are among the topics we address in this section.

DEFINING TERMS

Let's first define some terms. *Authority* is the *right* to influence others. It is conferred by the organization. *Power* is the *ability* to influence others. People in organizations may have power without authority, and they may have authority without power. *Influence* is the actual exertion of force on others. Influence is power put into action; power is latent influence. *Control* is the exertion of enough influence to change others' behaviors. We may have a lot of power and exert a lot of influence without getting people to do what we want.

THE NATURE OF POWER

The definitions just given suggest that power can be described in the following ways:

> **Latent:** Power is something that people have and may or may not choose to use. It is a weapon or tool; it may never be used, and just having it may make its use unnecessary.

> **Relative:** The power one person has over another depends largely on factors such as the expertise of one person relative to another and the hierarchical level of one relative to the other. As such, a manager may have considerable power relative to one person and little or none relative to another.

> **Perceived:** Power is based on one person's belief that another has certain characteristics. If I believe you have power over me, you've got it!

> **Dynamic:** Power relationships evolve over time as individuals gain or lose certain types of power relative to others.

USES OF POWER

We often think of power as something we can use to get others to do what we want. Although this view isn't necessarily wrong, it *is* incomplete. There are at least three general uses of power:[3]

> **Power over.** This is power used to make another person act in a certain way; it may be called *dominance*.

> **Power to.** This is power that gives others the means to act more freely themselves; it is sometimes called *empowerment*. We discuss empowerment in more detail later in this chapter.

> **Power from.** This is power that protects us from the power of others; it may be called *resistance*.

These uses of power suggest that power is more than just a way to change others' behaviors (although that function is certainly important). It may also be used to help others act more freely or to prevent others from forcing us to do things we don't want to do.

FORMS OF COMPLIANCE TO POWER

We can also think of power in terms of *why* people comply with it. Three power types can be identified, based on the mechanism by which others accede to the power:[4]

> *Coercive power* involves forcing someone to comply with our wishes.
> With *utilitarian power*, compliance results from desires for rewards. For example, an employee may do what the boss asks in order to get a raise.
> *Normative power* rests on the employees' belief that the organization has the right to govern their behavior.

BASES OF POWER

If we're going to use power, we first have to get it. Traditionally, a distinction has been made between how *people* get power (termed *interpersonal power bases*) and how *groups* or *organizational subunits* get power (termed *subunit power bases*). Although we retain this distinction for now, we must point out that it is murky; people may use the so-called subunit power bases, and groups or subunits may use the so-called interpersonal power bases.

Interpersonal Power Bases. John French and Bertram Raven have developed the best known scheme for classifying bases of interpersonal power.[5] They have identified the following five power bases:

1. **Legitimate power.** *Legitimate power* results when one person thinks it is legitimate, or right, for another to give orders or otherwise exert force. An employee who says, "I ought to do as my boss says" is reflecting belief in legitimate power. Legitimate power may have a variety of sources:
   > It may be culturally specified. In some cultures, it is considered right that older people or people of certain castes or with certain characteristics be given respect and obedience. This has been called "the power of the eternal yesterday."
   > It may come from acceptance of the social structure. If individuals accept the social structure as legitimate—whether it is the hierarchy of an organization, the status ranking in a street gang, or a country's governance system—they are likely to accept demands of their "superiors" as legitimate.
   > It may be designated by a legitimizing agent. Those with legitimate power may choose to share it with others. A firm's CEO may appoint an assistant. In democratic societies, the holders of legitimate power—we, the people—may pass on that power through elections.

   Legitimate power sounds a lot like authority. The difference is that authority is the *right* to exert force, whereas legitimate power resides in an individual's belief that someone else *has* that right. These aren't the same. For example, unless subordinates accept authority, a boss has no legitimate power. However, someone may have legitimate power without formal authority, perhaps because of personal characteristics such as age and experience.

2. **Reward power.** *Reward power* is power based on the perceived ability to reward. It depends on one person's perceived ability to administer desired outcomes to another and to decrease or remove outcomes that are not desired.

3. **Coercive power.** *Coercive power* (as discussed in our earlier presentation of types of power) is based on one person's perceived ability to affect punishment that another receives.

4. **Referent power.** *Referent power* comes from the feeling of identity, or oneness, that one person has for another, or the desire for such identity. The commercial picturing Michael Jordan and saying "Be like Mike" is a concise and direct appeal to referent power. As another example, a Duke University poll of graduating MBAs asked who the graduates most admired. After their own father, the person admired most—more than the president, the pope, or Gandhi— is Warren Buffett—who, you'll recall, headed *Fortune*'s "25 Most Powerful" list.[6] Warren Buffett clearly has referent power.

5. **Expert power.** *Expert power* is based on one person's perception that another has needed relevant knowledge in a given area. Doctors, lawyers, and computer specialists may all have expert power.

In addition to these interpersonal power bases, others have been suggested. For instance, possession of valuable information, persuasive abilities, and personal charisma may all be sources of power.[7] We touch on these potential sources later in the chapter, in our discussion of social influence.

The power bases aren't independent. For one thing, they may occur together; people at high levels in organizations are likely simultaneously to have a lot of legitimate, reward, and coercive power, and perhaps some other power bases, and thus can draw on an arsenal of power bases. The power bases are also interdependent in the sense that reliance on one power base may influence levels of other power bases. For example, if we regularly coerce our subordinates, we're unlikely to have much referent power relative to them.[8]

It may seem that some of the power bases we have identified are ethical and others are not. For instance, referent power seems fairly noble, whereas coercive power seems suspect and devious. However, this is an oversimplification; referent power may be used to get a teenager to use drugs or to induce a colleague to cheat on an expense account, and coercive power can be humanely employed as a last resort to stop an employee's self-destructive drug use. Instead of asking which interpersonal power bases are ethical, it may be more useful to ask how each power base can be developed and employed ethically. Some suggestions are summarized in Figure 9-1.[9]

Skills Practice 9-1 gives you a chance to develop skill in analyzing a work situation and identifying specific strategies for enhancing your arsenal of power bases.

Subunit Power Bases. In addition to these interpersonal power bases, at least two other power bases—control of critical resources and control over strategic contingencies—are important. As we said earlier, we discuss these as sources of power for subunits, such as departments, but they apply to individuals and groups as well.

Resource Dependence Approach. One source of subunit power is the ability to control the supply of important resources required by other subunits.[10] According

FIGURE 9-1
Guidelines for Ethically Attaining and Using Interpersonal Power

Characteristic	Guidelines
Legitimate	1. Make polite requests
	2. Make requests in a confident tone
	3. Make clear requests and check for comprehension
	4. Make sure that requests appear legitimate
	5. Explain reasons for the request
	6. Follow proper channels
	7. Exercise authority regularly
	8. Insist on compliance and check to verify it
	9. Be responsive to subordinate concerns
Reward	1. Make sure compliance can be verified
	2. Make sure the request is feasible
	3. Provide an attractive incentive
	4. Make it clear you can deliver on your promises
	5. Make sure your requests are proper and ethical
Coercive	1. Inform subordinates about rules and penalties for violations
	2. Administer discipline consistently and promptly
	3. Provide sufficient warning before resorting to punishment
	4. Get the facts before using reprimands or punishment
	5. Stay calm and avoid appearing hostile
	6. Maintain credibility
	7. Use appropriate punishments
	8. Administer warnings and punishments in private
Referent	1. Show consideration for subordinates' needs and feelings
	2. Treat each subordinate fairly
	3. Defend subordinates' interests when acting as a group representative
	4. Select subordinates who identify with you
	5. Show you would be personally pleased if the subordinate carried out a request for you
	6. Model appropriate behavior
Expert	1. Promote an image of expertise
	2. Maintain credibility
	3. Act confident and decisive in a crisis
	4. Keep informed
	5. Recognize subordinate concerns
	6. Avoid threatening the self-esteem of subordinates

to *the resource dependence approach,* those subunits that obtain the most critical and hard-to-get resources (such as human, material, financial, and information resources) acquire the most power because of the dependencies that are developed. For instance, the power of a university department is related to its ability to secure outside grants and contracts, thus bringing critical funds into the university.[11] Similarly, those units that are at the skin of the firm, so to speak, spanning the boundary between the organization and its environment, derive power from their ability to obtain critical information and other resources from the environment.[12]

Strategic Contingencies Approach. According to the *strategic contingencies approach,* summarized in Figure 9-2, a unit's power is based on three things:

FIGURE 9-2
The Strategic Contingencies Model

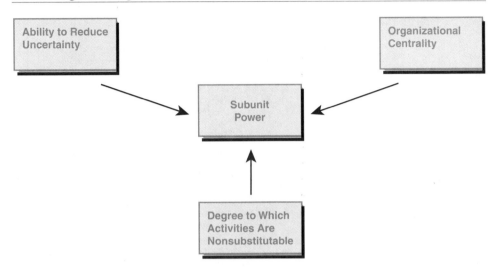

1. A unit will have more power if it is able to ***cope with uncertainty.*** That is, if the unit can reduce uncertainties faced by other units, it has power relative to those units. For example, there may be uncertainties about supply of funds or personnel, about market preferences, about changes in laws, or about the ability to produce enough goods to meet customer demands.
2. The unit will have more power if it is ***central*** in the flow of information and work between units. Units are more central if they have an immediate effect on the organization or if they have an impact on most other units.
3. Power increases with ***nonsubstitutability***; the harder it is for another unit to perform the activities of this unit, the more power this unit has.[13]

This perspective helps explain the power of people such as departmental administrative assistants. Even though they may have little formal power, everyone knows things would quickly grind to a halt if they left. They are the only ones who know where important documents are filed (so they cope with critical uncertainties), everyone depends on them (so they are central), and they keep all the information in their heads (so they can't be replaced).

The implications of the strategic contingencies approach for attaining power are straightforward:

1. Do something critical to the success of the organization.
2. Be in a position where many others depend on you.
3. And make sure you can't be replaced.

The ***and*** in this list is critical. According to the strategic contingencies approach, if ***any*** of these three conditions is lacking, your power will decrease dramatically.

SIGNS OF POWER
You will often want to know where power lies in the organization. For example, how can you tell who has power in an organization? Job titles may help; so may

status symbols. Still, we know these things can be deceptive and that some people with a lot of power don't have fancy titles or big offices. Some other signs of managers' power include the abilities to do the following:[14]

> Intercede favorably on behalf of someone in trouble with the organization
> Get a good placement for a talented subordinate
> Gain approval for expenditures beyond the budget
> Obtain above-average salary increases for subordinates
> Place items on the agenda at policy meetings
> Get fast access to top decision makers
> Have regular, frequent access to top decision makers
> Obtain early information about decisions and policy shifts

Signs of power may vary from one nation to another. For example, in Japanese organizations the appearance of equality is an important cultural value.[15] Because of this, salary, rank, and office space may have little to do with power. Instead, power can be gauged by studying patterns of interaction. Power flows from expertise, and those with power can be identified because others often consult with them.

SOCIAL INFLUENCE TACTICS

We said earlier that influence is power in action. Social influence is the use of power in interpersonal relationships. Here we discuss social influence approaches, consider how people might choose from among the approaches, and relate social influence to type of involvement.

SOCIAL INFLUENCE APPROACHES

People use a remarkable variety of approaches when attempting to influence others. Figure 9-3 lists some social influence tactics, arrayed from most popular to least popular.[16] It shows, for instance, that managers like to use participation, rational persuasion, and inspirational appeals to influence others. Tactics such as use of pressure

FIGURE 9-3
Social Influence Tactics

Rank	Tactic	Description
1	**Consultation**	Seeking participation in making or planning implementation of a decision
2	**Rational persuasion**	Using logical arguments and facts to persuade one another
3	**Inspirational appeals**	Making an emotional request or proposal that arouses enthusiasm by appealing to values and ideals or increasing confidence
4	**Ingratiating tactics**	Seeking to get someone in a good mood or to like you before asking for something
5	**Coalition tactics**	Seeking the aid of others to persuade someone, or using the support of others as an argument for agreement
6	**Pressure tactics**	Using demands, threats, or intimidation to get compliance
7	**Upward appeals**	Seeking to persuade someone that the request is approved at higher levels, or appealing to higher levels for help in getting compliance
8	**Exchange tactics**	Promising someone rewards or benefits in exchange for compliance

and formation of coalitions are less popular. Finally, promising something in return for compliance is an influence tactic of last resort; it's costly and may create expectations that there will *always* be rewards for compliance and compliance cannot be expected without such rewards. Let's look at some of the tactics in more detail.

Rational Persuasion. One way to get what you want is to make a compelling, persuasive argument. Persuasive communicators are well liked and eloquent and have high credibility. They gain credibility by their apparent expertise and by giving the impression that their motives are honorable.[17] Persuasive messages are clear and intelligible and moderately inconsistent with the message receiver's attitudes.[18] That is, a message entirely consistent with the receiver's prior attitudes makes no difference, whereas a message totally inconsistent with those attitudes is likely to be rejected out of hand.

Liking and Ingratiation. Quite simply, we're more willing to do something for people we like. Liking may be based on factors such as these:

> Physical attractiveness
> Compliments and flattery[19]
> Contact and cooperation (we tend to like people we know well, especially if we work with them on a common task or toward a cooperative goal)
> Association with other positive things (for instance, we like people who bring us good news and dislike those who bring us bad news)
> Social similarity (we like people who resemble us and are from the same social category)[20]

There may be a dark side to liking. For one thing, we said people like others who are similar to them. This may put minorities and women at a disadvantage in organizations populated primarily by white males. Some sources of bias can be consciously recognized and addressed, but we probably don't spend a lot of time thinking about why we first came to like someone, so the resulting bias may be hard to overcome. Perhaps as diverse people spend more time together in organizations they will recognize more similarities than are immediately apparent, and they will also see there are many other bases for liking.

Emotional Appeals. Anyone with a small child knows that emotional appeals can be effective. First, friendly emotions are a useful influence approach.[21] Researchers have studied how flight attendants maintain a cheerful attitude with customers,[22] how "cast members" at Disney display friendliness with "guests,"[23] and how salespeople present a positive "emotional front" to customers.[24] Such research shows that recipients of good cheer repay those positive emotions. They want to prolong the positive interaction and to ensure future interactions. As such, they tend to comply with the wishes of the cheerful person, and they are likely to see the person as credible (which, you'll recall, should enhance persuasiveness).

Negative or unpleasant emotions can also be tools of social influence, especially when the person displaying the emotions has more power than the target of the influence. For instance, some leaders use expressions of hostility and irritation to intimidate subordinates.[25] Similarly, bill collectors use negative emotions such as anger, irritation, and mild disapproval to get payments. These emotions create anxiety in debtors, and the debtors try to escape that anxiety by meeting the collector's demands.[26]

Finally, emotional contrast is often helpful; the presence of a nasty person makes a warm and friendly person seem even warmer and friendlier and makes compliance with this kind person's requests more likely. This is evidenced in "good cop, bad cop" routines, in which a suspect who has been interrogated by a mean and hostile officer is then treated warmly by a so-called good cop. The suspect is anxious to repay the kindness and may even feel compelled to confess.[27]

Social Proof. Another way we can influence people to take some action is by convincing them that others are taking the same action; this is called *social proof*. People are apt to follow the lead of others; for one thing, the fact that others are doing something suggests it is appropriate and socially acceptable. Many people are clearly aware of the principle of social proof. For example,

> *Our tendency to assume that an action is more correct if others are doing it is exploited in a variety of settings. Bartenders often salt their tip jars with a few dollar bills at the beginning of an evening to simulate tips left by customers and thereby to give the impression that tipping with folding money is proper barroom behavior. . . . Evangelical preachers are known to seed their audience with ringers, who are rehearsed to come forward at a specified time to give witness and donations. . . . The producers of charity telethons devote inordinate amounts of time to the . . . listing of viewers who have already pledged contributions.[28]*

As another example, recent research has examined social proof in the decisions of Wall Street analysts to initiate and abandon coverage of firms listed on the NASDAQ national market. The research showed that social proof creates "information cascades" in which decision makers initiate coverage of a firm when peers have recently begun coverage. Analysts that initiate coverage in the wake of a cascade are then prone to overestimate the firm's profitability and subsequently more likely than other analysts to abandon coverage of the firm. This creates a cycle of imitation-driven choice followed by disappointment and abandonment.[29]

CHOOSING FROM AMONG INFLUENCE APPROACHES

We've already said that people generally prefer some influence approaches, such as participation, to others, such as promising something in return for compliance. People also select influence approaches to fit the situation. For instance, individuals responding to authoritarian managers tend to use approaches such as blocking and ingratiation, whereas those responding to participative managers are more likely to rely on rational persuasion. Also, employees use different influence attempts with their superiors depending on the goals they are seeking. When they are trying to secure personal benefits, such as career advancement, employees tend to use ingratiation with their superiors. When they are trying to achieve organizational goals, they use a broader range of influence tactics.[30] This all suggests that even though people may have preferred strategies, they still recognize the need to choose from a broader arsenal of strategies if the situation calls for it.[31]

SOCIAL INFLUENCE AND TYPE OF INVOLVEMENT

People yield to influence through one of three processes—compliance, identification, and internalization.[32]

> **Compliance** occurs when people do something because they don't want to bear the costs of not doing it. For example, you may do what your boss tells you to do because you think you'll be punished if you don't.

> **Identification** results when influence flows from a person's attractiveness. Perhaps, for instance, the person is likable or charismatic or is in a position to which we aspire.

> **Internalization** takes place when we do something because we believe it is "the right thing to do."

This suggests that, although we may get what we want by relying on various power bases or employing diverse social influence tactics, we may get it in different forms and with different long-run consequences. A leader may have to use each of these processes at times, but it seems clear that identification and internalization will lead to better long-run consequences than compliance. Leaders who are credible and trustworthy are most likely to be able to use those processes.

EMPOWERING OTHERS

From the outside, the Thai Carbon Black factory appears nightmarish, as might be expected for a firm that produces the black powdery material used in tires and rubber products. Inside, though, you will see why the company was rated as one of the five best places to work in Asia as well as the winner of the Thai prime minister's Productivity Award. There is little emphasis on hierarchy; workers participate in decision making and have loose job descriptions that give them freedom to maneuver, and communications are open. Thai Carbon Black's CEO, S. Srinivasan, says, "Because there is no hierarchy, we work as a team."[33] He adds, "Knowledge gained and knowledge not shared is useless to the individual, to society, and to the organization. We seek to be a learning-based organization."[34] Workers are expected to be problem solvers; they participate in monthly management meetings and are encouraged to come up with new ideas for improving day-to-day operations. In 2002, the firm implemented over 650 different ideas offered by employees, and it credits the ideas for a large part of its recent 55 percent annual productivity gains. Each division of the company produces a monthly progress report, including everything from energy-saving production measures to a multiskill evaluation of each employee. An open-air tent outside the factory displays the results for all employees to view. Turnover at the firm is dropping, with one employee saying, "Here you are part of something bigger than just a job."[35]

Thai Carbon Black is a good example of the trend in many organizations toward employee empowerment. Other firms, ranging from TGI Fridays to Google, are also noteworthy for their empowerment programs.[36] Let's take a look at the need for empowerment and the process involved in establishing an empowered work force.

POWERLESSNESS

Carl Sandburg wrote, "I am the people—the mob—the crowd—the mass. Do you know that all the great work of the world is done through me?"[37] If the people are to do the world's work, they must have the power to do so. Unfortunately, many characteristics of traditional organizations create feelings of powerlessness and learned helplessness among employees; *learned helplessness* occurs when it appears one's behaviors simply don't make a difference.[38] Rules won't change, and we are bound to them. Bosses are set in their ways, and we must obey them. Things have always been done a certain way, and that's how we must do them. The assembly line is relentless, and we must follow it. And it seems there's nothing we can do about it. It's not surprising that many employees feel powerless and helpless.

Even high-level executives may feel they are helpless. For instance, managers are often encouraged to emulate successful behavior, even though it isn't clear to them (and perhaps to anyone else) why that behavior was successful. If the behavior turns out to work well, the manager still doesn't know why. If it fails, the manager is punished, even if he or she carried it out competently.[39] This is a pre-scription for powerlessness.

Powerlessness has many important and unfortunate consequences. For example, learned helplessness has been proposed as a mechanism resulting in—among other consequences—depression, burnout, academic failure, and susceptibility to illness.[40] Also, powerlessness leads to lowered self-efficacy. As we discussed in Chapter 2, self-efficacy is the belief that one can master a task, and it is critical for successful task accomplishment. Because powerlessness is pervasive in organizations, empower-ment is a rallying cry of the new millennium.[41]

THE EMPOWERMENT PROCESS

Empowerment seeks to break the spiral of powerlessness by giving employees a sense of real control. Empowerment gives people in organizations the ability to get things done, often at levels of the hierarchy where the power can be applied most directly and effectively. To gain a better understanding of empowerment, consider the empowerment process shown in Figure 9-4.[42]

Leaders empower by removing chains, developing subordinates' self-sufficiency, and employing empowering leadership practices. There are five stages to the empowerment process.

Stage 1 represents those conditions—bureaucratic climate; autocratic super-vision; rewards that aren't tied to performance; and routine, simplified jobs—that lead to powerlessness. In stage 1, the direct causes of powerlessness are identified. For example, unnecessary rules, supervisors who give employees no discretion, reward systems unrelated to things that employees can influence, and stultifying jobs are recognized as potential causes of powerlessness.

In *stage 2*, the manager draws on an arsenal of empowering managerial prac-tices. We consider each of these approaches, including participative management, goal setting, feedback, modeling, rewards based on behavior and competence, and job enrichment, in other chapters. For example,

> **Let the people who work for you participate in decision making.** They will gain a sense of control over their work lives, and they will be more enthu-siastic about implementing the decisions and selling them to others.

> **Offer control over work processes.** Toyota, Saturn, and Jaguar let workers on their assembly lines stop the lines at any time if they have a problem, immediately correcting errors and reducing the number of faulty products. The culture of Saturn is discussed in the Focus on Management feature. Similarly, many hotels now let their desk clerks respond directly to customers' concerns

FIGURE 9-4 [43]
The Empowerment Process

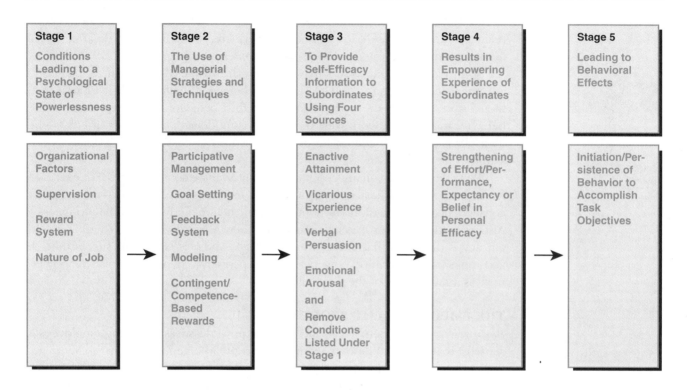

Stage 1	Stage 2	Stage 3	Stage 4	Stage 5
Conditions Leading to a Psychological State of Powerlessness	The Use of Managerial Strategies and Techniques	To Provide Self-Efficacy Information to Subordinates Using Four Sources	Results in Empowering Experience of Subordinates	Leading to Behavioral Effects
Organizational Factors Supervision Reward System Nature of Job	Participative Management Goal Setting Feedback System Modeling Contingent/ Competence-Based Rewards	Enactive Attainment Vicarious Experience Verbal Persuasion Emotional Arousal and Remove Conditions Listed Under Stage 1	Strengthening of Effort/Performance, Expectancy or Belief in Personal Efficacy	Initiation/Persistence of Behavior to Accomplish Task Objectives

without having to get supervisors' approval; they can even void customers' bills, granting them a free stay to compensate for a bad experience. Similarly, Disney World gives employees the authority to do whatever is necessary to deal with problems on the spot in order to make customers happy. Disney World believes front-line employees should be the first—and the last—contact with customers.[44]

> **Tie rewards to performance.** Employees naturally feel powerless when they see they aren't allowed to make a difference. When they see that their actions directly influence things they care about, they gain a sense of control—and they're more likely to do it again.

> **Express confidence, encouragement, and support.** Celebrate small wins and provide assurances that obstacles can be overcome.

Stage 3 is used to provide information to subordinates to increase their self-efficacies. This can be done in a variety of ways:[45]

> First, people may gain self-efficacy by actually mastering a task (called *enactive attainment*); initial success experiences make people feel more capable and strengthen their belief that they can handle more complex and difficult tasks. So giving employees goals they can attain successfully may be helpful.

> Second, *vicarious experience*—seeing that others who are similar can master a

FOCUS ON MANAGEMENT

AN EMPOWERING CULTURE AT SATURN CORP.

Saturn employees at plants in Spring Hill, Tennessee, and Wilmington, Delaware, don't punch time clocks. Labor and management (all called *team members* rather than *labor* and *management*) share the same cafeteria. Thanks to a unique agreement with the United Auto Workers union at the time of Saturn's creation, the union gave up rigid work rules, and GM (Saturn's parent corporation) abandoned most of its rigid hierarchy.

Saturn employees were grouped into small teams and given responsibility for everything from covering absent members to major production decisions.* The cooperative environment, focus on quality, and such concepts as no-haggle pricing have built a loyal customer base and provided an empowering work environment. When Cynthia Trudell, Saturn's chair and president, walks down the line, smiling workers ask her to pose with them for souvenir photos. The culture of Saturn is so unusual that a special team, called *Saturn Consulting Services,*

is available to provide consulting and training expertise to organizations wanting to learn from the Saturn experience. Go to the following site and click on "A Different Kind of Company" to learn more about Saturn's values, mission statement, philosophy, policies, and community activities.

http://www.saturn.com/

*To read more about Saturn and the challenges it currently faces, see I. Austen, "Problem Child," *Canadian Business,* March 26, 1999, pp. 22–31.

---

task—may enhance self-efficacy. As such, job training may involve showing someone completing the task.

> Third, employees may simply be convinced through *verbal persuasion,* words of encouragement and feedback that they can master tasks.

> Finally, techniques that create emotional support or foster a supportive and trusting group atmosphere may reduce the *emotional arousal* states that result from stress, fear, anxiety, and depression and lower self-efficacy.

In addition to these approaches, self-efficacy may be enhanced by removing the stage 1 conditions that led to powerlessness.[46] There is an old Abbott and Costello routine in which Costello, playing a patient, raises his arm and says to Abbott, playing a doctor, "Doc, it hurts when I do this." Abbott replies, "Don't *do* that!" So it is important to find the chains binding employees and then don't *do* that. Cut unnecessary red tape, rethink stifling rules, back off on overly close supervision, and treat your employees as capable and mature individuals.

In *stage 4,* the benefits of stages 2 and 3 are reaped as employees' self-efficacy is actually enhanced and employees gain a sense of power. Finally, in *stage 5*, the behavioral consequences of enhanced self-efficacy are seen: Empowered employees engage in task-oriented behavior.

The process model presented in the Bottom Line feature summarizes the basic steps associated with empowering employees in an organization. The Focus on Management feature discusses Fred Smith's actions to encourage empowerment at Federal Express.

Now use relevant material from this chapter to complete Skills Practice 9-2. Remember that your focus should be on how to translate the concept of empowerment into specific managerial action.

BOTTOM LINE

EMPOWERING EMPLOYEES

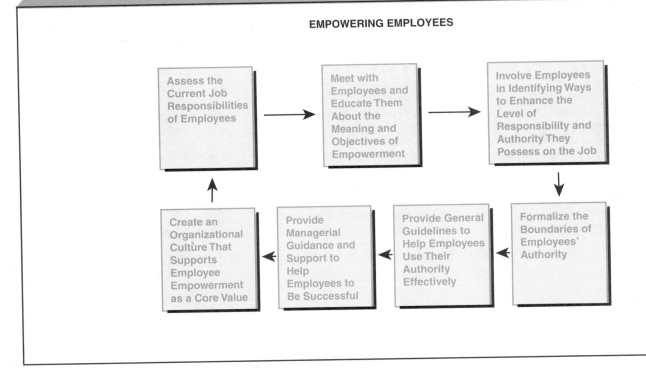

POLITICS

In this section we address organizational politics. We consider causes of political behaviors and the costs and benefits of politics. We then discuss specific political strategies and tactics and suggest guidelines for minimizing levels of political activity.

MANAGING POLITICS

When we hear someone speak of organizational politics, we probably think of such things as "passing the buck," "apple polishing," "backstabbing," and other "dirty tricks" we use to further our selfish interests. We use the term *organizational politics* more broadly, to refer to activities that people perform to acquire, enhance, and use power and other resources to obtain their preferred outcomes in a situation where there is uncertainty or disagreement.[47] Because the focus is on people's preferred outcomes, rather than organizational outcomes, this may or may not involve activities contrary to the best interests of the organization.

It is easy to condemn organizational politics as unethical (and we explore the ethics of politics later in the chapter). We need to remember, though, that the way in which an activity is labeled influences whether we see it as political. For example, what one person labels *blaming others* another may label *fixing responsibility*; passing the buck may be called *delegating responsibility*; forming coalitions may be labeled *facilitating teamwork*; apple polishing may be seen as *demonstrating loy-*

FOCUS ON MANAGEMENT

EMPOWERMENT AT FEDERAL EXPRESS[48]

The goal of Fred Smith, chairman and president of Federal Express, was to create a "power environment." Smith calls empowerment "the most important element in managing an organization." To create a power environment, Federal Express has a corporate philosophy that fosters respect for human dignity, ingenuity, and potential. There is a job-secure environment in which people aren't afraid to take risks. Jobs have been redesigned to increase employee power, and there are many opportunities for promotion from within. As an example of empowerment, when the company has badly mishandled an important shipment, the executive service employee handling the

order has the power to charter an airplane to handle the shipment. Customer service agents on the front line can make service credits on the spot to correct problems.[49]

Further, at Federal Express, there are many programs and processes designed to empower employees. An annual employee attitude survey, called *Survey Feedback Action,* is followed by an action phase in which managers meet with their staffs to develop an action plan for dealing with every concern. A *Guaranteed Fair Treatment* process is a three-stage avenue for airing employee grievances. An *Open-Door* process directs employees' questions to the people in the company best qualified to answer them. Unlike many such programs, the process at Federal Express is monitored to ensure that

each question is answered within 14 working days. A *Circle of Excellence* award is presented monthly to the best performing Federal Express station, underscoring teamwork, and other awards encourage employee service and achievement of quality. A *Bravo Zulu* (navy talk for "well done") program gives managers the chance to award dinner, theater tickets, or cash to any employee who has done an outstanding job. These philosophies, policies, and practices work together to create an environment in which employees feel valued and believe they can make a difference. FedEx is a winner of the Malcolm Baldrige National Quality Award and has continued to report steadily rising profitability.[50]

http://fedex.com/us/careers/

---

alty.[51] So we should be careful about condemning behavior as political until we ask whether the labeling itself was a political act![52]

People's ambivalence toward organizational politics is reflected in Figure 9-5. That figure shows, for example, that almost 90 percent of managers believe successful executives must be good politicians, but only about 40 percent feel politics helps the organization to function effectively. The figure also reflects a dilemma of sorts: Most managers believe those at the top got there because of politics, but about half want those at the top to get rid of politics. However, people like to dance with the ones they came with; they aren't likely to abandon the keys to their success.[53]

Further, even though you may be justifiably reluctant to use political tactics, it's probably true that everyone wants to avoid political gaffes, such as criticizing your boss in public, losing control of your emotions during meetings, or challenging sacred beliefs or values of the organization. So sensitivity to politics may be important, if only to be alert for the political actions of others and to avoid personal embarrassment. In the nearby Voice of Experience feature, Scott Finkelmeyer, an account executive at Siemens Medical Systems, provides suggestions for dealing with politics in organizations.

Skills Practice 9-3 will give you an opportunity to interview a management professional and to learn more about specific examples of effective and ineffective handling of politics in organizations.

In this section, we discuss factors that encourage political behavior and examine political strategies and tactics. We then consider some political games that are played

FIGURE 9-5
Managers' Feelings About Workplace Politics

Statement	% Expressing Strong or Moderate Agreement
The existence of workplace politics is common in most organizations.	93.2
Successful executives must be good politicians.	89.0
The higher you go in organizations, the more political the climate becomes.	76.2
Powerful executives don't act politically.	15.7
You have to be political to get ahead in organizations	69.8
Top management should try to get rid of politics in organizations.	48.6
Politics helps organizations function effectively.	42.1
Organizations free of politics are happier than those where there is a lot of politics	59.1
Politics in organizations is detrimental to efficiency.	55.1

Source: J. Gandz and V. V. Murray, "The Experience of Workplace Politics," *Academy of Management Journal,* 1980, p. 244.

in organizations. Finally, we look at the ethics of political behavior and its costs and benefits. If you decide that particular behaviors are self-serving at the expense of the organization or that the behaviors cost the organization more than they are worth, you can consider some guidelines we provide for minimizing political behavior.

FACTORS ENCOURAGING POLITICAL BEHAVIOR

Why does political behavior occur? It seems some people are prone to political behavior and some situations seem to foster such behavior. These are summarized in Figure 9-6.

Individual Factors. Four individual characteristics that influence political behavior are Machiavellianism, self-monitoring, need for power, and individual values. All have been discussed in previous chapters, so we look here only at their relationships to political behavior.

> **Machiavellianism.** As we discussed in Chapter 2, because Machiavellians believe ends justify means and they should always look out for number one, it's not surprising they are highly political. Al Neuharth, the founder of *USA Today* and author of *Confessions of an SOB,* has defended his view that "winning is the most important thing in life" by stating, "I'm simply describing a combination of techniques that most successful CEOs use but don't admit to" and adding, "Being Machiavellian, as a general offense, is not all bad." As these statements suggest, Machiavellians see political behavior as pragmatic and, as such, as appropriate. As an example, research has shown Machiavellianism to be related to the decision to offer illegal kickbacks to purchasing agents.[54] Students scoring higher on Machiavellianism have been shown to score lower on measures of ethical orientation and lower on corporate social responsibility orientation.[55] Further, marketers scoring higher on Machiavellianism have been shown to be less likely to consider ethical aspects of situations.[56]

> **Self-monitoring.** Recall that high self-monitors are like chameleons, adjusting their behaviors in ways to induce positive reactions from others. High self-

FIGURE 9-6
Some Determinants of Organizational Politics

monitors have been shown to be more apt than low self-monitors to engage in manipulation and filtering of the information that they transmit upward in order to create a favorable impression. For instance, they are more likely to transmit information that reflects positively on their decision processes and more likely to try to shift the blame for mistakes to others.[57]

> **Need for power.** Because politics is about the use of power, it makes sense that need for power should be related to political activity. In Chapter 4, we said the need for power is the desire to control other persons, to influence their behavior, and to be responsible for them. However, David McClelland

VOICE OF EXPERIENCE

MANAGING POWER, SOCIAL INFLUENCE, AND POLITICS
Scott Finkelmeyer, Account Executive, Siemens Medical Systems

1. What kinds of political issues do you face on your job and in your organization?

In my organization I was hired at the same time as six other individuals who had just graduated from college. We are all very achievement oriented and wanted to be successful and move up at Siemens. So we are competitive with each other in trying to make a good impression on our boss. This does not involve dirty tactics where we try to undermine each other, but rather a healthy sense of competitiveness that pushes each of us to be better.

At Siemens, the trainees in the account executive training program are strongly encouraged to work as a team and to do things that will reflect positively on the team as a whole because that is how we are viewed by others in the company. Two of my team members made some serious political errors during the first week on the job. First, when they arrived for a meeting at one of the corporate offices, one of them was rude to a receptionist. This receptionist informed management how she was treated, and it really tarnished the image of the entire team. What a way to start! Second, at a company-sponsored social event that week, another trainee from my team drank way too much beer, and it showed. This did not impress management very much either.

2. What advice would you give students regarding the effective handling of organizational politics in the real world?

First, always conduct yourself in a professional manner at all times when you are at work, including social events where people from your company are present. Never ever let your hair down! Remember that you are always being evaluated by others in your company, not just by your boss. Also, be aware of the grapevine in your organization. It can be nasty. Don't give people anything that can be processed through the rumor mill. Finally, I would say you should treat everyone in your organization as a customer, whether they are actually a customer or not.

identified two types of need for power.[58] ***Personalized power seekers*** try to dominate others for the sake of dominating, and they derive satisfaction from conquering others. ***Socialized power seekers*** satisfy their power needs in ways that help the organization. They may show concern for group goals, find goals to motivate others, and work with a group to develop and achieve goals. So we would probably expect more political behavior from personalized power seekers than from socialized power seekers.

> Finally, ***individual values*** may affect the levels of political behaviors or at least of unethical political behaviors. For example, the degree to which individuals have ***economic value orientations*** (interested in the production and consumption of goods and the uses or creation of wealth) or ***political value orientations*** (focusing on power, influence, and recognition) predicts unethical behavior.[59]

Organizational Factors. Several organizational factors are known to influence organization politics. These include organizational values, ambiguity, counternorms, competition among employees, and level in the organization.[60]

> **Organizational values.** One organizational influence on political behavior is the set of values dominant in the organization. As we discuss in Chapter 13, these values are central to organizational culture. The values of some organizations condemn political behavior. In these organizations, people believe "hard facts," "cool logic," and "objective criteria" should rule. In other organizations, political behavior is seen as valuable and necessary in the real world and as entirely appropriate. To the extent these values are widely accepted and communicated, political behavior is likely to vary accordingly. Some specific managerial values have been viewed as causes of unethical aspects of political activity:[61]
>   - A ***bottom-line mentality*** sees financial success as the only value to be considered; rules of morality are simply obstacles on the way to the bottom line.
>   - An ***exploitative mentality*** is a selfish perspective that encourages using people to benefit one's own immediate interests.
>   - A ***Madison Avenue mentality*** says, "It's right if I can convince you it's right." This public relations–oriented mentality focuses on making others believe our actions are moral, perhaps by hiding unethical behaviors or rationalizing them. As such, this mentality is a kind of organizational impression management; we look more at impression management later in the chapter.

> **Ambiguity.** Another key organizational determinant of political behavior is ambiguity. Politics thrives in ambiguous, uncertain situations. For instance, if goals are unclear, people may use political behaviors to define those goals to their advantage. If there is a lot of change in the organization, its markets, or its technology, people may exploit the resulting uncertainty to gain territory or otherwise serve self-interests. If there is ambiguity surrounding a decision, there is room for political maneuvering to define the decision and decision process to fit one's interests. Also, if there are limited resources, political behaviors may be used to maximize one's share of the pie.[62]

> **Counternorms.** Further, organizations may develop counternorms. ***Counternorms*** are accepted organizational practices that are contrary to the more

explicit, stated norms of the organization.[63] They are examples of the organization's "talking out of both sides of its mouth," saying one thing is appropriate but expecting another. Some of these counternorms are shown in Figure 9-7.[64]

> **Competition.** In addition, political behavior is nurtured by competition among employees. Competition fosters a zero-sum atmosphere, in which one person's gain is another's loss. In such an atmosphere, little incentive exists for cooperation and openness.

> **Level in the organization.** Finally, people at all levels of organizations share the view that political behavior increases with organizational level.[65] This may reflect the fact that at higher levels in organizations, the stakes are higher and decisions are often more ambiguous.

POLITICAL CAPABILITIES

David Butcher and Martin Clarke have discussed "smart politics," arguing for the idea of a "legitimate political mindset" that may be increasingly useful as managers must deal with a plethora of stakeholder interests.[66] They offered a listing of skills needed for "constructive politics," a sampling of which follows:

Conceptual Understanding

> **Power and politics**—evaluating the complexity of the influence process and the role of motives.
> **Relationships**—evaluating the different barriers to organizational relationships.
> **Political mechanisms**—recognizing the value of lobbying, stealth, and apparent adherence to formal procedure.

Self-Understanding

> **Balanced motives**—clarity about personal and organizational motivations.
> **Managerial irreverence**—a healthy skepticism about the limits of what is possible through the formal organization.

Awareness

> **Stakeholder knowledge**—knowing the agendas and motivations of key players.

FIGURE 9-7
Norms and Counternorms

Norms	Counternorms
Openness, honesty, candor	Secrecy and lying; "play your cards close to your chest"
Follow the rules	Break the rules to get the job done
Be cost-effective	"Spend it or burn it"
Take responsibility	Avoid responsibility; "pass the buck"
"All for one and one for all"	Achieve your goals at the expense of others
Maintain an appearance of consensus; support the team	Maintain high visibility; "grandstanding"
Take timely action	"Never do today what you can put off until tomorrow"

> **Organizational knowledge**—knowing who makes key decisions and how they are made.
> **Knowledge of the business environment**—knowing the issues critical for the organization.

Interpersonal Skills

> **Persuasive presentation**—developing collaborative outcomes through techniques such as personal enthusiasm and suggestion.
> **Reading others**—a continual observation and evaluation of the motives and actions of others.

POLITICAL STRATEGIES AND TACTICS

Jeffrey Pfeffer has described a variety of political strategies and tactics.[67] The strategies are general guidelines for the effective use of power for one's purposes. The tactics are specific ways in which those strategies can be carried out.

Political Strategies. Pfeffer identifies three general political strategies:

> **Make power unobtrusive.** Power is most effective when it is subtle. Blatantly employing power may create a backlash and use up "credits." It has been said of Michael Ovitz, founder of Creative Artists Agency, former president of Disney, and recognized Hollywood power broker, that he "exercises power like a Zen brush painter: delicate, deliberate strokes."[68] Ovitz realizes that a key to successful power use is not to appear to be using power.
> **Build legitimacy.** Power is most effective when the power itself and the decision process and outcomes that flow from it appear to be legitimate. For instance, if it can be shown that actions are consistent with the values of the organization or they were initiated by appropriate organizational actors (such as a committee broadly representing affected parties), legitimacy will be enhanced.
> **Build a base of support.** A final power strategy is to act in ways that either increase the actor's own power or obtain support or acquiescence from other powerful actors in the organization.

Political Tactics. The three strategies outlined by Pfeffer are general guidelines for effective power use. Here are some specific political tactics that are often employed to carry out those strategies successfully.

> **Use objective criteria selectively.** We've said that political tactics are likely to be employed in ambiguous, uncertain situations. In those situations, there is often room for disagreement over an appropriate criterion: Should we minimize cost, maximize quality, or what? In such cases, it's possible to decide which criterion makes your preferred alternative look best and then argue for that criterion. This is less obtrusive than simply arguing for the alternative; if the criterion is accepted, choice of the alternative will follow. Of course, in cases where you can simply specify criteria, you can essentially guarantee choice of your preferred alternative. For instance, you can say, "We need someone with at least 10 years of experience in this industry, and with an MBA, and with production experience, and who's familiar with our company. Go find the best person." Of course, through your specification of those criteria you have made the choice.
> **Use outside experts.** The ability to hire an outside expert, such as a con-

sultant, has many benefits. The expert is credible and authoritative because he or she appears objective, clearly has expertise, and is expensive—it's hard to disagree with someone whose advice costs thousands of dollars. However, Pfeffer sees outside experts as hired guns, brought in to support the position of the person who hired them. Although they appear objective, they in fact are not. They were selected on the basis of their past recommendations and views, they are fed information by the people who hired them, and they want to be hired again. As such, the appearance of objectivity is an illusion.

> **Control the agenda.** Those who control an agenda can take advantage of their position in at least three ways. First, they can simply decide what will and won't be considered. Second, they can decide what gets discussed when. Things placed early on an agenda tend to be carefully considered and endlessly debated. Things placed late tend to be considered casually, if at all; people are so tired of being in a meeting, they just want to get it over with. Third, the relative placement of proposals makes a difference. For instance, suppose you have a stronger and a weaker proposal. Which should you place first? The evidence suggests the weaker proposal should be placed first: It will be carefully considered and, if it is accepted, the stronger proposal will look even better and is also likely to be accepted. If the weaker proposal is rejected, the stronger proposal benefits in three ways: Its later placement means it will get less scrutiny, its placement after the weaker proposal lets it profit from contrast effects, and it may benefit from sympathy because the other proposal was defeated and you should get something. But what if you don't have a weaker proposal to place before the stronger proposal? Invent one! A weak dummy proposal may be designed and used specifically to make the later, real proposal look better, receive less scrutiny, and capture some sympathy.

> **Form coalitions.** A coalition is a set of individuals or organizations who join together to pursue a specific goal. For instance, people may pool their votes to defeat a common foe. In laboratory experiments, the coalition containing the fewest resources (dollars, votes, shares, or whatever) needed to win often forms. This is explained by the minimum-resource theory, which says the smaller the winning coalition, the more leverage you get from your resources (e.g., you may be able to win in a particular voting situation by having a plurality of perhaps 30 percent of the votes). And, with a small coalition, you don't have to share the spoils with so many others. In contrast to these laboratory findings, Pfeffer argues that real-world coalitions are often as large as possible—a maximum-resource theory. By forming a large coalition, there is a broader base of support and fewer losers who may hold grudges in the future. Further, this larger coalition may not really be costly; some members will be happy just to be on the winning side, and some may accept promises of future benefits.

Coalitions may be external or internal. An external coalition is formed with outside groups in contact with the organization, such as suppliers, creditors, or customers. An external coalition has the benefits of bringing in new resources and may have less conflict of interest with internal subunits. However, forming such coalitions may be seen as disloyal to the organization and its goals. An internal coalition is formed with others inside the organization with common interests. Internal allies are closer to the decision process and, therefore, may be more valuable in influencing decision outcomes.

One interesting internal coalition is formed through promotions. Suppose you're in a position to make or recommend a promotion. Of the handful of individuals who could possibly be selected, one seems clearly best qualified. Whom do you choose? Not that person. The reason: If you select the best qualified candidate, he or she will think, "I was chosen because I'm best qualified. I deserved it." If, however, you select someone who is a surprise, he or she will think, "I have this position because you gave it to me. I owe you." You have gained an ally. So the rule here is "promote the non-obvious choice."

Another innovative approach to formation of internal alliances is "everybody's a winner." With this tactic, people who don't get what they want may be given a fancy title or moved into a newly created supposedly higher level position as a consolation prize. This lets everyone save face, and the win-lose aspects of politics are downplayed.

> **Coopt others.** With cooptation, some dissenting element is brought into the unit. Cooptation involves giving a representative of the organization or subunit whose support is sought a position on the board, committee, or other body of the unit seeking the support. For example, a student who is constantly challenging decisions of a university committee may be asked to join the committee. The student will then be exposed to the social influence of the committee members and to conformity pressures and will be forced to justify his or her statements and actions. Also, the student will begin to have a stake in the success of the committee and begin to think about it differently.

When Douglas Fraser, then president of the AFL-CIO, was put on the board of directors of Chrysler, many hailed the event as a victory for labor. Others, though, felt Fraser had been coopted and he would now begin to identify more with management. One observer noted, "Fraser is now neither fish nor fowl." Of course, cooptation has its costs. For example, secrecy may be lost. In addition, the person who is coopted may actually persuade others.

> **Use committees.** Suppose I know whom I want chosen to fill a new position; let's say it's Janet. I know, though, that if I just appoint Janet, there may be some rumblings of dissent: I have been obtrusive, haven't developed an aura of legitimacy, and haven't built a base of support. Instead, I'll appoint a search-and-screen committee, made up of respected representatives of all the areas affected by the position to be filled. I'll widely publicize the committee and its distinguished members, and I'll give the committee the charge of providing me with a list of suitable candidates for the position. I'll somehow make sure Janet becomes one of those candidates (perhaps one of the committee members will be a plant who will argue for Janet's presence on the list, or perhaps I'll have to ask the committee to generate more names if Janet's name isn't included initially). When the committee gives me its list, I will thank it profusely, will broadly and visibly praise the committee members for their efforts, and will note the time and effort and expertise they have devoted to this important task. Then I'll pick Janet! Use of committees in this way nicely satisfies each of the general strategies just described: It is unobtrusive, it is seen as legitimate, and it builds a base of support.

QUESTIONING THE TACTICS

What makes Pfeffer's tactics so interesting is that they are all widely used and often appear socially desirable. And, of course, they may each be used for perfectly good and selfless reasons. Nevertheless, the discussion encourages us to at least question such tactics when they are used. We might ask, for instance,

> Why were these criteria specified in the posting of job requirements?
> Who selected the outside consultant who was brought in to make recommendations regarding changes in the reward system?
> Why wasn't a discussion of the proposed job redesign program on the agenda?
> Is this committee to which I've been appointed for real or is the decision it's dealing with a done deal?

Skills Practice 9-4 gives you a chance to apply the political strategies and tactics discussed in this section to a realistic organizational situation. Remember that this is the area about which recent graduates have consistently indicated they wish they had learned more while still in college, so challenge yourself and see what you can do.

Other Political Tactics. In addition to the tactics Pfeffer has presented, at least two others—defensive behaviors and impression management—deserve mention.

> **Defensive behaviors.** Just as power may be used to resist the influence attempts of others, political behavior may involve protecting one's self-interest.[69] As such, people may engage in *defensive behaviors* to avoid action, blame, or change. Some of these defensive behaviors are presented in Figure 9-8.[70] You have probably seen people use many of these defensive behaviors. Some of the behaviors, such as overconforming, passing the buck, depersonalizing, and buffing, probably come to mind when you think of a bureaucracy. Certainly, such behaviors are associated with many of the worst characteristics of bureaucratic organizations.

> **Impression management.** *Impression management* is behavior that people direct toward others to create and maintain desired perceptions of themselves.[71] The most prominent type of impression management behavior is self-presentation, which involves the manipulation of information about oneself.[72] Self-presentation can be verbal or nonverbal or involve displays of artifacts. There are at least eight types of verbal self-presentations, shown in Figure 9-9. One of those types—descriptions of the organization—is included because glowing descriptions of our organization are often used to reflect positively on ourselves. What the types have in common is that they each are intended to make us look better. Have you seen people use each of these impression management approaches? Do you think they worked?

In addition to verbal self-presentations, impression management may involve nonverbal behaviors. For example, erect body posture, a steady gaze, a confident tone of voice, facial expression, and gestures may all be used for impression management.[73] We might also try to create a favorable impression by the clothes we wear or how we decorate our offices.

Impression management may also involve creating other forms of impressions. For instance, Clark Molstad took a job as a brewery worker and studied

FIGURE 9-8
Defensive Behaviors

To Avoid Action

Overconforming—Avoiding action by resorting to a strict interpretation of one's responsibility ("The rules clearly say") and perhaps citing supportive precedents ("It's always been done this way")

Passing the buck—Foisting responsibility for execution of a task on another person ("I'm too busy"; "That's not my job")

Playing dumb—Attempting to avoid an unwanted task by falsely pleading ignorance or inability; "strategic helplessness"

Depersonalizing—Avoiding unwanted demands from others by treating them as objects or numbers rather than people

Smoothing and stretching—Smoothing refers to masking fluctuations in effort and output; fluctuations suggest inconsistency since peaks in performance suggest what is attainable and troughs thereby suggest a decline. Stretching refers to prolonging a task so one appears occupied.

Stalling—Appearing more or less supportive publicly while doing little or nothing privately; "foot-dragging"

To Avoid Blame

Buffing—Rigorously documenting activity or fabricating documents to project an image of competence and thoroughness

Playing safe—Evading situations that may reflect unfavorably on oneself

Justifying—Providing accounts that lessen one's responsibility for an event or apologies acknowledging at least partial responsibility for an event and including some expression of remorse

Scapegoating—Assigning blame for a negative outcome to someone or something that is not entirely (or not at all) blameworthy

Misrepresenting—Manipulating information about one's intentions, action, knowledge, performance, and so forth

Escalating Commitment—"Throwing good money after bad" in an attempt to recoup losses and vindicate the initial decision

To Avoid Change

Resisting change—A catch-all for a variety of behaviors, including some of the above behaviors such as overconforming, stalling, playing safe, and misrepresenting, when they are used to avoid change

Protecting turf—Defending the task domain against the encroachment of others in order to protect one's prestige and power

---

Source: Adapted from B. E. Ashforth and R. T. Lee, "Defensive Behavior in Organizations: A Preliminary Model," *Human Relations,* 1990, *43*, pp. 621–648.

how his coworkers reacted to the repetition and boredom of their jobs and to the total lack of freedom associated with being closely controlled by supervisors. Here is his description of the workers' impression management techniques:

> *The most effective of these worker tactics combine the acts of looking busy and disappearing into one process. When a worker is on foot and being observed, this procedure requires appearing busy and active, even preoccupied and harassed, and then managing to drop out of the supervisor's sight, either by going into the distance or by disappearing behind obstacles, such as machinery. The idea is to look intense and involved to the point that one can't be bothered with more work or with silly questions and conversation. . . . These ploys will not necessarily fool all experienced supervisors but, by disappearing, the worker can hope that something else will distract the supervisor's attention.*[74]

FIGURE 9-9
Verbal Self-Presentational Behaviors

Behavior	Definition	Example
Self-Descriptions	Statements describing oneself.	A job applicant tells a recruiter, "I'm a real go-getter. I tend to be a bit aggressive, but I always get results."
Organization Descriptions	Statements about the organization to which one belongs.	An acquaintance says, "I work for the best-respected firm in the industry."
Opinion Conformity	Expressions of agreement with the opinions of a target audience in order to gain audience approval	A manager says to his boss, "You're absolutely right. Government regulation is stifling industrial growth. I couldn't agree with you more."
Accounts	Explanations of a predicament-causing event that are designed to minimize the apparent severity of the predicament. Accounts may involve excuses, defenses of innocence, or justifications.	A worker complains to a supervisor, "I don't know what happened to the hydraulic press. I've kept up with maintenance, but it's not working correctly. It must have been defective."
Apologies	Admissions of blameworthiness for an undesirable event that are coupled with an attempt to obtain a pardon from the audience	A broker tells a client, "I'm sorry I'm late for our appointment. I'm almost always on time, but today's been an unusually hectic day. Please forgive me."
Acclaiming	Expressions of favorable events that are designed to maximize the desirable implications for the speaker.	A salesman informs a peer, "The sales in our division have nearly doubled since I was hired."
Other Enhancement	Efforts to increase one's attractiveness to an audience through the use of favorable evaluations of the target's attributes.	A junior executive tells a superior, "I really admire your style of management. You're decisive, fair, and opportunistic. It's a pleasure to work with you."
Rendering Favors	Doing something nice for a target audience in order to gain the target's approval.	A salesman informs a prospective client over lunch, "This is my treat. Order anything you like. Consider it a token of our esteem for your firm."

Source: Gardner and Martinko, p. 332.

For better or worse, evidence indicates that impression management works. For example, one study showed that those who engaged in impression management techniques, including other-enhancement, favorable self-descriptions, opinion conformity, and rendering favors, were given higher performance ratings than those who did not. Also, those who engaged in impression management had more supportive, positive communications with their supervisors than did others.[75] In addition, it has been shown that subordinates' engagement in various self-enhancing and other-enhancing impression management tactics with their superiors was related to greater liking by the superior, which in turn was related to more positive exchanges between the superior and subordinate.[76] Liking and the quality of the exchange relationship are often related to positive consequences for subordinates, such as greater influence in decisions and more supervisor support and guidance. Taken together, these findings show that impression management can have important consequences.

Skills Practice 9-5 will give you some practice in applying the impression management strategies discussed in the chapter to management situations.

POLITICAL GAMES

Our discussion of politics may suggest the picture of one or two political actors calmly choosing from among alternative strategies and tactics. In fact, politics often is going on all over the place in organizations. Henry Mintzberg has suggested that organizational politics is a "collection of goings on, a set of 'games' taking place . . . a kind of three ring circus."[77] He has identified four types of these games, as shown in Figure 9-10.[78]

It's clear that these games differ in many ways, such as their actors and purposes and their consequences for the organization. Also, some of the games, such as sponsorship games and whistle-blowing games, may be consistent with goals of the organizations; others, such as insurgency games and Young Turks games, may not. Further, some of the games appear to be more ethical than others. This is the issue to which we turn next.

Skills Practice 9-6 deals with an interesting way of looking at organizational politics—as a circus. It will also help you to understand how metaphors can be useful in conceptualizing organizational phenomena such as political behavior.

THE ETHICS OF ORGANIZATIONAL POLITICS

We began this section by saying it is hard to decide whether something is a political behavior and that the labeling of the behavior sometimes implies whether it is

FIGURE 9-10
Political Games

Game	Typical Players	Purpose
Authority Games		
Insurgency Game	Lower-level participants	To resist authority
Counterinsurgency Game	Upper-level managers	To fight back against resistance to formal authority
Power Base Games		
Sponsorship Game	Subordinate employees	To enhance power base by using superiors as sponsors
Alliance-Building Game	Peers—often line managers	To enhance power base by using peers to build alliances
Empire-Building Game	Line managers	To enhance power base by using subordinates to build empire
Rivalry Games		
Line vs. Staff Game	Line managers and staff personnel	To defeat each other in the quest for power
Rival Camps Game	Any groups at the same level	To defeat each other in the quest for power
Change Games		
Whistle-Blowing Game	Usually lower-level participant	To correct questionable or illegal behavior
Young Turks Game	Upper-level managers close to but not at center of power	To throw legitimate power into question, perhaps even overthrow it, and institute major power shift

unethical. It's not surprising, then, that people disagree so much over the ethics of political behavior in general and of specific political tactics in particular. To some extent, so-called dirty politics is like someone's definition of pornography: "I know it when I see it." And some behaviors—such as lying to or cheating others—would be labeled as unethical by almost anyone. Still, it would be helpful to have some guidelines we could apply to ask whether particular political behaviors are ethical. One set of such guidelines is presented in Figure 9-11.[79] According to those guidelines, an act must satisfy three conditions to be ethical. First, the act must improve the **welfare** of various parties involved rather than just favor narrow interests. Second, the act must respect the **rights** of all those involved, such as the rights of due process, free speech, and privacy. Finally, the act must be **just**. For instance, the act is unjust if it involves unequal treatment of individuals or inconsistent administration of rules. If any of these conditions are not satisfied, the act is unethical.[80]

These are useful guidelines, although they may be hard to apply. For instance, we may honestly believe an action considers everyone's interests, but others may see things very differently. Perhaps the best we can do is to try to ask and answer these questions consciously and honestly when considering our own actions—and we would do well to remember that self-serving biases and other perceptual errors may color our answers.

FIGURE 9-11
Asking Whether a Political Act Is Ethical

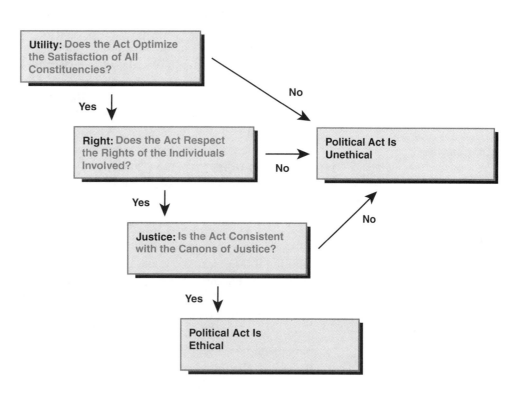

COSTS AND BENEFITS OF ORGANIZATIONAL POLITICS

In view of all that has been said, we could easily make the case we should just try to get rid of organizational politics. For instance, Henry Mintzberg has stated,

Politics is divisive and costly; it burns up energies that could go into operations. It can also lead to all kinds of aberrations. Politics is often used to sustain outmoded systems of power, and sometimes to introduce new ones that are not justified. Politics can also paralyze an organization to the point where its effective functioning comes to a halt and nobody benefits. The purpose of an organization, after all, is to produce goods and services, not to provide an arena in which people can fight with one another.[81]

Politics often does lead to such negative outcomes. For instance, it has been shown that political behaviors among managers are related to reduced interpersonal trust and enhanced feelings of alienation.[82] Also, perceptions of politics are related to reduced job satisfaction and increased job anxiety, stress levels, aggressive behavior, and intent to leave the firm.[83] Some evidence indicates that reactions to politics varies by culture. For example, one study found that reactions to organizational politics were stronger—in terms of higher intentions to leave the firm and lower levels of satisfaction and loyalty—for British employees than for Israelis.[84]

Nevertheless, before we address ways in which to get rid of political activity, we should recognize it may have some benefits. For example, Henry Mintzberg argues that political activity may:[85]

> Act in a Darwinian way to ensure that the strongest members of an organization are brought into positions of leadership.
> Ensure that all sides of an issue are fully debated. Politics encourages a variety of voices to be heard on any issue, and each voice is forced to justify its conclusions in terms of the broader good.
> Stimulate necessary change blocked by those currently in power. Because internal change is often blocked by the legitimate systems of influence, political power may be needed to bring it about.
> Ease the path for the execution of decisions. Managers may use politics to persuade, negotiate, and build alliances to smooth the path for the decisions they wish to make.

MINIMIZING POLITICAL ACTIVITY

Whatever you think of these potential benefits, you'll probably find yourself in situations in which you will want to minimize political activity. Here are some guidelines that follow from our discussion:

> **Don't close your eyes to politics.** Politics is important and pervasive; ignoring it doesn't make it less real. Think about the strategies and tactics we have discussed and ask whether, why, and by whom they are being used.
> **Challenge political behaviors.** We said in our discussion of learning theory in Chapter 4 that failure to respond to behaviors may be reinforcing. If we see behaviors we think are inappropriate, we should deal with them. If we have been rewarding them without meaning to, we should stop doing so. If it seems that employees believe only political behaviors can meet their objectives, we should try to help them find other, more legitimate ways to

reach their goals. If we ask employees to stop certain behaviors and they don't, we may have to use punishment; this, though, should be our last resort.

> **Reduce ambiguity.** Uncertainty fosters politics, so it follows that clarifying goals, minimizing unnecessary change, making decision processes clear, or otherwise minimizing ambiguity may discourage political activity.[86]

> **Make things visible.** Politics thrives in darkness, like mushrooms—and may have similar nutrients. So bringing activities out into the open may make some people more reluctant to play politics. Open meetings, published minutes of meetings, and public votes may all help. The key is to ensure that political activity can't be hidden.

> **Walk the talk.** If you argue against political behaviors but use them yourself, you're going to lose credibility. Instead, subordinates will assume that, whatever the talk, there are actually counternorms favoring politics.

> **Recognize that others may interpret your behaviors as political, even if you really weren't being political.** This reinforces the need for openness. Keep your actions visible and clearly explain them.

> **Reduce your own and others' vulnerability to political behavior.** People are often helpless in the face of political behavior because they lack options. They can't challenge such behavior because they can't afford to lose their jobs or jeopardize their careers. This suggests we should try to minimize our own vulnerability. We can do this by keeping our options open, minimizing secrecy, and fostering a climate in which politics is neither ignored nor rewarded.

BOTTOM LINE

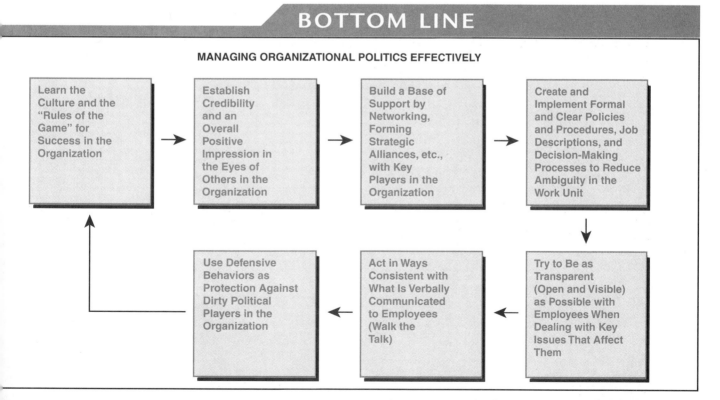

MANAGING ORGANIZATIONAL POLITICS EFFECTIVELY

Learn the Culture and the "Rules of the Game" for Success in the Organization →

Establish Credibility and an Overall Positive Impression in the Eyes of Others in the Organization →

Build a Base of Support by Networking, Forming Strategic Alliances, etc., with Key Players in the Organization →

Create and Implement Formal and Clear Policies and Procedures, Job Descriptions, and Decision-Making Processes to Reduce Ambiguity in the Work Unit

Use Defensive Behaviors as Protection Against Dirty Political Players in the Organization ←

Act in Ways Consistent with What Is Verbally Communicated to Employees (Walk the Talk) ←

Try to Be as Transparent (Open and Visible) as Possible with Employees When Dealing with Key Issues That Affect Them

We should also do all we can to ensure that others have ways to voice their concerns about politics without fear of reprisal and they are not placed in situations in which they have no choice but to submit to political pressures.

Skills Practice 9-7 gives you an opportunity to develop skill in analyzing situations involving political factors and developing strategies for reducing their influence on organizational effectiveness. The process model presented in the Bottom Line feature summarizes the basic steps associated with the general process of managing organizational politics effectively.

This chapter has presented some challenging topics. Power, social influence, and politics are inherently controversial and ambiguous. They are often employed in situations where it is unclear how an act may affect the various parties it touches, whether it is really well intentioned or manipulative, how others will view it, and whether its short-term impact may yield unforeseen long-term consequences. We've seen, as well, that power, social influence, and politics may be employed in ethical or unethical ways and may lead to everything from oppression to empowerment. Whatever the complexity of these issues, unquestionably you'll have to deal with them in the modern workplace. We hope the skills exercises and other content in this chapter will better arm you to face such difficult situations successfully.

TOP TEN LIST: KEY POINTS TO REMEMBER

MANAGING POWER, SOCIAL INFLUENCE, AND POLITICS

10. Recognize that power is latent, perceived, and relative.

9. Remember that power, influence, authority, and control are different things.

8. Focus more on developing and maintaining referent, expert, and reward bases of power rather than on the more traditional legitimate and coercive power bases.

7. Empower employees by removing conditions leading to powerlessness, using managerial strategies and techniques such as participative management, and taking steps to provide self-efficacy information.

6. Remember that empowering may actually enhance the power of a manager in many cases. Power is not a fixed pie.

5. Ensure that employees possess the job-specific knowledge, skills, and abilities as well as the maturity to benefit from an empowerment program.

4. Recognize that politics is a reality of organizations. The key is to manage it effectively.

3. Be sensitive to how your behavior influences others' impressions of you.

2. Consider the ethics of your political behavior by applying the utility, right, and justice tests.

1. Be proactive in taking actions to reduce political activity in your work unit or organization.

QUESTIONS FOR REVIEW AND REFLECTION

REVIEW QUESTIONS

1. Define authority, power, influence, and control.
2. Identify five characteristics of power.
3. Cite three general uses of power.
4. Distinguish among coercive power, utilitarian power, and normative power.
5. Define five interpersonal power bases.
6. Discuss the resource dependence approach and strategic contingencies approach to subunit power.
7. Identify five social influence approaches.
8. Do managers believe successful executives must be good politicians? Do they feel politics helps the organization function effectively?
9. What are four individual determinants of organizational politics? What are four organizational determinants of organizational politics?
10. Discuss three organizational values that may cause unethical political activity.

11. Identify at least five norms and their corresponding counternorms.
12. Discuss three general strategies for the effective use of power for one's own purposes.
13. Discuss six political tactics that may be used to carry out the general political strategies.
14. Identify defensive behaviors used to avoid action, avoid blame, and avoid change.
15. Describe at least five verbal self-presentational behaviors.
16. Discuss four types of political games, including their typical players and purposes.
17. What are three guidelines for determining whether a political act is ethical?
18. Discuss costs and benefits of organizational politics.
19. State seven guidelines for minimizing political activity.

CRITICAL THINKING QUESTIONS

1. A colleague says to you, "I would never use coercive power, period." How would you respond?
2. Consider the various forms of emotional appeals discussed in this chapter (that is, friendly emotions, negative or unpleasant emotions, and emotional contrast). Give one example of how each of these might be used ethically and one example of how each might be used unethically.

3. Pactiv Advanced Packaging Solutions (formerly Tenneco Packaging) is a world leader in packaging and automotive parts. Its credo is "Management with no fear, egos, or politics." Do you think this credo is feasible? Is it desirable? Defend your position.

4. Suppose you have a good test that could be used to determine which job candidates were likely to be Machiavellian. Would you use the measure as part of your selection process? Why or why not? If you would use the measure, what would you do with the information it provides?

5. As an employee of a management consulting firm, you have been assigned to a project involving a major corporation concerned about destructively high levels of political activity. After conducting interviews and focus groups with managers and other employees of the corporation, you have determined that a set of counternorms is in place. Those counternorms, which encourage secrecy, avoiding responsibility, and placing blame on others, are apparently widespread in the organization rather than being isolated in one or two units. What steps might you take to provide guidance to management on dealing with the counternorms?

6. After a serious disagreement about proposed changes in the company's pay systems, your boss announced in a meeting, "I've decided to call in an outside expert to get some objective advice on how we should proceed." What would you say or do in response to this announcement?

EXPERIENTIAL EXERCISES

WEB EXERCISE 9-1

Go to the Web site of the Leader to Leader Institute (formerly the Drucker Foundation) at **http://www.pfdf.org/leaderbooks/**. You will see a search box. Conduct searches on one or more terms from this chapter, such as *power*, *influence*, or *politics*. For instance, if you type *power* you will be given links to more than 200 articles or other materials relating to power. Select any two of the articles. For each article, write a one-page executive summary:

1. State the topic of the article and why that topic is important.
2. Summarize the author's key arguments.
3. Indicate what you see as the key management implications of the article.

WEB EXERCISE 9-2

Select one of the five individuals who topped *Fortune*'s 2003 "25 Most Powerful" list (or anyone else on the list), discussed at the beginning of the chapter. Do a search using Google or another Internet search engine to learn more about the individual and the ways he or she acquires and uses power. Try searches such as combining Buffett with "power or influence." This search, for example, yielded more than 6,400 hits in September 2003. Using *at least four* distinct Web sites, write a three- to five-page essay describing the bases of power employed by the individual. Include any other power-related information you feel is important, such as whether you believe the person employs various political strategies and tactics and whether he or she is ethical when using power.

CASE 9-1

EMPLOYEE EMPOWERMENT AT T.G.I. FRIDAY'S RESTAURANT

The Company

T.G.I. Friday's, a casual dining chain, opened its first location in New York City in 1965. The tremendous success of this first restaurant resulted in a long period of growth and expansion. As of July 2003, there were 723 T.G.I. Fridays located in 56 countries around the world.

The credo of T.G.I. Fridays is, "To treat every customer as an honored guest in our home." The company realizes this through a strong commitment to superior customer service in everything that it does. Customers tend to range in age from 21-49, with some college or a college degree, and a median annual income of $45,000-50,000.[87]

The restaurant has established itself as a leader in the industry through its unsurpassed selection of menu items served in a lively dining environment with entertaining and friendly bartenders and servers. Innovation has been a core value at T.G.I. Fridays through its unique atmosphere, and food and beverage presentation. It helped to popularize items such as the sports grill concept, potato skins, and frozen drinks.

T.G.I. Fridays has won numerous awards in the restaurant industry including the following:

- "Top 10 in Best Cheap Eats" (Miami/South Beach)
- "Top 10 Best After Work Bar" (Los Angeles)
- "Best Late Night Dining and Best Appetizers" (Las Vegas)
- "Best After Work Hangout" (Buffalo)
- "Top 3 in Best Happy Hours" (San Diego)
- "Employer of Choice" (Restaurant Business Magazine)

T.G.I. Fridays is owned by Carlson Restaurants Worldwide Inc., a global restaurant company based in Dallas, Texas. Carlson Restaurants is composed of three divisions: T.G.I. Fridays U.S.A., T.G.I. Friday's International, and Pick-Up Stix (a restaurant in the "fast-casual" segment of the market). The Carlson Credo is:[88]

> Whatever you do, do with INTEGRITY.
> Wherever you go, go as a LEADER.
> Whomever you serve, serve with CARING.
> Whenever you dream, dream with your ALL.
> And never, ever give up.

The Situation—Empowering Employees

T.G.I. Fridays creates an environment in which employees have opportunities to grow personally and professionally and to experience the gratification associated with success and excellence. Specifically, employees are empowered to do what is necessary and appropriate to bring about positive change to support the T.G.I. Friday's credo, to increase public awareness about the company, to improve its image, and to provide customers with incentives to continue returning to T.G.I. Fridays.

T.G.I. Fridays supports the empowerment of its employees by doing the following:[89]

- Each restaurant has a standardized décor and layout and has set times by which starters and main courses must reach the diner. The standardization is balanced with the provision of an extensive menu and opportu-

nities for the customer to choose combinations of items not listed on the menu.

- Staff must determine the "type" (e.g., the ones to leave alone, the ones to joke around with) of diner they serve and adjust their behavior accordingly. This helps employees to embrace the T.G.I. Friday value system and to feel a sense of ownership of this way of thinking and doing business.
- Staff are empowered to deal with customer complaints and even to take orders for food that is not on the menu. They can even offer some "give-aways" to customers when they feel it is necessary.
- Daily team meetings are held in which quality issues are discussed and important information is shared between staff members. This helps to build team spirit.
- The company uses a rigorous recruitment process in which prospective employees go through 3 or 4 intense interviews, role-playing exercises, and personality testing before being hired.
- New employees are thoroughly trained by experienced staff before starting the job.
- The top performing employees in a quarter are given responsibility for creating staff schedules. This gives each employee an incentive to become more efficient and it helps staff to better match schedules with individual preferences.

Results

The results of the employee empowerment program at T.G.I. Fridays have been mixed so far. On the positive side, the more experienced employees feel that they can act out spontaneously with customers (e.g., joking around, doing little things to make a customer's experience more positive) without having to wait for an authorization or intervention from a manager. However, they also complained that management itself was not empowered enough to solve various operational problems in the restaurants such as getting nonfunctioning equipment replaced (e.g., fryers). This problem was due to the bureaucracy in the larger T.G.I. Fridays corporate structure and system and the need for restaurant managers to obtain many authorizations before new equipment could be obtained at a given location.

Discussion Questions

1. Evaluate the empowerment program used at T.G.I. Fridays. What were its strengths? What were its weaknesses?
2. If you were hired as a consultant to conduct a formal evaluation of the empowerment program at T.G.I. Fridays, how would you proceed?

3. Based on the information in this case, what short-term recommendations would you make to management at T.G.I. Fridays regarding what it needs to do to enhance the effectiveness of the empowerment program? What actions would you take to maximize the likelihood that your recommendations were implemented?

4. Based on the information in this case, what long—term recommendations would you make to management at T.G.I. Fridays regarding what it needs to do to enhance the effectiveness of the empowerment program? What actions would you take to maximize the likelihood that your recommendations were implemented?

5. What are the practical implications of this case for you as a future manager in a real world organization?

CASE 9-2

MICROSOFT'S XBOX VIDEO GAME CONSOLE IN JAPAN

The Company

Microsoft is the world's leading software company, started by Bill Gates in 1975. The mission of the company is to enable people and businesses throughout the world to realize their full potential. The core values that support this mission include the following:[90]

Broad Customer Connection

Connecting with customers, understanding their needs and how they use technology, and providing valuable information and support to help them realize their potential.

A Global, Inclusive Approach

Thinking and acting globally, enabling a diverse workforce that generates innovative decision making for a spectrum of customers and partners, innovating to lower the costs of technology, and showing leadership in the communities in which we work and live.

Excellence

In everything that we do.

Trustworthy Computing

Deepening customer trust through the quality of our products and services, our responsiveness and accountability, and our predictability in everything that we do.

Great People with Great Values

Delivering on our mission requires great people who are bright, creative, energetic, and who share the following values:

- Integrity and honesty
- Passion for customers, partners, and technology
- Open and respectful with others and dedicated to making them better
- Willingness to take on big challenges and to see through them
- Self-critical, questioning, and committed to personal excellence and self-improvement
- Accountable for commitments, results, and quality to customers, shareholders, partners, and employees

Innovative and Responsible Platform Leadership

Expanding platform innovation, benefits, and opportunities for customers and partners; openness in discussing our future directions; getting feedback; and working with others to ensure that their products and our platforms work well together.

Enabling People to Do New Things

Broadening choices for customers by identifying new areas of business; incubating new products integrating new customer scenarios into existing businesses; exploiting acquisitions of key talent and experience; and integrating more deeply with new and existing partners.

As of 2003, Microsoft employed 55,000 people based on sales of over $32 billion and net income of over $9.9 billion.

The Situation—Development of Xbox

An internal review in the late 1990s conducted by Microsoft concluded that it had a huge opportunity to control the "living room of the future" but that Sony, the Japanese consumer electronics giant, was a major threat to achieving this objective. In addition, growth of PC sales was slowing while video game sales were skyrocketing. This led to a decision in 1999 for Microsoft to move from its traditional focus on software and get into the video game console business with a high-powered, cutting-edge machine called Xbox. The long-term objective of Xbox was to become the number-one selling video game console in the industry. In order to achieve this objective, Xbox was packed with a graphics processor, memory, and processing speed that far exceeded the two video game consoles against which it competed, the Sony Playstation 2 and the Nintendo Gamecube. Xbox included a hard drive for saving game information, DVD playback capabilities, a broadband-ready connection for online game play, and support for HDTV-quality (high-definition TV) game playback.

Microsoft partnered with leading computer hardware companies to develop the various components that would go into Xbox. For example, it worked with NVidia, a world leader in graphics processors and media communication devices, to manufacture the graphics processor unit for Xbox and Intel, the world's leading manufacturer of semiconductor memory products, to develop a Pentium III chip that provided the processing power behind Xbox. On the game side of the business, Xbox team worked with the company's Microsoft Games Studios as well as numerous third-party developers to create games that would take advantage of Xbox's superior technical capabilities.

Launch of Xbox

Xbox officially launched in the United States on November 15, 2001 in time for the holiday season. The initial portfolio of Xbox games included a racing game called Project Gotham Racing, a first-person shooter called Halo, and a football game called NFL Fever, all developed in partnership with Microsoft Game Studios. Xbox was well received by customers. It sold nearly 1.5 million units between its launch and the end of that holiday season. The launch was relatively smooth with the biggest challenge being the need to increase production to meet strong demand for the console.

Despite all of the critics who believed Microsoft had no chance of establishing Xbox as a viable competitor to the Playstation 2 and Game Cube, the early results in terms of sales were encouraging. However, Xbox team understood that the long-term success of their game console depended on technical superiority, but on the quantity and quality of games.

Xbox in Japan

One of the greatest challenges facing Xbox was to establish itself in the highly competitive Japanese video game market, the second largest in the world and home to many of the world's most innovative video game development companies including Sega, Konami, and Tecmo. In addition, it was the home turf of Sony and Nintendo. In order for Xbox to be successful in the long run, it had to do well in Japan so local game developers would be willing to support it.

The head of the Xbox Division in Japan was Pat Ohura, who joined Microsoft in 1986 and helped establish Microsoft Word as the dominant word processing program in Japan. However, Ohura had mixed feelings about accepting the position as head of the Xbox unit in Japan because many advised him the project was "too risky." On top of this, Ohura admitted he did not know much about the video game industry. He assembled a team of 180 employees composed of people recruited from Sony, Nintendo, game maker Square, and other top game developers to provide the foundation for Xbox Japan.

As plans for the Xbox launch moved forward, Ohura learned quickly that many Japanese game developers were skeptical about Microsoft and its plans to enter the video game business. In particular, many of them simply believed Microsoft was not truly committed to the video game business and that it lacked the discipline, patience, and passion for games needed to be a serious player in the industry. Some other developers said they were not willing to create games for Xbox because Microsoft was not a Japanese company. Others resisted because they feared Microsoft might take control of too much of their business. Finally, some were not interested simply because they disliked Microsoft and viewed it as a bully.

Microsoft's Strategy for Building the Credibility of Xbox in Japan[91]

Ohura tried to demonstrate to Microsoft's commitment to the video game business by setting up meetings between executives of Japanese game developers and Microsoft CEO Bill Gates in Tokyo. Although Gates discussed the technical aspects of Xbox, the Japanese executives were not impressed by him because they believed he knew little about the video game business.

Seamus Blackley, one of the architects of Xbox, also started flying to Tokyo every month to meet with Japanese game developers. He immersed himself in the game developer culture by partying with them until late at nightclubs and strip clubs. This helped Blackley to bond with them and to build their trust in him and Xbox. On another occasion, Japanese executives from Capcom, a major game developer, visited Microsoft's headquarters in Seattle. Some wild late-night drinking and partying between Microsoft and Capcom executives resulted in Capcom's decision to put the game "Onimusha" on Xbox.

Meanwhile, Ohura sacrificed weekends with his daughters to play more golf with game executives, He met with executives at game developers Tecmo and Square, pleading with them to put their games on Xbox. Ohura had to state he would "sacrifice his life" for Tecmo's Dead or Alive fighting game before the company's president agreed to bring the game to Xbox.

Initial Results in Japan

Xbox launched in Japan in February 2002. Initial sales were very disappointing with less than 200,000 units sold during the first weeks on the market. Some Japanese consumers were turned off by the size of the Xbox unit and the controller was too large for the hands of many Japanese children and adults. Some early quality problems with Xbox units caused scratches on game disks that damaged the console's image. Many Japanese consumers were also intensely loyal to their Playstation 2s and Game Cubes. However, arguably the most significant problem with Xbox in Japan was it lacked a portfolio of games that appealed to Japanese game players. The strength of the Xbox game portfolio was first-person shooters; many Japanese preferred role-playing games instead.

Recent Developments

In the fall of 2002, Microsoft announced that it was transferring Pat Ohura to the company's headquarters in Seattle where he would become part of Xbox's management team. Part of his role was to help Microsoft's American executives to understand the differences between the gaming markets in the United States and Japan.

In September 2003, Microsoft announced it had hired Yoshihiro Maruyama, the former chief operating officer of the U.S. unit of game maker Square, to head the Xbox division in Japan. Maruyama, a veteran in the gaming industry, was responsible for raising Square's U.S. revenue significantly. Microsoft is hopeful that he will be successful in improving relations with Japanese game developers and convincing more of them to create games for Xbox.

Discussion Questions

1. Why is Xbox experiencing problems in Japan?
2. Evaluate Microsoft's strategies for building credibility with Japanese game developers. In what ways was it effective? In what ways was it ineffective?
3. If you were hired as a consultant by Microsoft to help it address the issues raised in this case, what short-term recommendations would you make to management? What would you do to increase the likelihood that your recommendations actually get implemented?
4. If you were hired as a consultant by Microsoft to help them address the issues raised in this case, what long-term recommendations would you make to management? What would you do to increase the likelihood your recommendations actually get implemented?
5. What are the practical implications of this case for you as a future manager in the real world?

VIDEO CASE: LE MERIDIEN HOTEL

MANAGING POWER, SOCIAL INFLUENCE, AND POLITICS

Running Time: 16:25

Le Meridien Hotel, Boston

This video shows a day in the life of Le Meridien Hotel, Boston, focusing on the activities of the room services manager, Michiel Lugt, and the assistant general manager (resident manager), Bob van den Oord, including interactions with Glory Hippolite, executive housekeeper, and James Abaka, director of security. After viewing the video, answer the following questions:

1. What are some factors at Le Meridien (such as the nature of the work force, the unique demands of a hotel operation, and the hotel's ownership structure) that provide special challenges for management?
2. Which power bases seemed to be employed by Lugt and van den Oord? Which power bases were not apparent?
3. What social influence tactics were evident during the interactions with other managers?
4. What signs of power were displayed by Lugt and van den Oord? Did these managers take any steps to downplay power differentials?
5. Would you describe any of the behaviors displayed by Lugt and van den Oord as political? Why or why not?

http://www.lemeridienboston.com/

SKILLS PRACTICE

Developing an Effective Power Base

Skill Objective

To develop skill in analyzing a work situation and identifying specific strategies for enhancing one's managerial power base.

Procedure

Download the worksheet that was developed for this exercise from the text Web site.

1. Read the case that follows.
2. Assume you were the supervisor in the case, and develop a set of strategies for enhancing your overall power base.
3. Discuss your recommendations with a classmate or present them to the class.
4. Identify and discuss the practical implications of this case for you as a future manager or supervisor.

Case: Power and the Green Supervisor*

You are a 22-year-old recent graduate of a major university on the West Coast. You have just been hired as a project supervisor in an advertising firm. Your job is to lead a staff of 12 somewhat rebellious advertising specialists and support staff in creating new advertising campaigns for your firm's clients.

The ages of your staff range from 25 to 40 years.

These people have been with the firm for anywhere from 3 to 15 years. They've had no formal training in the development of advertising campaigns, but they do have 1 to 5 years of relevant advertising experience with the firm. Typically, the firm has followed a "promotion from within" policy, in which current employees are given preference over external candidates in filling position openings. However, the strength of your advertising training at the university, along with an advertising internship you completed while in school, impressed management at the firm so much, they offered you the job.

Your boss has arranged an initial meeting for you and your new staff. You walk into the room in which your staff has been chatting while waiting for you. Suddenly there is dead silence. Five pairs of eyes are now fixed on you. You know (1) it is critical to start off on the right foot (avoiding a negative first impression), and (2) you need to establish your credibility as their boss.

How would you begin to build a power base in relation to your staff?

*This case is based on the actual experiences of recent college graduates who have assumed supervisory positions.

SKILLS PRACTICE

Empowering Employees

Skill Objective

To develop skill in empowering employees in order to enhance their job satisfaction, work motivation, and job performance.

Procedure

Download the worksheet that was developed for this exercise from the text Web site.

1. This exercise may be done individually or in groups of three to five students.
2. Select a scenario from below on which to focus for this exercise.
3. Develop an action plan for empowering the employees in the scenario. Be specific and action oriented (i.e., indicate exactly what needs to be done).

4. Optional: Present the action plan to the class and defend it.
5. Discuss the questions that follow.

Discussion Questions

1. What are the general strengths and weaknesses of employee empowerment?
2. When is it most appropriate to use employee empowerment? When is it not appropriate?
3. What are the implications of this exercise for you as a future manager or supervisor?

Scenario 1: An Administrative Assistant

Beth Martin is the administrative assistant for Stacey Long, the director of human resources at the Marqwell Corporation. Beth's job is very routine but requires a tremendous amount of detail work (e.g., completing forms, typing letters and reports, answering the phone, filing, organizing, etc.). Unfortunately, Beth feels powerless in her job, because she is told everything must be done in a certain way. In addition, Beth must constantly get authorizations from Stacey before doing many things. Sometimes this creates inefficiencies when Stacey is out of the office or in meetings all day.

Beth is becoming increasingly dissatisfied with her job. She feels she can just "check her brain at the door" when she comes to work each day. What advice would you give to Stacey Long regarding strategies for empowering Beth?

Scenario 2: Sales Associates

Mike Anderson is the sales manager at Lord Foggington's Jewelry Store. Fifteen sales associates work for Mike. Their job duties include working with customers to identify their needs and to develop a variety of product options for satisfying these needs. Given that Lord Foggington's is in the business of selling jewelry, many customers come into the store wanting to negotiate or barter the best price possible for a given piece of jewelry. One problem with this is that the sales associates do not have the authority to negotiate prices with customers. Only Mike can authorize a price reduction from the official price on the tag attached to a given item.

Another problem is that the sales associates deal only with the sales process itself. After a purchase has been made, customers deal with the customer service department in getting jewelry repaired or cleaned. Sales associates feel this robs them of the opportunity to develop the long-term relationship with customers needed for repeat purchases and loyalty. What advice would you give Mike Anderson regarding strategies for empowering the sales associates?

SKILLS PRACTICE

9-3   *Skill Level: BASIC*

Fieldwork: Organizational Politics in the Real World

Skill Objective

To develop skill in analyzing political factors as they exist in actual organizational situations.

Procedure

Download the worksheet that was developed for this exercise from the text Web site.

1. Interview someone you know who is working in a managerial position. In your interview, be sure to ask the following questions:
   a. What is the most challenging political issue you have had to deal with on your job? How did you handle it, and what was the outcome?
   b. What is the biggest political mistake you or someone you know has made in your organization? Why was this such a serious mistake?
   c. Describe the person who you feel is the most effective at managing political issues in your organization. What is it about this person that makes him or her so skilled at organizational politics?
   d. What advice would you give to students about how to handle organizational politics when they start their first jobs in organizations after graduation?

2. Optional: Present a summary of your findings to the class.

3. Answer the following discussion questions.

Discussion Questions

1. Discuss the things you feel are associated with effective political players in organizations.
2. Discuss the things you feel are associated with ineffective political players in organizations.
3. What are the practical implications of this exercise for you as a future manager in a real-world organization?

SKILLS PRACTICE

Skill Level: CHALLENGING

Applying Political Strategies and Tactics

Skill Objective

To develop skill in formulating and implementing action plans for using political strategies and tactics effectively.

Procedure

Download the worksheet that was developed for this exercise from the text Web site.

1. This exercise can be done individually or in groups of three to five students.
2. Read the following scenario regarding a situation involving organizational politics.

    You are the vice president of marketing at a major insurance company based in Chicago, Illinois. The company offers a full line of insurance products for home, auto, business, and personal coverage. The company has approximately 5,000 employees in its corporate offices and another 2,500 insurance agents who serve as independent contractors to the company.

    The firm's financial performance has been very strong in the last five years, in particular. Although this is very encouraging, a major concern you have is that the growth potential for the markets in which your company operates is fairly limited. Given this, the strategic emphasis of the company has shifted from seeking new customers to retaining current customers.

    One of the keys to retaining customers successfully is the relationship between the agent and the customer. Specifically, agents who are especially good at building and maintaining a relationship with their customers tend to have much higher customer retention rates.

    On the basis of this situation, you would like to conduct a study of the service practices of agents to identify which service practices tend to be associ-

ated with higher customer retention. Although this sounds like a no-brainer in that the importance and value of the study would go unquestioned, you know you will encounter significant political hurdles if you pursue this study. For example, the agents are independent contractors (not employees), so they may resent the company checking up on them. The strained relationship between the company and the agent force in recent years will not help the situation either. In addition, the culture of the company tends to react very negatively to unfavorable results or information. This could also be a major problem in that some people may not see the need for the study and others don't want the study conducted because they are fearful of the results.

    Suppose you decided to move forward with your study of agent service practices despite concerns about the political ramifications. What actions could you take to manage the political factors associated with this scenario effectively?

3. Develop an action plan for applying political strategies and tactics effectively to this scenario. Be very systematic and specific in your recommendations.
4. Present your action plan to your class (optional).
5. Answer the discussion questions that follow.

Discussion Questions

1. Why is it important to manage political factors in organizations?
2. Evaluate your action plan. Why do you feel it would work? What are the barriers to its successful implementation? What could you do to overcome these barriers?
3. What are the practical implications of this exercise for you as a future manager in a real-world organization?

Skills Practice

Applying Impression Management Strategies

Skill Objective

To develop skill in applying impression management strategies in different types of organizational situations.

Procedure

Download the worksheet that was developed for this exercise from the text Web site.

1. This exercise can be done on an individual basis or in groups of three to five students.
2. Read the following organizational scenarios.

Scenario 1: Customer Rage at the Airport

You are the lead flight attendant for a major airline based in Chicago. It is the holiday season right now, and the number of air travelers is at an all-time high. At the worst time possible, your plane experiences a mechanical problem that will delay its departure for an unknown amount of time. You know the 300 passengers waiting impatiently at the gate will be absolutely furious when they hear the news.

What would you say to your customers in order to attempt to create a positive impression of you and your employer in handling this situation? Base your answer on the impression management techniques discussed in the chapter and be action oriented in terms of your recommendations.

Scenario 2: The New Employee

You are a brand-new employee working as merchandise trainee for a major retailer based in Cleveland. Although you graduated from an excellent university, majored in retail management, and earned a 3.9/4.0 GPA in school, you know this will not be enough for you to be successful in your real-world job.

As you start your new job, what kinds of strategies could you use to create and maintain a positive impression of yourself in the eyes of your boss and coworkers? Base your answer on the impression management techniques discussed in the chapter, and be action oriented in terms of your recommendations.

3. Identify actions that could be taken to implement impression management strategies effectively for each scenario. Be sure to base your action steps on the impression management strategies discussed in this chapter.
4. Answer the following discussion questions as a class.

Discussion Questions

1. Which strategies did you recommend for handling each scenario? Why do you feel they would be effective?
2. How would you respond to critics of impression management techniques who say they focus too much on appearance and image and not on the key issue of the real substance of what a person or company does?
3. What are the practical implications of this exercise for you as a future manager in a real-world organization?

Skills Practice

Politics as Circus

Skill Objective

To explore the metaphor of the organization as a circus.

Procedure

Download the worksheet that was developed for this exercise from the text Web site.

Henry Mintzberg compared organizational politics to a three-ring circus. Explore the metaphor of the organization as a circus. In particular, respond to each of the following questions.

1. What audiences is the circus trying to satisfy? How will it determine whether it has been successful?
2. What acts are playing in each of the three rings?
3. What mix of skills is needed in the circus?
4. Which acts require coordination?
5. What lions need to be tamed? What horses must be trained?
6. Who are the jugglers? The trapeze artists? The tightrope walkers? The animal trainers? The costume makers? The fire eaters?

7. Who are the clowns? Why are they clowning? Are they really happy?
8. Who wear masks? What are they covering up?

9. Who drives the circus train? Who cleans up after the elephants?
10. What acts are in the sideshow? Who is the shill?

SKILLS PRACTICE

9-7

Skill Level: CHALLENGING

Reducing Political Activity

Skill Objective

To develop skill in reducing the level of political activity in an organization.

Procedure

Download the worksheet that was developed for this exercise from the text Web site.

1. This exercise can be completed on an individual basis or in groups of three to five students.
2. Read the following scenario:

Management Development Specialists is a training firm that specializes in offering a variety of continuing education programs for business professionals in the areas of management, accounting, finance, and marketing. The company has been in existence for only two years, but it has quickly established itself as a high-quality provider of professional training services for many *Fortune* 500 clients.

The president of the company is Allison Warren, a training professional with a PhD in business administration and 20 years of corporate experience. Allison started the company on her own in 1997. As her customer base increased, the number of her employees has grown to over 25 training professionals.

Allison has a very informal but detail-oriented style of leading the company. She does not believe in creating structures and formalizing procedures because she feels these things will stifle the creativity of the organization. This approach is reflected in the lack of job descriptions, policies, and standard operating procedures in the company. Rather, employee responsibilities tend to blur together or overlap with each other in many cases. Oftentimes this creates confusion and frustration among employees and engenders conflict over who has ownership of certain tasks.

Allison tends to be very guarded in terms of sharing information with her employees regarding issues related to the company. In addition, she is involved in all significant decisions that affect the company. Because she uses her intuition (gut feeling) as a key driver of her decision-making process, this tends to promote a lot of competition and conflict among her employees who are fighting for her approval and financial support for their projects and programs. In many cases, the projects approved by Allison were not necessarily the best projects but rather the projects supported by the most skilled politicians in the company.

Recently, a growing number of employees have been complaining about the company's "hostile and back-stabbing culture." Employee morale has been declining, stress levels have increased dramatically, and many employees are talking about leaving the company if things don't change.

Using the general guidelines for reducing political activity discussed in the chapter, develop an action plan for Allison regarding the handling of this situation.

3. Discuss the following questions as a class.

Discussion Questions

1. What actions did you recommend that management take in order to reduce the level of political activity in the scenario? Why?
2. What barriers to success might exist in terms of implementing your recommendations?
3. Why is it problematic for a firm to have an excessively high level of political activity (i.e., what are the costs of political behavior in organizations)?
4. What are the practical implications of this exercise for you as a future manager in a real-world organization?

MANAGING CONFLICT

CHAPTER 10

Skills Objectives

> To apply the elements of the conflict process model to handle different types of conflict situations.

> To use various conflict-handling styles for dealing with different types of situations.

> To apply different types of strategies to resolve conflict situations.

> To apply strategies for generating productive conflict in organizations.

KNOWLEDGE OBJECTIVES

> Recognize the implications of a variety of conflict premises.

> Understand the causes and characteristics of organizational conflict.

> Discuss the elements of a conflict model.

> Identify conflict styles and the situations in which each is most appropriate.

> Discuss ways to resolve conflict.

> Specify ways to generate productive conflict.

Doug Williams was described by many of his workers at the Lockheed Martin plant in Meridian, Mississippi, as a ticking time bomb. He allegedly brimmed with rage, threatened coworkers, and made racist comments. In July 2003, he stormed out of work, got a shotgun and semiautomatic rifle from his pickup, and hunted down coworkers. When his rampage ended, Williams had killed five, injured nine more, and fatally shot himself in the chest. The trigger for his rage? He had been ordered to attend a course on ethics and sensitivity training.[1] Workplace homicide, the fastest growing type of homicide in the United States, is an extreme example of the 300,000 occurrences of workplace violence reported each year, with even more never documented.[2] Such violence is perhaps the most dramatic form of conflict at work, but employees are regularly dealing with conflict in some form. According to an American Management Association study, employees spend 25 percent of their time in some sort of dispute.[3]

Because managers are often the hub of organizational communications—in the middle of things—they must regularly deal with conflict. All organizations experience conflict. The way in which conflict is managed determines whether it is motivating or destructive. As we will see, conflict has many costs, but also many benefits. The challenge, then, is not to eliminate conflict but to manage conflict successfully.

In this chapter we examine organizational conflict, including its causes and characteristics. We see how conflict premises influence conflict processes and outcomes and discuss conflict management, including ways to resolve conflict and to generate productive conflict. To provide a foundation for reading the chapter, take a few minutes now to complete Self-Assessment 10-1, "Attitudes Toward Managing Conflict." After you are through, visit the text Web site to get feedback on the exercise.

SELF-ASSESSMENT 10-1

Attitudes Toward Managing Conflict

Answer the following questions regarding your attitudes toward managing conflict in organizations. Answer each question as honestly as possible using the following scale:

1 Disagree strongly
2 Disagree somewhat
3 Neither agree nor disagree
4 Agree somewhat
5 Agree strongly

____ 1. Too little conflict in an organization can be a problem rather than a strength.
____ 2. Compromising is always the best approach to use when dealing with conflict in organizations.
____ 3. Avoiding the conflict is always the least effective approach for handling conflict in organizations.
____ 4. It is never appropriate to resolve a conflict by only showing concern for achieving your objective.
____ 5. Conflict is always bad for an organization.
____ 6. There is one best approach for handling conflict in all situations.

_____ 7. Sometimes the best approach for handling conflict is to simply give in or accommodate the other individual in the conflict.

_____ 8. Conflict can sometimes be resolved by focusing on larger goals that all parties who are involved in the conflict have in common.

_____ 9. It is important to continue to manage the situation and the people who were involved in a conflict carefully after the conflict has been resolved.

_____ 10. The achievement of a win-win solution is always possible in a conflict situation.

As a way to introduce the material in this chapter and for you to assess your general conflict-handling skills, read the Pretest Skills Assessment and develop a plan for how you would handle the situation. After you are through, visit the text Web site to get feedback on the exercise.

Now complete Skills Practice 10-1. This exercise requires going out into the real world and interviewing managers about how they manage conflict, which should be an eye-opening experience for many of you. You may be surprised how challenging it is to handle this issue.

PRETEST SKILLS ASSESSMENT

Managing Conflict

Note: This exercise is based on actual events encountered by managers in real-world organizations. Some information may have been modified in order to maintain the anonymity of the people and organization involved in this situation.

You are the manager of a team of 12 financial analysts at a mutual fund company based on the East Coast. Your staff researches various companies and makes recommendations to fun managers to buy, hold, or sell various stocks in a given portfolio. You enjoy a good working relationship with all of your employees except for Joe McGraw. On the positive side, Joe is probably your best and brightest analyst. He possesses superior analytical skills and his drive and motivation are exceptional. However, Joe is also extremely abrasive and nearly impossible to work with on a team. He insists on doing things his way and he refuses to listen to anyone else's perspective on an issue. When you ask Joe to do something, he often decides unilaterally to do it in another way because he feels that he "knows best." Joe is a real "control freak" as well—he constantly sticks his nose into the work of his co-workers and tells them what to do and how to do it. He can be brutal in his criticism of his co-workers.

In the past, you have tried to accommodate Joe given that the overall quality of his work has been superior. However, now the situation has deteriorated to a point where you feel that something must be done to deal with Joe because many of your other employees have come to you to complain about him and some have threatened to quit if Joe's behavior does not change.

Develop an action plan for addressing the conflict in this situation. Be sure that your plan addresses both short-term and long-term issues. Be specific and be prepared to defend the feasibility and cost effectiveness of each element of your plan.

CONFLICT PREMISES

Conflict situations are generally emotion laden and, as such, they call for emotional intelligence. Here are some things to keep in mind as you think about and deal with conflict.

CONFLICT AND DISAGREEMENT ARE NORMAL IN HUMAN RELATIONSHIPS

Because of different life experiences, including upbringing, culture, education, and previous experience in relationships, people inevitably see the world in a variety of ways. Most of us think our view is the correct one because we interpret the world though our limited experience.

CONFLICT MAY BE GOOD

Conflict helps diagnose sources of problems and it motivates the search for new approaches. It provides an opportunity for people to recognize and value differences of opinion, open up their worldview, expand their perspective, and solve problems. It gives both parties the opportunity to learn, to improve, to practice tolerance, and to achieve satisfactory resolution of emotional tension that often hampers their creativity, productivity, trust, and communications both on and off the job.[4]

THE WAY CONFLICT IS FRAMED MAY INFLUENCE ITS NATURE AND OUTCOMES

Framing of conflict appears to vary along three dimensions, as follows:

> **Relationship/task.** First, do the parties to conflict focus on their relationships with the other party or on the task itself?

> **Emotional/intellectual.** Second, do the parties to conflict direct their attention to the emotional components of the dispute, such as hatred, anger, and jealousy, or to the actions that occur apart from those emotions?

> **Cooperate/win.** Finally, do the parties to conflict focus on maximizing joint outcomes or on maximizing their own gain, regardless of consequences for the other party?

Although it is hard to sort out fully how these perceptions influence outcomes, research provides some clues. For example, those parties adopting intellectual or relationship frames tend to be more satisfied with the conflict resolution process than those adopting task or emotional frames. Also, those parties adopting task or cooperation frames tend to attain higher personal and joint outcomes than those adopting a win-focused frame.[5] Thus our framing of the conflict situation is likely to affect satisfaction with the conflict process as well as conflict outcomes.[6]

A MUTUALLY ACCEPTABLE SOLUTION CAN OFTEN BE FOUND

If they can adopt an abundance mentality and communicate in an honest but considerate and respectful manner, people can often move from disagreement to compromise to collaboration.

CONFLICTING PARTIES CAN TAKE PERSONAL RESPONSIBILITY AND INITIATE COMMUNICATIONS

Consider the following:

> Your contribution to relationships is under your control; the part others choose to play is not under your control.

> When you change, your relationships change.

> Waiting for other persons or situations to change so you can change equals no change.
> The way you are treated by others depends partly on how you train them, as it were, to treat you.
> Risk taking is part of conflict management. You may be rejected.

TRUSTING BEHAVIOR CAN EVOKE TRUSTING BEHAVIOR.[7]

The principle of social reciprocity stipulates that you get back what you give to others: "What goes around, comes around." If you want others to trust you, listen to you, care for you, respect you, and the like, you must give these qualities first. You then stand a better chance of having them returned. You demonstrate trusting behavior by empowering others, being open to influence, taking some risks, and being willing to change when faced with new information. As Sitting Bull once said, "Offer your opponent the peace pipe first."

CONSENSUS AND SYNERGY ARE LIKELY ONLY WHEN PEOPLE CHOOSE TO COOPERATE RATHER THAN COMPETE

Sometimes, we must accommodate; other times, we must compete with all we have. Because of past experiences (often deprivations, rejections, and other painful emotional experiences), some people are compelled to compete, to win at all costs, even in personal relationships. When dealing with a battler on an unimportant issue, let the person win so you can gather social credits for later use. When dealing with a critical issue, as Sitting Bull continued, "Fight them with everything you have. And when it is over, let bygones be bygones."

SOME CONFLICTS ARE UNRESOLVABLE BECAUSE OF EMOTIONAL IMPAIRMENT

Most often, it is best to sidestep others' negativity, sarcasm, and malicious ridicule. Often people with low self-esteem ridicule others so they can feel better about themselves. Rather than taking such behavior personally, be assertive and honest regarding your convictions and your right to be treated with respect.

CAUSES OF CONFLICT

Some of the many potential causes of conflict are due to our perceptions, assumptions, and framing of conflict. Others, as we discuss next, are characteristics of the situation.

COMPETITION OVER SCARCE RESOURCES

The limit of resources in most organizations increases the potential for conflict. Individuals or units want to obtain the necessary money, facilities, personnel, and information to attain their goals. If resources appear scarce, efforts will be made to secure resources, often to the detriment of the goals of others. Inflating budgets, challenging the legitimacy of activities by others, and covert efforts to prevent budget cuts may all result from conflict over scarce resources.

AMBIGUITY OVER RESPONSIBILITY OR JURISDICTION

When it is not clear who is responsible for what, some things may not get done or there may be duplication of efforts.

TASK INTERDEPENDENCE

Task interdependence refers to the nature of the dependence among units for information or for financial, material, or human resources. The greater the interdependence among units, the greater the potential for conflict. There is substantial interdependence when units provide one another with inputs (this is called ***reciprocal interdependence***). For example, a legal department at a savings and loan may review borrowers' applications submitted to the loan department. After an application has been reviewed, it is sent back to the loan department so the request or denial of the loan can be processed. The output of the loan department becomes the input for the legal department, and the output of the legal department becomes the input of the loan department. That is, there is a two-way flow between departments.

Task interdependence is greatest in the case of team interdependence. ***Team interdependence*** exists when work is interactive or acted on jointly by members of different units rather than simply being transferred back and forth. Teamwork is the most important method of coordination in team interdependence.

GOAL INCOMPATIBILITY

Different individuals or units may have different, and perhaps incompatible, goals. Such differences may lead to conflict even when both parties agree on some overall goal for the organization. In the aftermath of a hijacking or bombing, for example, personnel responsible for airport security may institute more stringent and time-consuming procedures at security checkpoints. At the same time, personnel in the control tower are committed to the goal of maintaining takeoff and landing schedules. The delays caused by security may cause conflict between the two groups.

COMPETITIVE REWARD SYSTEMS

If individuals or units are given incentives that reward the attainment of the organizational goal, cooperation is likely to result. However, if the incentives are designed to reward those who attain their specific assigned goals without regard to coordination or the big picture, political behaviors are likely. For example, Ted Noble, vice president of sales at The Harter Group, an office furniture manufacturer, was offered a job by a fast-growing competitor. He would manage the New York region, another new hire would manage the Washington, D.C., region, and a third would manage a territory in Boston. The person with the most sales at the end of a designated period would become head of the Northeast division and oversee the other two. Noble declined the offer, reasoning, "Instead of engendering team work and camaraderie, it would create a divisive atmosphere, planning against the other guy. You wouldn't want to share information because it could forecast your own downfall. It would be a nice company to work for, but this would be like a gladiator pit, with all of us going after a piece of raw meat."[8]

DIFFERENTIATION

As each unit or department in an organization tries to cope with the unique demands of its own environment, it necessarily develops its own types of procedures, cherished values, and points of view. For example, a research department in a chemical firm might be run very democratically, and its personnel might develop a long-term time perspective because most of their projects will not reach fruition for years. In contrast, the production department might be run more autocratically, and its managers might be expected to put a much greater emphasis on immediate results. Because of these differences, communication and agreements about the sharing of resources will be difficult. Differentiation is a major source of conflict in mergers and acquisitions. The joined units may have different histories, values, time perspectives, risk preferences, and much else. The Focus on Management feature discusses the impact of differentiation at Litton Enterprise Systems.

Daniel Kovac, the Personal Lines Business Manager at the General Casualty Insurance Company, talks in the Voice of Experience feature about the conflict issues he encounters in his job and how he handles them.

A CONFLICT MODEL

Suppose someone says, "In a healthy company, you won't see conflict." We have already seen one reason to challenge such a statement: Some conflict enhances creativity and seeds change. Another basis for challenge is that the lack of visible conflict (i.e., what is manifested) doesn't imply tensions, hostilities, uncertainties, disagreements, or pressures don't exist. It simply means they have not been allowed to air. In a healthy relationship, we're likely to see some conflict from time to time. Such conflict, if not allowed to get out of control, can help vent frustrations, air concerns, and clear the air. But when conflict gets out of hand or a relationship is so fragile that people are afraid to voice their concerns, the situation becomes unhealthy.

Figure 10-1 presents a model of the conflict process. The model shows the several steps in the process and that a variety of factors may determine whether conflict ever becomes overt or manifest.[9]

FOCUS ON MANAGEMENT

DIFFERENTIATION AT LITTON ENTERPRISE SYSTEMS*

Litton Enterprise Solutions, a division of Litton Industries that provides information and technology services, provides a good example of the impact of differentiation. When Jeffrey Erle took over as president, the division was a loose confederation of East and West Coast operations that needed to be integrated in order to provide customers with a full range of services. The West Coast operation had been running call centers for more than 30 years, was hard working but resistant to change, and was led by an executive who thought he deserved Erle's position. The East Coast operation was pasted together from recent acquisitions and specialized in enterprise process consulting. The operation was led by a general manager who felt she should have been given the presidency. Her group was freewheeling and risk taking and cared little about Litton's culture and tradition. Because of these many differences, there was virtually no communication between the two operations, and there was no unified sense of direction. Both sides routinely engaged in covert sabotage in order to dilute the other's effectiveness.

http://www.litton.com/

*H. M. Guttman, "Conflict at the Top," *Management Review,* November 1999, pp. 49–53.

VOICE OF EXPERIENCE

Daniel J. Kovac, Personal Lines Business Manager, General Casualty Insurance Company

1. What types of conflicts do you experience in your job? How do you handle them?

Most conflict I encounter is related to differences in opinion on how to resolve a problem or achieve an objective. Because every organization must allocate limited resources to achieve its financial objectives, opinions vary widely on how best to use those resources. We are frequently forced to make decisions regarding which projects to pursue and which ones to abandon. When your time, talent and credibility are closely aligned with a project it is very difficult to give up your baby, so to speak. Most often, conflicts of resource allocation are resolved by direct, honest and sometimes confrontational discussions centered on corporate objectives and customer needs.

2. What is your experience with healthy conflict versus unhealthy conflict?

When I was a Market Strategist with MetLife Auto & Home, a consulting firm commented that the company's managers and leaders tended to be too nice to one another and hesitated to challenge ideas, plans or performance. As a consequence we were encouraged to create healthy conflict. Some people saw it as an opportunity to throw their weight around and accumulate power through intimidation or political maneuvering. And unfortunately, that can be an effective short-term technique. The best managers, however, focused their tough questions on underperforming products, processes, teams or individuals in an effort to reach the company's ambitious financial objectives.

3. How do you handle abrasive or difficult people that you have to deal with in your job?

I first figure out why I perceive that certain people are difficult or abrasive. Are they simply very direct and perhaps a little unpolished in their communication perspective? Are they abrasive because they're insecure or are they just downright mean? Once you pinpoint the motivation for their behaviors you can develop a strategy for working with them. Deal with direct people in a like manner. Flex your personality a little bit. Lean forward, make eye contact, stick to the business issue at hand and stand your ground.

When I do have to deal with people who are naturally combative or abrasive, I take a very, very tough stance. I'll pull them aside and tell them that their behavior or comments are unacceptable, disruptive, and unwelcome. That is very difficult to do and most people are afraid to take this approach. It's particularly difficult when the person is a peer. Chances are you won't permanently change behavior, but at least people know you won't tolerate it and they will direct their abuse elsewhere.

4. When entering the business world what advice can you give to students that will help them create healthy conflict?

Healthy conflict can be a source of tremendous innovation and positive change. However, recognize two things: First, you may be dealing with people who have decades of experience in an industry. If you want to challenge the status quo, ask tough questions, but at the same time acknowledge you're new to the industry and you're there to learn just as much as you are there to contribute. Secondly, don't back down if you don't get a reasonably good answer to your challenges. I've seen far more promising careers truncated because of fear than boldness.

LATENT CONFLICT

Latent conflict is essentially conflict waiting to happen. It is a situation in which the conditions are right for open conflict to develop. The aftermath of preceding conflict situations and environmental effects influence latent conflict. The latter are the conflict causes we discussed earlier, including scarcity of resources, ambiguous jurisdictions, incompatible goals, task interdependence, competitive reward systems, and differentiation.

FIGURE 10-1
The Conflict Process

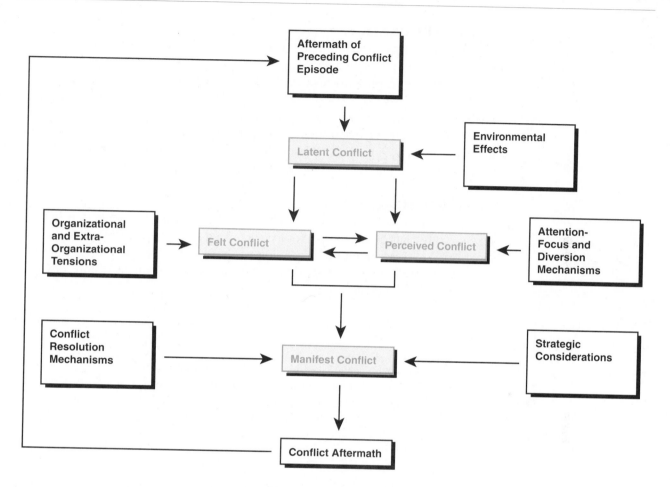

FELT CONFLICT

Felt conflict is experienced as discomfort and tension. Those people experiencing felt conflict are motivated to reduce those negative feelings. Other tensions inside or outside the organization may heighten felt conflict. For example, if we are also experiencing pressures at home or worried about losing our jobs, we may already be fragile. As such, we may feel even greater tension from further irritants.

PERCEIVED CONFLICT

Perceived conflict is the awareness we are in a conflict situation. For example, when we learn of budget cuts, we may realize a struggle over scarce resources is likely. Perceived conflict depends in part on mechanisms that may direct attention to or away from the conflict. For example, a sudden crisis may shift our attention from the current conflict situation. Conversely, if we know others are watching to see how we will do, we may be more conscious of the conflict. Note that felt conflict and perceived conflict are mutually reinforcing. When we perceive conflict, we are likely to experience tension, and when we feel conflict, we are likely to think about it.

MANIFEST CONFLICT

After conflict is perceived and felt, it may or may not become open, or manifest. As we saw in Figure 10-1, whether conflict becomes manifest depends on whether mechanisms are in place to resolve conflict as well as whether engaging in open conflict seems wise. Conflict resolution mechanisms might include a focus on larger goals, use of mediators, separation of parties, or use of negotiating techniques, as discussed later. Strategic considerations might include, for instance, a decision that the conflict "just isn't worth it." Although we may want a bigger share of the budget, we may decide fighting for it would lead to more costs than benefits.

CONFLICT AFTERMATH

Conflict is likely to breed more conflict and, when it does, that conflict is likely to take on a life of its own. Witness, for instance, long-standing feuds in which the original insult, misdeed, or misunderstanding has been long forgotten but the bitterness and even hatred continue unabated. The Focus on Management feature discusses the bitter legacy of conflict at the Dart Group.

CONFLICT STYLES

Recall that in Chapter 3 we discussed a set of five conflict styles that vary in terms of the degree to which they emphasize concern for satisfying our own needs and concern for satisfying needs of the other party.[10] In that chapter, we focused specifically on one of the styles: collaborating. Here we consider situations in which each style may be most appropriate.[11]

COMPETING

The competing, or forcing, conflict style involves trying to win at the other party's expense. The competing style generally leads to antagonism and festering resentment. It may be necessary when time is of the essence and we are sure we are correct or when the other party would take advantage of a more collaborative approach. In each of these cases, though, we should be sure to question our assumptions before resorting to competition. That is, is there really a time constraint? How can we be sure we are correct? What evidence do we have that the other party cannot be trusted?

AVOIDING

The avoiding style attempts to avoid or smooth over conflict situations. This style is generally unproductive, but it may be appropriate when conflicts are trivial. It may also be useful as a temporary tactic, to let parties cool down during heated disputes.

ACCOMMODATING

The accommodating style involves acceding completely to the other party's wishes or at least cooperating with little or no attention to one's own interests. This style may be acceptable when the other party has great power or the issue isn't really

FOCUS ON MANAGEMENT

THE LEGACY OF CONFLICT AT THE DART GROUP*

The legacy of conflict is seen in the saga of the Hafts, once called the "most feared family in retailing." Herbert Haft had founded the Dart Group (a retail empire including the Dart Drugs and Crown Books chains and Trak Auto, a national network of auto supply stores) in the 1950s. He was serving as CEO when, in early 1993, he read a newspaper article suggesting his clout was on the wane and his son, Robert, had become Dart's de facto head. Haft, a flamboyant executive whose small stature, trademark white pompadour, and feisty manner earned him comparison to "a cockatoo with a limo and driver," decided to make sure that wasn't going to happen. He quickly fired his corporate secretary (his wife Gloria) and his president (his son Robert), installing as president his younger son, Ronald, a shopping center developer with no experience in the business. His wife then filed for divorce, alleging—

among many other things—that Herbert was responsible for shady dealings designed to cheat her out of her share of the company's wealth. Robert sued for breach of contract and won, receiving a settlement of $40 million, and joined his sister Linda in a suit against Ronald. Then Herbert had a falling out with Ronald, who had purchased his father's voting shares to shelter them from Gloria in the divorce settlement, then sold those shares back to the company. The family subsequently battled for control of the empire, diverting attention from running the businesses and finally declaring bankruptcy and dismantling the company. In 1998, Richfood Holdings agreed to take over the financially troubled Dart Group. The feud, though, isn't over. After Herbert announced he was going to start an online health products venture, Healthquick.com, Robert started his own online business, Vitamins.com. The shootout in cyberspace was short lived, with both ventures falling prey to the bursting

of the Internet bubble. Still, people close to the family describe the ongoing saga as "never ending."

*This focus on management is based on M. Lewyn, "This Week on the Hafts . . . ," *Business Week,* November 22, 1993, p. 96; B. McMenamin, "Family Matters," *Forbes,* September 13, 1993, pp. 236–237; B. Dumaine, "America's Toughest Bosses," *Fortune,* October 18, 1993, pp. 38–45; K. Holland and A. Barrett, "Relief for a Poisoned Dart Group," *Business Week,* May 5, 1997, p. 48; D. Sparks, "Good Riddance, Herb," *Financial World,* May 20, 1997, pp. 32–34; S. Stoughton, "Writing a New Story Line for Crown Books," *Washington Post,* December 13, 1999, p. F18; S. Henry, "The Name Game," *Washington Post,* November 11, 1999, p. E01; and R. L. Dode, "Drugstore Cowboys: The Haft Family Rebuilds After an E-Commerce Shootout," *Business Forward,* May 2001.

http://www.bizforward.com /wdc/issues/2001-05/ drugstore.

important to us. However, appeasement may be seen as a sign of weakness and may lead to even greater demands rather than to "peace in our time." In the long term, it may generate rather than resolve conflict.

COMPROMISING

Compromising involves an attempt to find a satisfactory middle ground (i.e., to split the difference by reaching an agreement that, although not ideal for either party, seems equitable). Compromise may be necessary when there is little chance of agreement, both parties have equal power, and there are time constraints. Even when such conditions exist (and again, we should be sure to question whether they really do), compromising is unlikely to yield more than an equally unsatisfactory outcome.

COLLABORATING

This problem-solving style is mutually beneficial when the goal is a win-win solution that fully satisfies the interests of both parties. Collaborating (discussed in detail in Chapter 3) requires trust, open sharing of information, and creativity. It is the ideal style unless the parties to conflict have perfectly opposing interests.[12] Even in the latter case, though, we should be sure to examine whether those interests are truly opposing or whether in fact the apparent incompatibility is a misperception or failure to see the big picture.

As we've just discussed, some of these approaches generally work better than do others, but each may be appropriate in certain situations. We summarize the situations in which each style may be appropriate in Figure 10-2.

We should remember, of course, that the situation in which we find ourselves partly reflects our own actions. As such, along with considering the situation when choosing a style, we should anticipate how our choice of style may influence the future situation. For example, individuals using more collaborative styles tend to experience lower levels of subsequent conflicts relating to tasks and relationships as well lower stress than those adopting competing or avoiding styles.[13]

Also keep in mind that, whatever their actual impacts, others may perceive some styles as more or less appropriate and effective. For instance, the avoiding style is generally seen as ineffective and inappropriate, and the collaborative style is generally perceived as the most appropriate and effective style.[14] Perceptions are themselves important, so those choosing the avoidance style may be seen as weak, evasive, and uncooperative, even in situations where avoidance may be objectively appropriate.[15]

Now complete Self-Assessment 10-2 to better understand your conflict style. After you are through, visit the text Web site to learn more about your responses.

SELF-ASSESSMENT 10-2

Conflict Style

Answer each of the questions in this section using the following scale:

1 Disagree strongly
2 Disagree somewhat
3 Neither agree nor disagree
4 Agree somewhat
5 Agree strongly

When I'm faced with a conflict/bargaining situation,

____ 1. I generally try to keep a low profile.
____ 2. I find it's often best to seek the middle ground.
____ 3. I go for the win.
____ 4. I often focus more on satisfying the other person than on getting what I need.
____ 5. I'll back off rather than embarrass the other party.
____ 6. I usually try to split the difference, giving a little to get a little.
____ 7. I insist my position be accepted.
____ 8. I treat it as a mutual problem to be solved.
____ 9. I usually try to avoid controversial positions.
____ 10. I argue for my position as strongly as possible.
____ 11. I seek a solution that meets all our needs.
____ 12. I assume it wasn't important and back off.
____ 13. I'm willing to compromise if others will meet me halfway.
____ 14. I start by asking how we both can achieve our goals.
____ 15. I work hard to make sure there is a friendly, harmonious outcome.

FIGURE 10-2

Fitting Conflict Style to the Situation

Conflict Style	Appropriate Situation(s)
Competing	> Time is short and we're sure we are correct.
	> The other party would take advantage of a collaborative approach.
Avoiding	> The conflict is trivial.
	> We need a temporary cooling-off tactic.
Accommodating	> The other party has great power.
	> The issue isn't important to us.
Compromising	> There is little chance of agreement, both parties have equal power, and there are time constraints.
Collaborating	> This is the "ideal" style unless the parties to conflict have perfectly opposing interests.

Next complete Skills Practice 10-2. This exercise asks you to reflect on some of your most challenging past or current experiences with conflict and to develop some strategies to handle these situations more effectively in the future.

APPROACHES TO CONFLICT RESOLUTION

Several approaches to conflict resolution are shown in Figure 10-3. As we will see, some of these approaches involve changes to organizational processes, such as improving communications. Others entail specific actions in the conflict episode, such as using third parties. Still others focus on developing employees' skills, such as their ability to negotiate.[16]

FOCUS ON LARGER GOALS

Larger goals can often shift focus from conflict to cooperation. Threats of bankruptcy, loss of jobs, or deterioration of product quality can often encourage conflicting parties to cooperate to achieve a mutually beneficial goal. The need to save the company or to pull together to capture an opportunity encourages people to set aside hostilities.

IMPROVE COMMUNICATIONS

Because conflict often results from lack of communication or miscommunications, it follows that improving communications, in ways such as those we discussed in Chapter 7, may help prevent or reduce conflict. Communication is also critical in the midst of conflict. Here are some guidelines for communicating in a conflict situation. Try to come to agreement with your conflicting party to follow these guidelines in order to build more positive and productive, less stressful relationships.[17]

> Be honest; say what's on your mind now. Be open.
> Be specific; provide examples.

FIGURE 10-3

Approaches to Conflict Resolution

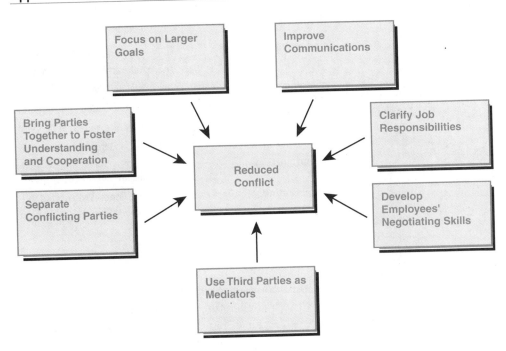

> Don't use the words *never* and *always.*
> Listen in depth; reflect and paraphrase what you hear.
> Ask questions to clarify the meaning of what the other person is saying.
> Focus on behavior the other person controls.
> Maintain good eye contact.
> Focus on only one specific issue or behavior at a time.
> Don't interrupt.
> Stay there. Don't walk away mentally, emotionally, physically, or psychologically.
> Be direct but tactful.
> Use *I* statements rather than *you* statements (e.g., "When this happens, I feel . . ." rather than "When you do this, it makes me feel . . .").
> Don't attack the other person by ridiculing, taunting, or otherwise being rude and hostile.
> Don't defend yourself by blaming others, avoiding, or withdrawing.

DEVELOP EMPLOYEES' NEGOTIATING SKILLS[18]

With training, employees can learn to reach constructive agreements. They can look beyond their own positions to consider the other party's interests, seek win-win solutions, and try to get past emotions when facing difficult decisions.[19]

USE THIRD PARTIES AS MEDIATORS

A neutral third party with expertise in human behavior can often facilitate the reduction of conflict. The third party can meet with both individuals or with representatives of both groups and help work out an agreement acceptable to both. Third parties can be especially useful when suspicion between groups has resulted in a deadlock. Because third parties have no vested interest in the conflict, the disputants are often willing to trust and abide by their recommendations.

Third-party mediators may play a variety of roles. The following are approaches the mediators may use to facilitate the conflict management process.[20]

> Help the protagonists express and understand their concerns, clarify the relative importance of issues, and search for underlying interests
> Examine the interrelations between interests and their degree of convergence or divergence. Parties to conflict sometimes assume incorrectly that their interests are incompatible.
> Facilitate the choice of the relevant approach for resolving the conflict. When interests are compatible, problem-solving approaches may be appropriate. When interests are primarily divergent, bargaining approaches may be preferable.
> Clarify the dynamics of interaction and implications for resolving the conflict.
> Identify assumptions and reframe the understanding of the conflict.
> Identify and reexamine mutual stereotypes and perceptions.
> Facilitate communications.
> Model appropriate communications through restating, reflecting, and summarizing.
> Identify inappropriate behaviors and propose more effective ones. If protagonists adopt competing or avoidance approaches in situations where they are not appropriate, suggest more effective approaches.
> Increase awareness of the conflict's real costs and benefits. Point out longer-term impacts on productivity, climate, and morale.

SEPARATE CONFLICTING PARTIES

The physical separation of conflicting parties is a quick and direct way to reduce conflict. Although it doesn't necessarily reduce the hostility felt between individuals or deal with the underlying causes of conflict, it prevents the conflict from flaring up. Obviously, this isn't an option when parties have to cooperate on a joint task.

BRING CONFLICTING PARTIES TOGETHER

Although separating conflicting parties is often useful, it may also be helpful to do just the opposite: bringing the parties together so they can get to know each other's perspectives and practice cooperation. Two Pacific Northwest nonprofit groups used this approach to smooth the waters between environmental and timber interests, battling over preservation of timberland for the spotted owl. Ten men central to the fight, including a mill owner, a logger, a scientist, and a government official, agreed to spend three days guiding an old wooden sailboat through the San Juan Islands in Puget Sound. According to one of the organizers, "It's a cooperative effort to be on the boat, and that spills over into any kind of discussion."[21]

Managers in all societies recognize that conflict must be managed, and the way it is managed depends on many cultural factors. For example, Koreans feel harmony is essential in all relationships and situations.[22] This belief is founded in Confucianism, which has influenced Korean thinking and culture for centuries. To help achieve harmony, the Confucians laid out a hierarchical societal structure and prescribed that individuals maintain their position. Further, individuals should exhibit piety toward parents, render loyalty to superiors, and preserve harmony with group members. Because harmony is an important goal, all parties should strive to attain it and, when it is disturbed, it should be restored through compromise. Those higher in status have an obligation to maintain or restore harmony among those below them, and they reap respect when they do so. Research shows that Korean leaders actively manage conflict, often intervening in their subordinates' disputes, and are quite assertive when dealing with their own subordinates. Korean subordinates tend to serve as deferential liaisons between the parties when assisting in their leaders' disputes.[23]

APPROACHES TO GENERATING PRODUCTIVE CONFLICT

Sometimes employee complacency, lethargy, and overconfidence are problems in an organization. In such cases, it may be useful to generate productive conflict. To foster constructive dissent:[24]

> Encourage norms that all employees, regardless of their position, should fully express their concerns, doubts, and ideas.
> Form task forces, made up of employees with various perspectives, outlooks, organizational positions, and backgrounds, to examine major problems and make recommendations.
> Form subgroups that take different sides of an issue.
> Emphasize that it is essential to examine issues critically and to find flaws and problems before competitors or customers do so.

To further encourage conflict, sales contests can create competition among marketing employees. Uncertainty can be induced by assigning different tasks, hiring new personnel, or changing the reward system. A devil's advocate can be given the task of finding faults in proposed solutions so as to avoid a situation in which a group fails to evaluate its choices critically. A scapegoat—someone who bears the blame for an unpopular action—may be needed to introduce needed changes. For example, a CEO who believes employees in one department are doing just enough to get by may assign a tough boss to the department, to shake things up. The new boss would introduce needed changes and take the heat from employees who may be upset. Once the changes have been implemented, the boss may be replaced. The Bottom Line feature presents a process model that summarizes the basic steps associated with the general conflict management process.

Skills Practice 10-3 requires you to find a partner. The exercise gives you an opportunity to practice the management of conflict by creating a simulation of an actual work situation and then applying different strategies for handling the conflict issues in the simulation.

Now complete Skills Practice 10-4, which involves analyzing a variety of conflict issues and conflict-handling strategies in the movie *Thirteen Days* with Kevin Costner.

BOTTOM LINE

APPLYING THE GENERAL CONFLICT MANAGEMENT PROCESS

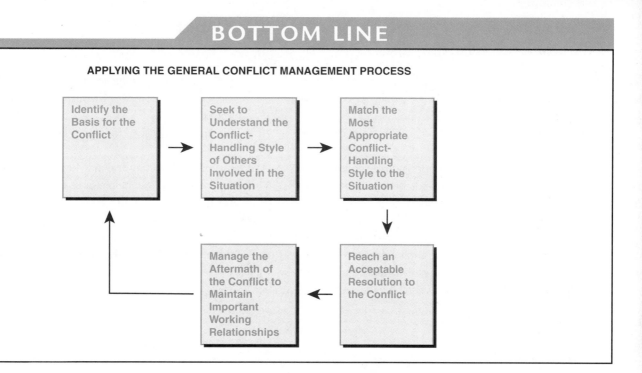

TOP TEN LIST: KEY POINTS TO REMEMBER

MANAGING CONFLICT

10. Recognize that some conflict may be good and no conflict at all may be very bad. Take action to stimulate healthy conflict in your work unit.
9. Adapt your approach for handling conflict to the nature of the situation.
8. View conflict situations as opportunities to learn. Take steps to achieve positive outcomes in the conflict aftermath (e.g., improved working relationships).
7. Accept conflict as a normal part of your job.
6. Remember that how you choose to frame a conflict greatly influences its nature and outcomes.
5. One valuable strategy for resolving conflict is to emphasize larger goals that overcome differences between various parties.
4. Use a competing style for handling conflict if you know you are correct or if you are under severe time constraints.
3. Use an avoiding style for handling conflict if the conflict is trivial.
2. Physically separating the individuals who are at odds with each other can help reduce conflict.
1. Any person involved in a conflict can contribute to its resolution by taking personal responsibility for finding a solution to the problem and by initiating communications with other parties involved in the situation.

QUESTIONS FOR REVIEW AND REFLECTION

REVIEW QUESTIONS

1. Discuss eight conflict premises.
2. Identify six causes of conflict.
3. Explain how framing of conflict influences conflict's nature and outcomes.
4. What is social reciprocity?
5. Define reciprocal interdependence.
6. Explain the stages of the conflict process.
7. Describe five conflict styles and indicate when each might be most effective.
8. Identify seven approaches to conflict resolution.
9. Discuss ways that communication with the conflicting party can build a more productive relationship.
10. Identify approaches to generating productive conflict.

CRITICAL THINKING QUESTIONS

1. We have seen that conflict may have benefits and costs. Describe a situation in which the benefits of conflict would be likely to far outweigh the costs. Then describe a situation in which the costs of conflict would be likely to dwarf the benefits.
2. Your golfing partner, the CEO of a local manufacturing firm, says to you, "I'm proud to say you won't see any conflict in our organization." How might you respond?
3. Defend a position for or against the following statement: "There is really no such thing as productive conflict. Any benefits potentially gained through conflict could have been achieved equally well in other, less destructive ways."
4. A colleague says, "I find the idea of bringing in an ax man as a scapegoat to be reprehensible." Do you agree? Why or why not?
5. Do you think a third party brought in from outside the firm to mediate a dispute can truly be neutral? What factors might prevent an outsider from being neutral? What factors would encourage neutrality?

EXPERIENTIAL EXERCISES

WEB EXERCISE 10-1

Go to the *Online Journal of Peace and Conflict Resolution* at: **http://ojpcr.trinstitute.org.master.com/texis/master/search/?q=conflict+styles&xsubmit=Search%3A&s=SS.**

This is a free "resource for students, teachers and practitioners in fields relating to the reduction and elimination of destructive conflict." Many examples are drawn from international settings. Click on "Search" near the top of the page. Conduct searches on one or more terms from this chapter, such as "conflict styles," "win-win," "framing," or "resolving conflict." For each search, you will be given a listing of Web resources dealing with the topic you have

chosen. For instance, you may find such resources as "An Analysis of Bloody Sunday," "Psychosocial Dynamics of the Armed Conflict in Colombia," "Instituting Problem-Solving Processes as a Means of Constructive Social Change," and "The Conflict Within: The Interpersonal Conflict Between Netanyahu and Arafat." Select any two of those resources. For each article, write a one-page executive summary:

1. State the topic of the resource and why that topic is important.
2. Summarize the author's key arguments.
3. Indicate what you see as key management implications of the resource.

WEB EXERCISE 10-2

University of Colorado Conflict Research Consortium

Go to the University of Colorado Conflict Research Consortium Web site at: **http://www.colorado.edu/conflict/**.

The site provides a rich set of resources relating to conflict. In the right-hand column, under the heading "CRInfo Editions," click on "Mediation" in the "Conflict

Processes" section. You will be taken to the "Mediation Edition" page. Click on the Web link for a topic that interests you in the "Mediation and Related Processes" section (for instance, "facilitation," "mediation," or "negotiation"). Select any three Web resources that interest you. Write a two- to three-page report summarizing what you learned from the resources.

CASE 10-1

THE CONFLICT OVER THE HEWLETT PACKARD–COMPAQ MERGER

The Company[25]

Hewlett Packard is a leading manufacturer and provider of personal imaging and printing, information technology infrastructure, access device, computing, and global service solutions for consumers and businesses. The company is headquartered in Palo Alto, California, and employs more than 141,000 people worldwide. The company's chief executive officer is Carly Fiorina. In 2003, Hewlett Packard had sales of over $73 billion and a net income of over $2.5 billion.

Hewlett Packard's major corporate objectives include the following:

- Customer Loyalty—To provide products, services, and solutions of the highest quality and deliver more value to our customers that earns their respect and loyalty.

- Profit—To achieve sufficient profit to finance our company growth, create value for our shareholders, and provide the resources we need to achieve our other corporate objectives.

- Market Leadership—To grow by continually providing useful and significant products, services, and solutions to markets we already serve—and to expand into new areas that build on our technologies, competencies, and customer interests.

- Growth—To view change in the market as an opportunity to grow; to use our profit and our ability to develop and produce innovative products, services, and solutions that satisfy emerging customer needs.

- Employee Commitment—To help HP employees to share in the company's success that they make possible; to provide people with employment opportunities based on performance; to create with them a safe, exciting, and inclusive work environment that values their diversity and recognizes individual contributions; and to help them gain a sense of satisfaction and accomplishment from their work.

- **Leadership Capability**—To develop leaders at every level who are accountable for achieving business results and exemplifying our values.
- **Global Citizenship**—Good citizenship is good business. We live up to our responsibility to society by being an economic, intellectual, and social asset to each country and community in which we do business.

The 2002 Hewlett Packard and Compaq Computer Merger

On September 3, 2001, Hewlett Packard announced a deal for it to acquire Compaq in a stock purchase valued at approximately $25 billion.[26] This deal would make Hewlett Packard one of the largest information technology companies in the world. Under the plan, Carly Fiorina would retain her position and Michael Capellas, the chairman and CEO of Compaq, would become president. The rationale for the merger was that the two companies would be able to combine their complementary strengths and products and services and reduce research and development costs.

Walter Hewlett's Position on the Compaq Merger [27, 28]

Walter Hewlett, son of Hewlett-Packard cofounder William Hewlett, was opposed to the merger of HP and Compaq because he believed HP should invest in the portion of the company where they had an obvious technological lead: the high-profit printing and imaging business. When deciding whether to go forward with the merger, Hewlett said in a board meeting that the plan "lacks strategic merit and substantially increases HP's exposure to the troubled commodity PC business." He came equipped with charts to support his stance on why the deal simply would not work. He also convinced his fellow board member, David Woodley Packard, son of cofounder Dave Packard, to support this view.

Critics say that Hewlett was against the merger because he wanted to preserve his father's company, but Hewlett denies this, explaining he had supported all of Fiorina's past decisions including her $1 billion acquisition of a high-end printer by Indigo Technologies, Inc. He also supported her decision to put in an $18 billion bid on a Pricewaterhouse Cooper consulting firm, before Fiorina abandoned the idea.

Fiorina's Position on the Compaq Merger

CEO Carly Fiorina believed that if HP merged with Compaq, together they could exploit economies of scale, compete more efficiently with Dell, and strengthen their service arm to compete with IBM.

She thought Hewlett lacked the credentials to be a deciding factor in this deal. Hewlett received his undergraduate degree from Harvard and then spent 12 years at Stanford completing a doctoral program in music and obtaining two master's degrees, in operations research and engineering. He had been on HP's board since 1987 and was chairman of a telephone company he started with a friend from Stanford, but this did not make him an expert on strategy. She said, "Walter Hewlett is a good man. But remember, it is he who is asking investors to accept his business judgment over that of HP's board and management team. We believe comparative business experience is germane."

A Timeline of the Feud[29]

November 2000:
Hewlett buys 200,000 shares of HP after CEO Carly Fiorina raises growth targets. But HP begins to falter as the economy slows. That begins the erosion of Hewlett's faith in top management, his colleagues say.

July 19, 2001:
Hewlett misses the first day of a two-day board meeting where the Compaq deal is discussed in detail. The next day, when all the other directors agree drastic action is needed, Hewlett says, "I don't know why you guys want to make a crisis out of this," according to a person at the meeting.

August 31, 2001:
Hewlett sees that the merger agreement claims unanimous board support and he protests. An HP lawyer tells him the deal will be done even if he votes against it. Hewlett concludes the terms may have to be renegotiated, possibly costing HP money. HP denies it suggested that.

September 1–2, 2001:
Hewlett considers resigning before the final vote is taken but decides not to. On September 3, he votes with the board but says he told the board he planned to vote his shares against the merger. In government filings, HP says Hewlett said no such thing.

November 6, 2001:
Hewlett goes public with his opposition to the Compaq deal. He gives Fiorina 30 minutes notice.

December 13, 2001:
Hewlett sends a letter to the board asking HP to scrap the

merger because 18 percent of its shares have been pledged against the deal.

December 16, 2001:

Because Fiorina and board member Richard Hackborn hint they may quit if the Compaq deal is scrapped, Hewlett's attorney asks HP to disclose whether they or others plan to resign.

January 7, 2002:

In a letter to the SEC, HP accuses Hewlett of lying in his SEC filings when he claimed to have been railroaded into voting for the Compaq merger. Hewlett says HP's filing is filled with "half-truths."

January 17, 2002:

HP runs print ads suggesting that HP founders "Bill and Dave" would have blessed the Compaq merger. Some HP insiders are irked. "There are a lot of people who are really offended by this," says Hewlett Foundation director Jim Gaither.

January 18, 2002:

HP sends a letter to shareholders characterizing Hewlett as an "academic and a musician" and questioning his business acumen.

January 23, 2002:

David Woodley Packard takes out an ad in the *Wall Street Journal* criticizing Fiorina's attempt to invoke the HP legacy in her pro-Compaq ads. The final sentence: "There is now a real danger that HP will die of a broken heart."

The Conflict Aftermath

Despite Hewlett's protests about HP's decision to merge with Compaq, he was still given the opportunity to work extensively on the integration process between the two firms. In sum, a million worker hours were spent on devel-

oping effective integration plans. So far, costs are down as projected, including a $1 billion savings from procurement. Layoffs totaled 15,000, but $55 million in bonuses were given to key staffers (split equally between Compaq and HP employees).

Although Wall Street initially did not seem to like this merger (with stock prices down almost 25 percent the day after it was announced), the stock could be recovering. It is worth almost twice as much now ($20.36/share) as it was at its all-time low in January 2003 ($10.92/share).

The current strategy of HP/Compaq is to emulate Dell's build-to-order direct sales model, to focus the Compaq products toward consumers wanting home offices and the HP brand for home entertainment and digital imaging. In addition, they plan to line up HP and Compaq products side by side and eliminate the weaker of the two to simplify product lines.

Discussion Questions

1. What type of conflict-handling style did Carly Fiorina use in dealing with Walter Hewlett over the Compaq merger issue? Was it effective? Why or why not? If not, what conflict-handling style should Fiorina have used instead?

2. What type of conflict-handling style did Walter Hewlett use in dealing with Carly Fiorina over the Compaq merger issue? Was it effective? Why or why not? If not, what conflict-handling style should Hewlett have used instead?

3. What, if anything, could have been done to avoid the conflict between Carly Fiorina and Walter Hewlett?

4. What are the practical implications of this case for you as a future manager in a real-world organization?

CASE 10-2

WORKPLACE AND DOMESTIC VIOLENCE AT MASSACHUSETTS GENERAL HOSPITAL

The Organization[30]

Massachusetts General Hospital (MGH) was founded in 1811. It is the third oldest general hospital in the United States. It admits 42,000 inpatients and handles more than 1.2 million patient visits each year. MGH is composed of a main campus and four health centers in Back Bay, Charlestown, Chelsea, and Revere. It possesses the largest hospital-based research program in the United States with

an annual budget of more than $300 million. MGH is the largest nongovernmental employer in Boston with a staff of over 16,000 employees. It is a part of the Harvard Medical School.

The Situation

MGH administrators were concerned that employees experiencing problems dealing with abusive and potentially violent individuals (e.g., patients, spouses, members of the general public) were not getting the help and support they needed. In addition, problems with violence in the workplace were creating a toxic work environment that demoralized other MGH employees who were not victims themselves, but who observed their coworkers dealing with these problems. Based on this, a formal workplace and domestic violence prevention program was created.

The Workplace and Domestic Violence Prevention Program[31, 32]

The program was developed through the extensive collaboration of MGH's security department and its employee assistance program (EAP). It focuses on providing short-term and long-term protection and solutions for MGH employees. The elements of the program are as follows:

- The program formally defines workplace violence as "Any incident that creates an environment in which employees feel unsafe." MGH staff are educated about warning signs of a potential problem.

  Warning Signs of Potentially Violent Individuals
  > A history of violence or criminal activity
  > A history of domestic violence
  > Verbally abusive or threatening behavior
  > Antisocial behavior
  > Negative changes in appearance and/or hygiene
  > Mood swings
  > Blaming others for problems
  > Romantic obsession
  > Alcohol or drug dependence
  > Depression
  > Failure to accept change
  > Excessive e-mails and voice mails that are derogatory in nature and unrelated to work

- The EAP is a benefit available to all MGH employees. It is managed by Partners Healthcare Systems, Inc. This firm is composed of five certified professional counselors who have an office in the hospital.

- EAP counselors provide emotional support, confidential counseling, referrals to victim advocates and support groups, legal resources, advocacy, education, and problem-solving skills for troubled MGH employees.

- Security department staff develop and implement protective plans to ensure the safety and security of MGH employees.

- The EAP provides consultation services to line supervisors and managers to assist them in identifying employees who may be suffering from the stress and

depression associated with workplace or domestic violence. Supervisors are encouraged to deal with the job-related problems employees may be experiencing and to inform them of the availability of EAP services.

- Utilization of the EAP is completely voluntary for MGH employees.

- When an employee seeks the assistance of the EAP, an assessment is conducted to determine whether the employee victim was verbally, emotionally, or physically abused. This is the basis for the development of an appropriate action plan to help an employee.

- Issues of domestic abuse are handled by referring employee victims to appropriate resources including legal services, support groups, and a victim's rights advocate. Services the security department can offer to protect the employee victim are also outlined.

- MGH employees who are the victims of violent domestic abuse work with staff from the security department to help them understand the problem and develop appropriate solutions.

- The security department's domestic violence prevention services include officer escorts, security surveys to assess risk factors, and referrals to legal services and resources.

- The EAP and the security department advertise their services to MGH employees in the form of newsletters and posters.

- The security department conducts workshops to educate employees about workplace and domestic violence as well as the services it provides for them. For example, some of the strategies for preventing workplace violence that are discussed include the following:
  > Review the Partners Workplace Violence policy.
  > Inform your supervisor immediately of a potentially violent situation.
  > Report any suspicious behavior to MGH Police and Security.
  > Take all threats seriously.
  > Wear your identification badge at all times.

Results

The Workplace and Domestic Violence Prevention Program at MGH has achieved a variety of benefits. First, employees who are victims of domestic/workplace violence or the threat of it learn how to handle their personal situations and relationships more effectively. Second, other MGH employees who have not experienced problems with abuse or violent people feel the work environment is safer for them. This helps increase the retention of valued members of the MHG staff. Finally, MGH staff are better able to focus on their work activities and are more productive when they don't have to worry about the issue of workplace or domestic violence.

Discussion Questions

1. Why are workplace and domestic violence growing problems in real-world organizations today?
2. Evaluate the Workplace and Domestic Violence Prevention Program being implemented at Massachusetts General Hospital. What are its strengths? Weaknesses?
3. How could an understanding of the conflict-handling styles discussed in this chapter be integrated into the Workplace and Domestic Violence Prevention Program? Be specific.
4. How could an understanding of the strategies for conflict resolution discussed in this chapter be integrated into the Workplace and Domestic Violence Prevention Program?
5. What recommendations would you make to MGH administrators about actions they should take to enhance the effectiveness of the Workplace and Domestic Violence Prevention Program? Be specific and action oriented, and justify each of your recommendations.
6. What are the key practical implications of this case for you a future manager in a real-world organization?

VIDEO CASE: MEDIATING CONFLICT RESOLUTION
MANAGING CONFLICT RESOLUTION

Running Time: 6:34

This video illustrates the process of conflict mediation. It suggests a systematic approach by which a neutral third party can intervene in a conflict situation. In the video, Alex and Katherine, two account executives at an advertising agency, are seen as being in conflict over issues relating to their clients.

The guidelines for effective mediation presented in the video refer to a "BCF statement." BCF is an acronym for:

B = **B**ehavior that bothers you
C = **C**onsequences of that behavior for you
F = Your **f**eelings about the situation

The form of the BCF statement is:

"When you [state behavior], I feel [state feelings] because [state consequences].

A BCF statement describes the problem from your point of view. It is not meant to propose solutions, and it should not attack the other party on a personal level.

Based on the video:

1. When should third-party mediation be used?
2. What is the proper role of the mediator?
3. What are the proposed steps in the conflict mediation process?
4. Based on the material in the video, give BCF statements for Alex and Katherine.
5. Indicate how participants in the conflict resolution process facilitated each proposed process step.
6. Do you feel the solution arrived at by Alex and Katherine was a "win-win" solution? Why or why not?

LIGHTEN UP

HUMOR AND CONFLICT

Humor can often defuse a tense situation. Sigmund Freud saw humor as an outlet for discharging psychic energy, thus providing relief from tension and rendering potentially damaging conflicts harmless. In addition, witty people are perceived to be more relaxed, better able to cope with stress, better able to change behaviors when necessary, far more intelligent, better problem solvers, and even more analytical. They are generally more articulate, better com- municators, better as motivators and decision makers, and more forgiving. And finally, those gifted with a sense of humor tend to be more open minded, less rigid in their beliefs, more hopeful and optimistic, more likely to see both sides of an issue, and far more accessible.[33] Here are two sites with humor resources on the Web:

Joke Central: http://www.joke-central.com, and Lots of Jokes: http://www.lotsofjokes.com/cat_ 101.htm.

SKILLS PRACTICE

10-1   *Skill Level: BASIC*

Field Experience: Interviews with Real-World Managers About Managing Conflict

Skill Objectives

1. To develop a better understanding of what management practitioners in the real world do to manage conflict effectively.

Procedure

1. Identify three managers who work in different busi- ness organizations. Ask the managers if you can inter- view each of them for approximately 30 minutes.

2. When you meet with each manager, ask the fol- lowing questions:

    a. Can you give me some examples of the types of conflict you encounter in your job?

    b. What types of strategies do you use to handle the conflict you experience in your job? Which ones tend to be the most effective? To what extent can you use the same approach to man- aging conflict when dealing with a variety of conflict situations?

    c. What actions can a manager take to stimulate positive conflict (conflict that enhances the effectiveness of people, a work unit, or an overall organization) in an organization?

    d. What advice would you give students regarding specific things they can do to manage conflict effectively in the real world?

3. Summarize the results of your interviews.

Discussion Questions

1. Based on the summary of your interviews, what are your key findings about managing conflict? Why?

2. What are the practical implications of this exercise for you as a future manager and leader of a real- world organization?

SKILLS PRACTICE

10-2   *Skill Level: BASIC*

Self-Generated Case Examples: Most Challenging Conflict Situations

Skills Objectives

1. To develop skill in reflecting on and analyzing current or past situations involving work conflict.

2. To identify conflict-handling strategies that can be used to manage conflict more effectively in the future.

Procedure

Note: Download the worksheet developed for this exer- cise from the Web site for the text.

1. Take a few minutes and brainstorm a list of at least five to seven examples of specific work (or school)- related situations in which you experienced an especially difficult conflict with one or more people. This can be a past or present conflict.

2. Select the one conflict situation you feel was the most challenging overall.

3. Write a thorough description of this situation on your worksheet. Be sure to include a description of

the nature of the conflict, your strategies for handling the conflict, and the outcome of your implementation of these strategies.

4. Now, using material from this chapter, evaluate your handling of the conflict situation you just described. Identify what you did well and what you did not do so well. Be as specific as possible.

5. Based on your evaluation of how you handled the conflict situation you selected, identify at least one specific action step you could take in the future to handle this kind of situation more effectively.

6. Optional: Repeat steps 2 through 5 using another conflict situation you select.

7. Optional: Work with another student to analyze

and evaluate one of your conflict situations. After you have completed the evaluation of your conflict situation, repeat the process with one of your partner's conflict situations.

Discussion Questions

1. What did this exercise reveal about how you manage conflict?

2. What can you do to ensure you actually implement the action steps you identified for managing conflict more effectively in this exercise?

3. What are the practical implications of this exercise for you as a future manager and leader of a real-world organization?

Skills Practice

10-3   *Skill Level:* **CHALLENGING**

Role Immersion Simulation: Managing the Conflict Process
Skill Objective
To develop skill in matching the appropriate conflict-handling style to different types of situations.
Procedure
1. Form pairs for this exercise.
2. Select one of the scenarios that follow. Each person should select one of the two roles in the situation used for this exercise.
3. Read the description for the role you selected and the overview of the situation. Do not read the role descriptions played by the other person.

Scenario 1: The Strained Relationship
StarCorp is a toy company that designs, manufactures, and markets educational toys for children between the ages of 0 and 15 years. The company's main headquarters are based in San Diego, California. Its current work force consists of 25,000 employees in the United States and another 5,000 in Latin America, Asia, and Europe. The company does the vast majority of its design and marketing work in the United States and outsources its manufacturing function to suppliers in low-wage countries in Asia and Latin America. The company's key strategic priorities are to support production innovation, customer service, and value.

StarCorp is a major player in the toy industry in terms of its product mix, distribution, and marketing expertise. However, the industry is intensely competitive, with cost the critical source of competitive advantage.

Role Description 1: Director of Marketing
You are the director of marketing. You have just been informed you will be working with the director of finance on a project that involves studying the cost effectiveness of a new process for distribution of your firm's products to retailers and individual consumers. You believe the new system may reduce costs, but that it will create huge inefficiencies and bottlenecks in the distribution process. This increases the risk that retailers and consumers may experience delays in obtaining hot-selling products you offer. Speed is critical in this industry, and with strong product offerings from other toy companies, StarCorp could lose out big if it can't respond to the demands of the market.

Your position is to keep the current distribution system because it is more flexible and responsive, although more costly to maintain. Your key concern is the customer and the market with a secondary concern for cost reduction. Use a *competing conflict-handling style* (demonstrate concern for your position, but little concern for the position of the director of finance). You may alter your conflict-handling style if you feel there is a legitimate basis for doing so, but do not give in easily!

Role Description 2: Director of Finance
You are the director of finance. You have a strong bottom-line mentality that stresses reducing costs and maximizing profits. You are a strong supporter of the new distribution system because you believe it will enable StarCorp to

reduce costs and operate more efficiently. Inflation, product development costs, and new competitors are driving costs up at an alarming rate (20 percent per year), and you must reverse this trend. Although you are most concerned about costs, you recognize the company needs to be responsive to its customer base as well. Attempt to use a *collaborating style* with the director of marketing. Try to find a common ground between your positions in which you both can fully achieve your objectives. See if there is a way to get the director of marketing to support the new system for its ability to reduce costs, but also attempt to get the marketing director's support by arguing the new system will not cause excessive inefficiencies in distribution. You may alter your conflict-handling style only if you feel there is a legitimate basis for doing so, but do not give in easily!

Scenario 2: Hardheaded and Pressed for Time

The Arlington assembly facility is owned by COMPELL, a major consumer electronics firm that designs and manufactures televisions, VCRs, DVD players, and stereo systems. This plant employs 1,500 employees who assemble various electronic products on assembly lines. COMPELL is known for innovative product design and superior product quality and durability. This reputation for quality has taken years for the company to establish so it is critical the firm's high-quality standards be maintained. However, as the company has taken action to improve product quality, its manufacturing processes have become more complex and costs have increased dramatically. This is a major concern for COMPELL management because the consumer electronics industry is extremely price sensitive.

Recently, COMPELL implemented a total quality management program that involved training managers and employees to use various quality tools (e.g., flow charts, scatter diagrams) and measures (e.g., customer satisfaction, process efficiency).

Role Description 1: Production Supervisor

You are the first-shift production supervisor for one of the assembly lines. You manage a team of 40 production employees. This has been your job for five years. The key measure of quality in your unit has always been the "defect rate" associated with products assembled in your area. You are not a big fan of the new total quality management program and you think measures such as customer satisfaction and process efficiency are not nearly as critical as the defect

rate measure. Use an *avoiding style of conflict* in responding to anyone who questions your position on this issue. Tell others you are doing fine on the defect measure and there is no problem as far as you are concerned. Although some of your employees have deviated from standard operating procedures in order to reduce product defects, you believe this is justified. The key here is to avoid acknowledging that any quality problem exists in your unit.

Role Description 2: Quality Supervisor

You are the quality supervisor at COMPELL's Arlington production facility. Your job is to implement total quality management principles in order to further enhance the company's reputation for product quality and durability. You have established a quality measurement system composed of 12 critical measures of quality you monitor on an ongoing basis. In reviewing the last six months of quality data, you have identified one production line that is well below average (25 percent below the plant average) on all of the quality measures (e.g., customer satisfaction, process efficiency, costs, productivity) except the defect measure. You decide to discuss this issue with the production supervisor. Use a *competing conflict–handling style* in dealing with the production supervisor by insisting the quality data clearly shows there are serious quality problems on his or her line. Insist the production supervisor improve on the other measures of quality and tell the person you are not interested in excuses. Explain to the production supervisor that he or she must improve quality on all 12 measures as part of the company's overall quality strategy. Maintain your position and do not give in!

4. Start the simulation and let it run for approximately 10 to 15 minutes.
5. After the simulation has been completed, answer the following questions with your partner.

Discussion Questions

1. When, if at all, did each of you become aware of the other person's conflict-handling style? How did you become aware of it?
2. Evaluate each person's handling of the conflict in the simulation. What could have been done differently to handle the conflict more effectively?
3. What are the practical implications of this exercise for you as a future manager in a real-world organization?

SKILLS PRACTICE

10-4

Skill Level: CHALLENGING

Conflict in Crisis Situations: **Thirteen Days**

Skill Objective

To develop skill in analyzing the nature and complexity of conflict in a major crisis and to understand the types of strategies used to handle this kind of situation.

Procedure

1. Obtain a copy of the movie *Thirteen Days* starring Kevin Costner. It is available on VHS and DVD and can be rented or purchased from a local video store or retailer.

2. Watch the movie (in class or at home on your own).

   Note: Download the worksheet developed for this exercise from the Web site for this book to help you develop a list of relevant scenes in the movie for answering the discussion questions.

   As you watch the film, use the conflict model discussed in the chapter to help you better understand the causes of the conflict and the strategies employed by both sides (the United States and the Soviet Union) to handle the situation. Document your notes from the film on your worksheet.

3. Discuss the following questions as a class:

   a. What were the causes of the conflict that occurred in the movie?

   b. What kinds of strategies were used by the U.S. government to handle the situation? What type of conflict-handling style best describes the approach used by the U.S. government? To what extent was the U.S. government effective in resolving the conflict? Why?

   c. What kinds of strategies were used by the Soviet Union to handle the situation? What type of conflict-handling style best describes the approach used by the Soviet Union? To what extent was the Soviet Union effective in resolving the conflict? Why?

   d. What would you have done differently if you were a member of the U.S. government in the situation shown in the movie? What would you have done differently if you were a member of the Soviet Union?

   e. What are the practical implications of this exercise for you as a future manager in a real-world organization?

MANAGING GROUPS

PART 3

MANAGING TEAMS

CHAPTER 11

Skills Objectives

> *To facilitate the movement of a team through the stages of group development.*

> *To design and implement effective plans to support the achievement of team objectives.*

> *To plan and conduct effective team meetings.*

> *To use team-building tools to make more effective team decisions.*

> *To use team-building tools to handle the most challenging problems facing teams in the workplace.*

> *To evaluate a team's functioning systematically and to develop action steps to enhance its effectiveness.*

KNOWLEDGE OBJECTIVES

> Discuss the importance of teams in the workplace.

> Identify and discuss the strengths and weaknesses of teams.

> Discuss when teams may be most useful and when they may not be needed.

> Identify and define the characteristics of effective teams and discuss specific actions that leaders can take to enhance a team's effectiveness.

> Identify and discuss guidelines for running team meetings effectively.

> Identify and describe team-building tools used to make team decisions and to handle other challenging problems that teams face in the workplace.

Headlines on July 26, 2003, heralded Lance Armstrong's dramatic victory at the Tour de France, his record-tying fifth-consecutive win.[1] In fact, although Armstrong's achievement was remarkable, the victory was very much a team effort, pitting riders of the U.S. Postal Service team against rival teams from around the world. The Postal Service Team was itself made up of riders from the United States, Russia, Canada, Spain, Luxembourg, Czechoslovakia, Norway, Colombia, Australia, and the Netherlands, and its efforts were focused on a single goal: victory for Lance Armstrong. In fact, when Armstrong's teammate, Victor Hugo Pena of Colombia, wore the yellow jersey—signifying overall leadership in the race—he continued to carry water bottles from his team car to deliver to his U.S. Postal Service teammates. Team members were selected for their unique skills, such as excellence in time trials or in mountain climbs, and for their willingness to work for the good of the team. Earlier in the year Armstrong had spoken of his pleasure that the 2002 team had stayed intact for 2003, noting, "For the first time in a long time, we have been able to retain everyone from the team in general. I think we have really started to hit our stride in terms of teamwork, communication and camaraderie. I'm looking forward to 2003 with these guys." Armstrong's words proved prescient, with teamwork contributing to a historic—and hard-earned—victory.

Teams are now pervasive in organizations of all kinds. At Harley-Davidson Motor Company, teams of workers machine aluminum castings into cylinder heads for motorcycles. The teams supervise themselves, with no bosses giving orders. The teams have the authority to purchase machines costing hundreds of thousands of dollars, to bargain with suppliers, and to decide the physical layout of the workplace. They set their own schedules and budgets, and they inspect the quality of their finished products. They hold meetings relating to productivity, quality, and other matters. In short, they manage themselves. These self-managing teams were a key factor in Harley's dramatic turnaround from the brink of bankruptcy in the early 1980s.[2] They represent a major trend in the modern workplace. Today, teams are everywhere, taking many forms, and handling many tasks. By one estimate, 80 percent of *Fortune* 500 companies now have half of their employees on teams.[3] Team-management skills are increasingly critical.

This chapter explores the management skills you will need to create and lead teams. You will learn the role of teams in today's business environment and strategies for building effective teams. Then we present techniques for running effective team meetings. We conclude the chapter by discussing self-managing teams and providing guidelines for use of special-purpose group techniques.

Answer the questions in Self-Assessment 11-1 as a way to assess your initial attitudes about teams. The self-understanding you gain from doing this will be helpful to you as you read the rest of the chapter. In addition, complete the Pretest Skills Assessment to develop a sense of your current skill in managing teams. After you are through, visit the text Web site to learn more about your responses. Before reading on, complete Skills Practice 11-1 to provide a real-world foundation for the topics to be discussed in this chapter.

SELF-ASSESSMENT 11-1

Attitudes Toward Teams

Answer the questions that follow regarding your attitudes toward working in teams. Try to respond to each question as honestly as possible using the following response scale:

1 Disagree strongly
2 Disagree somewhat
3 Neither agree nor disagree
4 Agree somewhat
5 Agree strongly

____ 1. Individuals are better than teams in generating creative solutions to business problems.

____ 2. Teams make better decisions than individuals when the task at hand is complex.

____ 3. Teams must have formal leaders in order to be successful.

____ 4. Teams should be used to complete all type of tasks and projects in organizations.

____ 5. Effective team management is primarily a matter of providing direction regarding the tasks a team must complete.

____ 6. There is little need to actively manage a well-designed team.

____ 7. All team meetings should have a written agenda.

____ 8. It is important for team members to get acquainted with one another when a new team is formed.

____ 9. Conflict among team members should always be avoided.

____ 10. Teams should have a clear idea of how they will evaluate their own effectiveness.

PRETEST SKILLS ASSESSMENT

Managing Teams

Note: This exercise is based on actual events encountered by managers in real-world organizations. Some information may have been modified in order to maintain the anonymity of the people and organization involved in this situation.

You are the new project leader at a medium-sized business software company based in San Francisco, California. The company has just completed a major restructuring that has resulted in some employee layoffs and reassignments. In addition, the company has implemented a pay freeze in order to reduce operating costs in the face of fierce competition from other U.S. and international firms. The primary areas of focus of the company are now on product innovation, productivity, and cost reduction.

Your project team was just created as part of the company's reorganization. Your objective is to work with your team to develop new business software that will dramatically enhance the productivity of business professionals and executives. You have 15 employees who are new to their jobs and relatively new to the company as well. Most of these new employees are inexperienced, and they do not know each other at all. In addition, their morale is low because of the stress associated with all of the changes taking place in the company.

Your task is to transform this group of individuals into a high-performing team that will create innovative and highly successful business software applications in the future. Develop an action plan for building your team in this situation. Be sure your plan addresses both short-term and long-term issues. Be very specific, and be prepared to defend each element of your plan in terms of its feasibility and cost effectiveness.

TEAMS IN THE WORKPLACE

Although teams may hold great promise in the workplace, it is important to recognize that teams can take different forms, depending on their purpose, and the use of teams is not without its costs. In this section we first consider types of teams.

Then we explore a variety of potential advantages and disadvantages of teams and provide guidelines for choosing between teams and individuals for addressing business issues.

TYPES OF TEAMS

You will be a member of many types of teams during your career. The teams will have a variety of purposes, forms, and members. Some of the teams will be functional, others cross-functional, and still others self-managing.

A *functional team*, also called a *command team* or *vertical team*, consists of a supervisor and his or her subordinates in the chain of command. This may be a manager and his or her direct reports, but it could also include members from more than two levels in the chain of command.

A *cross-functional team* is made up of members from different functional departments in the organization.[4] Such teams are formed to monitor, standardize, and improve work processes that cut across different parts of the organization, to develop products, or to otherwise address issues that call for broad representation and expertise. For example, representatives from the order entry, order processing, invoicing, inventory control, and shipping departments might form a cross-functional team to find ways to avoid delays in filling customers' orders. Cross-functional teams are becoming much more common as companies try to remove barriers that separate functions such as accounting, marketing, and production. In the quest to become boundaryless, companies are focusing on key processes and drawing team members from all over the organization to achieve process goals.

A *self-managing team*—such as the Harley-Davidson team in our chapter-opening example—is able to make key decisions about how its work is done. Members learn all tasks and rotate from job to job. Self-managing teams actually take over managerial duties, such as work and vacation scheduling, hiring new members, and ordering materials. Self-managing teams are increasingly important as companies must respond in prompt and creative ways to changes in customer demands, technology, economic conditions, and other factors. As we discuss later in this chapter, they also pose special challenges and require special skills.[5] In the Voice of Experi-

FOCUS ON MANAGEMENT

CROSS-FUNCTIONAL, CROSS-CULTURAL TEAMS AT MAXUS ENERGY

Maxus Energy, a subsidiary of Repsol-YPF S.A., based in Madrid, Spain, the world's eighth largest oil company, has built cross-functional teams that comprise different cultures, languages, sites, and even time zones.* Maxus views cross-cultural differences and cross-functional skills as strengths. A team at Maxus may consist of geophysicists, geologists, engineers, oil-drilling experts, and production experts. It may have members from the United States, Holland, Great Britain, and Indonesia. Team members may come from different religious, political, cultural, and functional backgrounds. This diversity brings in many perspectives and encourages creativity. Members must develop cross-cultural competencies and must learn to respect, trust, and value others' contributions.

http://www.repsol-ypf.com/
Note: This is a Spanish-language Web site.

*For a good discussion of teams at Maxus, see Charlene M. Solomon, "Global Teams: The Ultimate Collaboration," *Personnel Journal*, September 1995, pp. 49–53.

ence feature, Elizabeth Oberpriller discusses what she has learned about teams from her real-world experience.

THE ADVANTAGES OF TEAMS

Teams offer a variety of *potential* benefits. As we'll see later, these benefits will be realized *only if the teams are properly managed.* Some potential benefits include the following:

> Teams provide many perspectives, skills, and resources, especially if the group has diverse membership.

> Participation increases acceptance and understanding of the team's outcomes. When individuals feel they are real participants in the team, they are more willing to carry out the team's decisions and to endorse them enthusiastically to others.

> Participation is empowering. It is easy to feel helpless when you have little say in decisions affecting things that are important to you. Being part of a team that is making important decisions or carrying out other important tasks builds confidence and self-esteem, and it helps prevent a sense of powerlessness.

> Working in teams is stimulating. When we work in the presence of others, our adrenaline levels increase, stimulating us to greater performance. This

VOICE OF EXPERIENCE

WORKING IN REAL-WORLD TEAMS

Elizabeth Oberpriller, Assistant Buyer, Target Corporation, Minneapolis, Minnesota

1. What have you learned about working effectively in teams in the real world?

I've learned that to make a team effective in the real world, the key ingredient is communication. Each party must communicate thoughts and feelings about what is happening, to make a team work. Each party must also be perceptive not only to the environment surrounding them, but to the other parties as well. This will create an understanding and make the team more effective. Also, each party must value the opinions of others. Each party must ask for input from others even if she/he thinks her/his own idea is the best. Each party must

accept responsibility and allow for other leaders in the group instead of leading all the time. This will make everyone more comfortable, and ultimately the team will be the most effective.

2. What are the most challenging team experiences you have had so far?

Sometimes it's difficult to work with others when they don't share the same view as you do. Target is a very team-oriented organization and therefore I work with a lot of different people every day. I think the key to working with different views is to remain open minded and to understand that others have not had the same experiences you have had—that's why their opinions differ. In most cases, difference of opinion is good in a team because it makes you really concentrate on the issue or issues at

hand and forces you to think outside of the box. This is especially helpful in a retail-oriented environment, where being different is good—it separates you from the competition.

3. What kinds of things is your company doing to promote teamwork?

Target has come up with a few ways to help people work more effectively and successfully in teams. They have an individual incentive program as well as a group incentive program. Bonuses are given once a year on the company's performance as a whole, your particular department's performance, and individual performance. There are three bonuses total. This helps people work toward a common goal but also leaves room for individual achievement.

phenomenon—first noticed more than a century ago—is known as ***social presence effects***. IDEO Product Development, an organization that specializes in innovation, has a constant stream of backstage visitors, including clients, reporters, students, and others, even inviting them to join brainstorming sessions. IDEO believes this constant stimulation through social presence enhances the company's creative work.

Team decisions tend to be more reliable than those of individuals. Pooled judgments capture broader knowledge and dampen a variety of biases. For example, some people may be overconfident and others less confident than is appropriate. Team decisions may help balance out these biases. Reliable decisions are also likely to be better decisions.

Participation in teams is a developmental experience. Just as a backup quarterback may be put into a football game to gain valuable playing time and experience, an individual may be given playing time, so to speak, on a team to gain team-related skills.

These various potential benefits of teams are sometimes called ***process gains***. That is, they are gains that may be realized by appropriate use of group processes. When managing or participating in teams, we want to do all we can to capture these process gains.

THE DISADVANTAGES OF TEAMS

The benefits just presented help explain the tremendous appeal, and growing use, of teams in today's organizations. Note, though, that we were careful to call them *potential* benefits. Unfortunately, teams often suffer from serious drawbacks that may prevent those benefits from ever being realized. For example, these drawbacks may occur in teams:

> Dominant or stubborn members may control the process.
> Some members may be reluctant to participate.
> Some members may focus on personal goals. They may, for instance, try to use the meeting to gain resources for themselves, or they may simply want to win arguments, show off their knowledge, or bully another team member.
> Time and resources are taken from other activities.
> Some members may rely on others to carry the load, called ***social loafing***. This not only loses the contributions of those members, but angers others on the team who feel they're being treated as "suckers."[6]
> Team members may be afraid to rock the boat. That is, they may not want to seem like troublemakers, so they may suppress their concerns and simply agree with others.

These various potential drawbacks, sometimes called ***process losses***, are losses that may result from using group processes. Clearly, we want to minimize process losses.[7]

One difference between individuals and teams, which could be an advantage or disadvantage, is that groups tend to make riskier decisions than individuals—this is called the ***risky shift phenomenon***. The risky shift phenomenon is one manifestation of a more general phenomenon known as group polarization. ***Polarization*** is the tendency of groups to make initial group tendencies more polar—that is, more extreme.[8] So, if you as a leader feel people are being too cautious, using a team may encourage greater risk taking. If you're concerned that excessive risks are being taken, use of teams may be dangerous.

WHEN ARE TEAMS NEEDED?

When deciding whether or not to use a team to solve a business problem or achieve an organizational objective, managers will want to consider these advantages and disadvantages. Figure 11-1 offers guidelines—some of them based on material presented later in the chapter—for choosing between teams or individuals to address business issues.

BUILDING EFFECTIVE TEAMS

Once a decision has been made to use a team, there are several things to keep in mind in order to enhance team effectiveness. These include choosing team size and membership, defining the team's assignment, planning the team effort, managing the team through the stages of group development, and building team spirit.

CHOOSING A TEAM SIZE AND MEMBERS

A basic issue facing teams is the selection of its membership. This requires decisions about both team size and the mix of members.

Selecting a Team Size. How big should a team be? We'll start with the bottom line: Choose a five-person or seven-person team unless there are very compelling reasons to do otherwise. Any team with fewer than five members has its own unique set of problems.

The smallest team, with two members, is called a *dyad*. People in dyads tend to be anxious and uncomfortable. Members are reluctant to give opinions and

FIGURE 11-1
Deciding When to Use a Team

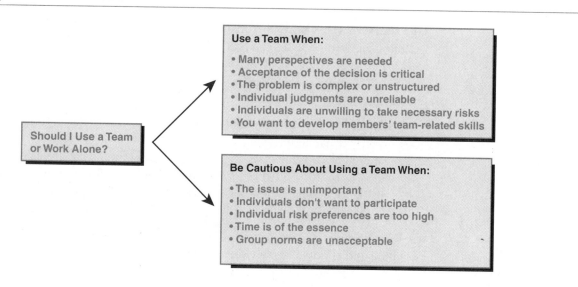

Should I Use a Team or Work Alone?

Use a Team When:

- Many perspectives are needed
- Acceptance of the decision is critical
- The problem is complex or unstructured
- Individual judgments are unreliable
- Individuals are unwilling to take necessary risks
- You want to develop members' team-related skills

Be Cautious About Using a Team When:

- The issue is unimportant
- Individuals don't want to participate
- Individual risk preferences are too high
- Time is of the essence
- Group norms are unacceptable

constantly ask for opinions. If the two members can't reach an agreement, there may be a stalemate, the team may break up, or one member may force the other to give in. Three-person teams, *triads,* have a special problem—if there is disagreement, the split is two to one. People generally don't like to be on the losing side, and it is especially upsetting to be an isolate, the *only* loser. In a triad, the member in the minority is *always* an isolate. Because of this, either one member is very unhappy or coalitions constantly have to shift, with associated tension and political activity. Four-person and six-person teams can lead to stalemates or power plays if the team is equally split—this is a problem with any even-sized group, but an even split is less likely as teams get larger.

Beyond size seven, team management becomes much more difficult. For instance, there are increased coordination problems and some members may be tempted to engage in social loafing.

When might you want to use larger or smaller groups than five or seven members? Quite simply, sometimes the problem or task isn't important enough to involve five members, or five people simply aren't available. Conversely, there may be political reasons for involving more than seven persons, or the problem or task may demand broad participation because of its great complexity. However, the problems associated with large teams are so great that we encourage you to do all you can to keep teams small. This may require breaking the team into subteams or using techniques (such as the nominal group technique, which we discuss later in the chapter) that restrict the degree of member interaction and the related problems.

Staffing the Team. The team's composition can have a major impact on how well it achieves its goals and how satisfied its members feel. Keep the following suggestions in mind:

> Vary team membership across tasks.
> Ensure availability of key information, skills, and resources.
> Ensure participation of affected parties.
> If you will not be leading the team, appoint a task-oriented leader with sufficient power to keep the team on track.
> Consider varying membership over the course of the task.

DEFINING THE TEAM'S ASSIGNMENT

Defining the team's assignment involves specifying—preferably, in writing—the team's purpose, responsibilities, and needs. Answers to the following questions make up the team's assignment.

> What is the issue the team must deal with? What is its scope?
> What is the team's responsibility? To perform a specific task? To make a decision? To exchange information?
> What are the constraints on the group? For example, what are its deadlines? What is its budget? What other resources (such as administrative support) are available to it? What should be the format of its final report or the nature of its final product? Will it have to give progress reports?

Now complete Skills Practice 11-2 in order to help develop basic skills in designing and conducting an effective team meeting.

PLANNING THE TEAM EFFORT

Once you define the team assignment, plan the overall team effort. This stage includes the following steps:

> Divide the team's overall assignment into parts. This overcomes psychological hurdles and makes it easier to develop estimates of total time and resource needs.
> Estimate the time and resources needed to complete each part of the assignment and the overall assignment.
> Determine the time and resources needed, and take necessary actions to reduce any gaps between what is needed and what is available. This may involve changing the assignment, getting deadlines extended, adding members to the team, seeking additional resources, or making other adjustments.

Skills Practice 11-3 provides an opportunity to develop skill in creating a team charter that formally specifies and documents a team's objectives, structure, process, and scope. Many high-performance teams in the real world use team charters, so it is very valuable for you to learn how to develop and use them. Be careful; it's not as easy as it looks!

MANAGING A TEAM THROUGH THE STAGES OF GROUP DEVELOPMENT

It is critical for leaders to understand how teams may change as they mature, and how different sets of behaviors are needed to manage teams through their various stages of development. In this section, we consider team expectations about appropriate behaviors for teams members in general (norms) and for specific team members (roles), and we see how these create needs for careful attention to the stages of group development.

Norms. *Norms* are the unwritten rules of the team. They are shared expectations about how team members should behave. For example, the team may have norms about how members should dress, how hard they should work, how much members should help one another, or whether team members should keep secrets from others in the organization. Norms may be *prescriptive*—dictating what should be done—or *proscriptive*—dictating what should not be done. Norms were quite evident in the 2003 Tour de France, discussed in the chapter-opening example. When Lance Armstrong fell after colliding with a spectator, other lead riders didn't take advantage of the fall to speed ahead and gain precious seconds. Instead, the group—including Armstrong's closest rival Jan Ullrich—waited for Armstrong to remount. This may have seemed remarkable to those not familiar with competitive cycling, but it represented a long-held, cherished tradition in competitive cycling.

Norms are powerful. Because we want to meet the expectations of our team members, norms control our behavior. This is sometimes called **clan control**, and such control may be even stronger than the control imposed by rules and orders. Further, once a team develops norms, those norms tend to persist—often, even after all the original members have eventually left the team and been replaced by new members.

Team members may import norms when they join the team. For example, members may bring with them the norms of their professions, or they may import the norms of other teams they've been on. For instance, if someone has been on a team that valued working extra hours to get a job done, she may bring that norm with her to a new team. Norms may also develop because of some critical event in the life of the team. For example, if a major client stops doing business with a firm because he was upset by an employee's rude behavior, norms may develop about the nature of appropriate interaction with clients. Often, though, norms develop gradually during the life of the team.

Our discussion of norms suggests the following guidelines for team management:

> Recognize the power of norms. Although unwritten, norms are just as real as, just as powerful as, and perhaps more enduring than written rules and regulations.
> Identify team norms; reinforce positive norms.
> Communicate expectations concerning performance and other goals.
> Recognize that norms develop gradually and are resistant to change.

Roles. We all wear many hats in life. We may be—at the same time—friends, neighbors, students, siblings, lovers, employees, and much more. Each of these hats carries with it a set of expectations for its wearer. Someone in a parent hat is expected to show concern for his or her children: to provide them with love, guidance, food, and shelter. Someone in a student hat is expected to attend classes, complete assignments, and be an active participant in class activities. These various hats are called *roles*.

As shown in Figure 11-2, team members can adopt many roles, not all of them positive. Two sets of roles—task-oriented roles and relations-oriented roles—are vital if the team is to be effective on a continuing basis. *Task-oriented roles* are needed to get the job done. Team members who initiate tasks, gather information for use by the team, offer suggestions, and help motivate others would be performing task-oriented roles. *Relations-oriented roles* are needed to keep the team healthy and its members satisfied. Team members who help keep the group harmonious, assist in helping members resolve disputes, and encourage members as they face barriers are engaging in relations-oriented roles. However, team members may also assume other, self-serving roles. *Self-oriented roles* are roles the member adopts for personal gain. These roles may often hamper team performance and cohesiveness. For instance, some team members gain a sense of power by dominating others or blocking others' attempts to get things done.

We said that roles carry with them sets of expectations. Sometimes, as discussed in Chapter 5, those expectations are unclear, conflicting, or overwhelming in number. Unclear expectations cause *role ambiguity*. Role ambiguity results when team members simply don't know what is expected of them. Conflicting expectations cause *role conflict*.[9] For example, you may experience role conflict if two colleagues tell you to do opposite things, or if your boss tells you to do one thing one day and the opposite the next. You may even feel role conflict if your own values—which carry their own role expectations—conflict with demands of a role. If, for instance, you are told to fire a long-term employee who is near retirement, which is contrary to your values, role conflict may result. Finally, when role expectations are simply overwhelming—we're expected to do too many things—*role overload* occurs. Role ambiguity, role conflict, and role overload cause *role stress*. Role stress causes dissatisfaction, absenteeism, turnover, poor performance, a host of illnesses, and many other problems.[10]

FIGURE 11-2
Team Roles

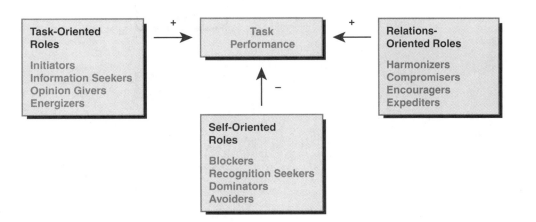

Especially when roles are in flux, careful attention to minimizing role stress is crucial. For instance, when the State Bank of India was developing ambitious expansion plans, top management recognized that new managerial roles would be a key to success. The bank needed a way to move experienced staff from their traditional hierarchical practices and relationships to new, more flexible and less formal roles. Part of the training process in anticipation of expansion was a series of seminars to discuss role concepts. Subsequently, close attention was paid to matching managers' personalities with the demands of their new roles.[11]

Managers can increase a team's productivity by understanding the different kinds of roles and adhering to the following guidelines:

> Encourage and reward members who adopt positive roles.
> Recognize that both task-oriented and relations-oriented roles are critical to team performance. A team that focuses only on relations-oriented roles may never get the job done. A team that emphasizes only task roles is likely to face growing member dissatisfaction, to lose team spirit, and to breed disruptive conflicts.
> Identify and discourage negative roles. Team leaders—and other team members—have a responsibility to make it clear that disruptive, self-serving behaviors will not be tolerated.
> Understand the roles you must play as a team leader—and those you need not play.
> Do all you can to minimize role ambiguity and role conflict. Make sure assignments are clear, messages are consistent and unambiguous, and responsibilities are not overwhelming.

Stages of Group Development. In fact, there are distinct stages of group development. As shown in Figure 11-3, these stages are called *forming, storming, norming, performing,* and *adjourning.*[12] As the names suggest, norms and roles don't become well developed until the team has experienced a lot of jockeying for position, testing of boundaries, and conflict.

FIGURE 11-3
Stages of Group Development

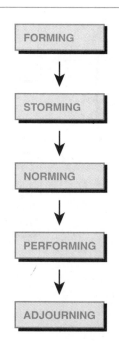

In the ***forming stage*** of group development, team members are getting acquainted and becoming oriented to the task. There is great uncertainty because expectations are unclear. Team members attempt to learn which behaviors are acceptable and which are not. At this stage, leaders can help members become comfortable and feel like part of the team. They can encourage quiet members to build relationships with others and can generally encourage communication and interaction among members.

During the ***storming stage***, conflict and disagreement among group members are likely. Members become more assertive in their roles, and their personalities begin to become clearer. The team lacks cohesiveness because there is jockeying for positions and subgroups form. This stage may be necessary to permit team members to resolve disagreements, uncertainties, and conflicts and to permit agreement and a common vision to develop. However, if the team doesn't get past the storming stage, it cannot become productive. As such, the leader must help the team work through this stage in ways that are ultimately constructive.

By the ***norming stage***, conflicts have largely been resolved, and the team becomes more cohesive. Members settle into roles, and team norms, values, and expectations develop. The leader should encourage communication among members at this stage and help team members as they agree on roles, values, and norms.

In the ***performing stage*** the team is mature. Members have learned the bounds of acceptable behavior, worked through their disagreements, developed norms, and settled in their roles. The focus now is on performance as team members constructively face new challenges, coordinate their activities, and pursue the team's vision. When the team is at this stage, it can largely manage its own affairs.

The leader can step back a bit, concentrating on helping the team with its self-management. Later in the chapter, we explore how the leader might do this.

Finally, in the *adjourning stage* the team dissolves, having accomplished its purposes or breaking up because of internal or external forces.

Again, development of norms and roles takes place over the course of the team development process. It is important to help shape positive norms and roles as early in the life of the team as possible. The nearby Bottom Line presents the basic steps involved in managing a team through the stages of group development.

Skills Practice 11-4 gives you an opportunity to analyze a highly successful football team as portrayed in the movie *Remember the Titans*. This is a great illustration of the stages of group development and is based on a true story.

BUILDING TEAM SPIRIT

Some teams stick together better than others. There is a real sense of team spirit, and members are proud to be associated with each other and with the team. Teams with

BOTTOM LINE

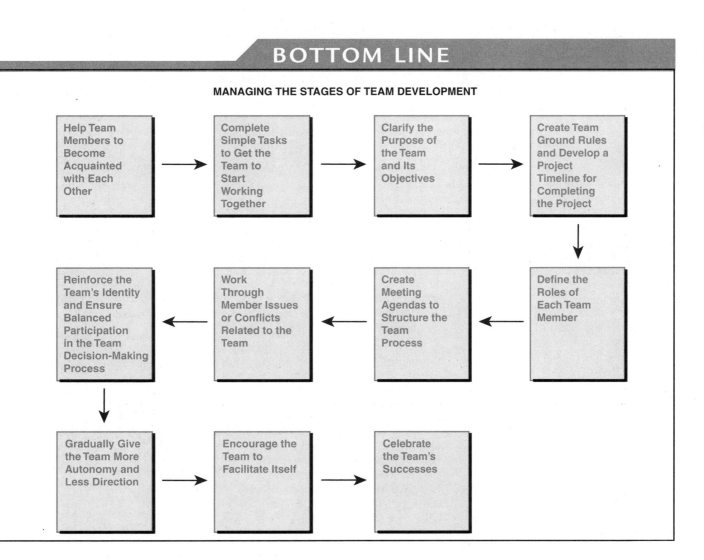

MANAGING THE STAGES OF TEAM DEVELOPMENT

Help Team Members to Become Acquainted with Each Other → Complete Simple Tasks to Get the Team to Start Working Together → Clarify the Purpose of the Team and Its Objectives → Create Team Ground Rules and Develop a Project Timeline for Completing the Project ↓

Reinforce the Team's Identity and Ensure Balanced Participation in the Team Decision-Making Process ← Work Through Member Issues or Conflicts Related to the Team ← Create Meeting Agendas to Structure the Team Process ← Define the Roles of Each Team Member

↓

Gradually Give the Team More Autonomy and Less Direction → Encourage the Team to Facilitate Itself → Celebrate the Team's Successes high levels of this team spirit—also called *cohesiveness*—generally are more effective in achieving their goals than teams that lack team spirit.[13] Members of cohesive teams also communicate relatively better with one another, are more satisfied, and feel less tension and anxiety.

Note that we said cohesive teams are more effective in achieving *their* goals. Because their goals may not always foster the best interests of the organization, it is important to make sure team members are aiming for the right sorts of things. If not, increasing team cohesiveness may help attain undesirable goals. So if a team has goals of high performance, creativity, and an honest day's work, greater cohesiveness is probably helpful. If it has goals of leaving work early, pilfering, doing as little as possible on the job, or padding the budget, increased cohesiveness may not be positive.

Several things help make teams more cohesive. For example, cohesiveness rises with increases in team status and team goal achievement. Cohesiveness also tends to increase when a clear outside threat requires the team to pull together to meet the challenge. As teams get bigger, cohesiveness declines.

Cohesiveness may be especially important at critical points in the life of an organization. For example, when GE Plastics, a division of General Electric Company, acquired rival company Borg-Warner Chemicals, the company faced the formidable task of integrating two very different work cultures. It was decided that some form of team-building experience was needed to make a lasting impression on the participants while serving some larger purpose. A project called "Share to Gain" was started in which GE Plastics employees from different departments and from the acquired company worked together to renovate five nonprofit facilities in San Diego. The project was credited with building corporate loyalty, enhancing team spirit, and smoothing the pains of integration.[14]

These characteristics suggest the following concrete guidelines for building team cohesiveness:[15]

FOCUS ON MANAGEMENT

HOT GROUPS

Extremely high levels of team spirit, excitement, and energy characterize what have been called "hot groups."* According to Jean Lipman-Blumen and Harold Leavitt, "A hot group is a special state of mind. It's not a name for some new team, task force, or committee. The hot group state of mind is task obsessed and full of passion, coupled with a distinctive way of behaving, a style that is intense, sharply focused, and full-bore. Any group can become a hot group—if it can get into that distinctive state of mind. . . . It is not the name, but that contagious single-mindedness, that all-out dedication to doing something important, that distinguishes a hot group from all others." Hot groups abound in Silicon Valley; the team that created the Macintosh computer is cited as a classic example. To encourage hot groups, according to Lipman-Blumen and Leavitt, it is important to make room for spontaneity, break down barriers, encourage intellectual exchange, select talented people and respect their self-motivation and ability, use information technology to build relationships, and value truth and the speaking of it.

*J. Lipman-Blumen and H. J. Leavitt, *"Hot Groups* (New York: Oxford University Press, 1999). See also J. Lipman-Blumen and H. J. Leavitt, "Hot Groups 'with Attitude': A New Organizational State of Mind," *Organizational Dynamics*, 1999, 27(4), pp. 63–72; and H. J. Leavitt and J. Lipman-Blumen, "Hot Groups: The Rebirth of Individualism," *Ivey Business Journal*, 2000, 65(1), pp. 60–65.

> Make it attractive to be a member of the team: Use logos and team names as appropriate. Emphasize team status. Make team membership an honor.
> Praise and publicize team accomplishments. Go for some small wins. That is, make sure the team has some projects and goals that can have clear, short-term consequences. Success on these may build cohesiveness and confidence as the team tackles larger tasks.
> Keep the team small.
> Identify outside threats and pressures. Communicate them to the team, and emphasize how teamwork can counter them.

The process model presented in the nearby Bottom Line provides a summary of the basic steps involved in developing team cohesion. Now complete Skills Practice 11-5, "Building Team Spirit."

DEALING WITH PROBLEM TEAM MEMBERS

Teams will never realize their potential if some team members fail to cooperate.[16] Unfortunately, team members sometimes behave in ways that detract from overall team performance.

TYPES OF PROBLEM BEHAVIORS

There are many forms of problem behaviors in teams. We consider four types of problem team members: freeloaders, complainers, bullies, and martyrs.

> **Freeloaders.** Some team members simply don't carry their fair share of the team's workload; they engage in social loafing. Such freeloaders detract

BOTTOM LINE

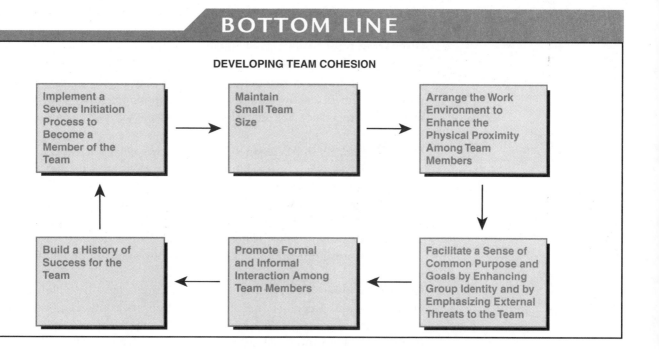

DEVELOPING TEAM COHESION

Implement a Severe Initiation Process to Become a Member of the Team → Maintain Small Team Size → Arrange the Work Environment to Enhance the Physical Proximity Among Team Members ↓ Facilitate a Sense of Common Purpose and Goals by Enhancing Group Identity and by Emphasizing External Threats to the Team ← Promote Formal and Informal Interaction Among Team Members ← Build a History of Success for the Team ↑

directly from team performance by their lack of contribution. In addition, they may provoke conflict in the team as other members refuse to carry an unproductive member.

> **Complainers.** These members constantly complain about the team's scheduling, activities, progress, or other matters. They see the project as a waste of time, feel they aren't being treated well, or simply hate to work in teams. Complainers damage team morale, and other members often spend an inordinate amount of time and energy trying to placate them.

> **Bullies.** Some members actively disrupt the team by pushing their opinions on others. Bullies seem to revel in making others feel inadequate or unintelligent. They may be better prepared or more knowledgeable than others and anxious to display their expertise, or they may use bullying to cover up their inadequacies. In either case, their insistence on controlling the team process leads to ill will and lack of team coordination.

> **Martyrs.** These are members who feel they are carrying the load for the team. They see themselves as being forced to cover for incompetent team members, having all the worst assignments, and doing far more than their fair share. Unlike complainers, they really don't want anything to change; they just want others to feel guilty and to acknowledge their burden. This often creates conflict as other team members chafe at the martyr's claims, attributions, and attitudes.

GUIDELINES FOR DEALING WITH PROBLEM BEHAVIORS

Many of these problem behaviors can be avoided or alleviated through proper planning and team management. For example,

> **Choose team members carefully.** Take team membership seriously. Think about whether potential members are likely to get along. Pick members who have a genuine interest in the task outcome. Make clear to each member why he or she is needed on the team.

> **Offer training.** Give members guidance on how to deal with problem behaviors. Members can, for instance, be shown videotapes of teams dealing successfully with problem members. Such videos may describe forms of potential problem behaviors, show team members' disappointment with such behaviors, make role expectations clear, and suggest specific ways to address problem behaviors.[17]

> **Provide clear goals.** Make sure the team knows what it is expected to do and why its task is important. Emphasize clear, well-defined goals and the consequences of the team's decision. Direction provided at the first team meeting is crucial and will establish lasting precedents for the team.

> **Define member responsibilities clearly.** Many problems in teams occur because members' responsibilities are unclear. Early agreement on a clear and equitable division of responsibilities will work wonders in preventing future conflict.

> **Use peer evaluations.** Team members and leaders must be willing and able to provide—and accept—honest feedback about their individual behaviors and the final outcome of the team's work.[18] Members are more willing to do their fair share and to curtail other problem behaviors if they know their

contributions will be evaluated. Approaches that employ peer evaluations, such as 360-degree feedback, are helpful in this regard.

> **Reward superior performance.** Team members who excel should somehow be rewarded for their contributions. This can take the form of positive peer evaluations, praise, or celebrations of accomplishments.

> **Don't let social considerations overwhelm concern with the task.** Many teams develop norms of peaceful coexistence—members are reluctant to confront others openly and to generate hurt feelings. As a result, social loafing and complaining is never challenged. Members must be willing to appeal to norms of fair participation and to deal openly with problem team members.

> **Appeal to the "shadow of the future."** Remind team members that they are likely to be working together on future tasks and inappropriate behavior on this task won't be forgotten.

> **Remove problem team members.** As a last resort, it may be necessary to remove an intransigent member from the team. Although this may be unpleasant, problem behaviors that sap team morale and performance cannot be allowed to continue unabated.

Skills Practice 11-6 will help you sharpen your team process analytical skills and link this with the identification of specific strategies for facilitating the effectiveness of a team based on watching the classic movie *Twelve Angry Men*. Good luck and pass the popcorn!

RUNNING TEAM MEETINGS

Meetings are a big part of the workday, and unless properly managed they can be frustrating, boring, and generally a waste of time. Alternatively, well-run meetings can reap the tremendous potential benefits of teams. As such, the ability to run a meeting well is a valuable skill. In this section, we provide guidelines for helping team members become acquainted, providing a facilitating setting, considering spatial arrangements, and giving structure to meetings.

HELPING TEAM MEMBERS BECOME ACQUAINTED

It's very important for team members to know and be comfortable with one another. If they aren't, meetings will be tense.[19]

> Before the first meeting, distribute members' biographical sketches, along with the team's assignment and other relevant materials.
> Before each meeting, give members a chance to socialize.
> At the first meeting, introduce each member or have the members introduce themselves.
> Use appropriate icebreaker exercises.[20] These might involve stories, exercises, or even jokes. Icebreakers can help overcome initial discomfort in teams. Until team members know who they are dealing with, they are uncomfortable and perhaps suspicious. However, icebreakers themselves can make team members nervous and uncomfortable if they aren't handled well.[21] Skills Practice 11-7 provides concrete suggestions for icebreaking.
> During long meetings, provide breaks.

Now complete Skills Practice 11-7 with a group of your classmates as a way to explore some basic strategies for getting acquainted with the other members of a new group.

PROVIDING A FACILITATIVE SETTING

Make sure the team can work in a comfortable space without distractions. Use a room large enough to accommodate the number of participants, but not so large as to make them feel lost. Provide flipcharts, whiteboards, and other writing surfaces. Avoid long, narrow tables, because they restrict eye contact and communication—a U-shaped seating arrangement works well. Try to have a comfortable lighting level. Offer flexibility in how team members can arrange themselves and their work.[22]

CONSIDERING SPATIAL ARRANGEMENTS

Sometimes the little things can make a big difference in teams. For example, when people come into a conference room for a meeting, they usually sit wherever they want. The team leader may—or may not—consciously choose a seat at the head of a conference table or in front of the group, but everything else is often left to chance. In fact, though, the way team members are arranged can make a big difference in how interaction takes place and, in turn, how well the team performs.

At least three aspects of spatial arrangements are important in teams: (1) how far apart team members are; (2) who is sitting in high-status positions; (3) how team members are arranged relative to one another. Let's look at these aspects in turn.

Interpersonal Distance. Suppose you meet a friend in the hallway and stop to chat. How close would you be likely to stand to your friend? Chances are you'd stand just far enough away that you could reach out and put your thumb in your friend's ear. The point is that we have certain comfortable distances for particular types of interactions. When people are too close to us or too far away, we tend to feel uneasy. Put another way, we have a sense of personal space, an area around us we treat as an extension of ourselves, and we want people to be in specific parts—or zones—of that personal space for particular activities. There are four zones of personal space, as shown in Figure 11-4.[23]

The ***intimate zone*** is a bubble extending, for Americans, to about 18 inches from the skin. As the name suggests, we let others enter this zone only for the very

FIGURE 11-4
Zones of Personal Space

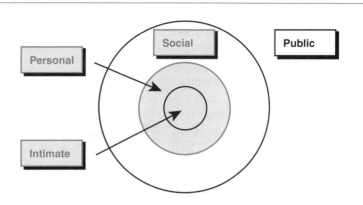

best of reasons, such as lovemaking, protecting, and comforting. When other circumstances—such as a crowded elevator—force us to allow people into the intimate zone, we tend to treat them as objects rather than persons.

The *personal zone* ranges from about 1.5 to 4 feet from the person. It is used for comfortable interaction with others and connotes closeness and friendship.

The *social zone*, from 4 to 12 feet, is used for most impersonal business. People working together use the inner part of the zone. The outer part is used for more formal interactions.

Finally, the *public zone*, more than 12 feet from the body, is beyond the range of comfortable interaction.

Interpersonal distances corresponding to the zones of personal space vary dramatically across cultures. For instance, in northern Europe, the bubbles tend to be quite large and people keep their distance. In southern France, Italy, Greece, and Spain, the bubbles are smaller. A distance seen as intimate in northern Europe overlaps normal conversational distance in southern Europe. As a result, Mediterranean Europeans get too close for the comfort of Germans, Scandinavians, English persons, and Americans of northern European ancestry.[24]

Businesspeople entering other cultures must be especially careful to learn appropriate zones for various interactions. Typically, people experience discomfort when their personal space is entered inappropriately. They may protest or leave the situation rather than accept it.[25]

Eye Contact. When leaders enter a room, where do they go? Often, they choose a position at the front of the room, or an elevated position, or a position at the head of a conference table. These positions have one thing in common: They each give the leader the chance to make direct eye contact with as many others as possible. In general, leaders tend to position themselves in a way that gives them a lot of potential eye contact with others. In turn, people who are in such positions (again, at the head of a conference table, in a central position in a room, or in an elevated position) are more likely to be seen as leaders. They are perceived (other things equal) to have more status and to be more leaderlike, and they have more communications directed toward them, than if they were in less visible positions.

Seating Arrangements. Suppose you and another individual were about to sit down at a conference table. Where would the two of you sit? Across from each other? Side by side? Corner to corner? Far apart? Your response probably depends on how the two of you would expect to be interacting, if at all. As shown in Figure 11-5, this is just what happens. If people expect to cooperate, they tend to sit side by side. If they expect to be in conflict, as in many bargaining situations, they tend to sit face to face. If they plan to engage in casual conversation, they sit corner to corner. If they don't plan to interact at all (for example, if they are each going to be working on their own homework), they tend to sit distant opposite.

Here's the more interesting finding: If people are *randomly* seated in these relative positions, they are more likely to interact in these ways than if seated differently. For example, people seated across from each other are more likely to get into an argument than if seated next to each other or corner to corner.

GIVING STRUCTURE TO MEETINGS

Team leaders are sometimes reluctant to provide structure. They don't want to be seen as bossy, and they believe (or hope) that things will somehow work themselves out. This is unfortunate, because meetings need—and team members welcome—structure. The key point here is that providing appropriate structure does not mean dominating the process. Instead, it gives team members clear bounds within which to operate.

> Prior to the meeting, distribute an agenda to all team members.
> At the beginning of the meeting, review progress to date and establish the task of the meeting.
> Early in the meeting, get a report from each member with a preassigned task.
> Manage the discussion to ensure fair participation. The team leader—and other team members—must make sure all members have the opportunity to participate. If one or a few members dominate the process, the benefits of using a team will quickly evaporate. Here are some tips for encouraging fair participation:
>   a. Establish norms for fair participation. For example, state early in the meeting, "Let's make sure we all have a chance to make our views known. I hope we'll all feel free to speak up, but also that we'll let others have their say."

FIGURE 11-5
Seating Arrangements for Different Activities

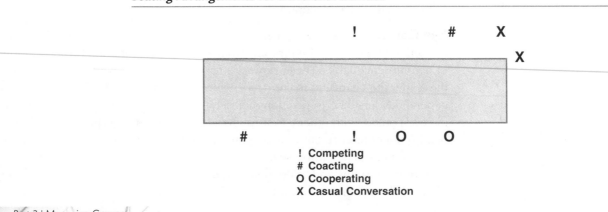

! Competing
Coacting
O Cooperating
X Casual Conversation

   b. Provide guiding comments. If someone has been dominating the process, say something to the effect of "Janet, I think you've done a good job of stating your position. Let's see if someone else has any comments." If someone hasn't been contributing, say something like "Donna, is there anything you'd like to add?" Often people are anxious to make a point but are reluctant to say anything unless they're asked directly to participate.

   c. Use a *round-robin process*, asking members directly to give their comments in turn. For example, the leader may simply say, "Let's go around the table and see what each of us has to say." Sometimes, when team members have made up lists of ideas, the round-robin technique may be used to have each member in turn give his or her first idea, then in turn give his or her second idea, and so on.

   d. Ask members to write down their ideas. This technique will result in more unique, clearly stated ideas.

> At the end of the meeting, summarize what was accomplished, where the group is on its schedule, and what will be the team's task at the next meeting. This wrapping up gives the team a sense of movement and accomplishment.

> Also, make public and clear each member's assignment for the next meeting. This creates a sense of responsibility. It also makes sure people know what they're expected to do, and that tasks don't either get duplicated by more than one team member or fall through the cracks, being ignored by all members.

The process model shown in the Bottom Line feature on the next page displays the general steps associated with planning and conducting an effective team meeting.

SELF-MANAGING TEAMS

We began this chapter with an example of the self-managing teams at Harley-Davidson. Harley's experience is not unique. According to one survey, more than two-thirds of *Fortune* 1,000 firms use self-managing teams with at least some employees, and they are one of the fastest growing forms of employee involvement.[26] Self-managing teams are common at such companies as Procter & Gamble, General Motors, Motorola, Ford, General Electric, AT&T, Xerox, American Express, and Prudential.[27]

WHY USE SELF-MANAGING TEAMS?

Everything about the new workplace suggests that self-managing teams will become increasingly important. For example, as organizations become flatter and more decentralized, decision making is pushed down to lower levels. With fewer supervisors, employees must learn to manage themselves. In addition, the modern work environment is dynamic and uncertain. In such an environment, firms must be agile, able to respond quickly to changes in markets and technologies. Placing responsibility at the level of the team, rather than at higher levels in the firm, permits rapid response—those closest to the customer and best able to meet customer demands have the authority to act. Further, employees generally value autonomy and opportunities to participate. As such, giving teams greater responsibility lets team members use their intellectual and creative capacities more fully and makes the job more interesting and intrinsically motivating. It should also help ensure that team

BOTTOM LINE

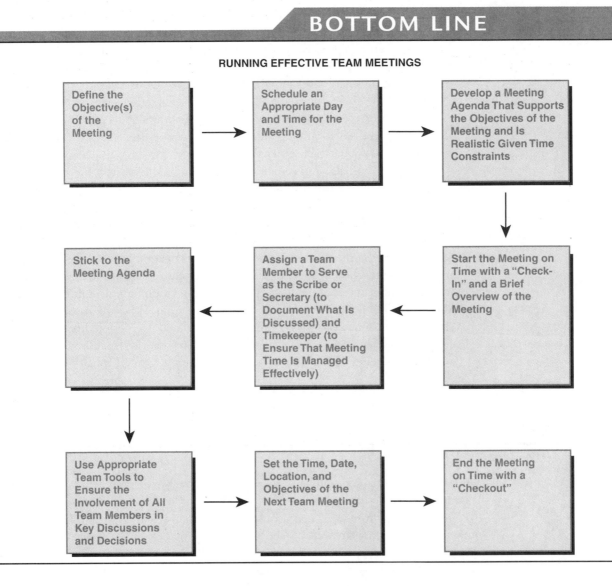

RUNNING EFFECTIVE TEAM MEETINGS

Define the Objective(s) of the Meeting

→

Schedule an Appropriate Day and Time for the Meeting

→

Develop a Meeting Agenda That Supports the Objectives of the Meeting and Is Realistic Given Time Constraints

↓

Stick to the Meeting Agenda

←

Assign a Team Member to Serve as the Scribe or Secretary (to Document What Is Discussed) and Timekeeper (to Ensure That Meeting Time Is Managed Effectively)

←

Start the Meeting on Time with a "Check-In" and a Brief Overview of the Meeting

↓

Use Appropriate Team Tools to Ensure the Involvement of All Team Members in Key Discussions and Decisions

→

Set the Time, Date, Location, and Objectives of the Next Team Meeting

→

End the Meeting on Time with a "Checkout"

members will take ownership of important organizational decisions and be more committed to implementing them enthusiastically.

HOW SELF-MANAGING TEAMS WORK

Quite simply, self-managing teams manage themselves. They take responsibility for their work, plan how they will carry it out, allocate duties among team members, monitor their own performance, seek resources, and make changes in their performance strategies as needed. In some cases, teams may also have responsibility for hiring, disciplining, and scheduling.[28] At Boeing, for instance, members of self-managing teams elect their own team leaders and interview prospective employees, looking especially for culture fit and attitude.[29]

Self-managing teams offer great promise, but they also pose special challenges. For one thing, of course, managing isn't easy. It would be naïve to think team members would be able to master easily the many tasks of management, including planning, organizing, motivating, and controlling. Our discussion of guidelines for self-management in Chapter 4 should be useful in this regard.

LEADER ROLES IN SELF-MANAGING TEAMS

What does it mean to be in charge of a self-managing team? It might seem that this is a contradiction in terms. In fact, though, the formally designated leader of a self-managing team has a variety of responsibilities. These include the following:[30]

> **Becoming a self-leader.** The leader must develop behavioral and cognitive self-management skills—discussed in Chapter 4—to achieve the self-motivation and self-direction needed to perform.

> **Modeling self-leadership.** The leader's own self-leadership behaviors serve as a model from which others can learn. When, for instance, self-managing team members see the leader setting goals for behavioral change, using self-reward to foster goal attainment, self-monitoring his or her performance, and then attaining the self-set goals, they are likely to initiate their own self-leadership actions.

> **Encouraging self-set goals.** As discussed in Chapter 4, goal setting is critical for effective motivation. Consistent with that discussion, leaders should encourage team members to set specific and challenging goals for themselves.

> **Creating positive thought patterns.** Constructive thought patterns are central to effective self-leadership. Leaders can attempt to transmit positive thought patterns to team members, and they can encourage positive self-expectations in them. Especially in the early stages of a new job or assignment, employees have doubts and fears, and a leader's words of confidence, praise, and support are crucial. This behavior often results in a self-fulfilling prophecy; those who believe they can do well are more likely to excel because of constructive thought patterns.

> **Developing self-leadership through reward and constructive reprimand.** Leaders of self-managing teams may use conventional rewards and reprimands to encourage self-leadership behaviors. However, use of reprimands is likely to discourage employees as they are in the transition to self-leadership and should be used only as a last resort for severe and chronic carelessness or underperformance. Beyond this, leaders should encourage and teach team members to reward themselves and build self-rewards into their work. That is, the leader should deemphasize externally administered rewards, emphasizing self-administered and natural rewards.

> **Promoting self-leadership through teamwork.** Quite simply, team members learn self-leadership through regular and varied experiences in team settings that place them in positions where self-management is necessary.

> **Facilitating a self-leadership culture.** Leaders must play a part in developing pervasive, integrated organizational cultures—as discussed in Chapter 13—which are conducive to high levels of self-management and performance.

Xerox uses many self-managing teams in its customer service division. Research on the teams has identified several factors that seem to characterize leaders of the most successful self-managing teams. For instance, leaders of the most successful teams give first priority to getting the team set up correctly and to arranging organizational support for it before turning to coaching.[31]

USING SPECIAL-PURPOSE GROUP TECHNIQUES

When we think of bringing people together to deal with problems, we probably envision a committee meeting, with people arranged—notebooks open and pens poised—around a conference table. In fact, though, there are more entrees on the group menu than just the committee du jour. Here we present four specific alternatives to traditional interacting groups: the devil's advocate, brainstorming, the affinity technique, and the nominal group technique. Each of these techniques is easy and effective to use, can be completed in a single session, and serves a specific purpose. Your mastery of these techniques can add valuable skills to your management arsenal.

TO ENCOURAGE HEALTHY DISSENT: THE DEVIL'S ADVOCATE

Beginning in the 12th century, the Roman Catholic Church instituted strict procedures to determine who was, or wasn't, worthy of sainthood. One barrier on the road to sainthood was the devil's advocate. The devil's advocate—a position that wasn't abolished until 1983—was a church officer whose role was to spot flaws in the arguments on behalf of a candidate for sainthood. Now the *devil's advocate* refers to an individual or group given the responsibility for challenging a proposal. The idea is to find flaws while they may still be remedied, or to recognize they are fatal, before competitors, customers, or others become aware of them.

The devil's advocate's role is to make sure the group takes a hard second look at its preferred alternative. Designating a devil's advocate makes it clear that dissent is legitimate. It brings out criticisms that might not otherwise be aired, and it highlights underlying assumptions.

However, devil's advocates must be used with caution. If they are employed too often or if they are overly severe in their criticisms, they may cause problems. Some people may become demoralized if their views are constantly criticized. As a result, they may come up with safe solutions, not especially risky or creative but able to stand up to criticism. Also, if the devil's advocate is successful in finding fatal problems with a plan or alternative, there is no new plan or alternative to take its place. That is, the devil's advocate approach focuses on what is wrong without pointing out what is right.

TO GENERATE CREATIVE IDEAS: GROUP BRAINSTORMING

People sometimes use the term *brainstorming* any time they sit around and try to come up with ideas. In fact, though, brainstorming is a specific technique with a set of rules. *Group brainstorming* seeks to create the right atmosphere for relaxed, spontaneous thinking. A small group of employees is brought together, presented with the problem, and told to follow four rules:

> **Don't criticize any ideas.** This creates a climate of psychological safety, reducing inhibitions.
> **Freewheel.** Any idea, no matter how wild, is fine.
> **Try to come up with as many ideas as possible.** The more ideas, the better.
> **Try to combine and improve.** Hitchhiking on others' ideas may create a chain of inspiration.

Many companies are using brainstorming to develop new product ideas, marketing approaches, and creative advertising strategies. For example, Honda's engineering team used a brainstorming approach to develop the highly fuel-efficient engine for the 1992 Honda Civic. Hallmark Cards has regular brainstorming sessions for its greeting card writers. Adaptec, a California semiconductor firm, believes it is difficult to build real consensus on important corporate decisions without an empathetic business organization. Employees at all levels of the organization attend interdepartmental brainstorming sessions. These sessions usually produce ideas that reflect the company's overall competencies better than ideas arising from any single department. Adaptec also engages in interdepartmental communications programs so each department is exposed to the elementary concepts used in other departments. For example, finance people attend sessions in marketing and operations. Employees at all levels appreciate seeing the whole picture and feeling involved.[32]

Diverse brainstorming groups, or groups that include members who hold minority views, typically produce not only more ideas but also higher quality ideas than homogeneous groups. As discussed in the nearby Focus on Management, some companies are now using idea centers to brainstorming and associated tools for enhancing group creativity.[33]

New electronic tools promise to make brainstorming even more effective. At IBM, meeting rooms are equipped with personal computers for each participant, and a large color monitor is located where everyone can see it. Participants type in their ideas, comments, or reactions on their keyboards. Their input, which is anonymous, appears simultaneously on the monitor as well as on each computer screen. Everyone gets a chance to contribute, and no one can dominate the process. One popular electronic tool for facilitating brainstorming and other group decision processes is Ventana Corporation's GroupSystems, described on the text Web site.[34]

As befits a technique meant to enhance creativity, there are some creative variants of brainstorming. With *stop-and-go brainstorming*, short periods of brainstorming (10 minutes or so) are interspersed with short periods of evaluation. *Reverse brainstorming* brings fresh approaches by turning the problem around. How could we stifle creativity? How could we decrease morale? How could we lower productivity? With large groups, the *Phillips 66 technique* can be used. Once the problem is clearly understood, small groups of six members brainstorm for six minutes. Then a member of each group presents the best ideas or all ideas to the larger group.

FOCUS ON MANAGEMENT

UNITED TECHNOLOGIES AUTOMOTIVE'S IDEA CENTER

In 1997, United Technologies Automotive, a subsidiary of Lear Corporation, added an Idea Center to its Dearborn, Michigan, headquarters. The center is a focal point for brainstorming and systems development, incorporating the latest technology and designed to stimulate the free flow of ideas. The center, which allows members from various product teams to meet in a supportive setting, aims at reducing costs, improving quality, and speeding up product development time.*

http://www.lear.com/

*See Dale Jewett, "Supplier Builds Itself an Incubator for Ideas," *Automotive News*, December 16, 1996, p. 20.

TO GENERATE CREATIVE IDEAS: THE AFFINITY TECHNIQUE

Brainstorming is a simple and useful tool for generating creative ideas. Another good creativity-enhancement tool is the *affinity technique*, a simple but powerful way for a team to enhance the effectiveness of its decision making. It can be used whenever a team is attempting to identify creative solutions to a problem. For example, the affinity technique can be used to identify ideas for improving customer service, product quality, or productivity. The affinity technique achieves its purpose by requiring a team to generate potential solutions to a problem systematically, clustering them in terms of their similarities, naming the clusters, and then using a voting procedure to identify which ideas should be given the highest priority.

Now use Skills Practice 11-8 to work in a group to apply the affinity technique for group decision making. Again, this is an excellent tool for addressing problems that require creative solutions.

TO GENERATE A GROUP SOLUTION: THE NOMINAL GROUP TECHNIQUE

Earlier in this chapter we pointed out benefits and drawbacks associated with using teams. Here's an important thing to recognize in looking at those lists—the benefits generally result simply from the many perspectives, skills, and resources brought to a group by its members, and the drawbacks usually result from the interaction of team members. For example, interaction may permit some people to dominate others, to block others' ideas, or to bully. Of course, interaction is often needed—we want the chance to air our views and to get others' ideas and reactions, and we often simply like to be able to talk with our colleagues. Still, there may be times when interaction really isn't needed and when, therefore, we might want to restrict it.

A nominal group (a group "in name only") is another name for a coacting (that is, noninteracting) group. For instance, if you and your roommates were all sitting around a table and writing down ideas on how to cut down on your food costs, without discussing your ideas or interacting in other ways, you would be members of a coacting group. With a coacting group, members are working together on the same task, but they aren't talking with one another or communicating in other ways.

The *nominal group technique* uses a blend of coacting and interacting stages in order to capture the benefits of groups while minimizing potential problems. It has the following goals:

> To encourage all members to make inputs
> To prevent dominant members from controlling the process
> To ensure that all ideas get a fair hearing
> To allow members to evaluate alternatives without fear of retribution.

To do all this, the nominal group technique uses the steps shown in Figure 11-6. Each of the steps in the figure is important, but one of them—the silent generation of ideas in writing without interaction—deserves further comment. By taking just 15 minutes or so to complete this step, you can achieve the following benefits:

> Ideas are generated without being evaluated.
> Members focus their time directly on the search for ideas.
> Nobody can dominate the process.
> Everyone makes inputs.
> Ideas are put in writing.

FIGURE 11-6

Steps in the Nominal Group Technique

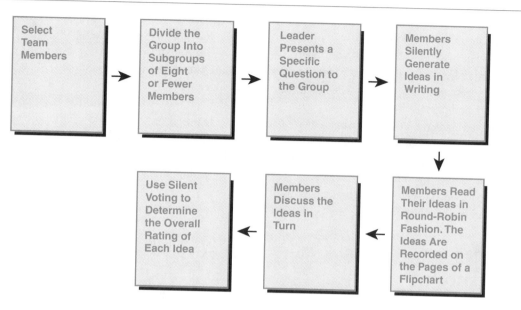

GAINING ACCEPTANCE OF NEW TECHNIQUES

Each of the tools we've just discussed works well and is widely used in modern organizations. Still, it sometimes seems difficult to try something different; people know what to expect in committees, and they're comfortable with them even as they lament the time they're wasting in one meeting after another. Here are some tips for gaining acceptance of new group processes:

> Just do it. Take charge and announce you're going to handle the meeting differently today. Your assurance in presenting and using these tools will go a long way toward ensuring their acceptance and enthusiastic use. As we discussed in Chapter 8, a forceful and assured leader is seen as charismatic and likely to have enthusiastic followers.

> Explain why you're doing something different. Point out that the tool you're going to use is the best available for the task you're about to undertake—coming up with good ideas, making sure concerns are aired, or coming up with a creative solution.

> Point out that these are widely used, effective techniques. Give specific examples of how they're used in companies such as IBM, American Express, Xerox, and Adaptec.

> Treat this as a skill-building experience both for yourself and for your colleagues. Point out to team members that they will all be team leaders, formal or informal, and learning these techniques may be of great value to them.

> Point out that mastering more group tools adds further to the team's resources. The tools don't have to be used all the time, but they're available when needed.

Now that you have learned about techniques for developing and managing teams, complete Skills Practice 11-9 as a way to understand how well your team is functioning and what can be done to enhance its effectiveness.

TOP TEN LIST: KEY POINTS TO REMEMBER

MANAGING TEAMS

10. Identify the objective(s) of your team.
9. Identify the expertise you will need on your team.
8. Select the members of your team based on the expertise needed *and* an appropriate diversity of team member work and personality styles.
7. Take the time to break the ice between team members in order to facilitate positive working relationships.
6. Work with team members to develop a timeline for achieving the goals of the project.
5. Define a role for each team member that aligns his or her needs and goals with those of the team.

4. Use ground rules and meeting agendas to structure the team process.
3. Ensure that all team members are participating in the team process.
2. Build quality checks into the team process that assess team progress in relation to the project timeline, and make adjustments as needed.
1. Balance the concerns for tasks and for people throughout all phases of the team process.

QUESTIONS FOR REVIEW AND REFLECTION

REVIEW QUESTIONS

1. Identify and describe three types of teams.
2. Discuss potential advantages and disadvantages of teams.
3. Discuss factors that help decide when a team should be used.
4. Provide guidelines for determining team size and membership.
5. Identify types of team roles, and indicate guidelines for enhancing a team's productivity by understanding these roles.
6. Give guidelines for defining the team's assignment and planning the team's effort.
7. Discuss ways to develop productive norms.
8. Describe team polarization and why it is important.
9. Identify causes and consequences of team cohesiveness.

10. Set out guidelines for helping team members become acquainted and for providing a facilitative setting for team meetings.
11. Discuss ways to give structure to meetings, including techniques to encourage fair participation.
12. Discuss how team member eye contact and seating arrangements influence team processes and outcomes.
13. Identify potential benefits of self-managing teams, as well as leader roles in self-managing teams.
14. Discuss special-purpose group techniques, including the devil's advocate, group brainstorming, the affinity technique, and the nominal group technique.
15. Provide guidelines for gaining acceptance of new techniques.

CRITICAL THINKING QUESTIONS

1. A manager says, "If I need a team, I'll form it. I don't want my employees to form informal groups, and I break up informal groups when I can." What might be some unintended consequences of the manager's actions?
2. Considering the potential advantages and disadvantages of teams, describe a situation in which a team would be *most* useful. Then describe a situation in which use of a team would clearly be undesirable.
3. Consider a group of which you are a member. Identify four norms of the group. How do you think each of

those norms developed? Discuss what you see as the consequences of each norm.
4. A colleague complains that every team he is in seems to start out fighting, stating, "I'm about to give up on teams." How might you respond?
5. Discuss how implementation of self-managing work teams might affect each of the following in organizations:
   a. Power relationships
   b. Selection and training
   c. Career mobility

6. Recall that polarization causes initial group tendencies to become more extreme. Discuss situations in which polarization might be desirable, as well as situations in which polarization is clearly undesirable. Are there any types of group tendencies for which polarization would *always* be harmful or would *always* be helpful?

7. The nominal group technique has been found to be very useful for generating large numbers of unique and creative ideas. What characteristics of the technique might limit the degree to which it is used?

8. Do you think the growing use of teams in organizations will continue? Why or why not?

EXPERIENTIAL EXERCISES

WEB EXERCISE 11-1

Go to the following URL and read the *ComputerWorld* article titled "Xerox: A Tough Culture to Duplicate."
http://www.computerworld.com/news/1998/story/0,11280,33384,00.html

Answer the following questions relating to the article:

1. How is dissent treated in Xerox Corp.'s information systems department? What are some consequences of that treatment?

2. How is diversity viewed in the department? What are some apparent benefits of diversity for the department?

3. What is the role of the annual employee motivation and satisfaction survey?

4. What might be some costs of the steps taken by the department to encourage expression of dissent?

WEB EXERCISE 11-2

Use a search engine such as Google to find Web sites containing the word *teamwork* as well as the name of a specific company of your choice. Review the selected sites to find material discussing teamwork (types, benefits, special characteristics, etc.) at the company. Write a one-page summary of your findings.

CASE 11-1

SELF-MANAGING WORK TEAMS AT CHEVRONTEXACO

The Company

The ChevronTexaco Corporation, headquartered in San Ramon, California, is a global petroleum company engaged in oil exploration, production, transportation, refining, retail marketing, chemical manufacturing and sales, and power generation.[35] It operates in more than 180 countries, with a work force of over 53,000 employees.

The vision of ChevronTexaco is "to be the global energy company most admired for its people, partnerships, and performance." The specific elements of this vision include the following:

- Providing energy products and services that are vital to society's quality of life
- Being known as people with superior capabilities and commitment, both as individuals and as an organization
- Thinking and behaving globally, and valuing the positive influence this has on our company

- Being the partner of choice because we best exemplify collaboration
- Delivering world-class performance
- Earning the admiration of all of our stakeholders—investors, customers, host governments, local communities, and our employees-not only for the goals we achieve but how we achieve them

The ChevronTexaco Way is composed of these elements:

- Performance (operational excellence, cost reduction, capital stewardship, and profitable growth)
- People (dynamic leaders, skilled employees, learning and innovation, recognition and accountability, world-class processes and organization, and technology and partnerships)
- Values (integrity, trust, diversity, partnership, high performance, responsibility and growth, protecting people and the environment)

- "Tracking Our Success" (being preferred as a place to work, being world class in safety, efficiency, reliability, and environmental stewardship; performing with speed, agility, and excellence; being the best partner of choice for the best business opportunities, being valued contributors to the quality of life in the communities where we work, having a sustained track record of earnings growth, and delivering superior long-term stockholder returns)

The Situation

The Kern River Asset Team (KRAT) is part of Chevron-Texaco's Western Production Business Unit and South Valley Profit Center. Its primary job is to produce oil from ChevronTexaco facilities in Bakersfield, California. The work force at this facility consisted of 80 field operators, craft personnel, technical support, clerical support, and management staff. In the past, the KRAT was composed of many asset teams that functioned within a traditional, hierarchical organization. This meant that power and authority was centralized at the top of the organization with frontline employees possessing little authority to make decisions about how to perform their jobs on their own.

Key Problems

Here are some of the problems associated with this approach:

- The teams had difficulty relating the processes associated with their asset to broad objectives. That is, workers did not understand how their work contributed to the achievement of the company's objectives.
- Teams had trouble developing a big picture perspective of the processes they managed. Workers only possessed a narrow view of their jobs and they could not see how their jobs fit into the larger system in their work unit.
- The small asset team structure encouraged accountability or ownership at the micro level. This resulted in redundancy of work processes that greatly reduced efficiency and increased operating costs.

The Self-Managing Work Team Structure

As part of an organizational restructuring, a self-managing work team structure was created in order to support continuous improvement. The new structure implemented at the Kern River Profit Center involved the organization of teams around specific work processes and quality management principles. Employee empowerment and labor–management cooperation were also important parts of the process.

To initiate the development of the self-managing work team concept at the company, a team of employees who represented various parts of the organization was formed. The objective of this team was to work with an external management consultant to identify and organize tasks into meaningful groupings and to define specific boundaries for each team. This design team kept employees updated regarding their progress on designing the new system. The guiding principles for this part of the development process were as follows:[36]

- The design provided for a natural business focus while accentuating the importance of the asset team's profits over those of individual process teams
- The design ensured a process improvement focus while stressing the importance of customer/supplier relationships
- The design was simple and flexible
- The design fostered an in-depth understanding among team members

The composition of the self-managing teams formed was diversified in terms of technical, interpersonal, and leadership skills. Each team had five to eight members. All the processes the teams would be managing were formally flowcharted as well. A total of 11 self-directed work teams were formed within the overall Kern River Asset Team organization. These included the following: reservoir management and planning team, well management team, production analyst team, oil and water separation team, steam team, and the energy management team.

At this point, the organization implemented the self-managing work team structure using an approach based on four key elements:

- Support from the organization in that employees were given adequate time to understand and support the new system
- The entire Kern River Asset Team work force was involved in resolving the issues that came up during the start-up
- Prior to start-up, the role, objectives, leadership model, and relationship expected from teams were clearly explained
- A training program to help teams prioritize their tasks in relation to assigned business processes and external constituents (suppliers, customers, etc.) was offered.

A coach was also assigned to each team to provide leadership support. The main purpose of this person was to monitor the progress of the team and to offer guidance as needed. Additional training was provided in the areas of general team building, problem solving, communication, conflict resolution, and so on.

In the beginning, the coach and each team made decisions together. However, the goal for the future was to transfer authority and responsibility for the business process from the coach to the team.

Some problems that occurred after the administration of the new team system included (1) employee frustration resulting from a lack of understanding of the system, (2) adopting a new system that required a fundamentally different mentality and way of doing things, (3) communication problems within the teams, and (4) personality and interpersonal conflicts.

Results

Here are the preliminary evaluations of the self-managing work team system:

- Product cycle time was reduced.
- Process improvements were identified and implemented.

- The use of process measures has helped the teams to enhance their knowledge and mastery of their process.

Discussion Questions

1. To what extent do you feel self-managing work teams are appropriate for this situation?
2. What were the strengths of the process for designing and implementing the self-managing work teams approach?
3. What were the weaknesses of the process for designing and implementing the self-managing work teams approach?
4. What recommendations would you give to Chevron-Texaco regarding the handling of this situation? What types of challenges might come up in implementing these recommendations? What could be done to overcome these challenges? Be specific.

Source: M. Attaran, "Succeeding with Self-Managed Work Teams," *Industrial Management*, July/August 1999, pp. 24–28.

CASE 11-2

THE SENIOR MANAGEMENT TEAM AT BIOCOM SCIENTIFIC INTERNATIONAL[37]

Note: This case is based on actual events that took place in a real-world organization. Some information may have been modified to ensure the anonymity of the team and organization.

The Company

Biocom Scientific International was formed by two entrepreneurs on the East Coast in 2000. The company develops a variety of cutting-edge systems and technologies for the biotechnology industry. The company's basic mission is to develop and market its technologies and systems to scientific research labs all over the world. The company currently employs approximately 100 people in the United States and another 50 in Europe and Asia. Annual sales have increased an average of 300 percent between 2001 and 2003.

The Senior Management Team at BioCom Scientific International is composed of five individuals:

William M. Connor, 52 years old, executive vice president and chief financial officer

William previously worked at a variety of other technology companies. He has a bachelor's degree in business adminis-

tration and a JD from major universities on the West Coast. He has been with the company since 2000.

Lisa Maxwell, 41 years old, vice president of business development and marketing

Lisa also possesses extensive experience with other technology companies. She has a bachelor's and master's degree in biology from an Ivy League school. She has been with the company since 2001.

Kenneth Rogers, 45 years old, senior vice president of systems development

Kenneth has held one position with another technology company before coming to Biocom International. He has a master's degree in chemical engineering from a major research university in the Midwest. He has been with the company since 2002.

Alan J. Foster, 51 years old, vice president of research and development

Alan is one of the founders of the company. He has a PhD in molecular biology from a major research university on the West Coast.

Josh C. Newman, 38 years old, vice president of bioinformatics

Josh is the newest member of the senior management

team. He has worked as a consultant in the bioinformatics field. He earned his bachelor's degree in computer science from a major university in the Southeast.

Methodology

Management consultants were hired by the senior management team at Biocom International to evaluate the functioning of the team and make recommendations for enhancing its effectiveness. Consultants conducted a series of interviews with members of the management team and administered an in-depth battery of paper-and-pencil self-assessments to capture their perceptions of the senior management team and its functioning. These questionnaires asked about each executive's perceptions of the team's management of conflict, meeting effectiveness, and overall team functioning (defining of roles and responsibilities, decision making, communicating, etc.) These data were supplemented with a series of ongoing observations of the management team during its meetings.

Results

The consultant's observations of the management team revealed the following:

- Each of Biocom's employees is working on a separate committee devoted to a specific part of the product development or marketing process.
- The company implements some cross-functional committees.
- The management team meets formally once a week.
- When the management team meets, it is usually the executive vice president that serves as the team leader.
- Members of the management team find the environment for meetings relaxed and informal.
- The main purpose of the management team is to coordinate the activities of the committees.

Overall results of the executive team's responses to the self-assessments revealed the following (the response scale ranged from 1 to 7 with higher scores reflecting greater degrees of team effectiveness):

Team Effectiveness Results: Mean Scores

Consultation with Each Other	Clarity of Team Goals	Amount of Member Participation	Communication	Decision Making	Clarity of Roles and Responsibilities
6.2	5.8	5.5	5.1	5.0	4.5

Procedures	Confronting Difficulties	Commitment to Goals	Quality of Work Atmosphere	Leadership	Support for Each Other
4.4	4.3	5.6	5.5	5.2	5.0

Risk Taking	Amount of Evaluation of Team Process	Meetings	Trust Among Team	Amount of Fun	
5.0	4.4	4.3	3.9	3.2	

Conflict Management Effectiveness Results—Mean Scores

Note: The response scale ranged from 1 to 7 with higher scores reflecting greater degrees of team effectiveness.

Consultation with Each Other	Acknowledging Other Views	Objectivity	Listening	Proper Approach to Conflict	Trust and Openness
5.2	4.6	4.6	4.3	4.1	4.2

Norms	Providing Closure to Issues	Appropriate Interpersonal Behaviors	Structure	Process Checking	Time Management
4.0	4.0	3.8	3.5	3.1	3.0

Dealing with Conflict Aftermath
3.0

Meeting Effectiveness Results: Mean Scores

Note: The response scale ranged from 1 to 7 with higher scores reflecting greater degrees of team effectiveness.

Good Setting for Meetings	Communication	Clarity of Meeting Objectives	Preparation for Meetings	Role Clarity During Meetings	Review of Meeting at End
6.4	5.0	4.6	4.5	4.2	4.0

Effective Meeting Process	Meetings Start on Time	Time Limits Set on Meetings	Warm-Ups Conducted at Beginning of Meetings	Participation in Meetings	Pace of Meetings
4.0	3.6	3.5	3.3	3.2	3.2

Dealing with Conflict During Meetings	Providing Closure on Meetings	Record Keeping During Meetings	Use of Agendas During Meetings
3.1	3.0	3.0	3.0

Conflict Handling Style Self-Assessment Results: Mean Scores

Note: Scores can range from 1 to 7 with higher scores indicating a higher degree of a given personality trait. More detailed explanations of the traits here can be found in Chapter 10, Managing Conflict.

	Avoiding Conflict Style	Collaborating Conflict Style	Compromising Conflict Style	Accommodating Conflict Style	Competing Conflict Style
William Connor	3.6	6.2	4.7	4.1	5.1
Lisa Maxwell	6.1	4.7	3.1	3.0	4.8
Kenneth Rogers	2.5	3.0	2.0	2.0	6.3
Alan Foster	3.5	5.8	6.4	5.0	3.0
Josh Newman	4.0	6.0	5.5	4.5	3.5

Discussion Questions

1. Now it's your turn to be the consultant. Based on the information provided here, analyze the results of the various assessments of the senior management team's functioning and identify the key findings. Download the worksheet created for this exercise from the Web site for this textbook to help you structure your approach to this exercise. Be sure to document your key findings on this worksheet.

2. Based on your key results, develop a set of *short-term recommendations* (tasks that should be done immediately or in the next few months) for the senior management team to help them enhance their effectiveness. Make sure that each of your recommendations is specific and action oriented. Be prepared to justify each of your recommendations to members of the senior management team in terms of merit, feasibility, and cost effectiveness. Also, make sure you address what senior management needs to do to ensure the effective execution of your recommendations.

3. Based on your key results, develop a set of *long-term recommendations* (tasks that should be implemented in the next three to five years) for the senior management team to help them enhance their effectiveness. Make sure each of your recommendations is specific and action oriented. Be prepared to justify each of your recommendations to members of the senior management team in terms of merit, feasibility, and cost effectiveness. Also make sure you address what senior management needs to do to ensure the effective execution of your recommendations.

4. Make a five- to ten-minute presentation of your results and recommendations to the class.

5. What did you learn from this case study in terms of the functioning of real-world teams and what must be done to enhance their effectiveness? Which concepts discussed in this chapter were helpful to you in conducting your analysis and in formulating your recommendations?

VIDEO CASE: NEXT DOOR FOOD STORE

A STUDY OF SELF-DIRECTED WORK TEAMS

Running Time: 11:36

Headquartered in Mount Pleasant, Michigan, Next Door Food Store is a family-run business with more than 30 outlets in Michigan and Indiana. The stores sell gasoline and a wide variety of grocery and general merchandise items. Next Door management faces many challenges, including a high turnover rate. Management believes it can address these challenges by motivating and empowering employees through the use of self-directed work teams. It is using self-directed work teams to encourage employees to shift from narrow individual goals to a focus on the business as a whole.

The video shows the first team in place at company headquarters, the audit department (called the DGIT Team). Next Door Food Store's training director, Brenda Henry-Coan, members of the DGIT Team, and others discuss the company's use of self-directed teams. After viewing the video, answer the following questions:

1. Why was the audit department selected as the company's first self-directed work team?
2. What are concerns that would interfere with DGIT Team members' motivation and ability to create a successful self-directed work team?
3. According to members of the DGIT Team, what must the team do to be successful?
4. Why are team-building exercises used at Next Door Food Store?
5. Is there any evidence that the DGIT Team has been successful?
6. How would being part of a self-directed work team, such as the DGIT Team, increase motivation?
7. The DGIT Team members are seeking ways to eliminate their own jobs. What would motivate them to do this?
8. According to DGIT Team members, what are the advantages of being out in the field?

http://www.nextdoor1.com/

LIGHTEN UP

"NORMS"

"Norm" is likely to bring to mind Norm Peterson, the jovial, rotund regular on *Cheers*. This long-running television program set in a Boston pub had a cast of characters that exchanged jokes, stories, and insults in the comfort of "a place where everybody knows your name." The characters on *Cheers* did, in fact, share a variety of norms. For example, members shared expectations about where the regulars should sit, how regulars entering the bar should be greeted, what subjects were acceptable for discussion, and how Cheers's patrons should react to challenges from outsiders. An ongoing gag was the "Normisms," Norm's replies to those greeting him when he entered the bar. For a collection of "Normisms," go to:

http://www.wort.org/normisms.html

LIGHTEN UP

CONCRETE CANOES AND SUBSURFACE PAINTBALL

Some team-building approaches move outside the office. For instance, many companies send their employees to outdoor challenge courses where team members must work together to complete tasks such as climbing walls, weaving their ways through webs of rope, and passing a hula hoop around a circle while holding hands. Other firms send their teams on caving, camping, sailing, or rock climbing outings. Some activities are even more innovative. For instance, companies may dispatch their teams to battle in a subsurface paintball complex or have them build and race concrete canoes.[38] These exercises encourage team members to develop team spirit by jointly facing adversity and overcoming challenges. Facilitators work with the teams to point out how the activities parallel the work environment.

SKILLS PRACTICE

11-1   *Skill Level:* CHALLENGING

Field Experience in Diagnosing Team Functioning

Skill Objectives

1. To provide exposure to the challenges facing real teams in organizations.

2. To develop the ability to evaluate the functioning of a team systematically.

3. To develop the ability to make recommendations for enhancing the functioning of a team.

Procedure

1. Identify the leader or manager of a work team in a local organization. Ask the manager or team leader

if you can interview him or her for approximately 30 to 45 minutes. If possible, interview two or three members of the team as well in order to obtain an employee perspective.

2. When you meet with the manager or team leader, ask the following questions:

   a. What does your team do? What are its key objectives?

   b. Describe the team's context in terms of the larger organization (its mission, goals, structure, culture) and industry (competitors, trends, customers, etc.).

   c. What is the composition of the team membership (size, skills, experience, education, work style)? What are the duties and responsibilities of each of the team members?

   d. What type of leadership style do you use in managing this team? Why?

   e. What are the major strengths of the team? Can you give me some examples of situations in which the team has demonstrated these strengths?

   f. What are the key opportunities for improvement for the team? Can you give me some examples of situations in which the team has demonstrated the need for improvement in these areas?

3. If you meet with some of the members of the team, ask the following questions:

   a. What are the major strengths of the team? Can you give me some examples of situations in which the team has demonstrated these strengths?

   b. What are the key opportunities for improvement for the team? Can you give me some examples of situations in which the team has demonstrated the need for improvement in these areas?

   c. What recommendations would you give to the leader of your team regarding specific actions that he or she could take to enhance the effectiveness of your team? Why would these recommendations be helpful?

4. Summarize the results of your interview(s).

Discussion Questions

1. Based on the results of your analysis, identify a set of specific recommendations you would make to the leader of the team you diagnosed that will enhance its effectiveness. Make sure each of your recommendations is action oriented and you could justify its merit to the leader of the team you diagnosed for this exercise.

2. What did you learn about the effective management of teams in the real world from doing this exercise?

SKILLS PRACTICE

11-2   *Skill Level:* **CHALLENGING**

Facilitating Effective Team Meetings

Skill Objective

To develop the skills needed to plan, facilitate, and evaluate a team meeting.

Procedure

1. Form groups of five to seven students.

2. Read the following brief overview of tips for running effective team meetings in this chapter and here.

   Brief Overview of Tips for Running Effective Team Meetings

   a. Assign one person to each of the following roles:

   Meeting Leader: This person is responsible for leading the team through the agenda.

   Facilitator: This person participates as a regular team member but also pays attention to the group process and ensures the ground rules are being followed (e.g., making sure everyone participates and the meeting starts and finishes on time).

   Scribe: This person takes notes regarding what was done in the meeting (e.g., issues discussed, decisions made).

   b. As a team, set specific ground rules that everyone on the team agrees to follow. These rules must be enforced consistently!

   Examples of Common Ground Rules

   - All meetings start and end on time.
   - All team members must come prepared.
   - One person talks at a time.
   - Everyone must participate.

- Differences in opinion should be valued and respected.

c. Criteria for evaluating a team process include the following:

- Were the objectives of the meeting achieved?
- Did the team stay on the agenda?
- Were the ground rules followed?
- Did all team members contribute to the team meeting?
- Was there balanced participation across team members during the meeting?
- Did all members of the team have a voice in any decisions that were made in the meeting?
- Was the team open to hearing opposing viewpoints on an issue before making a decision?
- Did the team summarize what each team member must do to meet their duties and responsibilities at the end of the meeting?
- Did the team discuss when the next meeting will be and what each team member must come prepared with to the next meeting?

3. Plan an agenda for a brief 15- to 25-minute meeting to complete a task or achieve an objective the group selects (e.g., planning a social get-together, creating a study group for an upcoming exam, creating a timeline for a team project in a class, etc.). Make sure your agenda has the following elements:

- Clear objectives
- An itemized listing of the issues to be covered
- A specific amount of time allocated for each agenda item

Note: You can download a meeting agenda worksheet developed for this exercise from the Web site for this book.

4. Conduct the meeting according to your agenda.
5. Evaluate your meeting process, and identify specific actions for improving future team meetings.

Discussion Questions

1. Why is it critical to plan meetings and to actively manage them? What is the cost of not doing so?
2. Why is the management of team meetings often much more challenging than it appears to be on the surface?
3. What are the key actions you need to take in order to conduct an effective team meeting, and how will you apply them once you are a manager in a real-world organization?

SKILLS PRACTICE

11-3 *Skill Level:* **BASIC**

Developing a Team Charter

Skill Objective

To develop skill in creating an effective team charter that specifies the basic objectives, structure, process, and scope of a team project.

Procedure

1. Form teams of five to seven individuals. Ideally, this exercise should be used with students who are at the beginning of a team project. Otherwise, you can brainstorm a project of your own to use for this exercise (e.g., a community service project, a fundraising project for a student organization).
2. Download the "Developing a Team Charter" worksheet developed for this exercise from the Web site for this textbook. It will provide a useful template for working through this exercise.
3. Working as a team, answer each of the diagnostic questions on the worksheet.

Team Charter Diagnostic Questions

1. Team name?
2. Team member names?
3. What is the team's purpose and mission?
4. What are the goals of this team?
5. What is the time frame for meeting these goals?
6. How will the team's success be measured?
7. Where can the team go for the information it needs?
8. What resources will be available to the team?
9. What are the roles and responsibilities of the team leader?
10. What are the roles and responsibilities of the team members?
11. How often will the team be expected to report progress and results?
12. What processes will be used to communicate with key stakeholders of the team?

13. What are the limits of the team's decision-making authority?
14. How and when will the team evaluate itself?
    4. Answer the discussion questions here as a class.
        a. What is the purpose of a team charter? How can it help a team to be more effective?
        b. What are the challenges associated with the development and implementation of a team charter? What can a team leader do to overcome these challenges?

SKILLS PRACTICE

| 11-4 | Skill Level: *CHALLENGING* |

Stages of Group Development: Case of **Remember the Titans**

Skill Objective

To develop skill in analyzing the progression of a team through the stages of group development.

Procedure

1. Obtain a copy of the movie *Remember the Titans.* It is available on VHS and DVD and can be rented or purchased from a local video store or retailer.
2. Watch the movie (in class or at home on your own). Be sure to note specific scenes and dialogue that demonstrate the football team in the movie is in a given stage of group development. Also, note the strategies used by the two coaches to facilitate the development of the team.

    Download the worksheet developed for this exercise from the Web site for this book. This will help you document your notes regarding the group's development over the course of the movie.

3. Discuss the following questions as a class.
    a. Identify and describe the evidence you obtained from the movie that demonstrates when the team was in the forming, storming, norming, and/or performing stage of group development.
    b. Evaluate the strategies used by the two coaches in the movie to facilitate the team's development. To what extent were they effective? Ineffective? Why?
    c. If you were the coach of this football team, what would you have done differently, if anything, to facilitate the development of this team? Why?
    d. What are the practical implications of this exercise for the management of work teams in real-world organizations?

SKILLS PRACTICE

| 11-5 | Skill Level: *BASIC* |

Building Team Spirit

Skill Objective

To develop skill in applying various tools to foster a sense of team identity and spirit.

Procedure

1. Form teams of five to seven students each. If you are working in teams for a class project, work with these people for this exercise.
2. Select one of the exercises here and work through it in your group.
    a. Team name and commercial
        Step 1: Brainstorm a list of names you feel might be appropriate for your team. Try to base your ideas on what you know about the various members of the team and, if applicable, the nature of the task the team is working on (e.g., a class project). Be creative and try to generate team names that are meaningful and motivating to your team.
        Step 2: Evaluate the various team names and decide on one for your team. Write this name down on a piece of paper.
        Step 3: Now try to develop a basic slogan that will go with your team name. The slogan should be one sentence in length and describe who the

team is, what it does, why it is important, or why it is good (or the best!) at what it does.

Step 4: Based on your team name and slogan, create a 10- to 30-second commercial for your team. The commercial should focus on communicating the team's goal, function, and/or strengths to others. This is an opportunity for the team to be highly creative and have some fun with the exercise. Note: Use any props you may have in your book bags, notebooks, and so on (e.g., cell phones, clothing,). Once the commercial has been developed, practice it a couple times and then present it to the class.

b. Human GPS

Note: Your instructor will bring one blindfold for each team and the list of locations your team will need to go to for this exercise.

Step 1: Place the blindfold over the eyes of one volunteer from your team.

Step 2: Look at the list of locations your instructor has given you. Everyone else on the team should now guide the blindfolded team member to the first location on your list (Note: All locations will be places your team will be familiar with) without physically holding or touching the blindfolded team member. It is okay for team members to provide basic verbal instructions, though. The best arrangement is for the nonblindfolded team members to walk in front of, beside, and behind the blindfolded team member.

Step 3: Once the blindfolded team member reaches the first location, he or she should stop and remove the blindfold. Now have another team member put on the blindfold. The rest of the team will now look at the second location on the list and then lead the blindfolded team member to that destination.

Step 4: This process continues until the team has found all of the locations on the list.

c. "That's What I Like About You"

Note: This exercise should ideally be used with a team that has been working together on a class project.

Step 1: This is an exercise that builds team spirit through the use of positive feedback. Give team members each an index card and ask them to write their name on it.

Step 2: Now ask everyone on the team to pass their index card to the team member on their right side. Each team member should now write something positive about the person whose name is on the index card in front of him or her.

Step 3: Once everyone is done with step 2, ask them to again pass their index card to the team member on their right and write a positive comment about that person on their index card.

Step 4: Keep repeating step 2 until all of the index cards have been circulated through all of the team members.

Step 5: Return the cards to team members based on whose name is at the top of the card and ask them to read the comments. What are their reactions to the comments that others made about them?

3. Discuss the following questions as a class.

a. What were your reactions to the exercise you just completed? What impact did it have on how you feel about your team members and team? Was it effective in building your team spirit?

b. What are the barriers to using these kinds of exercises with teams in real-world organizations? What actions could be taken to overcome these barriers?

c. What are the practical implications of this exercise for you as a manager and team leader in real-world organizations in the future?

SKILLS PRACTICE

11-6   *Skill Level: CHALENGING*

***Facilitating Team Development: The Case of* Twelve Angry Men**

Skill Objective
To develop skill in applying various strategies to facilitate the functioning of a team.
Procedure

1. Obtain a copy of the movie *Twelve Angry Men*. It is available on VHS and DVD and can be rented or purchased from a local video store or retailer.
2. Watch the movie (in class or at home on your own), but stop it each time you identify a situation in which you would have taken action to enhance the effectiveness of this group of jurors who are deliberating over a murder case with a potential death penalty for the defendant, if he is found guilty. As you are watching the movie, remember to analyze the patterns of communication, decision making, and conflict resolution among the various characters. In addition, watch for issues related to perception and attitudes in the film.

   Download the worksheet developed for this exercise from the Web site for this book. It will help you develop a list of scenes in the movie where you would take action to facilitate the group's functioning.
3. Discuss the following questions as a class:
   a. What is your overall evaluation of the functioning of the jurors in *Twelve Angry Men*? What were the strengths and weaknesses of the group?
   b. What is your evaluation of the jury foreman in facilitating the decision-making process of the jury? What were his strengths and weaknesses?
   c. If you were the jury foreman, what would you have done to enhance the effectiveness of the jury? Be very specific and action oriented.
   d. How are the group dynamics in this movie similar to teams in real-world organizations?
   e. What are the practical implications of this exercise for you as a future manager and team leader in a real-world organization?

SKILLS PRACTICE

11-7   *Skill Level: BASIC*

Team Management Skills: Breaking the Ice

Skill Objectives
1. To obtain information from your fellow team members so you can work more effectively with them during the course of the project.
2. To get acquainted with your fellow team members so you can begin to develop positive working relationships with one another.
Procedure

1. Form groups of four to six students each. Ideally, each group will work together for an actual class project. However, each group may be formed just for this exercise.
2. Go around the group and provide the following information to one another: your name, year in school, major, and where you are from.

3. Select one of the following ice-breaking activities to complete as a group:
   a. The Basic Q & A Exercise
      Step 1: State any one of the following questions to the team:
      > What's your favorite movie of all time? Why?
      > What's your favorite dessert? Why?
      > What's your favorite thing to do for relaxation? Why?

      Step 2: Give your team members 10 minutes to obtain the answers to the chosen question from each other.
   b. The Four Statements Exercise
      Step 1: Distribute one index card to each member of your team and ask him or her to write four

statements about themselves on the card. Three of these statements should be false and one should be true. Be creative and make this fun!!

Step 2: Bring the group back together and have each person read their statements and then ask the group which one he or she think is actually true.

c. The "Let's Do Lunch" Exercise

Step 1: Tell your team you would like to have an informal team meeting at a local restaurant.

Step 2: Ask your team for suggestions as to where to have lunch. Select the restaurant by vote or consensus.

Step 3: During the lunch, try not to talk about work issues. Rather, make small talk and try to get to know your team members as people.

d. The Pictionary Challenge Exercise

Note: Your instructor will bring the materials needed to conduct this exercise.

Step 1: Select a team leader for the exercise.

Step 2: Ask the team leader to take a marker or piece of chalk to the chalkboard (or dry erase board).

Step 3: The team leader will be given a Pictionary card from the instructor and told which

item or concept to focus on for the exercise.

Step 4: When the instructor says, "Go," the leader should attempt to draw the item or concept given to him or her without talking. The team should try to guess the correct answer.

Step 5: Team performance is based on the number of seconds it takes a team to guess the answer. This exercise can be repeated, if time permits.

4. Now brainstorm some ideas for a team name. Try to be creative.

5. Decide on a team name based on the list you generated.

Discussion Questions

1. What is the value of these simple activities? How do they help a group develop itself? What is the cost of not breaking the ice for the development and effectiveness of a team?

2. Can these ice-breaking exercises be used with working people in real-world organizations? If so, do they need to be modified in some way?

3. What are the practical implications of this exercise for you as a future manager of teams in real-world organizations?

SKILLS PRACTICE

11-8   *Skill Level:* **CHALLENGING**

Applying the Affinity Technique
Skill Objective
To develop skill in using the affinity technique to support team decision making.
Procedure

1. Form groups of four to six students each for this exercise.

2. Obtain the following items from your instructor:
   > one or two pieces of flipchart paper
   > one pad of self-sticking notes for each team member
   > one large felt-tip marker
   > four pieces of masking tape

3. Identify a problem or issue that requires a creative solution. Here are some examples:

   > How can a student organization increase the involvement of its members in its activities?

   > How can a fast-food restaurant make itself more attractive as a place of employment for college students?

   > How can an organization improve its customer service?

   > How can students best prepare themselves for a job in the real world?

   > How can a company (select one of interest to you) handle a problem or challenge it is facing?

   > How can a company (select one of interest to you) better market one of its products or services to its customers?

> How can a company (select one of interest to you) turn itself around and become more profitable, improve product/service quality, and enhance its overall effectiveness?

4. Using the issue you just identified, follow the steps associated with the affinity technique:

Step 1: State the problem: The first step is to state the problem by writing it on a flipchart or whiteboard clearly visible to the team. The problem should be an issue for which creative solutions are needed based on team member input. The team leader should make sure all team members understand the problem.

Step 2: Silent generation of ideas: Now each team member is given a packet of self-sticking notes. The team leader instructs each team member to generate ideas or potential solutions to the problem silently. Team members use one note for each idea. Again, this is done with no discussion between team members.

Step 3: Posting ideas: Once all team members have finished generating ideas on the notes, they stick them on a whiteboard or large piece of flipchart paper at the front of the room. They do not have to be put up in any order at this point. The key is simply to get all the team members' ideas together in one area.

Step 4: Clustering: Team members take a few steps back from the area with all the ideas posted and start looking for clusters of ideas. A cluster exists when the same or a highly similar idea is identified by two or more team members. When this happens, a team member (it makes no difference who) puts the notes together (i.e., sticks them next to each other). This should be done for all other ideas considered to be the same. Individual ideas that do not fit into any cluster are placed to the side for potential action later. A team may find any number of idea clusters, depending on their problem and the number of ideas initially generated.

Step 5: Naming: Finally, the team leader draws a circle around each cluster and asks the team to name it. When all the clusters have been named, the team leader checks to ensure all team members understand the meaning of every cluster. The final outcome from the affinity technique is a set of potential solutions (represented by the named clusters) for the problem in question.

Follow-up: Although not part of the formal affinity technique, team members are now in a position to vote for their favorite idea(s). This is useful in helping the team prioritize problem solutions in terms of which ones should be pursued first. A simple voting procedure could be used here: Team members each put a checkmark next to the three to five problem solutions they like the most (the team leader should decide the number to vote on based on the number of problem solutions that have been identified). The problem solutions with the highest number of votes are the ones the team should consider implementing first.

5. Discuss the following questions as a class.

a. How does this technique help a team make better decisions?

b. What are some other problems or issues that could be addressed with this technique?

c. What are some potential barriers to implementing this technique effectively? What can a team leader do to overcome these barriers?

d. What are the keys to applying this technique in a real-world organization?

SKILLS PRACTICE

Team Process Evaluation

Skill Objective

To perform an evaluation of each team's process in order to identify opportunities for improvement.

Directions

Answer each of the questions individually, then discuss them as a team. Based on your findings, identify specific strategies for enhancing the effectiveness of your team process. Download the worksheet developed for this exercise from the Web site for this book to help you structure your team evaluation more systematically. If possible, each team should make a brief presentation of its results.

Team Diagnostic Questions

1. List the specific things your team has been doing well so far in terms of managing its team process. Be sure to address evaluate your team in terms of the effectiveness of its planning and coordination of activities, time management, communication, decision making, conflict resolution, motivation, team meetings, and the execution of its plans. Be as frank as possible and try to identify specific examples to support each of your team's strengths.

2. List the specific things your team has *not* been doing well so far in terms of managing its team process. Be sure to address evaluate your team in terms of the effectiveness of its planning and coordination of activities, time management, communication, decision making, conflict resolution, motivation, team meetings, and the execution of its plans. Be as frank as possible and try to identify specific examples to support each of your team's opportunities for improvement.

3. List the specific team concepts, tools, or principles discussed in this chapter that you have applied to the management of your team process (e.g., agendas, timelines, ground rules). Have they been effective? Why or why not?

4. What opportunities for improvement exist in terms of enhancing the effectiveness of your team process? Be as specific as possible.

5. What actions can your team take to ensure that it actually implements the opportunities for improvement identified in question 4?

6. How can this exercise be used to enhance the effectiveness of teams in real-world organizations?

BUILDING HUMAN ASSETS

CHAPTER 12

Skills Objectives

> To design effective recruiting plans for filling job openings.

> To design an effective selection process for hiring qualified employees.

> To develop job-interviewing skills needed to assess job applicant qualifications.

> To conduct orientation training programs for new employees.

> To conduct efficient and humane termination sessions with employees.

> To design effective employee training programs to enhance job performance.

> To conduct effective performance appraisal sessions that provide appropriate feedback and identify goals and strategies for enhancing employee job performance.

KNOWLEDGE OBJECTIVES

> Describe the three stages of staffing.

> Discuss the trade-off between recruiting, selection, and placement on the one hand and training and development on the other.

> Identify sources of job applicants and describe the realistic job preview.

> Identify approaches to selection and hiring and explain their relative benefits and problems.

> Define placement and indicate what it includes.

> Discuss the need for training and development and identify training and development methods.

> Discuss why performance appraisal is important to the firm and how employee performance can be measured.

> Describe how job worth, employee performance, labor market conditions, and pay systems determine levels of employee compensation.

From the local delicatessen to the largest international bank, business firms are made up of people. It is critical to get good people into the right jobs and then to develop them properly. Recognizing this, companies have developed some novel staffing methods. For instance, it is said that retailer magnate J. C. Penney invited candidates to breakfast and served them eggs. If a candidate salted or peppered the eggs before tasting them, Penney concluded he or she was inclined to make decisions without enough information and was not suitable for the company.[1] As we will see, such salt-and-pepper approaches to human resources management are no longer viewed as acceptable or successful.

In a workplace that is dynamic, uncertain, stressful, and increasingly litigious, human resource skills are especially crucial. It is important, for instance, to maintain diversity in the workforce, to find good employees, to keep up with a bewildering array of employment laws relating to issues such as racial discrimination, sexual harassment, and advance notification of layoffs, and to see that employees continue to master new skills. Further, these activities are not solely the responsibility of human resource managers. Increasingly, line managers are working in partnership with HR managers and employees to ensure that the firm's human resource needs are met. In this chapter, we explore skills associated with attracting, selecting, and developing employees. We examine staffing and training and development. We also discuss approaches to appraising employee performance and to compensating employees.

Take a couple of minutes now to answer the questions in Self-Assessment 12-1. You will learn more from this chapter if you start off with a greater awareness of your beliefs and feelings about how to attract, select, and develop employees. After you are through, visit the text Web site to learn more about your responses. In the Voice of Experience feature, Jane Schumann, a recruiter with Kohl's Department Stores, talks about issues and challenges related to building human assets that managers face today.

SELF-ASSESSMENT 12-1

Attitudes Toward Building Human Assets

Answer the questions that follow regarding your attitudes toward building human assets. Answer each question as honestly as possible using the following response scale:

1 Disagree strongly
2 Disagree somewhat
3 Neither agree nor disagree
4 Agree somewhat
5 Agree strongly

____ 1. An abundance of high-quality workers is available in the external labor market.

____ 2. Promoting employees from within the organization is always the best approach to filling higher-level management positions.

____ 3. Job interviews have low validity as selection methods.

____ 4. Managers can ask just about any question they want to in a job interview.

____ 5. Managers should not check the work references of individuals who have applied for jobs with their organizations.

____ 6. Classroom training is generally the best training method for enhancing employee performance.

____ 7. The basis of a training program is its training objectives.

____ 8. An employee's manager is the only person who can legally evaluate the performance of that employee.

____ 9. Most managers do not need training in the conduct of performance appraisals.

____ 10. It is not critical for managers to develop an action plan for employees based on the performance appraisal.

As a way to assess your initial level of skill in attracting, selecting, and developing employees, read the scenario in the Pretest Skills Assessment and develop an action plan for how you would handle this situation. Be as specific as possible in stating your recommendations. After you are through, visit the text Web site to learn more about your responses.

VOICE OF EXPERIENCE

ATTRACTING, SELECTING, AND DEVELOPING EMPLOYEES

Jane Schumann, Corporate Recruiter, Kohl's Department Store

1. Why is HR important to the success of an organization in the "real world?"

All organizations have employees—and the HR function plays a key role in the acquisition, development, and productivity of those employees. How well the employee group performs is directly related to the success of the business.

2. What do you feel are the most difficult HR challenges that line managers face in today's business environment?

One of the most difficult challenges managers face today is recruiting qualified and motivated workers to perform jobs that can be somewhat routine and do not pay particularly well. Managers can try to train and motivate these workers so that they will be good performers, but the quality of the workers who are willing to take these jobs is highly variable.

3. There is a lot of talk about how HR professionals and line managers need to work together in a partnership in order to effectively handle HR issues. In terms of putting this idea into practice, what actions do line managers and HR professionals need to take to create and maintain an effective partnership?

They need to develop clear and productive lines of communication—as well as trust. Line managers have to trust the advice and assistance that HR provides.

4. What general advice would you give to new managers regarding the handling of HR issues?

New managers always try to give an immediate answer. They need to stop and consult HR. They should not feel pressure to give an answer right away—listen first and tell them they will get back to them. Then take the time to access a policy and procedure manual and human resources.

http://www.kohls.com/

Building Human Assets

Note: This exercise is based on actual events encountered by managers in real-world organizations. Some information may have been modified to maintain the anonymity of the people and organization involved.

You are the manager of a rental car company located near a major international airport on the East Coast of the United States. Your job is to manage overall operations and the 70 employees who work in customer service, maintenance, administration, and so on.

You are experiencing some significant challenges associated with your work force. It has become extremely difficult to find an adequate supply of qualified labor to fill position openings in your growing firm. You have been shocked by the low level of work skills (e.g., analytical, quantitative, computer) and poor attitudes (e.g., work ethic) exhibited by job applicants. You have also found it difficult to make the idea of working for a rental car company appealing to younger workers.

Many of the younger employees in their 20s feel that working for your company is a dead-end job with few opportunities to grow or advance in terms of a career. A recent employee attitude survey revealed that employees are not receiving any feedback on their job performance, and they feel management is not providing any support for them in terms of mastering new computer systems being integrated into their jobs and in understanding the company's new customer service concept.

Finally, the annual turnover rate for employees is 80 percent. This indicates you are not doing an effective job of finding the right kinds of people to fill various jobs. This has been especially problematic for customer service jobs.

Develop an action plan for addressing the human asset issues in this situation. Be sure your plan addresses both short-term and long-term issues. Be specific and be prepared to defend the feasibility and cost effectiveness of each element of the plan.

Let's get out into the real world again to gain some first-hand experience with issues related to building human assets. Complete Skills Practice 12-1 by interviewing managers about their perspectives on building human assets and suggestions for handling them more effectively.

STAFFING THE FIRM

Staffing is a vital part of human resource management. It involves bringing new people into the organization and then moving them through, and perhaps out of, the firm. Staffing consists of three stages: recruiting, selection and hiring, and placement. These staffing activities are coupled with the training and development function to match the abilities of the job candidate with the needs of the firm. We see this matching process most clearly when the new employee enters the firm or when the requirements of the job change.

STAFFING OR TRAINING?

Figure 12-1 illustrates the balancing act necessary between the staffing activities of recruiting, selection, and placement on the one hand and training and development

FIGURE 12-1
The Staffing/Training Balancing Act

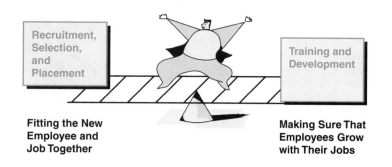

**Fitting the New
Employee and
Job Together**

**Making Sure That
Employees Grow
with Their Jobs**

on the other. In its personnel practices, should a firm tip the balance to one side or the other? More specifically, should a firm hire people who are ready to step into their jobs, or should it groom them through training programs?

Careful selection and placement certainly have their advantages. The new employees can begin work immediately, showing results right away rather than in six months, after a training program. For example, offshore drilling companies such as SEDCO hire undersea welders who are already competent and can do their jobs safely. Acquiring these skills takes years of experience. Individuals are hired because they already have proven skills; the firm does not have to gamble that they will learn them properly. Brokerage companies such as Prudential-Bache Securities offer big bonuses to brokers who come from other companies.[2] These brokers already have the needed skills and have proven their ability.

Training and development also has its advantages. For example, people can be hired at lower rates of pay if they come to the firm untrained. Also, training and development can be tailored exactly to the company's needs. For example, Westinghouse hires students with degrees in advertising and then retrains them completely. Ford, Bell Telephone, and McDonald's have similar training programs for employees who need special skills that cannot be obtained elsewhere. In addition, people are loyal to the firm that trained them. Sales and service personnel trained by IBM feel strong loyalty to their company; they are renowned for their dedication to IBM's interests. Bankers Trust New York Corp. placed ads in magazines for chess and bridge enthusiasts, in order to recruit trainees for bond trading positions. The company reasoned that bond traders, like bridge and chess players, make moves as part of a calculated game plan. One of the ads is shown in Figure 12-2. Bankers Trust believes it can teach individuals with these skills the specifics of bond trading.

In the remainder of this section, we will examine the three stages of staffing: recruiting, selection and hiring, and placement. In the next section, we will examine training and development.

RECRUITING

The first of staffing's three stages is recruiting. The term *recruiting* refers to all activities involved in finding interested and qualified applicants for a job opening.

FIGURE 12-2

Bankers Trust Ad in Chess Magazines Seeking Currency and Bond Traders

HERE'S A MOVE THAT COULD CHANGE YOUR LIFE.

Chess at its top level requires certain finely-honed skills.

The ability to predict an opponent's future moves.

Courage to take short-term risks for long-term gains.

Patience to assess every option available and strike accordingly.

Interestingly enough, these are the exact skills necessary to succeed as a trader in the global currency and securities markets.

Allow us to introduce ourselves.

We're Bankers Trust and this is basically a fancy 'Help Wanted' ad.

Bankers Trust is one of the most successful traders of foreign exchange and debt securities in the world.

Every day we trade over $35 billion in volume and we've made money doing this every year for the past twenty years.

Most of our competitors just hire MBAs right out of school but we're predicting that "a few good chess players" have what it takes to win in our highly competitive world.

The idea came to us from several of our best traders who are themselves, games players, one of our most successful in particular being an international master.

He is still moving pieces to form a calculated game plan, but now it is Yen and Deutchmarks as well as Rooks and Knights.

If you are interested in this quite unique job opportunity, send your resumé and/or a letter about yourself to Allen R. Beyer, Bankers Trust New York Corporation, 31st floor, One Bankers Trust Plaza, New York, New York, 10006. It doesn't really matter what your background is and it could be the best move you'll ever make.

No matter how employees are later selected, trained, and motivated, starting out with a good group of job applicants is crucial. The greater the number of applicants and the better their qualifications, the more likely the firm will build a solid personnel base.

Sources of Applicants. Job applicants can be found in many ways. Sources of applicants differ in ease of use, cost, and the quality of applicants obtained. Some primary sources are summarized in Figure 12-3.

CREATIVE RECRUITING

In the current tight job market, companies are trying some creative approaches to recruiting.[3] Consider the following.

> How tough is it to get high-tech help these days? Tough enough to send IBM to the beach. Big Blue is hitting three spring-break hot spots to get a jump on computer rivals in recruiting techno-savvy 18- to 20-year-olds. The company set up a booth at a job fair on the beach—even building a giant sand sculpture of an IBM ThinkPad and flying a plane over the beach with a banner promoting Big Blue's job Web site. At Lake Havasu in Arizona, IBM recruiters have rented jet skis to reach students tooling around in the water. Others will Rollerblade along the shore, giving out lava lamps and brochures to students.[4]

FIGURE 12-3
Sources of Applicants

Source	Benefits and Costs
Walk-ins to the company	Company must assign a contact person to greet walk-ins and set up procedures to store and use applications.
Newspaper and magazine ads	These bring in many applicants, but don't screen out unqualified applicants.
Referrals from current and past employees	Referring employees understand the firm's needs and may know good people in the industry.
Private employment agencies	These agencies are in the business of matching job seekers with suitable jobs. They charge a fee for their services.
Public employment agencies	Most cities have an office of the state employment agency. It finds jobs for unemployed people and may offer training programs.
Educational institutions	Universities, colleges, high schools, and other educational institutions are good sources of applicants. Companies may send recruiters to campus.
Labor unions	These are good sources of jobs for blue-collar and some professional jobs. Some have hiring halls where employers and job seekers are brought together.
Social service agencies	Various social service agencies provide training and assistance for the homeless, including help with job seeking.
Co-ops and internships	Students currently attending school may be available to work through co-ops and internships. With a co-op arrangement, the student attends school full time and works full time on an alternating basis. With an internship, the student works for an employer for a specified period of time, such as the summer.
Temporary help agencies	Contingent workers are workers who are employed by a firm on a temporary basis. Some are self-employed and others work for an agency that provides temporary workers to firms. They are used when work is of short duration and may give companies flexibility in responding to economic fluctuations.

> Where might companies find employees who were thinking about leaving their companies? Many firms—especially in high-tech industries—are linking their Web pages to the Dilbert Zone, the busiest site for frustrated programmers looking for a job change.[5] Check out the Dilbert List of the Day, a month of Dilbert, the Dilbert Travel Zone, Catbert's Anti-Career Zone, and other features at http://www.dilbert.com.

> The Internet is the hottest tool for recruiting.[6] Search engines such as Yahoo! and Excite as well as bulletin board systems and news groups provide job information. Job banks (which we discuss in the careers appendix) include the Career Resource Center, Career Mosaic, Job Trak, Monster Board, America's Job Bank, and many more. Cisco Systems, a computer network equipment manufacturer, hires as many as 1,200 people every three months. Its Internet job pages record as many as 500,000 hits a month.[7] Cisco gets 81 percent of its résumés from the Net, making 66 percent of its hires from the Net. Texas Instruments (TI) has updated its popular Web site with additional career development tools for engineering students and prospective hires. "Ask the Cyber Recruiter" is an interactive area where students can ask for career advice, post questions about TI, and learn how to use the Web for job searches. Cyber Recruiter also includes a "Career Mapper" that asks questions designed to

uncover what type of company or corporate culture would best suit an individual and "Fit Check" for assessing whether a user would be a good fit with the TI culture. Research shows Internet recruiting to offer cost savings and improve candidate quality.[8] Companies such as Staples Inc. find Internet recruiting makes it easier to locate employees with specific characteristics, such as title, gender, or ethnicity.[9]

Merits of Internal and External Recruiting Sources. There are costs and benefits to internal recruiting methods (such as internal job postings, referrals, and identifying internal candidates for promotion or transfer through skills inventories) and the various external recruiting methods. Internal sources generally benefit from the facts that employees are familiar with the organization, recruiting and training costs are relatively low, and internal recruiting enhances employee morale and motivation because it gives a signal that the organization offers opportunities for advancement. Internal recruiting, however, may lead to political infighting for promotions, inbreeding, and morale problems for those not promoted. External sources generally reverse these lists. They introduce new ideas and approaches, provide knowledge and skill not currently available in the organization, and permit new hires to start with clean slates. However, there may be less fit between the new hire and the organization, an increased adjustment period for the individual, and reduced morale and commitment for current employees.

Skills Practice 12-2 gives you the opportunity to develop a recruiting plan for a specific job. Remember to think strategically! That is, stay focused on using recruiting methods and sources appropriate to the job you are seeking to fill.

The Outsourcing Alternative. As we noted earlier in the chapter, outsourcing is one alternative available to firms.[10] In the face of increased demand, evolving needs, or cost considerations, firms may use outside parties to perform tasks that would otherwise be handled in-house.[11] This is a popular, rapidly growing option. By outsourcing some activities, firms can concentrate their resources on their core competencies, those things they do particularly well. A new biotechnology firm, for instance, may choose to outsource routine payroll functions because those functions do not require the firm's specialized expertise.

Controversy is currently raging over the outsourcing of millions of jobs from the United States to countries where labor costs are cheaper. Not just low-paying jobs but, increasingly, high-level, white-collar jobs are being outsourced to countries such as India, China, Taiwan, and Mexico.[12]

Realistic Job Preview. Most companies present a rosy picture of themselves and their job openings in order to attract job applicants. Partly as a result, many new employees experience "entry shock" and are dissatisfied when they learn the truth about the company. Many even quit after a short time. In addition, courts in recent years have ruled that employees can sue their companies if exaggerated claims or promises lured them into accepting a job.[13]

To avoid such outcomes, many companies now use realistic job previews. The *realistic job preview (RJP)* aims to give the recruit an accurate picture of what the company and the job are like.[14] For example, films of people on the job and uncensored comments of current employees may be used to acquaint new employees with the day-to-day reality of the job. ExxonMobil prints brochures describing the kinds of jobs available for people with varying educational backgrounds, the promotion and salary opportunities of the jobs, and where in the world an individual might work. Because of its highly developed preview, ExxonMobil has one of the lowest employee turnover rates in the petroleum industry. Research shows that RJPs lead to higher levels of employee satisfaction and lower levels of turnover. Further, presenting an honest, balanced picture doesn't appear to reduce the acceptance rate of jobs. The Focus on Management feature discusses the use of a realistic job preview by States News Service.

Try completing Skills Practice 12-3 on providing realistic job previews. Although as a concept this is not difficult to grasp, it takes real skill to present a balanced view of a job within the context of the recruiting process, where you are trying to attract prospective employees. The Bottom Line feature presents a process model summarizing the basic steps associated with implementation of the recruiting process.

SELECTION

The role of recruiting is to locate job candidates; the role of *selection* is to evaluate each candidate's qualifications and pick the one whose skills and interests best match requirements of the job and company.[15] Some firms use informal selection procedures, such as reviewing application blanks and résumés. Others ask their job candidates to take personality and ability tests. Still others have assessment centers, where procedures for selecting and hiring new employees are very systematic. The Focus on Management feature discusses selection at Toyota.

Careful selection procedures can be time consuming and costly. However, they are worthwhile if the costs of a wrong decision are high, if there are many applicants and few openings, and if selection tools are accurate. Some companies now use

FOCUS ON MANAGEMENT

WANTED: SOMEONE TO GO DOWN IN THE PERFECT STORM

States News Service, a Washington-based wire service hard strapped for funds and facing fierce competition from larger competitors, is struggling to stay alive. Further, it has trouble attracting new employees, and those who do join the service are quick to move on when better offers arrive; there were only three full-time reporters, down from 40 in 1993. Trying to maintain a sense of humor and borrowing from Sir Ernest Shackleton's famous ad that was posted in the *Times* of London in 1914 to recruit a shipping crew for a risky transatlantic journey on the

Endurance, States News Service editor and publisher Leland Schwartz posted the following job ad:

> "Reporters wanted for hazardous journey. Small wages. Bitter cold. Long months of complete darkness. Constant danger. Safe return doubtful. Honour and recognition in case of success."

The ad got an explosive response, drawing job seekers from all over the world. One applicant wrote, "Your description makes the position sound very attractive. One question though: Is the part about safe return negotiable?" Another wrote, "It would never better suit meself than to join along with your

band of high-seas ruffians. Rightly so I've earned me stripes on small expeditions, and I reckon a longer journey would befit me ever-growing foolhardiness." To undaunted applicants, Schwartz responded in his typical optimistic fashion, "[We] need reporters who can withstand being in a dinghy in the ocean in the perfect storm. The economy, Sept. 11, and the Internet explosion have crushed us."

Source: "Wanted, Someone to Go Down in the Perfect Storm," *American Journalism Review*, 2003, 25(4), p. 14.

BOTTOM LINE

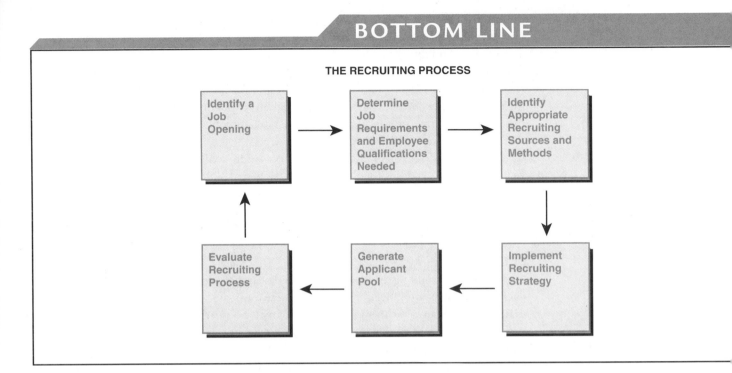

THE RECRUITING PROCESS

expensive selection procedures even for positions that would traditionally have been filled without much screening. Let's look at some of the ways in which firms determine whether the qualifications of a job candidate are in line with the requirements of the job.

Application Forms. The first source of information about a potential employee is the *application form*. It provides the hiring firm with information about educational background, work experience, and outside interests. Much of this information is especially useful for screening purposes. For example, an applicant for a position as a computer analyst should have had courses in data processing. The application

FOCUS ON MANAGEMENT

SELECTION AT TOYOTA

When Toyota Motor Corp. wanted to fill positions at its new auto assembly plant in Kentucky, it received 90,000 applications from 120 countries for its 2,700 production jobs and thousands more for the 300 office jobs. The company wanted to select workers who would conform to its emphasis on teamwork, loyalty, and versatility. Toyota

required applicants to spend as much as 25 hours completing written tests, workplace simulations, and interviews, in addition to undergoing a physical examination and a drug test. The tests examined not only literacy and technical knowledge, but also interpersonal skills and attitudes toward work. At each stage of the selection process, more applicants were screened out. Only 1 in 20 made it to the interview.*

http://www.toyota.com/

*R. Koenig, "Toyota Takes Pains, and Time, Filling Jobs at Its Kentucky Plant," Wall Street Journal, December 1, 1987, p. 1. See also N. Templin, "Dr. Goodwrench: Auto Plants, Hiring Again, Are Demanding Higher-Skilled Labor," Wall Street Journal, March 11, 1994, pp. A1, A4.

form would tell the employer right away whether the applicant had the needed training.

However, at least three problems are associated with application forms as sources of information about potential employees. First, the information provided by the applicant may not be relevant to performance on the job. Second, job applicants may give incorrect or misleading information on the forms or in résumés. The National Credit Verification Service has found that about one-third of the job applicants whose credentials it has investigated somehow misrepresented their educational backgrounds.[16] One survey found that 95 percent of college students are willing to make at least one false statement to get a job, and 41 percent have already done so.[17] Sometimes these misrepresentations are discovered many years later when employees are considered for promotion. When George O'Leary was hired as head football coach of Notre Dame in December 2001, it was discovered that he had been doctoring his résumé for at least two decades. O'Leary claimed to have a master's degree and to have played football in college, neither of which was true. Although almost everyone agreed O'Leary was a good football coach, such lies could not be tolerated, and he was fired immediately.[18] Third, the law places many restrictions on what can and cannot be asked on a job application.[19] Figure 12-4 lists questions considered to be unfair by the Washington State Human Rights Commission. Clearly, firms must be careful to avoid questions on application forms that violate state or federal law.

References. A *reference*, another popular selection tool, is information provided by previous employers, coworkers, teachers, or acquaintances concerning an applicant's credentials, past performance, or qualifications for the current position. The reference givers may be contacted in person, by phone, or by mail. Evidence sug-

FIGURE 12-4
Some Unfair Pre-Employment Inquiries

> Any inquiry that implies a preference for people under 40 years of age

> Whether applicant is a citizen; any inquiry into citizenship that tends to divulge applicant's lineage, ancestry, national origin, descent, or birthplace

> All inquiries relating to arrests

> Inquiries that would divulge convictions that do not reasonably relate to fitness to perform the particular job or that relate to convictions for which the date of conviction or release was more than seven years before the date of application

> Specific inquiries concerning spouse, spouse's employment or salary, children, child care arrangements, or dependents

> Any inquiries concerning handicaps, height, or weight that do not relate to the job requirements

> Whether the applicant is married, single, divorced, engaged, widowed, etc.

> Type or condition of military discharge

> Request that applicant submit a photograph

> Gender

> Any inquiry concerning race or color of skin, hair, eyes, etc.

> All questions as to pregnancy, and medical history concerning pregnancy and related matters

> Any inquiry concerning religious denomination, affiliations, holidays observed, etc.

> Requirement that applicant list all organizations, clubs, societies, and lodges to which the applicant belongs

> Inquiry into original name where it has been changed by court order or marriage

gests that references are generally of little value in the employee selection process. The people asked to provide references sometimes do not really know much about the person for whom they are providing the reference. Sometimes they are not frank because they do not want to say anything uncomplimentary about a person, especially in writing. And applicants usually carefully select references they think will write positive letters. As a result, references are generally biased in the applicant's favor.

References are probably most useful if a structured form is used so that all people providing references give the same information for each applicant. Also, standardized scoring keys can be used to arrive at quantitative scores relating to such factors as the applicant's mental ability, cooperation, dependability, and vigor.[20] In addition, it is often helpful to ask the references to in turn suggest other references. Although the job candidate might consciously choose references that would be likely to make positive comments, these secondary references may respond in a more balanced fashion.

Interviews. The hiring firm generally asks candidates that pass the initial screening process to participate in an *interview*, in which a representative of the hiring firm asks the candidate a series of questions. The goal of the interview is to determine how well the candidate's skills and interests match the job requirements. The interviewer may be a member of the firm's human resources department or a supervisor, team leader, or manager who has an open position. Some firms, such as Virginia Natural Gas and Philip Morris U.S.A., use panel interviewing, in which from two to six interviewers meet with job candidates as a team.[21]

Interviews can be conducted in many ways. Two types often used are structured interviews and unstructured interviews. In a *structured interview*, all candidates are asked the same list of questions in the same order. A structured interview helps ensure that all questions are related exclusively to job duties and requirements critical to job performance. By sticking to the questions in the structured interview, the interviewer gives each applicant the same chance as every other and makes it easier to compare candidates. Treating all applicants the same also makes it less likely that the company will be sued for discrimination in hiring.

An *unstructured interview*, in contrast, is a looser exchange between the interviewer and the job candidate. The interviewer often asks questions not on the planned list to follow up on the candidate's comments. This sometimes results in a more complete picture than would otherwise be possible. In general, though, unstructured interviews are less valid than structured interviews and, as already noted, more susceptible to legal challenges.[22]

Advantages of Interviews. Interviews are widely used. More than 90 percent of all people hired for industrial positions are interviewed at least once. Interviews are popular for many reasons, including the following:

> It is easier to ask someone a series of questions than to develop a test.

> Interviewing makes the selection process more personal and gives the interviewer an overall idea of whether the applicant is right for the job.

> Companies may use interviews to give the applicant information about the duties of the position to be filled and about the organization in general.

> Interviews may be used to sell the company to the applicant.

> Interviews may also be used to complete the information about job candidates.

> Good candidates might be unwilling to consider a job seriously unless they had the chance to ask questions and gather information.

Problems with Interviews. Despite the popularity of interviews, a successful interview does not always mean the recruit will perform well on the job. Interviewers sometimes show many biases, disagree with one another over which recruits are likely to do best, and ignore much of the information available. The success of an interview in identifying the best candidate for the job depends on the skill and good judgment of the individual interviewer.

Further, as with application forms, rather severe legal restrictions dictate what can be asked in interviews. These restrictions became even more severe after the Americans with Disabilities Act (ADA) was implemented in 1992.[23] For instance, questions about disabilities or medical histories are banned unless the applicant brings them up. The U.S. Equal Employment Opportunity Commission attempted in 1994 to clarify matters relating to the ADA by presenting lists of legal and illegal versions of similar interview questions. The legal versions are intended to focus on the ability to carry out the job rather than on disability per se. Unfortunately, as the questions presented in Figure 12-5 suggest, these distinctions are subtle and, some argue, confusing.[24]

There have been widely publicized cases in recent years relating to alleged discriminatory interview tactics, and studies show that most interviewers are unaware that certain types of questions may be discriminatory. For instance, questions about arrest records are inappropriate, because an individual must be considered innocent unless actually convicted of a crime. Even questions about the applicant's willingness to work on weekends could be seen as betraying religious discrimination, since orthodox Jews can't travel on Saturdays.

FIGURE 12-5
Discriminating Questions

Legal

1. Do you have 20/20 corrected vision?
2. How well can you handle stress?
3. Can you perform this function with or without reasonable accommodation?
4. How many days were you absent from work last year?
5. Are you currently illegally using drugs?
6. Do you regularly eat three meals a day?
7. Do you drink alcohol?

Illegal

1. What is your corrected vision?
2. Does stress ever affect your ability to be productive?
3. Would you need reasonable accommodation to do this job?
4. How many days were you sick last year?
5. What medications are you currently using?
6. Do you need to eat a small number of snacks at regular intervals throughout the day in order to maintain your energy level?
7. How much alcohol do you drink per week?

Improving Interviews. Steps can be taken to increase the likelihood of a successful interview. For example,

> Interviewers should always prepare for an interview by making a list of specific topics to cover and/or specific questions to ask.

> Interviewers should be trained in preparing questions that relate to the job requirements, probing for details, listening carefully, and avoiding discriminatory questions.

> Interviewers should use behavioral and situational questions. Behavioral questions ask candidates to recall and describe a specific behavior, such as a time when they had to deal with a hostile customer. Situational questions present a situation and ask how the candidate would deal with it. For instance, a question might be "Suppose a colleague yelled at you in front of a customer. What would you do?"

> Written records of the interview should be kept.

> Whenever possible, multiple interviewers should be used so the selection will depend on the judgment of more than one person.

> Interviews should never be the sole basis for selection of a candidate. They should be used along with other selection devices to provide additional information on candidates' strengths and weaknesses.[25]

Find a partner and complete Skills Practice 12-4, a role-immersion simulation exercise on job interviewing. The exercise will give you an opportunity to practice designing an interview process and developing interviewing skills. Remember to be systematic and focused in the questions you ask during the interview. The Bottom Line feature presents a process model summarizing the basic steps associated with implementation of the job-interviewing process.

Testing. A *test* is a systematic and standardized procedure for obtaining information from individuals. Testing is a relatively objective way to determine how well a person may do on the job. Many human resources experts and personnel managers believe testing is the single best selection tool. Tests yield more information about a person than does a completed application form, and they are generally less biased than interviews.[26]

Types of Tests. Human resources managers use many types of tests today. Let's examine seven types: ability tests, personality tests, interest tests, work sample tests, integrity tests, drug and impairment tests, and genetic testing.

> *Ability tests* measure whether the applicant has certain skills required to perform the job tasks. Mental ability tests assess memory, problem-solving speed, verbal comprehension, ability to deal with numbers, and so on.[27] The Focus on Management feature discusses the controversy surrounding use of mental ability testing in the New London Police Department. Mechanical ability tests measure spatial relations—the ability to see how parts fit together into a whole. Such spatial relations skills might be useful, for instance, in putting a carburetor back together or for drafting or interpreting blueprints. Psychomotor ability tests assess reaction time and dexterity. They might assess speed of limb movement, coordination, or finger dexterity. Psychomotor ability tests are given to people applying for jobs involving mostly physical tasks. Professional football teams use them to assess athletes.

BOTTOM LINE

THE JOB-INTERVIEWING PROCESS

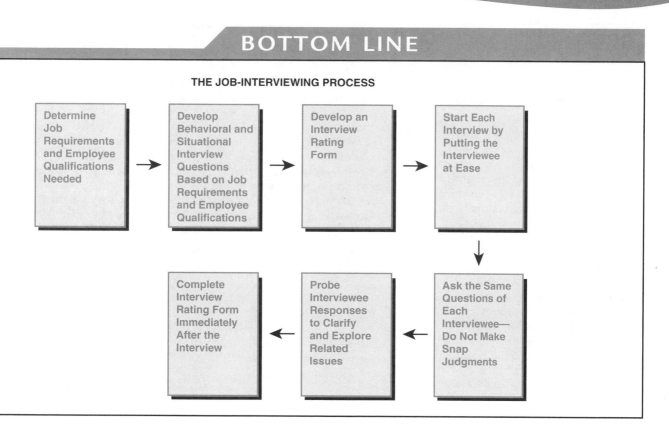

Determine Job Requirements and Employee Qualifications Needed → Develop Behavioral and Situational Interview Questions Based on Job Requirements and Employee Qualifications → Develop an Interview Rating Form → Start Each Interview by Putting the Interviewee at Ease

Complete Interview Rating Form Immediately After the Interview ← Probe Interviewee Responses to Clarify and Explore Related Issues ← Ask the Same Questions of Each Interviewee—Do Not Make Snap Judgments

> *Personality tests* measure the strength or weakness of personality character-istics considered important for good performance on the job. Job applicants are asked to describe themselves in terms of traits or behavior.[28]

Personality tests have been used for managerial jobs for a long time. They are now becoming more popular when hiring people for entry-level jobs, such as customer sales representatives and sales clerks, and for blue-collar posi-tions. This is especially true at companies that practice participatory manage-ment, where workers are given responsibility in running operations. Also, many financial service and insurance firms, trying to improve service in the face of competition, are looking harder for workers with people skills such as empathy, the ability to communicate, and motivation to please others. The Big 5 personality measures discussed in Chapter 2 have been shown to predict success across a variety of job types. More than 40 percent of *Fortune* 500 companies now use some form of psychological testing, and use is bur-geoning.[29]

> *Interest tests* measure a person's likes and dislikes for various activities. A person whose interests don't fit well with the characteristics of a particular job would probably find the job boring and unsatisfying.

> *Work sample tests* measure how well applicants perform selected job tasks. An applicant for a job that requires typing skills is usually given a typing test; a police officer candidate might be given judgment tasks involving realistic job situations. Work sample tests generally predict subsequent job performance quite well.

FOCUS ON MANAGEMENT

TOO SMART FOR THE NEW LONDON POLICE DEPARTMENT*

The former whaling village of New London, Connecticut, refused to grant Robert J. Jordan a job interview. The reason: He was *too* smart. The city of New London contends that applicants who score too high on a pre-employment test are likely to become bored in patrol jobs and will leave the force soon after the city has paid to train them. In 1996, Jordan scored 33 out of 50 on the exam, published by Wonderlic, Inc. The exam is used by 40,000 employers across the country, including the National Football League, and has been given to 125 million people since 1937. However, Jordan failed the test because his score was 8 points above the New London cutoff. Upon learning he had been denied an interview because of his high score, he sued the department. However, in September 1999, a federal judge in New Haven ruled that the practice of excluding too-bright applicants was constitutional, because the city treats all smart would-be officers the same and thus did not discriminate against Jordan.

The Wonderlic "User's Manual" warns clients about the costs of replacing workers who quit because they become dissatisfied with repetitive work, stating that "simply hiring the highest-scoring employee can be self-defeating." It offers the following suggested minimum and maximum cutoffs for selected professions, based on a scale from 1 to 50:

Administrator	27–35
Editor	29–35
Industrial engineer	28–34
Reporter	27–34
Teacher	27–34
Bookkeeper	24–29
Police, patrol officer	22–27
Telephone operator	22–26
Driver, bus or truck	20–24
Warehouseperson	17–21

Jordan has used up his savings in pursuing the case. He now supplements his insurance business by working as a state prison guard for $26,000 a year—$15,000 less than he would make as a New London patrol officer. New London says it will continue to use the test to screen out the overqualified. So "while those with badges and guns are called New York's finest, they will continue to be New London's fair to middling."†

*Based on M. Allen, "Ideas and Trends: Invoking the Not-Too-High-IQ Test," *New York Times*, September 19, 1999, p. D4; and T. Hughes, "Jordan v. The City of New London, Police Hiring and IQ: "When All the Answers They Don't Amount to Much," *Policing*, 2003, 26(2), pp. 298–312. See also K. S. Moustafa and T. R. Miller, "Too Intelligent for the Job? The Validity of Upper-Limit Cognitive Ability Test Scores in Selection," *S.A.M. Advanced Management Journal*, 2003, 68(2), pp. 4–9.

† Allen, "Ideas and Trends."

> *Integrity tests* measure an applicant's honesty. Dishonesty and theft can be major expenses for many firms. One form of honesty test is a polygraph (or lie detector) test, an electronic device used to detect lying. As a result of concerns about validity and invasion of privacy, a 1988 federal law outlawed most private uses of pre-employment polygraph tests aimed at assessing employee honesty.[30] Written "honesty" or "integrity" tests are now often given instead. These contain items concerning one's attitudes toward theft and other forms of dishonesty (such as "Do you ever think about cheating people?" or "Are there times when it's OK to be dishonest?") or about personality characteristics believed to be related to theft (such as "Do you consider yourself to be a trustworthy person?"). However, many of these written honesty tests may be even less valid than the polygraph tests they replace.[31] Further, it makes sense that dishonest employees might also be dishonest in responding to integrity test items. In addition, many individuals are offended when asked to take such tests. As a result, integrity testing should probably only be considered when the potential costs of dishonesty are very high.[32] Evidence does indicate that properly designed integrity tests can predict performance and counterproductive behavior at work.[33] One convenience store reported reducing its theft rate

by 60 percent after requiring potential hires to take an integrity test.[34] Further, courts have accepted performance on forms of integrity as an appropriate basis for employee dismissal.[35]

Many firms, including Abbott Laboratories, JCPenney, and Nordstrom Inc., are also trying to judge the integrity of applicants by performing credit checks.[36] Critics question the validity of credit checks and charge that firms may use them to obtain personal information they aren't supposed to consider, such as age or marital status.[37] Further, the Federal Fair Employment Reporting Act requires that if a company denies an applicant or employee a job or promotion based wholly or in part on information from a credit report, it must notify the person of the fact. The individual then has the right to review the entire report, demand a reinvestigation, and give his or her own version of statements in the report. In the case of some extensive credit checks, requirements are even stricter. Further, beginning in late 1997, employers were no longer able to obtain credit reports on employees without first advising them in writing and obtaining a written acknowledgment. Employees must then be informed that the credit check is being performed for purposes of retention.[38] Violations of the Fair Employment Reporting Act can result in civil and/or criminal penalties for the employer.[39]

> ***Drug and impairment tests*** measure abuse of alcohol or other drugs. The cost of alcohol and other drug abuse in the United States is estimated to be $60 billion per year. Substance abuse has been shown to be related to such behaviors at work as spending work time on personal matters, falling asleep, extra-long lunch and rest breaks, and theft.[40] Substance abuse also results in huge costs for sick time and health care. As a result, more than 80 percent of major U.S. corporations use drug tests, spending in excess of $250 million annually on the practice.[41] The tests may involve examining body fluids such as urine and blood, hair, or the reaction of the pupil to light.[42] The combined U.S. work force had a positive drug test rate of 4.6% in the first half of 2003, up from 4.4% the previous six months.[43] Focus on drug tests increased in 2003 with disclosures of widespread use of THG, a previously undetected steroid, among Olympic track stars, major league baseball players, and other athletes.[44]

In response to concerns that drug testing violates rights of privacy and may give false positive results, many firms have decided to use impairment testing, which involves using activities similar to a video game to measure an employee's ability to work.[45] One such test works on a PC coupled with a control panel and special software. During the test, a bar is centered on the computer screen. Below the bar is a vertical arrow that the computer sweeps back and forth at increasingly rapid speeds. Using a control knob, the employee tries to keep the arrow under the center mark of the bar. The focus of such tests is on actual impairment of motor skills and hand–eye coordination rather than on detecting chemicals. This permits employers to see immediately whether or not an employee is able to work on a given day. Further, impairment tests detect impairment because of illness, sleep deprivation, and emotional preoccupation that would be missed by drug tests.[46]

> ***Genetic testing***—a relatively new form of testing—may exclude employees with certain genetic characteristics.[47] Full of promise and peril, it applies the expanding science of genetics to the testing of workers for chromosomal

damage or susceptibility to disease. Genetic testing of workers comes in two varieties: monitoring and screening. They differ in their purposes and in the way they have been received.

Genetic monitoring involves testing groups of employees periodically to see whether they are showing any alarming chromosomal abnormalities that might have been caused by their environment. Monitoring has the approval of most observers, including labor leaders. It provides an early warning of danger from the work environment and indicates when workplaces need cleaning up.

Genetic screening is the onetime analysis of DNA taken from blood or other body fluids. It can find genetic markers that indicate a person may be especially susceptible to harm from a particular substance. Advocates of genetic screening say it could identify those with a special susceptibility to a disease and steer them away from work with dust or fumes that might trigger it. But screening worries many critics. They argue that if employers know certain workers are susceptible to a disease caused by workplace hazards, they will simply get rid of those workers rather than clean up the workplace. Critics also warn that such screening could be used to screen out employees who are likely to develop a debilitating or fatal genetic disease such as Huntington's chorea or Alzheimer's. If so, susceptible workers may find their privacy violated, their careers ruined, and their health insurance terminated.[48] More than 20 states, including Michigan and California, have passed legislation restricting the use of genetic testing for employment purposes.[49] Federal Executive Order 13145, signed into law in 2001, forbids federal employers from requesting or mandating genetic tests as conditions of hiring or receiving benefits, using such information in advancement decisions, and violating employee privacy rights with respect to such information.[50] Under a bill passed 95–0 in the U.S. Senate in late 2003 and awaiting consideration in the House, insurance companies would be banned from using people's genetic information or family histories to deny medical coverage or set premiums.[51]

Test Validity. Although testing works well, it is not perfect. First, the value of a test is based on its validity. *Validity* is the degree to which predictions from selection information are supported by evidence. Thus a test that accurately predicts employee performance is valid, and one that does not is invalid.[52] Valid tests are expensive to develop. Also, some jobs, such as those of top management, are hard to describe, and the abilities and interests required may be all but impossible to predict on the basis of test results. In general, ability tests and work sample tests are more valid than other selection tools.[53]

The issue of validity is demonstrated by the use of *graphology*, or handwriting analysis, to predict job performance.[54] Although still not widely used in the United States, graphology is very popular in western European countries, such as Britain and France. Most French companies require job applicants to provide handwritten letters. These are sent to graphologists, who analyze the handwriting and determine if the applicant is right for the job and has the proper character. Companies usually follow the graphologist's advice. The theory behind graphology is that handwriting reflects personality. For example, a high bar used to cross lowercase *t*'s is seen as reflecting strong willpower; a low bar is interpreted as revealing lack of self-confidence. Unfortunately, although graphology is difficult to fake, no solid evidence indicates it actually predicts job performance.[55]

Faking Tests. There is also the danger that tests can be faked (as we suggested may be the case with integrity tests). Tests are easiest to fake when it is obvious what they are measuring (that is, when the tests are *transparent*). As such, one way to discourage faking on tests is to make it hard to tell what the test is assessing. Unfortunately, tests that are not transparent tend to lack *face validity*. That is, because it isn't obvious what the test is measuring, people may be reluctant to accept its results.[56]

Test Fairness. Some tests may be unfair to certain groups, such as women and blacks. Everyone agrees tests should be fair, but few agree on a definition of fairness. To some people, a test is unfair if it includes questions about things that might be unfamiliar to some people because of their race or ethnic origin. For example, consider the following item to assess math skills: "Arnie bogeys all the odd-numbered holes and eagles all the even ones. What's Arnie's score for the entire round?"[57] Such an item reflects cultural bias, presuming background knowledge more likely in some social groups than in others. To other people, a test is unfair if it measures things that aren't needed on the job but serve to block some people from being hired. In the eyes of the law, a fair test does not underpredict or overpredict performance of one group of employees relative to another. For instance, if a test predicts white males will do better than black males on the job, when in fact both groups do equally well, the test is unfair.

Assessment Centers. Instead of just using an interview or a test, about 2,000 large companies approach the employee selection process more systematically. They use various procedures, combined in the form of an *assessment center*. Assessment centers are part of the firm; they are a collection of systematic procedures rather than a physical place. The centers employ psychologists and other experts on human behavior as well as providing tests, interviews, group discussions, and other approaches for evaluating job candidates. Often, managers from within the firm serve as assessors.

One approach used in assessment centers is *role playing*, where job recruits pretend to be actual employees in a real decision situation.[58] Another approach to discovering how recruits hold up under fire is the *in-basket*. The recruit is given a basket piled high with memos, phone messages, letters, and other matters requiring attention. Each person's performance is evaluated in terms of how the tasks are sequenced, how promptly they are completed, whether the most important ones in the pile are finished, and how good the proposed solutions are.

Assessment centers have many uses besides selection. They may help spot management potential early. They may pinpoint areas of weakness where employees should improve to enhance their career prospects. When the assessors are managers within the firm, the training they receive on how to run assessment centers is also valuable in helping them understand the firm, observe and rate behavior, and make judgments.

Assessment centers are expensive, but they may be worth the cost to the large firms that use them, such as AT&T, IBM, General Electric, and BellSouth, which can spread the costs over many employees.[59] AT&T alone runs more than 40,000 people through its center each year. Sprint created the University of Excellence, a corporate training operation combining assessment centers with executive development programs and other activities. The assessment centers establish an employee's readiness to accept initial or additional management responsibilities. The centers include challenging "day-in-the-life" simulations and then feed into management curricula.[60] Studies of assessment centers show them to make better predictions of employee performance than other approaches to selection.[61] Also, employees usually report that assessment centers have given them a fair chance to show their abilities.[62]

Selecting for Teams. As organizations rely more heavily on teams, they must carefully screen team candidates for their ability to work with other team members.[63] For example, at Delta Dental Plan, a self-directed team provides services for a contract providing dental insurance for 31,000 employees. This is Delta Dental's biggest contract, and the team must be staffed with qualified, motivated individuals. The Human Resources department spent more than six months recruiting and selecting team members. To ensure the team had balance, the company used a personality test called the Myers–Briggs Type Inventory to find members with complementary personality types. Also, because some customers of the new account were not English speaking, the company selected some bilingual team members. Finally, because Delta Dental wanted some team members who were familiar with the business and the company's culture and some who would bring fresh insight and perspectives, it selected members from both inside and outside the company. After ensuring that the mix of potential team members met these requirements for balance, candidates' interpersonal skills were assessed by interviews with members of the Human Resources department and other employees and managers. The Focus on Management feature discusses selection for teams at C&S Grocers. The process model shown in the Bottom Line feature summarizes the basic steps associated with implementation of the selection process.

FOCUS ON MANAGEMENT

SELECTION FOR SELF-DIRECTED TEAMS AT C&S GROCERS

At C&S Grocers, Inc., of Brattleboro, Vermont, the warehouse crew has worked in self-directed teams since 1989, a move credited with boosting employee morale and the company's profit margin.* Team members are involved in all hiring decisions, and they can recruit members from other teams, get rid of team members, or reassign job responsibilities. Teams with openings look to other teams for potential members. Employees are paid for each case order filled, and top-producing teams can handle 9,000 cases a day, which translates to about $20 an hour per employee. When a highly productive, and thus well-compensated, team finds that one member is not carrying his or her weight, it usually tries to help increase that member's productivity. If this fails, the team has the authority to pass the low performer off to another, typically less productive, team. For example, a team earning $20 an hour may trade a member who is producing at a level of $16 per hour to a team earning $14 an hour. The lower-performing team benefits, and the $20-per-hour team can then seek a superstar elsewhere in the firm.

*Based on S. Caudron, "Team Staffing Requires New HR Role," Personnel Journal, May 1994, pp. 88–94.

BOTTOM LINE

THE SELECTION PROCESS

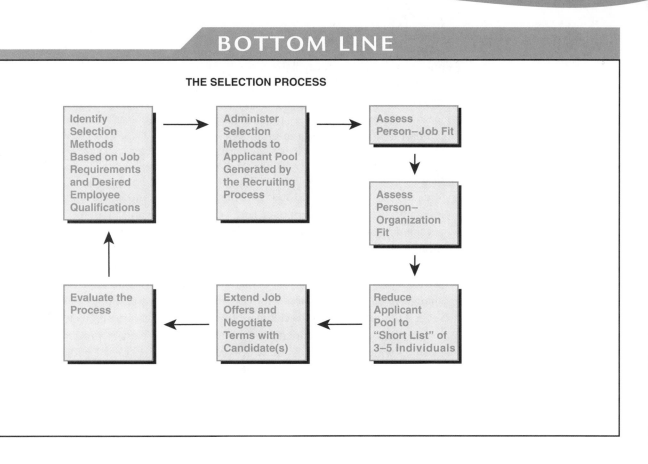

PLACEMENT

Placement means fitting people and jobs together after the people have become employees of the firm. It includes everything from helping new employees feel at home in the firm to promoting them to positions of greater pay and responsibility or demoting them to less demanding positions when necessary.

Orientation. *Orientation* involves introducing new employees to their jobs and to the company. It is their first inside look at the company, and it can make an important impression. The job orientation reduces uncertainties, makes company policies and expectations clear, and provides a good idea of what the firm, plant, and coworkers are like. Also, a thorough orientation sends a signal that the new employee has an important role to play in the organization.[64] Orientation also offers a bonding opportunity, ensuring that new hires don't feel alienated and helping instill in them a sense of pride and opportunity.[65]

Often, both the human resource department and the new employee's supervisor are involved in the orientation efforts. Orientation may include such elements as an explanation of job procedures and responsibilities, criteria for performance appraisal, organization and work unit rules, safety regulations, the chain of command for reporting purposes, and where to turn with problems or questions. Often, the new employee is given an orientation packet containing organization charts, maps of the facility, the company policy handbook, copies of performance appraisal forms, lists of holidays and employee benefits, phone numbers of key personnel, and copies of insurance plans.

Skills Practice 12-5 will give you a chance to develop an orientation program for new employees. Remember, this is an important part of the socialization process for new employees, as it sets the tone for the subsequent working relationship between the company and the employee.

Lateral Move. Firms sometimes move employees laterally—that is, neither up nor down in the organizational hierarchy, but sideways. One type of lateral move, systematic job rotation, may build worker skills. At Union Carbide, three executive vice presidents traded jobs to get a better feel for the total organization and to prepare for the presidency. Such lateral moves can provide valuable learning experiences, building a more solid base for later promotion.[66] Employees may welcome the change of pace and duties of job rotation, and those who learn a variety of skills may develop a greater sense of pride and self-worth.[67] Sometimes lateral moves are dictated by organizational changes. For instance, when IBM reorganized its staff to reduce costs, its plan required several thousand people to change jobs, often from staff positions to the sales force.[68]

W. R. Grace & Company, a chemical and consumer products company, has been moving managers laterally for years, some to special projects for the company's future, others to fill slots at locations far from their current posts, and still others to newly created jobs in other countries. According to the firm's vice president for corporate administration, "They get new challenges, and we get broadened managers—something a global, decentralized company must have."[69]

Promotion. The most pleasant job move is the promotion. A *promotion* is a move up, generally to a new title, more responsibility, and greater financial rewards. Most employees would like more status, challenge, and pay, so promotions are attractive to them. But good promotion decisions also benefit the firm. An individual who has demonstrated competence and loyalty to the firm and shows promise for further accomplishment is moved to a position with greater impact on the firm's success. Promotions also demonstrate to other employees that good performance and potential are rewarded, thus serving as a motivating device.

Promotions must be handled carefully. For one thing, the fact that the promoted individual did well at the old job is no guarantee he or she will do well at the higher-level job. Jobs at different levels may require vastly different skills and interests. All too often, a good salesperson or engineer becomes a poor manager. This tendency is called the *Peter Principle*, which asserts that good workers are repeatedly promoted to positions of greater authority.[70] Eventually, they reach their "level of incompetence" and will not be promoted again. Most managers can point to examples of the Peter Principle in their firms. Good promotion decisions prevent capable salespeople or engineers from becoming poor managers.

Promotions can also cause problems for the people promoted. Some employees may be happier in their current jobs than they would be in positions requiring greater responsibility, new skills, and geographic moves. Such changes can cause stress. To make the move a bit less scary, some firms have instituted fallback positions. Employees accepting promotions are guaranteed that if they are unhappy, they can fall back to their old positions or positions of equal stature.

However, most people certainly welcome promotions. Many employees may even experience an inverse Peter Principle, performing better as they take on increased responsibility and challenge.

Demotion. A move down in the organizational hierarchy to a lower title, less responsibility, and lower salary is called a *demotion*. Demotions are stressful for employees, of course, and they are likely to be resisted by unions. Still, demotions are often necessary. For example, companies may demote individuals who are performing poorly rather than fire them. Also, especially during recessions, employees may prefer demotion to unemployment. Some companies have experimented with demoting employees temporarily so they can relate better to their subordinates. Also, some employees ask for their old jobs back if they are unhappy with their promotions.

Termination. Another painful reality in business is the need to fire employees. Sometimes firings are necessary because employees have continued to perform poorly or because they have been unmotivated or uncooperative. Firings are traumatic for the terminated individual and costly for the firm. For instance, the firm will have to bear the costs of recruiting and training a replacement. Therefore, employees who are performing below standards should be counseled and given written performance goals and plans for meeting them. They should have a probationary period and receive regular feedback over that period. Firing should be used only if such corrective efforts fail, as a last resort.

In recent years, many employees have been fired as a result of factors having little to do with their motivation or performance. Due to technological changes, restructuring, mergers, changes in strategy, foreign competition, or other factors, firms may have to cut costs by reducing the size of their work force. As we have discussed in earlier chapters, such downsizing is taking place at unprecedented levels and rates.

It was probably inevitable that companies would come up with some innovative jargon to avoid using terms such as "firing" and "layoff." Employees who are terminated are now likely to hear their firms are engaging in a "skill mix readjustment," "rightsizing," or "work force imbalance correction." Other workers may find they have been subjected to "indefinite idling," "outplacing," "dehiring," "degrowing," "decruiting," or a "career-change opportunity."[71] Whatever they are called, firings are extremely stressful to individuals and firms. In some cases, the firm hires outplacement companies to assist people who are affected. These firms help the employer with the dismissal—offering advice and sometimes getting involved in the termination interview—and then counsel the individual on how to carry out a job search and cope with the period of transition between jobs. They may also actually help the individual find a job.

Because of recent changes in the law and its interpretation by the courts, companies can no longer fire employees anytime they want (called "termination at will"). Although courts generally recognize management's right to terminate employees who are incompetent, lazy, or uncooperative, they are increasingly attacking firings for certain other reasons.[72] For instance, courts have challenged firings for reasons of convenience, to make the employee a scapegoat, or to avoid pension costs. Also, the Worker Adjustment and Training Notification (WARN) Act requires U.S. employers with 100 or more employees to give 60 days' notice to employees who will be laid off as a result of a plant closing or a mass separation of 50 or more workers.

In some cases, terminated employees are claiming that firings defame their character, and they are filing defamation suits as well as claiming unlawful termination. For instance, a Texas jury awarded Don Hagler, a 41-year veteran of Procter & Gamble Co., $15.6 million in such a defamation case. Hagler said P&G fired him after publicly accusing him of stealing a $35 company telephone and posting notices accusing him of theft on company bulletin boards.[73] Clearly, companies planning to terminate employees should be certain of the facts in the case, avoid innuendo when discussing a firing, tell only those with a need to know the details of the firing, and avoid making an example of the fired employee. Here are some guidelines for effective termination:[74]

> Give as much warning as possible for mass layoffs.
> Be sure the employee hears of the termination from a manager, not a colleague.
> Sit down one on one in a private office with the person to be terminated.
> Tell the individual in the first sentence that he or she is terminated; leave no room for confusion.
> Express appreciation for the employee's past contributions if appropriate.
> Complete the firing session within 15 minutes. Make the session brief and to the point, not an opportunity for debate.
> Keep the conversation professional, avoiding personal comments.
> Briefly explain how much severance pay will be provided and for how long; provide written explanations of severance benefits.
> Provide outplacement services away from company headquarters.
> Unless security is an issue, don't rush the employee off site.

Skills Practice 12-6 will help you gain skill in what many managers say is the most challenging task they have had to perform in their jobs—terminating an employee. Most managers never receive any training whatsoever in how to terminate an employee in an appropriate, legal, and humane manner, so this exercise is important preparation for your future career.

TRAINING AND DEVELOPMENT

The training of employees and the development of their skills and careers have many advantages for the firm. First, training and development helps the firm meet its immediate human resource needs. Over the long run, training and development ensures that the firm's employees are ready to meet future challenges. As we'll see, training and development take a variety of forms.

Firms in the United States spend an estimated $30 billion a year to train employees.[75] Nevertheless, workers in the United States often receive far less training than their Japanese counterparts. For example, new production workers in Japan receive 380 hours of training, and new workers in Japanese-owned plants in the United States receive 370 hours. In contrast, new workers in U.S.-owned plants in North America receive only 47 hours of training, or about one-eighth as much.[76] This relative lack on emphasis on training is especially troubling in view of the fact that research shows training to have a strong positive impact on organizational outcomes.[77]

DETERMINING TRAINING AND DEVELOPMENT NEEDS

Training and development needs may arise for many reasons. In general, training and development should follow a systematic needs assessment. The needs assessment should consider three sets of factors:

1. *The organization*. What is the environment for training in terms of the organization's goals, resources, and climate for training?
2. *The task*. What is the work to be performed and the conditions under which it will be performed?
3. *The person*. What personal capabilities are needed to do the job, and what are the people like who will do the job?

The needs assessment may indicate a requirement for specific skills that are not readily available, such as computer programming, accounting, or mechanical skills. Or it may suggest needs for future career development among employees. Despite the importance of needs assessment, relatively few firms appear to conduct such an assessment in the design and development of training.[78] In addition, when determining training needs, firms often set up special training programs for women, minorities, and the disabled, in order to correct imbalances in management positions and meet affirmative action goals.[79]

ON-THE-JOB TRAINING

As the name says, *on-the-job training* is conducted while employees perform job-related tasks.[80] They are not taken out of the workplace or put in a classroom. Employees learn the job by doing it, with coaching and feedback from a supervisor or more experienced employees. On-the-job training is the most direct approach to training and development. It offers both employer and employee the quickest return in terms of improved performance. Such training is also conducted in anticipation of future job requirements. For example, many large companies rotate their employees through a variety of positions to broaden their knowledge of the company so they will be equipped to handle jobs in other areas. Other on-the-job training for employees includes regular coaching by a superior, committee assignments to involve individuals in decision-making activities, and staff meetings to broaden employee understanding of company activities outside their immediate areas.

OFF-THE-JOB TRAINING

It is often necessary to train employees away from the workplace. Such off-the-job training may take place elsewhere within the firm or outside the company. Role playing and in baskets, which we discussed in conjunction with assessment centers, are often used for training purposes. Let's consider other popular off-the-job training techniques.

Classroom Training. Some large organizations have sophisticated classrooms for training purposes; films, videotapes, and other audiovisual media are used. Classroom training might also include case studies. With case studies, information is presented about a business problem, such as how to finance the expansion of a new plant, and trainees are then asked to analyze the material and present recommendations. This may enhance their knowledge about specific issues and improve their decision-making skills. Classroom lectures have a poor public image as being a boring and ineffective delivery method, but research shows them to be a relatively effective training approach.[81]

Programmed Instruction. With *programmed instruction*, subject matter is broken down into organized, logical sequences. The trainee is presented with a segment of the information and responds by writing an answer or by pushing a button on a machine. When a correct response is given, the trainee is presented with the next segment of material. An incorrect response is met with an explanation and the suggestion to "try again." Computer-assisted instruction (CAI) is a more sophisticated version of programmed instruction in which the memory and computational ability of computers permit more complex topics to be taught.

Management Games. *Management games* present trainees with a simulated business situation. Trainees make a series of decisions, such as how much of a product to manufacture and what price to charge. Generally, trainees are members of teams competing with other teams. The performance of each team is evaluated, and trainees get feedback, often from a computer. The games give a feeling of real decision making and generate considerable enthusiasm. For example, in a three-day seminar on strategic planning, teams of four or five participants compete against each other in a simulation developed by Strategic Management Group.[82] Each team makes strategic business decisions that team members key into a computer. The computer calculates the effects of the decisions on bottom-line measures such as market share. Teams then adjust their strategies based on the feedback.

Behavior Modeling. With *behavior modeling*, trainees view videotapes in which a model supervisor is shown attempting to improve or maintain an employee's performance. The model shows specifically how to deal with the situation. Trainees then take the role of the supervisor and practice, in front of the trainer and other group members, the behaviors demonstrated by the models. As the trainee's behavior comes closer to that of the model, the trainer and other trainees provide praise, approval, encouragement, and attention. The behavior is videotaped to add feedback and reinforcement.

CORPORATE UNIVERSITIES

A major new development in company training is the growth of corporate universities, educational organizations established and run by a corporation to educate employees, customers, and suppliers.[83] There are now thousands of corporate universities, and their numbers are predicted to outstrip those of traditional universities by 2010. Corporate universities take a variety of forms. For instance, Dow Chemical—which has training expenditures of more than $90 million annually—is developing online learning over its company's intranet. In the first nine months, the company developed 31 classes across a broad range of topics, and over one-quarter of its 40,000 employees completed one or more classes. Dow expects to save more than $20 million in the first three years of the online university. We discuss corporate universities further in Chapter 15.

HIGH-TECH TRAINING

Sophisticated new tools are being used in training.[84] For instance, simulation in training once meant using expensive replicas of job situations. Now, 300 law enforcement agencies across the country use complex computer-based simulations. On a 10-foot video screen, patrol officers watch criminals respond to their actions. If officers use their laser guns to shoot a criminal, the attacker can die on the screen. If not, the suspect might escape or even shoot back, killing the officer. After the simulation is completed, the computer rates the officer on the accuracy of any shooting and the wisdom of the decision. Other computerized simulations are used as part of the training of airline pilots and operators of nuclear power plants.[85] In a sobering application, simulation is now being used to train commanders, pilots, and air defense crews to shoot down a commercial airliner to prevent a recurrence of the 9/11 scenario.[86]

The newest simulations employ *virtual reality*, which immerses the trainee in a simulated setting through the use of computer peripherals and stereographic imaging.[87] In one form of virtual reality, trainees wear fiber-optic helmets. They see 3-D images through the lenses of the helmet and hear stereophonic sound. As the trainee's head moves, the computer senses it and adjusts the image accordingly. In December 1993, NASA mounted an ambitious effort to repair the Hubble space telescope. The mission required six trips outside the space shuttle, each lasting more than six hours, during which astronauts removed, replaced, and repaired many telescope components. Their confidence and success were due in part to the fact that they had done it all before—in a virtual reality simulation back on Earth.[88] Although virtual reality techniques are expensive, they typically cost much less than training on real equipment.[89] Further, the cost of such technology is dropping while its sophistication is improving dramatically. In fact, using a specialized display system called a *haptic interface* (from the Greek *haptesthai*, meaning to grasp or touch), virtual reality can now simulate not just appearance but also touch.[90] The haptic interface transmits forces to the hand or fingers in a way that mimics the sensation of touching real objects. The trainee—such as a prospective surgeon—can actually feel objects created by the computer.[91]

CROSS-TRAINING

As firms make more use of cross-functional teams and generally seek employees with multiple skills, they are increasingly employing *cross-training*, training of employees to master one or more tasks in addition to their primary duties. Cross-training develops a versatile, flexible work force that is qualified and willing to work where the need arises.[92]

Often, cross-training includes training not just across multiple jobs but across jobs in different functional areas, such as accounting and sales. With such training, workers develop broader perspectives, enhancing cooperation and communication across functions.[93] As they develop breadth and their career prospects are enhanced, they often become more committed to the goals of the company as well as better able to provide quality service to customers.[94]

EVALUATING TRAINING OUTCOMES

Firms often fail to assess whether training programs have been effective in meeting their goals. Measures of training effectiveness might include participants' reactions to the training, learning of the content of the training, and use of new skills and knowledge on the job. It could also include the company's return on the training investment. For instance, personnel responsible for training at Allied Signal's Garrett Engine Division assessed its effectiveness on these dimensions. In assessing the return on training investment for programs aimed at maintenance workers, they considered the cost of the training and how equipment downtime subsequently differed between trained and untrained groups of workers. Using these figures, Garrett estimated that the training yielded a 126 percent return on investment.[95] The process model shown in the Bottom Line feature summarizes the basic steps associated with the implementation of the general training process.

Now complete Skills Practice 12-7 by watching *Top Gun*, the action film about training elite fighter pilots in the U.S. Navy. This is a great example of some very effective training methods and processes that can greatly benefit many organizations today. Enjoy!

Next complete Skills Practice 12-8. The purpose of this exercise is to give you a hands-on activity to practice applying the basic steps in the training process. Remember to base everything on the training objectives!

APPRAISING PERFORMANCE

Performance appraisal is the process of measuring employee performance against established goals and expectations. Before we look at techniques for performance appraisal, let's consider why performance should be appraised in the first place.

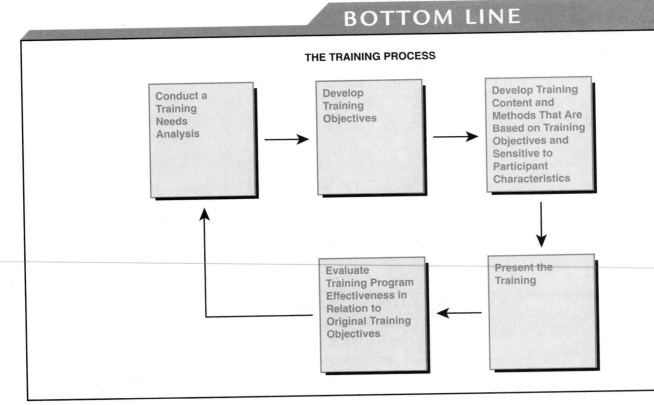

BOTTOM LINE

THE TRAINING PROCESS

Conduct a Training Needs Analysis → Develop Training Objectives → Develop Training Content and Methods That Are Based on Training Objectives and Sensitive to Participant Characteristics → Present the Training → Evaluate Training Program Effectiveness in Relation to Original Training Objectives → (back to Conduct a Training Needs Analysis)

WHY APPRAISE PERFORMANCE?

There are many reasons to measure how well employees are performing. First, if companies don't have good performance appraisals, they may make poor promotion, salary, and termination decisions. They may also find themselves vulnerable to lawsuits claiming unfair action on the part of the firm. Second, if employees are to do their jobs better in the future, they need to know how well they have done them in the past. Then they can make adjustments in their work patterns as necessary. Third, appraisal can have powerful motivating effects. When employees know their performance will be evaluated, they try harder to meet performance goals. For example, Northern States Power Company is committed to achieving the benefits of workplace diversity. As a result, its annual performance reviews now include an assessment of how well an individual creates an environment that cultivates work force diversity and measures each person's active participation in meeting departmental diversity goals.[96]

Finally, performance appraisal is necessary as a check on new policies and programs. For example, if a new pay system has been put into effect, it is useful to see whether it has had a positive effect on employee performance.

IMPROVING PERFORMANCE APPRAISALS

Performance appraisals are clearly very important, but many managers find the process difficult and unpleasant. They often have had little training or experience in conducting performance appraisals, and they are reluctant to make critical comments about their subordinates.[97] Here are some suggestions for improving performance appraisals:[98]

> Ensure that the performance appraisal measure is reliable and valid. For example, make sure the performance rating captures all the important aspects of performance and is not contaminated by nonperformance factors, such as personal liking.

> Provide training for raters. Such training can make the rater more knowledgeable and more comfortable with the process, and it may help reduce specific rating errors (such as halo error, discussed in Chapter 2).

> Involve employees in the process.

> Make sure performance ratings are discussed.

> Develop an action plan based on the discussion.

> Attempt to link merit increases to performance ratings.

> Integrate performance evaluation into the broader process of day-to-day performance management.

Some managers are turning to computer software programs and other high-tech tools to help make their appraisals more effective and constructive.[99] A typical program permits managers to type in goals they would like addressed and to select from categories to be included, such as professionalism, leadership, and job knowledge. Managers then grade employees by applying ratings to statements that appear on screen. Some programs also permit the manager to type in comments to be added to the employee's file and, if the comments are negative or contain inappropriate language, may suggest changes or call for more specific information.

Controversy has developed in recent years concerning the use of performance appraisals. For instance, W. Edwards Deming argued that performance appraisal and Total Quality Management are incompatible.[100] However, although it is true some performance appraisals are poorly planned or executed, much evidence substantiates their value. Indeed, all companies somehow appraise employees' performance; some just do it more systematically and openly than others. In fact, one survey showed that more than 20 percent of firms are tying performance appraisal directly to their Total Quality Management efforts.[101]

TYPES OF PERFORMANCE MEASURES

Performance may be appraised in at least three major ways. Appraisal can focus on employee traits, behavior, or accomplishments.

Trait Approaches. Under these approaches, a manager or performance appraiser rates an employee on such traits as friendliness, efficiency, and punctuality. The assumption is that these traits are related to performance. One such approach asks the appraiser to check the word or phrase (such as *outstanding*, *average*, or *poor*) that best describes how an employee rates on each trait.

Trait approaches are widely used in business, but they suffer from a number of problems. For instance, words such as *superior* and *average* may mean different things to different people. Also, the people appraising performance are sometimes biased in their ratings. They may also feel uncomfortable giving a coworker a low score on efficiency, decisiveness, or supervisory ability, especially if the ratings will be shown to the person being rated. As these problems suggest, trait approaches should never be used alone, if at all.

Behavioral Approaches. These approaches involve the rating or recording of specific employee actions. In the *critical incidents method*, for example, the performance appraiser keeps a list of all the employee's actions that were especially good or bad. A newer approach, the *behaviorally anchored rating scale*, presents a list of possible employee actions, rated on a scale ranging from very desirable to very undesirable. The rater checks the action on the scale in which the employee would be most likely to engage. By focusing on specific actions, this approach improves on the earlier trait approaches. However, behavioral approaches sometimes give employees the feeling that the rater is always looking over their shoulder.

Outcome Approaches. Rather than considering traits or actions, some appraisal techniques rate what the employee is supposed to accomplish on the job. This approach is time consuming and may cause people to focus only on objectives that can be easily expressed in numbers. However, it does get directly at what the company cares most about.[102]

Increasingly, firms are including a broad array of outcomes in their performance appraisal systems. As already noted, for example, some firms are tying performance appraisal to their efforts to increase diversity. At chemical giant Hoechst Celanese, four sets of outcomes are equally weighted in performance appraisals: attainment of work force diversity goals, financial success, customer satisfaction, and environmental and safety improvements.[103] As a result, managers at Hoechst Celanese pay attention to diversity, knowing the success of their diversity efforts will be reflected in their salaries and bonuses.

360-DEGREE FEEDBACK

In the past, the employee's immediate supervisor conducted the performance appraisal. Now firms such as British Airways, AT&T, Alberto Culver North America,

BOTTOM LINE

THE PERFORMANCE APPRAISAL PROCESS

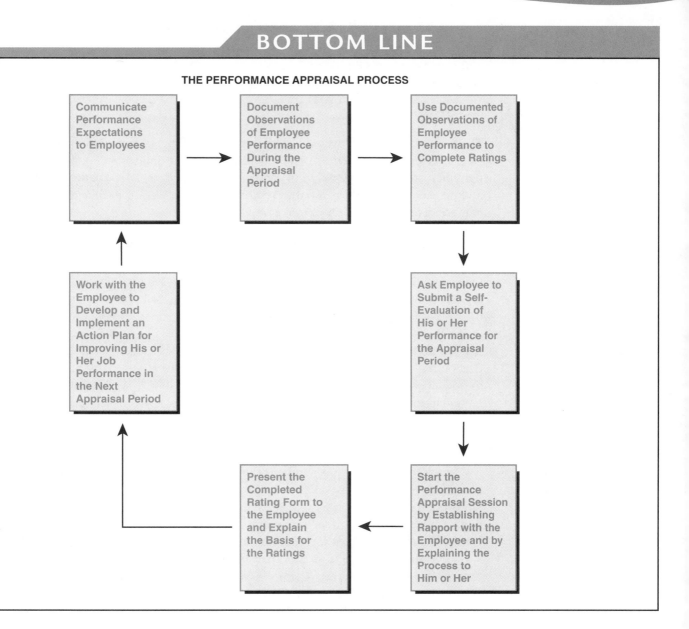

and General Electric are increasingly using 360-degree feedback.[104] With ***360-degree feedback***, the employee receives performance feedback from four sources: the supervisor, subordinates, peers or coworkers, and self-ratings. Using 360-degree feedback can potentially provide a fuller, more realistic picture of the employee's overall performance.[105] However, implementation of 360-degree feedback must be done carefully because, for instance, subordinates may be afraid to provide honest answers about their superiors' performance.[106]

Skills Practice 12-9 will give you a chance to experience the performance appraisal process from the perspective of the manager and the employee. This is a challenging process, so be prepared! The Bottom Line feature presents a process model summarizing the basic steps associated with implementation of the general performance appraisal process.

COMPENSATING EMPLOYEES

The wages paid to employees, as well as other job benefits, depend in part on how well those employees perform on the job. Other factors influencing employee compensation are the relative worth of each job within the firm, labor market conditions and prevailing wage rates, and the type of pay system used. Let's take a closer look at these determinants of employee compensation.

JOB ANALYSIS, SPECIFICATION, AND DESCRIPTION

The systematic study of a job to determine its characteristics is called *job analysis*. One common method of gathering information about a job is to observe workers on the job, noting which tasks they perform, the order in which the tasks are done, and the time it takes to perform each one. Another method is to interview employees about the nature of their work. Sometimes employees are asked to supply the needed information by filling out written questionnaires, which allows a job specification and job description to be written.[107] A *job specification* is a summary of the qualifications needed in a worker for a specific job. It is especially useful in recruiting job applicants and making hiring decisions. A job description is a short summary of the basic tasks making up a job. A *job description* usually includes the title of the job, the supervisor to whom the employee reports, all major categories of work activities involved in the job, and working conditions.

Job descriptions serve a number of important functions. First, they clarify organizational structure by specifying who is to perform each task. This also minimizes job overlap (in which two people are assigned the same task). Second, job descriptions can be used to introduce new employees to their jobs. In this way, they are given a good idea of what to expect on the job before they actually start work.

Job descriptions are also important in developing performance standards and criteria for job evaluations. *Performance standards* define the goals to be achieved by a worker over a specified period of time. The purpose of a *job evaluation* is to determine the relative worth of a job in the firm. In general, the more important the job, the higher should be the level of pay. The result of the job evaluation process is a rank ordering or rating of job importance, which is useful in setting wage and salary scales.

LABOR MARKET CONDITIONS

Supply and demand cause the wages for some jobs to be higher than the wages for others, even though the jobs may be of similar difficulty and responsibility. For example, in an area where many teachers but few nurses are looking for work, employers may have to pay more to hire a nurse than a teacher, even if the jobs are considered equally responsible. The level of wages is also influenced by what other local firms pay. For example, machine shops in the same town will tend to pay the same wage, especially if a union contract is in effect. Because of this tendency, some companies conduct surveys of local wage rates to make sure their own are in line.

PAY SYSTEMS

Even after the value of a job is determined and the local and regional wage differences are taken into consideration, one person may be paid more for the same job than another person. We can identify at least five other factors that account for wage differentials.

Seniority. The term *seniority* refers to the number of years spent with the company. Generally, the more years of service, the greater the level of pay. The idea is that seniority reflects loyalty to the company as well as valuable experience. In some countries, such as China, factories traditionally pay older employees more than younger workers on the same job, regardless of performance levels. When Volkswagen entered into a joint venture with Shanghai Automotive Industrial Corporation to form Shanghai Volkswagen Automotive Company, it found it had to adapt to this practice. So performance is not considered in setting pay, although it is a factor in promotion decisions.[108] However, Mitsubishi Motors Corp. announced in 2003 it was abandoning the seniority system that has long prevailed in Japan, replacing it with a performance-based system. Under the performance-based system, managers will rate employees each year and must designate one-fifth as less than satisfactory.[109]

Individual Performance. How much individual employees are paid is often based largely on how well they do on the job. Under a *piece-rate system* of compensation, total wages paid are tied directly to output. For example, a worker in a toy factory may get one dollar for every puppet produced. Piece-rate systems are often justified because they motivate employees. As we discussed in Chapter 4, rewards directly based on desired outcomes have the strongest motivating effects. Performance may be defined in various ways in compensation plans. For instance, at firms such as GTE and Sony, customer service representatives are rewarded on the basis of the speed and courtesy with which they respond to phone calls from customers.[110]

Group Performance. Workers performing similar or related tasks are sometimes organized into work groups, or teams. In such situations, pay scales are often tied to group performance. How much each person takes home is based on how well the group as a whole does. Such group performance systems encourage cooperation. Also, because wages for one worker are determined by the efforts of others, group members have an incentive to push slow workers to do better.

If rewards are to be based on individual or group performance, keep in mind the following guidelines:[111]

> **Link pay and performance appropriately.** Ensure that pay really is tied to performance under control of the individual or group and performance is fully assessed. For instance, it would make little sense to base pay on quantity produced for an assembly worker whose level of output is controlled by an assembly line. It would also be unwise to reward just one aspect of performance, such as quantity produced, if several aspects, including quality, are important.

> **Use pay for performance as part of a broader human resources management system.** Make sure performance appraisal systems are accurate and those conducting the appraisals are well trained.

> **Build employee trust and promote the belief that performance makes a difference.** Unless employees believe rewards will really be linked to good performance, they're unlikely to take pay for performance seriously.

> **Use multiple layers of rewards.** Pay based on individual performance lets employees see how their personal contributions lead to direct rewards, but it may encourage internal competition rather than cooperation. As such, it may help to base rewards on multiple performance measures. For instance, at AT&T credit bonuses are based on 12 measures, reflecting the performance of both regional teams and the entire business unit. Team members must meet their individual performance goals to be eligible for the bonuses.[112]

> **Increase employee involvement.** Because employees must view a pay plan as legitimate if they are to take it seriously, it helps to let employees participate in the design of the plan. This increases acceptance of the plan and provides a better fit of the plan to individual needs.

> **Include nonfinancial incentives.** Although pay is certainly important, remember that praise, honorary titles, increased job responsibility, and other nonfinancial incentives can also be provided as rewards for good performance.[113]

Plantwide or Companywide Productivity. Employee pay rates can be based in part on the productivity of the entire plant or organization. For instance, at Borden, 28,000 workers at 180 plants had the opportunity to win bonuses ranging from $250 to $800 each, depending on how their individual plants performed in relation to measures of attendance, safety, quality, production, and financial goals.[114]

At Monsanto's chemical plant in Luling, Louisiana, workers earned bonuses of $760 each when the plant met goals for reducing injuries and preventing pollutants from escaping into the outside air.[115] One form of productivity plan is the Scanlon Plan, under which groups of employees suggest to management how productivity might be improved. Then, at regular intervals, the productivity of the organization is evaluated. If productivity is up, each worker is rewarded with a bonus.[116] Some Japanese companies have adopted an interesting variation of this plan. They have annual picnics at which new ideas, inventions, and improvements devised by the employees are exhibited and demonstrated by the company president.

Organization-Based Plans. Many companies today feature profit-sharing plans. Under such plans, employees are given a bonus if company profits are high.[117] Although profit-sharing plans tend to be associated with large companies, they can also be useful at small firms. For instance, the Artful Framer Gallery, a small company in Fort Lauderdale, Florida, began a profit-sharing plan in 1987 when it employed only five people, and by 1993 the plan had amassed $150,000. The owner of the gallery states that "the plan makes employees happier and more committed to the company, which helps us produce better results than if they were uncertain about their benefits packages."[118]

Another way to link rewards to company performance is through employee stock option plans (ESOPs). ESOPs reward employees with company stock, either as an outright grant or at a price below market value. ESOPs give employees actual ownership of the firm.[119] ESOPs were initially an executive perk, but companies such as Procter & Gamble, General Electric, and Chase Manhattan now grant them at all levels.[120] Research shows that firms that have adopted ESOPs have subsequently done well, with total shareholder returns averaging almost 7 percent annually above those of similar companies without ESOPs.[121]

In some firms, employees' returns from ESOPs have been extraordinary. For instance, in one 12-year period, Charles Schwab and Co. contributed an average of 8,109 shares to each of its employees' ESOPs, which translated into $1.26 million per employee. As such, Schwab produced an estimated 2,000 new millionaires, many of whom took early retirement.[122]

ESOPs have come under attack recently due to cases, such as the Enron collapse, where employees found their savings decimated when the company's stock plummeted. Critics charge that ESOPs are prone to accounting abuses and employees often are granted only very limited disclosure of important financial information.[123]

A desirable feature of organization-based plans is that firms make payments only when the firm can best afford them. However, a problem with such plans is that employees are not rewarded on the basis of individual performance. Research clearly shows that the more closely rewards are tied to individual performance, the more strongly the employee will be motivated. Also, employees do not like to be penalized for things outside their control, such as low company productivity or profit or a fickle stock market. For instance, Du Pont introduced an ambitious "achievement sharing" plan, involving nearly 20,000 employees in its fiber plants. However, poor performance of Du Pont's fiber business, primarily due to a weak economy, caused employees to face pay losses, and the plan was ended two years later.[124] In general, plantwide productivity plans, profit-sharing plans, and ESOPs may result in more positive employee attitudes toward the company, but they may not have much impact on individual performance.

Figure 12-6 shows where each of the factors we have discussed fits into the process of setting employee wage and salary rates.

FIGURE 12-6
The Wage Determination Process

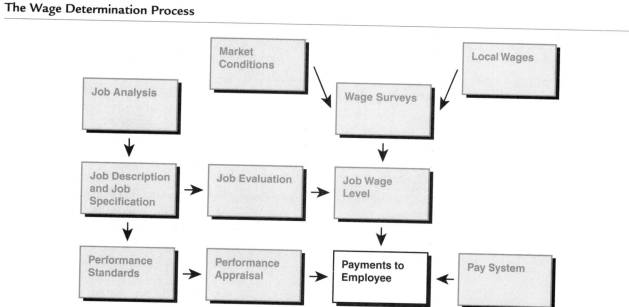

TOP TEN LIST: KEY POINTS TO REMEMBER

BUILDING HUMAN ASSETS

10. Make sure your recruiting strategy is based on a clear understanding of the requirements of the job and the type of person qualified for that job.

9. Use external recruiting methods when hiring for entry-level positions, and use internal recruiting methods (whenever possible) when hiring for higher-level positions.

8. Structure your job interview process so the questions are job-related and legal.

7. Focus on asking behavioral and/or situational types of interview questions, shown to be more valid in assessing the qualifications of job candidates.

6. Continually evaluate your recruiting and selection processes in order to enhance their effectiveness.

5. Use multiple valid selection methods in evaluating job candidates.

4. Be professional and humane when terminating employees.

3. Think strategically about training issues in your work unit by identifying specific training needs that support the achievement of your work unit's goals and objectives.

2. Make sure the performance appraisal method used reflects the key performance dimensions of the job performed by an employee.

1. Take steps to ensure that every performance appraisal leads to the development of a clear action plan for helping an employee to improve his or her job performance.

QUESTIONS FOR REVIEW AND REFLECTION

REVIEW QUESTIONS

1. What are the three stages of staffing?
2. What are the relative benefits of recruitment, selection, and placement versus training and development?
3. What is recruiting? Identify primary sources of job applicants.
4. Discuss relative costs and benefits of internal recruiting methods and external recruiting methods.
5. What is a realistic job preview?
6. What is the role of selection?
7. Discuss benefits and costs of alternative selection tools, including application forms, references, interviews, tests, and assessment centers.
8. Provide guidelines for improving interviews.
9. Identify and discuss seven types of tests.
10. Discuss each of the following aspects of testing: validity, faking, and fairness.
11. What is placement?
12. Explain the importance of orientation, lateral moves, promotions, and demotions.
13. Provide guidelines for effective termination.

14. What three sets of factors should you consider when conducting a training and development needs analysis?
15. Discuss five types of off-the-job training.
16. What are the reasons for appraising performance?
17. Identify guidelines for improving performance appraisals.
18. What are the relative merits of trait approaches, behavioral approaches, and outcome approaches to performance appraisal?
19. What is 360-degree feedback? How does it differ from traditional approaches to performance appraisal?
20. Define *job analysis*, *job specification*, and *job description*.
21. Identify guidelines for linking rewards to individual or group performance.
22. What are the relative benefits and costs of individual- or group-based rewards versus rewards based on plantwide or companywide outcomes?
23. Discuss the steps in the wage determination process.

CRITICAL THINKING QUESTIONS

1. A colleague states, "It's simply unfair to deprive people of jobs on the basis of their answers to some paper-and-pencil test." How would you respond?

2. As stated in the chapter, about one-third of job applicants whose credentials have been investigated by the National Credit Verification Service somehow misrepresented their educational backgrounds. You have learned that a current employee, hired in large part on the basis of her educational background, including a master's degree, falsified her application materials; she began a master's program but dropped out in the first semester. The employee has been doing extremely well on the job. What do you think should be done? Why?

3. A human resource manager presents the following argument: "The purpose of a rigorous selection process is to ensure we hire employees who will perform best on the job. When we use an ability test, for instance, we're looking for individuals who have the highest levels of skills required to do the job. It's not our concern *why* candidates developed, or didn't develop, those skills. They may have had a troubled childhood, inadequate education, poor training, or whatever, but the bottom line is that they haven't acquired needed skills. If that's the case, why should we be required to hire people that genetic screening shows are likely to develop health problems that will harm their productivity and sap company profits?" Take and defend a position for or against this argument.

4. Which of the various forms of integrity tests (e.g., polygraph tests, written honesty tests, credit checks) do you think is most defensible for selection purposes? Least defensible? Why?

5. The Peter Principle asserts that workers are promoted to positions of greater authority and responsibility as long as they perform well and that these promotions will continue until they reach their "level of incompetence." Taken to the extreme, the Peter Principle predicts that at steady state everyone in an organization will be incompetent. Present four arguments against this prediction of the Peter Principle.

6. Take and defend a position for or against the following statement: Performance appraisal is demeaning and has no place in modern organizations.

7. Your boss says, "In this environment, we have to become a team-based organization. To provide a clear and consistent message, all of our rewards will be team based." Discuss the potential benefits and costs of following your boss's suggestion.

8. An employee says, "Profit-sharing plans are just a way to shift risk from the company to employees. We accept lower pay with the promise of a share of profits, but if profits are poor for reasons out of our control, we're the ones left holding the bag." Do you agree? Why or why not?

EXPERIENTIAL EXERCISES

WEB EXERCISE 12-1

The Society for Human Resource Management (SHRM) is the world's largest human resource management association. It provides education and information services, conferences and seminars, government and media representation, online services, and publications to more than 120,000 professional and student members throughout the world. Go to the SHRM Web site at ***http://www.shrm.org/***.

The site contains a vast array of human resource information (some of it restricted to members). In the left-hand column, click on "HR Magazine." You will have access to articles in the latest issue of the magazine as well as articles from previous issues, a searchable index, and other features. Click on "Articles from Previous Issues." You will see articles arranged by category, such as Benefits, Compensation, Contingent Personnel, Diversity, Legal Issues, and Training and Development. Select any two articles. Write a two-page summary of each article, being sure to highlight how the article contributes to your knowledge as a potential manager.

WEB EXERCISE 12-2

HR-guide.com is a very extensive human resources Web site. It provides a wide variety of materials relating to such topics as personnel selection, job analysis, compensation, education programs, training and development, legal issues, and much more. Go to the site at **http://www.hr-guide.com/**.

Click on "Personnel Selection." This will take you to a page with information about tests, interviews, and other selection procedures and issues. At the bottom of the page are categories of interview questions (e.g., achievement, behaviors, creativity, interests, leadership, loyalty, self)—1,700 questions in total. Click on the "self" category (you will see 75 questions listed). Select five questions you think are particularly interesting or challenging. How would you answer each question?

CASE 12-1

CREATIVE RECRUITING STRATEGIES AT EDS CORPORATION

The Company[125]

EDS is a leading provider of management consulting, information, and technology services that help clients enhance their long-term performance in the areas of customer service, quality assurance, and product development. It is a global leader in providing these services to 35,000 business and government clients in 55 countries around the world. Its business clients come from industries such as communications, health care, financial services, energy and chemicals, and retailing.

The company is headquartered in Plano, Texas, and employs more than 137,000 worldwide (as of 2002). In 2002, the company generated $1.1 billion in net income based on $21.5 billion in sales.

The strategic intent of EDS is to "be the premier global outsourcing services company.[126] This position will be built on providing the industry's most cost-effective, high-value IT outsourcing services."

The company seeks to achieve its strategic intent by valuing the following:[127]

- **People.** EDS people are dedicated to ensuring every client is well served. Our highly skilled IT professionals are recognized the world over for their innovation, responsiveness, and flexibility.
- **Service Excellence Commitment.** Service excellence is our heart and soul, the gene in the EDS culture. It's how we continue to meet-and exceed-our commitments.
- **Consortium Approach.** Unlike conglomerates tied to in-house products, our consortium approach enables clients to receive best-of-thought EDS solutions combined with best-of-bred technologies from like-minded hardware and software providers.
- **Industry Expertise.** We deliver compelling value propositions that demonstrate we understand our clients' businesses and have deep expertise in their industries.

- **A Focus on Value.** Delivering value for clients drives everything we do.
- **Our Clients and Our People.** Our passion for client success is why we come to work. As a global outsourcing leader, our success begins with our people, who are absolutely the industry's best.
- **Serving Your World.** EDS manages more than 350 customer relationships and more than 2.4 billion customer interactions in 41 languages. Our help-desk agents respond to more than 27 million support calls each year and serve clients in 24 languages.
- Our Communities-EDS employees volunteered over 30,000 hours of community service in 2002.

Creative Recruiting Practices[128]

EDS has developed a reputation for being especially adept at using innovative strategies to recruit high-quality employees, even in an increasingly tight labor market. For example, EDS is a major sponsor for the U.S. Sunrayce, an intercollegiate competition involving the design and racing of solar-powered cars. The company provides equipment and its own engineers to support the competition. In the end, this has proven to be an extremely valuable strategy for attracting top-notch college graduates to fill a variety of technical positions within the company.

EDS also recruits employees by sending company representatives to ski lodges around the country and passing out flyers and T-shirts to skiers as they are flying down the slopes. This strategy has helped the company build name recognition among its target populations.

The company maintains a strong commitment to developing long-term partnerships with 50 colleges and universities throughout the United States. This includes offering résumé writing and other career services to college students and a national case study competition in which EDS executives serve as judges. Finalists earn the opportunity to visit EDS corporate headquarters and to win scholarships.

EDS has a large college internship program that hires 500 to 700 students each year. Interns are given numerous opportunities to learn about the company and its culture. If a manager is sufficiently impressed with an intern, he or she may offer that individual a job up to 9 to 10 months before graduation.

An employee referral program is also a major component of the EDS overall recruiting system. Employees receive a variety of rewards for making referrals. In addition, any employee who makes a referral gets his or her name placed in a drawing to win prizes such as vacations and laptop computers.

When it comes to career fairs, EDS differentiates itself from other employers by using a traveling EDS mobile station equipped with interview rooms and satellite links to the Internet. The company even inserts its recruiting ads into a direct-mail envelope called Val Pak that includes coupons for discounts on products and services.

The company's Web site provides extensive resources on career opportunities that describe the benefits of working for EDS, which include the following:

- Employees can work in any of 60 countries in a wide variety of industries to which the company provides services (e.g., energy, health care, manufacturing, and retail).

- The company provides the tools and support needed to empower employees to develop themselves personally and professionally. These include a "Career Mobility Policy," which encourages lateral and upward job mobility, and a "Self-Directed Career Planning Process," which helps employees develop formal long-term career development plans.

- Employees can participate in a mentoring program, which promotes a mutual learning process that supports the achievement of career objectives.

- EDS's corporate university offers a wide range of courses that can be accessed anyplace and anytime by employees.

- The company's generous employee benefit package includes flexible benefit options, a company-funded pension plan, a 401(k) plan with the employer matching up to 25 percent of employee contributions, employee stock options, flexible work arrangements (e.g., job sharing, telecommuting), and a Diversity paid holiday so each employee can observe his or her unique cultural or religious practices.

- Finally, EDS hires a large number of college graduates with backgrounds in music and the humanities and then trains them through its own development programs.

Summary

Clearly, EDS uses a multifaceted recruiting strategy that enhances its attractiveness as an employer among students at leading colleges and universities. It also effectively develops long-term partnerships with sources of qualified labor and uses creative recruiting methods to tap into nontraditional populations.

Discussion Questions

1. Evaluate EDS's various recruiting strategies. What are their strengths? Weaknesses? Be specific.

2. What type of selection system would you recommend to EDS to support its recruiting practices? Identify and describe the elements of the system.

3. What recommendations would you make to EDS to improve its overall recruiting efforts? Be specific and action oriented.

4. What are the practical implications of this case for you as a future manager?

CASE 12-2

UPWARD APPRAISAL AT FEDEX

Overview[129]

Most people are all too familiar with the concept of the annual review: An employee and supervisor sit down together to evaluate the employee's performance over the past year. In most cases, the score on the evaluation directly correlates with the raise or bonus the individual receives for the following year. The system is common practice for most companies and allows supervisors to demonstrate they are dedicated to developing their employees and encouraging them to grow.

However, you may not be as familiar with the reverse, a form of evaluation called upward appraisal. This technique provides employees with an opportunity that may exist to some only in fantasy: a confidential way to grade one's boss. Upward appraisal is becoming more and more popular within the business community, with some companies believing it is vital to their success.

FedEx and Its Upward Appraisal Process

FedEx is dedicated to the use of upward appraisal, or Survey Feedback Action (SFA) as they like to call it.[130] The FedEx Corporation provides strategic leadership and consolidated financial reporting results for its independent companies including FedEx Express, FedEx Ground, FedEx Freight, FedEx Custom Critical, FedEx Trade Networks, and FedEx Services.[131] The mission of the company is as follows:

> *FedEx Corporation will produce superior financial results for its shareowners by providing high value-added logistics, transportation, and relation information services through focused operating companies. Customer service requirements will be met in the highest quality manner appropriate to each market segment served. FedEx Corporation will strive to develop mutually rewarding relationships with its employees, partners, and suppliers. Safety will be the first consideration in all operations. Corporate activities will be conducted to the highest ethical and professional standards.*[132]

The worldwide corporate headquarters of FedEx is in Memphis, Tennessee. In 2003, the company's revenue was $16.5 billion. Fedex provides services to 215 countries. It employs more than 190,000 people worldwide.

Fred Smith, FedEx founder and CEO, believes FedEx's most important asset is its people. He claims that if you develop employees to be the best they can be, they develop your business. Thus FedEx's business philosophy can be boiled down to these three aspects: People–Service–Profit (PSP). If your people are stretched to reach their fullest potential, they will provide good service. If a company consistently provides good service, it is bound to grow and flourish, making a profit. So how does a company as large as FedEx (with employees located in more than 100 countries) work to develop its people? FedEx found that SFA is an effective way to do this.

The Survey Feedback Action (SFA) process is explained within its name. First, FedEx *surveys* all of its employees (once a year) to get their *feedback* on their managers and the company in general. Then it works to translate feedback into *action*, which usually means working to improve the performance and quality of management itself.

Even though the formula for SFA is simple, two principles must be enforced in order to make this concept effec-

tive in practice. The first is that SFA must be universal. It needs to be applied to every employee at every level. Second, management needs to accept it. Because SFA directly impacts the careers of managers, some are intimidated by the idea of being evaluated by subordinates. Some managers have suggested this could be a way for employees to bully them. Others propose the reverse could happen. To illustrate the latter, a number of supervisors have been known to practice the "Pizza Party Phenomenon": They take their employees out for dinner and/or drinks the night before appraisals to create a last-minute positive impression (playing off the recency effect). However, in general, good managers usually embrace SFA and view the evaluation as an opportunity to improve and become better managers.

In order for SFA (or any form of upward appraisal) to be successful, employees need to believe in the concept. To get employees to take SFA seriously, they must be sold on the idea. This entails having senior management behind the philosophy, supporting it and practicing it. They must sell it to people at all levels. Then they need to demonstrate that SFA provides actual results. People are more willing to offer their feedback if they think it will be valued and used.

Persuading employees to provide honest feedback means assuring them their opinions will remain confidential. This is especially important in the case of upward appraisals because employees are evaluating a supervisor who has power over them. This requires a two-step process. First, the evaluation system must be secure enough that the survey cannot be traced back to the individual who took it. Second, it is imperative that severe disciplinary measures are enforced if anyone attempts to breach confidentiality. The survey can be designed to ask questions such as sex, age, or department, but these factors cannot be used to identify employees. They should only be utilized to gain a better understanding of general trends. For example, if the survey asked each employee about the length of time he or she had been with the organization, this information could help determine if new employees felt alienated or if older employees felt unappreciated.

FedEx uses surveys to obtain employee feedback, and it also uses discussion as another method to gain information. FedEx breaks employees into workgroups that usually consist of around 15 people. All of these people work in the same department and report to the same manager. Once a year, the groups are surveyed on their opinions regarding the organization as a whole, their supervisors, and a variety of local issues. Once a month the team gets together to discuss everyday issues and the progress they have seen as a result of SFA. They evaluate whether the action points based on SFA are being implemented. They are also free to discuss the topic mentioned within the survey itself.

Once a survey is completed, it is scored. This process provides a personal score for each manager. The score can then be used for developmental purposes throughout the following year. It will show managers the areas where employees felt they were strong and areas that could use some improvement. The key to making this portion of the process successful is to convince managers to see this as a development tool and not a way to expose weaknesses. If the score is used for development, the manager can set up a meeting with his or her supervisor to designate certain action steps he or she plans to take to improve on weaker points and, in turn, become a better manager.

Discussion Questions

1. What are the objectives of upward appraisal? How does this process differ from a traditional approach to performance appraisal?

2. Do you think upward appraisal is an effective approach for enhancing the effectiveness of a manager? Why or why not?

3. What are the barriers to implementing an effective upward appraisal process in an organization? What can be done, in general, to overcome these barriers?

4. Evaluate the elements of the upward appraisal process used at FedEx. What are its strengths? Weaknesses? Justify your evaluation using information from the case and this chapter.

5. What recommendations would you give FedEx management for enhancing the effectiveness of its upward appraisal system? What barriers to implementing your recommendations might exist at FedEx, and what would you do to overcome them?

6. What are the practical implications of this case for you as a future manager in a real-world organization?

VIDEO CASE: NEXT DOOR FOOD STORE

MANAGING HUMAN RESOURCES

Running Time: 14:09

Headquartered in Mount Pleasant, Michigan, Next Door Food Store is a family-run business with more than 30 outlets in Michigan and Indiana. The stores sell gasoline and a wide variety of grocery and general merchandise items. Along with many other challenges, Next Door must deal with a diverse customer base as well as the convenience store industry's remarkable 100 percent average annual turnover rate.

The video shows Next Door Food Store's president and CEO, Dave Johnson, as well as Human Resource managers Barry Chapman and Diane McKenna, Training Director Rich Evanoff, and other Next Door Food Store personnel as they discuss how Next Door seeks to develop loyal and competent employees while controlling costs. After viewing the video, answer the following questions.

1. What does Next Door Food Store see as its target market? How does the nature of that target market influence the sorts of employees needed by Next Door?

2. What are some costs of turnover to Next Door? According to the video, what has been a primary cause

of employee turnover at Next Door? What are the four main elements of Next Door's efforts to reduce turnover?

3. What is Next Door doing to facilitate hiring of qualified employees?

4. What are the goals of training at Next Door? What is the nature of that training?

5. What is the nature of the compensation system at Next Door?

6. What is the purpose of the performance evaluation system at Next Door? What is the company doing to help ensure that performance evaluations are carried out on a timely basis?

7. What factors does Next Door weigh in deciding whether to offer particular benefits, such as medical benefits for all employees?

http://www.nextdoor1.com/

LIGHTEN UP

ROTTEN RÉSUMÉS

Here are some unintentional bloopers from actual job seekers' résumés:

- "I am extremely loyal to my present firm, so please don't let them know of my immediate availability."
- "Note: Please don't misconstrue my 14 jobs as 'job hopping.' I have never quit a job."
- "Marital status: Often. Children: Various."
- "Wholly responsible for two (2) failed institutions."
- "Terminated after saying, 'It would be a blessing to be fired.'"
- "I am writing to you, as I have written to all *Fortune* 1000 companies every year for the past three years, to solicit employment."

- "Insufficient writing skills, thought processes have slowed down some. If I am not one of the best, I will look for another opportunity."
- "It's best for employers that I not work with people."
- "Excellent memory; strong math aptitude; excellent memory; effective management skills; and very good at math."

To check out more résumé bloopers and other résumé information, go to Resumania at

http://www.resumania.com

LIGHTEN UP

YO! I'M YOUR CEO

When Ben & Jerry's Homemade Inc. wanted to find a successor for cofounder and CEO Ben Cohen, it held a "Yo! I'm your CEO" essay contest. Aspiring CEOs were asked to mail in 100-word essays on "Why I Would Be a Great CEO for Ben & Jerry's." The first-place finisher got to run Ben & Jerry's; the runner-up got a lifetime supply of ice cream. Even the losers were to receive rejection letters "suitable for framing." Although the approach is whimsical, the task is a serious one. Cohen said, "I feel really stretched trying to run an organization this size." To make the job more attractive, the company lifted a salary cap that limited the CEO's pay to seven times that of the lowest paid employee.

Response to the contest was overwhelming, with 22,500 entries arriving in less than two months from as far away as London and India. One applicant took out a full-page ad in the *New York Times* offering his services. Another attached his résumé to a Superman costume.

To help make the decision regarding the new CEO, Ben & Jerry's hired an executive search firm. Fourteen search firms were considered. The winning firm, Russell Reynolds Associates Inc., included a list of employees' 19 favorite Ben & Jerry's flavors with its presentation. The firm learned of the victory with the arrival of 19 gallons of those ice cream flavors.[133]

The choice for CEO, Robert Holland, subsequently supervised Ben & Jerry's expansion into France and helped professionalize the company's management. He has since left Ben & Jerry's to purchase WorkPlace Interiors, an office-furniture dealership established by Steelcase Inc.[134] To learn about Ben & Jerry's progress under its new owner, Unilever, and its latest CEO, Yves Couette, visit Ben & Jerry's on the Web at:[135]

http://www.benandjerrys.com/

LIGHTEN UP

UNUSUAL INTERVIEWS

Human resource professionals at 100 major American corporations were asked for stories of unusual job applicant behavior they had experienced. Here are some they shared.

- Said he was so well qualified that if he didn't get the job, it would prove the company's management was incompetent.

- She wore a Walkman and said she could listen to music and me at the same time.
- Balding candidate abruptly excused himself, returned to office a few minutes later wearing a hairpiece.
- Asked to see interviewer's résumé to see if the personnel executive was qualified to judge the candidate.

- Said if he were hired, he would demonstrate his loyalty by having the corporate logo tattooed on his forearm.
- Interrupted to phone his therapist for advice on answering specific interview questions.
- Wouldn't get out of chair until I would hire him. I had to call the police.
- Took a brush out of my purse, brushed his hair, and left.

- Candidate asked me if I would put on a suit jacket to ensure that the offer was formal.
- Candidate said he didn't really want the job, but the unemployment office needed proof he was looking for one.
- Asked if I wanted some cocaine before starting the interview.

SKILLS PRACTICE

12-1   *Skill Level: BASIC*

Field Experience: Interviews with Real-World Managers About Building Human Assets

Skill Objective

To develop a better understanding of what management practitioners in the real world do to build human assets effectively.

Procedure

1. Identify one or two managers who work in different business organizations. Ask the manager(s) if you can interview each of them for approximately 30 minutes.

2. When you meet with each manager, ask the following questions:

   a. What kinds of challenges do you experience in attracting qualified people to your organization? What actions do you take to address these challenges effectively?

   b. What kinds of challenges do you experience in selecting the most qualified person for a given job in your organization? What actions do you take to address these challenges effectively?

   c. What type of training does your organization provide for its employees? Do you feel it is effective? Why or why not?

   d. Please describe how the performance appraisal process works in your organization. Do you feel it is effective? Why or why not?

   e. What advice would you give students regarding specific actions they can take to handle the issues we just discussed once they enter the real world?

3. Summarize the results of your interviews.

Discussion Questions

1. Based on the summary of your interviews, what are your key findings about building human assets? Why are these findings so significant?

2. What are the practical implications of this exercise for you as a future manager and leader of a real-world organization?

SKILLS PRACTICE

12-2   *Skill Level: CHALLENGING*

Developing a Strategic Recruiting Plan

Skill Objective

To develop skill in designing and implementing a recruiting plan for a specific job.

Procedure

Note: Download from the text Web site the worksheet developed for this exercise.

1. Select one of the following scenarios (or you can select a job based on your current real-world job).

   Scenario 1: Recruiting Web Page Designers at an Internet Retailer

   You work at an upstart Internet retailer that sells books, videos, CDs, and so on. Due to the explosive growth of your firm, you must hire 10 high-level Web page designers who can continually develop and maintain the company's Web site in order to attract, satisfy, and retain customers. Currently, only two people are performing this function. No formal job description yet exists for this job, but you need experienced people who are creative, enthusiastic, and team oriented and can work in a self-directed manner. What would you do to recruit people for this job?

Scenario 2: Recruiting New Agents at an Insurance Company

You work as a district manager at a major insurance company based in the Midwest. Your company sells a full line of insurance through an agent force that works as an independent contractor for the company. Recently, you have noticed the following few trends:

a. The company's long-term growth potential in current and new markets is excellent.

b. The five-year success rate (agents who are profitable after five years of operation) has plummeted to below 50 percent.

c. Interest in becoming an insurance agent has fallen to an all-time low among people in their 20s.

In terms of the job of insurance agent, ideally you need someone with these qualities:

- Excellent interpersonal skills
- Good management and organizational skills
- The ability to develop trust in the eyes of customers
- Strong ties with the local community in which he or she is doing business

- The ability to work in a self-directed manner
- Perseverance and the ability to delay gratification

You need to hire a large number of new agents who can support the company's expansion strategy. Given this situation, develop a recruiting plan to increase the hiring of new insurance agents at the company.

2. Develop a plan for recruiting qualified candidates to fill the job openings in the scenario you selected. This plan should include the following elements:

   a. The job that needs to be filled
   b. The objectives of this recruiting initiative
   c. Job requirements (duties and responsibilities)
   d. Desired applicant qualifications
   e. Where you will look for appropriate candidates to fill this job (recruiting sources)
   f. The methods you will use to recruit from the sources you have selected
   g. How you will evaluate the effectiveness of your recruiting process

3. Answer the following discussion questions.

Discussion Questions

1. Evaluate your recruiting plan in terms of its relative strengths and weaknesses.

2. What are the key actions you must take to implement your recruiting plan effectively?

3. What are the barriers to the success of your recruiting plan? What steps would you take to overcome these barriers?

4. What are the practical implications of this exercise for you as a future manager or supervisor?

SKILLS PRACTICE

12-3

Skill Level: BASIC

Conducting Realistic Job Preview

Skill Objective

To develop skill in identifying and effectively communicating a balanced perspective (positive and negative characteristics) of a job to candidates during the recruiting process.

Procedure

Note: Download from the text Web site the worksheet developed for this exercise.

1. Find a partner for this exercise.

2. Select a job you are familiar with. This can be your current part-time job or a job you held in the past.

3. Make a list of the positive aspects of the job (e.g., type of work, compensation, work environment, coworkers, opportunities for advancement, benefits).

4. Make a list of the negative aspects of the job (e.g.,

type of work, compensation, work environment, coworkers, opportunities for advancement, benefits).

5. Practice communicating the positive and negative aspects of the job to your partner as if you were interviewing that person for your job. Be careful not to oversell the positive aspects of the job. Also, take care not to be overly negative about the less desirable aspects of the job either.

Discussion Questions

1. Although this may be a basic exercise, why is it important to provide realistic job previews during the recruiting process? What are the costs of not doing this?

2. What could you do to further apply the concept of a realistic job preview in other aspects of the hiring process? Try to be as specific as possible.

3. What should the appropriate balance be in terms of discussing the positive and negative aspects of a position with job candidates?

4. What are the practical implications of this exercise for you as a future manager or supervisor?

SKILLS PRACTICE

12-4   *Skill Level:* **CHALLENGING**

Role-Immersion Simulation Exercise: Conducting an Effective Job Interview

Skill Objective
To develop skill in designing and implementing an effective job interview.

Procedure

Note: Download from the text Web site the worksheet developed for this exercise.

1. Select one of the following scenarios or a job you are familiar with to use for this exercise.

Situation 1

You are the manager of customer sales and service for a major catalog retail firm based in northern Wisconsin. It is time to start hiring help for the holiday season. You are interested in hiring customer service representatives who can answer customer calls, take orders accurately, answer questions about catalog merchandise intelligently, and provide service to customers in a friendly and professional manner. You need people who are hard working, trustworthy, and dependable. You will be interviewing job applicants for these positions.

Situation 2

You are the current president of the general management student organization at your university. It is the end of the school year and time to select your successor. When you took over as president of the organization last year, it was literally in shambles. There were only a handful of active members, low attendance at meetings, no funds in the organization's bank account, and very few activities in terms of speakers and social

events. Since then, you have rebuilt the membership to more than 100. The organization has over $2,000 in the bank, it has sponsored many events and socials, which have been a great success, and it was even recognized by the university as the best student organization of the year. Your goal at this point is to maintain the positive momentum of the organization by selecting a strong leader who can build on what you have done. You have decided to interview a person who has indicated an interest in being president of the organization.

2. Design your interview process. Make sure you address the following issues:

a. List the key duties and responsibilities of this job.

b. List the key employee qualifications (knowledge and skills) needed for this job.

c. Given the job responsibilities and applicant qualifications you just listed, what kinds of behavioral or situational interview questions would be appropriate for assessing the degree to which the candidate is qualified for the job? Make a list of four to six interview questions.

3. Conduct a mock interview with a partner in the class, with you playing the role of the interviewer. Your job is to assess the qualifications of the interviewee with respect to the job you are using for this exercise. Summarize your evaluation of the candidate in terms of the following three areas:

a. Strengths of the candidate

b. Weaknesses of the candidate

c. Overall evaluation of the candidate

The person being interviewed (your partner) should play himself or herself and use personal background as a basis for answering the interview questions.

4. Switch roles and repeat steps 1 through 3. When you are done, answer the following discussion questions.

Discussion Questions

1. Evaluate the effectiveness of the interviews you and your partner conducted with each other. What went well? What didn't go so well?

2. If you were to conduct your interviews again, what would each of you do differently?

3. What are the practical implications of this exercise for you as a future manager or supervisor?

SKILLS PRACTICE

12-5
Skill Level: BASIC

Conducting New Employee Orientations

Skill Objective
To develop skill in designing orientation programs for new employees.

Procedure
Note: Download from the text Web site the worksheet developed for this exercise.

1 Select a job and organization you are familiar with. This may be your current job or a job you had in the past.

2. Develop a plan for conducting an effective new-employee orientation for this job and the company as a whole. At a minimum, be sure to address parts a, b, and c that follow.

   a. List the major issues the employee needs to be informed of about the job (e.g., duties, responsibilities, procedures, policies, performance standards and expectations)

   b. List the major issues the employee needs to be informed of about the work unit (e.g., breaks, procedures, policies, meeting coworkers, meetings, culture)

   c. List the major issues the employee needs to be informed of about the organization (e.g., company history, mission, culture, benefits, general policies)

3. Answer the following discussion questions.

Discussion Questions

1. Describe the process you would use for implementing your orientation program.

2. What is the value of conducting new-employee orientation programs? What is the cost of not providing an orientation for new employees?

3. Why do so many companies fail to conduct any kind of orientation program for new employees? What kinds of problems may result from not having an orientation program?

4. What are the practical implications of this exercise for you as a future supervisor or manager?

SKILLS PRACTICE

12-6
Skill Level: CHALLENGING

Role-Immersion Simulation: Conducting Effective Employee Terminations

Skill Objective
To develop skill in conducting employee terminations in a professional, humane, and legal manner.

Procedure
Note: Download from the text Web site the worksheet developed for this exercise.

   1. Find a partner for this exercise. One person should

assume the role of the manager; the other person should play the role of the employee.

2. Read the following scenario to provide a context for the exercise.

The Manager Role

You are a sales manager for a struggling construction equipment manufacturing firm based in Indiana. Top management has issued a directive for all managers to reduce their staff by 20 percent effective immediately. After a grueling decision-making process, you have decided to lay off an employee who has been a solid performer as a sales representative and has been with the company for over 20 years.

The Employee Role

Your role is to listen to what the manager has to say and to evaluate it after he or she has completed the termination meeting. Try to react as you would if this were actually happening to you.

3. The manager should now conduct the employee termination. After it is completed, the two partners should evaluate the process in terms of how effec-

tively the student playing the manager role applied the managerial guidelines for handling employee terminations.

4. Optional: Once this round of the exercise has been completed, the two partners can change roles and repeat the process.

Discussion Questions

1. What did you find most difficult about conducting your mock employee termination?

2. If you were to do this exercise again, what would you do the same in terms of conducting the employee termination? What would you do differently?

3. Many real-world managers do a poor job of handling employee terminations. Why do you think this is the case? What can companies do to support managers better in handling this difficult issue?

4. What are the practical implications of this exercise for you as a future supervisor or manager?

SKILLS PRACTICE

12-7   *Skill Level: CHALLENGING*

Training in the Real World: **Top Gun**

Skill Objective

To develop skill in analyzing and evaluating the application of training methods and processes in an organizational setting.

Procedure

1. Obtain a copy of the movie *Top Gun* starring Tom Cruise and Val Kilmer. It is available on VHS and DVD and can be rented or purchased from a local video store or retailer.

2. Watch the movie (in class or at home on your own). Be sure to note specific scenes and dialogue that illustrate various training methods.

Note: Download the worksheet developed for this exercise from the Web site for this book. This will help you document your notes regarding relevant scenes from the movie.

3. Discuss the following questions as a class.

a. What were the training objectives of the Top Gun program? To what degree were these objectives appropriate?

b. What types of training methods were used in the Top Gun program? To what degree were they appropriate given the objectives of the program? Use specific scenes and dialogue from the movie to support your answer.

c. How would go about evaluating the effectiveness of the Top Gun training program?

e. What are the practical implications of this exercise for you in dealing with training issues in real-world organizations?

SKILLS PRACTICE

Developing a Training Program

Skill Objective
To develop skill in designing a training program for a job.

Procedure
Note: Download from the text Web site the worksheet developed for this exercise.

1. Select a job you are familiar with, for instance, a current or previous part-time job, a summer job, or an internship.
2. Design a training program for new employees in this job consisting of the following elements:
   a. Training objectives (1–3) for your training program
   b. Training content for the training program
   c. Training methods for delivering your content
   d. An evaluation plan for assessing the effectiveness of your training program
3. Present a brief summary of your training program to the class.

SKILLS PRACTICE

Role-Immersion Simulation: Conducting an Effective Employee Performance Appraisal

Skill Objective
To develop skill in conducting an effective employee performance review.

Procedure
Note: Download from the text Web site the worksheet developed for this exercise.

1. Find a partner for this exercise. One person will play the role of the manager; the other person will play the role of Lisa, the employee.
2. Read the following role descriptions.

Role 1: The Manager

You are the supervisor of a team of sales associates who work in the TV and video department at a major consumer electronics retailer. The sales associates all work on a sales commission. An ideal sales associate has a strong customer service orientation, excellent sales figures, and consistent attendance, comes to work on time, works well with others, and is mature and professional.

It is time for Lisa's performance review. She has been working in her current job as a sales associate for about three years now. Lisa's sales per day average $1,200. The average daily sales figure for all of your sales associates is $1,000.

Lisa used a total of seven sick days this year. She was also marked "late" (more than 30 minutes late for the beginning of her shift) twice.

Lisa tries to help others out with their work (e.g., stocking merchandise, cleaning) when she is not busy. Generally, she has a positive attitude, although sometimes she is rather moody and short with her coworkers and even with customers on occasion. Lisa has demonstrated an excellent understanding of the products you carry in your department. How would you rate Lisa's performance based on the performance evaluation form that follows?

Performance Appraisal Form

Performance Evaluation Form: Sales Associate
Department: TV/Video
Employee: Lisa

	Poor	Fair	Satisfactory	Good	Excellent
1. Customer Orientation	1	2	3	4	5
2. Sales Productivity	1	2	3	4	5
3. Attendance	1	2	3	4	5
4. Punctuality	1	2	3	4	5
5. Teamwork	1	2	3	4	5
6. Attitude	1	2	3	4	5

Role 2: Lisa, the Employee

Your job is to listen to what the manager says to you about your job performance and to react as you would if this were actually happening to you. Be sure to read the foregoing information about Lisa to guide you in determining what to do and say during this exercise.

3. The manager should now sit down with the employee and conduct a performance appraisal session in which Lisa's performance ratings are discussed.

4. After the performance ratings have been discussed, the manager and Lisa should develop an action plan. This plan should include the following:

a. Performance goals: specific ends that the employee should accomplish in the next year

b. Supporting action steps: specific actions that should be taken to support the achievement of the performance goals

c. Training needs: any training needed to support the achievement of the performance goals

Discussion Questions

1. Evaluate the performance appraisal process conducted by the manager. What was done well? How could the process have been improved?

2. What are the practical implications of this exercise for you as a future supervisor or manager?

ORGANIZATIONAL CULTURE

Skills Objectives

> To assess the culture of an organization and to identify its strengths and weaknesses.

> To develop skill in designing and creating an organizational culture that supports the goals and strategies of a firm.

> To formulate strategies for enhancing the effectiveness of an existing organizational culture.

KNOWLEDGE OBJECTIVES

> Understand the nature and functions of organizational culture.

> Identify elements of organizational culture and discuss ways in which organizations can use those elements to achieve desired organizational outcomes.

> Know how to assess organizational culture and bring about desired changes.

> Understand how organizational culture may be related to performance and other outcomes.

Millions of Americans watched horrified as the space shuttle *Columbia* disintegrated 16 minutes before its scheduled landing on February 1, 2003. In the months following the disaster, attention focused on a chunk of foam that fell from the shuttle's external fuel tank and put a hole in a wing. When the Columbia Accident Investigation Board issued its report, though, a more fundamental, systemic cause was isolated—a culture of complacency at NASA. In that culture, people who suspected potential safety problems were pressured by peers and managers to keep doubts to themselves, reliance on past success was seen as a substitute for sound engineering practices, top management failed to receive critical communications, and professional differences of opinion were stifled.[1] Culture, although subtle and difficult to assess, can have powerful consequences, for better or worse. Culture shapes attitudes and behavior in organizations and affects many important personal and organizational outcomes.

We have seen that many changes in the modern workplace are likely to increase employees' levels of stress, insecurity, and frustration. It seems that many companies are chasing short-term financial gains at awful human costs. At the same time, other organizations are taking positive steps to ensure that they offer employees humane, supportive, empowering workplaces. Firms with strong, positive cultures may have major competitive advantages in the new world of work. They will offer attractive environments, thus improving attraction and retention of good employees, and will have the potential for enhanced performance.

In this chapter, we address organizational culture, including its functions, elements, and impact on performance. We also offer guidelines for assessing culture and, as appropriate, for managing cultural change. We see how such companies as Southwest Airlines, Quad/Graphics, GE, and Disney have used organizational culture to foster employee satisfaction and motivation as well as organizational performance.

Read the Pretest Skills Assessment and develop an action plan for dealing with the situation effectively. This will help you assess how much you already know about handling issues related to organizational culture.

PRETEST SKILLS ASSESSMENT

Organizational Culture

Note: This exercise is based on actual events encountered by managers in a real-world organizations. Some information may have been modified in order to maintain the anonymity of the people and organization involved in this situation.

You are a management consultant hired by a major manufacturing company to help it enhance its long-term effectiveness. This is a traditional organization in that its structure is very hierarchical, the culture of the firm values respect for authority, employee jobs are very narrowly defined, and communication flows from management to employees (i.e., from the top down) and not vice versa. In addition, management emphasizes a "bottom-line mentality" that puts tremendous pressure on employees to meet difficult production targets.

The result of this is an environment in which employees fear and mistrust management. Many employees resort to cutting corners in terms of quality and safety in order to meet their production targets. Employees do as they are directed by management and do not ask questions. Overall, the morale of employees is quite low.

The organization's performance has been in decline for some time now. Profits have fallen more than 70 percent this year. Product costs are up while quality is down dramatically.

Senior management recognizes the urgency of the situation. Specifically, they want you to assess the situation and develop an action plan that provides specific recommendations regarding actions that should be taken to foster a more appropriate culture in the organization. This would be a culture that gives employees the authority to make decisions regarding their jobs and encourages them to meet efficiency goals without engaging in unethical behavior. Be sure your plan addresses both short-term and long-terms issues. Be very specific and be prepared to defend each element of your plan in terms of its feasibility and cost effectiveness. Remember that increasing worker pay is not an option and more parties for workers would just make the problem worse in this case. After you are done, you can check to get feedback on your results by visiting the Web site for this text.

Now answer the questions in Self-Assessment 13-1 as a way to gauge your initial attitudes about organizational culture. The self-understanding you gain from doing this will be helpful to you as you read the rest of the chapter. After you are done, visit the text Web site to learn more about your responses. In the Voice of Experience feature, Aaron Kennedy, the founder of fast-growing Noodles and Company, discusses the importance of culture at Noodles.

SELF-ASSESSMENT 13-1

Attitudes Toward Organizational Culture

Answer the following questions regarding your attitudes toward organizational culture. Try to respond to each question as honestly as possible using the following response scale:

1 Disagree strongly
2 Disagree somewhat
3 Neither agree nor disagree
4 Agree somewhat
5 Agree strongly

____ 1. The culture of an organization is something that just naturally occurs—it cannot be managed.

____ 2. Organizational culture may influence employee satisfaction but otherwise has little to do with the long-term performance of a firm.

____ 3. Organizational culture can be an important mechanism for shaping the behavior of employees.

____ 4. Most organizations have just one culture that prevails throughout the firm.

____ 5. Organizational culture represents a company's values, norms, rituals, and beliefs in terms of how it does business.

____ 6. Organizational culture should be compatible with the strategy being followed by a company.

____ 7. Organizational culture is relatively easy to change.

____ 8. Management plays a key role in defining the culture in an organization.

____ 9. Multiple cultures cannot coexist in one organization.

____ 10. Every organization has some type of culture.

VOICE OF EXPERIENCE

AARON KENNEDY

Founder, Noodles and Company

1. Is maintaining and strengthening the culture at Noodles an important part of your role?

About five years into building Noodles & Company (15 restaurants), I realized that one of the things making our company so successful was the uniquely appealing culture we had created. I also recognized that this was perhaps our most defensible competitive advantage. I then proposed to the board that we hire another person to manage the day-to-day management of the company so I could focus more exclusively on the culture, brand, and culinary evolution of the company.

2. Is culture fit considered in the Noodles selection process?

We don't hire anyone that we don't think will fit and be a positive influence on our culture. Historically, any time we went against the cultural screen, it inevitably was a painful experience.

3. Do you use any sorts of rites or ceremonies to reinforce the culture at Noodles?

We continue the tradition of having lunch together as a whole team once every couple of weeks—now the office team is 70 people and it takes quite a few tables. But it's still fun to hang out together and chat. We also have an annual mountain "summit" where we take the general manager from every restaurant and all of our central support personnel to the mountains for a big cultural infusion once a year—Vail, Breckenridge, Keystone, etc.

4. Does organizational culture play a role in your decision of whether to open new restaurants?

We determine how fast we can grow (open new restaurants) based on the availability of cultural heroes who can step in to manage the new units . . . and bring the Noodles & Company culture to life there. In cities where our culture is thriving and we have an abundant supply of managers, we will focus our expansion efforts there and endeavor to open new restaurants more rapidly.

5. Are there other examples of how culture is important at Noodles?

Within our organization, we have inverted the typical organizational pyramid. To us, this means our team members who connect with the customers (cashiers and servers) are at the top of our org chart. Everyone else is here to support them and provide them the food and tools to delight the customer. Sometimes we hire people who have worked their way up in their career and feel they are entitled to just boss people around. They never fit in and thus end up being ineffective and leaving. Culture is rooted in the way you view the world.

BUILDING A CONSTRUCTIVE ORGANIZATIONAL CULTURE

Organizational culture consists of the values, symbols, stories, heroes, and rites that have special meaning for a company's employees. Culture represents the emotional, intangible part of the organization. If structure is the organization's skeleton, culture is its soul.

Many firms are now attempting to develop organizational cultures that are helpful in motivating their employees and keeping them committed to the firm. Companies such as Southwest Airlines, Quad/Graphics, Nordstrom, Disney, and General Electric credit their distinctive cultures for much of their success. Of 400 CEOs in North America and Europe interviewed by Price Waterhouse, 47 percent said that reshaping culture and related employee behavior took up a great deal of their time and was as important as monitoring financial information.[2] At General Motors, executives carry "culture cards" to remind them of their new missions. Japanese firms make heavy use of organizational culture for controlling member behavior through such strategies as songs, uniforms, and team-building exercises.

It is relatively easy to document a new machine's costs and benefits or even to demonstrate the short-term savings of slashing the work force. Because these things can be measured, managers tend to focus on them.

But what are the true costs of a reorganization that leaves workers overburdened, angry, and stressed? What are the hidden costs of a merger that, although attractive on paper, leads to internal clashes over core values and assumptions about "the right way to do things"? Conversely, what would be the benefits of a culture that instills values of cooperation and creativity, fosters loyalty, and people see as a "great place to be"? Because these things are difficult to measure, managers tend to overlook them. Culture, though, is real, and it is important. A study of 200 mergers found incompatible cultures to be *the* primary cause of failures.[3]

If something is to provide competitive advantage for a firm, it must be valuable, rare, and difficult to imitate. Unlike new technology, a pricing strategy, or a product design, an organizational culture is unique and impossible to duplicate. As such, it has the potential to yield great and enduring strategic advantage. But a strong culture can be destroyed overnight through an ill-advised redesign, an ill-planned merger, or a rash downsizing.

FUNCTIONS OF AN ORGANIZATIONAL CULTURE

Culture may serve many important functions in organizations, as shown in Figure 13-1:[4]

> **Cooperation.** By providing shared values and assumptions, culture may enhance goodwill and mutual trust, encouraging cooperation.
> **Decision making.** Shared beliefs and values give organizational members a consistent set of basic assumptions and preferences. This may lead to a more efficient decision-making process, because there are fewer disagreements about which premises should prevail.

FIGURE 13-1

Functions of an Organizational Culture

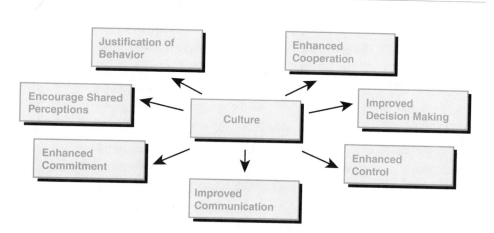

> **Control.** Culture serves as a subtle organizational control system, informally approving or prohibiting some patterns of behavior. Control in organizations is provided by three mechanisms, referred to as *markets, bureaucracies,* and *clans.*[5] The *market control mechanism* relies on price. If results fall short of goals, prices (not only those charged to customers but those paid to suppliers

FOCUS ON MANAGEMENT

ORGANIZATIONAL CULTURE AT QUAD/GRAPHICS*

Selected as one of the "100 Best Companies to Work for in America," Quad/Graphics is a remarkable success story. In 1971, Harry Quadracci bought a small abandoned factory for $150,000 and paid for it with a rubber check for $10,000 as a deposit, a second mortgage on his home, and the hope he could arrange more financing by the time the deal closed. Now Quad/Graphics is the ninth-largest printer in the United States and has more than 10,000 employees at 16 plants in Wisconsin, New York, Georgia, California, Japan, and elsewhere. The company prints more than 100 million magazines a month.

The company's philosophy is "Have fun, make money, and don't do business with anyone you don't like." Quadracci, who has been called the P. T. Barnum of printing, described the company as a circus, a continuous performance of highly creative and individualistic troupes who retained the childlike ability to be surprised and the flexibility to thrive on change.

Once a year, in May, the annual Quad University is held: Managers gather for a two-day conference, leaving nonmanagement personnel in charge. Others in the industry call this practice of leaving employees unsupervised a huge gamble, because a small slip-up could cost the firm hundreds of thousands of dollars on a single print run.

Quadracci disagreed. There have been few problems with this "management by walking away," he maintained. This attitude of trust permeates the company.

When Harry Quadracci founded the company, he said it would be "run by employees for employees," and one of his strongest beliefs is that people need to be free to do their best, without a lot of rules or fear of being punished if they make mistakes. When one unit spent three years and $1 million developing a new folding machine that didn't work, Quadracci threw a champagne party and awarded a medal to the project leader, saying, "You've got to have a perfect zero once in a while as well as a perfect success if you've explored alternatives." When Quadracci was warned that giving employees full responsibility for their presses would fragment management, he responded, "I think that's a good idea. Let's fragment management."

Unlike other printers, there are no time clocks at Quad/Graphics—workers are trusted to show up and to fill out their own time cards. Quad/Graphics has never been unionized, and there are no rigid lines between management and workers. A common saying is, "No one is ever done learning at Quad/Graphics." More than three of every four employees attend training sessions annually, and customers are welcome to sit in as well.

The company offers a variety of benefits. Every Quad/Graphics loca-

tion has a fitness center and child-care center. The company has a 40-acre nature preserve, lets employees purchase take-out food from its cafeterias (one of the nation's few company cafeterias with a liquor license), and maintains facilities for baseball, volleyball, basketball, and archery. Pay is augmented 15 percent by a combination of a profit-sharing plan and a savings program in which the company matches every dollar saved by an employee with 30 cents of its own, up to 6 percent of pay. There is even free popcorn that's always available. The popcorn is a constant reminder of Quadracci's philosophy that employees should generate a steady flow of new ideas, like kernels of corn in a popcorn popper.

In July 2002, Quad/Graphics was jolted by news of the death of Harry Quadracci by accidental drowning. Some wondered whether Quad/Graphics' culture could survive the demise of its visible and passionate founder. But one industry observer observed, "The legacy there is deeply rooted. It will go on."

http://www.qg.com/

*The discussion of Quad/Graphics is based on D. Kehrer, "The P. T. Barnum of Printing," *Across the Board,* May 1989, pp. 53–54; D. Kehrer, "The Miracle of Theory Q," *Business Month,* September 1989, pp. 44–49; R. Ganzel, "Putting Out the Welcome Mat," *Training,* March 1998, pp. 54–62; and K. O'Brien, "Harry, We Hardly Knew Ye," *American Printer,* September 2002, p. 10.

and employees for the organization's inputs) are adjusted to stimulate necessary change. The *bureaucratic control mechanism* relies on formal authority. The control process consists of adjusting rules and regulations and issuing directives. Finally, the *clan control mechanism* relies on shared beliefs and values.[6] These shared beliefs and values essentially provide a map that members can rely on to choose appropriate courses of action. Clan control derives from culture.

> **Communication.** Culture reduces communication problems in at least two ways. First, there is no need to communicate in matters for which shared assumptions already exist; such things "go without saying." Second, shared assumptions provide guidelines and cues to help interpret messages that are received.

> **Commitment.** People feel committed to an organization when they identify with it and feel emotional attachment to it. Strong cultures foster strong identification and feelings through beliefs and values that the employee can share with others.

> **Perception.** Organizational reality is socially constructed; what an individual sees is conditioned by what others sharing the same experience say they are seeing. Shared beliefs and values influence this process by providing organization members with shared interpretations of their experience.

> **Justification of behavior.** Finally, culture helps organization members make sense of their behavior by providing justification for it. For example, it may be possible to justify expenditures on family-sensitive work practices on the basis of shared values relating to the value of people in the organization. The Focus on Management feature describes the unique, strong culture of Quad/Graphics.

ELEMENTS OF ORGANIZATIONAL CULTURE

As a manager, you will be a creator, shaper, guardian, and communicator of organizational culture. You will play these roles through the behaviors you model, the things you expect and reward, the policies you set, the messages you send, and the cultural elements you employ. Let's consider some key elements of organizational culture.[7]

VALUES

Values are deep-seated, personal standards that influence our moral judgments, responses to others, and commitment to personal and organizational goals. Values—the bedrock of organizational culture—let employees know how they are expected to behave and what actions are acceptable. For example, Procter & Gamble has core values of leadership, integrity, trust, passion for winning, and ownership, and it works to communicate those values and instill them in employees.

The sharing of values is key to the development of a successful organizational culture. The functions of culture listed earlier all relate somehow to the impact of shared values and assumptions. This suggests that the degree to which those values and assumptions are shared should be important. For instance, we might go into one organization and find everyone shares the same values, tells the same stories, and points to the same heroes. Such a culture, in which there is sharing and acceptance of core values, is sometimes called a *strong culture*.[8]

In view of the various functions of culture, we might expect that the nature and strength of organizational culture would ultimately affect quality, productivity, and profitability. This view was bolstered by the work of Tom Peters and Robert Waterman, described in their best seller, *In Search of Excellence*. Peters and Waterman concluded on the basis of their research on a variety of "excellent" companies that:

> *Without exception, the dominance and coherence of culture proved to be an essential quality of the excellent companies. Moreover, the stronger the culture and the more it was directed toward the marketplace, the less need was there for policy manuals, organization charts, or detailed procedures and rules. In these companies, people way down the line know what they are supposed to do in most situations because the handful of guiding values is crystal-clear.*[9]

We consider the impacts of organizational culture later in the chapter. However, it seems clear that a sharing of values may have important consequences for organizations and their members.[10] The values at Hewlett-Packard are discussed in the Focus on Management feature.

FOCUS ON MANAGEMENT

VALUES AT HEWLETT-PACKARD

At Hewlett-Packard, there is a clear focus on the five values of the "HP Way":

> We have trust and respect for individuals.

> We focus on a high level of achievement and contribution.

> We conduct our business with uncompromising integrity.

> We achieve our common objectives through teamwork.

> We encourage flexibility and innovation.

If values are to have a positive impact on the culture of the organization, they must become part of the daily working lives of employees. At Hewlett-Packard, units are kept small. There are no time clocks. Employees can choose which shift to work. Offices are separated by open partitions to increase accessibility and foster teamwork. In addition, Hewlett-Packard has an unwritten policy never to lay people off.* Thus the company's policies and practices support its values.

Carly Fiorina, the president and CEO of Hewlett-Packard and the first woman to head a company listed on the Dow Jones Industrial Average, addressed the COMDEX convention on November 15, 1999. In her address Fiorina said, "I will argue that the challenge for the Net, as we enter the new millennium, the challenge to make the Net warm, intimate, friendly, pervasive, personal, is not about technology. It's first about culture, and the culture in our companies, in all of our companies, as we wrestle with what's next on the Net. I believe companies to succeed in this new era, to really fulfill the promise of the Net, must build a new culture." Fiorina envisioned that culture as based on radical ideas, inventiveness, and synthesis of "the best of the old and the new, of the dot-com and the bricks and mortar, of the young Turks and the old guard." To read Fiorina's full speech to Comdex, and to view a video of the speech, go to:

http://www.hp.com/ghp/ceo/ speeches/comdex99.html

Following the controversial merger of Hewlett-Packard with Compaq, Fiorina was faced with a new challenge: merging the two corporate cultures while reinforcing the impression that Hewlett-Packard was retaining its historic focus on innovation. Although early results seemed positive, observers warned that the cultural integration would take years and Fiorina was in for challenging times. To visit the Hewlett-Packard Web site, go to:

http://www.hp.com/

*See "Best Practices at Hewlett-Packard," *Dealerscope,* March 2000, p. 57; E. Nee, "Hewlett-Packard's New E-vangelist," *Fortune,* January 10, 2000, pp. 166–167; R. Faletra, "Fiorina's Progress So Far in HP-Compaq Integration Does Not Guarantee Success," *CRN,* May 5, 2003, p. 112; and J. Markoff, "Innovation at Hewlett Tries to Evade the Ax," May 5, 2003, p. C1.

SYMBOLS

Symbols stand for or suggest something else. Office assignments signal status. Dress codes suggest the level of formality. A logo can influence customer and employee perceptions. Mary Kay Ash of Mary Kay Cosmetics chose the bumblebee as a symbol for her organization because "Aerodynamically the bumblebee shouldn't be able to fly, but the bumblebee doesn't know that so it goes on flying anyway."[11] And, an action can be symbolic. Consider the "Lambeau Leap," where a Green Bay Packers player leaps into the arms of hometown fans in the stands at Lambeau Field after scoring a touchdown, symbolizing oneness with the Green Bay faithful.

When General Motors decided to overhaul its organizational culture to regain competitiveness, then GM president John F. Smith closed the executive dining room on the 14th floor of corporate headquarters and dispensed with neckties on Fridays—symbolic actions to reflect the company's moves toward being more democratic and responsive.[12]

Similarly, when Cincinnati Milacron wanted to regain its position as a world leader in factory machinery, it adopted as its symbol the wolf pack. The company logo depicted a circle of wolves flanked on each side by a fierce wolf's head. "It's not a joke to us," said Milacron's president Daniel J. Meyer. "Wolves are survivors. They work in teams, and they go out to kill."[13] The wolf pack symbol was meant to convey an image both to the company's employees and to its external constituencies. The importance of logos is illustrated by the Focus on Management feature.

NARRATIVES

Narratives are written or spoken accounts used by members of the organization to make sense of their experiences and express their feelings and beliefs. Narratives may take a variety of forms, including stories, legends, myths, and sagas.[14]

Stories dramatize relatively ordinary, everyday events within organizations in order to convey important cultural meanings. They often combine truth and fiction, are spread by word of mouth, and convey important values. Stories often reflect basic themes—whether, for example, the organizational culture supports equality or inequality, security or insecurity, and control or lack of control.

FOCUS ON MANAGEMENT

THE LAND O'LAKES LOGO

The importance of company symbols to those outside the firm is seen in a study of customers' ratings of 47 firms on such characteristics as quality and reputation.* Six hundred customers were asked to rate the firms on the basis of their names, and 600 others were provided with the company logos. Those logos often had a strong influence on the ratings. For example, Motorola's logo improved its score by 55 percent and Buick's by 53 percent. But the Travelers umbrella reduced the insurer's score by 6 percent, and Land O'Lakes' kneeling Native American woman—perhaps because of its politically incorrect connotations—dropped the company's approval rating by 12 percent. To see the Land O'Lakes logo and read its history, go to:

http://www.landolakes.com/new/ourCompany/LandOLakesHistory.cfm

*"When Company Logos Detract from Image," *Wall Street Journal*, June 18, 1993, p. B1. See also P. W. Henderson and J. A. Cote, "Guidelines for Selecting or Modifying Logos," *Journal of Marketing*, April 1998, *62(2)*, pp. 14–30.

As an example, a story widely repeated at IBM tells of how founder and CEO Tom Watson praised a security guard who required him to go back for his identification. A similar story is told at Revlon, differing in just one detail: When a Revlon receptionist refused to let CEO Charles Revson walk off with a sign-in sheet, he fired her. The first story conveys a sense of egalitarianism, saying, "We all obey the rules." The second conveys the opposite, saying, "We obey the rulers."[15] The importance of stories at 3M is described in the Focus on Management feature.

Legends are more uplifting than stories and portray events that defy explanation by ordinary circumstances. Here's a legend at Procter & Gamble:

> *Just before the turn of the century, Harley Procter, a son of the founders of Procter & Gamble Company, became concerned that the company's candle business was declining. One Sunday morning, while attending church services, he had a revelation as the minister read a passage about ivory palaces from the 45th Psalm. He went to the company's board of directors, composed of very religious men, and told them of his revelation. Using it, he persuaded them to call a new white bath soap Ivory.*[16]

Myths are dramatic, unquestioned narratives about imagined events. They are often used to explain the origins or transformations of things of great importance. The explanations are placed beyond doubt and argument. Although myths are largely inventions, they have a kind of ingrained integrity and truth; they have been called "things that never happened, but always are."[17]

FOCUS ON MANAGEMENT

STORIES AT 3M

The eleventh commandment at 3M is "Never kill a new product idea." The importance of innovation as a 3M value is supported by a story often repeated throughout the organization. According to the story, an employee accidentally developed cellophane tape but was unable to get his superiors to accept the idea. Persistent in his belief in the new product, the employee found a way to sneak into the corporate boardroom and tape down the board members' copies of the minutes with the transparent tape. The board was impressed enough with the novelty to give it a try, and the product was incredibly successful.* This story not only reinforces the importance of innovation but encourages 3M

employees who believe strongly in their ideas never to take no as a final answer.

3M's Web site introduces its "Innovation Chronicles" as follows: *Stories have always been an important part of 3M's culture. This compilation presents some of the important milestones in 3M's history, based on recollections of those who were major participants in these milestones. Stories such as these can help us in understanding the many sources of our innovative culture—and the importance of our continuing desire to challenge and encourage each other as we look for innovative new ways to meet customer needs and solve customer problems. They*

can help to inspire all 3Mers to participate in the stories of our future.

Go to the "Innovation Chronicles" at the following address to read more about the importance of stories to 3M's culture and tales about the invention of masking tape, cellophane tape, and Post-It® Notes and about 20 other 3M stories:

http://www.3m.com/about3m/pioneers/innovChron.jhtml

*A. Wilkins, "The Creation of Company Cultures: The Role of Stories and Human Resource Systems," *Human Resource Management,* 1984, 23, p. 21. See also J. Collins, "The 10 Greatest CEOs of All Time," *Fortune,* July 21, 2003, *148(2),* pp. 54–58, 62, 64, 68.

Finally, *sagas* are a form of narrative that describes heroic exploits performed in the face of adversity. They help perpetuate culture by anchoring the present in the past and lending meaning to the future. They intermix historical facts (sometimes in embellished and altered form), justifications of past events, and wishful thinking. Many sagas celebrate the organization's founders and their ideas. The tale of how Bill Hewlett and Dave Packard began Hewlett-Packard in Hewlett's garage using Hewlett's oven and of how they subsequently dealt with adversity without laying off workers is such a saga. When Hewlett-Packard's CEO, Carly Fiorina, wanted to reinvigorate the company, she chose the slogan "Back to the Garage."[18]

HEROES

Heroes are company role models. In their actions, character, and support of the existing organizational culture, they highlight the values a company wishes to reinforce. Heroes are often the main characters of organizational narratives. CEOs such as Steve Jobs at Apple Computer, Anita Roddick of the Body Shop, Sam Walton of Wal-Mart, and Jack Welch of GE are heroes in their firms; as these examples suggest, some people remain heroes even after leaving their firms. But heroes may come from all levels, such as an employee who persevered to champion an important new product or who provided extraordinary effort when the company faced a crisis.[19]

FOCUS ON MANAGEMENT

HERB KELLEHER OF SOUTHWEST AIRLINES*

Herb Kelleher is cofounder, chairman, and former CEO of Southwest Airlines. Irreverent, Elvis-impersonating, arm-wrestling, chain-smoking, bear-hugging, rap tune-singing, Harley Davidson–riding, Wild Turkey–drinking Kelleher plays many roles, among them coach, quarterback, cheerleader, sage, cultural icon, father figure, friend, and legend. Much of Southwest's folklore recounts Kelleher's outrageous antics and comments. Kelleher could be found singing "Tea for Two" for Southwest employees, walking plane aisles dressed as the Easter Bunny, tossing luggage with baggage handlers, or having a beer with an off-hours flight crew. Under his guidance, Southwest has been remarkably successful. It has been profitable every year since 1973 (the

only airline able to make that claim), yet maintains the lowest fares. It is the safest airline in the world and ranks number one in the industry for service, on-time performance, and lowest employee turnover rate. It has been named the most admired airline and the best place to work in the United States by *Fortune* magazine. One thousand dollars invested in Southwest in 1971 is worth more than $250,000 today. Here's Kelleher's take on Southwest's recipe for success: "First, employees are number one. The way you treat your employees is the way they will treat your customers. Second, have fun at work. Third, take the competition seriously but not yourself. Fourth, think of the company as a service organization that happens to be in the airline business. Last, always practice the Golden Rule, internally and externally." Kelleher crafted a unique culture at Southwest Airlines through

a mix of humor, altruism, concern for others, and straight talk. Southwest looks for these qualities in prospective employees, saying, "But what are their values? We'll take the one with the less experience if he has the values we're looking for; someone else can take the expert." Learn more about Kelleher and Southwest at:

http://www.iflyswa.com/

*Based on J. C. Quick, "Crafting an Organizational Culture: Herb's Hand at Southwest Airlines," *Organizational Dynamics*, Autumn 1992, pp. 45–56; K. Melymuka, "Sky King: Down-to-Earth Technology Helps Make Herb Kelleher's Southwest Airlines a Soaring Success," *Computerworld*, September 28, 1998, pp. 68–71, and "Interview: Herbert Kelleher Discusses the Airline Industry," *Weekend Edition*, April 26, 2003, p. 1.

The founder and former CEO of Southwest Airlines, Herb Kelleher, is clearly a hero at Southwest. Read more about him in the Focus on Management feature.

RITES

Rites combine cultural forms into a public performance. *Rites of passage* mark important transitions. For instance, employees who complete a rigorous management training program off site may be welcomed back with a speech, a certificate, and perhaps a cocktail party.

Rites of enhancement celebrate accomplishments of members, enhancing their status. The enhanced individuals often receive some concrete symbol of their enhanced status. Mary Kay Cosmetics (http://www.marykay.com/) is famous for its rites of enhancement. It gives its high-performing members a variety of awards and titles. Diamond pins, furs, and pink Cadillacs (and other luxury cars) are awarded to its top performers at elaborate meetings called Mary Kay Seminars. Participants, dressed in fancy evening clothes, receive their awards on the stage of an auditorium to the cheers of a large audience.[20] Rites of enhancement both provide public recognition of a person's personal accomplishments and serve to motivate others to similar efforts.

FOCUS ON MANAGEMENT

CULTURE AT WALT DISNEY COMPANY

Walt Disney Company is a good example of an organization in which elements of culture are apparent. The employees in Disney's theme parks—primarily high school and college students—are critical to the company's success. Disney's challenge is to get them to convey the Disney fantasy and create happiness while carrying out repetitive work at low pay. To make the challenge even greater, Disney is heavily unionized, with 24 unions at Disneyland alone. Disney meets this challenge by careful attention to its organizational culture.

For one thing, Disney uses language to reinforce the culture. Employees are called *cast members*, and they don't work—they're "cast" in "roles." Cast members are employed "onstage" or "backstage," and they wear "costumes" rather than uniforms.

Further, Disney uses selection, training, and socialization to create a sense of community and shared values. The company's clean-cut and conservative image generally attracts the kind of employees Disney wants. In addition, the company shows prospective employees a film about the kind of discipline, grooming, and dress code the company demands. Cast members participate in an ongoing orientation program that continually reinforces the firm's values, philosophies, and guest service standards. During orientation, teachers at Disney University dress in full uniform as they lead new employees through the park.

To encourage commitment and enthusiasm, Disney uses service recognition awards, peer recognition programs, and banquets for 10, 15, or 20 years of service. Informal recognition parties help boost morale. During the Christmas holiday, the parks open one night just for cast members and their families,

and management dresses in costumes and operates the parks. All events are designed to build a sense of camaraderie and identification with the Disney organization.*

http://disney.go.com/ disneycareers/index.html

*Based on C. M. Solomon, "How Does Disney Do It?" *Personnel Journal,* December 1989, pp. 50–57; and L. Rubis, "Show and Tell," *HR Magazine,* April 1998, pp. 110–117. See also H. Allerton, "Professional Development the Disney Way," *Training and Development,* May 1997, pp. 50–56; M. Gunther, "Eisner's Mouse Trap," *Fortune,* September 6, 1999, pp. 106–118; L. Lynch, "Sustaining Innovation: Walt Disney Instilled How," *T&D,* June 2001, *55(6),* pp. 44–49; and "How to Manage a Dream Factory—the Entertainment Industry," *The Economist,* January 18, 2003, *366(8307),* pp. 73–75.

Rites of integration bring people together to revive shared feelings that bind and commit them to the organization. An annual holiday party is a rite of integration. So is the Wal-Mart annual meeting, where 20,000 shareholders come together to see featured celebrities, hear inspiring stories, watch videos about Wal-Mart's accomplishments, and join in the Wal-Mart cheer.[21] The nearby Focus on Management describes rites and other elements of culture at Walt Disney Company.

RITUALS

Rituals are relatively simple combinations of repetitive behaviors, often carried out without much thought and often brief in duration. Rituals guide behavior in daily organizational life. There may be rituals, for instance, about how organizational members greet one another, how visitors are met at airports, who eats where and with whom, and how a phone conversation should proceed. These rituals often are more important for their expressive, emotional consequences than for more practical reasons.

Now complete Skills Practice 13-1. This will help you better describe the culture of an organization by thinking about its characteristics in a variety of unusual ways.

ASSESSING CULTURE

If we are to describe, understand, and perhaps influence culture, we need to be able to somehow assess it. For example, how do we tell whether we are likely to fit well in a culture or whether the culture seems to foster healthy interactions among employees? One way to do this is with careful observation and questioning. This yields a rich, relatively unconstrained view of the organization's culture and provides compelling, concrete examples.

Here are some suggestions for learning about an organization's culture:

> Look around—what do the headquarters and other buildings look like? How are people dressed? Is there much interaction? Who is talking with whom? How does the place feel?

> Ask to see newsletters and other internal documents. What values are emphasized? Who are the heroes held up for praise? Are parties, celebrations, or other ceremonies mentioned? What sorts of things are discussed?

> Look at annual reports or other communications to those outside the firm. What face is being presented to the world?

> Ask, "Can you tell me anything about what the culture is like here? Are there any stories that people here tell about the firm?"

> Ask, "What values are stressed here? How are they communicated? How are they reinforced?"

> Ask, "Who is looked up to here?"

> See what you can learn about rites and ceremonies in the organization. What happens when people accomplish something? Are there rites of passage, such as promotion ceremonies and retirement parties? Are there regular get-togethers, such as holiday parties, social events, and company sporting events?

> Ask, "What sorts of behaviors are expected and rewarded here? What sorts of behaviors are punished?"

> Ask people outside the firm what they think of it.
> Check magazines, newspapers, and other sources to get clues about the culture of the organization.

These sorts of steps to assess culture are valuable, but observation alone cannot answer some important questions about culture. For instance, observation doesn't permit systematic examination of the strength of relationships among culture-related variables or rigorous comparisons across cultures. Further, it is difficult with observation to sort out the relative roles of multiple variables. A complementary approach to observation is to score culture on various dimensions using questionnaires. Such measures permit comparison of culture across organizations. They also make it possible to assess relationships between characteristics of culture and other organizational characteristics, including performance and other outcomes.

Now let's get out into the real world and examine organizational culture in an actual organization. By completing Skills Practice 13-2, you will be able to better see the role of organizational culture in determining the success of a firm.

It's movie time again. Complete Skills Practice 13-3 by watching the movie *Gung Ho*. This is a comedy about clashing organizational cultures involving a Japanese auto company that acquires an American auto company. This exercise will give you an opportunity to assess organizational culture issues and to have a few laughs along the way.

SUBCULTURES AND COUNTERCULTURES

Our discussion of organizational culture to this point may give the impression that a single culture pervades an entire organization. In fact, though, there will almost certainly be many subcultures: distinctive clusters of ideologies, cultural forms, and other practices within the larger culture. *Subcultures* may develop among members of the organization who have common training or duties, similar personal characteristics, frequent interaction, or shared experiences.

In fact, there may even be countercultures in organizations. *Countercultures* are subcultures that contradict the dominant culture. The dominant culture and these countercultures may exist in uneasy symbiosis, taking opposite positions on value issues that are critically important to each of them.[22] Several situations may give rise to countercultures.[23] For example, determined innovators in old, established organizations may feel they must oppose the dominant culture to permit change. Or a counterculture may arise as a way to handle severe shared employee discontents, as when employees oppose a threatening new program or policy. Further, when firms with differing cultures combine through mergers or acquisitions, the culture of the acquired organization may represent a counterculture for the acquiring firm.

It may seem that a single strong culture would be best, as suggested by the earlier quotation by Peters and Waterman. There are certainly costs to subcultures and countercultures. For example, differences in perspectives and goals may lead to conflict and misunderstanding. Nevertheless, subcultures may be useful.

John Jermier and his colleagues have provided a fascinating glimpse into subcultures of a police organization.[24] They used questionnaires, participant observation, and interviews to identify five distinct subcultures of the organization, such as "crime-fighting commandos," "peace-keeping moral entrepreneurs," and "anti-military social workers." The subcultures differed in how they were organized and acted and in their performance and commitment to the organization; only one of the subcultures seemed in close conformance with the "official" culture. The researchers concluded that the police organization was actually a "soft bureaucracy," with a rigid exterior appearance symbolizing what key stakeholders expect but with less rigid internal practices. In this way, an external face could be presented while subcultures were free to develop and meet specific demands.

Just as subcultures may have value to the organization, countercultures may serve useful functions for the dominant culture. For example, countercultures may help clarify the boundaries between acceptable and unacceptable behavior and may provide a safe haven for the development of innovative ideas.[25] Further, countercultures may encourage the questioning of old, and perhaps outmoded, values.

Here are some concrete suggestions for deviating constructively from the dominant culture:[26]

> **Self-insurance.** Using self-insurance means going against the culture on the basis of one's credibility and acceptance in the culture. The more deviance required by the proposed action, the more credits have to be cashed in, and the more that must somehow be replenished. The nonconformist who is able to get away with murder, at it were, often successfully applies this tactic, as seen in the following example:

> *Over the years, Smallwood had gone out on a limb to stake his business reputation on ideas and products that others had described as "crazy." Several of these had eventually turned out to be stars in the corporate constellation. As his reputation grew and spread in the industry (he became the industry "godfather"), he continued to go against the grain of the prevailing culture when he felt his business convictions, based on in-depth industry knowledge, justified this. A certain amount of such nonconformity gradually became expected of Smallwood, and even after once engaging in insubordination, his internal credibility and ability to buck culture remained intact.*[27]

> **Culture insurance.** This approach calls for the support of others with high status, particularly those known to be "good soldiers" in the organization. This spreads the risk of nonconformity among the "old faithful."
> **Counterculture clout.** Lower-status people in the organization can also provide the support needed to permit deviation from culture, as long as there are enough of them. This is the tactic used by John DeLorean at General Motors to challenge GM's values of respect for authority, fitting in, loyalty, and teamwork. The tactic generally requires a charismatic leader who is able to create a new ideology and new symbols to weld a subunit into a counterculture. Often, the counterculture and its leader eventually are granted some legitimacy, resources, and autonomy. In return, it agrees to follow certain rules and to limit the scope of its rebellion.[28]

CULTURE AND EFFECTIVENESS

Does organizational culture affect important organizational outcomes, such as quality and productivity? The many functions of organizational culture we discussed at the beginning of the chapter would certainly suggest that culture is important and could reasonably be expected to influence organizational outcomes. Further, much of the tremendous interest in organizational cultures was spawned by a few best-selling business books that provided prescriptions for "effective" cultures that would lead to quality and productivity. As shown in Figure 13-2, there are at least four positions concerning how culture might influence organization performance.[29]

The first of these approaches attempts to identify particular cultural characteristics associated with success. For example, William Ouchi in his book *Theory Z* presented comparative studies of Japanese and American management techniques. Ouchi reported that many successful Japanese companies have strong cultures that emphasize such values as employee participation, open communication, security, and equality.[30] Ouchi's comparison of typical Japanese (type J), typical American (type A), and type Z American organizational cultures is presented in Figure 13-3. Ouchi saw the type Z culture as incorporating individual achievement and advancement but as having a dedication to developing a sense of community in the workplace. He believed the type Z organization's emphasis on new cultural values in the work environment would reduce the negative influences of norms by fostering individuality and individual responsibility. Ouchi argued that the cultures of Japanese firms and American type Z firms would help them outperform type A firms. Such arguments led managers and consultants to embrace many Japanese ideas and practices, such as quality circles. Although such approaches are associated with many potential benefits, as we discuss in other chapters, their success has been mixed.[31]

The most popular writing on the relationship between organizational culture and effectiveness was presented by Tom Peters and Robert Waterman in *In Search of Excellence*.[32] Based on their observation of 62 successful firms, including Hewlett-

FIGURE 13-2

Views of How Organizational Culture Affects Performance

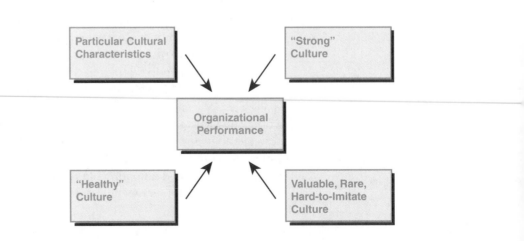

FIGURE 13-3
Type A, Type J, and Type Z Organizations

Cultural Value	U.S. (Type A)	Japan (Type J)	U.S. (Type Z)
Commitment to Employees	Short-term employment	Lifetime employment	Long-term employment
Decision Making	Individual	Group and consensus	Group and consensus
Responsibility	Individual	Collective	Individual
Evaluation	Rapid and quantitative	Slow and qualitative	Slow and qualitative
Control	Explicit and formal	Implicit and informal	Implicit and informal
Career Paths	Narrow	Broad	Moderately broad
Concern for People	Narrow	Holistic	Holistic

Packard, McDonald's, Disney Productions, Levi Strauss, and Johnson & Johnson, the authors concluded that eight key attributes of the organizational culture contributed to their success:

1. **A bias for action.** Although the companies may be analytical in their approach to decision making, they prefer to "do it, fix it, try it." That is, problems are not talked to death, nor is time wasted developing elaborate models for solving problems.

2. **Closeness to the customer.** Learning from customers is important for success. Customer satisfaction becomes a dominant value and can be achieved through excellent customer service and high product quality and reliability.

3. **Autonomy and entrepreneurship.** Excellent companies encourage innovativeness through the development of structures that foster innovation and change. Work units are kept small so employees have a sense of belonging and feel comfortable about making suggestions.

4. **Productivity through people.** Rank-and-file employees are viewed as valued resources of the organization, the main source of quality and productivity. "We-versus-them" labor attitudes are avoided.

5. **Hands-on, value-driven.** Managers of excellent companies have clearly defined the value system of the firm. Both managers and employees understand what values guide the activities of the firm. For example, McDonald's incorporates quality, service, cleanliness, and value in all aspects of the company's activities.

6. **Stick to the knitting.** Successful companies stay close to the business they know. This may mean a focus on a single product line or a related group of product lines rather than a diverse mix of products.

7. **Simple form, lean staff.** Keeping the company simple in its structure with few staff positions was found to be important to company success. In general, no more than five layers of management are encouraged. When

the company increases in size, divisions are broken down into subdivisions to avoid additional layers of management.

8. **Simultaneous loose-tight properties.** Excellent companies are both centralized and decentralized. They apply centralized or tight controls to the company's core values. In other areas, such as innovation and creativity, controls on employees are loose or decentralized.

Not every company studied by Peters and Waterman scored high on all eight attributes. However, success in promoting some of the attributes and a desire to score well on others were part of the organization culture.

Let's take a look at this framework in a real-world organization. Complete Skills Practice 13-4. This will give you an opportunity to assess the Peters and Waterman's attributes of excellent organizations in an organization and to critically evaluate the framework.

The Peters and Waterman findings have received widespread attention, but they have not gone without challenge.[33] For example, Peters and Waterman focused on successful companies, but what if the characteristics of "excellent" companies were also found in companies that are poor performers? Also, measures of excellence were limited to the financial performance of the company.[34] Were the organizations also successful in terms of customer satisfaction and social responsibility? Subsequent developments haven't been encouraging. For instance, in the years following publication of *In Search of Excellence,* several of the "excellent" companies suffered financially.[35] Further, one study found no significant five-year performance differences between a representative subset of 14 of the Peters and Waterman "excellent" companies and 162 firms representative of the *Fortune* 1,000 industrials.[36] In fact, average performance was lower for the "excellent" firms than for the comparison group. Further, no significant differences were found between the two groups of firms in the extent to which they adhered to measured attributes that Peters and Waterman associated with excellence. And there were no significant relationships between the degree to which firms in either group adhered to those attributes and their performance.[37] Tom Peters himself has now stated, "We faked the data," although it's unclear whether that statement was meant to be taken seriously.[38]

Perhaps such findings shouldn't be too surprising. After all, organizations operate in different environments, under different strategic conditions, and with different structures and technologies. It seems unreasonable that the same type of culture would be appropriate for all these differing conditions. Continuing to search for "one best way" may be futile. Instead, it may be more important to ensure that cultural elements are internally consistent and in tune with demands of particular internal and external environments.[39]

A second position concerning the relationship of culture to performance is that strong cultures lead to success. Terrence Deal and Allen Kennedy in their book *Corporate Cultures: The Rites and Rituals of Corporate Life* took this position, titling their first chapter "Strong Cultures: The New 'Old Rule' for Business Success."[40] Similarly, earlier in the chapter we provided a quote from Peters and Waterman stating that strong cultures typified their excellent organizations. As such, this approach focuses not just on the nature of cultural characteristics, but also (or instead) on their strength.

Unfortunately, some confusion surrounds just what a strong culture *is*. The term *strong culture* is sometimes used in different ways. Some see strong cultures as cultures where values and ideologies are widely shared and clearly ordered in terms of their relative importance. Others use the term to mean extremity of culture, with a strong culture reflecting strong commitment to certain positions, such as strong emphasis on personal worth. In general, it seems simplistic to assume that strength of culture per se would necessarily lead to success. Certainly some strong cultures are inconsistent with the demands of their environments, and a strong culture may discourage change. So it may be necessary that a culture be "right"—fitting the needs of its members and the demands of its environment—as well as strong.

A third position, as seen in Figure 13-4, focuses on sick cultures.[41] It sees some cultures as deriving unhealthy modes of functioning from the psychopathological problems of their chief executives. Such so-called neurotic firms would be unlikely to attain long-term success.

The fourth position on the relationship of culture to performance tries to identify conditions under which cultures are more important for and conducive to success. For instance, if a culture is to contribute to sustained financial performance (as we suggested earlier in the chapter), it must (1) be valuable in the sense it leads the firm to behave in ways that result in high sales, low costs, high margins, and other factors adding financial value to the firm; (2) be rare in the sense that other firms don't have the same or very similar cultures; and (3) be difficult to imitate so competitors can't readily change their cultures to include the same advantageous characteristics.[42] A strategic advantage of a unique and valuable culture, once developed, is that the third of these conditions is likely to follow: Competitors are likely to find it impossible to duplicate. The Bottom Line feature presents a process model summarizing the basic steps associated with development of an effective organizational culture.

FIGURE 13-4
Neurotic Leaders and Their Firms

Form of Neurosis	Chief Executive	Culture
Dramatic	Needs attention, excitement; feels a sense of entitlement	Dependency needs of subordinates complement "strong leader" tendencies of chief executive
Suspicious	Vigilantly prepared for counter attacks and personal threats	"Fight-or-flight" culture, including dependency, fear of attack, lack of trust
Detached	Withdrawn and not involved; lacks interest in present or future	Lack of warmth or emotions; conflicts; jockeying for power; insecurity
Depressed	Lacks self-esteem, self-confidence, or initiative; fears success and tolerates mediocrity or failure	Lack of initiative; passivity; negativity; lack of motivation; ignorance of markets; leadership vacuum
Compulsive	Tends to dominate organization from top to bottom; dogmatic or obstinate; perfectionist	Rigid, inward-directed, insular; subordinates are submissive, uncreative, insecure

BOTTOM LINE

DEVELOPING AN EFFECTIVE ORGANIZATIONAL CULTURE

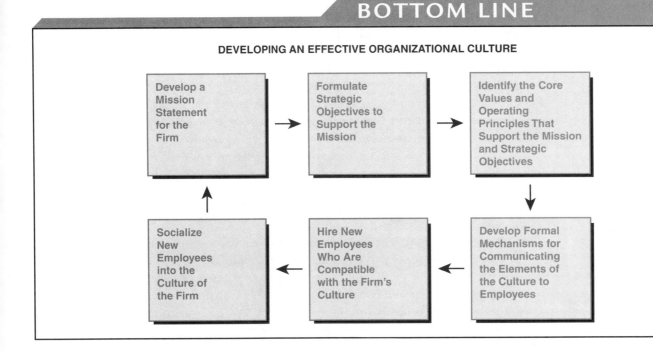

Develop a Mission Statement for the Firm	→	Formulate Strategic Objectives to Support the Mission	→	Identify the Core Values and Operating Principles That Support the Mission and Strategic Objectives

Socialize New Employees into the Culture of the Firm	←	Hire New Employees Who Are Compatible with the Firm's Culture	←	Develop Formal Mechanisms for Communicating the Elements of the Culture to Employees

CHANGING CULTURES

Our discussion of managing culture may give the impression that culture can easily be molded to fit some image. In fact, though, change may be very difficult; values, stories, heroes, and rituals develop over time and are enduring.

This is nicely illustrated by the case of a *Fortune* 500 manufacturer saddled with a history of low productivity, poor quality, and hostile labor relations.[43] When a consultant hired by the company began talking with the employees, they told him many stories about Sam, the 300-pound plant manager with the personality of King Kong. When Sam saw a transmission that displeased him, he smashed it with a sledgehammer. A worker called to Sam's office vomited on the way. Once Sam drove his car into the plant, got on the roof, and began screaming at his workers. One fed-up worker poured a line of gasoline to Sam's car and lit it.

Hearing these stories, the stunned consultant made an appointment to see the plant manager. When he entered the plant manager's office, the consultant was surprised to see a slim, pleasant-looking man behind the desk; his name was Paul. "Where's Sam?" the consultant asked. Paul, looking puzzled, replied, "Sam has been dead for nine years." Paul's claim notwithstanding, Sam was clearly very much alive in the minds of the employees. Paul's efforts of almost a decade to instill a sense of fairness and participation were thwarted by the plant's nightmarish history. To change a company's culture, leaders in an organization should consider these recommendations:[44]

> **Understand the current culture.** It is hard to chart a course without knowing where you are now. Similarly, it is folly to attempt to change culture without first understanding the current culture.

> **Change at the right time.** Culture change is most likely to be successful when, as with any other change, there is a felt need. This may occur when there is a problem (a "burning platform"), opportunity, or change in circumstances.

> **Value diversity.** We often hear the cure for a rare disease may be found in the cells of an obscure creature in the depths of a rain forest or that a threatened plant may prove to be an unimagined energy source. We are warned that loss of ecological variety may forever cut off opportunities: Diversity offers potential. Similarly, organizations with many distinct subcultures may have better chances for successful change. Rather than starting from scratch, such organizations can select subcultures that best fit the vision of the desired culture, nourish them, and diffuse them throughout the organization. Similarly, those employees who have been bucking the old culture and who have ideas for a better one can be encouraged.

> **Understand resistance to culture change.** People resist changes for many reasons, such as fear of the unknown, threats to personal security, habit, threats to power and influence, lack of trust, and disruption of social relationships. Whether or not these fears and concerns are justified, their impact is real. Sources of resistance to culture change must be recognized and sensitively dealt with; we address this issue in Chapter 14.

> **Recognize the importance of implementation.** Many change efforts fail because of flaws in implementation. Quite simply, changes don't implement themselves. It is critical that adequate human and financial resources be provided for implementation and those responsible for the implementation accept the need for change and are motivated to pursue their task enthusiastically. Such acceptance and enthusiasm are unlikely unless top management clearly and visibly supports the cultural change.

> **Use appropriate cultural forms.** Cultural change can be facilitated by appropriate use of symbols, rites, narratives, and other cultural forms. For example, managers can employ symbolic tools, such as being present at meetings relating to the change and visibly spending time related to the values they preach. New logos and slogans can be developed. Rites can be modified to incorporate new values, or new rites can combine elements of the old and the new. Stories reinforcing the change can be publicized.

> **Give it some time.** Everything we've said suggests that changing organizational culture will be difficult and time consuming. There will almost certainly be resistance. Those who resist the change will be quick to point to problems that arise during the change process, and there will always be a period during which costs of change are obvious but benefits are still on the horizon. However, as Rosabeth Moss Kanter has said, "Everything looks like a failure in the middle." It is critical to focus on the horizon and to recognize it takes time to reach it. Significant organizationwide improvements may take five to ten years.[45]

The Bottom Line feature presents a process model summarizing the basic steps associated with changing the culture of an organization. A major challenge facing

BOTTOM LINE

CHANGING THE CULTURE OF AN ORGANIZATION

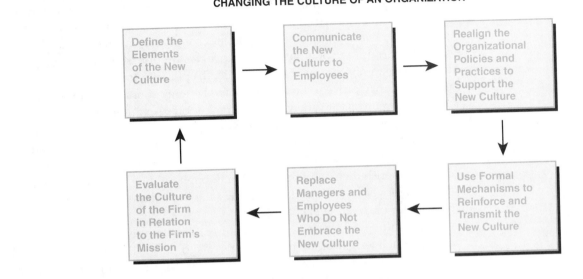

many managers is how to change the existing culture at a firm to one that better supports the mission, goals, and strategies of the organization. Completing Skills Practice 13-5 will help you develop skill in creating action plans for transforming the culture of an organization.

Organizational culture may be dismissed by some as soft and idealistic. They are not. You say you don't have the time to deal with cultural issues? In engineering a remarkable turnaround at General Electric, CEO Jack Welch went to Crotonville, GE's Leadership Development Center, *every two weeks for more than 15 years* to run leadership training programs, teach the GE Management Values statement, and reinforce the GE culture. Jack Welch found the time.

TOP TEN LIST: KEY POINTS TO REMEMBER

ORGANIZATIONAL CULTURE

10. Develop and maintain an organizational culture that reinforces the core values of the firm.
9. Align the culture of an organization with its mission and strategic objectives.
8. Use a variety of methods (e.g., stories, rites and ceremonies, heroes, and symbols) to communicate organizational culture to employees.
7. Allow subcultures and even countercultures to coexist with the dominant corporate culture when they support the strategic objectives of the firm.
6. Assess the current culture of a firm as the first step in developing a plan for maintaining or changing it.
5. Identify the underlying causes of resistance to changing corporate culture as a basis for developing a plan for ultimately transforming it.
4. Recognize that cultural change in organizations will take time.
3. Develop and implement a formal process (e.g., orientation training program) for socializing new employees into the culture of an organization.
2. Document a description of an organization's culture in employee handbooks, annual reports, newsletters, and so on, to maintain employee awareness of the culture.
1. Ensure that appropriate actions are taken to support the implementation of an organization's culture.

QUESTIONS FOR REVIEW AND REFLECTION

REVIEW QUESTIONS

1. What is organizational culture?
2. Discuss seven important functions of organizational culture.
3. Define values, symbols, narratives, heroes, rites, and rituals.
4. What is a strong culture? Why does it matter?
5. Discuss four types of narratives.
6. Discuss rites of enhancement and rites of integration.
7. Provide guidelines for assessing organizational culture.
8. What are subcultures and countercultures? Why are they important?
9. Identify four suggestions for deviating constructively from the dominant culture.
10. Discuss four views of how organizational culture is related to performance and other organizational outcomes.
11. Provide seven guidelines for changing organizational cultures.

CRITICAL THINKING QUESTIONS

1. Do you think organizational cultures are more important in some types of firms than others? Defend your position. If your answer is yes, describe the characteristics of the firm, environment, employees, or other factors that might influence the importance of organizational culture.
2. A CEO tells her top management team, "I want a strong, unified culture. There's no place for subcultures in this organization." Do you agree that subcultures are inconsistent with a strong culture? Why or why not?
3. The chapter has considered four perspectives concerning how organizational culture might affect a firm's performance. Which of these perspectives do you feel is most useful? To what extent can the perspectives complement one another? Be as specific as possible.
4. A colleague says, "I can understand how having a strong culture might help management. Still, words such as *brainwashed* and *robot* come to mind when I think of cultures where everyone is encouraged to think alike. That doesn't sound like a place I want to be." What might you say to reassure your colleague?
5. A concern is sometimes raised that by focusing on issues such as culture companies may lose sight of the bottom line. Based on the material presented in this chapter and your own experience and perspectives, discuss ways that *failure to pay attention* to organizational culture and related issues may harm a firm's financial performance.

EXPERIENTIAL EXERCISES
WEB EXERCISE 13-1: ORGANIZATIONAL CULTURES

1. Do a Web search using a search engine such as Google to find information about a firm's corporate culture. In the search engine, type "corporate culture" and the name of the firm for which you'd like information. Some firms with noteworthy cultures, and for which there are many Web resources, include GE, Disney, IBM, Apple, Nike, Harley-Davidson, Southwest Airlines, and Johnson & Johnson, but you do not have to limit your search to those companies. Select at least four Web sites that provide information about the corporate culture of the firm you have chosen.

2. In addition, do a Web search to find the company's Web page (some of these are given in this chapter).

Go to that page and find links to information about the company's culture.

3. Based on the information on the company's Web page and the other four (or more) sites, how would you describe the company's culture? Do you expect it to be effective? Would you like to work for the company? Are there things about the culture that need to be changed or should be zealously reinforced? In your answers, be sure to note any inconsistencies between the culture as described on the company's Web page and on the other sites you have selected.

WEB EXERCISE 13-2: CORPORATE ANTHEMS

1. Go to the following Web site to find a large compilation of corporate anthems:

http://insight.zdnet.co.uk/business/ 0,39020481,2122414,00.htm

The site provides, for instance, anthems for Honeywell, Apple, Texas Instruments, IBM, Ernst & Young,

Fujitsu, and Hewlett-Packard. For each anthem, you'll find a discussion of the anthem, the lyrics, and a link to an audio file of the anthem.

Select two anthems. Discuss what the anthem suggests about the culture of the corresponding organization.

Based on the anthems, compare and contrast the cultures of the two organizations.

CASE 13-1
GLOBALIZING THE GE WAY
The Company[46]

Thomas Edison founded General Electric as the Edison Electric Light Company on October 15, 1878. In its early years, the company played a key leadership role in creating the lighting and power generation businesses. Since that time, General Electric, or GE, has grown into a diversified services, technology, and manufacturing company in businesses including aircraft engines, appliances, commercial equipment, financial services, medical systems, plastics, and entertainment. In 2002, its total revenues were $131.7 billion. The company operates in over 100 countries around the world. It has 315,000 employees (197,000 in the United States). The chairman and chief executive officer between 1981 and 2001 was Jack Welch. On September 7, 2001, Jeffrey Immelt took over as the ninth CEO in GE's history.

General Electric has developed and maintained a reputation for being one of the best corporations in the world.

The awards it has received include the following:

> Global Most Admired Company: *Fortune*, 1999, 2000, 2001, 2002
> World's Most Respected Company: *Financial Times*, 1999, 2000, 2001, 2002, 2003
> America's Most Admired Company: *Fortune*, 1999, 2000, 2001, 2002

Strategic Initiatives

> General Electric's business strategy focuses on four key "Growth Initiatives":
>> *Technology—GE wants to lead the next generation of technology by achieving technical excellence in each business through developing global technical capability, increasing new product growth, and investing in global research.*
>> *Services—The new GE vision involves investing in businesses and technology to improve the perfor-*

mance of its installed base and the way it is served.

> *Customer Centricity—This involves ensuring that everything that is done provides value to customers.*
> *Globalization—This refers to an attempt to grow revenues by selling goods and services in global markets.*

The GE Culture[47]

The core values that provide the foundation for GE's culture are as follows:

> *A Passion for Our Customers—Success is measured in terms of the success of customers, driven by Six Sigma and a spirit of innovation.*
> *Meritocracy—Creating opportunities for the best people from around the world to grow and live their dreams.*
> *Growth-Driven, Globally Oriented—Growing people, markets, and businesses around the world.*
> *Every Person, Every Idea Counts—Respect for the individual and valuing each employee's contributions.*
> *Playing Offense—Using the advantages of size to take risks and to try new things . . . never allowing size to be a disadvantage.*
> *Embracing Speed and Excellence—Using the benefits of the digital age to accelerate our success and to build a faster and smarter GE.*

Business Strategies[48]

The most significant long-term challenge facing GE is how to transform itself into a truly global corporation that embraces the GE culture or "GE Way" (i.e., its value system) throughout all of its businesses, managers, and employees around the world. A major focus in achieving this objective has been GE's multitude of businesses throughout Asia. The strategy GE has been implementing in recent years in Asia has emphasized taking GE's universal corporate culture, transplanting it in a range of Asian countries, nurturing the development of local talent, and letting the businesses evolve and grow to suit local market conditions.

Each GE business group possesses a strategic plan for the Asian countries in which it operates. However, GE's overall organizational structure for Asia is based on business needs and not geographic location.

GE maintains a highly centralized organizational structure in terms of the key elements of its business model (e.g., core values, financial targets, performance evaluation and promotion, globalization, Six sigma quality). Beyond these issues, GE's system emphasizes adapting business and management practices to local conditions. For ex-

ample, when GE acquired such firms as Toho Mutual Life Insurance in Japan, it changed the Japanese company's books to the "GE format" and eliminated the "seniority-based" employment system. The rest of the company, however, tailored much of its strategy and operations to the Japanese market.

GE provides employees in its Asian business units with opportunities to have a voice in identifying opportunities for additional revenue growth. For example, one manager at its GE Capital operations in Thailand believed there was a huge opportunity for the company to finance consumer auto loans. Although Jack Welch was initially skeptical, the employee made a compelling case to support his proposal and it was supported. The bottom line is that many of the best ideas at GE are initiated by lower-level employees.

GE has used American expatriates to staff key positions in Asian operations in the past. However, the company has been sending many of these American expatriates home and replacing them with Asian managers and executives. The rationale for this practice has been to empower local managers who understand their home markets with the authority to manage their businesses effectively. In addition, using expatriates was not viewed as an appropriate strategy for supporting the company's overall globalization strategic initiative.

Results and Future Challenges

So far, General Electric's various Asian businesses have been growing twice as fast as those in other parts of the company. In addition, GE has achieved superior margins in its Asian operations.

According to Jack Welch, one of the most critical challenges facing GE is what he calls the "globalization of intellect." This will require the creation of a system and corporate culture that fully leverage the knowledge and expertise of GE employees in the United States as well as in the diversity of countries where GE does business. One example of an attempt to move in this direction was the creation of a corporate research and development unit in Bangalore, India, that may eventually employ 1,000 scientists and engineers. The company's only other research and development unit is based in Schenectady, New York, where it employs about 1,600 professionals. Other similar types of actions will be needed if GE is truly serious about realizing its vision of becoming a global corporation.

Discussion Questions

1. Describe the organizational culture at General Electric.
2. Evaluate the effectiveness of the organizational culture at General Electric.

3. What recommendations would you make to Jeffrey Immelt regarding how to address the globalization of intellect challenge?

4. What recommendations would you make to Immelt in terms of how to handle the other challenges facing GE?

5. What are the practical implications of this case for you as a future manager?

http://www.ge.com

CASE 13-2

ENRON'S DARWINIAN DOWNFALL

The Rise of Enron[49]

Enron was formed in 1985 when Houston Natural Gas and InterNorth merged to create a nationwide natural gas pipeline system. Ken Lay, the chief executive officer at Houston Natural Gas, was named to the positions of chairman and chief executive officer in 1986. In 1989, Jeff Skilling joined the company as the head of trading. Skilling became a critical member of Lay's team, responsible for hiring many people who were skilled at making big business deals for the company. Skilling gave his employees tremendous autonomy to do whatever they needed to do to improve the performance of the company.

Meanwhile, Enron continued to expand aggressively throughout the 1980s and early 1990s. It opened overseas offices in London in 1998, acquired Transportadora de Gas del Sur to spearhead its South American expansion in 1992, and began construction of a power plant in India in 1996.

In 1996, Skilling became the president and chief operating officer. The company continued to make acquisitions: It bought the Portland General Electric Corporation to expand its electricity business in 1997 and Wessex Water United Kingdom to support the creation of its water subsidiary. By the year 2000, Enron had become the sixth largest energy company in the world. In February 2001, Skilling replaced Ken Lay as chief executive officer with Lay staying on as chairman.

The Collapse of a Corporate Giant

In March 2001, Enron unexpectedly jettisoned its plan to create a service that would deliver movies to people's homes through the Internet. The following month, Enron announced that a bankrupt utility company called Pacific Gas and Electric Co. owed it $570 million.

This was just the beginning of the end for Enron. Four months later, Skilling made the shocking announcement that he was stepping down as chief operating officer for "personal reasons." Ken Lay took over for Skilling.

In October, the company announced its third-quarter earnings including over $1 billion in charges and $35 million based on investment partnerships headed by Andrew Fastow, the company's chief financial officer. As a result, the Securities and Exchange Commission initiated a formal investigation into these partnerships. The next month, Enron announced it was restating its earnings for 1997–2000 and the first three quarters of 2001. At this point, Enron's stock closed at $8.63, an 89 percent drop for the year.

On December 2, 2001, Enron filed for Chapter 11 bankruptcy, which not only left thousands of employees jobless, but also led to many losing their retirement savings in 401(k) plans tied to the company's stock. Clearly, unethical accounting and auditing practices played a significant role in the downfall of this energy empire. However, Enron's culture was also a driving force that influenced executives to behave unethically.

The Enron Culture[50, 51]

Enron strove for an entrepreneurial culture. It tried to create an image of its executives as smart, sassy, creative, and risk takers. One way to do this was by hiring a lot of young employees. Enron would heavily recruit people just out of their undergraduate or MBA programs, enticing them to come on board with a promise of independence and a large amount of responsibility. These recent grads were given extraordinary authority, despite their lack of experience in the business world. For example, they could make a $5 million decision without higher approval. In addition, young people were promoted quickly. Turnovers from promotions were close to 20 percent. Finally, there were not enough older workers with industry experience to serve as mentors. Many new employees were left to make it on their own, without proper training or guidance from management. This was a typical symptom of Enron's survival of the fittest mindset.

Using this Darwinian approach, they rewarded stars, who generally possessed very individualistic characteristics:

highly competitive people who disliked sharing power, authority, or information. Little value was linked to team building. There was no reward system in place for those who were team players. To get ahead, every person had to be out for himself or herself.

Getting promoted at Enron meant demonstrating an ability to positively impact stock price. Because stock price is earnings driven, Enron promoted whoever provided quick earnings. Moreover, there was little scrutiny about whether these numbers were legitimate or how they were booked. Executives were compared to their peers in their ability to drive up earnings. This made many employees feel that in order to get ahead, they needed to do whatever it took to keep up with their peers, even if it meant unethical means like cheating or cutting corners.

Management at Enron was hands off, without tight controls. The organizational structure was considered flat, but Enron employees knew CEO Jeff Skilling was in charge. Top executives claimed that Skilling surrounded himself with yes-men. Gaining Skilling's trust, which often meant agreeing with him, won employees a lot of freedom. Skilling echoed the "All that matters is money!" philosophy by giving employees hefty rewards for increasing earnings. He pushed employees to make deals that created earnings now rather than creating solid assets for the long term. Suggesting the latter often resulted in being ostracized by Skilling and other top managers.

Finally, Enron had an ineffective performance review system. A performance review committee was comprised of 20 people who ranked approximately 400 vice presidents, then directors, and finally managers. Those awarded a superior rating (top 5 percent) were given bonuses 66 percent higher than those given an excellent rating (next 30 percent). Top management experts used to believe this system promoted creativity. At Enron, the intent of this system was to ensure that employees were not getting rewarded by getting on the good side of one or two people. Skilling believed it would be difficult to "suck up" to 20 different people. Unfortunately, this system had the opposite effect. Employees were then very concerned about getting on the bad side of anyone that could damage their review; therefore they did not want to raise objections about managerial decisions. This not only promoted a "yes-man" culture, but in retrospect, it seemed to promote greed and financial impropriety at the expense of Enron's shareholders.

Discussion Questions

1. Based on the discussion of elements of organizational culture from the chapter, assess Enron's culture.
2. Identify and discuss how Enron's culture contributed to the collapse of the company.
3. Identify and describe actions that management might have taken to foster a more effective organizational culture at Enron.
4. What are the practical implications of this case for you as a future manager in a real-world organization?

VIDEO CASE: W. B. DONER & CO.

CULTURE IN AN ORGANIZATION

Running Time: 15:30

W. B. Doner & Company is an international advertising agency with offices worldwide. The company, which has won awards for its work for such clients as Red Roof Inns and British Petroleum, prides itself on its creative work. However, as a medium-sized agency in an industry dominated by huge firms, Doner had to develop a unique culture. The video shows Doner CEO Alan Kalter and others as they discuss the nature and purposes of this culture. After viewing the video, answer the following questions:

1. What behaviors does the Doner culture aim to stimulate and enhance?
2. How does Doner's culture contribute to its success?
3. What does Doner look for in employees who would best fit the culture? What sorts of people would be unlikely to fit well in the Doner culture?
4. What are some important characteristics of the Doner culture?
5. What are the core values established by the company's founder, Broad Doner?
6. What are some unacceptable behaviors in the Doner culture?
7. What is the purpose of the Head, Heart, and Funny Bone Award?
8. Based on the Doner experience, what role can a strong culture play in a time of crisis?

SKILLS PRACTICE

13-1   *Skill Level:* CHALLENGING

Images of Organizations

Skill Objective
To develop skill in describing an organizational culture by thinking about its characteristics in a variety of unusual ways.

Procedure
Answer the following questions regarding an organization of which you are currently a member. Download from the text Web site the worksheet developed for this exercise.

1. What are the principal images or metaphors that people use to describe your organization? Provide at least three such images or metaphors.
2. What does your organization look like? Sketch a picture that represents your view of your organization. You don't need to be an artist to do this. Just draw something that conveys to you what the organization is like. Does the organization seem to you like a vehicle? An animal or mix of animals? A person or persons?
3. What does your organization sound like? Give the name of a song or songs or some song lyrics (or write your own lyrics) that represent your organization.
4. What does your organization feel like? List words or phrases (happy, comfortable, frightening, exciting, or whatever) that best capture what your organization feels like.

Discussion Questions
1. How would you describe the culture of the organization you studied for this exercise?
2. Based on completing this exercise, how would you describe the culture of your organization?
3. How could this exercise be used to deal with culture issues in real-world organizations?
4. What are the practical implications of this exercise for you as a future manager in a real-world organization?

SKILLS PRACTICE

13-2   *Skill Level:* CHALLENGING

Fieldwork Experience: Assessing Organizational Culture

Skill Objective
To develop skill in assessing organizational culture.

Procedure
1. Identify an organization in your local community. Try to use an organization in which you already know someone, if possible. This will facilitate gaining access to the organization.
2. Visit your organization and take a tour of its operations. Again, this part of the process will be greatly enhanced if you have a contact in the organization. As you conduct your tour, look for the following types of things (review the section on assessing organizational culture for more ideas):
   > Use of corporate symbols
   > The corporate mission statement
   > The physical work environment
   > Attire worn by employees versus management
   > The employee parking lot: Are there reserved spots for executives?

In addition, ask your contact at the organization the following questions:
   > How would you describe the culture in this organization?
   > Can you give me specific examples of things that reflect the culture of this organization (e.g., employee handbook, general policy statements, annual company events)?

Discussion Questions
1. Do you think the culture of this organization supports the overall mission and goals of the firm? Why or why not?
2. If you could change the culture of this organization, what would you do?
3. What kinds of barriers to change might you experience if you attempted to change the culture of the organization you analyzed for this exercise?
4. What are the practical implications of this exercise for you as a future manager?

SKILLS PRACTICE

13-3   *Skill Level:* BASIC

Assessing Organizational Culture: **Gung Ho**

Skill Objective
To develop skill in assessing the various elements of an organizational culture.

Procedure

1. Obtain a copy of the movie *Gung Ho* starring Michael Keaton. It is available on VHS or DVD and can be rented or purchased from a local video store or retailer.

2. Watch the movie (in class or at home on your own). Note: Download the worksheet developed for this exercise from the Web site for this book. This will help you record your notes from various scenes in the movie.

   As you watch the film, assess the various elements of the organizational cultures of the Japanese and American companies portrayed in the film. Document your notes about these scenes on your worksheet.

3. Discuss the following questions as a class.

   a. Describe the organizational cultures of the companies portrayed in the film. What were their key elements? Use specific scenes from the film to support your assessment.

   b. Was there a dominant culture in the companies portrayed in the film? What about subcultures or countercultures? Use specific scenes from the film to support your assessment.

   c. Why did a clash of organizational cultures occur in the film? What strategies could have been taken to overcome this problem more effectively?

   d. What are the practical implications of this exercise for you as a future manager and leader in a real-world organization?

SKILLS PRACTICE

13-4   *Skill Level:* CHALLENGING

Field Experience: Assessing Organizational Culture Using the Peters and Waterman Attributes of Excellent Organizations

Skill Objective
1. To develop skill in assessing an organization's culture using the Peters and Waterman attributes of excellent organizations

Procedure

1. Identify a manager who works in an organization. Try to obtain a member of upper management for this interview because he or she may have a better global perspective of the organization and its culture. Ask the manager if you can interview him or her for approximately 30 to 45 minutes. Note: Download the interview worksheet developed for this exercise from the Web site for this textbook.

2. When you meet with the manager, give him or her a copy of the worksheet for this exercise (it contains a list of Peters and Waterman's attributes of excellent organizations). Ask the person to read the definition of each attribute and assess the degree to which he or she feels the organization possesses this attribute. Ask for specific examples to support the manager's assessment of each attribute.

3. Now ask the manager to comment on the degree to which the manager feels a high level of each attribute has a positive impact on the overall performance of the organization.

4. Ask the manager what actions could be taken to increase the degree to which his or her organization possesses the attributes of Peters and Waterman's excellent organizations.

5. Summarize the results of your interview.

Discussion Questions

1. Based on the summary of your interview, to what degree does the organization you studied for this exercise possess Peters and Waterman's attributes of excellent organizations?

2. Evaluate the culture of the organization you studied

for this exercise. What are its strengths? Weaknesses? What actions would you recommend to management of this organization to enhance the effectiveness of its culture?

3. What types of actions did your manager suggest for increasing the degree to which the organization

possesses Peters and Waterman's attributes of excellent organizations? Do you agree with these actions? Why or why not?

4. Based on the summary of your interview, what are the practical implications of this exercise for you as a real-world manager?

SKILLS PRACTICE

13-5 *Skill Level:* CHALLENGING

Transforming Organizational Cultures

Skill Objective

To develop skill in formulating action plans for changing organizational culture.

Procedure

Note: Download the worksheet developed for this exercise from the Web site for this textbook.

1. This exercise can be completed on an individual basis or in groups of three to five students.
2. Read the descriptions of organizational cultures that follow. Select one of the organizations to focus on for this exercise.
3. Develop an action plan for changing the culture of the selected firm.
4. Optional: Present your action plan to the class and defend its logic. Be sure to discuss why you feel your plan would work.
5. Answer the discussion questions that follow.

Discussion Questions

1. Which guidelines for changing organizational culture (from the chapter) did you incorporate into your action plan? Why?
2. What are some general obstacles to changing an organization's culture? What would you do to address these obstacles?
3. What are the practical implications of this exercise for you as a future manager?

Organizational Cultures: Mini-scenarios

Note: The scenarios described here are based on actual companies.

Scenario 1: Creating a Team-Based Culture

The Micro-X Corporation, a major computer hardware manufacturer, is a very traditional organization in many ways. It is very hierarchical, and managers tend to be highly authoritarian in their leadership styles. The organization is functionally structured, meaning that work tends to be

organized by functional area (e.g., marketing, human resources, finance, etc.). Thus, little interaction occurs across functional areas in the company. Employees' jobs tend to be highly specialized and relatively narrow.

In response to competitive pressures and the need to design and manufacture better computer components more efficiently, the company has adopted a team-based approach in which cross-functional teams are formed and given the responsibility for product development. Early indications from the new team-based approach are that its employees are not embracing it. A key barrier is that the culture of the organization still emphasizes functional thinking and individual effort as opposed to the cross-functional and team-oriented mentality needed now. What would you do to change the culture of Micro-X?

Scenario 2: Creating a Learning Organization Culture

Wilson Motor Company, a global leader in the design and manufacture of a full line of sport-utility vehicles and trucks, is experiencing extreme competitive pressures from other automotive companies in the United States and in Germany and Japan. The company's major problem is that it seems to make the same mistakes again and again. For example, the redesigns of its current models tend to be consistently off in relation to the needs and desires of its target customers. The exterior styling of the vehicles themselves is viewed as "weird" or "boring." The interiors of many vehicles use an excessive amount of cheap-looking plastic material.

One of the major reasons for the company's inability to learn from its mistakes is an ingrained corporate culture that emphasizes good news: Management is not interested in hearing about problems or weaknesses in the organization. Positive results tend to be emphasized at management meetings. Bad news results in a shoot-the-messenger ritual that makes people fearful of discussing anything negative with management. Although management perceives that everything is okay, their view does not match reality. If you were a consultant, what would you do to change the culture at Wilson Motor in order to create a learning organization that learns from good and bad news?

Scenario No. 3: Creating a Merit-Based Culture

North American Air, one of the major airlines in the United States, has always possessed a culture that emphasized being a family and taking care of employees. Traditionally, this culture was reflected in the company's employment practices, such as pay and promotion-from-within policies based on length of service to the company. This has led to the creation of an "entitlement" culture in which employees felt it was their right to receive generous pay increases each year independent of actual job performance.

Unfortunately, North American Air's performance has dropped significantly in the last three years. Profitability, customer satisfaction, and operating efficiency have all declined.

The CEO of North American Air realizes the company must focus more on achieving bottom-line results. This will require a major cultural shift for the company in terms of moving from an entitlement culture to a merit-based culture that emphasizes and rewards employees on the basis of their actual contributions to the success of the company. What would you do to create a merit-based culture in this firm?

MANAGING CHANGE

CHAPTER 14

Skills Objectives

> To design and implement organizational change effectively.

> To apply strategies for handling various forms of resistance to change.

> To design and implement organizational development interventions effectively.

> To design and implement effectively the principles for creating a learning organization.

KNOWLEDGE OBJECTIVES

> Identify forces for change, the nature of the change process, and targets of change.

> Understand sources of resistance to change and approaches to overcoming resistance.

> Recognize the special challenges associated with major organizational transitions.

> Describe organization development (OD), including OD assumptions, the OD process, and conditions for OD success.

> Describe the learning organization, including the disciplines, learning disabilities, and approaches to applying the disciplines.

Heraclitus is quoted as saying in about 513 B.C., "All is flux" and "The only constant is change." Although the statement "The only constant is change" has become a cliché, unquestionably organizations and their members are now facing remarkable levels of change. Product life cycles, markets, the nature of competition, the composition of the work force, the keys to strategic advantage, and much else are changing at accelerating levels. For example, in 1950, 10,000 companies failed. Today about eight times that number fail annually. The number of new product introductions has doubled in the last decade. The average tenure of a *Fortune* 300 CEO is now only four years, down from eight years two decades earlier.[1]

In this chapter, we address organizational change, including forces for change, the nature of the change process, and targets for change. We consider sources of resistance to change and approaches that can be taken to deal effectively with such resistance. Then we examine the set of change approaches known as *organization development* and conclude with a discussion of ways to develop change-oriented learning organizations.

Take a few minutes now to complete Self-Assessment 14-1. You will learn more from this chapter if you start off with a greater awareness of your beliefs and feelings about organizational change. After you are through, visit the text Web site to get feedback on your results.

SELF-ASSESSMENT 14-1

Attitudes Toward Managing Change

Answer the following questions regarding your attitudes toward change in organizations. Answer each question as honestly as possible using the response scale that follows.

1 Disagree strongly
2 Disagree somewhat
3 Neither agree nor disagree
4 Agree somewhat
5 Agree strongly

_____ 1. Management shouldn't have to take an active role in overcoming employees' resistance to change.

_____ 2. Organizational change often fails because management does not provide support to employees in implementing the change.

_____ 3. For the most part, resistance to change is irrational.

_____ 4. Because change is stressful, management when preparing for a major organizational change should be careful not to give the impression a crisis exists.

_____ 5. In general, employees will accept a change if the reasons for it are carefully explained to them.

_____ 6. In major change efforts, such as downsizings, management's time and energy are best used by focusing just on those people directly affected by the change, such as those who will be laid off.

_____ 7. In the modern business environment, planning for change is generally infeasible so emphasis should be directed toward reacting to change.

_____ 8. The complex and dynamic environments facing modern organizations requires that they become more predictable and efficient.

_____ 9. In all the uncertainty associated with major organizational change, it is best for management to wait until it has full information about the probable impact of the change before communicating about the change with employees.

_____ 10. Over the last 25 years, the pace of change has leveled off.

_____ 11. The only effective way to bring about change is to try to change people's behavior directly.

_____ 12. Just as individual employees may become smarter, it may be possible for organizations to "learn."

As a way to assess your initial level of skill in managing change in organizations, complete the Pretest Skills Assessment. Read the scenario and develop an action plan for how you would handle this situation. Be as specific as possible in stating your recommendations. After you are through, visit the text Web site to get feedback on your results.

PRETEST SKILLS ASSESSMENT

Managing Change

Note: This exercise is based on actual events encountered by managers in a real-world organization. Some information may have been modified in order to maintain the anonymity of the people and organization involved in this situation.

You are the manager of Miller Automotive Group, a network of dealerships of domestic and imported automobiles. You oversee the activities of more than 50 salespeople in these dealerships. Many of these individuals have been salespeople for more than 20 years. Their average age is 53 years old.

Recently, you decided to implement a new computerized customer relationship management system designed to help salespeople better manage information abut their current, prospective, and past customers. This system is far superior to the traditional method that salespeople have used to keep track of customer information (physical files). Although you were certain the new system would be a hit with the salespeople, you were surprised that many of them said they did not like it and refused to use it.

As the manager of these salespeople, develop an action plan for effectively implementing the new customer relationship management system in this organization. Be sure your plan is specific and addresses both short-term and long-term issues. Be prepared to defend the feasibility and cost effectiveness of each element of your plan.

Leaders make change happen, initiate improvements, make the world different. Most people tend to seek pleasure and avoid pain, but almost all change involves disruption of safe, comfortable routines. That's one reason why leaders meet resistance.

The ability to manage change is a valuable skill. Change is a critical uncertainty facing the organization. Environments of organizations are becoming increasingly dynamic. Organizations are becoming more change oriented, responding to various forces. Still, change is difficult, and not all change is good. Change may often be necessary, but it shouldn't be pursued blindly. It may be rewarding, but it may also be painful. Further, people may differ in the degree to which they resist change and in their motivations to change.

FORCES FOR CHANGE

We discussed in Chapter 1 and elsewhere the many forces for change in the modern workplace. Globalization, the growing diversity of the work force, the explosion of the Internet, the changing psychological contract, new legislation, political changes, shifting consumer and employee desires and expectations, and heightened levels of competition are among the many external forces for change. Internal forces for change might include performance gaps, new leadership, a new mission, and employee pressures. These forces for change are pervasive and accelerating in both frequency and magnitude. They demand that companies and their employees develop the capability, motivation, and mindset to succeed in a radically changed—and radically changing—new world of work.

PLANNED VERSUS REACTIVE CHANGE

Managers can respond to pressures for change either by planning or reacting. *Planned change* occurs when managers develop and install a program intended to alter organizational activities in a timely and orderly way. In many instances, planned change is instigated because managers anticipate the development of a force for change and thus seek to prepare the organization to adjust activities with minimal disruption. *Reactive change* occurs when managers simply respond to the pressure for change when it comes to their attention. Usually this is a piecemeal approach because managers are facing problems needing immediate resolution.[2]

Planned change is typically regarded as superior to reactive change. It is often used when change in the organization is extensive and lengthy. As such, it requires a greater commitment of time and resources and additional expertise in formulating and implementing the change. However, planned change can also be very effective when only modest change in organizational activities is required. The key to planned change is the ability of managers to anticipate what's needed.

Reactive change is usually hurried and less expensive to carry out than planned change. It is most effective when applied to small or day-to-day problems in the organization. Examples would include postponing production activities in response to shipping delays, altering a dress code policy to enable office workers to help move belongings to new headquarters, or deciding to hire computer consultants when it becomes clear that recently purchased computers are in some ways incompatible with current systems. These changes usually require minimal planning and are best handled by managers when a problem occurs. Reactive change also may be appropriate when external and internal forces are themselves changing so rapidly that planning is virtually impossible.

Now let's get out into the real world. Complete Skills Practice 14-1 by interviewing some real-world managers about how they deal with change issues in their organizations.

THE CHANGE PROCESS

Whether managers engage in planned or reactive change, understanding and implementing the steps in the change process increase the chances for success. Kurt

Lewin's change model includes three general stages of the change process (see Figure 14-1).

Figure 14-1 shows that successful change requires first creating a situation in which change is seen as necessary and desirable, then taking steps to bring about the change, and finally ensuring that conditions are appropriate to reinforce the change. Clearly, change is multifaceted. We address these steps throughout the remainder of the chapter.

Skills Practice 14-2 will help you develop skill in applying Lewin's change process model to a realistic organizational situation. Remember to address all three phases.

TARGETS OF CHANGE

As shown in Figure 14-2, we might want to change many things in organizations, including people's attitudes or behaviors, the nature of technology, structural relationships, and even ultimate goals.

STRUCTURAL CHANGE

Structural change involves altering a firm's formal authority structure or job definitions. Examples include changes in communication patterns, the way in which rewards are given, how the firm is departmentalized, or the decisions employees can make. Job enrichment, self-managing teams, and empowerment all involve structural change.

FIGURE 14-1

The Change Process—Lewin's Change Model

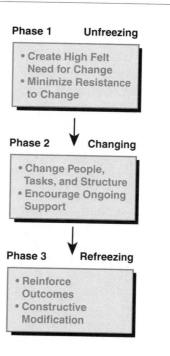

FIGURE 14-2
Targets of Change

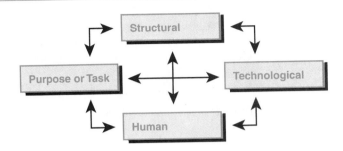

As an example of structural change, at the aircraft engine factories of Rolls-Royce, workshop managers were not allowed to change shop assignments or give out rewards. Therefore, workers tended to ignore the workshop managers. The factory managers, who made the decisions and gave out rewards, spent very little time in the workshops and could not make good decisions on giving rewards. When upper management decided to let workshop managers determine shop assignments and give out rewards, productivity and quality increased dramatically.

TECHNOLOGICAL CHANGE

Technological change occurs when a new method is used to transform resources into a product or service. An organization's technology consists of machinery, knowledge, tools, techniques, and actions necessary to complete the transformation process. The installation of robots on an automobile assembly line is a good example of a technological change as is the rapid computerization of the workplace.

HUMAN CHANGE

Human change involves changing employee attitudes, skills, knowledge, or behavior. Persuading employees to support the United Way or view diversity more positively, to learn how to use a computer, or to prepare for a new team assignment requires human change. We considered human approaches to change in Chapter 12. In addition, organization development, discussed later in this chapter, relies heavily on human change.

PURPOSE OR TASK CHANGE

With a *purpose* or *task change*, the goal of the organization is changed. At one time, the goal of the March of Dimes was to conquer polio. When an effective polio vaccine was introduced, the March of Dimes changed its organizational goal to conquering birth defects.

SOURCES OF RESISTANCE TO CHANGE

Niccolò Machiavelli wrote, "There is nothing so difficult as to implement change, since those in favor of the change will be small in number and those opposing the change will be numerous and enthusiastic in their resistance to change." As such, it is important to recognize that resistance to change is likely and to prepare to deal with it.

It is often tempting to dismiss resistance to change as irrational or petty. In fact, though, people often have many reasons to resist a particular change, some of them very reasonable. Sources of resistance to change are shown in Figure 14-3.[3]

SELF INTEREST

It is natural for organization members to have interests in benefiting themselves directly. Recall that the theories of motivation we have considered, such as expectancy theory and learning theory, are based on the idea that we seek positive outcomes and try to avoid negative outcomes. Resistance is likely to occur if a proposed change threatens those interests. Being assigned to manage a new product may increase one's prestige while lessening the prestige of those who did not receive the assignment. Changes may threaten—among other things—skills, power, relationships with others, social status, and self-esteem.

UNCERTAINTY

Change brings uncertainty. Organization members may resist a change because they cannot see how the change will affect their work and lives. Often they expect the worst. And they know that change may predict future change. As such, even those who expect to emerge unscathed from a major change (e.g., a reorganization, merger, or implementation of new technology) may wonder about what further changes it may precipitate and how they will be affected. This can lead to a dogged resistance and a preference for the status quo.

LACK OF UNDERSTANDING AND TRUST

Many proposed changes are not adequately explained to those who will be affected by the change. For example, Ciba Geigy employees learned on their car radios as they drove to work one day that their company was merging with Sandoz and the combined company would probably employ at least 10 percent fewer workers.

F I G U R E 1 4 - 3
Sources of Resistance to Change

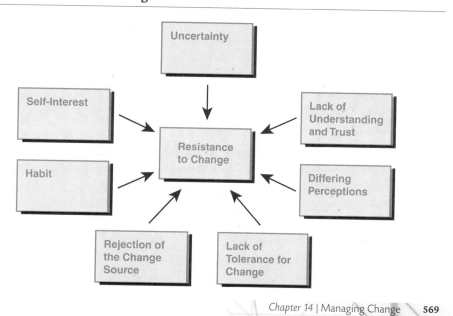

FOCUS ON MANAGEMENT

TRUST BUILDING AT EASTMAN CHEMICAL*

Earnest Deavenport, CEO of Eastman Chemical, a spin-off from Eastman Kodak, credits the company's substantial success to the way in which Eastman has retooled the traditional contract between company and employees. Deavenport says; "We have to capture the heart and spirit of the individual before we can capture market share or our competition's customers." Eastman has pursued a trust-building strategy by moving

decision making further down in the organization, enhancing the company's role as a provider of information, and developing an incentive and compensation program that encourages employees worldwide to become stewards of the company. Through the latter program, called the *Eastman Performance Plan,* Eastman employees will soon own 20 percent of the company's stock. Eastman Chemical was a winner of the 1993 Malcolm Baldrige National Quality Award. It is the only major chemical company to receive the

award. "The Eastman Way" states that Eastman people are the key to the company's success and its values and principles are aimed at treating them with fairness and respect. Read about those values and principles at:

http://www.eastman.com/ About_Eastman/Our_ Commitment_To_You/ Our_Values.asp

*See K. Ohlson, "Leadership in an Age of Mistrust," *Industry Week,* February 2, 1998, pp. 37–46.

Failure to understand the change increases the chances that members or departments will resist the change. Unfortunately, in a recent study, only 28 percent of surveyed workers reported that their managers do a good job of explaining decisions to them, and only 27 percent reported they're involved in decisions that affect them.[4]

Lack of trust can also support resistance to change. Prior experiences with those supporting or initiating change may have involved misrepresentations or deceit. In this case, resistance may be based simply on who supports the proposed change in the organization. The Focus on Management feature discusses Eastman Chemical's efforts to build the trust of its employees.

DIFFERING PERCEPTIONS

Differences of opinion about the need for change and what the change will accomplish can be a cause of resistance. People tend to see situations and events differently because of prior experiences and training. An engineer is likely to view a change in the production process differently than an accountant views it. The engineer may perceive the change in terms of increasing efficiency in the production of a good. The accountant may perceive the change in terms of the cost increase that will be reflected in the price of the product. Thus, resistance may result from legitimate disagreements over the outcome of change based on the differing perceptions.

LACK OF TOLERANCE FOR CHANGE

Some people feel comfortable with change; others feel uncomfortable. Even when organization members are shown that the change will not threaten their self-interest, the results are certain, full understanding and trust exist, and perceptions agree, they may still resist change. For example, some people prefer to drive the same route to work even when they agree a different route is quicker, safer, and less crowded. They are unwilling to change because they like the comfortable familiarity of the old route.

Now, complete Self-Assessment 14-2, Assessing Your Readiness for Change, and go to the Web site for this text to learn more about your responses.

SELF-ASSESSMENT 14-2

Assessing Your Readiness for Change

Use the following scale to respond to each of the statements listed here. Write the appropriate number in the blank in front of each statement.

1. Disagree strongly
2. Disagree somewhat
3. Neither agree nor disagree
4. Agree somewhat
5. Agree strongly

____ 1. It frustrates me when I don't quickly know how well I've done my job.

____ 2. In an ideal world, I'd know in advance the exact consequences of each of my actions.

____ 3. Few things upset me more than to have to do a job without a clear understanding of what has to be done.

____ 4. On my job, I look forward to changes.

____ 5. I prefer to find my own ways to do my job.

____ 6. I generally find surprises on my job to be undesirable.

____ 7. I dislike ambiguous situations.

____ 8. I like to know exactly what others expect of me on my job.

APPROACHES TO OVERCOMING RESISTANCE TO CHANGE

What can leaders do to reduce human inertia and encourage participation, cooperation, or at least compliance? Some primary approaches to dealing with resistance to change are summarized in Figure 14-4.[5]

Aristotle argued that all attempts to encourage others to change their minds, feelings, and behavior can be summarized in terms of the ***rhetorical triangle***, shown in Figure 14-5. It is useful to consider the change approaches in the context of the rhetorical triangle.

Here *logos* refers to convincing another person to accept a change through reason, logic, and data; *ethos* through the strength of your moral character and the trust that followers have in you; and *pathos* through appeals to your target audience's emotional and psychological needs.

LOGOS

When people are told about a change at work that will affect them, they normally react by first asking "Why?" When you initiate change, be prepared to provide a clear rationale in a direct, well-supported manner, using education and communication as your persuasive method. To accomplish this:

> **Do your homework**, gathering relevant facts that prove that a real problem exists. Identify potential causes and pinpoint probable causes. Thoroughly describe on paper the problem or opportunity, its causes, the need to do

FIGURE 14-4
Change Approaches

Tactic	Characteristics
Education and Communication	Explaining the need for and logic of the change
Participation and Involvement	Having members participate in the planning and implementation of the change
Facilitation and Support	Gradual introduction of the change process and provision of support to people affected by the change
Negotiation and Agreement	Negotiating and bargaining to win acceptance or reduce resistance to change
Manipulation and Co-optation	Covertly steering individuals or groups away from resistance to change through selective use of information, or assigning potential resisters to a desired position in the change process
Coercion	Demanding that members support the change or be threatened with the loss of rewards and resources

something about it, alternative solutions, and the cost benefits of each. Communicate clearly the advantages and disadvantages of the change you are selling.

> **Identify sources of help.** Who could help you sell the change? Staff, managers, inside/outside experts? Idea champions, venture teams, and innovation departments (each discussed in Chapter 3) may all prove useful, as may external change agents (discussed later in this chapter).

> **Anticipate questions and objections.** Think about the change from others' point of view. Identify the questions you would have and the objections you would raise if you were the target of this change.

> **Sell the benefits** of the change in terms of the perspective of those who will have to go through it. How will the change help to make things better and avoid or reduce bad consequences? It is easiest to sell the need for change when there is a *burning platform*, a dramatic, vivid demonstration that the current situation is unacceptable. Plummeting profits, competitive threats, irate

FIGURE 14-5
The Rhetorical Triangle

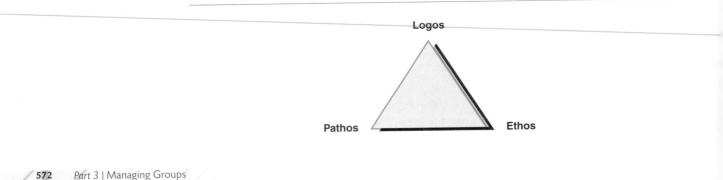

FOCUS ON MANAGEMENT

THE BURNING PLATFORM AT ALLIED SIGNAL

Larry Bossidy, former CEO of Allied Signal, said about that company's burning platform, "In 1991, we were hemorrhaging cash. That was the issue that needed focus. I traveled all over the company with the same message and the same charts, over and over. 'Here's what I think is good about us. Here's what I'm worried

about. Here's what we have to do about it. And if we don't fix this cash problem, none of us is going to be around. You can keep it simple: We're spending more than we're taking in. If you do that at home, there will be a day of reckoning.' In the first 60 days, I talked to probably 5,000 employees. . . . Also, there was a context to our burning platform. . . . People here had

observed difficulties at IBM, Kodak, and other companies, so the environment was ripe for change."[6] Bossidy capped his career at Allied Signal in grand fashion, retiring in April 2000 after completing another major change effort—the acquisition of Honeywell.[7]

http://www.honeywell.com/

customers, or lawsuits may all serve as burning platforms. In the Focus on Management feature, Larry Bossidy discusses the burning platform he addressed at Allied Signal. General Dennis Reimer, the U.S. Army's chief of staff, spoke of the army's attempts at change. He explained that with the end of the Cold War and the fall of the Berlin Wall, the army is in a different world and that it has to be able to change to serve the nation's needs. However, General Reimer noted that the army is a conservative organization and it believes in the "first rule of wingwalking: You don't let go of what you've got in your hands until you've got something else in your hands."[8] As such, change can best be sold when the present situation is unacceptable and there is something else to hold on to—some promising new beginning.

> **Use catalytic mechanisms** to reinforce the change.[9] *Catalytic mechanisms* help translate objectives into performance by making stretch goals reachable. They generally involve a dramatic policy that turns normal corporate practice on its head, requiring people to act in new ways that further the overarching corporate goal.[10] Granite Rock's unique catalytic mechanism is discussed in the Focus on Management feature on the following page.

> **Listen in depth** to concerns, questions, and fears.

> **Create an implementation plan** that answers the key questions most people have when faced with change: who, what, where, when, why, and how.

ETHOS

People cooperate with a leader who has high credibility, a combination of competence and trustworthiness. We tend to believe someone who demonstrates *expertise* and *authoritativeness*, has the requisite qualifications, and comes across to them as experienced, informed, skilled, and intelligent. When faced with a persuasive argument, the audience asks, "Does this person *know* the truth?" The other dimension is *trustworthiness*: one's character, moral fiber, and personal integrity. When faced with a persuasive argument, the audience asks, "Does this person *tell* the truth?"

FOCUS ON MANAGEMENT

SHORT PAY AT GRANITE ROCK

As an example of a catalytic mechanism, Granite Rock is a century-old California company that sells crushed gravel, concrete, sand, and asphalt. A dozen years ago, the company's copresidents, Bruce and Steve Woolpert, set an audacious goal for the company: Granite Rock would provide total customer satisfaction and achieve a reputation for service that met or exceeded Nordstrom, an upscale department store world famous for delighting its customers. To achieve this goal, the Woolperts implemented a radical new policy:

"short pay." The bottom of every Granite Rock invoice contains the words, "If you are not satisfied for any reason, don't pay us for it. Simply scratch out the line item, write a brief note about the problem, and return a copy of this invoice along with your check for the balance." Note that Granite Rock customers don't have to ask for a refund or return the product or even call and complain. They have the complete discretion to decide whether and how much to pay based on their satisfaction level. Short pay serves as a warning system, pro-

viding specific feedback about quality. It impels managers to track down the root causes of problems to prevent repeated short payments. It signals to employees and customers the sincerity of the company's commitment to customer satisfaction. Since Granite Rock implemented short pay, it has had remarkable success. The small firm has been able to compete successfully with huge rivals, has significantly improved its profit margins, and won the 1992 Malcolm Baldrige Quality Award.

http://www.graniterock.com/

PATHOS

You may have a rational idea for change, one that has a great cost-benefit ratio. You also may be seen as a trusted person of strong moral character and technical competence. That's not enough to persuade people to change, however. You also must attend to your target audience's emotional and psychological needs.

If the change you are initiating threatens people's emotional safety and security—if it lowers their self-confidence or self-esteem—you may get begrudging compliance or none at all. One effective way to satisfy people's emotional needs and to stimulate high motivation is to get them actively involved in the change itself. When people feel they have had a voice and a hand in shaping the change and its implementation, they tend to adopt ownership of it. Now it isn't just you; *I* has turned to *we*. Such participation and involvement can be sought at stages in the process or throughout, depending on the skills and interests of the players and the needs of the situation.

Using *participation* in planning and implementing changes simultaneously enriches people's work, raises self-esteem and self-confidence, and hones their problem-solving skills. In this way, you may turn what at first looks like win-lose into a win-win proposition for all.

Some changes, however—despite your best efforts—create winners and losers. Productivity improvements, for example, sometimes result in unneeded staff. You initiate such painful change by providing *facilitation and emotional support* and by *negotiating, compromising, and compensating* the individuals for their loss. Here the leader pays special attention to people's emotional needs and concerns and to their pocketbooks. Eliminating a job but transferring the person to a less desirable but higher-paying job is an example. Providing a generous severance-pay package is another.

MANIPULATION AND COERCION

As a leader, you can use other forms of persuasion: manipulating people through misinformation and downright lies; demanding change in a forceful, dictatorial manner; or threatening people with punishments if they fail to comply. Do these tactics work? Sometimes, but usually at high costs to morale, to positive working relationships, to willing cooperation, and to your trustworthiness as a leader. The best advice? Sit closer to Aristotle.

Figure 14-6 provides a summary of situations in which the various change approaches are likely to be selected. The Bottom Line feature identifies the steps associated with overcoming resistance to change effectively. Now, please complete Skills Practice 14-3. This exercise is designed to give you some practice in analyzing situations in which employee resistance to change exists and in developing action plans for dealing with these issues appropriately.

Now, watch the movie *Hoosiers* and complete Skills Practice 14-4. It is the story of a losing high school basketball team and what happens after a controversial new head coach is brought in to turn the team members into champions. Will they make it? You'll just have to watch and find out for yourself.

MANAGING DIFFICULT TRANSITIONS

Organizations, and we as individuals inside and outside organizations, are continually dealing with transitions. Many of these are difficult and painful. Obviously, a

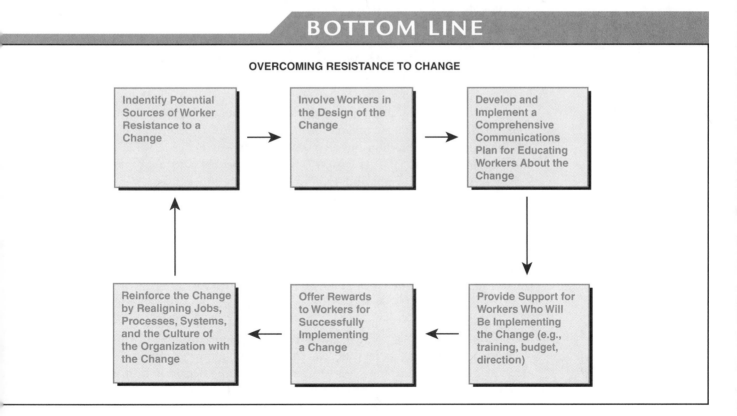

BOTTOM LINE

OVERCOMING RESISTANCE TO CHANGE

Indentify Potential Sources of Worker Resistance to a Change → Involve Workers in the Design of the Change → Develop and Implement a Comprehensive Communications Plan for Educating Workers About the Change → Provide Support for Workers Who Will Be Implementing the Change (e.g., training, budget, direction) → Offer Rewards to Workers for Successfully Implementing a Change → Reinforce the Change by Realigning Jobs, Processes, Systems, and the Culture of the Organization with the Change → (back to Indentify Potential Sources of Worker Resistance to a Change)

FIGURE 14-6

Deciding When to Use the Change Approaches

Tactic	Best When
Education and Communication	Resistance to change is due to lack of information or inaccurate information and analysis.
Participation and Involvement	The initiators of change don't have all the information they need to design the change, and others have considerable power to resist.
Facilitation and Support	People are resisting change because of fear or adjustment problems.
Negotiation and Agreement	Someone or some group will clearly lose out in the change and that party has considerable power to resist.
Manipulation and Co-optation	Other tactics won't work or are too expensive.
Coercion	The initiator of change has power, and change must occur quickly.

major layoff is a painful transition, but so is a major technological change (valued skills are lost, status relationships may change, uncertainty is introduced, social relationships change), or a major reorganization, or a move to a new location, or simply the voluntary leaving of a friend and colleague, perhaps due to retirement or taking a new job elsewhere. Certainly some currently popular practices, such as reengineering, implementing TQM, and trying to change organizational culture, involve major, and perhaps painful, transitions.

It is critical to think about managing transitions before they occur. This is needed to help successfully carry out the transition but also to think through the full consequences of the transition, and *thus to see if it is really desirable*.

In cases where transitions involve some people leaving, as in some reorganizations, it is important to take actions not only for the people who are leaving, but also for those who are staying, and for those who are affected, or even those just watching. The latter might include others elsewhere in the organization, friends, or users of services, among others.

It is especially important to think about losses that may result from the transition and how they will be dealt with. This is because we tend to focus on the gains of a proposed course of action. It is comforting to say that cutting back jobs or reorganizing or introducing a new technology will save $X per year. It is uncomfortable to think about potential losses; that is dissonance inducing. So we tend not to do it.

The following is a listing—a checklist of sorts—of things to keep in mind during transitions. The listing is not meant to imply all of these things will be done unilaterally by management. It may be especially important when dealing with major emotional issues such as transitions to get employee participation in managing the change, and perhaps to form teams of workers to help manage the transitions.

CLEARLY EXPLAIN THE REASONS FOR THE TRANSITION: SHOW HOW ENDINGS ENSURE CONTINUITY

Critical to any change is the process of unfreezing, where people are shown that a proposed change is preferable to the current situation. Make sure people first understand the problem or opportunity dictating the change. It is necessary to sell the problem before selling the solution. Then explain how the change will improve the situation.

It is especially important to show how the change assures continuity, how it is not just uncertainty inducing but also protective and maintaining. This may include appeals to organizational culture: How is the change consistent with important *values* that firm members hold? How would past heroes in the organization have felt about the change?

EXPLAIN WHY THE TRANSITION IS OCCURRING *IN THE WAY IT IS OCCURRING*

It's not enough to say the competitive situation demands changes. Why *these* changes? Why me? Procedural fairness is critical. If a change is presented as a way to deal with a problem or opportunity, but there is no evidence that other alternatives, perhaps less painful, have been considered, those hurt by the change will understandably be suspicious and angry (even more than otherwise). This is also important strategically; if we haven't in fact considered alternatives, we may be presenting a poor solution.

MINIMIZE UNCERTAINTY: DEFINE WHAT IS OVER AND WHAT IS NOT

Give people information, and do it again and again. There are many rationalizations for not communicating. Here are some common ones:

1. They don't need to know it yet. We'll tell them when the time comes. It'll just upset them now.
2. They already know it. We announced it.
3. I told the supervisors. It's their job to tell the rank and file.
4. We don't know all the details ourselves, so there's no point in saying anything until everything has been decided.

Of course, sometimes laws or competitive situations may preclude passing on some information. But most of the time information is withheld simply because managers are afraid to give it.

IDENTIFY WHO IS LOSING WHAT

In the case of a layoff or a major restructuring, it sometimes seems obvious that those laid off or those faced with an increased workload or those forced into a less desirable working situation are losing a lot. But beyond that, we have to recognize that their colleagues and peers may also be losers: social support networks, empty desks, survivor guilt; they may be stuck with a lot more work. And perhaps *all* employees are losing something: a culture of certainty, an implicit guarantee of permanent employment. So who are the obvious losers? Who are the secondary losers? What does the firm lose? What do all of us—employees and the firm—lose? What are the losses to our customers and members of interorganizational networks?

ACKNOWLEDGE LOSSES OPENLY AND SYMPATHETICALLY

It is important to bring the losses out into the open—acknowledge them and show your concern for the affected people, for example: "I'm sorry we have to make these transfers; we're losing good people." Some people feel that talking openly about losses stirs up trouble. Usually it is pretending the losses don't exist that causes trouble. Honest and open display of concern often defuses feelings of inequitable treatment.

EXPECT AND ACCEPT SIGNS OF GRIEVING

When endings take place, people get angry, sad, frightened, depressed, and confused, as shown in Figure 14-7.[11] These emotions are sometimes taken as signs of poor morale, but they are most appropriately seen as signs of grieving. You find them in a family that has lost a member, and you find them in an organization where an ending has taken place. At first, there may be none of these signs. Instead, there may first be denial. But they will come.

Expect these signs and be ready to deal with them. And it's not enough in a layoff or reorganization to say, "These people are to be gone by tomorrow morning. We don't have to deal with their grieving." Those leaving are not the only grievers. And the grief of those who leave may still have serious consequences for the organization.

PROVIDE FAIR COMPENSATION FOR LOSSES

What can I give to balance, or help balance, what I've taken away? First, you must consider carefully the nature of the losses. For instance, is there loss of status, turf, team membership, recognition, or pleasant working conditions?

Sometimes compensation can be concrete, such as a severance package in the case of layoffs. Often, though, symbolic actions are important to show respect. Help ensure continuity of pay and benefits.

FIGURE 14-7
Signs of Grieving

FACILITATE THE COPING OF THOSE WITH LOSSES

Firms must consider what they can do to reduce employee stress or to reduce its negative effects. In the case of layoffs, this would involve doing all one can to ease the stress of termination and facilitate movement to a new position. For instance,

> Provide counseling
> Allow for gradual transition to the new situation
> Publicize reasons for termination—make it clear the people are not to blame
> Help with job search; permit continued access to phone and fax

MARK THE ENDINGS

There is a sense of incompleteness and emptiness when endings are not marked. This is one reason we have wakes and funerals. But we also have going-away parties or a ceremony to retire an athlete's number. These ceremonies recognize loss but also reaffirm the value of what is lost. They are symbols of worth. To simply end something without recognition is demeaning. Symbolic actions are often as important as any actions that can be taken.

TREAT THE PAST WITH RESPECT

Never denigrate the past. Sometimes managers, in trying to make the future appear promising, ridicule or demean the old way of doing things. They engage in what are known as *rites of degradation*, finding scapegoats for blame and implying that by banishing the scapegoat, things will be better. This attitude often enhances resistance to change because many people identify with the so-called good old days and feel their self-worth is at stake when the past is attacked.

If the desire is to point out the positive features of the new situation as compared with the past, do it in ways that are not judgmental. Unless there is a compelling and concrete reason to criticize the past, don't.

PLAN FOR NEW BEGINNINGS

It is critical that those who remain can look forward to new beginnings, that there is not just a sense of loss but also a sense of promise.

Beginnings are typically wonderful and awful. An Italian writer, Cesare Pavese, wrote, "the only joy in the world is to begin," but Walter Bagehot, an English political scientist, wrote, "one of the greatest pains of human nature is the pain of a new idea." Beginnings are exciting and scary. But without planning for new beginnings, there is only a sense of ending.

In the Voice of Experience feature, Kathleen Rowe, the Chief Information Officer at Winterthur North America, discusses the strategies she uses to manage organizational change effectively.

ORGANIZATION DEVELOPMENT

Organization development (OD) has been defined as "an effort (1) planned, (2) organization-wide, and (3) managed from the top, to (4) increase organizational effectiveness and health through (5) planned interventions in the organization's 'process,' using behavioral science knowledge."[12] In this definition, we find the key ideas to the organization development approach to change. First, the OD approach

VOICE OF EXPERIENCE

MANAGING ORGANIZATIONAL CHANGE

Kathleen Rowe, Chief Information Officer, Winterthur North America

1. What kinds of changes do you have to deal with in your job? How do you cope with them?

A CIO always faces changes in technology, but beyond that is organizational change, changes in the business landscape, and changing expectations from one's customers—both internal and external.

One copes with change through a combination of agility, love of challenge, and planning. I tell my staff they need to embrace change because it is the only constant. To do that, you need to have a framework, whether it is in technology or in organizational planning, that supports moving products and processes in and out of the plan as needed without disrupting everything else.

2. What are some of the major challenges your organization has faced in terms of change? How do you deal with them?

The major challenges have been in organization structure and process. For example, we reorganized the Information Services Department. In some areas, we began changing the expectations of some positions, emphasizing analytical skill, moving some higher-level skills away from consultants to the staff, and moving some programming requirements to outside providers. This allows an increase in capacity to deliver projects while keeping expenses flat. We added, deleted, and changed positions. We focus on results, not just on quantity of effort.

Soon after, we decided to consolidate the corporate services of three U.S. companies, so we introduced new change before the staff had become fully comfortable with the earlier changes. Now there is staff in multiple locations, different reporting relationships, a need to think of oneself as belonging to a larger corporate entity while remaining committed to the success of each individual operation. We are consolidating technology, requiring common standards and processes across the companies, and looking for synergies that reduce cost, enhance our independent agents' interactions with us, and improve productivity.

Some of the staff has accepted change more readily than others. That is not a surprise. I believe the initial round of organizational change actually made the second event less stressful than it would have been, partly because of the changes themselves, and partly because change is not quite the enemy it was at the beginning. Additionally, the HR consultant who supports the department enjoys the trust of the staff. She helps as we go through change and is available to the staff as they need her.

There always will be some people who cannot accept change. They may look for different roles, either inside or outside of the company. And there are those who blossom. If you are willing to be a change agent, you learn to accept the first and to enjoy the second.

3. What are some of the most common mistakes that organizations make in the design and implementation of change?

I don't think any of us introduce change perfectly, but the most common mistakes are underestimating how human beings respond to change and undercommunicating. People do not need to hear just the facts; they want to know, "How does this affect me?" People are particularly threatened by anything that is perceived as a negative impact on another person, even those with whom they do not have collegial bonds.

Undercommunicating is another common mistake. We need to communicate what is changing, the rationale and benefits, the timetable, the kinds of impacts, and so on. At the same time we need to tell people when we're going to tell them more—and then follow through on that promise. This needs to continue all the way through implementation, and even after as we evaluate the actual results.

4. What are the most important strategies for managing the design and implementation of organizational changes effectively in the real world?

Communicate, communicate. Take the time to plan. Have people you trust review your design and implementation plans and find the flaws. Engage with experts such as marketing and human resources to improve how you articulate the plan and the plan benefits, and to ensure that human issues and concerns receive a high level of attention. Tell people how it's going. Get ideas (and use them) from your subordinates and get them on board. Don't forget to communicate with your colleagues and customers who may be impacted by the change. Be visible and available.

VOICE OF EXPERIENCE (continued)

5. What advice would you give students regarding what they need to learn about the effective management of change in real-world organizations?

They need to understand where change brings value, rather than implementing change for its own sake. The implementer of change in the real world needs to show that he or she is comfortable with ambiguity and can embrace and support change that is good for the organization even if it isn't particularly good for that individual.

Most of all, they need to recognize that change is mostly about people. Even when the change is to reduce expenses, increase profit share, consolidate the client base, or enhance the company's image, people are the ones who design, plan, implement, explore, and succeed or fail.

is planned. Change is based not on spontaneity but on careful consideration of the goal of the change and the methods that will lead to the achievement of that goal. Second, OD is an approach to human change that considers and includes all members of the organization, not just certain individuals or groups. Third, OD is a change approach supported by top management. Generally, this requires a firm commitment of resources to the change process. Fourth, the change is designed to increase organizational effectiveness and improve the working conditions of its members. Increased effectiveness at the cost of deteriorating working conditions is to be avoided. Finally, OD uses behavioral science approaches to create a more open and honest atmosphere in organizations. Emphasis is on the use of techniques that facilitate communication and problem solving among members.

OD ASSUMPTIONS AND VALUES

The practice of OD is based on several assumptions about people as individuals, as group members, and as members of the organization. These assumptions guide OD practitioners in their efforts to bring about change in the organization.

> **People as individuals.** OD practitioners make three basic assumptions concerning people as individuals. First, people in the organization seek to satisfy higher needs, such as personal development and growth in their jobs. Second, people desire to make a contribution to the organization. Third, people have not only the desire to contribute to the organization but the potential to do so. The OD approach seeks to overcome organizational barriers that discourage members from satisfying higher needs and making a contribution to the organization through their work.

> **People as group members.** OD practitioners assume the nature of group relationships will determine the satisfaction and contribution of the individual members of the group. It is important to the OD approach that group members feel acceptance in a work group is meaningful and the group is capable of generating trust, support, and cooperation among the members. Finally, the nature of the group should be such that members are capable of acting both as leaders and as followers in the group when necessary.

> **People as members of the organization.** OD practitioners assume organizational structures have an impact on member attitudes and behaviors. For

instance, if a new policy on dress were communicated to organizational members, there would be an effort to abide by the policy. A second assumption is that win-lose conflict strategies—in which one member wins at the expense of another—are not healthy in the organization. A third assumption is that upper management must have a long-term commitment to change within the organization.

These assumptions of the OD approach are critical to the OD practitioner's success. If a practitioner of OD were to try to improve the effectiveness and health of an organization in which members did not want to participate in the change and upper management did not support the change, the chances of success would be slim.

THE OD PROCESS

Several important steps can be identified in the OD process. OD is typically started by what is termed a *change agent,* usually an individual outside the organization who intervenes to start the change process. The steps involved in the intervention are to identify a need for change, to select a technique for change, to gather top management support, to overcome resistance to change, and to evaluate the change process. We have already discussed some of these steps, but it is useful to consider them in the OD context.

> **Identify a need for change.** The first step of an OD intervention occurs when the change agent identifies a need for change. This step may, for example, be the result of work with managers or employees in trying to understand why productivity or satisfaction is low. The change agent must determine whether the situation is temporary or may have long-lasting effects on organization and member effectiveness. If the situation appears to be long lasting, the change agent will want to identify a change process that will solve the problem.

> **Select a technique for change.**[13] A broad arsenal of intervention techniques is available to change agents.

  • **Diagnostic techniques.** Once the change agent has identified a need for change, an effort to get more information about the situation is necessary. This can be accomplished through diagnostic techniques that may include such methods as administering questionnaires and surveys, conducting interviews, attending meetings, or reviewing reports and minutes of the organization.

  • **Team building.** Team building (discussed in Chapter 11) consists of a series of activities designed to help individuals who work in groups develop a sense of teamwork. Teams may consist of members who work alongside one another daily or are together on a project only for a short time. The change agent introduces exercises that help communication among members of the team and teaches problem-solving techniques (as discussed in Chapter 3).

  • **Survey feedback.** The survey feedback technique of organization development starts with administering a questionnaire designed to gauge attitudes and perceptions of members. The information is then collected by the change agent and fed back to members. The feedback may present the results of the survey with time set aside for the group to discuss their meaning and explore possible interpretations. Members may be actively involved in the solution to problems through the use of the survey feedback technique.

- **Education.** Educational techniques usually consist of classroom training. The classroom can be used for both the development of skills in relating to others and the exploration of material on specific topics. Emphasis is on the development of human skills rather than of technical skills.
- **Intergroup activities.** The change agent may want to focus on techniques designed to improve relationships between groups. These may include techniques that increase communication between groups, develop understanding of one another's goals and problems, and promote cooperation.
- **Third-party peacemaking.** The change agent may want to use mediation or negotiation between parties engaged in conflict (as discussed earlier in this chapter). The parties to conflict may be groups, individuals, or organizations or a mix of the three.
- **Sociotechnical activities.** The term *sociotechnical* refers to the way in which members relate to the organization technology. The change agent may examine the technology of the organization to see whether it is compatible with existing structures. If not, a structural change, such as a move toward decentralization, may be necessary. Or the change agent may want to change the number and composition of tasks for which an employee has responsibility.
- **Process consultation.** Process consultation is a popular technique in which the change agent observes individuals or groups in the organization to develop an understanding of their attitudes and behaviors. The change agent provides immediate feedback to members so they can readily understand how certain processes shape their relationships.
- **Life and career planning.** Life and career planning is particularly useful when the goals of members and the goals of the organization are incompatible. The change agent may help individuals formulate personal goals that mesh with those of the organization or identify specific career maps and training opportunities.
- **Coaching.** Coaching is an effective technique when individuals need feedback to understand how others are responding to them. The information provided is usually nonevaluative and constructive.
- **Planning and goal setting.** Time management, goal setting, and activity planning are important managerial tasks. The change agent can help managers improve their performance in these areas. Increasingly, computer software is being made available to managers for these purposes.

> **Gather top management support.** The successful implementation of any OD technique directed at human change requires the support of top management. Top management should communicate support of the OD change technique to those organizational members who will be involved in the change process. Communication from top management should identify the goals, purpose, and expected results of the change effort. In this way, members will more fully understand why the change effort is taking place and know that top management supports its implementation. Without the support of top management or in situations in which top management has not announced its

support, members are likely to treat the change effort as frivolous or inconsequential. If this occurs, the change effort is doomed.

> **Plan the change process.** The change process must be well conceived from start to finish. The change agent should break down the change process into subparts, and then each subpart should be carried out sequentially. This will enable the change agent to check and evaluate progress. If some techniques do not work, the change agent can substitute a more effective technique without a large loss of organizational resources invested in the change process.

> **Overcome resistance to change.** As noted earlier in the chapter, resistance to change may come from many directions. Top management may get cold feet partway through the change process and begin to withdraw support. Managers of divisions or departments directly affected by the change may feel their competence or power is under attack. In addition, managers of divisions or departments left out of the change process may, because of uncertainty, feel the change will weaken their position. Employees may feel the change process is an effort to increase their work performance without a commensurate increase in pay. Or they may feel the change is simply an effort to check their work and that management will use the information to decide about firings or layoffs. Whatever the source or nature of the resistance, the change agent should have a well-thought-out plan to counter the resistance and apply the techniques for overcoming resistance to change (discussed earlier).

> **Evaluate the change process.** Evaluation of the change process is the final step in an OD program. Measures of the effectiveness of the program can be established through observation of activities, discussions with participants and nonparticipants, and collection of performance data to determine whether the change process achieved its goal. Evaluation of the change process can be difficult. Many factors outside the control of the change agent may affect the intended outcome of the process. As such, change agents should look beyond their own efforts in evaluating the causes of success or failure of the change process.

CONDITIONS FOR SUCCESSFUL OD PROGRAMS

Although many factors may contribute to the success or failure of an OD program, several important conditions are thought necessary for an OD program to succeed:[14]

> **Recognition by managers and members that the organization has problems.** Without such recognition, it is unlikely a change process will receive the required resources to make the effort successful.

> **Use of an external change agent to start the process.** The change agent should not be a member of the organization. Internal change agents often lack the objectivity and autonomy to carry out necessary changes, and their efforts may be hampered by political infighting.

> **Support from top management for the change process.** As noted, the lack of top management support can seriously jeopardize the successful implementation of a change program.

> **Involvement of work group leaders.** Where change is directed at work groups or teams, the work group leaders must have an active role in the change process. Without their involvement, implementation of the change process is unlikely to occur.

> **Early success with the OD effort.** Success breeds success. Generally, change agents should strive initially to carry out a change process that has a high chance of success. Success motivates members to continue with the process and gives them confidence that more ambitious efforts can also be successful.

> **Understanding of the change process and its goals.** Generally, people will not respond positively to a change process unless they understand why the change is being made. Articulation of the purpose and goals of the change process should be made frequently.

> **Support of managerial strengths.** Change agents often become so focused on the process, they ignore the positives that exist in the organization. Effective managers should be acknowledged and reinforced. The change agent should be wary of overplaying the expert role in an organization.

> **Inclusion of human resource managers in the OD program.** The change agent should include managers from the personnel or human resources department in the planning and implementation of the change process. Human resources managers can provide valuable information and insight into members' performance, development, and rewards.

> **Development of internal OD resources.** One goal of an OD program is to make change an ongoing and comfortable process in the organization. The change agent should involve and train organization managers at all levels in OD skills and techniques so managers of the organization can plan and carry out change long after the change agent has left.

> **Effective management of the OD program.** The change agent should watch and respond to situations to optimize the chances of success. This often requires careful coordination and control of activities to ensure the change process is carried out correctly and members support the program.

> **Measurement and evaluation of results.** Measurement and evaluation of results provide the change agent and members of the organization with important information about the effectiveness of the change program. This information can be the basis for planning and implementing future change programs.

Now complete Skills Practice 14-5. This will give you a chance to develop skill in creating OD programs to handle different types of organizational problems.

THE LEARNING ORGANIZATION

As organizations face environments that are increasingly competitive, complex, uncertain, and dynamic, they must develop the capacity to change on an ongoing basis.[15] Adaptability and flexibility require the ability to learn continually. According to Arie De Geus, head of planning for Royal Dutch/Shell, "The ability to learn faster than your competitors may be the only sustainable competitive advantage." Peter Senge, in his book *The Fifth Discipline,* discusses learning organizations. According to Senge, in learning organizations "people continually expand their capacity to create the results they truly desire, where new and expansive patterns of thinking are nurtured, where collective aspiration is set free, and where people are continually learning how to learn together."[16] Learning organizations develop specific learning capabilities not present in traditional organizations.[17] The five disciplines of the learning organization are presented in Figure 14-8.[18]

FIGURE 14-8
The Five Disciplines of Learning Organizations

Discipline	Description
Personal Mastery	This discipline of aspiration involves formulating a coherent picture of results that people most desire (their personal vision) alongside a realistic assessment of the current state of their lives (their current reality).
Mental Models	This discipline of reflection and inquiry skills focuses on being aware of the personal attitudes and perceptions that influence thought and interaction. By reflecting upon, discussing, and reconsidering these internal pictures, people gain capability in governing their actions and decisions.
Shared Vision	This collective discipline involves building a common sense of purpose. People learn to nourish a sense of commitment by developing shared images of the future that they seek to create and the principles and guiding practices by which they hope to get there.
Team Learning	This discipline of group interaction requires reflecting on action as a team and transforming collective thinking skills so the team can develop intelligence and ability greater than the sum of the individual members' talents.
Systems Thinking	This discipline involves understanding the language of interrelationships that shape the behavior of the systems in which people exist and thereby being better able to deal with the forces that shape the consequences of our actions.

Source: P. Senge, A. Kleiner, C. Roberts, R. Ross, G. Roth, and B. Smith. *The Dance of Change: The Challenges to Sustaining Momentum in Learning Organizations,* (New York: Doubleday, 1999), pp. 32–33. These disciplines are discussed in detail in P. M. Senge, *The Fifth Discipline: The Art & Practice of the Learning Organization* (New York: Doubleday, 1990), pp. 139–269.

Senge argues that these five disciplines must develop as an ensemble. Systems thinking is the "fifth discipline" that integrates the disciplines, fusing them into a coherent body of theory and practice. Without systems thinking, Senge reasons, the other disciplines may become "separate gimmicks or the latest organization change fads."[19] For example, unless we adopt a systems perspective, vision paints enticing pictures of the future without adequate regard for the forces that must be mastered to achieve them.

THE SEVEN LEARNING DISABILITIES

Senge has identified seven "learning disabilities" that interfere with organizational learning. Before these disabilities can be cured, we must recognize them.[20]

1. "I am my position." People often identify with their jobs rather than with the purpose of the larger enterprise of which they are a part. They tend to see themselves as having little or no influence over the larger system and thus see their responsibilities as limited to the boundaries of their position. As a result, they have little sense of responsibility for overall results.

2. "The enemy is out there." We have a tendency to "externalize"—to find someone or something outside ourselves to blame when things go wrong. So when a company loses market share, it is tempted to blame foreign governments, unions, unfair competitors, disloyal customers, or anyone

but itself. Unfortunately, if we refuse to consider that our actions—our failure to stay focused on our customers, to take actions to retain our valued employees, or to treat our suppliers with respect—may be the true source of our problems, we will never learn from our mistakes and never correct them. We would do well to remember the words of Pogo: "We have met the enemy and he is us."

3. "The illusion of taking charge." According to Senge, all too often, "proactiveness" is just reactiveness in disguise; people just become more aggressive in fighting the "enemy out there." True proactiveness, he argues, requires seeing how we contribute to our own problems; it is a product of our way of thinking rather than of an emotional state.

4. "The fixation on events." We are conditioned to see life as a series of events and to believe there is one obvious cause for each event. However, Senge argues, "Today, the primary threats to our survival, both of our organizations and of our society, come not from sudden events but from slow, gradual processes."[21]

5. "The parable of the boiled frog." A frog placed in a pot of boiling water will quickly try to jump out. However, if the frog is placed in water at room temperature and the heat is very gradually turned up to the point of boiling, the frog will stay in place and ultimately be killed. The reason: Its internal apparatus for sensing threats to survival is geared to sudden changes in the environment, not to gradual changes. Similarly, the U.S. auto industry initially paid little attention to Japanese competition because Japanese market share eased up gradually. Thus, it is critical to remain attuned to the gradual processes that often pose the greatest threats.[22]

6. "The delusion of learning from experience." We learn best from experience. Unfortunately, we never experience the consequences of our most important decisions. The most important decisions made in organizations have systemwide consequences that play out over years or decades.

7. "The myth of the management team." Senge argues that members of management teams, instead of working together to battle these disabilities, fight for turf, try to avoid blame, and work to give the appearance of a cohesive team. They squelch disagreement, discourage questioning, and reward those who express their views rather than inquire into complex issues. This all leads to a situation that psychologist Chris Argyris calls "skilled incompetence," teams full of people who are very proficient at keeping themselves from learning.

DEVELOPING LEARNING ORGANIZATIONS

To develop a learning organization successfully, it is necessary to instill the five disciplines while overcoming learning disabilities. This requires a variety of elements:[23]

> **Learning leaders.** Leadership in a learning organization begins with the principle of creative tension.[24] Creative tension comes from recognizing the gap between where we want to be—our "vision"—and the truth about where we are—our "current reality." The leadership task of generating creative tension without causing defensiveness means leaders must be able to see leaps of abstraction, to balance inquiry and advocacy, to recognize the difference

between the views that they espouse and those they act out, and to recognize and defuse defensive routines. Learning leaders must also help others see the big picture. To do this, they must see interrelationships rather than things and processes rather than snapshots. They must be able to move beyond blame, using systems thinking to see how the cause of problems is part of an interrelated system. They must focus on areas of high leverage, using small, focused actions to produce significant, enduring improvements. That is, properly placed small actions may serve as levers, bringing important change with a minimum of effort. In addition, learning leaders must look beyond symptoms to underlying causes in the system.

> **Leadership communities.**[25] In learning organizations, the leaders are those building the new organization and its capabilities.[26] Such leadership is collective, and it is based on the idea of *servant leadership*: People lead because they want to serve one another as well as a higher purpose. In addition to executive leaders, two other types of leaders are important in these leadership communities: local line leaders and internal networkers, or community builders. Local line leaders are individuals with significant business responsibility and bottom-line focus. They have units large enough to be meaningful microcosms of the organization, yet they have enough autonomy to undertake meaningful change. Local line leaders create subcultures that may be quite different from the mainstream culture. They sanction significant practical experiments aimed at connecting new learning capabilities to business results. Internal networkers, or community builders, have no positional authority, but they bring about change through the strength of their convictions and the clarity of their ideas. Internal networkers understand informal networks, and they move freely, with high accessibility. They identify local line managers who have the power to take action and who are inclined to develop new learning capabilities. Internal networkers then serve as "seed carriers," linking people of like minds in varied settings to one another's learning efforts. They may subsequently help develop formal coordination and steering mechanisms needed to leverage from local experiments to organizationwide learning. Executive leaders, local line leaders, and internal networkers are all important parts of leadership communities in learning organizations.

> **Learning infrastructures.**[27] Learning organizations weave basic tools and methods for reflective thinking throughout the firm. They create virtual learning spaces or "managerial practice fields" in which learning arises through performance and practice.[28] For example, such companies as Royal Dutch/Shell, AT&T, Federal Express, and Ford Motor Company use such tools as scenario planning, learning laboratories, and learning forums. At Shell, planners produce multiple plans for multiple possible scenarios. As they plan for multiple futures, assumptions have to be articulated, and mental models become explicit. At Ford Motor Company, learning laboratories are part of the product development process. Groups involved in product design ask how the design process can be redesigned so they are not just designing new products but continually developing better ways to develop products. In this way, the learning process and the product development process are interwoven. At AT&T, teams meet regularly in learning sessions called *forums* to discuss

strategic issues. At the chairman's forum, the top 150 people meet twice a year to discuss basis strategy of the firm. In a sense, these various learning tools are all experiments sharing common elements: (1) they connect the learning agenda to core management processes and business imperatives; (2) they involve key players; and (3) they respect freedom of choice, permitting learning to occur in different ways.

> **Learning cultures.**[29] A learning organization represents a shift in culture. The learning organization embodies new capabilities and is grounded in a rein-forcing culture based on transcendent human values of love, wonder, humility, and compassion. The culture of a learning organization treats surprises as opportunities to grow and differing behaviors, assumptions, and viewpoints as valid. In addition, it is a culture that recognizes the limitations of our knowl-edge and perspectives and thus the need and opportunity for improvement.

The Bottom Line feature identifies the steps associated with developing a learning organization effectively.

We began this chapter by saying change is pervasive and important and the ability to deal with change will be increasingly vital. Your ability to manage change will be a major factor in your success as a manager and in the effectiveness of your organization. In addition, this is a skill that will serve you well in life in general. Take it seriously.

BOTTOM LINE

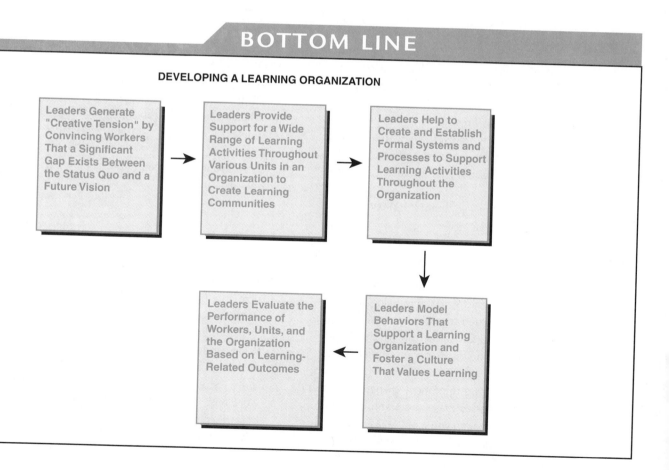

DEVELOPING A LEARNING ORGANIZATION

Leaders Generate "Creative Tension" by Convincing Workers That a Significant Gap Exists Between the Status Quo and a Future Vision → Leaders Provide Support for a Wide Range of Learning Activities Throughout Various Units in an Organization to Create Learning Communities → Leaders Help to Create and Establish Formal Systems and Processes to Support Learning Activities Throughout the Organization → Leaders Model Behaviors That Support a Learning Organization and Foster a Culture That Values Learning → Leaders Evaluate the Performance of Workers, Units, and the Organization Based on Learning-Related Outcomes

Top Ten List: Key Points to Remember

MANAGING CHANGE

10. Expect to spend a lot of time trying to get others in your organization to see the need for a specific change.

9. Aggressive and thorough education and communication will be needed on an ongoing basis to get people in an organization to understand a change and to support it.

8. The most effective strategy to use for managing change varies depending on the nature of the situation.

7. Provide the support needed by those who will be implementing change to enable them to be successful in making the change work.

6. Reinforce any change that is implemented by modifying job descriptions, policy statements, flow charts, organizational charts, and/or mission statements to support the change.

5. Recruit, hire, train, and reward employees who are able to function effectively in a changing work environment.

4. Foster an organizational culture that values and embraces change.

3. Involve all key organizational players (e.g., senior management, line managers, human resources personnel, and affected employees) in the design and implementation of any OD program.

2. Work to build learning organizations. A key is the "Fifth Discipline," the ability to view and manage organizations as systems of interrelated parts.

1. Any major organizational change must have the support of top management in order to be successful.

Questions for Review and Reflection

REVIEW QUESTIONS

1. Differentiate between planned and reactive change.
2. Discuss the three stages of the change process.
3. Describe four primary targets of change.
4. Discuss seven sources of resistance to change.
5. Discuss six approaches to overcoming resistance to change, including when each is most effective.
6. What is the rhetorical triangle? What are the three points on that triangle?
7. What is organization development (OD)? What are its assumptions and values?
8. Discuss the stages of the OD process.
9. Identify factors that contribute to success or failure of OD programs.
10. What is a learning organization? What are the five disciplines of learning organizations? What are the seven learning disabilities?
11. Discuss four approaches to developing learning organizations.

CRITICAL THINKING QUESTIONS

1. After a serious disagreement about proposed changes in the company's pay systems, at a meeting your boss announced, "I've decided to call in an outside expert to get some objective advice on how we should proceed." What would you say or do in response to this announcement?

2. You have led a task force to propose changes in company policies in order to make the workplace more "family friendly." Although you feel the task force did a thorough job in soliciting inputs and gathering other information to ensure the proposed changes were feasible and in line with employee preferences, the task force's recommendations were met with widespread foot shuffling and comments of "flavor of the day." What would be your next steps?

3. As part of a discussion of a proposed major restructuring, you point out that major change attempts work best when there is a "burning platform." Your boss disagrees, saying, "That's motivating with fear. We need to change *before* the platform is on fire."

Take a position for or against your boss's argument.

4. After a presentation on targets of change, your colleague says to you, "Any attempt to change people directly is unethical, period. What right does management have to try to toy with people's values or attitudes? What's next?" Do you agree with your colleague? Why or why not?

5. Consider the rhetorical triangle. Think about a partic- ular change with which you are quite familiar that affected more than one person; this could be a personal change, a change at work, or any other sort of change that interests you. Discuss how logos, pathos, and ethos did or did not play roles in the change process. Were there ways in which these elements of the triangle could have been used to make the change process more successful?

EXPERIENTIAL EXERCISES

WEB EXERCISE 14-1

Go to the Web site of the Leader to Leader Institute (formerly the Drucker Foundation) at *__http://www.pfdf.__ __org/ leaderbooks/__*. You will see a search box. Conduct searches on one or more terms from this chapter, such as *change, trust,* or *learning organization.* For instance, if you type *change,* you will be given links to almost 500 articles or other materials relating to change. Select any two of the articles. For each article, write a one-page executive summary:

1. State the topic of the article and why that topic is important.
2. Summarize the author's key arguments.
3. Indicate what you see as the key management implications of the article.

WEB EXERCISE 14-2

Go to the "United Parcel Service and the Management of Change" site at *__http://cbpa.louisville.edu/bruce__ __/cases/ups/htm/ups.htm__*.

The case presented on the site is a student team project, written for a management class of Professor Reginald Bruce at the University of Louisville. It provides a comprehensive discussion of successful and unsuccessful change efforts at UPS. Read the case and answer the following questions:

1. What were the burning platforms that convinced UPS of the need for change?

2. What were the change efforts? Why was each change effort undertaken?
3. What were some of the sources of resistance to change at UPS? How were they addressed?
4. Which change efforts were successful and which were unsuccessful? What factors contributed to the success, or lack of success, of each effort?
5. Overall, how would you characterize the effectiveness of attempts to change at UPS?

__http://www.ups.com__

CASE 14-1

IMPLEMENTING A PARADIGM SHIFT AT THE BAYFIELD MENTAL HEALTH INSTITUTE[30]

Note: This case is based on actual events in a real-world organization. Because of concerns regarding the potential sensitivity of issues presented in this case, some information has been modified to protect the anonymity of the company and its employees.

The BMHI Organization

The Bayfield Mental Health Institute (BMHI), located in Seattle, Washington, is a residential facility for people who have been diagnosed with a variety of severe mental illnesses. The institute has over 1,200 patients living in its complex. BMHI currently employs over 2,700 part-time and full-time employees who develop and implement a variety of services and programs (e.g., psychological testing, counseling, physical and occupational therapy, and direct care services) at the institute.

Although the overall BMHI work force is committed to its work and the organization, the work environment is very demanding both physically and mentally. Many of the residents are subject to violent outbursts against staff members. Moreover, many of the direct care jobs that provide maintenance services for residents are routine low-status jobs that pay poorly. This has resulted in an annual turnover rate in excess of 100 percent for these jobs. In addition, increased competition from other health care organizations and ever increasing costs that have exerted pressure on BMHI to find ways to remain competitive.

The Paradigm Shift (Change)

Recently, top administrators at BMHI held a week-long strategic planning meeting at an off-site location to discuss current opportunities, threats, and the future direction of the institute. The result was the development of a new paradigm for BMHI that specified a new set of fundamental goals, underlying principles, and values that would ideally provide the future direction for the organization. This new paradigm is displayed in Figure 1.

This framework was designed to focus on everything BMHI does in relation to its customer, the resident, and to outline the key operating principles by which all members of the organization would operate on a daily basis in caring for each resident at the institute.

Although the top administration was thrilled with the new paradigm they had devised, they recognized one of the most difficult challenges they would face would be how to get the rest of the BMHI work force (lower-level managers and supervisors and front-line employees) to understand it and to change their behavior to support it in the future. Clearly, the administration did not want the new BMHI paradigm to be nothing but a fancy-looking conceptual framework that nobody understood, cared about, or put into practice.

The new BMHI paradigm was unveiled at a recent town hall meeting held by the head administrator of the institute. Many of the employees in attendance had no reaction to the new paradigm. Some commented, "This is just another fad from administration"; others said, "The paradigm has nothing to do with those who are in the trenches on the front lines caring for the residents." Later, an employee survey conducted by the human resources department revealed that 65 percent of employees were suspicious of the new paradigm, and 82 percent of them indicated they preferred the status quo over the new paradigm.

Discussion Questions

1. Now it's your turn to be the consultant. Based on the information provided here, develop an action plan for

FIGURE 1

The New BMHI Paradigm: Resident Quality of Life and Functioning

Resident Quality of Life
- Psychological Well-Being
- Physical Well-Being
- Life Skills
- Work Skills

↑ ↑ ↑

The BMHI Value System
- Caring for the Resident
- A Supportive Environment
- A Committed Staff
- Responsive to Resident Needs
- A Professional Orientation
- Collaboration Among All Staff
- Integrity

building short-term (now or in the next few months) understanding and commitment to the BMHI paradigm among its employees. Download the worksheet created for this exercise from the Web site for this textbook to help you structure your approach to this exercise. Document your key actions on this worksheet. Make sure each of your recommendations is specific and action oriented. Be prepared to justify each of your recommendations to the administration in terms of merit, feasibility, and cost effectiveness. Also, make sure you address what the administration needs to do to ensure the effective execution of your recommendations.

2. Based on your key results, develop a set of *long-term recommendations* (goals to be accomplished in the next three to five years) to help top administrators at BMHI build understanding and commitment to the BMHI paradigm among its employees. Make sure each of your recommendations is specific and action oriented. Be prepared to justify each of your recommendations to the top administrators in terms of merit, feasibility, and cost effectiveness. Also, make sure you address what top administration needs to do to ensure the effective execution of your recommendations.

3. (Optional) Make a five- to ten-minute presentation of your results and recommendations to the class.

4. What did you learn from this case study about implementing change issues in real-world organizations?

CASE 14-2

REINVENTING XEROX CORPORATION

The Company

The Xerox Corporation, based in Stamford, Connecticut, is a document solutions, systems, and services provider including color and black-and-white printers, digital presses, multifunction devices, digital copiers, related supplies, software, and support. The company was founded in Rochester, New York, as the Haloid Company. It was renamed the Xerox Corporation in 1961.

The mission of the Xerox Corporation is to "help people find better ways to do great work—by constantly leading in document technologies, products, and services that improve our customers' work processes and business results." The company's core values include the following:

> We succeed through satisfied customers.
> We deliver quality and excellence in all we do.
> We require premium return on assets.
> We use technology to develop market leadership.
> We value and empower employees.
> We behave responsibly as a corporate citizen.

In 2002, the company had earnings of $0.02 per share based on revenue of $15.8 billion. It had 67,800 employees worldwide with 40,100 of them in the United States.[31] In the early 1980s, Xerox faced intense competition from Japanese rivals such as Canon, Minolta, and Ricoh in the copier industry. This raised concerns among analysts that Xerox may not survive. David T. Kearns, the CEO at that time, executed a brilliant turnaround strategy that focused on improving the company's products, technology, and after-sales service. Six years later, Xerox was a strong and profitable company again.

The Current Situation

In the year 2000, history appeared to repeat itself as Xerox faced stiff competition combined with falling earnings and a severe cash crunch. The resignations of CEO Richard Thoman and his replacement, Paul Allaire, failed to help the company, and its stock price went from $64 in May 1999 to $8 as of October 2000. Questions again emerged regarding whether Xerox would survive this crisis.[32]

The Turnaround Strategy

In July 2001, Xerox announced it was promoting Anne Mulcahy, a more than 25-year veteran with the company who started as a field sales representative, from president to chief executive officer. Her tenure as CEO started on August 1, 2001.

Mulcahy implemented a wide range of changes aimed at helping turn around the company's fortunes. These included the following:[33]

> Restructuring the company to cut annual expenses by $1.7 billion.
> Selling $2.3 billion worth of noncore assets to reduce the company's debt from $15.6 billion to $9.2 billion.
> Cleaning up the company's accounting problems. The Securities and Exchange Commission (SEC) had accused Xerox of distorting its numbers in order to meet Wall Street's expectations
> Logging more than 100,000 miles visiting Xerox locations to talk with employees during her first year as CEO, which boosted employee morale.
> Meeting with 50 CEOs of client companies and lowering prices based on their feedback.
> Introducing new products and services that offer customers higher productivity at a lower cost.
> Investing $1 billion in research and development each year.
> Expanding the company into services (e.g., helping companies better manage the flow of documents and setting up computer networks).

Other qualities that helped Mulcahy implement the various elements of the turnaround strategy included her ability to stay focused, be decisive, understand Xerox's customers, and be open to criticism from customers. She also believes her ability to develop and nurture a motivated work force is a critical part of her job.

Results

Up through August 2003, Xerox reported a 9 percent increase in cash generated despite weakness in the overall copier market. Aggressive pricing enabled the company to increase its share in key markets. Cash on hand stood at $2.3 billion due to the company's success in raising money from bondholders, equity investors, and banks.[34]

Overall, Xerox's turnaround strategy has been successful in achieving some short-term objectives including eliminating noncore assets, reducing costs by $1 billion, and growing revenue by pursuing the office environment, production environment (e.g., commercial printers), and the document management process.

Despite these short-term successes, some significant barriers still face Mulcahy and others at the Xerox. These include the following:[35]

> Intense competition in the copier market from Canon, HP, Ricoh, and others.
> The presence of an insider culture that makes the company resistant to change.
> An ineffective board that has been too passive in dealing with critical issues such as the sales force reorganization and the cash crunch the company experienced.
> Accounting scandals: ongoing SEC probes into alleged irregularities in Xerox's accounting practices.
> Weak economy: Many corporate buyers have stopped purchases of nonessential goods.

> Maintaining employee morale: This will be a challenge given that Xerox has already laid off more than 13,000 employees.
> Money: Xerox's cash position has improved, but it is not secure yet. The company will need to work hard to continue raising additional cash.

Discussion Questions

1. What are the key opportunities and threats facing Xerox now?
2. To what extent do you believe Mulcahy's strategies for changing Xerox are appropriate for this situation? Why?
3. What recommendations would you give to Mulcahy regarding the handling of this situation? What types of challenges might arise as a result of implementing these recommendations? What could be done to overcome these challenges? Be specific.

VIDEO CASE: CENTRAL MICHIGAN COMMUNITY HOSPITAL

MANAGING CHANGE

Running Time: 12:00

Central Michigan Community Hospital (CMCH), named one of the top 100 hospitals in the United States, is riding a tidal wave of change. Faced with growing governmental regulation and scrutiny, heightened competition, controls on costs, increased patient load, and many other fundamental changes, CMCH must respond quickly and appropriately if it is to survive and prosper.

The video shows the hospital's president/CEO, medical director, patient care services administrator, chief financial officer, surgeons, and others as they discuss the situation at CMCH. After viewing the video, answer the following questions:

1. What are specific environmental changes to which CMCH must respond?
2. What are some of the constraints CMCH faces as it attempts to deal with change?

3. What are some of the changes CMCH is undertaking to meet environmental challenges?
4. How does the traditional nature and training of health care workers impact on resistance to change at CMCH?
5. What are some specific things CMCH is doing to help make its change efforts successful?
6. Do the various actions CMCH is taking to deal with its changing environment appear consistent with the guidelines for managing change presented in this chapter? Why or why not?

http://www.cmhs.org/cmhsframe.asp?action =cmchinfo

LIGHTEN UP

BAD FADS

Although change is often desirable, people may also implement change for questionable reasons. For example, some change efforts are essentially impression management, attempts to give the appearance of progress or to detract

attention from other problems. In addition, change may sometimes take the form of blind following of fads.[36] In a Dilbert cartoon, when the boss announces at a meeting that "companies must learn to embrace change," the employees sitting around the conference table collectively think, "Uh-oh. It's another management fad. Will it pass quickly or will it linger like the stench of a dead woodchuck under the porch?" When the boss continues, "I think we should do a 'change' newsletter," they collectively think

"woodchuck." Check out fashion, collectible, activity, and event fads of the last 100 years:

http://www.badfads.com

LIGHTEN UP

TERRIBLE PREDICTIONS

Charles Duell, then the commissioner of the U.S. Office of Patents, stated in 1899, "Everything that can be invented has been invented." For this and other terrible predictions,

as well as for more quotes regarding inventions, go to:

http://www.chemistrycoach.com/invention.htm

SKILLS PRACTICE

14-1   *Skill Level:* **BASIC**

Field Experience: Interviews with Managers About Managing Organizational Change

Skill Objective

1. To develop a better understanding of what management practitioners in the real world do to manage change effectively.

Procedure

1. Identify two managers who work in different business organizations. Ask the manager(s) if you can interview each of them for approximately 30 to 45 minutes.

2. When you meet with each manager, ask the following questions:

   a. Why is the issue of change so important to organizations in today's business environment?

   b. Can you give me an example of a change you implemented in your organization that was met with resistance from employees? Why did they

   resist this change? What did you do to overcome this resistance to change?

   c. What do you think a manager needs to do to manage change effectively in organizations?

   d. What advice would you give students regarding specific things they can do to manage change effectively in the real world?

3. Summarize the results of your interviews.

Discussion Questions

1. Based on the summary of your interviews, what are your key findings about managing change? Why?

2. What are the practical implications of this exercise for you as a future manager and leader of a real-world organization?

SKILLS PRACTICE

14-2   *Skill Level:* **CHALLENGING**

Applying Lewin's Change Process Model

Skill Objective

To develop skill in applying Lewin's change process model in order to manage the overall change process in an organization effectively.

Procedure

1. This exercise may be completed on an individual basis or in groups of three to five students.

2. Read the scenario that follows.

Coopers owns and operates 75 department stores in North America, Europe, Latin America, and Asia. It specializes in high-end apparel and accessories for adults and children. It employs over 50,000 people across its worldwide operations.

Coopers entered the retail business in 1890 when

it opened its first store in New York City. Since then, Coopers has been a major force in the retail industry. Its name has always been synonymous with the concepts of value, variety, quality, and service.

In recent years, Coopers' overall performance measured in terms of sales, profits, and customer satisfaction has declined significantly as aggressive new competitors have entered the retailing industry. Some industry analysts now view Coopers as a retailer whose merchandise mix and service concept are out of touch with its customer base. Other analysts have said Coopers is too slow and conservative to compete in today's volatile and dynamic retailing environment. Finally, customers are becoming increasingly dissatisfied with the unprofessional service they are receiving in Coopers stores by sales associates who are rude and don't know anything about the products they are selling. Despite these warning signs regarding the current state of affairs at Coopers, senior management appears unfazed. Their attitude is that "Coopers is still the number one retailer in the world and it will come back." They have explained away criticism of the company's performance as being attributable to

unforeseen changes in market conditions or to weak economies in some countries in which Coopers does business. The bottom line is that senior management intends to continue to "do business as usual."

3. Use Lewin's change process model to develop an action plan for addressing the key challenges in the situation described.

   Note: Please download the worksheet for completing this exercise from the Web site for this textbook.

4. Answer the following discussion questions.

Discussion Questions

1. What are the key activities and outcomes associated with the three phases of Lewin's change process model?

2. How does your action plan successfully apply Lewin's change process model? Be specific.

3. What kinds of problems or "barriers to success" might you encounter in implementing your action plan? What steps could you take to overcome them?

4. What are the practical implications of this exercise for you as a future manager in a real-world organization?

SKILLS PRACTICE

14-3
Skill Level: **CHALLENGING**

Overcoming Resistance to Change

Skill Objective
To develop skill in effectively managing and overcoming employee resistance to change.

Procedure

1. This exercise can be done individually or in groups of three to five students.

2. Select one of the following scenarios.

Scenario 1: Total Quality Management

Meritron Corporation is a major provider of wireless communication services based in Palo Alto, California. It employs about 2,000 workers at its world headquarters and another 1,200 workers at various regional offices around the United States. Owing to concerns regarding inefficiencies and ineffectiveness (e.g., poor quality) in administrative processes at the corporate office (e.g., customer service, order processing, etc.), senior management

has decided to implement a total quality management (TQM) program. This new initiative will entail implementing fundamentally new ways of thinking and doing things, including (1) a process orientation, (2) identifying and tracking critical measures of success, (3) benchmarking, and (4) the use of data-based decision making.

When senior management sent out a brief memo to employees informing them of the new TQM program, the response was one of skepticism and frustration. Many employees felt this was just another "management fad" that would pass quickly. Others felt TQM was applicable only to manufacturing settings. One employee even commented that he thought TQM was a "Japanese management method" and therefore could not work in a very different culture such as that of the United States.

Scenario 2: Teamwork

TBM Medical Products is a major manufacturer of medical diagnostic equipment used for performing computed axial tomographic (CAT) scans, ultrasounds, and blood analysis. The product development process at the firm involves researchers, engineers, and marketing professionals working independently to develop appropriate technologies and then to design products that use these technologies. This means there tends to be little interaction among the three groups of individuals during the overall product development process.

A recent internal evaluation of the firm's operations revealed that the product development process was inefficient relative to other companies in the industry. Senior management has concluded that transitioning into a "team-based organization" would help enhance the efficiency and effectiveness of the product development process. However, the problem with this was that the researchers, engineers, and marketing people involved in the process were accustomed to working only with others in their area; they did not like the idea of having to work in "cross-functional teams." In addition, the work styles of the researchers, engineers, and marketers all differed from one another in fundamental ways. For example, the concepts of

"customers" and "markets" were critical to marketers, but many engineers and researchers did not focus on them. Moreover, the marketers did not understand the technical aspects of the products as the researchers and engineers did.

3. Develop an action plan for dealing with the employee resistance to change in the scenario you selected. Be sure to base your plan on the strategies for dealing with resistance to change discussed in the chapter.

   Note: Download the worksheet developed for this exercise from the Web site for this textbook.

4. Answer the following discussion questions as a class.

Discussion Questions

1. What were the causes of the resistance to change in your scenario?

2. Which strategies did you propose to use to handle the resistance to change in your scenario? Why do you feel they will be effective?

3. What barriers to success would your action plan face in relation to the scenario? What could you do to overcome them?

4. What are the practical implications of this exercise for you as a future manager?

SKILLS PRACTICE

14-4   *Skill Level:* **BASIC**

Change Analysis: **Hoosiers**

Skill Objective

To develop skill in analyzing change and resistance to change issues as seen in the movie *Hoosiers*.

Procedure

1. Obtain a copy of the movie *Hoosiers* starring Gene Hackman. It is available on VHS and DVD and can be rented or purchased from a local video store or retailer.

2. Watch the movie (in class or at home on your own). Note: Download the worksheet developed for this exercise from the Web site for this book. This will help you record your notes from various scenes in the movie.

   As you watch the film, take notes regarding the forces to change, resistance to change, and strategies for overcoming resistance to change seen throughout the movie. Be sure to document your notes about all relevant scenes on your worksheet.

3. Discuss the following questions as a class.

   a. What were the forces to change that existed in the situation when the new basketball coach took over as leader of the team?

   b. What kinds of resistance to change existed throughout the movie? What was the impact of this resistance on the effectiveness of the basketball team?

   c. What kinds of strategies did the basketball coach use to overcome resistance to change? Were they effective? Why or why not?

   d. What kinds of change issues shown in this movie are similar to the types of issues many people face in real-world business organizations?

   e. What are the practical implications of this exercise for you as a future manager and leader in a real-world organization?

SKILLS PRACTICE

14-5
Skill Level: CHALLENGING

Developing an Organizational Development Program

Skill Objective
To develop skill in designing and implementing organizational development programs.
Procedure
Note: Download the worksheet developed for this exercise from the Web site for this textbook.

1. Select one of the following work scenarios to use for this exercise. You may work in groups of three to five individuals for this exercise if you wish. You should assume you all are organizational development consultants who will be attempting to address the issues in your situation.

Scenario 1: Employee Morale Problems After a Major Reorganization

A manufacturing company has just implemented a major reorganization in order to streamline its processes and to reduce costs. Some divisions have been merged together; others were completely eliminated. Approximately 20 percent of the company's work force was laid off as well. These changes have caused tremendous morale problems for employees. There is a lot of negativity in the work environment, and productivity has declined dramatically. Nobody seems to care much about anything anymore. Management has hired you to come in, to conduct a diagnosis of the organization, and to develop and implement appropriate interventions to enhance the effectiveness of the organization.

Scenario 2: Individualistic Attitudes in a Teamwork-Based Organization

Management at a financial services firm wants to shift the organization from a traditional (hierarchical, bureaucratic) organization to a team-based organization that will foster collaboration between staff in different parts of the organization and result in improved customer service and reduced costs. However, this may not be easy considering that the culture and reward system of the firm have encouraged competition and individual performance over teamwork for decades. Management has hired you to conduct a diagnosis of the organization and to develop and implement an appropriate intervention for encouraging teamwork.

Scenario 3: Toxic Work System

The customer service department at a major airlines is suffering from a "toxic work environment." The 124 customer service representatives are paid low wages; their work is very routine and provides no stimulation. Supervisors are unsupportive and verbally abusive toward employees at times. Customer service representatives regularly report they hate their jobs and they hate dealing with all of the whining and complaining from customers. The nature of this work environment puts everyone in a sour mood most of the time. Recently, the airline received the worst customer service ratings in the industry by a wide margin. This prompted management to hire you to conduct a diagnosis of the customer service unit and to develop and implement an intervention to dramatically improve the service it provides for the airline's customers.

2. Based on the situation you selected here and the discussion of organizational development in this chapter, describe the steps you would take to design and implement an OD program to address the issue(s) in your scenario.

Discussion Questions
1. Evaluate the effectiveness of your OD program. What are its strengths and weaknesses?
2. What are the keys to the effective implementation of your OD program?
3. What are the practical implications of this exercise?

MAINTAINING AND BUILDING SKILLS

CHAPTER 15

Skills Objectives

> To perform a self-evaluation of the management skills acquired in this book.

> To develop a personal management skills mastery plan for the future.

> To apply management skills from a systematic and integrated approach.

KNOWLEDGE OBJECTIVES

> Explain steps involved in planning ongoing skills learning.

> Identify opportunities for management skills learning while still in school.

> Explain how an organization is a marketplace for skills.

> Discuss how reading of popular management books and journals can enhance learning.

> Understand how professional associations, participation in local business and community activities, and networking can facilitate ongoing skill development.

> Describe some approaches to finding stretching assignments at work.

> Identify alternative ways to foster your formal continuing education.

Now that you are nearing completion of this textbook, you may be tempted to believe you can put aside thoughts of developing management skills and move onto other things. Resist the temptation. Management skills require lifelong learning and constant practice. The growing importance and awareness of lifelong skills learning is becoming increasingly clear, as seen in Al Gore's proposal during his 2000 presidential campaign for a tax credit to foster "lifelong learning accounts" for education and training.[1]

This text has used as its foundation a social learning approach, consisting of skills assessment, skills awareness, skills attainment, and skills application. This approach differs from many conventional texts in its strong skills emphasis and from experiential exercise texts in its provision of conceptual underpinnings for skills. The text's strong skills emphasis is consistent with a chorus of calls from business-people, educators, and politicians for greater skills focus in business education. As we have discussed in previous chapters, social learning approaches have been used very successfully in business and other settings. In addition, experimental evidence in classroom settings shows social learning approaches to be superior to experiential education that emphasizes applying skills before learning about their conceptual foundations.[2]

We have used the social learning process to help you develop an array of important management skills. To be successful in the workplace, you will both have to apply those skills properly and continually update your skills portfolio. To facilitate that process, we use this chapter to encourage you to look ahead toward your career and its associated opportunities and demands. We begin with a discussion of planning for ongoing skills learning, offer tips for how you can continue to develop management skills while still in school, and encourage you to think of organizations as skills marketplaces and incubators. We then provide some guidelines for continued reading for ongoing skills development and give you suggestions for participating in professional associations and networks. We conclude with advice for seeking stretching assignments at work, making use of Web resources, and exploring continuing education options.

PLAN FOR ONGOING SKILLS LEARNING

When asked about his presidential ambitions, former New York governor Mario Cuomo once said, "I have no plans, and no plans to plan." If you are going to build a strong and sustaining management skills portfolio, you will need to plan, and to plan to plan on an ongoing basis.

MAP AND TRACK YOUR SKILLS PORTFOLIO

Your skills portfolio will be critical to your career. Be aware of what is in the portfolio and what is needed. On a regular basis, stop and conduct a self-assessment of your management skills. As a starter, complete Self-Assessment 15-1; download the worksheet for this exercise from the text Web site. Then go back and redo the Self-Assessment Exercises in previous chapters to see whether your before and after scores differ and to pinpoint those areas that need more work. Maintain a written record of your skill development activities and of skills in which you are proficient. When writing or updating your résumé, be sure to highlight your skill proficiencies.

Skills Portfolio

Answer each of the questions in this section using the following scale:

1 Disagree strongly
2 Disagree somewhat
3 Neither agree nor disagree
4 Agree somewhat
5 Agree strongly

I have a good basic mastery of the following skills:

____ 1. Active listening
____ 2. Time management
____ 3. Developing an action plan
____ 4. Self-management
____ 5. Developing a strategic plan
____ 6. Using tools for creativity enhancement
____ 7. Setting goals
____ 8. Developing a power base
____ 9. Applying the general problem-solving process
____ 10. Managing informal communication
____ 11. Empowering employees
____ 12. Managing undesired employee behaviors
____ 13. Assessing organizational culture
____ 14. Designing and implementing employee attitude surveys
____ 15. Handling ethical dilemmas
____ 16. Applying job design principles to enhance employee motivation
____ 17. Personal stress management
____ 18. Effective speaking
____ 19. Using transformational leader behaviors
____ 20. Becoming an effective mentor
____ 21 Reducing political activity
____ 22. Conflict management
____ 23. Managing change
____ 24. Evaluating a team process
____ 25. Developing a mission statement
____ 26. Assessing employee job satisfaction
____ 27. Sensitivity to cross-cultural differences
____ 28. Applying the balanced scorecard
____ 29. Understanding and managing nonverbal communications
____ 30. Conducting a job interview
____ 31. Conducting a performance appraisal
____ 32. Critical thinking
____ 33. Facilitating effective team meetings
____ 34. Diagnosing team functioning
____ 35. Applying impression management techniques

DEVELOP A SKILLS ACTION PLAN

Develop a plan for maintaining and reinforcing your current skills and for developing new skills. In developing your plan, recognize that you have to be aiming at a moving target. In an interview, one young woman was asked what she thought she would be doing in 20 years. She replied, "That job hasn't been invented yet."[3] Hockey great Wayne Gretzky is credited with explaining his success by saying, "I skate to where the puck is going, not to where it is."[4] Similarly, Margaret Schweer, director of human resources for information systems at Kraft Foods, says of training programs that "It's not just giving people skills for where they are now but for where they're going."[5] You will need to learn the skills "where the puck is going." Fortunately, the puck appears to be going in generally predictable directions, although with increasing speed. For example, demands for interpersonal skills, problem-solving skills, and communication skills will almost certainly become even more important in future decades. Nevertheless, be alert to new developments in your company, industry, or society in general that may place value on new, perhaps now unimaginable, skills and perspectives.

IDENTIFY ROLE MODELS

One good way to recognize desirable skills and behaviors is to identify role models whose skills you would like to emulate.[6] A role model could be anyone whose behaviors and accomplishments you've admired, such as a boss, a famous executive, someone from an annual listing of best managers, a teacher, or a parent. Once you've decided you want to "be like Mike" or like Steve, or Fiorina, or Jack, focus on the behaviors of the role model. Recall from our discussions of social learning in previous chapters that when modeling others, you do not want to simply mimic them; rather, you want to learn *from* them. They may be in different contexts, have different backgrounds, be attending to different goals, and so on. Your task is to develop skills based on their examples and to apply those skills in the ways that are required in your unique situation.

USE SELF-MANAGEMENT FOR SKILL LEARNING

Once you have identified skills you would like to develop or maintain, apply the self-management principles you learned in Chapter 4. That is, treat each skill as a behavior to be changed or reinforced. Pinpoint the specific behavior, set specific goals for behavior change, and set up a system of rewards to reinforce skill learning. Monitor the behavior systematically to track your progress, and develop contingency plans in case your initial attempts at skill learning or maintenance are unsuccessful.

PRACTICE, PRACTICE, PRACTICE

There is an old joke about a person who gets into a cab in New York City and asks the driver, "Do you know how to get to Carnegie Hall?" The driver's reply of "Practice, practice, practice" also provides the directions to mastering a job, moving toward the executive suite, or having a fulfilling career. Use every chance you get to practice your management skills.

COORDINATE YOUR SKILLS

We have talked about skills as being in a portfolio or tool kit. As with any tools, you must both learn how to use them and then use them together in proper ways. Resist the temptation to simply apply a new skill to every problem you find: It has been said that "If all you have is a hammer, everything looks like a nail." Just as each construction job requires a specific combination of tools, often used in a particular order and in concert with one another, organizational tasks require a proper balance and combination of skills. So take advantage of opportunities for learning, practicing, and using management skills that require you to employ them together. Skills Practice 15-1 is an in-class exercise that will give you the opportunity to immerse yourself in a fun and hands-on activity that requires the use of a variety of management skills.

SEEK OUT LEARNING OPPORTUNITIES WHILE IN SCHOOL

Although much of your ongoing skill learning will take place once you've entered a work environment, many good opportunities to acquire management skills are also available while you are still in school. Here are some options to consider:

INTERNSHIPS[7]

Most business schools have internship opportunities to give students the chance to experience realistic business environments. According to the National Society for Internships and Experiential Education, an internship is "any carefully monitored work or service experience in which an individual has intentional learning goals and reflects actively on what he or she is learning throughout the experience."[8] Participants in internships receive hands-on training while contributing real productive work to the organization. Often, the internship serves as a trying-out period in which companies and individuals see whether they fit one another before making a longer term commitment. Some internships now provide competitive salaries and benefits.[9]

INDEPENDENT STUDIES

Many colleges and universities offer students the opportunity to take independent studies. These typically permit students to earn credits for working one to one with a faculty member to explore an interesting issue. If, for example, you want to learn more about team building or conflict management, you might approach a faculty member who has an interest in one of those areas. Requirements for the independent study will vary but generally are tailored to fit a student's particular needs and interests.

STUDENT ORGANIZATIONS

Student organizations provide the opportunity to participate in many management-related activities, develop management skills, and adopt leadership roles. Two such organizations are Sigma Iota Epsilon and AIESEC. Sigma Iota Epsilon is both an honorary and a professional management society. Its goals are to stimulate interest and achievement in the field of management, to stimulate scholarship in management, and to gain recognition of the contribution and value of scholastic achievement in the management discipline. For more information, visit http://sienational.colostate.edu/.

The world's largest student organization, AIESEC is a global network of 50,000 members across more than 83 countries and territories at more than 800 universities worldwide.[10] AIESEC's primary activity is facilitating work-abroad exchange programs between its member countries. AIESEC in the United States sends students from the United States to work abroad and receives students from around the world to work for companies in the United States. For more information, visit http://www.aiesec.org/.

TEAM PROJECTS

In the Voice of Experience feature, the members of a high performance student team that completed a semester-long class project talk about what they learned about managing teams.

Skills Practice 15-2 is actually a project that gives you an opportunity to step out into the real world and examine how many of the issues related to management exist in actual organizations. This will require some extra work on your part, but it will definitely be worth it when you see how many management concepts and

VOICE OF EXPERIENCE

WHAT WE LEARNED ABOUT WORKING IN TEAMS!

Team Quint Eastwood (+1), A High-Performing Student Team: Matt Berres, Justin Farr, Kristi Eastwood, Chris Domach, Rob Pesch, Kate Peterson

1. **What steps did you take to develop the skills necessary to become an effective team?**

   Probably the most important element of our team's success was open communication. Everyone listened to each other and valued each other's input. From the start, we set goals and deadlines. We made sure the workload was evenly distributed to all members. Another key element of our team's success was positive feedback and reinforcement, which made members want to do their best.

2. **What are the biggest challenges you experienced in working on your team project? What did**

you do to overcome these challenges?

   The biggest challenge was trying to work around our busy schedules. With six people in our group, it sometimes seemed impossible to agree on a time to meet. We overcame this challenge by communicating frequently. Group e-mails were sent out to make sure everyone could meet at a certain time and place. Flexibility also played a large role in helping our team overcome this problem. When a group meeting was cancelled or postponed, we all were willing to work around it and adjust our schedules accordingly. Another problem our team experienced was feeling like the project would never end, that it was just too much work. We were able to overcome this problem by setting short-term goals to make the project seem a little bit more manageable. We also supported each other every step of the way,

which definitely helped when we couldn't see the light at the end of the tunnel.

3. **What has been the most rewarding part about working on a semester-long team project?**

   Our team worked long hours to make sure the finished project was the best it could be. Knowing we all helped produce such a quality product and feeling like all the hard work paid off was definitely very rewarding. It was also great getting to know people who share the same goals.

4. **What advice would you give students who say managing a team is easy?**

   Managing a team *is not easy!* Finding times to meet and learning to work with people who have different personalities and work habits can be very challenging. The key is to respect each other and stay positive every step of the way.

issues discussed earlier in this book come to life. In addition, completing this project will help you develop self-management skills (and teamwork skills, if you do this project with another student).

VIEW ORGANIZATIONS AS MARKETPLACES FOR—AND INCUBATORS OF—SKILLS

In seeking a job, be sure to gather information on which skills are especially valued in the firms you consider and what the firm does to help employees develop and reinforce the skills; the answers will give you valuable insights about your fit to the firms and may also speak volumes about the firms' cultures. Some firms may value certain skills because of their unique cultures, histories, and environments. If your skills are similar to those valued, you are likely to achieve *supplementary fit*. That is, your skills will match those already prevalent in the firm. Alternatively, firms may be seeking particular skills because they are now lacking in the firm, perhaps because of a new strategic direction. In such cases, you may achieve *complementary fit*; your skills, although different from those currently found in the firm, are now needed and valued. You may be especially valuable in such situations, although you may be viewed by others, at least initially, as "different."

You can sometimes glean information about valued skills from job interviews, observation, and reading articles about firms. As an example of the latter, much has been written about how Southwest Airlines values employees who have the skills and attitudes needed to fit well into its environment of fun. In addition, some firms may make their skills preferences and requirements explicit, such as through tests given during selection or after hiring. At Sears, Roebuck & Co., for example, new employees are tested not just on technical skills but on such specific soft skills as the abilities to manage projects, work with people outside the firm (e.g., vendors), build teams, and lead others.[11]

Some firms, such as AT&T, British Airways, BP, Siemens, and The World Bank, even have "ideal profiles" of skills for future executives.[12] For example, Siemens has defined 22 desirable management characteristics under 5 basic competencies of understanding, drive, trust, social competence, and what it terms a "sixth sense." PepsiCo's desired competency profile has 18 key dimensions defining how individuals see the world, think, and act. Such firms typically use systematic training and development programs to develop managers in ways that fit the ideal profiles. Many companies now recognize as well that strong skills training programs do more than just develop employees; in an age when skills portfolios are the key to career success, strong company training programs are an important tool for recruiting and retaining employees.[13] In the Voice of Experience feature, Brenda Schauf discusses management skills needed to succeed in the real world.

READ WIDELY AND BUILD A MANAGEMENT SKILLS LIBRARY

The amount of material we have asked you to digest in this book may seem daunting. The thought of doing even more extensive reading on an ongoing basis may appear overwhelming. Here's the good news to keep in mind: Life is an open-

VOICE OF EXPERIENCE

MANAGEMENT SKILLS NEEDED IN THE REAL WORLD

Brenda Schauf, Assistant Store Manager and Human Resources Manager, Marshall Field's

1. What do you see as the key management challenges you face in your job?

Offering prospective and current team members a positive work experience has been a significant challenge in recent years. We need to find ways to make our team members' work experience enjoyable so they will want to remain employed with us. Part of the reason for this concern is increasing competition in the retail industry and challenges associated with finding qualified workers who have the skills needed to provide high-quality service to our customers.

Another significant challenge is how to create a work environment that is performance driven. We need to continue to find ways to provide better service to our customers. So the bottom line here is a paradox: How do we make work more enjoyable for our team members and at the same time ask them to work harder?

2. What kinds of strategies are you implementing in addressing these challenges?

We make sure we provide top-notch training for all of our team members. This is critical so they feel they possess the knowledge and skills needed to be successful in their jobs. New employees also buddy up with a team trainer who helps them learn the ropes associated with their new jobs. Managers of new employees make sure they maintain regular interaction with employees during their first 90 days of employment. This involves coaching, providing feedback, and clarifying performance expectations with employees.

In the recruiting and selection process, we try to provide job candidates with a realistic job preview so there are no surprises later. If we oversell a job in order to hire a given employee, we will probably just lose that person later when he or she realizes the job is not consistent with his or her expectations (i.e., not as good as he or she thought it would be).

We spend a lot of time on employee recognition. We have tried some creative and fun types of events, such as employee luncheons, treats, and morning rallies before the store opens. The rallies are especially interesting in that we try to communicate a point about customer service to our employees by presenting skits based on game shows, such as *Who Wants to Be a Millionaire?* or the *Price Is Right*. Our team members have responded very favorably to these kinds of events.

3. What do you feel are the most critical management skills needed for success in today's business environment?

I would have to say being responsive and managing change are the most critical skills. We have a saying around here that "speed is life." To us, this reflects the importance of adapting to a changing business environment (e.g., technological, customer, economic) as a critical skill for success.

Leadership is still a critical skill as well. Managers absolutely must have the ability to provide a vision and to get their team to respond effectively to their directives.

4. What advice would you give to college students regarding their preparation for a job as a supervisor or manager in an organization?

I would strongly recommend getting some experience running or leading something while you are still in school. Becoming a leader or running a committee in a student organization really helps develop exactly the kinds of leadership skills we look for in the retailing industry. I'm sure many other employers feel the same way.

If you are able to become a supervisor in a restaurant or become a resident adviser in a dormitory, these are other fantastic ways to develop leadership skills. The key here is that even though the context is different in the business world, the management skills you acquire from your college learning experiences transfer very well to a wide variety of real-world management jobs.

5. What advice would you give to students who obtain nonmanagerial jobs immediately after graduation but want to be promoted to a managerial position in the future?

Be prepared to work your way up in an organization. If you are interested in getting promoted to a management position, be sure to make it known to your boss and others in your organization. Don't expect them to be able to read your mind! Work to develop relationships with people in your organization who can help you achieve your career goals. Ask to take on additional responsibilities that go beyond your regular job duties and responsibilities. Volunteer to take on new projects. This

VOICE OF EXPERIENCE (continued)

will give you an opportunity to show what you can do and to develop the right kinds of skills needed for advancement to a management position.

6. **What advice would you give to students who are first-time managers in real-world business organizations regarding the key things they should do to be successful?**

Again, be sure to work on establishing strong working relationships with others in your organization. Recognize that you do not know everything—take the time to learn the ropes. Be sensitive to how people with more experience may perceive you. Don't act like you know everything. Finally, be open to honest feedback, both positive and nega-

tive. This is what you will need in order to improve your performance as a manager and ultimately to grow as a business professional.

http://www.marshallfields
.com/

book test. If you're aware of concepts and information sources and know how to access them, memorization usually isn't necessary.

READ POPULAR MANAGEMENT BOOKS

Such books as *In Search of Excellence* and *Theory Z* helped spawn a remarkable number of tomes offering practical advice to managers. The popularity of such books is evidenced by their regular appearance on the *New York Times* bestseller list. The books may focus on a particular topic, such as organizational culture or reward systems; may provide guidance for specific career issues, such as entering a management position or making career moves; or may offer the philosophies and perspectives of particular executives, consultants, or business professors. Some of these books provide excellent advice, and we have quoted from, or otherwise referenced, many of them in this text. We encourage you to sample broadly from such sources. You will learn about particular firms and individuals and may see how popular management tools are being applied.

In reading such books, though, maintain a critical eye. For instance, recognize that issues are complex, and question such flat statements as "change is good" or "money doesn't motivate." Be skeptical as well of argument by assertion, where the author simply states something to be the case with no support other than his or her personal authority. Also, be cautious when an author relies heavily on argument by anecdote, using supporting examples instead of logically convincing arguments or data. The fact that a particular characteristic or practice is seen in successful firms doesn't necessarily mean it caused that success. The characteristic or practice may, for instance, be just as common—or even more common—in unsuccessful firms. To really learn anything about whether something is important to success, it would be necessary to consider successful and unsuccessful firms with and without the characteristic or practice. Unfortunately, anecdotes are powerful; we tend to believe a specific example more than statistics. As such, be especially alert to the seduction of anecdotes.

READ PRACTITIONER-ORIENTED MANAGEMENT JOURNALS

We have drawn from many sources in developing this text, including many practitioner-oriented journals. For example, we have regularly used examples and information from such sources as *Across the Board, Business Week, Chief Executive, Executive Excellence, Forbes, Fortune, HR Focus, HRMagazine, INC., Incentive, Industry Week, Personnel Journal, Quality, Supervision, Supervisory Management, Management Review, Management Today, Training, Training & Development,* and *Workforce.* Other journals from which we've cited, such as *Black Enterprise* and *Working Woman,* are aimed at specific audiences. Still others, such as *Business Europe, Business Mexico,* and *China Business Review,* focus on particular geographic areas. These are all worthwhile outlets; when you get a chance, go to a library or bookstore and look through some of the issues to see which journals best fit your interests and style preferences.

The following journals are noteworthy in their efforts to bring recent research and theory to practitioner audiences. As such, they are in a sense hybrids between scholarly journals that report research and theory primarily aimed at academics and more popular press management magazines. If you are really interested in keeping up on the latest developments in management, we encourage you to consider them.

> *Academy of Management Executive (AME).* A publication of the Academy of Management, *AME* aims to provide practicing executives with relevant management tools and information based on recent advances in management theory and research. *AME* directly supports the Academy of Management's main objectives, which are to foster the general advancement of research, learning, teaching, and practice in the management field and to encourage the extension and unification of management knowledge. See http://www.aom.pace.edu/ame/.

> *California Management Review (CMR).* *CMR* serves as a vehicle of communication between those who study management and those who practice it. *CMR* publishes articles that are both research based and address issues of current concern to managers. The journal emphasizes three areas of critical importance to both practicing managers and academic researchers: strategy and organization, global competition and competitiveness, and business and public policy. See http://www.haas.berkeley.edu/News/cmr/.

> *Harvard Business Review (HBR).* The goal of *HBR* is to be the source of the best new ideas for people who are creating, leading, and transforming business. Features in *HBR* help business leaders establish an intellectual agenda for discussion—and change—within their companies. They give firsthand insight into how companies operate and how senior-level managers respond to demanding workplace challenges, describe best practices and hands-on management techniques, report on cutting-edge research and its application in real organizations, and draw on the experiences of executives, consultants, and other experts. See http://www.hbsp.harvard.edu/products/hbr/index.html.

> *Journal of Management Inquiry (JMI).* *JMI* publishes the latest research and practice written by today's top management scholars and professionals from a wide variety of areas within the management and organization field.

Sponsored by the Western Academy of Management, *JMI* seeks to provide an outlet for creative, frame-challenging work. See http://www.sagepub.com/journal.aspx?pid=172.

> **Organizational Dynamics**. The domain of *Organizational Dynamics* is organizational behavior and development, human resource management, and strategic management. The journal's objective is to link leading-edge thought and research with management practice. *Organizational Dynamics* publishes articles that embody both theoretical and practical content, showing how research findings can help deal more effectively with the dynamics of organizational life. See http://www.elsevier.nl/locate/issn/00902616.

> **Sloan Management Review**. *Sloan Management Review* bridges the gap between management research and practice, evaluating and reporting on new research to help readers identify and understand significant trends in management. Published by the MIT Sloan School of Management, the journal covers all management disciplines, although its particular emphasis is on corporate strategy, leadership, and management of technology and innovation. See http://Mitsloan.mit.edu/smr/index.html.

You may read an article or book and want to know more about its topic. One good way to do this is simply to go straight to the source and contact the author. Authors are generally very pleased to learn of interest in their work and to share information. Many articles provide contact information for authors, often including e-mail addresses. To find e-mail addresses and other information for authors, you can often locate their web sites through a simple Internet search. Alternatively, many professional associations, including some of those listed in the following pages, have searchable membership pages. For instance, the Academy of Management Member Search page is located at http://apps.aomonline.org/MemberDirectory/main.asp. You can access that page to get contact information for the more than 13,000 members of the Academy of Management.

READ BROADLY

We don't mean to imply you should restrict your reading to management books and journals. To the contrary, we encourage you to read broadly, whether Shakespeare, Steinbeck, Sartre, or Spillane. In doing so, though, keep some part of your mind open to skills learning opportunities. One of the many rewards of reading is the insights that literature reveals about the varieties, causes, and consequences of human behavior (i.e., about the stuff of management).

Now see what you can do with the management knowledge and skills you have developed from reading this book. Skills Practice 15-3 gives you a chance to analyze a real-world organization of interest to you. Complete the exercise and then evaluate your analysis and recommendations.

PARTICIPATE IN PROFESSIONAL ASSOCIATIONS, LOCAL ACTIVITIES, AND NETWORKS

Professional associations and networking offer a wealth of opportunities for ongoing skills development. In this section, we discuss some primary professional associations you might want to explore, suggest ways to get involved in business and community activities, and provide some guidelines for developing and using physical and virtual networks.

GET INVOLVED IN PROFESSIONAL ASSOCIATIONS

Many prominent professional associations deal with management and related areas. Participation in these organizations provides contacts, information about new developments, opportunities for interaction at meetings and events, and, in some cases, the chance to adopt leadership roles. We encourage you to think about membership in one or more of the following professional associations. By visiting the associations' Web pages, you will get a better sense of what they offer (including many benefits for nonmembers). In some cases, there are also local and regional branches of the professional associations. Some of the associations offer special student memberships at reduced rates. In addition to these organizations, consider joining associations, such as Toastmasters, that focus on developing specific skills.

> **Academy of Management.** With more than 13,000 members in 90 countries, the Academy of Management is a professional society composed of professors who conduct research and teach management in colleges, universities, or research institutions and of doctoral students who are pursuing degrees in management. Members also include management consultants and managers from a variety of business settings. The purpose of the Academy of Management is to foster the general advancement of research, learning, teaching, and practice in the management field. The academy publishes scholarly papers, conducts forums for the exchange of knowledge, and provides services that enhance the science and practice of management. See http://www.aom.pace.edu/.

> **American Management Association (AMA).** AMA is the world's leading membership-based management development organization. More than 700,000 customers and members each year in the Americas, Europe, and Asia learn business skills and best management practices through seminars, conferences, and special events; e-learning and self-study courses; customized corporate and government services; and publications. See http://www.amanet.org/index.htm.

> **American Psychological Association (APA).** APA is the largest scientific and professional organization representing psychology in the United States. With more than 159,000 members, APA is also the largest association of psychologists worldwide. APA works to advance psychology as a science, a profession, and a means of promoting human welfare. See http://www.apa.org/.

> **American Psychological Society (APS).** To better aid and support its members, APS offers a wide range of benefits designed to meet the specific needs of scientific psychologists. There is an APS Student Caucus for student members. See http://www.psychologicalscience.org/.

> **American Society for Training and Development (ASTD).** ASTD is the world's premier professional association and leading resource on workplace learning and performance issues. ASTD's membership includes more than 70,000 people working in the field of workplace performance in 100 countries worldwide. Its leadership and members work in more than 15,000 multina-

tional corporations, small- and medium-sized businesses, government agencies, colleges, and universities. See http://www.astd.org/.

> **Society for Industrial and Organizational Psychology (SIOP).** SIOP is a division within the American Psychological Association that is also an organizational affiliate of the American Psychological Society. The society's goal is to promote human welfare through the various applications of psychology to all types of organizations providing goods and services, such as manufacturing concerns, commercial enterprises, labor unions or trade associations, and public agencies. See http://www.siop.org/.

> **Society for Human Resource Management (SHRM).** SHRM is the world's largest human resource management association. SHRM provides education and information services; conferences and seminars; government and media representation; online services; and publications to more than 145,000 professional and student members throughout the world. See http://www.shrm.org/.

> **WorldatWork.** WorldatWork, formerly the American Compensation Association and Canadian Compensation Association, is a 48-year-old global not-for-profit professional association dedicated to knowledge leadership in disciplines associated with attracting, retaining, and motivating employees. More than 25,000 human resources professionals, consultants, educators, and others are members of the association. WorldatWork emphasizes total rewards, specifically focusing on compensation and benefits and on other components of the work experience, such as work/life balance, recognition, culture, professional development, and work environment issues. In addition to membership, WorldatWork offers certification and education programs, online information resources, publications, conferences, research, and networking opportunities. See http://www.worldatwork.org/.

PARTICIPATE IN LOCAL BUSINESS AND COMMUNITY ACTIVITIES[14]

Participation in local business and community activities offers many opportunities for skills development and practice, for developing professional contacts, and for personal satisfaction. In addition, many firms now include community service components in their performance appraisals. Here are five volunteer opportunities to explore:

> **Rotary International.** Rotary is an association of business and professional leaders who are united worldwide and provide humanitarian service, encourage high ethical standards in all vocations, and seek to help build world peace and goodwill. There are more than 29,000 Rotary clubs in 161 countries, with a total of 1.2 million members. See http://www.rotary.org/.

> **Chamber of Commerce.** The U.S. Chamber of Commerce is the world's largest not-for-profit business federation, representing 3 million businesses, 3,000 state and local chambers, 830 business associations, and 87 American chambers of commerce abroad. Managers interested in community service might offer to represent their companies at chamber meetings and perhaps take a leadership position on a working committee in the chamber.[15] See http://www.uschamber.org/default.htm.

> **Junior Achievement (JA).** JA's mission is to ensure that children have an understanding of the free enterprise system. With the help of approximately 150,000 volunteers nationwide, JA currently reaches nearly 4 million students across America through programs in grades from kindergarten through high school. The American Management Association and JA have formed a partnership to promote volunteerism and lifelong learning. In appreciation for volunteer efforts, JA will give its volunteers a complimentary membership in the AMA. See http://www.ja.org/.

> **Big Brothers/Big Sisters.** Big Brothers/Big Sisters of America is the nation's largest youth-mentoring organization. Programs match kids with mentors who provide meaningful friendship and share fun experiences. See http://www.bbbsa.org/.

> **Ronald McDonald Houses.** Ronald McDonald Houses provide a "home-away-from-home" for the families of seriously ill children receiving treatment at nearby hospitals. There are now 206 Ronald McDonald Houses in 19 countries. The houses are supported by nearly 25,000 volunteers, who donate 1 million hours annually. See http://www.rmhc.com/.

Many other organizations and opportunities will be specific to your city, state, or region. In addition, newspapers and other news media often issue calls for volunteers to help with various activities. Managers can also contribute by serving on the board of trustees of schools or on advisory boards of colleges.[16]

DEVELOP AND MAINTAIN NETWORKS

As we discussed in the context of careers, networking can be critical to success and personal fulfillment. However, networking is about much more than amassing a set of names of people who can be called if you're looking for work. Networks may help with job contacts, but they serve many other important roles, particularly for skill development. Networks may be physical (made up of people with whom you physically interact from time to time), or virtual (consisting of members linked electronically).[17]

Physical Networks. Physical networks offer many advantages, such as the opportunity for personal face-to-face interaction and social support. To develop such networks, start by keeping up with former classmates and coworkers. Attend local association chapter meetings and seminars.[18] Consider joining a management reading club.[19] Check to see whether there are local networking groups that fit your needs and interests.

Virtual Networks. Virtual networks offer the benefits of ease and immediacy of access and broad membership. You may decide to join one or more formal virtual networks. In addition, you may want to develop your own, more specialized virtual networks.

A ready-made form of virtual network is the electronic mailing list. Typically, for example, professional associations maintain listservers for member interaction. Sign on to several of these lists (we discuss some on the text Web site) and see which best fit your needs and interests. You are likely to learn a lot by simply lurking on these lists (i.e., by passively reading comments exchanged among list members). However, we encourage you to take full advantage of these resources by actively seeking out information. List members tend to be glad—even eager—to provide information. Such specific questions as "Can anyone tell me about their experiences with applying team-based rewards?" or "What are some pros and cons of using formal suggestion systems?" or "Can anyone recommend a good recent article on nonverbal communications?" are likely to generate many responses.

In addition to such formal electronic networks, you may want to develop virtual networks of your own. For example, Webgrrls was founded by Aliza Sherman. Sherman wanted to network with other women, located the personal Web pages of women around the world, and started e-mailing them on a regular basis.

Some Guidelines for Developing Networks. If you're thinking of developing a network, whether physical or virtual, treat the process much like a team-building exercise. For instance, include members with important skills, perspectives, and contacts. Work to build diversity of all kinds into the network. Especially with virtual networks, incorporate members from varying cultures. Update the network over time to ensure it is viable and responsive to emerging needs. As the network founder, you have the chance, if you wish, to maintain a central network position and thus to take on leadership roles. And, whether you're founding a network or a network member, be sure to contribute your skills, time, and insights to other members. View the networks as a place to give as well as to get.

EXPLORE STRETCHING ASSIGNMENTS

Once in a company, find ways to stretch so as to learn, test, and apply new skills. Set difficult goals for yourself and don't stay in one position so long that you're no longer learning. Try to work outside your job description and seek varied assignments.

WORK OUTSIDE YOUR JOB DESCRIPTION

Your job description defines the required scope of your work activities, but it is not meant as a cage. As discussed in previous chapters, such extra-role behaviors as organizational citizenship behaviors are increasingly important in organizations. Although such behaviors go beyond the formal requirements of the job, they are often crucial to organizational performance and member satisfaction, and they are likely to be viewed favorably. As such, find ways to take on additional responsibilities. Search for new learning opportunities at work and look for projects that would be enjoyable and provide valuable information.[20] Make sure your boss and others are aware of your interest in learning and be proactive in pursuing skill-enhancing opportunities.[21]

SEEK VARIED ASSIGNMENTS[22]

Remember from our discussion of careers that organizational mobility can take many forms, not just vertical but radial and circumferential. Moves at the same level in an organization can yield fresh perspectives, new insights into how the firm functions, heightened visibility, and skill-learning opportunities. For these reasons, many firms groom their future leaders by systematically moving them between jobs to acquire needed competencies, often in different departments, locations, and even countries. As such, explore options for job rotation, especially to positions that offer the potential to add skills to your portfolio. Depending on your personal circumstances and the nature of your organization, global assignments may provide especially rich learning opportunities.

MAKE USE OF THE RESOURCES OF THE WORLD WIDE WEB

We hope the text's Exercises and other Web links and the Web-Wise boxes on the text Web site have encouraged you to make greater use of the Web as a learning resource. Continue experimenting with the Web's potential. As a first step, you may want to take the time to go back and try Web exercises in this book that you haven't had an opportunity to complete. Beyond that, explore management-related professional associations, journals, and other resources as discussed in this chapter. Using search engines (we like Google, although your preferences may vary), try some searches on specific management topics. Beyond that, if you have access through your school or business to such journal databases as ABI/Inform and Proquest, practice with them. Using such databases, you can search for information about specific topics, companies, or individuals or about some combination (such as leadership at GE). These databases include most management-oriented journals and often provide full articles rather than just abstracts.

EXPLORE CONTINUING EDUCATION OPTIONS

An important part of your lifelong learning will be formal continuing education. Fortunately, the opportunities for continuing education have exploded in number and form. For example, while pursuing advanced degrees once required difficult trade-offs, such as the need to take months or years off from work, colleges and universities have become more flexible in their offerings. Many, for example, offer full evening MBA programs or weekend programs, sometimes in the form of executive MBA programs for more experienced managers. In addition, about 2 million students worldwide are enrolled in distance education courses from providers in the United States and Canada.[23] An estimated 80 percent of U.S. colleges and universities were offering online classes in 2001. Online learning is flexible and accessible, removing barriers of time and distance.

Along with universities that offer continuing education offerings, companies are taking a much more active role in determining their employees' learning needs and in finding or developing appropriate educational options. Some firms now have full learning centers. Others have started full corporate universities.[24] There were 1,600 corporate universities by 2000, and the number is projected to grow to 37,000 by 2010—exceeding the number of traditional universities. Corporate universities such as the Disney Institute, Saturn Consulting Services, the Xerox Center, the RCA Campus, and Holiday Inn University provide a diverse set of educational programs for their own employees, and they often open their doors to employees of other firms. Companies believe that by operating their own corporate universities they can tailor offerings to the specific needs of their work forces, ensure continued skill development, and enhance employee loyalty.

We have certainly covered a lot of material in this book. To increase the likelihood that the knowledge and skills you have acquired are applied in the future, complete your last exercise, Skills Practice 15-4, now. This activity is especially important because it focuses on having you assess how much progress you have made in developing important management skills and what you can do in the future to develop these skills further as part of your overall professional development.

One of the key objectives of this chapter was to encourage you to think about the big picture in relation to all the management knowledge and skills you have acquired since you began this journey back in Chapter 1. Given this, the final Top Ten List draws from the entire book in providing a list of critical points about management we hope you will remember (and ideally you will act on!) in your future careers. We hope you have enjoyed your management skills learning journey with us. We wish you all success with your careers as future leaders and managers!

TOP TEN LIST: KEY POINTS TO REMEMBER

MAINTAINING AND BUILDING SKILLS

10. Learn the business strategy, culture, rules for success, and industry associated with the organization where you are employed.

9. Develop a clear sense of your objectives as a manager, the specific actions you will take to achieve those objectives, and how you will measure your effectiveness and that of your employees and overall work unit.

8. Understand differences (e.g., perceptions, personality, decision-making style) among those with whom you work and to whom you report. Use this information as a basis for adapting your management style to the situation.

7. Actively manage communication with your employees to keep them on the same page (i.e., encourage mutual understanding) and in the loop (i.e., up to date) on issues that affect them.

6. Use a systematic and data-driven process that incorporates the input of relevant players (e.g., employees, customers) to identify and implement the best possible alternatives given time and resource constraints.

5. There is no single best way to lead others: Understand the needs of the situation first and then match the appropriate leadership style to that situation.

4. Achieve and sustain employee motivation by clarifying your performance standards, providing support (e.g., training, feedback, guidance) to employees in achieving those standards, and appropriately rewarding employees for meeting these standards successfully using a combination of valued financial and nonfinancial rewards.

3. Establish and maintain your credibility and authority as the leader of a team by building and using appropriate personal bases of power (i.e., traits, knowledge, and skills you possess) and position bases of power (i.e., resources that come with your management title and job) to influence your employees in supporting the implementation of desired work behaviors.

2. Great teams must be created. Manage your team actively by establishing effective working relationships, building a team structure and supporting process, and ensuring the ongoing growth and development of each member of the team and the team as a whole.

1. You need more than common sense to become a great manager. Translate what you know about good management into actual management practice.

QUESTIONS FOR REVIEW AND REFLECTION

REVIEW QUESTIONS

1. What are the primary steps in planning for ongoing skills learning?
2. Identify at least four ways you can develop management skills while still in school.
3. In what sense are organizations marketplaces for skills?
4. What are the benefits of reading popular management books? What are some related cautions?
5. Identify six journals that attempt to bring recent management theory and research to practitioner audiences.
6. What are eight major professional associations that might facilitate lifelong learning of management skills?
7. Discuss five community organizations in which you might participate to foster networking and skills practice and development.
8. Discuss physical and virtual networks, and provide guidelines for developing networks.
9. Identify four ways to stretch at work so as to learn new skills.
10. How can the Internet be used to enhance ongoing management skills development?
11. Discuss continuing education options for ongoing management skills development.

CRITICAL THINKING QUESTIONS

1. Do you think management skills learned in school activities (e.g., team projects) can transfer to the real world? Why or why not?

2. Which of the management skills that you have learned will be most important in your future career? Why? Do you think the same skill will also be most important for life in general?

3. Some virtual networking groups, such as the Webgrrls network discussed in a Web-Wise on the text Web site, are aimed at the interests and needs of specific types of people (e.g., women, gays and lesbians, older workers, and so on). What are the advantages of such specialized networking groups? What do you see as potential disadvantages?

4. In today's turbulent business environment, do you think it is possible to "skate to where the puck is going"? What might be some difficulties in doing this? In answering this question, try to expand on the puck metaphor. For example, what if the ice itself is melting? What if someone changes the rules of the game?

5. In general, do you think physical or virtual networks are more important to your ongoing success and learning? Why?

6. Stretch your imagination to think of three radical changes that might occur in the workplace in the next two decades. Discuss the implications of those changes for the nature of needed management skills.

EXPERIENTIAL EXERCISES

WEB EXERCISE 15-1

Use an Internet search engine, such as Excite or Google, to conduct a search for "Management Skills." You'll find many links to related topics (a recent Google search yielded 1,260,000 "hits" for "Management Skills"!), so you may want to limit your search further by adding such terms as "exercises," "examples," "readings," or "assessment." Some of the sites will be commercial; others will be associated with universities, professional associations, governmental agencies, journals, and so on. Some sites will offer skill-specific information, such as "change management skills," "project management skills," "career management skills," or "time management skills," and others will be broader. *Select two noncommercial sites.* For each site, complete the following activities:

1. Indicate why you selected the site.
2. Describe what features the site provides.
3. Discuss at least two things you learned from the site, in terms of specific information about topics, additional sources of information, new perspectives, and so on.

WEB EXERCISE 15-2

Select *three* of the eight professional associations discussed in this chapter. Go to the association Web sites and answer the following questions for each association:

1. Identify at least five offerings provided by the association to its members (e.g., newsletters, journals, meeting opportunities, education programs).
2. Determine whether there are local chapters and, if so, the nature of their activities.
3. Determine whether there are special student memberships and, if so, what benefits they provide.

Following your exploration of the three association sites, indicate which of the associations appears to fit your interests best, and explain why you have made that choice.

Case 15-1

VERIZON COMMUNICATIONS: BUILDING A WORLD-CLASS COMPANY

The Background: The Merging of Two Companies
In June 2000, GTE and Bell Atlantic Corp. merged to form the largest local telephone company in the United States: Verizon Communications. Charles Lee, CEO of GTE, and Ivan Seidenberg, CEO of Bell Atlantic Corp, decided to share temporarily the position of CEO for the newly merged company. Not only were they able to handle this difficult task with ease, they also ensured that the merger went smoothly. Moreover, while other telecom companies saw their stock prices plummet as a result of the soured economy in late 2001, Verizon experienced a 4 percent increase in its stock price. Both CEOs were named in *Business Week*'s list of top 25 managers. Lee remained co-CEO until his retirement in June 2002, at which point Seidenberg took over the sole responsibility.

"The Verizon Promise" provides a broad framework that identifies the core purpose and values of the company. Specifically, it says the following:[25]

The Verizon Promise

Our Core

Purpose

We bring the benefits of communications to everybody

Our Core **Values**

Veritas Values

Integrity

Respect

Service

Imagination

Passion

Horizon Values

Our Core Goal

We will create the most respected brand in communications

Our **Future**

We will be a successful company when we make and keep our promise to our customers, communities, shareholders, and our employees

As of early 2003, the company employed more than 229,000 people. Its 2002 net income was over $4 million, based on approximately $67.6 billion in sales. Verizon is the number-one local telephone company in the United States and the number-two telecom service provider. In addition, Verizon Wireless, its joint venture with Vodafone, is the number-one U.S. wireless provider with 34.6 million subscribers.[26]

Verizon's Vision[27]
Over the next 10 to 15 years, Verizon plans to spend $20 to $40 billion in developing an incredibly fast fiber-optic Internet connection, which it hopes to make available to every home and office across the country. This connection is expected to be at least 10 times faster than broadband services available today. Not only will it be fast, but it is also predicted to be capable of carrying everything from old-fashioned phone service to high-definition television. Verizon plans to remake digital communication. Think Jetson-style phone service, where companies can provide face-to-face service, except through the Web. Verizon is the only telecom company pursuing this type of project. Other companies plan to provide this type of service only if Verizon proves first that it is profitable.

This is not the only tactic that Verizon CEO Seidenberg is aggressively pursuing. Currently, Verizon is running a trial in Manhattan for a new product called Wi-Fi. So far, Verizon has planted almost 1,000 Wi-Fi locations, allowing broadband subscribers near Verizon phone booths to be able to surf the Web wirelessly. In September 2003, Verizon rolled out a service known as 3G, which allows customers to connect to the Internet from their mobile phones. No other telecom company has pursued either one of these initiatives. Again, competitors are waiting to see how profitable these products are for Verizon before they make the decision to invest in such services.

Seidenberg also hopes to redefine the telecom industry by providing "cable-like" services, but to a different crowd. The cable industry focuses primarily on entertainment and games. Seidenberg believes Verizon can provide technology that centers on education, health care, financial services, and governmental services. This would allow for options like easy access to video conferencing between doctors and sick patients. Students could view a class lecture they missed if they were sick and unable to attend.

Verizon plans to compete directly with the cable industry by providing products such as TV programming or video services. These would be available on demand. The idea has gained the support of Sumner Redstone, the CEO of Viacom (whose holdings include MTV Networks and Paramount Pictures).

How Verizon Achieves Competitive Advantage

One way that Verizon is able to achieve competitive advantage is by its pricing strategies. Verizon is often capable of offering high quality products for the lowest price. For instance, Verizon was the first telecom company to cut the cost of broadband services 30 percent to $35 a month. Verizon was also the first to provide unlimited local and long-distance calling for one flat fee of $55 per month. Customers loved this plan, and every other phone company soon adopted it. Verizon's capacity for maintaining first mover's advantage keeps its growth consistently above its competitors.

This high growth leads to high revenues, another one of Verizon's competitive advantages. Verizon has the third largest capital budget in the country. Verizon generates 50 percent more in revenues than even its closest competitor (SBC). Seidenberg claims he can sink $12.5 to $13.5 billion in capital expenditures without needing to raise funding.

Verizon has several advantages regarding its fiber-optics initiative. The cost of installing a fiber-optic connection in a home or business continues to decrease. The cost of one line four years ago ran about $4,000. At present, it is close to $2,000 per line. In approximately five years, analysts expect the cost to decrease to only $1,000 per line. In addition, about 45 percent of Verizon's clients are wired via telephone poles (compared to 28 percent for SBC and 13 percent for Qwest). It is approximately 30 percent cheaper to upgrade a line if the customer is already wired though a telephone pole.

Finally, Verizon prides itself on being a great place to work for talented and motivated professionals. Its advertised benefits include excellent salary and benefits, performance-based incentive awards, tuition assistance, outstanding career and growth opportunities, and a unique environment of talented and diverse people.

Beware of Barriers: Verizon Is Not Completely Home Free

Verizon's CEO and top executives are enthusiastic about the direction Verizon is heading, but skeptics still remain. Some experts question whether Verizon's investments in fiber-optic connections make good financial sense. Competitors point out that, if Verizon's ventures prove prof-itable, they can adopt such procedures and technological advances at only a fraction of the cost that Verizon initially needed to invest. If this initiative fails, Verizon is admittedly too invested in this project to bail out (i.e., they are not utilizing a test market). Some say the bigger question is whether the market is even ready for such advances.

Cable companies may also pose a threat for Verizon, since they are working to break into the telephone market. Analysts suggest that cable players may win 3.7 million phone lines nationwide by 2005, which would give them 30 percent of the total market share (versus the 2 percent market share they currently have). Also, Verizon faces tough competition from other wireless companies, like AT&T, which seized 3.7 percent of Verizon's phone lines in 2002.

Another concern for Verizon is the amount of debt it is carrying compared to competitors. Verizon's debt-to-earning ratio is 1.6, compared with SBC's 0.8 and BellSouth's 1.1. Verizon has ample cash to cover such payments but will need to reduce debt if it plans on making new investments. This may require the sale of some of its assets.

Discussion Questions

1. Identify and discuss the management skills needed to lead Verizon Communications effectively. Why are they important?
2. What are the most significant management challenges at Verizon Communications? Why are these challenges so important?
3. What recommendations would you give to management at Verizon Communications to enable the company to achieve its long-term vision?
4. What are the practical implications of this case for you as a future manager in a real-world organization?

Case 15-2

CRISIS AT THE BOEING COMPANY

The Company[28]

The Boeing Company is the world's largest aerospace company: the number-one manufacturer of large commercial jets and the number-three defense contractor. The company is composed of two major business units, Commercial Airplanes and Integrated Defense Systems. As of early 2003, Boeing employed 166,000 people. Its 2002 net income was $492 million based on sales of $54 billion. Boeing's vision statement is as follows:

> *People working together as a global enterprise for aerospace leadership.*

Strategies

- *To run healthy core businesses*
- *To leverage strengths into new products and services*
- *To open new frontiers*

Core Competencies

- *Detailed customer knowledge and focus*
- *Large-scale systems integration*
- *Lean enterprise*

Values

- *Leadership*
- *Integrity*
- *Quality*
- *Customer satisfaction*
- *People working together*
- *A diverse and involved team*
- *Good corporate citizenship*
- *Enhancing shareholder value*

The Crisis[29, 30]

"Accountability begins at the top." These words were written by Phil Condit, former Boeing CEO, to his staff approximately one week before his resignation. This phrase was used to explain why Boeing CFO, Mike Sears, had been forced out. Both Sears and manager Darleen A. Druyun were fired for ethics violations in negotiating a tanker contract with the U.S. government. Boeing claims that Condit's resignation was unrelated to the scandal. Despite Boeing's statement that Condit's resignation was voluntary, others doubt that and insist it was long overdue.

Condit has been called a bold visionary, a superior engineer, a creative designer, a brilliant problem solver. Unfortunately, "great manager" may not be the phrase that comes to mind when describing Condit. Although his strong vision resembled those of Boeing's CEOs of old, his other qualities did not. Unlike past leaders who were known for their ability to make fast, unwavering decisions, Condit was indecisive. Whereas others led conservative lifestyles, Condit earned the reputation of being a womanizer and indulged in extravagant living. All of these aspects contributed to his management style conflicting with traditional ways of doing things at Boeing.

Technical Wizard, But Strategically Inept?

Most people would admit Condit was a technical wizard, but he could not seem to conjure up the ability to make sound strategic decisions. Condit started his career with Boeing in 1965 as a recent graduate from Princeton's aeronautics master's program. Shortly after coming on board, he solved a problem that enabled the Federal Aviation Administration to develop rules on spacing between jumbo and smaller aircrafts. This ability impressed Boeing's CEO at the time, Thornton A. "T" Wilson, who was confident that Condit was not only a great engineer, but a great person as well. Condit was on his way up the corporate ladder.

Before becoming CEO, Condit was best known for his design leadership on the 757 and 777 programs. Again, Condit was commended for his engineering ability. His work stimulated notable breakthroughs in the industry. Yet his decisions from a management perspective were considered subpar. For instance, he overshot his budget 100 percent (which translated into $6 billion). Boeing declined to comment on this topic.

Condit's inadequacies as a manager became a greater concern when he rose to the position of CEO in 1997. During his first year in office, he decided Boeing needed to accelerate airline production, even though the company was moving toward an automated process. The assembly lines almost broke down, which resulted in not only humiliation for Condit, but a punishing decrease in stock price from Wall Street and a damaged relationship with shareholders. Condit took full responsibility and vowed to improve his performance in the future.

Unfortunately, this was not Condit's only strategic flop. One of Condit's biggest mistakes as CEO was underestimating Airbus, Boeing's European competitor. Not only did Condit give his personal guarantee that Airbus would not launch the now successful A380 program, but he was trigger shy when it came time to act. Boeing's programs, the 747x, the super-sized 747, and later the Sonic Cruiser, were ready to be launched in response. Despite marketing efforts and strong suggestions to move forward with these initiatives, Condit backed out at the last minute. He later admitted this was the wrong decision.

The High Life or a Low Life?

In addition to these strategic failures, Condit was also criticized for his decision to live the high life. He had a reputation for extravagant living—for example, the custom miniature train that circulated through his entire medieval-style mansion delivering drinks to guests. The parties he hosted included such features as poetry readings and Camelot themes displaying characters from King Arthur. Still it was less his desire for lavish living that got him into trouble and more his relationships with women.

Condit had the reputation of being a womanizer. Throughout his tenure with Boeing, he was married four times. His second wife was a Boeing secretary. Shortly after they split, he started dating Boeing receptionist Laverne Hawthorne. They dated for six months. Then he was promoted to president and the company decided it needed to downsize. Hawthorne was terminated. Allegedly, she filed a wrongful termination suit. Several Boeing executives claim there was a settlement; however, both Hawthorne and Condit refused to comment.

After Condit's third marriage (to his first cousin) dissolved, the company started to raise concerns about his personal life. It is said that several Boeing executives confronted Condit about his lifestyle, expressing concern about his behavior. One Boeing lawyer compared him to former president Bill Clinton.

A Time to Plant, A Time to Uproot

Strategic failures can be forgiven. So can a playboy lifestyle. But when a company is faced with allegations of scandal and corrupt ethics from its biggest client (which also happens to be the U.S. government), something must change. In this case, the change came in the form of a new CEO.

Although Condit is not accused of having any involvement in the alleged scandals that led to the termination of Sears and Druyun, he claims it was in the company's best interest for him to step down. The position of CEO has been awarded to Harry C. Stoneciper.

Discussion Questions

1. What types of management problems is the Boeing Company experiencing? Why are these problems occurring?

2. Which management topics discussed in this textbook are illustrated in this case?

3. Evaluate Phil Condit's effectiveness as chief executive officer at Boeing Company using material from the textbook. Based on this, what are Condit's managerial strengths? Weaknesses? Support your answer using material from this case study.

4. What recommendations would you give to Harry Stoneciper, the new chief executive officer, in order to enhance Boeing's effectiveness in the short and long term?

5. What are the practical implications of this case for you as a future manager in a real-world organization?

Video Case: Yahoo!

A STUDY OF ENTREPRENEURSHIP AND INNOVATION: YAHOO!

Running Time: 15:50

Yahoo! is the world's number-one Web site, as it has been for most of the Web's existence.[31] Founded in 1994 by David Filo and Jerry Yang, two Stanford University doctoral students, Yahoo! is now a global organization with more than 3,000 employees. Yahoo! helps people to find everything from stamp collecting information to the latest stock quotes. In this video, cofounder Jerry Yang, director of brand management Karen Edwards, senior producer John Briggs, and others discuss the need for innovation and critical thinking at Yahoo! After viewing the video, answer the following questions:

1. What does John Briggs mean when he says, "We're essentially in the tornado right now"? What are some implications of the fact that Yahoo! is "in the tornado"?

2. In what sense is Yahoo! a learning organization?

3. How does Yahoo! combine strategy, leadership, culture, organization design, and information sharing to develop a learning organization?

4. What are the elements of Yahoo!'s strategy?

5. What are the important cultural values at Yahoo!?

6. How does Yahoo!'s organization design facilitate learning?

7. Why do Yahoo! employees say they enjoy working in a learning organization?

8. To what degree could Yahoo!'s approaches to becoming a learning organization provide guidance for people attempting to achieve lifelong learning?

http://www.yahoo.com/

LIGHTEN UP

PETWORKING[32]

Just below the Eleanor Roosevelt statue in the West 72nd Street entrance to Riverside Park is a 16,000-square-foot space that might be New York City's best kept networking secret. This is the dog-meet-dog world of "petworking," where people look for work as they walk their pets. The pet walkers include such celebrities as Conan O'Brien, Al Franken, and Elaine Boosler and realtors, surgeons, journalists, architects, and many others, but "it's mostly people who know people who know other people who know of an opening or opportunity." In this and other dog-gathering spots in the city, leads about jobs are shared along with dog biscuits.

Bash Dibra, author of *Dogspeak*, explains that "Dogs are social creatures and thus they force interaction." The dogs act as catalysts in breaking down barriers and opening communication. The first remark is about the dog and then "maybe the next comment is 'I had a really bad day and I think I need to look for another job.'" One pet worker pointed out that "It's the oldest way young men and women pick each other up in the city. Why not leverage a winning formula?"

http://www.urbanhound.com

SKILLS PRACTICE

15-1   *Skill Level:* CHALLENGING

You Be the Manager!

Skill Objective

To develop an integrated and systematic approach for using personal, interpersonal, and management skills for the completion of an unstructured group task.

Procedure

Note: Download the worksheet for this exercise from the text Web site.

1. You will need to work in groups of six to eight students for this exercise.

2. After you have formed your groups, your instructor will randomly select a formal leader for this exercise.

3. Once the leader has been selected, read the description of the group task that follows.

Overview of the Group's Task

Your task is to work with your team leader to develop and present a *highly creative 20- to 30-second TV advertisement to sell a product or service* with which you all are familiar. Some teams in the past have selected cars, famous restaurants, airlines, hotels, food, or beverages for this activity. The specific product or service you select is not critical so long as at least some of the members of the team have some familiarity with it. *Note that every member of your team must play some role or part in the presentation of the advertisement.*

Your instructor will have flip chart paper and markers if you want to use them for your advertisement. You will have 30 minutes to develop and practice your advertisement before you must present it to the class. Your classmates will evaluate the quality of your advertisement in terms of whether the length of your advertisement was within the 20- to 30-second range, the degree to which all members of the team participated in the advertisement, and the degree of originality reflected in your advertisement. Good luck and have fun!

4. Your instructor will now tell you to start working on your task. He or she will keep track of time and stop you after 30 minutes, so watch your time!

5. Remember that you will need to develop *and* present your advertisement to the class and everyone on the team must be involved in presenting the advertisement to the rest of the class.

6. After time has been called, present your advertisement to the class, ask your classmates to evaluate it, and then discuss the following questions as a class.

Discussion Questions

1. Describe your team's process in terms of how you approached the task you were given to complete. What were the key challenges you faced in completing this task? What did you do to try to overcome them?

2. Evaluate your team's process. In what ways was it effective? Ineffective? What did the team leader do to try to facilitate the process?

3. What types of general skills were needed to be successful in completing this task? Why?

4. What types of management skills were needed to be successful in completing this task?

5. Suppose you were asked to repeat this exercise again by developing another creative advertisement for the same product or service you used the first time. What would you do the same to enhance your success the second time? What would you do differently?

6. What are the practical implications of this exercise for you as a future manager?

SKILLS PRACTICE

15-2   *Skill Level:* CHALLENGING

Field Work Experiences in Management and Organizational Behavior

Skill Objectives

1. To use management knowledge and analytical skills to study and evaluate management problems and challenges in real-world organizational settings.

2. To develop the management skills needed to complete complex projects.

Procedure

1. Decide whether you want to complete this project as an individual or in a group. (Many students in the past have preferred working in teams.)

2. Identify a manager who might be willing to work with you for this project. If you don't know someone personally, ask your instructors, alumni office, career placement service, friends, and family for the names of working managers who might be willing to help you out. Not-for-profit organizations are often very willing to work with students on these kinds of projects as well.

3. Once you have found a manager willing to work with you, discuss what you would like to do with that person.. Some examples of projects that students have completed in the past include the following:

   > Evaluating the functioning of a work team and developing recommendations for enhancing its effectiveness.

   > Evaluating the design and implementation of a specific change in an organization and making recommendations for improving the process in the future.

   > Assessing employee job satisfaction, identifying key areas of dissatisfaction, and developing recommendations for enhancing job satisfaction.

   > Assessing the culture of an organization and evaluating its effectiveness in relation to the organization's mission and objectives.

   > Assessing levels of job stress of employees and formulating action steps to reduce or eliminate the causes of stress.

   > Analyzing the reasons why employees choose to leave an organization and developing recommendations for increasing retention behavior.

   > Evaluating a management process or system (e.g., customer service, sales, production, product development) and developing recommendations for enhancing its effectiveness.

Note: These are just examples of the types of projects students have completed in the past. The best one for you will be based on what you and the manager you are working with are interested in and the amount of time you are expected to devote to this project. Visit the text Web site to see additional examples of appropriate projects for this exercise.

4. Once you have selected an appropriate topic and focus for your project, work with your instructor and the manager to develop a basic plan for completing the project. Be sure you have a clear and

fairly tight focus for this project. Also, be clear how you will go about achieving your objective. How will you collect your data? Personal interviews? A survey? Reviewing documents and data given to you by the manager? Finally, have a clear idea of how your final product will look. At a minimum, you would want to present a written summary of your project to your instructor and manager, describing what you did, what you found, and what you recommend.

5. After you have completed this project, discuss the following questions as a class.

Discussion Questions

1. What are the key concepts you learned about management in organizations, based on completing this project?

2. Which management concepts, principles, and issues discussed in this book were most relevant and valuable to you in conducting your analysis and in making your recommendations to management? Why?

3. What were the most significant challenges you faced in completing this project?

4. What types of management skills did you need to complete this project successfully?

5. If you were to repeat this process, what would you do in the same way as you did the first time? What would you do differently? Why?

6. What are the practical implications of this project for you as a future manager?

SKILLS PRACTICE

15-3   *Skill Level: BASIC*

Self-Generated Case in Management

Skill Objective

To apply your management analytical skills to a case study of an organization that is of particular interest to you.

Procedure

1. Search the print media (e.g., *New York Times, Washington Post, Business Week, Fortune, Wall Street Journal*) or the Internet for an article (or articles) about an especially successful or unsuccessful organization of interest to you. For example, this may be a *Fortune 500* company, a global company, or a not-for-profit organization. The key here is that you are interested in the organization.

2. Read the article(s) and identify what management has done to contribute to the effectiveness (or ineffectiveness) of the organization. Try to be very specific.

3. Now assume you are a member of management at the organization discussed in your article(s) and develop a basic action plan (set of recommenda-

tions) for addressing the current situation. If the organization is doing well, focus on what would have to be done to sustain its success. If the company is doing poorly, focus on what has to be done to address the key problems it is facing.

4. Write a memo to the CEO of the company making an argument for why he or she should implement your recommendations. Use the knowledge you have acquired in earlier chapters to support your case.

Discussion Questions

1. Evaluate the process you used to analyze the organization on which you focused for this exercise. What did you do well? What did you not do so well?

2. Evaluate the action plan you developed. What are its strengths and weaknesses?

3. Evaluate your memo to the CEO of the organization. What are its strengths and weaknesses?

4. What are the practical implications of this exercise for you as a future manager?

SKILLS PRACTICE

15-4   *Skill Level:* CHALLENGING

Revisiting My Management Skills Mastery Plan

Skill Objective

1. To reflect on the management knowledge and skills you have acquired in relation to the goals you set for yourself in Skills Practice 1-5 ("Developing My Management Skills Mastery Plan").

2. To identify your own Top Ten List of key points about management skills you will take away from reading this book.

3. To identify specific action steps you can take to develop your management knowledge and skills further while you are still in school and when you obtain your first real-world job after graduation.

Procedure

Note: Download the worksheet for this exercise from the text Web site.

1. Use the management skills mastery plan you developed in Skills Practice 1-5 ("Developing My Management Skills Mastery Plan") as a reference for working through this activity. Use the worksheet you downloaded to record all of your responses to steps 2 through 7 that follow.

2. Review the areas that you identified as your Key Personal Strengths in Skills Practice 1-5. Assess the degree to which you feel you further developed your key personal strengths based on what you learned in this book. Why do you feel this way?

3. Review the areas that you identified as your Key Personal Weaknesses in Skills Practice 1-5. Assess the degree to which you feel that you improved in the areas of your key personal weaknesses. Although you may not have completely eliminated these areas as concerns, the key is the progress you made in overcoming them. Why do you feel this way?

4. Review the Knowledge Objectives you identified in Skills Practice 1-5. Assess the degree to which you feel you achieved your knowledge objectives. Why do you think you were successful (or unsuccessful) in achieving these objectives?

5. Review the Skill Objectives you identified in Skills Practices 1-5. Assess the degree to which you feel you achieved your skill objectives. Why do you think you were successful (or unsuccessful) in achieving these objectives?

6. Now, reflecting on everything that you have learned about management knowledge and skills in Chapters 1 through 14, brainstorm your own Top Ten List of the things you have learned about management and can use in the future.

7. Finally, think about what kinds of specific actions you can take to further enhance your management knowledge and skills in the future. If you still have some time before you graduate, focus more on what you can do as a student to acquire management knowledge and skills. If you are graduating very soon, focus more on what you can do once you start your new job (managerial or nonmanagerial) to acquire management knowledge and skills.

8. Create a written summary of your responses to steps 2 through 7, and talk about it with your instructor or present it to your class for discussion purposes. Although this step is optional, it is highly beneficial to take some time to process your answers and hear what other students came up with based on their assessments.

APPENDIX A
STRATEGIC MANAGEMENT

When IBM chose Louis V. Gerstner, Jr., then CEO of RJR Nabisco, as its Chairman and CEO, it handed him a monumental task. Critics of IBM argued it was too bureaucratic, too slow in shifting its emphasis from the declining mainframe computer market to personal computers, had a labor force that should be cut by 80,000 to 100,000 employees, and was preoccupied with its own view of the world. As an outsider to the computer industry, Gerstner was seen as lacking technical knowledge, but a tough manager who could provide fresh perspectives and would not be constrained by the tradition and culture of IBM. The business world waited anxiously to see what strategies Gerstner would pursue. In taking over the reins of IBM in 1993, Gerstner faced many of the key issues considered in this appendix. He said, "What IBM needs right now is a series of very tough-minded, market-driven, highly effective strategies in each of its businesses." Gerstner is credited with rescuing IBM, showing that it is possible to "teach elephants to dance."[1] Gerstner worked to change IBM's insular culture, halt the proposed breakup of the company, streamline repetitive processes, refocus energies on the mainframe market, focus employee attention on customer needs and changing markets, and significantly reduce the workforce throughout IBM's worldwide locations. Gerstner retired from IBM in December 2002 and the following month accepted the position of chairman of the Carlyle Group, a global private equity firm.[2] His successor at IBM, Sam Palmisano, an IBM veteran of more than 25 years, quickly moved to build on Gerstner's successes, implementing an "e-business on demand" strategy, flattening the organization structure, placing more emphasis on teams, and creating a more egalitarian culture.[3] According to one observer, "He has taken Gerstner's strategy to the next level."[4]

In this appendix, we consider the big picture facing firms, including how highly effective strategies are developed in the face of environmental demands. Just as athletic coaches must develop a game plan to guide their team during competition, leaders of organizations, such as Lou Gerstner and Sam Palmisano, need a game plan that will enable the firm to meet its goals over the course of several years. In developing a strategic plan, leaders must consider the firm's past performance, current position, and goals and answer four strategic questions:

> How do we respond to new opportunities in the environment, lessen the impact of threats from the environment, and strengthen the mix of the organization's activities by doing more of some things and less of others?

> How do we assign resources among the various subunits, divisions, and activities of the organization?

> How do we compete with other organizations for customers through allocation of existing or new products and services?

> How do we effectively manage organizational activities at the departmental, divisional, and corporate levels of the organization?

We begin this appendix with a look at domains and characteristics of the organizational environment. We then consider approaches to determining organizational effectiveness and discuss the strategic planning process. Next, we offer guidelines for conducting a strategic analysis, for establishing a purpose, vision, and mission, and for defining strategic objectives. Following this, we discuss approaches for choosing corporate-level strategies and business-unit-level strategies. We conclude with suggestions for implementing and evaluating the strategic plan.

THE ORGANIZATIONAL ENVIRONMENT

Although managers' decisions are often made at a micro level, dealing with individuals and small groups, it is important to recognize that organizations operate within environments that largely dictate what policies and practices are feasible, desirable, and even necessary. In this section we consider key environmental domains and environmental characteristics.

ENVIRONMENTAL DOMAINS

As shown in Figure A-1, organizations operate in the context of six key environmental domains: economic, political, social, technological, competitive, and physical. The natures of these domains help define appropriate organizational strategies and practices.

The Economic Domain. Many economic factors, such as interest rates, trade deficits, inflation rates, gross domestic product indicators, and the money supply, may influence an organization's activities. Factors in the economic domain influence

FIGURE A-1
Environmental Domains of an Organization

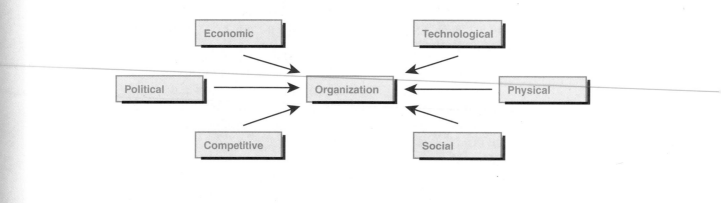

the ability of managers to get resources needed to produce goods and services and distribute those goods and services to a market. In addition, employees are likely to behave very differently depending on the nature of the economic environment. For instance, dissatisfied employees might stay with a company in a poor economy but may decide to leave the firm if the economy is good and other jobs are plentiful.[5]

The Political Domain. The political domain of the organization environment rests on laws and regulations passed by governmental agencies and legislative bodies. Legislation has been directed toward the elimination of discrimination based on gender, race, and age. Other legislation has been designed to bring about an end to sexual harassment in the workplace, prevent unfair pricing in markets, restrict pollution, protect consumers, discourage unethical behaviors, and regulate corporate taxation. However, the enforcement of these laws and regulations often varies because of differing beliefs by both political incumbents and the electorate about the need for such enforcement.

As companies are increasingly going global, a big consideration is the political risk associated with foreign governments. Political risk refers to the possibility that political decisions, conditions, or events in a country will affect the business climate in such a way that investors will lose money or will make less than they expected when the investment was made. For example, if there is a strong possibility that a country's government may suddenly change its policies, political risk is high. As such, examination of country political factors and associated risk is an important part of the decision process of multinational firms.[6]

The Social Domain. The social domain of an organization's environment consists of societal values, attitudes, norms, customs, and demographics. Every society incorporates values and attitudes that may be uniform across a population or may vary by regional or ethnic groupings. Values are what people believe to be proper goals for members of the society to maintain or achieve. Attitudes reflect what individuals think about issues and behaviors that occur within a society.

In the United States, most citizens value freedom of speech as a necessary feature of their daily lives. They may, however, believe that other citizens are abusing that right. Citizens in other countries may think freedom of speech is unnecessary or is a value that only leads to disruption in their daily lives. Other values and attitudes that may differ by regions within a country or between countries concern the role of the family, the importance of clean air, and the role of religion in political institutions. Values and attitudes are often expressed in the legal codes of countries. The First Amendment of the U.S. Constitution, for example, guarantees the right of free speech to all citizens.

Values and attitudes, however, can change over time. For instance, events following the attacks of September 11, 2001 on the World Trade Center have led to controversy regarding whether the rights of privacy, due process, and freedom of speech should be limited to enhance national security.[7] As another example, fifty years ago in the United States many people viewed the role of "mother" as taking precedence over the mother's desire to work outside the home. This attitude has changed, despite some resistance, and over 50 percent of women with children under the age of six are now active in the workforce, up from just 12 percent in 1950. As another example, the idea of providing benefits to same-sex partners would have been considered radical until recently. However, as of mid-2003, more than 5,600 firms, including 4 percent of the *Fortune* 500 firms, provided domestic-partner benefits for lesbian and gay employees. Several of the largest companies—including General Motors, Ford, IBM, Citigroup Inc., AT&T, Procter & Gamble, Chevron Texaco, Boeing, and Sears, Roebuck, and Co.—offer the benefits.[8]

The Technological Domain. The technological domain, or technology, refers to the application of knowledge to the production and distribution of goods and services. Technology is often viewed as a major source of environmental change for an organization. Technology is greatly affected by innovation. *Innovation* is the creation or modification of a process, product, or service. Innovation can occur at different rates, as can its transfer throughout the environment. *Technology transfer* involves the application of innovation to processes, products, or services either within or between industries.

The many ways that technology and technological change are transforming organizations are evident throughout the text. In early 2004, the Mars Exploration Rover Spirit was sending panoramic images of the Red Planet to earth, cloning was becoming commonplace, huge advances had been made in genome mapping, machine-to-machine communication was increasing, and it was possible to "taste" food—including the sounds and sensations of eating—with use of a food simulator.[9] Other major technological changes include the growing use of personal computers and the explosion of the Internet. By one estimate, the Internet Revolution will result in 40 million people working from home in 2004.[10] Accompanying these technological developments are fundamental changes in the way business is done, including the emergence of Web-based dot.com companies such as Amazon.com.[11]

The Competitive Domain. Organizations can face a wide variety of competitive conditions in their environment. Some large organizations compete only with small organizations, often giving them an advantage in pricing of their products. Other competitive conditions arise from different mixes in the strategies that competitors pursue, as we discuss later in this appendix.

Within a capitalistic system, organizations can compete in one of four competitive market structures: monopoly, oligopoly, monopolistic competition, or perfect competition. A *monopoly* exists when an organization has sole access to the market for its goods and services. In a monopoly situation, competitors either have been restricted from access to customers or have voluntarily chosen not to compete in the market. Restrictions to markets may occur when regulatory agencies or governments grant a single organization the right to provide a good or service to the market, such as in the case of utility agencies or police departments. An *oligopoly* exists when only a few firms are in competition to provide goods and services to a market. In this situation the number of firms producing a good or service is so small that actions by any single firm in the industry concerning price, output, product style, or terms of sale have a perceptible impact on the sales of the other firms. *Monopolistic competition* exists when many firms offer a similar good or service with only minor price differentials. For example, gasoline stations operate under conditions of monopolistic competition; customers may willingly spend a few cents more a gallon to avoid inconvenience, but they will probably balk at a big price difference.

Perfect competition exists when many organizations offer essentially the same good or service; price thus becomes the primary discriminator for the customer. Some agricultural commodities, such as wheat, operate in a market closely resembling perfect competition.

The competitive market structure is a major influence on a firm's strategies and practices. For example, a company in a monopoly position may have little need for flexibility and adaptability, and it may be able to offer its employees a stable and secure work environment. *Deregulation*—the relaxing of government controls on firms to permit greater competition—has transformed such industries as energy delivery, telecommunications, and financial services. Firms that were once in secure market positions now find themselves facing strong competition and pressured to be more responsive to market demands. This may require them to alter their structures, policies, and practices.

The Physical Domain. All organizations must respond in some manner to factors in their physical domain. Weather conditions, for instance, may greatly influence the activities of a firm. Airlines must follow the location and movement of storm systems, construction companies in the upper Midwest must schedule their activities to avoid outside work during harsh winter months, and orange growers must make quick decisions about harvesting when frost warnings are issued.

The physical domain may also influence things such as availability of a large pool of qualified talent. For example, companies located in one of the "Best Places to Live," as identified, for instance, by *Money* magazine, may find themselves at an advantage. See http://money.cnn.com/best/bplive/.

ENVIRONMENTAL DIMENSIONS

An organization's environment may vary on some important dimensions. Three such dimensions are *munificence*, *dynamism*, and *complexity.*[12]

Munificence. The *munificence* of an organization's environment refers to the level of resources available to the organization. The degree of munificence may range from rich to lean. Rich environments usually exist where resources are plentiful. However, a rich environment attracts other organizations, and, over time, environments will move from rich to lean. As such, rich environments usually exist in the early stages of industry development or under conditions of a monopoly market structure. When environments become lean, organizations may have to be more efficient in their use of resources or employ other tactics in order to survive.

Dynamism. *Dynamism* refers to the rate of change in environmental factors. When environmental factors remain basically unchanged, the environment is stable. When those factors change rapidly, the environment is dynamic.

Complexity. *Complexity* is the number of components in an organization's environment and the degree to which they are similar or different. An environment with few and similar components is less complex than one with many and varied components.

Together, dynamism and complexity influence the degree to which managers in an organization see the environment as unpredictable; this unpredictability is called *perceived environmental uncertainty.*[13] In conditions where the environment is relatively uncertain, firms may have to emphasize flexibility and creativity over efficiency. Such an environment demands that managers and employees have sophisticated training and problem-solving skills. Conversely, a relatively certain environment may permit a firm to rely more heavily on standard routines and procedures. Because the environment holds few surprises, employees need fewer skills and ongoing training is less important. A recurring theme throughout the text is that organizational environments are increasingly dynamic and complex and thus that sophisticated skills and ongoing learning are crucial.

THE EFFECTIVE ORGANIZATION AND THE STRATEGIC PLANNING PROCESS

A key task of strategic planning is to make the organization more effective. But what *is* an effective organization? *Organizational effectiveness* is the degree to which the organization achieves its goals, maintains its health, secures resources needed for survival, and satisfies parties that have a stake in it.[14]

This definition suggests that effectiveness has several dimensions. On one dimension, an organization is effective if it attains its goals. The approach to defining organizational effectiveness that focuses on this dimension is called the *goal assessment* approach. It is concerned with whether the organization reaches the growth, sales, profitability, or other goals management has set for it.

However, the effectiveness of an organization can be measured in other ways. For instance, is an organization effective if it is profitable but its workforce is unhappy? Is it effective if it has captured large markets this year but is faced with threats to its supplies of raw materials, labor, or capital? Is it effective if it boosts production capacity with new technology but in so doing upsets the local community or customers? These questions suggest three criteria, besides goal accomplishment, for measuring organizational effectiveness.

First, *internal process assessment* focuses on organizational health. According to this approach, an unhealthy organization cannot be called effective, regardless of profitability. This approach considers such measures of organizational health as employee satisfaction, levels of conflict, coordination of department activities, and production efficiency. Second, *systems resource assessment* considers whether an organization is able to acquire the resources it needs to survive and prosper. Social service agencies must acquire federal, state, or municipal funding to continue offering their services. Manufacturing firms must acquire labor and raw materials to continue operating. Biotechnology firms must have access to start-up capital and qualified scientists.

Finally, *strategic constituencies assessment* of effectiveness looks at groups inside or outside the organization that have a stake in it, such as customers, stockholders, the community, creditors, suppliers, and employees. According to this approach, an organization is effective when it has satisfied these important constituencies. The Focus on Management feature discusses the relative importance given to its constituencies by Alagasco, a natural gas distributor.

The different approaches for assessing organizational effectiveness are shown in Figure A-2. In determining whether an organization is effective, it is important to

ALAGASCO PUTS CUSTOMERS SECOND

Alagasco, Alabama's largest utility—and the only utility on *Fortune* magazine's 100 Best Companies to Work for in America list—is proud of its philosophy of "putting customers second."* Alagasco believes that by putting employees first and treating them well, good service to customers will naturally follow. As one sign of commitment to its employees, each year Alagasco employees at all levels meet to refine the corporate strategic plan for the coming year. Everyone then receives a copy of the final plan so at follow-up meetings they can ask questions about the plan and learn more about their individual roles in helping Alagasco meet its objectives. Training in both work skills and corporate activities and philosophies is also a priority.

http://www.alagasco.com/

*S. Delenne, "Putting Customers Second," American Gas, March 1999, pp. 36–37.

consider these various perspectives. Doing so highlights the fact that an organization, whatever its profits or losses this year or next, cannot be seen as truly effective if its workforce is dissatisfied and uncoordinated, if its sources of labor, materials, or finances are drying up, or if it is alienating important constituencies.

Every year *Fortune* magazine surveys more than 10,000 executives, directors, and securities analysts. They are told to choose the companies they admire most, regardless of industry. To create separate lists by industry, *Fortune* asked ballot recipients to rank companies in their own industry on eight criteria, ranging from long-term investment value to social responsibility. The result is a guide to the best corporate reputations in the United States and worldwide. The results for 2003 are listed in Figure A-3. Wal-Mart's ascent to the top spot on the U.S. list marks the first time in the survey's history that the nation's largest company was also the most

FIGURE A-2

Approaches to Assessing Organizational Effectiveness

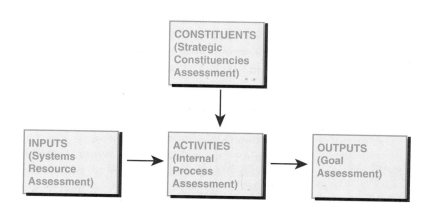

FIGURE A-3
The Most Admired Companies

Top Ten in the U.S.	Top Ten Outside the U.S.	Country
1. Wal-Mart	1. Toyota Motor	Japan
2. Southwest Airlines	2. BNW	Germany
3. Berkshire Hathaway	3. Sony	Japan
4. Dell Computer	4. Nokia	Finland
5. General Electric	5. Nestlé	Switzerland
6. Johnson & Johnson	6. Singapore Airlines	Singapore
7. Microsoft	7. L'Oréal	France
8. FedEx	8. Honda Motor	Japan
9. Starbucks	9. BP	Britain
10. Procter & Gamble	10. Royal Dutch Shell Group	Netherlands/Britain

Source: N. Stein, "America's Most Admired Companies," *Fortune*, March 3, 2003, pp. 81–82.

admired. Warren Buffett—whose company, Berkshire Hathaway, was third on the list—cast his first-place vote for Wal-Mart, stating, "[Wal-Mart] is the largest company around, and it hasn't lost a bit of the dynamism that it had back when Sam [Walton] started it. I think that's enormously impressive."[15] See http://www.fortune.com/fortune/mostadmired.

Another way organizational effectiveness is assessed along multiple dimensions is with the Malcolm Baldrige National Quality Award. The award was established in 1987 to enhance U.S. competitiveness by promoting quality awareness, recognizing quality and business achievements of U.S. companies, and publicizing these companies' successful performance.[16] The award is based on rated performance on seven criteria: leadership, information and analysis, strategic planning, human resource development and measurement, process management, business results, and customer focus and satisfaction. Specific questions relating to each criterion are presented in Figure A-4. Since 1988, 58 organizations have received the award. The seven 2003 winners of the award were Medrad (a medical imaging firm), Boeing Aerospace Support, Caterpillar Financial Services Corp., Stoner Inc. (a small privately owned manufacturer of specialized cleaners, lubricants, and coatings), Community Consolidated School District 15 of Palatine, Illinois, Baptist Hospital, Inc. of Pensacola, Florida, and Saint Luke's Hospital of Kansas City. See http://www.quality.nist.gov/.

In working to make their organizations effective, managers must develop strategic plans. *Strategies* are simply methods of competition. The *strategic plan* of an organization is a comprehensive plan that reflects the longer term needs and directions of the organization or subunit. Strategic planning consists of several key components. Figure A-5 shows those components and how they are linked together into the process of strategic planning.[17]

MTM, Inc. is a firm whose mission is to help create competitive advantages for its customers by offering comprehensive analysis, solutions, and support services to provide for the capture, storage, retrieval, sharing, and management of information. In the Voice of Experience feature on page A-12, Daniel Nordloh, MTM's chief operating officer, discusses strategy development and implementation.

Organizational Effectiveness Index—The Baldrige Award Criteria

Leadership

1. Executives in the organization create and maintain a leadership system based on clear values and high expectations.
2. The values, expectations, and directions of the organization are effectively communicated and reinforced throughout the workforce.
3. Executives in the organization seek to identify future opportunities for the company and its stakeholders.
4. The organization takes action to promote legal and ethical conduct in all that it does.
5. The organization looks ahead to anticipate public concerns and to assess possible impacts on society of our products and services.

Information and Analysis

1. The organization's performance measurement system is designed to align operations with company objectives.
2. The organization's performance management system was developed based on customer needs and how these needs are met.
3. The organization uses competitive comparisons and benchmarking to set stretch targets that are consistent with the firm's competitive strategy.
4. The organization analyzes and integrates information and data from all relevant operations to support business decisions and planning.
5. The organization has a set of criteria that are used to identify appropriate information and data to be used for competitive comparisons and benchmarking.

Strategic Planning

1. Strategy development in the organization considers present and future customer requirements and expectations.
2. Strategy development in the organization assesses the relationship between the competitive environment and company capabilities.
3. The organization aligns work-unit and partner plans and targets.
4. Productivity, cycle time improvement, and waste reduction are included in the organization's plans and targets.
5. The organization generates two- to five-year projections regarding its operational performance compared with key competitors and benchmarks over this time period.

Human Resource Development and Management

1. The human resource planning and evaluation in the organization is aligned with the firm's strategic and business plans.
2. Reliable, valid, and complete HR information is available for company planning.
3. The design of jobs in the organization fosters flexibility and rapid response to changing requirements.
4. The compensation and recognition policies in our region reinforce the effectiveness of the design of jobs.
5. The company's training function helps to build company and employee capabilities.

Process Management

1. The organization translates service requirements into efficient and effective delivery processes.
2. The organization uses a measurement plan to maintain process performance.
3. The organization's key support service processes are designed and maintained so that current requirements are met and operational performance is continuously improved.
4. The organization works to improve its relationship with suppliers.
5. The organization uses feedback from suppliers to improve internal processes.

Business Results

1. The organization tracks current levels and trends in key measures of quality for products and services.
2. The organization uses current levels and trends in key measures of operational and financial performance to drive performance improvement efforts.
3. The organization tracks current levels and trends in key measures of employees' well-being and satisfaction.
4. The organization tracks current levels and trends in key measures of supplier performance.

Customer Focus and Satisfaction

1. The organization employs an effective process for understanding which product and service features are most important to current and prospective customers.
2. The organization uses listening and learning strategies to address the future requirements and expectations of current and potential customers.
3. The organization has systems in place to resolve all customer complaints effectively and promptly.
4. The organization compares the satisfaction levels of customers with those at competing firms.
5. The organization analyzes current levels and trends in key measures of customer satisfaction and dissatisfaction segmented by customer groups and service types.

The Strategic Planning Process

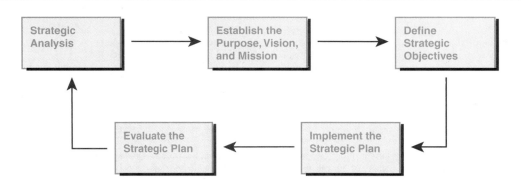

CONDUCT A STRATEGIC ANALYSIS

To formulate a strategic plan, managers must conduct a *strategic analysis* in order to understand the external environment and internal capabilities of the organization. One technique for doing this is the *SWOT analysis*.[18] *SWOT* is an acronym for **s**trengths and **w**eaknesses of an organization's internal capabilities and **o**pportunities and **t**hreats in the organization's environment. SWOT analysis permits managers to develop a strategic profile of the organization and assumes an organization will achieve strategic success by increasing strengths and opportunities and lessening weaknesses and threats. Figure A-6 lists key questions to guide managers in a SWOT analysis.

SWOT analysis provides managers with a logical framework for assessing their organization's current and future positions. This assessment permits managers to identify a set of alternative strategies. SWOT analysis can be conducted periodically to keep managers informed about changes in important internal or external factors. It wasn't until Chrysler Corporation conducted a SWOT analysis after near bankruptcy that managers fully understood what environmental threats and internal weaknesses they faced. The SWOT analysis enabled Chrysler's management to reassess its situation clearly and to successfully turn the company around. The Focus on Management feature on page A-13 discusses use of a SWOT analysis at Ruby Tuesday.

ESTABLISH THE PURPOSE, VISION, AND MISSION

Following strategic analysis, the next step in formulating a strategic plan is specifying the purpose, vision, and mission of the organization. The *purpose* of the organization is the reason for the organization's existence. For example, the purpose of an organization might be to earn a profit, preserve wetlands, or provide social services for citizens of a state. *Vision* is a vivid description of a preferred future. The vision can be simple or complex, concise or elaborate, but it must be clear, engaging, compelling, sincere, and stretching. In Martin Luther King's famous "I have a dream" speech, he was presenting his vision of a preferred future. Here are some *vision statements*:[19]

Questions to Guide Managers in a SWOT Analysis

INTERNAL

Strengths	Weaknesses
A distinctive competence?	No clear strategic direction?
Adequate financial resources?	A deteriorating competitive position?
Good competitive skills?	Obsolete factories?
Well thought of by buyers?	Subpar profitability?
An acknowledged market leader?	Lack of managerial depth and talent?
Well-conceived functional area strategies?	Missing any key skills or competencies?
Access to economies of scale?	Poor track record in implementing strategy?
Insulated from strong competitive pressures?	Plagued with internal operating problems?
Technology leader?	Vulnerable to competitive pressures?
Cost advantages?	Falling behind in research?
Competitive advantages?	Too narrow a product line?
Product innovation abilities?	Weak market image?
Proven management?	Competitive disadvantages?
Other?	Below-average marketing skills?
	Unable to finance needed changes in strategy?
	Other?

EXTERNAL

Opportunities	Threats
Serve additional customer groups?	Likely entry of new competitors?
Enter new markets or segments?	Rising sales of substitute products?
Expand product line to meet broader range of customer needs?	Slower market growth?
Diversify into related products?	Adverse government policies?
Vertical integration?	Growing competitive pressures?
Ability to move to better strategic group?	Vulnerability to recession and business cycle?
Complacency among rival firms?	Growing power of customers or suppliers?
Faster market growth?	Changing buyer needs and tastes?
Other?	Adverse demographic changes?
	Other?

Source: Adapted from A. A. Thompson, Jr., and A. J. Strickland, *Strategic Management: Concepts and Cases* (Plano, TX: Business Publications, Inc., 1990), 91.

> "A dynamic community, prosperous, environmentally committed, with boundless opportunity" (Singleton Shire, New South Wales, Australia).
> "The best people providing the best technologies for the world's best air force" (U.S. Air Force Research Laboratory).
> "To be recognized as the industry leader in total quality and customer service and to set the standard by which all others are judged in the aerospace industry" (Superior Forge, Inc.).
> "A healthier Nigeria in a healthier world" (Association of Nigerian Physicians in the Americas [ANPA]).

The organizational **mission** is the path managers choose to achieve the purpose and vision. The mission is often written down in the form of a **mission statement**.[20] Selecting a mission is a critical decision. The Focus on Management feature discusses the mission statement for Ben & Jerry's.

CORPORATE STRATEGY

Daniel A. Nordloh, Chief Operating Officer, MTM, Inc.

1. What is the overall mission of your organization? What are the related strategic objectives?

MTM's mission is to help organizations gain competitive advantages by offering comprehensive analysis, solutions, and support services to provide for the efficient capture, storage, retrieval, sharing, and management of information.

Our services and solutions help ensure business *continuity*, enable *collaboration*, help ensure legal and regulatory *compliance*, and reduce operating costs. A current strategic objective is to help business leaders understand the importance and value of the information that comprises organizations.

2. What are the biggest challenges you are encountering in developing and implementing strategies in your company? How are you handling the challenges?

MTM is evolving from the mindset of simply selling hardware and software to a culture that is collectively passionate about offering organizations the knowledge and services that will help them better themselves. Our strategy involves getting together with business leaders to discuss their objectives and learning how our services and solutions might help them accomplish their objectives.

The challenge lies in aligning MTM resources to ensure we are properly positioned with clients in terms of sales, marketing, and support efforts. We are responding to these challenges in a number of ways, but simply put, we are working to ensure we have the right people in the right opportunity within MTM and we clearly define responsibilities and manage expectations.

The following is a core value of MTM employees, emphasizing how important each of us is in helping one another: "We value that a quality group of employees, committed and accountable to a common goal, results in people needing to rely on one another to succeed. Such reliance builds trust, and from trust develops an environment in which we can all count on one another to confidently set our sights ever higher and work together to achieve our goals."

3. How rapidly do you need to adjust your strategies?

Ongoing planning provides the opportunity for us, for the most part, to anticipate proactively the need for strategic change. Once we determine the need for change, the resultant strategy is communicated and implemented rather quickly.

4. How does your strategy change as organic growth slows? When demand lessens, how will you transition to a strategy aligned with a mature market?

Our acquisition strategy continually provides opportunities to grow through additional geographic and/or industry markets. The technological solutions we use to solve customer problems evolve rather rapidly, thus frequently offering the opportunity for existing customers to realize additional benefits. We provide ongoing support of solutions and biannual report cards to our clients that indicate the value of deploying additional and/or more robust solutions. Such a market position provides both recurring and net new revenue opportunities.

5. What advice would you give students regarding the development of overall management skills?

Take personal responsibility for recognizing and honing your leadership skills. Such qualities are paramount in developing as a successful manager. Surround yourself with people that share similar values but have various backgrounds and interests. We can learn a great deal from one another. My experience consistently demonstrates that people who take a sincere interest in others tend to be infinitely more successful and fulfilled versus those who look out for only their own well-being.

Stuckey's Inc., a restaurant chain, saw its mission as providing "convenient, moderately priced home cooking" to travelers along the interstates. The company enjoyed huge success until the late 1970s, when interstate travel decreased and consumer taste shifted toward gourmet cuisine. By defining its mission as servicing interstate customers rather than dine-out customers in general, Stuckey's was forced to close most of its interstate facilities. By 1998, the chain had only 51 facilities—

SWOT Analysis at Ruby Tuesday

Ruby Tuesday operates and franchises more than 600 casual-dining restaurants in 38 states. As the first step in a thorough strategic management process, Ruby Tuesday conducted a SWOT analysis. Strengths identified included "growth rate of 20 percent," "strong technical skills," and "fast reaction time from management team." Among weaknesses were "lack of proactive approach (need outside help in developing)," "internal communications could be improved," and "need comprehensive review of compensation system." Some opportunities identified were "small markets are viable with smaller units," "delivery and takeout potential good," and "technology development in units and at headquarters." Finally, threats included "competition—direct: Chili's, T.G.I. Fridays, Bennigan's; indirect: Taco Bell, grocery stores, specialty markets," "difficulty in finding new sites (need population of 200,000 to support new site)," and "lack of differentiation in markets."

The SWOT analysis results were then used throughout the remainder of the strategic planning process.*

http://www.ruby-tuesday.com

*This example is from R. H. Woods, "Strategic Planning: A Look at Ruby Tuesday," *Cornell Hotel and Restaurant Administration Quarterly,* June 1994, pp. 41–50. See also C. D. Waters, "Ruby Tuesday to Divest Sister Chains in Favor of Core Product," *Nation's Restaurant News,* April 24, 2000, pp. 1–2.

down from 360 at its peak in the 1970s.[21] Thus the choice of a mission can have a significant and long-lasting effect on an organization's ability to achieve its purpose.

Most large firms have developed mission statements, and some develop separate mission statements for their subunits. For instance, Marriott International Inc. developed separate mission statements for the corporation and for the hotel division and then asked each of its 250 hotels to craft mission statements of their own.[22] Read about Marriott's core values, culture, brands, and other corporate information at http://marriott.com/corporateinfo/default.mi. The process model presented in the Bottom Line feature on page A-15 summarizes the basic steps associated with the development of an effective mission statement.

DEFINE STRATEGIC OBJECTIVES

Strategic objectives are needed to support the purpose, vision, and mission. Strategic objectives specify desired long-run and short-run results. Objective setting is an essential part of strategic planning, in that it specifies performance targets for managers at all levels of the organization. The setting of objectives is derived directly from the purpose, vision, and mission of the organization.

Existing objectives are often the result of prior strategic plans and are reset when they have been achieved or have gone unmet or the context of the organization has changed substantially. For instance, events such as governmental deregulation of the industry, emergence of new competitors, unionization of workers, lowered demand for products or services, and the retirement of top executives can each necessitate such reevaluation. When this occurs, managers must examine the organization's purpose, vision, and mission and determine whether strategic objectives need to be reset or the existing objectives are desirable and achievable. The Focus on Management feature on page A-16 discusses strategic objectives at Dana Corporation.

Setting objectives provides managers with a base for formulating strategies. Objectives also provide managers with criteria for selecting and rejecting alternative strategies based on an evaluation of each strategy's potential for achieving goals at all levels of the organization. As we discuss in the following sections, strategic objectives can be set at both the corporate and business-unit levels.

CHOOSE CORPORATE-LEVEL STRATEGIES

Corporate-level strategies provide direction for the total organization. Managers at the corporate level define a strategic direction that includes business units and departments within those business units. Managers often select either grand strategies or portfolio strategies for guiding their company.

GRAND STRATEGIES

A *grand strategy* is a broad plan to guide the organization toward reaching its goals. Depending on the size of the organization and the nature of the goals to be achieved, managers may choose to implement one of three grand strategies: growth, stability, or retrenchment.

A *growth strategy* is common in new emerging industries or industries that are undergoing rapid growth and gaining new external opportunities. Growth strategies can be appealing and may lead to great success, but they can also be risky. By focusing on growth, firms may fail to pay proper attention to efficiency, the needs of current customers, or even safety. The latter danger is vividly illustrated in the Focus on Management feature on page A-17.

A *stability strategy* is selected when managers want to protect the existing market share of the firm from external threats or have just completed a phase of rapid growth or divestment. A stability strategy allows managers to concentrate on

DEVELOPING A MISSION STATEMENT

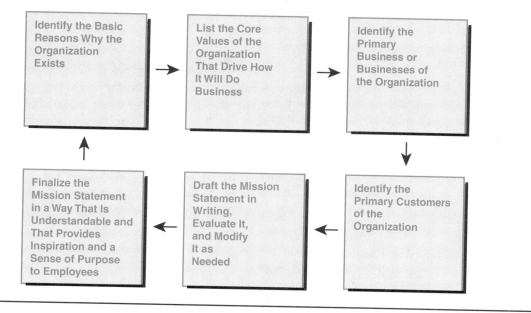

increasing the internal strengths of the firm. After many years of growth, Holiday Inn chose to stabilize its operations by curtailing growth and focusing on upgrading its hotels to compete more effectively.

Finally, a *retrenchment strategy* is often selected when managers are faced with declining performance due to internal weaknesses and external threats. Many firms, including General Motors and IBM, have dramatically cut back on hiring, laid off workers, reduced salaries, and sold off units in recent years.[23] As another example of retrenchment, Procter & Gamble had lost market share in recent years to such rivals as Unilever, in part because of its large size and slow response to competitors' actions.[24] In June 1999, P&G announced a major cost cutting as part of its Organization 2005 restructuring program. The initiative aimed to cut 15,000 staff, including 6,000 from Europe, the Mideast, and Africa. Designed to improve the speed of decision making and innovation and to set the foundation for future growth, the initiative also included a restructuring of operations to permit tailoring to the needs of local markets. Organization 2005 ran into problems, including substantial costs, leading to the resignation of P&G CEO Durk Jager. Ultimately, 17,400 positions were cut and the effort was terminated in June 2003. Nevertheless, Organization 2005 appears to have yielded long-term benefits, with sales climbing sharply in late 2003.[25] See http://www.pg.com.

Figure A-7 shows how a SWOT analysis can help with the choice of a grand strategy. After conducting a SWOT analysis, managers can locate the cell that best describes their present position and choose a suitable strategy. For example, if there are many opportunities in the firm's environment and the firm has substantial internal strengths, a growth strategy is appropriate. In contrast, if there are major

STRATEGIC OBJECTIVES AT DANA CORPORATION*

Dana Corporation, one of the world's largest independent suppliers to vehicle and engine manufacturers, operates hundreds of technology, manufacturing, and customer service facilities in 30 countries. Dana was selected in 1999 as a "Most-Admired Manufacturer" in the United States by *Start Magazine*, a business publication focused on technology issues, and two of its units have received the Malcolm Baldrige National Quality Award, one for manufacturing excellence and the other for service excellence. In recognizing Dana, *Start Magazine* emphasized Dana's strategic objectives, focus on technology, employee involvement, and reputation. Among Dana's strategic objectives are to have a return 15 percent on invested capital after tax, 25 percent of sales from products less than 2 years old, 40 hours of education per person annually, and 65 percent of business opportunity outside the United States. Read Dana's strategic plan at

http://www.dana.com/overview/strategic/

* For recent discussions of Dana Corporation, see D. Drickhamer, "Picking Up the Reins," *Industry Week*, November 2003, p. 15; and "Dana's Latest Tack: Shed After-market Business Units," *Automotive News*, December 15, 2003, p. 32.

---

threats in the environment and the firm has critical internal weaknesses, a retrenchment strategy may be needed.

PORTFOLIO STRATEGIES

A ***portfolio strategy*** considers the business mix of the firm—that is, the types of business units and product lines the firm controls. The BCG matrix and the GE matrix are two models many corporations use in selecting a portfolio strategy.

BCG Matrix. The ***BCG matrix*** model of strategy, developed by the Boston Consulting Group, emphasizes the nature of the internal mix of business units that are under the control of management. The BCG matrix views the overall investment a

---

FIGURE A-7
Grand Strategy Selection Matrix

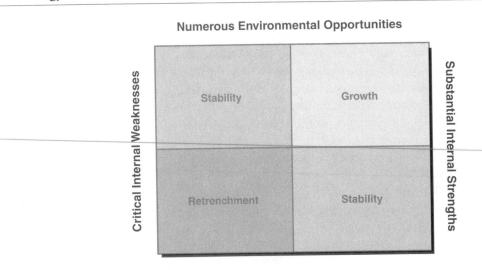

THE RISKS OF "GROWTH AT ANY COST"

The danger of "growth at any cost" was dramatically evident when ValuJet Flight 592 crashed shortly after takeoff from Miami International Airport on May 11, 1996, disappearing beneath the Florida Everglades and killing all 110 people aboard. Remarkably, ValuJet—which had grown since its inception to serve 17 states—was only two years old. ValuJet had attempted to achieve growth through aggressive efforts to maintain low costs. To pursue this strategy, it paid low salaries, used planes averaging older than 26 years (versus the industry average of 10 years), turned planes around in 20 minutes from arrival to departure (in the process making it difficult for Federal Aviation Administration [FAA] inspectors to do their jobs), and relied heavily on maintenance.* ValuJet pictured itself as the Wal-Mart of airlines. However, as noted by one writer, "The problem: Wal-Mart does not conduct business 35,000 feet above the ground."† A National Transportation Safety Board report, issued in August 1997, cited ValuJet for failing to oversee properly its contract maintenance program and ensure that contractors complied with maintenance, training, and hazardous material requirements. One of those contractors—SabreTech Inc.—was charged in July 1999 with murder and manslaughter for its part in the disaster. The FAA grounded ValuJet after the crash.

The airline later merged with discount carrier AirTran and now flies under the name AirTran.#
http://www.airtran.com/

* See, for instance, D. Greising, "Growing Pains at ValuJet," *Business Week*, May 15, 1995, pp. 50–51; and J. T. McKenna, "FAA Inspection Cites ValuJet Oversight Lapses," *Aviation Week and Space Technology*, March 9, 1998, p. 59.

† M. Merzer and I. P. Cordle, "Seeds of ValuJet Disaster Found Fertile Soil," *Miami Herald*, May 4, 1997, p. A1.

C. Haddad, "Catch Him If You Can: Joe Leonard's Low Costs Have AirTran Outflying Delta," *Business Week*, September 15, 2003, p. 93.

---

firm has made in various lines of business. Its objective is to help managers decide about the deployment of resources to each business unit or product line.[26]

In the BCG matrix, business units or product lines are classified according to two dimensions: overall market growth rate and market share held by the business unit. The classification of business units within the matrix leads to identification of the four strategic types shown in Figure A-8: stars, cash cows, question marks, and dogs.[27]

> A *star* is a business unit that has both a high market growth rate and a relatively large share of the market. Typically, this is a product line or business that has high potential for growth and needs large amounts of short-run cash to support rapid growth. Stars are attractive to organizations because they have the potential to increase sales and therefore to generate large amounts of profit in the future.

> A *cash cow* has a large share of the market, but there is little growth. Large amounts of surplus cash can be milked from a cash cow and channeled into stars.

> *Question marks* exist in a rapidly growing market but have a small market share. Managers must decide whether to invest more capital into the business unit or product to take advantage of the high growth opportunity (that is, to transform it into a star) or to divest it to emphasize other business units and products in the portfolio. Either way, managers are faced with some risk—in making a large investment that may result in failure or in passing up an opportunity that may later turn out to be highly profitable.

FIGURE A-8
The BCG Portfolio Matrix

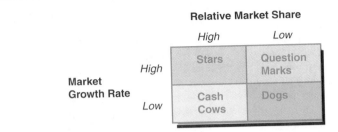

Relative Market Share

	High	Low
High	Stars	Question Marks
Low	Cash Cows	Dogs

Market Growth Rate

> A **dog** is a poor performer because of little growth in the market and a small market share. Usually, dogs are a cash drain on the organization because they are unable to support themselves with the small amount of revenue they can generate. Management must either try to sell the unit to another company or liquidate its assets.

GE Matrix. The *GE matrix*, sometimes called the *GE nine-cell matrix*, provides upper managers with a way to evaluate existing business units and those they might like to acquire. Developed by General Electric with the help of the consulting firm McKinsey and Company, the GE matrix introduces multiple factors for evaluating business units. As shown in Figure A-9, business units are plotted in the matrix on two dimensions: industry attractiveness and business strength. *Industry attractive-*

FIGURE A-9
The GE Matrix

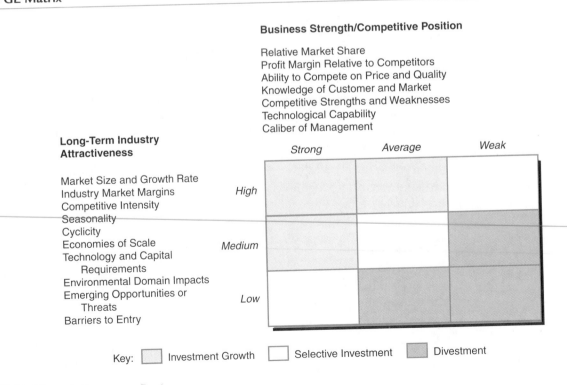

Business Strength/Competitive Position

Relative Market Share
Profit Margin Relative to Competitors
Ability to Compete on Price and Quality
Knowledge of Customer and Market
Competitive Strengths and Weaknesses
Technological Capability
Caliber of Management

Long-Term Industry Attractiveness

Market Size and Growth Rate
Industry Market Margins
Competitive Intensity
Seasonality
Cyclicity
Economies of Scale
Technology and Capital
    Requirements
Environmental Domain Impacts
Emerging Opportunities or
    Threats
Barriers to Entry

	Strong	Average	Weak
High			
Medium			
Low			

Key: ☐ Investment Growth ☐ Selective Investment ☐ Divestment *ness* includes such factors as market size, market growth rate, seasonality, types of competitors, and technical complexity of products. *Business strength* is determined by such factors as profit margins, market share, quality of management, and manufacturing technology.

Based on where the business unit is located on the two dimensions, one of three basic strategies is recommended: investment growth, selective investment, or divestment. Business units falling in the lightly shaded cells of Figure A-9 are candidates for investment and growth, because they rank high in both industry attractiveness and business strength. Business units falling in the white cells should only be invested in selectively. Investments should be cautious until a change in the unit's strength or degree of industry attractiveness occurs. Business units in the dark cells are candidates for divestment because they rank low in both industry attractiveness and business strength.

Grand strategies and portfolio strategies are useful for corporate strategists whether they seek to build the organization through internal growth or through acquisitions. Since the 1980s portfolio strategies have been used extensively to evaluate business units as candidates for acquisition.

CHOOSE BUSINESS-UNIT-LEVEL STRATEGIES

Several models have been developed for describing and explaining different types of business-unit-level strategies. Two such models useful to managers in understanding how the strategy of their business units relates to their industry are the *adaptation model* and the *competitive model*. Each model makes different assumptions about the relationships among strategy, organization, and the environment. The following discussion of each strategic type focuses on its assumptions, alternative strategies that managers can consider, and the way the strategy can be implemented for success.

ADAPTATION MODEL

Raymond Miles and Charles Snow developed the adaptation model of organizational strategy.[28] The *adaptation model* contends that a major thrust of strategic management should be the alignment of organizational activities with key dimensions of the organization's environment. To accomplish this end, managers must set up a strategy that will adapt to environmental conditions and also manage internal activities of the organization to support the selected strategy. Adaptation of the organization to the environment is accomplished by simultaneously solving three critical strategic problems: the entrepreneurial problem, the engineering problem, and the administrative problem.

> The *entrepreneurial problem* considers what managers believe to be their market. It is solved by determining what goods or services the organization will produce for a defined product-market domain.

> The *engineering problem* is one of deciding which methods are appropriate for the production and distribution of goods and services. The solution to the engineering problem is determined by the solution of the entrepreneurial problem, or management's decision on what products or services will be provided to a market. The solution usually involves implementing systems for pro-

ducing, controlling, and distributing the goods or services that support the organization's mission. Using robots on the production line, providing employees with authority to decide on the pace of work, and distributing goods or services to specific markets can be solutions to the engineering problem.

> The *administrative problem* addresses the need to develop an appropriate administrative system within the organization. It is solved by designing an organizational system that will enhance the coordination of activities to achieve the solutions to the entrepreneurial and engineering problems. Decisions about the degree of bureaucracy of the organization, number of employees supervised by each manager, and methods of hiring employees may be questions that must be answered to solve the administrative problem.

The adaptation model of organizational strategy contends that managers must interrelate the three solutions to the entrepreneurial, engineering, and administrative problems. Organizations that are most successful, according to this strategic model, are those that have correctly matched the solutions to the conditions of the organization's environment. Four types of organizations, classified by the ways they solve these problems, are identified by Miles and Snow: defenders, prospectors, analyzers, and reactors.

Defenders. The *defender strategy* is carried out when management seeks or creates an environment that is stable. Managers will emphasize protecting the market share they have gained. A defender solves the entrepreneurial problem by defining a narrow market segment and producing only a few products or services to provide to the market. It solves the engineering problem by emphasizing efficiency, thus lowering costs and permitting a price that competitors cannot match. It uses rigid bureaucratic controls to solve the administrative problem, thus reducing errors and increasing efficiency. The defender strategy is similar to the stability strategy we discussed previously. McDonald's exemplifies a defender organization by focusing on a narrow market segment (fast-food consumers), maximizing efficiency in production (cooking methods that lead to product uniformity), and enforcing strict employee controls (dress and behavior codes for employees). See *http://www .mcdonalds.com/*.

Prospectors. The *prospector strategy* is the opposite of the defender strategy. The prospector seeks or creates an unstable environment in the form of rapid change and high growth in the market. Management tries to locate and exploit new product opportunities. It solves the entrepreneurial problem by defining the environment in broad terms to encourage innovation and diversity in activities. Because internal activities must be diverse and adaptable to new opportunities, managers solve the engineering problem by avoiding long-term commitments to any single method of production. Instead, large capital investments are avoided and multiple methods of production that can be changed as necessary are used. Administratively, managers encourage flexibility in member activities through loose controls to maximize growth and change.

Johnson & Johnson represents a prospector organization by broadly defining its market (home and personal products), employing multiple methods of production (more than 200 operating companies that are continually changing), and setting loose administrative controls (each division manager selects the administrative structure believed to be appropriate for his or her employees). See *http://www .johnsonandjohnson.com/home.html*.

Analyzers. An analyzer is an organization that exists between the two extremes of defender and prospector. The *analyzer strategy* involves adapting solutions from both the defender and prospector strategies to the three problems. Consistency is maintained by identifying two areas of activity for the organization. One is a stable market, where a defender strategy is pursued. The other is an unstable market, where a prospector strategy is pursued. The major concern of managers is to maintain a balance between organizational subunits that are defender oriented and subunits that are prospector oriented. The entrepreneurial problem is solved by identifying two market segments—one stable and the other changing. The engineering problem is solved by managers who emphasize methods of efficiency in production for the stable subunits and methods of flexibility for those subunits oriented to a changing market. The administrative problem is solved by setting up a structure with tight controls over stable subunit activities and loose controls for subunits engaged in developing new products.

Reactors. A reactor organization is basically one that has suffered strategic failure. This may be due to poor managerial decisions about the strategic plan. Miles and Snow note that use of the *reactor strategy* may be due to causes such as the following.

> Top management has not clearly articulated the organization's strategy.

> Management has not fully shaped the organization's structure and processes to fit a chosen strategy.

> Management has not changed the organization's strategy/structure relationship in the face of major environmental changes.

If an organization wants to end the reactor mode of strategy, management must develop either new solutions to the entrepreneurial, engineering, or administrative problem or solutions to all three, depending on what caused the failure.

COMPETITIVE MODEL

The competitive model of organizational strategy was developed by Michael Porter.[29] The *competitive model* contends that the nature and degree of competition in an industry determine the strategy appropriate for managers to formulate and implement.

Industry Forces. Porter identified five industry forces that determine the degree of competition within an industry. Thus his model is sometimes called the *Five Forces Model of Industry Competition*.

> *The threat of new entrants to compete in the industry.* New competitors entering an industry often bring with them large resources with the goal of gaining market share and profits. This may be achieved through the creation of a new company, as was the case with Kmart in the retail industry, or by diversification of a firm in one industry into another industry through acquisition, as Philip Morris did with the purchase of Miller Brewing. How serious the threat of entry is depends on barriers to entry that exist in the industry and on the reaction the new entrant can expect from existing competitors.

> *The bargaining power of suppliers in the industry.* In some industries, suppliers of materials to competing organizations can gain power by either raising prices for their materials or lowering quality. Thus powerful suppliers can squeeze profitability out of an industry by dictating the price and quality of the materials that are bought by the competing firms. Suppliers should not be thought of solely as firms that manufacture a product to provide to an industry. Labor unions can also be a supplier group. For instance, in the sports industry, players' unions can exert a strong influence over the profit of team owners, since the unions are more concentrated, there are few substitutes, the product is important to the buyer's business, products are differentiated (e.g., fan loyalties), and players could conceivably start their own league.

> *The bargaining power of customers in the industry.* The conditions that make customers powerful are similar to those that make suppliers powerful. Customers can force down prices, demand higher quality goods and services, and play competitors against each other—all of which serve to lower profitability in the industry. Customers, of course, include individual customers as well as organizations. Looking again at the sports industry, two types of customers for sports entertainment can be identified: fans who attend games and television networks that provide games to viewers in their homes. It is easy to understand why television networks have more bargaining power over team owners than do fans attending the games.

> *The threat of substitute products or services from potential competitors.* Substitute products limit the potential prices of goods or services in an industry. If the price of a product is too high, buyers will seek substitutes. Producers of sugar have been faced with many substitutes that have greatly eroded profits and kept the price of sugar low. Saccharin, corn syrup, and aspartame have been introduced as substitutes for sugar and marketed at lower prices. As a result, sugar producers have been forced to accept a smaller share of the sweetener market.[30]

> *Competitive rivalry among existing firms.* Rivalry among existing competitors takes the form of such tactics as price competition, advertising battles, new product introductions, and increased customer service or warranties. Rivalry occurs because managers of competing organizations believe they can improve their position in the industry by implementing one or more of these tactics.

The goal of a competitive strategy is to find a position in the industry where the organization can best defend itself against those forces or can influence them in its favor. Managers of organizations who best understand these forces, according to Porter, will have greater success at selecting a strategy that will be suited to conditions in the industry.

The competitive model provides a mapping of industry conditions that managers can examine to develop a strategy that will improve organizational performance. Once management has assessed the factors that influence competition within the industry, competitive opportunities and threats can be determined. Identification of organizational strengths and weaknesses will then enable management to identify a strategy that will help the organization compete effectively.

Competitive Strategies. Porter identified three strategies that managers can implement to compete against other organizations in the industry: (1) overall cost leadership, (2) differentiation, and (3) focus. The degree of success of each competitive strategy depends on the amount of commitment members have to the strategy and the effectiveness of managers in implementing the strategy.[31]

> **Overall cost leadership.** The *overall cost leadership strategy* requires management to formulate and implement a strategic plan that will lead to construction of efficient facilities; attainment of cost reductions; tight cost and overhead control; avoidance of marginal customer accounts; and minimal costs in areas such as research and development, service, sales, and advertising. By maintaining an efficient and low-cost organization, management can attain above-average returns in the industry and make it difficult for less efficient competitors to match the price of the product. If less efficient competitors are successful at matching the product price of the overall cost leader, their returns will be much lower because of their higher costs.

The ability to achieve a position of overall cost leadership often requires a high market share, favorable access to raw materials, design of products for ease in manufacturing, maintenance of a wide line of related products, and service to all major customers to build volume. Briggs & Stratton, Du Pont, and Texas Instruments are among firms that have employed this strategy successfully.[32]

> **Differentiation.** The *differentiation strategy* recognizes that a firm's product is unique in relation to other products produced in the industry. Management cannot ignore costs in implementing the differentiation strategy; however, costs are a secondary rather than a primary consideration. A differentiation strategy is successful through emphasis on strong marketing abilities, creative product engineering, strong commitment to research and development, a reputation for quality or technological leadership, and a long tradition in the industry for having skilled employees.

Often the adoption of a differentiation strategy means a high market share must be sacrificed. When the product is perceived to be superior, margins can be raised. However, customers may recognize the superiority of the product but be unwilling to pay the high price. Smaller retailers competing with giant Wal-Mart have turned to differentiation strategies to survive.[33]

> **Focus.** The *focus strategy* pursues either an overall cost leadership strategy or a differentiation strategy by focusing on a narrow customer group, product line, or geographic market. The focus strategy provides products or services to a narrow segment, or niche, in the industry. Examples of successful focus strategies are Illinois Tool Works, which designs fasteners, and Fort Howard Paper, which provides industrial-grade paper. Gap, with its limited product lines and concentration on traditional sources of success, is another example of successful use of a focus strategy.[34]

The competitive model identifies five industry forces that managers must consider in formulating and implementing strategies that will lead to organizational effectiveness. Analysis of these five forces by management should enable it to devise a strategic plan that will lead to efficiency in operations (overall cost leadership), uniqueness of product (differentiation), or targeting a narrow market segment and developing efficiency or uniqueness (focus). Those organizations that develop the best methods for achieving these goals will be the most successful in the industry.

IMPLEMENT THE STRATEGIC PLAN

Vince Lombardi, the famous coach of the Green Bay Packers football team, once said, "The best game plan in the world never blocked or tackled anybody." Like football coaches, managers must see that strategic plans are converted into action. To do this, they must effectively communicate the plan; assign responsibility and authority for activities within the plan; motivate employees to achieve the plan; develop methods for measuring the results of activities; and develop procedures for taking any necessary corrective action. These are among the skills we discuss throughout the text.

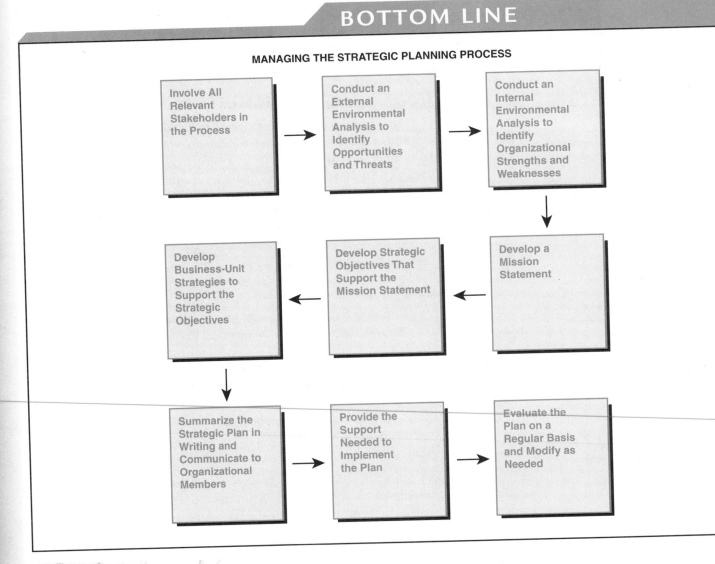

BOTTOM LINE

MANAGING THE STRATEGIC PLANNING PROCESS

Involve All Relevant Stakeholders in the Process → Conduct an External Environmental Analysis to Identify Opportunities and Threats → Conduct an Internal Environmental Analysis to Identify Organizational Strengths and Weaknesses

Develop Business-Unit Strategies to Support the Strategic Objectives ← Develop Strategic Objectives That Support the Mission Statement ← Develop a Mission Statement

Summarize the Strategic Plan in Writing and Communicate to Organizational Members → Provide the Support Needed to Implement the Plan → Evaluate the Plan on a Regular Basis and Modify as Needed

EVALUATE THE STRATEGIC PLAN

We began this appendix with a discussion of ways to examine organizational effectiveness. That discussion suggested that effectiveness has many facets. If so, we must assess effectiveness of the strategic plan on those multiple facets. The *balanced scorecard (BSC)* is a conceptual framework for translating an organization's vision into a set of performance indicators distributed among four perspectives: financial, customer, internal business processes, and learning and growth.[35] Using the BSC, companies can monitor their current performance (finances, customer satisfaction, and business process results) and their efforts to improve processes, motivate and educate employees, and enhance information systems—that is, their ability to learn and improve. The Bottom Line feature presents a process model summarizing the basic steps associated with managing the strategic planning process.

As the information and examples throughout this appendix make clear, careful attention to strategy is critical to organizational success. Unfortunately, one survey showed that 85 percent of management teams spend less than one hour each month discussing strategy.[36] We hope that you as a manager will give these crucial skills the attention they deserve.

LIGHTEN UP

AMBUSHES AND GOLDEN PARACHUTES*

Here is some of the colorful language used by corporate strategists in discussing mergers and acquisitions:

Afterglow: Postmerger euphoria of acquirer and/or acquiree, usually soon lost.

Ambush: Swift and premeditated takeover attempt.

Big-game hunting: Planning and executing takeovers of large companies.

Big-hat boys: Texas moneymen interested in "big-game hunting."

Cyanide pill: Antitakeover finance strategy in which the potential target arranges for long-term debt to fall due immediately and in full if it is acquired.

Double Pac-Man strategy: Target firm makes tender offer for the stock of its would-be acquirer.

Golden parachutes: Provision in the employment contracts of top executives that ensures them a lucrative financial landing if the firm is acquired in a takeover.

Hired guns: Merger and acquisition specialists, other investment bankers, and lawyers employed by either side in any takeover.

Mushroom treatment: Postmerger problems from an acquired executive's standpoint: "First they buried us in manure, then they left us in the dark awhile; then they let us stew; and finally they canned us."

Pirates or raiders: Hostile acquirers.

Sharks: Takeover artists.

Shark repellent: Protective strategies for preventing or combating a hostile tender offer.

White knight: Acceptable acquirer sought by a potential acquiree to forestall an unfriendly takeover; the preferred suitor.

Wounded list: Executives of an acquired firm who develop health or career problems from the deal.

*Excerpted and adapted from P. M. Hirsch, "From Ambushes to Golden Parachutes: Corporate Takeovers as an Instance of Cultural Framing and Institutional Integration," *American Journal of Sociology*, 1986, 91(4), pp. 830–835.

APPENDIX B
MANAGING CAREERS

These are interesting times to be embarking on a career. Each year, hundreds of thousands of business graduates enter the job market. Fortunately, business is one field that offers a rich diversity of interesting job opportunities and a relatively favorable job market. Nevertheless, as we have seen throughout this book, business is changing rapidly, and jobs and careers are changing with it. Downsizing, mergers, market and technological changes, new perspectives on the psychological contract, and shifting patterns and levels of global competition are creating unprecedented levels of uncertainty, challenge, and opportunity.

In the midst of this new world of work, people are rethinking the meaning of careers and of career success, and they are less inclined than in the past to pursue a lifelong career with a single firm. Only about a third of all careers in the United States are traditional (i.e., vertical careers in corporations), and this figure continues to fall.[1] Employees regularly report concerns about losing their jobs. Remarkably, Labor Department statistics project that the average person entering the work force in the United States will have three and a half careers and work for 10 employers, keeping each job for only about three and a half years. Given this reality, employees must prepare themselves for a *portfolio career*: one in which people develop a portfolio of their accomplishments in different companies. They can then carry that portfolio with them to help to secure new jobs.[2] These are times that call for energy, careful and intelligent career planning, and active career self-management.

In this appendix, we examine approaches to managing your career. We discuss the protean career, career stages in organizations, fitting people to careers, and guidelines for self-management of careers, and we close with a focus on career issues relating to diversity and mentoring. In the Voice of Experience feature, Kerry Snyder, a manager at Met Life Auto & Home, talks about the importance of career management issues in real world organizations.

THE PROTEAN CAREER

Let's begin by discussing what we mean by a career. Certainly, a career has to do with getting jobs, and perhaps with moving between jobs, places, and levels of responsibility and challenge. However, a career means more than that.

Proteus was a character in Greek mythology who could change shape in any way he wanted—from fire to lion to dragon to tree. Only when Proteus was held down was such change impossible. Douglas Hall has drawn on this myth to coin the term *protean career.* According to this view of careers, there is much more to a career than just moving up the hierarchies of organizations:

MANAGING CAREERS

Kerry Snyder, Manager, Met Life Auto & Home

1. Why is it important for organizations to help employees with their career development?

Employees are a company's greatest asset. Their development is paramount for growth in the organization. It is an important relationship because the organization grows only if employees continue to develop. A unified vision for the future is needed so the growth can begin and can be sustained within the organization.

2. What does your company do to support the development of its employees?

The opportunity to cross-train within different departments, job rotations, and special projects are available for employees for ongoing career development. Additionally, the organization encourages employees to enroll in industry-related courses and promotes community volunteer involvement programs as well. Participants are then recognized within their departments and the organization for their completed activities.

3. What do you do to support the career development of your employees?

I have held coaching sessions with employees on how their contributions impact the organization and what types of educational courses or specific job-related training would benefit them and help them achieve their development needs. I have helped advance employees, to meet their career development goals through new position assignments, outside of my management scope.

4. What advice would you give to students about what they should do to enhance their career development once they obtain a job in a real-world organization?

Continue to read, to learn, and to stay in touch with events occurring throughout the world not only in business but in the political and cultural arenas as well. These trends will shape how business will be conducted in the future.

A job is obtained, but a career is built. Too many students jump into their first job assignment within a particular industry and work at mastering their job but fail to hone skill sets needed to take the next step in building their careers. Organizations view employees as resources and expect their employees to contribute value to the organization.

Employees must maximize their contribution to the organization by adding value. They can increase their value by investing in ongoing learning and improving their competencies. The investment will pay off in the form of career advancement.

The protean career is a process which the person, not the organization, is managing. It consists of all of the person's varied experiences in education, training, work in several organizations, change in occupational field, etc. The protean career is not what happens to the person in any one organization. The protean person's own personal career choices and search for fulfillment are the unifying or integrative elements in his or her life. The criterion of success is internal (psychological success), not external.[3]

Viewed in this light, a career is an ongoing sequence of events, some of which may have little or nothing to do with money or prestige. Also, according to this view, a career extends over the entire work life. What happens in one year or in one corporation is just a small piece of the rich career mosaic. Finally, determining whether a career is successful is up to the individual. If people are happy with the way their careers turn out, how can anyone say their careers are failures? Figure B-1 summarizes key differences between the traditional view of careers and the protean view.

FIGURE B-1
The Protean Versus the Traditional Career

Issue	Protean Career	Traditional Career
Who's in charge?	Person	Organization
Core values	Freedom; growth	Advancement; power
Degree of mobility	High	Lower
Important performance dimensions	Psychological success	Position level; salary
Important attitude dimensions	Work satisfaction; professional commitment	Work satisfaction; organizational commitment
Important personality dimensions	Do I respect myself? (self-esteem);	Am I respected in this organization? (esteem from others);
	What do I want to do? (self-awareness)	What should I do? (organizational awareness)
Important adaptability dimensions	Work-related flexibility; current competence (measure: marketability)	Organization-related flexibility (measure: organizational survival)

CAREER IDENTITY

The protean view of careers also highlights the fact that much more than one's company and hierarchical level change throughout a career. There may, for instance, be changes in *career identity*, the integration of individuals with the requirements of their career environments.[4] Our identities define who we are, and the sort of work we do plays a large part in establishing an identity. Hall points out that "The question, 'What do you do?' is often a more acceptable way of asking, 'Who are you?'"[5] As such, one measure of career success is whether our work is consistent with our self-identity. If you think of yourself as a creative, responsible individual but you spend your days doing routine, low-level tasks, you probably don't think of your career as successful.

CAREER ADAPTABILITY

Similarly, *career adaptability* may change over the course of one's career. Such terms as *managerial obsolescence* suggest that, after a while on the job, managers may become inflexible in their attitudes, outdated in their knowledge, and less intrinsically motivated to do the job. As such, career adaptability is the ability to respond successfully to new job demands. Adaptability may result from training in technical and interpersonal skills; working with new, young employees who provide a fresh perspective and knowledge of new concepts; job rotation; and independent study. Another measure of career success, then, is the degree to which you have been able to stay current, fresh, and responsive.

CAREER ATTITUDES

Finally, *career attitudes* may change over the course of careers. These attitudes, such as satisfaction with work and commitment to the organization, are shaped by many factors inside and outside the organization. Clearly, if you are dissatisfied with your job and company, you probably don't think of your career as successful.

CAREER STAGES IN ORGANIZATIONS

Many writers have drawn parallels between the life cycle and career stages. Although social changes are calling into question whether such a perspective is appropriate, it probably is the case that careers do have a series of stages and those stages are linked in part to life stages. Figure B-2 shows roles associated with four career stages.

As an apprentice, the individual is directed by others and concerned with helping and learning. Colleagues become independent contributors to the organization. At the mentor stage, individuals assume responsibility for others, spending time on such activities as training and guidance. Finally, sponsors are concerned with directing the organization as a whole and shaping its direction. As people pass through these stages in their early, middle, and late careers, their task needs and socioemotional needs change. Figure B-3 presents a summary of these evolving needs. Let's consider some important aspects of each of these stages.

EARLY CAREER ISSUES

Early in their careers, people often experience great uncertainty about their competence and performance potential.[6] They are likely to need guidance and support to get their careers moving. This stressful time can have a major influence on the remainder of their careers.

Career Problems of Young Managers. Young managers commonly face a variety of problems. An awareness of these problems may help you to deal with them when they occur.

> **Early frustration and dissatisfaction.** As our discussion of socialization processes suggested, young managers' job expectations often exceed reality. Their academic training may have focused on cases in which they took the roles of top-level executives. So they may now expect to get a lot of responsibility quickly. Instead, they are often placed in routine, boring jobs until they have proven themselves. As a result, young managers may experience severe reality shock, become frustrated, and perhaps leave the firm. If the company has painted an overly bright picture when recruiting, this reality shock may be especially great.

FIGURE B-2
Roles Associated with Four Career Stages

	Stage 1	Stage 2	Stage 3	Stage 4
Central Activity	Helping Learning Following directions	independent Contributor	Training Interacting	Shaping the direction of the organization
Primary Relationship	Apprentice	Colleague	Mentor	Sponsor
Major Psychological Issues	Dependence	Independence	Assuming responsibility for others	Exercising power

FIGURE B-3
Developmental Needs in Careers

Stage	Task Needs	Socioemotional Needs
Early Career	• Develop action skills • Develop a specialty • Develop creativity, innovation • Rotate into a new area after 3–5 years	• Support • Autonomy • Deal with feelings of rivalry, competition
Middle Career	• Develop skills in training and coaching others (younger employees) • Train for updating and integrating skills • Develop broader view of work and organization • Job rotation into new job requiring new skills	• Opportunity to express feelings about midlife (anguish, defeat, limited time, restlessness) • Reorganize thinking about self (mortality, values, family, work) • Reduce self-indulgence and competitiveness • Support and mutual problem solving for coping with midcareer stress
Late Career	• Shift from power role to one of consultation, guidance, wisdom • Begin to establish self in activities outside the organization (start on a part-time basis)	• Support and counseling to help see integrated life experiences as a platform for others • Acceptance of one's one-and-only life cycle • Gradual detachment from organization

> **Insensitivity and passivity.** Organizations are political. Young managers often are insensitive to the political aspects of organizations and may resent them. They may also be passive, hoping things will turn out for the best. As a result, they may not actively explore the organizational environment to understand relationships and attitudes and to clarify their own positions.

> **Loyalty dilemmas.** Most people in authority value subordinates' loyalty. One survey asked chief executives what they value most in subordinates. Fully 86 percent said they value loyalty most, distantly followed by sense of humor (6 percent), capacity for hard work (5 percent), and integrity (3 percent).[7] However, there are many versions of loyalty. Some see loyalty as obedience: Subordinates are loyal if they do what they are told. Others interpret loyalty as putting in effort and long hours to prove concern for the company. To still others, loyalty is successful completion of tasks or protection of the superior from ridicule and adverse evaluation by others or giving the superior honest information about mistakes and potential failures. Unfortunately, young managers often do not know which version of loyalty the organization or superior expects. These uncertainties and conflicts may cause the young manager to conform to power and authority, to try to change the superior's expectations, or to leave.[8]

> **Personal anxiety.** Young managers may experience anxiety. They often find that just at the time they are beginning to reap the rewards of their jobs, they question the value of what they are doing. They may say, "I am making $70,000 a year, but I don't think what the company produces has much value to society." As a result, young managers may fear they are selling out. Young managers may also feel anxiety about commitment to the organization. They may feel they would benefit from conforming to the norms of the organization and having a sense of certainty about their careers, but they don't want to close doors and shatter illusions about possibilities. Finally, young managers

may feel anxious about being dependent on others in the organization or they may also feel anxiety because others in the organization—subordinates, peers, and even superiors—are dependent on them.[9]

> **Ethical dilemmas.** Most young managers face unexpected career dilemmas that force them to think about what is ethical and unethical.[10] In one survey, 30 percent of new employees admitted to feeling pressure to compromise their company's ethical standards because of deadlines, overly aggressive goals, concerns about the company's survival, and other factors. Thirty percent reported personally observing conduct that violated the law or their company's standards in the last year. Frequently mentioned types of misconduct included falsifying reports or records, lying to supervisors, theft, and sexual harassment. However, less than half the employees said they tried to report what they saw to others in the company.[11] In trying to resolve ethical dilemmas, the young manager may consider economic self-interest, obedience to the law, observance of religious principles, obedience to a superior, or doing the greatest good for the greatest number.[12]

> **Job security.** Job security has always been a concern for new managers. Recognizing this, some companies are using security as a lure.[13] For example, Electronic Data Systems offers three-year contracts, although it requires a payback of a portion of new hires' training costs if they bail out early.[14] Similarly, probably few careers offer less job security than professional sports, where an injury or poor year can mean the end of a promising career. The Cleveland Indians used this knowledge as part of their rebuilding strategy. The Indians signed on more than a dozen young players at less pay than they might get elsewhere but with assurances they'd be employed for at least two or three years.[15]

> **Organizational seduction.** Anyone who has read John Grisham's novel *The Firm* or has seen the movie knows about another early-career danger: organizational seduction.[16] This occurs when the organization provides new employees with jobs that are very enticing, in terms of pleasant work environment, stimulating tasks, chances to satisfy status needs, and so on. When this happens, employees sometimes become so committed to the organization that their longer-term career interests—and perhaps their nonwork lives—are hurt. The employees may, for instance, feel guilt about leaving the firm for a better opportunity, may burn out through overwork, may pass up professional development opportunities, may neglect their families, and so on. Seduction is, of course, difficult to deal with precisely because it's so pleasant. However, employees in early career would be wise to listen to the counsel of others about whether the energy and focus they are giving the job are appropriate and to ask whether the short-term pleasures of organizational seduction are worth the longer-term costs.

The Importance of Early Career Challenge and Success. Our discussion of organizational seduction suggests that stimulating, challenging jobs may have some inherent dangers. At the same time, though, considerable evidence indicates that, kept in proper balance, early job challenge can be very helpful. A model of the career-growth cycle suggests the importance of this early career challenge.[17]

According to this model, shown in Figure B-4, a job that provides challenging, stretching goals triggers the process of career growth. The clearer and more challenging the goals and the more support the job provides, the more effort the employee will exert and the greater the chance of good performance. A person who does a good job and receives positive feedback will feel successful. These feelings of psychological success will enhance self-esteem and increase job involvement. This will lead, in turn, to the setting of future stretching goals and continued career growth.[18]

MIDDLE CAREER ISSUES

By midcareer, individuals are becoming fully independent contributors. They have learned the ropes of organizational life and focus on exposure and advancement. There can be many new stresses at this stage, and some individuals may find their movement thwarted.

Coping with Midcareer Stress.[19]
At midcareer, the employee experiences many physiological, attitudinal, occupational, and family changes. There is an awareness of aging and recognition that many ambitious career goals will never be attained. New life goals may be sought. A disturbing sense of obsolescence may develop, coupled with a feeling that one is becoming less mobile and less attractive in the job market.

Having realistic expectations about midcareer crises and transitions seems to ease the stress and pain of this period. In addition, midcareer employees can receive training to provide exposure to new skills and ideas. They may also be trained to help younger employees, thereby remaining fresh and up to date. Midcareer employees can be encouraged to face their feelings of restlessness and insecurity, to

FIGURE B-4
The Career-Growth Cycle

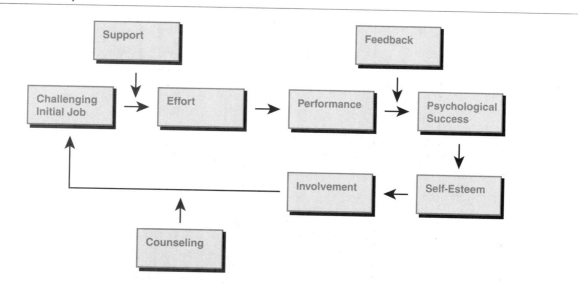

reexamine their values and life goals, and to set new goals or recommit themselves to old ones. Life-planning and career-planning exercises may be especially valuable. The company can take steps to deal with obsolescence through seminars, workshops, degree programs, and other forms of retreading. It can also try to prevent obsolescence in the first place by providing challenging job assignments that force the individual to build new skills and learn about new developments in the professional field.

The Career Plateau. Historically, the *career plateau* was defined as the point in a career where the likelihood of further promotions is very low.[20] More recently, it has been suggested that plateauing may take two forms, hierarchical and content. A *hierarchical plateau* is consistent with the initial definition. That is, it results when an individual has little chance of further vertical movement in the organization. A *content plateau* occurs when the individual is no longer challenged by his or her job responsibilities. Employees experiencing content plateaus report less favorable job attitudes than those experiencing hierarchical plateaus. Not surprisingly, those facing both sorts of plateaus report the least favorable job attitudes.[21]

Employees often experience plateaus at midcareer. Some people may hierarchically plateau because they simply don't want any more promotions. Perhaps they enjoy their current jobs, do them well, and simply don't want to move out of them. Or perhaps they just don't want more responsibility at this point in their lives. Others may have plateaued because of poor performance. Still others find there is no place they can go; there are no openings at higher levels. So, the fact that an employee is plateaued doesn't necessarily say anything about his or her performance.

Figure B-5 presents a model of managerial career states. The model classifies four principal career states on the basis of current performance and likelihood of future promotion.

Learners have high potential for advancement but are now performing below standards. Trainees or employees recently promoted into new positions that they have not yet mastered would be examples. *Stars*, performing well and having high potential for continued advancement, are on a fast track. *Solid citizens* have good current performance but little promotion potential. Finally, *deadwood* are poor performers with little potential for advancement.

FIGURE B-5
Performance and Promotability

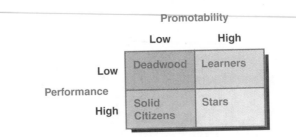

The solid citizens and deadwood have plateaued, although for different reasons. Deadwood are "ineffective plateauees." Solid citizens are "effective plateauees." Some are organizationally plateaued because of lack of openings. Because organizations are typically pyramid shaped, such organizational plateauing is common. Others are personally plateaued either because they do not desire higher level jobs or because they are not seen as having the abilities needed for such jobs.

This model raises some interesting issues. For instance, firms may want to take steps to ensure their solid citizens are not neglected. They can appraise, counsel, and develop career paths for solid citizens and provide them with training, skill upgrading, and development. They can try to identify deadwood early and act to restore performance through a variety of means. For instance, they might employ education programs to upgrade technical skill; development programs focusing on emotional and intellectual recharging; and job rotation through new duties, skill demands, or location. Individuals reporting their companies to employ such practices are relatively unlikely to report being plateaued. Research also shows that people who engage in active career planning and goal setting are less likely to experience hierarchical or content plateaus than those who do not.[22]

Workers who have plateaued because of slack demand for labor or because of poor performance often have little to do. Japanese white-collar excess workers are called *madogiwazoku*, or "sitting by the window tribe," because they have little to do but stare out the window. They may be assigned to lawn or maintenance work. In the United States, executives whose careers have stagnated have been called *shelf sitters*; they have been "put on the shelf" in make-work, dead-end positions.[23]

Many plateaued managers apparently can cope with and adapt to the career plateau.[24] As we have said, some genuinely may not want promotions. Others who did not receive desired promotions may rationalize, emphasizing the longer hours and increased pressure that promotions would bring. Still others may divert their energies to activities outside the job. Finally, some plateaued managers may move to new jobs within the firm to hide their embarrassment from their peers.

Whatever the satisfaction level of plateaued managers, plateauing may cause problems for more than just the plateaued employee. One survey found that younger employees were often demoralized by the stalled careers of older, plateaued employees, thinking this might be a vision of what the future holds for them. Plateaued employees were also seen as clogging promotion channels, lowering morale of coworkers and subordinates, and harming relationships with customers and clients.[25]

Further, there is some disturbing evidence about the health consequences of plateauing. For example, one study (which examined data for subjects tracked over a period of 70 years, from 1922 to 1992) found mortality rates to be significantly higher for men whose careers plateaued after early rapid progress than for those whose career progress continued unabated.[26] Although the causes of such mortality may be complex, the findings provide further evidence that career plateaus should be taken very seriously.

LATE CAREER ISSUES

By late career, many individuals have already experienced considerable advancement and may turn their attentions to aiding and developing others. If their careers have been fulfilling, this can be a satisfying and rewarding time. If the career was frustrating, this can be a difficult period of trying to cope with disappointments. In late career, individuals also begin to turn their thoughts toward separation from the organization.

Mentoring. In late career, many older, more experienced managers serve as mentors for less experienced protégés and contribute to their career development. We consider mentoring in more depth later in the appendix.

Adjustment into Retirement. Retirement gives some individuals a sense of loss and finality. Many workers fantasize that they will die soon after retirement. For other people, retirement is a chance to escape a frustrating or high-pressure job and to enjoy free time and pursue hobbies. In any case, this is a major transition. As we discussed earlier in the text, life change—whether desirable or undesirable—is stressful. Retirement combines changes in work patterns with personal, financial, and perhaps health changes. Those happiest in retirement have prepared for it over time and have made plans for their retirement years. They have considered not just finances but also values, priorities, and the sort of legacy they want to leave at work.[27]

MOVING UP AND DOWN, IN AND OUT, AND AROUND

The view of stages we have just considered focused primarily on upward movement in the organization. However, movement may be more complex. As shown in the model seen in Figure B-6, movement through the organization may take place in three dimensions, making up a *career cone*.[28]

> **Vertical.** Vertical movement is up and down the organizational hierarchy, such as a promotion or demotion. This is the traditional way to view movement in organizations.
> **Radial.** Radial career movement includes moves toward or away from the inner circle or the core of the system. Radial movement takes the individual closer to or further from central tasks, people, or power. Generally, radial movement is related to vertical movement. However, some individuals may experience vertical movement while remaining on the periphery. Others may stay on a level but move closer to the core as they gain experience and trust.
> **Circumferential.** Circumferential movement means moving to a different function, program, or product in the organization, such as to production from sales. Such moves may be a useful broadening experience, providing the base for future vertical moves.

Different organizations have different structures and boundaries relating to these dimensions and thus offer different types of mobility to employees. The boundaries that correspond to the types of movement are three:

> **Hierarchical boundaries**, separating the hierarchical levels from one another
> **Inclusion boundaries**, separating individuals or groups who differ in their degree of centrality

The Career Cone

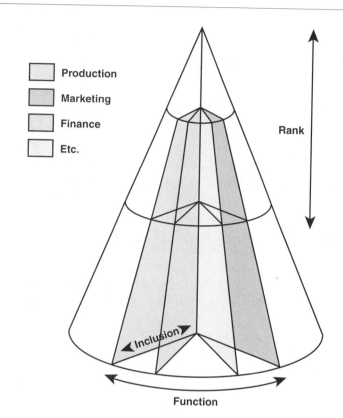

Legend:
- Production
- Marketing
- Finance
- Etc.

Rank

Inclusion

Function

> **Functional or departmental boundaries**, separating departments or different functional groupings from each other.

Organizations differ in terms of the number of each type of boundary, how difficult it is for members to cross those boundaries, and the criteria for movement across boundaries.

This view has some important implications. It suggests, for instance, that promotions may actually hinder subsequent career progress if they result in moves away from the core (as when people are kicked upstairs, receiving so-called promotions to powerless, peripheral—and perhaps newly created—positions). Lateral moves toward the core or across functions to gain visibility and expertise or to get out of a clogged channel, however, may be valuable.[29]

As employees and companies recognize this, more attention is being given to lateral moves, and many large firms, including American Greetings, Corning, and Eastman Kodak, are encouraging them.[30] At some firms, such as FMC Corporation and Whirlpool Inc., cross-functional training—including international experience—is being touted as critical.[31] Similarly, companies are trying some interesting new approaches to lateral moves. For example, Corning Inc., which has long attracted recruits by promising them they can "change careers without changing companies," now offers a 5 percent raise to managers who make lateral moves, and it encourages managers not to block subordinates' lateral moves. Also, American Greetings Corporation redesigned 400 jobs in its creative division and asked workers and managers to reapply. Everyone was guaranteed a job, without a pay cut. With the restructuring completed, employees work in teams instead of assembly-line fashion, and they can freely transfer between teams that make different products.[32]

FITTING PEOPLE TO CAREERS

We have discussed what careers are, and we have explored some of the key issues you may face at various career stages. But how do people choose careers and then make other career-related decisions? Several theories try to answer these questions by examining the fit of individuals to careers. Such theories might help organizations select appropriate individuals and tailor programs to their particular needs. They might also help individuals find suitable positions. Let's consider three models that focus on individual differences in the way people view occupations or jobs: career anchors, occupational personality types, and career concept types. As we review models, think about the things that you value and find of interest and how those values and interests may shape your career.[33]

CAREER ANCHORS

On the basis of his research, Edgar Schein has presented the idea of *career anchors*.[34] These anchors are "a syndrome of motives, values, and self-perceived competencies which function to guide and constrain an individual's entire career."[35] An anchor can be thought of as a "master motive" or the thing the person will not give up under any circumstances. Schein's study led him to conclude there are at least five career anchors, as follows.

> **Anchor 1: managerial competence.** The career is organized around the competencies and values inherent in the management process. The most important components of this concept are the ability to influence and supervise, the ability to analyze and solve complex problems, and emotional stability.

> **Anchor 2: technical-functional competence.** The career is organized around the challenge of the actual work being done, whether it is related to marketing, financial analysis, corporate planning, or some other area. The anchor is the technical field or functional area rather than the managerial process itself. Individuals with this anchor don't want to be promoted out of the kind of work they are doing.

> **Anchor 3: security.** The individual has an underlying need for security and tries to stabilize the career by tying it to the given organization. More than others, individuals with this anchor are likely to let the organization define their careers. They rely on the organization to recognize their needs and competencies and to do what is best for them.

> **Anchor 4: creativity.** Individuals with this anchor have a strong need to create something. This anchor is most evident among entrepreneurs, but corporate employees may also hold it.

> **Anchor 5: autonomy and independence.** The concern is with freedom and autonomy. Individuals with this anchor often find organizational life too

restrictive or intrusive into their personal lives and seek careers that offer more autonomy.

Career anchors have been used, for instance, to examine the career motivations of self-employed individuals. For the self-employed, autonomy and independence was found to be the most common anchor, followed by creativity and then security. Further, the career anchors were associated with career outcomes. Those with a career anchor of creativity were relatively more satisfied with the job and had greater psychological well-being. Those with the autonomy and independence anchor reported the highest levels of skill utilization and intent to remain self-employed. Those self-employed individuals pursuing the security career anchor had the least positive career outcomes, including lower job and life satisfaction, lower psychological well-being, and lower intent to remain self-employed.[36]

Can you think of people who appear to hold each of these career anchors? The anchors reflect predominant concerns. An employee may still care about other things, but the anchor is overriding. It is important that companies recognize these anchors and create appropriate career opportunities. For example, a person with a technical-functional anchor may not welcome a promotion to a management position. Organizations must think about the contributions that people with various anchors can make. They will also have to develop multiple reward systems and career paths to permit the full development of diverse kinds of individuals. Recognizing this, some companies—such as Texas Instruments at its information systems and services division—use career anchors for counseling and evaluation in their career development programs.[37]

OCCUPATIONAL PERSONALITY TYPES

John Holland reasoned that people gravitate toward environments that match their personal orientations. He proposed a hexagonal model, with six personality types and six matching occupational environments:[38]

> **Realistic.** This type involves aggressive behavior and physical activities requiring skill, strength, and coordination. Examples include forestry, trucking, and farming.

> **Investigative.** The investigative type involves cognitive (thinking, organizing, understanding) rather than affective (feeling, acting, or interpersonal and emotional) activities. Examples include biology, mathematics, and oceanography.

> **Social.** The social type involves interpersonal rather than intellectual or physical activities. Examples include clinical psychology, foreign service, and social work.

> **Conventional.** This type involves structural, rule-regulated activities and subordination of personal needs to an organization or person of power and status. Examples include accounting and finance.

> **Enterprising.** The enterprising type involves verbal activities to influence others and to attain power and status. Examples include management, law, and public relations.

> **Artistic.** The artistic type involves self-expression, artistic creation, expression of emotions, and individualistic activities. Examples include art and music education.

Research shows that when people choose a career consistent with their personality, they are more likely to be satisfied with their career choice and not to change professions. They are also more likely to remain excited by the nature of the work they do and to be satisfied with their colleagues at work.[39]

CAREER CONCEPT TYPES

We all know that people differ in terms of how they move from job to job and the degree to which they are active or passive in that movement, initiating moves or going with the flow. Michael Driver described four basic *career concept types*:[40]

> **Transitory.** There is no clear pattern of career movement. Some transitory individuals may drift in a relatively passive way from job to job. Others may be entrepreneurial types who innovate new activities but move on as soon as stabilization sets in.
> **Steady state.** The individual chooses a lifetime occupation. Steady state types settle into an organization and prefer stability rather than change.
> **Linear.** Career choice is made early, and there is emphasis on steady upward movement on a career ladder.
> **Spiral.** There is a planned search for increasing self-development and creative growth. The career choice may change periodically.

Driver has linked his career concept types to Schein's career anchors. For instance, individuals having security as the career anchor might fit the steady-state career concept. Those with autonomy as the career anchor might adhere to the transitory or spiral career concepts.

Driver reasons that organizations might be categorized in terms of the four career concept types. A transitory organization is loose, temporary, and entrepreneurial, with few formal procedures. Both linear and steady state organizations have classic pyramidal structures with tight controls. However, there is stress on vertical movement in linear organizations and units of great stability in steady state organizations. Some high-technology or artistic organizations may show spiral patterns. Some departments in linear or steady state organizations may also operate in a spiral mode.

An employee would generally best fit into an organization of a corresponding type—a transitory individual in a transitory organization, and so on. A linear individual, for instance, would be uncomfortable in a transitory organization. However, Driver also takes a dynamic view of the career concept types. He reasons that career concepts may evolve during a lifetime, owing to work or other social learning or to the inner dynamic of human development. Therefore, organizations must do more than simply be concerned with fit to an unchanging employee; they must also cultivate staff planning systems, employee development programs, and even strategies and structures that recognize transitions among career concept types.

SELF-MANAGEMENT OF CAREERS

Many forces affect career development. Organizational practices clearly play a role, and luck may even be important.[41] Certainly, though, as the workplace becomes more dynamic and uncertain, employees are forced to be more proactive, acting to manage their own careers. Research shows that career self-management strategies have positive effects on career outcomes, especially in the absence of mentoring support.[42] Further, research suggests that individuals who actively manage their own careers also receive more career management help from their employers, creating a "virtuous circle" of career management in which individual and organizational activities complement each other.[43]

GUIDELINES FOR SELF-MANAGEMENT OF CAREERS

Here are some guidelines for the self-management of careers:[44]

> **Develop basic career competencies.** There are at least five basic career competencies, and each can be developed:[45]

- **Self-appraisal.** Successful career development requires self-awareness. The counseling, guidance, career planning, or personnel offices on most campuses can help at this stage. Counseling interviews, aptitude and interest tests, and career-planning exercises may all be useful. Also, just asking others, such as an instructor or boss, to give you feedback about your performance can be enlightening.

- **Occupational information.** Career development requires a fit between you and your job, so it's important to learn about potential jobs. Some sources that provide information about types of work, skill requirements, occupational developments, worker trait requirements, and other relevant factors include the *Dictionary of Occupational Titles*, the U.S. Department of Labor's *Occupational Outlook Handbook*, and the *Occupational Outlook Quarterly*. Also, some interactive computer methods for providing career information are now available.[46]

- **Goal selection.** Career success, according to the approach taken in this appendix, means achieving one's goals, so the process of properly setting goals is crucial. It is generally best if goals are challenging, consistent with career capabilities, set by the individual (alone or in collaboration with another), and implemented by the person's independent effort.

- **Planning.** Once a goal is set, it is necessary to specify the steps to meet that goal and to determine the order of those steps. Both counseling and career-planning exercises may be helpful at the planning stage.[47]

- **Problem solving.** Because problems constantly arise during careers, competence in problem solving can be crucial to successful movement through a career.

> **Choose an organization carefully.** Your choice of an organization to work for is extremely important. The organization will control many important rewards, may determine where you live, and may even influence the sorts of competencies you develop and the kinds of skills you exercise. Also, your initial choice of an employer may have lasting consequences in terms of your chances for future moves to other organizations.

> **Get a challenging initial job.** In choosing a first job, generally give such short-term considerations as starting salary and location less weight than you give to challenge and potential for career growth. If you do take a job that

offers little challenge, you should probably try either to make a later job change or to redefine your job to assume more responsibility.

> **Be an outstanding performer.** Good performance enhances your esteem both in the eyes of others, such as your boss, and in your own eyes. Ask your boss to help you to set challenging goals, to give feedback, and to coach you.

> **Develop professional mobility.** More options are better than fewer. Mobility and potential mobility (not just upward mobility, but mobility of all kinds) are crucial to career success. Active networking offers the potential for greater mobility.[48]

> **Plan your own and your spouse's careers collaboratively.** By the end of the 20th century, both spouses were employed at least part time in more than half of U.S. married couples with children.[49] When both spouses are working or may work, severe strains can result unless careful career planning takes place. It is unrealistic and unfair to assume one partner will go along passively when the other takes a job transfer.[50]

> **Get help in career management.** Seek advice from experts in your school or organization. Consider using professional job counselors or placement specialists.

> **Anticipate chance events.** No matter how precisely you plan, chance will play a role. Develop contingency plans that specify what you will do if various things—good or bad—happen.

> **Continually reassess your career.** Midcourse corrections may be needed. You will have to make career choices all your life, not just when you first leave school. Continually ask where you are, where you want to be, and how you are going to get there.

The process model presented in the Bottom Line feature summarizes the basic steps associated with implementation of the general career development process.

GLOBAL PERSPECTIVES ON CAREERS

As companies take seriously the fact that business is becoming more global, they must also develop global perspectives on careers. For one thing, as firms increasingly enter global markets and send employees to foreign assignments, they must consider whether prospects for transfer have the skills, flexibility, and tolerance for uncertainty required to perform successfully in foreign settings. Also, the costs of sending and maintaining an employee abroad have been estimated at three to seven times that person's salary, so mistakes can be costly.[51]

The number of expatriates—employees who take assignments in foreign countries—is increasing. Expatriates may enjoy the experience of international assignments, and they may be able to take on levels of responsibility not otherwise possible. However, expatriates also face difficulties and frustrations.[52] There are a variety of financial hassles relating to taxes, housing expenses, and often costs of sending children to private English-speaking schools. More spouses are reluctant to give up their careers to be with their mates. There are heightened concerns about safety in the face of terrorist threats. There is also a reluctance to be "out of sight and out of mind." Recognizing these issues, more companies are taking steps to ease expatriates' frustrations. They may, for instance, tie global assignments directly to

MANAGING THE CAREER DEVELOPMENT PROCESS

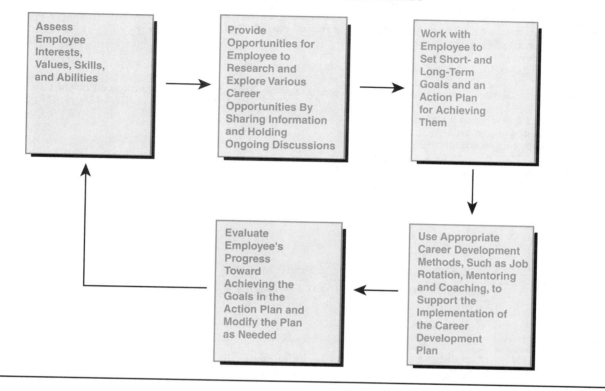

career planning programs, and they may pick up more costs; about 15 percent compensated for lost wages of spouses. Some companies send employees abroad for relatively short periods of time. The Eli Lilly Company, for example, introduced the International Switch Program, with managers going abroad for stints of just a few months.[53]

Figure B-7 presents some questions asked by AT&T when screening candidates for overseas transfer. How would you respond to the questions? Also, multinational firms must recognize that foreign nationals may have different career experiences, expectations, and aspirations than U.S. workers. National cultures shape the way in which people think of careers and the way in which they perceive the world of work.[54]

VALUING DIVERSITY: ENHANCING CAREERS FOR WOMEN AND MINORITIES

Women and minorities may still face an invisible but real *glass ceiling* that acts as a subtle barrier to promotions into high-level executive jobs.[55] As of 2003, women held 15.7 percent of corporate officer positions in Fortune 500 companies, up from

FIGURE B-7

Questions Asked by AT&T When Screening Candidates for Overseas Transfer

- Would your spouse be interrupting a career to accompany you on an international assignment? If so, how do you think this will [affect] your spouse and your relationship with each other?
- Do you enjoy the challenge of making your own way in new situations?
- Securing a job on re-entry will be primarily your responsibility. How do you feel about networking and being your own advocate?
- How able are you in initiating new social contracts?
- Can you imagine living without television?
- How important is it for you to spend significant amounts of time with people of your own ethnic, racial, religious, and national background?
- As you look into your personal history, can you isolate any episodes that indicate a real interest in learning about other peoples and cultures?
- Has it been your habit to vacation in foreign countries?
- Do you enjoy sampling foreign cuisine?
- What is your tolerance for waiting for repairs?

Source: "Consultants for International Living," *The Wall Street Journal*, January 9, 1992, p. B1.

12.5 percent in 2000 and 8.7 percent in 1995. Of top-earning corporate officers, 5.2 percent are women, up from 1.2 percent in 1995. Although these increases are encouraging, it is clear that women are still substantially underrepresented, especially at the tops of organization.[56] Only one of the top-40 companies in terms of revenue has a female CEO: Hewlett-Packard, with Carly Fiorina.[57] And, as if glass ceilings aren't bad enough, there may be "glass walls" as well.[58] The glass walls keep women and minorities in staff or support positions in such areas as public relations and human resources and away from jobs in such core areas as marketing, production, and sales. As such, women face hierarchical, functional, and inclusion barriers.[59]

The reasons why women have not made greater progress are complex. Certainly, the old boys' network and associated gender stereotypes may play roles.[60] In addition, women appear to be less inclined to play "the promotion game," preferring to rely on high performance and commitment for visibility to their seniors rather than the networking, ingratiation, and self-promotion strategies used more by males.[61] Also, research suggests that women are much less likely than men to negotiate for pay, promotions, and recognition.[62] Further, women's disproportionate responsibilities for child rearing detract from time that can be devoted to the career. This is certainly true both for lone mothers and for women in dual-career situations.[63] Getting to the top often appears to require women to give up children and spouses. Forty-two percent of female corporate executives aged 41 to 55 and 49 percent of women earning more than $100,000 a year are childless.[64]

There are some signs of change. As noted, the percentage of management jobs held by women has increased dramatically over the last quarter century. In addition, annual earnings of full-time women workers are now about 80 percent of comparable male earnings, up from 60 percent in 1979.[65] Still, companies recognize that there is a long way to go and they must take active steps to further the career development of women and minorities. In this section, we consider some of the steps now being taken.

WOMEN'S CAREER DEVELOPMENT

The growing number of women in management presents opportunities and challenges to organizations. If women's potential is to be fully realized and used, companies must take active steps to foster their career development. As shown in Figure B-8, companies have chosen several routes to such development.

Some of these routes take traditional forms, such as posting of job opportunities, career counseling, and training programs. Training programs and other developmental opportunities are crucial, and evidence suggests that women have fewer developmental opportunities relating to high-responsibility positions than do men.[66] Other approaches are more innovative, such as opportunities for part-time jobs at advanced levels in the hierarchy and a variety of family-sensitive work practices, which we discuss next. Mentoring also can be critical to women's career development, discussed later in the appendix.

> **Family-Sensitive Work Practices.** Many companies are using a variety of family-sensitive work practices (also called family-friendly work practices) to permit managers to better balance work and family demands. Some of these practices, such as flexible work hours, job sharing, compressed workweeks, family-leave policies, and work-at-home arrangements, provide needed flexibility. Others, such as on-site child care facilities, reduce distraction and such concerns as baby-sitting.

> Research shows that firms that use family-sensitive practices often reap gains in greater loyalty, increased job satisfaction, and lower turnover.[67] Some firms also report productivity increases, and family-sensitive practices are a powerful recruiting tool.[68]

> Ironically, though, it appears that firms offering family-friendly policies are sometimes the slowest in promoting women to management positions.[69] Further, some women feel that if they use such family-friendly policies as flextime, their chances of promotion are reduced. Some observers feel that

FIGURE B-8
Company Practices to Enhance Women's Career Development

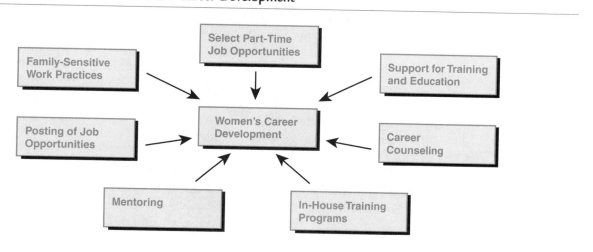

family-sensitive work practices may emphasize the differences between genders, making it harder for women to overcome stereotypes and get serious consideration for top jobs.

> **Job-Pathing.** Job-pathing involves a carefully planned sequence of job assignments aimed at developing minorities into certain job-related skills.[70] The paths are designed to ensure that important skill-building experiences are provided in increments small enough not to overwhelm the individual but large enough to require stretching. The goal is to minimize the career time needed to reach a target job. Through the use of job-pathing, one large retail organization feels it can reduce the time to develop a store manager from fifteen years to five. Plotting career paths not only speeds employee growth but forces the organization to think about the career paths it is now using. It may find that some potential paths are not being used and perhaps that paths can be plotted through different functional areas to develop managers with broader views.

> **Talent Development Among Hourly Employees.** Companies are trying to find new ways to attract more female and minority hourly workers into presupervisory programs. One problem is perceptual: Females and minorities sometimes feel that opportunities for upward mobility are lacking or that barriers exist to their upward mobility. Some also do not perceive themselves as fitting into supervisory roles. Firms must act to alter these perceptions. Some firms are also relying on training programs conducted by professional or trade organizations to develop female and minority employees. Many of these employees see training provided by such associations as being less competitive and more supportive than company-sponsored programs.

> **Layoff Policies.** Women and minorities have historically faced a major hurdle in corporations. Because the movement of women and minorities in management positions has been primarily a recent phenomenon, they have suffered from companies' "last hired, first fired" rules. That is, when layoffs have occurred, white men, with longer tenure, have been most likely to keep their jobs. As such, promising women and minorities have often found their management careers cut short.[71] Now, many large firms, such as Du Pont, AT&T, and Honeywell, are using criteria other than seniority to make job-cut decisions.[72] For example, Honeywell bases its decisions on performance appraisals, and AT&T has used early-retirement sweeteners to encourage older managers—primarily white men—to leave. These policies are welcomed by women and minorities but often are very stressful for white men, who sometimes say they feel abandoned.[73] As such, companies are in a precarious situation, hoping to increase diversity but wanting to avoid a white male backlash and charges of reverse discrimination. At some firms such courses as one at AT&T titled "White Males: The Label, the Dilemma" are offered in which employees, male and female, white and minority, learn about work force changes and can express their feelings.

CAREER DEVELOPMENT OF MINORITIES

Many firms have developed special programs for minorities. For example, American Airlines offers English as a second language for minority employees, and it sponsors an Asian Cultural Association and an Organization of African Americans. To encourage minority development, American has a Walk-a-Mile Program, a systematic method of establishing career goals and receiving guidance in choosing career paths. In the program, minority employees can nominate themselves for a position and then work for a day in that position with the person currently holding the job.

American Express Company has a Black Employee Network and the East-West Exchange (an Asian employee network), which act as support groups to aid in networking and self-help programs. The organizations bring in speakers, host career panels, and sponsor events around Black History Month and other special holidays.[74]

McDonald's offers career development programs tailored to its diverse work force, including seminars on such topics as black career development, Hispanic career development, and managing cultural differences. In addition, affirmative action training is given to thousands of employees each year at McDonald's employee management training school, Hamburger University. The company also supports organized minority employee networking groups that have representatives meet periodically with company management. McDonald's maintains close ties to minority colleges and students through its scholarships and contributions. It also has a program that develops minority entrepreneurs.[75]

Companies are also beginning to recognize the special career needs, interests, and challenges of employees with alternative sexual orientations. Gay, lesbian, and bisexual (GLB) employees rank low on workplace assimilation—in fact, they are rated lowest of any group in terms of how well they fit in at work—and feel they aren't given the same career opportunities or support as are heterosexuals.[76] Reported levels of employment discrimination and hate crimes against lesbians have increased in recent years.[77] Perhaps as a result of such factors, GLB employees who are not open about their sexual identity at work are more satisfied with their incomes and generally have higher incomes than those who disclose their sexual orientation to employers and coworkers.[78]

MENTORING

In Homer's *The Odyssey*, Mentor was the trusted adviser of Odysseus, king of Ithaca. When Odysseus went to fight in the Trojan War, he entrusted the care of his kingdom to Mentor, who served as the teacher and overseer of Odysseus's son, Telemachus. Today a *mentor* is generally defined as one who is an experienced, well-established member of a profession or firm and takes a personal interest in the career of a less experienced member and attempts to facilitate that individual's career advancement. As we'll see, though, the nature of mentoring is evolving, and this definition will evolve with it.

PHASES IN THE MENTORING RELATIONSHIP[79]
There are four phases in the mentoring relationship:

> **Initiation.** This is a period of six months to a year during which the relationship gets started and begins to take on importance for both individuals. Both parties develop expectations and engage in work-related interactions. The mentor coaches and provides challenging work and visibility. The protégé provides technical assistance, shows respect, and demonstrates the desire and

willingness to be coached. It is important to recognize that the relationship between mentor and protégé may be initiated by the protégé. Indeed, it may be increasingly important for protégés to take proactive roles, seeking out appropriate mentors. Research shows that protégés do influence the nature and amounts of mentoring they receive and that protégés who have internal loci of control, are high self-monitors, and have high emotional stability are especially likely to initiate mentoring relationships.[80]

> **Cultivation.** After initiation, there is a phase of two to five years during which the mentor provides many career-related and psychosocial functions. There are frequent interactions and many mutual benefits. Both parties become emotionally linked.

> **Separation.** This phase may begin when the protégé feels it is time to assert autonomy and independence or when something external to the relationship, such as a promotion for the protégé or a transfer for the mentor, is marked by significant changes in the functions provided by the mentor relationship and in the affective experiences of the mentor and protégé. There may be feelings of turmoil, anxiety, and loss, and both parties reassess the value of the relationship as it becomes a less central part of their work lives. The period is especially stressful if the protégé feels abandoned by the mentor or if the mentor resents the protégé's growing independence. Nevertheless, this phase is critical to development; it gives the young manager a chance to demonstrate the ability to perform independently from the mentor, and it enables the mentor to demonstrate success in developing new management talent.

> **Redefinition.** If the separation stage has been negotiated successfully, the relationship enters a final, redefinition stage characterized primarily by friendship. The parties continue to have some informal contact and to provide mutual support. The relationship takes on a more equal footing, although the mentor may continue to take pride in the protégé's accomplishments and the protégé may continue to feels gratitude and appreciation for the support of earlier years.

BENEFITS AND COSTS OF MENTORING[81]

The mentoring relationship is critical to career development. Precisely because it is so important, mentoring may generate both costs and benefits for both the mentor and protégé.

Benefits and Costs to Protégés. Benefits and costs of mentoring from the perspective of the protégé are shown in Figure B-9. There are clearly many potential benefits of the mentoring relationship to protégés. Mentors bring the strengths and accomplishments of their protégés to the attention of others, nominating them for positions and increasing their visibility. They take protégés under their wing, helping protect them from various consequences of errors and warning them of the dangers associated with certain actions. They provide valuable emotional support and guidance. In general, evidence suggests that mentoring is crucial to protégés' career development.[82]

At the same time, mentoring may entail costs for protégés. For one thing, protégés may have an increased workload and work under heightened scrutiny on their

Benefits and Costs of Mentoring for the Protégé

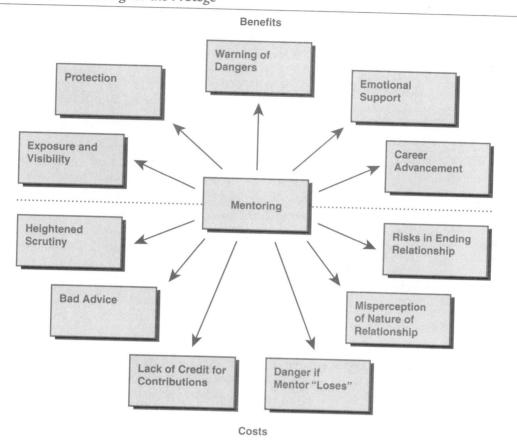

jobs. Further, if the mentor lacks talent or has mistaken ideas about the company, the protégé may be hurt. The protégé may also toil in the shadow of the mentor and thus fail to receive proper credit for his or her contributions. Further, being attached to a mentor may be a problem if the mentor loses in a major political contest. Also, others may misperceive the nature of the relationship. For example, if the mentor is of the opposite gender, others may assume the professional relationship has turned personal.[83] Protégés may also run risks if they terminate the relationship but stay with the organization. Further, if coworkers think the protégé is getting special treatment that they are not, resentment is likely. As one manager noted, "No one likes the teacher's pet."[84]

Benefits and Costs to Mentors. Mentors also face various benefits and costs in the mentoring relationship. On the plus side, protégés are generally loyal to mentors and put in time and effort on assigned tasks. Mentors receive recognition from others in the firm for their mentoring efforts, and they are associated with achievements of the protégé. Further, many mentors get great personal satisfaction from mentoring: It causes them to feel needed and gives them a sense of accomplishment.

However, mentoring demands considerable time and effort. Further, if the protégé lacks talent or motivation and fails to perform well, the mentor may be blamed. And, like the protégé, the mentor may suffer from others' misperceptions of the basis of a mixed-gender relationship. Finally, mentors often feel deserted and betrayed when a protégé breaks off the mentoring relationship.

CURRENT ISSUES IN MENTORING

As evidence of the value of mentoring mounts, companies are exploring new approaches to make mentoring more effective and more readily and uniformly available.

Formal versus Informal Mentoring. Mentoring may be formal, in which the company matches mentor and protégé and provides guidelines for the relationship, or informal, with mentor and protégé connecting through personal interactions or other informal means.[85] Informal mentoring often works well, but some worthy individuals may not get the chance to serve as protégés, and various biases may lead to favoritism in mentoring.[86] Formal mentoring programs help ensure that everyone in the company is supported by someone who shares the goal of helping the protégé maximize his or her potential.[87] These programs seem to work best when mentors have received training, the programs have visible top management support, and there is a supportive corporate culture. In addition, assigned mentors must be willing and able to take their roles seriously.

Matching Mentors and Protégés. Companies are paying increasing attention to matching of mentors with protégés. Rather than simply pair a protégé with a more experienced mentor, firms are considering such factors as matches of personalities and interests. They sometimes also consider minority status, age, and gender in the matching process. Further, as discussed in the Focus on Management feature

FOCUS ON MANAGEMENT

REINVENTING MENTORING AT INTEL[88]

Intel is reinventing the old approach to mentoring in order to teach, inspire, and reconnect its employees. Intel matches mentors and protégés not on the basis of job title or years of service but of required skills. So 12-year veteran Ann Otero, a senior administrative assistant who is a master at tapping into the company's informal people networks, finds herself providing mentoring on the Intel culture and the ways to navigate its internal networks to a manager who outranks her. In turn, she is being mentored by a senior-level executive to learn enough about leadership to be comfortable speaking up in the high-level meetings she attends.

At Intel, mentoring isn't always face to face. Instead, Intel uses an intranet and e-mail to perform matchmaking, yielding relationships that span state and national borders. The matching system uses an employee database to create an intranet-based questionnaire to match mentors with partners. Once a match is made, partners—not mentors—set up meetings and decide what they want to work on. The details of the relationship are put into a mentoring contract. Although not binding, the contract creates accountability. The limits of what can be discussed are set not by the company but by the mentor and partner; there are no mentoring police.

addressing mentoring at Intel, matching may be based on needed skills, regardless of the job title and seniority of the mentor and protégé.

Multiple Mentoring. The traditional mentoring model is one mentor working with one protégé, but multiple mentoring may sometimes be appropriate.[89] Multiple mentoring may involve mentoring in peer groupings, mentoring within teams, or mentoring circles, where a single leader mentors several protégés at one time. Multiple mentoring involves an employee in a *developmental network*, a set of people who take an active interest in and action to advance the protégé's career by providing developmental assistance.[90] In peer or team mentoring groups, the members themselves usually provide mentoring to each other. They may form temporary pairs or subgroups to address a specific issue, then disband and reform around a different issue. Mentoring circles involve one mentor working with a group of protégés. Such circles typically feature a single mentor who focuses the group and provides technical and organizational guidance. The mentor helps the group use their combined energies and experiences to help one another, thus generating many perspectives.

Long-Distance and Virtual Mentoring. IKEA U.S. is described by the company's learning and development manager as "very much an old Swedish male organization."[91] To increase diversity, IKEA is relying on mentoring. In its pilot program, 50 employee pairs were brought together, with no pairs from the same department. The pairs went through a three-day training session and then commenced a one-year relationship via e-mail, phone, and videoconferencing; the program required three face-to-face meetings as well. This heavy reliance on electronic means for the bulk of the mentoring relationship is characteristic of long-distance or virtual mentoring. With *virtual mentoring* mentor and protégé interact via e-mail, the Internet, or other electronic media. Virtual mentoring is cost effective and permits broader access to mentors than would otherwise be possible. It may be an effective way to transmit information, but might not work well for building and refining interpersonal skills.[92] Virtual mentoring may pair e-mail for posting questions and responses that are not time urgent, reviewing conclusions, and maintaining contact, with phone conversations to exchange impressions on sensitive issues and permit listening for nonverbal cues such as raising or lowering of voice, change in tone, silence, quickening or slowing of speech, and sighs or pauses.[93]

Mentoring of Women and Minorities.[94] Firms are taking formal steps to ensure that qualified women and minorities have mentors. Dozens of large firms, including AT&T, Johnson & Johnson, and Xerox, have hired full-time diversity managers, one of whose roles is to establish mentoring relationships.[95] At many companies, such as Pacific Bell, promising women—often nominated by their department heads—are paired with senior executives who offer one-to-one career counseling. And many women who attain high positions reach out to help younger women—some of them still in school. For example, a University of Pennsylvania alumnae group called the *Trustees' Council of Penn Women* gives female students a list of about 70 distinguished women on whom they can call for career advice. The council also runs a shadowing program that lets students spend a workday with a female executive. The process model in the Bottom Line feature

THE FORMAL MENTORING PROCESS

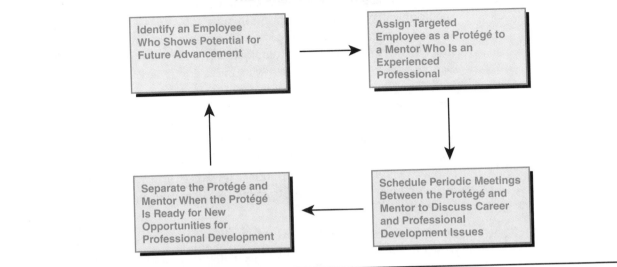

summarizes the basic steps associated with the implementation of the formal mentoring process.

We began this appendix by warning you to prepare for interesting times, and we hope we have helped with that preparation. Those who will survive and prosper in the modern workquake will actively seek to understand their organizations and professions and their own career goals and capabilities and will be proactive in managing their work lives and careers. We encourage you not only to take seriously the information in this appendix when thinking about and planning for your career but to continue to seek information about careers and career management. Good luck in the coming interesting times!

NOTES

CHAPTER 1. THE MANAGEMENT CHALLENGE: CRITICAL SKILLS FOR THE NEW WORKPLACE

1. G. Hanson, "Determinants of Firm Performance: An Integration of Economic and Organizational Factors," Ph.D. diss., University of Michigan Business School, 1986.

2. "Poor Managers Cause Failures," *Credit Management*, July 1999, p. 7.

3. For a study of causes of small business failure in developing countries and a review of research on determinants of small firm performance, see F. N. Al-Shaikh, "Factors for Small Business Failure in Developing Countries," *Advances in Competitiveness Research*, 1998, *6*, pp. 75–86.

4. A. Zagorin, "The Fruit of Its Labor," *Time*, November 1, 1999, pp. 50–51; J. Birger, "Toys R Cheap," *Money*, September 2000, pp. 42–44; K. Popovich, "Gateway Moves to Stem Wounds," *eWeek*, February 5, 2001, p. 34; "Pointing the Blame," *Scholastic News*, September 29, 2003, p. 2; M. Spiro and S. Hamm, "The Fall of Baan," *Business Week*, August 28, 2000, pp. 247–252; and N. Stein, "Yes, We Have No Profits," *Fortune*, November 26, 2001, pp. 182–190.

5. M. Warner, "Fallen Idols," *Fortune*, October 30, 2000, pp. 108–121; R. Monk, "Why Small Businesses Fail," *CMA Management*, July–August 2000, pp. 12–13; and J. A. Nickell, "Thought for Food," *Ziff Davis Small Business*, February 2002, p. 25.

6. S. R. Sabo, "Skills for the Next Century," *Association Management*, December 1999, pp. 37–41.

7. M. Messmer, "Skills for a New Millennium," *Strategic Finance*, August 1999, pp. 10–12.

8. C. Kaydo, "The New Skills of Top Managers," *Sales and Marketing Management*, May 2000, p. 16.

9. P. B. Thomas, "The Competency-Based Preprofessional Curriculum: A Key Component of Vision Success," *Journal of Accountancy*, October 2000, pp. 128–131.

10. For similar findings relating to critical skills of chief investment officers, see L. K. Singh, "Investment DNA," *Institutional Investor*, June 2001, p. 146.

11. P. M. Buhler, "Managing in the New Millennium," *Supervision*, August 2000, pp. 16–18.

12. The following examples are drawn in part from L. Secretan, "Learning Fuels the Soul," *Industry Week*, August 21, 2000, p. 29.

13. M. K. McGee and J. Mateyaschuk, "Educating the Masses," *Informationweek*, February 15, 1999, pp. 61–81.

14. B. Leonard, "Basic Skills Training Pays Off for Employers," *HRMagazine*, October 1999, pp. 32–33.

15. "Survey Shows Fundamental Managerial Skills Lacking," *Management Services*, January 1999, p. 3.

16. "In-House Solution to Skills Shortage," *Works Management*, March 2000, p. 7.

17. "Survey Shows," p. 3.

18. G. Fleming and E. Emde, "Creating the Future: Developing the Critical Skills Is Everybody's Business," *Information Executive*, April 1998, p. 7.

19. W. J. Morin, "You Are Absolutely, Positively on Your Own," *Fortune*, December 9, 1996, p. 222.

20. B. Hall, "The Top Training Priorities for 2003," *Training*, February 2003, pp. 38–41.

21. L. Tischler, "IBM: Manager Jam," *Fast Company*, October 2002, p. 48.

22. *Human Capital: Key Principles from Nine Private Sector Organizations*, GAO/GGD-00-28, Report to Congressional Requesters by the U.S. General Accounting Office, January 2000.

23. Buhler, "Managing in the New Millennium"; and J. R. Thompson and

C. W. LeHew, "Skill-Based Pay as an Organizational Innovation," *Review of Public Personnel Administration*, Winter 2000, pp. 20–40.

24. T. J. Wallis, "Skills Every Employer Wants," *Career World*, November–December 2001, p. 15. For similar finding among employers in Hong Kong, see S. Kanwerayotin, "The Search for 'Soft' Skills," *Far Eastern Economic Review*, June 28, 2001, p. 72.

25. J. Palmer, "Marry Me a Little," *Barron's*, July 24, 2000, pp. 25–27.

26. For more on key competencies in the new world of work, see L. T. Eby, M. Butts, and A. Lockwood, "Predictors of Success in the Era of the Boundaryless Career," *Journal of Organizational Behavior*, 2003, *24(6)*, pp. 689–708.

27. R. V. Gilmartin, "Diversity and Competitive Advantage at Merck," *Harvard Business Review*, January–February 1999, p. 146. See also T. Vinas, "Merck's Rx: People First," *Industry Week*, August 13, 2001, pp. 42–44; and E. McGirt, "Corporate America's Best Benefits," *Money*, December 2002, p. 158.

28. N. Brodsky, "Becoming the Boss," *Inc*, October 2000, pp. 29–30.

29. R. A. Baron and G. D. Markman, "Beyond Social Capital: How Social Skills Can Enhance Entrepreneurs' Success," *Academy of Management Executive*, February 2000, pp. 106–116.

30. W. McKinley, J. Zhao, and K. G. Rust, "A Sociotechnical Interpretation of Organizational Downsizing," *Academy of Management Review*, 2000, *25(1)*, pp. 227–243. See also E. Arnold and M. Pulich, "Managing Effectively in the Downsized Organization," *The Health Care Manager*, January–March 2003, pp. 56–62.

31. R. Ault, R. Walton, and M. Childers, *What Works: A Decade of Change at Champion International* (San Francisco: Jossey Bass, 1998).

32. R. Dzinkowski, "Mission Possible," *CMA Management*, February 2000, pp. 36–40.

33. See, for instance, M. Weinreb, "Power to the People," *Sales and Marketing Management*, April 2003, pp. 30–35.

34. See G. M. Spreitzer, S. G. Cohen, and G. E. Ledford, Jr., "Developing Effective Self-Managing Work Teams in Service Organizations," *Group & Organization Management*, September 1999, pp. 340–366; M. Attaran and T. T. Nguyen, "Succeeding with Self-Managed Work Teams," *Industrial Management*, July–August 1999, pp. 24–28; and P. A. Chansler, P. M. Swamidass, and C. Cammann, "Self-Managing Work Teams: An Empirical Study of Group Cohesiveness in 'Natural Work Groups' at a Harley-Davidson Motor Company Plant," *Small Group Research*, 2003, *34(1)*, pp. 101–120.

35. D. Domeyer, "Enhance Your PEOPLE Skills," *Women in Business*, September–October 2000, p. 34.

36. See J. Walsh, "The Portable Manager," *Electric Perspectives*, January–February 1999, pp. 16–20.

37. K. Ellis, "Making Waves," *Training*, 2003, *40(6)*, p. 16.

38. For one extensive review, see P. A. Cohen, "College Grades and Adult Achievement: A Research Synthesis," *Research in Higher Education*, 1984, *20*, pp. 281–291.

39. L. W. Porter and L. E. McKibbin, *Management Education and Development: Drift or Thrust into the 21st Century?* (New York: McGraw-Hill, 1988).

40. J. Pfeffer, J. Sutton, and R. I. Sutton, *The Knowing-Doing Gap: How Smart Companies Turn Knowledge into Action* (Boston: Harvard Business School Press, 2000), p. 22.

41. Ibid., pp. 246–262.

42. A. Bandura, *Social Foundations of Thought and Action* (Englewood

Cliffs, NJ: Prentice-Hall, 1986); T. R. Davis and F. Luthans, "A Social Learning Approach to Organizational Behavior," *Academy of Management Review*, 1980, *5*, pp. 281–290; and A. P. Brief and R. J. Aldag, "The Self in Organizations: A Conceptual Review," *Academy of Management Review*, 1981, *6(1)*, pp. 75–88.

43. For example, see D. B. Curtis, J. L. Winsor, and D. Stephens, "National Preferences in Business and Communication Education," *Communication Education*, 1989, *38(6)*, pp. 6–15; F. Luthans, S. A. Rosenkrantz, and H. W. Hennessey, "What Do Successful Managers Really Do? An Observation Study of Managerial Activities," *Journal of Applied Behavioral Science*, 1985, *21*, pp. 255–270; and O. Nordhaug, "Competence Specificities in Organizations," *International Studies of Management & Organization*, 1998, *28(1)*, pp. 8–29.

44. D. B. K. Lyons and S. Stuart, "International CEOs on the Rise," *Chief Executive*, February 2000, pp. 51–53.

45. Ibid. See also M. Goldsmith, C. Walt, and K. Doucet, "New Competencies for Tomorrow's Global Leader," *CMA Management*, December 1999–January 2000, pp. 20–24; J. P. Neelankavil, A. Mathur, and Y. Zhang, "Determinants of Managerial Performance:

A Cross-Cultural Comparison of the Perceptions of Middle-Level Managers in Four Countries," *Journal of International Business Studies*, First Quarter 2000, pp. 121–140; and C. A. Bartlett and S. Ghoshal, "What Is a Global Manager?" *Harvard Business Review*, 2003, *81(8)*, pp. 101–108.

46. G. A. Yukl, *Leadership in Organizations*, 4th ed. (Englewood Cliffs, NJ: Prentice-Hall, 1998).

47. C. M. Pavett and A. W. Lau, "Managerial Work: The Influences of Hierarchical Level and Functional Specificity," *Academy of Management Journal*, 1983, *12*, pp. 170–177.

48. These definitions are based on Nordhaug, "Competence Specificities in Organizations," pp. 8–29.

49. See C. Gourley, "A Change for the Better: How to Write an Action Plan," *Writing*, April–May 2003, pp. 8–10; W. Webb, "Winds of Change," *Training*, July 2002, pp. 40–43.

50. J. Helyar, "Hooter's," *Fortune*, September 1, 2003, p. 140.

51. http://www.hooters.com/company/mission_statement.

52. L. Tischler, "IBM: Manager Jam," *Fast Company*, October 2002, p. 48.

CHAPTER 2. UNDERSTANDING AND VALUING DIFFERENCES

1. P. Digh, "Coming to Terms with Diversity," *HRMagazine*, November 1998, pp. 117–120.

2. For instance, see T. H. Cox, "Managing Cultural Diversity: Implications for Organizational Competitiveness," *Academy of Management Executive*, 1991, *5(3)*, pp. 45–56; and K. E. Joyce, "Lessons for Employers from *Fortune*'s '100 Best,'" *Business Horizons*, 2003, *46(2)*, pp. 77–84.

3. F. Rice, "How to Make Diversity Pay," *Fortune*, August 8, 1994, p. 79. For discussions of IBM's recent diversity efforts, see M. Shum and J. W. Moss, "IBM: A Case Study in Affirmative Action Best Practices," *Diversity Factor*, 2002, *10(2)*, pp. 10–14; and "Louis V. Gerstner, Jr.: IBM," *Business Week*, January 14, 2002, p. 54.

4. Ibid.

5. Digh, "Coming to Terms with Diversity," p. 120. Betsy Holden, CEO of Kraft Foods, was chosen as one of the recipients of *Working Woman*'s Champions of Diversity award; see A. Finnegan, "Champions 2001," *Working Woman*, 2001, *26(4)*, p. 50.

6. J. Hickman, C. Tkaczyk, E. Florian, J. Stemple, and D. Vasquez, "50 Best Companies for Minorities," *Fortune*, July 7, 2003, pp. 103–104, 108, 110, 112, 119–120.

7. D. Kirkpatrick, J. J. Phillips, and P. P. Phillips, "Getting Results from Diversity Training—in Dollars and Cents," *HR Focus*, October 2003, p. 3.

8. Rice, "How to Make Diversity Pay," p. 84. For more on training for tolerance, see "Diversity Trends: Global Focus, Mainstream Training, Age Issues," *HR Focus*, 2003, *80(3)*, p. 8; S. T. Brathwaite, "Denny's: A Diversity Success Story," *Franchising World*, July–August 2002, pp. 28–29.

9. J. H. Lucas and M. G. Kaplan, "Unlocking the Corporate Closet," *Training & Development*, January 1994, pp. 35–38.

10. L. L. Castro, "More Firms 'Gender Train' to Bridge the Chasms That Still Divide the Sexes," *Wall Street Journal*, January 2, 1992, pp. 11, 14.

11. D. Berta, "Operators' Training Focuses on Ending Harassment," *Nation's Restaurant News*, February 10, 2003, p. 18.

12. Rice, "How to Make Diversity Pay," pp. 78–86.

13. B. McKay, "Coca-Cola's Daft Says Salaries Will Be Tied to Diversity Goals," *Wall Street Journal Interactive Edition*, March 10, 2000.

14. "The Diversity Initiative at US WEST Dex," *Successful Meetings*, March 1998, pp. 55–57.

15. For recent discussions of company programs to enhance diversity, see "Driving Diversity," *Hispanic*, 2003, *16(5)*, p. 46; W. J. Mott, Jr., "Developing a Culturally Competent Workforce: A Diversity Program in Progress," *Journal of Healthcare Management*, 2003, *48(5)*, pp. 337+; K. Gray, "Enterprise Rent-a-Car: Recruiting Program Is a Driving Force Behind Enterprise's Success," *NACE Journal*, 2003, *63(3)*, p. 19; and "Communications, Funding, Affinity Groups Fuel Diversity Programs," *HR Focus*, 2003, *80(4)*, p. 9. For a critical perspective on the business case for diversity, see F. Hansen, "Diversity's Business Case Doesn't Add Up," *Workforce*, 2003, *82(4)*, pp. 28–32.

16. Rice, "How to Make Diversity Pay," p. 84; and L. Egodigwe, *Black Enterprise*, 2003, *33(7)*, pp. 70–74.

17. Rice, "How to Make Diversity Pay," pp. 84, 86. See also K. Crow, "Staying Focused on Diversity Goals in Harder Times," *New York Times*, October 28, 2003, p. G2.

18. For evidence on the stability of personality, see J. G. Vaidya, E. K. Gray, J. Haig, and D. Watson, "On the Temporal Stability of Personality: Evidence for Differential Stability and the Role of Life Experiences," *Journal of Personality and Social Psychology*, 2002, *83(6)*, pp. 1469+; and B. J. Small, C. Hertzog, D. F. Hultsch, and R. A. Dixon, "Stability and Change in Adult Personality over 6 Years: Findings from the Victoria Longitudinal Study," *Journals of Gerontology: Series B*, 2003, *58B(3)*, pp. P166–P170.

19. Aristotle, *The Nichomachean Ethics*. For more on the relevance of Aristotle's views to behavior in organizations, see T. Morris, *If Aristotle Ran General Motors: The New Soul of Business* (New York: Henry Holt, 1997); B. Dyck and R. Kleysen, "Aristotle's Virtues and Management Thought: An Empirical Exploration of an Integrative Pedagogy," *Business Ethics Quarterly*, 2001, *11(4)*, pp. 561–574; and R. Duska and J. DesJardins, "Aristotelian Leadership and Business," *Business & Professional Ethics Journal*, 2001, *20(3–4)*, pp. 19–38.

20. D. Goleman, *Emotional Intelligence* (New York: Bantam Books, 1995). For a review incorporating this concept, see Q. N. Huy, "Emotional Capability, Emotional Intelligence, and Radical Change," *Academy of Management Review*, 1999, *24*, pp. 325–345. See also D. Goleman, *Working with Emotional Intelligence* (New York: Bantam Books, 1998); H. A. Elfenbein and N. Ambady, "Predicting Workplace Outcomes from the Ability to Eavesdrop on Feelings," *Journal of Applied Psychology*, 2002, *87(5)*, pp. 963–971; and M. D. Akers and G. L. Porter, "Your EQ Skills: Got What It Takes?" *Journal of Accountancy*, 2003, *195(3)*, pp. 65–69.

21. H. Gardner, *Frames of Mind* (New York: Basic Books, 1993). Also see J. Collins, "How to Make a Better Student: Seven Kinds of Smart," *Time*, October 19, 1998, pp. 94–96; and J. L. Nolen, "Multiple Intelligences in the Classroom," *Education*, 2003, *124(1)*, pp. 115–119.

22. See Goleman, *Emotional Intelligence* and *Working with Emotional Intelligence*.

23. See Goleman, *Working with Emotional Intelligence*.

24. S. Freud, "Civilization and Its Discontents," in J. Strachey (ed. and trans.), *The Standard Edition of the Complete Psychological Works*, vol. 2 (New York: Macmillan, 1962). For a summary of Freud's work and life, see P. Gay, "Psychoanalyst: Sigmund Freud," *Time*, March 29, 1999, pp. 66–69.

25. See Z. Shapira, *Risk Taking: A Managerial Perspective* (New York: Russell Sage Foundation, 1995). For a cross-cultural comparison of risk taking, see H. Lobler and J. Bode, "Risk Taking Under Transition: An Empirical Comparison Between Chinese, Western-, and Eastern-German Managers," *Thunderbird International Business Review*, January–February 1999, pp. 69–81.

26. See, for instance, L. V. Ryan and A. K. Buchholtz, "Trust, Risk, and Shareholder Decision Making: An Investor Perspective on Corporate Governance," *Business Ethics Quarterly*, 2001, *11(1)*, pp. 177–194; and W. H. Stewart, Jr., J. C. Carland, J. W. Carland, and S. Sweo, "Entrepreneurial Dispositions and Goal Orientations: A Comparative Exploration of United States and Russian Entrepreneurs," *Journal of Small Business Management*, 2003, *41(1)*, pp. 27–46.

27. R. C. Becherer and J. G. Maurer, "The Proactive Personality Disposition and Entrepreneurial Behavior Among Small Company Presidents," *Journal of Small Business Management*, 1999, *37*, pp. 28–36; J. M.

28 See, for instance, M. Kemmelmeier, Burnstein, Krumov, and Genkova, "Individualism, Collectivism, and Authoritarianism in Seven Societies," pp. 304–322.

29 For instance, see R. A. Bernardi, "The Relationships Among Locus of Control, Perceptions of Stress, and Performance," *Journal of Applied Business Research*, 1997, *13*, pp. 1–8; G. M. Spreitzer, "Psychological Empowerment in the Workplace: Dimensions, Measurement, and Validation," *Academy of Management Journal*, 1995, *38*, pp. 1442–1465; M. C. Reiss and K. Mitra, "The Effects of Individual Difference Factors on the Acceptability of Ethical and Unethical Workplace Behaviors," *Journal of Business Ethics*, 1998, *17*, pp. 1581–1593; and O. C. Hansemark, "Need for Achievement, Locus of Control and the Prediction of Business Start-Ups: A Longitudinal Study," *Journal of Economic Psychology*, 2003, *24(3)*, pp. 301–320.

30 For a recent study of the effects of Machiavellianism, see K. Bass, T. Barnett, and G. Brown, "Individual Difference Variables, Ethical Judgments, and Ethical Behavioral Intentions," *Business Ethics Quarterly*, 1999, *9*, 183–205.

31 For recent examinations of self-monitoring, see W. S. Long, E. J. Long, and G. H. Dobbins, "Correlates of Satisfaction with a Peer Evaluation System: Investigation of Performance Levels and Individual Differences," *Journal of Business and Psychology*, 1998, *12*, pp. 299–312; and D. B. Turban and T. W. Dougherty, "Role of Protégé Personality in Receipt of Mentoring and Career Success," *Academy of Management Journal*, 1994, *37*, pp. 688–702.

32 M. Kilduff and D. V. Day, "Do Chameleons Get Ahead? The Effects of Self-Monitoring on Managerial Careers," *Academy of Management Journal*, 1994, *37*, pp. 1047–1060.

33 D. V. Day, D. J. Schleicher, A. L. Unckless, and N. J. Hiller, "Self-Monitoring Personality at Work: A Meta-analytic Investigation of Construct Validity," *Journal of Applied Psychology*, 2002, *87(2)*, pp. 390–401. See also P. F. Hewlin, "And the Award for Best Actor Goes to . . . Facades of Conformity in Organizational Settings," *Academy of Management Review*, 2003, *28(4)*, pp. 633–642.

34 See, for instance, T. A. Judge, C. A. Higgins, and C. J. Thoresen, "The Big Five Personality Traits, General Mental Ability, and Career Success Across the Life Span," *Personnel Psychology*, 1999, *52*, pp. 621–652; F. De Fruyt and I. Mervielde, "RIASEC Types and Big Five Traits as Predictors of Employment Status and Nature of Employment," *Personnel Psychology*, 1999, *52*, pp. 701–727; and F. Lievens, F. De Fruyt, and K. Van Dam, "Assessors' Use of Personality Traits in Descriptions of Assessment Centre Candidates: A Five-Factor Model Perspective," *Journal of Occupational and Organizational Psychology*, 2001, *74(5)*, pp. 623–635.

35 T. A. Judge and R. Ilies, "Relationship of Personality to Performance Motivation: A Meta-analytic Review," *Journal of Applied Psychology*, 2002, *87(4)*, pp. 797–807; J. F. Salgado, "Predicting Job Performance Using FFM and Non-FFM Personality Measures," *Journal of Occupational and Organizational Psychology*, 2003, *76(3)*, pp. 323–346; and T. A. Judge, D. Heller, and M. K. Mount, "Five-Factor Model of Personality and Job Satisfaction: A Meta-Analysis," *Journal of Applied Psychology*, 2002, *87(3)*, pp. 530–541.

36 Ibid.

37 A. S. Grove, "A High-Tech CEO Updates His Views on Managing and Careers," *Fortune*, September 18, 1995, p. 229.

38 B. Beasley-Murray, "Mergers Make Slow Comeback," *Global Finance*, 2003, *17(4)*, pp. 31–32.

39 J. H. Prager, "Managing Cultural Diversity—on the Pitcher's Mound," *Wall Street Journal*, September 30, 1998, pp. B1+.

40 See G. Hofstede, *Culture's Consequences: International Differences in Work-Related Values* (Beverly Hills, CA: Sage, 1980). For studies using the framework, see D. N. Ross, "Culture as a Context for Multinational Business: A Framework for Assessing the Strategy-Culture 'Fit,'" *Multinational Business Review*, 1999, *7*, pp. 13–19; and Kemmelmeier, Burnstein, Krumov, and Genkova, "Individualism, Collectivism, and Authoritarianism in Seven Societies," pp. 304–322.

41 The following examples are based on R. E. Axtell, *Gestures* (New York: Wiley, 1991); and R. E. Axtell, *Do's and Taboo's Around the World*, 3rd ed. (New York: Wiley, 1993).

42 B. Berelson and G. A. Steiner, *Human Behavior: An Inventory of Scientific Findings* (Englewood Cliffs, NJ: Harcourt, Brace, & World, 1964).

43 D. C. Dearborn and H. A. Simon, "Selective Perception: A Note on the Departmental Identifications of Executives," *Sociometry*, 1958, *21*, pp. 140–144. See also M. J. Waller, G. P. Huber, and W. H. Glick, "Functional Background as a Determinant of Executives' Selective Perception," *Academy of Management Journal*, 1995, *38*, pp. 943–974.

44 S. S. Zalkind and T. W. Costello, "Perception: Some Recent Research and Implications for Administration," *Administrative Science Quarterly*, 1962, *7*, pp. 218–235.

45 M. Haire, "Role Perceptions in Labor-Management Relations: An Experimental Approach," *Industrial and Labor Relations Review*, 1955, *8*, pp. 204–216.

46 J. R. Terborg and D. R. Ilgen, "A Theoretical Approach to Sex Discrimination in Traditionally Masculine Occupations," *Organizational Behavior and Human Performance*, 1975, *13*, pp. 352–376.

47 A. Stirn, "Body Piercing: Medical Consequences and Psychological Motivations," *The Lancet*, 2003, *361(9364)*, pp. 1205–1215.

48 For a recent study of gender stereotypes, see D. L. Vogel, S. R. Wester, M. Heesacker, and S. Madon, "Confirming Gender Stereotypes: A Social Role Perspective," *Sex Roles*, 2003, *48(11–12)*, pp. 519–528.

49 See, for instance, H. Rheem, "Effective Leadership: The Pygmalion Effect," *Harvard Business Review*, 1995, *73*, p. 14.

50 See D. Howard, "The Hiring Game," *Canadian Business*, September 26, 1997, p. 136; T. H. Feeley, "Evidence of Halo Effects in Student Evaluations of Communication Instruction," *Communication Education*, 2002, *51(3)*, pp. 225–236; and C. E. Naquin and R. O. Tynan, "The Team Halo Effect: Why Teams Are Not Blamed for Their Failures," *Journal of Applied Psychology*, 2003, *88(2)*, pp. 332–340.

51 For a discussion of weight halo effects, see T. J. Wade and C. DiMaria, "Weight Halo Effects: Individual Differences in Perceived Life Success as a Function of Women's Race and Weight," *Sex Roles*, 2003, *48(9–10)*, pp. 461–466.

52 For one example, see M. F. R. Kets de Vries, "The Anatomy of the Entrepreneur: Clinical Observations," *Human Relations*, 1996, *49*, pp. 853–883.

53 M. Haire and W. F. Grunes, "Perceptual Defenses: Processes Protecting an Organized Perception of Another Personality," *Human Relations*, 1950, *3*, pp. 403–412.

54 Based on the *Wall Street Journal*, March 1, 1989, and March 10, 1989.

55 For a thorough discussion of implicit theories, see R. J. Sternberg, "Implicit Theories of Intelligence, Creativity, and Wisdom," *Journal of Personality and Social Psychology*, 1985, *49*, pp. 607–627. For a more recent example, see J. S. Beer, "Implicit Self-Theories of Shyness," *Journal of Personality and Social Psychology*, 2002, *83(4)*, pp. 1009–1024.

56 H. H. Kelley, "The Processes of Causal Attribution," *American Psychologist*, 1973, *28*, pp. 107–128. For an application of causal attribution to discrimination, see P. Corrigan, F. E. Markowitz, A. Watson, D. Rowan, and M. A. Kubiak, "An Attribution Model of Public Discrimination Towards Persons with Mental Illness," *Journal of Health and Social Behavior*, 2003, *44(2)*, pp. 162–179.

57 S. Shellenbarger, "Dad Takes Home a Tough Day at Work," *Wall Street Journal*, June 29, 1994, p. B1.

58 Ibid.

59 For a discussion of job satisfaction and its determinants across nations, see J. A. Ritter and R. Anker, "Good Jobs, Bad Jobs: Workers' Evaluations in Five Countries," *International Labour Review*, 2002, *141(4)*, pp. 331–358.

60 P. C. Smith, L. M. Kendall, and C. L. Hulin, *The Measurement of Satisfaction in Work and Retirement* (Chicago: Rand McNally, 1969). See also A. J. Kinicki, F. M. McKee-Ryan, C. A. Schriesheim, and K. P. Carson, "Assessing the Construct Validity of the Job Descriptive Index: A Review and Meta-Analysis," *Journal of Applied Psychology*, 2002, *87(1)*, pp. 14–32.

61 A. H. Brayfield and H. F. Rothe, "An Index of Job Satisfaction," *Journal of Applied Psychology*, 1951, *35*, pp. 307–311.

62 See, for instance, M. A. Griffin, "Dispositions and Work Reactions: A Multilevel Approach," *Journal of Applied Psychology*, 2001, *86(6)*, pp. 1142–1151.

63 Although there has been some concern that satisfaction and affectivity might simply be measures of the same thing, rigorous statistical procedures show satisfaction, positive affectivity, and negative affectivity to be distinct constructs. For instance, see A. O. Agho, J. L. Price, and C. W. Mueller, "Discriminant Validity of Measures of Job Satisfaction, Positive Affectivity and Negative Affectivity," *Journal of Occupational and Organizational Psychology*, 1992, *65*, pp. 185–196.

64 B. M. Staw, N. E. Bell, and N. A. Clausen, "The Dispositional Approach to Job Attitudes: A Lifetime Longitudinal Perspective," *Administrative Science Quarterly*, 1986, *31*, pp. 56–77.

65 For instance, see D. Seligman, "Genes on the Job," *Fortune*, January 13, 1992, p. 87.

66 See J. Adler, "The Happiness Meter," *Newsweek*, July 29, 1996, p. 78.

67 On this point, see B. Gerhart, "How Important Are Dispositional Factors as Determinants of Job Satisfaction? Implications for Job Design and Other Personnel Programs," *Journal of Applied Psychology*, 1987, *72*, pp. 366–373; and T. C. Murtha, R. Kanfer, and P. L. Ackerman, "Toward an Interactionist Taxonomy of Personality and Situations: An Integrative Situational-Dispositional Representation of Personality Traits," *Journal of Personality and Social Psychology*, 1996, *71*, pp. 193–207.

68 These items are drawn from T. M. Lodahl and M. Kejner, "The Definition and Measurement of Job Involvement," *Journal of Applied Psychology*, 1965, *49*, pp. 24–33.

69 For a discussion of this issue, see A. W. Schaef and D. Fassel, *The Addictive Organization* (New York: Harper & Row, 1988).

70 "Taking Stock of Our Fundamental Traits," *The Kiplinger Letter*, 2001, *78(52)*, p. 1.

71 R. T. Mowday, R. M. Steers, and L. W. Porter, "The Measurement of Organizational Commitment," *Journal of Vocational Behavior*, 1979, *14*, pp. 224–247; and A. Cohen, *Multiple Commitments at Work* (Mahwah, NJ: Erlbaum, 2003).

72 See, for instance, J. Meyer and N. Allen, "Testing the 'Side-Bet' Theory of Organizational Commitment: Reexamination of the Continuance and Affective Scales," *Journal of Applied Psychology*, 1984, *69*, pp. 372–378; and E. Snape and T. Redman, "An Evaluation of a Three-Component Model of Occupational Commitment: Dimensionality and Consequences Among United Kingdom Human Resource Management Specialists," *Journal of Applied Psychology*, 2003, *88(1)*, pp. 152–159.

73 See, for instance, S. A. Wasti, "Organizational Commitment, Turnover Intentions and the Influence of Cultural Values," *Journal of Occupational and Organizational Psychology*, 2003, *76(3)*, pp. 303–320; and J. B. Thatcher, L. P. Stepina, and R. J. Boyle, "Turnover of Information Technology Workers: Examining Empirically the Influence of Attitudes, Job Characteristics, and External Markets," *Journal of Management Information Systems*, 2002–2003, *19(3)*, pp. 231+.

74 See A. Cohen, "Age and Tenure in Relation to Organizational Commitment: A Meta-Analysis," *Basic and Applied Social Psychology*, 1993, *14*, pp. 143–159; and A. Cohen, "Organizational Commitment and Turnover: A Meta-Analysis," *Academy of Management Journal*, 1993, *36*, pp. 1140–1157.

75 R. J. Vandenberg and C. E. Lance, "Examining the Causal Order of Job Satisfaction and Organizational Commitment," *Journal of Management*, 1992, *18*, pp. 153–167.

76 For interesting discussions of this issue, see A. Rafaeli and R. I. Sutton, "Expression of Emotion as Part of the Work Role," *Academy of Management Review*, 1987, *12*, pp. 23–37; and J. J. Sallaz, "The House Rules: Autonomy and Interests Among Service Workers in the Contemporary Casino Industry," *Work and Occupations*, 2002, *29(4)*, pp. 394–427.

77 For more on the regulation of emotions, see J. Van Maanen and G. Kunda, "'Real Feelings': Emotional Expression and Organizational Culture," in L. L. Cummings and B. M. Staw (eds.), *Research in Organizational Behavior*, vol. 11 (Greenwich, CT: JAI Press, 1989), pp. 43–103; and J. M. Diefendorff and E. M. Richard, "Antecedents and Consequences of Emotional Display Rule Perceptions," *Journal of Applied Psychology*, 2003, *88(2)*, pp. 284–294.

78 R. T. LaPiere, "Attitudes and Actions," *Social Forces*, 1934, *13*, pp. 230–237.

79 Ibid.

80 This listing is based primarily on A. L. Weber, *Social Psychology* (New York: HarperCollins, 1992), pp. 129–130.

81 This figure is the sum of the monthly quit rates for 2002 as reported by the Bureau of Labor Statistics. Some writers consider all job changes, including movements within an organization, as turnover. We are maintaining the more traditional use of the term. For a discussion of the consequences of voluntary turnover, see C. R. Taylor, "Focus on Talent," *T + D*, 2002, *56(12)*, pp. 26–31.

82 See C. O. Trevor, "Interactions Among Actual Ease-of-Movement Determinants and Job Satisfaction in the Prediction of Voluntary Turnover," *Academy of Management Journal*, 2001, *44(4)*, pp. 621–638.

83 W. H. Mobley, S. O. Horner, and A. T. Hollingsworth, "An Evaluation of Precursors of Hospital Employee Turnover," *Journal of Applied Psychology*, 1978, *63*, pp. 408–414. See also E. G. Lambert, N. L. Hogan, and S. M. Barton, "The Impact of Job Satisfaction on Turnover Intent:

A Test of a Structural Measurement Model Using a National Sample of Workers," *Social Science Journal*, 2001, *38(2)*, pp. 233–250.

84 See, for instance, J. K. Sager and A. Menon, "The Role of Behavioral Intentions in Turnover of Salespeople," *Journal of Business Research*, 1994, *29*, pp. 179–188; P. W. Hom and A. J. Kinicki, "Toward a Greater Understanding of How Dissatisfaction Drives Employee Turnover," *Academy of Management Journal*, 2001, *44(5)*, pp. 975–987; and R. D. Iverson and D. B. Currivan, "Union Participation, Job Satisfaction, and Employee Turnover: An Event-History Analysis of the Exit-Voice Hypothesis," *Industrial Relations*, 2003, *42(1)*, pp. 101–105.

85 P. M. Muchinsky and P. C. Morrow, "A Multidisciplinary Model of Voluntary Employee Turnover," *Journal of Vocational Behavior*, 1980, *17*, pp. 263–290; and L. Lavelle, "After the Jobless Recovery, a War for Talent," *Business Week*, September 29, 2003, p. 92.

86 Bureau of National Affairs, "Absenteeism Policy Guide," *BNA Policy and Practices Manual no. 518*, 1981, p. 223.

87 "Last Minute Absences Cost Big Bucks," *Business and Health*, November 1998, p. 56; "Absenteeism Sickens Bottom Line," *HR Focus*, January 1999, p. 4; "Unplanned Absenteeism Adds Up," *Global Cosmetic Industry*, 2003, *171(1)*, p. 18; and "New Figures Suggest That Flexible Working Could Be the Solution to Rising Employee Absence," *Women in Management Review*, 2003, *18(3–4)*, p. 163.

88 K. Dow Scott and G. S. Taylor, "An Examination of Conflicting Findings on the Relationship Between Job Satisfaction and Absenteeism: A Meta-Analysis," *Academy of Management Journal*, 1985, *28*, pp. 599–612. See also "Unplanned Absenteeism Adds Up."

89 For a discussion of why people believe that satisfaction and performance are strongly related, see C. D. Fisher, "Why Do Lay People Believe that Satisfaction and Performance Are Correlated?" *Journal of Organizational Behavior*, 2003, *24(6)*, pp. 753–777.

90 For instance, see F. Herzberg, B. Mausner, R. O. Peterson, and D. F. Capwell, *Job Attitudes: Review of Research and Opinion* (Pittsburgh: Psychological Service of Pittsburgh, 1957); and A. H. Brayfield and W. H. Crockett, "Employee Attitudes and Employee Performance," *Psychological Bulletin*, 1955, *52*, pp. 396–424.

91 M. T. Iaffaldano and P. M. Muchinsky, "Job Satisfaction and Job Performance: A Meta-Analysis," *Psychological Bulletin*, 1985, *97*, pp. 251–273. A meta-analysis is essentially a statistical summary of past research.

92 D. W. Organ, "A Reappraisal and Reinterpretation of the Satisfaction-Causes-Performance Hypothesis," *Academy of Management Review*, 1977, *2*, pp. 46–53; L. Van Dyne, J. W. Graham, and R. M. Dienesch, "Organizational Citizenship Behavior: Construct Redefinition, Measurement, and Validation," *Academy of Management Journal*, 1994, *37*, pp. 765–802; and D. W. Organ and K. Ryan, "A Meta-analytic Review of Attitudinal and Dispositional Predictors of Organizational Citizenship Behavior," *Personnel Psychology*, 1995, *48*, pp. 775–802.

93 For a discussion of organizational citizenship behaviors, see J. A. LePine, A. Erez, and D. E. Johnson, "The Nature of Dimensionality of Organizational Citizenship Behavior: A Critical Review and Meta-Analysis," *Journal of Applied Psychology*, 2002, *87(1)*, pp. 52–65.

94 T. S. Bateman and D. W. Organ, "Job Satisfaction and the Good Soldier: The Relationship Between Affect and Employee 'Citizenship,'" *Academy of Management Journal*, 1983, *26*, pp. 587–595.

95 T. F. O'Boyle, "Disgruntled Workers Intent on Revenge Increasingly Harm Colleagues and Bosses," *Wall Street Journal*, September 15, 1992, p. B1; and M. Solomon, "Rage in the Workplace," *Computerworld*, July 30, 2001, pp. 32–34.

96 S. V. Magyar, Jr., "Preventing Workplace Violence," *Occupational Health & Safety*, 2003, *72(6)*, pp. 64–69; "Workplace Violence Remains a Threat in Many Settings," *Professional Safety*, 2003, *48(10)*, p. 16; and V. Sanderford-O'Connor, "Violence Prevention Techniques for Over-Stressed Workplaces," *Occupational Health and Safety*, 2002, *71(7)*, pp. 102–104.

97 F. Barringer, "Postal Officials Examine System After Two Killings," *New York Times*, May 8, 1993, p. 7.

98 D. L. Johnson, "Manager's Journal: The Best Defense Against Workplace Violence," *Wall Street Journal*, July 19, 1993, p. A10.

99 J. E. Rigdon, "Companies See More Workplace Violence," *Wall Street Journal*, April 12, 1994, p. B1.

100 P. H. Mirvis and E. E. Lawler, III, "Measuring the Financial Impact of Employee Attitudes," *Journal of Applied Psychology*, 1977, *62*, pp. 1–8. This article provides a very nice tutorial on behavioral accounting.

101 R. B. Dunham, *Organizational Behavior: People and Processes in Management* (Homewood, IL: Irwin, 1984), pp. 90–91.

102 See, for instance, A. P. Brief, A. H. Butcher, and L. Roberson, "Cookie, Disposition, and Job Attitudes: The Effects of Positive Mood-Inducing

Events and Negative Affectivity on Job Satisfaction in a Field Experiment," *Organizational Behavior and Human Decision Processes*, 1995, *62*, pp. 55–62; J. M. George and J. Zhou, "Understanding When Bad Moods Foster Creativity and Good Ones Don't: The Role of Context and Clarity of Feeling," *Journal of Applied Psychology*, 2002, *87(4)*, pp. 687–714; D. Goleman, R. Boyatzis, and A. McKee, "Primal Leadership: The Hidden Driver of Great Performance," *Harvard Business Review*, 2001, *79(11)*, pp. 42–53; and R. E. Boyatzis, "Positive Resonance," *Education Week*, 2002, *21(32)*, p. 52.

103 N. Gueguen and M.-A. De Gail, "The Effect of Smiling on Helping Behavior: Smiling and Good Samaritan Behavior," *Communication Reports*, 2003, *16(2)*, pp. 133+.

104 D. G. Myers, *Social Psychology*, 4th ed. (New York: McGraw-Hill, 1993), p. 528; and J. M. George and A. P. Brief, "Feeling Good–Doing Good: A Conceptual Analysis of the Mood at Work–Organizational Spontaneity Relationship," *Psychological Bulletin*, 1992, *112*, pp. 310–329.

105 L. Festinger, *A Theory of Cognitive Dissonance* (Evanston, IL: Row, Peterson, 1957). See also E. Harmon-Jones and C. Harmon-Jones, "Testing the Action-Based Model of Cognitive Dissonance: The Effect of Action Orientation on Postdecisional Attitudes," *Personality and Social Psychology Bulletin*, 2002, *28(6)*, pp. 711–723.

106 Dissonance theory is one of a family of balance theories, each of which argues that people wish to maintain a state of balance—here, that various thoughts should be consistent, or in balance—and will take actions to restore balance. We explore another balance theory, called equity theory, in chapter 6.

107 For an interesting example, see A. D. DeSantis, "A Couple of White Guys Sitting Around Talking," *Journal of Contemporary Ethnography*, 2003, *32(4)*, pp. 432–467.

108 Weber, *Social Psychology*, p. 131.

109 Ibid., pp. 131–132.

110 Ibid., p. 132.

111 "Protecting Growth: The Business Case for Diversity Today," *Business Week Online*, http://www.businessweek.com/adsections/2002/diversity/diversity.htm.

112 http://www.Pfizer.com.

113 http://www.Pfizer.com.

114 L. Dagberg, "The Top Diversity Employer Profiles and Role Models of 2002: Pfizer," *The Black Collegian Online*, http://www.black-collegian.com/issues/1stsem02/pfizer2002-1st.shtml.

115 http://www.achievement.org/autodoc/page/win0bio-1.

116 L. Clementson, "Oprah on Oprah," *Newsweek*, January 8, 2001, pp. 38–44.

117 P. Sellers, "The Business of Being Oprah," *Fortune*, October 11, 2003, pp. 50–64.

CHAPTER 3. PROBLEM SOLVING

1 See J. S. Lublin and M. Maremont, "Boss Talk: Taking Tyco by the Tail; After a Tumultuous First Year, Breen Discusses His Strategy to Clean House, Restore Trust," *Wall Street Journal*, August 6, 2003, p. B1.

2 See, for instance, "Toys 'R' Us Official to Quit as President of U.S. Toy Stores," *Wall Street Journal*, January 21, 2003, p. D7.

3 See, for instance, M. L. Wald and J. Schwartz, "NASA Management Failings Are Linked to Shuttle Demise," *New York Times*, July 12, 2003, p. A1; S. R. Morrissey, "Repairing NASA," *Chemical and Engineering News*, July 14, 2003, p. 27; and "Houston, You Have a Problem," *Scientific American*, August 2003, p. 10.

4 This listing is drawn primarily from G. P. Huber, *Managerial Decision Making* (Glenview, IL: Scott, Foresman, 1980).

5 For more on problem definition, see G. H. Wedberg, "But First, Understand the Problem," *Journal of Systems Management*, June 1990, pp. 20–28; and R. Hamlin, "Improved Problem Solving," *Supervisory Management*, October 1991, p. 7. See also S. Tomas, "Creative Problem-Solving: An Approach to Generating Ideas," *Hospital Materiel Management Quarterly*, May 1999, *20(4)*, pp. 33–45.

6 In fact, one alternative dominates another if it is at least as good as the other on all attributes and better on even one.

7 See, for instance, R. T. Clemen, *Making Hard Decisions: An Introduction to Decision Analysis*, 2nd ed. (Belmont, CA: Duxbury Press, 1996).

8 B. A. Stein and R. M. Kanter, "Leadership for Change: The Rest of the Story," *Frontiers of Health Services Management*, Winter 1993, p. 29.

9 This listing is based on B. M. Staw and J. Ross, "Understanding Behavior in Escalation Situations," *Science*, October 1986, pp. 216–220. See also G. McNamara, H. Moon, and P. Bromiley, "Banking on Commitment: Intended and Unintended Consequences of an Organization's Attempt to Attenuate Escalation of Commitment," *Academy of Management Journal*, April 2002, *45*, pp. 443–452.

10 See M. Keil and R. Montealegre, "Cutting Your Losses: Extricating Your Organization When a Big Project Goes Awry," *Sloan Management Review*, Spring 2000, pp. 55–68; and M. Mandell, "Knowing When to Quit," *World Trade*, April 1999, p. 95.

11 For instance, see J. Zaslow, "Moving On—You've Got to Know When to Fold 'Em: The Science of a Well-Timed Exit," *Wall Street Journal*, January 2, 2003, p. D1. See also S. D. Moore, "Failure Is No Stranger in Drug Research—Problems at Glaxo, Roche Highlight Problems of Discovery," *Wall Street Journal*, June 15, 1998, p. 1.

12 J. Barr, "A Disaster Plan in Action: How a Law Firm in the World Trade Center Survived 9/11 with Vital Records and Employees Intact," *The Information Management Journal*, May/June 2003, pp. 28–29. See also P. Kennedy, C. Perrottet, and C. Thomas, "Scenario Planning After 9/11: Managing the Impact of a Catastrophic Event," *Strategy and Leadership*, 2003, *31*, pp. 4–13.

13 This cycle is sometimes referred to as the PDSA cycle, for Plan-Do-Study-Act. For discussions of PDCA, see P. R. Scholtes, *The Leader's Handbook: Making Things Happen, Getting Things Done* (New York: McGraw-Hill, 1998), pp. 33–34. C. N. Johnson, "The Benefits of PDCA," *Quality Progress*, May 2002, p. 120, and D. L. Kelley and Paul Morath, "How Do You Know the Change Worked?" *Quality Progress*, July 2001, pp. 68–74.

14 See, for instance, H. A. Simon, "A Behavioral Model of Rational Choice," in M. Alexis and C. Wilson (Eds.), *Organizational Decision Making* (Englewood Cliffs, NJ: Prentice-Hall, 1967); P. Slovic, "Psychological Study of Human Judgment: Implications for Investment Decision Making," *Journal of Finance*, 1972, *27*, pp. 779–800; R. N. Taylor, "Psychological Determinants of Bounded Rationality," *Decision Sciences*, 1975, *6*, pp. 409–429; and W. B. Arthur, "Inductive Reasoning and Bounded Rationality," *The American Economic Review*, 1994, *84*, pp. 406–411.

15 For more on framing effects, see G. Whyte, "Decision Failures: Why They Occur and How to Prevent Them," *Academy of Management Executive*, August 1991, pp. 23–31; D. Frisch, "Reasons for Framing Effects," *Organizational Behavior and Human Decision Processes*, 1993, *54*, pp. 399–429; and H. Mano, "Risk-taking, Framing Effects, and Affect," *Organizational Behavior and Human Decision Processes*, 1994, *57*, pp. 38–58.

16 P. Wright, "The Harassed Decision Maker: Time Pressures, Distractions, and the Use of Evidence," *Journal of Applied Psychology*, 1974, *59*, pp. 555–561. See also E. W. Farmer, J. Hunter, and A. J. Belyavin, "Performance Under Time Constraints: The Role of Personality," *Perceptual and Motor Skills*, 1984, *59*, pp. 875–884; T. V. Paul, "Time Pressure and War Initiation: Some Linkages," *Canadian Journal of Political Science*, 1995, *28*, pp. 255–276.

17 I. L. Janis and L. Mann, *Decision Making: A Psychological Analysis of Conflict, Choice, and Commitment* (New York: Free Press, 1977), provide a thorough discussion of these situations. See also J. E. Driskell and E. Salas, "Group Decision Making Under Stress," *Journal of Applied Psychology*, 1991, *76*, pp. 473–478; "Managing Under Stress," *Supervision*, September 1993, p. 25; N. R. Augustine, "Managing the Crisis You Tried to Prevent," *Harvard Business Review*, November/December 1995, pp. 147–158; and R. P. Weiss, "Crisis Leadership," *TD*, March 2002, pp. 28–33.

18 C. M. Peterson and L. R. Beach, "Man as an Intuitive Statistician," *Psychological Bulletin*, 1967, *68*, pp. 29–46, provide one good early review supporting this view.

19 For instance, see R. M. Hogarth, "Beyond Discrete Biases: Functional and Dysfunctional Aspects of Judgmental Heuristics," *Psychological Bulletin*, 1981, *90*, pp. 197–217.

20 See A. Tversky and D. Kahneman, "Judgment Under Uncertainty: Heuristics and Biases," *Science*, 1974, *185*, pp. 1124–1131, for a good discussion. For a thorough recent review and discussion, see C. R. Sunstein, "Hazardous Heuristics," *The University of California Law Review*, 2003, *70*, pp. 751–782.

21 See T. A. Stewart, "Thinking Rationally About Irrational Thinking," *Harvard Business Review*, July 2003, p. 8. See also J. E. Hilsenrath,

"Nobel Winners Are a New Breed," *Wall Street Journal*, October 10, 2002, p. B1.

22 J. G. March and H. A. Simon, *Organizations* (New York: Wiley, 1958).

23 Tversky and Kahneman, "Judgment Under Uncertainty."

24 On this specific point, see S. Lichtenstein et al., "Judged Frequency of Lethal Events," *Journal of Experimental Psychology: Human Learning and Memory*, 1978, *4*, 551–578. For a detailed discussion of the availability heuristic, see A. Tversky and D. Kahneman, "Availability: A Heuristic for Judging Frequency and Probability," *Cognitive Psychology*, 1973, *5*, pp. 207–232. See also M. Manis, J. Shedler, and J. Jonides, "Availability Heuristic in Judgments of Set Size and Frequency of Occurrence," *Journal of Personality and Social Psychology*, 1993, *65*, pp. 448–457.

25 This example is from Tversky and Kahneman, "Judgment Under Uncertainty."

26 E. Valenzi and I. R. Andrews, "Individual Differences in the Decision Process of Employment Interviewers," *Journal of Applied Psychology*, 1973, *58*, pp. 49–53.

27 M. Roig and L. DeTommaso, "Are College Cheating and Plagiarism Related to Academic Procrastination?" *Psychological Reports*, 1995, *77*, pp. 691–698. For more on procrastination, see N. N. Harris and R. I. Sutton, "Task Procrastination in Organizations: A Framework for Research," *Human Relations*, 1983, *36*, pp. 987–995; N. A. Milgram, W. Dangour, and A. Raviv, "Situational and Personal Determinants of Academic Procrastination," *The Journal of General Psychology*, 1992, *119*, pp. 123–133; and C. Senecal, R. Koestner, and R. J. Vallerand, "Self-Regulation and Academic Procrastination," *The Journal of Social Psychology*, 1995, *135*, pp. 607–619.

28 See, for instance, R. McGarvey, "Now or Never," *Entrepreneur*, October 1995, pp. 75–77; J. P. Zane, "Some Advice to Heed, If Not Now, Tomorrow: Procrastination's Toll on the Job," *New York Times*, February 11, 1996, Sec. 3, p. 11; and H. Lancaster, "Procrastinators: Mend Your Ways Before Your Job Stalls," *Wall Street Journal*, May 7, 1996, p. B1.

29 L. S. Richman, "Rekindling the Entrepreneurial Fire," *Fortune*, February 21, 1994, p. 112.

30 This choice mode was first proposed by C. E. Lindblom, "The Science of Muddling Through," *Public Administration Review*, 1959, *19*, pp. 79–88. See also C. W. Park, "Joint Decisions in Home Purchasing: A Muddling-Through Process," *The Journal of Consumer Research*, 1982, *9*, pp. 151–162.

31 See Edwards, "Human Information Processing," and H. J. Einhorn, "Overconfidence in Judgment," *New Directions for Methodology of Social and Behavioral Science*, 1980, *4*, pp. 1–16, for discussions of explanations for this tendency. See also M. Bjorkman, "Internal Cue Theory: Calibration and Resolution of Confidence in General Knowledge," *Organizational Behavior and Human Decision Processes*, 1994, *58*, pp. 386–405.

32 For a discussion of decision confirmation, see D. J. Power and R. J. Aldag, "Soelberg's Job Search and Choice Model: A Clarification, Review, and Critique," *Academy of Management Review*, 1985, *10*, pp. 48–58.

33 Janis and Mann, *Decision Making: A Psychological Analysis of Conflict, Choice, and Commitment*.

34 Ibid.

35 This is based primarily on O. Behling and N. L. Eckel, "Making Sense out of Intuition," *Academy of Management Executive*, 1991, *5(1)*, pp. 46–54. For a discussion of ways that executives view intuition, see L. A. Burke and M. K. Miller, "Taking the Mystery Out of Intuitive Decision Making," *Academy of Management Executive*, 1999, *13(4)*, pp. 91–99. See also I. Clarke and W. Mackaness, "Management 'Intuition': An Interpretive Account of Structure and Content of Decision Schemas Using Cognitive Maps," *The Journal of Management Studies*, March 2001, *38(2)*, pp. 147–172; and E. Bonabeau, "Don't Trust Your Gut," *Harvard Business Review*, May 2003, *81(5)*, pp. 116–131.

36 M. W. McCall, Jr., and R. E. Kaplan, *Whatever It Takes* (Englewood Cliffs, NJ: Prentice-Hall, 1985), p. 32.

37 H. Simon, "Making Management Decisions: The Role of Intuition and Emotion," *Academy of Management Executive*, 1987, *1*, pp. 57–64. See also R. Frantz, "Herbert Simon. Artificial Intelligence as a Framework for Understanding Intuition," *Journal of Economic Psychology*, April 2003, *24(2)*, pp. 265–278.

38 J. Adair, "Why Managers Need to Develop Their Intuition," *International Management*, November 1984, pp. 34, 39–40.

39 S. A. Mednick, "The Associative Basis of the Creative Process," *Psychological Review*, 1962, *69*, p. 221. For a discussion of creative prod-

ucts, see S. P. Besemer and D. J. Treffinger, "Analysis of Creative Products: Review and Synthesis," *Journal of Creative Behavior*, 1981, *15*, pp. 158–178.

40 For discussions of the impact of motivation on creativity, see G. Halpin and G. Halpin, "The Effect of Motivation on Creative Thinking Abilities," *Journal of Creative Behavior*, 1973, *7*, pp. 51–53; T. Stevens, "Creativity Killers," *Industry Week*, January 23, 1995, p. 63; and K. Vergoth, "Head Trips," *Psychology Today*, November/December 1995, p. 12.

41 G. Wallas, *The Art of Thought* (New York: Harcourt, Brace, 1926). For a good discussion of the stages of the creative process, see J. D. Couger, *Creative Problem Solving and Opportunity Finding* (Danvers, MA: Boyd & Fraser, 1995), pp. 230–236.

42 Quoted in G. A. Davis, *Creativity Is Forever* (Dubuque, IA: Kendall/Hunt, 1983), p. 9.

43 W. J. J. Gordon, *Synectics* (New York: Harper & Row, 1961).

44 Davis, *Creativity Is Forever*, p. 67.

45 See "Four Ways to Boost Creativity," *Training*, December 1991, pp. 16+.

46 Gordon, *Synectics*, p. 42. For more on direct analogy, see L. Okagaki and B. Koslowski, "Another Look at Analogies and Problem Solving," *The Journal of Creative Behavior*, 1987, *21*, pp. 15–21; and D. Offner, "'Hitch-Hiking' on Creativity in Nature," *The Journal of Creative Behavior*, 1990, *24*, 199–204.

47 See the Synectics, Inc. Web site included on the text Web site for examples.

48 For more on the use of analogies, see "Keep Those Great Ideas Coming," *Executive Female*, January–February 1993, pp. 46–50; T. Pollock, "Strategies for Creative Thinking," *Supervision*, 1995, *56*, pp. 21–22; and T. Proctor, "Paradigm Shift: A New Perspective Involving Analogical Thinking," *Management Decision*, 1996, *34(7)*, pp. 33–38.

49 See Davis, *Creativity Is Forever*, for a fuller discussion.

50 A. F. Osborne, *Applied Imagination: Principles and Procedures of Creative Problem Solving*, 3rd ed. (Buffalo, NY: Creative Education Foundation, 1993). See also M. Michalko, "Four Steps Toward Creative Thinking," *The Futurist*, May/June 2000, pp. 18–21.

51 R. P. Crawford, "The Techniques of Creative Thinking," in G. A. Davis and J. A. Scott (Eds.), *Training Creative Thinking* (Huntington, NY: Krieger, 1978).

52 Davis, *Creativity Is Forever*.

53 This example is from J. E. Arnold, "Useful Creative Techniques," in S. Parnes (Ed.), *A Sourcebook of Creative Thinking* (New York: Scribner's, 1962), pp. 251–268.

54 For studies on morphological analysis, see E. P. Stratton and R. Brown, "Improving Creative Training by Training in the Production and/or Judgment of Solutions," *Journal of Educational Psychology*, 1970, *61*, pp. 16–23; T. F. Warren and G. A. Davis, "Techniques for Creative Thinking: An Empirical Comparison of Three Methods," *Psychological Reports*, 1969, *25*, pp. 207–214; F. Zwicky, *Discovery, Invention, Research Through the Morphological Approach* (New York: Macmillan, 1969); and "Four Ways to Boost Creativity," *Training*, 1991, *28*, pp. 16+.

55 See, for instance, D. M. Ricks, "Challenging Assumptions That Block Learning," *Training*, August 1997, pp. 56–62.

56 A. K. Naj, "Hey, Get a Grip! Your Basic Paper Clip Is Like a Mousetrap," *Wall Street Journal*, July 24, 1995, pp. A1, A8.

57 See B. Olmo, "Retroduction: The Key to Creativity," *Journal of Creative Behavior*, 1977, *11*, pp. 216, 221.

58 D. Stipp, "Patrick Gunkel Is an Idea Man Who Thinks in Lists," *The Wall Street Journal*, June 1, 1987, pp. 1, 11.

59 This example is drawn from M. Michalko, *Thinkertoys* (Berkeley, CA: Ten Speed Press, 1991), pp. 45–46. For an interesting discussion of assumption challenging, see E. McFadzean, "What Can We Learn from Creative People? The Story of Brian Eno," *Management Decision*, 2000, *38(1/2)*, pp. 51–56.

60 See R. J. Sternberg, L. A. O'Hara, and T. I. Lubart, "Creativity as Investment," *California Management Review*, Fall 1997, pp. 8–21; A. Cummings and G. Oldham, "Enhancing Creativity: Managing Work Contexts for the High Potential Employee," *California Management Review*, Fall 1997, pp. 22–38; N. Madjar, G. R. Oldham, and M. G. Pratt, "There's No Place Like Home? The Contributions of Work and Nonwork Creativity Support to Employees' Creative Performance," *Academy of Management Journal*, August 2002, *45(4)*, pp. 757–767; and P. Tierney and S. M. Farmer, "Creative Self-Efficacy: Its Potential Antecedents and Relationship to Creative Performance," *Academy of Management Journal*, December 2002, *45(6)*, pp. 1137–1148.

61 This example is drawn from S. Yoder, "Japan's Scientists Find Pure

Research Suffers Under Rigid Life Style," *The Wall Street Journal*, November 31, 1988, p. A1. See also E. Thornton, "Japan's Struggle to Be Creative," *Fortune*, April 19, 1993, pp. 129+; and J. S. Jun and H. Muto, "The Hidden Dimensions of Japanese Administration: Culture and Its Impact," *Public Administration Review*, March/April 1995, pp. 125–134. For discussions of efforts to enhance creativity in Japan, see M. Kitaura, "Japanese Vocational Training Under the Microscope," *Human Resource Management International Digest*, March/April 1997, *5(2)*, pp. 32–34; and J. Watts, "Seeking More Creativity, Japan Overhauls IP Laws," *Research Technology Management*, September/October 2000, *43(5)*, pp. 4–5.

62   The *Wall Street Journal*, January 5, 1985, p. 3.

63   For more on venture teams, see K. Murphy, "Venture Teams Help Companies Create New Products," *Personnel Journal*, March 1992, pp. 60–63+; and B. Frost, T. Gannarelli, and C. Hunt, "Venture Teams: Not Improving What Is, But Creating What Isn't," *Public Management*, 1995, *77*, pp. 17–21.

64   The name "skunk works" is borrowed from "Skonk Works," the name of the still used to make Kickapoo Joy Juice in the late Al Capp's comic strip *Li'l Abner*.

65   J. B. White and O. Suris, "How a 'Skunk Works' Kept the Mustang Alive —On a Tight Budget," *Wall Street Journal*, September 21, 1993, pp. A1, A12.

66   For more examples, see D. A. Fulghum, "Stealth UAV Goes to War," *Aviation Week and Space Technology*, July 7, 2003, p. 20; and B. Parks, "The Garage That Saved Whirlpool's Soul," *Business 2.0*, February 2003, pp. 50–52.

67   T. J. Peters and R. H. Waterman, Jr., *In Search of Excellence: Lessons for America's Best-Run Companies* (New York: Harper & Row, 1982), 203–204. For more on idea champions, see J. M. Howell and C. A. Higgins, "Champions of Change: Identifying, Understanding, and Supporting Champions of Technological Innovations," *Organizational Dynamics*, Summer 1990, pp. 40–55; and P. G. Greene, C. G. Brush, and M. M. Hart, "The Corporate Venture Champion: A Resource-Based Approach to Role and Process," *Entrepreneurship Theory and Practice*, Spring 1999, pp. 103–122.

68   For discussions of intrapreneurship, see "How Can Big Companies Keep the Entrepreneurial Spirit Alive?" *Harvard Business Review*, November/December 1995, pp. 183–186+; M. H. Peak, "Turning Entrepreneurial Ideas Inside Out," *Management Review*, 1996, *85*, p. 7; T. D. Schellhardt: "David and Goliath: Some Giant Companies Are Particularly Good at Fostering an Entrepreneurial Spirit. Here's How They Do It," *Wall Street Journal*, May 23, 1996, p. R14; S. A. Zahra, A. P. Nielsen, and W. C. Bogner, "Corporate Entrepreneurship, Knowledge, and Competence Development," *Entrepreneurship Theory and Practice*, Spring 1999, pp. 169–189; and B. Antoncic and R. D. Hirsch, "Intrapreneurship: Construct Refinement and Cross-Cultural Validation," *Journal of Business Venturing*, September 2001, *16(5)*, pp. 495+.

69   This section is based on B. Bird, *Entrepreneurial Behavior* (Glenview, IL: Scott, Foresman, 1989), p. 28. See also L. Prasad, "The Etiology of Organizational Politics: Implications for the Intrapreneur," *Advanced Management Journal*, Summer 1993, pp. 35–41; and J. E. Woodilla, "From Intrapreneurship to Entrepreneurship: Is Technical Expertise Sufficient? —A Case Study," *New England Journal of Entrepreneurship*, September 2003, pp. 55–61.

70   These are based on G. F. Pinchot, III, *Intrapreneuring* (New York: Harper & Row, 1985), pp. 198–256. For more on Pinchot's views, see J. Pickard, "A Fertile Grounding," *People Management*, October 24, 1996, pp. 28–34.

71   "Intrapreneurship at Bell Atlantic," *Business Quarterly*, Spring 1993, pp. 46–47.

72   R. Loutfy and L. Belkhir, "Managing Innovation at Xerox," *Research Technology Management*, July/August 2001, pp. 15–24. See also N. Valery, "Survey: Innovation in Industry: Adopting Orphans," *The Economist*, February 20, 1999, pp. S21–S22.

73   T. Cox, Jr., *Cultural Diversity in Organizations: Theory, Research, and Practice* (San Francisco: Berrett-Koehler, 1994), pp. 31–35. See also G. F. Shea, "Learn How to Treasure Differences," *HRMagazine*, December 1992, pp. 34–37.

74   R. M. Kanter, *The Change Masters* (New York: Simon & Schuster, 1983), p. 167.

75   P. L. McLeod, S. A. Lobel, and T. Cox, Jr., *Cultural Diversity and Creativity in Small Groups: A Test of the Value-in-Diversity Hypothesis*. Unpublished working paper, University of Michigan, Ann Arbor, 1993.

76   C. J. Nemeth, "Dissent, Group Process, and Creativity," in *Advances in Group Processes*, Vol. 2, (1985), pp. 57–75.

77   J. E. McGrath, *Groups: Interaction and Performance* (Englewood Cliffs, NJ: Prentice-Hall, 1984). See also I. Dodds, "Differences Can Also Be Strengths," *People Management*, April 20, 1995, pp. 40–41+.

78   See T. Cox, Jr., *Cultural Diversity in Organizations*, pp. 36–39.

79   For more on this issue, see J. M. Ivancevich and J. A. Gilbert, "Diversity Management: Time for a New Approach," *Public Personnel Management*, Spring 2000, pp. 75–92; K. Melymuka, "Indulging Our Differences: 100 Best Places to Work," *Computerworld*, June 19, 2000, pp. 56–57; and J. T. Polzer, L. P. Milton, and W. B. Swann, Jr., "Capitalizing on Diversity: Interpersonal Congruence in Small Work Groups," *Administrative Science Quarterly*, June 2002, *47(2)*, pp. 296–324.

80   J. E. Rigdon, "More Companies Send Staffs on Retreats to Spur Creativity and Jolt Thinking," *Wall Street Journal*, October 16, 1991, pp. B1, B8. See also R. Barker, "The Art of Brainstorming," *Business Week*, August 26, 2002, p. 168.

81   L. Bannon, "Think Tank in Toyland —Freewheeling Group Activities of Mattel's 'Project Platypus' Aim at Hatching Playthings," *Wall Street Journal*, June 6, 2002, p. B1. See also L. Miles, "How to Spark the Creative Process," *Marketing*, March 20, 2003, pp. 23–24.

82   This section is based on E. Thornton, "Japan's Struggle to Be Creative," *Fortune*, April 19, 1993, pp. 129–134.

83   These guidelines are based in part on R. Fisher, W. Ury, and B. Patton, *Getting to Yes: Negotiating Agreement without Giving In*, 2nd ed. (New York: Penguin Books, 1991). That book is an excellent, readable discussion of guidelines for attaining win-win outcomes.

84   These guidelines for planning negotiations are based primarily on J. H. Hopkins, "Negotiations and the Credit Professional," *Business Credit*, June 1999, pp. 16–17.

85   To learn more about BATNA, see R. Fisher, W. Ury, and B. Patton, *Getting to Yes: Negotiating Agreement Without Giving In*, 2nd ed. (New York: Penguin Books, 1991), pp. 97–106. See also T. Gile, "Big Deal," *Journal of Property Management*, May/June 2003, *68*, pp. 28–32.

86   R. Fisher et al., *Getting to Yes*, p. 38.

87   These strategies were proposed by D. G. Pruitt, "Achieving Integrative Agreements," in M. H. Bazerman and R. J. Lewicki, *Negotiating in Organizations* (Beverly Hills, CA: Sage, 1983), pp. 35–50.

88   This section is based on M. H. Bazerman, *Judgment in Managerial Decision Making*, 3rd ed. (New York: Wiley, 1994), pp. 141–144.

89   Based on D. Eisenberg. Can McDonald's Shape Up? *Time*, September 30, 2002.

90   Source: www.mcdonalds.com/corporate/index.html.

91   Based in part on J. Fox, "Nokia's Secret Code," *Fortune*, May 1, 2000, pp. 160–168.

92   Source: www.nokia.com/nokia/0,6771,33005,00.html.

93   Source: eet.com/pressreleases/bizwire/88204.

94   Source: www.emergic.org/archives/indi/003018.php.

95   Source: www.matr.net/article-6738.html.

CHAPTER 4.   MOTIVATING EFFECTIVELY

1   For a review of research on seven motivation theories, see M. L. Ambrose and C. T. Kulik, "Old Friends, New Faces: Motivation Research in the 1990s," *Journal of Management*, 1999, *25(3)*, pp. 231–292.

2   A. H. Maslow, "A Theory of Human Motivation," *Psychological Review*, 1943, *50*, pp. 370–396. For more on Maslow's views, see E. Hoffman, "The Last Interview of Abraham Maslow," *Psychology Today*, January 1992, pp. 68–73; M. R. Hagerty, "Testing Maslow's Hierarchy of Needs: National Quality-of-Life Across Time," *Social Indicators Research*, March 1999, *46(3)*, pp. 24–271; and J. Iachini,

"Starting the 'Fire' Under an Undermotivated Employee," *Occupational Health & Safety*, March 2003, *72(3)*, pp. 18, 20.

3   D. C. McClelland, "Business Drive and National Achievement," *Harvard Business Review*, July–August 1962, pp. 99–112. For an interesting discussion of McClelland and his work, including how McClelland built on the work of psychologist Henry Murray, see N. Lemann, "Is There a Science of Success?" *Atlantic Monthly*, February 1994, pp. 82–98.

4   McClelland, "Business Drive," p. 103.

5   Lemann, "Is There a Science of Success?" p. 92.

6 For more on the impact of need for achievement on economic development, see C.-M. Lau and L. W. Busenitz, "Growth Intentions of Entrepreneurs in a Transitional Economy: The People's Republic of China," *Entrepreneurship Theory and Practice*, Fall 2001, *26(1)*, pp. 5–20; A. Walter, M. Auer, and H. G. Gemunden, "The Impact of Personality, Competence, and Activities of Academic Entrepreneurs on Technology Transfer Success," *International Journal of Entrepreneurship and Innovation Management*, 2002, *2(2,3)*, pp. 268+; and L. Yu, "Rates of Takeoff in Europe," *MIT Sloan Management Review*, Summer 2003, *44(4)*, p. 10.

7 D. C. McClelland and D. H. Burnham, "Power Is the Great Motivator," *Harvard Business Review*, March–April 1976, pp. 100–110. For evidence concerning need for power and need for affiliation, see D. G. Winter, "Power, Affiliation, and War: Three Tests of a Motivational Model," *Journal of Personality and Social Psychology*, September 1993, pp. 532–545.

8 For a recent discussion of learning theories in organizations, see R. Zemke, "Who Needs Learning Theory Anyway?" *Training*, September 2002, *39(9)*, pp. 86–91.

9 I. P. Pavlov, *The Work of the Digestive Glands*, trans. W. H. Thompson (London: Charles Griffin, 1902).

10 B. F. Skinner, *Contingencies of Reinforcement: A Theoretical Analysis* (East Norwalk, CT: Appleton-Century-Crofts, 1969).

11 S. L. Myers, "Russia Punishes Commanders for Copter Crash That Killed 119," *New York Times*, September 8, 2002, p. A13. See also S. L. Myers, "Russia Charges Officer in Chechen Copter Crash," *New York Times*, May 8, 2003, p. A8.

12 W. Nord, "Beyond the Teaching Machine: The Neglected Area of Operant Conditioning in the Theory and Practice of Management," *Organizational Behavior and Human Performance*, 1969, *4*, pp. 375–401.

13 W. C. Hamner and E. P. Hamner, "Behavior Modification on the Bottom Line," *Organizational Dynamics*, 1976, *4*, pp. 3–21.

14 This listing is drawn from E. A. Locke and G. P. Latham, *Goal Setting for Individuals, Groups, and Organizations* (Chicago: Science Research Associates, 1984).

15 For an interesting discussion of the psychological impact of working in a situation where the mission is unclear, see T. W. Britt, "Black Hawk Down at Work," *Harvard Business Review*, January 2003, *81(1)*, pp. 16–17.

16 J. F. Bryan and E. A. Locke, "Goal Setting as a Means of Increasing Motivation," *Journal of Applied Psychology*, 1967, *51*, pp. 274–277.

17 See, for instance, G. P. Latham, M. Erez, and E. A. Locke, "Resolving Scientific Disputes by the Joint Design of Crucial Experiments by the Antagonists: Application to the Erez-Latham Dispute Regarding Participation in Goal Setting," *Journal of Applied Psychology*, 1988, *73*, pp. 753–772.

18 G. P. Latham and J. J. Baldes, "The 'Practical Significance' of Locke's Theory of Goal Setting," *Journal of Applied Psychology*, 1975, *60*, pp. 122–124.

19 R. Rodgers and J. E. Hunter, "Impact of Management by Objectives on Organizational Productivity," *Journal of Applied Psychology*, 1991, *76*, pp. 322–336.

20 M. Castaneda, T. A. Kolenko, and R. J. Aldag, "Self-Management Perceptions and Practices: A Structural Equations Analysis," *Journal of Organizational Behavior*, 1999, *20(1)*, pp. 101–120.

21 See S. Kerr and J. M. Jermier, "Substitutes for Leadership: Their Meaning and Measurement," *Organizational Behavior and Human Performance*, 1978, *22*, pp. 375–403; and P. M. Podsakoff, S. B. McKenzie, and W. H. Bommer, "Meta-analysis of the Relationships Between Kerr and Jermier's Substitutes for Leadership and Employee Job Attitudes, Role Perceptions, and Performance," *Journal of Applied Psychology*, 1996, *81*, pp. 380–399.

22 T. Petzinger, Jr., "Self-Organization Will Free Employees to Act Like Bosses," *Wall Street Journal*, January 3, 1997, p. B1.

23 See T. A. Stewart, "Looking Ahead: The Search for the Organization of Tomorrow," *Fortune*, May 18, 1992, pp. 92–98; J. J. Laabs, "Ben & Jerry's Caring Capitalism," *Personnel Journal*, November 1992, pp. 50–57; and R. Wageman, "Case Study: Critical Success Factors for Creating Superb Self-Managing Teams at Xerox," *Compensation and Benefits Review*, September–October 1997, pp. 31–41.

24 D. B. Jeffrey, "A Comparison of the Effects of External Control and Self-Control on the Modification and Maintenance of Weight," *Journal of Abnormal Psychology*, 1974, *83*, pp. 404–410.

25 T. M. Hout and J. C. Carter, "Getting It Done: New Roles for Senior Executives," *Harvard Business Review*, November–December 1995, pp. 133–141; and "New *Fortune*/Hay Group Ranking of 'The World's Most Admired Companies' Published," *PR Newswire*, November 30, 1999.

26 For one review, see F. Andrasik and J. S. Heimberg, "Self-Management Procedures," in L. W. Frederiksen (ed.), *Handbook of Organizational Behavior Management* (New York: Wiley-Interscience, 1982), pp. 219–247.

27 See, for instance, M. E. Gist, A. G. Bavetta, and C. K. Stevens, "Transfer Training Method: Its Influence on Skill Generalization, Skill Repetition, and Performance Level," *Personnel Psychology*, 1990, *43*, pp. 501–523; and G. P. Latham and C. A. Frayne, "Self Management Training for Increasing Job Attendance: A Follow-up and a Replication," *Journal of Applied Psychology*, 1989, *74*, pp. 411–416.

28 The examples of self-management goals, monitoring, modifying of cues and consequences, and reordering of behaviors were provided in former students' self-management exercises.

29 This section is based on C. C. Manz and H. P. Sims, Jr., "SuperLeadership: Beyond the Myth of Heroic Leadership," *Organizational Dynamics*, Spring 1991, pp. 18–35. See also "Science and Technology: The Power of Negative Thinking," *The Economist*, December 18, 1999, pp. 127–128; and D. Sullivan, "Clear Thinking for Scary Times," *Advisor Today*, September 2002, *97(9)*, p. 108.

30 For instance, see "Stress-Busters," *Credit Union Management*, June 1999, p. 8.

31 V. H. Vroom, *Work and Motivation* (New York: Wiley, 1964). For more recent discussions of expectancy theory, see Ambrose and Kulik, "Old Friends," pp. 231–292; R. G. Isaac, W. J. Zerbe, and D. C. Pitt, "Leadership and Motivation: The Effective Application of Expectancy Theory," *Journal of Managerial Issues*, 2001, *13(2)*, pp. 212–226; and A. Erez and A. M. Isen, "The Influence of Positive Affect on the Components of Expectancy Motivation," *Journal of Applied Psychology*, 2002, *87(6)*, pp. 1055–1067.

32 Both expectancies and instrumentalities are also sometimes expressed as correlations. Unlike probabilities, correlations can take on negative values. Outcomes would be restated accordingly.

33 See D. Sauey, "Group Life Insurance Is Backbone of Cafeteria Plans," *Credit Union Magazine*, October 2001, p. 60; and C. Lee, "Customized Compensation Packages," *Journal of Property Management*, September–October 2001, *66(5)*, pp. 30–38.

34 See E. Walster, G. W. Walster, and E. Berscheid, *Equity: Theory and Research* (Boston: Allyn & Bacon, 1978), for a review of studies on this issue.

35 See R. S. Allen and C. S. White, "Equity Sensitivity Theory: A Test of Responses to Two Types of Under-Reward Situations," *Journal of Managerial Issues*, 2002, *14(4)*, pp. 435–451; K. G. Wheeler, "Cultural Values in Relation to Equity Sensitivity Within and Across Cultures," *Journal of Managerial Psychology*, 2002, *17(7–8)*, pp. 612–627; and I. Yamaguchi, "The Relationships Among Individual Differences, Needs and Equity Sensitivity," *Journal of Managerial Psychology*, 2003, *18(4)*, pp. 324–344.

36 G. S. Leventhal, "Fairness in Social Relationships," in J. Thibaut, J. T. Spence, and R. Carson (eds.), *Contemporary Topics in Social Psychology* (Morristown, NJ: General Learning Press, 1976).

37 This listing is based on G. S. Leventhal, "The Distribution of Rewards and Resources in Groups and Organizations," in L. Berkowitz and E. Walster (eds.), *Advances in Experimental Social Psychology*, vol. 9 (New York: Academic Press, 1976).

38 M. W. Miller, "As IBM Losses Mount, So Do the Complaints About Company Perks," *Wall Street Journal*, October 27, 1993, p. A1.

39 C. Farrell, "Stock Options for All!" *Business Week Online*, September 20, 2002.

40 E. Krell, "Getting a Grip on Executive Compensation," *Workforce*, February 2003, *82(2)*, pp. 30–34; J. Useem, "Have They No Shame?" *Fortune*, April 28, 2003, pp. 57–60, 64; and A. Borrus and M. Arndt, "Executive Pay: Labor Strikes Back; Recent Union-Led Proxy Victories Could Curb Corner-Office Excesses," *Business Week*, May 26, 2003, p. 46.

41 T. Leander, "The Global Shakeup in Executive Comp," *Global Finance*, August 1998, pp. 12–14; and D. Bilefsky, "Mad About Money: The Outrage over CEO Pay Isn't Only a U.S. Phenomenon; Just Ask Shareholders in Europe," *Wall Street Journal*, April 14, 2003, p. R3.

42 J. S. Adams, "Inequity in Social Exchange," in L. Berkowitz (ed.), *Advances in Experimental Social Psychology*, vol. 2 (New York: Academic Press, 1965).

43 Although there are some more sophisticated equity theory formulations, this version is adequate in most cases.

44 For instance, see E. Jaques, *Equitable Payment* (New York: Wiley, 1961), and R. D. Pritchard, M. D. Dunnette, and D. O. Jorgenson,

"Effects of Perceptions of Equity and Inequity on Worker Performance and Satisfaction," *Journal of Applied Psychology Monograph*, 1972, *56*, pp. 75–94.

45 See Walster, Walster, and Berscheid, *Equity*, for a review of related studies.

46 Ibid.

47 J. Greenberg, "Employee Theft as a Reaction to Underpayment Inequity: The Hidden Cost of Pay Cuts," *Journal of Applied Psychology*, October 1990, pp. 561–568.

48 Adams, "Inequity in Social Exchange."

49 For a review of evidence concerning forms of fairness, see J. A. Colquitt, D. E. Conlon, W. J. Wesson, C. O. L. H. Porter, and K. Y. Ng, "Justice at the Millennium: A Meta-analytic Review of 25 Years of Organizational Justice Research," *Journal of Applied Psychology*, 2001, *86(3)*, pp. 425–445.

50 M. C. Kernan and P. J. Hanges, "Survivor Reactions to Reorganization: Antecedents and Consequences of Procedural, Interpersonal, and Informational Justice," *Journal of Applied Psychology*, 2002, *87(5)*, pp. 916–928.

51 M. L. Ambrose and R. Cropanzano, "A Longitudinal Analysis of Organizational Fairness: An Examination of Reactions to Tenure and Promotion Decisions," *Journal of Applied Psychology*, 2003, *88(2)*, pp. 266–275.

52 See also J. Kickul, S. W. Lester, and J. Finkl, "Promise Breaking During Radical Organizational Change: Do Justice Interventions Make a Difference?" *Journal of Organizational Behavior*, June 2002, *23(4)*, pp. 469–488.

53 For an examination of the impacts of fairness perceptions on organizational outcomes, see T. Simons and Q. Roberson, "Why Managers Should Care About Fairness: The Effects of Aggregate Justice Perceptions on Organizational Outcomes," *Journal of Applied Psychology*, 2003, *88(3)*, pp. 432–443.

54 F. W. Taylor, *The Principles of Scientific Management* (New York: Harper & Brothers, 1911). See also A. Harrington, "The Big Ideas," *Fortune*, November 22, 1999, pp. 152–154.

55 C. Argyris, *Integrating the Individual and the Organization* (New York: Wiley, 1964).

56 M. S. Myers, *Every Employee a Manager: More Meaningful Work Through Job Enrichment* (New York: McGraw-Hill, 1970).

57 See R. Bénabou and J. Tirole, "Intrinsic and Extrinsic Motivation," *Review of Economic Studies*, 2003, *70*, pp. 489–520.

58 J. S. Hirsch, "Now Hotel Clerks Provide More than Keys," *Wall Street Journal*, March 5, 1993, p. B1.

59 K. Kelly, "The New Soul of John Deere," *Business Week*, January 31, 1994, pp. 64–66.

60 L. M. Grossman, "Truck Cabs Turn into Mobile Offices as Drivers Take on White-Collar Tasks," *Wall Street Journal*, August 3, 1993, pp. B1, B9.

61 J. R. Hackman and E. E. Lawler, III, "Employee Reactions to Job Characteristics," *Journal of Applied Psychology Monograph*, 1971, *55*, pp. 259–286; and J. R. Hackman and G. R. Oldham, "The Job Diagnostic Survey: An Instrument for the Diagnosis of Jobs and the Evaluation of Job Redesign Projects," Technical Report No. 4, Department of Administrative Sciences, Yale University, 1974. For other discussions of this model, see R. J. Aldag, S. H. Barr, and A. P. Brief, "Measurement of Perceived Task Characteristics," *Psychological Bulletin*, 1981, *90*, pp.

415–431; R. J. Aldag and A. P. Brief, *Task Design and Employee Motivation* (Glenview, IL: Scott, Foresman, 1979); K. H. Roberts and W. Glick, "The Job Characteristics Approach to Task Design: A Critical Review," *Journal of Applied Psychology*, 1981, *66*, pp. 193–217; and Y. Fried and G. R. Ferris, "The Validity of the Job Characteristics Model: A Review and Meta-Analysis," *Personnel Psychology*, 1987, pp. 287–322.

62 For discussions of the importance of autonomy at work, see M. D. Burdi and L. C. Baker, "Physicians' Perceptions of Autonomy and Satisfaction in California," *Health Affairs*, July–August 1999, *18(4)*, pp. 134–145; and G. Wang and R. G. Netemeyer, "The Effects of Job Autonomy, Customer Demandingness, and Trait Competitiveness on Salesperson Learning, Self-Efficacy, and Performance," *Journal of the Academy of Marketing Science*, 2002, *30(3)*, pp. 217–228.

63 R. B. Dunham, R. J. Aldag, and A. P. Brief, "Dimensionality of Task Design as Measured by the Job Diagnostic Survey," *Academy of Management Journal*, 1977, *20*, pp. 209–223. See also Y. Fried and G. R. Ferris, "The Dimensionality of Job Characteristics: Some Neglected Issues," *Journal of Applied Psychology*, 1986, *71*, pp. 419–426.

64 Aldag, Barr, and Brief, "Task Characteristics," pp. 415–431.

65 Ibid.

66 Ibid.

67 For instance, consider a simple two-characteristics case where characteristic A has a score of 0 on a scale of 0 to 5 and characteristic B has a score of 3. If an employee combines the scores with an additive model, the job would have a score of $0 + 3 = 3$. With a multiplicative model, the job would have a score of $0 \times 3 = 0$. That is, it would not motivate at all. Suppose then that job changes were made to improve the score on characteristic B to 5. If an employee combines those scores with an additive model, the score becomes $0 + 5 = 5$, an improvement of 2. With a multiplicative model, the score remains at $0 \times 5 = 0$.

68 E. F. Stone, "Some Personality Correlates of Perceptions of and Reactions to Task Characteristics," Working Paper, Purdue University, 1977.

69 See Aldag and Brief, *Task Design and Employee Motivation*, pp. 93–95, for more on this issue.

70 J. R. Hackman and G. R. Oldham, *Work Redesign* (Reading, MA: Addison-Wesley, 1980).

71 See, for instance, L. P. Wilbur, "The Value of On-the-Job Rotation," *Supervisory Management*, November 1993, p. 6; and M. A. Campion, L. Cheraskin, and M. J. Stevens, "Career-Related Antecedents and Outcomes of Job Rotation," *Academy of Management Journal*, 1994, *37*, pp. 1518–1542. See also J. Ortega, "Job Rotation as a Learning Machine," *Management Science*, October 2001, *47(10)*, pp. 1361–1370.

72 Aldag and Brief, *Task Design and Employee Motivation*, pp. 62–70.

73 Source: Based on a management consulting project completed by M. Wegner, August 2002.

74 http://www.gymboree.com/our_company/cs_home.jsp?FOLDER%3C%3Efolder_id=754517&bmUID=1061391814046.

75 http://www.gymboree.com/our_company/cs_home.jsp?FOLDER%3C%3Efolder_id=980081&bmUID=1061391591530.

76 http://www.gymboree.com/our_company/cs_home.jsp?FOLDER%3C%3Efolder_id=754529&bmUID=1061392095904.

77 Source: S. C. Lundin, J. Christensen, and H. Paul, *FISH! A Remarkable Way to Boost Morale and Improve Results* (New York: Hyperion Books, 2000).

CHAPTER 5. MANAGING STRESS

1 See C. M. Solomon, "Stressed to the Limit," *Workforce*, September 1999, pp. 48–54; and C. Koch, "Personal Management: Are You Putting on a Little Weight? Do You Think No One Understands You? Do You Feel Out of Control? Of Course You Do. Why Should You Be Any Different from Any Other CIO? Here's Why You Need to Stop, Take a Look Around and Change Your Ways," *CIO*, August 1, 2003, pp. 1+.

2 See, for instance, J. Corville and L. M. Bernardi, "Helping Employees Manage Stress," *The Canadian Manager*, Fall 1999, p. 11; "Workplace Violence: Gaining Ground on 'Going Postal'?" *Security*, December 1998, pp. 9–13; and M. P. Magyar, "Preventing Workplace Violence," *Occupational Health and Safety*, June 2003, pp. 64–68.

3 P. Rosch, president of the American Institute of Stress, as reported in *ManpowerArgus*, December 1998, p. 11.

4 "Stress: Japanese Killer," *Psychology Today*, September/October 2000, pp. 10–11.

5 For more on stress at Microsoft, as well as about other extremely stressful jobs, see "Stressed Out: Extreme Job Stress: Survivors' Tales," *Wall Street Journal*, January 17, 2001, p. B1.

6 "Stress: Japanese Killer," pp. 10–11.

7 This section is based in part on K. L. Miller, "Now, Japan Is Admitting It: Work Kills Executives," *Business Week*, August 3, 1992, p. 35; S. Arai, "Rethinking Japan's Work Ethic," *Japan 21st*, June 1994, p. 25; Z. Abdoolcarim, "Executive Stress: A Company Killer," *Asian Business*, August 1995, pp. 22–26; S. Long, "Culture of Long Hours Inexcusable," *Australian Financial Review*, October 20, 1999, p. 19; and P. Hadfield, "If You Think You're Overworked, Think Again," *New Scientist*, December 8, 2001, p. 15.

8 H. Cass, "Sleep: The Feel Good Prescription," *Total Health*, May/June 2000, pp. 28–32. See also "The Risks of Tranquility," *Health Letter*, August 2000, pp. 9–10.

9   D. Mills, "Time Out," *OH & S Canada*, September 1999, p. 62. See also B. Saporito, "The Most Dangerous Job in America," *Fortune*, May 31, 1993, pp. 130–140.

10 The term *building-related illness* is used when a particular building problem is related to a particular illness. The term *sick building syndrome* is used when a specific illness cause cannot be identified.

11 This Focus on Management is based on L. Lagnado, "FDNY Tries to Rescue Its Own," *Wall Street Journal*, March 5, 2002, p. B1+; E. Christenson, "Firefighters: Looking for Ways to Stop the Exodus," *Newsweek*, October 7, 2002, p. 8; and D. France, "Now, 'WTC Syndrome,'" *Newsweek*, November 5, 2001, p. 10.

12 B. A. Wood and M. A. Al, "Sick Building Syndrome: A Potpourri Analysis," *Federation of Insurance & Corporate Counsel Quarterly*, Spring 1999, pp. 347–378. See also "Sick Building Syndrome Affects Productivity and Health," *Professional Safety*, January 2003, p. 15; and M. Conlin and J. Carey, "Is Your Office Killing You? Sick Buildings Are Seething with Molds, Monoxide—and Worse," *Business Week*, June 5, 2000, p. 114.

13 T. F. Segalla, "'Sick Building' and 'Indoor Air Quality,'" *Federation of Insurance & Corporate Counsel Quarterly*, Spring 1999, pp. 321–332.

14 Ibid. See also A. Chen and E. Vine, "It's in the Air," *Best's Review*, January 1999, pp. 79–80; A. Mann, "This Place Makes Me Sick," *Time*, December 21, 1998, pp. 38–40; and S. Cullen, "Your Office May Be Hazardous to Your Health," *Office Solutions*, November/December 2002, pp. 18–21.

15 For instance, see L. M. Andersson and C. M. Pearson, "Tit for Tat? The Spiraling Effect of Incivility in the Workplace," *Academy of Management Review*, July 1999, pp. 452–471.

16 P. Urs Bender, "Powerful Presentations," *CMA Management*, April 1999, p. 31; and T. Simons, "Scared Speechless: Understanding and Conquering Stage Fright," *Presentations*, September 1998, pp. 39–46.

17 J. A. Rolls, "Facing the Fears Associated with Professional Speaking," *Business Communication Quarterly*, June 1998, pp. 103–106.

18 N. James, "Emotional Labour: Skill and Work in the Social Regulation of Feelings," *Sociological Review*, 1988, *37*, pp. 15–42.

19 J. Van Maanen and G. Kunda, "'Real Feelings': Emotional Expression and Organizational Culture," in L. L. Cummings and B. M. Staw (Eds.), *Research in Organizational Behavior* (Greenwich, CT: JAI Press, 1989), pp. 43–103. See also J. A. Morris and D. C. Feldman, "The Dimensions, Antecedents, and Consequences of Emotional Labor," *Academy of Management Review*, October 1996, pp. 986–1010; J. Martin, K. Knopoff, and C. Beckman, "An Alternative to Bureaucratic Impersonality and Emotional Labor: Bounded Emotionality at the Body Shop," *Administrative Science Quarterly*, June 1998, pp. 429–469; and J. Diefendorff and E. M. Richard, "Antecedents and Consequences of Emotional Display Rule Perceptions," *Journal of Applied Psychology*, 2003, *88(2)*, pp. 284–294.

20 T. H. Holmes and R. H. Rahe, "Social Readjustment Rating Scale," *Journal of Psychosomatic Research*, 1967, *11*, pp. 213–218.

21 L. Bronte, "Is Retirement Dangerous to Your Health?" *Across the Board*, March/April 2002, pp. 53–54.

22 T. H. Holmes and M. Masuda, "Life Change and Illness Susceptibility," in B. S. Dohrenwend and B. P. Dohrenwend (Eds.), *Stressful Life Events: Their Nature and Effects* (New York: Wiley, 1974), pp. 45–72. See also J. G. Rabbin and E. L. Strunening, "Life Events, Stress and Illness," *Science*, 1976, pp. 1013–1020.

23 See, for instance, L. K. Savery and M. Wooden, "The Relative Influence of Life Events and Hassles on Work-Related Injuries: Some Australian Evidence," *Human Relations*, March 1994, pp. 283–305; and D. Zohar, "When Things Go Wrong: The Effect of Daily Hassles on Effort, Exertion and Negative Mood," *Journal of Occupational and Organizational Psychology*, September 1999, pp. 265–283.

24 C. Aaron-Corbin, "The Multiple-Role Balancing Act," *Management Review*, October 1999, p. 62.

25 D. White, "It's a Dog's Life," *Psychology Today*, November/December 1998, p. 10.

26 "FYI," *Incentive*, October 1999, p. 79.

27 See, for instance, M. M. Robinson, A. P. Barbee, M. Martin, T. L. Singer, and B. Yegidis, "The Organizational Costs of Caregiving: A Call to Action," *Administration in Social Work*, 2003, *27(1)*, p. 63.

28 E. Kaplan-Leiserson, "Generation Sandwich," *TD*, February 2003, pp. 16–17.

29 For a discussion, see R. Schickel, "Living with the Dead," *Time*, October 25, 1999, p. 118.

30 See P. Frost and S. Robinson, "The Toxic Handler: Organizational Hero and Casualty," *Harvard Business Review*, July/August 1999, pp. 96–106. See also P. J. Frost, "Why Compassion Counts!" *Journal of Management Inquiry*, June 1999, pp. 127–133; and P. J. Frost, *Toxic Emotions at Work* (Boston: Harvard Business School Press, 2003).

31 For more on the link between stress and heart attacks, see "Work Stress Doubles Heart Attack Death Risk," *Worklife*, 2003, *14(4)*, pp. 9, 11. See also T. Parker-Pope, "Stress in Aftermath of Terrorism May Boost Risk of Heart Attack," *Wall Street Journal*, September 28, 2001, p. B1.

32 See R. Kalimo, K. Pahkin, and P. Mutanen, "Work and Personal Resources as Long-Term Predictors of Well-Being," *Stress and Health*, December 2002, *18(5)*, pp. 227–234.

33 Tension discharge rate is a construct presented in R. M. Rose, C. D. Jenkins, and M. W. Hurst, *Air Traffic Controller Health Study: A Prospective Investigation of Physical, Psychological, and Work-Related Changes* (Austin: University of Texas Press, 1978).

34 These examples, based on the work of Martin Seligman, are drawn from G. Cowley, "Stress-Busters: What Works," *Newsweek*, June 14, 1999, pp. 60–61.

35 S. Caminiti, "The Big Business of Burnout," *Working Woman*, November 1998, pp. 50–54.

36 See R. Cropanzano, D. E. Rupp, and Z. S. Byrne, "The Relationship of Emotional Exhaustion to Work Attitudes, Job Performance, and Organizational Citizenship Behaviors," *Journal of Applied Psychology*, 2003, *88(1)*, pp. 160–169.

37 For more on burnout, see "How to Beat Burnout," *Healthcare Executive*, July/August 2003, p. 40; L. Browning, "A Burnout Cure That Few Companies Prescribe," *New York Times*, July 6, 2003; and J. L. Haughorn, "How to Pass the Stress Test: An IT Executive Tells the Story of His Own Stress-Related Breakdown and Recovery, and Reveals What You Can Do to Avoid the Abyss," *CIO*, May 1, 2003, p. 1.

38 These are based in part on R. J. Aldag and B. Joseph, *Leadership & Vision: 25 Keys to Motivation* (New York: Lebhar-Friedman, 2000), pp. 15–18.

39 "Making Time to Manage," *Agency Sales*, February 1999, pp. 40–44.

40 See L. R. Dominguez, "Putting an End to Putting It Off," *HRMagazine*, February 1999, pp. 124–129.

41 P. Bolt, "A Question of Balance," *British Journal of Administrative Management*, July/August 1999, pp. 17–18.

42 See S. Folkman and R. S. Lazarus, "An Analysis of Coping in a Middle-Aged Community Sample," *Journal of Health and Social Behavior*, 1980, *21*, pp. 219–239; and J. C. Latack, "Coping with Stress: Measures and Future Directions for Scale Development," *Journal of Applied Psychology*, 1986, *71*, pp. 377–385.

43 D. C. Knight, "Wake Up! Employee Sleep Deprivation Is Costing You Big," *Office Solutions*, December 2000, *17(12)*, pp. 29–31. For useful suggestions on improving sleep habits, see R. Davidhizar and R. Shearer, "Your Best Preparation for a Good Day's Work: A Good Night's Sleep." *Health Care Manager*, December 2000, *19(2)*, 38–49.

44 Davidhizar and Shearer, "Your Best Preparation for a Good Day's Work." This article also provides very useful suggestions for improving sleep habits.

45 J. Sandberg, "As Bosses Power Nap, Cubicle Dwellers Doze Under Clever Disguise," *Wall Street Journal*, July 23, 2003, p. B1; and T. F. Shea, "The 'Power Nap' as Workplace Training Aid," *HRMagazine*, September 2002, p. 27.

46 See, for instance, C. Chatterjee, "Life Support," *Psychology Today*, May/June 1999, p. 24; D. R. Deeter-Schmelz and R. P. Ramsey, "Considering Sources and Types of Social Support: A Psychometric Evaluation of the House and Wells (1978) Instrument," *Journal of Personal Selling and Sales Management*, Winter 1997, pp. 49–61; and J. Schaubroeck and L. S. Fink, "Facilitating and Inhibiting Effects of Job Control and Social Support on Stress Outcomes and Role Behavior: A Contingency Model," *Journal of Organizational Behavior*, March 1998, pp. 167–195.

47 T. Miyazaki, T. Ishikawa, H. Iimori, A. Miki, M. Wenner, I. Fukunashi, and N. Kawamura, "Relationship Between Perceived Social Support and Immune Function," *Stress and Health*, 2003, *19(1)*, pp. 3–7.

48 B. Herbert and M. F. Klipper, *The Relaxation Response* (New York: Avon, 1995).

49 See J. Schmidt-Wilk, "TQM and the Transcendental Meditation Program in a Swedish Top Management Team," *TQM Magazine*, 2003, *15(4)*, p. 219.

50 M. Oz, "Say 'Om' Before Surgery," *Time*, January 20, 2003, p. 71.

51 M. Der Hovanesian, "Zen and the Art of Corporate Productivity," *Business Week*, July 28, 2003, p. 56.

52 For further discussion of the steps of progressive muscle relaxation, visit http://caregiver-information.com/Relaxation/muscle_relaxation.htm.

53 See, for instance, T. M. Begley, "Coping Strategies as Predictors of Employee Distress and Turnover After an Organizational Consolidation: A Longitudinal Analysis," *Journal of Occupational and Organizational Psychology*, December 1998, pp. 305–329.

54 For a discussion of how Wall Street traders are making use of counseling, see D. Lugo, "Analyze This! Traders Turn to Shrink to Do Better During Tough Times," *Investment Dealers' Digest: IDD*, March 17, 2003, p. 1.

55 G. Hinderyckx, "Creative Process Often Starts with a Good Massage," *Marketing News*, April 15, 1991, pp. 8–9.

56 For more on employee health costs, see M. Prince, "Employers Focus on Cost Control for Health Savings," *Business Insurance*, July 7, 2003, p. 20; and B. Cryer, R. McCraty, and D. Childre, "Pull the Plug on Stress," *Harvard Business Review*, July 2003, 81(7), pp. 102–107.

57 D. R. Powell, "Characteristics of Successful Wellness Programs," *Employee Benefits Journal*, September 1999, pp. 15–21; and S. Bean, "Making Well-Being a Team Effort," *Occupational Health*, April 2003, pp. 22–24.

58 Ibid.

59 For more on the benefits of company programs to address employee health care costs, see E. Vernarec, "Making the Case to Top Manage-ment," *Business and Health*, July 1999, pp. 20–25; and W. Atkinson, "Healthy Choice," *Incentive*, June 2003, p. 48+.

60 Vernarec, "Making the Case to Top Management."

61 Except where otherwise specified, the following material is drawn from D. R. Powell, "Characteristics of Successful Wellness Programs," *Employee Benefits Journal*, September 1999, pp. 15–21.

62 Ibid.

63 J. Burns, "Health Promotion Programs Produce Measurable Results," *Managed Healthcare*, May 1999, p. 42.

64 Atkinson, "Healthy Choice."

65 K. Hein, "The Boiling Point," *Incentive*, September 1998, pp. 26–32.

66 A. G. Lipold, "Home Depot Opens the Door to New Healthy Lifestyles," *Business and Health*, December 2001, p. 20.

67 "EAPs Adopt Broad Brush Approach to Helping Employees," *Employee Benefit Plan Review*, October 1999, p. 44.

68 P. R. Johnson and J. Indvik, "The Organizational Benefits of Assisting Domestically Abused Employees," *Public Personnel Management*, Fall 1999, pp. 365–374.

69 M. B. Scott, "Deloitte and Touche Programs Work to Retain Employees in a Competitive Industry," *Employee Benefits Review*, September 1998, 53(3), pp. 32–33.

CHAPTER 6. FOSTERING ETHICAL BEHAVIOR

1 R. Lacayo and A. Ripley, "Persons of the Year," *Time*, January 6, 2002, 160(27), p. 32. See also C. C. Verschoor, "Are 'Whistle-Blowers' Heroes or Just Doing Their Jobs?" *Strategic Finance*, March 2003, pp. 18–19.

2 For discussions of these companies, see, for instance, K. Eichenwald, "Former Enron Executive Pleads Guilty," *New York Times*, October 31, 2003, p. C1; R. Randall, "The Fall of Arthur Andersen," *Strategic Finance*, 2003, 85(1), p. 21; J. S. Lublin and M. Maremont, "Boss Talk: Taking Tyco by the Tail," *Wall Street Journal*, August 6, 2003, p. B1; R. F. Worth, "Ex-Official of WorldCom Pleads Guilty to Fraud," *New York Times*, October 8, 2002, p. C9. For discussions of the erosion of employee and public trust, see S. Shellenbarger, "Rash of Corporate Scandals Is Eroding Worker Confidence," *Wall Street Journal*, July 25, 2002, p. 1; and D. Schorr, "Is There Anybody Else We Can Trust?" *The Record*, June 15, 2003, p. O.05.

3 See, for instance, C. L. Hays, "Prosecutors Ask Judge to Keep Stewart Charges Intact," *New York Times*, November 7, 2003, p. C9; and J. Steinberg, "*Time*'s 2 Top Editors Resign After Furor on Writer's Fraud," *New York Times*, June 6, 2003, p. A1.

4 For a related discussion see R. Zemke, "A Matter of Trust," *Training*, 2002, 39(12), p. 12.

5 M. Peyser, "Dysfunction Junction," *Newsweek*, November 3, 2003, p. 74.

6 On the shaming of white-collar criminals, see D. M. Kahan and E. A. Posner, "Shaming White-Collar Criminals: A Proposal for Reform of the Federal Sentencing Guidelines," *Journal of Law and Economics*, 1999, 42(1), pp. 365–391; and K. I. Schacter and D. K. Stern, "Bringing Out the Rough Stuff," *National Law Journal*, August 11, 2003, p. 15.

7 For a discussion of the constructs of ethics and business ethics, see G. Svensson and G. Wood, "The Dynamics of Business Ethics: A Function of Time and Culture—Cases and Models," *Management Decision*, 2003, 41(4), pp. 350–361.

8 J. P. Keenan and C. A. Krueger, "Whistleblowing and the Professional," *Management Accounting*, August 1992, pp. 21–24.

9 "American Workers Do the Right Thing," *HR Focus*, March 1999, p. 4.

10 For discussions of employee theft, see M. Malone, "Hands in the Till," *Restaurant Business*, April 15, 2003, pp. 20–23; and "Ethics Programs Help Curb Employee Theft," *USA Today Magazine*, December 2002, p. 10.

11 J. R. Morse, "The Economic Costs of Sin," *The American Enterprise*, 2003, 14(7), p. 14.

12 D. Berta, "Employee Behavior Study Alarms Operators," *Nation's Restaurant News*, August 4, 2003, p. 1.

13 See M. J. Weinstein and A. C. George, "New OECD Treaty Fights Corruption," *National Law Journal*, 1999, 21(27), pp. B5–B8; E. Mekay, "Development: Ethical Guidelines Proposed for Multinationals," *Global Information Network*, December 13, 2002, p. 1; and P. Reina, "Some Countries Are Bad to the Bone on Bribery But New Initiatives and Laws May Be Leading to a Global Cleanup," *ENR*, 2003, 25(41), pp. 41–43.

14 "A War on Global Corruption," *New York Times*, May 11, 1993, p. D2.

15 See, for instance, "The Destructive Costs of Greasing Palms," *Business Week*, December 6, 1993, pp. 133, 136, and 138.

16 See, for instance, S. Chester and D. Selley, "Giving Kickbacks the Boot," *CA Magazine*, August 1999, pp. 20–24; "Kicking the Kick-backs," *The Economist*, May 31, 1997, pp. 61–62; and D. Paletta, "ZNet Latest to Settle Kickback Charges," *American Banker*, September 30, 2003, p. 4.

17 "The Americas: IBM's Last Tangle in Argentina," *The Economist*, August 1, 1998, p. 31. For another example of kickbacks, see C. Becker, "Partners in Crime?" *Modern Healthcare*, June 9, 2003, p. 8.

18 B. Barnhart, "What's Down on Farm Should Be What's Up in Seattle," *Chicago Tribune*, November 26, 1999, p. 1.

19 B. Pearson, "WTO: Enemy Number One," *Australian Financial Review*, November 25, 1999, p. 13.

20 M. Hood, "Hundreds Protest Ahead of WTO Meeting," *Agence France-Presse*, November 29, 1999; and L. McShane, "Nike Suit," *Associated Press Newswires*, November 20, 1999.

21 A. W. June, "In Its First Major Report, Anti-Sweatshop Group Cites Violations," *Chronicle of Higher Education*, July 4, 2003, p. A23.

22 "Nike Agrees to Pay $1.5 Million to Anti-Sweatshop Group," *Chronicle of Higher Education*, September 26, 2003, p. A44.

23 C. C. Verschoor, "A Study of the Link Between a Corporation's Financial Performance and Its Commitment to Ethics," *Journal of Business Ethics*, October 1998, pp. 1509–1516. See also L. Wah, "Ethics Linked to Financial Performance," *Management Review*, July/August 1999, p. 7.

24 T. Mason, "The Importance of Being Ethical," *Marketing*, October 26, 2000, p. 27.

25 R. van der Merwe, L. Pitt, and P. Berthon, "Are Excellent Companies Ethical? Evidence from an Industrial Setting," *Corporate Reputation Review*, 2003, 5(4), pp. 343–356.

26 R. J. Costa-Clarke, "The Costly Implications of Terminating Whistle-blowers," *Employment Relations Today*, 1994–1995, pp. 447–454; and S. Seidenberg, "States Passing Whistleblower Statutes," *National Law Journal*, 2003, 25(21), pp. A24+.

27 W. Zellner, "Was Sherron Watkins Really So Selfless?" *Business Week*, December 16, 2002, p. 110.

28 P. Jackson, "Whistles and Safety Valves," *CA Magazine*, April 1999, pp. 43–44.

29 C. Daniels, "'It's a Living Hell,'" *Fortune*, April 15, 2002, pp. 367–368.

30 Ibid.

31 L. A. Skillen, "A New Breed of Whistleblower," *Pharmaceutical Executive*, August 2003, p. 114.

32 For recent discussions of Hammurabi and ethics, see J. W. Butler, "Hammurabi, Hippocrates & Business Ethics," *Executive Speeches*; August/September 1994, pp. 67–68; G. Zajac, "Beyond Hammurabi: A Public Service Definition of Ethics Failure," *Journal of Public Administration Research and Theory*, 1996, 6, pp. 145–190; and F. E. Greenman and J. F. Sherman, "Business School Ethics—An Overlooked Topic," *Business and Society Review*, Summer 1999, pp. 171–177.

33 To read the full Code of Hammurabi, go to: http://elsinore.cis.yale.edu/lawweb/avalon/hamframe.htm.

34 Quoted in P. A. French, *Collective and Corporate Responsibility* (New

York: Columbia University Press, 1984), p. 187. See also G. Moore, "Corporate Moral Agency: Review and Implications," *Journal of Business Ethics*, October 1999, pp. 329–343.

35 For a discussion of corporate liability for criminal acts, see T. Brief and T. McSweeny, "Corporate Criminal Liability," *American Criminal Law Review*, 2003, *40(2)*, pp. 337–365.

36 W. M. Rexroad, T. J. F. Bishop, J. A. Ostrosky, and L. M. Leinicke, "The Federal Sentencing Guidelines for Organizations," *CPA Journal*, February 1999, pp. 26–31.

37 D. R. Dalton, M. B. Metzger, and J. W. Hill, "The 'New' U.S. Sentencing Commission Guidelines: A Wake-Up Call for Corporate America," *Academy of Management Executive*, February 1994, pp. 7–13. See also T. Hatcher, "New World Ethics," *T + D*, August 2003, p. 42+; and J. E. Scuro, Jr., "Trends in Federal Sentencing Guidelines," *Law & Order*, 2003, *51(2)*, pp. 8–9.

38 L. M. Franze, "The Whistleblower Provisions of the Sarbanes-Oxley Act of 2002," *Insights; the Corporate & Securities Law Advisor*, 2002, *16(12)*, pp. 12–21. See also "Analysis: Sarbanes-Oxley Act Impact on Corporate America," *All Things Considered*, July 30, 2003, p. 1.

39 For this review of four decades of findings on trust in leadership, see K. T. Dirks and D. L. Ferrin, "Trust in Leadership: Meta-Analytic Findings and Implications for Research and Practice," *Journal of Applied Psychology*, 2002, *87(4)*, pp. 611–628.

40 J. M. Kouzes and B. Z. Posner, *The Leadership Challenge* (San Francisco: Jossey-Bass, 1995), pp. 20–24.

41 "How to Help Reinvigorate Your Organization's Ethics Program," *HR Focus*, 2003, *80(6)*, p. 7. See also E. Neuborne, "Incentive Ethics Under Fire," *Potentials*, 2003, *36(3)*, p. 5.

42 For a thorough discussion of the evolution and development of codes of ethics and surrounding controversies, see B. J. Farrell, D. M. Cobbin, and H. M. Farrell, "Codes of Ethics: Their Evolution, Development and Other Controversies," *Journal of Management Development*, 2002, *21(2)*, pp. 152–163.

43 C. H. Deutsch, "Proper Conduct in the Workplace," *New York Times*, July 29, 1990, p. F25.

44 M. M. Clark, "Corporate Ethics Programs Make a Difference, But Not the Only Difference," *HRMagazine*, 2003, *48(7)*, p. 36.

45 G. R. Weaver, L. K. Treviño, and P. L. Cochran, "Corporate Ethics Programs in the Mid-1990's: An Empirical Study of the *Fortune* 1000," February 1999, pp. 283–294. For more evidence of the importance of communications and reward systems to guide ethical behavior, see L. K. Treviño, M. Brown, and L. P. Hartman, "A Qualitative Investigation of Perceived Executive Ethical Leadership: Perceptions from Inside and Outside the Executive Suite," *Human Relations*, 2003, *56(1)*, pp. 5–37.

46 M. Moran, "Coaches, NCAA Agree to Chart New Course; Group Working on Ethics Codes, Drafting Sanctions for Misconduct," *USA Today*, October 16, 2003, p. C07.

47 "How to Help Reinvigorate Your Organization's Ethics Program," *HR Focus*, 2003, *80(6)*, p. 7.

48 W. E. Shafer, "Ethical Pressure, Organizational-Professional Conflict, and Related Work Outcomes Among Management Consultants," *Journal of Business Ethics*, 2002, *38(3)*, pp. 263–275.

49 J. West, E. Berman, and S. Bonczek, "Frontiers in Ethics Training," *PM, Public Management*, June 1998, pp. 4–9.

50 V. J. Callan, "Predicting Ethical Values and Training Needs in Ethics," *Journal of Business Ethics*, 1992, *11(10)*, pp. 761–769.

51 P. J. Dean, "Making Codes of Ethics Real," *Journal of Business Ethics*, 1992, *11(4)*, pp. 285–290.

52 G. McDonald, "Business Ethics: Practical Proposals for Organizations," *Journal of Business Ethics*, April 1999, pp. 143–158.

53 A. K. Naj, "GE's Drive to Purge Fraud is Hampered by Workers' Mistrust," *Wall Street Journal*, July 22, 1993, p. A1.

54 See B. J. Farrell, D. M. Coggin, and H. M. Farrell, "Codes of Ethics: Their Evolution, Development and Other Controversies," *Journal of Management Development*, 2002, *21(2)*, pp. 152–163, for figures on the percentages of organizations using a variety of approaches to encouraging ethical behavior.

55 S. N. Mehta, "MCI: Is Being Good Good Enough?" *Fortune*, October 27, 2003, p. 117.

56 McDonald, "Business Ethics: Practical Proposals for Organizations." For a discussion of ethics hotlines in which individuals can contact experts trained in ethics, including ethics professors, see L. A. Peck, "The Search for Sound Advice," *The Quill*, September 2001, pp. 59–60.

57 For a comprehensive discussion of corporate ombudsmen, see M. P. Rowe, "The Corporate Ombudsman: An Overview and Analysis," *Negotiation Journal*, April 1987, pp. 127–140.

58 See J. Blalock, "Informal Harassment Policies Key to Prevention," *Workforce*, October 1998, pp. 9–11; and O. Isachson, "Do You Need an Ombudsman?" *HR Focus*, September 1998, p. 6.

59 C. Hirschman, "Someone to Listen," *HRMagazine*, 2003, *48(1)*, pp. 46–51.

60 Ibid.

61 G. Graham, "If You Want Honesty, Break Some Rules," *Harvard Business Review*, 2002, *80(4)*, pp. 42–46. See also "Building a Culture of Honesty," *Healthcare Executive*, 2002, *17(4)*, p. 29; and R. R. Sims and J. Brinkmann, "Enron Ethics (or Culture Matters More than Codes)," *Journal of Business Ethics*, 2003, *45(3)*, pp. 243–256.

62 http://www.levisstrauss.com/about.

63 http://www.levisstrauss.com/responsibility/conduct.

64 N. Munk, "How Levi's Trashed a Great American Brand," *Fortune*, April 12, 1999, pp. 83–90.

65 http://www.tyco.com/tyco/index.asp.

66 http://www.forbes.com/2003/09/29/cx_da_0929topnews.html.

67 M. Warner, "Exorcism at Tyco," *Fortune*, April 28, 2003, pp. 106–110.

Chapter 7. Communicating Effectively

1 T. R. Peters and R. H. Waterman, *In Search of Excellence: Lessons from America's Best-Run Companies* (New York: Harper & Row, 1982).

2 N. Thompson, "More Companies Pay Heed to Their 'Word of Mouse' Reputation," *New York Times*, June 23, 2003, p. C4.

3 H. Mintzberg, *The Nature of Managerial Work* (Englewood Cliffs, NJ: Prentice-Hall, 1973).

4 W. G. Scott and T. R. Mitchell, *Organization Theory: A Structural and Behavioral Analysis* (Homewood, IL: Irwin, 1976).

5 E-mail from Glenn F. Tilton, chairman, president, and CEO of United, to Mileage Plus members, December 9, 2002.

6 This section is based in part on J. W. Newstrom and K. Davis, *Organizational Behavior: Human Behavior at Work*, 9th ed. (New York: McGraw-Hill, 1993), pp. 93–96.

7 This listing of channel characteristics is drawn from R. B. Dunham, *Organizational Behavior: People and Processes in Management* (Homewood, IL: Irwin, 1984).

8 H. J. Leavitt, *Managerial Psychology*, rev. ed. (Chicago: University of Chicago Press, 1964), pp. 138–152.

9 R. L. Daft and R. H. Lengel, "Information Richness: A New Approach to Managerial Behavior and Organization Design," in B. Staw and L. L. Cummings (Eds.), *Research in Organizational Behavior* (Greenwich, CT: JAI Press, 1984), pp. 191–233.

10 This section is based in part on Newstrom and Davis, *Organizational Behavior*.

11 J. Steinberg, "Time's 2 Top Editors Resign After Furor on Writer's Fraud," *New York Times*, June 6, 2003, p. A1.

12 *Wall Street Journal*, November 12, 1982, p. 1.

13 M. Master, "Could you be a BDU?" *Across the Board*, May 1999, p. 71.

14 M. Rowh, "Cy*ber*speak (si ber spek) n. language or terms related to computers or digital technology," *Office Systems*, April 1999, p. 8.

15 J. D. Glater, "Holy Change Agent! Consultants Edit Out Jargon," *Wall Street Journal*, June 14, 2003, p. C1.

16 *Wall Street Journal*, September 30, 1988, p. 23.

17 *Wirtschaftswoche* (Germany), as reported in *ManpowerArgus*, July 1997, *346*, p. 11.

18 For discussions of handbooks and manuals, see G. Flynn, "Take Another Look at the Employee Handbook," *Workforce*, March 2000, pp. 132–134; G. Levine, "Q&A: The Power of Employee Handbooks," *Bobbin*, July 1998, pp. 78–82; and J. London, "Bring Your Employee Handbook into the Millennium," *HR Focus*, January 1999, p. 6.

19 See S. Solo, "Japanese Comics Are All Business," *Fortune*, October 9, 1989, pp. 143–149. For more on mangas, see C. Reid, "American Manga Breaks Out," *Publishers Weekly*, February 24, 2003, pp. 18–19.

20 Weidlich, "The Corporate Blog Is Catching On," *New York Times*, June 22, 2003, p. C12.

21 See T. Love, "Back to the Old Suggestion Box," *Nation's Business*, May 1998, p. 11; and P. Lilienthal, "If You Give Your Employees a Voice, Do You Listen?" *Journal for Quality and Participation*, Fall 2002, *25(3)*, pp. 38–40.

22. See M. I. Lurie, "The 8 Essential Steps in Grievance Processing," *Dispute Resolution Journal*, November 1999, pp. 61–65.

23. For a good discussion of organizational surveys, see R. B. Dunham and F. J. Smith, *Organizational Surveys: An Internal Assessment of Organizational Health* (Homewood, IL: Irwin, 1979). See also R. J. Sahl, "Creating a Company-Specific Attitude Survey," *The Human Resource Professional*, September/October 1999, pp. 23–27; and L. Simpson, "What's Going on in Your Company? If You Don't Ask, You'll Never Know," *Training*, June 2002, pp. 30–34.

24. This section, including the listing of guidelines for effective speaking, is based primarily on W. P. Galle, Jr., B. H. Nelson, D. W. Luse, and M. F. Villere, *Business Communication: A Technology-Based Approach* (Chicago: Irwin, 1996), pp. 447–458.

25. For discussions of listening, see S. Caudron, "Listen Up!" *Workforce*, August 1999, pp. 25–27; R. C. Boyle, "A Manager's Guide to Effective Listening," *Manage*, July 1999, pp. 6–7; and R. A. Prince and K. M. File, "Listen Then Talk: The Difference Between Top Financial Advisors and the Rest Is That the Top Advisers Really, Really, Really Listen," *Financial Planning*, November 1, 1998, pp. 167–168.

26. See C. Crossen, "The Crucial Question For These Noisy Times May Just Be: 'Huh?'" *Wall Street Journal*, July 19, 1997, pp. A1, A6.

27. This section is based on Galle et al., *Business Communication* , pp. 444–447.

28. For instance, see P. Buhler, "Are You Really Saying What You Mean?" *Supervision*, September 1991, pp. 18–20; B. J. Sparks, "Make the Right Moves with Body Language," *Real Estate Today*, June 1994, pp. 35–38; and S. Martin, "The Role of Nonverbal Communications in Quality Improvement," *National Productivity Review*, Winter 1995–1996, pp. 27–39.

29. This section is based on Galle et al., *Business Communication*.

30. "Experts Can Read in the Eyes Whether Person Is Telling Lies," *Tulsa World*, January 26, 1987.

31. This discussion of types of nonverbal communication is based in part on G. B. Davis and M. H. Olson, *Management Information Systems: Conceptual Foundations, Structure, and Development*, 2nd ed. (New York: McGraw-Hill, 1985).

32. This discussion of paralanguage is based on Galle et al., pp. 534–535. See also J. P. T. Fatt, "It's Not What You Say, It's How You Say It," *Communication World*, June/July 1999, *16(6)*, pp. 37–40; and L. H. Chaney and C. G. Green, "Presenter Behaviors: Actions Often Speak Louder Than Words," *American Salesman*, April 2002, *47(4)*, pp. 22–27.

33. J. R. Davitz and L. Davitz, "Nonverbal Vocal Communication of Feeling," *Journal of Communication*, 1961, *11*, pp. 81–86.

34. J. Sterrett, "Body Language and Job Interviews," *Journal of Business Education*, 1977, *53*, pp. 122–123.

35. J. L. Waltman and S. P. Golen, "Detecting Deception During Interviews," *The Internal Auditor*, August 1993, pp. 61–63. See also L. Koller, "To Catch a Liar," *Internal Auditor*, October 2002, pp. 42–47.

36. R. L. Birdwhistell, "*Kinesics in Context: Essays on Body Motion Communications*" (Philadelphia: University of Pennsylvania Press, 1970).

37. For discussions of the importance of eye contact, see M. Brody, "Delivering Your Speech Right Between Their Eyes," *Supervision*, June 1994, p. 18; S. A. Miller, "Controlling How Others See You Is Good Business," *CPA Journal*, October 1994, pp. 75–76; and T. Nichols, "Smart Talk," *CA Magazine*, January–February 1995, pp. 60+.

38. See, for instance, D. Booher, "Executive Presence," *Executive Excellence*, May 2003, *20(5)*, p. 19.

39. J. Hornik, "Tactile Stimulation and Consumer Response," *Journal of Consumer Research*, December 1992, pp. 449–458. See also N. Gueguen, "The Effect of the Influence of Touch on the Behaviour of Consumers: Two External Experimental Illustrations," *La Revue des Sciences de Gestion: Direction et Gestion*, July–October 2001, p. 150; and S. C. Mooy and H. S. J. Robben, "Managing Consumers' Product Evaluations Through Direct Product Experience," *Journal of Product and Demand Management*, 2002, *11(6/7)*, pp. 432–458.

40. For instance, see T. Walker, "Discrimination and the Law: What Supervisors Should Know," *Supervisory Management*, August 1992, pp. 10–11.

41. W. P. Galle et al., p. 532. See also A. Griswold, "How to Dress the Part: Work Wardrobes Convey Department and Rank," *Adweek*, May 19, 2003, *44(20)*, p. 37

42. M. Lefkowitz, R. Blake, and J. Mouton, "Status of Actors in Pedestrian Violations of Traffic Signals," *Journal of Abnormal and Social Psychology*, 1955, *51*, pp. 704–706.

43. As an interesting example, see "Britain's Judges May Flip Wigs over Makeover," *Wall Street Journal*, May 14, 2003, p. B5.C.

44. D. Keenan, "Does Your Dress Suit Your Job?" *Accountancy*, May 1995, p. 94.

45. See, for instance, B. Ziegler, "IBM Goes Casual, Drops White Shirts, and Plans a Woodsier Headquarters," *Wall Street Journal*, February 3, 1995, p. A3; G. Button, "No Bathrobes, Please," *Forbes*, November 6, 1995; and L. Himelstein and N. Walster, "Levi's vs. the Dress Code," *Business Week*, April 1, 1996, pp. 57–58.

46. See L. Lee, "Some Employees Just Aren't Suited for Dressing Down," *Wall Street Journal*, February 3, 1995, pp. A1, A6.

47. This section is based in part on A. C. Filley, *Interpersonal Conflict Resolution* (Glenview, IL: Scott, Foresman, 1975).

48. K. C. Laudon and J. P. Laudon, *Management Information Systems: Organization and Technology*, 3rd ed. (New York: Macmillan, 1994), p. 291.

49. J. C. Sipior and B. T. Ward, "The Dark Side of Employee Email," *Association for Computing Machinery: Communications of the ACM*, July 1999, pp. 88–95.

50. R. F. Rohan, "Say 'So Long' to Snail Mail," *Black Enterprise*, September 1998, pp. 37–38.

51. See E. Schwartz, "Lotus Moving on Language Conversion for Messages," *InfoWorld*, May 29, 2000, p. 8; and "Wearable PCs: Where Sci-Fi Fantasy Meets Modern Power, Practicality," *Security*, May 1999, pp. 9–10.

52. See C. Taylor, "Moving Targets," *Far Eastern Economic Review*, June 8, 2000, pp. 42–54; and J. Guyon, "The World Is Your Office," *Fortune*, June 12, 2000, pp. 227–234.

53. P. B. Carroll, "Computer Confusion," *Wall Street Journal*, June 4, 1990, pp. R28–R29. See also A. Markels, "Managers Aren't Always Able to Get the Right Message Across with E-Mail," *Wall Street Journal*, August 6, 1996, p. B1.

54. B. N. Meeks, "The Privacy Hoax," *Association for Computing Machinery, Communications of the ACM*, February 1999, pp. 17–19.

55. M. A. Nusbaum, "New Kind of Snooping Arrives at the Office," *New York Times*, July 13, 2003, p. C12.

56. Y. J. Dreazen, "The Best Way To Guard Your Privacy," *Wall Street Journal*, November 18, 2002, p. R4.

57. For a discussion of ethical issues relating to e-mail privacy, see P. S. L. Flanagan, "Cyberspace: The Final Frontier?" *Journal of Business Ethics*, March 1999, pp. 115–122.

58. See Y. J. Dreazen, "The Best Way to Guard Your Privacy," *Wall Street Journal*, November 18, 2002, p. R4.

59. G. Blake, "E-mail with Feeling," *Research Technology Management*, November/December 1999, pp. 12–13; and "Express Yourself; Emoticons Let Hackers Share Their Feelings," *Morning Star*, October 23, 2000, p. 5B.

60. G. P. Zachary, "Tech Shop: Can Autodesk's Latest CEO Survive A Cabal of Programmers Who Send 'Flame Mail'?" *Wall Street Journal*, May 28, 1992, p. A1; and K. Zhivago, "Dance of the Flamers," *MC Technology Marketing Intelligence*, April 2000, p. 108.

61. J. C. Sipior and B. T. Ward, "The Dark Side of Employee Email," *Association for Computing Machinery: Communications of the ACM*, July 1999, pp. 88–95; M. Schrage, "Flaming Ideas," *Technology Review*, March 2003, *106(2)*, p. 23; and J. Wagstaff, "Fear and Loathing on the Web," *Far Eastern Economic Review*, July 24, 2003, *166(29)*, pp. 38–39.

62. J. C. Sipior and B. T. Ward, "The Dark Side of Employee Email," *Association for Computing Machinery: Communications of the ACM*, July 1999, pp. 88–95.

63. See G. Colombo, "Polish Your E-Mail Etiquette," *Sales and Marketing Management*, June 2000, p. 34; and E. R. Blume, "The Etiquette Advantage," *Electric Perspectives*, May/June 2000, pp. 54–67.

64. L. Woellert, "Out, Out Damned Spam: Junk E-mail Accounts for Roughly Half of All Network Traffic. Here are Five Ways to Beat It Back," *Business Week*, August 11, 2003, p. 54. See also M. Mangalindan, "Didn't Get E-Mail? That Could Be Spam's Fault, Too; Vigilant Blockers Toss Out the Good with the Bad; Artist Misses Own Show," *Wall Street Journal*, August 4, 2003, p. A1.

65. T. Reiss and R. McNatt, "You've Got Mail, and Mail, and Mail . . . ," *Business Week*, July 20, 1998, p. 6.

66. D. Beckman and D. Hirsch, "Triage for E-mail Clutter," *ABA Journal*, February 2000, p. 66; and G. R. Notess, "Filtering the Email Storm," *Online*, November/December 1998, pp. 64–66. For a discussion of telephonic robots that juggle fax, e-mail, and telephone calls, see J. R. Garber, "Phobot Phone Home," *Forbes*, December 14, 1998, p. 238.

67. L. Bongiorno and R. Brandt, "Nuns on the Internet, Software in the Souk," *Business Week*, January 30, 1995, p. 39.

68. C. C. Sanford, "The Internet: An Electronic Global Village," *Decision Line*, May 1994, pp. 3–6.

69 T. A. Stewart, "Boom Time on the New Frontier," *Fortune*, Autumn 1993, pp. 153–161.

70 E. Richard, "Anatomy of the World-Wide Web," *Internet World*, April 1995, pp. 28–30.

71 P. H. Lewis, "Companies Rush to Set Up Shop in Cyberspace," *New York Times*, November 2, 1994, p. D1.

72 A. Cortese, J. Verity, R. Mitchell, and R. Brandt, "Cyberspace," *Business Week*, February 27, 1995, pp. 78–86.

73 S. Konicki, "Powerful Portals," *Informationweek*, May 1, 2000, pp. 44–66. See also T. Campbell, "A Portal to Productivity," *Sales and Marketing Management*, April 2000, p. 34.

74 For instance, M. Davids, "Smiling for the Camera," *Journal of Business Strategy*, May/June 1999, pp. 20–24; G. Baker, "Does Videoconferencing Really Increase Business Efficiency," *New Zealand Management*, August 2003, p. 52; and M. Hamblen, "Vendors Vie to Boost Videoconferencing Market," *Computerworld*, July 21, 2003, *37(29)*, p. 14.

75 See also S. Neuman, "SARS leaves a Silver Lining: Companies Save by Videoconferencing," *Wall Street Journal*, July 8, 2003, p. A14; and B. Caulfield, "Burn Your Boarding Pass," *Business 2.0*, July 2003, p. 114.

76 B. Ziegler, "Video Conference Calls Change Business," *Wall Street Journal*, October 12, 1994, p. B1; and L. Wood, "Videoconferencing Shows It's Ready for Prime Time," *Internet Week*, July 12, 1999, p. 26.

77 N. Gross and J. Carey, "In the Digital Derby, There's No Inside Lane," *Business Week*, Special Issue on 21st Century Capitalism, 1994, pp. 146–154. See also S. Fister, "Videoconferencing: Good, Fast, and Cheap," *Training*, April 2000, pp. 30–32; and R. Evans, "The Value of Voice," *Communications International*, June 2000, pp. 43–48.

78 V. Zwass, "Electronic Commerce: Structures and Issues," *International Journal of Electronic Commerce*, Fall 1996, pp. 3–23.

79 F. J. Riggins and H.-S. Rhee, "Toward a Unified View of Electronic Commerce," *Association for Computing Machinery, Communications of the ACM*, October 1998, pp. 88–95.

80 "Survey: E-Commerce: Something Old, Something New," *The Economist*, February 26, 2000, pp. 15–27.

81 S. J. Takacs and J. B. Frieden, "Changes on the Electronic Frontier: Growth and Opportunity of the World-Wide Web," *Journal of Marketing Theory and Practice*, Summer 1998, pp. 24–37.

82 "Help Wanted, Inquire Within," *Fortune*, Summer 2000, pp. 101–102.

83 M. Mendoza, "Opening Up with Extranets," *Computer-Aided Engineering*, February 2000, pp. 20–26.

84 "Heineken Redefines Collaborative Planning Through the Internet," *Beverage Industry*, September 1998, p. 47.

85 "Multinational Monitor," *Business Europe*, May 17, 2000, p. 3; "A High-Tech Surprise from Japan," *Business Week*, January 17, 2000, p. 118; I. M. Kunii and S. Baker, "Amazing DoMoCo," *Business Week*, January 17, 2000, p. 24; and A. Reinhardt, "Europe Is Going Mad for I-Mode; Telecoms Across the Continent Are Offering DoCoMo's Service," *Business Week*, July 28, 2003, p. 29.

86 See, for instance, J. D. Johnson, "Approaches to Organizational Communication Structure," *Journal of Business Research*, 1992, *25*, pp. 99–113; and J. D. Johnson, W. A. Donohue, and C. K. Atkin, "Differences Between Formal and Informal Communication Channels," *Journal of Business Communication*, 1994, *31*, pp. 111–122.

87 I. Adler, "Inside the Rumor Mill," *Business Mexico*, November 1997, pp. 14–15.

88 See L. Sierra, "Tell It to the Grapevine," *Communication World*, June/July 2002, pp. 28–29; and G. Michelson and V. S. Mouly, "'You Didn't Hear It from Us But . . .': Towards an Understanding of Rumour and Gossip in Organizations," *Australian Journal of Management*, 2002, *27*, pp. 57–65.

89 These guidelines are based in part on P. M. Buhler, "A New Role for Managers: The Move from Directing to Coaching," *Supervision*, August 1998, pp. 17–19; S. A. Mobley, "Judge Not: How Coaches Create Healthy Organizations," *Journal for Quality and Participation*, July/August 1999, pp. 57–60; W. J. Rinke, "Be a Coach, Not a Cop," *Executive Excellence*, June 1998, p. 17; B. Rosner, "How Do You Coach the Best from Your Employees?" *Workforce*, November 1998, pp. 24–25; and P. Simonsen and L. Davidson, "Do Your Managers Have the Right Stuff?" *Workforce*, August 1999, pp. 47–52.

90 L. Beamer, "Teaching English Business Writing to Chinese-Speaking Business Students," *Bulletin of the Association for Business Communication*, 1994, *57(1)*, pp. 12–18.

91 W. B. Gudykunst and Y. K. Kim, *Communicating with Strangers: An Approach to Intercultural Communication* (New York: Random House, 1984), pp. 12–13.

92 D. Clark, "Hey, #!@*% Amigo, Can You Translate The Word 'Gaffe'?" *Wall Street Journal*, July 8, 1996, p. B6.

93 "Asian Language Exams Getting Popular Among Japanese," Japan Economic Newswire via DowVision, December 29, 1994.

94 L. J. Iandoli, "Italian for Business and Communication: Research Methodology and Creation of a Syllabus," *Journal of Language for International Business*, 1993, *5(1)*, pp. 14–24.

95 See L. Beamer, "Learning Intercultural Communication Competence," *Journal of Business Communication*, 1992, *29(3)*, pp. 285–303; N. Zaidman, "Stereotypes of International Managers: Content and Impact on Business Interactions," *Group and Organization Management*, March 2000, pp. 45–66; and J. S. Osland, A. Bird, and J. Delano, "Beyond Sophisticated Stereotyping: Cultural Sensemaking in Context," *The Academy of Management Executive*, February 2000, pp. 65–79.

96 *Wall Street Journal*, December 29, 1987, p. 15.

97 These are based in part on M. W. Miller, "A Story of the Type That Turns Heads in Computer Circles," *Wall Street Journal*, September 15, 1992, pp. A1, A6.

CHAPTER 8. LEADING EFFECTIVELY

1 The discussion of Steve Jobs is based in part on P. Burrows, "Apple," *Business Week*, July 31, 2000, pp. 102–113; P. Nesbitt, "The Lazarus of the PC World," *Accountancy*, May 2000, pp. 60–61; S. Berglas, "What You Can Learn from Steve Jobs," *Inc*, October 1999, pp. 29–32; M. Krantz, "Steve's Two Jobs," *Time*, October 18, 1999, pp. 62–68; and "A Boss's Life," *Business Week*, January 11, 1999, p. 63.

2 For instance, see D. Leonard, "Songs in the Key of Steve," *Fortune*, May 12, 2003, p. 54+; P.-W. Tam, "Pixar Finds Jump of 87% in Profit, Lifted by 'Nemo,'" *Wall Street Journal*, August 8, 2003, p. B4; and S. Alsop, "I've Bitten the Apple: Steve Jobs Keeps Rocking My World," *Fortune*, June 9, 2003, p. 188.

3 W. G. Bennis and B. Nanus, *Leaders: The Strategies for Taking Charge* (New York: Harper & Row, 1985), p. 221.

4 T. A. Mahoney, T. H. Jerdee, and A. N. Nash, *The Identification of Management Potential: A Resource Approach to Management Development* (Dubuque, IA: W. C. Brown, 1961).

5 See W. O. Jenkins, "A Review of Leadership Studies with Particular Reference to Military Problems," *Psychological Bulletin*, 1947, *44*, pp. 54–79; R. M. Stogdill, "Personal Factors Associated with Leadership: A Survey of the Literature," *Journal of Psychology*, 1948, *25*, pp. 35–71; and C. A. Gibb, "Leadership," in G. Lindzey and E. Aronson (Eds.), *Handbook of Social Psychology*, vol. 4, pp. 205–282 (Reading, MA: Addison-Wesley, 1969.).

6 C. Bird, *Social Psychology* (New York: Appleton-Century, 1940).

7 L. F. Carter and M. Nixon, "An Investigation of the Relationship Between Four Criteria of Leadership Ability for Three Different Tasks," *Journal of Psychology*, 1949, *23*, pp. 245–261.

8 T. A. Judge, J. E. Bono, R. Ilies, and M. W. Gerhardt, "Personality and Leadership: A Qualitative and Quantitative Review," *Journal of Applied Psychology*, 2002, *87(4)*, pp. 765–780. See also T. A. Judge and J. E. Bono, "Five-Factor Model of Personality and Transformational Leadership," *Journal of Applied Psychology*, 2000, *85(5)*, pp. 751–765.

9 A. C. Filley, R. J. House, and S. Kerr, *Managerial Process and Organizational Behavior*, 2nd ed. (Glenview, IL: Scott, Foresman, 1976), p. 226.

10 S. Kerr, C. Schriesheim, C. J. Murphy, and R. M. Stogdill, "Toward a Contingency Theory of Leadership Based upon the Consideration and Initiating Structure Literature," *Organizational Behavior and Human Performance*, 1974, *12*, pp. 62–82.

11 R. J. House, "A Path-Goal Theory of Leader Effectiveness," *Administrative Science Quarterly*, 1971, *16*, pp. 321–338; and M. G. Evans, "The Effects of Supervisory Behavior on the Path-Goal Relationship," *Organizational Behavior and Human Performance*, 1970, *5*, pp. 277–298. See also A. W. Joshi and S. Randall, "The Indirect Effects of Organizational Controls on Salesperson Performance and Customer Orientation," *Journal of Business Research*, October 2001, *54(1)*, pp.

1+; and C. Silverthorne, "A Test of Path-Goal Theory in Taiwan," *Leadership & Organization Development Journal*, 2001, *22(4)*, pp. 151–158.

¹² For a recent analysis of substitutes for leadership, see S. D. Dionne, F. Y. Yammarito, L. E. Atwater, and L. R. James, "Neutralizing Substitutes for Leadership Theory: Leadership Effects and Common-Source Bias," *Journal of Applied Psychology*, 2002, *87(3)*, pp. 454–464.

¹³ See G. B. Graen and M. Uhl-Bien, "Relationship-Based Approach to Leadership: Development of Leader-Member Exchange (LMX) Theory of Leadership over 25 Years: Applying a Multi-Level, Multi-Domain Perspective," *Leadership Quarterly*, 1995, *6*, pp. 219–247; K. J. Dunegan, M. Uhl-Bien, and D. Duchon, "LMX and Subordinate Performance: The Moderating Effects of Task Characteristics," *Journal of Business & Psychology*, Winter 2002, *17(2)*, pp. 275–285; and K. Carson and P. P. Carson, "LMX Reflections: An Interview with George Graen," *Journal of Applied Management and Entrepreneurship*, 2002, *7(2)*, p. 91. For a discussion of the roles of coworker exchanges (CWXs) in understanding leadership processes, see K. M. Sherony and S. G. Green, "Coworker Exchange: Relationships Between Coworkers, Leader-Member Exchange, and Work Attitudes," *Journal of Applied Psychology*, 2002, *87(3)*, pp. 542–548.

¹⁴ G. B. Graen and M. Uhl-Bien, "The Transformation of Professionals into Self-Managing and Partially Self-Designing Contributions: Toward a Theory of Leader-Making," *Journal of Management Systems*, 1991, *3(3)*, pp. 33–48.

¹⁵ R. E. Byrd, "Corporate Leadership Skills: A New Synthesis," *Organizational Dynamics*, 1987, *16(1)*. pp. 34–43.

¹⁶ For example, see D. E. Elenkov, "Effects of Leadership on Organizational Performance in Russian Companies," *Journal of Business Research*, June 2002, pp. 467+; T. Dvir, D. Eden, B. J. Avolio, and B. Shamir, "Impact of Transformational Leadership on Follower Development and Performance: A Field Experiment," *Academy of Management Journal*, August 2002, *45(4)*, pp. 735+; and B. M. Bass, B. J. Avolio, D. I. Jung, and Y. Berson, "Predicting Unit Performance by Assessing Transformational and Transactional Leadership," *Journal of Applied Psychology*, 2003, *88(2)*, pp. 207–218.

¹⁷ This is based on J. A. Conger, "Inspiring Others: The Language of Leadership," *Academy of Management Executive*, February 1991, pp. 31–45.

¹⁸ R. K. Greenleaf, *The Servant as Leader* (Indianapolis : Robert K. Greenleaf Center for Servant Leadership, 1970).

¹⁹ Source: Based on a management consulting project completed by A. Klima, August 2001.

²⁰ Source: http://media.ford.com/newsroom/release_display.cfm?article_id=15865.

²¹ Source: http://www.ford.com/en/company/about/overview.htm.

²² http://www.ford.com/en/company/about/leadership/WilliamClayFord.htm.

²³ Sources: K. Kerwin, J. Muller, and D. Welch, "Bill Ford's Long Hard Road. He Was Happy as Chairman. Now, His Burden Is Huge. Is He Up to It?" *Business Week*, October 7, 2002, pp. 88–92; K. Kerwin, "Can Ford Pull Out of Its Skid?" *Business Week*, March 31, 2003, pp. 70–72; J. Muller, "Bill Ford's Next Act," *Forbes*, June 23, 2003, pp. 74–80.

²⁴ Sources: B. Morris, "Can Ford Save Ford?" *Fortune*, November 18, 2002, pp. 53–63; and K. Naughton, "Bill Ford's Rainy Days," *Newsweek*, June 16, 2003, pp. 38–40.

²⁵ These examples are drawn from B. Fryer, "Bosses from Heaven—and Hell," *ComputerWorld*, August 9, 1999, pp. 46–47; T. Carvell, "By the Way—Your Staff Hates You," *Fortune*, September 28, 1998, pp. 200–212; S. Caudron, "The Boss from Hell," *Industry Week*, September 4, 1995; and M. Greilsamer, "The Dilbert Barometer," *Across the Board*, March 1995, pp. 39–41.

CHAPTER 9. MANAGING POWER, SOCIAL INFLUENCE, AND POLITICS

¹ J. Useem, "Power," *Fortune*, August 11, 2003, pp. 56+.

² Ibid.

³ E. P. Hollander and L. R. Offermann, "Power and Leadership in Organizations," *American Psychologist*, 1990, *45*, pp. 179–189.

⁴ A. Etzioni, *Modern Organizations* (Englewood Cliffs, NJ: Prentice-Hall, 1964).

⁵ J. R. P. French and B. Raven, "The Bases of Social Power," in D. Cartwright and A. F. Zander (Eds.), *Group Dynamics*, 2nd ed. (Evanston, IL: Row Peterson, 1960), pp. 259–269.

⁶ Useem, "Power."

⁷ These power bases were proposed by G. Yukl and C. M. Falbe, "Importance of Different Power Sources in Downward and Lateral Relations," *Journal of Applied Psychology*, 1991, *76*, pp. 416–423.

⁸ For an empirical examination of relationships among power bases, see M. A. Rahim, D. Antonioni, and C. Psenicka, "A Structural Equations Model of Leader Power, Subordinates' Styles of Handling Conflict, and Job Performance," *International Journal of Conflict Management*, 2001, *12(3)*, pp. 191–211.

⁹ These guidelines are based on Gary A. Yukl, *Leadership in Organizations* (Englewood Cliffs, NJ: Prentice-Hall, 1981), pp. 44–58.

¹⁰ E. Yuchtman, and S. E. Seashore, "A System Resource Approach to Organizational Effectiveness," *American Sociological Review*, 1967, *32*, pp. 891–903; J. Pfeffer and G. Salancik, *The External Control of Organizations* (New York: Harper & Row, 1978); D. D. Phan and N. M. Stata, "E-Business Success at Intel: An Organization Ecology and Resource Dependence Perspective," *Industrial Management + Data Systems*, 2002, *102(3/4)*, pp. 211–217; and A. J. Hillman and T. Dalziel, "Boards of Directors and Firm Performance: Integrating Agency and Resource Dependence Perspectives," *Academy of Management Review*, 2003, *28(3)*, pp. 383–396.

¹¹ G. R. Salancik and J. Pfeffer, "The Bases and Uses of Power in Organizational Decision Making: The Case of a University," *Administrative Science Quarterly*, 1974, *19*, pp. 453–473.

¹² H. Aldrich and D. Herker, "Boundary Spanning Roles and Organizational Structure," *Academy of Management Review*, 1977, *2*, pp. 217–230; R. E. Spekman, "Influence and Information: An Exploratory Investigation of the Boundary Role Person's Basis of Power," *Academy of Management Journal*, 1979, *22*, pp. 104–117; and G. S. Russ, M. C. Galang, and G. R. Ferris, "Power and Influence of the Human Resources Function Through Boundary Spanning and Information Management," *Human Resource Management Review*, 1998, *8(2)*, pp. 125–148.

¹³ For applications of the strategic contingencies perspective, see M. A. Carpenter and W. M. G. Sanders, "Top Management Team Compensation: The Missing Link Between CEO Pay and Firm Performance?" *Strategic Management Journal*, 2002, *23(4)*, pp. 367–375; and D. K. Datta, N. Rajagopalan, and Y. Zhang, "New CEO Openness to Change and Strategic Persistence: The Moderating Role of Industry Characteristics," *British Journal of Management*, 2003, *14(2)*, pp. 101–114.

¹⁴ R. M. Kanter, "Power Failure in Management Circuits," *Harvard Business Review* (July–August 1979), pp. 31–54. See also D. Rynecki, T. Smith, M. Shanley, and A. Wheat, "Field Guide to Power," *Fortune*, August 11, 2003, pp. 126–127.

¹⁵ This discussion is drawn from Pfeffer, *Managing with Power*, pp. 64–66.

¹⁶ G. Yukl and C. M. Falbe, "Influence Tactics and Objectives in Upward, Downward, and Lateral Influence Attempts," *Journal of Applied Psychology*, 1990, *75*, pp. 132–140.

¹⁷ For instance, see R. E. Petty and J. T. Cacioppo, *Attitudes and Persuasion: Central and Peripheral Routes to Persuasion* (New York: Springer-Verlag, 1984); and S. Moscovici, "Social Influence and Conformity," in G. Lindzey and E. Aronson (Eds.), *Handbook of Social Psychology*, 3rd ed., Vol. 2 (New York: Random House, 1985), pp. 347–412.

¹⁸ W. J. McGuire, "Attitudes and Attitude Change," in Lindzey and Aronson, *Handbook of Social Psychology*, pp. 233–346.

¹⁹ For more on ingratiation techniques, see S. H. Appelbaum and B. Hughes, "Ingratiation as a Political Tactic: Effects Within the Organization," *Management Decision*, 1998, *36(2)*, pp. 85–95.

²⁰ These bases for liking are drawn from Pfeffer, *Managing with Power*, p. 213.

²¹ This discussion of emotional appeals is based on A. Rafaeli and R. I. Sutton, "Emotional Contrast Strategies as Means of Social Influence: Lessons from Criminal Interrogators and Bill Collectors," *Academy of Management Journal*, 1991, *34*, 749–775.

²² A. R. Hochschild, *The Managed Heart* (Berkeley: University of California Press, 1983).

²³ J. V. Van Maanen and G. Kunda, "Real Feelings: Emotional Expression

and Organizational Culture," in L. L. Cummings and B. M. Staw (Eds.), *Research in Organizational Behavior*, Vol. 11 (Greenwich, CT: JAI Press, 1989), pp. 43–104.

24 R. I. Sutton and A. Rafaeli, "Untangling the Relationship Between Displayed Emotions and Organizational Sales: The Case of Convenience Stores," *Academy of Management Journal*, 1988, *31*, pp. 461–487.

25 D. Kipnis, "The Use of Power in Organizations and in Interpersonal Settings," in S. Oskamp (Ed.), *Applied Social Psychology Annual*, Vol. 5 (Beverly Hills, CA: Sage, 1984), pp. 179–210; and D. Kipnis and S. M. Schmidt, "An Influence Perspective on Bargaining," in M. Bazerman and R. Lewicki (Eds.), *Negotiating in Organizations* (Beverly Hills, CA: Sage, 1983), pp. 303–319.

26 R. I. Sutton, "Maintaining Norms About Expressed Emotions: The Case of Bill Collectors," *Administrative Science Quarterly*, 1991, *36*, pp. 245–268.

27 For a discussion of the importance of emotional appeals in promoting organizational change, see S. Fox, Y. Amachai-Hamburger, and E. A. Evans, "The Power of Emotional Appeals in Promoting Organizational Change Programs," *Academy of Management Executive*, 2001, *15(4)*, pp. 84–95.

28 These examples are drawn from R. B. Cialdini, *Influence: Science and Practice*, 2nd ed. (Glenview, IL: Scott, Foresman, 1988), p. 112.

29 H. Rao, H. R. Greve, and G. R. Davis, "Fool's Gold: Social Proof in the Initiation and Abandonment of Coverage by Wall Street Analysts," *Administrative Science Quarterly*, 2001, *46(3)*, pp. 502–526.

30 M. A. Ansari and A. Kapoor, "Organizational Context and Upward Influence Tactics," *Organizational Behavior and Human Decision Processes*, 1987, *40*, pp. 39–49.

31 See also L. Sussman, A. J. Adams, F. E. Kuzmits, and L. E. Raho, "Organizational Politics: Tactics, Channels, and Hierarchical Roles," *Journal of Business Ethics*, 2002, *40(4)*, pp. 313–329.

32 H. C. Kelman, "Processes of Opinion Change," *Public Opinion Quarterly*, 1961, *25*, pp. 57–78.

33 S. W. Crispin, "Workers' Paradise," *Far Eastern Economic Review*, 2003, *166(15)*, pp. 40–41.

34 Ibid.

35 Ibid.

36 "TGI Fridays Champion Empowerment Through Involvement," *Measuring Business Excellence*, 2002, *6(2)*, pp. 65–67; and F. Warner, "How Google Searches Itself," *Fast Company*, July 2002, pp. 50–51.

37 C. Sandburg, *Chicago Poems* (New York: Henry Holt, 1916), p. 172.

38 M. E. P. Seligman, *Helplessness: On Depression, Development, and Death* (San Francisco: Freeman, 1975); L. Y. Abramson, M. E. Seligman, and J. D. Teasdale, "Learned Helplessness in Humans: Critique and Reformulation," *Journal of Abnormal Psychology*, 1978, *87*, 49–74. See B. E. Ashforth, "The Experience of Powerlessness in Organizations," *Organizational Behavior and Human Decision Processes*, 1989, *43*, pp. 207–242, for a model in which powerlessness leads to helplessness and work alienation. See also C. R. Campbell and M. J. Martinko, "An Integrative Attributional Perspective of Empowerment and Learned Helplessness: A Multimethod Field Study," *Journal of Management*, 1998, *24(2)*, pp. 173–200; and S. B. Schepman and L. Richmond, "Employee Expectations and Motivation: An Application of the 'Learned Helplessness' Paradigm," *Journal of the American Academy of Business, Cambridge*, September 2003, *3(2)*, pp. 405–408.

39 C. Mellow, "Gloom and Doom at the Top," *Business Month*, December 1989, p. 11.

40 J. Garber and M. E. P. Seligman (Eds.), *Human Helplessness* (New York: Academic Press, 1980).

41 Although empowerment may be a rallying cry for the new millennium, it has deep historical roots. For instance, the rise of the city-state of Athens 2,500 years ago has been attributed to the empowerment of its citizens. See B. Manville and J. Ober, "Beyond Empowerment: Building a Company of Citizens," *Harvard Business Review*, 2003, *81(1)*, pp. 48–53.

42 These are based primarily on J. A. Conger and R. N. Kanungo, "The Empowerment Process: Integrating Theory and Practice," *Academy of Management Review*, 1988, *13*, pp. 471–482; and J. A. Conger, "Leadership: The Art of Empowering Others," *Academy of Management Executive*, 1989, *3*, pp. 17–24.

43 Source: Conger and Kanungo, p. 475.

44 J. Tschohl, "Empowerment: The Key to Customer Service," *American Salesman*, November 1997, pp. 12–15.

45 A. Bandura, "Self-Efficacy Mechanism in Human Agency," *American Psychologist*, 1982, *37*, pp. 122–147.

46 A. Bandura, "Self-Efficacy: Toward a Unifying Theory of Behavioral Change," *Psychological Review*, 1977, *84*, pp. 191–215; and A. P. Brief and R. J. Aldag, "The 'Self' in Work Organizations: A Conceptual Review," *Academy of Management Review*, 1981, *6*, pp. 75–88.

47 J. Pfeffer, *Power in Organizations* (Marshfield, MA: Pitman, 1981), pp. 137–177.

48 Based in part on F. W. Smith, "Empowering Employees," *Small Business Reports,* January 1991, pp. 15–20.

49 "Empowering Employees to Delight Customers at FedEx," *Management Development Review*, 1997, *10(3)*, p. 12.

50 See J. R. Deliz, "Lessons Learned from Baldrige Winners," *Computers and Engineering*, 1997, *33 (1/2)*, pp. 171–174; and A. G. Keane, "Profits, Profits, Profits," *Traffic World*, June 30, 2003, p. 1.

51 T. C. Krell, M. E. Mendenhall, and J. Sendry, "Doing Research in the Conceptual Morass of Organizational Politics," paper presented at the Western Academy of Management Conference, Hollywood, CA, April 1987.

52 For more on the labeling of behavior as political, see "The Longest Climb," *Psychology Today*, November 1994, pp. 40–43; "What Is Terrorism?" *The Economist*, March 2, 1996, pp. 23–25; M. C. Bolino, "Citizenship and Impression Management: Good Soldiers or Good Actors?" *Academy of Management Review*, January 1999, pp. 82–98; and D. S. Scott and K. A. Jehn, "Ranking Rank Behaviors," *Business and Society*, September 1999, pp. 296–325.

53 J. Gandz and V. V. Murray, "The Experience of Workplace Politics," *Academy of Management Journal*, 1980, *23*, p. 244.

54 W. H. Hegarty and H. P. Sims, Jr., "Organizational Philosophy, Policies, and Objectives Related to Unethical Decision Behavior: A Laboratory Experiment," *Journal of Applied Psychology*, 1979, *64*, pp. 331–338.

55 J. M. Rayburn and L. G. Rayburn, "Relationship Between Machiavellianism and Type A Personality and Ethical-Orientation," *Journal of Business Ethics*, November 1996, pp. 1209–1219; and B. K. Burton and W. H. Hegarty, "Some Determinants of Student Corporate Social Responsibility Orientation," *Business and Society*, June 1999, pp. 188–205.

56 A. Singhapakdi, "Ethical Perceptions of Marketers: The Interaction Effects of Machiavellianism and Organizational Ethical Culture," *Journal of Business Ethics*, May 1993, pp. 407–418. See also R. C. Erffmeyer, B. D. Keillor, and D. T. LeClair, "An Empirical Investigation of Japanese Consumer Ethics," *Journal of Business Ethics*, January 1999, pp. 35–50; and K. Bass, T. Barnett, and G. Brown, "Individual Difference Variables, Ethical Judgments, and Ethical Behavioral Intentions," *Business Ethics Quarterly*, April 1999, pp. 183–205.

57 P. M. Fandt and G. M. Ferris, "The Management of Information and Impressions: When Employees Behave Opportunistically," *Organizational Behavior and Human Decision Processes*, 1990, *67*, pp. 140–158.

58 D. C. McClelland, W. N. Davis, R. Kalin, and E. Wanner, *The Drinking Man: Alcohol and Human Motivation* (New York: Free Press, 1972). See also D. Buchanan and R. Badham, "Politics and Organizational Change: The Lived Experience," *Human Relations*, May 1999, pp. 609–629.

59 Hegarty and Sims, "Organizational Philosophy."

60 For further discussion on situational antecedents of politics, see J. M. L. Poon, "Situational Antecedents and Outcomes of Organizational Politics Perceptions," *Journal of Managerial Psychology*, 2003, *18(1/2)*, pp. 138–155.

61 D. M. Wolfe, "Is There Integrity in the Bottom Line: Managing Obstacles to Executive Integrity," in S. Srinivastava (Ed.), *Executive Integrity: The Search for High Human Values in Organizational Life* (San Francisco: Jossey-Bass, 1988), pp. 140–171.

62 R. Miles, *Micro Organizational Behavior* (Glenview, IL: Scott, Foresman, 1980); C. Leana, "Power Relinquishment Versus Power Sharing: Theoretical Clarification and Empirical Comparison of Delegation and Participation," *Journal of Applied Psychology*, 1987, *72*, pp. 228–233.

63 E. Jansen and M. A. Von Glinow, "Ethical Ambivalence and Organizational Reward Systems," *Academy of Management Review*, 1985, *10*, pp. 814–822.

64 This figure is adapted from Jansen and Von Glinow, "Ethical Ambivalence," p. 817.

65 J. Gandz and V. V. Murray, "The Experience of Workplace Politics," *Academy of Management Journal*, 1980, *23*, pp. 237–251.

66 D. Butcher and M. Clarke, "Redefining Managerial Work: Smart Politics," *Management Decision*, 2003, *41(5)*, pp. 477–487.

67 Pfeffer, *Power in Organizations*, pp. 137–177.

68 R. Grover, M. Landler, and M. Oneal, "Ovitz: How Many Fields Can the King of Hollywood Conquer?" *Business Week*, August 9, 1993, p. 50;

C. Booth, "Chalk One Up for Ovitz," *Time*, November 1, 1999, p. 34; and P. Plagens and C. Brown, "Hollywood's Big Art Deal," *Newsweek*, December 6, 1999, pp. 78–80.

[69] This section is primarily based on B. E. Ashforth and R. T. Lee, "Defensive Behavior in Organizations: A Preliminary Model," *Human Relations*, July 1990, pp. 621–648. For more on defensive behaviors, see A. D. Brown, "Narcissism, Identity, and Legitimacy," *Academy of Management Review*, July 1997, pp. 643–686; and E. Peirce, C. A. Smolinski, and B. Rosen, "Why Sexual Harassment Complaints Fall on Deaf Ears," *Academy of Management Executive*, August 1998, pp. 41–54.

[70] This figure is adapted from B. E. Ashforth and R. T. Lee, "Defensive Behavior in Organizations: A Preliminary Model," *Human Relations*, 1990, *43*, pp. 621–648. See also V. S. Folkes and Y. O. Whang, "Account-Giving for a Corporate Transgression Influences Moral Judgment When Those Who 'Spin' Condone Harm-Doing," *Journal of Applied Psychology*, 2003, *88(1)*, pp. 79–86; and J. C. Shaw, E. Wild, and J. A. Colquitt, "To Justify or Excuse? A Meta-Analytic Review of the Effects of Justifications," *Journal of Applied Psychology*, 2003, *88(3)*, pp. 444–458.

[71] D. J. Schneider, "Tactical Self-Presentations: Toward a Broader Conception," in J. T. Tedeschi (Ed.), *Impression Management Theory and Social Psychological Research* (New York: Academic Press, 1981), pp. 23–40; and S. Caudron, "The Fine Art of Ingratiation," *Industry Week*, February 17, 1997, pp. 41–48.

[72] This section is primarily based on W. L. Gardner and M. J. Martinko, "Impression Management in Organizations," *Journal of Management*, 1988, *14*, pp. 321–338. See also L. Chaney and J. Lyden, "Impression Management: The Office Environment," *Supervision*, April 1996, pp. 3–5; M. C. Bolino, "Citizenship and Impression Management: Good Soldiers or Good Actors?" *Academy of Management Review*, January 1999, pp. 82–98; and A. P. J. Ellis, B. J. West, A. M. Ryan, and R. P. DeShon, "The Use of Impression Management Tactics in Structured Interviews: A Function of Question Type?" *Journal of Applied Psychology*, 2002, *87(6)*, pp. 1200–1208.

[73] B. R. Schlenker, *Impression Management: The Self-Concept, Social Identity, and Interpersonal Relations* (Monterey, CA: Brooks/Cole, 1980).

[74] C. Molstad, "Control Strategies Used by Brewery Workers: Work Avoidance, Impression Management and Solidarity," *Human Organization*, 1988, *4*, p. 357.

[75] S. J. Wayne and K. M. Kacmar, "The Effects of Impression Management on the Performance Appraisal Process," *Organizational Behavior and Human Decision Processes*, 1991, *48*, pp. 70–88.

[76] S. J. Wayne and G. R. Ferris, "Influence Tactics, Affect, and Exchange Quality in Supervisor-Subordinate Interactions: A Laboratory Experiment and Field Study," *Journal of Applied Psychology*, 1990, *75*, pp. 487–499.

[77] H. Mintzberg, *Power In and Around Organizations* (Englewood Cliffs, NJ: Prentice-Hall, 1983), p. 187.

[78] Mintzberg, *Power In and Around Organizations;* and H. Mintzberg, *Mintzberg on Management* (New York: Free Press, 1989).

[79] M. Velasquez, D. J. Moberg, and G. F. Cavanagh, "Organizational Statesmanship and Dirty Politics: Ethical Guidelines for the Organizational Politician," *Organizational Dynamics*, August 1983, pp. 65–80.

[80] Velasquez, Moberg, and Cavanagh suggest there may be "overwhelming factors" that justify setting aside one or all of the criteria. These might include conflicts between criteria, conflicts within criteria, or lack of capacity to employ the criteria.

[81] Mintzberg, *Mintzberg on Management*, pp. 248–249.

[82] P. Kumar and R. Ghadially, "Organizational Politics and Its Effects on Members of Organizations," *Human Relations*, 1989, *42*, pp. 305–314.

[83] G. R. Ferris and K. M. Kacmar, "Perceptions of Organizational Politics," *Journal of Management*, 1992, *18*, pp. 93–116; R. Cropanzano, J. C. Howe, A. A. Grandey, and P. Toth, "The Relationship of Organizational Politics and Support to Work Behaviors, Attitudes, and Stress," *Journal of Organizational Behavior*, March 1997, pp. 159–180; K. M. Kacmar, D. P. Bozeman, D. S. Carlson, and W. P. Anthony, "An Examination of the Perceptions of Organizational Politics Model: Replication and Extension," *Human Relations*, March 1999, pp. 383–416; E. Vigoda, "Stress-Related Aftermaths to Workplace Politics: The Relationships Among Politics, Job Distress, and Aggressive Behavior in Organizations," *Journal of Organizational Behavior*, 2002, *23(5)*, pp. 571–592; and J. M. L. Poon, "Situational Antecedents and Outcomes of Organizational Politics Perceptions," *Journal of Managerial Psychology*, 2003, *18(1/2)*, pp. 138–155.

[84] E. Vigoda, "Reactions to Organizational Politics: A Cross-Cultural Examination in Israel and Britain," *Human Relations*, 2001, *54(11)*, pp. 1483–1518.

[85] These are drawn from Mintzberg, *Mintzberg on Management*, pp. 249–250. For a discussion of a political perspective on leadership, in which politics is defined as the constructive management of shared meaning, see A. P. Ammeter, C. Douglas, W. L. Gartner, W. A. Hochwarter, and G. R. Ferris, *Leadership Quarterly*, 2002, *13(6)*, pp. 751–796.

[86] See, for instance, "Avoid Politics by Establishing Objective Criteria for Capital Budget Decision Making," *Health Care Strategic Management*, December 1999, pp. 18–19.

[87] http://www.tgifridays.com/News/fri_bg.htm.

[88] http://www.tgifridays.com/News/carlsoncredo.htm.

[89] "TGI Fridays: Champion Empowerment Through Involvement," *Measuring Business Excellence*, 2002, *6(2)*, p. 65.

[90] http://www.microsoft.com/mscorp/mission.

[91] R. A. Guth and K. L. Tran, "Microsoft Must Woo Game Makers from Japan if Its Xbox is to Thrive." *Wall Street Journal*, March 26, 2002, p. A1.

CHAPTER 10. MANAGING CONFLICT

[1] A. Campo-Flores, K. Peraino, and J. Raymond, "A Nightmare on the Job," *Newsweek*, July 21, 2003, p. 42.

[2] S. V. Magyar, Jr., "Preventing Workplace Violence," *Occupational Health & Safety*, June 2003, *72(6)*, pp. 64, 66–68.

[3] B. Campbell, "Has Your Workplace Become a Battlefield?" *Black Enterprise*, November 2002, *33(4)*, p. 67.

[4] See, for instance, K. M. Eisenhardt, J. L. Kahwajy, and L. J. Bourgeois, III, "How Management Teams Can Have a Good Fight," *Harvard Business Review*, July/August 1997, pp. 77–85; and T. K. Capozzoli, "Conflict Resolution— A Key Ingredient in Successful Teams," *Supervision*, November 1999, pp. 14–16.

[5] V. L. Huber, M. A. Neale, and G. Northcraft, "Decision Bias and Personnel Selection Strategies," *Organizational Behavior and Human Decision Processes*, 1987, *40*, pp. 136–147; R. Pinkley, "Dimensions of Conflict Frame: Disputant Interpretations of Conflict," *Journal of Applied Psychology*, 1990, *75*, pp. 117–126; and R. L. Pinckley and G. B. Northcraft, "Conflict Frames of Reference: Implications for Dispute Processes," *Academy of Management Journal*, February 1994, pp. 193–205.

[6] For more on the nature and consequences of conflict frames, see M. E. Schweitzer and L. A. DeChurch, "Linking Frames in Negotiations: Gains, Losses and Conflict Frame Adoption," *International Journal of Conflict Management*, 2001, *12(2)*, pp. 100–113; and J. M. Livingood, "Reframing and Its Uses," *Dispute Resolution Journal*, November 2002–January 2003, *57(4)*, pp. 42–50.

[7] For a discussion of antecedents of managerial trustworthy behavior and the challenge of initiating trust, see E. M. Whitener, S. E. Brodt, M. A. Korsgaard, and J. M. Werner, "Managers as Initiators of Trust: An Exchange Relationship Framework for Understanding Managerial Trustworthy Behavior," *Academy of Management Review*, July 1998, pp. 513–530.

[8] S. Lorge, "Political Animals," *Sales and Marketing Management*, February 1999, pp. 50–55.

[9] For one discussion of this model, see G. H. Johnson, T. Means, and J. Pullis, "Managing Conflict," *The Internal Auditor*, December 1998, pp. 54–59.

[10] Various names have been used to describe these styles. As one example, one classification of styles is turtle (avoiding), shark (forcing), teddy bear (accommodating), fox (compromising), and owl (collaborating). See "Are You an Animal?" *Incentive*, September 1996, pp. 56–57.

[11] Use of these styles also appears to be related to personality, with preferred style varying depending on the degree to which the manager exhibits various combinations of the "Big Five" personality dimensions. See P. J. Moberg, "Linking Conflict Strategy to the Five-Factor Model: Theoretical and Empirical Foundations," *International Journal of Conflict Management*, 2001, *12(1)*, pp. 47–68.

[12] For research linking collaborative style to job performance, see, for instance, M. A. Rahim, D. Antonioni, and C. Psenicka, "A Structural Equations Model of Leader Power, Subordinates' Styles of Handling

Conflict, and Job Performance," *International Journal of Conflict Management,* 2001, *12(3),* pp. 191–211.

[13] R. A. Friedman, S. T. Tidd, S. C. Currall, and J. C. Tsai, "What Goes Around Comes Around: The Impact of Personal Conflict Style on Work Conflict and Stress," *International Journal of Conflict Management,* 2000, *11(1),* pp. 32–55.

[14] M. A. Gross and L. K. Guerrero, "Managing Conflict Appropriately and Effectively: An Application of the Competence Model to Rahim's Organizational Conflict Styles," *International Journal of Conflict Management,* 2000, *11(3),* pp. 200–226.

[15] The styles may also be used in combination. See E. van de Vliert, S. E. Huismans, and M. C. Euwema, "Managing Conflict with a Subordinate or a Supervisor: Effectiveness of Conglomerated Behavior," *Journal of Applied Psychology,* 1995, *80(2),* pp. 271–281.

[16] See also M. P. Angelica, "Eight Steps to Managing Conflict," *Nonprofit World,* July/August 2002, *20(4),* pp. 29–32.

[17] These guidelines are drawn from R. J. Aldag and B. Joseph, *Leadership & Vision: 25 Keys to Motivation* (New York: Lebhar-Friedman Books, 2000), p. 86.

[18] For discussions of negotiating skills and conflict, see P. Jacobs, "Negotiating for Success," *InfoWorld,* December 7, 1998; pp. 131–132; and D. Strutton and L. E. Pelton, "Negotiation: Bringing More to the Table Than Demands," *Marketing Health Services;* Spring 1997, pp. 52–58.

[19] See also K. Kiser, "The New Deal," *Training,* October 1999, pp. 116–126.

[20] Drawn from P. S. Nugent, "Managing Conflict: Third-Party Interventions for Managers," *Academy of Management Executive,* 2002, *16(1),* p. 147.

[21] P. L. Stepanowsky, "Some Swimming Lessons Could Be Best Way to Prepare for This Cruise," *Wall Street Journal,* October 17, 1990, p. B1.

[22] This example is based on N.-H. Kim, D. W. Sohn, and J. A. Wall, Jr., "Korean Leaders' (and Subordinates') Conflict Management," *International Journal of Conflict Management,* April 1999, pp. 130–152. For more on cross-cultural comparison of conflict resolution tactics, see R. Cropanzano, H. Aguinas, M. Schminke, and D. L. Denham, "Disputant Reactions to Managerial Conflict Resolution Tactics: A Comparison Among Argentina, the Dominican Republic, Mexico, and the United States," *Group and Organization Management,* June 1999, pp. 124–154; and L.-C. Chang, "Cross-Cultural Differences in Styles of

[23] Negotiation Between North Americans (U.S.) and Chinese," *Journal of American Academy of Business,* March 2002, 1(2), pp. 179–187.

For additional discussions of cross-cultural differences in conflict styles and attitudes, see C. Tinsley, "Models of Conflict Resolution in Japanese, German, and American Cultures," *Journal of Applied Psychology,* 1998, *83(2),* pp. 316–323; M. J. Gelfand, L. H. Nishii, K.-I. Ohbuchi, and F. Fukuno, "Cultural Influences on Cognitive Representations of Conflict: Interpretations of Conflict Episodes in the United States and Japan," *Journal of Applied Psychology,* 2001, *86(6),* pp. 1059–1074; and D. Tjosvold, C. Hui, D. Z. Ding, and J. Hu, "Conflict Values and Team Relationships: Conflict's Contribution to Team Effectiveness and Citizenship in China," *Journal of Organizational Behavior,* 2003, *24(1),* pp. 69–88.

[24] Based on D. Tjosvold, "Putting Conflict to Work," *T + D,* 1988, *42(12),* pp. 61–64.

[25] http://www.hp.com.

[26] http://www.computerworld.com/hardwaretopics/story/ 0,10801,63509,00.html.

[27] C. Edwards and A. Park, "HP and Compaq: It's Showtime: The Cost-Cutting Looks Doable, But Other Synergies May Be More Elusive Than Expected," *Business Week,* June 17, 2002, p. 76.

[28] "Business: Carly v Walter: Hewlett-Packard and Compaq," *The Economist,* January 26, 2002, p. 74.

[29] P. Burrows, "What's the Truth About Walter Hewlett?" *Business Week,* February 11, 2002, -. 74.

[30] http://www.massgeneral.org/news/for_reporters/overview.htm.

[31] B. S. Michelman, N. P. Robb, and L .M. Coviello, "A Comprehensive Approach to Workplace Violence," *Security Management,* 1998, *42(7),* pp. 28–35.

[32] http://www.massgeneral.org/depts./pubaffairs/issues/08170violence.htm.

[33] L. Farrell, "You've Got to be Kidding: Humor as a Fundamental Management Tool," *Information Management Journal,* July 1998, pp. 3–8+. See also J. W. Newstrom, "Making Work Fun: An Important Role for Managers," *S.A.M. Advanced Management Journal,* Winter 2002, *67(1),* pp. 4–9; and F. Sala, "Laughing All the Way to the Bank," *Harvard Business Review,* September 2003, *81(9),* pp. 16–17.

CHAPTER 11. MANAGING TEAMS

[1] See J. Leicester, "Teamwork in Trial Puts Armstrong in Second," *Augusta Chronicle,* July 10, 2003, p. C1; and F. Thomazeau, "Famous Five But Armstrong Turns Attention to Joy of Six; American Says Strength of Ullrich and Beloki Will Drive Him On," *The Herald* [Glasgow, UK], July 28, 2003, p. 3.

[2] For more on teams at Harley-Davidson, see Tim Minahan, "Harley-Davidson Revs Up Development Process," *Purchasing,* May 7, 1998, pp. 44S18, 44S20, 44S22–23; and Clyde Fessler, "Rotating Leadership at Harley-Davidson: From Hierarchy to Interdependence," *Strategy & Leadership,* July/August 1997, pp. 42–43. See also R. Teerlink and L. Ozley, *More Than a Motorcycle: The Leadership Journey at Harley-Davidson* (Boston: Harvard Business School Press, 2000); and P. Chansler, P. M. Swamidass, and C. Cammann, "Self-Managing Work Teams: An Empirical Study of Group Cohesiveness in 'Natural Work Groups' at a Harley-Davidson Motor Company Plant," *Small Group Research,* 2003, *34(1),* pp. 101–120.

[3] C. Joinson, "Teams at Work," *HRMagazine,* 44(5), pp. 30–36.

[4] For discussions of cross-functional teams, see M. A. Brunelli, "How Harley-Davidson Uses Cross-Functional Teams," *Purchasing,* 1999, *127(7),* p. 148; A. R. Jassawalla and H. C. Sashittal, "Building Collaborative Cross-Functional New Product Teams," *Academy of Management Executive,* 1999, *13(3),* pp. 50–63; and M. A. Clark, S. D. Amundson, and R. L. Cardy, "Cross-Functional Team Decision-Making and Learning Outcomes: A Qualitative Illustration," *Journal of Business and Management,* Summer 2002, *8(3),* pp. 217–236.

[5] For an interesting discussion of the self-managing team approach taken by Team New Zealand for the 2003 America's Cup, see V. Jayne, "Managing the America's Cup: Using a Characteristic Kiwi Approach: Small, Non-Hierarchical, and Non-Specialized," *New Zealand Management,* February 2003, pp. 26–32.

[6] See D. R. Comer, "A Model of Social Loafing in Real Work Groups," *Human Relations,* 1995, *48,* pp. 647–667; J. M. George and G. R. Jones, "Experiencing Work: Values, Attitudes, and Moods," *Human Relations,* 1997, *50,* pp. 393–416; and S. Murphy, S. J. Wayne, R. C.

Liden, and B. Erdogan, "Understanding Social Loafing: The Role of Justice Perceptions and Exchange Relationships," *Human Relations,* January 2003, *56(1),* pp. 61–84.

[7] See, for instance, M. Erez and A. Somech, "Is Group Productivity Loss the Rule or the Exception? Effects of Culture and Group-Based Motivation," *Academy of Management Journal,* 1996, *39(6),* pp. 1513–1537.

[8] For in-depth discussions of polarization, see D. Isenberg, "Group Polarization: A Critical Review and Meta-Analysis," *Journal of Personality and Social Psychology,* 1986, *50,* pp. 1141–1151; and "Deliberative Trouble? Why Groups Go to Extremes," *Yale Law Review,* October 2000, *110,* pp. 71–119.

[9] For discussions of role conflict and ambiguity, see Y. Fried, H. A. Ben-David, R. B. Tiegs, N. Avital, and U. Yeverechyahu, "The Interactive Effect of Role Conflict and Role Ambiguity on Job Performance," 1998, *71(1),* pp. 19–27; and T. C. Tubre and J. M. Collins, "Jackson and Schuler (1985) Revisited: A Meta-Analysis of the Relationships Between Role Ambiguity, Role Conflict, and Job Performance," *Journal of Management,* 2000, *26(1),* pp. 155–169.

[10] See Tubre and Collins, "Jackson and Schuler (1985) Revisited." See also K. Y. Au and J. Fukuda, "Boundary Spanning Behavior of Expatriates," *Journal of World Business,* Winter 2002, *37(4),* pp. 285–296.

[11] T. K. Das, "Training for Changing Managerial Role Behavior: Experience in a Developing Country," *Journal of Management Development,* 2001, *20(7),* pp. 579–603.

[12] These stages were first proposed by Bruce W. Tuckman, "Developmental Sequence in Small Groups," *Psychological Bulletin,* 1965, *63,* pp. 384–399. For a recent discussion, see C. Joinson, "Teams at Work," *HRMagazine,* 1999, *44(5),* pp. 30–36.

[13] For discussions of cohesiveness, see C. W. Langfred, "Is Group Cohesiveness a Double-Edged Sword?" *Small Group Research,* 1998, *29,* pp. 124–143; and A. V. Carron and L. R. Brawley, "Cohesion: Conceptual and Measurement Issues," *Small Group Research,* 2000, *31,* pp. 89–106.

[14] D. Bollier, "Building Corporate Loyalty While Rebuilding the Community," *Management Review*, October 1996, pp. 17–22.

[15] For more on team building, see J. R. Hackman, "New Rules for Team Building," *Optimize*, July 2002, pp. 50+; and G. Smith, "Group Development: A Review of the Literature and a Commentary on Future Research Directions," *Group Facilitation*, Spring 2001, pp. 14–45.

[16] This section is based in part on D. S. Jalajas and R. I. Sutton, "Feuds in Student Groups: Coping with Whiners, Martyrs, Saboteurs, Bullies, and Deadbeats," *Organizational Behavior Teaching Review*, 1984–1985, *9(4)*, pp. 94–102. See also C. C. Manz, J. Mancuso, C. P. Neck, and K. P. Manz, *For Team Members Only: Making Your Workplace Productive and Hassle-Free* (New York, AMACOM, 1997); and T. Schulte, "Facilitating Skills: The Art of Helping Teams Succeed," *Hospital Materiel Management Quarterly*, 1999, *21(1)*, 13–26.

[17] See L. Summers and B. Rosen, "Mavericks Ride Again," *Training and Development*, 1994, *48(5)*, pp. 119–123.

[18] W. F. Cascio, "Managing a Virtual Workplace," *Academy of Management Executive*, 2000, *14(3)*, pp. 81–90.

[19] See J. Sansing, "Tips for Building Rapport at That Crucial First Meeting," *American Agent & Broker*, May 2003, pp. 20, 22; and J. Lynn, "Life Styles: First Impressions, You Can't Do Them Over," *Commercial Law Bulletin*, July/August 2001, *16(4)*, pp. 32–33.

[20] See, for instance, B. W. Mattimore, "Imagine That!" *Training & Development*, July 1994, *48(7)*, pp. 28–32; and Virginia Johnson, "Judy's Question: Heard Any Good Jokes Lately?" *Training & Development*, October 1996, p. 16.

[21] Bart Dahmer, "Kinder, Gentler Icebreakers," *Training & Development*, August 1992, pp. 46–49.

[22] For a variety of guidelines on running meetings, including layout, see K. Tyler, "The Gang's All Here," *HRMagazine*, 2000, *45(5)*, pp. 104–113; K. Lalli, "Creating Team Spaces That Work," *Facilities Design and Management*, Spring 1998, pp. 22–24; and L. R. Hudak, "Space Odyssey," *Successful Meetings*, September 2002, pp. 31–32, 42–43.

[23] These zones were first presented by Edward T. Hall in *The Hidden Dimension* (New York: Doubleday, 1968).

[24] See Edward T. Hall and Mildred Reed Hall, *Understanding Cultural Differences* (Yarmouth, ME: Intercultural Press, 1990).

[25] See M. Skinner, "Avoid a Culture Clash Overseas," *Successful Meetings*, May 2001, p. 38.

[26] Edward E. Lawler, III, Susan A. Mohrman, and G. E. Medford, Jr., *Creating High Performance Organizations: Practices of Employee Involvement and TQM in Fortune 1000 Companies* (San Francisco: Jossey Bass, 1995).

[27] Charles C. Manz, "Bossasaurus," *Financial Executive*, November/December 1994, p. 64.

[28] For instance, see Mary Uhl-Bien and George B. Graen, "Individual Self-Management: Analysis of Professionals' Self-Managing Activities in Functional and Cross-Functional Work Teams," *Academy of Management Journal*, June 1998, *41(3)*, pp. 340–350.

[29] C. Joinson, "Teams at Work," *HRMagazine*, 1999, *44(5)*, pp. 30–36.

[30] This listing is from C. C. Manz and H. P. Sims, Jr., "SuperLeadership: Beyond the Myth of Heroic Leadership," *Organizational Dynamics*, 1991, *19(4)*, pp. 18–35. See also S. G. Cohen, L. Chang, and G. E. Ledford, Jr., "A Hierarchical Construct of Self-Management Leadership and Its Relationship to Quality of Work Life and Perceived Work Group Effectiveness," *Personnel Psychology*, 1997, *50(2)*, pp. 275–308; and R. Wageman, "How Leaders Foster Self-Managing Team Effectiveness: Design Choices Versus Hands-On Coaching," *Organization Science*, September/October 2001, *12(5)*, pp. 559–578.

[31] See Ruth Wageman, "Critical Success Factors for Creating Superb Self-Managing Teams," *Organizational Dynamics*, Summer 1997, pp. 49–60. See also M. Moravec, "Self-Managed Teams," *Executive Excellence*, 1999, *16(10)*, p. 18; and M. Attaran and T. T. Nguyen, "Succeeding with Self-Managed Work Teams," *Industrial Management*, 1999, *41(4)*, pp. 24–28.

[32] See Paul G. Hansen, "Getting Your Team on the Same Side," *Financial Executive*, March/April 1994, pp. 43–45.

[33] See J. Sorcher, "New Gains," *Home Textiles Today*, February 2000, pp. 38–41; and A. M. Moss, "Idea Center Inspires Laminate Design," *FDM, Furniture Design & Manufacturing*, June 2000, *72(2)*, pp. 62–65.

[34] See W. H. Cooper, R. B. Gallupe, and S. Pollard, "Some Liberating Effects of Anonymous Electronic Brainstorming," *Small Group Research*, 1998, *29*, pp. 147–178.

[35] Source: http://www.chevrontexaco.com/about/company_profile

[36] Source: M. Attaran and T. T. Nguyen, "Design and Implementation of Self-Directed Process Teams," *Management Decision*, 1999, *37(7)*, p. 563.

[37] Source: Based on a management consulting project completed by V. Anozie, J. Hyche, J. Phillips, R. Ranm, M. Treble, and T. San Filippo, May 2003.

[38] For examples, see "Team Building: All at Sea?" *Management Services*, October 1997, *41(10)*, p. 8; and "Concrete Canoe Racing: How Did It Get Where It Is Today?" *Civil Engineering*, September 1998, *68(9)*, p. 78. For an interesting example of use of the "theater of the oppressed" for team building, see W. P. Ferris, "Theater Tools for Team Building," *Harvard Business Review*, December 2002, *80(12)*, 24–25.

CHAPTER 12. BUILDING HUMAN ASSETS

[1] R. S. Reynolds, Jr., "How to Pick a New Executive," *Fortune*, September 1, 1986, p. 113.

[2] See A. Bennett, "Firms Toss Around Big Signing Bonuses to Coax Executives to Change Loyalties," *Wall Street Journal*, June 15, 1990, p. B1.

[3] For instance, see P. J. Kiger, "Search and Employ," *Workforce*, 2003, *82(6)*, pp. 64–66, 68.

[4] See "Where the Fortune 500 Hit the Beach: Spring Break Career Expo 2000," *PR Newswire*, February 11, 2000, p. 1; and L. Williams, "Bayou Classic Offers Job Fair; Annual Event About More Than Football," *Times-Picayune*, November 25, 2003, p. 1.

[5] M. F. Cook, "Choosing the Right Recruitment Tool," *HR Focus*, October 1997, pp. S7–S8.

[6] P. W. Braddy, L. F. Thompson, K. L. Weunsch, and W. F. Grossnickle, "Internet Recruiting," *Social Science Computer Review*, 2003, *21(3)*, pp. 374–385.

[7] Cook, "Choosing the Right Recruitment Tool."

[8] "Research Demonstrates the Success of Internet Recruiting," *HR Focus*, April 2003, p. 7.

[9] "Searching for the One," *InformationWeek*, February 17, 2003, p. 58. For more on high-tech recruiting, see R. Munger, "Technical Communicators Beware: The Next Generation of High-Tech Recruiting Methods," *IEEE Transactions on Professional Communication*, 2002, *45(4)*, pp. 276–290.

[10] See, for instance, J. B. Quinn, "Strategic Outsourcing: Leveraging Knowledge Capabilities," *Sloan Management Review*, Summer 1999, pp. 9–21.

[11] See J. McMorrow, "Future Trends in Human Resources," *HR Focus*, September 1999, pp. 7–9; and J. Chutchian-Ferranti, "The Virtual Corporation," *Computerworld*, September 13, 1999, p. 64.

[12] "The Worst Case Business Scenario," *Boston Globe*, November 9, 2003, p. D10; R. B. Reich, "High-Tech Jobs Are Going Abroad! But That's Okay," *Washington Post*, November 2, 2003, p. B3; P. G. Gosselin, "Nation Losing More Than Unskilled Labor," *Los Angeles Times*, October 20, 2003, p. C1; and K. Madigan and M. J. Mandel, "Outsourcing Jobs: Is It Bad?" *Business Week*, August 25, 2003, p. 36.

[13] E. J. Pollock, "Ruling Frowns on Employers' False Promises," *Wall Street Journal*, October 7, 1992, p. B1.

[14] J. P. Wanous, *Recruitment, Selection, Orientation, and Socialization of Newcomers*, 2nd ed. (Reading, MA: Addison-Wesley, 1992). See also B. Pappas, "Accentuate the Negative," *Forbes*, December 28, 1998, p. 47; and B. R. Kupperschmidt, "Unlicensed Assistive Personnel Retention and Realistic Job Previews," *Nursing Economics*, 2002, *20(6)*, pp. 279–283.

[15] For a thorough recent review relating to personnel selection, see I. T. Robertson and M. Smith, "Personnel Selection," *Journal of Occupational and Organizational Psychology*, 2001, *74*, pp. 441–472.

[16] A 1993 survey by Accountemps, a temporary staffing firm, came to a similar conclusion, showing that executives involved in hiring suspect one-third of job applicants lie or omit relevant information from their résumés. See J. Martin, "Employees Are Fighting Back," *Fortune*, August 8, 1994, p. 12.

[17] E. McShulskis, "Beware College Grads Willing to Lie for a Job," *HRMagazine*, August 1997, pp. 22–24. See also M. Dolliver, "Giving Dishonesty a Bad Name," *Adweek*, February 8, 1999, p. 16; and M.

Sweet, "Our Brilliant Careers: You Wouldn't Believe the Things People Put on Their CVs, Says Matthew Sweet, But Employers Are Starting to Check on Them," *The Guardian*, July 21, 1999, p. T6.

[18] M. Kinsman, "Who Gets Hurt By Those Fibs on the Résumé?" *San Diego Union-Tribune*, December 24, 2001, p. E1.

[19] See Y. Y. Chung, "The Validity of Biographical Inventories for the Selection of Salespeople," *International Journal of Management*, 2001, 18(3), pp. 322–329; and H. T. Phan and B. H. Kleiner, "How to Hire the Best People Without Breaking the Law," *Nonprofit World*, 2002, 20(5), pp. 17–18.

[20] M. G. Aumodt, D. A. Bryan, and A. J. Whitcomb, "Predicting Performance with Letters of Recommendation," *Public Personnel Management*, 1993, 22, pp. 81–90.

[21] D. L. Warmke and D. J. Weston, "Success Dispels Myths About Panel Interviewing," *Personnel Journal*, April 1992, pp. 120–126; and M. Dixon, S. Wang, J. Calvin, B. Dineen, and E. Tomlinson, "The Panel Interview: A Review of Empirical Research and Guidelines for Practice," *Public Personnel Management*, 2002, 31(3), pp. 397–428.

[22] For more on the merits of structured and unstructured interviews, and on reasons why structured interviews are rarely used, see K. I. van der Zee, A. B. Bakker, and P. Bakker, "Why Are Structured Interviews So Rarely Used in Personnel Selection?" *Journal of Applied Psychology*, 2002, 87(1), pp. 176–184.

[23] J. Woo, "Job Interviews Pose Rising Risk to Employers," *Wall Street Journal*, March 11, 1992, p. B1.

[24] W. Lambert, "Have You Ever? New EEOC Guidelines for Job Interviewing Baffle Employers," *Wall Street Journal*, July 15, 1994, pp. B1, B10.

[25] D. C. Feldman, *Managing Careers in Organizations* (Glenview, IL: Scott, Foresman, 1988), pp. 53–55.

[26] For one summary of business applications of testing, see M. P. Cronin, "This Is a Test," *INC.*, August 1993, pp. 64–68.

[27] See K. R. Murphy, B. E. Cronin, and A. P. Tam, "Controversy and Consensus Regarding the Use of Cognitive Ability Testing in Organizations," *Journal of Applied Psychology*, 2003, 88(4), pp. 660–671; and J. F. Salgado, N. Anderson, S. Moscoso, C. Bertua, F. de Fruyt, and J. P. Rolland, "A Meta-Analytic Study of General Mental Ability Validity for Different Occupations in the European Community," *Journal of Applied Psychology*, 2003, 88(6), pp. 1068–1081.

[28] For one discussion, see W. Arthur, Jr., D. J. Woehr, and W. G. Graziano, "Personality Testing in Employment Settings: Problems and Issues in the Application of Typical Selection Procedures," *Personnel Review*, 2001, 30(5/6), pp. 657–676.

[29] B. Clements, "Psychological Testing Is Gaining Adherents as More Companies Seek Tools for Enhancing Productivity," *News Tribune*, May 14, 2001, p. C14.

[30] The Employee Polygraph Protection Act of 1988 does not apply to public employers such as local governments. However, even in the case of government employers, courts have ruled polygraph tests to be "unreasonably intrusive" and have banned their use. For instance, see "Polygraph Tests," *Monthly Labor Review*, August 1990, p. 39. See also D. T. Lykken, *A Tremor in the Blood: Uses and Abuses of the Lie Detector* (New York: Plenum, 1998); and D. L. Faigman, S. E. Fienberg, and P. C. Stern, "The Limits of the Polygraph," *Issues in Science and Technology*, 2003, 20(1), pp. 40–46.

[31] G. Fuchsberg, "Prominent Psychologists Group Gives Qualified Support to Integrity Tests," *Wall Street Journal*, March 7, 1991, p. B8. See also G. M. Lousig-Nont, "Nobody Works Here," *The CPA Journal*, April 1998, p. 59; and G. M. Alliger and S. A. Dwight, "A Meta-Analytic Investigation of the Susceptibility of Integrity Tests to Faking and Coaching," *Educational and Psychological Measurement*, 2000, 60(1), pp. 59–72.

[32] See D. R. Dalton and M. B. Metzger, ""Integrity Testing" for Personnel Selection: An Unsparing Perspective," *Journal of Business Ethics*, 1993, 12, pp. 147–156.

[33] N. Luther, "Integrity Testing and Job Performance Within High Performance Work Teams: A Short Note," *Journal of Business and Psychology*, 2000, 15(1), pp. 19–25.

[34] Clements, "Psychological Testing Is Gaining Adherents."

[35] L. Cadiz, "Appeals Court Upholds the Firing of Officer; Corporal Was Dismissed After Failing Integrity Test," *The Sun*, February 2, 2001, p. 3B.

[36] E. E. Stewart, "Detecting and Deterring Employee Theft," *Healthcare Financial Management*, February 1997, pp. 72, 74.

[37] G. Fuchsberg, "More Employers Check Credit Histories of Job Seekers to Judge Their Character," *Wall Street Journal*, May 30, 1990, p. B1.

[38] E. E. Stewart, "Detecting and Deterring Employee Theft," *Healthcare Financial Management*, February 1997, pp. 72, 74.

[39] S. S. Moore and A. K. Burwell, "How To Avoid Credit-Check Hazards," *Nation's Business*, May 1993, p. 56.

[40] W. E. K. Lehman and D. D. Simpson, "Employee Substance Abuse and On-the-Job Behaviors," *Journal of Applied Psychology*, 1992, 77, pp. 309–321.

[41] E. R. Greenberg, "Drug-Testing Now Standard Practice," *HR Focus*, September 1996, p. 24; and D. May, "Testing by Necessity," *Occupational Health & Safety*, April 1999, pp. 48–51. See also S. Overman, "Splitting Hairs," *HRMagazine*, August 1999, pp. 42–48.

[42] See, for instance, J. Meyer, "Tampering with the Truth: Lab Devises New Tests," *Denver Post*, November 24, 2003, p. C1.

[43] "Drug Abuse; Drug Use Climbed in the U.S. Workforce in the First Half of 2003," *Drug Week*, December 5, 2003, p. 113.

[44] See, for instance, "Belarus Shot Putter Banned for Steroids," *Milwaukee Journal Sentinel*, November 26, 2003, p. 2C; "IAAF to Punish Doping Offenders," *Houston Chronicle*, November 24, 2003, p. 7; T. J. Quinn, "Steroid Debate Leaves Baseball Players Divided," *Knight Ridder Tribune News and Service*, November 24, 2003, p. 1; and "THG Detected in Track Stars," *Deseret News*, November 23, 2003, p. D6.

[45] C. R. Fine, "Video Tests Are the New Frontier in Drug Detection," *Personnel Journal*, June 1992, pp. 149–161.

[46] D. R. Comer, "A Case Against Workplace Drug Testing," *Organization Science*, 1994, 5, pp. 259–271.

[47] For instance, see D. Stipp, "Genetic Testing May Mark Some People as Undesirable to Employers, Insurers," *Wall Street Journal*, July 9, 1990, p. B1; and R. L. Rundle, "What Should I Do? The More We Know About Our Genes, the More Difficult the Ethical Questions We Will Face," *Wall Street Journal*, October 18, 1999, p. R16.

[48] Based on K. Zeitz, "Employer Genetic Testing: A Legitimate Screening Device or Another Method of Discrimination?" *Labor Law Journal*, April 1991, pp. 230–238; N. A. Jeffrey, "A Change in Policy: Genetic Testing Threatens to Fundamentally Alter the Whole Notion of Insurance," *Wall Street Journal*, October 18, 1999, p. R15; P. Recer, "Experts Warn of Biases Linked to Gene Mapping; They Say Genetic Research Could Lead to Discrimination in Hiring and Insurance," *Grand Rapids Press*, February 12, 2001, p. A3; M. K. Zachary, "Recent Developments in Employment Testing—Part 1—Genetic Testing," *Supervision*, 2001, 62(2), pp. 22–26; and R. A. Curley, Jr., and L. M. Caperna, "The Brave New World Is Here: Privacy Issues and the Human Genome Project," *Defense Counsel Journal*, 2003, 70(1), pp. 22–35.

[49] "Harassment of Contract Workers Banned," *Associated Press Newswires*, October 11, 1999; and "Legislation to Protect People on Genetic Testing Advances," *Associated Press Newswires*, October 19, 1999.

[50] Zachary, "Recent Developments in Employment Testing."

[51] J. Abrams, "Genetic Prejudice Banned," *Columbian*, October 15, 2003, p. A6.

[52] For a discussion of Equal Employment Opportunity Commission requirements for test validity, and suggestions for demonstrating validity, see V. Frazee, "Do Your Job-Applicant Tests Make the Grade?" *Workforce*, Fall 1996, p. 16. See also F. L. Schmidt and J. E. Hunter, "The Validity and Utility of Selection Methods in Personnel Psychology: Practical and Theoretical Implications of 85 Years of Research Findings," *Psychological Bulletin*, 1998, 124(2), pp. 262–274.

[53] See J. Krohe, Jr., "Outsmarting the Outsmarters," *Across the Board*, January 1998, pp. 20–26; and L. Marsh, "By Their Actions Shall Ye Know Them," *Works Management*, November 1997, pp. 52–53.

[54] See R. Persaud, "You Are What You Write," *New Scientist*, March 9, 2002, pp. 40–42.

[55] For more on handwriting analysis, see J. Zweig and J. M. Clash, "Show Your Hand," *Forbes*, June 21, 1993, p. 240; B. Leonard, "Reading Employees," *HRMagazine*, April 1999, pp. 67–73; and R. J. Tripician, "Confessions of a (Former) Graphologist," *The Skeptical Inquirer*, 2000, 24(1), pp. 44–47.

[56] For more on test faking, see R. Mueller-Hanson, E. D. Heggestad, and G. C. Thornton, III, "Faking and Selection: Considering the Use of Personality from Select-In and Select-Out Perspectives," *Journal of Applied Psychology*, 2003, 88(2), pp. 348–355.

[57] D. Rubin, "Cultural Bias Undermines Assessment," *Personnel Journal*, May 1992, pp. 47–52.

[58] Role playing can also be useful for training negotiators and preparing students and employees to deal with critical events. See, for instance, "Indiana U. Role-Play Program Drills M.B.A. Students in Worst-Case Scenarios," *Chronicle of Higher Education*, 2001, 48(6), p. A37; and A. A. Slatkin, "Structured Role-Play for Negotiators," *Law & Order*, 2001, 49(3), pp. 74–76.

59 For a discussion of the assessment center at BellSouth, see "BellSouth Expands Services Offered Through Its State-of-the-Art Technology Assessment Center," *PR Newswire*, June 20, 2003, p. 1.

60 K. Mailliard, "Sprint: Retention via Training," *HR Focus*, October 1997, p. S6.

61 See C. Caldwell, G. C. Thornton, III, and M. L. Gruys, "Ten Classic Assessment Center Errors: Challenges for Selection Validity," *Public Personnel Management*, 2003, *32(1)*, pp. 73–88.

62 For more on assessment centers, see G. C. Thornton, *Assessment Centers in Human Resource Management* (Reading, MA: Addison-Wesley, 1992); "We Don't Just Want to Meet the Captain of the Hockey Team," *Management Today*, December 1997, p. 64; and G. H. Harel, A. Arditi-Vogel, and T. Janz, "Comparing the Validity and Utility of Behavior Description Interview Versus Assessment Center Ratings," *Journal of Managerial Psychology*, 2003, *18(1/2)*, pp. 94–104.

63 This section is based on S. Caudron, "Team Staffing Requires New HR Role," *Personnel Journal*, May 1994, pp. 88–94.

64 C. Mahaffey, "The First 30 Days: The Most Critical Time to Influence Employee Success," *Employment Relations Today*, Summer 1999, pp. 53–60.

65 J. Gioia, "Use Orientation Process to Bond with New Employees," *HR Focus*, June 1999, p. S9.

66 J. S. Lublin, "Strategic Sidling: Lateral Moves Aren't Always a Mistake," *Wall Street Journal*, August 4, 1993, p. B1.

67 L. P. Wilbur, "The Value of On-the-Job Rotation," *Supervisory Management*, November 1993, p. 6.

68 For more on job rotation, see A. Brown, "Job Rotation Program Turns Heads," *Canadian HR Reporter*, 2003, *16(1)*, p. 12; and B. Bennett, "Job Rotation," *Training Strategies for Tomorrow*, 2003, *17(4)*, pp. 7+.

69 C. H. Deutsch, "Keeping the Talented People," *New York Times*, August 12, 1990, p. F25.

70 For a recent discussion, see J. A. Fairburn and J. M. Malcomson, "Performance, Promotion, and the Peter Principle," *Review of Economic Studies*, 2001, *68(234)*, pp. 45–66. To read about the "Peter Principle moment" of Scott Cook, co-founder of Intuit, see J. Solomon, "The Secrets of His Success," *FSB: Fortune Small Business*, 2001, *11(8)*, pp. 34–38.

71 G. Fuchsberg, "Well, at Least "Terminated with Extreme Prejudice" Wasn't Cited," *Wall Street Journal*, December 7, 1990, p. B1.

72 For one discussion, see D. E. Newton and B. H. Kleiner, "Termination at Will vs. Termination for Just Cause: Where Are We Today?" *Managerial Law*, 2002, *44(1/2)*, pp. 75–80.

73 G. Stern, "Companies Discover That Some Firings Backfire into Costly Defamation Suits," *Wall Street Journal*, May 5, 1993, p. B1.

74 These guidelines are based on L. R. Gomez-Mejia, D. B. Balkin, and R. L. Cardy, *Managing Human Resources*, 2nd ed. (Upper Saddle River, NJ: Prentice Hall, 1998), pp. 190–194.

75 O. Port, "Lev Landa's Worker Miracles," *Business Week*, September 21, 1992, pp. 72–73.

76 R. A. Faidley, "Build a Lean, Clean Training Machine," *Training & Development*, October 1993, pp. 69–70.

77 W. Arthur, Jr., W. Bennett, Jr., P. S. Edens, and S. T. Bell, "Effectiveness of Training in Organizations: A Meta-Analysis of Design and Evaluation Features," *Journal of Applied Psychology*, 2003, *88(2)*, pp. 234–245. See also S. E. Lockyer, "Does Training Pay? It's Hard to Measure," *American Banker*, July 8, 2003, p. 7A.

78 Ibid.

79 For a discussion of the McJobs program, which McDonald's uses to train individuals with disabilities to work in its restaurants, see J. J. Laabs, "The Golden Arches Provide Golden Opportunities," *Personnel Journal*, July 1991, pp. 52–56.

80 See "Eight Steps to Better On-the-Job Training," *HR Focus*, July 2003, pp. 11, 13–14; and K. Crompton, "On-the-Job Training Fortifies Nursing Ranks Here," *Journal of Business*, 2002, *17(9)*, p. B1.

81 W. Arthur, Jr., W. Bennett, Jr., P. S. Edens, and S. T. Bell, "Effectiveness of Training in Organizations: A Meta-Analysis of Design and Evaluation Features," *Journal of Applied Psychology*, 2003, *88(2)*, pp. 234–245.

82 K. Slack, "Training for the Real Thing," *Training & Development*, May 1993, pp. 79–89. See also C. M. Solomon, "Simulation Training Builds Teams Through Experience," *Personnel Journal*, June 1993, pp. 100–108; and B. Lierman, "How to Develop a Training Simulation," *Training & Development*, February 1994, pp. 50–52.

83 See, for instance, H. A. Suzik, "Corporate Universities on the Rise," *Quality*, April 1999, p. 22; J. N. Mottl, "Corporate Universities Grow," *Internetweek*, March 15, 1999, p. 23; J. Vitiello, "New Roles for Corporate Universities," *Computerworld*, April 9, 2001, p. 42; K. Ellis, "Corporate U's: High Value or Hot Air?" *Training*, 2002, *39(9)*, pp. 60–64; and G. Johnson, "9 Tactics to Take Your Corporate University from Good to Great," *Training*, 2003, *40(7)*, pp. 38, 40–42.

84 S. Greengard, "How Technology Is Advancing HR," *Personnel Journal*, September 1993, pp. 80–90; "Army Sponsors "Virtual" Machinist Training," *Manufacturing Engineering*, March 1999, pp. 28–29; and J. Barbrian, "High-Tech Times," *Training*, 2003, *40(10)*, pp. 52–55.

85 For instance, see J. Bone, "It's Only an Illusion with Simulator Training," *Safety & Health*, January 1992, pp. 32–35; and P. Taylor, "Education Tool of the Future: Simulation," *Financial Times*, November 24, 2003, p. 4.

86 M. Kelley, "Planning the Unthinkable: Shooting Down an Airliner," *The Commercial Appeal*, October 3, 2003, p. A9.

87 See, for instance, A. Rosenbloom, "Toward an Image Indistinguishable from Reality," *Association for Computing Machinery, Communications of the ACM*, August 1999, pp. 28–31; D. Orenstein, "Virtual Reality Saves on Training," *Computerworld*, March 8, 1999, p. 44; and M. C. Whitton, "Making Virtual Environments Compelling," *Association for Computing Machinery, Communications of the ACM*, July 2003, pp. 40–47.

88 B. Delaney, "Virtual Reality Lands the Job," *NewMedia*, August 1994, p. 45; see also C. Covault, "Virtual Reality Utilized in Station, Shuttle Ops," *Aviation Week & Space Technology*, September 28, 1998, p. 74.

89 See B. Geber, "Simulating Reality," *Training*, April 1990, pp. 41–46; J. Holusha, "Technology: Carving Out Real-Life Uses for Virtual Reality," *New York Times*, October 31, 1993, p. C11; and F. Moody, *The Visionary Position: The Inside Story of the Digital Dreamers Who Are Making Virtual Reality a Reality* (New York: Times Books, 1999).

90 J. K. Salisbury, Jr., "Making Graphics Physically Tangible," *Association for Computing Machinery, Communications of the ACM*, August 1999, pp. 74–81; R. Hercz, "Seeking Computers That Can Feel," *New York Times*, November 9, 2000, p. G19; and R. Kay, "The Sensual Computer: High Touch, High-Tech," *Computerworld*, October 9, 2000, p. 78.

91 I. Amato, "Helping Doctors Feel Better," *Technology Review*, 2001, *104(3)*, pp. 64–70; and P. D. Thacker, "Fake Worlds Offer Real Medicine," *JAMA*, 2003, *290(16)*, pp. 2107, 2111–2112.

92 J. E. Santora, "Keep Up Production Through Cross-Training," *Personnel Journal*, June 1992, pp. 162–166; and B. Gill, "Cross Training Can Be a Win-Win Plan," *American Printer*, October 1997, p. 88.

93 M. Messmer, "Cross-Discipline Training: A Strategic Method to Do More with Less," *Management Review*, May 1992, pp. 26–28; and J. Ross, "Cross Training," *Computer Reseller News*, April 21, 1997, pp. 127–128.

94 M. Leshner and A. Browne, "Increasing Efficiency Through Cross-Training," *Best's Review*, December 1993, pp. 39–40; and M. A. Marks, M. J. Sabella, C. S. Burke, and S. J. Zaccaro, "The Impact of Cross-Training on Team Effectiveness," *Journal of Applied Psychology*, 2002, *87(1)*, pp. 3–13.

95 J. Pine and J. Tingley, "ROI of Soft Skills Training," *Training*, February 1993, pp. 55–60.

96 N. Weidenfeller, "Celebrating Diversity," *Public Utilities Quarterly*, June 15, 1992, pp. 20–22.

97 See, for instance, A. Simmons, "When Performance Reviews Fail," *T+D*, 2003, *57(9)*, pp. 47–51; "Low Marks for Performance Appraisal," *Worklife*, 2003, *14(4)*, p. 8.

98 See also "A Simple Approach to Annual Reviews," *HR Focus*, November 2003, pp. 6–7, 10; K. Fritscher-Porter, "Positive Performance Appraisals," *OfficePro*, October 2003, pp. 6–7, 10, 12.

99 E. C. Baig, "So You Hate Rating Your Workers?" *Business Week*, August 22, 1994, p. 14; and M. Cohn, "Best Buy Beefs Up Customer Value at the Call Center," *Internet World*, June 2002, pp. 42–43.

100 For instance, see P. R. Scholtes, "Total Quality or Performance Appraisal: Choose One," *National Productivity Review*, Summer 1993, pp. 349–363; and T. Juncaj, "Do Performance Appraisals Work?" *Quality Progress*, 2002, *35(11)*, pp. 45–49.

101 J. J. Laabs, "Specialized Pay Programs Link Employees" TQM Efforts to Rewards," *Personnel Journal*, January 1994, p. 17. For a discussion of how performance appraisals can be used in ways consistent with the teachings of TQM, see D. Antonioni, "Improve the Management Process Before Discontinuing Performance Appraisals," *Compensation & Benefits Review*, 26(3), 1994, pp. 29–37. See also K. A. Aldakhilallah and D. H. Parente, "Redesigning a Square Peg: Total Quality Management Performance Appraisals," *Total Quality Management*, 2002, *13(1)*, pp. 39–52.

102 For some recent attempts to integrate MBO effectively with other human resource functions, see J. Pickard, "Motivate Employees to Delight Customers," *Transportation & Distribution*, July 1993, p. 48; P. Palvia, S. Sullivan, and S. Zeltman, "PRISM Profile: An Employee-Oriented System," *HR Focus*, 1993, *70(6)*, p. 19; and D. Daley, "Pay for Performance, Performance Appraisal, and Total Quality Management," *Public Productivity & Management Review*, Fall 1992, pp. 39–51.

103 F. Rice, "How to Make Diversity Pay," *Fortune*, August 8, 1994, pp. 78–86; and M. Hayes, "Goal Oriented," *Information Week*, March 10, 2003, pp. 34–36, 40–42.

104 A. Murdoch, "Going Full Circle," *Accountancy*, November 1998, pp. 48–49; G. D. Huet-Cox, T. M. Nielsen, and E. Sundstrom, "Get the Most From 360-Degree Feedback: Put It on the Internet," *HRMagazine*, May 1999, pp. 92–103; C. L. Bernick, "When Your Culture Needs a Makeover," *Harvard Business Review*, 2001, *79(6)*, pp. 53–64; and K. Clark, "Judgment Day; It's Survival of the Fittest as Companies Tighten the Screws on Employee Performance Reviews," *U.S. News and World Report*, January 13, 2003, pp. 31–32.

105 See A. Evans, "From Every Angle," *Training*, 2001, *38(9)*, p. 22; and T. A. Beehr, L. Ivanitskaya, C. P. Hansen, D. Erofeev, and D. M. Gudanowski, "Evaluation of 360 Degree Feedback: Relationships with Each Other and with Performance and Selection Predictors," *Journal of Organizational Behavior*, 2001, *22(7)*, pp. 775–788.

106 See D. A. Waldman, L. E. Atwater, and D. Antonioni, "Has 360 Degree Feedback Gone Amok?" *Academy of Management Executive*, May 1998, pp. 86–94; and S. Wimer, "The Dark Side of 360-Degree Feedback," *T + D*, 2002, *56(9)*, pp. 37–42.

107 See E. C. Dierdorff and M. A. Wilson, "A Meta-Analysis of Job Analysis Reliability," *Journal of Applied Psychology*, 2003, *88(4)*, 635–646.

108 "Merging Management Methods," *China Business Review*, September–October 1992, p. 13.

109 J. B. Treece, "Mitsubishi Ends Seniority-Based Promotions," *Automotive News*, March 31, 2003, p. 16.

110 J. E. Rigdon, "More Firms Try to Reward Good Service, But Incentives May Backfire in Long Run," *Wall Street Journal*, December 5, 1990, p. B1; and D. Anderson, "How to Run an Incentive," *Occupational Health & Safety*, 2003, *72(6)*, pp. 38, 40, 42, 44–46, 48–49.

111 This listing is based on Gomez-Mejia et al., *Managing Human Resources*, pp. 333–336. See also V. Mahajan and S. Sarin, "Teamwork, Incentives Give Managers New Challenges," *Marketing News*, 2001, *35(6)*, p. 21.

112 "AT&T Credit: Continuous Improvement as a Way of Life," *Work in America Institute*, October 1991, p. 2.

113 For some examples, see "Motivating Without Money," *Boardwatch*, 2002, *16(1)*, p. 12.

114 "All Pulling Together, to Get the Carrot," *Wall Street Journal*, April 30, 1990, p. B1.

115 J. Greenwood, "Workers: Risks and Rewards," *Time*, April 15, 1991, pp. 42–43.

116 See D. Collins, *Gainsharing and Power: Lessons from Six Scanlon Plans* (Ithaca, NY: Cornell University Press, 1998); and J. B. Arthur and G. S. Jelf, "The Effects of Gainsharing on Grievance Rates and Absenteeism over Time," *Journal of Labor Research*, Winter 1999, pp. 133–145.

117 See M. A. Conte, "Contingent Compensation: (How) Does It Affect Company Performance?" *Journal of Economic Issues*, June 1992, pp. 583–592.

118 J. A. Fraser, "Profit Sharing?" *INC.*, November 1993, p. 137.

119 See, for instance, C. Higley, "ESOPs—Fable or Fairy Tale?" *Landscape Management*, 2003, *42(10)*, pp. 4–5; and D. K. Rubin and M. B. Powers, "Through Ownership, More Employees Are Pumping Up the Company; Workers At All Levels Buy Into Their Firms' Futures—and Their Own," *ENR*, August 18, 2003, pp. 24–31.

120 K. Smith and L. Luciano, "America's Best Company Benefits," *Money*, October 1999, pp. 116–126.

121 G. Koretz, "ESOP Benefits Are No Fables," *Business Week*, September 6, 1999, p. 26.

122 C. Pickering, "Meet the Schwillionaires," *Forbes*, August 23, 1999, p. 34.

123 A. J. Maggs, "Enron, ESOPs, and Fiduciary Duty," *Benefits Law Journal*, 2003, *16(3)*, pp. 42–52; and E. MacDonald, "Microsoft's Lonely Parade," *Forbes*, August 11, 2003, p. 044a.

124 R. Koenig, "Du Pont Plan Linking Pay to Fibers Profit Unravels," *Wall Street Journal*, October 25, 1991, p. B1.

125 http://www.hoovers.com/eds.

126 http://www.eds.com/about_eds/en_about_eds.shtml.

127 http://www.eds.com/about_eds/en_about_eds.shtml.

128 Source: C. M. Solomon, "Stellar Recruiting for a Tight Labor Market," *Workforce*, August 1998, pp. 66–70.

129 J. S. Lublin, "It's Shape-Up Time for Performance Reviews," *Wall Street Journal*, October 4, 1994, p. B1.

130 T. Dignall, "The Power of Upward Appraisal," *Executive Development*, 1993, *6(1)*, p. 7.

131 http://www.fedex.com/us/about/overview/companie/corporation.

132 http://www.fedex.com/us/about/today/mission.html.

133 Based on G. Smith, "Life Won't Be Just a Bowl of Cherry Garcia," *Business Week*, July 18, 1994, p. 42; and J. S. Lublin, "Ben & Jerry's Scoffs at Tradition, Hires Some Suits to Find a CEO," *Wall Street Journal*, August 10, 1994, p. B1.

134 See "Ben & Jerry's Former CEO Buys Furniture Dealership," *Facilities Design & Management*, May 1997, p. 24; and D. Kadlec, "A New Flavor at Ben & Jerry's," *Time*, October 14, 1996, p. 72.

135 See A. Serwer, "Ben & Jerry's Is Back: Ice Cream and a Hot Stock," *Fortune*, August 2, 1999, pp. 267–268.

CHAPTER 13. ORGANIZATIONAL CULTURE

1 See R. Cowen, "After the Tragedy," *Science News*, 2003, *164(13)*, p. 203; T. Reichhardt, "NASA Braced for Culture Shock as *Columbia* Inquiry Reaches Verdict," *Nature*, 2003, *424(6951)*, p. 863; and B. Dickey, "Shuttle Shakeup," *Government Executive*, 2003, *35(11)*, pp. 54–56, 58–61.

2 G. W. Dauphinais and C. Price, "The CEO as Psychologist," *Management Review*, September 1998, pp. 10–15.

3 "Incompatible Cultures Cause Merger Failures," *Workforce*, November 1998, p. 9. For more on the role of culture in mergers and acquisitions, see S. F. Gale, "Memo to AOL Time Warner: Why Mergers Fail," *Workforce*, 2003, *82(2)*, pp. 60–63; I. Dackert, P. R. Jackson, S.-O. Brenner, and C. R. Johannson, "Eliciting and Analysing Employees' Expectations of a Merger," *Human Relations*, 2003, *56(6)*, pp. 705–725; and M. Schraeder and D. R. Self, "Enhancing the Success of Mergers and Acquisitions: An Organizational Culture Perspective," *Management Decision*, 2003, *41(5/6)*, pp. 511–527.

4 These functions are drawn primarily from V. Sathe, *Culture and Related Corporate Realities* (Homewood, IL: Irwin, 1985), pp. 25–31; J. Martin and C. Siehl, "Organizational Culture and Counterculture: An Uneasy Symbiosis," *Organizational Dynamics*, August 1983, pp. 52–64; and J. C. Picken and G. G. Dess, "Out of (Strategic) Control," *Organizational Dynamics*, 1997, *26(1)*, pp. 35–48.

5 W. G. Ouchi, "A Conceptual Framework for the Design of Organizational Control Mechanisms," *Management Science*, 1979, pp. 833–848.

6 For more on clan control, see J. R. Deckop, R. Mangel, and C. C. Cirka, "Getting More Than You Pay For: Organizational Citizenship Behavior and Pay-for-Performance Plans," *Academy of Management Journal*, August 1999, pp. 420–428; S. Maguire, "The Discourse of Control," *Journal of Business Ethics*, March 1999, pp. 109–114; and "Context and Control in Foreign Subsidiaries: Making the Case for the Host Country National Manager," *Journal of Leadership and Organizational Studies*, 2003, *10(1)*, pp. 93–105.

7 For excellent discussions of culture and cultural elements, see H. M. Trice and J. M. Beyer, *The Cultures of Work Organizations* (Englewood Cliffs, NJ: Prentice Hall, 1993); and J. Martin, *Organizational Culture: Mapping the Terrain* (Thousand Oaks, CA: Sage, 2002).

8 For instance, see V. Sathe, *Culture and Related Corporate Realities* (Homewood, IL: Irwin, 1985), p. 15. See also R. Jacob, "Corporate Reputations," *Fortune*, March 6, 1995, pp. 54–59; and J. B. Sorensen, "The Strength of Corporate Culture and the Reliability of Firm Perfor-

mance," *Administrative Science Quarterly*, 2002, *47(1)*, pp. 70–91.

9   T. J. Peters and R. H. Waterman, Jr., *In Search of Excellence* (New York: Harper & Row, 1982), pp. 75–76.

10 See H. English, "Hiring for Values," *Executive Excellence*, May 2000, p. 19; and A. E. M. Van Vianen, "Person-Organization Fit: The Match Between Newcomers' and Recruiters' Preferences for Organizational Cultures," *Personnel Psychology*, 2000, *53*, pp. 113–149.

11 For instance, see J. A. Conger, "Inspiring Others: The Language of Leadership," *Academy of Management Executive*, February 1991, pp. 31–45; and K. Klenke, "Cinderella Stories of Women Leaders: Connecting Leadership Context and Competencies," *Journal of Leadership and Organizational Studies*, 2002, *9(2)*, pp. 18–28.

12 J. B. White, "GM Is Overhauling Corporate Culture in an Effort to Regain Competitiveness," *Wall Street Journal*, January 13, 1993, p. A3.

13 R. E. Winter, "Milacron Wolfpack Goes In for the Kill," *Wall Street Journal*, August 14, 1990, p. A6.

14 See R. F. Dennehy, The Executive as Storyteller," *Management Review*, March 1999, pp. 40–43, and C. Collison and A. Mackenzie, "The Power of Story in Organizations," *Journal of Workplace Learning*, 1999, *11(1)*, p. 38, for discussions of the importance of narratives in organizations. For a discussion of narratives told by employees in a 160-year-old newspaper company, see M. O'Leary, "From Paternalism to Cynicism: Narratives of a Newspaper Company," *Human Relations*, June 2003, *56(6)*, pp. 685–704.

15 See T. A. Stewart, "The Cunning Plots of Leadership," *Fortune*, September 7, 1998, pp. 165–166.

16 From Trice and Beyer, *The Cultures of Work Organizations*, p. 103, adapted from A. Wilkins, "Organizational Stories As an Expression of Management Philosophy." Ph.D. thesis proposal, Stanford University, June 1977.

17 L. Pondy, "Union of Rationality and Intuition in Management Action," in S. Srivastva and Associates (Eds.), *The Executive Mind* (San Francisco: Jossey-Bass, 1983), p. 159.

18 G. Anders, "The Carly Chronicles," *Fast Company*, February 2003, *67*, pp. 66–72.

19 See K. E. Mills-LeBlanc and C. LeBlanc, "Heroes are Not Just Sandwiches; They Are the Main Ingredients of Healthy Foodservice Cultures," *Nation's Restaurant News*, November 6, 2000, p. 30.

20 For instance, see M. Boyd, "Gender Benders," *Incentive*, September 1995, p. 92.

21 See, for example, "Neurosis, Arkansas-Style," *Fortune*, April 17, 2000, p. 8; and J. Collins, "Bigger, Better, Faster (What I Saw at Wal-Mart—and What It Means for the Future of Your Company)," *Fast Company*, 2003, *71*, pp. 74–76, 78.

22 Martin and Siehl, "Organizational Culture and Counterculture."

23 These and other causes for countercultures are discussed in greater detail in Trice and Beyer, *The Cultures of Work Organizations*, pp. 244–252.

24 J. M. Jermier, J. W. Slocum, Jr., L. W. Fry, and J. Gaines, "Organizational Subcultures in a Soft Bureaucracy: Resistance Behind the Myth and Facade of an Official Culture," *Organization Science*, *2*, 1991, pp. 170–194.

25 Martin and Siehl, "Organizational Culture and Counterculture."

26 V. Sathe, *Culture and Related Corporate Realities* (Homewood, IL: Irwin, 1985), pp. 280–295.

27 Ibid., p. 286.

28 To read more about subcultures and countercultures, see H. M. Trice, *Occupational Subcultures in the Workplace* (Ithaca, NY: ILR Press, 1993); G. Hofstede, "Identifying Organizational Subcultures: An Empirical Approach," *Journal of Management Studies*, January 1998, pp. 1–12; I. Brookes, "Managerial Professionalism: The Destruction of a Non-Conforming Subculture," *British Journal of Management*, March 1999, pp. 41–52; and S. Liu, "Cultures Within Culture: Unity and Diversity of Two Generations of Employees in State-Owned Enterprises," *Human Relations*, 2003, *56(4)*, pp. 387–417.

29 This categorization is provided by Trice and Beyer, *The Cultures of Work Organizations*, pp. 21–23.

30 W. G. Ouchi, *Theory Z: How American Business Can Meet the Japanese Challenge* (Reading, MA: Addison-Wesley, 1982).

31 For instance, see E. E. Lawler and S. A. Mohrman, "Quality Circles: After the Honeymoon," *Organizational Dynamics*, Spring 1987, pp. 42–54. See also G. N. Flores and D. R. Utley, "Management Concepts in Use—a 12-Year Perspective," *Engineering Management Journal*, September 2000, pp. 11–17.

32 T. J. Peters and R. H. Waterman, Jr., *In Search of Excellence* (New York: Harper & Row, 1982), pp. 257–258.

33 D. Carroll, "A Disappointing Search for Excellence," *Harvard Business Review*, November–December 1983, pp. 78–88.

34 B. Johnson, A. Natarajan, and A. Rappaport, "Shareholder Returns and Corporate Excellence," *Journal of Business Strategy,* Fall 1985, pp. 52–62.

35 "Who's Excellent Now?" *Business Week*, November 5, 1984, pp. 76–88.

36 M. A. Hitt and R. D. Ireland, "Peters and Waterman Revisited: The Unended Quest for Excellence," *Academy of Management Executive*, May 1987, pp. 91–98.

37 For further discussions of *In Search of Excellence* and of its prescriptions, see T. Merriden, "The Eight Pillars of Wisdom," *Management Today*, April 1998, pp. 119–120; S. Crainer and D. Dearlove, "Excellence Revisited," *Business Strategy Review*, 2002, *13(1)*, pp. 13–19; and J. W. Newstrom, "*In Search of Excellence*: Its Importance and Effects," *Academy of Management Executive*, 2002, *16(1)*, pp. 53–56. For interviews with Tom Peters and discussions of his recent writings, see S. Crainer, "The Gurus: Tom Peters," *Management Today*, May 1997, pp. 74–75; and B. Rosner, "Tom Peters Sounds Off," *Workforce*, 2000, *79(8)*, pp. 56–60.

38 T. Peters, "Tom Peter's True Confessions," *Fast Company*, 2001, *53*, pp. 78–81, 84, 86, 88–90, 92. See also T. Galvin, "No Laughing Matter," *Training*, 2002, *39(2)*, p. 6.

39 For more on the links of cultural characteristics to firm performance, see E. E. Christensen and G. G. Gordon, "An Exploration of Industry, Culture and Revenue Growth," *Organization Studies*, 1999, *20*, pp. 397–422; C. P. M. Wilderom, U. Glunk, and R. Maslowski, "Organizational Culture as a Predictor or Organizational Performance," in N. M. Ashkanasy, C. P. M. Wilderom, and M. F. Peterson (Eds.), *Handbook of Organizational Culture and Climate* (Thousand Oaks, CA: Sage), pp. 193–209; and C. J. Fisher and R. J. Alford, "Consulting on Culture: A New Bottom Line," *Consulting Psychology Journal: Practice and Research*, 2000, *52(3)*, pp. 206–217.

40 T. Deal and A. Kennedy, *Corporate Cultures: The Rites and Rituals of Corporate Life* (Reading, MA: Addison-Wesley, 1982). See also T. E. Deal and A. A. Kennedy, *The New Corporate Cultures: Revitalizing the Workplace after Downsizing, Mergers, and Reengineering* (Cambridge, MA: Perseus, 2000).

41 For instance, see M. F. R. Kets de Vries and D. Miller, *The Neurotic Organization* (San Francisco: Jossey-Bass, 1984). See also M. Punch, "Suite Violence: Why Managers Murder and Corporations Kill," *Crime, Law & Social Change*, 2000, *33(3)*, pp. 243–280; and H. Lindborg, "Lessons from Prairie Dogs," *Quality Progress*, 2003, *36(9)*, p. 81.

42 J. B. Barney, "Organizational Culture: Can It Be a Source of Sustained Competitive Advantage?" *Academy of Management Review*, 1986, *2*, pp. 656–665.

43 B. Duhaime, "Creating a New Company Culture," *Fortune,* January 15, 1990, p. 128.

44 These are based in part on Trice and Beyer, *The Cultures of Work Organizations*, pp. 393–426, and B. Dumaine, "Creating a New Company Culture," *Fortune*, January 15, 1990, pp. 127–131.

45 For a detailed discussion of employee reactions to culture change, including the roles of culture strength and subcultures, see L. C. Harris and E. Ogbonna, "Employee Responses to Culture Change Efforts," *Human Resource Management Journal*, 1998, *8(2)*, pp. 78–92. See also I. Dackert, P. R. Jackson, S.-O. Brenner, and C. R. Johansson, "Eliciting and Analysing Employees' Expectations of a Merger," *Human Relations*, 2003, *56(6)*, pp. 705–725.

46 http://www.ge.com/en/microsite/company/companyinfo/at_a_glance/fact_sheet.htm.

47 http://www.ge.com/en/microsite/company/companyinfo/at_a_glance/ge_values.

48 J. Rowher, "GE Digs into Asia," *Fortune*, October 2, 2000, pp. 164–170.

49 http://www.chron.com/cs/CDA/story.hts/special/enron/1127125.

50 John A. Byrne, with Mike France in New York and Wendy Zellner in Dallas, "The Environment Was Ripe for Abuse: Enron's Unrelenting Stress on Growth and Its Absence of Controls Helped Push Execs into Unethical Behavior," *Business Week* (Industrial/technology edition), February 25, 2002, p. 118.

51 Wendy Zellner in Dallas with Christopher Palmeri in Houston, Mike France in New York, Joseph Weber in Chicago, and Dan Carney in Washington, "Jeff Skilling: Enron's Missing Man: The CEO Who Created Its In-Your-Face Culture Has Been Largely Absent from the Inquiry," *Business Week* (Industrial/technology edition), February 11, 2002, p. 38.

Chapter 14. Managing Change

1. These examples are drawn from "The New Business Imperative: The Capacity to Respond," *Chief Executive*, May 2003, pp. 2–13.
2. See C. J. G. Gersick, "Pacing Strategic Change: The Case of a New Venture," *Academy of Management Journal*, 1994, *37(1)*, pp. 9–45.
3. One framework for considering forces for and against change, proposed by Kurt Lewin, is called force field analysis, which involves considering forces arrayed for and against change in order to help determine whether a proposed change is feasible and what steps are needed to facilitate the change. For discussions, see G. Brager and S. Holloway, "Assessing Prospects for Organizational Change: The Uses of Force Field Analysis," *Administration in Social Work*, 1992, *16(3,4)*, pp. 15–28; and G. L. Duffy, J. Bauer, and J. W. Moran, "Solve Problems with Open Communication," *Quality Progress*, 2001, *34(7)*, p. 160.
4. M. Boles and B. P. Sunoo, "Three Barriers to Managing Change," *Workforce*, January 1998, p. 25.
5. For a discussion of helping employees accept and adapt to change, see J. L. Bennett, "Change Happens," *HR Magazine*, September 2001, pp. 149–156; and S. Simmerman, "Square Wheels," *Executive Excellence*, June 2003, *20(6)*, pp. 15–16. For research on sources of resistance to change, see M. Pardo del Val and C. M. Fuentes, "Resistance to Change: A Literature Review and Empirical Study," *Management Decision*, 2003, *41(2)*, pp. 148–155.
6. "Bossidy's Burning Platform," *Journal of Business Strategy*, September/October 1996, p. 10. See also S. Sherman, "A Master Class in Radical Change," *Fortune*, December 13, 1993, pp. 82–86; and M. Z. Strub, "Quality at Warp Speed: Reengineering at AT&T," *Bulletin of the American Society for Information Science*, April/May 1994, pp. 17–19.
7. J. P. Donlon, "The CEO's CEO," *Chief Executive*, July/August 1998, pp. 28–37; and T. A. Stewart, "How to Leave It All Behind," *Fortune*, December 6, 1999, pp. 345–348.
8. A. J. Vogl, "The Army After Next," *Across the Board*, June 1999, pp. 43–47.
9. See J. Collins, "Turning Goals into Results: The Power of Catalytic Mechanisms," *Harvard Business Review*, July/August 1999, pp. 70–82.
10. See also "Discipline and Desire," *Harvard Business Review*, July/August 1999, p. 10.
11. For a discussion of organizational change processes as resembling death and dying, see D. Zell, "Organizational Change as a Process of Death, Dying, and Rebirth," *Journal of Applied Behavioral Science*, March 2003, pp. 73–96.
12. R. Beckhard, *Organization Development: Strategies and Models* (Reading, MA: Addison-Wesley, 1969), p. 9.
13. This listing of OD techniques was proposed by W. L. French and C. H. Bell, Jr., *Organization Development: Behavioral Science Interventions for Organization Improvement*, 2nd ed. (Englewood Cliffs, NJ: Prentice-Hall, 1978).
14. Ibid., pp. 215–218.
15. For example, see P. A. McLagan, "The Change-Capable Organization," *TD*, January 2003, pp. 50–58.
16. P. M. Senge, *SW* (New York: Doubleday, 1990), p. 3.
17. P. Senge, "Sharing Knowledge," *Executive Excellence*, September 1999, pp. 6–7.
18. P. Senge, A. Kleiner, C. Roberts, R. Ross, G. Roth, and B. Smith, *The Dance of Change: The Challenges to Sustaining Momentum in Learning Organizations* (New York: Doubleday, 1999), pp. 32–33. These disciplines are discussed in detail in Senge, *The Fifth Discipline*, pp. 139–269.
19. Senge, *The Fifth Discipline*, p. 12.
20. Drawn from Senge, *The Fifth Discipline*, pp. 18–25.
21. Senge, *The Fifth Discipline*, pp. 21–22; italics in original.
22. See also P. M. Senge, "Slow Threats," *Executive Excellence*, April 1994, pp. 5–7.
23. See also C. R. James, "Designing Learning Organizations," *Organizational Dynamics*, 2003, *32(1)*, pp. 46–61.
24. P. Senge, "Creative Tension," *Executive Excellence*, January 1999, pp. 12–13.
25. P. Senge, "Leading Learning Organizations," *Executive Excellence*, April 1996, pp. 10–11.
26. P. M. Senge, "Creating Quality Communities," *Executive Excellence*, June 1994, pp. 11–13.
27. This section is based primarily on P. Senge, "Learning Infrastructures," *Executive Excellence*, February 1995, p. 7.
28. Senge, "Creating Quality Communities."
29. Ibid.
30. Based on a consulting project completed by R. Ferrarese, Summer 2002.
31. http://www.xerox.com.
32. knowledge@wharton, October 26, 2000.
33. O. Kharif, "Anne Mulcahy Has Xerox by the Horns," *Business Week Online*, May 29, 2003.
34. A. Newman, "More Black Ink at Xerox," *Business Week*, August 11, 2003, p. 40.
35. T. Datz, "Can Xerox Duplicate Its Past Success?" http://www.darwinmag.com, April 2002.

Chapter 15. Maintaining and Building Skills

1. See G. F. Seib and B. Davis, "Independence Day: New Economy Leaves Mark on Every Facet Of Campaign 1000—As Loyalties Fray, Voters Seek Government They Can Click On and Off—Riding a 'Major Anxiety Shift,'" *Wall Street Journal*, November 7, 2000, p. A1. See also R. D. Schwartzman, "Transforming Leader Development Through Lifelong Learning," *Military Review*, 2003, *83(3)*, p. 63.
2. G. M. McEviy, "Answering the Challenge: Developing the Management Action Skills of Business Students," *Journal of Management Education*, 1998, *22*, pp. 655–670. See also J. Bigelow, "Teaching Action Skills: A Report from the Classroom," *Exchange: The Organizational Behavior Teaching Journal*, 1983, *8(2)*, pp. 28–34.
3. L. Perlman, "View from the Top on Lifelong Learning," *Star Tribune*, July 5, 1999, p. 03D.
4. There are quite a few variations on this quote. In fact, the quote appears to have originated not with Wayne Gretzky but with his father, Walter. On this point—and how metaphors and quotes often get twisted—see J. Rosenfeld, "CDU to Gretzky: The Puck Stops Here!," at www.fastcompany.com/online/36/cdu.html. Regardless of the source, the quote offers good advice.
5. S. Gittlen, "Training at its Best," *Network World*, November 13, 2000, p. 123.
6. For discussions of role models, see J. Collins, "The 10 Greatest CEOs of All Time," *Fortune*, July 21, 2003, pp. 54–58, 62, 64, 68.; B. Higgins, "Female Agents Need More Role Models," *National Underwriter*, July 21, 2003, p. 41; and I. Portsmouth, "A Time for Heroes," *Profit*, June 2003, p. 6.
7. For example, see C. Ryan and R. H. Krapels, "Organizations and Internships," *Business Communication Quarterly*, December 1997, pp. 126–131; "Internships Prove Valuable in Poor Job Market," *Black Issues in Higher Education*, 2003, *20(15)*, p. 13; and J. Chatzky, "Interns, Get Moving," *Time*, October 27, 2003, p. 82.
8. S. D. Gilbert, *Internships 1997*, 2nd ed. (New York: Simon & Schuster, 1997), p. 2.
9. See, for instance, B. Weinstein, "Internships Offer Solid Pay, Experience," *Los Angeles Times*, October 20, 2000, p. E4; and "Renewed Questions About Internships," *USA Today*, August 2003, p. 5.
10. AIESEC was formerly a French acronym for *Association Internationale des Etudiants en Sciences Economiques et Commerciales*. Today, the association no longer uses this acronym because its membership has grown to encompass a much wider range of disciplines than only economics and commerce.
11. S. Gittlen, "Training at Its Best," *Network World*, November 13, 2000, p. 123. For more on hiring for soft skills, see "Report Says Students Lack 'Soft' Work Skills," *What Works in Teaching and Learning*, January 12, 2002, pp. 1–2; and D. Dubie, "Mining for a Diamond in the Rough," *Network World*, September 15, 2003, p. 47.
12. C. A. Bartlett and S. Ghoshal, "The Myth of the Generic Manager: New Personal Competencies for New Management Roles," *California Man-*

agement Review, Fall 1997, pp. 92–116. See also S. F. Gale, "Putting Job Candidates to the Test," *Workforce*, 2003, *82(4)*, pp. 64–67.

13 S. Gittlen, "Training at Its Best," *Network World*, November 13, 2000, p. 123; and M. Olesen, "What Makes Employees Stay," *Training & Development*, October 1999, pp. 48–52.

14 See, for instance, P. M. Buhler, "Managing in the New Millennium," *Supervision*, August 2000, pp. 16–18.

15 Ibid.

16 For discussions of how companies are working with schools to provide advice, encourage skills training, and help recruit future talent, see M. K. McGee and J. Mateyaschuk, "Educating the Masses," *Information-week*, February 15, 1999, pp. 61–81.

17 For discussions of the importance of networking for job search and career management, see "Making Connections Can Lead to a Job," *USA Today*, April 2003, pp. 5–6; and F. Windisch, *Fire Chief*, August 2003, p. 116.

18 J. T. Chyna, "Climbing the Ladder: What it Takes to Succeed in Health-care Management," *Healthcare Executive*, November/December 2000, pp. 12–17.

19 D. Bonner and L. Tarner, "Once Upon an HRD Book Club," *Training & Development*, December 1999, pp. 45–51. See also P. Houser, "Books n Clubs: Reading for Support," *Black Issues Book Review*, May/June 2003, p. 43.

20 J. T. Chyna, "Climbing the Ladder: What It Takes to Succeed in Health-care Management," *Healthcare Executive*, November/December 2000, pp. 12–27.

21 J. L. Kennedy, "7 Steps will Show Boss You're Ready for New Chal-lenge," *Milwaukee Journal Sentinel*, November 12, 2000, p. 1. See also N. E. Betz, "A Proactive Approach to Midcareer Development," *Coun-seling Psychologist*, March 2003, p. 205.

22 See J. LLoyd, "Changing Workplace Requires You to Alter Your Career Outlook," *Milwaukee Journal Sentinel*, July 4, 1999, p. 1; A. LaPlante, "Serving Up Hot Projects," *Computerworld*, June 28, 1999; pp. CW29–CW33; and W. C. Byham, "Grooming Leaders," *Executive Excellence*, June 1999, p. 18.

23 T. McDonald, "Learning on the Line," *Successful Meetings*, August 2000, p. 37; and W. W. Conhaim, "Education Ain't What It Used to Be," *Infor-mation Today*, December 2003, 20(11), pp. 37–38.

24 S. Dillich, "Corporate Universities," *Computing Canada*, August 4, 2000, p. 25; and E. E. Gordon, "Bridging the Gap," September 2003, 40(8), p. 30.

25 http://www22.verizon.com/about/car/eers/codeofconduct.

26 http://www.hoovers.com/verizon.

27 Steven Rosenbush, Tom Lowry, Roger Crockett, and Irene Kunii, "Ver-izon's Gutsy Bet: Will Its Massive Rollout of Fiber-Optic Cable—Right to Customers' Homes and Offices—Keep It Ahead of the Pack?" *Busi-ness Week*, August 4, 2003, p. 52.

28 http://www.hoovers.com/boeing.

29 Stanley Holmes, "Boeing: What Really Happened," *Business Week*, December 15, 2003, p. 45.

30 "Boeing, Boeing, Gone," *Economist.com/Global Agenda*, London, December 2, 2003, p. 1.

31 For recent discussions of Yahoo! see T. Semel, "Yahoo!" *Business Week*, January 12, 2004, p. 64; and J. M. Pethokoukis, "Seeking an Edge Google Aims to Stay No. 1 in Search Engines as Big-Bucks Competi-tors Circle Around," *U.S. News & World Report*, November 3, 2003, 135(15), p. 38.

32 L. Pedersen, "Petworking," *New York Times*, October 22, 2000, p. CY.1.

APPENDIX A. STRATEGIC MANAGEMENT

1 For Gerstner's account of the revival of IBM, see L. V. Gerstner, Jr., *Who Says Elephants Can't Dance? Inside IBM's Historic Turnaround* (New York: HarperBusiness, 2002).

2 See, for instance, "The Nine Lives of Lou Gerstner," *The Economist*, June 7, 2003, p. 65; and, S. E. Ante, "The New Blue: Lou Gerstner Saved Big Blue. Now It's Up to New CEO Sam Palmisano to Restore It to Greatness," *Business Week*, March 17, 2002, pp. 80–87.

3 See "We Have Reinvented Ourselves Many Times," *Business Week*, March 17, 2003, p. 88; and J. O'Heir, "Sam I Am: Getting Down to E-Business at IBM," *CRN*, November 17, 2003, pp. 52–54, 56.

4 O'Heir, "Sam I Am," p. 54.

5 See, for instance, H. Dolezalek, "Don't Go," *Training*, July/August 2003, p. 52; J. Saba, "Preparing for Better Times," *Potentials*, January 2003, p. 6; D. Berta, "Wane in Hourly Workers' Turnover," *Nation's Restaurant News*, November 17, 2003, p. 16; and L. Lavelle, "After the Jobless Recovery, a War for Talent," *Business Week*, September 29, 2003, p. 92.

6 For discussions of political risks in Asia, Central America, and Europe, see "Calculating Risk," *Asiamoney*, November 2000, pp. 64–66; C. A. Rarick, "Determinants and Assessment of Political Risk in Central America," *S.A.M. Advanced Management Journal*, Summer 2000, pp. 41–46; and H. Ramcharran, "Foreign Direct Investments in Central and Eastern Europe: An Analysis of Regulatory and Country Risk Fac-tors," *American Business Review*, June 2000, pp. 1–8.

7 For example, see T. Powers, "Liberty and Justice for Almost All," *The Weekly Standard*, June 16, 2003, pp. 12–15; R. H. Bork, "Civil Liberties After 9/11," July/August 2003, pp. 29–35; and K. Shora and T. Edgar, "After 9/11, An Assault on Civil Liberties," *Trial*, October 2003, pp. 56–61.

8 See, for instance, C. Tejada, "A Special News Report About Life on the Job—and Trends Taking Place There," *Wall Street Journal*, October 10, 2000, p. A1; "More Companies Offering Same-Sex-Partner Benefits," *New York Times*, September 26, 2000, p. C2; A. C. Costello, "Domestic Partner Benefits in the Workplace," *Journal of Pension Benefits*, Autumn 2002, pp. 10–14; "Health Care Benefits of Domestic Partners," *The Kiplinger Letter*, July 25, 2003, p. 1; and "Benefits Boon," *The Advocate*, June 24, 2003, p. 34.

9 For example, see "New and Puzzling Images from the Mars Rover Spirit," *All Things Considered*, January 6, 2004, p. 1; "Stem-Cell Therapy; Therapeutic Clonic Generates Cloned, Compatible Stem Cells in Bovine Model," *Drug Week*, January 2, 2004, p. 586; "Chimp Genome; Draft Chimp Sequence Aligned with Human Genome,"

Drug Week, January 2, 2004, p. 165; E. Schwartz, "When Machines Speak," *InfoWorld*, November 17, 2003, p. 20; and "Taste Food Without Cooking," *Popular Mechanics*, December 2003, p. 28.

10 J. T. A. Gabel and N. R. Mansfield, "The Information Revolution and Its Impact on the Employment Relationship: An Analysis of the Cyberspace Workplace," *American Business Law Journal*, Winter 2003, pp. 301–353.

11 For views on the status and future of dot-coms, see R. Burton, "Future Trends," *Futurics*, 2002, *26(3/4)*, pp. 86–89; M. Veverka, "New Dot.Com Deal Signals Changing Times," *Barron's*, January 14, 2002, p. T3; T. Wasserman, "Dot-Com Survivors Build Brands," *Brandweek*, June 23, 2003, p. S66; and D. Kirkpatrick, "They're Back! Get Ready for Another Wave of Net IPOs," *Fortune*, September 15, 2003, pp. 216–217.

12 See T. A. Stetz and T. A. Beehr, "Organizations' Environment and Retirement: The Relationship Between Women's Retirement, Envi-ronmental Munificence, Dynamism, and Local Unemployment Rate," *Journals of Gerontology*, July 2000, pp. S213–S221; and D. R. DeTi-enne and C. R. Koberg, "The Impact of Environmental and Organiza-tional Factors on Discontinuous Innovation Within High Technology Industries," *IEEE Transactions on Engineering Management*, November 2002, pp. 352–364.

13 For discussions of the nature and roles of environmental uncertainty, see J. A. Parnell, D. L. Lester, and M. L. Menefee, "Strategy as a Response to Organizational Uncertainty: An Alternative Perspective on the Strategy-Performance Relationship," *Management Decision*, 2000, *38(8)*, pp. 520–530; P. Kreiser and L. Marino, "Analyzing the Historical Development of the Environmental Uncertainty Con-struct," *Management Decision*, 2002, *40(9)*, pp. 895–905; L. Bstieler and C. W. Gross, "Measuring the Effect of Environmental Uncertainty on Process Activities, Project Team Characteristics, and New Product Success," *Journal of Business & Industrial Marketing*, 2003, *18(2/3)*, pp. 146–161; and O. O. Sawyer, J. McGee, and M. Peterson, "Per-ceived Uncertainty and Firm Performance in SMEs: The Role of Per-sonal Networking Activities," *International Small Business Journal*, 2003, *21(3)*, pp. 269–288.

14 For recent applications of models of organizational effectiveness, see M. Zairi and Y. F. Jarrar, "Measuring Organizational Effectiveness n the NHS: Management Style and Structure Best Practices," *Total Quality Management & Business Excellence*, December 2001, pp. 882–889; G. B. Jordan, L. D. Streit, and J. S. Binkley, "Assessing and Improving the Effectiveness of National Research Laboratories," *IEEE Transactions on Engineering Management*, May 2003, pp. 228–235; and P. D.

Nobbie and J. L. Brudney, "Testing the Implementation, Board Performance, and Organizational Effectiveness of the Policy Governance Model in Nonprofit Boards of Directors," *Nonprofit and Voluntary Sector Quarterly*, December 2003, pp. 571–595.

[15] N. Stein, "America's Most Admired Companies," *Fortune*, March 3, 2003, p. 81.

[16] See "The Malcolm Baldrige Award—at a Glance," *Journal for Quality and Participation*, January/February 1999, p. 25; K. Sandrick, "Tops in Quality," *Trustee*, September 2003, pp. 12–16; and D. Hopen, "The Message Is Clear," *Quality Progress*, October 2003, pp. 50–58.

[17] For thorough discussions of strategic planning and the strategic planning process, see M. A. Hitt, R. D. Ireland, and R. E. Hoskisson, *Strategic Management: Competitiveness and Globalization*, 5th ed. (Cincinnati: South-Western, 2003); J. S. Harrison and C. H. St. John, *Foundations in Strategic Management*, 2nd ed. (Cincinnati: South-Western, 2002); and R. A. Pitts and D. Lei, *Strategic Management: Building and Sustaining Competitive Advantage*, 3rd ed. (Cincinnati: South-Western, 2003).

[18] See M. F. Turner, "How Does Your Company Measure Up?" *Black Enterprise*, November 2001, p. 52; P. Huxley, "The Contribution of Social Science to Mental Health Services Research and Development: A SWOT Analysis," *Journal of Mental Health*, April 2001, pp. 117–120; D. C. Barson, "Competing Intelligently," *Global Cosmetic Industry*, June 2002, pp. 26, 28; and J. S. Harrison, "Strategic Analysis for the Hospitality Industry," *Cornell Hotel and Restaurant Administration Quarterly*, 2003, *44(2)*, pp. 139–152.

[19] For more on vision statements, see "Vision Statement of the United States Marine Corps," *Leatherneck*, December 2000, p. 17; M. Jacobs, "Lonza's Vision," *Chemical & Engineering News*, April 29, 2002, p. 14; and "Preparing a Vision Statement," *The Futurist*, July/August 2002, p. 59.

[20] For discussions of mission statements, see E. Tarnow, "A Recipe for Mission and Vision Statements," *IEEE Transactions on Professional Communication*, 2001, *44(2)*, pp. 138–141; D. Ingman, J. Kersten, and T. Brymer, "Strategic Planning That Uses an Integrated Approach," *PM. Public Management*, May 2002, pp. 16–18; and G. A. Berg, M. Csikszentmihalyi, and J. Nakamura, "Mission Possible?" *Change*, September/October 2003, pp. 40–47.

[21] For instance, see G. Andrews, "Stuckey's Staples and Souvenirs Still Draw Traveling Customers," *Indianapolis Star News*, January 24, 1998. Pet, Inc., which purchased the Stuckey's chain in 1964, sold it back to William Stuckey, Jr., the son of the founder, in 1985. Stuckey's website says there are now over 200 franchised locations on interstate highways in 19 states.

[22] G. Fuchsberg, "'Visioning' Missions Becomes Its Own Mission," *Wall Street Journal*, January 7, 1994, pp. B1, B4. See also "It Pays to Give Employees a Personal Stake in Customer Care," *PHC Profit Report*, December 2000, p. 4.

[23] See, for instance, J. Laabs, "Has Downsizing Missed Its Mark?" *Workforce*, April 1999; R. Spiegel, "Are Distributors Cutting Muscle?" *Electronic News*, August 19, 2002, p. 4; and R. Pallium and Z. K. Shalhoub, "Rationalizing Corporate Downsizing with Long-Term Profitability—an Empirical Focus," *Management Decision*, 2002, pp. 436–447.

[24] S. Bell, "P&G Forced by Rivals to Change Old Habits," *Marketing*, June 17, 1999, p. 15.

[25] See R. Madapati, "Procter & Gamble: Organization 2005 and Beyond," *Global CEO*, May 2003, pp, 51–62; and J. Neff, "P&G Outpacing Unilever in Five-Year Battle," *Advertising Age*, November 3, 2003, p. 1.

[26] For discussions of the BCG model, see N. K. Taneja and G. R. Stearns, "Product Portfolio Planning for Airlines," *Transportation Journal*, Spring 1989, pp. 50–55; and J. H. Taggart and M. S. Harding, "The Process of Subsidiary Strategy: A Study of Ciba-Geigy Classical Pigments," *Management Decision*, 1998, *36(9)*, pp. 568–579.

[27] For a related discussion, see N. Shore, "Find the 'Seabiscuit' in Your Portfolio," *Brandweek*, September 15, 2003, pp. 23–24.

[28] R. E. Miles and C. C. Snow, *Organizational Strategy, Structure, and Process* (New York: McGraw-Hill, 1978). See also B. Burnes, "Organizational Choice and Organizational Change," *Management Decision*, 1997, *35(10)*, pp. 753–759; D. W. Vorhies and N. A. Morgan, "A Configuration Theory Assessment of Marketing Organization Fit with Business Strategy and Its Relationship with Marketing Performance," *Journal of Marketing*, 2003, *67(1)*, pp. 100–128; and N. G. Castle, "Strategic Groups and Outcomes in Nursing Facilities," *Health Care Management Review*, 2003, *28(3)*, pp. 217–227.

[29] For more on the model, see G. M. Stewart, "Put Yourself in a Strategic Position," *Industrial Engineer*, June 2001, pp. 30–32; S. Slater and E. Olson, "A Fresh Look at Industry and Market Analysis," *Business Horizons*, January/February 2002, pp. 15–22; and H. Barth, "Fit Among Competitive Strategy, Administrative Mechanisms, and Performance: A Comparative Study of Small Firms in Mature and New Industries," *Journal of Small Business Management*, 2003, *41(2)*, pp. 133–147. To learn more about Michael Porter and his views, see "Ranking the Gurus," *Electric Perspectives*, March/April 2003, p. 10; and K. H. Hammonds, "Michael Porter's Big Ideas," *Fast Company*, March 2001, pp. 150–155.

[30] For more on this issue, see D. Buss, "Sweet Success," *Brandweek*, May 12, 2003, pp. 22, 24; and "Sweeten Up Your Summer with Stevia," *Total Health*, June/July 2003, p. 48.

[31] See, for instance, D. Marlin, J. W. Huonker, and M. Sun, "An Examination of the Relationship Between Strategic Group Membership and Hospital Performance," *Health Care Management Review*, 2002, *27(4)*, pp. 18–29.

[32] C. Malburg, "Competing on Costs," *Industry Week*, October 16, 2000, p. 31.

[33] A. Z. Cuneo, "Rival Retailers Devise Ways to Compete Against Giant," *Advertising Age*, October 6, 2003, p. 35.

[34] B. Stone, "Back to Basics," *Newsweek*, August 4, 2003, p. 42.

[35] See R. S. Kaplan and D. P. Norton, *The Strategy-Focused Organization: How Balanced Scorecard Companies Thrive in the New Business Environment* (Boston: Harvard Business School Publishing, 2001); W. N. Zelman, G. H. Pink, and C. B. Matthias, "Use of the Balanced Scorecard in Health Care," *Journal of Health Care Finance*, 2003, *29(4)*, pp. 1–16; and "The Balanced Scorecard: One Approach to HR Metrics," *HR Focus*, October 2003, pp. S2–S3.

[36] Kaplan and Norton, The Strategy-Focused Organization.

Appendix B. Managing Careers

[1] S. Caudron, "HR Revamps Career Itineraries," *Personnel Journal*, April 1994, pp. 64A–64P.

[2] Charles Handy proposed the idea of the portfolio career. For discussions, see C. Rapoport, "Charles Handy Sees the Future," *Fortune*, October 31, 1994, pp. 155–160; A. Rogers, "Self Promotion," *Works Management*, March 1999, pp. 30–33; and C. G. Wagner, "The New Meaning of Work," *The Futurist*, September/October 2002, pp. 16–17.

[3] From D. T. Hall, *Careers in Organizations* (Glenview, IL: Scott-Foresman, 1976).

[4] For more on career identity, see A. S. M. Leung and S. R. Clegg, "The Career Motivation of Female Executives in the Hong Kong Public Sector," *Women in Management Review*, 2001, *16(1)*, pp. 12–20; B. H. Drake, M. Meckler, and D. Stephens, "Transitional Ethics: Responsibilities of Supervisors for Supporting Employee Development," *Journal of Business Ethics*, 2002, *38(1/2)*, pp. 141–155; D. M. Tokar, J. R. Withrow, R. J. Hall, and B. Moradi, "Psychological Separation, Attachment Security, Vocational Self-Concept Crystallization, and Career Indecision: A Structural Equation Analysis," *Journal of Counseling Psychology*, 2003, *50(1)*, pp. 3–19; and R. M. Orange, "The Emerging Mutable Self: Gender Dynamics and Creative Adaptations in Defining Work, Family, and the Future," *Social Forces*, 2003, *82(1)*, pp. 1–34.

[5] Hall, *Careers in Organizations*, p. 135.

[6] The first five of these problems are based primarily on R. A. Webber, "Career Problems of Young Managers," *California Management Review*, 1976, *18(4)*, pp. 11–33.

[7] "Blind Devotion Wanted?" *Wall Street Journal*, July 22, 1997, p. A1.

[8] For more on loyalty dilemmas, see M. Steen, "Loyalty Is a Two-Way Street, Readers Say, and the First Priority Is Your Own Career," *InfoWorld*, December 27, 1999/January 3, 2000, p. 73; and J. Wajcman and B. Martin, "My Company or My Career: Managerial Achievement and Loyalty," *British Journal of Sociology*, 2001, *52(4)*, pp. 559–578.

[9] For discussions of early career stress, see F. M. Weinstein, C. C. Healy, and P. E. Ender, "Career Choice Anxiety, Coping, and Perceived Control," *The Career Development Quarterly*, 2002, *50(4)*, pp. 339–349; and J. LaBeau, "Chronic Career Stress: What It Looks Like and What to

Do About It," *PM. Public Management*, 2003, *85(10)*, pp. 8–13.

10 See, for instance, "Ethical Decision Rewind," *Career World*, October 2003, p. 11; M. M. Ezarik, "Getting it Right," *Career World*, October 2003, pp. 6–11; and T. B. Orr, "What Would You Do If . . . ," *Career World*, April/May 2002, pp. 26–28.

11 L. A. Tansey, "Right vs. Wrong," *National Business Employment Weekly*, Spring/Summer 1994, pp. 11–12.

12 For more on ethical issues in careers, see J. W. Gauss, "Integrity Is Integral to Career Success," *Healthcare Financial Management*, August 2000, p. 89; H. Walls, "The Dog Ate My Ethics," *IIE Solutions*, September 2002, p. 24; and J. Schettler, "Just Like Starting Over," *Training*, December 2002, p. 78.

13 See C. D. Marsan, "Help Wanted: Uncle Sam Is Hiring," *Network World*, October 7, 2002, p. 57; J. Pont, "Leaps of Faith," *Potentials*, September 2003, p. 13; and J. A. Challenger, "The Coming Labor Shortage," *The Futurist*, September/October 2003, pp. 24–28.

14 G. Fuchsberg, "Canadian Firm Gives New Hires Job Guarantees," *Wall Street Journal*, July 16, 1991, pp. B1, B6.

15 E. Norton, "Young Indians Help Tribe Hit Comeback Trail," *Wall Street Journal*, October 5, 1992, p. B1. For more on job security, see J. S. Chatzky, "How Safe Is Your Job?" *Money*, December 2001, pp. 130–138; and K. Clark, "No Pink Slips at This Plant; Private Practices; St. Joe, Ind.," *U.S. News & World Report*, February 18, 2002, p. 40.

16 R. J. Lewicki, "Organizational Seduction: Building Commitment to Organizations," *Organizational Dynamics*, 1981, *10(2)*, pp. 5–22. For tips on maintaining healthy work/life balance, see "Achieving a Healthy Work/Life Balance," *Healthcare Executive*, May/June 2002, p. 38; and A. Cohen, "Survey Says: Workers Want Balance," *Sales and Marketing Management*, September 2002, p. 13.

17 D. T. Hall and D. S. Hall, "What's New in Career Management?" *Organizational Dynamics*, Summer 1976, pp. 17–33.

18 J. S. Livingston, "Pygmalion in Management," *Harvard Business Review*, 1969, *47(4)*, pp. 81–89, presents an interesting discussion of the powerful role that early career challenge and superiors' high expectations play in career growth. This was reprinted by the *Harvard Business Review* in 2003 as a "Best of *Harvard Business Review* article." For an intriguing presentation of the role of the self-fulfilling prophecy in careers and life, see R. Wiseman, "The Luck Factor," *The Skeptical Inquirer*, May/June 2003, pp. 26–30.

19 This discussion is based primarily on Hall, *Careers in Organizations*. See also B. P. Buunk and P. P. M. Janssen, "Relative Deprivation, Career Issues, and Mental Health Among Men in Midlife," *Journal of Vocational Behavior*, 1992, *40(3)*, pp. 338–350; J. Broady-Preston and S. Bell, "Motivating Mid-Career LIS Professionals: The Aberystwyth Experience," *New Library World*, 2001, *102(10)*, p. 372–381; and N. E. Betz, "A Proactive Approach to Midcareer Development," *Counseling Psychologist*, March 2003, pp. 205–211.

20 See T. P. Ference, J. A. Stoner, and E. K. Warren, "Managing the Career Plateau," *Academy of Management Review*, 1977, *2(4)*, p. 602; C.-T. Chau, "Career Plateaus," *The Internal Auditor*, October 1998, pp. 48–52; G. L. Cronin, "Looking Beyond the Career Plateau," *Safety & Health*, December 2001, p. 56; and J. A. Duffy, "The Application of Chaos Theory to the Career-Plateaued Worker," *Journal of Employment Counseling*, 2000, *37(4)*, pp. 229–236.

21 T. A. Allen, M. L. Poteet, and J. E. A. Russell, "Attitudes of Managers Who Are More or Less Career Plateaued," *The Career Development Quarterly*, 1998, *47(2)*, pp. 159–172.

22 T. A. Allen, J. E. A. Russell, M. L. Poteet, and G. H. Dobbins, "Learning and Development Factors Related to Perceptions of Job Content and Hierarchical Plateauing," *Journal of Organizational Behavior*, 1999, *20(7)*, pp. 1113–1137.

23 E. Jennings, *The Mobile Manager: Study of the New Generation of Top Executives* (Ann Arbor: Bureau of Industrial Relations, Graduate School of Business Administration, University of Michigan, 1967). See also J. R. Lincoln and Y. Nakata, "The Transformation of the Japanese Employment System: Nature, Depth, and Origins," *Work and Occupations*, February 1997, pp. 33–55.

24 J. Near, "Reactions to the Career Plateau," *Business Horizons*, July–August 1984, pp. 75–79; and N. Nicholson, "Purgatory or Place of Safety? The Managerial Plateau and Organizational Age Grading," *Human Relations*, 1993, *46(12)*, pp. 1369–1389. See also D. L. Montgomery, "Happily Ever After: Plateauing as a Means for Long-Term Job Satisfaction," *Library Trends*, 2002, *50(4)*, pp. 702–718.

25 M. J. McCarthy, "Plateaued Workers Cause Big Damage," *Wall Street Journal*, August 17, 1988, p. 21.

26 E. L. Pavalko, G. H. Elder, Jr., and E. C. Clipp, "Worklives and Longevity: Insights from a Life Course Perspective," *Journal of Health and Social*

Behavior, 1993, *34(4)*, pp. 363–380. This study also found sharply elevated mortality rates for individuals who experienced a period in which they moved through a series of unrelated jobs.

27 For discussions, see C. Jack, "Life Stages: A Successful Roadmap to Pre-Retirement Planning," *National Underwriter*, October 27, 2003, pp. 21, 39; and K. Isaacson, "Retirement: One Size Doesn't (and Shouldn't) Fit All," *Women in Business*, November/December 2003, pp. 12–13.

28 E. H. Schein, *Career Dynamics: Matching Individual and Organizational Needs* (Reading, MA: Addison-Wesley, 1978). For an extension of this model, see J. A. Katz, "Modelling Entrepreneurial Career Progressions: Concepts and Considerations," *Entrepreneurship Theory and Practice*, Winter 1994, pp. 23–29.

29 For more on moving into the inner circle, see R. W. Shrader, "Earning a Place in the Inner Circle: Truth and Trust," *Vital Speeches of the Day*, September 1, 2002, pp. 717–720.

30 J. S. Lublin, "Strategic Sidling: Lateral Moves Aren't Always a Mistake," *Wall Street Journal*, August 4, 1993, p. B1.

31 A. Bennett, "Path to Top Job Now Twists and Turns," *Wall Street Journal*, March 15, 1993, p. B1.

32 These examples are from J. E. Rigdon, "Using Lateral Moves to Spur Employees," *Wall Street Journal*, May 26, 1992, p. B1. For more on lateral moves, see J. Sweat, "Staying Put," *InformationWeek*, January 21, 2002, pp. 36–40.

33 For discussions of person-career fit, see J. Arenofsky, "Creating Your Career Path," *Career World*, September 2001, pp. 6–10; T. J. Wallis, "Be Creative in Choosing a Career," *Career World*, 2002, *31(1)*, pp. 17–19; D. DeMan, "Know When to Bail," *Pharmaceutical Executive*, November 2002, pp. 102–105; D. M. Cable and D. S. DeRue, "The Convergent and Discriminant Validity of Subjective Fit Perceptions," *Journal of Applied Psychology*, 2002, *87(5)*, pp. 875–884; and F. Bartolome and P. A. L. Evans, "Managerial Misfits," *Harvard Business Review*, 2003, *81(5)*, p. 132.

34 For more on Schein's career anchors, see D. C. Feldman, *Managing Careers in Organizations* (Glenview, IL: Scott, Foresman, 1988), pp. 101–106; P. R. Sparrow, "Reappraising Psychological Contracting," *International Studies of Management & Organization*, Spring 1998, pp. 30–63; P. Simonsen and L. Davidson, "Do Your Managers Have the Right Stuff?" *Workforce*, August 1999, pp. 47–52; and H.-H. Tan and B.-C. Quek, "An Exploratory Study on the Career Anchors of Educators in Singapore," *Journal of Psychology*, 2001, *135(5)*, pp. 527–544.

35 E. H. Schein, "Career Anchors and Career Paths: A Panel Study of Management School Graduates," in J. Van Maanen (Ed.), *Organizational Careers: Some New Perspectives* (London, Wiley-Interscience, 1977), p. 63.

36 D. C. Feldman, and M. C. Bolino, "Career Patterns of the Self-Employed: Career Motivations and Career Outcomes," *Journal of Small Business Management*, 2000, *38(3)*, pp. 53–67.

37 S. Overman, "Weighing Career Anchors," *HRMagazine*, March 1993, pp. 56, 58.

38 J. Holland, *The Psychology of Vocational Choice* (Waltham, MA: Blaisdell, 1966); J. Holland, *Making Vocational Choices: A Theory of Vocational Personalities and Work Environments* (Odessa, FL: Psychological Assessment Resources, 1985). See also F. D. Fruyt and I. Mervielde, "RIASEC Types and Big Five Traits as Predictors of Employment Status and Nature of Employment," *Personnel Psychology*, Autumn 1999, pp. 701–727; and A. A. Helwig, "The Measurement of Holland Types in a 10-Year Longitudinal Study of a Sample of Students," *Journal of Employment Counseling*, 2003, *40(1)*, pp. 24–32.

39 See D. C. Feldman and H. J. Arnold, "Personality Types and Career Patterns: Some Empirical Evidence on Holland's Model," *Canadian Journal of Administrative Sciences*, 1985, *2(2)*, pp. 192–210, for one supportive study. For a analysis on the issue, which raises some questions about the links of congruence to satisfaction, see M. Tranberg, S. Slane, and S. E. Ekeberg, "The Relation Between Interest Congruence and Satisfaction: A Meta-Analysis," *Journal of Vocational Behavior*, 1993, *42(3)*, pp. 253–264. See also D. R. Pietrzak and B. J. Page, "An Investigation of Holland Types and the Sixteen Personality Factor Questionnaire, Fifth Edition," *The Career Development Quarterly*, 2001, *50(2)*, p. 179–188.

40 The following discussion is based largely on M. J. Driver, "Career Concepts and Career Management in Organizations," in C. L. Cooper (Ed.), *Behavioral Problems in Organizations* (Englewood Cliffs, NJ: Prentice-Hall, 1979). For more on career concept types, see F. A. E. McQuarrie and E. L. Jackson, "Transitions in Leisure Careers and Their Parallels in Work Careers: The Effect of Constraints on Choice and Action," *Journal of Career Development*, 2002, *29(1)*, pp. 37–53; and

R. N. Llewellyn, "The Four Career Concept Types," *HR Magazine,* September 2002, pp. 121–124. In the latter article, steady state individuals are referred to as "experts" and transitory individuals as "roamers."

41 D. Seligman, "Luck and Careers," *Fortune,* November 16, 1981, pp. 60–66, 70, 72, and R. Wiseman, "The Luck Factor," *The Skeptical Inquirer,* May/June 2003, pp. 26–30, present interesting discussions of the role of luck in careers.

42 S. E. Murphy and E. A. Ensher, "The Role of Mentoring Support and Self-Management Strategies on Reported Career Outcomes," *Journal of Career Development,* 2001, *27(4),* pp. 229–246.

43 J. Sturges, D. Guest, N. Conway, and K. M. Davey, "A Longitudinal Study of the Relationship Between Career Management and Organizational Commitment Among Graduates in the First Ten Years at Work," *Journal of Organizational Behavior,* 2002, *23(6),* pp. 731–748.

44 Hall, *Careers in Organizations,* pp. 179–189. For more on self-management of careers, see E. H. Fram, "Today's Mercurial Career Path," *Management Review,* November 1994, pp. 40–43; S. R. Covey, "The New Contract," *Executive Excellence,* January 1996, pp. 3–5; C. Maxey, "No More Mr. Nice Guy," *Training & Development,* 1999, *53(6),* pp. 17–18; and Z. King, "Career Self-Management: A Framework for Guidance of Employed Adults," *British Journal of Guidance & Counselling,* 2001, *29(1),* pp. 65–78.

45 J. O. Crites, *Theory and Research Handbook, Career Maturity Inventory* (Monterey, CA: McGraw-Hill, 1973). For more on career competencies, see L. T. Eby, M. Butts, and A. Lockwood, "Predictors of Success in the Era of the Boundaryless Career," *Journal of Organizational Behavior,* 2003, *24(6),* pp. 689–708.

46 See the Web-Wise materials on the text website for related resources. See also G. Brong, "Fact Based Career Decisions," *Quality Progress,* August 2003, p. 88.

47 For guidelines for career planning, see K. Daly, "Directing Your Future," *Career World,* November/December 2003, pp. 5–7.

48 See, for instance, "Not Asking for Help Is Top Networking Mistake," *USA Today,* August 2003, p. 6; and B. McLean, "Networking Lessons," *Fortune,* November 10, 2003, p. 192.

49 "Families with Both Parents Employed Are Now a U.S. Majority," *Work & Family Life,* January 2001, p. 1.

50 For challenges faced by dual-career couples, see D. M. Doumas, G. Margolin, and R. S. John, "The Relationship Between Daily Marital Interaction, Work, and Health-Promoting Behaviors in Dual-Career Couples: An Extension of the Work-Family Spillover Model," *Journal of Family Issues,* 2003, *24(1),* pp. 3–20; R. Batt and P. Valcour, "Human Resources Practices as Predictors of Work-Family Outcomes and Employee Turnover," *Industrial Relations,* April 2003, pp. 189–220; and K. C. Gareis, R. C. Barnett, and R. T. Brennan, "Individual and Crossover Effects of Work Schedule Fit: A Within-Couple Analysis," *Journal of Marriage and Family,* 2003, *65(4),* pp. 1041–1054.

51 S. F. Gale, "Taxing Situations for Expatriates," *Workforce,* 2003, *82(6),* pp. 100–107.

52 C. Butler, "A World of Trouble," *Sales and Marketing Management,* September 1999, pp. 44–50.

53 Ibid. For more on expatriates, see Y. Paik and C. M. Vance, "Evidence of Back-Home Selection Bias Against US Female Expatriates," *Women in Management Review,* 2002, *17(2),* pp. 68–79; A. Halcrow, "Expats: The Squandered Resource," *Workforce,* 1999, *78(4),* pp. 42–46; and E. Janush, "Management of the Cross Border Employees Function," *Employee Benefits Journal,* 2003, *28(2),* pp. 50–54.

54 For instance, see V. Skorikov and F. W. Vondracek, "Career Development in the Commonwealth of Independent States," *The Career Development Quarterly,* June 1993, pp. 314–329; and A. Yan, G. Zhu, and D. T. Hall, "International Assignments for Career Building: A Model of Agency Relationships and Psychological Contracts," *Academy of Management Review,* 2002, *27(3),* pp. 373–391.

55 For discussions of the glass ceiling and companies' attempts to break it, see L. E. Wynter and J. Solomon, "A New Push to Break the 'Glass Ceiling,'" *Wall Street Journal,* November 15, 1989, pp. B1, B10; and J. S. Lublin, "Firms Designate Some Openings for Women Only," *Wall Street Journal,* February 7, 1994, p. B1. Although the dearth of women in top management positions supports the idea of a glass ceiling, research specifically addressing the phenomenon is lacking. For one study (which failed to find support for the phenomenon in a government setting), see G. N. Powell and D. A. Butterfield, "Investigating the 'Glass Ceiling' Phenomenon: An Empirical Study of Actual Promotions to Top Management," *The Academy of Management Journal,* 1994, *37(1),* pp. 68–86.

56 L. Koss-Feder, "U.S. Women: Number of Women in Top Corporate Jobs Rises," *Global Information Network,* February 14, 2003, p. 1. See also M. Bertrand and K. F. Hallock, "The Gender Gap in Top Corporate Jobs," *Industrial & Labor Relations Review,* 2001, *55(1),* pp. 3–21.

57 G. Epstein, "Breaking the Glass," *Barron's,* May 26, 2003, pp. 17–19. For more on the glass ceiling, see R. H. Chernesky, "Examining the Glass Ceiling: Gender Influences on Promotion Decisions," *Administration in Social Work,* 2003, *27(2),* pp. 13–16; G. H. Dreher, "Breaking the Glass Ceiling: The Effects of Sex Rations and Work-Life Programs on Female Leadership at the Top," *Human Relations,* 2003, *56(5),* pp. 541–562; and B. Kiviat, "The Partnership Glass Ceiling," *Time,* November 3, 2003, p. 103.

58 See J. A. Lopez, "Study Says Women Face Glass Walls as Well as Ceilings," *Wall Street Journal,* March 3, 1992, p. B1; D. L. Collins, A. Reitenga, A. B. Collins, and S. Lane, "'Glass Walls' in Academic Accounting? The Role of Gender in Initial Employment Position," *Issues in Accounting Education,* 2000, *15(3),* pp. 371–391; B. Kerr, W. Miller, and M. Reid, "Sex-Based Occupational Segregation in U.S. State Bureaucracies, 1987–1997," *Public Administration Review,* 2002, *62(4),* pp. 412–423; and M. Hultin, "Some Take the Glass Escalator, Some Hit the Glass Ceiling? Career Consequences of Occupational Sex Segregation," *Work and Occupations,* 2003, *39(1),* pp. 30–61.

59 For discussions of the status of women in management, see D. R. Dalton and C. M. Daily, *Across the Board,* November/December 1998, pp. 16–20; and S. Mavin, "Women's Career in Theory and Practice: Time for a Change?" *Women in Management Review,* 2001, *16(4),* pp. 183–192.

60 See D. L. Vogel, S. R. Wester, M. Heesacker, and S. Madon, "Confirming Gender Stereotypes: A Social Role Perspective," *Sex Roles,* 2003, *48(11/12),* pp. 519–528; and N. Lane and N. F. Piercy, "The Ethics of Discrimination: Organizational Mindsets and Female Employment Disadvantage," *Journal of Business Ethics,* 2003, *44(4),* pp. 313–326.

61 V. Singh, S. Kumra, and S. Vinnicombe, "Gender and Impression Management: Playing the Promotion Game," *Journal of Business Ethics,* 2002, *37(1),* pp. 77–89.

62 L. D. Tyson, "New Clues to the Pay and Leadership Gap," *Business Week,* October 27, 2003, p. 36.

63 S. Gill and M. J. Davidson, "Problems and Pressures Facing Lone Mothers in Management and Professional Occupations—a Pilot Study," *Women in Management Review,* 2001, *16(7/8),* pp. 383–399.

64 L. D. Tyson, "New Clues to the Pay and Leadership Gap," *Business Week,* October 27, 2003, p. 36.

65 A. L. Otten, "Gender Pay Gap Eased over Last Decade," *Wall Street Journal,* April 15, 1994, p. B1; K. T. Greenfield, "What Glass Ceiling?" *Time,* August 2, 1999, p. 72; and L. Stein, "Glass Ceiling News Business," *U.S. News and World Report,* December 15, 2003, p. 14.

66 P. J. Ohlott, M. N. Ruderman, and C. D. McCauley, "Gender Differences in Managers' Developmental Experience," *The Academy of Management Journal,* 1994, *37(1),* pp. 46–67.

67 B. P. Noble, "At Work: Making a Case for Family Programs," *New York Times,* May 2, 1993, p. 25; and A. L. Saltzstein, Y. Ting, and G. H. Saltzstein, "Work-Family Balance and Job Satisfaction: The Impact of Family-Friendly Policies on Attitudes of Federal Government Employees," *Public Administration Review,* 2001, *61(4),* pp. 452–467.

68 M. Galen, A. T. Palmer, A. Cuneo, and M. Maremont, "Work and Family," *Business Week,* June 28, 1993, pp. 80–88; J. Kiser, "Behind the Scenes at a 'Family Friendly' Workplace," *Dollars & Sense,* January/February 1998, pp. 19–21.

69 R. Sharpe, "Being Family Friendly Doesn't Mean Promoting Women," *Wall Street Journal,* March 29, 1994, pp. B1, B5. See also G. H. Albrecht, "How Friendly Are Family Friendly Policies?" *Business Ethics Quarterly,* 2003, *13(2),* pp. 177–192.

70 See P. Symons, "The Career Pathing Question," *Credit Union Management,* April 1994, pp. 11–12; and C. Caggiano, "A Path for Employee Growth," *Inc,* August 1998, p. 11.

71 See, for instance, M. M. Elvira and C. D. Zatzick, "Who's Displaced First? The Role of Race in Layoff Decisions," *Industrial Relations,* 2002, *41(2),* pp. 329–361.

72 J. A. Lopez, "Companies Alter Layoff Policies to Keep Recently Hired Women and Minorities," *Wall Street Journal,* September 18, 1992, pp. B1, B16.

73 See M. Galen and A. T. Palmer, "White, Male, and Worried," *Business Week,* January 31, 1994, pp. 50–55.

74 See P. Fagerberg, "American Express," *Black Collegian,* October 2003, pp. 74–75; and A. Finnegan, "Leading from the Top: American Express," *Working Mother,* June/July 2003, pp. 52–53.

75 A. Zuber, "Minority Franchisees Prosper with Help from McD Support Groups," *Nation's Restaurant News,* February 14, 2000, pp. 26–27; M. Lord, "They're Online and on the Job; Managers and Hamburger Flip-

pers Are Being E-Trained at Work," *U.S. News and World Report*, October 15, 2001, p. 72; and D. Berta, "McD Offers Philadelphia Managers College Credits," *Nation's Restaurant News*, March 19, 2001, p. 18.

76 "The Benefit of Inclusion," *The Advocate*, June 10, 2003, p. 171; and M. M. Naula, A. M. Saucier, and L. E. Woodard, "Interpersonal Influences on Students' Academic and Career Decisions: The Impact of Sexual Orientation," *The Career Development Quarterly*, 2001, *49(4)*, pp. 352–373.

77 S. Degges-White and M. F. Shoffner, "Career Counseling with Lesbian Clients: Using the Theory of Work Adjustment as a Framework," *The Career Development Quarterly*, 2002, *51(1)*, pp. 87–96.

78 Ibid. See also Y. B. Chung, "Career Counseling with Lesbian, Gay, Bisexual, and Transgendered Persons: The Next Decade," *The Career Development Quarterly*, 2003, *52(1)*, pp. 78–86.

79 K. E. Kram, "Phases in the Mentor Relationship," *Academy of Management Journal*, 1983, *26(4)*, pp. 608–625; and K. E. Kram, "Mentoring in the Workplace," in D. T. Hall and associates (Eds.), *Career Development in Organizations* (San Francisco: Jossey-Bass, 1986), pp. 160–201. See also G. T. Chao, "Invited Reaction: Challenging Research in Mentoring," *Human Resource Development Quarterly*, Winter 1998, pp. 333–338.

80 D. B. Turban and T. W. Dougherty, "Role of Protégé Personality and Receipt of Mentoring and Career Success," *Academy of Management Journal*, 1994, *37(3)*, pp. 688–702..

81 This discussion is based largely on R. J. Burke and C. A. McKeen, "Mentoring in Organizations: Implications for Women," *Journal of Business Ethics*, 1990, *9(4–5)*, pp. 317–332. See also D. C. Feldman, "Toxic Mentors or Toxic Protégés? A Critical Re-Examination of Dysfunctional Mentoring," *Human Resource Management Review*, 1999, *9(3)*, pp. 247–278; B. R. Ragins and T. A. Scandura, "Burden or Blessing? Expected Costs and Benefits of Being a Mentor," *Journal of Organizational Behavior*, May 1999, pp. 493–509; and J. Perrone, "Creating a Mentoring Culture," *Healthcare Executive*, May/June 2003, pp. 84–85.

82 G. Dreher and R. Ash, "A Comparative Study of Mentoring Among Men and Women in Managerial, Professional and Technical Positions," *Journal of Applied Psychology*, 1990, *75(5)*, pp. 525–535; E. A. Fagenson, "The Mentor Advantage: Perceived Career/Job Experiences of Protégés vs. Non-Protégés," *Journal of Organizational*

Behavior, 1989, *10(4)*, pp. 309–320; and J. Conklin, "The Benefits of Mentoring," *Quality Progress*, 2002, *35(11)*, p. 91.

83 See, for instance, R. M. O'Neill and S. D. Blake-Beard, "Gender Barriers to the Female Mentor-Male Protégé Relationship," *Journal of Business Ethics*, 2002, *37(1)*, pp. 51–63.

84 J. A. Lopez, "Being Your Boss's Pal May Be Hazardous to Your Career," *Wall Street Journal*, June 8, 1994, p. B1.

85 B. Raabe and T. A. Beehr, "Formal Mentoring versus Supervisor and Coworker Relationships: Differences in Perceptions and Impact," *Journal of Organizational Behavior*, 2003, *24(3)*, pp. 271–294.

86 Ibid.

87 B. Goldsmith, "Creating a Company Mentoring Program," *Office Solutions*, January/February 2003, pp. 42–43.

88 F. Warner, "Inside Intel's Mentoring Movement," *Fast Company*, April 2002, pp. 116–120.89. This section is from L. Ambrose, "Multiple Mentoring," *Healthcare Executive*, July/August 2003, pp. 58–59.

90 M. C. Higgins and K. E. Kram, "Reconceptualizing Mentoring at Work: A Developmental Network Perspective," *Academy of Management Review*, 2001, *26(2)*, pp. 264–288.

91 E. Neuborne, "Mentors as Motivators," *Potentials*, March 2003, p. 16.

92 S. B. Knouse, "Virtual Mentors: Mentoring on the Internet," *Journal of Employment Counseling*, 2001, *38(4)*, pp. 162–169.

93 L. Ambrose, "Long-Distance Mentoring," *Healthcare Executive*, March/April 2003, pp. 62–63. See also A. Field, "No Time to Mentor? Do It Online. E-mail Offers Busy Professionals a Way to Give Back," *Business Week*, March 3, 2003, p. 126.

94 For summaries of issues relating to mentoring for women and minorities in organizations, see R. J. Burke and C. A. McKeen, "Mentoring in Organizations: Implications for Women," *Journal of Business Ethics*, 1990, *9(4–5)*, pp. 317–332; D. A. Thomas, "The Truth About Mentoring Minorities: Race Matters," *Harvard Business Review*, 2001, *79(4)*, pp. 98–112; and J. Barbian, "The Road Less Traveled," *Training*, May 2002, pp. 38–40.

95 A. B. Fisher, "When Will Women Get to the Top?" *Fortune*, September 21, 1992, pp. 44–56; M. B. White, "A Day in the Life of a Diversity Manager," *Diversity Factor*, Winter 1999, pp. 42–43; and L. Stansky, "Corporate Counsel Push for Diversity," *National Law Journal*, 2003, *25(34)*, p. A14.

COMPANY INDEX

SUBJECT INDEX

functions of, *535*, 535–37
GE case study, 554–56
heroes, 541–42
importance of, 532, 534–35
learning cultures, 589
narratives, 539–41
rites, 542–43
subcultures and countercultures, 544–45
symbols, 539
values, 537–38
W. B. Doner case study, 557
culture insurance, 545
cultures, national
    communication and, 55, 302, 304–6, *306*
    conflict resolution and, 421–22
    cross-cultural differences, 53–55, *56*
Cuomo, Mario, 600
customer focus and satisfaction, in Baldrige Award criteria, A-9
customers, bargaining power of, A-22

D

Daft, Douglas, 43
databases, journal, 614
De Geus, Arie, 585
"deadwood," B-8–B-9
Deal, Terrence, 548
dealing with others, in job characteristics model, 194
death march, 218
Deavenport, Earnest, 570
decision confirmation, 110
decision control, 100–101
decision making, 99, 100, 139, 535. *See also* problem solving
decoding, in communication process, 279, *280*
deep breathing, 243
defamation suits, 504
defender strategy, A-20
defense mechanisms, and job size, 192, *193*
defensive avoidance, 110
defensive behaviors, as political tactics, 387, 388
delayering, and managerial skills, 11
DeLorean, John, 545
"The delusion of learning from experience," 587
Deming, W. Edwards, 509
Deming cycle, 102
democratic leaders, 330, *330*, 332
demotion, 503
Denardo, Dan, 300
departmental boundaries, B-11
depersonalizing, 388
deregulation, A-5
development and training. *See* training
developmental needs in careers, *B-5*
developmental networks, B-25
devil's advocate, and teams, 460
Dibra, Bash, 622
differentiation, and conflict, 412–13
differentiation strategy, A-23

the Dilbert Zone, 487
dilemmas, and problem solving, 97
direct analogy, 116
direct experience, in attitude formation, 71
directive leadership, 335
Disclosure (film), 12, 30
discrimination. *See* diversity and differences
discriminatory questions in interviewing, 493
discussion management, in teams, 456–57
displacement, 73
dispositional determinants of job satisfaction, 68–69
dissatisfaction, *73*, 73–74, B-4. *See also* satisfaction
dissonance reduction, 79–80, 110
distance, interpersonal, 454–55, *455*
distraction, as barrier to communication, 284
distress, 221, *222*
distributive approaches to negotiation, 128, *128*
distributive fairness, 184–85, 190
divergent thinking, 97
diversity and differences
    attitude-behavior relationships, 64, *65*, 71–80
    attitudes, *63*, 63–65, 71
    attitudes, changing, 43–44
    career development for women and minorities, B-17–B-21
    creativity and, 125–26
    cross-cultural, 53–55, *56*
    cultural change and, 551
    definition of diversity, 38
    mentoring of women and minorities, B-25
    minorities, best companies for, 41
    personality, 45–53
    personnel policies, 44–45, *45*
    Pfizer case study, 83–84
    rewarding efforts, 43
    training for tolerance, 42–43
    value and benefits of, 40, 83
DNA screening, 498
dogmatism, 50
"dogs," A-17
Dogspeak (Dibra), 622
domains, environmental, *A-2*, A-2–A-5
dominance, as use of power, 366
dominating alternative, 98
dotcoms, 301
downsizing
    causes of, 503
    commitment and, 71
    delayering, 11
    diversity and, 44
    identifying losses, 577
    managerial skills and, 11
    women and minorities, and layoff policies, B-20
downward communication, 288
dress, as nonverbal communication, 296–97

Drew, Ernest H., 41
Driver, Michael, B-14
Drucker Foundation, 396, 591
drug testing, 497
Druyun, Darleen A., 620
Duell, Charles, 595
duplication of communication channels, 280
dyads, 443–44
dynamism, A-5

E

e-commerce, 300–302
e-mail, 297–98, 314, 612–13
e-tailers, 301
EAPs (employee assistance programs), 235–36
Eastman Performance Plan, 570
economic domain of organizational environment, A-2–A-3
economic value orientation, 382
Edison, Thomas, 554
education. *See* skills learning and development; training
educational techniques for change, 583
Edwards, Karen, 621
effect, law of, 160
effectiveness
    employee, work-unit, and organizational levels, *20*, 21
    organizational, A-6–A-8, *A-7*, A-9
    organizational culture and, *546*, 546–49, *550*
effort, in expectancy theory, 181
Einstein, Albert, 119
eldercare, as stressor, 226
electronic communication, 297–303
electronic mailing lists, 612–13
elimination by aspects, 98
Emerson, Ralph Waldo, 85
emoticons, 314
emotional appeals, 372–73
emotional arousal, 377
emotional exhaustion, 228
emotional frame for conflict, 410
emotional intelligence (EQ), 45–48
emotional labor, 224
emotional stability, 52
emotions, controlling in negotiations, 130
emotive function of communication, 279
empire-building game, 390
employee assistance programs (EAPs), 235–36
employee attitude surveys, 289, 317–18
employee effectiveness, in management skills framework, *20*, 21
employee stock option plans (ESOPs), 514–15
empowerment
    at Federal Express, 379
    managerial skills and, 11
    powerlessness, 374–75
    process model, *378*
    process of, 375–78, *376*

social responsibility and, at Levi
    Strauss, 265
trends, 53–54
GNS (growth-need strength), 197
goal acceptance, 170
goal assessments approach, A-6
goal commitment, 170
goal selection, and career manage-
    ment, B-15
goal-setting theory, 151, *168,* 168–70,
    171, 209–10
goals
    conflict and, 412, 419
    path–goal theory, 334–36, *336*
    self-management and, 174
    team problems and, 452
    unethical behavior and, 259–60
Goleman, Daniel, 46
golfing, 355
Gordon, J. J., 116
Gordon technique, 116, *120*
Gore, Al, 600
Gore, Bill, 176
governments, foreign, A-3. *See also*
    globalization
graduates, hiring criteria for, 9–10
Graham, Ginger, 261
grand strategies, A-14–A-16, *A-16,*
    A-19
grapevine, 302
graphology, 498–99
Greenleaf, Robert K., 349
Greer, George, 110
Gretzky, Wayne, 602
grievances, 288–89
grieving, signs of, 578, *578*
group brainstorming, 460–61
groups. *See* teams
GroupSystems software, 461
Grove, Andrew, 53
"growth at any cost," A-17
growth-need strength (GNS), 197
growth needs, 155, 158
growth strategy, A-14
Gung Ho (film), 544, 559

H

Haas, Robert, 265–66
Hackborn, Richard, 427
Haft family, 417
Hagler, Don, 504
Hall, Douglas, B-1–B-3
Halo effect, 59–60, 285
Hammurabi, Code of, 256
hand movements, 295
handbooks, 288
handoffs, 124
handwriting analysis, 498–99
haptic interface, 507
hardiness, and stress, 227
Harvard Business Review (HBR), 608
hassles, as stressors, 225
Hawthorne, Laverne, 621
health consequences of plateauing,
    B-9
health risk appraisal, 234
Henry-Coan, Brenda, 471
Heraclitus, 564

Hering Illusion, 58, *59*
heroes, 541–42
Herrman, Jack, 314
heuristics, 107–9
Hewlett, Bill, 541
Hewlett, Walter, 426
hierarchical boundaries, B-10–B-11
hierarchical plateaus, B-8
hierarchy of needs (Maslow), 153–54,
    154
high-context cultures, 55, 305
high-tech training, 506–7
Hippolite, Glory, 400
hiring and selection. *See also*
    staffing
    application forms, 490–91
    assessment centers, 499–500
    forward-looking approach, 12
    interviews, 492–94, *495*
    managerial skills and, 9–10
    online recruiting, 301
    process model, *501*
    references, 491–92
    résumé bloopers and unusual
        interviews, 522–23
    role of, 489–90
    teams, selection for, 500
    testing, 494–99
    at Toyota, 490
Hofstede, Geert, 54
Holland, Robert, 522
home-run philosophy, 124
Homer, B-21
homicide, workplace, 408
honesty, 258, 284–85, 496–97
Hoosiers (film), 575, 597
hot groups, 450
hotlines, ethics, 261
hourly employees, talent develop-
    ment among, B-20
House, Robert, 334–35
Housman, A. E., 115
HR-guide.com, 517–18
human change, 568
human resources management
    in Baldrige Award Criteria, A-9
    compensation, 43, 512–15, *515*
    demotion, 503
    importance of, 482
    lateral moves, 502
    Next Door Food Store case study,
        521
    organizational development and,
        585
    orientation, 501–2
    performance appraisal, 43, 508–12
    placement, 501–4
    promotion, 502–3
    recruiting, 485–89, *490*
    recruiting case study (EDS), 518–19
    résumé bloopers, 522
    selection (*See* hiring and selection)
    staffing vs. training, 484–85, *485*
    termination, 503–4
    training and development (*See*
        training)
    upward appraisal case study
        (FedEx), 519–21

human skills, in management skills
    framework, 19, *20*
humanistic-existential theories, 48
humor, and conflict, 430
hypertext, 299

I

"I am my position," 586
"I Have a Dream" speech (King),
    344–46
I-mode cell phones, 301–2
idea champions, 122–23
idea checklists, 117–18
idealized influence, 342
identification, and social influence,
    374
identity, career, B-3
Ig Nobel Prizes, 139–40
"The illusion of taking charge,"
    587
immediacy of communication chan-
    nels, 280
Immelt, Jeffrey, 342, 554
impairment testing, 497
implicit theories, 61
impression management, 387–90
"in basket" test, 499
in-groups and out-groups, 338–39
In Search of Excellence (Peters and
    Waterman), 276, 538, 546–48,
    607
incentives. *See* motivation; rewards
inclusion boundaries, B-10–B-11
incrementalizing, 109, 116
incubation, in creative process, 115
independence, as career anchor,
    B-12–B-13
independent studies, 603
individualistic cultures, 54
individualized consideration, 342
indoctrination, 80
industry attractiveness, in GE matrix,
    A-18–A-19
industry forces, in competitive model,
    A-21–A-22
influence. *See also* power
    definition, 366
    idealized, 342
    leadership as, 326
    Microsoft Xbox case study,
        398–400
    social influence tactics, 371–74
informal mentoring, B-24
information
    in Baldrige Award Criteria, A-9
    communication and, 278–79
    conservatism in processing, 109–10
    defensive avoidance, 110
    equity rules and, 189
    "perfect," 104
    problem solving, influence on, 104
    retention of, 285, 287
    sharing of, in negotiations, 131–32
    subordinate need for, 333
ingratiation, 371, 372
initiating structure, 332, *333*
initiation phase, in mentoring, B-
    21–B-22

innovation, and technological domain, A-4
input-outcome equation, in equity theory, 186
insensitivity, in young managers, *B-5*
insight, in creative process, 115
inspirational appeals, 371
inspirational leadership, 342
instrumentality, in expectancy theory, 180–81, 182
insurgency game, 390
integration, rites of, 543
integrative approach to negotiation, *128,* 128–29, 131
integrity tests, 496–97
intellectual frame for conflict, 410
intellectual stimulation, and leadership, 342
intelligence, emotional (EQ), 45–48
intelligence quotient (IQ), 46
interests, negotiating from, 130
interests tests, 495
intergroup activities, and change, 583
internal coalitions, 385
internal competition. *See* competition
internal monopolies, 125
internal networkers, 588
internal process assessment, A-6
internalization, and social influence, 374
international assignments. *See* globalization
Internet and the World Wide Web
    corporate portals, 299
    description of, 298–99
    e-mail, 297–98, 314, 612–13
    as learning resource, 614
    Netiquette, 298, 308
    recruiting on, 487–88
    virtual networks, 612–13
internships, 603
interpersonal conflict. *See* conflict
interpersonal dimensions, in job characteristics model, 194–95
interpersonal distance, and teams, 454–55, *455*
interpersonal intelligence, 46
interpersonal power bases, 367–68
interpersonal skills, 19, *20,* 384
interpersonal space, 297
interpretation of stimuli, in perceptual process, *57,* 58–60
interviews, 67, 492–94, *495,* 522–23. *See also* hiring and selection
intimate zone, in personal space, 454–55, *455*
intracapital, 125
intrapersonal intelligence, 46
intrapreneurship, 123–25
intrinsic motivation, 192
intuition, and problem solving, 111–12, 114
investigative occupational type, B-13
involvement, job, 70
involvement, work, 70
IQ, 46
Ivester, Douglas, 312

J

JA (Junior Achievement), 612
Jager, Durk, A-15
Japan
    "A Beginner's Guide to Japan," 308
    comic books as communication, 288
    e-commerce, 301–2
    equality, appearance of, 371
    madogiwazoku ("sitting by the window tribe"), B-9
    Microsoft Xbox in, 399–400
    organizational culture in, 546, *547*
    overwork and *karoshi,* 218
    smile training, 314
    uncreative environment, 121–22, 126
jargon, 284, 313–14
JDI (Job Descriptive Index), 66, 67
Jermier, John, 544–45
Jerry Maguire (film), 172, 211
job analysis, and compensation, 512
job analysis technique, 242–43
job characteristics model and job design. *See also* careers
    overview, 152, 190–91
    conditions for successful redesign, 196–97
    dimensions, 193–95, *194, 195*
    empowerment, redesign for, 379
    evidence on the model, 195–96
    growth-need strength (GNS), 197
    guidelines for managing, 228–32
    implementing principles, 196, *197*
    job size, 191–93
    perceptions and, 196
    process model, *198*
    specialization issues, 191, *192*
job demands, as stressor, 223–24
job depth, 191
job descriptions, 512, 613
Job Descriptive Index (JDI), 66, 67
job enlargement, 191
job enrichment
    implementing principles, 196, *197*
    job characteristics model and, 191, 192–93
    managerial skills and, 11
job evaluations, 512
job facet satisfaction, 65, *66*
job involvement, 70
job-pathing, B-20
job rotation, 196
job satisfaction. *See* satisfaction
job scope, 191–92
job security issues, for young managers, B-6
job specifications, and compensation, 512
jobs, identification with, 586
Jobs, Steve, 324
Johnson, Dave, 521
Jones, Linda, 272
Jordan, Robert J., 496
journal databases, 614
Journal of Management Inquiry (JMI), 608–9
journals, practitioner-oriented, 608–9

Junior Achievement (JA), 612
just actions, 258
just-in-time, 117
justifying, 388

K

Kadokawa, Yoshiko, 314
Kahneman, Daniel, 107–8
Kalter, Alan, 557
Kanter, Rosabeth Moss, 100
karoshi and overwork, 218
Kasparov, Gary, 105
Kelleher, Herb, 541
Kelley, Harold, 62
Kennedy, Aaron, 534
Kennedy, Allen, 548
kickbacks, 252, 253, 254
King, Martin Luther, Jr., 344–46, A-10
knowing–doing gap, 14–17
knowledge, tacit, 15
knowledge management, 15
Koiso, Yurchiro, 314
Korea, 421–22
Korhonen, Pertti, 138
Koslowski, Dennis, 267–68
Kouzes, Jim, 258
Kovac, Daniel J., 414
Kroc, Ray A., 134
Kruszelnicki, Karl, 140
Kwon, Hyuk-ho, 140

L

labor market conditions, and compensation, 512
labor unions, as supplier group, A-22
LaNeve, Mark, 25
language of leadership, 344–46
languages, and cross-cultural communication, 305
LaPiere, R. T., 72
latent conflict, 414, *415*
lateral moves, 502, B-11–B-12
law of effect, 160
laws and legislation, 256–57, A-3
Lay, Kenneth, 250, 556
layoffs. *See* downsizing
Leader to Leader Institute, 396, 591
leader–member exchange (LMX) theory, 337–41, *339, 340*
leadership
    overview, 324, 346–47
    autocratic and democratic styles, 330, *330,* 332
    in Baldrige Award Criteria, A-9
    best and worst managers of 2002, 327
    Biocom senior management team, 467–70
    changing approach to, 326–28, *327*
    communities of, 588
    consideration and initiating structure, 332, *333*
    definition, 326
    Ford case study, 352–54
    knowing–doing gap and, 16–17
    language of, 344–46

equity theory and fairness, 152, 184–90

expectancy theory and, 151, 178–83

FISH! philosophy, 198

goal-setting theory and, 151, 168–72

Gymboree case study, 202–4

intrinsic and extrinsic, 192

job characteristics model and job design, 152, 190–98

learning theories and, 151, 159–67

management by objectives (MBO), 170–72

need theories, 152–58

path–goal theory and, 335

self-management, 172–78

USA International Insurance Company case study, 201–2

Valassis Communications case study, 204–5

movement, career, 502–3, B-10–B-12, B-11

movies

Apollo 13, 112, 144

The Breakfast Club, 42, 87

Bringout out the Dead, 226

Disclosure, 12, 30

Ghandi, 347, 360

Gung Ho, 544, 559

Hoosiers, 575, 597

Jerry Maguire, 172, 211

Lifeboat, 315

Mother Teresa, 347, 360

October Sky, 143

Office Space, 5, 29

The Perfect Storm, 100–101

Pushing Tin, 236, 244–45

Remember the Titans, 449, 474

Thirteen Days, 423, 433

Top Gun, 508, 527

Twelve Angry Men, 453, 476

Wall Street, 254, 269–70

Mulcahy, Anne, 593–94

multiple mentoring, B-25

munificence, A-5

Murrah Federal Building bombing, 281

Muruyama, Yoshihiro, 400

Myers, M. Scott, 192

"The myth of the management team," 587

myths, 540

N

Nanus, Burt, 326

Napoleon, 342

narratives, 539–41

NASA, 507, 532

Nasser, Jacques A., 352, 353

National Business Ethics Survey, 259

National Society for Internships and Experiential Education, 603

NBA (National Basketball Association), 101

NCAA (National Collegiate Athletic Association), 259

need theories. *See also* motivation

overview, 151, 152–53

Alderfer's ERG theory, 155, *156*

implications of, 157–58

Maslow's need hierarchy, 153–54, *154*

McClelland's manifest needs, 155–57

need satisfaction process, 152, *153*

process model, *158*

satisfaction progression, 154

needs assessment, for training, 505

needs rule, in equity theory, 189

negative affectivity, 68

negotiating and bargaining

BATNA (Best Alternative to a Negotiated Agreement), 129

conflict and, 420

information-sharing tactics, 131–32

integrative agreements, techniques for, 131

postsettlement settlements, 132

strategies and styles, *127,* 127–29

win-win solutions, 129–31

Netiquette, 298, 308

networkers, internal, 588

networks, and skills development, 612–13

networks, communication, 282–83, *283*

networks, developmental, B-25

Neuharth, Al, 380

neurotic firms, 549

neutralizers and substitutes, 336–37, *338, 339*

new entrants, threat of, A-21

New London Police Department, 496

new work environment, managerial skills in, 10–12

New York City Fire Department (FDNY), 223

New York Times, 283–84

New York Yankees, 54

Newman, Josh C., 467, 470

newsletters, 288

The Nicomachean Ethics (Aristotle), 45

Noble, Ted, 412

nominal group technique, 462, *463*

nonreinforcement, 161

nonspecific compensation, in integrative agreements, 131

nonverbal communication

cultural differences, 55

forms of, *295,* 295–97

functions of, 294–95

gestures, appropriate, 290–91

listening cues, 293

self-presentation and, 387–89

in teams, 455

Nordloh, Daniel A., A-12

normative power, 367

norming stage of group development, 448

norms, in teams, 445–46, 471

norms and counternorms, 382–83

O

O magazine, 85, 86

OB (organizational behavior), 13

Oberpriller, Elizabeth, 441

objectives, strategic, A-13–A-14, A-16

OBM (organizational behavior modification), 165–67, *167*

O'Brien, Karen, 42

obsolescence, managerial, B-3

occupational information, and career management, B-15

occupational personality types, B-13–B-14

October Sky (film), 143

OD (organizational development), 579, 581–85

The Odyssey (Homer), B-21

Office Space (film), 5, 29

Oklahoma City bombing, 281

O'Leary, George, 491

oligopoly, A-4

Ollila, Jorma, 137

ombudsmen, 261, 264

on-the-job training, 505

1001 Ways to Reward Employees (Nelson), 206–7

one-way communication, 280–82

Online Journal of Peace and Conflict Resolution, 425

online retail sales, 301

openness to experience, 52

operant (Skinnerian) conditioning, 160, *160*

opinion conformity, 389

The Oprah Winfrey Show, 85, 86

optimism, and stress, 227

organization-based compensation plans, 514–15

organization descriptions, self-presentational, 389

organization of stimuli, in perceptual process, *57, 58*

organizational audit groups, 287

organizational behavior (OB), 13

organizational behavior modification (OBM), 165–67, *167*

organizational citizenship behaviors, 78

organizational culture. *See* culture, organizational

organizational development (OD), 579, 581–85

Organizational Dynamics, 609

organizational effectiveness, *20, 21,* A-6–A-8, *A-7,* A-9

organizational environment, A-2–A-6

organizational levels, *13, 383*

organizational politics. *See* politics, organizational

organizational seduction, B-6

organizations, creative, *121,* 121–27

orientation (training), 501–2

Osborne, Alex, 118

Oshima, Ichiro, 218

other enhancement, 389

Ouchi, William, 546

out-groups and in-groups, 338–39

outcome approaches to performance appraisal, 510

outcomes, first-order and second-order, 179, *179*

workplace community portals, 299
World Trade Center, 101
World Wide Web. *See* Internet and
    the World Wide Web
WorldatWork, 611
Wozniak, Steve, 324
written communication, 287–89, 290

X

X-GAMES, 358

Y

Y networks, 282–83, *283*
Yang, Jerry, 621
Young, Roy, 268–69
young managers, career problems of,
    B-4–B-6
Young Turks game, 390